Johnson & Johnson
One Johnson & Johnson Plaza
New Brunswick, New Jersey
08933

K mart Corporation
3100 West Big Beaver Road
Troy, Michigan 48084

Kellogg Company
One Kellogg Square
P.O. Box 3599
Battle Creek, Michigan
49016-3599

Kimberly-Clark Corporation
P.O. Box 619100
DFW Airport Station
Dallas, Texas 75261-9100

The Kroger Co.
1014 Vine Street
Cincinnati, Ohio 45201

L.A. Gear, Inc.
4221 Redwood Avenue
Los Angeles, California
90066

The Limited, Inc.
Two Limited Parkway
P.O. Box 16000
Columbus, Ohio 43216

MCI Communications
Corporation
1133 19th Street, N.W.
Washington, D.C. 20036

Marriott Corporation
Marriott Drive
Washington, D.C. 20058

Maytag Corporation
403 West Fourth Street North
Newton, Iowa 50208

McDonald's Corporation
McDonald's Plaza
Oak Brook, Illinois 60521

McDonnell Douglas
P.O. Box 516
St. Louis, Missouri
63166-0516

Midway Airlines
5959 South Cicero Avenue
Chicago, Illinois 60638

Mobil Corporation
150 East 42nd Street
New York, New York 10017-5666

Monsanto Company
800 North Lindberg Boulevard
St. Louis, Missouri 63167

The New York Times Company
229 West 43d Street
New York, New York 10036

NIKE, Inc.
3900 S.W. Murray Blvd.
Beaverton, Oregon 97005

Pacific Gas and Electric Company
77 Beale Street
San Francisco, California 94106

Penney, J.C. Company
14841 North Dallas Parkway
Dallas, Texas 75240-6760

PepsiCo, Inc.
Purchase, New York 10577

Philip Morris Companies, Inc.
120 Park Avenue
New York, New York 10017

Polaroid Corporation
549 Technology Square
Cambridge, Massachusetts
02139

The Quaker Oats Company
P.O. Box 9001
Chicago, Illinois 60604-9001

Quaker State Corporation
255 Elm Street
Oil City, Pennsylvania
16301

Ralston Purina Company
Checkerboard Square
St. Louis, Missouri 63164

Reebok International Ltd.
150 Royall Street
Canton, Massachusetts
02021

Rubbermaid Incorporated
1147 Akron Road
Wooster, Ohio 44691

Sara Lee Corporation
Three First National Plaza
Chicago, Illinois 60602-4260

Scott Paper Company
Scott Plaza
Philadelphia, Pennsylvania 19113

Sears, Roebuck and Co.
Sears Tower
Chicago, Illinois 60684

Squibb Corporation
P.O. Box 4000
Princeton, New Jersey 08543-4000

Texas Instruments
Post Office Box 655474
Dallas, Texas 75265

The Toro Company
8111 Lyndale Avenue South
Bloomington, Minnesota 55420

Turner Broadcasting System, Inc.
One CNN Center
100 International Boulevard
Atlanta, Georgia 30303

Unisys Corporation
P.O. Box 500
Blue Bell, Pennsylvania
19424-0001

United Technologies
United Technologies Building
Hartford, Connecticut 06101

USAir Group, Inc.
2345 Crystal Drive
Arlington, Virginia 22227

Wendy's International, Inc.
P.O. Box 256
4288 West Dublin-Granville Road
Dublin, Ohio 43017-0256

Westinghouse Electric
Corporation
Westinghouse Building
Gateway Center
Pittsburgh, Pennsylvania 15222

Woolworth, F.W. Co.
233 Broadway
New York, New York
10279-0001

Zenith Electronics Corporation
1000 Milwaukee Avenue
Glenview, Illinois 60025

# Accounting Principles

THIRD EDITION

# About the Authors

**Lanny M. Solomon** is currently a professor of accounting at the University of Texas at Arlington. He holds a Ph.D. in accounting and information systems from Case Western Reserve University and is a certified management accountant. Professor Solomon has published articles in *The Accounting Review, Journal of Accountancy, Cost and Management,* and various journals of state CPA societies. In addition, he has presented numerous papers at technical accounting meetings. Professor Solomon is an active member of the American Accounting Association and the Institute of Certified Management Accountants, has public and industrial accounting experience, and has been the recipient of several outstanding teaching awards.

**Richard J. Vargo,** currently a professor at the University of the Pacific, received his doctorate in accounting from the University of Washington. He has experience with an international public accounting firm. Articles by Professor Vargo have appeared in the *Journal of Accountancy, CPA Journal,* and other professional publications. He is the author of several other accounting and business books, including one prepared for the American Institute of Certified Public Accountants. Professor Vargo is actively involved in the American Accounting Association, and has served as a member of the editorial board of *The Accounting Review* and the Professional Examinations Committee. In addition, he has acted as a consultant to a number of businesses on accounting and financial reporting matters.

**Larry M. Walther** is an associate professor of accounting at the University of Texas at Arlington. He received his doctorate in accounting from Oklahoma State University and has experience with an international public accounting firm. Professor Walther is both a certified public accountant and a certified management accountant. Articles by Professor Walther have appeared in *The Accounting Review, Journal of Accountancy, Management Accounting, The Practical Accountant,* and other professional journals. He is a member of the American Accounting Association, Texas Society of Certified Public Accountants, and other professional organizations. Professor Walther has provided consulting services to a number of businesses on accounting and financial reporting matters and serves as a director of a corporation that operates in the Dallas-Fort Worth area.

THIRD EDITION

# Accounting Principles

**Lanny M. Solomon**
*The University of Texas at Arlington*

**Richard J. Vargo**
*University of the Pacific*

**Larry M. Walther**
*The University of Texas at Arlington*

**West Publishing Company**
*Saint Paul ■ New York ■ Los Angeles ■ San Francisco*

**Production Credits**

Illustrations: Rolin Graphics
Proofreading: Lynn Reichel
Composition: Bi-Comp, Inc.
Cover Design: Roslyn M. Stendahl, Dapper Design
Cover Image: © David Bishop
Index: Patricia A. Lewis
Photos: p. 6 (bottom middle) Gary Gladstone, (bottom right) David Wagenaar.


50 W. Kellogg Boulevard
P.O. Box 64526
St. Paul, MN 55164–1003



Printed in the United States of America

97 96 95 94 93 92 91 8 7 6 5 4 3 2

**Library of Congress Cataloging-in-Publication Data**

Solomon, Lanny M., 1946–
Accounting principles/Lanny Solomon, Richard Vargo, Larry Walther.—3rd ed.
p. cm.
ISBN 0-314-66635-4
1. Accounting. I. Vargo, Richard J. II. Walther, Larry M. III. Title.
HF5635.S688 1990
657—dc20 89-70584
CIP

# Contents in Brief

# Contents

## Chapter 9 Inventory 303



## Chapter 10 Property, Plant, and Equipment: Acquisition and Depreciation 343

## Chapter 15 Introduction to Corporations 511



## Chapter 16 Corporations: Additional Equity Issues and Income Reporting 541

## Chapter 17 Long-Term Liabilities 579



## Chapter 18 Long-Term Investments 621

## Chapter 19 Statement of Cash Flows 659



## Chapter 20 Financial Statements: Analysis and Further Disclosures 709

## Chapter 21 Introduction to Managerial and Cost Accounting 753



## Chapter 22 Job Order Costing Systems 791



## Chapter 23 Process Costing Systems 827

# Preface

## To the Instructor

Accounting education has undergone considerable change in recent years. Students have been asked to comprehend a growing number of complex pronouncements; professorial complaints regarding students' reading and analytical abilities have increased; and there is evidence that we are losing our brightest classroom performers to other disciplines on campus. Furthermore, classes often contain a substantial number of students who quickly lose interest in the subject matter, which is often regarded as time-consuming and somewhat dry and boring. It is these very problems that prompted us to write the first edition of *Accounting Principles* in 1983 and to develop many of the refinements in this, the third edition.

Although we cannot perform miracles, we are confident that our text can arouse students' interest in accounting, thereby creating a more dynamic instructional environment. This ability grows out of the text's heavy emphasis on real-world experience. We make extensive use of data from corporate financial reports to illustrate important points, along with interesting excerpts from periodicals and a decision-oriented approach to management accounting. In short, our aim is to add pizzazz to the study of the subject. However, we do not lose sight of our main objective as accounting educators: *to provide a well-balanced presentation of the measurement and reporting of financial activity.* Users of the first two editions have indicated that our objectives have been met. Both faculty *and* students were enthusiastic about the book's clarity, readability, accuracy, and comprehensiveness.

Not only have we tried to meet diverse readership needs, but we have also addressed diverse instructional philosophies. Flexibility has been a prime consideration in the design of this book. For those instructors who desire to reinforce learning of basic accounting procedures via reversing entries, work sheets, special journals, and other similar tools, such topics are covered in ample depth. However, this coverage may be omitted without any loss of continuity if a more conceptual presentation is preferred. Discussions of the concepts and rationale that underlie accounting practices are integrated at appropriate points throughout the text. The result, we believe, is an enlightening presentation—one that will create a stimulating educational experience.

## Significant Changes in the Third Edition

On the basis of user feedback and market studies, we have made various changes in the organization and content of the third edition. The major changes include:

**1** A new appendix has been added to Chapter 3 concerning the initial recording of prepaid expenses and unearned revenues in income statement accounts.

**2** Instructors can now satisfy personal preferences by covering either the closing-entry method or the adjusting-entry method of end-of-period inventory amounts. (Chapter 5)

**3** The presentation on special journals has been streamlined (Chapter 6). In addition, the discussion of computers in accounting has been totally rewritten to reflect the increased use of microcomputers in data processing and data analysis.

**4** The coverage of perpetual inventory systems (Chapter 9) has been expanded to include the LIFO and moving-average costing methods.

**5** The coverage of inflation accounting has been significantly reduced. (Chapter 13)

**6** Long-term bond investments (Chapter 18) are now accounted for by using the effective-interest amortization method.

**7** Chapter 19, which covers the statement of cash flows, was totally rewritten to reflect *Statement of Financial Accounting Standards No. 95.* Discussion of both the direct and indirect methods of computing the cash flows from operating activities is provided.

**8** A discussion of the various types of financial statement footnotes has been added to Chapter 20.

**9** The second edition's coverage of job order and process cost accounting has been split into two chapters (Chapters 22 and 23). This arrangement has allowed us to add the following topics: cost drivers in the new manufacturing environment; job costing systems in service organizations; and discussion of both FIFO and weighted-average process costing, with the instructor being free to cover one method or the other.

**10** The presentation of federal income taxes for individuals has been shortened and now appears in Appendix A at the end of the text.

**11** A new appendix (D) covers the timely topic of ethics and the accountant.

**12** Each chapter contains four new pedagogical features. In addition to appearing at the beginning of the chapter, learning objectives are duplicated in the margin at the appropriate point in the chapter's narrative. Also throughout the discussion are various "Tips & Techniques," which are hints and pitfalls to avoid when dealing with selected subjects. Finally, all chapters conclude with a summary that is tied to the learning objectives, and a multiple-choice quiz for student solution.

**13** For those instructors who may want to provide an extra challenge to their students, a new problem section entitled "Beyond the Basics" has been designed. These problems/cases involve more application (and mind stretching) than the problems that appear in Series A and Series B. All requirements are answerable, however, from either the text's presentation or good common sense.

**14** The use of graphic illustrations has been greatly expanded in terms of both quality and quantity.

## Second Edition Features Retained

Many features in the second edition proved popular with users. Those features, repeated in this edition, include a heavy use of real-world firms and data, excerpts from periodicals, a truly managerial section, solid problem material, and clarity and readability of presentations.

### Heavy Real-World Emphasis

Many accounting texts use hypothetical firms in their illustrations and examples. The authors have found that students show an increased interest in the subject matter when exposed to the accounting and financial reporting practices of real businesses. Thus, we include annual report data and "war stories" of over 100 different companies, including McDonald's, American Airlines, Apple Computer, the Toronto Blue Jays, and The Coca-Cola Company. We have carefully selected firms from industries with which students themselves have contact. All examples were screened for appropriateness at the introductory level.

### Excerpts from Periodicals

The authors have integrated excerpts from journal and newspaper articles into topical discussions in an effort to bridge the gap between academia and the business world. The selected articles relate to the subject matter at hand and were chosen (and adapted) to focus on practical, interesting applications. Excerpts are from such popular periodicals as *The Wall Street Journal*, *Forbes*, and *Business Week*. Typical examples include:

"Depreciation: Is Nothing Sacred?"
"Freebies Create a Growing Liability"
"The Grateful Dead: Planning + Control + Decision Making"

### A Truly Managerial Section

The final chapters of an accounting principles text are normally devoted to cost and managerial accounting topics. The usual approach is to have students calculate this and calculate that, while paying very little attention to the use or impact of the data they are generating. Our approach is to focus on the how *and* why of planning, control, performance evaluation, and decision making, and to show practical applications whenever possible. This balanced presentation should appeal to a wide variety of instructors, including those who currently use a separate text for managerial coverage.

### Solid Problem Material

All problem material contained in this text was carefully designed to reflect current accounting principles and practices. Questions, exercises, and problems range in scope from the simple to the complex; all were written and solved by the authors to assure total coordination with the text presentation. To further ensure accuracy and reliability, we have triple-checked the *Instructor's Solutions Manual.* We are confident that the end-of-chapter materials are as trouble-free as repeated multiple checking can make them; they will provide a solid, well-rounded foundation for accounting students and a varied resource for instructors.

As noted earlier, the problem material is divided into Series *A* and Series *B*. Instructors can therefore use one problem for illustration purposes and assign another as homework, or use different problem sets in alternating semesters or quarters. Although duplication is important, the authors have not lost sight of the need for variety. There is ample variety of material within both sets that allows instructors to approach a given topic from varying perspectives.

### Clarity and Readability of Presentations

We have monitored readability throughout the text and have strived to make troublesome topics (such as adjusting entries, corporate equity, bonds, and the statement of cash flows) especially understandable to students. To eliminate differences in writing styles, one of the authors has spent countless hours integrating the same tone, approach, and manner of presentation in all 28 chapters. Accounting is a rigorous subject for most individuals. The authors recognize this fact and have worked hard to produce a clear and usable volume. Comments from users (instructors *and* students) indicate that we have, in fact, generated a readable book.

## Supplementary Materials

A complete set of supplementary materials for both student and instructor accompanies this text to help facilitate the learning and teaching of accounting.

### For the Student

- **Study Guide.** A study guide, available in two volumes, has been written by Larry Walther to reinforce the material presented in the text. The study guide contains chapter learning objectives; a chapter synopsis; multiple-choice, two-response, and completion questions; exercises; and answers *with explanations*, as well as computer software that provides step-by-step instruction on key accounting topics.
- **Working Papers.** Two volumes of working papers have been prepared: Volume I covers Chapters 1–14; Volume II covers Chapters 14–28 and Appendix A. The inclusion of Chapter 14 (Partnerships) in both volumes recognizes that coverage of this topic occurs in the first Principles course at some schools and in the second course at others. Many of the working papers are partially filled in, thereby allowing students to concentrate on accounting concepts as opposed to the pencil pushing associated with problem setup.
- **Practice Sets.** The authors have written a number of practice sets that tie together various issues discussed in the text.

*Valley Nutrition Center* (1A): Covers Chapters 1–6 and focuses on the accounting cycle.

*Island Surfwear* (1B): An alternative version to practice set 1A; uses a different setting and data.

*Lap Top Computers Company* (1C): Written by James Weglin of North Seattle Community College; a business papers practice set.

*Classic Auto* (2): Accompanies Chapters 7–12; reinforces concepts and interrelationships via a typical year-end situation faced by an accountant.

*The Thompson Corporation* (3): Covers Chapters 15–17; helps the student understand and integrate the principles and practices of corporate accounting.

*United Manufacturing Company* (4): Designed to accompany Chapters 21–27;

focuses on cost and managerial accounting including job order and process costing, budgeting, variance analysis, and decision making.

*Newport Angling Gear* (5): A computerized practice set; a description appears in the section entitled "Computer Software."

## For the Instructor

- **Annotated Instructor's Edition.** An annotated instructor's version of the text has been prepared by Laurie Walther and Mary Lee Hodge, both from The University of Texas at Arlington. This special printing contains various types of aids to improve teaching effectiveness. The aids, which appear in the text's margins, include Points to Emphasize, Teaching Ideas, and Ethics Issues.
- **Instructor's Solutions Manual.** A comprehensive, two-volume manual is available that contains the solutions to all questions, exercises, and problems. In addition, a suggested completion time and difficulty index is provided for each problem. Solutions to the practice sets are available in separate booklets.
- **Instructor's Resource Manual.** The instructor's resource manual contains detailed lecture outlines that parallel the text's discussion. These outlines are especially useful for part-time instructors and graduate teaching assistants. The manual also includes suggested homework assignments and a cross-referencing of all exercises and problems to chapter learning objectives.
- **Transparencies.** A set of transparencies is free to adopters. Packaged in two boxes, the transparencies contain solutions to all exercises and problems. All are prepared in large, easy-to-read type.
- **Teaching Transparencies.** A set of over 100 teaching transparencies is free to adopters. These helpful color acetates include summaries of key narrative discussions raised in the chapter and various examples, with an emphasis on those that are too time-consuming to present on a chalkboard. A special group of "layered" transparencies is included; these consist of overlays, allowing the instructor to demonstrate, one step at a time, the completion of a work sheet, the construction of a production cost report, and other troublesome tasks.
- **Lecture Outline Transparencies.** The lecture outlines contained in the instructor's resource manual are available on transparencies. These helpful tools add structure to a classroom presentation and allow students to focus on key points raised in each chapter.
- **Test Banks.** Two thoroughly revised and expanded test banks have been prepared. Each chapter of the text is covered via an ample selection of multiple-choice, true-false, and matching questions, along with a series of multi-part exercises. The test banks are available in printed and microcomputer versions.
- **Achievement Tests.** A set of objective achievement tests is available in bulk in alternate forms. These tests take 40 to 60 minutes to complete and examine a student on approximately three chapters at a given sitting. In addition, we offer two comprehensive tests in alternate forms for Chapters 1–14 and Chapters 15–28; these require approximately 100 to 120 minutes to administer.

## Computer Software

We also offer a variety of microcomputer software to help both student and instructor.

- **Westest.** Westest is a microcomputer test-generation package that consists of item banks on disks and the software necessary to turn them into instructor-customized examinations. Random selection of questions is available and, if desired, multiple tests may be generated simultaneously. Westest can be used on the IBM PC and compatible machines, the Apple IIe family of computers, and the Macintosh.
- **Computer-Assisted Accounting Tutorials.** Contained in the Study Guide, these tutorials present essential accounting material on a step-by-step basis. As they proceed through the lesson, students are queried on subject matter presentations via a series of two-response (e.g., yes/no, agree/disagree, logical/illogical), multiple-choice, and computational questions. The tutorials are designed for use on an IBM PC or compatible machines.
- **Computerized Practice Set.** Newport Angling Gear, a computerized practice set compatible with the IBM PC, covers Chapters 1–9 in two separate modules. The set illustrates the ability of the computer to process transactions and prepare financial statements; some "what if" analysis may be employed. An instructor's manual is available.
- **Lotus 1-2-3 Spreadsheet Exercises.** Approximately three exercises and one problem from each chapter have been adapted to microcomputers by John Bedient of Albion College. These exercises, denoted by a diskette symbol, are solved by use of Lotus 1-2-3 (IBM) templates. The related instructor materials are available to text adopters.

## Acknowledgments

A project of this nature and magnitude is a team effort, entailing much cooperation, thoughtfulness, and patience. To our team members we owe a tremendous debt of gratitude. Those persons who class-tested our material and reviewed chapters were especially helpful with their comments and suggestions. Therefore, many thanks to the following people: Sallie Branscom, Virginia Western Community College; Jeanne David, University of Detroit; Robert DeFilippis, Fairleigh Dickinson University; Daniel Galvin, Diablo Valley College; Carolyn King, Old Dominion University; Edward Krohn, Miami-Dade Community College; Sondra Laemmle, University of Louisville; Jim Patten, California State College—Bakersfield; Beverly Piper, Ashland College; Robbie Sheffy, Tarrant County Junior College; Larry Roman, Cuyahoga Community College; Barbara Shiarappa, Trenton State College; Sammie Smith, Stephen F. Austin State University; and Steven Wong, San Joaquin Delta College.

A special thank you for various chores related to the text's development goes to Mary Lee Hodge, Debra Hopkins, Don McConnell, Richard Mark, Vicki Peden, and Hemendra Vartak, all of The University of Texas at Arlington.

The assistance from West Publishing in developing this manuscript was extremely helpful. We especially appreciate the work of Ken Zeigler, Bob Horan, Sharon Kavanagh, Andi Peters, Bill Stryker, Lucinda Gatch, Mary Verrill, and Kristen McCarthy—all of whom offered numerous suggestions and provided constant encouragement during the period that the text and ancillary materials were under development.

And finally, we are deeply appreciative of the support of our families that enabled us to pursue this project. In view of the time commitment and constant deadlines, their patience went above and beyond the call of duty. To Nancy, Scott, and Deborah Solomon; Melinda, Matthew, Blaine, and Mike Vargo; and Laurie, Corbett, and Russell Walther—we love you.

Comments from users are welcomed and appreciated.

Lanny M. Solomon
Richard J. Vargo
Larry M. Walther

# A Message to Our Readers. . . .

You are about to begin the study of accounting, which has frequently been called the language of business. Accounting concepts and terminology are used in conversations among managers and often appear in business periodicals. A day doesn't go by, for example, without metropolitan newspapers reporting the financial happenings of major U.S. corporations.

Ask almost any professional (e.g., a company president, engineer, marketing manager, or the owner of a local restaurant) and he or she will likely cite an improvement in job performance and/or lifestyle by having a reasonable understanding of accounting and financial matters. The importance of accounting is perhaps best seen via the following statistics. A survey performed by the major accrediting agency of U.S. business schools asked managers to evaluate various courses to determine which ones students should stress in their studies. Accounting ranked first. (Finance and economics placed second and third, respectively.) Another study performed by *Fortune* magazine found that many corporations preferred their chief executive officers (CEOs) to have a heavy accounting and financial background. Approximately 25% of the 800 highest paid CEOs in this country followed a financial career path while climbing to the top of the corporate hierarchy.

Over the years, many businesses have flourished because of entrepreneurial spirit and innovative ideas and products. Some companies, of course, have met with more success than others. Those organizations that have outpaced the competition have done so, in part, from their executives' ability to understand and analyze basic accounting information. Careful study of this text will give you the foundation for developing that ability. You will be exposed to principles, practices, and procedures—all of which are necessary to gain a fundamental understanding of the subject matter.

Accounting is a discipline characterized by growth and challenge. Although the introductory course in which you are enrolled may be more time consuming and rigorous than other courses on campus, understand that the effort you put forth today will have significant long-term benefits. The time that you spend is an investment in the future, with high returns in the years to come.

# An Introduction to Accounting

CHAPTER 1

## Learning Objectives

After reading this chapter you should:

**1** Be familiar with the users, uses, and limitations of accounting information.

**2** Be familiar with the accounting profession and accounting-related careers.

**3** Understand the use of accounting principles in financial reporting.

**4** Understand the meaning of assets, liabilities, and owner's equity and the relationship of these components in the accounting equation.

**5** Be aware of the four items that cause owner's equity to change: specifically, owner investments, owner withdrawals, net income, and net loss.

**6** Understand the impact of various transactions on the accounting equation.

**7** Understand the content of and be able to prepare an income statement, a statement of owner's equity, and a balance sheet.

Most professionals recognize that accounting plays a major role in the management of any business. Companies require a system that summarizes past financial activity and communicates selected information to interested parties. Accounting is such a system. By reporting output (e.g., ending cash balances, earnings for the period, and the manufactured cost of finished products) to the appropriate individual(s), accounting gives its users the ability to make more informed economic decisions.

This process is better understood if we develop a definition of accounting, which, in itself, is not an easy task. The field is broad and the work that an accountant performs is varied. Accountants are typically involved with such diverse activities as the review of business transactions and client computer systems, tax planning, budgeting, and the analysis of long-term investment proposals. A publication from an accounting firm notes:

> Historically, [accounting] suffered from an image problem—the Bob Cratchit syndrome—which portrayed it as dull, routine work. If this view were ever true, it certainly isn't today.[1]

Observing the accountants' work and the profession of which they are members, few would find fault with the following definition: **Accounting** is a set of concepts and techniques that collectively measure, summarize, and report financial information about an economic unit. To expand, most disciplines are based on some type of theoretical framework. Accounting is no exception. The foundation for much of what accountants do is a set of underlying principles, assumptions, and practices that have been generally accepted by the accounting profession. These items are used to measure the financial activities of numerous business units including Boeing Corporation, the family-owned corner market, and even the local art museum. Once derived, the measurements are processed, summarized, and communicated to interested parties in the form of financial reports and statistics, allowing users to make judgments about a wide variety of business matters.

## Users and Uses of Accounting Information

**OBJECTIVE 1**
**Be familiar with the users, uses, and limitations of accounting information.**

The audience for accounting information is large and diverse. Numerous user groups within and outside of an enterprise attempt to satisfy their needs by relying on financial disclosures (see Exhibit 1-1). For example:

*Owners* have invested their precious funds into a business organization. This group requires information concerning investment profitability and whether continuance in an ownership role is economically justified. Potential owners have similar information needs. These individuals desire insight about a firm's past earnings trends, future growth prospects, and overall operations, perhaps in comparison with other enterprises in the same industry.

*Creditors* are those parties that provide a firm with goods, services, and financial resources by either extending credit or making loans. Included in this group are suppliers, banks, loan companies, and other lending institutions. Creditors are interested in knowing whether an organization can settle its obligations (including related interest charges) in a timely manner and on scheduled dates. Consequently, an enterprise's existing cash position, outstanding debts, and present and projected earnings are of utmost concern.

*Managers* are charged with the responsibility of meeting a company's goals and objectives. To achieve this end, managers must select from and implement various

[1] Peat Marwick Main & Co., *Your Career in Professional Accounting,* p. 12.

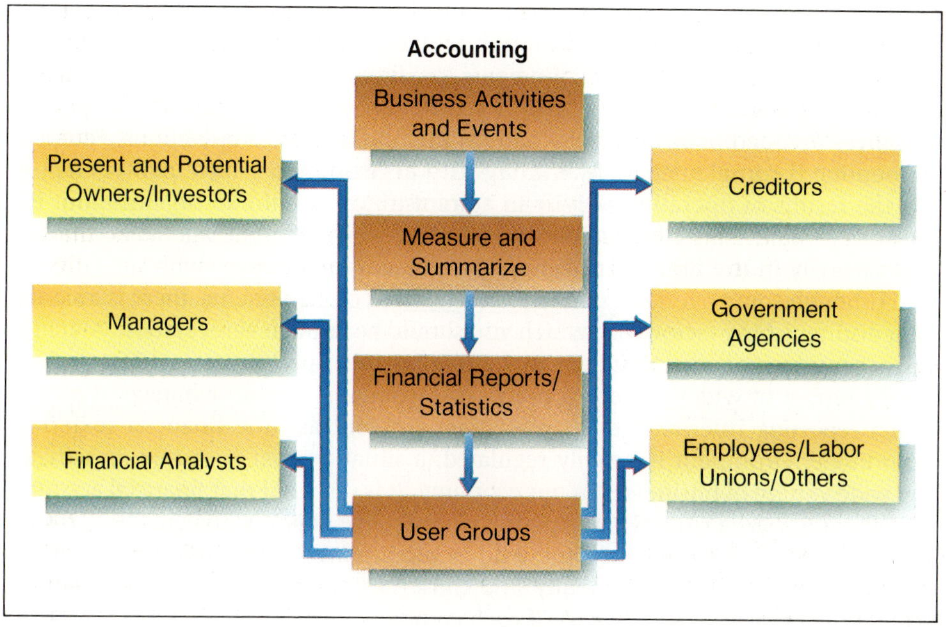


**Exhibit 1-1**
**Accounting and the Communication Process**

projects, evaluate performance, and, if necessary, take corrective action to bring an organization back on target. Depending on the firm involved, information needs will vary and may include product cost data, manufacturing resource requirements, and cash flow projections.

*Government agencies* also employ accounting information. Governmental units, along with various programs (such as social security and unemployment), are financed from the taxes that are paid by businesses and individuals. These taxes are frequently based on income as defined by numerous tax statutes and rulings. In addition to serving as a funding source, businesses must often comply with the financial reporting directives of certain regulatory agencies. These agencies are charged with administering a variety of legislative enactments and include the Securities and Exchange Commission (SEC), the Interstate Commerce Commission, and the U.S. Department of Labor, to name just a few.

Finally, other users include *financial analysts,* who advise their clients or employers about the relative attractiveness of various investment alternatives; *employees and labor unions,* who need information to properly evaluate salary and fringe benefit packages; and customers, lawyers, and trade associations.

Suffice it to say that accountants strive to satisfy the diverse needs of these users; sometimes, however, the needs conflict. Disclosures and reporting techniques that are relevant for one user group may be inappropriate for others. For this reason the basic financial reports produced by accountants are general purpose in orientation; namely, the reports are neutral when communicating information to the broad spectrum of interested parties.

## Financial and Managerial Orientation

Accounting encompasses extensive subject matter and consists of many component parts. Two of the field's major segments are financial accounting and managerial accounting.

**Financial accounting** is primarily concerned with external reporting, that is, communicating the results of economic activities to parties outside the firm. Included in this group are potential owners, creditors, and some government agencies. The financial reporting function centers on a fair presentation of (1) the resources invested in an enterprise and (2) the profitability of operations. Financial accounting is complemented by **managerial accounting,** which involves reporting the results of operating activity to administrators within an organization. Because of its nature and the audience to which it is directed, managerial accounting deals heavily in the areas of planning, control, and decision making.

Although some overlap exists between these two components, there is a significant distinguishing factor with which you should be familiar—regulation. Managerial accounting is characterized by an "anything goes" philosophy. Although there are a number of widely accepted practices, a company can do whatever it pleases when reporting internally to its executives. In contrast, the financial (external) reporting environment is heavily regulated, a situation that is caused, in part, by the wide variety of businesses in our economy. It is essential that financial accounting be standardized somewhat to permit comparative analysis. Imagine the difficulties faced by a potential investor who is attempting to evaluate the economic activities of Ford Motor Company and those of The Gap, Inc. (a much smaller retailer of casual and activewear). If each company were allowed to account for its activities by employing unique, self-prescribed methods, the investor would surely face a formidable task.[2]

The private sector agency that currently oversees external reporting is the **Financial Accounting Standards Board (FASB).** Beginning operation in 1973, the FASB has studied a number of important topics and has issued various pronouncements that detail specific accounting practices. These pronouncements, called *Statements of Financial Accounting Standards,* constitute generally accepted accounting principles and are followed by virtually all large businesses in the United States. The work of the FASB will be cited throughout this text; at this point simply understand the FASB's existence and basic function.

## Limitations of Accounting Information

Although widely disseminated and relied upon, accounting information contains several inherent limitations. Because accounting involves the computation of dollar amounts, many people assume a great degree of precision in financial reports. As you progress through the study of accounting, you will see that numerous estimates, assumptions, and subjective judgments are required in the reporting of business activity. Further, the accountant must frequently select from among various acceptable accounting practices when determining how well an organization has performed over a period of time. Collectively, these factors contribute to a general lack of "exactness" in the financial information disclosed by a business enterprise.

Another limitation associated with accounting information is that certain events are not conducive to monetary measurement. For example, the loss of a key manager and low employee morale often have undesirable consequences for a firm; however, placing a dollar value on these items is extremely difficult. How is

[2] Although standardization is suggested here, businesses are given some leeway when selecting and implementing accounting practices. This fact will become apparent in later chapters.

an organization's profit affected, for instance, if a sales manager suddenly resigns in favor of a new position with a strong competitor? Accountants are unable to express an event such as this in economic terms and therefore use the **monetary unit assumption** when assessing performance. This assumption holds that only events and activities measurable in dollars are entered and recognized in a company's records.

A further limitation of accounting information is the fact that the measures employed do not necessarily portray true value. As we will see shortly, accounting measures are often based on cost rather than on current worth.

The preceding criticisms should not be interpreted as an indictment of accounting. There are logical explanations that underlie the need for these restricting factors. In addition, the accounting profession has prescribed certain standards to partially offset the limitations' negative impact. The accountant, for example, often prepares a narrative discussion describing certain nonfinancial events that have a significant bearing on the business organization. Furthermore, the profession is continually reevaluating its position to determine if changes in practices would improve the relevancy and reliability of a firm's information disclosures.

### The Accountant: A Glorified Bookkeeper?

Many people tend to confuse bookkeeping with accounting. They often express the opinion that these two occupations are identical, or that the accountant is nothing more than a glorified bookkeeper. Both of these notions are incorrect.

**Bookkeeping** is concerned with record keeping and is composed of numerous mechanical tasks. Accountants may become involved with this type of work at times, but usually their duties are more complex and sophisticated. Accounting focuses primarily on the *use and interpretation* of information as opposed to repetitive data accumulation. In other words, the bookkeeper assists the accountant in generating the figures needed for reporting and analysis.

## The Accounting Profession

OBJECTIVE 2
**Be familiar with the accounting profession and accounting-related careers.**

The profession of accounting can be traced back almost 500 years and has had considerable time for growth and development. Accounting and its financial and managerial reporting functions have matured considerably in response to a changing, dynamic business environment.

With this maturity comes an opportunity for well-paid and challenging careers—careers that have blossomed in the last decade for sharp and dedicated individuals. To better understand these career opportunities, a brief overview of the profession's various facets is helpful. (See Exhibit 1-2 for an accompanying pictorial presentation.)

### Public Accounting

Firms engaged in **public accounting** render accounting services to all types of enterprises (e.g., hotels, publishers, equipment manufacturers, and professional sports clubs). In view of the size and multiple locations of many of their clients, several public accounting firms have offices from coast to coast and in foreign countries; others operate on a much smaller scale and are established on a regional or local basis.

Using a computer to improve efficiency . . .

Reviewing an automated manufacturing process . . .

Studying a fast-food operation . . .

Advising a client on financial matters . . .

Helping a small business with an inventory problem . . .

Attending a professional development class . . .

**Exhibit 1-2**
**A Day in the Life of an Accountant**

All of these firms, regardless of scope, employ certified public accountants (CPAs). **CPAs** are individuals who, like doctors, dentists, and lawyers, are licensed to practice their profession. The CPA certificate is granted to those who pass a rigorous multi-part examination and meet certain accounting experience and educational requirements.

Public accounting firms perform numerous services for their clients. Most often their work is in the fields of auditing, income tax, and management advisory services (MAS).

## Auditing

Audit work represents the major source of business for most public accounting firms, particularly those organized on the national or international level. **Auditing** involves the investigation and examination of the transactions that underlie an organization's financial reports. The investigation is conducted by an auditor, who studies the controls that have been built into a client's information-processing system for purposes of error detection and fraud prevention. In addition, the auditor performs statistical tests on accounting data to verify the data's reasonableness.

A major purpose of the audit process is to increase the credibility of the financial statements (reports) prepared by a business. The statements are sent to the owners of the business, to financial analysts, and frequently to government agencies. These parties are vitally concerned that the reports result in a neutral and complete presentation of the enterprise's financial activities. The employment of an *external independent* auditor, who performs certain investigative tasks, enhances this process.

### Income Tax

Public accounting firms also perform **income tax services.** These services are very specialized and include much more than the preparation and filing of tax returns. In fact, many of the mechanical procedures associated with tax returns have been computerized, thus eliminating considerable drudgery for the accountant.

Tax accountants must be well versed in the many and often confusing tax laws. Not only do they determine the amount of taxes owed to federal, state, and local authorities, but tax accountants also ensure compliance with tax laws and plan for the future. They advise clients on various alternatives that might minimize taxes. The suggested courses of action are within the legal boundaries of the tax statutes and therefore center on techniques of tax avoidance, not tax evasion.

### Management Advisory Services

**Management advisory services (MAS)** are the broadest of the services performed by public accounting firms. MAS essentially involve the operation of a management consulting practice for clients. Often the work is only indirectly related to traditional accounting matters, leading some of the larger firms to hire nonaccounting specialists for selected practice areas. Examples include physicians (if a firm has extensive involvement with hospitals), educators (if the firm does considerable work in university administration), computer experts, and engineers.

It is an impossible task to list all the advisory services performed by accountants. However, the following projects seem fairly representative: inventory control, analysis and design of information-processing systems, implementation of production-scheduling systems, cost analysis of lease-versus-buy alternatives, and assistance in product pricing.

## Private Accounting

**Private accounting,** sometimes referred to as industrial accounting, is another major branch of the profession. Rather than perform accounting services for many different clients, a private accountant is employed by an individual business to render services exclusively for that organization. As you can imagine, there is considerable variety within this field. Typical opportunities for employment include jobs with retailers, manufacturers (in such diverse industries as petroleum and filmmaking), and service enterprises (such as airlines, lending institutions, and ski resorts).

There are several other significant distinctions between public and private accounting. Although many CPAs are employed in the private sector, there is no specific licensing procedure for private accountants. The only accounting "license" is the CPA. There are, however, examinations and programs designed to measure competence in the private field. One of the most prominent is the *Certified Management Accountant* (*CMA*) program, which requires candidates to pass a broad two-and-a-half-day examination. This test covers such disciplines as managerial finance and economics, principles of organizational behavior, business ethics, financial and managerial accounting practices, and quantitative methods. Another program has been designed to measure proficiency in internal auditing. Individuals passing an examination and meeting work experience requirements may receive the *Certified Internal Auditor* (*CIA*) designation.

Much of the work performed in the private field can be subdivided into specialized areas, including the following:

## Cost Accounting

**Cost accounting,** an important facet of managerial accounting, deals with the collection, assignment, and interpretation of costs. Cost data are captured by an organization's information system and then assigned to various business segments and activities. Examples of such segments include territories, departments, and products. Activities, on the other hand, may encompass the design of a new advertising campaign, the operation of a summer recreation program by a city, or the implementation of a new all-day ticket plan by an amusement park. The purpose of the assignment process is to answer the age-old question, "How much does it cost?" Once cost is determined, management can proceed with an analysis of:

- Anticipated costs for various planning needs.
- Budgeted versus actual costs for control and evaluation.
- Relevant costs of different alternatives for use in decision making.
- Costs of producing goods and services for use in pricing and inventory valuation.

## Internal Auditing

Large organizations often have their own personnel to review and monitor established accounting procedures and controls. The review process, which determines whether the procedures and controls are functioning as originally intended, helps to (1) safeguard the company's resources and (2) check the reliability and accuracy of the accounting information being produced. The individuals performing this work are known as **internal auditors.** Although their duties and responsibilities are similar to those of auditors employed in public accounting (i.e., external auditors), the internal-audit orientation is somewhat different. The internal auditor focuses mainly on controls and procedures. The independent external auditor, while also investigating accounting controls, is concerned primarily with the fairness of the financial statements that are prepared by a business.

## Other Activities

Depending on size, many companies engage in accounting activities other than cost accounting and internal auditing. Larger businesses maintain separate *systems departments* to design the methods, procedures, and forms needed to process accounting data. Frequently, computers are involved. In addition, many organizations have established *planning departments* that deal heavily with budgeting and forecasting. Finally, large businesses often operate their own *tax departments.* These departments offer in-house advice on various issues and engage in tax-planning activities.

### Governmental Accounting

The last major segment of the profession is composed of those accountants employed by governmental agencies. Like profit-seeking businesses, the government has many financial and managerial accounting needs that must be satisfied. Records must be kept, reports prepared, monies accounted for, and operations controlled and reviewed. Governmental accountants assist in all of these tasks—at the local, state, and federal levels. More specifically, the accountant's duties may range from helping the Federal Bureau of Investigation in a fraud case, to assisting in local property tax collections, to auditing defense contracts for the U.S. Department of Defense.

The accounting work performed by three agencies, the Internal Revenue Service (IRS), the Securities and Exchange Commission (SEC), and the General Accounting Office (GAO), is especially well-known and widely publicized. The *IRS* is responsible for processing the millions of tax returns that are filed each year, as well as administering the tax laws that are passed by Congress and handed down by the courts. The *SEC,* on the other hand, was established to oversee the Securities Act of 1933 and the Securities Exchange Act of 1934. This agency reviews the financial statements of businesses that offer securities for sale to the public and has the authority to impose certain reporting standards. Finally, the *GAO* has often been called the "watchdog" of Congress because it evaluates other governmental agencies and programs. Its work is sometimes far removed from conventional accounting and has included investigations of NASA's space shuttle program and pilots' medical standards.

## Key Underlying Concepts

**OBJECTIVE 3**
**Understand the use of accounting principles in financial reporting.**

Earlier in the text we noted that accounting is supported by a set of underlying principles and concepts. These concepts are presented throughout the text, with an in-depth discussion contained in Chapter 13. At this particular time it is helpful to introduce the entity assumption and the principles of historical cost and objectivity. We will then expand our discussion to focus on an entity's "financial position" and its relevance to the fundamental accounting equation. In short, the following sections provide an introduction to the manner in which accounting measures financial activity.

### Entity Assumption

The **entity assumption** holds that an organization must be viewed as a unit that is separate and apart from its owners and from other firms. If this assumption were not made, personal economic activities of the owners (e.g., the purchase of a home, the payment of a child's college tuition) would be merged with the transactions of their businesses, thus combining the affairs of two separate and distinct units. The resulting financial statements constructed to report the business's financial health and profitability, therefore, would not be meaningful.

The entity assumption also notes that a firm should be viewed aside and apart from other firms. Imagine the difficulty of performing a detailed analysis of the computer industry if the operations of IBM could not be distinguished from those of Apple. These are two separate units and their activities must be accounted for accordingly. The entity assumption thus requires the establishment of segregated accounting systems and individual sets of financial records for each business enterprise.

There are three popular entity forms in this country. The simplest in structure is the **sole proprietorship,** which is a business owned by one individual. A step above the proprietorship is the **partnership**—an organization owned by two or more individuals and managed according to a contractual agreement among them. The third basic form of entity is the **corporation,** in which the owners are its stockholders. Most enterprises are operated as proprietorships; accordingly, our initial discussions will focus on this widespread organizational form.

## Historical-Cost Principle

Accounting is based on the **principle of historical cost.** This principle holds that acquisitions of goods, services, and other resources by a business are initially entered in the accounting records at acquisition cost. For example, if Stadium Manufacturing pays $200,000 to purchase a parcel of land for use as a future plant site, the land is established in the records at $200,000. Further, if the company had financed the acquisition, not only would the land be set up at this amount, but the accounting records would also reveal a $200,000 bank loan (i.e., mortgage).

The use of historical cost, while beneficial in some respects, creates an interesting accounting problem. Entering a long-term resource in the accounting records at cost at the time of acquisition is satisfactory. Maintaining that resource over its lifetime at cost, however, can result in a severe misstatement of financial condition and profitability. Picture, for instance, what has happened to the real estate market in many parts of the country over the past 10 to 15 years. Prices have soared because of inflation; yet the historical-cost basis of accounting ignores these increases in valuation. As an example, suppose the land purchased for $200,000 is now worth $350,000. The land, nevertheless, will continue to be carried and reported at $200,000. Because of this treatment, the cost basis is criticized by many users of financial reports as not being in accord with economic reality.

Accountants have taken various steps in recent years to help overcome this deficiency, including the supplemental publication of selected inflation-adjusted data. Despite the problem with historical cost, it continues to serve as the primary valuation base in accounting. One of the underlying reasons is the objectivity principle.

## Objectivity Principle

Accountants strive to produce financial reports that are unbiased, thereby reducing (or eliminating) various user interpretations that may arise. One way of achieving this goal is to follow the **objectivity principle,** which holds that accounting valuations be both definite and verifiable. Although subject to a great deal of criticism, historical cost is said to meet these twin criteria.

Consider, for instance, the parcel of land in our earlier example that Stadium Manufacturing acquired for $200,000. The parcel may have cost the seller

$110,000 and, at the time of Stadium's acquisition, may have been assessed for property taxes at $150,000. Further, the land may have been appraised by three independent appraisal services at $180,000, $210,000, and $230,000 to determine its "worth" when negotiations were about to occur. Which of these figures is correct? They all are. The cost of $200,000 was entered in Stadium's accounting records, however, because Stadium and the seller negotiated a transaction, agreeing that the land was to be exchanged at a price of $200,000. The use of definite cost figures helps to make accounting reports and information more objective. Conversely, appraisal or market figures can vary and often incorporate personal opinion and bias.

In addition to being definite, historical cost is also verifiable by financial experts. In our discussion of the accounting profession, we noted that auditors examine the financial reports of an enterprise to determine whether the reports result in a fair presentation of economic activity. The use of objective, cost-based information lends itself to this process. Evidence of the cost of goods, services, and resources normally exists in the form of contracts, accounting documents, and canceled checks. Furthermore, objective cost data allow different accountants who may be examining a complex transaction to reach essentially the same conclusions and report the same facts. When subjective market and appraisal values are used, this outcome would probably not occur.

## Financial Position and the Entity

Let us begin our study of the entity (and proprietorships) by focusing on a popular accounting concept called financial position. An entity's **financial position** reveals the resources owned by the business and the claims on those resources by specified parties at a particular point in time. The specified parties are the firm's creditors and owner, resulting in the relationship shown in Exhibit 1-3.

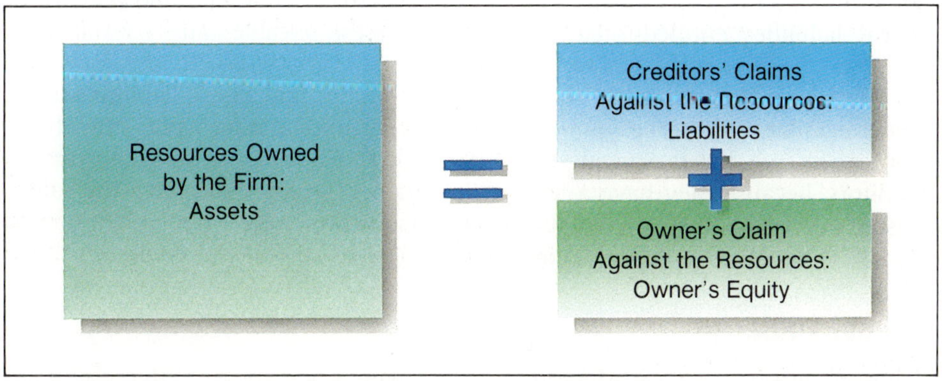


**Exhibit 1-3**
**Financial Position**

OBJECTIVE 4
Understand the meaning of assets, liabilities, and owner's equity and the relationship of these components in the accounting equation.

We will now expand on this relationship which, in its shortened form, is commonly referred to as the fundamental **accounting equation.** The shortened form is:

Assets = Liabilities + Owner's Equity

## Assets

**Assets** are the economic resources owned by a company that are expected to benefit future time periods. These resources are controlled by the entity and have arisen from past transactions and events.

An organization can possess many different types of assets. Some assets, such as the cash that a business has on hand and in the bank, inventories of goods maintained for sale, buildings, land, and equipment, have a definite physical existence. In contrast, other business resources lack physical substance but are able to render benefits because they represent valuable legal rights and/or claims. Two examples are patents and receivables.

A patent, which is granted by the federal government, gives its owner the exclusive right to manufacture, use, and sell a particular product or process. Receivables, on the other hand, are the amounts that a business expects to collect on some future date. The most commonly encountered receivable, *accounts receivable,* represents the amounts due a company from its customers. This asset generally arises from the sale, on credit, of goods and services.

## Liabilities

The economic obligations of an entity are known as **liabilities.** Such obligations are owed to creditors and, like assets, are created from a variety of past transactions and events. Consider, for instance, that many businesses buy goods and services on credit, with the amounts owed to be paid on a future date. These transactions give rise to a liability known as *accounts payable.* In addition, an entity may borrow funds via a loan (thereby creating a loan payable) and use the funds to acquire equipment, expand a warehouse, or purchase other assets.

Still other liabilities arise when a company has obligated itself to pay certain costs connected with normal business activities. Suppose, for example, that on December 31, the Hernandez Company owes $2,000 of employee salaries, $500 of interest, and $300 for payroll taxes. Assuming that all amounts will be paid on some future date, the company's accounting records at the end of the year would reveal liabilities entitled salaries payable, interest payable, and payroll taxes payable.

Businesses that use credit too liberally sometimes find that a liability's future settlement date approaches more quickly than desired. In other words, the obligation comes due, but the paying firm may be strapped for cash. In such cases the creditors, because they have a legal claim against the firm, can force the sale of business assets to satisfy the amounts due. As shown on page 11, it should now be clear that liabilities represent creditor claims against an entity's resources.

## Owner's Equity

**Owner's equity, or capital,** represents the owner's net worth or "interest" in the assets of a business. It is equal to the company's net assets (i.e., assets minus liabilities).

The concept of owner's equity is best explained by resetting the accounting equation in the following format:

Assets − Liabilities = Owner's Equity

Now, assume that Colorado Enterprises has assets of $50,000 and liabilities of $30,000, resulting in $20,000 ($50,000 − $30,000) of owner's equity. These figures indicate that the firm has resources that amount to $50,000 and creditor claims against those resources of $30,000. As noted earlier, should Colorado experience financial difficulties and be unable to settle its obligations, the creditors can force the sale of business assets. Law dictates that distributions be made first to the creditors, with any remaining amounts going to the owner. The owner, then, is said to have a $20,000 *residual* interest in the assets of the entity.

**TIPS & TECHNIQUES**

Owner's equity is the mathematical difference between total assets and total liabilities, nothing more, nothing less. Many people are under the impression that "capital" is equivalent to cash, to be used for future spending and acquisitions. This notion is incorrect; there is *no* direct relationship between capital and a company's cash balances.

## A Further Look at Owner's Equity

The three components of the fundamental accounting equation—assets, liabilities, and owner's equity—change throughout the year in response to various transactions and events. To illustrate, assume the following data apply to Mansfield Builders as of December 31, 19X1:

| | |
|---|---|
| Assets | $100,000 |
| Liabilities | $ 30,000 |
| Owner's equity | 70,000 |
| Total liabilities and owner's equity | $100,000 |

Suppose that Mansfield desires to purchase a new machine that costs $25,000. Because of insufficient cash balances, the company has arranged to finance the purchase by obtaining a $25,000 loan from the equipment dealer. This transaction results in the following figures:

| | |
|---|---|
| Assets ($100,000 + $25,000) | $125,000 |
| Liabilities ($30,000 + $25,000) | $ 55,000 |
| Owner's equity | 70,000 |
| Total liabilities and owner's equity | $125,000 |

Assets have increased because of the machine, while liabilities have risen from the loan. It is important to notice that owner's equity has remained at $70,000. We can conclude that any transaction or event that affects both assets *and* liabilities by an equal amount has no impact on owner's equity. Similarly, a transaction that affects *only* assets (such as an acquisition of machinery for a cash payment) or *only* liabilities will leave owner's equity intact. What, then, causes this third component of the accounting equation to rise or fall?

**OBJECTIVE 5**
**Be aware of the four items that cause owner's equity to change: specifically, owner investments, owner withdrawals, net income, and net loss.**

Owner's equity will change during a time period because of four factors:

| *Factor* | *Impact on Owner's Equity* |
|---|---|
| Investments by the owner | Increase |
| Withdrawals by the owner | Decrease |
| Net income | Increase |
| Net loss | Decrease |

## Investments by the Owner

The owner of an enterprise often takes personal assets and puts (invests) them in a business. Since the investment causes company assets to increase, the owner's net "interest" or equity in these assets will also increase.

## Withdrawals by the Owner

A withdrawal is just the opposite of an investment; the owner is removing assets from the business (usually cash) for personal use. Withdrawals therefore decrease the equity of the owner in the firm's assets.

## Net Income/Net Loss

The earnings of a company will also affect owner's equity, with earnings being defined in accounting by the term "net income." **Net income** is the excess of a company's revenues over expenses for a given time period. When an individual states that a business is "making money," he or she normally means that a net income is being generated. Like owner investments, net income causes the owner's equity in the assets of the enterprise to rise.

Companies do not always operate in a profitable manner, perhaps because of a lack of cost control or a depressed economy. Operating in an unprofitable manner means an entity's expenses exceed its revenues, creating a **net loss** for the period. A net loss has the opposite effect of net income and causes owner's equity to decrease.

To comprehend the concepts of net income and net loss, it is necessary to understand the meaning of revenues and expenses. These terms are introduced here and will be discussed more fully throughout the text.

### Revenues and Expenses

Businesses pursue a variety of activities in an attempt to earn a profit. Such profit-related activities give rise to **revenues,** which are the amounts charged to customers for goods sold or services rendered. Revenues may take many different forms, as the following list shows:

| *Entity* | *Revenue Form* |
|---|---|
| Toys "R" Us, Inc. | Toy sales revenue |
| Ryder System, Inc. | Vehicle-leasing revenue |
| Los Angeles Dodgers | Ticket revenue |
| Law firm | Fees earned |

**Expenses,** on the other hand, are the costs incurred in producing revenue. Unlike assets, expenses do not benefit future time periods; rather, the related benefits are received currently. Examples of expenses include the salaries and wages incurred for employee services, utility costs incurred for natural gas and electricity, interest costs incurred for the use of borrowed money, advertising, repairs, and taxes. Notice that owner withdrawals are absent from this listing. Expenses must be related to the revenue-generating process of the firm; withdrawals, in contrast, arise from a totally different situation (i.e., the personal use of business assets by the owner).

> **TIPS & TECHNIQUES**
>
> Revenues and expenses should not be equated with the cash inflows and outflows of a firm. Consider, for instance, that a company may receive cash from its owner as an investment or pay cash to acquire land (an asset). Both of these transactions affect cash; in neither case, however, is any revenue or expense involved.

## The Accounting Equation: An Extended Illustration

**OBJECTIVE 6**
Understand the impact of various transactions on the accounting equation.

To tie together a number of the concepts introduced in this chapter, we will focus on the operations of Vista Transit. Vista, a small proprietorship that provides charter transportation in the town of Oceanside, was founded on January 2 of the current year. The firm's January transactions are described in the following sections and their effect on the accounting equation is shown.

**Investment by the Owner**—Ted Barto began the operation of Vista Transit on January 2 by investing $40,000 in the firm. As a result of this transaction, the company now has an asset, Cash, of $40,000. In addition, Barto has obtained a $40,000 interest (i.e., owner's equity) in the firm's assets. The items that affect owner's equity are listed individually for the sake of clarity, with revenues and expenses to be entered in the net income/net loss column.

| | Assets | = | Liabilities | + | Owner's Equity | | |
|---|---|---|---|---|---|---|---|
| Date | Cash | | | | (+) Investments | (−) Withdrawals | (+) Net Income (−) Net Loss |
| 1/2 | +$40,000 | | | | +$40,000 | | |

**Purchase of Assets for Cash**—Vista acquired two used vans for the business at a total cost of $34,000 on January 6. The company paid cash, thereby decreasing its remaining funds to $6,000 ($40,000 − $34,000). Notice, however, that this transaction merely shifts dollar amounts from one asset to another, leaving the total assets intact at $40,000.

| | Assets | | = Liabilities + | Owner's Equity | | |
|---|---|---|---|---|---|---|
| Date | Cash | Vans | | (+) Investments | (−) Withdrawals | (+) Net Income (−) Net Loss |
| | $40,000 | $ — | | $40,000 | | |
| 1/6 | −34,000 | +34,000 | | | | |
| | $ 6,000 | $34,000 | | $40,000 | | |

**Generation of Revenue on Account**—The firm completed two charter trips on January 12 and billed clients a total of $1,700. This transaction is representative of Vista's earnings process, causing an increase in total revenue (and income) for the entity. Furthermore, the clients have been billed and will pay at a later date. An asset, Accounts Receivable, has therefore been created because Vista has a claim against these individuals. This type of transaction is commonly known as a sale of services on account.

| | Assets | | | = Liabilities + | Owner's Equity | | |
|---|---|---|---|---|---|---|---|
| Date | Cash | Accounts Receivable | Vans | | (+) Investments | (−) Withdrawals | (+) Net Income (−) Net Loss |
| | $6,000 | $ — | $34,000 | | $40,000 | | $ — |
| 1/12 | | +1,700 | | | | | +1,700 (Charter revenue) |
| | $6,000 | $1,700 | $34,000 | | $40,000 | | $1,700 |

*Note:* Assets are normally listed in order of liquidity, or nearness to cash. Receivables appear before vans because collections from customers are forthcoming in a relatively short period of time. Vans, conversely, will render services for a number of years before being disposed of or sold.

**Recognition of Expense on Account**—Westside Auto performed miscellaneous repairs on one of the vans on January 16. The repairs amounted to $750; Vista agreed to pay the balance due in 30 days. This transaction involves an increase in Vista's liabilities (Accounts Payable) because of the balance owed to the repair shop. In addition, $750 of expense must be recognized, which reduces the company's profitability for the month.

| | Assets | | | = Liabilities + | Owner's Equity | | |
|---|---|---|---|---|---|---|---|
| Date | Cash | Accounts Receivable | Vans | Accounts Payable | (+) Investments | (−) Withdrawals | (+) Net Income (−) Net Loss |
| | $6,000 | $1,700 | $34,000 | $ — | $40,000 | | $1,700 |
| 1/16 | | | | +750 | | | −750 (Repairs) |
| | $6,000 | $1,700 | $34,000 | $750 | $40,000 | | $ 950 |

**Collection of Accounts Receivable**—A $600 check from a client who was previously billed on January 12 arrived in the mail of January 21. Is this revenue for Vista? The answer is no. Vista performed the service earlier in the month, and revenue was recorded at the time the billing took place. To record the $600 as revenue again would result in a double counting. The client is paying the balance due, requiring a reduction in Accounts Receivable. This type of transaction is frequently referred to as a receipt on account.

| | Assets | | | = Liabilities + | Owner's Equity | | |
|---|---|---|---|---|---|---|---|
| Date | Cash | Accounts Receivable | Vans | Accounts Payable | (+) Investments | (−) Withdrawals | (+) Net Income (−) Net Loss |
| | $6,000 | $1,700 | $34,000 | $750 | $40,000 | | $950 |
| 1/21 | +600 | −600 | | | | | |
| | $6,600 | $1,100 | $34,000 | $750 | $40,000 | | $950 |

**Payment of Accounts Payable**—Vista paid $400 to Westside Auto on January 27, partial payment for the repairs performed on January 16. The repairs were initially established as a liability, to be paid on a future date. Because payment is now occurring, the related account payable must be eliminated. Transactions of this nature are commonly known as payments on account.

| | Assets | | | = Liabilities + | Owner's Equity | | |
|---|---|---|---|---|---|---|---|
| Date | Cash | Accounts Receivable | Vans | Accounts Payable | (+) Investments | (−) Withdrawals | (+) Net Income (−) Net Loss |
| | $6,600 | $1,100 | $34,000 | $750 | $40,000 | | $950 |
| 1/27 | −400 | | | −400 | | | |
| | $6,200 | $1,100 | $34,000 | $350 | $40,000 | | $950 |

**Payment of Expenses**—On January 29, Vista paid $500 to its drivers, subdivided as follows: John Warren, $300; Ben Richards, $200. Each driver earned $200 of wages during the month. Warren received an extra $100 to cover the cost of advertising materials that he designed and distributed to Oceanside residents. The wage and advertising expenditures are expenses for Vista—costs incurred to generate revenue.

| | Assets | | | = Liabilities + | Owner's Equity | | |
|---|---|---|---|---|---|---|---|
| Date | Cash | Accounts Receivable | Vans | Accounts Payable | (+) Investments | (−) Withdrawals | (+) Net Income (−) Net Loss |
| | $6,200 | $1,100 | $34,000 | $350 | $40,000 | | $950 |
| 1/29 | −300 | | | | | | −200 (Wages) |
| | | | | | | | −100 (Advertising) |
| | −200 | | | | | | −200 (Wages) |
| | $5,700 | $1,100 | $34,000 | $350 | $40,000 | | $450 |

**Sale of an Asset**—Because of the entry of a new competitor in the Oceanside market, Vista decided to sell one of its vans on January 30. The van, acquired on January 6 for $14,000, was sold to a charter client for the same amount. The client paid Vista $10,000 down, with the balance owed to be remitted in two weeks. This transaction affects three different assets, calling for an increase to both Cash and Accounts Receivable and a decrease to Vans.

| | Assets | | | = Liabilities + | Owner's Equity | | |
|---|---|---|---|---|---|---|---|
| Date | Cash | Accounts Receivable | Vans | Accounts Payable | (+) Investments | (−) Withdrawals | (+) Net Income (−) Net Loss |
| | $ 5,700 | $1,100 | $34,000 | $350 | $40,000 | | $450 |
| 1/30 | +10,000 | +4,000 | −14,000 | | | | |
| | $15,700 | $5,100 | $20,000 | $350 | $40,000 | | $450 |

**Withdrawal by the Owner**—Ted Barto withdrew $250 from the company on January 31 to meet personal living expenses. This $250 outlay, while increasing the firm's total withdrawals, results in a reduction of both Cash and owner's equity.

| | Assets | | | = Liabilities + | Owner's Equity | | |
|---|---|---|---|---|---|---|---|
| Date | Cash | Accounts Receivable | Vans | Accounts Payable | (+) Investments | (−) Withdrawals | (+) Net Income (−) Net Loss |
| | $15,700 | $5,100 | $20,000 | $350 | $40,000 | $ — | $450 |
| 1/31 | −250 | | | | | +250 | |
| | $15,450 | $5,100 | $20,000 | $350 | $40,000 | $250 | $450 |
| | | $40,550 | | = $350 + | | $40,200* | |

* $40,000 − $250 + $450.

**TIPS & TECHNIQUES**

As you have seen, business transactions affect the accounting equation in many different ways. Assets, liabilities, and owner's equity can each remain the same or change; there are numerous possibilities. Stated bluntly (and honestly), if your approach to learning this and subsequent material is memorization, you will be fighting a losing battle. *Successful accounting students are those who develop the abilities to reason and analyze, not memorize.*

## Financial Statements

OBJECTIVE 7
Understand the content of and be able to prepare an income statement, a statement of owner's equity, and a balance sheet.

Owners, managers, lenders, and analysts use accounting information for a variety of purposes. Much of this information is contained within formal financial reports that are compiled and distributed by companies. These reports are commonly referred to as **financial statements.**

The financial statements prepared by a business reveal various insights about the entity's operations and financial position, with one of the most important disclosures being net income. Most businesses are organized with a profit objective and strive to generate a return for their owners. Income measurement is a complex task; at this point you should understand that income is probably the single most important barometer of economic success and of utmost interest to financial statement users.

In addition to profit generation, companies seek to maintain a healthy financial position. This means that an entity has the ability to pay its debts when due, along with the potential of generating future positive cash flows. Statement users therefore pay close attention to a firm's cash and near-cash assets (i.e., liquidity) in relation to the amounts owed to creditors. Put simply, if a company is unable to meet its maturing obligations, the firm's survival as an ongoing entity could be threatened.

An entity's financial information is disclosed via four financial statements (and accompanying footnotes): the income statement, statement of owner's equity, balance sheet, and statement of cash flows. Discussion of the last statement, which shows the cash flows related to a company's operating, investing, and financing activities, is postponed until Chapter 19 because of its complex nature.

### Income Statement

The **income statement** summarizes the results of operations by disclosing an entity's net income or net loss. This statement, like its counterparts, is divided into two sections: heading and body. The heading reveals the company's name, the name of the statement, and the period of time covered by the statement. The period is usually a month, a quarter, or a year. The statement's body contains detailed accounting information, in this case an itemized listing of revenues and expenses.

The income statement for Vista Transit appears on the top of Exhibit 1-4. Observe how the statement is developed from the net income/net loss column of the accounting equation. Because revenues exceeded expenses, the business was profitable during its first month of operation.

## HIGHLIGHT

# "Creative" Financial Reporting

Companies spend thousands of dollars in related design and publication costs. There are awards for the best and the worst and some are even considered legends. They go out by the millions and are the target of hungry dogs. Yet, the majority are filed in the wastebasket without ever being opened. What are we talking about? Each year, large corporations produce an annual report—a brochure-type item containing financial statements, photographs, and marketing hype of the company's business activities, resources, and products.

These glossy production jobs often provide interesting—and surprisingly candid—insights into a firm's philosophy and personality. Pfizer Inc., for example, the giant drug producer, discusses its disillusionment with annual reports in its own report by noting that the yearly releases "are getting out of hand . . . Sometimes design overwhelms message." The Pfizer executives might have been referring to H. J. Heinz Inc., which produced an award winner not too long ago with its 40-page salute to the tomato. And then there's the case of GE's computer technicians, who grew so tired of posing for pictures that they programmed their consoles, shown in the background of the pictures, to read "TILT." The subtle protests were pictured in the company's 1960 offering. [1]

Most annual reports tend to look the same. Every so often, however, one comes over the horizon and seems to stand out like a shining star. A few years ago, for instance, Pizza Time Theatre Inc., came out with an annual report for children. It had cartoons and games and was generally a lot of fun—which is more than could be said for the company. Within a year or so, Pizza Time had filed for bankruptcy, and investors of all ages "took a bath." In contrast, Ashton-Tate, a microcomputer software firm, had much to celebrate in a recently concluded successful year. The results were mailed to shareholders on—you guessed it—floppy diskettes. [2]

Creative reporting surfaces in its fullest when businesses try to downplay bad times. Take the case of General Dynamics Corp., which had various run-ins with Defense Department auditors about overcharges on defense contracts. The company's annual report contained a lengthy discussion about ethics. Similarly, Bank of Boston Corp., which recently pleaded guilty to failing to report over $1 billion of cash transactions, proudly published a 22-page spread that detailed the firm's civic commitment to Boston. [3]

And what about the hungry dog noted in the first paragraph? Spice maker McCormick & Co., follows a tradition by lacing its report with a different scent each year. One reader noted that the report smelled so good that his dog ate it. [4] If such a practice continues and grows and the SEC allows it, just think of where all this might lead. Maybe we'll be seeing enclosures of other products, such as cassette tapes, coupons for ice cream and vacation stays, and so forth.

Interestingly, a new trend in financial reporting may make the design and glitz even more important. A new "slimmed-down" look is now being used—one that focuses on a summary annual report without all the numbers and facts of the past. As a foundation that studies these public-relations jobs concludes, "Annual reports will have to be skillfully written and designed if they are to gain the reader's attention and hold it for five or 10 minutes." [5]

SOURCES: Adapted from "Annual Reports Take on a New, Slimmed-Down Form," *The Wall Street Journal,* July 2, 1987, p. 1; "Annual Reports: the Good, the Bad, and the Ridiculous," *Business Week,* April 7, 1986, p. 40 [3]; "The Creative Writing in This Year's Annual Reports," *Business Week,* April 15, 1985, p. 48 [4]; "Here is Our Report on a Report About Corporate Annual Reports," *The Wall Street Journal,* October 23, 1986, p. 39 [1, 5]; and "Selling Investors on the Business," *Inc.,* May, 1986, p. 155 [2]. The fourth article listed is reprinted by permission of *The Wall Street Journal,* 

**Exhibit 1-4**
**Financial Statements of Vista Transit**

**VISTA TRANSIT**
**Income Statement**
**For the Month Ended January 31, 19XX**

| | | |
|---|---|---|
| Charter revenue | | $ 1,700 |
| Less expenses | | |
| Repairs | $ 750 | |
| Wages | 400 | |
| Advertising | 100 | |
| Total expenses | | 1,250 |
| Net income | | $ 450 |

**VISTA TRANSIT**
**Statement of Owner's Equity**
**For the Month Ended January 31, 19XX**

| | | |
|---|---|---|
| Beginning balance, Jan. 1 | | $ — |
| Increases | | |
| Owner investments | $40,000 | |
| Net income | 450 | 40,450 |
| | | $40,450 |
| Decreases | | |
| Owner withdrawals | | 250 |
| Ending balance, Jan. 31 | | $40,200 |

**VISTA TRANSIT**
**Balance Sheet**
**January 31, 19XX**

| | |
|---|---|
| Assets | |
| Cash | $15,450 |
| Accounts receivable | 5,100 |
| Vans | 20,000 |
| Total assets | $40,550 |
| Liabilities | |
| Accounts payable | $ 350 |
| Owner's equity | |
| Ted Barto, capital | 40,200 |
| Total liabilities & owner's equity | $40,550 |

### Statement of Owner's Equity

The **statement of owner's equity** discloses the causes of change in owner's equity during the accounting period. Consequently, the following items comprise the heart of this financial report: owner investments, owner withdrawals, and net income (or net loss). Vista's statement of owner's equity appears in the middle of Exhibit 1-4. The January 31 balance of $40,200 will carry over to become the beginning owner's equity balance on February 1, 19XX.

### Balance Sheet

The **balance sheet** focuses on a measure that was introduced earlier in the chapter. By revealing the resources owned by the entity and the claims on those resources by the creditors and owner of the business, the statement's emphasis is on financial position. Appropriately, the balance sheet is sometimes called the statement of financial position.

To become more specific, the balance sheet is a formalized listing of the accounting equation's components: assets, liabilities, and owner's equity. This financial report shows that the sum of the individual equity interests, the owner's and creditors', is equal to and in balance with the firm's assets; that is, assets = liabilities + owner's equity. This equality is shown for some particular *point* in time. The statement's heading, therefore, reflects a single date rather than a time period.

The balance sheet of Vista Transit, which appears at the bottom of Exhibit 1-4, is based on the January 31 final balances of the accounting equation illustration with one minor exception. So that the information already contained in the income statement and statement of owner's equity is not duplicated, the January 31 (ending) owner's equity balance is reported as a single amount labeled Ted Barto, Capital.

### Statement Interrelationships

The three statements that we discussed are distinct, with each presenting different types of financial information. Although they do differ, the statements are also interrelated. The income statement furnishes the necessary net income figure for the statement of owner's equity, which, in turn, provides the ending capital amount for the balance sheet.

The statements are also interrelated in another sense. The balance sheet depicts a company's financial position as of a specific date, for example, January 31 in the Vista Transit illustration. Going one step further, the company would subsequently prepare an income statement and a statement of owner's equity for February to disclose monthly activity. To complete the reporting cycle, a new balance sheet would be constructed as of February 28. It is apparent, then, that the income statement and the statement of owner's equity bridge the gap between successive balance sheets when reporting financial information.

## Chapter Review

### Learning Objectives—The Key Points

**1 Be familiar with the users, uses, and limitations of accounting information.** Many groups use accounting information, including owners, creditors, managers, government agencies, financial analysts, and employees and labor unions. These groups study a company's earnings, the ability of an organization to settle its debts on a timely basis, the progress of a business toward meeting stated objectives, and other key issues. The information under review, however, suffers from certain inherent limitations. Accounting, for example, is based on various estimates, assumptions, and subjective judgments; lacks the ability to express all events in monetary terms; and sometimes fails to portray true value.

**2 Be familiar with the accounting profession and accounting-related careers.** The profession and its career options tend to be segmented into public, private, and governmental accounting. Public accountants render accounting services, such as external auditing, tax planning, and management consulting, to other businesses. With private accounting, an individual provides accounting services for a specific organization, the work often centering on cost accounting or internal auditing. Finally, governmental accountants are employed by a variety of local, state, and federal agencies. The accounting functions performed by three of these agencies, the Internal Revenue Service (IRS), the Securities and Exchange Commission (SEC), and the General Accounting Office (GAO), are fairly well-known and widely publicized.

**3 Understand the use of accounting principles in financial reporting.** Because of the wide variety of businesses in our economy, some standardization is necessary when reporting to external parties. Financial accounting is therefore governed by a set of accounting principles that includes the monetary unit assumption, the entity assumption, and the principles of historical cost and objectivity. The monetary unit assumption holds that only events and activities measurable in dollars are recognized in a company's accounting records. The entity assumption holds that a business is viewed as a unit that is separate and distinct from its owners and from other businesses. There are three types of business entities: sole proprietorships, partnerships, and corporations. The historical-cost principle requires that goods, services, and other resources be entered in the accounting records at acquisition cost. This procedure results in an objective valuation amount at the time of acquisition; however, the meaningfulness of cost-based amounts can deteriorate over time, especially in inflationary economies. Historical cost is consistent with the objectivity principle, which holds that accounting valuations be definite and verifiable.

**4 Understand the meaning of assets, liabilities, and owner's equity and the relationship of these components in the accounting equation.** Assets are the economic resources of a firm that are expected to benefit future time periods. Typical examples of assets include cash, land, buildings, inventories, and equipment. Certain parties have claims on these resources. Liabilities, for instance, measure the claims on the resources by creditors; such amounts therefore represent the economic obligations owed by a company to suppliers, lenders, and others. In contrast, the owner's equity is the owner's net worth or "interest" in the assets of the business. The owner has a residual claim against business resources, that is, a secondary claim after the creditors. The three components are related, as shown by the accounting equation: assets = liabilities + owner's equity.

**5 Be aware of the four items that cause owner's equity to change: specifically, owner investments, owner withdrawals, net income, and net loss.** An investment by the owner occurs when the owner relinquishes personal assets to the enterprise. Such an event causes the owner's equity of an entity to increase. Conversely, an owner may remove assets from a business for personal use, causing owner's equity to fall. Owner's equity will also change from the earnings of a business which, in turn, are dependent on revenues and expenses. Revenues are the amounts charged to customers for goods sold or services rendered; in contrast, expenses are the costs incurred to produce revenues (e.g., salaries, advertising, utilities, and other similar items). If revenues exceed expenses a net income is generated and owner's equity will increase. The opposite case, expenses in excess of revenues, creates a net loss and causes a reduction in owner's equity.

**6 Understand the impact of various transactions on the accounting equation.** A company's transactions and events affect the accounting equation in many different ways. The purchase of an asset on account, for example, will increase both assets and liabilities.

The acquisition of that same asset for cash, however, will leave total assets, liabilities, and owner's equity unchanged. Finally, a withdrawal of cash out of the business will decrease both assets and owner's equity. Memorization of the impact of these transactions and events should not be attempted. Instead, it is best to reason and analyze the ultimate effect on the equation's components.

**7 Understand the content of and be able to prepare an income statement, a statement of owner's equity, and a balance sheet.** The income statement reveals an entity's revenues and expenses (and associated net income or net loss) for a particular period of time. The statement of owner's equity shows the amount of change in owner's equity during the same time period covered by the income statement. This change is caused by the firm's net income or net loss and any owner investments and withdrawals. Finally, the balance sheet details a company's assets and liabilities as of a specific date. As its name implies, this financial statement shows that the sum of the assets is equal to and in balance with the individual equity interests, that is, assets = liabilities + owner's equity.

## Chapter Quiz

The five questions that follow relate to several issues raised in the chapter. Test your knowledge of these issues by selecting the best answer. (The answers appear on p. 38.)

**1** The principle of historical cost:
- a holds that acquisitions of goods and services should be entered in the accounting records at acquisition cost.
- b results in the development of subjective financial statements.
- c is ideal for use in periods of high inflation.
- d is not acceptable when constructing general-purpose financial statements.

**2** Apex Company had owner's equity of $32,000 on January 1, 19X2. During January, owner investments and withdrawals amounted to $15,000 and $9,000, respectively. In addition, the company generated net income of $2,000. The amount of owner's equity on January 31 was:
- a $8,000.
- b $36,000.
- c $40,000.
- d $58,000.

**3** John Davis recently withdrew $1,000 cash from the Davis Repair Shop, a sole proprietorship. This transaction would:
- a decrease both assets and liabilities.
- b decrease both assets and owner's equity.
- c decrease assets and increase owner's equity.
- d increase both assets and owner's equity.

**4** A company's ending accounts receivable balance and the period's advertising expense would be found on which respective financial statements?
- a Balance sheet and statement of owner's equity.
- b Balance sheet and income statement.
- c Income statement and balance sheet.
- d Income statement and statement of owner's equity.

**5** X Company had revenues, expenses, owner investments, and owner withdrawals of $45,000, $35,000, $4,000, and $1,000, respectively. The firm's net income was:
- a $9,000.
- b $10,000.
- c $13,000.
- d $14,000.

## Summary Problem

On October 2, 19XX, John Gilbert opened the Gilbert Realty Company. The following transactions occurred during the month:

Oct. 2 Received $25,000 cash from Gilbert as an investment in the business.
6 Received a $3,600 cash commission for services rendered on the sale of a home.
10 Paid $400 of transportation expenses. (Gilbert uses his personal auto for business matters and bills the firm for all business expenses.)
14 Sold another home. The commission on this sale was $3,200, but Gilbert will not receive the cash until November.
18 Paid $900 of advertising expenses.
23 Purchased furniture for the office at a cost of $6,500. Paid a down payment of $2,000 and agreed to remit the balance owed next month.
24 Paid utility bills of $350 for the month.
27 Returned $600 of office furniture to the supplier. The supplier deducted the return from the amount that Gilbert owes.
29 Paid $1,700 of salaries expense.
30 Processed a $500 cash withdrawal for personal use.

### Instructions

**a** Analyze the effects of these transactions on the individual elements of the accounting equation.

**b** Prepare an income statement for the month ended October 31.

**c** Prepare a statement of owner's equity for the month ended October 31.

**d** Prepare a balance sheet as of October 31.

### Solution

**a**

| | Assets | | | = Liabilities + | Owner's Equity | | |
|---|---|---|---|---|---|---|---|
| Date | Cash | Accounts Receivable | Office Furniture | Accounts Payable | (+) Investments | (−) Withdrawals | (+) Net Income (−) Net Loss |
| 10/2 | +$25,000 | | | | +$25,000 | | |
| 10/6 | +3,600 | | | | | | +$3,600 (Commissions) |
| 10/10 | −400 | | | | | | −400 (Transportation) |
| 10/14 | | +$3,200 | | | | | +3,200 (Commissions) |
| 10/18 | −900 | | | | | | −900 (Advertising) |
| 10/23 | −2,000 | | +$6,500 | +$4,500 | | | |
| 10/24 | −350 | | | | | | −350 (Utilities) |
| 10/27 | | | −600 | −600 | | | |
| 10/29 | −1,700 | | | | | | −1,700 (Salaries) |
| 10/30 | −500 | | | | | +$500 | |
| | $22,750 | $3,200 | $5,900 | $3,900 | $25,000 | $500 | $3,450 |

b

**GILBERT REALTY**
**Income Statement**
**For the Month Ended October 31, 19XX**

| | | |
|---|---|---|
| Commissions | | $6,800 |
| Less expenses | | |
| Transportation | $ 400 | |
| Advertising | 900 | |
| Utilities | 350 | |
| Salaries | 1,700 | |
| Total expenses | | 3,350 |
| Net income | | $3,450 |

c

**GILBERT REALTY**
**Statement of Owner's Equity**
**For the Month Ended October 31, 19XX**

| | | |
|---|---|---|
| Beginning balance, Oct. 1 | | $ — |
| Increases | | |
| Owner investments | $25,000 | |
| Net income | 3,450 | 28,450 |
| | | $28,450 |
| Decreases | | |
| Owner withdrawals | | 500 |
| Ending balance, Oct. 31 | | $27,950 |

d

**GILBERT REALTY**
**Balance Sheet**
**October 31, 19XX**

| | |
|---|---|
| Assets | |
| Cash | $22,750 |
| Accounts receivable | 3,200 |
| Office furniture | 5,900 |
| Total assets | $31,850 |
| Liabilities | |
| Accounts payable | $ 3,900 |
| Owner's equity | |
| John Gilbert, capital | 27,950 |
| Total liabilities & owner's equity | $31,850 |

## Questions

**Q1-1** Identify typical users of accounting information.

**Q1-2** How does financial accounting differ from managerial accounting?

**Q1-3** What are several of the limitations of accounting information?

**Q1-4** How does bookkeeping differ from accounting?

**Q1-5** Paul Martin is contemplating an investment in the Indiana Company. He has secured the firm's audited financial statements, which have been examined by a certified public accountant. How can Martin be satisfied that the statements do not present false and incorrect information to purposely mislead investors?

**Q1-6** Differentiate between internal and external auditing.

**Q1-7** Explain the entity assumption.

**Q1-8** Mr. P, the president of Fairwood Company, recently purchased a new car solely for personal use. He asked Mr. A, Fairwood's accountant, to record the car as a miscellaneous expense of the company's current accounting period. Mr. A refused. Explain the reason behind A's action.

**Q1-9** Discuss the use of historical cost in the accounting process. Why is historical cost used, and what is one of its chief limitations?

**Q1-10** What is meant by the term "financial position"?

**Q1-11** Define the term "owner's equity."

**Q1-12** What factors cause owner's equity to change during an accounting period?

**Q1-13** Gifford's December income statement is in the process of being prepared. Through December 30 the firm has generated a $2,600 net income. The only transaction on December 31 is a withdrawal by the owner of $3,000. Would it be correct to say that Gifford incurred a $400 net loss during December? Why?

**Q1-14** The Harter family owns a service station in Vermont. After his first lecture in accounting principles, the youngest of the Harter sons, Teddy, decided to review the accounting records for the year just ended. He noted that net income of $15,800 was generated. At the same time the balance in the station's checking (i.e., cash) account had decreased by $5,300. Teddy felt that this situation was not possible and that a mistake had been made. Is Teddy correct? Explain and cite several examples to support your answer.

**Q1-15** Thomas and Rodriguez are having a heated debate regarding the order in which certain items should be listed on the balance sheet. Their views are as follows:

*Thomas*—Cash, Accounts Receivable, Equipment, Rent Expense
*Rodriguez*—Equipment, Accounts Receivable, Rent Expense, Cash

Who is correct? Why?

**Q1-16** The text suggests that the income statement should be prepared first, the statement of owner's equity second, and the balance sheet last. Explain how this order of preparation facilitates the accounting process.

## Exercises

**E1-1** ***Basic concepts***

Pants Palace is a firm that specializes in the sale of jeans and related accessories. Stores are operated in shopping malls throughout the country. Identify the items that follow as an asset, a liability, a revenue, or an expense from Pants Palace's viewpoint.

a Monthly rental charges paid to a mall.
b The inventory of jeans and tops owned by the firm.
c A loan that is owed to Second Federal Savings.
d Daily sales that are made to customers.
e Advertising costs incurred for a back-to-school promotion.
f Amounts due from customers.
g Land that is held by the company for future development of a new national headquarters.
h Cash on hand in each store for paying small miscellaneous expenses.

**E1-2** ***Basic computations***

The following selected balances were extracted from the accounting records of Rossi Enterprises on December 31, 19X3:

| | | | |
|---|---|---|---|
| Accounts payable | $ 3,200 | Interest expense | $ 2,500 |
| Accounts receivable | 14,800 | Land | 18,000 |
| Auto expense | 1,900 | Loan payable | 40,000 |
| Building | 30,000 | Utilities expense | 4,100 |
| Cash | 7,400 | Tax expense | 3,300 |
| Fee revenue | 56,900 | Wage expense | 37,500 |

a Determine Rossi's total assets as of December 31.
b Determine the company's total liabilities as of December 31.
c Compute 19X3 net income or loss.

**E1-3** ***Impact of business transactions***

The items that follow describe the impact of a business transaction or event on the components of the accounting equation. Present an example of a transaction or event that correctly matches the described impact.
a Increase an asset and increase a liability.
b Increase one asset and decrease another asset.
c Increase an asset and increase in owner's equity from a transaction or event not related to income-producing activities.
d Increase an asset and increase in owner's equity from a transaction or event related to income-producing activities.
e Decrease an asset and decrease a liability.
f Decrease an asset and decrease in owner's equity from a transaction or event not related to income-producing activities.

**E1-4** ***Analysis of transactions***

Write the accounting equation on a piece of paper. By using "+" and "−," indicate the effect of each of the following transactions on total assets, liabilities, and owner's equity:
a Rendered services on account.
b Purchased a new machine for cash.
c Recorded customer receipts on account.
d Recorded the receipt of an electric bill, to be paid next month.
e Paid the weekly salaries of the employees.
f Purchased land that cost $18,000 by paying $6,000 down and securing a loan payable for the remaining balance.
g Paid the electric bill that was previously recorded in (d).
h Returned a new desk purchased earlier in the month on account. The bill had not as yet been paid.

**E1-5** ***Accounting equation; analysis of owner's equity***

Sportscar Repair revealed the financial data that follow on January 1 and December 31 of the current year.

| | *Assets* | *Liabilities* |
|---|---|---|
| January 1 | $45,000 | $20,000 |
| December 31 | 49,000 | 31,000 |

a Compute the change in owner's equity during the year by using the fundamental accounting equation.
b Assume there were no owner investments or withdrawals during the year. What is the probable cause of the change in owner's equity from part (a)?
c Assume there were no owner investments during the year. If the owner withdrew $17,000, determine and compute the company's net income or net loss. Be sure to label your answer.
d If owner investments and withdrawals amounted to $13,000 and $2,000, respectively, determine whether the company operated profitably during the year. Show appropriate calculations.

**E1-6** ***Financial statement content***
You are in the process of reviewing the income statement, statement of owner's equity, and balance sheet of the Weissman Company. On which financial statement(s) would the following information be found?
a The amount of equipment owned.
b Withdrawals by the owner.
c Interest incurred on loan payable.
d Beginning owner's equity.
e Ending owner's equity.
f Amounts owed to creditors.
g Fees earned for services rendered.
h Amounts due from customers.

**E1-7** ***Balance sheet preparation***
The following data relate to Preston Company as of December 31, 19XX:

| | | | |
|---|---|---|---|
| Building | $44,000 | Accounts receivable | $24,000 |
| Cash | 17,000 | Loan payable | 30,000 |
| J. Preston, capital | 65,000 | Land | 21,000 |
| Accounts payable | ? | | |

Prepare a balance sheet in good form as of December 31, 19XX.

**E1-8** ***Income statement concepts***
Evaluate the comments that follow as being True or False. If the comment is false, briefly explain why.
a An income statement reveals the net income or net loss of an entity for a period of time as opposed to a specific date.
b Withdrawals are properly classified as an expense of doing business.
c If a company has $50,000 of revenues for March, it stands to reason that cash receipts for March must total $50,000.
d If expenses exceed revenues, a net loss has been generated.
e A computer acquired late in the year for use in the business should be disclosed on a firm's income statement.

**E1-9** ***Financial statement relationships***
The following information appeared on the financial statements of Upstate Technical Services:

| | |
|---|---|
| Income statement | |
| Total revenues | $ 58,500 |
| Net income | 7,200 |

| | |
|---|---|
| Statement of owner's equity | |
| Beginning owner's equity balance | $ 89,700 |
| Owner investments | 5,000 |
| Ending owner's equity balance | 70,800 |
| Balance sheet | |
| Total assets | $145,000 |

By picturing the content of and the interrelationships among the financial statements, determine:

a Total expenses for the year.
b Total owner withdrawals.
c Total liabilities.

## Problems

### Series A

**P1-A1** ***Identification of transactions***

The following tabulation summarizes several transactions of the Boston Company:

| | *Assets* | | | = *Liabilities* + | *Owner's Equity* | | |
|---|---|---|---|---|---|---|---|
| | *Cash* | *Accounts Receivable* | *Computers* | *Accounts Payable* | *(+) Investments* | *(−) Withdrawals* | *(+) Net Income (−) Net Loss* |
| Balances | $5,000 | $13,000 | $29,000 | $17,000 | $26,000 | $11,000 | $15,000 |
| (a) | −800 | | | | | | −800 |
| (b) | +1,900 | −1,900 | | | | | |
| (c) | −2,000 | | | | | +2,000 | |
| (d) | −3,000 | | +10,000 | +7,000 | | | |
| (e) | | +1,500 | | | | | +1,500 |
| (f) | | | +2,500 | | +2,500 | | |
| (g) | | | | +900 | | | −900 |
| | $1,100 | $12,600 | $41,500 | $24,900 | $28,500 | $13,000 | $14,800 |

**Instructions**

Write a brief explanation of each transaction (*a*)–(*g*).

**P1-A2** ***Basic transaction processing***

On September 1 of the current year, John McCarthy established a sole proprietorship. The following transactions occurred during the month:

1 Received $25,000 from McCarthy as an investment in the business.
2 Purchased $4,000 of office equipment on account.
3 Rendered $1,900 of services on account.
4 Paid $500 of office salaries.
5 Received a $300 electric bill, to be paid next month.
6 Paid $7,000 to acquire a used truck.
7 Processed a $900 withdrawal for McCarthy.
8 Received $650 from clients who were previously billed in (3).
9 Received $200 from clients for services rendered.
10 Paid $450 on account to the supplier of office equipment in (2).
11 Sold $350 of extra office equipment to a neighboring business for $350 cash.

### Instructions

a Arrange the following asset, liability, and owner's equity components of the accounting equation in a manner similar to that shown on page 16: Cash, Accounts Receivable, Office Equipment, Truck, Accounts Payable, Investments, Withdrawals, and Net Income/Net Loss. Note: This step is not necessary if you are using the preprinted working papers that accompany the text.
b Record each transaction on a separate line. After all transactions have been recorded, compute the balance in each of the preceding items.
c Answer the following questions for McCarthy:
  (1) What is the total of the company's assets at month-end? On which financial statement(s) would this information be found?
  (2) What is the owner's equity of the business at month-end? On which financial statement(s) would this information be found?

**P1-A3** ***Statement preparation***

The following balances are taken from the accounting records of Rawhide Enterprises at the close of its year on June 30, 19X2:

| | | | |
|---|---|---|---|
| Accounts payable | $19,200 | Land | $11,000 |
| Accounts receivable | 13,500 | Loan payable | 48,000 |
| Advertising expense | 8,000 | Miscellaneous expense | 1,000 |
| Building | 50,000 | Repair expense | 3,000 |
| Cash | 10,000 | Service revenue | 70,000 |
| Chuck Day, capital | 14,000* | Utilities expense | 12,000 |
| Equipment | 11,200 | Wage expense | 33,000 |

* This amount represents Day's capital balance on July 1, 19X1. Owner withdrawals and investments during the year totaled $4,500 and $6,000, respectively.

The building, equipment, and land were acquired just before the close of business on June 30.

### Instructions

a Prepare the income statement for Rawhide Enterprises in good form.
b Prepare the statement of owner's equity for Rawhide in good form.
c Prepare Rawhide's balance sheet in good form.

**P1-A4** ***Transaction analysis and statement preparation***

The transactions that follow relate to Frisco Enterprises for March 19X1, the company's first month of activity.

Mar. 1 Received $20,000 cash from Joanne Burton, the owner, as an investment in the business.
4 Rendered $2,400 of services on account.
7 Acquired a small parcel of land by paying $6,000 cash.
12 Received $700 from a client, who was billed previously on March 4.
15 Paid $800 to the *Journal Herald* for advertising that ran during the first half of the month.
18 Acquired $9,000 of equipment from Park Central Outfitters by paying $7,000 down and agreeing to remit the balance owed within the next two weeks.
22 Received $300 from clients for services performed on this date.
24 Paid $1,500 on account to Park Central Outfitters in partial settlement of the balance due from the transaction on March 18.
28 Rented a car from United Car Rental for use on March 28. Total charges amounted to $75, with United billing Frisco for the amount due.

31 Paid $900 for March wages.
31 Processed a $600 cash withdrawal from the business for Joanne Burton.

**Instructions**

a Determine the impact of each of the preceding transactions on Frisco's assets, liabilities, and owner's equity. Use the following format:

| *Assets* | | | | = *Liabilities* + | *Owner's Equity* | | |
|---|---|---|---|---|---|---|---|
| *Cash* | *Accounts Receivable* | *Land* | *Equipment* | *Accounts Payable* | *(+) Investments* | *(−) Withdrawals* | *(+) Net Income (−) Net Loss* |

Record each transaction on a separate line. Calculate balances only after the last transaction has been recorded.

b Prepare an income statement, a statement of owner's equity, and a balance sheet in good form.

**P1-A5** ***Financial statement preparation***

On January 1, 19X3, Mike Jeffcote opened the Jeffcote Advertising Agency, a sole proprietorship. Mike was able to begin operations with $90,000 cash, one-third of which was acquired via a bank loan. The remaining amount was obtained from an owner investment. A review of the accounting records for January revealed the following:

- *Asset purchases* Land, $15,000; building, $40,000; and office equipment, $9,000. These amounts were paid in cash; however, the firm still owes $3,000 for the equipment acquisition.
- *Services performed* Total billings on account, $29,500. Clients have remitted a total of $8,400 in settlement of their balances due.
- *Expenses incurred* Salaries, $21,000; utilities, $300; taxes, $150; interest, $800; and miscellaneous, $400. These amounts had been paid by month-end with the exception of $250 of the miscellaneous items.

Further information revealed that Jeffcote withdrew $3,100 of cash from the business on January 31.

**Instructions**

a Prepare an income statement for the month ended January 31, 19X3.
b Prepare a statement of owner's equity for the month ended January 31, 19X3.
c Prepare a balance sheet as of January 31, 19X3.

**P1-A6** ***Identification of income statement errors***

The following income statement was prepared by the bookkeeper of the Action Tree Service:

| ACTION TREE SERVICE<br>Profit and Loss Statement<br>June 30, 19XX | | |
|---|---|---|
| Revenue | | |
| Services rendered | $34,900 | |
| Accounts receivable | 6,100 | $41,000 |
| Owner investments | | 16,000 |
| Total revenue | | $57,000 |
| Less: | | |
| Salaries expense | $15,600 | |
| Advertising expense | 3,400 | |
| Down payment on truck | 1,000 | |
| Utilities expense | 900 | |
| Rent expense | 1,200 | |
| Tree trimming equipment | 1,500 | |
| Loan payment (includes $600 interest) | 1,900 | |
| Miscellaneous expense | 12,000 | |
| Supplies used | 800 | |
| Owner withdrawals | 2,000 | |
| Total deductions | | 40,300 |
| Net loss | | $16,700 |

**Instructions**

Identify and explain the errors in Action's income statement. Tell what should be done to correct the errors. (*Note:* A corrected income statement is not required.)

## Series B

**P1-B1** ***Identification of transactions***

The following tabulation summarizes several transactions of the McLendon Company:

| | *Assets* | | | = *Liabilities* + | *Owner's Equity* | | |
|---|---|---|---|---|---|---|---|
| | *Cash* | *Accounts Receivable* | *Equipment* | *Accounts Payable* | *(+) Investments* | *(−) Withdrawals* | *(+) Net Income (−) Net Loss* |
| Balances | $9,000 | $11,000 | $10,000 | $7,000 | $15,000 | $6,000 | $14,000 |
| (a) | | +900 | | | | | +900 |
| (b) | −1,000 | | +1,500 | +500 | | | |
| (c) | +800 | | | | | | +800 |
| (d) | −1,200 | | | −1,200 | | | |
| (e) | +4,000 | | | | +4,000 | | |
| (f) | | | | +700 | | | −700 |
| (g) | −2,000 | | | | | +2,000 | |
| | $9,600 | $11,900 | $11,500 | $7,000 | $19,000 | $8,000 | $15,000 |

**Instructions**

Write a brief explanation of the nature of each transaction (*a*)–(*g*).

**P1-B2** ***Basic transaction processing***

On November 1 of the current year, Victor Rigotti established a sole proprietorship. The following transactions occurred during the month:

1 Received $19,000 from Rigotti as an investment in the business.
2 Paid $9,000 to acquire a used minivan.
3 Purchased $1,800 of office furniture on account.
4 Rendered $2,100 of consulting services on account.
5 Paid $300 of repair expenses.
6 Received $800 from clients who were previously billed in (4).
7 Paid $500 on account to the supplier of office furniture in (3).
8 Received a $150 electric bill, to be paid next month.
9 Processed a $600 withdrawal for Rigotti.
10 Received $250 from clients for consulting services rendered.
11 Returned a $450 office desk to the supplier. The supplier agreed to reduce the balance due from Rigotti.

**Instructions**

a Arrange the following asset, liability, and owner's equity components of the accounting equation in a manner similar to that shown on page 16: Cash, Accounts Receivable, Office Furniture, Van, Accounts Payable, Investments, Withdrawals, and Net Income/Net Loss. Note: This step is not necessary if you are using the preprinted working papers that accompany the text.
b Record each transaction on a separate line. After all transactions have been recorded, compute the balance in each of the preceding items.
c Answer the following questions for Rigotti:
  (1) How much does the company owe to its creditors at month-end? On which financial statement(s) would this information be found?
  (2) Subsequent to the initial $19,000 investment, did owner's equity increase or decrease during the month? By how much? On which financial statement(s) would this information be found?

**P1-B3** ***Statement preparation***

The following balances are taken from the accounting records of Essex and Associates at the close of its year on December 31, 19XX:

| | | | |
|---|---|---|---|
| Accounts payable | $ 8,700 | Miscellaneous expense | $ 3,800 |
| Accounts receivable | 18,350 | Postage expense | 8,400 |
| Advertising expense | 3,850 | Repair expense | 5,600 |
| Cash | 15,000 | Salaries expense | 34,000 |
| Gloria Essex, capital | 26,800* | Service revenue | 65,000 |
| Land | 9,000 | Utilities expense | 2,500 |
| Loan payable | 5,500 | Van | 8,000 |

* This amount represents Essex's capital balance on January 1, 19XX. Owner investments and withdrawals during the year totaled $10,000 and $7,500, respectively.

The van was acquired just before the close of business on December 31.

**Instructions**

a Prepare Essex's income statement in good form.
b Prepare Essex's statement of owner's equity in good form.
c Prepare Essex's balance sheet in good form.

**P1-B4** ***Transaction analysis and statement preparation***

The transactions that follow relate to R. David Enterprises for August 19X2, the company's first month of activity.

| | | |
|---|---|---|
| Aug. | 1 | Received $22,000 cash from Roland David as an investment in the business. |
| | 6 | Acquired a small parcel of land by paying $9,000 cash. |
| | 9 | Rendered $2,400 of services, $300 of which were for cash and the remainder were on account. |
| | 13 | Paid $900 to WBGH radio for ads that had run the previous week. |
| | 16 | Received $200 from a client, who was billed previously on August 9. |
| | 19 | Acquired $6,500 of computing equipment from Master Computer; made a down payment and agreed to remit the remaining $1,800 balance by September 10. |
| | 23 | Received $150 from clients for services performed on this date. |
| | 26 | Returned $600 of the computing equipment purchased on August 19. Master Computer agreed to reduce the balance due on September 10. |
| | 28 | Processed a $700 withdrawal from the business for Roland David. |
| | 31 | Paid $1,000 for August wages. |
| | 31 | Received a $100 electric bill, to be paid next month. |

**Instructions**

a Determine the impact of each of the preceding transactions on the company's assets, liabilities, and owner's equity. Use the following format:

| *Assets* | | | | = *Liabilities* + | *Owner's Equity* | | |
|---|---|---|---|---|---|---|---|
| *Cash* | *Accounts Receivable* | *Land* | *Computing Equipment* | *Accounts Payable* | *(+) Investments* | *(−) Withdrawals* | *(+) Net Income (−) Net Loss* |

Record each transaction on a separate line. Calculate balances only after the last transaction has been recorded.

b Prepare an income statement, a statement of owner's equity, and a balance sheet in good form.

**P1-B5** ***Financial statement preparation***

On October 1, 19X6, Susan Thompson opened Thompson Decorating Services, a sole proprietorship. Susan was able to begin operations with $50,000 cash, 60 percent of which was acquired via an owner investment. The remaining amount was obtained from a bank loan. A review of the accounting records for October revealed the following:

- *Asset purchases* Van, $16,000; office equipment, $4,000; and decorator (household) furnishings, $17,000. These amounts were paid in cash except for $2,100 that is still owed for the furnishings acquisition.
- *Services performed* Total billings on account, $18,300. Clients have remitted a total of $14,200 in settlement of their balances due.
- *Expenses incurred* Salaries, $8,700; advertising, $2,500; postage, $1,800; utilities, $100; taxes, $150; interest, $450; and miscellaneous, $200. These amounts had been paid by month-end with the exception of $700 of the advertising expenditures.

Further information revealed that Thompson withdrew $5,500 of cash from the business on October 31.

**Instructions**

a Prepare an income statement for the month ended October 31, 19X6.
b Prepare a statement of owner's equity for the month ended October 31, 19X6.
c Prepare a balance sheet as of October 31, 19X6.

**P1-B6** ***Identification of income statement errors***

The following income statement was prepared by the bookkeeper of the Christy Pet Grooming Service:

| CHRISTY PET GROOMING<br>Profit and Loss Statement<br>June 30, 19XX | | |
|---|---|---|
| Revenue | | |
| Services rendered | $37,000 | |
| Amounts due from clients | 6,500 | $43,500 |
| Bank loan | | 20,500 |
| Total revenue | | $64,000 |
| Less: | | |
| Salaries expense | $11,200 | |
| Accounts payable | 2,100 | |
| Personal clothing | 1,600 | |
| Utilities expense | 1,000 | |
| Advertising expense | 1,800 | |
| Office equipment | 200 | |
| Loan payment (includes $400 interest) | 1,700 | |
| Miscellaneous expense | 12,000 | |
| Tax expense | 450 | |
| Owner withdrawals | 2,400 | |
| Total deductions | | 34,450 |
| Net worth | | $29,550 |

**Instructions**

Identify and explain the errors in Christy's income statement. Tell what should be done to correct the errors. (*Note:* A corrected income statement is not required.)

## Beyond the Basics

**BB1-1** ***Income and asset determination***

Rose Jacobson desires to borrow money to expand her one-year-old consulting practice, which is organized as a sole proprietorship. In an effort to satisfy the request of a local banker, Jacobson's bookkeeper (Vivian Stoddard) was asked to prepare a list of cash receipts and cash disbursements for the first twelve months of operation. The banker also requested a determination of the practice's total assets as of the end of the year.

Stoddard supplied the following information:

| Cash receipts | |
|---|---|
| Fees from cash-paying clients | $ 78,000 |
| Client receipts on account | 36,000 |
| First National Bank loan | 10,000 |
| Owner investment | 141,000 |
| Total | $265,000 |

| | |
|---|---|
| Cash disbursements | |
| Salary payments | $ 38,000 |
| Purchase of land | 45,000 |
| Utilities expense | 3,000 |
| Tax expense | 2,000 |
| Owner withdrawals | 70,000 |
| Total | $158,000 |
| Total assets | $212,000 |

Additional data follow:

1 Fees still due from clients total $8,000. These fees were not considered by Stoddard when generating the preceding figures.
2 Interest of $150 is owed to the bank on the First National loan.
3 Salaries not yet paid but owed to employees amount to $5,000.
4 Jacobson's personal art collection, on display in the client reception area, was included in the asset total at $40,000 (the present fair market value). The collection cost Jacobson $25,000.
5 Land, acquired by the practice for $45,000, was included in the asset total at $65,000. Jacobson had recently received offers of the latter amount from potential purchasers.

**Instructions**

a The banker desires to know whether the firm was profitable during the first year of operation. Furnish him with the necessary information by preparing an income statement in good form for the year ended December 31, 19XX.
b Assuming the use of generally accepted accounting practices, compute the correct valuation of the firm's assets. Briefly justify your answer.

**BB1-2** ***Accounting information: Uses and reporting***

Frank Bell is an outdoors enthusiast. While employed as a personnel manager at Hansen Engineering in Denver, Frank often helped friends on camping trips and had even built a canoe for river exploration. Luckily, Frank's brother owned a sporting goods store in a neighboring suburb. This was a nice arrangement because it gave Frank access to wholesalers' catalogues, thereby allowing acquisitions of specialized equipment at great savings.

Frank's love for camping, coupled with his friends' support, soon led to his resignation from Hansen Engineering and the opening of The Outdoors Store. Frank rented space in a local shopping center and purchased an extensive supply of maps and outdoor equipment. He also acquired some materials and hired a laborer to expand his canoe-building activities. The entire operation was financed from various investments that Frank had made over the years.

An extensive advertising campaign for the store's opening proved very beneficial, with business being much better than expected. However, as the winter months approached, store traffic slowed. Frank soon realized that his operation faced a problem shared by many other firms—seasonality. In an effort to boost sales during fall and winter, Frank conducted some market research and decided to add ski equipment and accessories to his product line.

Having resolved that issue, Frank still faced several other problems. An emergency withdrawal had left the store's cash balance at a dangerously low level. Recent canoe-building costs appeared to be skyrocketing, although Frank could not be certain because of the absence of a formal costing system. In addition, upon signing the original lease at the shopping center, Frank anticipated conducting business only in the camping field. With a new venture into skiing, however, he rapidly found himself cramped for space. Finally, there was a financing issue. The outlays required for the purchases of ski equipment were more than the store's checking account could bear, creating the need for a bank loan.

In an effort to minimize operating costs, Frank had maintained the financial records for The Outdoors Store himself. Fortunately, he had completed two accounting courses at a local university before being employed by Hansen Engineering. In his own words, however, Frank admitted that "partying came before studying and I really wasn't a serious student." The bank's loan officer, in a preliminary conversation with Frank, had suggested that the store's financial statements be audited by a CPA.

**Instructions**

a How can accounting help Frank in the management of The Outdoors Store?
b The loan officer had suggested that the store's financial statements be audited by a CPA. Briefly explain the audit process and the rationale behind the banker's request.
c Assume the role of the loan officer. What information would she like to see before making a decision on a loan for The Outdoors Store?
d What are the basic financial statements of a business and what information is reported by these statements?

## Answers to Chapter Quiz

**1** a

**2** c ($32,000 + $15,000 − $9,000 + $2,000)

**3** b

**4** b

**5** b ($45,000 − $35,000)

# Processing Accounting Information

CHAPTER 2

## Learning Objectives

After reading this chapter you should:

1 Understand accounts, debits and credits, journals, the chart of accounts, and their interrelationships.

2 Be able to post transactions.

3 Understand what a trial balance is and how it is constructed.

4 Be aware of the impact of errors on the trial balance and the various steps necessary to locate an error.

The businesses that operate in our economy are involved with a multitude of financial events and transactions, such as the sale of goods and services to customers, the payment of cash to creditors and employees, the acquisition of merchandise and equipment, and owner investments and withdrawals. These examples, while not all-inclusive, illustrate the variety of transactions that a company must be capable of handling and recording. Add to this variety the frequency with which these transactions occur and a genuine record-keeping problem is created.

The Vista Transit example in Chapter 1 showed that a business could process transactions by increasing and decreasing the components of the fundamental accounting equation. Although this processing method was satisfactory for illustrative purposes, some modification is necessary in a more realistic environment. It is not uncommon for an enterprise to process thousands of transactions each day. In addition, complex organizations may have dozens of asset, liability, and owner's equity elements that must be updated on a timely basis.

To illustrate the record-keeping problems of real firms, consider the Atlanta Braves and PepsiCo, Inc. The Braves, a professional baseball team owned by Turner Broadcasting System, Inc., is certainly not a giant organization by today's standards. Operating in one primary location, the club generates revenues of around $24 million and fields a team for approximately two-thirds of a year. At first glance, accounting for the Braves would not appear much more complex than the accounting required for Vista Transit. However, a deeper probe into the operations of a professional baseball club discloses the following:

- Multiple sources of revenue from gate receipts, concession operations, and the sale of broadcast rights.
- Guaranteed salaries under long-term player contracts.
- Participation in the Major League Baseball Players' Benefit Plan.

In addition, the Braves lease sports facilities. Rentals are dependent on paid attendance or revenues at sports events, subject to specified minimum amounts.

PepsiCo, considerably larger than the Atlanta Braves, has annual revenues of about $13 billion and conducts activities in three different business segments. PepsiCo's holdings and operations include the following:

| ***Business Segment*** | ***Company*** |
|---|---|
| Soft drinks | Pepsi-Cola Co. |
| Snack foods | Frito-Lay, Inc. |
| Restaurants | Pizza Hut, Inc., Taco Bell, Kentucky Fried Chicken |

Manufacturing soft drinks, feeding thousands of people in restaurants, and producing snack foods are only a small part of PepsiCo's daily activities that need summarization for inclusion in its financial statements. Furthermore, management must have ready and efficient access to operating information for use in planning, control, and decision-making activities.

## The Accounting System

Whether large like PepsiCo or small like Vista Transit, all companies need the capability to produce financial statements, generate information for executives, and satisfy numerous governmental reporting requirements (such as the filing of an income tax return). In an effort to perform these varied tasks, businesses have found it beneficial to establish formalized accounting systems that operate in the following manner:

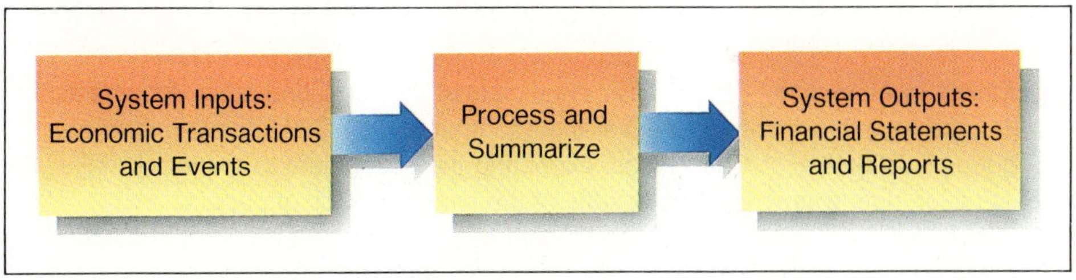


Economic transactions and events are input to an entity's system. The inputs are then translated into a specialized processing "language" (to be discussed shortly) and later summarized. These processes result in the production of numerous financial reports and outputs that are useful to various parties.

Such accounting systems have long been recognized as a key ingredient to effective management. This fact was stated very succintly by Franklin Roosevelt, who over 50 years ago noted:

> A good system of accounting, by indicating weaknesses in the structure of the business, may save thousands of dollars to investors and may even save the business itself. The development of natural resources, the exploitation of new fields of commerce, . . . keener competition, higher standards of living and greater complexities of modern business . . . have brought about a condition where an effective accounting system is as essential to the continued life of a business as production and distribution.[1]

The accounting systems found in practice today range in scope from the simple to the sophisticated. No matter how complex, virtually all systems employ four basic tools to process transactions into financial information. These tools, which improve efficiency and reduce the cost of the input-to-output conversion, are accounts, debits and credits, journals, and the chart of accounts.

## Accounts

**OBJECTIVE 1**
**Understand accounts, debits and credits, journals, the chart of accounts, and their interrelationships.**

As we explained earlier in the text, transactions and events affect the fundamental accounting equation. To accumulate the information necessary for financial statement and report construction, a business must keep detailed records of its assets, liabilities, and owner's equity. Assets, for example, should be subdivided into more specific elements such as cash, accounts receivable, and equipment, with individual accountings made for each element.

The records that are kept for the individual asset, liability, and owner's equity components are known as **accounts.** If a company employs manual accounting methods, the record keeping for each account is normally performed on a separate sheet of paper. If electronic data processing is utilized, the account is located somewhere in a computer's memory or on a floppy diskette. No matter which medium is employed, however, the purpose of the account is the same: to accumulate (record) the increases and decreases that result from transactions. All the accounts taken

[1] Letter from Franklin Roosevelt to the president of the American Institute of Accountants, October 12, 1937.

HIGHLIGHT

# Small Business Accounting: Bag It!

"Homer, if you don't get those invoices and checks to the office in Baton Rouge this week, you can just hang it up." Ed Simpson, the owner of a construction firm, was talking to his superintendent, Homer Huntley. Simpson had come to the construction site after repeated phone calls had failed to produce the documents needed to record expenditures and the extent of progress on the job Homer was supervising.

By the time Simpson had left the construction shack, Homer was furious. "Bookkeepers! Don't they have anything better to do than to ruin my day?" Homer then started yanking invoices, check stubs, handwritten notes, and other papers off the nails that he had driven into the shack's walls as a filing system for job records. Homer stuffed the papers into a brown grocery bag he'd been using as a trash container, folded the bag's top and fastened it with a nail, and mailed the records to the home office that night.

The preceding story is true, although the names have been changed to protect the not-so-innocent. The conflict between good accounting practice and the speedy completion of related procedures is a very real one, made more difficult by the attitudes of people like Homer Huntley. Traditional corrective efforts have sought to educate personnel about the need to keep reliable records. To a large extent, though, the efforts have been relatively unsuccessful in small enterprises like Simpson Construction.

Brown bag bookkeeping, a small business accounting system, is alive and popular. Many small businesses today save check stubs, invoices, and other documents and deliver them to their trusted CPA at year end in grocery bags, expecting the accountant to somehow make heads or tails of the jumbled mass of papers.

One consultant has gone so far as to suggest that three classes of brown baggers exist. The Class I brown bagger, a rare commodity, uses the system in the proper manner by keeping separate bags or containers for each type of document. The documents are neatly filed in the bags in chronological order, with appropriate handwritten notes attached (e.g., a receipt from a business luncheon might contain a note such as "Ate with Tim Smith of Smith Radiator—tried to get more of his business").

A Class II bagger does not organize the documents but does annotate them properly and at least keeps them together for the accountant. Finally, there's the Class III bagger, or the ultimate in sloppiness. Documentation of business activity is generally inadequate and/or missing. Even the most skilled accountants experience trouble here, with trouble being translated into added hours on the job. Added hours, of course, generate more revenues for the CPA.

To conclude, many organizations have taken steps to ensure the adequacy of their systems, some, naturally, more than others. How does brown bag bookkeeping fit in? Although microcomputers are playing an important role in making the bagger obsolete, this type of bookkeeping system will always exist. Class I and II baggers are, as a minimum, preferable to a constant and ineffectual struggle to get the Homer Huntleys of the world to do detailed and disciplined accounting work.

SOURCE: Adapted from "Brown Bag Bookkeeping," *Journal of Accountancy*, July, 1986, pp. 122, 124, 126, 128. Reprinted with permission from *Journal of Accountancy*, copyright © 1986 by American Institute of Certified Public Accountants, Inc. Opinions of the authors are their own and do not necessarily reflect policies of the Institute.

together comprise a firm's **general ledger.** Essentially, the general ledger is a book that contains separate listings for each account that appears on an organization's financial statements.

The account may assume several different forms. One form is the **T-account,** so named because of its shape. A Cash T-account appears as follows:

| *Cash* | | | |
|---|---|---|---|
| 19XX | | | |
| 2/1 | 1,000 | 2/4 | 450 |
| 2/12 | 200 | 2/18 | 290 |
| 2/24 | 600 | | **740** |
| (1,060) | **1,800** | | |

Observe that the T-account has both a left and a right side. The left side of any account is known as the *debit* side, and the right side is known as the *credit* side. In this particular case, Cash has entries that total $1,800 on the debit side (debits) and $740 on the credit side (credits).[2] The Cash account therefore has a debit balance of $1,060 ($1,800 − $740). If a given account has credits in excess of debits, the account would possess a credit balance.

The T format presents a concise picture of the various transactions affecting a given account and is useful for understanding how transactions increase or decrease assets, liabilities, and owner's equity. For these reasons the T-account is used throughout the text. In actual practice, however, the **running balance form of account** is encountered more frequently. Using the same information that appeared in the preceding example, we can illustrate the running balance form as follows:

| Cash | | | | | Account No. 110 |
|---|---|---|---|---|---|
| Date | Explanation | Post Ref | Debit | Credit | Balance |
| 19XX | | | | | |
| Feb. 1 | | | 1,000 | | 1,000 |
| 4 | | | | 450 | 550 |
| 12 | | | 200 | | 750 |
| 18 | | | | 290 | 460 |
| 24 | | | 600 | | 1,060 |

Entries on the left side of the T-account are recorded in the debit column; entries on the right side appear in the credit column.

The running balance account form offers the advantage of maintaining an up-to-date balance after each transaction. In addition, an explanation column is provided for descriptive purposes should an unusual entry arise. Normally, however,

[2] The small boldface figures are commonly known as *footings*.

this column is left blank. The use of the posting reference (Post Ref) column will be explained shortly.

At this point you should understand the concepts of establishing an account and determining the related balance. However, two important questions have probably occurred to you:

1 Should the dollar amounts be entered as debits or credits?
2 Which amounts in the Cash account represent increases in cash and which are decreases?

The answers to these questions will become clear in the explanation of a second key accounting mechanism, debits and credits.

## Debits and Credits

**Debits and credits** are tools used by the accountant to increase and decrease account balances. Certain accounts are debited to record an increase; that is, entries are made on the debit (left) side or in the debit column. These accounts, in turn, are credited when a reduction is needed, with entries being made on the right side (credit) or in the credit column. To keep the accounting equation balanced, other accounts employ the opposite rule; namely, increases are recorded by credits and decreases are recorded by debits. Exhibit 2-1 summarizes the debit/credit rules used in accounting.

To understand the rules, remember that the elements of the accounting equation are assets, liabilities, and owner's equity. In addition, recall that owner's equity changes, in part, from net income and/or net loss. Given that these latter two items are derived by comparing an entity's revenues and expenses, it is safe to say there are five basic account types: assets, liabilities, owner's equity, revenues, and expenses.

The balance of each account is obtained by offsetting or netting the total debits against the total credits. Certain account types tend to contain more debits than credits and will almost always possess a debit balance. Their **normal balance,** then, is a debit balance. According to Exhibit 2-1, assets and expenses fall in this category. In contrast, liabilities, owner's equity, and revenue accounts generally have more credits than debits and usually possess a credit balance.

The normal balances of accounts correspond to the fundamental accounting equation: assets = liabilities + owner's equity. An enterprise's assets (debit balances) are matched against their ownership interests—the creditors' (credit balances) and the owner's (credit balance). Because revenues increase owner's equity, such accounts normally possess a credit balance. Expenses, conversely, have the

**Exhibit 2-1**
**Debit/credit Rules**

| *Account Type* | *Normal Balance* | *To Increase* | *To Decrease* |
|---|---|---|---|
| Assets | Debit | Debit | Credit |
| Liabilities | Credit | Credit | Debit |
| Owner's equity | Credit | Credit | Debit |
| Revenues | Credit | Credit | Debit |
| Expenses | Debit | Debit | Credit |

opposite effect and generally maintain a debit balance. These relationships are shown in Exhibit 2-2.

> **▶ TIPS & TECHNIQUES**
>
> The preceding discussion should *not* be taken to mean that accounts always contain a normal balance. Certain accounts may, at times, carry opposite balances; for example, Accounts Receivable (an asset) could have a credit balance if a customer overpaid the amount due a business. In other cases, however, an opposite balance generally means that an error has arisen. For instance, a credit balance in Machinery (also an asset) is not possible because a company cannot have "negative" equipment.

## Application of the Rules

A review of Exhibits 2-1 and 2-2 will show that to increase the balance of any asset or expense, the account must be debited. Let us focus for a moment on Six Flags, Inc., which operates a chain of amusement parks. The salaries earned by the firm's employees would be debited to the Salaries Expense account because the company's total salary expense is increasing. In contrast, credits are used to record increases in liabilities, owner's equity, and revenues. Thus, Six Flags would credit an Amusement Revenue account to record the admission fees received from visitors who enter the corporation's various facilities.

The observant accounting student should note that *the procedures to increase any account match perfectly with the account's normal balance.* Consequently, once the normal balance is mastered, all you need remember is to give the account "more of the same" to record an increase. The rules to decrease, of course, would be just the opposite.

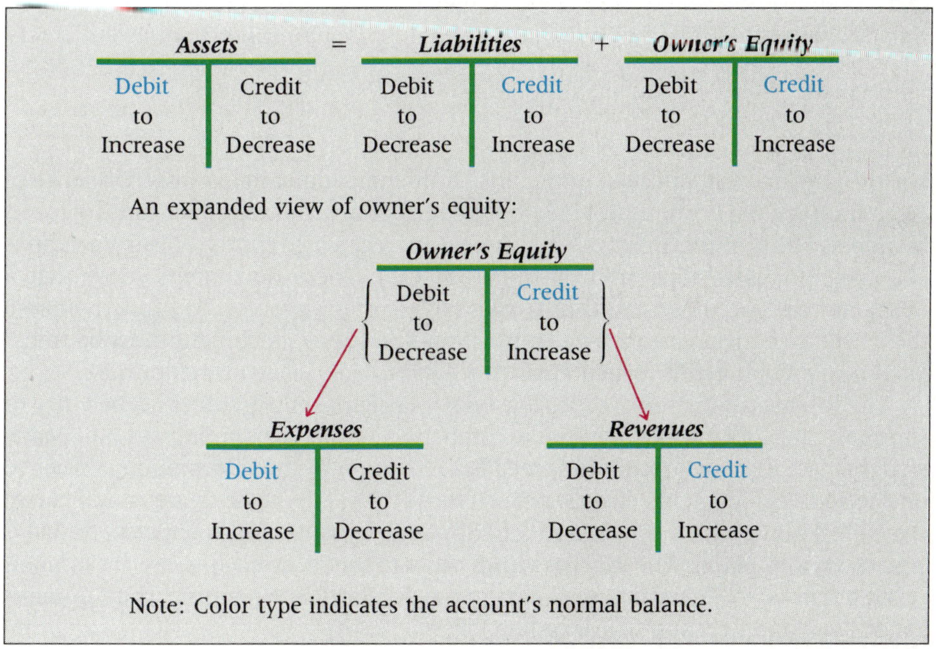


**Exhibit 2-2**
**Relationship of Normal Balances and the Accounting Equation**

Let us return now to the two questions raised on page 44 that relate to the Cash account illustration. The answers are as follows:

**1** The dollar amounts will be entered as debits or credits depending on whether the amounts increase or decrease the account. Because Cash is an asset, receipts or increases are recorded as debits. Conversely, decreases to Cash are entered on the right side as credits, or in the credit column.

**2** This question has really been answered above. Debits of $1,800 ($1,000 + $200 + $600) represent increases to the Cash account, while the credits ($450 and $290) are reductions.

### Misconceptions about Debits and Credits

There are two common misconceptions about debits and credits. From their experiences with retail stores, many people believe that credits *always* reduce account balances. When they pay on account or return merchandise, customers are often told that their account will be credited. Because the amounts due from customers are an asset to the retail establishment, these transactions will generate credits to reduce Accounts Receivable. Keep in mind, however, that credits also increase certain account balances, specifically, liability, owner's equity, and revenue accounts.

A second misconception is that credits are good and debits are bad. This notion is incorrect. Although credits reduce your account on someone else's books ("good"), credits also increase the amounts you owe as shown in your Accounts Payable account ("bad"). Overall, then, it is a matter of perspective. Generally stated, the "good/bad" relationship has no validity and is best forgotten.

At this juncture it would be wise to thoroughly learn (repeat, *thoroughly learn*) the rules presented in Exhibits 2-1 and 2-2. These rules are used throughout the study of accounting, as they form the basis for the proper recording and processing of all business transactions. The sooner that you master the exhibits, the better off you will be.

## Journals

The transactions that affect an entity arise from many different sources. Evidence of these transactions is often provided by the receipt or issuance of accounting forms known as **source documents** (e.g., inventory receiving reports, bills from suppliers, customer sales slips, and customer checks). These documents show that a transaction has occurred and thus trigger the recording process. To properly record the account changes caused by a transaction, the source document must be translated into a debit/credit format. This translation takes place in the journal.

The **journal,** sometimes called the book of original entry, serves as the entry or starting point for transactions into a company's formal accounting system. Many students feel that the journal is a needless repetition of the information contained on the source documents. This is not so. Frequently, transactions are complicated; they affect numerous accounts and are supported by voluminous paperwork that is filed in various places. The journal brings order to the recording process by summarizing a transaction's key financial data in one location. Furthermore, the summarization is done in chronological order.

## The Recording Process

To record its many transactions, a business may utilize different types of journals. For example, sales transactions may be entered in a specialized sales journal, purchases in a purchases journal, cash receipts in a cash receipts journal, and so forth. The journal illustrated in this chapter is commonly referred to as a *two-column general journal.* It has two amount columns (debit and credit) and is used to record a variety of transactions.

Recording transactions in the journal is a three-step process known as **journalizing.** The transactions are first analyzed in terms of the accounts that are affected. Next, the appropriate debits and credits are determined. Finally, in their new debit/credit format, the transactions are formally entered in the journal.

To illustrate these procedures, let us examine the following transaction of the Wise Advertising Agency. The agency was founded on May 1 of the current year when Gary Wise invested $9,000 of personal savings into the business. Analyzing the effect of this transaction, we see that the investment increased the agency's cash balance and also owner's equity. Using the format introduced in Chapter 1, the investment would appear as follows:

| *Assets* | = *Liabilities* + | *Owner's Equity* |
|---|---|---|
| *Cash* | | *Investments* |
| +$9,000 | | +$9,000 |

Once the proper accounts are determined, the transaction is next translated into debits and credits. Because Cash is an asset, a $9,000 debit is needed to record the appropriate increase. As we just noted, the investment has also increased owner's equity, namely, the Gary Wise, Capital account. According to the debit/credit rules, increases to owner's equity are recorded by credits. This analysis is summarized in the following general journal entry:

| *Date* | *Accounts* | *Post Ref* | *Debit* | *Credit* |
|---|---|---|---|---|
| 19XX | | | | |
| May 1 | Cash | | 9,000 | |
| | Gary Wise, Capital | | | 9,000 |
| | Owner investment | | | |

Observe that the debits are recorded first and appear next to the date column. Credits are entered next by using a slight indentation. Finally, a short description of the transaction is prepared because the general journal will eventually contain a variety of transactions. The explanation notes the purpose of the entry; that is, to record an investment by the owner. The posting reference (Post Ref) column is left blank at the time the entry is made.

Upon completion of the recording process, debits of $9,000 equal credits of $9,000, and the entry is said to be in balance. *In any transaction, the total dollar amount of the debits must equal the total dollar amount of the credits.* Naturally, this equality would not be possible if a transaction affected only one account. Accountants, however, prevent this situation from arising by employing a double-entry system of bookkeeping. With such a system, a transaction always affects a minimum of two general ledger components.

> **TIPS & TECHNIQUES**
>
> Observe that we are really performing the same operation that was illustrated in Chapter 1—increasing and decreasing the various components of the accounting equation. Now, however, the increases and decreases are recorded by using a system of debits and credits. The overall objective of effecting account balance changes has remained the same; only the methodology differs.

## Chart of Accounts

Accounts in the general ledger are usually arranged in the following order: assets, liabilities, owner's equity, revenues, and expenses. Within each grouping the individual accounts are assigned a number according to the **chart of accounts**—a detailed listing of a company's accounts and associated account numbers. For example, the asset portion of a chart of accounts may appear as follows:

| Assets (100s) | |
|---|---|
| Cash | 101 |
| Accounts receivable | 110 |
| Inventory | 120 |
| Land | 130 |
| Building | 140 |
| Equipment | 150 |

Liabilities might be numbered in the 200s, owner's equity accounts in the 300s, and so on. The determination of a suitable numbering scheme is an important issue in systems design work. Sufficient gaps should be left when assigning account numbers for the possible insertion of additional accounts at a later date.

The chart of accounts is very useful in helping to determine proper transaction recording. For instance, suppose Binkert Company paid an electric bill of $1,800 on March 31. The correct analysis should reveal that Binkert's total electrical costs have increased, calling for a debit to an expense account. Also, Cash has decreased. Therefore the following entry appears to be needed:[3]

| | | | |
|---|---|---|---|
| Mar. 31 | Utilities Expense | 1,800 | |
| | Cash | | 1,800 |
| | Paid utilities bill | | |

However, a review of the chart of accounts might reveal that Binkert does not use a Utilities Expense account. Rather, in view of the large sums expended for energy costs, the firm has established separate accounts for:

- Electricity expense
- Natural gas expense

[3] This entry is recorded in general journal format. Observe the manner in which the account titles and amounts are staggered, thus duplicating the appearance of the entry in the general journal. It is not necessary to write the words "debit" and "credit" next to the accounts or amounts because this format is well recognized and understood by accountants.

- Fuel oil expense
- Telephone expense
- Water and sewer expense

Separate accounts furnish management with more detailed information. The proper entry, then, which could only be made after inspecting the chart of accounts, requires a debit to Electricity Expense.

In addition to assisting with transaction recording, the chart of accounts also reveals how organizations can differ. While virtually every company has accounts such as Cash, Accounts Receivable, Loans Payable, Sales, and Salaries Expense, businesses often establish accounts that are attuned to their specific area of operation. A review of corporate annual reports revealed the specialized accounts listed in Exhibit 2-3.

## Posting: Interaction of the Basic Tools

OBJECTIVE 2
Be able to post transactions.

The journal alone is not sufficient to handle the recording process. Many transactions have affected the same account and must be grouped together (i.e., summarized) to allow for the eventual preparation of financial statements. This summarization is achieved through **posting,** a process by which transactions in the journal are transferred to accounts in the ledger. The necessary posting for the entry on May 1 of Wise Advertising appears in Exhibit 2-4. The circled numbers represent the order in which the posting steps are performed.

To explain: (1) The transaction recorded in the journal requires a debit to Cash of $9,000. This amount is transferred to the debit column of the Cash account. (2) Next, the date of the transaction (May 1) is indicated. (3) J1 is then entered in the posting reference column of the Cash account to signify that the debit was transferred from page 1 of the general journal (as opposed to one of the other journals noted earlier). This procedure is performed should the need arise to trace a ledger entry back to its origin. (4) The account number, 101, is next placed in the posting reference column of the journal. This step serves two purposes:

1 The posting reference facilitates the tracing process by showing the accountant the account to which the debit was actually transferred.

2 The posting reference signifies completion of the posting process. Consequently, a blank in this column is interpreted to mean that an entry has not yet been transferred. This procedure is important; should an interruption occur, the person performing the posting can easily find the proper place to resume his or her work.

| *Firm* | *Account* | *Account Type* |
|---|---|---|
| Philip Morris Companies, Inc. | Leaf tobacco inventory | Asset |
| Delta Air Lines, Inc. | Advance payments for new equipment | Asset |
| Kimberly-Clark Corporation | Timberlands | Asset |
| The New York Times Company | Unexpired subscriptions | Liability |
| Chevron Corporation | Exploration costs | Expense |

**Exhibit 2-3**
**Specialized Business Accounts**

**Exhibit 2-4**
**Posting Transactions from the Journal to the Ledger**

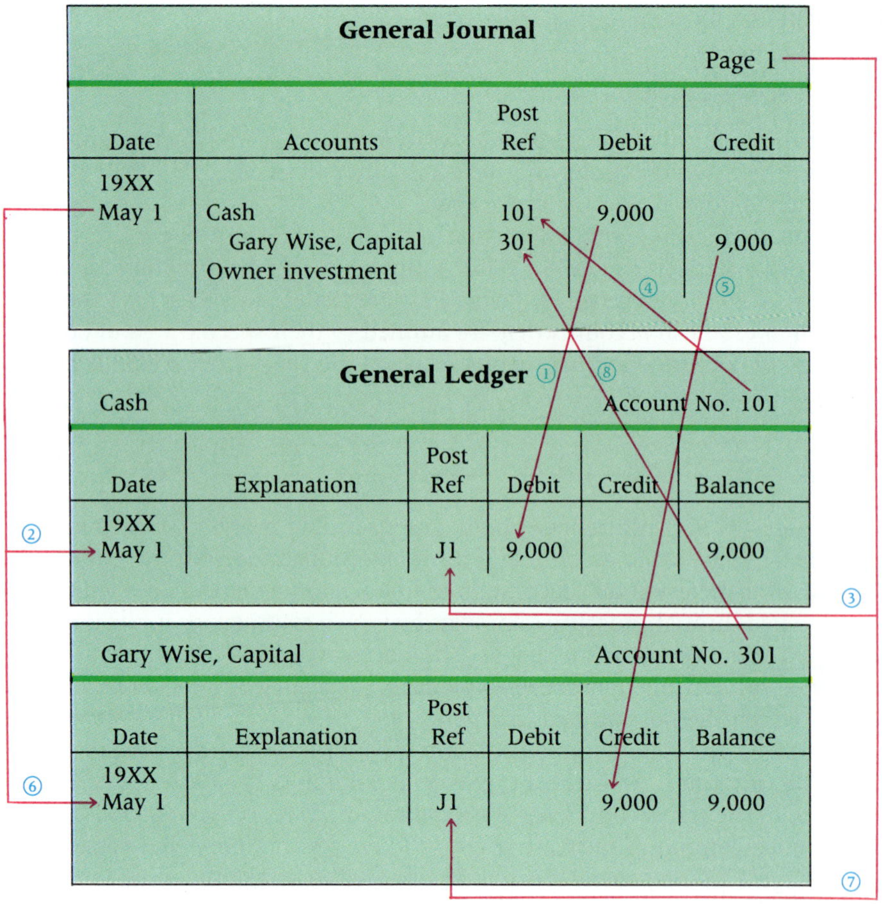


The Cash account has now been increased by $9,000. If there were additional debits in the journal entry, they, too, would be posted in this fashion.

Once the debit is posted, the credit is transferred in a similar manner. ⑤ The investment generated a credit to Gary Wise, Capital. Therefore $9,000 is posted from the journal to this account. ⑥ Next, May 1 is transferred to the date column. ⑦ The source of the entry, J1, is then entered in the ledger account. ⑧ Finally, the account to which the credit was transferred (301) is entered in the journal. The credit has now been posted and the process is complete.

## An Extended Illustration

The interrelationships among debits and credits, journal entries, and ledger accounts are best viewed by means of an extended illustration. Transactions of the Wise Advertising Agency are now presented, along with the proper journal entries. You should concentrate on each transaction and its analysis *prior* to viewing the correct entry. Again, follow the process of reasoning, not memorizing. Account numbers appear in the journal, indicating that the entries have already been posted to the general ledger accounts.

***May 1*** Gary Wise invested $9,000 in the business.

***Analysis*** See page 47.

***Entry***

| | | | | Page 1 |
|---|---|---|---|---|
| 19XX<br>May 1 | Cash<br>Gary Wise, Capital<br>Owner investment | 101<br>301 | 9,000 | <br>9,000 |

***May 5*** Paid $800 of marketing and promotional costs related to the agency's opening.

***Analysis*** Expenses have increased; thus, Marketing Expense is debited. The Cash account (an asset) has decreased from the payment, requiring a credit.

***Entry***

| | | | | |
|---|---|---|---|---|
| 5 | Marketing Expense<br>Cash<br>Paid promotional costs | 520<br>101 | 800 | <br>800 |

***May 10*** Acquired a small parcel of land for $5,500 from Knox Developers. Paid $1,000 down, with the remaining balance due in 10 days.

***Analysis*** Land is debited to record the appropriate increase. Cash is credited due to the payment. In addition, Accounts Payable is credited for $4,500 ($5,500 − $1,000), because the amount owed to Knox, a liability, has increased.

***Entry***

| | | | | |
|---|---|---|---|---|
| 10 | Land<br>Cash<br>Accounts Payable<br>Acquired parcel of land;<br>balance payable in 10 days | 130<br>101<br>210 | 5,500 | <br>1,000<br>4,500 |

Note: All necessary debits are recorded first, followed by the required credits. Observe that total debits of $5,500 equal total credits of $5,500.

***May 14*** Billed clients for services rendered, $1,700.

***Analysis*** The amounts due from clients have increased; Accounts Receivable, an asset, is therefore debited. The revenues earned by the agency have also increased, calling for a credit to Agency Revenue.

***Entry***

| | | | | |
|---|---|---|---|---|
| 14 | Accounts Receivable<br>Agency Revenue<br>Billed clients | 120<br>410 | 1,700 | <br>1,700 |

***May 20*** Paid the $4,500 balance due Knox Developers from the transaction on May 10.

***Analysis*** The $4,500 payment has reduced Wise Advertising's cash balance and the amounts owed to creditors. Accounts Payable, a liability, is debited and Cash is credited.

***Entry***

| | | | | |
|---|---|---|---|---|
| 20 | Accounts Payable | 210 | 4,500 | |
| | Cash | 101 | | 4,500 |
| | Paid Knox Developers on account | | | |

***May 23*** Received $950 from clients on account.

***Analysis*** Two assets are involved in this transaction: Cash and Accounts Receivable. Cash has increased and must be debited. Because the amounts due from clients have decreased, Accounts Receivable is credited.

***Entry***

| | | | | |
|---|---|---|---|---|
| 23 | Cash | 101 | 950 | |
| | Accounts Receivable | 120 | | 950 |
| | Received cash from clients on account | | | |

***May 25*** Received a $125 electric bill, due in June.

***Analysis*** Total expenses have increased, requiring a debit to Electricity Expense. Accounts Payable is credited to record the increase in the amounts owed to creditors.

***Entry***

Page 2

| | | | | |
|---|---|---|---|---|
| 19XX | | | | |
| May 25 | Electricity Expense | 530 | 125 | |
| | Accounts Payable | 210 | | 125 |
| | Received May's electric bill; due in June | | | |

***May 27*** Received a call from Kathy Howard, a client, stating that she had not paid her bill of May 14 because of a $100 overcharge. Wise checked the agency's records and found the client was correct.

***Analysis*** Refer to the entry of May 14. Accounts Receivable and Agency Revenue were each overstated by $100 and must therefore be reduced. The original entry is left intact to improve accountability.

***Entry***

| | | | | |
|---|---|---|---|---|
| 27 | Agency Revenue | 410 | 100 | |
| | Accounts Receivable | 120 | | 100 |
| | Corrected error on 5/14 pertaining to Kathy Howard | | | |

***May 28*** Paid office salaries of $825.

***Analysis*** Similar to the transaction of May 5.

**Entry**

| | | | | |
|---|---|---|---|---|
| 28 | Salaries Expense | 510 | 825 | |
| | Cash | 101 | | 825 |
| | Paid May salaries | | | |

***May 30*** Gary Wise withdrew $200 from the business for personal use.

***Analysis*** Recall that withdrawals decrease owner's equity. Rather than debit Gary Wise, Capital, many companies use a separate **drawing account** to accumulate such amounts. The drawing account normally possesses a debit balance and, as such, gives rise to the entry that follows.

**Entry**

| | | | | |
|---|---|---|---|---|
| 30 | Gary Wise, Drawing | 320 | 200 | |
| | Cash | 101 | | 200 |
| | Owner withdrawal | | | |

***May 31*** Billed clients for services rendered, $2,500.

***Analysis*** Similar to the transaction of May 14.

**Entry**

| | | | | |
|---|---|---|---|---|
| 31 | Accounts Receivable | 120 | 2,500 | |
| | Agency Revenue | 410 | | 2,500 |
| | Billed clients | | | |

The general ledger accounts relevant to the foregoing journal entries are illustrated in Exhibit 2-5. Trace each transaction from the journal to the ledger to understand how information is processed through an accounting system.

**Exhibit 2-5**
**General Ledger Accounts for Wise Advertising Agency**

Cash — Account No. 101

| Date | Explanation | Post Ref | Debit | Credit | Balance |
|---|---|---|---|---|---|
| 19XX | | | | | |
| May 1 | | J1 | 9,000 | | 9,000 |
| 5 | | J1 | | 800 | 8,200 |
| 10 | | J1 | | 1,000 | 7,200 |
| 20 | | J1 | | 4,500 | 2,700 |
| 23 | | J1 | 950 | | 3,650 |
| 28 | | J2 | | 825 | 2,825 |
| 30 | | J2 | | 200 | 2,625 |

| Accounts Receivable | | | | | Account No. 120 |
|---|---|---|---|---|---|
| Date | Explanation | Post Ref | Debit | Credit | Balance |
| 19XX | | | | | |
| May 14 | | J1 | 1,700 | | 1,700 |
| 23 | | J1 | | 950 | 750 |
| 27 | | J2 | | 100 | 650 |
| 31 | | J2 | 2,500 | | 3,150 |

| Land | | | | | Account No. 130 |
|---|---|---|---|---|---|
| Date | Explanation | Post Ref | Debit | Credit | Balance |
| 19XX | | | | | |
| May 10 | | J1 | 5,500 | | 5,500 |

| Accounts Payable | | | | | Account No. 210 |
|---|---|---|---|---|---|
| Date | Explanation | Post Ref | Debit | Credit | Balance |
| 19XX | | | | | |
| May 10 | | J1 | | 4,500 | 4,500 |
| 20 | | J1 | 4,500 | | — |
| 25 | | J2 | | 125 | 125 |

| Gary Wise, Capital | | | | | Account No. 301 |
|---|---|---|---|---|---|
| Date | Explanation | Post Ref | Debit | Credit | Balance |
| 19XX | | | | | |
| May 1 | | J1 | | 9,000 | 9,000 |

| Gary Wise, Drawing | | | | | Account No. 320 |
|---|---|---|---|---|---|
| Date | Explanation | Post Ref | Debit | Credit | Balance |
| 19XX | | | | | |
| May 30 | | J2 | 200 | | 200 |

| Agency Revenue | | | | | Account No. 410 |
|---|---|---|---|---|---|
| Date | Explanation | Post Ref | Debit | Credit | Balance |
| 19XX | | | | | |
| May 14 | | J1 | | 1,700 | 1,700 |
| 27 | | J2 | 100 | | 1,600 |
| 31 | | J2 | | 2,500 | 4,100 |

| Salaries Expense | | | | | Account No. 510 |
|---|---|---|---|---|---|
| Date | Explanation | Post Ref | Debit | Credit | Balance |
| 19XX | | | | | |
| May 28 | | J2 | 825 | | 825 |

| Marketing Expense | | | | | Account No. 520 |
|---|---|---|---|---|---|
| Date | Explanation | Post Ref | Debit | Credit | Balance |
| 19XX | | | | | |
| May 5 | | J1 | 800 | | 800 |

| Electricity Expense | | | | | Account No. 530 |
|---|---|---|---|---|---|
| Date | Explanation | Post Ref | Debit | Credit | Balance |
| 19XX | | | | | |
| May 25 | | J2 | 125 | | 125 |

## Trial Balance

**OBJECTIVE 3**
**Understand what a trial balance is and how it is constructed.**

Earlier in the chapter we noted that total debits must equal total credits in any given transaction. Because journal entries are transferred (posted) to the ledger, the ledger accounts (taken collectively) should contain equal debit/credit totals as well. To determine whether this equality does in fact exist, the accountant constructs a trial balance. A **trial balance** is a listing of the general ledger accounts, along with the dollar balances contained therein. Unlike the balance sheet, income statement, and statement of owner's equity, the trial balance is not a formal financial statement that is distributed to owners, creditors, and other interested parties. Simply stated, its sole use is within an organization to determine whether the accounting records are in balance.

**Exhibit 2-6**
**Trial Balance for Wise Advertising Agency**

| WISE ADVERTISING AGENCY<br>Trial Balance<br>May 31, 19XX | | |
|---|---|---|
| Cash | $ 2,625 | |
| Accounts receivable | 3,150 | |
| Land | 5,500 | |
| Accounts payable | | $ 125 |
| Gary Wise, capital | | 9,000 |
| Gary Wise, drawing | 200 | |
| Agency revenue | | 4,100 |
| Salaries expense | 825 | |
| Marketing expense | 800 | |
| Electricity expense | 125 | |
| | $13,225 | $13,225 |

The trial balance of the Wise Advertising Agency appears in Exhibit 2-6. This two-column report lists debit balances in the left column and credit balances in the right column. The trial balance shows that the required equality is maintained at $13,225.

OBJECTIVE 4
Be aware of the impact of errors on the trial balance and the various steps necessary to locate an error.

## Equality Does Not Ensure Accuracy

Unfortunately, a trial balance with equal debit/credit totals does not always mean the accounting process was free from error. Several errors can occur that have no effect on the required equality. To illustrate, examine the transaction recorded by Wise on May 31:

| | | | |
|---|---|---|---|
| May 31 | Accounts Receivable | 2,500 | |
| | Agency Revenue | | 2,500 |
| | Billed clients | | |

As shown by the ledger accounts, this entry increased the balance in Accounts Receivable from $650 to $3,150. Furthermore, Agency Revenue rose from $1,600 to $4,100.

Consider, for a moment, the effect of a transaction omission. If Wise's bookkeeper had failed to record and post this entry, the two accounts just cited would each be understated by $2,500. Nevertheless, the trial balance will continue to balance. Although Accounts Receivable and Agency Revenue would both be incorrect, the debit/credit equality is still maintained, now at $10,725 ($13,225 − $2,500). To be more specific, any type of error in which debits and credits are equal will have no impact on the trial balance's balancing. In addition to transaction omission, other such errors include transaction duplication, the posting of entries to the wrong accounts, and journalizing errors (e.g., incorrect accounts and amounts within a journal entry).

## Unequal Totals

Unlike the errors just noted, other errors may occur that create unequal trial balance totals. The resulting out-of-balance condition is naturally unacceptable, and the debit/credit equality must be restored.

Locating the source of an error is often very troublesome, as the trial balance is really a summarization of both the journalizing and posting processes. Mistakes can be made when (1) transactions are placed in the journal, (2) journal entries are posted to the ledger, and (3) the trial balance is constructed. It is generally suggested that one work backward through this sequence of procedures in attempting to pinpoint problems. The following steps may prove helpful:

1 Re-add the trial balance columns.
2 Calculate the difference between the debit and credit totals. If the difference is divisible by 9, there is a good chance that a transposition or a slide has occurred. A **transposition** means that two digits of a given number have been accidentally reversed (e.g., the number 560 is listed as 650, 125 as 152, and so on). With a **slide,** the decimal point of a number is improperly moved to the left or the right (e.g., the number 895 is recopied as 8,950).
3 Calculate one-half the difference between the debit and credit totals, and then look for that amount in the trial balance. If the amount can be located, a debit balance may have been entered in the credit column or vice versa. This type of error always causes the trial balance totals to differ by twice the amount of the improperly placed account balance.
4 After thoroughly checking the trial balance, return to the ledger. Examine individual accounts by recomputing balances and looking for transpositions, slides, and debit/credit reversals.
5 Return to the journal and inspect individual entries. Trace the entries to the ledger accounts to verify the accuracy of posting.

It should now be evident that a variety of errors can occur in the preparation of a trial balance. Error detection for a business of even modest complexity and size can be extremely frustrating because of the number of accounts and transactions involved. In addition, the possibility exists that several errors may have occurred that have counterbalancing effects on one another. Indeed, error determination and location is often more challenging than the recording and processing of transactions and the preparation of financial statements.

## A Brief Overview

The concepts presented in this chapter have laid the groundwork for comprehending the manner in which accounting information is produced. A transaction (or event) starts the entire process in motion. The transaction triggers the generation of a source document, which is translated into debits and credits and recorded in the journal. The entries in the journal are then transferred to accounts in the ledger by posting. Next, the trial balance is prepared to determine whether the ledger accounts are in balance. This sequence of events can be summarized as shown in Exhibit 2-7.

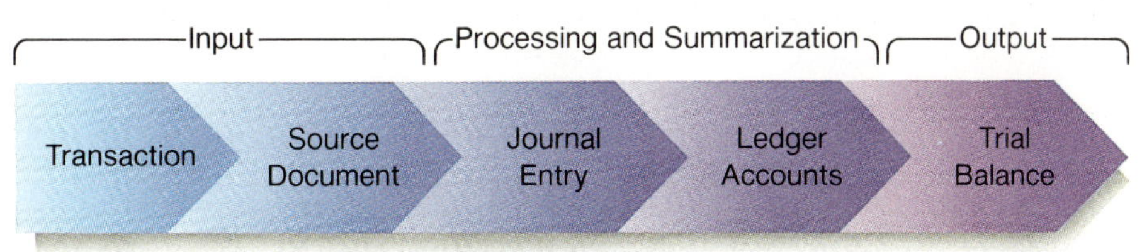


**Exhibit 2-7**
**Basic Sequence in the Accounting Process**

The trial balance is not the end of the process; it is only an intermediate step in the processing cycle. The next two chapters will illustrate the remaining procedures that must be performed for a transaction to find its way into a company's financial statements.

## Chapter Review

### Learning Objectives—The Key Points

**1 Understand accounts, debits and credits, journals, the chart of accounts, and their interrelationships.** The transactions and events that affect a firm trigger the generation of various types of source documents such as sales slips and receiving reports. These documents are recorded in the journal by using a debit/credit format. The debits and credits, based on the following rules, are employed to increase and decrease the individual records that are kept for accounts (e.g., Cash, Accounts Payable, Agency Revenue, and so forth).

| *Account Type* | *Normal Balance* | *To Increase* | *To Decrease* |
|---|---|---|---|
| Assets | Debit | Debit | Credit |
| Liabilities | Credit | Credit | Debit |
| Owner's equity | Credit | Credit | Debit |
| Revenues | Credit | Credit | Debit |
| Expenses | Debit | Debit | Credit |

The entries in the journal are then transferred to the general ledger by the posting process. The possible accounts to use when constructing journal entries are contained in a listing called the chart of accounts.

**2 Be able to post transactions.** The posting process encompasses various procedures that involve the transfer of information contained in the journal to the proper accounts in the general ledger. The major objective of posting is to summarize in one place the various transactions that may affect a given account.

**3 Understand what a trial balance is and how it is constructed.** A trial balance is a two column report that is used to check the equality of debits and credits in the general ledger. The necessary procedures for construction involve classifying an account's end-of-period balance as either a debit or a credit. These amounts are then totaled to determine if the required debit/credit equality holds true.

**4 Be aware of the impact of errors on the trial balance and the various steps necessary to locate an error.** Numerous errors can occur when constructing a trial balance. Several of these errors, including transaction omission and transaction duplication, continue to allow total debits to equal total credits. Others, such as transpositions, slides, and debit/credit reversals, destroy the required equality. Locating an error involves performing certain mathematical tests on the trial balance figures (e.g., determining whether the difference between the debit and credit totals is divisible by 9) and, if needed, on the ledger account data. As a final step, it may be necessary to work backward to the journal to examine individual journal entries.

## Chapter Quiz

The five questions that follow relate to several issues raised in the chapter. Test your knowledge of the issues by selecting the best answer. (The answers appear on p. 75.)

**1** A credit is used in accounting to:
a increase an asset account.
b decrease a liability account.
c increase a revenue account.
d increase an expense account.

**2** Popcorn, Inc., recently purchased some office equipment on account. The proper entry would involve a:
a debit to Office Expense and credit to Accounts Payable.
b debit to Office Equipment and credit to Accounts Payable.
c debit to Office Equipment and credit to Accounts Receivable.
d debit to Accounts Payable and credit to Office Equipment.

**3** Which of the following statements is incorrect?
a Transactions are initially recorded in the journal and then transferred to the general ledger.
b A company's accounts are housed in the general ledger.
c Posting is a process by which accounting information is transferred from one record to another.
d A source document is initially translated into a debit/credit format in the general ledger.

**4** The trial balance:
a is prepared at the beginning of an accounting period.
b checks the equality of debits and credits contained in the general ledger.
c is prepared by extracting information directly from the journal.
d is a formal financial statement like the balance sheet.

**5** Sofa Company's trial balance will not balance if:
a the $2,900 debit balance in the Cash account is entered in the trial balance's credit column.
b the bookkeeper accidentally forgets to record a payment of rent in the journal.
c a credit to Accounts Receivable is posted as a credit to Accounts Payable.
d a $460 purchase of equipment is accidentally entered in the accounting records as $640.

## Summary Problem

A chart of accounts and a list of transactions for operations of the Drake Company during March follow.

| | | | |
|---|---|---|---|
| Cash | 110 | John Drake, drawing | 320 |
| Accounts receivable | 120 | Service revenue | 410 |
| Office equipment | 130 | Salaries expense | 510 |
| Accounts payable | 210 | Utilities expense | 520 |
| John Drake, capital | 310 | | |

Mar. 1 Received $40,000 cash from John Drake, the owner, as an investment in the business.
18 Services rendered to date: cash, $15,500; on account, $12,200.
20 Paid employees' salaries of $10,500.
24 Purchased $4,000 of office equipment from Peach Equipment Company. Paid $3,200 down and agreed to remit the balance owed in 10 days.
30 Paid the March electric bill of $175.
31 Processed a $1,000 cash withdrawal to John Drake.

**Instructions**

**a** Record the transactions in a general journal.

**b** Post the transactions from the journal to the ledger.

**c** Prepare a trial balance as of March 31.

**Solution**

**a**

| | | | | Page 1 |
|---|---|---|---|---|
| Date | Accounts | Post Ref | Debit | Credit |
| 19XX | | | | |
| Mar. 1 | Cash | 110 | 40,000 | |
| | John Drake, Capital | 310 | | 40,000 |
| | Owner investment | | | |
| 18 | Cash | 110 | 15,500 | |
| | Accounts Receivable | 120 | 12,200 | |
| | Service Revenue | 410 | | 27,700 |
| | Recorded service revenue from operations | | | |
| 20 | Salaries Expense | 510 | 10,500 | |
| | Cash | 110 | | 10,500 |
| | Paid employees' salaries | | | |
| 24 | Office Equipment | 130 | 4,000 | |
| | Cash | 110 | | 3,200 |
| | Accounts Payable | 210 | | 800 |
| | Purchased office equipment; balance due in 10 days | | | |
| 30 | Utilities Expense | 520 | 175 | |
| | Cash | 110 | | 175 |
| | Paid March electric bill | | | |
| 31 | John Drake, Drawing | 320 | 1,000 | |
| | Cash | 110 | | 1,000 |
| | Owner withdrawal | | | |

**b**

| Cash | | | | | Account No. 110 |
|---|---|---|---|---|---|
| Date | Explanation | Post Ref | Debit | Credit | Balance |
| 19XX | | | | | |
| Mar. 1 | | J1 | 40,000 | | 40,000 |
| 18 | | J1 | 15,500 | | 55,500 |
| 20 | | J1 | | 10,500 | 45,000 |
| 24 | | J1 | | 3,200 | 41,800 |
| 30 | | J1 | | 175 | 41,625 |
| 31 | | J1 | | 1,000 | 40,625 |

Accounts Receivable — Account No. 120

| Date | Explanation | Post Ref | Debit | Credit | Balance |
|---|---|---|---|---|---|
| 19XX Mar. 18 | | J1 | 12,200 | | 12,200 |

Office Equipment — Account No. 130

| Date | Explanation | Post Ref | Debit | Credit | Balance |
|---|---|---|---|---|---|
| 19XX Mar. 24 | | J1 | 4,000 | | 4,000 |

Accounts Payable — Account No. 210

| Date | Explanation | Post Ref | Debit | Credit | Balance |
|---|---|---|---|---|---|
| 19XX Mar. 24 | | J1 | | 800 | 800 |

John Drake, Capital — Account No. 310

| Date | Explanation | Post Ref | Debit | Credit | Balance |
|---|---|---|---|---|---|
| 19XX Mar. 1 | | J1 | | 40,000 | 40,000 |

John Drake, Drawing — Account No. 320

| Date | Explanation | Post Ref | Debit | Credit | Balance |
|---|---|---|---|---|---|
| 19XX Mar. 31 | | J1 | 1,000 | | 1,000 |

| Service Revenue | | | | | Account No. 410 |
|---|---|---|---|---|---|
| Date | Explanation | Post Ref | Debit | Credit | Balance |
| 19XX Mar. 18 | | J1 | | 27,700 | 27,700 |

| Salaries Expense | | | | | Account No. 510 |
|---|---|---|---|---|---|
| Date | Explanation | Post Ref | Debit | Credit | Balance |
| 19XX Mar. 20 | | J1 | 10,500 | | 10,500 |

| Utilities Expense | | | | | Account No. 520 |
|---|---|---|---|---|---|
| Date | Explanation | Post Ref | Debit | Credit | Balance |
| 19XX Mar. 30 | | J1 | 175 | | 175 |

**c**

**DRAKE COMPANY**
**Trial Balance**
**March 31, 19XX**

| | | |
|---|---|---|
| Cash | $40,625 | |
| Accounts receivable | 12,200 | |
| Office equipment | 4,000 | |
| Accounts payable | | $ 800 |
| John Drake, capital | | 40,000 |
| John Drake, drawing | 1,000 | |
| Service revenue | | 27,700 |
| Salaries expense | 10,500 | |
| Utilities expense | 175 | |
| | $68,500 | $68,500 |

## Questions

**Q2-1** Briefly explain how a typical accounting system operates.

**Q2-2** What is a general ledger?

**Q2-3** In terms of debits and credits, assets are decreased by ______________, expenses are increased by ______________, and revenues are increased by ______________.

**Q2-4** Explain how Accounts Payable could have a debit balance.

**Q2-5** Explain the relationship between the fundamental accounting equation and normal account balances.

**Q2-6** Les Howard accidentally debited an expense account rather than an asset account. As a result of this error, determine whether the following items will be overstated, understated, or unaffected.
a Total assets will be ______________.
b Total expenses will be ______________.
c Net income will be ______________.

**Q2-7** What is a source document? How are source documents used in the accounting process?

**Q2-8** Explain the functions of the chart of accounts.

**Q2-9** A student once commented: "I don't understand the purpose of the ledger account. It seems as though the account is an unnecessary duplication of the journal." Is the student correct? Why?

**Q2-10** Why is the posting reference column in the journal left blank at the time an entry is recorded?

**Q2-11** What is the purpose of a trial balance?

**Q2-12** What types of errors will not affect the equality of the trial balance totals?

**Q2-13** The general journal of the Sprint Company contained the following entry:

| Date | Accounts | Post Ref | Debit | Credit |
|---|---|---|---|---|
| May 19 | Accounts Payable | 210 | 800 | |
| | Cash | | | 800 |

Will the totals of the trial balance be in agreement? Why?

## Exercises

**E2-1** ***Recognition of normal balances***
Classify each of the following as an asset, liability, revenue, or expense. Also indicate the normal account balance of each item.
a Salary costs incurred and paid by a flower shop.
b Amounts due from customers.
c Amounts owed to creditors.
d Property taxes incurred by a muffler shop.
e Long-term loan owed to a bank from the borrower's point of view.
f Admission charges to games from a football team's viewpoint.
g Goods held for resale by a retail store.
h Land held as an investment.
i Fuel costs of an airline.
j Sales of a department store.

**E2-2** ***Transaction analysis, classification***
On February 3, 19X3, Charles Lowry invested $18,000 cash in a new business called the Lowry Service Organization (LSO). Shortly thereafter, LSO purchased $6,700 of

office equipment on account from a local supplier. An examination of the accounting records for February revealed that wage expenses totaled $2,200, all of which were paid in cash. LSO rendered $4,100 of services during the month and billed clients for this amount. By the end of February, clients still owed $450.

A review of the preceding data will reveal that five transactions and events occurred during the month. You are to identify these transactions and events and determine the accounts that are affected. Then, determine the account type (asset (A), liability (L), owner's equity (OE), revenue (R), or expense (E)); whether the accounts have increased or decreased; and whether the accounts must be debited or credited to record the impact of the transaction. Fill in the chart that follows (the first transaction is done as an example):

| *Brief Transaction Description* | *Accounts Affected* | *Account Type* | *Increase or Decrease* | *Debit or Credit* |
|---|---|---|---|---|
| Owner investment | Cash | A | Increase | Debit |
| | Lowry, Capital | OE | Increase | Credit |

**E2-3** ***Debits and credits, journals, ledgers, the chart of accounts***

The comments that follow were taken from the test of an accounting principles student. Do you agree with these comments or disagree? For those comments with which you disagree, briefly state the reason behind your position.

a Debits are used to decrease liability accounts.
b A trial balance with equal debit/credit totals indicates that a firm's transactions have been recorded properly.
c Transactions are normally recorded in the ledger and then posted to the journal.
d The chart of accounts is a useful device in trying to determine the appropriate titles of accounts to debit and credit.
e Failure to credit a revenue account will overstate total revenues on the income statement.

**E2-4** ***General journal and general ledger content***

St. James Services uses a general journal and general ledger to process transactions. Assume that the volume of transactions has grown in recent months and that all posting procedures have already been performed. A manager has requested that you provide the following data:

a The total amounts that clients owe the firm as of May 31.
b The accounts that were increased or decreased by a particular transaction on a specific date.
c The total cash received during May.
d The reason for a cash disbursement on May 14.
e A listing, by date, of all transactions that decreased Accounts Payable during the month.

Evaluate the data requests of the manager independently and determine whether the requests can be answered most efficiently by a review of the company's general journal *or* the company's general ledger.

**E2-5** ***Basic journal entries***

Record the following transactions in general journal form. Include explanations.

a Paid advertising expenses, $600.
b Rendered $280 of services to customers on account.
c Purchased $2,600 of office equipment on account.
d Processed a $400 cash withdrawal for Angie McDonald, the company's owner.
e Received $100 from customers who were previously billed in part (b).
f Purchased land in exchange for $25,000 cash.

**E2-6** ***Basic journal entries***

The following transactions pertain to Monarch Company:

| | | |
|---|---|---|
| June | 4 | Received a $10,000 cash investment from James Wharton, the company's owner. |
| | 9 | Borrowed $6,000 from the First National Bank. |
| | 12 | Paid salaries expense, $1,500. |
| | 17 | Purchased $3,200 of office equipment on account. |
| | 23 | Billed clients for services rendered, $2,800. |
| | 28 | Returned $500 of the office equipment purchased on June 17 and paid the remaining balance owed. |
| | 30 | Recorded a $75 water bill, to be paid next month. |

Prepare journal entries (and explanations) to record Monarch's transactions.

**E2-7** ***Trial balance preparation***

Brighton Company began operation on March 1 of the current year. The following account balances were extracted from the general ledger on March 31; all accounts have normal balances.

| | | | |
|---|---|---|---|
| Accounts payable | $12,000 | Interest expense | $ 300 |
| Accounts receivable | 8,800 | Land | ? |
| Advertising expense | 5,700 | Loan payable | 26,000 |
| Bob Brighton, capital | 30,000 | Salaries expense | 11,100 |
| Cash | 22,500 | Utilities expense | 700 |
| Fees earned | 18,900 | | |

a Determine the cost of the company's land by preparing a trial balance.
b Determine the firm's net income for the period ended March 31.

**E2-8** ***Error detection***

The bookkeeper of the Tulsa Towing Company is attempting to locate an error in the trial balance. Which of the following figures was probably listed incorrectly? Why?

| *Debit* | *Credit* |
|---|---|
| $ 650 | |
| 200 | |
| 460 | |
| | $ 780 |
| | 250 |
| 270 | |
| 370 | |
| $1,950 | $1,030 |

**E2-9** ***Trial balance errors***

Consider each of the following errors individually:

a Incorrectly overstated the balance in the Wage Expense account by $1,000.
b Recorded a $93 electric bill due next month as a $39 debit to Salaries Expense and a $39 credit to Accounts Payable.
c Failed to record the payment of a $400 account payable.
d Recorded the $200 purchase of equipment on account as a credit to Equipment and a credit to Accounts Payable.
e Recorded a $600 cash receipt on account as a debit to Cash and a credit to Fee Revenue.
f Recorded the $4,500 balance of Accounts Payable in the debit column of the trial balance.

Determine (1) which of the preceding errors would cause the trial balance totals to be unequal and (2) which total (debit or credit) would be smaller.

## Problems

### Series A

**P2-A1** ***Transaction analysis and trial balance preparation***
The T-accounts that follow were taken from the books of the Cary Company on December 31 of the current year. Letters in the accounts reference specific transactions of the firm.

| *Cash* | | | |
|---|---|---|---|
| (a) | 20,000 | (d) | 500 |
| (h) | 800 | (f) | 300 |
| (i) | 1,000 | (g) | 600 |
| (j) | 400 | | |

| *Accounts Receivable* | | | |
|---|---|---|---|
| (c) | 1,400 | (h) | 800 |

| *Tools* | | | |
|---|---|---|---|
| (b) | 700 | (g) | 100 |

| *Equipment* | | | |
|---|---|---|---|
| (a) | 6,000 | (i) | 1,000 |
| (e) | 5,000 | | |

| *Accounts Payable* | | | |
|---|---|---|---|
| (g) | 700 | (b) | 700 |
| | | (e) | 5,000 |

| *Cary, Capital* | | | |
|---|---|---|---|
| | | (a) | 26,000 |

| *Fees Earned* | | | |
|---|---|---|---|
| | | (c) | 1,400 |
| | | (j) | 400 |

| *Advertising Expense* | | | |
|---|---|---|---|
| (d) | 500 | | |

| *Utilities Expense* | | | |
|---|---|---|---|
| (f) | 300 | | |

**Instructions**

a Write a brief explanation of each of the transactions (a)–(j).
b Determine the balance in each account and prepare a trial balance.

**P2-A2** ***T-account and trial balance preparation***
Consider the following transactions of the Lopez Service Organization:

| | | |
|---|---|---|
| May | 1 | The owner, José Lopez, opened a bank account in the name of the business by depositing $12,500. |
| | 8 | Rendered services on account, $4,000. |
| | 16 | Paid $1,000 for employee salaries. |
| | 19 | Customers, previously billed, paid $2,500 on account. |
| | 24 | Purchased $400 of office equipment on account. |
| | 25 | Rendered services for cash, $750. |
| | 27 | Paid 60% of the amount due for the equipment purchased on May 24. |
| | 28 | Purchased land for a future building site. Paid $6,000 down and secured a $14,000 loan for the remaining balance. |
| | 28 | Recorded the receipt of the May electric bill of $115. The bill will be paid in June. |
| | 31 | Paid $800 for May rent of office space. |

**Instructions**

a Show how the transactions would appear in the following T-accounts: Cash; Accounts Receivable; Office Equipment; Land; Accounts Payable; Loan Payable; Lopez, Capital; Service Revenue; Rent Expense; Salaries Expense; and Utilities Expense. Then determine the balance of each account.
b Prepare a trial balance.

**P2-A3** ***Entry and trial balance preparation***
A review of the records of Sun & Fun revealed the following trial balance as of January 31, the end of the first month of activity. Account numbers appear in parenthesis.

| | | |
|---|---|---|
| Cash (110) | $22,700 | |
| Accounts receivable (120) | 2,500 | |
| Land (130) | 20,000 | |
| Accounts payable (210) | | $ 5,800 |
| Mary Hodge, capital (310) | | 37,000 |
| Professional fees (410) | | 29,500 |
| Salaries expense (510) | 15,000 | |
| Advertising expense (520) | 8,200 | |
| Utilities expense (530) | 3,900 | |
| | $72,300 | $72,300 |

The following transactions occurred during February:

Feb. 2 Paid $800 to creditors on account.
5 Billed customers $4,000 for services rendered.
9 Paid $1,500 for advertising and $2,200 for salaries.
16 Received February's electric bill of $600, to be paid in March.
23 Received $750 from customers on account.
27 Sold 25% of the land to a neighboring business for $5,000.

**Instructions**

a Record the necessary journal entries for February on page 2 of the company's general journal.
b Open the firm's running balance ledger accounts by entering account titles, account numbers, and January 31 balances. *Note:* This step is not necessary if you are using the preprinted working papers that accompany the text.
c Post the journal entries to the ledger.
d Prepare a trial balance as of February 28.

**P2-A4** ***Journal entries, posting, trial balance preparation***
AAA Furniture Leasing was founded on February 1 of the current year to rent furniture and decorative accessories, primarily to apartment residents. The following transactions occurred during the first month of operation:

Feb. 1 James Larkin, the owner, invested $28,000 of personal funds into the business.
4 Acquired $35,000 of rental inventory from Trendsetters, Inc. Paid $10,000 down, with the remaining balance due in five equal monthly installments beginning on February 28.
10 Received $7,000 of additional financing by securing a short-term loan with United Bank & Trust.
19 Returned $2,200 of furniture to Trendsetters that was shipped in error. Trendsetters agreed to reduce the amount of the first installment due; the other installments would remain as originally negotiated.
23 Paid operating expenses as follows: salaries, $1,900; utilities, $600; and marketing, $950.

28 Paid the first installment due to Trendsetters, Inc.

28 Recorded February rental revenues as follows: cash, $2,900; on account, $3,700.

AAA has established the following accounts and account numbers:

| | | | |
|---|---|---|---|
| Cash | 110 | James Larkin, capital | 300 |
| Accounts receivable | 120 | Rental revenue | 400 |
| Rental inventory | 130 | Marketing expense | 510 |
| Accounts payable | 210 | Salaries expense | 520 |
| Loan payable | 220 | Utilities expense | 530 |

**Instructions**

a Record AAA's transactions in the general journal.

b Post the transactions to running balance ledger accounts.

c Prepare a trial balance.

**P2-A5** ***Journal entry preparation***

On January 1 of the current year, MuniServ began operations with $100,000 cash. The cash was obtained from an owner investment by Peter Houston of $70,000 and a $30,000 bank loan. Shortly thereafter the company acquired selected assets of a bankrupt competitor. The acquisition included land ($15,000), a building ($40,000), and vehicles ($10,000). MuniServ paid $45,000 at the time of the transaction and agreed to remit the remaining balance due of $20,000 (an account payable) by February 15.

During January, the company had additional cash outlays for the following items:

| | |
|---|---|
| Purchases of store equipment | $4,600 |
| Loan payment, including $100 interest | 500 |
| Salaries expense | 2,300 |
| Advertising expense | 700 |

The January utilities bill of $200 was received on January 31 and will be paid on February 10.

MuniServ rendered services to clients on account amounting to $9,400. All customers have been billed; by month-end, $3,700 had been received in settlement of account balances.

**Instructions**

a Present journal entries that reflect MuniServ's January transactions, including the $100,000 raised from the owner investment and loan.

b Compute the total debits, total credits, and ending balance that would be found in the company's Cash account.

c Determine the amount that would be shown on the January 31 trial balance for Accounts Payable. Is the balance a debit or a credit?

**P2-A6** ***Preparation of corrected trial balance***

Nettles Company was founded on January 1, 19X3. The bookkeeper was having difficulty with the December 31, 19X3, trial balance, which follows.

| | | |
|---|---|---|
| Cash | $ 31,300 | |
| Accounts receivable | 26,100 | |
| Building | 50,000 | |
| Accounts payable | | $ 13,200 |
| Loan payable | | 55,000 |
| Ralph Nettles, capital | | 25,600 |
| Ralph Nettles, drawing | 6,900 | |
| Service revenue | | 71,000 |
| Salaries expense | | 38,900 |
| Utilities expense | 4,100 | |
| Advertising expense | 7,600 | |
| | $126,000 | $203,700 |

The following facts have been called to his attention:

a All accounts have normal balances.

b Receipts of $2,900 from customers on account were debited to Cash and credited to Ralph Nettles, Drawing.

c Debits in the Accounts Receivable account were incorrectly stated as $5,500 rather than $4,500.

d The Building account includes the land on which the building is sitting. Correspondence indicates that 80% of the complex's cost is attributed to the building.

e The December electric bill of $500, due in January, was not recorded.

f A withdrawal of $1,200 in December was accidentally debited to Ralph Nettles, Capital. The credit was recorded correctly.

g A $2,900 salary payment was debited to Cash and credited to Salaries Expense.

h A $3,200 advertising bill was inadvertently recorded and paid as $2,300. The advertising agency agreed to accept the balance due in January, 19X4.

i The Miscellaneous Expense account of $1,900 was accidentally omitted from the trial balance.

j Credits of $1,000 to the Service Revenue account were overlooked when calculating the account's balance.

### Instructions

Prepare a corrected December 31, 19X3, trial balance for the Nettles Company.

## Series B

### P2-B1 *Transaction analysis and trial balance preparation*

The T-accounts that follow were taken from the records of Bruner Enterprises on December 31 of the current year. Letters in the accounts reference specific transactions of the firm.

| *Cash* | |
|---|---|
| (a) 20,000 | (b) 500 |
| (e) 2,400 | (c) 900 |
| (i) 1,900 | (d) 10,000 |
| (j) 3,000 | (h) 1,300 |

| *Accounts Receivable* | |
|---|---|
| (g) 4,000 | (i) 1,900 |

| *Land* | |
|---|---|
| (d) 10,000 | (j) 3,000 |

| *Machinery* | | | |
|---|---|---|---|
| (b) | 4,000 | (f) | 2,000 |

| *Accounts Payable* | | | |
|---|---|---|---|
| (f) | 2,000 | (b) | 3,500 |
| (h) | 1,300 | | |

| *Bruner, Capital* | | | |
|---|---|---|---|
| | | (a) | 20,000 |

| *Service Revenue* | | | |
|---|---|---|---|
| | | (e) | 2,400 |
| | | (g) | 4,000 |

| *Utilities Expense* | | | |
|---|---|---|---|
| (c) | 600 | | |

| *Salary Expense* | | | |
|---|---|---|---|
| (c) | 300 | | |

**Instructions**

a Write a sentence or two describing the nature of transactions (a)–(j).
b Determine the balance in each account and prepare a trial balance.

**P2-B2** ***T-account and trial balance preparation***

Consider the following transactions of the Estrada Service Organization:

| | | |
|---|---|---|
| July | 1 | The owner, Vincent Estrada, opened a bank account in the name of the business by depositing $10,000. |
| | 6 | Rendered services for cash, $3,700. |
| | 11 | Purchased $450 of tools on account. |
| | 15 | Rendered services on account, $1,900. |
| | 21 | Paid office salaries of $1,400. |
| | 22 | Purchased $9,000 of office equipment by paying $1,800 down and securing a loan payable for the remaining balance. |
| | 24 | Returned $50 of the tools purchased on July 11. |
| | 27 | Customers, previously billed, paid $1,550 on account. |
| | 29 | Recorded the receipt of the July electric bill of $140. The bill will be paid in August. |
| | 31 | Paid $1,000 for July rent of office space. |

**Instructions**

a Establish T-accounts for Cash; Accounts Receivable; Tools; Office Equipment; Accounts Payable; Loan Payable; Estrada, Capital; Service Revenue; Office Salaries Expense; Utilities Expense; and Rent Expense. Enter the transactions in the T-accounts and determine the balance of each account.
b Prepare a trial balance.

**P2-B3** ***Entry and trial balance preparation***

A review of the records of Service City revealed the following trial balance as of October 31, the end of the first month of activity. Account numbers appear in parenthesis.

| | | |
|---|---|---|
| Cash (110) | $31,800 | |
| Accounts receivable (120) | 4,600 | |
| Land (130) | 28,000 | |
| Accounts payable (210) | | $15,700 |
| Roger Gates, capital (310) | | 42,500 |
| Service revenue (410) | | 39,900 |
| Wage expense (510) | 19,300 | |
| Marketing expense (520) | 10,300 | |
| Repairs expense (530) | 4,100 | |
| | $98,100 | $98,100 |

The following transactions occurred during November:

Nov. 3 Received $1,800 from customers on account.
7 Paid $900 of wages and $1,200 of marketing expenses.
12 Sold 75% of the land to a client for $21,000 cash.
16 Had $400 of repair work performed; agreed to pay the balance due in early December.
20 Rendered $3,500 of services on account.
28 Paid $3,900 to creditors on account.

**Instructions**

a Record the necessary journal entries for November on page 3 of the company's general journal.
b Open the firm's running balance ledger accounts by entering account titles, account numbers, and October 31 balances. *Note:* This step is not necessary if you are using the preprinted working papers that accompany the text.
c Post the journal entries to the ledger.
d Prepare a trial balance as of November 30.

**P2-B4** ***Journal entries, posting, trial balance preparation***

CompuVision was founded on August 1 of the current year to rent microcomputers to college students and business establishments. The following transactions occurred during the first month of operation:

Aug. 1 Jim Norwood, the owner, invested $50,000 of personal funds into the business.
2 Received $10,000 of additional funding by securing a short-term loan with the Second National Bank.
11 Acquired $42,000 of computer equipment from Klein Wholesale. Paid $12,000 down, with the remaining balance due in three equal monthly installments beginning on August 31.
22 Paid operating expenses as follows: advertising, $1,500; salaries, $2,400; and utilities, $300.
26 Returned $3,600 of defective computer equipment to Klein Wholesale. Klein will reduce the amount of the first installment due; the second and third installments would remain as originally negotiated.
31 Recorded August rental revenues as follows: cash, $1,900; on account, $2,700.
31 Paid the first installment due to Klein Wholesale.

CompuVision has established the following accounts and account numbers:

| | | | |
|---|---|---|---|
| Cash | 110 | Jim Norwood, capital | 310 |
| Accounts receivable | 120 | Rental revenue | 410 |
| Computer equipment | 130 | Advertising expense | 510 |
| Accounts payable | 210 | Salaries expense | 520 |
| Loan payable | 220 | Utilities expense | 530 |

**Instructions**

a Record CompuVision's transactions in the general journal.
b Post the transactions to running balance ledger accounts.
c Prepare a trial balance.

**P2-B5** ***Journal entry preparation***

On August 1 of the current year, Eclipse Enterprises began operations with $60,000 cash. The cash was obtained from a $40,000 bank loan and a $20,000 owner investment by Suzanne Peters. Shortly thereafter the company acquired selected assets of a bankrupt competitor. The acquisition included land ($18,000), a van ($12,000), and computer equipment ($7,000). Eclipse paid $24,000 at the time of the transaction and agreed to remit the remaining balance due of $13,000 (an account payable) by September 10.

The firm rendered services to clients that amounted to $13,600, subdivided as follows: cash, $4,000; on account, $9,600. By month-end, customers still owed Eclipse $2,400. Cash outlays during August in addition to those previously mentioned were:

| | |
|---|---|
| Wage expense | $2,100 |
| Repairs expense | 300 |
| Loan payment, including $150 interest | 700 |

The August utilities bill of $250 was received on August 31 and will be paid on September 3.

**Instructions**

a Present journal entries that reflect Eclipse's August transactions, including the $60,000 raised from the loan and owner investment.
b Compute the total debits, total credits, and ending balance that would be found in the company's Cash account.
c Determine the amount that would be shown on the August 31 trial balance for Accounts Receivable. Is the balance a debit or a credit?

**P2-B6** ***Preparation of corrected trial balance***

Sandberg Company was founded on January 1, 19X6. The bookkeeper was having difficulty with the December 31, 19X6, trial balance, which follows.

| | | |
|---|---|---|
| Cash | $ 25,800 | |
| Accounts receivable | 45,700 | |
| Land | 30,000 | |
| Accounts payable | 21,300 | |
| Loan payable | | $ 42,000 |
| R. Sandberg, capital | | 75,800 |
| R. Sandberg, drawing | 24,000 | |
| Professional fees | | 65,100 |
| Rent expense | 18,000 | |
| Advertising expense | 16,400 | |
| Salaries expense | 28,600 | |
| | $209,800 | $182,900 |

The following facts have been called to his attention:

a All accounts have normal balances.
b A $2,000 cash withdrawal by the owner was not recorded.
c A $3,200 billing to a client was recorded as a debit to Accounts Receivable and a debit to Professional Fees.
d Debits of $4,800 were overlooked when computing the balance of the Salaries Expense account.

e The Interest Expense account, which contained a $2,700 balance, was accidentally overlooked when constructing the trial balance.
f Debits in the Cash account were computed as $5,600 rather than the correct amount of $8,600.
g A $5,400 rent payment was credited to Cash; no debit was recorded.
h Sandberg recently sold one-quarter of the land to his brother for cash. The company originally paid $60,000 for the entire parcel; the sale was made at cost, with Cash and R. Sandberg, Capital, being debited for $15,000 each and the Land account credited for $30,000. No other land transactions have occurred.
i A $2,100 bill from the company's advertising agency was inadvertently recorded and paid as $1,200. The agency agreed to accept the balance due in early January, 19X7.
j An examination of the Accounts Receivable account in the general ledger revealed that a $3,100 debit was improperly placed in the credit column.

**Instructions**
Prepare a corrected December 31, 19X6, trial balance for the Sandberg Company.

## Beyond the Basics

**BB2-1** ***Trial balance analysis and journal entry preparation***
Palm Beach Enterprises renders various types of repair services. Eighty percent of the services are on account; the remaining 20% are for cash. The company purchases the equipment necessary to provide the services and finances its acquisitions via bank loans. The following information was extracted from trial balances that were prepared on April 30 and May 31 of the current year:

| | *April 30* | *May 31* |
|---|---|---|
| Accounts receivable | $25,900 | $23,000 |
| Equipment | 63,500 | 70,800 |
| Loans payable (for equipment) | 45,000 | 46,700 |
| Repair revenue, year-to-date | 55,600 | 68,800 |
| Interest expense, year-to-date | 2,900 | 3,600 |

Palm Beach sold $8,000 of equipment during May at cost and received cash in return. All interest charges owed to the firm's banks were paid by month-end.

**Instructions**
a Determine the revenues generated during May from repair services.
b Prepare journal entries to record the following:
(1) Repair services rendered for cash during May.
(2) Repair services rendered on account during May.
(3) Collections on account from customers during May.
c Calculate the cost of equipment acquired during May.
d Prepare journal entries to record the following:
(1) The equipment acquired during May.
(2) The equipment sold during May.
(3) May's loan payments, including interest.

**BB2-2** ***System development; journal entry and trial balance preparation***
Tom Todd has just completed his first year as a cotton farmer. During the past 12 months he leased a farm and the necessary equipment and found that he thoroughly enjoyed the experience. He now desires to pursue a farming career in earnest, and is negotiating to buy land and equipment of his own.

Todd has approached Martha Deller, a loan officer at Farmers Bank and Trust, about the possibility of obtaining funding for the proposed acquisitions. Deller has requested certain financial information about Todd's farming venture. Todd, in turn, supplied a small notebook that he had kept, detailing various transactions and events that occurred during the year. Relevant excerpts from this notebook follow.

Jan. 2 Today I contacted Otto Hanna and leased his 100 acre farm. We agreed that I would pay him one-fourth of the gross proceeds from the sale of my cotton. The crop is to be sold as soon as possible after harvest.

5 I opened a bank account for the farm and deposited $20,000.

8 Went to town and bought fertilizer that cost $2,400; also rented a tractor from the fertilizer dealer for $900. I paid one-half of the total amount due and agreed to pay the remaining balance later.

9 Fuel for the tractor cost $80; paid in cash.

15 Went to town to return the tractor; paid the balance owed to the fertilizer dealer. While in town I wrote a $65 check on the farm's bank account to pay for family groceries.

Mar. 1 Bought cotton seed for $480 (a new hybrid kind) and rented a tractor and planter for $1,200; paid in full.

4 Returned the tractor. Fuel cost another $640 (cash).

July 29 No rain again—65 days and still counting.

Aug. 27 Had the cotton sprayed in preparation for harvest (cost $1,800). The sprayer company gave extended terms—don't have to pay until the end of next month.

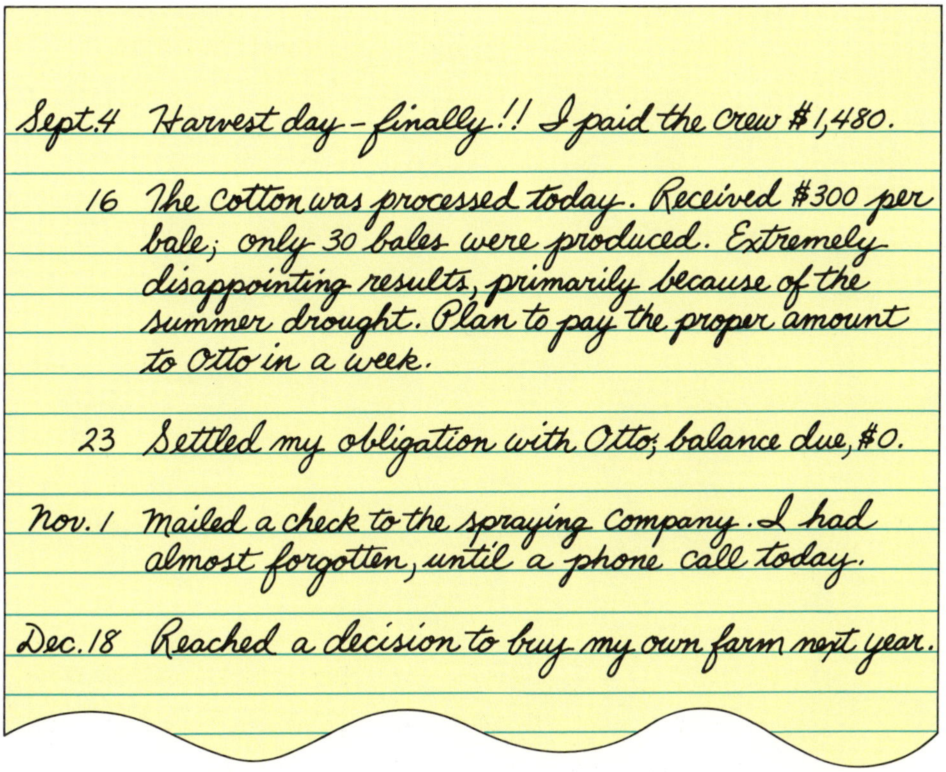

Sept. 4 Harvest day—finally!! I paid the crew $1,480.

16 The cotton was processed today. Received $300 per bale; only 30 bales were produced. Extremely disappointing results, primarily because of the summer drought. Plan to pay the proper amount to Otto in a week.

23 Settled my obligation with Otto; balance due, $0.

Nov. 1 Mailed a check to the spraying company. I had almost forgotten, until a phone call today.

Dec. 18 Reached a decision to buy my own farm next year.

Deller examined the notebook and returned it to Todd, indicating as politely as she could that his records needed improvement. She went on to say that in view of the bank's lending policy, formalized accounting records were necessary before the board would consider any loan application. Todd has approached you, notebook in hand, with a request to "set up some accounting records."

**Instructions**

a Specify the components of a simplified accounting system that Todd could use to process transactions. Include in your response a chart of accounts numbering scheme.

b Use this system to record and process the farm's transactions for the year. *Hint:* Hanna's share of the sale proceeds should be recorded as a liability of the farm and not be treated as farm revenue.

c Prepare a trial balance and comment on the success or failure of the first year of operation.

d In light of your response to part (c), should Deller exclude Todd from consideration for a loan? Briefly explain.

## Answers to Chapter Quiz

**1** c

**2** b

**3** d

**4** b

**5** a

# Income Measurement and Adjusting Entries

CHAPTER 3

## Learning Objectives

After reading this chapter you should:

**1** Understand the impact of the periodicity assumption on accounting and income measurement.

**2** Understand the principle of revenue recognition.

**3** Know when to record expenses and understand the significance of the matching principle.

**4** Understand the underlying differences between the accrual basis and the cash basis of accounting.

**5** Know why the adjusting process is needed and which items typically require adjustment.

**6** Be able to prepare adjusting entries and understand their impact on the financial statements.

**7** Be able to prepare an adjusted trial balance.

**8** (Appendix) Be familiar with the "income statement approach" of accounting for prepaid expenses and unearned revenues.

As we move into Chapter 3, you should have some familiarity with the tools accountants use to process transactions. We saw that debits and credits record increases and decreases in the accounts that are kept by a business. In addition, we observed that entries are posted from the journal to the ledger to summarize the effect of various transactions on a given account. Finally, we noted a trial balance proves the equality of the account balances in the ledger.

You may think that we can now generate financial statements by using the information contained in the trial balance. Unfortunately, we cannot. The preparation of statements at this particular point could result in misleading reports of financial position and profitability. Although daily transactions have been entered in the journal and posted to the proper accounts, the accounting records may still not reflect the correct status of a company's financial affairs at the end of the period.

As a very simple example, consider the procedures that accompany the acquisition of, say, $300 of office supplies. Initially, the $300 purchase price is recorded in the accounting system via a journal entry and the supplies are placed in a storage closet. The supplies are then slowly consumed—a pen here, a box of paper clips there, and so forth. Theoretically, this usage should be recorded on a daily basis, with constant reductions being made to the Supplies account (an asset). From a practical viewpoint, however, virtually all companies keep the amount of bookkeeping at a manageable level and opt for an end-of-period update that reflects the *total* amount of consumption. Unless this updating (i.e., adjusting) procedure is performed, the ledger accounts and the resulting financial statements will be incorrect.

The updating procedure is a key issue in accounting and forms the basis for part of this chapter's discussion. Before presenting the related details, however, it is more appropriate to focus on the underlying rationale for the process, namely, income measurement.

## Income Measurement

Financial statement users have a keen interest in firm performance, particularly the results of operations as expressed by the net income figure. Consequently, a major objective of accounting is to derive a fair and "proper" determination of an organization's earnings for a given reporting period. Earnings measurement is a complicated task—one that accountants must wrestle with on a daily basis. Complex questions arise that relate to the identification of accounting periods, the proper point in time to recognize revenue, the appropriate moment to record an expense, and other important issues. Perhaps the best place to begin is with a discussion of income from the accountant's perspective.

### The Meaning of Income

Almost all businesses are started with the objective of producing a profit, or "making money." These phrases, when put into accounting terms, mean the generation of net income.

The quest for profits is an integral part of the capitalist system. Profits (or losses) are the result of managers using the economic factors of production—land, labor, and capital—in an effective (or ineffective) manner. Economists say that we can measure the outcome of this process in terms of being "better off." That is, profit constitutes the amount by which a business is better off at the end of a period compared to the beginning of the period. Profit would therefore represent a comparison of worth or value at two different points in time.

A determination of the degree of "better-offness" normally entails a number of subjective assumptions. For example, assume that an entity's key competitor has recently gone out of business. Presumably, the surviving entity is "better off"; however, quantifying the event involves obvious difficulties. For instance, will the surviving company attract new customers and increase its market share? Will a new business take advantage of the situation and begin operation? These events will naturally affect the survivor; determining their impact in dollars, however, is extremely troublesome. Generally stated, the economist's definition of profit is beyond the realm of what the accountant can objectively measure.

In an effort to overcome this problem, accountants have developed a different definition of income (or profit). Accounting income is measured by subtracting an organization's expenses from its revenues. Expenses and revenues arise from *transactions and events,* which are happenings that have economic consequences for a firm and are measurable in dollars. (This latter criteria is consistent with the monetary unit assumption discussed in Chapter 1.) Examples of typical transactions and events include the rendering of services to clients, the sale of merchandise to customers, and the incurrence of business expenses such as salaries and taxes. In summary, the accountant downplays the economic concept of profit and employs a more objective **transactions approach** when computing net income.

## The Accounting Period

OBJECTIVE 1
**Understand the impact of the periodicity assumption on accounting and income measurement.**

The accountant's approach to income measurement is complicated because the transactions and events that affect the financial well-being of an enterprise occur continually over the enterprise's lifetime. An in-depth analysis will find that most economic activities are ongoing; they do not cease and restart at specific times. In view of this situation, how can performance be measured? Owners, creditors, and financial analysts naturally cannot wait until the conclusion of an entity's life to assess whether a firm was successful or unsuccessful in its business endeavors. To address this situation, the accounting profession has adopted a periodicity assumption.

The **periodicity assumption** holds that for reporting purposes, an organization's life can be divided into discrete accounting periods (e.g., months, quarters, years, and so forth). If the year is selected, several different alternatives are available:

| *Type of Year* | *Explanation* |
|---|---|
| Calendar year | Runs from January 1–December 31 |
| Fiscal year | Any one-year period other than the above (e.g., July 1–June 30) |
| Natural business year | Ends at the conclusion of the natural business year (e.g., October 31 for a professional baseball club, which is after the play-offs and World Series) |

Although the periodicity assumption seems practical and logical, an allocation problem arises when breaking the life of a company into divisible "chunks." This problem is an outgrowth of the continuous nature of operating activity: many financial events relate to more than a single reporting period. The accounting implications of this situation are highlighted in the following case of Hilton Hotels Corporation.

Hilton generates the bulk of its revenues from furnishing room, gaming, food, and beverage services. Concentrating on the first service listed, suppose that the company received a room reservation request from a customer toward the end of an accounting period. The customer occupied the room for several days during the following period and, upon departure, charged the entire amount owed on a national credit card. The credit card company paid Hilton in the reporting period *after* the stay was completed. Further, assume that Hilton contracted for linen and maid services during the first accounting period, received those services during the second period, and paid its bill in the third period.

In view of these events, two basic questions arise for purposes of measuring financial activity. First, in which period should the revenue from services be recognized? In period 1 when the reservation was secured, in period 2 when the room was provided, or in period 3 when cash was received from the credit card company? Also, in which period should the cost of linen and maid service be recorded as an expense? In period 1 when Hilton committed to the service, in period 2 when the service was received, or in period 3 when Hilton paid the amount due? To answer these questions, one must possess an understanding of the principles of revenue recognition and matching—the foundation for income measurement.

## Revenue Recognition

OBJECTIVE 2
Understand the principle of revenue recognition.

The segmentation of an entity's life into artificial reporting periods forces the accountant to address the issue of **revenue recognition.** Stated differently, the accountant must determine the proper point in time to enter revenue into the accounting records. An obvious solution might be to recognize revenue when it is earned; but exactly when does the earnings process occur? Before deciding for certain, let us explore an example with which you may be familiar. Recall that several years ago, Coleco (a manufacturer of games and toys) introduced the Cabbage Patch Kids dolls. This particular item was such a hit that Coleco could sell the dolls even before production took place. In this case, was revenue *earned* as production occurred, or when the company went through the "routine formality" of making a sale? The correct answer is debatable.

To avoid the confusion introduced by the preceding situation, the accounting profession has settled on a well-accepted guideline: *revenue is generally recognized at the time services are rendered or when goods are sold and delivered to a customer.* At this particular point a company has concluded a major part of the economic activity related to the transaction. This point-of-sale recognition rule applies whether the customer pays cash on the spot or promises to pay in the future (or even if the customer has paid in advance).

Recall our Hilton hotel illustration. Now you can see that the revenue should be recognized in period 2, when the room was occupied (and the service was provided).

## Expense Recognition—The Matching Principle

OBJECTIVE 3
Know when to record expenses and understand the significance of the matching principle.

As noted earlier, a fair measurement of income is an important accounting objective. Because revenues *and* expenses are significant elements in this process, it logically follows that business expenses be recognized in the same period as the revenues that they helped to produce. This concept is known as the **matching principle.**

The application of the matching principle is usually straightforward, especially when there is a direct cause and effect relationship between costs and revenues. In our Hilton hotel example, for instance, the costs for linens and maid service should be expensed during period 2 when the customer occupied the room, utilized these services, and generated revenue for the company. The fact that the costs were paid in period 3 does not alter the analysis. In fact, recognition in period 3 would create a mismatch, with revenues appearing on one income statement and the associated expenses on another.

Application of the matching principle can become troublesome when the relationship between costs and revenues is less direct or less strong. Consider, for instance, an entity's use of long-term assets such as equipment, machinery, and buildings. These assets render benefits for a number of years; by the end of their lives they are "fully consumed" because of wear and tear, obsolescence, and other factors. Consistent with the matching principle, each period benefited should be charged with an appropriate amount of expense. How much to charge is another matter—it is obviously difficult to figure the exact portion of a long-term asset (e.g., a building) that is used up in, say, one year.

To overcome this computational problem, accountants employ a systematic approach and gradually expense the cost of such assets over an estimated service life. Known as *depreciation,* the mechanics of this process will be introduced shortly. Significantly, this approach is still rooted in a desire to adhere to the matching principle; however, the level of precision is not as great when compared with those costs that demonstrate strong causal relationships with associated revenues.

## Accrual Basis Accounting

OBJECTIVE 4
Understand the underlying differences between the accrual basis and the cash basis of accounting.

The revenue and expense recognition principles just presented are fundamental to the **accrual basis of accounting.** Under the accrual basis, revenues are recognized when goods are sold or when services are rendered, and expenses are recognized when incurred. Related expenses are thus matched against revenues, regardless of whether such amounts (i.e., expenses) have been paid. As an example, consider the following data of Denton Enterprises that relate to January of the current year:

- *Services rendered*—The firm rendered $30,000 of services to clients, subdivided as follows: cash, $8,000; on account, $22,000. Customers paid $12,000 of the latter amount after being billed.
- *Operating expenses*—Denton incurred $10,000 of operating expenses, of which $7,000 were paid.
- *Rental payment*—At the beginning of January, Denton paid $6,000 for the next three months' rent.
- *Loan*—In the middle of the month the company secured a $20,000 loan. As of January 31, $100 of interest had been incurred; the interest will be paid to the bank in February.

Denton's accrual basis income statement appears in Exhibit 3-1.

Service revenue is $30,000 because the firm rendered services and earned $30,000 in January. The expenses incurred in producing this revenue are deducted to determine the month's net income. Note that only $2,000 ($\frac{1}{3}$ of the rental payment) is deducted as an expense; the remaining portion is applicable to future

**Exhibit 3-1**
**Accrual Basis Income Statement for Denton Enterprises**

**DENTON ENTERPRISES**
**Income Statement—Accrual Basis**
**For the Month Ended January 31, 19XX**

| | | |
|---|---|---|
| Service revenue | | $30,000 |
| Less expenses | | |
| Operating | $10,000 | |
| Rent | 2,000 | |
| Interest | 100 | |
| Total expenses | | 12,100 |
| Net income | | $17,900 |

periods and will be written off in subsequent months.[1] Finally, interest of $100 is recognized because Denton had use of the loan proceeds to help finance January operations.

## Cash Basis Accounting

When measuring income, some companies select another method of accounting known as the **cash basis.** With the cash basis, revenues are recognized in the period of *receipt,* and expenses are recognized in the period of *payment.* Examine Denton's cash basis income statement, which is shown in Exhibit 3-2.

Note that the statement concentrates on cash flows. Services rendered during the month, for example, total $30,000. Cash receipts from services, however, amount to only $20,000 ($8,000 + $12,000), and this is the amount recorded as revenue. Only $7,000 of the operating expenses are recognized in January; the remaining $3,000 will be recognized in future months when paid. Turning to the rental payment, the entire outflow of $6,000 is treated as January rent expense. Although $4,000 applies to February and March, this fact is ignored under the cash basis. The loan, which is a cash receipt, is not considered revenue because it has not been generated by Denton's earnings process. The $100 of interest, applicable to January, can also be ignored, because payment will not take place until February.

The cash basis of accounting is criticized as not being in accord with economic reality. Stated simply, the receipt and disbursement of cash do not adequately measure financial activity within a given time period. This fact is apparent when examining Denton's transactions. Although the company rendered services amounting to $30,000, only those services for which cash is received in January are recognized as January revenue. As far as expenses are concerned, the firm incurred and became legally liable for $10,100 of operating and interest expense. Under cash basis accounting, however, only $7,000 is recognized. Finally, expensing the entire $6,000 rental payment in the current month overstates Denton's "true" rent expense, because $4,000 really relates to February and March.

Overall, the cash basis does not properly match revenues and expenses. In Denton's case, for instance, several expenses that helped to generate January revenues will not be deducted until paid in future months. Furthermore, certain expenses were deducted (e.g., two months' rent) that failed to produce any revenue for the current period.

[1] Accounting for such "prepayments" is explored in more depth in a later section of this chapter.

**DENTON ENTERPRISES**
**Income Statement—Cash Basis**
**For the Month Ended January 31, 19XX**

| | | |
|---|---|---|
| Service revenue | | $20,000 |
| Less expenses | | |
| Operating | $7,000 | |
| Rent | 6,000 | |
| Total expenses | | 13,000 |
| Net income | | $ 7,000 |

**Exhibit 3-2**
**Cash Basis Income Statement for Denton Enterprises**

## Cash and Accrual Methods in Practice

Because of the possible mismatch of revenues and expenses and the resulting misstatement of financial position, few businesses utilize a strict cash basis of accounting. The cash basis is probably employed most frequently in the preparation of income tax returns for individual taxpayers. The problem faced by businesses is that many companies have substantial investments in long-term assets such as buildings, machinery, and equipment. Under a strict cash basis these resources would be expensed when acquired and paid for despite the fact that benefits are rendered for a number of years. In light of the amount of dollars involved, the cash basis would severely distort reported earnings.

Most businesses that desire to use the cash basis adopt a **modified cash basis** system, which is really a combination of both the cash and accrual methods. The cash basis is followed; however, significant expenditures that benefit more than one accounting period are established as assets when acquired. As an asset's benefits are consumed or used up, the asset's cost is transferred to the income statement and treated as a business expense. The modified cash basis is often employed by professional practices (e.g., medical and law) and by small service organizations.

In contrast, virtually all large companies use the accrual basis of accounting. Usually, the majority of these firms' purchase, sale, and expense transactions are made on account, creating the likelihood that event occurrence and subsequent payment will take place in different periods. In view of the possible mismatch that can occur with the cash basis, the accrual method is preferred by accountants and is therefore featured throughout this text.

# Adjusting Entries

OBJECTIVE 5
Know why the adjusting process is needed and which items typically require adjustment.

Financial statements that fairly present and measure economic activity cannot be produced by relying solely on information contained in the trial balance. As explained in the introduction to this chapter, many accounts need additional updating to reflect their correct status. Because of this situation, a process known as adjusting takes place at the end of the reporting period. In the **adjusting process** the accountant analyzes the various accounts that are maintained by a business. If updating is necessary, adjusting entries (adjustments) are recorded in the journal and posted to the ledger.

## HIGHLIGHT

# Cash-Basis Accounting and Uncle Sam

The problem with the federal government, Rep. Joseph J. DioGuardi says, is that it has too many lawyers and too few accountants. Mr. DioGuardi is an accountant. Recently, after a career spent poring over the books of private corporations, he won a seat in Congress and began studying the books of the federal government. "I'm appalled at the way we account for government spending around here," he said, his voice rising with indignation. "We're using a Mickey Mouse, cash-basis accounting system."

The New York Republican is more emphatic than most of his fellow accountants, but he isn't alone in his critique. The government's top accountant agrees. So do various other accountants, budget officials, and economists both inside and out of government. Bad accounting methods, critics say, can produce bad government policy. Because Washington focuses primarily on the cash it spends and gets each year—and the difference, or deficit, between them—its drives to cut immediate outlays can lead to actions that turn out to be penny-wise and pound-foolish.

Consider the following: Government budget proposals often include the sale of massive amounts of federal assets. Under the accounting methods used by large businesses, such asset sales would not necessarily increase income. For instance, if the assets were sold for less than the amount invested in them, a loss could arise. In contrast, under government accounting conventions, the cash raised by those asset sales would help to reduce the federal deficit, regardless of the sale price. "It's like selling your house to pay for your current spending," a Stanford University economist notes.

Further, a combination of deficit reduction goals and a cash basis accounting system may drive Congress to raise cash or cut spending in the short run but increase costs over the long run. As an example, getting approval to buy or construct federal office space has become nearly impossible because of the big initial outlays that are involved. Such amounts, of course, would further increase the deficit now, a not-so-wise political move. The outcome is that the government's rent bill runs about a billion dollars a year. An accountant with the General Services Administration argues that because the government pays lower interest rates than private builders do and because it is almost certain to need the office space indefinitely, it would usually save money by owning rather than leasing. "The way it is [. . .], at the end of 20 years you end up with nothing but a bunch of canceled rent checks," he complains.

As one CPA observes about the cash basis, "Basically, the government is like someone who uses only a checkbook. That's not a complete picture of [. . .] financial affairs. It doesn't reflect assets, liabilities, commitments in the future. How can you run a trillion-dollar business without knowing what [the] financial position is?"

Whatever the merits of arguments for accounting reform, they don't seem to be carrying the day in Washington. As Mr. DioGuardi has observed with regard to accountants in the Senate and the House, "I can't identify more than a handful in the entire history of Congress!" And, as an official from the Commerce Department notes, accounting changes aren't likely to alter the way Washington works. "[It's] politics," he says.

SOURCE: Adapted from "Government's System of Accounting Comes Under Rising Criticism," *The Wall Street Journal*, February 3, 1986, pp. 1, 11. Reprinted by permission of *The Wall Street Journal*, © Dow Jones & Company, Inc., 1986. All rights reserved worldwide.

Frequently, the adjusting process centers on two specific situations:

1 Previously-recorded multiperiod costs and revenues that must be split among two or more accounting periods.
2 Expenses and revenues that have been incurred or earned in a given period but not as yet entered in the accounts.

The adjusting process is really an outgrowth of the accrual basis of accounting, with a focus on the revenues *earned* (as opposed to those received) and the expenses *incurred*.

## Multiperiod Costs and Revenues

Given the continuous nature of business activity, many of the costs and revenues encountered by a company pertain to more than a single accounting period. The three month rental payment in the Denton Enterprises illustration is one such example. In order to correctly measure financial activity, these items must be split or allocated among the periods affected. The next few pages focus on the related allocation procedures for prepaid expenses, depreciation, and unearned revenues—common examples of multiperiod costs and revenues.

### Prepaid Expenses

OBJECTIVE 6
Be able to prepare adjusting entries and understand their impact on the financial statements.

**Prepaid expenses** are goods and services purchased for future consumption and paid for in advance. Typical examples include such items as insurance, supplies, and rent. It is important to understand that prepaid expenses are *assets* because such amounts will benefit future accounting periods. As these assets are consumed in the process of producing revenue for a business, a portion of their cost must be written off as expense. This write-off occurs in the adjusting process and ensures a proper match of expense and revenue on the income statement.

To illustrate the required accounting, we will continue the Wise Advertising Agency example from Chapter 2. Wise had transactions during May that involved prepaid insurance and supplies.

***Prepaid Insurance*** On May 1, the agency paid $480 for a two-year insurance policy. The transaction, which creates an asset known as prepaid insurance, is recorded by the following journal entry:

| | | | |
|---|---|---|---|
| May 1 | Prepaid Insurance | 480 | |
| | Cash | | 480 |
| | Purchased two-year policy | | |

As each day passes, a portion of the insurance policy expires. Thus, at the end of the period, the Prepaid Insurance account must be updated by an adjusting entry.

The policy acquired provides protection for two years at a cost of $20 per month ($480 ÷ 24 months). By the end of May, $20 of the policy has been consumed; consequently, Wise must credit Prepaid Insurance. This amount represents an expense and, accordingly, total expenses are increased by a debit to Insurance Expense. Here is the necessary adjusting entry:

| | | | |
|---|---|---|---|
| May 31 | Insurance Expense | 20 | |
| | Prepaid Insurance | | 20 |
| | Adjusting entry | | |

These accounts now appear as follows:

| *Prepaid Insurance* | | | |
|---|---|---|---|
| 5/1 | 480 | 5/31 | 20 |
| | **460** | | |

| *Insurance Expense* | | | |
|---|---|---|---|
| 5/31 | 20 | | |

The Prepaid Insurance balance of $460 represents the 23 months of insurance that are still prepaid and is disclosed on the May 31 balance sheet in the asset section. The Insurance Expense account, which contains the one month of expired insurance at $20, appears on the May income statement.

The transfer of prepaid insurance to expense will continue in later periods. Eventually, by the end of two years, Wise will have a zero balance in the asset account. The cost of the entire policy will have been removed from the balance sheet, indicating that the firm expects no additional future benefits from its May 1 payment. The proper accounting for prepaid expenses is shown in a generalized format in Exhibit 3-3.

**Exhibit 3-3**
**Accounting for Prepaid Expenses**

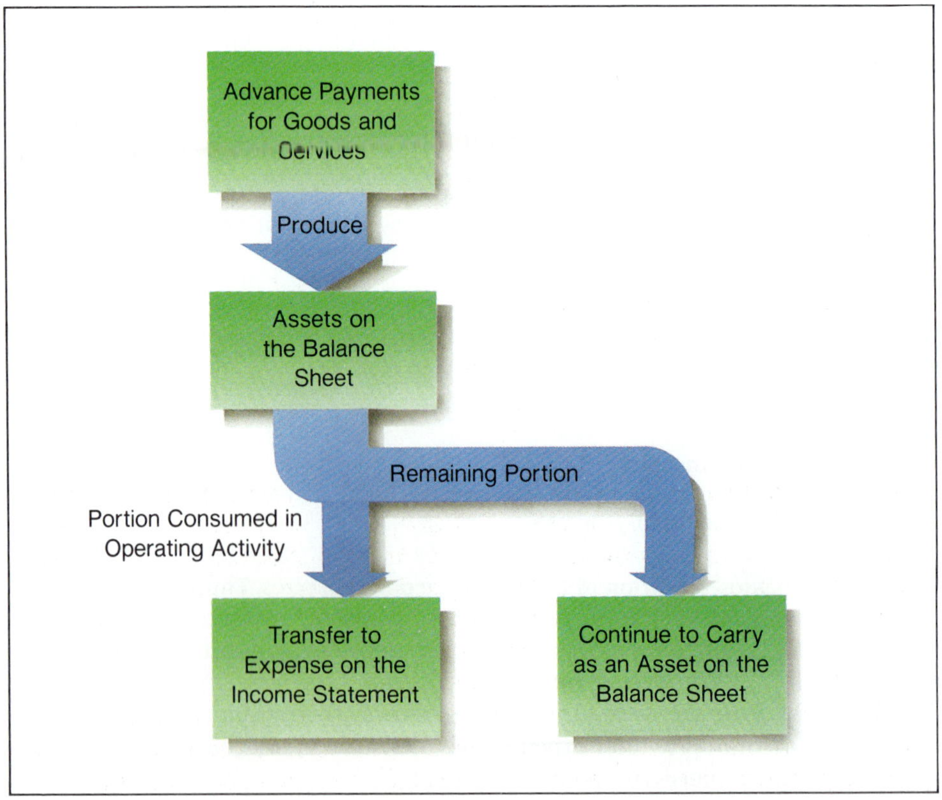

***Supplies*** On May 4, the agency purchased $340 of supplies for cash. Because these items will be used in future periods, the purchase is recorded in an asset account as follows:

| | | | |
|---|---|---|---|
| May 4 | Supplies | 340 | |
| | Cash | | 340 |
| | Purchased supplies for cash | | |

On May 31, Wise determined that various supplies had been consumed in operations and that items costing $260 remained on hand.

An adjusting entry must reduce the asset Supplies from $340 to $260 to reflect the amount owned at the end of the period. Because this account presently has a debit balance of $340, a credit of $80 yields the desired result. The $80 figure, which represents the portion used during May, is an expense and must be debited to Supplies Expense. The necessary adjusting entry follows.

| | | | |
|---|---|---|---|
| May 31 | Supplies Expense | 80 | |
| | Supplies | | 80 |
| | Adjusting entry | | |

Similar to Wise's insurance transaction, the Supplies Expense balance of $80 would appear on the May income statement. The Supplies account contains a balance of $260 ($340 − $80) after adjustment and would be disclosed on the May 31 balance sheet.

**TIPS & TECHNIQUES**

The rationale that underlies the adjustment for prepaid expenses is easy to understand if you picture the nature of the expenditure. Prepaid expenses are goods and services that render future benefits to a company. Such items, which are properly considered assets, are eventually consumed in business activity and must be written off as expense. The recognition of expense and the reduction of the prepaid item is achieved by an adjusting entry that tends to parallel that shown below.

| | | |
|---|---|---|
| Expense | XXX | |
| Prepaid Item | | XXX |

The entry's dollar amount represents the portion of the prepaid expense *used or consumed* during the period.

## Depreciation

The amount of money spent by most businesses for prepaid expenses is relatively small. Considerable sums are expended, however, for the acquisition of other assets, such as buildings, machinery, and equipment, that benefit multiple accounting periods. Although these assets normally assist in the revenue-producing process for a longer period of time than the typical prepaid expense, the same basic accounting practice is followed: the asset's balance is written off to expense upon consumption. This expense is called **depreciation.**

Generally speaking, accountants are unable to determine the exact portion of a long-term asset that is consumed in a given period. As a result, it is common practice to systematically expense a fraction of the asset's cost each year the asset is used. One possible approach for doing this, called the *straight-line method,* takes an equal amount of depreciation during each year of service life.

To illustrate, assume that Wise acquired a used car for cash on May 1 for use in the business. The car cost $4,500 and was estimated to have a service life of three years. The following entry was made:

| | | | |
|---|---|---|---|
| May 1 | Car | 4,500 | |
| | Cash | | 4,500 |
| | Purchased used car | | |

Annual depreciation will total $1,500 ($4,500 ÷ 3 years). On a monthly basis this amounts to $125 ($1,500 ÷ 12), giving rise to the following adjusting entry on May 31:

| | | | |
|---|---|---|---|
| May 31 | Depreciation Expense | 125 | |
| | Accumulated Depreciation: Car | | 125 |
| | Adjusting entry | | |

Depreciation Expense is debited and increases the agency's total expenses. Notice that the Car account is *not* credited, as accountants prefer to leave the cost of a long-term asset intact in the account where initially recorded. Thus, a separate account is established—Accumulated Depreciation: Car. This account appears as a *reduction* in the asset section of the balance sheet and is appropriately termed a **contra asset.** As its name implies, the Accumulated Depreciation account keeps a running total of the depreciation taken during the various accounting periods. The car would appear on the May 31 and June 30 balance sheets as follows:

| | ***May 31*** | ***June 30*** |
|---|---|---|
| Assets | | |
| ⋮ | | |
| Car | $4,500 | $4,500 |
| Less: Accumulated depreciation | 125 | 250 |
| | $4,375 | $4,250 |

The net figures ($4,375 and $4,250) represent the car's **book value,** or the amount that the car is carried at on the books of the business. Book value is simply the numerical difference between an asset's cost and the depreciation taken to date and should not be equated with the true value of the asset in the marketplace.

## Unearned Revenues

The last of the multiperiod items to be discussed is unearned revenue. **Unearned revenue** represents future revenue that has been collected but not as yet earned. The earnings process, often called *realization,* will occur when some type of service is performed.

At the time of collection, unearned revenue represents a liability to the recipient, because goods or services are owed in return. Magazine publishers, for example, often establish an Unearned Subscription Revenue account. On receipt of a subscription, the publisher owes the subscriber a specified number of issues. As another example, airlines often report unearned revenue accounts on their balance sheets. Consider USAir Group, Inc., for instance, which owns USAir and several commuter airlines. Recently, the company reported $319 million in a liability account entitled Traffic Balances Payable and Unused Tickets. An explanation of this account was found in the following footnote that accompanied the financial statements:

> Passenger ticket sales are recognized as revenue when the transportation service is rendered. At the time of sale, a liability is established (Traffic Balances Payable and Unused Tickets) and subsequently eliminated either through carriage of the passenger, through billing from another carrier which renders the service or by refund to the passenger.

Returning to the Wise Advertising Agency example, assume that the firm received $10,400 on May 16 to design and run a 52-week advertising program for McConnell and Associates. The necessary work on the program began immediately. The following entry records the receipt of cash:

| | | | |
|---|---|---|---|
| May 16 | Cash | 10,400 | |
| | Unearned Agency Revenue | | 10,400 |
| | Receipt for 52-week program | | |

Unearned Agency Revenue is a liability account, because Wise owes McConnell a service (advertising work). Observe that the credit increases the agency's obligations to its clients.

By the end of May, two weeks of work had been performed on the contract. Because revenue is earned at the rate of $200 per week ($10,400 ÷ 52), $400 must be recorded as Agency Revenue for inclusion on the May income statement. In addition, the amount of advertising work owed to McConnell has been reduced to $10,000 ($10,400 − $400) and will appear in the liability section of Wise's balance sheet. The proper updating is achieved by the following adjusting entry:

| | | | |
|---|---|---|---|
| May 31 | Unearned Agency Revenue | 400 | |
| | Agency Revenue | | 400 |
| | Adjusting entry | | |

The impact of the entry is shown by these T-accounts:[2]

**Unearned Agency Revenue**

| | | | |
|---|---|---|---|
| 5/31 | 400 | 5/16 | 10,400 |
| | | | (10,000) |

**Agency Revenue**

| | | | |
|---|---|---|---|
| | | 5/31 | 400 |

The preceding accounting treatment parallels that shown earlier for prepaid expenses. In this case, an appropriate amount of the liability becomes earned as services are performed, requiring a transfer of dollars from the unearned account to Agency Revenue. This process is illustrated in a generalized format in Exhibit 3-4.

## Unrecorded Expenses and Revenues—Accruals

**Accruals** are expenses and revenues that gradually accumulate throughout an accounting period. Unlike the multiperiod costs and revenues just presented, accruals have not as yet been recorded in the accounts. As a result, an adjusting entry is

[2] In Chapter 2, the Agency Revenue account was affected by transactions on May 14, 27, and 31. These transactions are omitted here, allowing us to focus solely on the unearned revenue concept.

**Exhibit 3-4**
**Accounting for Unearned Revenues**

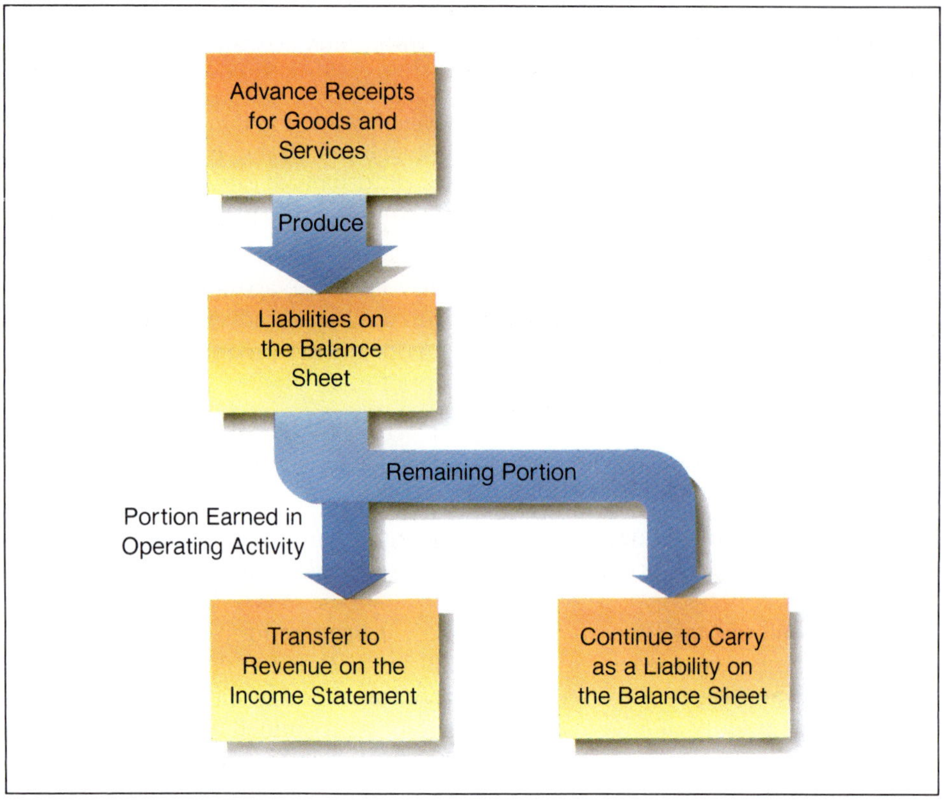


needed so that these items are properly considered when the financial statements are prepared.

Accruals are consistent with the accrual basis of accounting. **Accrued expenses** are expenses that have been incurred but not as yet paid. Examples include the wages incurred by businesses during the last few days of a month and the interest owed to creditors on loans. Both of these expenses gradually accumulate and are likely to be paid in the next reporting period. **Accrued revenues,** on the other hand, have been earned although not as yet received. Common examples of accrued revenues include the interest just mentioned (from the creditors' viewpoint), commissions earned, and unbilled revenues. As you can see, we are focusing on revenues *earned* and expenses *incurred* and *not* on the related cash receipt or disbursement. These concepts are explored by returning to the Wise Advertising illustration.

## Accrued Expenses

On May 1, the agency obtained a $6,000 loan. Payments are due on the first of each month; interest is computed at the rate of 1 percent per month on the unpaid balance. The proceeds from the loan are recorded in the following entry:

| | | | |
|---|---|---|---|
| May 1 | Cash | 6,000 | |
| | Loan Payable | | 6,000 |
| | Recorded loan proceeds | | |

As of May 31, interest charges have been incurred because Wise has had use of the borrowed funds during the month. Although the interest will not be remitted until the first payment date on June 1, the charges arose in May and should appear on May's financial statements. Consequently, an adjusting entry is needed to update the accounts.

Interest is computed at the rate of 1 percent per month on the unpaid balance of the loan. May's interest thus amounts to \$60 (\$6,000 × 0.01). This amount represents an increase in Wise's total borrowing costs for the accounting period, requiring a debit to Interest Expense. Further, because payment does not occur until the following month, \$60 must also be placed in a liability account to show the firm's obligation as of May 31. Interest Payable is therefore credited, and the adjusting entry follows.

| | | | |
|---|---|---|---|
| May 31 | Interest Expense | 60 | |
| | Interest Payable | | 60 |
| | Adjusting entry | | |

***Accrued Salaries*** Focusing on another accrued expense (salaries), assume that Wise's employees work a five-day week. Employees are paid on the last Friday of each month, and payday for May occurred on the 28th (see p. 53). As shown in the accompanying diagram, the company has incurred one day of expense (May 31) that will not be paid until the end of June.

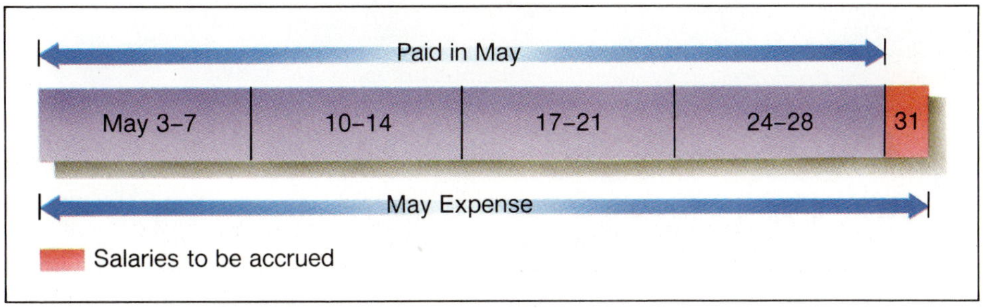


This expense properly belongs to May and must be accrued (i.e., recorded) at the end of the month by an adjustment. If salaries for May 31 amount to \$50, the necessary adjusting entry is:

| | | | |
|---|---|---|---|
| May 31 | Salaries Expense | 50 | |
| | Salaries Payable | | 50 |
| | Adjusting entry | | |

The expense is debited because the agency's total salary cost has increased. Salaries Payable, a liability, is credited to reflect the added obligation of the firm as of month-end.

## Accrued Revenues

To illustrate accrued revenue, assume that on May 14, Wise agreed to provide services for Holmes Corporation during the next five months. As of May 31, the agency had rendered services totaling \$710. The \$710 is properly considered May revenue because the service was provided during May; yet, to date, no entry has been made in the accounting records. The correct adjusting entry is as follows:

| | | | |
|---|---|---|---|
| May 31 | Accounts Receivable | 710 | |
| | Agency Revenue | | 710 |
| | Adjusting entry | | |

Accounts Receivable is debited because the amounts due from clients have increased. In addition, Agency Revenue is credited to record the increase in the revenue earned from business activity.

### ▶ TIPS & TECHNIQUES

The adjustments required for accruals are an extension of two simple definitions. An accrued expense has been *incurred but not as yet paid*, and an accrued revenue has been *earned though not as yet received*. Given that both of these items must be entered in the accounting records at the end of the period, the adjustments may be pictured as follows:

| Accrued Expense | | | Accrued Revenue | | |
|---|---|---|---|---|---|
| Expense | XXX* | | Receivable | XXX† | |
| Payable | | XXX | Revenue | | XXX |

* Amount incurred
† Amount earned

## Adjusted Trial Balance

OBJECTIVE 7
Be able to prepare an adjusted trial balance.

Recall from Chapter 2 that a trial balance is constructed to check the equality of debits and credits in the general ledger. To reflect the account changes that result from the adjusting entries, many companies go one step further and prepare an **adjusted trial balance.** Before we illustrate the necessary construction procedures, we must update the records of the Wise Advertising Agency for the additional transactions of May introduced in this chapter. For the required computations, study Exhibit 2-6 and then review the tabulation that follows.

| | |
|---|---|
| Cash: $2,625 + $10,400 (unearned revenue) + $6,000 (loan) − $480 (insurance) − $340 (supplies) − $4,500 (car) | $13,705 |
| Prepaid insurance: $0 + $480 (purchase on 5/1) | $480 |
| Supplies: $0 + $340 (purchase on 5/4) | $340 |
| Car: $0 + $4,500 (purchase on 5/1) | $4,500 |
| Unearned agency revenue: $0 + $10,400 (receipt on 5/16) | $10,400 |
| Loan payable: $0 + $6,000 (obtained on 5/1) | $6,000 |

The double underlined figures (and others) are carried forward to the first two columns of Exhibit 3-5, where preparation is shown. Note that the "regular" trial balance summarizes daily transaction information only; adjusting entries are not considered. Columns 3 and 4, on the other hand, reveal the adjustments presented in the preceding discussion.

**Exhibit 3-5**
**Preparation of Adjusted Trial Balance**

| Account Title | Trial Balance Debit | Trial Balance Credit | Adjustments Debit | Adjustments Credit | Adjusted Trial Balance Debit | Adjusted Trial Balance Credit |
|---|---|---|---|---|---|---|
| Cash | 13,705 | | | | 13,705 | |
| Accounts receivable | 3,150 | | (*g*) 710 | | 3,860 | |
| Prepaid insurance | 480 | | | (*a*) 20 | 460 | |
| Supplies | 340 | | | (*b*) 80 | 260 | |
| Land | 5,500 | | | | 5,500 | |
| Car | 4,500 | | | | 4,500 | |
| Accounts payable | | 125 | | | | 125 |
| Unearned agency revenue | | 10,400 | (*d*) 400 | | | 10,000 |
| Loan payable | | 6,000 | | | | 6,000 |
| Gary Wise, capital | | 9,000 | | | | 9,000 |
| Gary Wise, drawing | 200 | | | | 200 | |
| Agency revenue | | 4,100 | | (*d*) 400<br>(*g*) 710 | | 5,210 |
| Salaries expense | 825 | | (*f*) 50 | | 875 | |
| Marketing expense | 800 | | | | 800 | |
| Electricity expense | 125 | | | | 125 | |
| | 29,625 | 29,625 | | | | |
| Insurance expense | | | (*a*) 20 | | 20 | |
| Supplies expense | | | (*b*) 80 | | 80 | |
| Depreciation expense | | | (*c*) 125 | | 125 | |
| Accumulated depreciation: car | | | | (*c*) 125 | | 125 |
| Interest expense | | | (*e*) 60 | | 60 | |
| Interest payable | | | | (*e*) 60 | | 60 |
| Salaries payable | | | | (*f*) 50 | | 50 |
| | | | 1,445 | 1,445 | 30,570 | 30,570 |

Observe that both halves of each adjustment (i.e., debit and credit) are keyed or referenced by a letter, the letter (*a*) in the case of insurance. The purpose of this procedure is to facilitate an examination of the adjustments by anyone who so desires. There are no rules regarding the assignment of specific letters to particular accounts.

In several cases an account that is needed in an adjusting entry does not appear in the trial balance. When this situation occurs, the account is simply written on the lines below the trial balance. After all the adjustment information is entered, the columns are totaled to check the equality of debits and credits.

Next, the trial balance data and the adjustments are combined to yield the desired outcome. As an example, the $3,150 balance in Accounts Receivable is combined with a $710 debit (increase) from an adjusting entry, and the result ($3,860) is placed in the debit column of the adjusted trial balance. Similarly, the Prepaid Insurance balance of $480 is credited or reduced by a $20 adjustment. The account's $460 ending balance, a debit, is thus also entered in the debit column. After all appropriate extensions have been made, the columns are totaled to verify mathematical accuracy. The completed product is shown in Exhibit 3-6. Notice that for presentation purposes, all similar account types have been grouped together.

**Exhibit 3-6**

| WISE ADVERTISING AGENCY<br>Adjusted Trial Balance<br>May 31, 19XX | | |
|---|---|---|
| Cash | $13,705 | |
| Accounts receivable | 3,860 | |
| Prepaid insurance | 460 | |
| Supplies | 260 | |
| Land | 5,500 | |
| Car | 4,500 | |
| Accumulated depreciation: car | | $ 125 |
| Accounts payable | | 125 |
| Unearned agency revenue | | 10,000 |
| Interest payable | | 60 |
| Salaries payable | | 50 |
| Loan payable | | 6,000 |
| Gary Wise, capital | | 9,000 |
| Gary Wise, drawing | 200 | |
| Agency revenue | | 5,210 |
| Salaries expense | 875 | |
| Marketing expense | 800 | |
| Electricity expense | 125 | |
| Insurance expense | 20 | |
| Supplies expense | 80 | |
| Depreciation expense | 125 | |
| Interest expense | 60 | |
| | $30,570 | $30,570 |

Once an adjusted trial balance is prepared, the accountant has an excellent springboard for the construction of the financial statements. As you will see in Chapter 4, the data just developed serve as the foundation for a *work sheet*—a columnar form that aids in the generation of the income statement, statement of owner's equity, and balance sheet.

## Adjustment Errors

The adjusting process is very important as far as the accountant is concerned. Failure to properly adjust the books at the end of the period will produce errors in the financial statements. To illustrate, assume that Wise's accountant failed to consider the expiration of a prepaid expense. As a result, an expense account was not debited, nor was an asset account credited. The company's expenses were not increased and are therefore understated. Because such amounts are subtracted from revenues on the income statement, the reported net income figure will be too high. Unfortunately, the problem does not stop here, given the manner in which the financial statements are linked together (see Exhibit 3-7). The overstated net income is carried forward to both the statement of owner's equity and the balance sheet. The exhibit reveals, however, that the required equality between assets and the total of liabilities and owner's equity is still maintained because of Wise's failure to credit (reduce) the appropriate asset account.

Should the adjustment error involve an accrual, a similar type of analysis can be performed. Assume, for instance, that Wise's accountant failed to make the $710

**Exhibit 3-7**
**Prepaid Expense Adjustment Errors**

Entry omitted:

| | | |
|---|---|---|
| Expense | XXX | |
| Prepaid Expense* | | XXX |
| To record the expiration of a prepaid expense | | |

* An asset account

**Income Statement**

| | | |
|---|---|---|
| Revenues | | $ OK |
| Less expenses | | Understated |
| Net income | | $ Overstated |

**Statement of Owner's Equity**

| | | |
|---|---|---|
| Beginning balance, Jan. 1 | | $ OK |
| Add: Net income | $Overstated | |
| Deduct: Withdrawals | OK | Overstated |
| Ending balance, Dec. 31 | | $Overstated |

**Balance Sheet**

| | |
|---|---|
| Assets | $Overstated |
| Liabilities | $ OK |
| Owner's equity | Overstated |
| Total liabilities & owner's equity | $Overstated |

adjustment for accrued revenues. The failure to credit Agency Revenue will understate revenues on the income statement. If revenues are understated, net income will be too small. This, in turn, depresses ending owner's equity on both the statement of owner's equity and the balance sheet. The balance sheet will balance, however, because the accountant also failed to debit (increase) Accounts Receivable.

## APPENDIX An Alternative Accounting Treatment for Prepaid Expenses and Unearned Revenues

The accounting treatments illustrated in the body of this chapter for prepaid expenses and unearned revenues are used by many businesses. These treatments could be called the "balance sheet approach" because the initial recording of insurance, supplies, and revenues received in advance took place in balance sheet accounts. More specifically, the acquisition of prepaid expenses entailed a debit to an asset account, while the receipt of unearned revenue generated a credit to a liability.

OBJECTIVE 8
Be familiar with the "income statement approach" of accounting for prepaid expenses and unearned revenues.

Under an alternative accounting practice followed by some firms (i.e., the "income statement approach"), prepaid expenses and unearned revenues are recorded initially in income statement accounts. Prepaid expenses are immediately charged to expense when acquired, and unearned revenues are credited to revenue accounts upon collection. To illustrate these accounting alternatives, we will continue to use data from the Wise Advertising Agency example.

## Accounting for Prepaid Expenses

Recall from page 85 that Wise acquired a two-year insurance policy on May 1. The $480 policy cost was recorded in an asset account entitled Prepaid Insurance, indicating use of the balance sheet method. One month of the policy expired during May, requiring a transfer of $20 ($480 ÷ 24 months) from Prepaid Insurance to Insurance Expense via an adjusting entry. These events and the resulting financial statement disclosures are summarized at the top of Exhibit 3-8.

This exhibit also reveals the proper accounting had the agency used the income statement approach. Upon acquisition, the cost of the entire policy is placed in the

**Exhibit 3-8**
**Alternative Accounting Methods for Prepaid Expenses**

On May 1, Wise Advertising paid $480 for a two-year insurance policy. The policy expires at the rate of $20 per month ($480 ÷ 24 months).

***Balance Sheet Approach***

| Date | Account | Debit | Credit |
|---|---|---|---|
| 5/1 | Prepaid Insurance | 480 | |
| | Cash | | 480 |
| | Purchased two-year policy | | |
| 5/31 | Insurance Expense | 20 | |
| | Prepaid Insurance | | 20 |
| | Adjusting entry | | |

***Prepaid Insurance***

| | | | |
|---|---|---|---|
| 5/1 | 480 | 5/31 | 20 |
| | 460 | | |

***Insurance Expense***

| | | | |
|---|---|---|---|
| 5/31 | 20 | | |

Balance sheet disclosure, May 31:
Prepaid insurance, $460

May income statement disclosure:
Insurance expense, $20

***Income Statement Approach***

| Date | Account | Debit | Credit |
|---|---|---|---|
| 5/1 | Insurance Expense | 480 | |
| | Cash | | 480 |
| | Purchased two-year policy | | |
| 5/31 | Prepaid Insurance | 460 | |
| | Insurance Expense | | 460 |
| | Adjusting entry | | |

***Prepaid Insurance***

| | | | |
|---|---|---|---|
| 5/31 | 460 | | |

***Insurance Expense***

| | | | |
|---|---|---|---|
| 5/1 | 480 | 5/31 | 460 |
| | 20 | | |

Balance sheet disclosure, May 31:
Prepaid insurance, $460

May income statement disclosure:
Insurance expense, $20

Insurance Expense account. It is naturally incorrect to show the full policy cost of $480 on May's income statement because the actual expense to the firm is only $20. In view of this situation, an adjusting entry is needed at the end of the month.

To achieve the desired $20 balance in Insurance Expense, this account must be reduced, or credited, by $460 ($480 − $460 = $20). The $460 figure represents the cost of the policy's forthcoming 23 months (i.e., the prepaid portion as of May 31) and is therefore debited to Prepaid Insurance. In effect, the adjustment transfers the *unused* portion of the prepayment from the expense account to an asset, resulting in one month of cost on the income statement and the remaining 23 months of cost on the balance sheet.

## Accounting for Unearned Revenues

The alternative accounting treatment for unearned revenues is similar to that shown for prepaid expenses. We will once again utilize data from the Wise Advertising example, this time focusing on the May 16 receipt of $10,400 from McConnell and Associates for a 52-week advertising program. The analysis shown earlier in the text on page 89 is summarized at the top of Exhibit 3-9.

**Exhibit 3-9**
**Alternative Accounting Methods for Unearned Revenues**

Wise received $10,400 on May 16 to design and run a 52-week advertising program for McConnell and Associates. Two weeks of work had been performed by the end of the month, resulting in $400 of revenue [($10,400 ÷ 52 weeks) × 2].

***Balance Sheet Approach***

| | | | |
|---|---|---|---|
| 5/16 | Cash | 10,400 | |
| | Unearned Agency Revenue | | 10,400 |
| | Receipt for 52-week program | | |
| 5/31 | Unearned Agency Revenue | 400 | |
| | Agency Revenue | | 400 |
| | Adjusting entry | | |

*Unearned Agency Revenue*

| | | | |
|---|---|---|---|
| 5/31 | 400 | 5/16 | 10,400 |
| | | | 10,000 |

*Agency Revenue*

| | | | |
|---|---|---|---|
| | | 5/31 | 400 |

Balance sheet disclosure, May 31:
Unearned agency revenue, $10,000

May income statement disclosure:
Agency revenue, $400

***Income Statement Approach***

| | | | |
|---|---|---|---|
| 5/16 | Cash | 10,400 | |
| | Agency Revenue | | 10,400 |
| | Receipt for 52-week program | | |
| 5/31 | Agency Revenue | 10,000 | |
| | Unearned Agency Revenue | | 10,000 |
| | Adjusting entry | | |

*Unearned Agency Revenue*

| | | | |
|---|---|---|---|
| | | 5/31 | 10,000 |

*Agency Revenue*

| | | | |
|---|---|---|---|
| 5/31 | 10,000 | 5/16 | 10,400 |
| | | | 400 |

Balance sheet disclosure, May 31:
Unearned agency revenue, $10,000

May income statement disclosure:
Agency revenue, $400

Wise originally recorded the receipt by crediting Unearned Agency Revenue, a liability account. Because two weeks of work had been performed by month-end, the adjusting entry reflected the earnings process and transferred $400 from the liability account to Agency Revenue for inclusion on the income statement. The remaining amount of advertising work to be performed ($10,000) is disclosed on the balance sheet.

Had Wise employed the income statement method, the $10,400 collection would have been entered in an income statement account on May 16, namely, Agency Revenue. By May 31, the firm had earned a total of $400—the proper amount to disclose on the income statement. An adjusting entry is therefore needed that reduces (debits) the Agency Revenue account by $10,000 ($10,400 − $10,000 = $400). This amount is a liability for Wise because the firm owes McConnell $10,000 of future services. Appropriately, then, the adjusting entry removes the amount *yet to be earned* from the Agency Revenue account and places it in Unearned Agency Revenue. The resulting financial statement disclosures reveal the agency's liability and revenue earned at $10,000 and $400, respectively.

### A Comparison of the Two Approaches

Careful study of the balance sheet and income statement approaches shows that the resulting financial statement presentations are identical. Both of these methods are found in practice, with the income statement approach being extremely popular for those items that will be *totally* consumed (or earned) in the accounting period of payment (or receipt). Such items would not require adjusting entries at the end of the period, given the income statement's adjustment focus on the amounts *unused* or *unearned.* Less work at this busy time of the processing cycle normally, in turn, leads to greater efficiencies in the generation of financial information.

## Chapter Review

### Learning Objectives—The Key Points

**1 Understand the impact of the periodicity assumption on accounting and income measurement.** The periodicity assumption holds that for reporting purposes, an entity's life be divided into discrete accounting periods. These periods allow feedback to interested parties at specified intervals of time, such as a month, quarter, or a year. Because of the continuous nature of economic activities (e.g., the generation of revenue), the assumption requires that economic activities be allocated or apportioned among the periods affected.

**2 Understand the principle of revenue recognition.** Accountants generally use a point-of-sale rule to determine the proper time to recognize revenue in the accounting records. Revenues are usually entered in the accounts when goods are sold or when services are rendered. Both of these situations signify completion of a major part of the economic activity related to the transaction.

**3 Know when to record expenses and understand the significance of the matching principle.** Expenses are entered in the accounting records in the same period as the revenues that they helped to produce. This concept, known as the matching principle, is relatively straightforward when a strong cause and effect relationship exists between revenue and expense. When a weak relationship is present, allocation methods (e.g., depreciation) may be necessary to charge each period with an appropriate amount of expense.

**4 Understand the underlying differences between the accrual basis and the cash basis of accounting.** With the accrual basis, revenues are recognized in the accounts when goods are sold or when services are rendered, and expenses are recognized when incurred. This method of accounting results in a better matching of revenue and expense than the cash basis. Under the cash basis, revenues are recorded in the accounts in the period of receipt, and expenses are recognized when paid.

**5 Know why the adjusting process is needed and which items typically require adjustment.** The adjusting process is needed because many accounts are not up-to-date at the end of the accounting period. The items that often need adjustment include previously-recorded costs and revenues that must be split among two or more accounting periods, for example, prepaid expenses, long-term assets, and unearned revenues. Other items that require adjusting entries are accrued revenues and expenses, or revenues and expenses that have been earned or incurred in a given period but not as yet entered in the accounts.

**6 Be able to prepare adjusting entries and understand their impact on the financial statements.** Adjustments introduced in this chapter were those for prepaid expenses, depreciation, unearned revenues, accrued expenses, and accrued revenues. The proper entries for these items are generalized in the following chart:

| | *Type of Account* | |
|---|---|---|
| ***Type of Adjustment*** | ***Debited*** | ***Credited*** |
| Prepaid expense | Expense | Asset |
| Depreciation | Expense | Contra asset |
| Unearned revenue | Liability | Revenue |
| Accrued expense | Expense | Liability |
| Accrued revenue | Asset | Revenue |

The omission of any of these entries would affect both the balance sheet and the income statement. The failure to debit an expense, for example, would understate expenses, overstate net income, and overstate owner's equity.

**7 Be able to prepare an adjusted trial balance.** The adjusted trial balance is prepared at the end of an accounting period by combining the trial balance and a company's adjusting entries. This document is used to assist in the construction of financial statements.

**8 (Appendix) Be familiar with the "income statement approach" of accounting for prepaid expenses and unearned revenues.** Under the income statement approach, prepaid expenses are recorded initially in expense accounts and unearned revenues are entered in revenue accounts. The adjusting process moves the unconsumed part of the prepaid expense from the expense account to an asset account. Similarly, the yet-to-be-earned portion of the unearned revenue is transferred from the revenue account to a liability.

## Chapter Quiz

The five questions that follow relate to several issues raised in the chapter. Test your knowledge of the issues by selecting the best answer. (The answers appear on p. 114.)

1 The accrual basis of accounting:
  a is less popular than the cash basis with respect to use by large businesses.
  b better matches expenses and revenues than does the cash basis of accounting.
  c recognizes revenues when earned and expenses when paid.
  d recognizes revenues when received and expenses when paid.

**2** Joe Hamilton contacted Denver Painting Contractors in July to paint his office building. The price was agreed on in August, the painting took place in September, and Hamilton paid Denver in October. In which month would Hamilton recognize an expense under the accrual basis of accounting? Under the cash basis of accounting?

| | *Accrual Basis* | *Cash Basis* |
|---|---|---|
| a | July | September |
| b | August | September |
| c | September | October |
| d | August | October |

**3** The Supplies account of Design Limited contained a $3,200 balance before adjustment on December 31. If $2,400 of supplies remain on hand at year-end, the proper adjusting entry would be:

| | *Debit* | *Credit* | *Amount* |
|---|---|---|---|
| a | Supplies Expense | Supplies | $2,400 |
| b | Supplies Expense | Supplies | $800 |
| c | Supplies | Supplies Expense | $2,400 |
| d | Supplies | Supplies Expense | $800 |

**4** Kip's Appliances sells three-month service contracts to buyers of new appliances. The $32,800 balance in the company's Unearned Service Contract Revenue account is properly classified as:

a an expense.
b revenue.
c an asset.
d a liability.

**5** As of August 31, Sun Shade Auto Tinting owes $600 of interest (as yet unrecorded) to First Bank and Trust. If payment will take place on September 5, Sun Shade would classify the interest on August 31 as:

a a prepaid expense.
b an unearned revenue.
c an accrued expense.
d an accrued revenue.

## Summary Problem

Gottom Company began operation on January 1 of the current year. The company's December 31 trial balance follows.

| GOTTOM COMPANY<br>Trial Balance<br>December 31, 19XX | | |
|---|---|---|
| Cash | $ 65,000 | |
| Accounts receivable | 4,200 | |
| Office supplies | 800 | |
| Prepaid insurance | 2,000 | |
| Office furniture | 16,000 | |
| Accounts payable | | $ 10,000 |
| Paul Gottom, capital | | 30,000 |
| Paul Gottom, drawing | 7,400 | |
| Service revenue | | 85,000 |
| Salaries expense | 24,000 | |
| Rent expense | 3,000 | |
| Utilities expense | 2,000 | |
| Other expense | 600 | |
| | $125,000 | $125,000 |

The following adjustment information has come to your attention:
1 Ending office supplies on hand: $300.
2 Prepaid insurance expired during the period: $1,600.
3 Depreciation expense on the furniture: $2,000.
4 Accrued salaries owed to employees: $150.

**Instructions**

**a** Prepare Gottom's required adjusting entries.

**b** Prepare an adjusted trial balance similar to that shown in Exhibit 3-6.

**Solution**

| | | | |
|---|---|---|---|
| **a** Dec. 31 | Office Supplies Expense | 500 | |
| | Office Supplies | | 500 |
| | Adjusting entry | | |
| 31 | Insurance Expense | 1,600 | |
| | Prepaid Insurance | | 1,600 |
| | Adjusting entry | | |
| 31 | Depreciation Expense | 2,000 | |
| | Accumulated Depreciation: Office Furniture | | 2,000 |
| | Adjusting entry | | |
| 31 | Salaries Expense | 150 | |
| | Salaries Payable | | 150 |
| | Adjusting entry | | |

**b**

| GOTTOM COMPANY<br>Adjusted Trial Balance<br>December 31, 19XX | | |
|---|---|---|
| Cash | $ 65,000 | |
| Accounts receivable | 4,200 | |
| Office supplies | 300 | |
| Prepaid insurance | 400 | |
| Office furniture | 16,000 | |
| Accumulated depreciation: | | |
| office furniture | | $ 2,000 |
| Accounts payable | | 10,000 |
| Salaries payable | | 150 |
| Paul Gottom, capital | | 30,000 |
| Paul Gottom, drawing | 7,400 | |
| Service revenue | | 85,000 |
| Salaries expense | 24,150 | |
| Rent expense | 3,000 | |
| Utilities expense | 2,000 | |
| Office supplies expense | 500 | |
| Insurance expense | 1,600 | |
| Depreciation expense | 2,000 | |
| Other expense | 600 | |
| | $127,150 | $127,150 |

## Questions

**Q3-1** Why aren't financial statements prepared directly from the account balances reported in the trial balance?

**Q3-2** Explain the transactions approach to the measurement of a company's net income or net loss.

**Q3-3** Differentiate between a fiscal year and a natural business year.

**Q3-4** What basic accounting problem arises from dividing the life of a business into discrete periods for reporting purposes?

**Q3-5** When is revenue generally recognized in the accounting records?

**Q3-6** Explain the matching principle.

**Q3-7** Explain when expenses and revenues are recognized under both the accrual basis and the cash basis of accounting.

**Q3-8** Explain, by citing several examples, how the cash basis can result in a mismatch of revenues and expenses in a given accounting period.

**Q3-9** Explain why virtually all large businesses use the accrual basis of accounting.

**Q3-10** Fuller Company uses a calendar year and prepares quarterly reports for its owner. On August 1, the firm prepaid a six-month, $600 insurance premium. What is the proper amount of insurance expense to recognize for the third quarter under the (a) cash basis, (b) accrual basis, and (c) modified cash basis?

**Q3-11** What types of items frequently require adjusting entries?

**Q3-12** In reviewing the records of Yager Company, you find that three months' rent of $750 was prepaid to Savage Property Management on November 1. Both companies use the accrual basis of accounting. In view of this transaction,

a What account and amount would you show on Yager's income statement for the month ended November 30? On Savage's income statement for the month ended November 30?

b What account and amount would you show on Yager's November 30 balance sheet? On Savage's November 30 balance sheet?

**Q3-13** What is meant by the term "depreciation"? What is the purpose of recording depreciation in the accounting records?

**Q3-14** A large retailer offers service contracts with the purchase of major appliances by customers. When a contract is sold, the following entry is made:

| | | |
|---|---|---|
| Cash | XXX | |
| Unearned Service Contract Revenue | | XXX |
| To record sale of service contract | | |

On which financial statement and in what section would the Unearned Service Contract Revenue account appear? What is the rationale behind your answer?

**Q3-15** How does an accrued expense differ from a prepaid expense?

**Q3-16** Why is an adjusted trial balance prepared?

***Q3-17** Modular Products, Inc., recently charged an outlay for prepaid advertising costs to the Advertising Expense account. Describe the adjusting entry that would be required at the end of the period.

## Exercises

**E3-1** ***Revenue and expense recognition: accrual basis***

Dave Morris began a law practice several years ago, shortly after graduating from law school. During 19X1 he was approached by Delores Silva, who had recently suffered a back injury in an automobile accident. Morris accepted Silva as a client, and in 19X2 proceeded with a lawsuit against Maddox Motors. The suit alleged that Maddox had knowingly sold Silva an automobile with defective brakes. Late in 19X2 the courts awarded Silva $240,000 in damages. Morris was entitled to 40% of this settlement for his fees. In 19X3, Maddox Motors paid Silva and Morris their respective shares of the judgment.

Morris incurred secretarial and photocopy charges in 19X2 of $12,000—all related to the Silva case. Of this amount, $8,000 was paid in 19X2 and the balance was paid in 19X3.

Assuming that Morris uses the accrual basis of accounting, in what year(s) should the revenue and expense amounts be recognized? Why?

**E3-2** ***Accrual basis and cash basis income computation***

Campbell's Cooking Clinic furnished the following information about its first year of operation:

- *Revenue from Cooking Classes*—The firm provided 14,000 hours of classroom instruction at $5 per hour. Students paid $18,000 at the time of enrollment; an addi-

* An asterisk preceding an item indicates that the material is covered in an appendix to this chapter.

tional $40,000 was subsequently collected prior to the end of the year. The remaining balance is still outstanding.

- *Lesson Booklets*—The clinic purchased 1,000 lesson booklets at $4 each for use in its classes. Eighty percent of the total purchase price had been paid by year-end. A count on December 31 revealed that 400 booklets were still on hand.
- *Operating Expenses*—Rent, salary, advertising, and office expenses of $15,600 had been incurred by December 31. Of this amount, $3,100 will be paid in the following accounting period.

a Compute Campbell's accrual basis net income for the year ended December 31.
b Compute Campbell's cash basis net income for the year ended December 31.

**E3-3** ***Recognition of concepts***

Consider the items that follow and classify as (1) prepaid expense, (2) unearned revenue, (3) accrued expense, (4) accrued revenue, or (5) none of the foregoing.

a May season ticket sales of a professional hockey club.
b Supplies on hand at the end of an accounting period.
c Interest owed on a loan payable and due in the following month.
d The loan payable in item (c).
e The interest in item (c) from the bank's viewpoint.
f Monies generated from sales of one-year service contracts on new appliances.
g Service fees earned but unbilled at month-end.
h Repair costs, incurred and paid in August.
i Advertising costs paid in May that pertain to a June promotional campaign.
j Wages owed on March 31, to be paid on April 2.

**E3-4** ***Analysis of prepaid account balance***

The following information relates to Auto City Enterprises for 19XX:

| | |
|---|---|
| Supplies expense | $ 9,500 |
| Supplies on hand, December 31 | 3,200 |
| Cost of supplies purchased during 19XX | 10,700 |

Compute the balance in Auto City's Supplies account on January 1, 19XX.

**E3-5** ***An overview of the adjusting process***

Evaluate the comments that follow as being True or False. If the comment is False, briefly explain why.

a Adjusting entries are normally recorded on the last day of the accounting period.
b The balance in an account entitled Prepaid Art Supplies would most likely be disclosed on a company's income statement.
c If $700 of a $2,900 insurance policy expired during the period, the Prepaid Insurance account should contain a $2,200 balance after adjustment.
d The Oxnard Aristocrats, a minor league baseball team, records receipts of season ticket revenue in the Unearned Season Ticket Revenue account. The proper adjusting entry to reflect revenue earned during the period would involve a credit to this account.
e An adjustment for an accrued expense involves an increase to a liability account.

**E3-6** ***Basic adjusting entries***

Record the adjusting entries necessary for King Company as of December 31, the end of the current accounting period.

a Accrued interest owed to the bank, $2,400.
b Insurance purchased during the year totaled $1,200. Of this amount, $800 is applicable to the next accounting period. The original $1,200 payment was recorded as a debit to Prepaid Insurance.
c King earned $200 of an $800 receipt from a client for consulting services. The receipt was initially recorded in the Unearned Consulting Revenue account.

d Sales of $224,000 were made during December. King pays the sales force a 10% commission; no commissions had been paid by the end of the month.
e Accrued interest on various amounts due King totaled $580 at year-end.

**E3-7** ***Unearned revenue, journal entries***
Malibu Tan, a tanning salon, opened its doors on October 1 of the current year and was an instant success. Patrons could use the salon's services by purchasing a special 12-month membership for $180, 10-visit coupon books for $50, or individual visits for $6. The following data relate to October operations:

| | |
|---|---|
| 12-month memberships sold | 35 |
| 10-visit coupon books sold | 120 |
| Coupons redeemed during the month | 90 |
| Individual visits | 270 |

The 12-month membership was a grand opening special and was offered for sale only on October 1. Assume that all sales and individual visits were for cash and that Malibu uses the accrual basis of accounting. The company records sales of memberships and coupon books in an account entitled Unearned Customer Revenue.
a Present the necessary journal entries to record the sale of 12-month memberships and 10-visit coupon books.
b Present the necessary journal entries to record the coupons redeemed during the month and the individual visits.
c Present any other entries that are necessary to properly reflect Malibu's financial status as of October 31.

**E3-8** ***Adjustment error***
The accountant for Stringer Services failed to adjust the Supplies account to recognize the amount consumed during March. As a result of this error, will the following items be overstated, understated, or unaffected?
a March revenues will be ______________________.
b March expenses will be ______________________.
c March net income will be ______________________.
d Ending owner's equity as of March 31 will be ______________________.
e Assets as of March 31 will be ______________________.
f Liabilities as of March 31 will be ______________________.

***E3-9** ***Income statement approach, adjusting entries***
Quality Food Products, Inc., had the following transactions on April 1:

- Paid $960 to acquire a one-year liability insurance policy.
- Received $3,900 to render consulting services to Midtown Hospital over the next three months. The services were to begin immediately.

Quality records prepaid expenses and unearned revenues initially in income statement accounts.
a Record the proper journal entries on April 1.
b Record the necessary adjusting entries on April 30.

## Problems

### Series A

**P3-A1** ***Accrual and modified cash basis***
The following information pertains to Beta Company for October:

| | |
|---|---|
| Services rendered during October to customers on account | $14,380 |

| | |
|---|---|
| Cash receipts from | |
| Owner investment | 7,000 |
| Customers on account | 5,650 |
| Cash customers for services rendered in October | 6,800 |
| Cash payments to | |
| Creditors for expenses incurred during October | 4,400 |
| Creditors for expenses incurred prior to October | 2,100 |
| Monroe Equipment for purchase of new machinery on October 1 | 8,400 |
| Expenses incurred during October, to be paid in future months | 3,725 |

The machinery is expected to have a service life of five years.

**Instructions**

Calculate Beta's net income for October, using the following methods:

a Accrual basis of accounting

b Modified cash basis of accounting

**P3-A2** ***Journal entries and adjustments***

The Jarman Company was formed on September 1 of the current year. The following transactions occurred during the first month of operation:

| | | |
|---|---|---|
| Sept. | 1 | Received $20,000 from James Jarman, the owner, as an initial cash investment. |
| | 2 | Purchased office equipment having a five-year life for $2,400 cash. |
| | 6 | Billed clients for services rendered, $4,000. |
| | 9 | Received $2,700 from clients on account. |
| | 11 | Purchased advertising space in a local newspaper for $2,100 cash. The ads will run four times in September and eight times in October. (Charge this expenditure to the Prepaid Advertising account.) |
| | 15 | Rendered services to a client for $1,400 cash. |
| | 21 | Received $600 from clients for services to be performed in October. The company records such transactions in the Unearned Service Revenue account. |
| | 25 | Paid staff salaries of $1,250. |
| | 27 | Applied for and received a $200,000 loan, to be used for business expansion. |

As of September 30, Jarman owes staff salaries of $400. Furthermore, accrued interest on the loan totals $260 and the firm has rendered unbilled services to clients in the amount of $5,430.

**Instructions**

a Prepare journal entries to record the September transactions of the Jarman Company.

b Prepare the adjusting entries necessary at the end of September. Be sure to analyze *all* data presented.

**P3-A3** ***Adjusting entries***

You have been called in to examine the records of the Gem Company as of December 31, 19X2, the close of the current reporting period. In the course of your examination you discover the following:

a Accrued interest on loans owed by Gem totals $15,800 as of December 31.

b On January 1, 19X2, the Supplies account had a balance of $1,470. Additional purchases made during the year amounted to $4,420. As of December 31, supplies of $1,950 remain on hand.

c Prepaid Advertising contains a debit balance of $1,080 on December 31. The balance represents the amount Gem paid on August 1 for a series of ads in a monthly magazine. The ads will run over six months, beginning with the magazine's November issue.

d During the accounting period Gem paid insurance premiums as follows, each time debiting Prepaid Insurance:

| *Date Paid* | *Policy No.* | *Length of Policy* | *Amount Paid* |
|---|---|---|---|
| Jan. 1 | 168AQ4 | 1 year | $450 |
| July 1 | 77462J | 2 years | 400 |
| Dec. 1 | AB14492 | 2 years | 360 |

e The Unearned Agency Revenue account contains a balance of $4,800, which represents payments from two clients during 19X2. The first client paid $3,600 on March 1 for services to be performed from April through November. The second payment of $1,200 was received on August 1 for six months of services to be performed starting in September.

f Gem rendered services to clients in December amounting to $6,400. The services have not as yet been entered in the accounting records.

g Depreciation on equipment amounted to $8,500 for the year.

### Instructions

The accounts were last adjusted on December 31, 19X1. Present the adjusting entries required on December 31, 19X2, under the accrual basis of accounting.

**P3-A4** ***Preparation of adjusted trial balance***

The trial balance of the Chapin Company as of December 31, 19XX, follows.

**CHAPIN COMPANY**
**Trial Balance**
**December 31, 19XX**

| | | |
|---|---|---|
| Cash | $ 6,000 | |
| Accounts receivable | 14,400 | |
| Prepaid insurance | 1,200 | |
| Equipment | 18,500 | |
| Accumulated depreciation: equipment | | $ 2,250 |
| Accounts payable | | 9,840 |
| Unearned service revenue | | 1,800 |
| Loan payable | | 6,000 |
| Keith Chapin, capital | | 7,500 |
| Keith Chapin, drawing | 4,000 | |
| Service revenue | | 43,710 |
| Salaries expense | 14,800 | |
| Utilities expense | 1,200 | |
| Rent expense | 11,000 | |
| | $71,100 | $71,100 |

The following adjustment information has come to your attention:

1 Services provided but not yet billed, $500.

2 Prepaid insurance expired during the period, $800.

3 Depreciation expense on the equipment, $750.
4 Unearned service revenues that have been earned during the period, $400.
5 Accrued interest on the loan payable, $75.
6 Salaries incurred but not yet paid, $900.

**Instructions**

a Prepare Chapin's required adjusting entries in general journal form.
b Prepare an adjusted trial balance, using an approach similar to that demonstrated in Exhibit 3-5.
c Suppose that you were asked to prepare the financial statements of Chapin Company. Would the trial balance or the adjusted trial balance be more useful in completing this assignment? Briefly explain.

**P3-A5** ***Adjustment errors***

Accounting personnel for the Napa Valley Company discovered the following errors after the financial statements had been prepared. Napa's fiscal year ended on June 30, 19XX.

a Overlooked $500 of accrued salaries that are owed by the firm.
b Recorded and posted the $3,900 depreciation entry twice.
c A $2,000 receipt for services to be rendered over the next five months was recorded in the Unearned Service Revenue account on May 1, 19XX. The account has yet to be adjusted.
d The company enters all rental prepayments in the Prepaid Rent account. No adjusting entry has been recorded for $700 of rental charges that expired during the period.
e Recorded $3,000 of interest that is owed to the firm as follows:

| | | |
|---|---|---|
| Interest Revenue | 3,000 | |
| Interest Receivable | | 3,000 |

**Instructions**

Using a tabular format similar to the following, determine the effect of each error, individually, on Napa Valley's financial statements. *Hint:* Remember that net income affects owner's equity. Error (*a*) is done as an example.

| | *19XX Income Statement* | | | *Balance Sheet as of June 30, 19XX* | | |
|---|---|---|---|---|---|---|
| ***Error*** | ***Revenue*** | ***Expense*** | ***Net Income*** | ***Assets*** | ***Liabilities*** | ***Owner's Equity*** |
| (*a*) | | −$500 | +$500 | | −$500 | +$500 |

***P3-A6** ***Adjustment alternatives***

Creative Management (CM) began operations on January 1 of the current year. A review of the company's accounting records on December 31 discovered the following:

- All advertising for the year had been prepaid. On March 1, CM paid $3,600 for space in six issues of *Artists' Monthly,* with displays to begin on May 1. In addition, on September 1, CM paid $4,800 for ads in 24 issues of *Theater Guild.* By year-end, ads had appeared in 11 issues of the latter publication.
- The company agreed to manage a popular rock group's financial affairs for a 12-month period beginning on April 1 for a fee of $18,000. CM received the entire fee on March 1.

The firm's general ledger revealed accounts entitled Prepaid Advertising, Advertising Expense, Management Revenue, and Unearned Management Revenue. CM uses the accrual basis of accounting and adjusts its accounting records at the end of the year.

**Instructions**

a Assume that Creative Management initially records prepaid expenses and unearned revenues in balance sheet accounts. Present the necessary journal entries to:
  (1) Record the transactions of March 1 and September 1.
  (2) Adjust the accounting records on December 31.

b Repeat part (a), assuming that prepaid expenses and unearned revenues are initially recorded in income statement accounts.

c Determine the amounts that would be disclosed on the company's year-end financial statements for Advertising Expense, Prepaid Advertising, Management Revenue, and Unearned Management Revenue. Base your answers on the initial recording of the preceding transactions in:
  (1) Balance sheet accounts.
  (2) Income statement accounts.

## Series B

**P3-B1** ***Accrual and modified cash basis***

The following information pertains to the Milsap Company for June:

| | |
|---|---|
| Services provided during June to customers on account | $34,450 |
| Cash receipts from | |
| Bank loan | 6,600 |
| Cash customers for services rendered during June | 16,640 |
| Customers on account | 28,500 |
| Cash payments to | |
| Milan Furniture for purchase of new office furniture on June 1 | 9,000 |
| Creditors for expenses incurred during June | 36,000 |
| Creditors for expenses incurred prior to June | 6,000 |
| Expenses incurred during June, to be paid in future months | 7,400 |

The furniture is expected to have a service life of six years.

**Instructions**

Calculate Milsap's net income for June, using the following methods:

a Accrual basis of accounting

b Modified cash basis of accounting

**P3-B2** ***Journal entries and adjustments***

The Lee Company was formed on June 1 of the current year. The following transactions occurred during the first month of operation:

June 1 Received $10,000 from Sharon Lee, the owner, as an initial cash investment.

2 Purchased computer equipment having a three-year life for $1,800 cash.

5 Billed clients for services rendered, $2,000.

9 Purchased advertising space in a local newspaper for $1,600 cash. The ads will run twice in June and six times in July. (Charge this expenditure to the Prepaid Advertising account.)

12 Received $600 from clients on account.

16 Rendered services to a client for $400 cash.

19 Received $950 from clients for services to be performed in August. The company records such transactions in the Unearned Service Revenue account.
26 Paid employee wages of $800.
28 Applied for and received a $100,000 loan, to be used for business expansion.

As of June 30, Lee owes employee wages of $250. Furthermore, accrued interest on the loan totals $80, and the firm has rendered unbilled services to clients in the amount of $2,500.

**Instructions**

a Prepare journal entries to record the June transactions of the Lee Company.
b Prepare the adjusting entries necessary at the end of June. Be sure to analyze *all* data presented.

**P3-B3** ***Adjusting entries***
You have been called in to examine the records of Holiday Company as of November 30, 19X7, the close of the current reporting period. In the course of your examination you discover the following:

a Building depreciation totaled $7,500 for the year.
b Prepaid Advertising has a debit balance of $6,500 on November 30, which represents payment on August 18 for uniform space in 26 issues of a weekly magazine. As of November 30, advertisements had appeared in 12 issues.
c Salaries earned by employees but unpaid by year-end amounted to $3,900.
d Holiday agreed that Auto Express could lease some extra space in Holiday's parking lot for $300 per month, effective September 1. Auto Express has yet to pay Holiday and, to date, no entry has been made in the accounting records. (Holiday uses an account entitled Lease Receivable to record such transactions.)
e The beginning balance in the Office Supplies account on December 1, 19X6, was $2,570. The account was increased during the year for purchases that amounted to $4,420, and a year-end count revealed that supplies costing $4,800 had been consumed by November 30.
f On March 1, an entry was made in the Unearned Service Revenue account for $24,000. This amount represents a receipt for eight months of services to be rendered beginning on June 1.
g A review of the Prepaid Insurance account discovered that Holiday had acquired a two-year liability insurance policy for $960 on February 1, 19X7. Another policy that cost $1,320 for six months' coverage of building contents was acquired one month later.

**Instructions**

The accounts were last adjusted on November 30, 19X6. Present the adjusting entries required on November 30, 19X7, under the accrual basis of accounting.

**P3-B4** ***Preparation of adjusted trial balance***
The trial balance of the Logo Company as of December 31, 19XX, follows.

# Completion of the Accounting Cycle

CHAPTER 4

## Learning Objectives

After reading this chapter you should:

**1** Be able to prepare a work sheet and the accompanying financial statements.

**2** Know how to close a set of books and how to prepare a post-closing trial balance.

**3** Be able to describe the various steps in the accounting cycle.

**4** Be familiar with the concept of an operating cycle and the construction of a classified balance sheet.

**5** Be able to compute the current ratio and working capital for a company.

**6** (Appendix) Understand the concept and mechanics of reversing entries.

In the previous chapter we examined the adjusting process, which is used to update selected accounts upon conclusion of the reporting period. Chapter 3 also included an illustration showing how adjusting entries are combined with account data to derive an adjusted trial balance.

Because an entity's records now reflect all measurable activity that has occurred, we can begin to concentrate on disclosure of this activity via a formal income statement, statement of owner's equity, and balance sheet. The construction of these reports involves the simple reorganization of the information contained in the adjusted trial balance.

A natural inclination might be to assume that statement preparation is the final step in the financial reporting cycle. As you will soon see, a few additional tasks must be performed to ready a company's records for the next accounting period. These tasks include closing entries and the preparation of a post-closing trial balance. This chapter examines financial statement construction along with the preceding "housekeeping" chores. Our presentation concludes with an in-depth discussion of balance sheets, including the need for added captions within the body of this statement.

## Work Sheet

**OBJECTIVE 1**
**Be able to prepare a work sheet and the accompanying financial statements.**

Most businesses have a large number of accounts in their general ledgers that require adjustment. To help accountants to better organize their work for this process, a series of *working papers* is often prepared. These documents are used for preliminary calculations when deriving financial statement data (e.g., the cost of supplies consumed during the reporting period, a company's depreciation expense, and so forth). Generally speaking, working papers provide evidence of related computations and are useful in answering questions of auditors concerning the validity of the figures being reported.

There are many different types of working papers, with one of the most popular being the work sheet. The **work sheet** is a large columnar form that assists in the formation of an entity's financial statements. The design of the work sheet not only helps to detect mathematical errors, but it also highlights certain types of discrepancies *before* such discrepancies are entered in the journal and posted to the ledger. In effect, one could view the work sheet to be the accountant's "scratch pad." Proper completion of this important document ensures that many end-of-period accounting procedures have been performed correctly.

### Work Sheet Construction

The work sheet and the procedures for preparation will be shown by continuing the Wise Advertising Agency example from the previous chapter. The starting point for preparation is the trial balance and the end-of-period adjusting entries. These data are reproduced in Exhibit 4-1.

The amounts in the trial balance are combined with the adjustments to produce an adjusted trial balance. Notice, for instance, that the $3,150 debit balance in Accounts Receivable is increased by $710, yielding an ending account balance of $3,860. This procedure should be familiar to you; it is identical to that described in the previous chapter. A review of Exhibit 3-5 and the accompanying discussion that begins on page 92 may be helpful at this time. The review will not only serve as a refresher, but it also shows that the Chapter 3 illustration coincides precisely with the first six columns of the work sheet. The numbers that appear in colored type (the income statement and balance sheet data) are really the only new elements to master.

## Income Statement and Balance Sheet

The data in the adjusted trial balance serve as the "raw material" for a company's financial statements. Thus, each amount listed in the adjusted trial balance is transferred to either the work sheet's income statement section or balance sheet section.

**Exhibit 4-1**
**Work Sheet for Wise Advertising**

**WISE ADVERTISING AGENCY**
**Work Sheet**
**For the Month Ended May 31, 19XX**

| Account Title | Trial Balance Debit | Trial Balance Credit | Adjustments Debit | Adjustments Credit | Adjusted Trial Balance Debit | Adjusted Trial Balance Credit | Income Statement Debit | Income Statement Credit | Balance Sheet Debit | Balance Sheet Credit |
|---|---|---|---|---|---|---|---|---|---|---|
| Cash | 13,705 | | | | 13,705 | | | | 13,705 | |
| Accounts receivable | 3,150 | | (g) 710 | | 3,860 | | | | 3,860 | |
| Prepaid insurance | 480 | | | (a) 20 | 460 | | | | 460 | |
| Supplies | 340 | | | (b) 80 | 260 | | | | 260 | |
| Land | 5,500 | | | | 5,500 | | | | 5,500 | |
| Car | 4,500 | | | | 4,500 | | | | 4,500 | |
| Accounts payable | | 125 | | | | 125 | | | | 125 |
| Unearned agency revenue | | 10,400 | (d) 400 | | | 10,000 | | | | 10,000 |
| Loan payable | | 6,000 | | | | 6,000 | | | | 6,000 |
| Gary Wise, capital | | 9,000 | | | | 9,000 | | | | 9,000 |
| Gary Wise, drawing | 200 | | | | 200 | | | | 200 | |
| Agency revenue | | 4,100 | | (d) 400<br>(g) 710 | | 5,210 | | 5,210 | | |
| Salaries expense | 825 | | (f) 50 | | 875 | | 875 | | | |
| Marketing expense | 800 | | | | 800 | | 800 | | | |
| Electricity expense | 125 | | | | 125 | | 125 | | | |
| | 29,625 | 29,625 | | | | | | | | |
| Insurance expense | | | (a) 20 | | 20 | | 20 | | | |
| Supplies expense | | | (b) 80 | | 80 | | 80 | | | |
| Depreciation expense | | | (c) 125 | | 125 | | 125 | | | |
| Accumulated depreciation: car | | | | (c) 125 | | 125 | | | | 125 |
| Interest expense | | | (e) 60 | | 60 | | 60 | | | |
| Interest payable | | | | (e) 60 | | 60 | | | | 60 |
| Salaries payable | | | | (f) 50 | | 50 | | | | 50 |
| | | | 1,445 | 1,445 | 30,570 | 30,570 | 2,085 | 5,210 | 28,485 | 25,360 |
| Net income | | | | | | | 3,125 | | | 3,125 |
| | | | | | | | 5,210 | 5,210 | 28,485 | 28,485 |

This process is performed on a line-by-line basis, starting at the top of the work sheet. *Revenues and expenses go to the income statement. Assets, liabilities, and owner's equity accounts, the last of which includes the drawing account, are extended to the balance sheet.* Although the drawing account does not appear on a formal balance sheet,[1] extension is necessary because withdrawals reduce owner's equity.

### Financial Statement Totals

As a final step, after all amounts have been extended, the income statement and balance sheet columns are totaled. Focusing on the income statement, the credit column contains the accounts with credit balances, namely, the revenues. In contrast, the debit column contains the expense accounts. Therefore:

| | |
|---|---|
| Total revenues (credits) | $5,210 |
| Total expenses (debits) | 2,085 |
| Net income | $3,125 |

The net income figure is placed beneath the debit total and is added to bring both columns into agreement with each other.

Turning to the balance sheet, the firm's net income is entered in the credit column because net income increases owner's equity. The income of $3,125 is then combined with the other balance sheet credits, yielding a total of $28,485.

Wise generated net income during May; if the agency had operated at a loss, the procedure for balancing the statements would have been slightly different. With expenses in excess of revenues, the loss would be entered in the credit column of the income statement to achieve the desired equality. On the balance sheet the net loss must reduce owner's equity. Appropriately, then, the loss would be listed in the debit column to produce the necessary impact.

**TIPS & TECHNIQUES**

Students often take a quick glance at a finished work sheet and conclude that it is extremely complex and beyond their comprehension. As you have seen, work sheet construction is *not* difficult if viewed as a logical step-by-step process. In fact, the most troublesome elements are those introduced in Chapters 2 and 3—the generation of a trial balance that balances and the determination of the proper adjusting entries.

## Uses of the Work Sheet

The work sheet performs several useful functions for the accountant. As is evident from its form, the work sheet lays the groundwork for formal financial statement preparation. In addition, it serves as the basis for completing the adjusting process and assists in closing at the end of the accounting period.

[1] Withdrawals appear on the statement of owner's equity.

## Financial Statements

Once the work sheet is completed, the preparation of financial statements is a relatively easy task. Virtually all the information needed for this process is found in the work sheet's income statement and balance sheet sections. The income statement, for example, is simply a formalized listing of the income statement debit and credit columns.

The statement of owner's equity cannot be constructed by relying solely on the work sheet. Any investments made by the owner are already buried in the capital account, which appears in the adjusted trial balance. Consequently, it is necessary to return to the general ledger and examine the underlying detail of owner's equity (see Gary Wise, Capital, in Exhibit 2-5).

Finally, the balance sheet is prepared by compiling the asset and liability figures that are listed in the balance sheet section. The drawing account of $200 is ignored; it was used when constructing the statement of owner's equity. As you know, the balance sheet reflects end-of-period amounts; thus, the ending figure on the statement of owner's equity is carried over and labeled as Gary Wise, Capital. This procedure was discussed in Chapter 1 and is illustrated in Wise's financial statements, which are shown in Exhibit 4-2.

## Adjusting Entries

In the previous chapter we first introduced the concept of adjustments via formal journal entries (see pages 87 and 88 as examples). We later used the information contained in these adjustments for purposes of completing the adjusted trial balance and the work sheet. The presentation in Chapter 3 was for illustrative purposes only. In practice, accountants would first prepare the work sheet and then record data from the adjustment columns into the journal. The work sheet, therefore, serves as the basis for the updating process at the end of the period.

Like other journal entries, the adjustments are posted to the general ledger. This procedure achieves consistency with the balances that appear in the agency's financial statements. We will assume that all adjustments presented in the Wise Advertising illustration have already been journalized and posted.

## The Closing Process

**OBJECTIVE 2**
**Know how to close a set of books and how to prepare a post-closing trial balance.**

Discussion of the **closing process** should help to tie together several loose ends. As we emphasized earlier in the text, four factors cause owner's equity to change during the accounting period: investments, withdrawals, net income, and net loss. The statement of owner's equity of Wise Advertising (see Exhibit 4-2) reveals an ending balance of $11,925 from these items. Interestingly, however, the capital *account* in the general ledger contains a balance of $9,000. This latter amount reflects only the investment on May 1, which was recorded directly in the account. Withdrawals, on the other hand, are located in Gary Wise, Drawing, and net income is composed of the various revenue and expense accounts. It is naturally desirable that the ending balance reported on the statement of owner's equity (and the balance sheet) be consistent with the ending balance found in the ledger. This consistency is achieved by placing a set of *closing entries* in the accounting records at the end of the period.

**Exhibit 4-2**
**Financial Statements of Wise Advertising Agency**

**WISE ADVERTISING AGENCY**
**Income Statement**
**For the Month Ended May 31, 19XX**

| | | |
|---|---|---|
| Agency revenue | | $5,210 |
| Less expenses | | |
| Salaries expense | $875 | |
| Marketing expense | 800 | |
| Electricity expense | 125 | |
| Insurance expense | 20 | |
| Supplies expense | 80 | |
| Depreciation expense | 125 | |
| Interest expense | 60 | |
| Total expenses | | 2,085 |
| Net income | | $3,125 |

**WISE ADVERTISING AGENCY**
**Statement of Owner's Equity**
**For the Month Ended May 31, 19XX**

| | | |
|---|---|---|
| Beginning balance, May 1 | | $ — |
| Increases | | |
| Owner investments | $9,000 | |
| Net income | 3,125 | 12,125 |
| | | $12,125 |
| Decreases | | |
| Owner withdrawals | | 200 |
| Ending balance, May 31 | | $11,925 |

***Purpose*** The purpose of the closing process is twofold. First, closing corrects the just mentioned lack of agreement between the capital account and the owner's equity statement. Second, closing reduces the balances in certain accounts to zero. The income statement and the statement of owner's equity each report economic activity for a span of time. On conclusion of a given period, a business must start anew in its accumulation of information for these two financial reports. *Thus, revenue, expense, and drawing accounts must be closed, or reduced to zero, so there is no carry-over from one period to the next.* These accounts are appropriately known as **temporary** or **nominal accounts.**

Because the balance sheet reports information at a particular point in time as opposed to a period, *balance sheet components (assets, liabilities, and ending owner's equity) are never closed.* Wise, for example, reported a cash balance of $13,705 on May 31. It would not make any sense to reduce this account to zero so that the firm could start accounting all over again on June 1. The agency has $13,705 of cash to

| WISE ADVERTISING AGENCY<br>Balance Sheet<br>May 31, 19XX | | |
|---|---|---|
| **Assets** | | |
| Cash | | $13,705 |
| Accounts receivable | | 3,860 |
| Prepaid insurance | | 460 |
| Supplies | | 260 |
| Land | | 5,500 |
| Car | $4,500 | |
| Less: Accumulated depreciation | 125 | 4,375 |
| Total assets | | $28,160 |
| **Liabilities** | | |
| Accounts payable | | $ 125 |
| Unearned agency revenue | | 10,000 |
| Loan payable | | 6,000 |
| Interest payable | | 60 |
| Salaries payable | | 50 |
| Total liabilities | | $16,235 |
| **Owner's equity** | | |
| Gary Wise, capital | | 11,925 |
| Total liabilities & owner's equity | | $28,160 |

begin June operations, not zero. Accounts whose balances are carried forward from period to period are commonly called **real accounts.**

***Technique*** Most companies close their books only once a year. For illustrative purposes, however, we will demonstrate the necessary closing process for Wise Advertising on May 31, the conclusion of the agency's first month of activity.

Closing is a four-step process that requires the establishment of a new account entitled **Income Summary.** As its name implies, the Income Summary account is used to summarize the net income or net loss of a business. The four steps to closing are as follows:

**1** Close all revenue accounts.
**2** Close all expense accounts.
**3** Close the Income Summary account.
**4** Close the drawing account.

The information needed to perform these steps is obtained from the work sheet.

***Closing Revenue Accounts*** Revenue accounts normally possess credit balances. To reduce the accounts to zero, the closing entry debits revenue accounts for the amount of their balance and credits Income Summary. This process transfers all revenues earned to the credit side of Income Summary and is shown in Exhibit 4-3.

**Exhibit 4-3**
**Closing Revenue Accounts**

| | | | |
|---|---|---|---|
| May 31 | Agency Revenue | 5,210 | |
| | Income Summary | | 5,210 |
| | To close revenues | | |

*Agency Revenue*

| | | | |
|---|---|---|---|
| 5/27 | 100 | 5/14 | 1,700 |
| 5/31 Closing | 5,210 | 5/31 | 2,500 |
| | **5,310** | 5/31 Adj | 400 |
| | | 5/31 Adj | 710 |
| | | | **5,310** |

*Income Summary*

| | | | |
|---|---|---|---|
| | | 5/31 | 5,210 |

To explain, the Agency Revenue account contains charges from May 14, 27, and 31 (see Exhibit 2-5) and two adjusting entries (see Exhibit 4-1). The balance *prior* to closing is $5,210 ($5,310 − $100). The closing entry debits Agency Revenue for $5,210, thereby equalizing total debits and credits and reducing the account's balance to zero.

***Closing Expense Accounts*** The closing of expense accounts is performed in essentially the same manner. Each expense account is credited to eliminate its debit balance. The closing entry's corresponding debit, then, is to Income Summary, which transfers the expenses incurred to the debit side of this account. Rather than close the expense accounts individually, a combined or *compound journal entry* is usually employed to reduce posting. Exhibit 4-4 illustrates the proper entry and the related postings.

***Closing the Income Summary Account*** The Income Summary account presently contains revenues (credits) of $5,210 and expenses (debits) of $2,085. The resulting credit balance of $3,125 ($5,210 − $2,085) represents Wise's net income for May.

The next step in the closing process is to reduce, or close, the Income Summary account to zero. This is achieved by debiting Income Summary for $3,125. To complete the entry, Gary Wise, Capital, is credited because net income causes owner's equity to increase. The necessary entry is shown in Exhibit 4-5.

In the case of a net loss, the Income Summary account would possess a debit balance prior to closing. The required closing entry, therefore, is the opposite of that just described.

***Closing the Drawing Account*** The final step in the closing process is to close the drawing account. From information that is shown in the adjusted trial balance columns of the work sheet, Wise's drawing account contains a $200 debit balance. A credit is therefore needed to reduce the account to zero. Because withdrawals decrease owner's equity, the required entry appears as shown in Exhibit 4-6.

By entering and posting this final journal entry, one completes the closing process. Observe that the revenue, expense, and drawing accounts all contain zero balances and are ready to accumulate June transactions. In addition, note that the

**Exhibit 4-4**
**Closing Expense Accounts**

| | | | |
|---|---|---|---|
| May 31 | Income Summary | 2,085 | |
| | Salaries Expense | | 875 |
| | Marketing Expense | | 800 |
| | Electricity Expense | | 125 |
| | Insurance Expense | | 20 |
| | Supplies Expense | | 80 |
| | Depreciation Expense | | 125 |
| | Interest Expense | | 60 |
| | To close expenses | | |

*Income Summary*

| | | | | | |
|---|---|---|---|---|---|
| 5/31 | | 2,085 | 5/31 | | 5,210 |

*Salaries Expense*

| | | | | | |
|---|---|---|---|---|---|
| 5/28 | | 825 | 5/31 | Closing | 875 |
| 5/31 | Adj | 50 | | | |
| | | **875** | | | |

*Supplies Expense*

| | | | | | |
|---|---|---|---|---|---|
| 5/31 | Adj | 80 | 5/31 | Closing | 80 |

*Marketing Expense*

| | | | | | |
|---|---|---|---|---|---|
| 5/5 | | 800 | 5/31 | Closing | 800 |

*Depreciation Expense*

| | | | | | |
|---|---|---|---|---|---|
| 5/31 | Adj | 125 | 5/31 | Closing | 125 |

*Electricity Expense*

| | | | | | |
|---|---|---|---|---|---|
| 5/25 | | 125 | 5/31 | Closing | 125 |

*Interest Expense*

| | | | | | |
|---|---|---|---|---|---|
| 5/31 | Adj | 60 | 5/31 | Closing | 60 |

*Insurance Expense*

| | | | | | |
|---|---|---|---|---|---|
| 5/31 | Adj | 20 | 5/31 | Closing | 20 |

**Exhibit 4-5**
**Closing the Income Summary Account**

| | | | |
|---|---|---|---|
| May 31 | Income Summary | 3,125 | |
| | Gary Wise, Capital | | 3,125 |
| | To close Income Summary | | |

*Income Summary*

| | | | |
|---|---|---|---|
| 5/31 | 2,085 | 5/31 | 5,210 |
| 5/31 Closing | 3,125 | | |
| | **5,210** | | |

*Gary Wise, Capital*

| | | | |
|---|---|---|---|
| | | 5/1 | 9,000 |
| | | 5/31 | 3,125 |

$11,925 ending balance in Wise's capital account now agrees with the firm's financial-statement disclosures as shown on pages 120 and 121.

**TIPS & TECHNIQUES**

Notice that the drawing account is closed to Gary Wise, Capital, and *not* to Income Summary. The latter account is used to summarize and collect only those elements that affect a company's earnings. Withdrawals of business assets are not expenses and are thus excluded from income computations.

***An Overview*** The closing process is overviewed in Exhibit 4-7. Throughout a period an entity's revenues, expenses, and owner withdrawals are accumulated in separate, temporary accounts for presentation in the financial statements. Upon conclusion of the reporting period these accounts have all served their temporary purposes and, accordingly, are closed. Closing transfers such balances to owner's capital, a permanent (real) element of the accounting equation.

**Exhibit 4-6**
**Closing the Drawing Account**

| | | | |
|---|---|---|---|
| May 31 | Gary Wise, Capital | 200 | |
| | Gary Wise, Drawing | | 200 |
| | To close drawing account | | |

*Gary Wise, Drawing*

| | | | |
|---|---|---|---|
| 5/30 | 200 | 5/31 Closing | 200 |

*Gary Wise, Capital*

| | | | |
|---|---|---|---|
| 5/31 | 200 | 5/1 | 9,000 |
| | | 5/31 | 3,125 |
| | | | (11,925) |

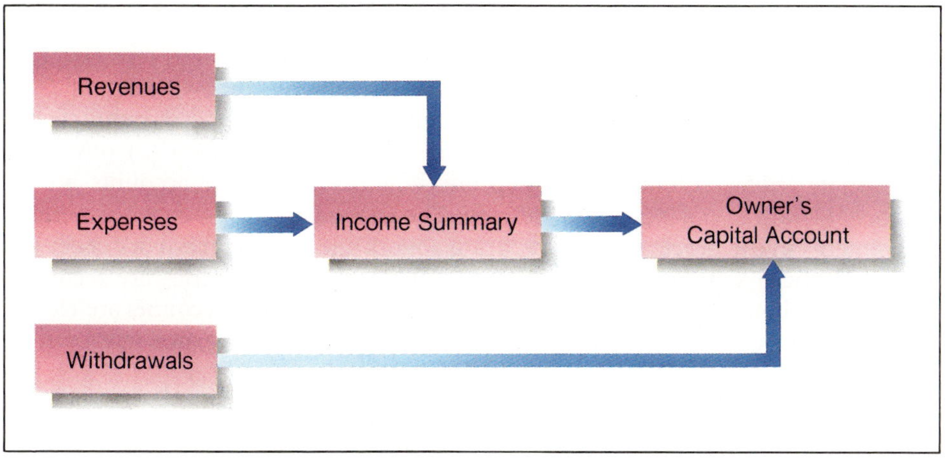


**Exhibit 4-7**
**An Overview of the Closing Process**

***Post-Closing Trial Balance*** Errors can occur during the closing process, just as they can in other accounting procedures. To determine whether the accounts are still in balance after the closing entries have been journalized and posted, accountants often prepare a **post-closing trial balance.** The post-closing trial balance examines ledger balances to determine if total debits equal total credits. Because this report is constructed after completion of the closing process, no balances remain in the drawing, revenue, and expense accounts. In addition, the capital account has been increased (decreased) by any net income (net loss) that has been generated and decreased by owner withdrawals. The post-closing trial balance for Wise Advertising appears in Exhibit 4-8.

**Exhibit 4-8**
**Post-Closing Trial Balance**

**WISE ADVERTISING AGENCY**
**Post-Closing Trial Balance**
**May 31, 19XX**

| | | |
|---|---|---|
| Cash | $13,705 | |
| Accounts receivable | 3,860 | |
| Prepaid insurance | 460 | |
| Supplies | 260 | |
| Land | 5,500 | |
| Car | 4,500 | |
| Accumulated depreciation: car | | $ 125 |
| Accounts payable | | 125 |
| Unearned agency revenue | | 10,000 |
| Loan payable | | 6,000 |
| Interest payable | | 60 |
| Salaries payable | | 50 |
| Gary Wise, capital | | 11,925 |
| | $28,285 | $28,285 |

## A Look Back: The Accounting Cycle

OBJECTIVE 3
Be able to describe the various steps in the accounting cycle.

A review of the material presented in this chapter and the previous two chapters reveals that we have been studying the **accounting cycle.** The cycle encompasses the various tasks performed during an accounting period to process transactions. Specifically, (1) transactions are recorded in the journal and then (2) posted to appropriate ledger accounts. To determine whether the ledger accounts are in balance, (3) a trial balance is constructed. The trial balance is updated by certain adjustments in the process of (4) preparing a work sheet. From the work sheet (5) formal financial statements are produced, and (6) adjusting entries are recorded in the journal and posted to the ledger. Finally, (7) temporary accounts are closed and (8) a post-closing trial balance is prepared. The entire sequence is shown in Exhibit 4-9.

## The Balance Sheet

The past few chapters have shown how transactions and events eventually find their way to an entity's financial statements. Recall that financial statements comprise the output of an accounting system and, in fact, are considered by many people to be the primary objective of the accounting function. Because of their importance, we now begin an in-depth probe of the various reports prepared by a

**Exhibit 4-9**
**The Accounting Cycle**

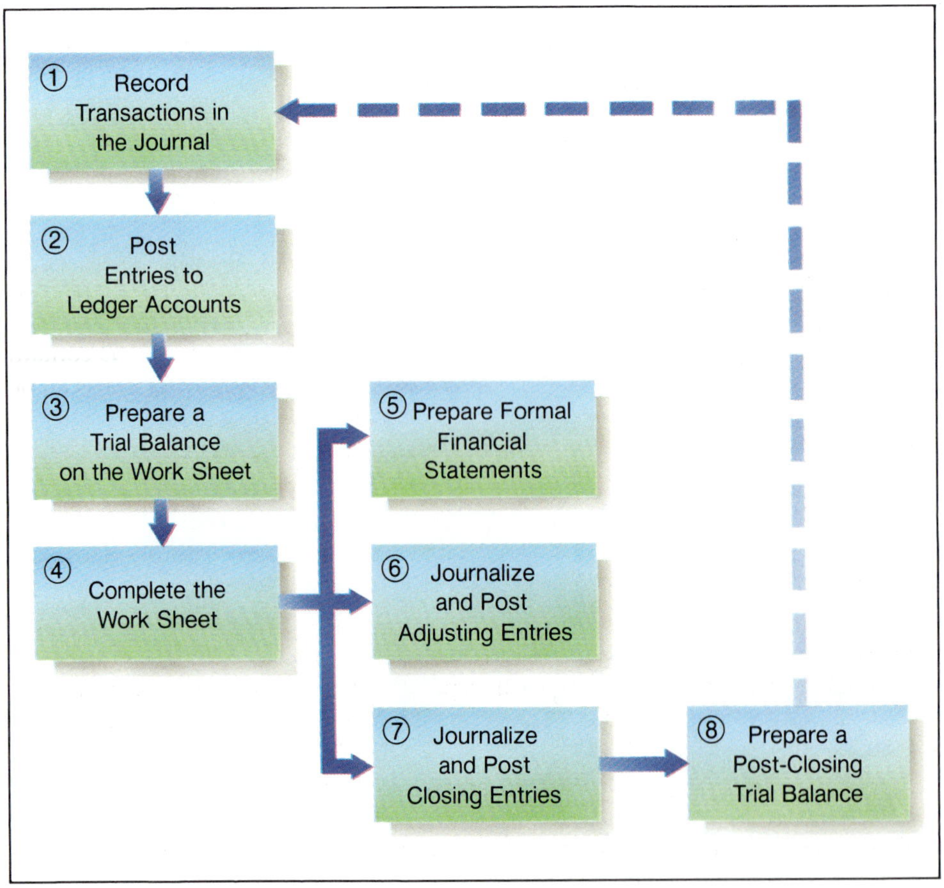

business that disclose economic activity. Our initial focus is on the balance sheet, with discussions of the other financial statements to follow in later chapters.

The balance sheet provides information about a company's assets, liabilities, and owner's equity. Such information is useful in many ways to different groups of individuals. For example, the manager of a slumping company can study the level of merchandise inventory at the end of an accounting period to judge the effectiveness of a new ordering policy. Stable inventory levels may prompt the manager to question why the ordering policy has not paralleled significant declines in sales. Creditors review the asset and liability relationships on a balance sheet to determine the adequacy of cash balances for settling a firm's current and upcoming obligations. Creditors also analyze this financial statement to determine if the owners are investing their own capital in the business or relying on other creditors, such as banks, to finance operations. Lenders, in particular, want the owners to have a sizable stake in the business should financial problems develop.

Although the balance sheet is extremely useful, it suffers from several limitations. First, current values are seldom employed for asset valuation. As noted earlier in the text, accounting is based on the historical-cost principle. Assets are recorded in the accounts at acquisition cost and, generally, cost remains in the records until disposal (i.e., sale). Consequently, a company that acquired a parcel of land 10 years ago for $50,000 would continue to report a valuation of $50,000 even though the parcel may be currently worth several times that figure.

A second problem is that many of the assets important to the profitability and future existence of a business are not measurable in dollars. These assets, which include a good management, a skilled work force, a prime location, and business contacts and relationships, are therefore omitted from the balance sheet. No one would dispute the value of these items to a firm; yet an objective valuation for accounting purposes is extremely difficult to derive.

## Statement Classification

**OBJECTIVE 4**
**Be familiar with the concept of an operating cycle and the construction of a classified balance sheet.**

The balance sheet portrayed in Exhibit 4-2 is adequate for an entity such as the Wise Advertising Agency. The business activities of "real world" firms, however, tend to be more complex and involve numerous and varied accounts. Appropriately, balance sheets (and other financial statements, too) virtually always contain account classification schemes so that important relationships and subtotals can be obtained. Standard classifications improve statement utility because users can better analyze the financial relationships that are relevant and significant to them.

The balance sheet's classifications are discussed on the next few pages.

### Assets

***Current Assets*** **Current assets** are those assets that management intends to convert into cash or consume in the normal course of business within a relatively short period of time. The time period depends on the **operating cycle** of the entity, that is, how long it takes a company to obtain goods for sale (i.e., inventory), sell the inventory, and ultimately collect the related receivables. For companies selling goods on credit, the operating cycle appears as shown in Exhibit 4-10.

Most businesses have numerous operating cycles within an accounting period and use one year as the minimum time frame for classifying current assets. Be aware, however, that some firms have operating cycles well over one year in

**Exhibit 4-10**
**Operating Cycle**

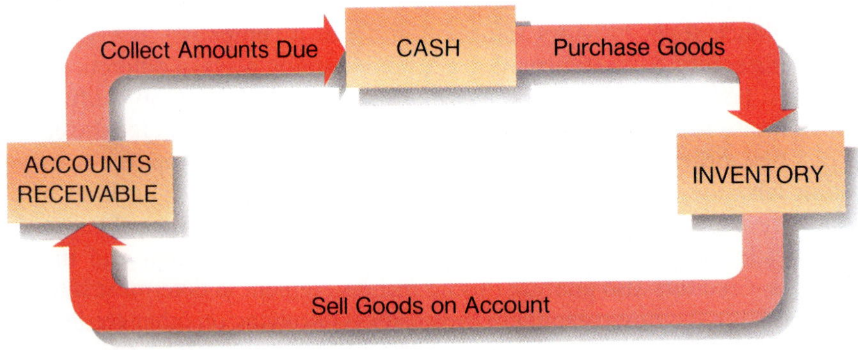


length. Examples include tobacco companies, which must cure their tobacco leaf, and liquor producers, which must age their inventory. Thus, the time period for purposes of the current asset definition is *one year or the operating cycle, whichever is longer.*

Current assets include cash, short-term investments and receivables, inventories, and prepaid expenses. These accounts are sequenced on the balance sheet in order of **liquidity,** or how close a current asset is to becoming cash. To illustrate, examine the balance sheet of The Williamsburg Company in Exhibit 4-11. Presented directly after cash is a short-term investment, the certificate of deposit. Although the certificate matures six months from the time of origination, it can be converted into cash immediately if necessary. Accounts receivable is listed next and represents claims against customers for inventory already sold or services rendered. The receivables are normally collected in a month or two, depending on the credit and collection practices of the firm. The merchandise inventory has yet to be sold and is presented next. Depending on the type of business involved, several months could elapse before the existing goods are purchased by customers and cash is ultimately collected. Prepaid expenses, such as rent, insurance, and supplies, commonly appear as the final current asset. Unlike receivables and inventory, prepaid expenses will not be converted to cash; they will, however, be consumed within a relatively short time.

***Long-Term Investments*** The next asset classification on the balance sheet is **long-term investments.** These investments are made with the intention of being retained for a prolonged period of time. Examples include land purchased either for speculation or as a future plant site, funds set aside for a company's expansion program, and investments made to acquire other entities.

***Property, Plant, and Equipment*** **Property, plant, and equipment** consists of assets that are used in the operation of a business and not held for resale to customers. These assets are tangible and have a long-term usefulness to a firm. Examples of property, plant, and equipment include land, buildings, machinery, furniture and fixtures, and vehicles. With the exception of land, the costs of assets in this category are gradually charged to expense via the depreciation process discussed in Chapter 3. Items of property, plant, and equipment are normally listed on the balance sheet in order of the length of their service lives, from the longest to the shortest. A typical presentation is shown in Exhibit 4-11.

Exhibit 4-11

**THE WILLIAMSBURG COMPANY**
**Balance Sheet**
**December 31, 19X1**

| *Assets* | | | |
|---|---|---|---|
| Current assets | | | |
| Cash | | $ 181,000 | |
| Certificate of deposit (six-month maturity) | | 50,000 | |
| Accounts receivable | | 1,389,000 | |
| Merchandise inventory | | 2,375,000 | |
| Prepaid expenses | | 36,000 | |
| Total current assets | | | $ 4,031,000 |
| Long-term investments | | | |
| Land (held for future use) | | | 1,000,000 |
| Property, plant, & equipment | | | |
| Land | | $2,000,000 | |
| Buildings | $3,000,000 | | |
| Less: Accumulated depreciation | 1,250,000 | 1,750,000 | |
| Equipment | $1,000,000 | | |
| Less: Accumulated depreciation | 175,000 | 825,000 | |
| Vehicles | $ 45,000 | | |
| Less: Accumulated depreciation | 40,000 | 5,000 | |
| Total property, plant, & equipment | | | 4,580,000 |
| Intangible assets | | | |
| Patents on inventions | | | 40,000 |
| Other assets | | | |
| Long-term receivables (due 19X6) | | | 850,000 |
| Total assets | | | $10,501,000 |
| *Liabilities & Owner's Equity* | | | |
| Current liabilities | | | |
| Accounts payable | | $3,000,000 | |
| Salaries payable | | 500,000 | |
| Unearned revenues | | 400,000 | |
| Current portion of mortgage payable | | 100,000 | |
| Total current liabilities | | | $ 4,000,000 |
| Long-term liabilities | | | |
| Mortgage payable (due 19X9) | | | 1,500,000 |
| Total liabilities | | | $ 5,500,000 |
| Owner's equity | | | |
| Rudy Williams, capital | | | 5,001,000 |
| Total liabilities & owner's equity | | | $10,501,000 |

***Intangible Assets*** **Intangibles** are assets that lack physical existence; at the same time, however, these items represent valuable long-term rights to the business that has acquired or developed them. Examples include franchises, patents, copyrights, trademarks, and product formulas. Each year a portion of an intangible's cost is expensed as the asset's rights are used up or expire. This process and other issues related to intangibles are discussed further in Chapter 11.

***Other Assets*** Any asset account that cannot be placed in one of the previous classifications is presented in the other assets category. For instance, The Williamsburg Company lists long-term receivables as an other asset.

## Liabilities

***Current Liabilities*** Generally stated, liabilities that will be liquidated within one year or the operating cycle, whichever is longer, are called **current liabilities.** Observe the consistency with the current asset definition. Examples of current liabilities include payables to suppliers and utilities, wages payable to employees, taxes payable to governmental units, and interest payable to banks. Another type of current liability is the unearned revenue discussed in Chapter 3. Unearned revenues represent cash received in advance of goods or services provided. These prepayments are liabilities until the goods or services are given in return, which usually occurs in less than a year's time.

**OBJECTIVE 5**
**Be able to compute the current ratio and working capital for a company.**

Current liabilities are normally paid or reduced by current assets. Consequently, the relationship between current assets and current liabilities is important, especially from a creditor's point of view. Creditors and other financial statement users periodically study this relationship by dividing the total current assets by the total current liabilities. The result, called the **current ratio,** provides insight into a firm's ability to pay short-term obligations on time and maintain its credit rating. Bankers and other lenders often prefer to see total current assets at least twice as large as total current liabilities. This 2 : 1 ratio essentially means that for every $1 owed and payable in the near future, a business has $2 of current assets available or soon available that can be used for payment.[2] Usually, a high current ratio is preferable to a low one. However, an abnormally high ratio may indicate that too much cash or inventory is held for the volume of business being generated. As a result, a company may be forced to forgo other more profitable investment opportunities.

The relationship between current assets and current liabilities can also be studied by calculating **working capital,** the mathematical difference between total current assets and total current liabilities. Working capital is the amount that would remain if all current obligations were paid immediately. Thus, this figure provides an assessment of a company's ability to pay debts as the obligations come due. The amount of working capital should be sufficient to meet day-to-day expenses and provide for some expansion.

From the data shown in Exhibit 4-11, we see The Williamsburg Company's current ratio and working capital appear somewhat tenuous. The firm's current ratio is 1.01 : 1 ($4,031,000 : $4,000,000), while working capital stands at only

[2] Remember that current assets include cash *and* assets that will be converted into cash in the near future (e.g., accounts receivable, inventories, and short-term investments). The exception is prepaid expenses.

$31,000 ($4,031,000 – $4,000,000). Should an unexpected event arise, management may be forced to scramble for cash. Why? Although Williamsburg's current assets do exceed its current liabilities, observe the current asset composition. Approximately 93.4% of the current asset total is comprised of receivables and inventory, both of which will require some time until ultimate conversion into cash. Creditors may therefore be reluctant to conduct business with the firm for fear of nonpayment.

***Long-Term Liabilities*** Obligations that are expected to be paid after one year or the operating cycle, whichever is longer, are classified as **long-term liabilities.** Examples of such liabilities include certain bank loans and mortgages payable. Many long-term obligations are paid in annual installments, that is, $X per year. As a result, the portion of a long-term liability that will be paid within one year or the operating cycle is properly disclosed under the heading of "current." To illustrate, notice that Williamsburg owes $1,600,000 from a mortgage due in 19X9. The liability is split according to its payment dates: $100,000 within one year and $1,500,000 after one year.

## Owner's Equity

As explained in Chapter 1, owner's equity represents the owner's net worth (or "interest") in the assets of a business. The owner's equity section of the balance sheet varies with the three forms of business organization: sole proprietorship, partnership, and corporation.

***Sole Proprietorship*** A **sole proprietorship** is an enterprise owned by one person in which owner investments and withdrawals, as well as the net income (or net loss), are merged into a single account at the end of the period. For The Williamsburg Company, the account is labeled Rudy Williams, Capital. The proprietorship's balance sheet, then, will contain only one owner's equity account: the name of the owner followed by the term "Capital."

***Partnership*** A **partnership** is a business owned by two or more persons, with a separate capital account established for each partner. Similar to what occurs in the proprietorship, each capital account after closing will contain a partner's investments, withdrawals, and an appropriate share of the entity's net income or net loss. Net income or net loss can be divided among the partners in any fashion. Generally, a written agreement stipulates the profit-sharing arrangements; if no written agreement exists, profits and losses are usually divided equally. Accounting problems for partnerships are presented later in the text, in Chapter 14.

***Corporation*** A third form of business organization is the **corporation.** The owners, called *stockholders,* are the investors who have purchased the firm's transferable units of ownership—known as **shares of capital stock.**

Unlike sole proprietorships and partnerships, corporations do not combine owner investments, net income and net losses, and withdrawals in one capital account. Instead, shareholder investments are recorded in a Capital Stock account, and a separate account called **Retained Earnings** is used to keep track of the profits generated by management. Just as sole proprietorships and partnerships permit owner withdrawals, corporations follow a similar practice. Corporate withdrawals are termed **dividends** and represent distributions of income to the stock-

HIGHLIGHT

# All Balance Sheets Are Not Created Equal

The balance sheet of The Williamsburg Company is very representative of those prepared by many "real world" businesses. There are notable exceptions, however, which often arise because of unique industry characteristics. Consider the following examples:

**Banks—**If you have occasion to review the balance sheet of a commercial bank, don't snicker because the accountants forgot to establish current and noncurrent categories. Omitting these classifications is appropriate because of the nature of a bank's assets and liabilities. For example, a financial institution's largest asset is its loans to customers (a receivable). How does one differentiate between current and noncurrent—the loans have varying terms and when the due date arrives, there is a likelihood of renewal. As a result, loans are frequently classified by purpose—energy-related, agricultural, real estate, and so forth.

Customer deposits (a liability to a bank because such amounts are owed to clientele) also present a problem. Typically the institution's largest liability, these amounts are normally payable on demand by the customer. It therefore becomes difficult, if not impossible, to identify such sums as current or noncurrent.

**Utilities—**To an untrained eye, it would seem that utility companies prepare "upside down" balance sheets. In the asset section, plant and equipment is listed first, followed by current assets. On the liability side, "capitalization" (i.e., stockholders' equity and long-term obligations) heads the list and is followed by current liabilities.

The rationale for this arrangement is that utility companies have substantial investments in their plant and equipment, sometimes in the billions of dollars because of nuclear power plants. For a local or regional business, the amount of money is indeed significant. This investment is normally financed through permanent and long-term capital, such as stock issuances and various types of long-term debt. Financial statement users are particularly interested in an analysis of these sizable components over time. Evaluations of current assets and current liabilities therefore take a back seat and are positioned accordingly.

**Insurance Companies—**Many insurance companies prepare two balance sheets. Are these firms trying to pull a fast one? Hardly! One balance sheet will likely be constructed to comply with generally accepted accounting principles. A second balance sheet, however, may be required for compliance with the various state laws that regulate the company (termed statutory accounting principles). Significant differences may arise in both asset and liability valuations.

Another interesting facet of insurance companies can be observed by reviewing the owners' equity section of the balance sheet. Frequently, the account titles would indicate that the customers own the firm. This is in fact the case. Many insurance businesses are organized as "mutual companies," meaning they are owned and controlled by the existing policyholders.

Unique—yes! Unusual—no! Those companies that have balance sheets with a special flavor invariably have financial statement users with special needs. The accounting profession has managed to tailor its reports to satisfy these users, resulting in a variety of presentations and disclosures. Stated simply, no two balance sheets are created equal.

holders. At any point in time, then, the balance in Retained Earnings represents undistributed profits that are left (retained) in the firm.

A simplified owners' (stockholders') equity section of a corporate balance sheet would appear as follows:

| | |
|---|---|
| Stockholders' equity | |
| Capital stock, 10,000 shares authorized and issued | $100,000 |
| Retained earnings | 42,500 |
| Total stockholders' equity | $142,500 |

In practice, accounting for corporate equity can become quite complex. Further discussion of corporations is presented in Chapters 15 and 16.

## Footnotes and the Principle of Disclosure

The balance-sheet classifications just discussed improve a company's presentation of financial information. For most organizations, however, further enhancement is needed. Many business activities are complex and require some explanation, that is, an explanation that goes beyond the numbers shown on the income statement, statement of owner's equity, and balance sheet.

In recognition of this fact, the financial statements are normally accompanied by a series of **footnotes** that provide an expansion on selected company information. Footnotes are employed to describe the details of significant accounting policies, major business events that occurred during the period, pending lawsuits, and various other facets of operation. Such information is used extensively by analysts and investors to better understand the figures being reported. See Appendix B at the end of the text, which contains the footnotes and financial statements of the Alberto-Culver Company.

The use of footnotes is an example of the accounting principle of disclosure. **Disclosure** means that the financial statements result in a fair presentation of the facts that influence the decisions and judgment of an informed user of financial information. Such facts must be presented in a timely manner and be unbiased and understandable.

## APPENDIX Reversing Entries

**OBJECTIVE 6**
**Understand the concept and mechanics of reversing entries.**

Our presentation of the accounting cycle concluded with the construction of a post-closing trial balance. Some companies add a further step to the cycle by using reversing entries. To explain, a **reversing entry** is the exact opposite of an adjusting entry. The same accounts are involved, but the debits and credits are reversed. Reversing entries are journalized on the first day of the following accounting period and, it is important to note, are an optional bookkeeping procedure.

To illustrate the concept and purpose of reversals, assume that Houston Enterprises has a $15,000 payroll for a five-day work week. Employees are paid every Friday, giving rise to the following journal entry:

| | | |
|---|---|---|
| Salaries Expense | 15,000 | |
| Cash | | 15,000 |
| Paid salaries for the week | | |

It is now December and the last payroll of the month falls due on Friday, the 26th. The journal entry just shown is recorded once again when cash is disbursed to the employees. By December 31, an additional three working days will have elapsed (Monday, December 29, through Wednesday, December 31). Houston must therefore record the following adjusting entry to properly reflect the salary expense incurred during this period:

| | | | |
|---|---|---|---|
| Dec. 31 | Salaries Expense | 9,000 | |
| | Salaries Payable | | 9,000 |
| | Adjusting entry | | |

The $9,000 adjustment is based on salaries of $3,000 per day ($15,000 ÷ 5 days).

Shortly after the adjusting process is completed, the books would be closed and the balance in the Salaries Expense account reduced to zero. The relevant expense and liability accounts would appear as follows:

| Salaries Expense | | | |
|---|---|---|---|
| 12/31 Adj | 9,000 | 12/31 Closing | 9,000 |

| Salaries Payable | | | |
|---|---|---|---|
| | | 12/31 Adj | 9,000 |

*Note:* For illustrative purposes we have omitted the weekly $15,000 debits to Salaries Expense.

## Case A—No Reversing Entries

At this point Houston must decide whether it wants to utilize reversing entries. Let us first assume that the firm does *not* use reversals. As a result, our example can be completed by focusing on Friday, January 2—the next payday. Houston's $15,000 payroll would be recorded in the following manner:

| | | | |
|---|---|---|---|
| Jan. 2 | Salaries Payable | 9,000 | |
| | Salaries Expense | 6,000 | |
| | Cash | | 15,000 |
| | Paid salaries for the week | | |

Salaries Payable is debited to eliminate the salaries owed from the previous accounting period. In addition, Salaries Expense is debited to recognize the payroll costs (i.e., an expense) related to the first two days of January ($3,000 × 2 days = $6,000).

## Case B—Using Reversing Entries

We will now assume that Houston elects to use reversals. On January 1, the first day of the new accounting period, the firm will reverse the December 31 adjustment in the following manner:

| | | | |
|---|---|---|---|
| Jan. 1 | Salaries Payable | 9,000 | |
| | Salaries Expense | | 9,000 |
| | Reversing entry | | |

The impact of this entry is best seen by studying the accompanying T-accounts:

| Salaries Expense | | | |
|---|---|---|---|
| 12/31 Adj | 9,000 | 12/31 Closing | 9,000 |
| | | 1/1 Rev | 9,000 |

| Salaries Payable | | | |
|---|---|---|---|
| 1/1 Rev | 9,000 | 12/31 Adj | 9,000 |

The Salaries Payable account is reduced to zero; Salaries Expense, on the other hand, contains an abnormal credit balance of $9,000. Because of its zero balance, there is no need to debit Salaries Payable when payment takes place on January 2. Instead, the *entire* disbursement is expensed, as follows:

| | | | |
|---|---|---|---|
| Jan. 2 | Salaries Expense | 15,000 | |
| | Cash | | 15,000 |
| | Paid salaries for the week | | |

The $15,000 debit, when combined with the account's existing credit balance, leaves $6,000 in Salaries Expense. This amount correctly reflects Houston's salary costs for the first two days of January: $3,000 per day × 2 days = $6,000.

## An Overview

A comparison of the two approaches reveals identical outcomes. Specifically, the expense is split between the accounting periods affected: $9,000 of expense is recognized in December (3 days) and $6,000 in January (2 days). Further, no balance remains in Salaries Payable, indicating that Houston has completely settled its year-end salary obligation.

As the end result is the same, why would a company use reversing entries? Although an extra journal entry is involved, reversals facilitate the bookkeeping process and reduce the chance for errors. To illustrate, briefly review Case A (no reversing entries). Observe the need to reference the year-end accrual to determine the amount of the January 2 cash disbursement that was expensed in the previous period ($9,000). In contrast, the use of reversals (Case B) allows the bookkeeper to record the normal payroll entry (namely, a debit to Salaries Expense and a credit to Cash). The possibility is therefore eliminated that errors will creep into the accounts on the subsequent payment date from the bookkeeper's failure to consider a previously recorded adjustment.

The basic reversing procedures that were shown for salaries apply to other accrued expenses as well. Reversing entries are also used with accrued revenues. Generally speaking, reversals are applied to those adjusting items that involve future cash flows. In some cases the reversing process can be employed with prepaid expenses and unearned revenues; these cases are somewhat unusual, however, and will not be discussed here.

# Chapter Review

### Learning Objectives—The Key Points

**1 Be able to prepare a work sheet and the accompanying financial statements.** A work sheet is a columnar form that aids in the construction of financial statements. An entity's trial balance data are combined with appropriate adjustments to yield the adjusted trial balance. Each account in the adjusted trial balance is then extended to one of the work sheet's financial statement sections, with assets, liabilities, and owner's equity accounts going to the balance sheet and revenues and expenses being transferred to the income statement.

**2 Know how to close a set of books and how to prepare a post-closing trial balance.** At the end of a reporting period, a company's temporary accounts (revenues, expenses, and drawing) are closed, or reduced to zero. Revenue accounts are debited, with a corresponding credit being made to Income Summary. Next, the individual expenses are credited and the Income Summary is debited. The Income Summary, now containing the income or loss of the firm, is closed to the owner's capital account. As a final step, the drawing account is credited and charged against owner's capital. The post-closing trial balance is constructed after the closing process is completed by extracting account balances from the general ledger.

**3 Be able to describe the various steps in the accounting cycle.** The accounting cycle consists of the various tasks performed during a period to process transactions. These tasks include journalizing, posting, construction of a trial balance, and preparation of a work sheet and formal financial statements. Also included are the recording and posting of adjusting entries, the closing process, and preparation of a post-closing trial balance.

**4 Be familiar with the concept of an operating cycle and the construction of a classified balance sheet.** An operating cycle is the amount of time that it takes a business to buy inventory, sell that inventory to customers, and collect the related receivables. Statement classifications, such as those for current assets; long-term investments; property, plant, and equipment; intangible assets; other assets; current liabilities; long-term liabilities; and owner's equity, help make a balance sheet more useful for purposes of financial analysis.

**5 Be able to compute the current ratio and working capital for a company.** The current ratio is a measure that indicates a company's ability to pay short-term debts as the obligations come due. It is computed by dividing total current assets by total current liabilities. Working capital, on the other hand, is the difference between total current assets and total current liabilities and shows the amount that would remain if all current obligations were paid immediately.

**6 (Appendix) Understand the concept and mechanics of reversing entries.** Reversing entries are employed to reduce the possibility of errors in an accounting system. These entries are made on the first day of a new accounting period and are the exact opposite of previously-recorded adjustments for accrued expenses and accrued revenues. It is important to note that reversals are an optional bookkeeping procedure.

## Chapter Quiz

The five questions that follow relate to several issues raised in the chapter. Test your knowledge of the issues by selecting the best answer. (The answers appear on p. 151.)

**1** When preparing a work sheet, the balance in the Accounts Payable account should be extended from the adjusted trial balance column to the:
a income statement debit column.
b income statement credit column.
c balance sheet debit column.
d balance sheet credit column.

**2** Which of the following statements about the closing process is correct?
a Balances in income statement accounts are reduced to zero.
b The owner's capital account is updated to reflect the period's net income and owner withdrawals.
c Temporary accounts are given different treatment than real accounts.
d All of the above statements are correct.

**3** Which of the following is the correct closing entry for Joe Salem's drawing account?
a Debit Joe Salem, Drawing; credit Joe Salem, Capital
b Debit Joe Salem, Drawing; credit Income Summary
c Debit Joe Salem, Capital; credit Joe Salem, Drawing
d Debit Income Summary; credit Joe Salem, Drawing

**4** Which of the following accounts would not appear on a post-closing trial balance?
a Accounts Receivable
b Rent Expense
c Loan Payable
d Al Jarvis, Capital

**5** The balance sheet's current asset classification:
a is normally disclosed after the property, plant, and equipment classification.
b includes cash and other assets expected to be realized or consumed within one year of the balance sheet date or the operating cycle, whichever is longer.
c includes cash and other assets expected to be realized or consumed within one year of the balance sheet date or the operating cycle, whichever is shorter.
d reports the patents and copyrights owned by a firm.

## Questions

**Q4-1** What are the key benefits of preparing a work sheet?

**Q4-2** Why is the net income amount (as derived from the income statement columns of the work sheet) also entered as a credit in the balance sheet columns?

**Q4-3** Why are the adjusting entries that appear on the work sheet also recorded in the general journal?

**Q4-4** What are the objectives of the closing process?

**Q4-5** Which accounts are closed at the end of the accounting period and which are not closed?

**Q4-6** What are the differences between the adjusted trial balance and the post-closing trial balance?

**Q4-7** What is meant by the term "accounting cycle"?

**Q4-8** Discuss the limitations of the balance sheet.

**Q4-9** Define the operating cycle. Should businesses attempt to shorten the cycle or lengthen it? Why?

**Q4-10** How should current assets be organized on the balance sheet?

**Q4-11** What is an intangible asset? Present three examples of intangible assets.

**Q4-12** Discuss the use of the current ratio in making credit decisions.

**Q4-13** Are all pertinent facts about a company disclosed directly in the body of a balance sheet and other financial statements? If not, what additional technique is used?

**Q4-14** An accountant recently stated that a company's balance sheet lacked adequate disclosure. Explain the accountant's comment.

***Q4-15** What is a reversing entry? Are reversing entries a required or an optional bookkeeping procedure?

## Exercises

**E4-1** ***Work sheet extensions***

The bookkeeper of Micro Shack is in the process of completing the company's work sheet for the year just ended. The following accounts appear in the adjusted trial balance:

a Accounts receivable
b Fee revenue
c Long-term payable due Lincoln Credit Corporation
d Utilities expense
e Frank Bush, drawing

* An asterisk preceding an item indicates that the material is covered in the appendix to this chapter.

f Unearned client fees
g Display equipment
h Prepaid store rent
i Frank Bush, capital

For each of the preceding items, indicate whether the account should be extended to the income statement debit column, income statement credit column, balance sheet debit column, or the balance sheet credit column. Assume that all accounts have normal balances.

**E4-2** ***Preparation of financial statements***
The adjusted trial balance of the Driftwood Boat Repair Company as of December 31, 19XX, appears as follows:

| | | |
|---|---|---|
| Cash | $36,000 | |
| Accounts receivable | 4,000 | |
| Supplies | 7,000 | |
| Equipment | 24,000 | |
| Accumulated depreciation: equipment | | $ 3,000 |
| Accounts payable | | 19,200 |
| Salaries payable | | 3,500 |
| George Leny, capital | | 41,300 |
| George Leny, drawing | 800 | |
| Service revenue | | 17,200 |
| Rent expense | 1,800 | |
| Supplies expense | 1,200 | |
| Salaries expense | 6,400 | |
| Depreciation expense | 3,000 | |
| | $84,200 | $84,200 |

George Leny organized Driftwood on January 2, 19XX, with an initial cash investment of $41,300.

Prepare Driftwood's income statement and statement of owner's equity for the year ended December 31, 19XX. Also prepare the company's December 31 balance sheet, using a format similar to that shown in Exhibit 4-2.

**E4-3** ***Overview of the closing process***
Evaluate the comments that follow as being True or False. If the comment is false, briefly explain why.

a The closing process is performed after adjusting entries have been journalized and posted.
b Because they both possess a debit balance, Salaries Expense and Susan Franklin, Drawing, are treated in the same manner when accounts are closed at the end of the period.
c The Equipment account is closed at the end of the period by a debit to Income Summary and a credit to Equipment.
d If MultiTech incurred a net loss for the period just ended, the Income Summary account would contain a debit balance after the revenue and expense accounts have been closed.
e If a $4,900 balance is listed in the adjusted trial balance for Dave Miller, Capital, it stands to reason that Miller's capital account in the post-closing trial balance would be listed at $4,900 as well.

**E4-4** ***Understanding the closing process***
Examine the following list of accounts:

| | |
|---|---|
| Interest payable | Accumulated depreciation: equipment |
| Alex Kenzy, drawing | Accounts payable |
| Service revenue | Cash |
| Accounts receivable | Supplies expense |
| Interest expense | |

Which of the preceding accounts:
a Appear on a post-closing trial balance?
b Are commonly known as temporary, or nominal, accounts?
c Generate a debit to Income Summary in the closing process?
d Are closed to the capital account in the closing process?

**E4-5** ***Closing entries***
Sharp Company had the following adjusted trial balance on December 31:

| | | |
|---|---|---|
| Cash | $ 8,700 | |
| Accounts receivable | 15,500 | |
| Prepaid rent | 4,900 | |
| Land | 33,000 | |
| Accounts payable | | $ 19,400 |
| Salaries payable | | 3,000 |
| Vicki Sharp, capital | | 45,600 |
| Vicki Sharp, drawing | 12,000 | |
| Service revenue | | 48,300 |
| Rent expense | 7,200 | |
| Advertising expense | 5,000 | |
| Salaries expense | 24,000 | |
| Utilities expense | 6,000 | |
| | $116,300 | $116,300 |

Prepare the closing entries that Sharp would record on December 31.

**E4-6** ***Steps in the accounting cycle***
Organize the following steps in the correct sequence of occurrence.

| *Step* | *Procedure* |
|---|---|
| A | Formal financial statements are produced. |
| B | Transactions are posted to appropriate ledger accounts. |
| C | Closing entries are journalized and posted. |
| D | Daily transactions are recorded in the journal. |
| E | A post-closing trial balance is prepared. |
| F | Adjusting entries are entered in the journal and posted to the ledger. |
| G | The trial balance is updated by certain adjustments in the process of preparing a work sheet. |
| H | A trial balance is constructed. |
| I | A work sheet is completed. |

**E4-7** ***Balance sheet account classification***

The balance sheet of Bull & Bear is similar to that appearing in Exhibit 4-11. Under which classification would each of the following accounts appear?

a Supplies
b Copyrights
c Unearned commission revenue
d Charles Foster, capital
e Receivable from Mark Sedlack, due in two years
f Land purchased for speculation
g Portion of long-term loan payable due in three months
h Machinery
i Patents
j Accounts receivable

**E4-8** ***Current ratio and working capital calculations***

Selected accounts of Stereo Warehouse, with current balances, are presented in the list that follows.

| | |
|---|---|
| Accounts payable | $41,300 |
| Steve Ralston, capital | 80,000 |
| Accounts receivable | 36,800 |
| Salary expense | 30,500 |
| Cash | 14,500 |
| Patents | 49,000 |
| Prepaid expenses | 1,900 |
| Interest payable | 700 |
| Merchandise inventory | 55,800 |
| Loan payable, due in five months | 22,500 |
| Loan payable, due in three years | 45,000 |

a Determine the current ratio.
b Calculate the company's working capital.
c How will working capital be affected if Stereo Warehouse has a crash program to collect its receivables?

***E4-9** ***Reversing entries***

Burger Palace, which uses reversing entries, incurred $6,000 of wage and salary expenses during the last few days of 19X1. The company will pay these expenses on January 4, 19X2, as part of the $15,000 weekly payroll.

a Present the adjusting entry that is needed at the end of 19X1.
b Assuming a $740,000 balance in the Wage and Salary Expense account prior to the adjustment, present the necessary entry to close this account.
c Record the company's reversing entry on January 1, 19X2.
d Present the entry needed on January 4, 19X2.
e How much of the January 4 payroll is considered expense of 19X2?

## Problems

### Series A

**P4-A1** ***Closing entries***

The income statement of the Gourmet Cooking School for the year ended December 31, 19XX, follows.

**GOURMET COOKING SCHOOL**
**Income Statement**
**For the Year Ended December 31, 19XX**

| | | |
|---|---|---|
| Tuition revenue | | $89,600 |
| Less expenses | | |
| Salaries expense | $39,700 | |
| Rent expense | 13,800 | |
| Advertising expense | 5,400 | |
| Food & supplies expense | 14,200 | |
| Transportation expense | 1,100 | |
| Utilities expense | 2,500 | |
| Total expenses | | 76,700 |
| Net income | | $12,900 |

Mary Winslow, the school's owner, had a beginning capital balance of $44,500 on January 1, 19XX. During the year she invested an additional $12,000 into the firm and withdrew $5,100.

**Instructions**

a Prepare the necessary closing entries for the year ended December 31.
b Compute the December 31, 19XX, balance of Winslow's capital account.

**P4-A2** ***Abbreviated work sheet, financial statements, closing entries***
Holly Knight is employed in the accounting department of Expert Systems Company. She was in the process of completing the firm's work sheet for the year ended December 31 and had progressed through the adjusted trial balance columns. A portion of her work follows.

| | *Adjusted Trial Balance* | |
|---|---|---|
| | *Debit* | *Credit* |
| Cash | $ 29,200 | |
| Accounts receivable | 25,800 | |
| Supplies | 2,600 | |
| Prepaid insurance | 1,400 | |
| Equipment | 42,700 | |
| Accumulated depreciation: equipment | | $ 10,400 |
| Accounts payable | | 18,000 |
| Ray Vogel, capital | | 65,200 |
| Ray Vogel, drawing | 3,900 | |
| Service revenue | | 56,200 |
| Wages expense | 32,100 | |
| Advertising expense | 2,400 | |
| Rent expense | 5,900 | |
| Miscellaneous expense | 1,300 | |
| Supplies expense | 800 | |
| Insurance expense | 1,100 | |
| Depreciation expense | 3,300 | |
| Wages payable | | 2,700 |
| | $152,500 | $152,500 |

Additional information revealed that owner investments in the firm amounted to $7,000 during the year.

Holly was recently called out of town because of a family emergency. You are her assistant and recognize that the various year-end accounting procedures must be performed on a timely basis.

**Instructions**

a Complete the work sheet that Holly had begun. *Note:* The preceding data should be entered in the adjusted trial balance columns. We have omitted the company's trial balance and adjustments for the sake of simplicity.
b Prepare an income statement, statement of owner's equity, and balance sheet in good form. The balance sheet should parallel the format used in Exhibit 4-2.
c Prepare the firm's closing entries.

**P4-A3** ***Cycle starting with work sheet***
Trimcraft Company has the following trial balance as of December 31, 19XX:

| | | |
|---|---|---|
| Cash | $ 5,800 | |
| Accounts receivable | 8,200 | |
| Prepaid insurance | 2,000 | |
| Supplies | 2,700 | |
| Equipment | 89,800 | |
| Accumulated depreciation: equipment | | $ 10,000 |
| Accounts payable | | 7,250 |
| Loan payable | | 18,500 |
| Lori Metcalf, capital | | 56,850 |
| Lori Metcalf, drawing | 4,000 | |
| Service revenue | | 72,000 |
| Salaries expense | 30,500 | |
| Rent expense | 12,000 | |
| Advertising expense | 6,600 | |
| Interest expense | 3,000 | |
| | $164,600 | $164,600 |

Additional accounts maintained by the business include Salaries Payable, Interest Payable, Income Summary, Insurance Expense, Supplies Expense, and Depreciation Expense. Trimcraft's accountant has derived the following adjustment data:
1 Insurance applicable to future periods: $700.
2 Supplies used: $1,800.
3 Depreciation on the equipment: $3,500.
4 Accrued interest on the loan: $400.
5 Accrued salaries incurred but not yet paid: $1,200.
6 Unrecorded service revenue, to be collected in future months: $2,200.

On March 9, 19XX, Metcalf invested $10,000 cash in the business. This event is already reflected in the figures reported in the trial balance.

**Instructions**

a Complete a work sheet in good form for Trimcraft Company for the year ended December 31.
b Prepare an income statement, statement of owner's equity, and balance sheet in good form. The balance sheet should be similar in format to that shown in Exhibit 4-2.
c Record Trimcraft's adjusting entries in the journal.
d Record Trimcraft's closing entries in the journal.
e Prepare a post-closing trial balance.

**P4-A4** ***Accounting cycle***

Classic Company, which began operations on May 1, had the following transactions:

| | | |
|---|---|---|
| May | 1 | Bruce Sim, the owner, invested $9,000 cash, $12,000 of office equipment, and a building valued at $75,000 in the business. The office equipment has a service life of five years and the building has a service life of 25 years. |
| | 1 | Paid $240 for a four-month insurance policy. |
| | 4 | Received $660 from a client to render services over the next four weeks. |
| | 11 | Paid $400 for computer services. |
| | 15 | Billed clients for services rendered, $3,800. |
| | 21 | Received $2,200 from clients on account. |
| | 24 | Borrowed $7,000 from the bank. |
| | 26 | Purchased $12,000 of new office equipment; paid $7,000 down and agreed to pay the balance in June. This office equipment will not be depreciated until June. |
| | 29 | Paid wages of the office staff, $4,700. |
| | 31 | Recorded $1,000 of miscellaneous expenses that were incurred in May but will be paid during June. |

Classic's chart of accounts follows.

| | | | |
|---|---|---|---|
| Cash | 110 | Unearned service revenue | 240 |
| Accounts receivable | 120 | Loan payable | 250 |
| Prepaid insurance | 130 | Bruce Sim, capital | 310 |
| Office equipment | 140 | Bruce Sim, drawing | 320 |
| Accumulated depreciation: | | Income summary | 330 |
| office equipment | 141 | Service revenue | 410 |
| Building | 150 | Computer service expense | 510 |
| Accumulated depreciation: | | Wage expense | 520 |
| building | 151 | Insurance expense | 530 |
| Accounts payable | 210 | Depreciation expense | 540 |
| Wages payable | 220 | Interest expense | 550 |
| Interest payable | 230 | Miscellaneous expense | 560 |

As of May 31, accrued interest on the loan amounted to $40, while accrued wages totaled $300. In addition, since the last billing to clients on May 15, the firm had rendered $2,480 of services. Finally, Classic has earned three weeks of revenue from the prepayment received on May 4.

**Instructions**

a Record the transactions of May in the general journal.

b Post the journal entries to the proper ledger accounts.

c Complete a work sheet for the month ended May 31. Be certain to analyze *all* data presented to correctly determine Classic's adjustments.

d Prepare an income statement, statement of owner's equity, and balance sheet in good form. The balance sheet should be similar in format to that shown in Exhibit 4-2.

e Record Classic's adjusting entries in the journal and post to the proper ledger accounts.

f Record Classic's closing entries in the journal and post to the proper ledger accounts.

g Prepare a post-closing trial balance.

**P4-A5** ***Classified balance sheet***

Assume that Case Company has the following balance sheet accounts at the end of 19X1:

| | |
|---|---|
| Building | $82,000 |
| Accumulated depreciation: office furniture | 800 |
| Loan receivable (due May 19X9) | 4,200 |
| Cash | 5,150 |
| Merchandise inventory | 41,570 |
| Loan payable (due 19X8) | 74,560* |
| Office furniture | 8,000 |
| Land held for speculation | 18,320 |
| Receivable from employee (due 19X5) | 3,355 |
| Short-term investments | 22,000 |
| J. Case, capital | 40,835 |
| Salaries payable | 750 |
| Accounts receivable | 31,500 |
| Accounts payable | 52,100 |
| Accumulated depreciation: building | 19,000 |
| Land | 37,500 |
| Payable to finance company (due June 19X2) | 71,800 |
| Patents | 10,000 |
| Prepaid insurance | 900 |
| Office supplies | 750 |
| Taxes payable | 5,400 |

* Of this amount, $2,000 is payable within the next 12 months.

**Instructions**

Prepare a classified balance sheet as of December 31, 19X1, similar in format to that shown in Exhibit 4-11.

***P4-A6** ***Reversing entries***

Greenery, which began business on January 3 of the current year, renders landscaping services to both residential and commercial clients. The company's total wage expense through the most recent payday, June 26, totals $34,750. Greenery pays its employees every Friday for a five-day week; data for the next pay period (June 29–July 3) follow.

| *Date* | *Wage Cost Incurred* |
|---|---|
| Monday, June 29 | $280 |
| Tuesday, June 30 | 300 |
| Wednesday, July 1 | 300 |
| Thursday, July 2 | 300 |
| Friday, July 3 | 315 |

Greenery uses reversing entries.

**Instructions**

a Compute the company's total wage expense through June 30.
b Present the journal entries needed on June 30 to adjust and close the Wage Expense account.
c Prepare the necessary reversing entry on July 1.
d Prepare the necessary journal entry to disburse Greenery's weekly payroll on July 3.
e Repeat part (d), assuming that Greenery does not use reversing entries.
f Is it mandatory that Greenery use reversing entries? Briefly explain.

## Series B

**P4-B1** ***Closing entries***

The income statement of Morton's Taxi Service for the year ended December 31, 19XX, follows.

| MORTON'S TAXI SERVICE<br>Income Statement<br>For the Year Ended December 31, 19XX | | |
|---|---|---|
| Taxi revenue | | $144,360 |
| Less expenses | | |
| Salaries expense | $41,640 | |
| Auto rental expense | 12,400 | |
| Gasoline expense | 14,430 | |
| Maintenance expense | 1,500 | |
| License expense | 6,200 | |
| Tires expense | 970 | |
| Total expenses | | 77,140 |
| Net income | | $ 67,220 |

Daniel Morton, the service's owner, had a beginning capital balance of $37,300 on January 1, 19XX. During the year he invested an additional $10,000 into the firm and withdrew $26,000.

**Instructions**

a Prepare the necessary closing entries for the year ended December 31.
b Compute the December 31, 19XX, balance of Morton's capital account.

**P4-B2** ***Abbreviated work sheet, financial statements, closing entries***

Paul Cohen is employed in the accounting department of Crossroads Repair Company. He was in the process of completing the firm's work sheet for the year ended December 31 and had progressed through the adjusted trial balance columns. A portion of his work follows.

| | Adjusted Trial Balance | |
|---|---|---|
| | Debit | Credit |
| Cash | $ 25,400 | |
| Accounts receivable | 20,700 | |
| Repair supplies | 4,300 | |
| Prepaid rent | 1,800 | |
| Machinery | 65,300 | |
| Accumulated depreciation: machinery | | $ 15,900 |
| Accounts payable | | 20,800 |
| Loan payable | | 16,900 |
| Bob Goodson, capital | | 62,200 |
| Bob Goodson, drawing | 6,800 | |
| Service revenue | | 74,600 |
| Wages expense | 40,400 | |
| Insurance expense | 2,500 | |
| Interest expense | 1,300 | |
| Miscellaneous expense | 900 | |
| Repair supplies expense | 5,200 | |
| Rent expense | 10,800 | |
| Depreciation expense | 5,300 | |
| Interest payable | | 300 |
| | $190,700 | $190,700 |

Additional information revealed that owner investments in the firm amounted to $4,000 during the year.

Paul was recently called out of town because of a family emergency. You are his assistant and recognize that the various year-end accounting procedures must be performed on a timely basis.

**Instructions**

a Complete the work sheet that Paul had begun. *Note:* The preceding data should be entered in the adjusted trial balance columns. We have omitted the company's trial balance and adjustments for the sake of simplicity.

b Prepare an income statement, statement of owner's equity, and balance sheet in good form. The balance sheet should parallel the format used in Exhibit 4-2.

c Prepare the firm's closing entries.

**P4-B3** ***Cycle starting with work sheet***

Detroit Maintenance Service has the following trial balance as of December 31, 19XX:

| | | |
|---|---|---|
| Cash | $ 8,200 | |
| Accounts receivable | 19,900 | |
| Prepaid advertising | 3,100 | |
| Maintenance supplies | 10,800 | |
| Building | 77,500 | |
| Accumulated depreciation: building | | $ 15,700 |
| Accounts payable | | 14,800 |
| Loan payable | | 54,700 |
| Larry Bishop, capital | | 33,100 |
| Larry Bishop, drawing | 12,000 | |
| Fee revenue | | 78,200 |
| Wage expense | 42,400 | |
| Utilities expense | 8,900 | |
| Insurance expense | 7,300 | |
| Interest expense | 6,400 | |
| | $196,500 | $196,500 |

Additional accounts maintained by the business include Wages Payable, Interest Payable, Income Summary, Advertising Expense, Maintenance Supplies Expense, and Depreciation Expense. Detroit's accountant has derived the following adjustment data:

1 Prepaid advertising applicable to future periods: $1,200.
2 Maintenance supplies used: $2,900.
3 Accrued interest on the loan: $500.
4 Accrued wages incurred but not paid: $1,800.
5 Unrecorded fee revenue, to be collected in future months: $3,400.
6 Depreciation on the building: $5,100.

On March 10, 19XX, Bishop invested $9,500 cash in the business. This event is already reflected in the figures reported in the trial balance.

**Instructions**

a Complete a work sheet in good form for Detroit Maintenance Service for the year ended December 31.
b Prepare an income statement, statement of owner's equity, and balance sheet in good form. The balance sheet should be similar in format to that shown in Exhibit 4-2.
c Record Detroit's adjusting entries in the journal.
d Record Detroit's closing entries in the journal.
e Prepare a post-closing trial balance.

**P4-B4** ***Accounting cycle***

Uptown Company, which began operations on August 1, had the following transactions:

| | | |
|---|---|---|
| Aug. | 1 | Received $20,000 from Kent Gibson, the owner, as an investment in the business. |
| | 1 | Purchased $6,000 of office equipment for cash; the equipment has a service life of five years. |
| | 1 | Paid $360 for a three-month insurance policy. |
| | 7 | Received $440 from a client to render services over the next eight weeks. |
| | 11 | Paid rent expense, $900. |
| | 14 | Billed clients for services rendered, $4,500. |
| | 19 | Received $780 from clients on account. |
| | 23 | Borrowed $5,500 from the bank. |

24 Purchased $9,000 of new office equipment; paid $5,500 down and agreed to pay the balance in September. This office equipment will not be depreciated until September.
27 Paid salaries of the office staff, $2,100.
29 Recorded $650 of miscellaneous expenses that were incurred in August but will be paid during September.

Uptown's chart of accounts follows.

| | | | |
|---|---|---|---|
| Cash | 110 | Kent Gibson, capital | 310 |
| Accounts receivable | 120 | Kent Gibson, drawing | 320 |
| Prepaid insurance | 130 | Income summary | 330 |
| Office equipment | 140 | Service revenue | 410 |
| Accumulated depreciation: | | Rent expense | 510 |
| office equipment | 150 | Office salaries expense | 520 |
| Accounts payable | 210 | Insurance expense | 530 |
| Office salaries payable | 220 | Depreciation expense | 540 |
| Interest payable | 230 | Interest expense | 550 |
| Unearned service revenue | 240 | Miscellaneous expense | 560 |
| Loan payable | 250 | | |

As of August 31, accrued interest on the loan amounted to $50, while accrued salaries totaled $180. In addition, since the last billing to clients on August 14, the firm had rendered $1,900 of services. Finally, Uptown has earned three weeks of revenue from the prepayment received on August 7.

**Instructions**

a Record the transactions of August in the general journal.
b Post the journal entries to the proper ledger accounts.
c Complete a work sheet for the month ended August 31. Be certain to analyze *all* data presented to correctly determine Uptown's adjustments.
d Prepare an income statement, statement of owner's equity, and balance sheet in good form. The balance sheet should be similar in format to that shown in Exhibit 4-2.
e Record Uptown's adjusting entries in the journal and post to the proper ledger accounts.
f Record Uptown's closing entries in the journal and post to the proper ledger accounts.
g Prepare a post-closing trial balance.

**P4-B5** ***Classified balance sheet***

Assume that Novak Company has the following balance sheet accounts at the end of 19X1:

| | |
|---|---|
| Land held as a future plant site | $ 45,810 |
| Loan receivable (due in 19X6) | 21,200 |
| Delivery equipment | 10,000 |
| Accumulated depreciation: building | 74,000 |
| Accounts receivable | 34,560 |
| Prepaid insurance | 1,800 |
| Prepaid rent | 1,200 |
| Office supplies | 700 |
| Loan receivable (due in one month) | 9,400 |
| Certificate of deposit (matures in two months) | 10,000 |
| Accumulated depreciation: store equipment | 14,700 |
| Trademark | 520 |
| Accounts payable | 47,000 |

| | |
|---|---|
| Bank loan payable (due in nine days) | 25,000 |
| William Novak, capital | 127,890 |
| Store equipment | 52,100 |
| Cash | 6,200 |
| Payable to State Corporation (due in 19X9) | 52,000* |
| Taxes payable | 18,500 |
| Accumulated depreciation: delivery equipment | 8,500 |
| Merchandise inventory | 52,600 |
| Salaries payable | 2,500 |
| Building | 124,000 |

* Of this amount, $4,500 is payable within the next year.

**Instructions**

Prepare a classified balance sheet as of December 31, 19X1, similar in format to that shown in Exhibit 4-11.

***P4-B6** ***Reversing entries***

Air Shuttle, which began business on February 10 of the current year, provides a shuttle service to DFW International Airport in Dallas. The company's total wage expense through the most recent payday, August 26, totals $54,720. Air Shuttle pays its employees every Friday for a five-day week; data for the next pay period (August 29–September 2) follow.

| *Date* | *Wage Cost Incurred* |
|---|---|
| Monday, Aug. 29 | $400 |
| Tuesday, Aug. 30 | 425 |
| Wednesday, Aug. 31 | 425 |
| Thursday, Sept. 1 | 450 |
| Friday, Sept. 2 | 425 |

Air Shuttle uses reversing entries.

**Instructions**

a Compute the company's total wage expense through August 31.
b Present the journal entries needed on August 31 to adjust and close the Wage Expense account.
c Prepare the necessary reversing entry on September 1.
d Prepare the necessary journal entry to disburse Air Shuttle's weekly payroll on September 2.
e Repeat part (d), assuming that Air Shuttle does not use reversing entries.
f Determine Air Shuttle's wage expense for the first two days of September assuming the company:
  (1) Uses reversing entries.
  (2) Does not use reversing entries.

## Beyond the Basics

**BB4-1** ***Identification of balance sheet errors***

The following balance sheet was prepared by a staff assistant of the Orlando Company:

**ORLANDO COMPANY**
**Balance Sheet**
**For the Year Ended December 31, 19X1**

| *Assets* | | |
|---|---|---|
| Current assets | | |
| Accounts receivable | $ 68,500 | |
| Cash | 27,000 | |
| Short-term investments (cost, $20,000), at current market value | 22,000 | |
| Merchandise inventory | 157,500 | |
| Receivable from supplier (due in 19X7) | 8,000 | $283,000 |
| Property, plant, & equipment | | |
| Buildings and land | $164,000 | |
| Equipment | 59,200 | |
| | $223,200 | |
| Plus: Accumulated depreciation | 45,600 | 268,800 |
| Other assets | | |
| Prepaid insurance | $ 4,100 | |
| Estimated value of top management personnel | 350,000 | 354,100 |
| Total assets | | $905,900 |
| *Liabilities & Owner's Equity* | | |
| Current liabilities | | |
| Accounts payable | $ 43,600 | |
| Salaries payable | 18,900 | |
| Owner withdrawals | 28,000 | |
| Patents | 27,700 | $118,200 |
| Long-term liabilities | | |
| Mortgage payable (payable $10,000 per year for 35 years) | $350,000 | |
| Owner investments | 53,600 | 403,600 |
| Owner's equity | | |
| Brenda Adams, capital | $200,000* | |
| Total payments to suppliers | 184,100 | 384,100 |
| Total liabilities & owner's equity | | $805,900 |

* Excludes owner investments and withdrawals during 19X1.

**Instructions**

Indicate the deficiencies in the preceding financial statement. *Note:* A corrected balance sheet is not required.

**BB4-2** ***Analysis of liquidity***

The following selected account data have been extracted from the financial records of General Industries and American Products, two distributors of consumer goods:

| | *General Industries* | *American Products* |
|---|---|---|
| Accounts payable | $ 75,000 | $ 29,000 |
| Prepaid expenses | 5,000 | 7,000 |
| Property & equipment | 300,000 | 190,000 |
| Accounts receivable | 60,000 | 42,000 |
| Interest payable | 7,000 | 8,000 |
| Short-term investments | 30,000 | 14,000 |
| Long-term loan payable | 140,000 | 120,000 |
| Salaries payable | 18,000 | 13,000 |
| Cash | 40,000 | 14,000 |
| Inventory | 65,000 | 63,000 |

**Instructions**

a Prepare the current asset and current liability sections of both companies' balance sheets in good form.

b Briefly discuss the meaning of the current ratio and then compute the current ratio for both firms.

c Assume that you are a supplier and you are considering doing business with these firms. Based on the current ratio computations, would you prefer to do business with General Industries or American Products? Briefly explain.

d Repeat part (c), now basing your decision on an analysis of each firm's current asset composition. Show appropriate calculations.

## Answers to Chapter Quiz

**1** d

**2** d

**3** c

**4** b

**5** b

CHAPTER 5

# Accounting/ Reporting for Merchandising Operations

## Learning Objectives

After reading this chapter you should:

1. Understand the importance of inventories to business enterprises.
2. Be able to account for typical transactions of sellers and buyers of merchandise.
3. Understand the difference between the gross and net methods of accounting for purchases.
4. Be able to compute cost of goods sold and gross profit and prepare the financial statements and work sheet for a merchandising concern.
5. Be able to prepare the adjusting and closing entries for a merchandising enterprise.
6. Understand the differences between single- and multiple-step income statements.

The bulk of the material presented in the first four chapters has focused on accounting for service enterprises. These firms are engaged in a wide variety of activities and include such entities as repair shops, advertising agencies, airlines, theaters, and professional sports clubs. Service enterprises charge a fee or commission for their services and are a rapidly growing and significant factor in our economy.

We now turn our attention to a different type of operation: the merchandising business. A merchandising firm acquires goods for resale to others (i.e., **merchandise inventory**) and is exemplified by the retailer and wholesaler. Accounting for retailers and wholesalers is not completely different from accounting for service businesses; thus, most of the material presented earlier is still applicable. The purchase and sale of inventory, however, are accompanied by and create several added complexities for the accountant, which form the basis for this chapter's discussion. Before proceeding, a few words are necessary about the nature and importance of inventory.

## Inventory: A Cause for Concern

OBJECTIVE 1
Understand the importance of inventories to business enterprises.

Inventories have a far-reaching impact on several different areas within an organization. The marketing department, for example, is concerned that a business carry sufficient quantities of the "right" goods in order to attain a high level of customer service. Marketing desires to avoid out-of-stock situations, which could result in lost sales and, even worse, an occasional lost customer.

The finance department also has a keen interest in inventory, with financial personnel having the responsibilities of securing operating funds and overseeing investments. Inventories represent the investment of a significant portion of these funds for a merchandising entity. As an example, consider the data that appear in Exhibit 5-1.

In addition to the money tied up in inventory, the basic commitment to a merchandising operation gives rise to storage costs, insurance, and local inventory taxes. And, frequently, companies must raise the funds necessary to finance inventory purchases by obtaining short-term loans. These loans, in turn, obligate a firm to substantial interest payments. Overall, then, an investment in inventory is very costly. Thus, unlike the marketing department, the finance department generally wants as little inventory on hand as possible.

**Exhibit 5-1**
**Inventory Disclosures of Merchandising Firms**

| *Firm* | *Inventory Valuation ($000 omitted)* | *Inventory as a Percent of Total Assets* |
|---|---|---|
| F.W. Woolworth Co. | $1,715,000 | 48.5% |
| J.C. Penney Company, Inc. | 2,201,000 | 18.0 |
| K mart Corporation | 5,671,000 | 46.8 |
| Sears, Roebuck and Co. | 3,715,500 | 4.8 |
| The Limited, Inc. | 407,006 | 19.0 |

Note: Several alternatives are available to a company to arrive at an inventory valuation. These alternatives produce differing results and partially account for the wide variation in inventory as a percentage of total assets. Inventory valuation is discussed in more detail later in the text.

Lost sales, lost customers, and the funds committed to an investment in merchandise eventually affect a company's net income. For this reason (and others) inventory is also a primary concern for the accountant.

## Measuring Merchandising Income

The success of a business organization is often judged by the size of its "bottom line," or net income. A merchandising entity will be profitable if the amounts charged to customers (i.e., sales revenue) exceed the cost of merchandise sold and the operating expenses of the business. The income statement that appears in Exhibit 5-2, simplified for purposes of illustration, shows that Mid Cities Auto Parts earned 7¢ on every sales dollar ($7,000 ÷ $100,000). Further, by purchasing goods from suppliers and then selling the goods at a higher price to its customers, Mid Cities was able to generate a $52,000 gross profit.

Given this brief overview of merchandising profitability, we now present a detailed discussion of sales revenue, cost of goods sold, gross profit, and inventory accounting. In so doing, we will focus on the operations of Peachtree Jeans, an Atlanta-based wholesaler of pants, shirts, and related accessories.

### Sales Revenue

OBJECTIVE 2
Be able to account for typical transactions of sellers and buyers of merchandise.

The revenues of a merchandising concern are generated from its sales of inventory. The timing and measurement of these revenues are of major importance in accounting; incorrect recognition will result in inaccurate reports of financial position and earnings. An entity should record revenue in the accounting records when ownership of the goods is transferred from the seller to the buyer. Normally, this transfer occurs at the time of sale. The amount of revenue to be recognized is determined by the transaction price, which is usually the amount of cash received or to be received.

To properly account for its revenues, a business will establish an account entitled Sales. If desired, an entity could utilize separate accounts to determine revenues by product line (e.g., Pants Sales, Shirt Sales, and Accessories Sales). Understand that the Sales account is used *strictly* to record revenues that relate to the sale

**Exhibit 5-2**
**Income Statement of a Merchandising Firm**

**MID CITIES AUTO PARTS**
**Income Statement**
**For the Year Ended December 31, 19XX**

| | | |
|---|---|---|
| Sales | | $100,000 |
| Cost of goods sold | | 48,000 |
| Gross profit | | $ 52,000 |
| Expenses | | |
| Salaries | $30,000 | |
| Rent | 12,000 | |
| Utilities | 3,000 | |
| Total expenses | | 45,000 |
| Net income | | $ 7,000 |

of merchandise; the sale and/or disposal of other assets are recorded elsewhere. As an example, if Peachtree Jeans sold some extra office supplies for cash, Cash would be debited and Office Supplies would be credited. The Sales account is not affected.

A business must properly record both cash and credit sales. Although the exact procedures vary, the following description is representative of the practices of many companies. When a cash sale is made, a sales slip or *invoice* is completed by a clerk, who also enters the transaction into a cash register (or other similar device). At the end of the day the register is closed out, and the following entry is made (amount is assumed):

| | | | |
|---|---|---|---|
| Apr. 3 | Cash | 325 | |
| | Sales | | 325 |
| | Daily cash sales | | |

Credit sales are handled in much the same fashion. Depending on the system employed, either the sales invoices or register can provide the basis for the necessary journal entry. The use of the latter device may seem somewhat surprising; however, more and more businesses have transaction entry terminals that are linked to a computer (in essence, an electronic cash register). These terminals are used to record both cash and credit sales and, as transactions occur, are capable of updating merchandise inventory records of units on hand.

To illustrate the required accounting for credit sales, assume that Peachtree Jeans sold $700 of merchandise on account to Marty's Outpost on April 7. The following entry would be needed:

| | | | |
|---|---|---|---|
| Apr. 7 | Accounts Receivable | 700 | |
| | Sales | | 700 |
| | Sale on account to Marty's Outpost | | |

## Sales Returns and Allowances

Sales of merchandise often give rise to returns. Customers frequently change their minds, find that merchandise does not fit well once they get it home, or notice defects. If an exchange of goods is neither possible nor desired, most merchandisers will grant a refund or reduce the customer's account balance. Sometimes, particularly in the case of defects or damaged goods, the seller will grant the buyer an *allowance,* that is, a price reduction as incentive to keep the item.

Once a return or allowance is authorized, the seller documents the transaction on a form known as a **credit memorandum.** For a sale on account, a copy is given to the customer and a copy is forwarded to the accounts receivable department. The credit memo informs accounts receivable to credit, or reduce, a particular customer's balance.

The proper accounting treatment for sales returns and allowances is shown by the following example. Suppose that on April 16, Marty's Outpost returned $180 of shirts for credit that it had purchased on April 7. Peachtree Jeans, the seller, would record the transaction as follows:

| | | | |
|---|---|---|---|
| Apr. 16 | Sales Returns & Allowances | 180 | |
| | Accounts Receivable | | 180 |
| | Merchandise returned by Marty's Outpost | | |

The net amount of the sale is $520 ($700 − $180). Rather than reduce the Sales account by a debit, one can establish a separate account entitled Sales Returns & Allowances. The use of a separate account is preferable because it allows management and other readers of financial statements to easily see the amount of returns and allowances in comparison with sales volume. This relationship, particularly if returns and allowances are significant, provides insight regarding customer satisfaction (or dissatisfaction) with merchandise. In addition, an abnormally high level of returns may reveal the presence of shipping problems, such as merchandise being damaged or mishandled while en route to customers.

The sales on April 3 and 7 and the return on April 16 would appear on an income statement as follows:

| | |
|---|---|
| Revenues | |
| Sales | $1,025 |
| Less: Returns & allowances | 180 |
| Net sales | $ 845 |

In view of this treatment (i.e., a deduction from Sales), Sales Returns & Allowances is commonly referred to as a **contra revenue** account.

## Trade Discounts

Sellers frequently offer discounts to purchasers, more so to businesses than to individual consumers. One type of discount is a **trade discount.** To explain, manufacturers and wholesalers spend considerable time and money to publish catalogs of the merchandise they offer for sale. These publications often show the merchandise at a basic catalog price, or **list price.** Purchasers, however, are normally entitled to a reduction in cost and ultimately pay **invoice price,** that is, list price minus an applicable trade discount.

This procedure may seem somewhat strange. Why not just publish the invoice price in the first place? The use of trade discounts does offer several distinct benefits. If a change in market conditions dictates price changes, it is much easier (and cheaper) to quote a different trade discount than to update and reprint an entire catalog. Further, trade discounts can be altered as needed to give customers more incentive to purchase larger quantities (e.g., the larger the quantity purchased, the greater the discount).

Trade discounts are *not* entered in the accounting records; in effect, such amounts are already reflected in the actual selling prices charged by the merchant. To illustrate the proper record keeping, assume that Peachtree stocks a particular style of shirt having a list price of $25. If Peachtree received an order for 600 shirts and granted a 30% trade discount, the purchaser would be charged $10,500, computed as follows:

| | |
|---|---|
| List price (600 shirts × $25) | $15,000 |
| Less: 30% trade discount | 4,500 |
| Invoice price | $10,500 |

An invoice would be prepared for this amount, and $10,500 would be recorded in the Accounts Receivable and Sales accounts. A separate trade discounts account is not established.

## Cash Discounts

When merchandise is sold on account, the seller usually gives the buyer a certain period of time to settle his or her account balance. Often, sales on account are

**Exhibit 5-3**
**Example of Invoice**

INVOICE
**Peachtree Jeans**
5130 Meridian Parkway
Atlanta, Georgia 30309

Sold to: Expressway Chic
2200 Madison Blvd.
Birmingham, Alabama 36296

Invoice no.: 6708
Invoice date: 4/10/X7
Your order no: B-1403
Sales representative: 32

Ship to: Same
Shipped via: Overnight Freight
Shipping terms: F.O.B. Birmingham

Terms of sale: 2/10, n/30

| QUANTITY | DESCRIPTION | UNIT PRICE | AMOUNT |
|---|---|---|---|
| 40 | Jeans--#1630 | 25.00 | 1,000.00 |
| 25 | Blouse--#5800 | 20.00 | 500.00 |
| | | | 1,500.00 |

expected to be paid within 30 days of the invoice date. Sellers, however, normally desire to collect the amounts due more rapidly to cover expenses and for purposes of investment. Consequently, to encourage prompt payment, they sometimes offer incentives called **cash discounts.** From the seller's point of view the cash discount is termed a **sales discount.**

Cash discounts are normally stated on the invoice and expressed in the following format: 2/10, n/30 or perhaps 3/10, n/eom (see Exhibit 5-3). In both examples the first set of numbers indicates the discount rate and the discount period. The second set discloses the invoice due date. The terms of sale are read as follows:

- *2/10, n/30*—A 2% discount from the invoice price is allowed if payment is made within 10 days of the invoice date; otherwise the total invoice price is due within 30 days.
- *3/10, n/eom*—A 3% discount is allowed if payment is made within 10 days of the invoice date; otherwise the total invoice price is due by the end of the month (eom).

There are several alternatives available to account for sales discounts. The most popular approach is to record both Accounts Receivable and Sales at the total (gross) invoice price. The underlying rationale is that at the time of sale, the seller has no idea whether the discount will be taken. Later, if the buyer takes advantage of the offered price reduction, the difference between the cash received and the original amount due is recorded as a discount. In contrast, if the discount is not utilized, the amount paid by the customer is recorded in the same manner as any other receipt on account.

For instance, assume that Peachtree sold $1,500 of merchandise on account to a customer on April 10, terms 2/10, n/30. The sale and subsequent cash receipt are handled as follows:

| | | | |
|---|---|---|---|
| Apr. 10 | Accounts Receivable | 1,500 | |
| | Sales | | 1,500 |
| | Sale on account: terms 2/10, n/30 | | |

***Case A: Customer Pays on April 19 and Takes the Discount***

| | | | |
|---|---|---|---|
| Apr. 19 | Cash | 1,470 | |
| | Sales Discounts | 30 | |
| | Accounts Receivable | | 1,500 |
| | Collection on account; discount taken | | |

***Case B: Customer Pays on April 26 and Forgoes the Discount***

| | | | |
|---|---|---|---|
| Apr. 26 | Cash | 1,500 | |
| | Accounts Receivable | | 1,500 |
| | Collection on account; discount missed | | |

Observe that the sale is recorded at the total invoice price of $1,500. If the customer settles the amount due by April 20, a $30 discount ($1,500 × 0.02) can be taken and the customer will pay $1,470 ($1,500 − $30). Although only $1,470 is received, Accounts Receivable is credited for the full $1,500. This procedure reduces Accounts Receivable to zero, thereby indicating the purchaser has no further obligation to Peachtree. The $30 is debited to Sales Discounts, a contra revenue that is disclosed on the income statement as a reduction from the Sales account.

## Cost of Goods Sold

Recall from Chapter 3 that accountants use the matching concept when measuring income. To explain, a business incurs various costs and expenses in the process of generating revenue. In an effort to judge profitability, the costs and expenses are matched against (i.e., subtracted from) the revenues that they helped to create (see Exhibit 5-2 as an example).

Keeping this fact in mind, let us now focus on the merchandising enterprise. A merchandising business has many different types of expenditures; perhaps the most significant is for the cost of products offered for sale. To achieve a proper matching on the income statement, the cost of units sold to customers during the accounting period must be deducted from net sales. This deduction is appropriately termed **cost of goods sold** and is dependent on three underlying items: (1) beginning inventory, (2) net purchases, and (3) ending inventory.

Most entities will begin an accounting period with a certain amount of merchandise held for resale to customers (termed the *beginning inventory*). Subsequently, the stock of inventory on hand is supplemented by purchases from suppliers. Combined, these two amounts represent a "pool" of **goods available for sale.** If an entity is in the very fortunate position of being able to sell all of its merchandise, the goods available for sale would correspond to the firm's cost of goods sold. In a more realistic situation, however, some inventory normally remains on hand (i.e., unsold) upon conclusion of the reporting period. Known as the *ending inventory,*[1] this amount would have to be considered in computing the proper amount to match against net sales on the income statement. The manner in which this is done is shown in the following example.

Assume that Peachtree Jeans had $67,000 of inventory on hand at the start of the current accounting period. Throughout the year the firm acquired $146,000 of

[1] The ending inventory of one accounting period becomes the beginning inventory of the following period.

goods, meaning that $213,000 ($67,000 + $146,000) of merchandise was available for resale to customers. On conclusion of activity on December 31, accounting personnel checked existing stock levels in the warehouse and determined an ending inventory of $48,000. As shown in Exhibit 5-4, Peachtree has apparently sold inventory that cost the company $165,000.

**Exhibit 5-4**
**Determining Cost of Goods Sold**

***In pictorial terms:***

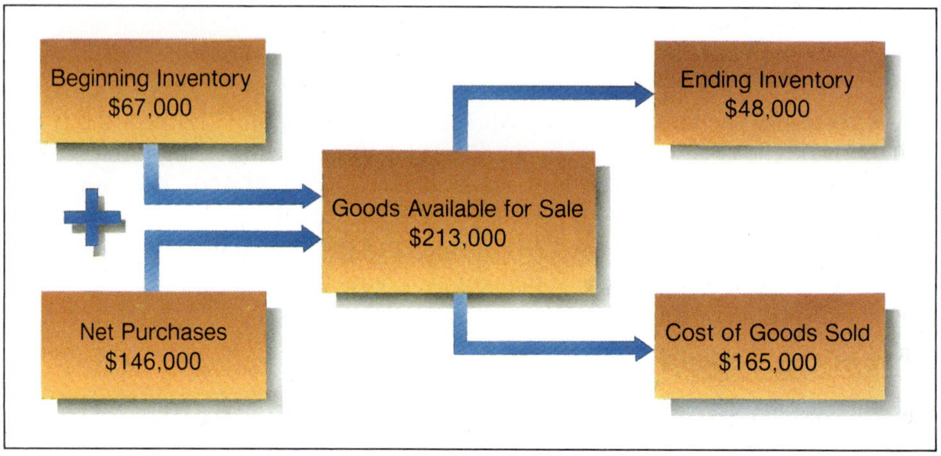


***In mathematical terms:***

| Cost of goods sold | |
|---|---|
| Beginning inventory | $ 67,000 |
| Add: Net purchases | 146,000 |
| Goods available for sale | $213,000 |
| Less: Ending inventory | 48,000 |
| Cost of goods sold | $165,000 |

The concepts presented in this exhibit have important financial statement implications. More specifically, the ending inventory figure will appear on Peachtree's December 31 balance sheet in the current asset section. Cost of goods sold, on the other hand, is deducted from net sales on the income statement. Both of these financial statements will be illustrated shortly.

## Accounting for Merchandise Acquisitions

Our study of cost of goods sold introduced the underlying components of beginning inventory, ending inventory, and net purchases. An in-depth discussion of the first two components is more appropriately deferred until Chapter 9. At this point, however, you should begin to understand the financial measurement and reporting problems related to merchandise acquisitions. Such acquisitions are entered in the records in accordance with the historical-cost principle.

To illustrate the necessary accounting, assume that Peachtree Jeans purchased $9,000 of merchandise on account on April 16. The entry would be as follows:

| | | | |
|---|---|---|---|
| Apr. 16 | Purchases | 9,000 | |
| | Accounts Payable | | 9,000 |
| | Purchased merchandise on account | | |

The Purchases account is used to record acquisitions of goods for resale to customers. It normally has a debit balance and appears on the income statement in the cost of goods sold section. The correct manner of disclosure will be shown shortly.

**▶ TIPS & TECHNIQUES**

Be aware that Purchases is used *solely* for merchandise. As shown earlier in the text, acquisitions of items that will be used in the business (e.g., equipment and supplies) are recorded in their own respective accounts. The acquisition of supplies, for instance, results in a debit to Supplies and has no impact on the Purchases account.

## Purchases Returns and Allowances

As was true for sales, purchase transactions often involve returns and allowances. Returns and allowances are caused by many factors, including the arrival of merchandise (1) in a damaged condition, (2) much later than a requested delivery date, or (3) in error. Before a return or allowance is formally recorded in the accounts, the purchaser prepares documentation of the transaction in the form of either a letter or a **debit memorandum.** The debit memo informs the seller that its account, an account payable, has been debited (reduced) by the purchaser.

Proper accounting for purchases returns and allowances is shown by continuing the previous example. Suppose that $650 of the goods purchased on April 16 arrived past a requested delivery date. On April 30, Peachtree received authorization from the supplier and returned this merchandise. The following entry would be recorded:

| | | | |
|---|---|---|---|
| Apr. 30 | Accounts Payable | 650 | |
| | Purchases Returns & Allowances | | 650 |
| | Returned merchandise to supplier | | |

The net amount of the purchase is $8,350 ($9,000 − $650). Rather than credit the Purchases account for the reduction, it is preferable to establish a separate account for returns and allowances. This procedure allows management to better examine the percentage relationship between returns and allowances and gross purchases, thus providing some insight into the effectiveness of the purchasing department. A large percentage of returns could be caused by sloppy ordering or by dealings with unreliable suppliers.

The purchase and return would appear on Peachtree's income statement as follows:

| | |
|---|---|
| Cost of goods sold | |
| ⋮ | |
| Purchases | $9,000 |
| Less: Returns & allowances | 650 |
| Net purchases | $8,350 |
| ⋮ | |

### Purchases Discounts

Recall that sellers frequently offer a cash discount for prompt payment of invoices. From the buyer's perspective this discount is commonly known as a **purchases discount.** If at all possible, buyers should take advantage of this potential reduction in the cost of merchandise acquired. Why? The reason becomes apparent in the example that follows.

Suppose that Peachtree acquired $10,000 of merchandise subject to terms of 2/10, n/30. Management has two options:

**1** Pay $9,800 [$10,000 − 0.02 ($10,000)] within 10 days of the invoice date.

**2** Pay $10,000 within 30 days of the invoice date.

If Peachtree forgoes the discount and settles the transaction when due, the firm must pay an additional $200. The $200 outlay allows management to have the use of $9,800 for a period of 20 days (30 − 10) and may be construed as interest. For the 20-day period, then, the effective interest rate is 2.04% ($200 ÷ $9,800). Most interest rates are expressed on an annual basis of 360 days, meaning that the supplier's terms are equivalent to 36.72% ($\frac{360}{20}$ × 2.04%)! In view of the cost, purchasers should take advantage of cash discounts even if it means borrowing money from the bank. Much cheaper financing is generally available via short-term loans.

**OBJECTIVE 3**
**Understand the difference between the gross and net methods of accounting for purchases.**

***Gross Method*** A popular approach to accounting for purchases discounts corresponds to the previously illustrated method for sales discounts. Under the **gross method,** both purchases and accounts payable are recorded at the total invoice cost of the merchandise acquired. This technique is logically sound, because at the time of purchase the buyer does not always know whether the discount will be taken.

Using the gross method, let us assume Peachtree purchased $4,000 of sportswear on account from Wrangler Corporation on April 14, subject to terms of 2/10, n/30. The purchase and subsequent payment would be recorded as follows:

| | | | |
|---|---|---|---|
| Apr. 14 | Purchases | 4,000 | |
| | Accounts Payable | | 4,000 |
| | Purchase on account; terms 2/10, n/30 | | |

***Case A: Peachtree Pays on April 23 and Takes the Discount***

| | | | |
|---|---|---|---|
| Apr. 23 | Accounts Payable | 4,000 | |
| | Purchases Discounts | | 80 |
| | Cash | | 3,920 |
| | Paid on account; discount taken | | |

***Case B: Peachtree Pays on April 27 and Forgoes the Discount***

| | | | |
|---|---|---|---|
| Apr. 27 | Accounts Payable | 4,000 | |
| | Cash | | 4,000 |
| | Paid on account; discount missed | | |

While Case B is straightforward, Case A needs some explanation. By paying the invoice before the 10-day discount period expires, Peachtree is entitled to an $80 discount ($4,000 × 0.02). Although only $3,920 is remitted to Wrangler, Accounts

Payable is debited for the entire $4,000 because the balance is paid in full. The Purchases Discounts account is credited for the reduction in cost and is later used in deriving the net cost of merchandise acquired. It is therefore deducted from the Purchases account in the income statement's cost of goods sold section.

In this particular example the discount was calculated on the basis of the $4,000 invoice cost. If any of the merchandise acquired had been returned to Wrangler prior to payment, the discount would have been figured on the net purchase only. Furthermore, discounts are computed on merchandise cost only; they are not permitted on freight charges incurred by the buyer to acquire goods.

***Net Method*** Because of the high interest costs associated with missing discounts, many companies follow a policy of taking all discounts offered. In anticipation of securing these reductions in cost, businesses may follow an alternative recording procedure for purchases called the **net method.** Under this approach, both purchases and accounts payable are recorded at the net cost of the purchase, that is, total invoice cost minus the anticipated cash discount. If the discount is taken, the liability is removed from the books in similar fashion to other payments on account. Any discounts missed, on the other hand, are entered in an account entitled Purchases Discounts Lost.

To illustrate the net method, we will use the same transaction that appeared in the previous discussion—a $4,000 purchase subject to terms of 2/10, n/30. The April 14 acquisition and subsequent payment on account would be recorded as follows:

| | | | |
|---|---|---|---|
| Apr. 14 | Purchases | 3,920 | |
| | Accounts Payable | | 3,920 |
| | Purchase on account; terms 2/10, n/30 | | |

***Case A: Peachtree Pays on April 23 and Takes the Discount***

| | | | |
|---|---|---|---|
| Apr. 23 | Accounts Payable | 3,920 | |
| | Cash | | 3,920 |
| | Paid on account; discount taken | | |

***Case B: Peachtree Pays on April 27 and Forgoes the Discount***

| | | | |
|---|---|---|---|
| Apr. 27 | Accounts Payable | 3,920 | |
| | Purchases Discounts Lost | 80 | |
| | Cash | | 4,000 |
| | Paid on account; discount missed | | |

Under Case A, since the liability is already established at the net figure of $3,920, no additional discount is recorded. Under Case B, $4,000 must be paid: $3,920 for the merchandise acquired and an $80 penalty for late payment.

The Purchases Discounts Lost account appears on the income statement as an expense. The presence of a large balance in this account means that a business has missed a considerable number of discounts and often raises questions concerning managerial effectiveness. The discounts may have been lost because of carelessness in paying invoices and allowing discount periods to lapse or perhaps because of a very tight cash position. Whatever the cause, the firm is incurring extremely high interest costs as a result, and corrective action may be needed.

## Freight Charges

The acquisition of merchandise by retailers and wholesalers often gives rise to transportation charges. These charges can be significant, especially when a company deals in bulky or heavy items. Freight costs are borne by either the seller of the goods or the buyer, the exact party being determined by an order's freight terms.

Freight terms are usually expressed as F.O.B. shipping point or F.O.B. destination. **F.O.B.,** or free on board, means the seller will place the merchandise sold on board a freight carrier at no charge. Whether the seller or buyer incurs the transportation costs thereafter is dependent on "shipping point" or "destination." For example, if the terms are **F.O.B. shipping point,** the seller's responsibility for freight stops when the goods are loaded for shipment. Thus, the buyer incurs all freight charges. In contrast, under **F.O.B. destination,** the seller's responsibility ceases when the goods arrive at their ultimate destination (e.g., the buyer's warehouse). Consequently, the seller is liable for transportation costs. These points are summarized as follows:

| *Terms of Shipment* | *Where Seller's Responsibility Ceases* | *Who Incurs Freight Charges* |
|---|---|---|
| F.O.B. shipping point | At point of shipment | Buyer |
| F.O.B. destination | At goods' destination | Seller |

The preceding treatment is consistent with the ownership of goods during the in-transit period. With F.O.B. shipping point, for example, title to merchandise legally shifts from the seller to the buyer at the time of shipment. In contrast, under F.O.B. destination, transfer of title occurs at the time of the goods' receipt.

***Freight-In and Freight-Out*** As a logical outgrowth of the historical-cost principle, freight charges incurred on the *acquisition* of merchandise are treated as part of the purchase cost. Rather than bury these charges in Purchases, however, many firms maintain a separate account entitled Freight-in. Used only for transportation on incoming goods, Freight-in is added to the Purchases account on the income statement (see p. 166) to arrive at a net delivered cost of merchandise acquired.

To illustrate accounting for the purchaser under terms of F.O.B. shipping point, assume that Peachtree Jeans purchased $3,000 of footwear on account from Sport Shoe Company on April 22, F.O.B. shipping point. If freight charges amounted to $80, Peachtree would record the following entry:

| | | | |
|---|---|---|---|
| Apr. 22 | Purchases | 3,000 | |
| | Freight-in | 80 | |
| | Accounts Payable | | 3,080 |
| | Purchased merchandise; terms F.O.B. shipping point | | |

The credit of $3,080 to Accounts Payable shows that Peachtree owes the footwear dealer for the freight. Apparently, as a matter of convenience to the purchaser, Sport Shoe prepaid the transportation costs and expects to be reimbursed. If the costs were not prepaid, Peachtree would disburse $80 to the freight company upon receipt of the goods, requiring a credit to the Cash account.

The preceding treatment applies strictly to freight on incoming merchandise; transportation charges related to outgoing shipments (i.e., sales) are debited to a different account entitled Freight-out. Generated under terms of F.O.B. destination, such charges bear no connection to an entity's purchases and, hence, are excluded from the cost of goods sold computation. Freight-out is a selling cost and is properly listed among a company's typical business expenses (such as salaries, advertising, utilities, and rent).

## Inventory Accounting

Merchandising businesses stock a variety of goods for resale to customers. The cost of these goods is carried in an account called Inventory or Merchandise Inventory. Interestingly, however, when we look back at the methods of recording purchases and sales that were presented earlier in the chapter, we never debited or credited the Inventory account. All merchandise acquisitions were debited to Purchases, and all sales were recorded in the Sales account. Apparently, then, the balance found in the Inventory account at the beginning of the period remains there throughout the year.[2] This type of record-keeping system is known as a **periodic inventory system.** At the end of the accounting period, the Inventory account must be updated to reflect the proper amount of goods owned by the firm.

The periodic system is in contrast to a **perpetual inventory system,** in which the Inventory account is directly increased for each purchase and also decreased for every sale. Many entities employ a perpetual (running) count of the units on hand to closely monitor and better control stock levels. This practice often results in improved customer service and production efficiency, as costly stockouts of merchandise and/or raw materials are avoided (or reduced). Although the perpetual method of accounting for *units* is simple, the maintenance of a running count of *dollar* values in the Inventory account creates several unique record-keeping problems. We will therefore use the periodic system for the remainder of this chapter.

## Financial Statements of a Merchandising Concern

Thus far in the text we have concentrated on three financial statements: the income statement, statement of owner's equity, and the balance sheet. The income statement is prepared first and ties together a number of the concepts discussed in this chapter. It is therefore an appropriate place to begin.

### Income Statement

OBJECTIVE 4
Be able to compute cost of goods sold and gross profit and prepare the financial statements and work sheet for a merchandising concern.

The income statements of a service business and a merchandising entity differ considerably. While both statements measure net income, the introduction of inventory gives rise to several modifications. See Exhibit 5-5, for example, which contains the income statement of Peachtree Jeans. (*Note:* The account balances that appear in Exhibit 5-5 through 5-8 were obtained from Peachtree's general ledger as of December 31, 19XX.)

Consistent with the matching concept, observe that the costs incurred in producing sales are deducted from the sales revenues generated. These costs are operating expenses and cost of goods sold. **Operating expenses** are expenses that arise from the principal selling and administrative activities of a business and include such items as rent, advertising, wages, utilities, and repairs.

[2] We will soon illustrate how a balance gets into the Inventory account.

**Exhibit 5-5**
**Income Statement of a Merchandising Firm**

**PEACHTREE JEANS**
**Income Statement**
**For the Year Ended December 31, 19XX**

| | | | | |
|---|---|---|---|---|
| Revenues | | | | |
| Sales | | | | $307,000 |
| Less: Sales discounts | | | $ 5,000 | |
| Sales returns & allowances | | | 2,000 | 7,000 |
| Net sales | | | | $300,000 |
| Cost of goods sold | | | | |
| Beginning inventory, Jan. 1 | | | $ 67,000 | |
| Add: Purchases | | $148,000 | | |
| Freight-in | | 5,000 | | |
| | | $153,000 | | |
| Less: Purchases discounts | $3,000 | | | |
| Purchases returns & allowances | 4,000 | 7,000 | | |
| Net purchases | | | 146,000 | |
| Goods available for sale | | | $213,000 | |
| Less: Ending inventory, Dec. 31 | | | 48,000 | |
| Cost of goods sold | | | | 165,000 |
| Gross profit | | | | $135,000 |
| Operating expenses | | | | |
| Rent expense | | | $ 15,000 | |
| Salaries expense | | | 61,000 | |
| Utilities expense | | | 11,000 | |
| Freight-out | | | 7,000 | |
| Advertising expense | | | 13,000 | |
| Depreciation expense | | | 10,000 | |
| Insurance expense | | | 9,000 | |
| Total operating expenses | | | | 126,000 |
| Net income | | | | $ 9,000 |

Notice that cost of goods sold is subtracted from net sales to arrive at **gross profit** (sometimes called gross margin). Gross profit represents the profit that a company produces from the sale of inventory. A review of the figures in Exhibit 5-5 will show that for every dollar of net sales, Peachtree was able to earn $0.45 ($135,000 ÷ $300,000) from merchandise. This amount was used to cover operating expenses and produce a net income.[3]

[3] In more precise terms, the "average" sales dollar was used as follows:

| | | |
|---|---|---|
| Sales revenue | | $1.00 |
| Recovery of merchandise cost ($165,000 ÷ $300,000) | $0.55 | |
| Selling and administrative expenses ($126,000 ÷ $300,000) | 0.42 | 0.97 |
| Net income | | $0.03 |

## HIGHLIGHT

# Gross Profit: From Little or None to "Are You Serious?"

Gross profit, computed by subtracting cost of goods sold from net sales, varies greatly from business to business and from product to product. As evidence, consider the highly successful Toys "R" Us, which controls close to 20% of the nation's toy market. Aggressive growth and attractive earnings have made this firm a dominant force in retailing. Part of the success arises from a clever gross profit strategy.

Toys "R" Us believes in cultivating new customers. Management lures new parents to its stores by stocking a wide selection of baby products (e.g., disposable diapers and formula), with some being sold at little or no profit. Selling baby products cheap, the company's chairman says, is a shrewd marketing move. "If you have a new baby, you're the most important customer we have. You're going to stay with us 12 to 15 years."

This same lack-of-profit strategy is also followed when it comes to selling hot products. In 1977, for instance, an electronic game called "Simon" was nearly as popular as Cabbage Patch Kids have been. It was also in short supply. One retailing executive notes that "some stores took advantage of the demand and charged more than $30." Toys "R" Us, though, charged less than $20, figuring that shoppers would believe that everything else in its stores was as good a bargain. [1]

Let's now go to the movies. Hershey's chocolate bars consistently rank among the top ten sellers in the U.S. But you won't find them at many of your neighborhood theaters. The sweet tooth stars at the movies are a strange mix that includes surprisingly few of the most popular candies, although Snickers does make the list. The movie house hot sellers instead include such things as Milk Duds, Sno Caps, and Jujyfruits, which are rare birds indeed at the supermarket.

Do movie goers have different tastes in candy from the rest of the population? Not at all. It's the movie house operators who prefer the obscure brands, which tend to be more profitable. The candy counter delivers up to 75% of the theater's profit, so the owners, with limited space for candy, peddle only those sweets that deliver the highest margin.

There is no standard markup for concessions at movie theaters. But typically, a soft drink that costs the theater 10 cents will sell for about 75 cents—a gross profit of 650% of cost. And a candy bar that is 35 cents will be sold for at least $1—a markup of 186%. Says one wholesaler, "The Hershey Bar isn't there because of the cost factor. A large bar made especially for movie goers would run the theater about 71 cents, which means they'd have to get $2.25 for it. And at that price it wouldn't sell."

New products occasionally surface at the concession stand. A Tex-Mex concoction called Nachos has become one of the fastest growing new items. This cheese, hot pepper, and chips snack is no more trouble to prepare than popcorn and provides the same delicious 300% (plus) gross profit. Also, because they're so spicy, Nachos usually increase soft drink sales 12% to 20%. As one executive notes, "In time, you're going to see a lot more innovations." Until then, please pass the Milk Duds and other high profit items. [2]

SOURCES: Adapted from "Founder Lazarus is a Reason Toys 'R' Us Dominates Its Industry," *The Wall Street Journal*, November 21, 1985, pp. 1, 22 [1]; and "Those Peculiar Candies That Star at the Movies," *Forbes*, May 19, 1986, pp. 174, 176 [2]. 

Finally, you can now see the income statement's expansion to include the various concepts and accounts that we have been discussing. Observe that net sales is derived by subtracting discounts and returns and allowances from the Sales account. Net purchases, a key component of the cost-of-goods-sold calculation, is subdivided into its elements of purchases, freight-in, purchases discounts, and purchases returns and allowances. Furthermore, freight-out, an expense related to the sale of merchandise, is listed among the operating expenses.

### Statement of Owner's Equity

The statement of owner's equity summarizes the changes in the capital account during the reporting period. This financial statement is identical for both a service business and a merchandising concern and is shown in Exhibit 5-6.

### Balance Sheet

The balance sheets of a service business and a merchandiser are also similar, with the exception of inventory. The inventory of a merchandising firm is an asset and, accordingly, an Inventory account appears in the statement's current asset section. The balance reported in this account represents the amount of merchandise owned upon conclusion of the reporting period ($48,000 in Peachtree's case—see Exhibit 5-4). The company's balance sheet as of December 31, 19XX, is shown in Exhibit 5-7.

## Going Behind the Scenes: The Work Sheet

The work sheet is the underlying foundation for the preparation of financial statements. Recall that trial balance data are combined with the entries in the adjustment columns. These "updated" figures are listed in the adjusted trial balance columns and then extended on a line-by-line basis to the appropriate financial statement section (e.g., income statement or balance sheet).

It is important to note that with the exception of Inventory (and Capital), all of the accounts listed in the trial balance reflect the transactions that occurred during the period. Remember that the Inventory account under a periodic system is not

**Exhibit 5-6**
**Statement of Owner's Equity of a Merchandising Firm**

**PEACHTREE JEANS**
**Statement of Owner's Equity**
**For the Year Ended December 31, 19XX**

| | |
|---|---|
| Beginning balance, Jan. 1 | $147,200 |
| Add: Net income* | 9,000 |
| | $156,200 |
| Deduct: Owner withdrawals | 6,000 |
| Ending balance, Dec. 31 | $150,200 |

* From Exhibit 5-5.

affected by sales and purchases; thus, the account's balance represents the goods on hand at the start of the year. For Peachtree Jeans this figure amounts to $67,000.

Two different approaches may be used when handling the beginning inventory (and also the ending inventory) on a work sheet: the closing entry method and the adjusting entry method. Both approaches produce the same end result in the financial statements and both are widely used by accountants. The closing entry method is illustrated on the next few pages; a discussion of the adjusting entry method appears in an appendix to this chapter. Be sure to ask your instructor which approach he or she prefers.

## The Closing Entry Method

As we will soon show, the **closing entry method** is so named because the Inventory account is updated in the closing process. Please refer to Peachtree's work sheet, which appears in Exhibit 5-8. (*Note:* New accounts presented in this chapter are shown in capital letters.) A careful study of the exhibit will reveal that Peachtree has extended the $67,000 beginning inventory from the adjusted trial

**Exhibit 5-7**
**Balance Sheet of a Merchandising Firm**

**PEACHTREE JEANS**
**Balance Sheet**
**December 31, 19XX**

| | | |
|---|---|---|
| ***Assets*** | | |
| Current assets | | |
| Cash | $ 25,700 | |
| Accounts receivable | 19,600 | |
| Inventory | 48,000 | |
| Prepaid insurance | 4,800 | |
| Total current assets | | $ 98,100 |
| Property, plant, & equipment | | |
| Equipment | $124,800 | |
| Less: Accumulated depreciation | 34,800 | 90,000 |
| Total assets | | $188,100 |
| ***Liabilities & Owner's Equity*** | | |
| Current liabilities | | |
| Accounts payable | $ 36,400 | |
| Salaries payable | 1,500 | |
| Total current liabilities | | $ 37,900 |
| Owner's equity | | |
| Valerie Bain, capital* | | 150,200 |
| Total liabilities & owner's equity | | $188,100 |

* From Exhibit 5-6.

balance to the income statement debit column. This procedure is performed because of the inventory's use in the computation of cost of goods sold. A review of the debit column will show that, in effect, the beginning inventory is being added to net purchases to arrive at goods available for sale.

Next, as indicated by the shaded numbers, the $48,000 ending inventory count is inserted in both the income statement credit column and the balance sheet debit column. The credit allows the goods available for sale figure to be reduced by the ending inventory, to yield cost of goods sold. In contrast, the debit is needed so that Peachtree can report the year-end inventory on its balance sheet, along with the other assets owned by the firm.

**Exhibit 5-8**
**Work Sheet of a Merchandising Firm: Closing Entry Method**

**PEACHTREE JEANS**
**Work Sheet**
**For the Year Ended December 31, 19XX**

| | *Trial Balance* | | *Adjustments* | | *Adjusted Trial Balance* | | *Income Statement* | | *Balance Sheet* | |
|---|---|---|---|---|---|---|---|---|---|---|
| *Account Title* | *Debit* | *Credit* | *Debit* | *Credit* | *Debit* | *Credit* | *Debit* | *Credit* | *Debit* | *Credit* |
| Cash | 25,700 | | | | 25,700 | | | | 25,700 | |
| Accounts receivable | 19,600 | | | | 19,600 | | | | 19,600 | |
| INVENTORY | 67,000 | | | | 67,000 | | 67,000 | 48,000 | 48,000 | |
| Prepaid insurance | 13,800 | | | (b) 9,000 | 4,800 | | | | 4,800 | |
| Equipment | 124,800 | | | | 124,800 | | | | 124,800 | |
| Accumulated depreciation: equipment | | 24,800 | | (a) 10,000 | | 34,800 | | | | 34,800 |
| Accounts payable | | 36,400 | | | | 36,400 | | | | 36,400 |
| Valerie Bain, capital | | 147,200 | | | | 147,200 | | | | 147,200 |
| Valerie Bain, drawing | 6,000 | | | | 6,000 | | | | 6,000 | |
| SALES | | 307,000 | | | | 307,000 | | 307,000 | | |
| SALES DISCOUNTS | 5,000 | | | | 5,000 | | 5,000 | | | |
| SALES RETURNS & ALLOWANCES | 2,000 | | | | 2,000 | | 2,000 | | | |
| PURCHASES | 148,000 | | | | 148,000 | | 148,000 | | | |
| FREIGHT-IN | 5,000 | | | | 5,000 | | 5,000 | | | |
| PURCHASES DISCOUNTS | | 3,000 | | | | 3,000 | | 3,000 | | |
| PURCHASES RETURNS & ALLOWANCES | | 4,000 | | | | 4,000 | | 4,000 | | |
| Rent expense | 15,000 | | | | 15,000 | | 15,000 | | | |
| Salaries expense | 59,500 | | (c) 1,500 | | 61,000 | | 61,000 | | | |
| Utilities expense | 11,000 | | | | 11,000 | | 11,000 | | | |
| FREIGHT-OUT | 7,000 | | | | 7,000 | | 7,000 | | | |
| Advertising expense | 13,000 | | | | 13,000 | | 13,000 | | | |
| | 522,400 | 522,400 | | | | | | | | |
| Depreciation expense | | | (a) 10,000 | | 10,000 | | 10,000 | | | |
| Insurance expense | | | (b) 9,000 | | 9,000 | | 9,000 | | | |
| Salaries payable | | | | (c) 1,500 | | 1,500 | | | | 1,500 |
| | | | 20,500 | 20,500 | 533,900 | 533,900 | 353,000 | 362,000 | 228,900 | 219,900 |
| Net income | | | | | | | 9,000 | | | 9,000 |
| | | | | | | | 362,000 | 362,000 | 228,900 | 228,900 |

## Adjusting Entries

OBJECTIVE 5
Be able to prepare the adjusting and closing entries for a merchandising enterprise.

The work sheet not only assists in the construction of financial statements, but is also useful in the preparation of adjusting entries. When the beginning and ending inventories are treated in the manner just described, the adjusting entries for a merchandising concern parallel those shown earlier in the text for a service business. In Peachtree's case, for instance, the three adjusting entries for depreciation, prepaid insurance, and accrued salaries would be recorded in the journal and posted to the ledger. Please refer to Chapters 3 and 4 should you need a refresher of the proper procedures.

## Closing Entries

As before, all temporary accounts must be closed at the end of the reporting period. Such accounts would include those listed in the work sheet's income statement section, along with the drawing account. The income statement accounts with debit balances are closed in a combined journal entry by crediting each account and debiting Income Summary. New accounts introduced in this chapter that have debit balances are Sales Discounts, Sales Returns & Allowances, Purchases, Freight-in, and Freight-out. Next, income statement accounts that contain credit balances are debited, with a corresponding credit to Income Summary. New accounts that fall in this category include Sales, Purchases Discounts, and Purchases Returns & Allowances.

Because Inventory is listed in both the income statement debit *and* credit columns, the account is afforded special treatment. Inventory is credited in the first entry for $67,000, a procedure that reduces the balance in the account to zero. It is then debited for $48,000 in the second entry, thereby recording (inserting) the ending balance of goods owned by the firm.

These two closing entries, along with the Inventory and Income Summary accounts, follow. Notice (1) the manner in which the Inventory account has been updated and (2) how the journal entries eventually place the company's $9,000 net income (from Exhibit 5-5) in Income Summary.

| | | | |
|---|---|---|---|
| Dec. 31 | Income Summary | 353,000 | |
| | Inventory | | 67,000 |
| | Sales Discounts | | 5,000 |
| | Sales Returns & Allowances | | 2,000 |
| | Purchases | | 148,000 |
| | Freight-in | | 5,000 |
| | Rent Expense | | 15,000 |
| | Salaries Expense | | 61,000 |
| | Utilities Expense | | 11,000 |
| | Freight-out | | 7,000 |
| | Advertising Expense | | 13,000 |
| | Depreciation Expense | | 10,000 |
| | Insurance Expense | | 9,000 |
| | To remove beginning inventory and close income statement accounts having debit balances | | |
| 31 | Inventory | 48,000 | |
| | Sales | 307,000 | |
| | Purchases Discounts | 3,000 | |
| | Purchases Returns & Allowances | 4,000 | |
| | Income Summary | | 362,000 |
| | To record ending inventory and close income statement accounts having credit balances | | |

| *Inventory* | | | |
|---|---|---|---|
| 1/1/XX | 67,000 | 12/31/XX | 67,000 |
| 12/31/XX | 48,000 | | |

| *Income Summary* | | | |
|---|---|---|---|
| 12/31/XX | 353,000 | 12/31/XX | 362,000 |
| | | | 9,000 |

To complete the closing process, the Income Summary and drawing accounts are both closed to capital.

| | | | |
|---|---|---|---|
| Dec. 31 | Income Summary | 9,000 | |
| | Valerie Bain, Capital | | 9,000 |
| | To close Income Summary | | |
| 31 | Valerie Bain, Capital | 6,000 | |
| | Valerie Bain, Drawing | | 6,000 |
| | To close drawing account | | |

## Income Reporting

The preceding sections of this chapter have focused primarily on various facets of income measurement as related to a merchandising entity. We now turn our attention to income *reporting,* namely, financial statement presentation of operating results. A review of income statements of large U.S. companies will find considerable variation in both formats and disclosures.

### Single- and Multiple-Step Statements

OBJECTIVE 6
Understand the differences between single- and multiple-step income statements.

Many business enterprises prepare a **single-step income statement,** which has one section for revenues and another section for costs and expenses.[4] The single-step approach offers the advantage of simplicity, since income (or loss) before tax is determined with one step (i.e., one subtraction). Because many unsophisticated users of financial information may be confused by a detailed presentation of earnings, a large number of companies opt for this type of format. A single-step income statement of Bristol-Myers Company, known for such products as Clairol hair-coloring, Excedrin, and Windex, appears in Exhibit 5-9.

Many other business enterprises use a **multiple-step income statement,** where accounts are presented by association so that important relationships can be easily seen by readers. Merchandising firms, for example, deduct cost of goods sold from net sales to arrive at gross profit. In addition, operating expenses, other revenues and expenses, and income taxes are all segregated. Many accountants believe that specific placements and the disclosure of important subtotals (such as gross profit) make the multiple-step format more informative and useful.

The multiple-step income statement of The Waikiki Trading Company, Inc., appears in Exhibit 5-10. Note the grouping of accounts by association and the number of steps involved before net income is shown. We will now highlight several new features that relate to the firm's presentation.

[4] Corporate entities are subject to federal income taxes, while sole proprietorships and partnerships are not. If desired, such amounts may be shown separately.

**BRISTOL-MYERS COMPANY**
**Consolidated Statement of Earnings**
**For the Year Ended December 31, 1988**
**(in Millions)**

| | | |
|---|---|---|
| Net sales | | $5,972.5 |
| Expenses | | |
| Cost of products sold | $1,803.6 | |
| Marketing, selling, and administrative | 1,606.5 | |
| Advertising and product promotion | 978.8 | |
| Research and development | 394.1 | |
| Other | (95.8) | 4,687.2 |
| Earnings before income taxes | | $1,285.3 |
| Provision for income taxes | | 456.3 |
| Net earnings | | $ 829.0 |

**Exhibit 5-9**
**Single-Step Income Statement of Bristol-Myers**

## Selling and Administrative Expenses

Observe that operating expenses (i.e., those that relate to normal business activities and operations) are subdivided into selling and administrative components. Selling expenses are those associated with the sale of merchandise; administrative costs, on the other hand, are incurred in the management of business affairs. Certain individual expenses may need to be split between the two categories because they relate to both functional areas. An example would be depreciation on a building that houses both selling activities and executive offices.

## Other Revenues and Expenses

Companies frequently incur expenses (and generate revenues) that are not directly related to normal business operations. For instance, assume that a retail store leased some extra space to a charitable organization for use as an office. The retail store would earn rental revenue and may incur some added expense (such as maintenance) as a result of the lease. On the single-step income statement, the revenue and expense would be presented as part of total revenues and total expenses, respectively. On the multiple-step statement, however, items related to the lease that affect net income would be shown in a separate nonoperating (other) category.

A careful review of Exhibit 5-10 will reveal the disclosure of interest expense in the "other" classification. The rationale for this placement is that interest (be it revenue or expense) is not derived from operating activities, such as selling a product or rendering a service. Instead it arises from a situation of either providing or securing some type of financing and is shown accordingly.

## Income Tax Expense

Income tax expense is deducted separately from other corporate business expenses when using the multiple-step format. This treatment is justified because the amount of tax is dependent on the calculation of a company's income before tax. In

**Exhibit 5-10 Multiple-Step Income Statement**

**THE WAIKIKI TRADING COMPANY, INC.**
**Income Statement**
**For the Year Ended December 31, 19XX**

| | | | | |
|---|---|---|---|---|
| Revenues | | | | |
| Sales | | | | $510,000 |
| Less: Sales discounts | | | $ 10,000 | |
| Sales returns & allowances | | | 5,000 | 15,000 |
| Net sales | | | | $495,000 |
| Cost of goods sold | | | | |
| Beginning inventory, Jan. 1 | | | $100,000 | |
| Add: Purchases | | $120,000 | | |
| Freight-in | | 5,000 | | |
| | | $125,000 | | |
| Less: Purchases discounts | $4,000 | | | |
| Purchases returns & allowances | 1,000 | 5,000 | | |
| Net purchases | | | 120,000 | |
| Goods available for sale | | | $220,000 | |
| Less: Ending inventory, Dec. 31 | | | 50,000 | |
| Cost of goods sold | | | | 170,000 |
| Gross profit | | | | $325,000 |
| Operating expenses | | | | |
| Selling expenses | | | | |
| Advertising | | $ 45,000 | | |
| Sales salaries | | 27,000 | | |
| Depreciation expense: building | | 10,000 | | |
| Depreciation expense: store equipment | | 13,000 | | |
| Depreciation expense: delivery vans | | 14,000 | | |
| Miscellaneous | | 8,000 | | |
| Total selling expenses | | | $117,000 | |
| General & administrative expenses | | | | |
| Executive salaries | | $ 95,000 | | |
| Office salaries | | 43,000 | | |
| Insurance | | 18,500 | | |
| Depreciation expense: building | | 5,000 | | |
| Miscellaneous | | 12,500 | | |
| Total general & administrative expenses | | | 174,000 | |
| Total operating expenses | | | | 291,000 |
| Income from operations | | | | $ 34,000 |
| Other revenues (expenses) | | | | |
| Interest expense | | | | (4,000) |
| Income before income taxes | | | | $ 30,000 |
| Income taxes | | | | 10,000 |
| Net income | | | | $ 20,000 |

Waikiki's case, for example, the company is subject to a $33\frac{1}{3}\%$ tax rate. Income taxes amounting to $10,000 ($30,000 × $33\frac{1}{3}\%$) are therefore subtracted to yield a final profit figure of $20,000.

### Gains and Losses

Businesses enter into a variety of earnings transactions. Many transactions are routine, such as sales to customers and payments for salaries and supplies; others, however, are not. For instance, a business may only occasionally sell a piece of equipment, a building, or a long-term investment. Market and economic conditions change over time, and management may decide that disposal is the proper course of action to follow.

Transactions that involve the sale of property, plant, and equipment or investments, as well as other events, often give rise to a gain or loss. For example, suppose that a firm purchased a parcel of land for $56,000 for use as a future plant site in a companywide expansion program. At some later date the company may sell the land because of a change in plans. If the land is sold for, say, $100,000, there is a gain of $44,000 ($100,000 − $56,000) on the sale.

Gains and losses affect profitability and are therefore disclosed on the income statement. Gains increase net income, and losses cause a reduction. For businesses that use a multiple-step income statement, such gains and losses are usually placed in the other revenue (expense) category. As an example, a recent income statement of NWA Inc. (Northwest Airlines) contained the following presentation (figures are in thousands):

| | | |
|---|---|---|
| Operating income | | $205,159 |
| Other income (expense) | | |
| Interest expense, net | $(50,497) | |
| Investment income | 7,119 | |
| Gain on disposition of assets | 40,077 | |
| Other—net | 11,824 | 8,523 |
| Earnings before income taxes | | $213,682 |

## APPENDIX The Adjusting Entry Method for Merchandise Inventory

As noted in the body of the chapter, an Inventory account maintained under a periodic system is not affected by the period's purchase and sales transactions. With Peachtree Jeans, for example, the $67,000 inventory balance from January 1 continues to be found in the account on December 31. It is therefore necessary that some updating be done to reflect the cost of goods owned by the firm at year-end. This process may be performed by a series of two adjustments under the so-called **adjusting entry method.**

### Adjusting Entries for a Merchandising Business

Focus for a moment on Exhibit 5-11, the work sheet for Peachtree Jeans. (*Note:* New accounts presented in this chapter are shown in capital letters.) Three of the company's adjustments, namely those for depreciation (c), prepaid insurance (d), and accrued salaries (e), should look familiar. They are identical to the types of adjustments that are recorded by service businesses, a subject that was discussed in Chapters 3 and 4. A review of this material is in order should you need a refresher of the logic and procedures that underlie the entries.

**Exhibit 5-11**
**Work Sheet of a Merchandising Firm: Adjusting Entry Method**

**PEACHTREE JEANS**
**Work Sheet**
**For the Year Ended December 31, 19XX**

| Account Title | *Trial Balance* | | *Adjustments* | | *Adjusted Trial Balance* | | *Income Statement* | | *Balance Sheet* | |
|---|---|---|---|---|---|---|---|---|---|---|
| | *Debit* | *Credit* | *Debit* | *Credit* | *Debit* | *Credit* | *Debit* | *Credit* | *Debit* | *Credit* |
| Cash | 25,700 | | | | 25,700 | | | | 25,700 | |
| Accounts receivable | 19,600 | | | | 19,600 | | | | 19,600 | |
| INVENTORY | 67,000 | | (b) 48,000 | (a) 67,000 | 48,000 | | | | 48,000 | |
| Prepaid insurance | 13,800 | | | (d) 9,000 | 4,800 | | | | 4,800 | |
| Equipment | 124,800 | | | | 124,800 | | | | 124,800 | |
| Accumulated depreciation: equipment | | 24,800 | | (c) 10,000 | | 34,800 | | | | 34,800 |
| Accounts payable | | 36,400 | | | | 36,400 | | | | 36,400 |
| Valerie Bain, capital | | 147,200 | | | | 147,200 | | | | 147,200 |
| Valerie Bain, drawing | 6,000 | | | | 6,000 | | | | 6,000 | |
| SALES | | 307,000 | | | | 307,000 | | 307,000 | | |
| SALES DISCOUNTS | 5,000 | | | | 5,000 | | 5,000 | | | |
| SALES RETURNS & ALLOWANCES | 2,000 | | | | 2,000 | | 2,000 | | | |
| PURCHASES | 148,000 | | | | 148,000 | | 148,000 | | | |
| FREIGHT-IN | 5,000 | | | | 5,000 | | 5,000 | | | |
| PURCHASES DISCOUNTS | | 3,000 | | | | 3,000 | | 3,000 | | |
| PURCHASES RETURNS & ALLOWANCES | | 4,000 | | | | 4,000 | | 4,000 | | |
| Rent expense | 15,000 | | | | 15,000 | | 15,000 | | | |
| Salaries expense | 59,500 | | (e) 1,500 | | 61,000 | | 61,000 | | | |
| Utilities expense | 11,000 | | | | 11,000 | | 11,000 | | | |
| FREIGHT-OUT | 7,000 | | | | 7,000 | | 7,000 | | | |
| Advertising expense | 13,000 | | | | 13,000 | | 13,000 | | | |
| | 522,400 | 522,400 | | | | | | | | |
| Income summary | | | (a) 67,000 | (b) 48,000 | 67,000 | 48,000 | 67,000 | 48,000 | | |
| Depreciation expense | | | (c) 10,000 | | 10,000 | | 10,000 | | | |
| Insurance expense | | | (d) 9,000 | | 9,000 | | 9,000 | | | |
| Salaries payable | | | | (e) 1,500 | | 1,500 | | | | 1,500 |
| | | | 135,500 | 135,500 | 581,900 | 581,900 | 353,000 | 362,000 | 228,900 | 219,900 |
| Net income | | | | | | | 9,000 | | | 9,000 |
| | | | | | | | 362,000 | 362,000 | 228,900 | 228,900 |

Adjustments (a) and (b), on the other hand, are new and unique to the merchandising entity. As noted, the Inventory account must be updated to reflect the goods owned on December 31—$48,000 in Peachtree's case. In addition, because both the beginning and ending inventories are found in the cost-of-goods-sold computation on the income statement, these amounts have a direct bearing on gross profit and earnings. Recall from Chapter 4 that when end-of-period procedures are performed, the Income Summary account will eventually contain a company's net income (or net loss). Thus, in order to achieve the desired results, the two adjustments that follow are needed.

| | | | |
|---|---|---|---|
| Dec. 31 | Income Summary | 67,000 | |
| | Inventory | | 67,000 |
| | To remove beginning inventory balance | | |
| 31 | Inventory | 48,000 | |
| | Income Summary | | 48,000 |
| | To record ending inventory balance | | |

After posting, the Inventory and Income Summary accounts would appear as shown.

| *Inventory* | | | |
|---|---|---|---|
| 1/1/XX | 67,000 | 12/31/XX | 67,000 |
| 12/31/XX | 48,000 | | |

| *Income Summary* | | | |
|---|---|---|---|
| 12/31/XX | 67,000 | 12/31/XX | 48,000 |

Let us complete our discussion of the merchandising company's work sheet by viewing the Inventory and Income Summary lines.

Adjustment data continue to be combined with the trial balance figures to produce the adjusted trial balance. With Inventory, the $67,000 debit in the trial balance is merged with adjustments (b) and (a), a $48,000 debit and a $67,000 credit, to yield a $48,000 debit balance. This amount is extended to Peachtree's balance sheet, as the figure represents the company's ending inventory. Turning to the Income Summary line, notice that both adjusting entry amounts are entered in the adjusted trial balance columns and then extended to the income statement section. These latter procedures are necessary because the figures represent the beginning and ending inventory balances, which, as explained earlier, are both needed in cost-of-goods-sold calculations.

## Closing Entries

Once the adjusting entries are journalized and posted, the accounting records may be closed. Similar to a service business, the merchandising firm closes all temporary accounts (i.e., those listed in the work sheet's income statement columns, and also the drawing account). The income statement accounts with debit balances are closed in a combined journal entry by crediting each account and debiting Income Summary. New accounts introduced in this chapter that have debit balances are Sales Discounts, Sales Returns & Allowances, Purchases, Freight-in, and Freight-out. Next, income statement accounts that contain credit balances are debited, with a corresponding credit to Income Summary. New accounts that fall in this category include Sales, Purchases Discounts, and Purchases Returns & Allowances. These journal entries and the Income Summary T-account (after posting) follow.

| | | | |
|---|---|---|---|
| Dec. 31 | Income Summary | 286,000 | |
| | Sales Discounts | | 5,000 |
| | Sales Returns & Allowances | | 2,000 |
| | Purchases | | 148,000 |
| | Freight-in | | 5,000 |
| | Rent Expense | | 15,000 |
| | Salaries Expense | | 61,000 |
| | Utilities Expense | | 11,000 |
| | Freight-out | | 7,000 |
| | Advertising Expense | | 13,000 |
| | Depreciation Expense | | 10,000 |
| | Insurance Expense | | 9,000 |
| | To close income statement accounts having debit balances | | |
| 31 | Sales | 307,000 | |
| | Purchases Discounts | 3,000 | |
| | Purchases Returns & Allowances | 4,000 | |
| | Income Summary | | 314,000 |
| | To close income statement accounts having credit balances | | |

**Income Summary**

| | | | |
|---|---|---|---|
| 12/31/XX | 67,000 | 12/31/XX | 48,000 |
| 12/31/XX | 286,000 | 12/31/XX | 314,000 |
| | **353,000** | **(9,000)** | **362,000** |

Observe that the Income Summary account now contains Peachtree's $9,000 net income (from Exhibit 5-5). To complete the closing process, the Income Summary and drawing accounts are both closed to Valerie Bain, Capital, in the following manner:

| | | | |
|---|---|---|---|
| Dec. 31 | Income Summary | 9,000 | |
| | Valerie Bain, Capital | | 9,000 |
| | To close Income Summary | | |
| 31 | Valerie Bain, Capital | 6,000 | |
| | Valerie Bain, Drawing | | 6,000 |
| | To close drawing account | | |

## Chapter Review

### Learning Objectives—The Key Points

**1 Understand the importance of inventories to business enterprises.** Inventories affect many different areas of business operations including marketing, finance, and accounting. To avoid stockouts and provide reliable customer service, marketing personnel generally desire to carry high levels of goods. Because of the money tied up in inventory and the associated carrying costs, the finance department usually takes an opposing point of view and prefers low inventory levels. Finally, the accountant has a keen interest in inventory because sales and related inventory financing costs affect a company's net income.

**2 Be able to account for typical transactions of sellers and buyers of merchandise.** The chapter presents a variety of merchandising transactions, many of which are summarized in the following chart:

| Type of Transaction | Journal Entry: Debit | Journal Entry: Credit |
|---|---|---|
| Sale of merchandise on account | Accounts Receivable | Sales |
| Return on account of previously-sold goods | Sales Returns & Allowances | Accounts Receivable |
| Receipt on account, minus cash discount | Cash, Sales Discounts | Accounts Receivable |
| Purchase of merchandise on account | Purchases | Accounts Payable |
| Return on account of previously-acquired goods | Accounts Payable | Purchases Returns & Allowances |
| Payment on account, minus cash discount (gross method) | Accounts Payable | Cash, Purchases Discounts |
| Purchase of merchandise on account, F.O.B. shipping point, freight prepaid | Purchases, Freight-in | Accounts Payable |

Be sure to remember that the Purchases and Sales accounts are used solely for merchandise transactions and not for acquisitions or disposals of other assets.

**3 Understand the difference between the gross and net methods of accounting for purchases.** Under the gross method, the Purchases and Accounts Payable accounts are established at the gross invoice price of merchandise acquired. Any discounts taken are credited to Purchases Discounts. With the net method, transactions are recorded at the invoice price minus any discounts that could be taken. If a discount is missed, it is charged to the Purchases Discounts Lost account.

**4 Be able to compute cost of goods sold and gross profit and prepare the financial statements and work sheet for a merchandising concern.** Cost of goods sold is calculated as follows: beginning inventory + net purchases − ending inventory. The net purchases figure is derived by adding freight-in to gross purchases and then subtracting any purchases discounts and purchases returns and allowances that occurred during the period. Gross profit, or profit from the sale of merchandise, is computed as net sales minus cost of goods sold.

The preceding items all appear on the income statement, with the ending inventory also being disclosed in the current asset section of the balance sheet. The work sheet that underlies these statements is constructed in the normal fashion, with the only new procedure involving the beginning and ending inventory figures. The procedure depends on whether a company uses the closing entry method of handling inventories or the adjusting entry method (appendix).

**5 Be able to prepare the adjusting and closing entries for a merchandising enterprise.** The adjusting and closing processes update selected accounts and reduce the balance in temporary accounts to zero. With regard to inventory, the Inventory account is updated through the closing process under the closing entry method to reflect the ending balance of goods owned by the firm. This same procedure is performed with adjusting entries under the adjusting entry method. The Inventory and Income Summary accounts are used with both approaches.

**6 Understand the differences between single- and multiple-step income statements.** The single-step income statement normally discloses all revenues in one section and all expenses (except income taxes) in another. This arrangement is said to be very easy to understand. In contrast, the multiple-step statement contains various classifications such as operating expenses and other revenues and expenses, as well as significant subtotals (e.g., gross profit). The multiple-step's format is often more informative because of added captions and disclosures.

## Chapter Quiz

The five questions that follow relate to several issues raised in the chapter. Test your knowledge of the issues by selecting the best answer. (The answers appear on p. 194.)

**1** Which of the following statements is incorrect?
- a Sales Discounts is commonly known as a contra revenue account.
- b Net sales minus cost of goods sold equals gross profit.
- c The balance in an Inventory account that is maintained under a periodic inventory system remains constant throughout the year.
- d A trade discount is a specialized type of cash discount.

**2** Which of the following accounts would not be used if a company employed the net method of recording purchases?
- a Purchases
- b Purchases Discounts
- c Purchases Discounts Lost
- d Purchases Returns

**3** Harris Company reported the following information for the period just ended: Net sales, $5,000; net purchases, $2,900; beginning inventory, $1,700; and ending inventory, $2,000. The company's cost of goods sold is:
- a $1,800.
- b $2,400.
- c $2,600.
- d $3,200.

**4** Hospital Supply purchased $8,000 of merchandise on July 9 from Rosen Manufacturing, F.O.B. shipping point, terms 2/10, n/30. Freight charges of $200 were paid by Rosen and appear on the invoice. If Hospital Supply settled the transaction on July 17, the company would pay:
- a $7,840.
- b $8,036.
- c $8,040.
- d $8,200.

**5** Which of the following accounts would most likely appear in the operating expense section of a multiple-step income statement?
- a Freight-out.
- b Freight-in.
- c Sales Discounts.
- d Interest Expense.

## Summary Problem

The Breakfast Bar reported the following information for the period just ended:

| | |
|---|---|
| Freight-in | $ 8,800 |
| Purchases | 349,000 |
| Purchases discounts | 6,600 |
| Purchases returns & allowances | 3,800 |
| Sales | 573,600 |
| Sales discounts | 4,000 |
| Sales returns & allowances | 11,400 |

An examination of the firm's Inventory account, which is maintained under a periodic system, revealed a beginning balance on January 1 of $77,200. A hand count revealed that $95,800 of inventory was owned by the company on December 31.

**Instructions**

**a** Compute the company's (1) net sales, (2) cost of goods sold, and (3) gross profit.

**b** Determine the normal balance (debit or credit) of the following accounts: Sales, Purchases Discounts, Freight-in, and Sales Returns & Allowances.

**c** When The Breakfast Bar makes a charge to the Freight-in account, would the transaction being recorded involve a purchase with terms of F.O.B. shipping point or F.O.B. destination? Why?

**Solution**

| | | | | |
|---|---|---|---|---|
| **a** (1) | Sales | | | $573,600 |
| | Less: Sales discounts | | $ 4,000 | |
| | Sales returns & allowances | | 11,400 | 15,400 |
| | Net sales | | | $558,200 |
| (2) | Beginning inventory, Jan. 1 | | | $ 77,200 |
| | Add: Purchases | | $349,000 | |
| | Freight-in | | 8,800 | |
| | | | $357,800 | |
| | Less: Purchases discounts | $6,600 | | |
| | Purchases returns & allowances | 3,800 | 10,400 | |
| | Net purchases | | | 347,400 |
| | Goods available for sale | | | $424,600 |
| | Less: Ending inventory, Dec. 31 | | | 95,800 |
| | Cost of goods sold | | | $328,800 |
| (3) | Net sales | | | $558,200 |
| | Cost of goods sold | | | 328,800 |
| | Gross profit | | | $229,400 |

**b** Credit, credit, debit, debit

**c** F.O.B. shipping point. The Freight-in account is used for transportation charges incurred by the buyer of merchandise, which occurs under terms of F.O.B. shipping point. With F.O.B. destination the seller incurs the charges, requiring a debit to Freight-out on the seller's accounting records.

## Questions

**Q5-1** The vice-presidents of marketing and finance of the Rucker Company are having a debate regarding the proper levels of inventory to carry. Explain the probable position of each vice-president and why she favors that position.

**Q5-2** Explain the function and use of a credit memorandum.

**Q5-3** Rather than publish catalogs that contain invoice prices, many companies follow the practice of printing list prices and then granting a trade discount to purchasers. What advantages are associated with this procedure?

**Q5-4** Distinguish between a trade discount and a cash discount.

**Q5-5** Explain why a purchaser should normally take advantage of cash discounts even if it means obtaining a bank loan to do so.

**Q5-6** Contrast the gross and net methods of recording purchases. What is an important advantage associated with the latter approach?

**Q5-7** The Gomez Company sells an item that has a list price of $1,000. Management is contemplating whether to ship the item F.O.B. shipping point or F.O.B. destination. Compare the trade discounts that would probably be quoted under the two alternatives. Which trade discount would probably be smaller? Why?

**Q5-8** A student once commented: "The Freight-in account is very similar to the Purchases Returns account. Both appear in the cost-of-goods-sold section of the income statement as a reduction to determine net purchases." Evaluate the student's comment.

**Q5-9** What is the basic difference between a periodic and a perpetual inventory system?

**Q5-10** Explain the difference between gross profit and net income.

**Q5-11** The Ames Company sells its products at approximately 35% above cost; yet, at the end of the current year, a net loss of $15,000 was incurred. Explain how this situation is possible.

**Q5-12** Systems, Inc., recently disclosed interest charges in the operating expense section of its income statement. Do you agree or disagree with the company's reporting treatment? Why?

**Q5-13** Where are gains and losses normally reported on a multiple-step income statement?

## Exercises

**E5-1** ***Trade and sales discounts***

Master Built Auto Parts had the following credit sales during June:

| *Date of Sale* | *List Price* | *Applicable Trade Discount* | *Credit Terms* | *Date Paid* |
|---|---|---|---|---|
| June 6 | $1,500 | 20% | 2/10, n/30 | June 11 |
| 8 | 2,500 | — | 3/10, n/eom | 26 |
| 11 | 800 | — | 2/10, n/30 | 19 |
| 12 | 1,300 | 25% | 1/10, n/20 | 24 |

For each of the four transactions, compute the proper credit to Master Built's Sales account. Also determine the amount of cash received in full settlement of each sales invoice.

**E5-2** ***Gross and net methods of accounting for purchases***

Fashion Corner purchased $2,700 of merchandise on account on May 10, terms 2/10, n/30.

a Assuming that Fashion Corner uses the gross method of accounting for purchases, present entries to record the following:
   (1) The purchase on May 10.
   (2) Payment of the invoice if payment was made on May 19.
   (3) Payment of the invoice if payment was made on May 31.

b Repeat instruction (a), assuming that Fashion Corner uses the net method of accounting for purchases.

**E5-3** ***Gross and net methods of accounting for purchases: An analysis***

The Software Shoppe purchased $265,000 of merchandise during the year subject to terms of 2/10, n/30. Returns to suppliers amounted to $12,000; all returns took place prior to any payments on account. An analysis of the company's records revealed a balance in the Purchases Discounts account of $1,050 at year-end. The Software Shoppe uses the gross method of accounting for purchases.

a Determine the balance in the Purchases Discounts Lost account had The Software Shoppe used the net method of accounting for purchases rather than the gross method.

b What are some possible causes of lost discounts?

c Given the company's situation, would use of the net method have been more beneficial? Briefly explain.

**E5-4** ***Purchases discount computations; freight terms***

Lombardi made the following purchases of merchandise during the current accounting period:

| | *Original Amount of Purchase* | *Purchases Returns* | *Shipping Terms* | *Freight Charges* |
|---|---|---|---|---|
| a | $1,000 | $150 | F.O.B. destination | $100 |
| b | 600 | — | F.O.B. shipping point | 90 |
| c | 750 | — | F.O.B. destination | 60 |
| d | 1,200 | 300 | F.O.B. shipping point | 150 |

All purchases returns were made immediately upon receipt of the goods; freight charges were initially paid by the sellers and, when appropriate, were billed to Lombardi.

The preceding transactions were settled within 10 days to take advantage of a 2% discount. Determine the amount of cash Lombardi paid to the seller in full settlement of each of the merchandise acquisitions.

**E5-5** ***Journal entries for buyer and seller of merchandise***

On October 4, Matlock Company purchased $18,000 of merchandise from Nevada Wholesale, terms 3/10, n/30. The goods were shipped F.O.B. destination, with Nevada paying the freight company $95. Because of a shipping error, Matlock returned $700 of the merchandise on October 9. Finally, on October 13, Matlock paid the proper amount due to Nevada.

a Record all necessary journal entries on Matlock's books, assuming that Matlock uses the gross method of accounting for purchases.

b Record all necessary journal entries on Nevada's books.

**E5-6** ***Merchandising concepts***

Evaluate the comments that follow as being True or False. If the comment is false, briefly explain why.

a Soft Rock Cafe acquired $42,000 of restaurant equipment on account for use in the business. The company should debit Purchases and credit Accounts Payable to correctly record the transaction.

b The balance in the Freight-out account should be added to the balance in Purchases to arrive at the net delivered cost of merchandise acquired.

c Cash discounts should be computed on merchandise cost only, excluding any applicable freight charges incurred on the transaction.

d The balance in an Inventory account that is maintained under a periodic system tends to fluctuate during an accounting period from an entity's purchase and sale transactions.

e Cash discounts and trade discounts are a convenient means to reduce a catalog price to invoice price.

**E5-7** ***Basic merchandising computations***

A review of the records of Gamma Distributing revealed the following information:

| | | | |
|---|---|---|---|
| Purchases | $232,200 | Freight-in | $ 3,800 |
| Rent expense | 11,300 | Sales | 461,300 |
| Salaries expense | 24,000 | Inventory, Jan. 1 | 19,400 |
| Freight-out | 4,300 | Inventory, Dec. 31 | 26,900 |
| Utilities expense | 8,400 | Sales returns | 1,100 |

Compute cost of goods sold, gross profit, and net income for Gamma Distributing.

**E5-8** ***Merchandising computations: Working backward***

The following information was obtained from the records of Companies A, B, and C:

| | *A* | *B* | *C* |
|---|---|---|---|
| Sales | $90,300 | $51,200 | $ (g) |
| Sales discounts | (a) | 3,700 | 2,000 |
| Net sales | 88,400 | (d) | 60,700 |
| Beginning inventory | 70,000 | 39,500 | (h) |
| Net purchases | 99,800 | (e) | 15,600 |
| Ending inventory | (b) | 30,000 | 10,000 |
| Cost of goods sold | 62,000 | 33,200 | (i) |
| Gross profit | 26,400 | (f) | 36,800 |
| Total expenses | (c) | 11,200 | 41,800 |
| Net income (loss) | 9,100 | 3,100 | (j) |

Compute the amounts that are indicated by the letters (a)–(j).

**E5-9** ***Updating the Inventory account; closing entries (closing entry method)***

The following selected balances were extracted from the accounting records of Design Fantastic:

| | | |
|---|---|---|
| Karen Jackson, capital | | $87,500 |
| Karen Jackson, drawing | $18,000 | |
| Sales | | 99,300 |
| Sales discounts | 2,100 | |
| Purchases | 55,400 | |
| Purchases returns | | 3,000 |
| Wage expense | 22,900 | |
| Marketing expense | 5,600 | |
| Rent expense | 12,000 | |
| Utilities expense | 3,700 | |

The company's Inventory account contains a balance of $21,800, reflecting the cost of the beginning inventory. Goods costing $27,400 remain on hand at the end of the period, December 31, 19XX.

Using the closing entry method, prepare the journal entries that are needed to update the Inventory account and close the accounting records for the period just ended.

**E5-10** ***Income statement computations***

Selected account balances from Marshall Company for the current year include the following:

| | | | |
|---|---|---|---|
| Sales | $372,000 | Sales discounts | $ 1,000 |
| Purchases | 206,000 | Beginning inventory | 98,700 |
| Advertising expense | 11,500 | Salesmen's salaries | 12,600 |
| Administrative salaries | 26,300 | Insurance expense | 4,000 |
| Ending inventory | 94,400 | Depreciation expense | 15,000 |
| Sales returns | 2,800 | | |

Forty percent of the insurance and depreciation expense relates to Marshall's sales activities. Calculate the following:

a Net revenues
b Cost of goods sold
c Gross profit
d Total selling expenses
e Total general and administrative expenses
f Net income (loss)

***E5-11** ***Updating the Inventory account; closing entries (adjusting entry method)***
Refer to Exercise 5-9. Replace the last paragraph with the following and solve the exercise:

> Using the adjusting entry method, prepare adjustments to update the Inventory account. Then, close the accounting records for the period just ended.

## Problems

### Series A

**P5-A1** ***Merchandising journal entries***
The Patrick Company had the following transactions during April:

Apr. 1 Sold $4,000 of merchandise on account to Campbell Company, terms 2/10, n/30.
3 Purchased $2,500 of merchandise on account from West Enterprises, terms 3/10, n/30. The merchandise was shipped F.O.B. shipping point; freight charges amounted to $80 and were paid by West.
7 Issued a credit memorandum for $200 to the Campbell Company for defective merchandise sold on April 1.
8 Received the proper amount due from Campbell Company.
10 Purchased a computer on account for business use from Bell Resources for $11,400, terms n/eom.
12 Paid the proper amount due to West Enterprises.
18 Received a purchase order from Gibbons Distributing for merchandise having a list price of $6,000. The order was subject to a 40% trade discount and terms of 1/10, n/30. Patrick shipped the merchandise F.O.B. destination and paid $40 of freight charges.
29 Received the proper amount due from Gibbons Distributing.
30 Paid the amount due to Bell Resources.

**Instructions**

Prepare journal entries for the April transactions, assuming Patrick uses the gross method of accounting for purchases. All terms of sale are strictly followed.

**P5-A2** ***Gross versus net purchases methods***
Interstate Photo sells cameras and video equipment in Georgia. The company had the following purchases transactions in March:

Mar. 3 Purchased $2,400 of merchandise on account from Photography Wholesale, terms 1/10, n/30.

* An asterisk preceding an item indicates that the material is covered in the appendix to this chapter.

8 Purchased $4,500 of goods on account from Import Video, terms 2/10, n/30. The goods were shipped F.O.B. shipping point; freight charges of $175 were prepaid by Import and appear on the invoice.
11 Paid the proper amount due to Photography Wholesale.
13 Returned $250 of the merchandise purchased on March 8 because of a shipping error made by Import Video.
22 Paid the proper amount due to Import Video.
28 Purchased $380 of office supplies on account from Main Street Office Supply.

**Instructions**

a Record the preceding transactions, assuming that Interstate Photo uses the gross method of accounting for purchases. All terms of sale are strictly followed.
b Record the preceding transactions, assuming that Interstate Photo uses the net method of accounting for purchases. All terms of sale are strictly followed.

**P5-A3** ***Work sheet, adjusting entries, closing entries (closing entry method)***
Vicki Glazer was in the process of completing the work sheet of Runner's Supply for the year ended December 31, 19X4, when she was suddenly called out of town. Her work follows.

| | *Trial Balance* | | *Adjustments* | |
|---|---|---|---|---|
| *Account Title* | *Debit* | *Credit* | *Debit* | *Credit* |
| Cash | 18,200 | | | |
| Accounts receivable | 25,900 | | | |
| Inventory | 63,100 | | | |
| Prepaid insurance | 4,200 | | | (a) 1,400 |
| Equipment | 20,900 | | | |
| Accumulated depreciation: equipment | | 7,600 | | |
| Accounts payable | | 23,500 | | |
| Loan payable | | 30,000 | | |
| Robert Edwards, capital | | 67,700 | | |
| Robert Edwards, drawing | 18,000 | | | |
| Sales | | 169,800 | | |
| Sales returns & allowances | 900 | | | |
| Purchases | 87,300 | | | |
| Freight-in | 2,000 | | | |
| Purchases discounts | | 1,500 | | |
| Advertising expense | 5,000 | | | |
| Wage expense | 44,400 | | (b) 1,000 | |
| Rent expense | 9,600 | | | |
| Interest expense | 600 | | | |
| | 300,100 | 300,100 | | |
| Insurance expense | | | (a) 1,400 | |
| Wages payable | | | | (b) 1,000 |

A piece of paper labeled "Work Sheet Data" was found on Vicki's desk and contained the following:

1 Insurance applicable to future periods, $2,800.
2 Wages incurred but not yet paid, $1,000.

3 Depreciation on the equipment, $2,000.
4 Loan interest incurred but not yet paid, $300.
5 Unbilled customer sales, $700.
6 Ending inventory, $59,800.

**Instructions**

a Complete the work sheet that Vicki had started. Runner's Supply uses the closing entry method for handling end-of-period inventory.
b On the basis of the work sheet that you have prepared, journalize the company's (1) year-end adjusting entries and (2) year-end closing entries.

**P5-A4** ***Work sheet, financial statements, and closing entries (closing entry method)*** Phoenix Appliance has the following trial balance as of December 31:

| | | |
|---|---|---|
| Cash | $ 37,200 | |
| Accounts receivable | 49,300 | |
| Merchandise inventory | 41,800 | |
| Prepaid rent | 6,400 | |
| Store supplies | 3,950 | |
| Equipment | 38,500 | |
| Accumulated depreciation: equipment | | $ 11,100 |
| Accounts payable | | 16,820 |
| Mark McGarry, capital | | 119,850 |
| Mark McGarry, drawing | 7,500 | |
| Sales | | 227,880 |
| Sales returns | 1,570 | |
| Sales discounts | 4,360 | |
| Purchases | 91,720 | |
| Freight-in | 1,970 | |
| Purchases returns | | 970 |
| Purchases discounts | | 1,750 |
| Salaries expense | 51,800 | |
| Marketing expense | 11,820 | |
| Insurance expense | 10,800 | |
| Utilities expense | 3,180 | |
| Delivery expense | 16,500 | |
| | $378,370 | $378,370 |

Additional accounts maintained by the business include Salaries Payable, Income Summary, Rent Expense, Store Supplies Expense, and Depreciation Expense. Phoenix's accountant has derived the following data:
1 Rental prepayments expiring during the current period: $4,000.
2 Store supplies used during the period: $1,800.
3 Depreciation on the equipment: $3,700.
4 Accrued salaries: $1,900.
5 Ending inventory: $31,500.

McGarry's capital account includes $15,000 of owner investments made during the year.

**Instructions**

a Complete a work sheet in good form for Phoenix Appliance for the year ended December 31. The company uses the closing entry method of accounting for inventory.
b Prepare a multiple-step income statement, statement of owner's equity, and a classified balance sheet in good form. The firm's selling activities account for

70% of the salaries cost and 40% of the insurance, utilities, rent, and depreciation expense.

c Record Phoenix's adjusting entries in the journal.

d Record Phoenix's closing entries in the journal.

**P5-A5** ***Income statement classification***

Welder's Supply Company sells its own inventory to area factories in addition to selling products for other companies on a commission basis. Presented below are the categories used on a multiple-step income statement.

1 Revenue
2 Cost of goods sold
3 Selling expenses
4 General & administrative expenses
5 Other revenue (expense)
6 Income taxes

The following accounts were taken from the firm's general ledger:

a Depreciation expense: office
b Freight-in
c Purchases discounts
d Depreciation expense: delivery equipment
e Sales returns
f Sales commissions (paid by Welder's Supply)
g Office supplies expense
h Inventory (ending)
i Interest expense
j Customer entertainment expense
k Sales
l Purchases
m Payroll taxes payable
n Loss from spring flood
o Freight-out
p Warren Robb, capital
q Interest revenue
r Advertising expense
s Miscellaneous expense (relates to management of the business)

**Instructions**

Classify the accounts of Welder's Supply as to their proper placement on the income statement. If any of the accounts do not appear on the income statement, determine whether they appear on the balance sheet or the statement of owner's equity.

**P5-A6** ***Income statement preparation***

Presented below is financial information of the Juarez Corporation for 19XX.

| | |
|---|---:|
| Sales | $587,400 |
| Freight-in | 10,800 |
| Loan interest expense | 5,950 |
| Interest revenue | 3,800 |
| Sales returns | 4,200 |
| Purchases returns | 7,310 |
| Gain on sale of land | 18,900 |
| Merchandise inventory (ending) | 54,700 |
| Merchandise inventory (beginning) | 58,200 |
| Loss on sale of building | 24,300 |
| Purchases | 226,900 |
| Sales discounts | 9,400 |
| Administrative expenses | |
| Executive salaries | 61,800 |
| Depreciation expense: buildings | 23,600 |
| Insurance expense | 6,300 |
| Miscellaneous expense | 3,100 |
| Selling expenses | |
| Delivery expense | 17,900 |
| Sales commissions | 31,500 |

| | |
|---|---|
| Selling expenses (cont.) | |
| Advertising expense | 7,250 |
| Depreciation expense: delivery equipment | 10,400 |
| Insurance expense | 3,090 |

The corporation is subject to a 40% income tax rate.

**Instructions**

a Prepare a multiple-step income statement for the year ended November 30, 19XX.

b Explain what you would have done differently if instruction (a) had called for the preparation of a single-step income statement. What benefits are available to financial statement users from the multiple-step approach?

***P5-A7** ***Work sheet, adjusting entries, closing entries (adjusting entry method)***
Refer to Problem 5-A3.

**Instructions**

Complete the requirements as stated on page 187. Assume, however, that Runner's Supply uses the adjusting entry method for handling end-of-period inventory rather than the closing entry method.

***P5-A8** ***Work sheet, financial statements, and closing entries (adjusting entry method)***
Refer to Problem 5-A4.

**Instructions**

Complete the requirements as stated on pages 187 and 188. Assume, however, that Phoenix Appliance uses the adjusting entry method of accounting for inventory rather than the closing entry method.

## Series B

**P5-B1** ***Merchandising journal entries***
The Nolan Company had the following transactions during March:

Mar. 2 Purchased $9,200 of merchandise on account from Thomas Company, terms 1/10, n/eom. The merchandise was shipped F.O.B. shipping point; freight charges amounted to $120 and were paid by Thomas.

4 Sold $4,100 of merchandise on account to Moritz Company, terms 2/10, n/30.

9 Purchased office furniture on account for business use from Victory Office Equipment for $5,800, terms n/eom.

10 Issued a credit memorandum for $500 to Moritz Company for merchandise shipped in error on March 4.

11 Paid the proper amount due to Thomas Company.

13 Received the proper amount due from Moritz Company.

19 Received a purchase order from USA Imports for merchandise having a list price of $7,700. The order was subject to a 20% trade discount and terms of 2/10, n/30. Nolan shipped the merchandise F.O.B. destination and paid $110 of freight charges.

30 Received the proper amount due from USA Imports.

31 Paid the amount due to Victory Office Equipment.

**Instructions**

Prepare journal entries for the March transactions, assuming Nolan uses the gross method of accounting for purchases. All terms of sale are strictly followed.

**P5-B2** ***Gross versus net purchases methods***

Beautiful Face operates several small cosmetics stores in shopping malls. During July, store no. 108 had the following purchases transactions:

July 7 Purchased $950 of cosmetics on account from Lovely Lady, terms 2/10, n/30. The goods were shipped F.O.B. shipping point; freight charges of $25 were prepaid by Lovely Lady and appear on the invoice.

12 Purchased $125 of store supplies on account from Atlas Office Supplies.

17 Purchased $1,400 of cosmetics on account from the Charles Norman Company, terms 1/10, n/30.

20 Paid the proper amount due to Lovely Lady.

21 Returned $200 of the cosmetics purchased on July 17 because of a shipping error made by the Charles Norman Company.

26 Paid the proper amount due to the Charles Norman Company.

**Instructions**

a Record the preceding transactions, assuming Beautiful Face uses the gross method of accounting for purchases. All terms of sale are strictly followed.

b Record the preceding transactions, assuming Beautiful Face uses the net method of accounting for purchases. All terms of sale are strictly followed.

**P5-B3** ***Work sheet, adjusting entries, closing entries (closing entry method)***

Steve Harper was in the process of completing the work sheet of Party Supply for the year ended January 31, 19X2, when he was suddenly called out of town. His work follows.

| | *Trial Balance* | | *Adjustments* | |
|---|---|---|---|---|
| *Account Title* | *Debit* | *Credit* | *Debit* | *Credit* |
| Cash | 12,500 | | | |
| Accounts receivable | 25,900 | | | |
| Inventory | 47,400 | | | |
| Prepaid advertising | 2,000 | | | (a) 1,300 |
| Equipment | 15,500 | | | |
| Accumulated depreciation: equipment | | 4,700 | | |
| Accounts payable | | 20,900 | | |
| Loan payable | | 20,000 | | |
| Debbie Hunt, capital | | 46,200 | | |
| Debbie Hunt, drawing | 12,000 | | | |
| Sales | | 140,300 | | |
| Sales discounts | 2,100 | | | |
| Purchases | 66,800 | | | |
| Freight-in | 900 | | | |
| Purchases returns | | 1,200 | | |
| Insurance expense | 3,100 | | | |
| Salary & wage expense | 37,500 | | | |
| Rent expense | 7,200 | | | |
| Interest expense | 400 | | (b) 100 | |
| | 233,300 | 233,300 | | |
| Advertising expense | | | (a) 1,300 | |
| Interest payable | | | | (b) 100 |

A piece of paper labeled "Work Sheet Data" was found on Steve's desk and contained the following:

1 Advertising applicable to future periods, $700.
2 Interest incurred but not yet paid, $100.
3 Unbilled customer sales, $1,900.
4 Salaries and wages incurred but not yet paid, $1,400.
5 Depreciation on the equipment, $1,500.
6 Ending inventory, $36,000.

**Instructions**

a Complete the work sheet that Steve had started. Party Supply uses the closing entry method for handling end-of-period inventory.

b On the basis of the work sheet that you have prepared, journalize the company's (1) year-end adjusting entries and (2) year-end closing entries.

**P5-B4** ***Work sheet, financial statements, and closing entries (closing entry method)***
The Wheaton Company has the following trial balance as of December 31:

| | | |
|---|---|---|
| Cash | $ 24,900 | |
| Accounts receivable | 36,800 | |
| Merchandise inventory | 38,000 | |
| Prepaid advertising | 6,400 | |
| Supplies | 3,700 | |
| Equipment | 72,000 | |
| Accumulated depreciation: equipment | | $ 13,400 |
| Accounts payable | | 30,600 |
| Jerry Wheaton, capital | | 140,200 |
| Jerry Wheaton, drawing | 16,600 | |
| Sales | | 285,900 |
| Sales returns & allowances | 5,700 | |
| Sales discounts | 2,000 | |
| Purchases | 175,100 | |
| Freight-in | 4,400 | |
| Purchases returns & allowances | | 1,800 |
| Purchases discounts | | 4,300 |
| Wage expense | 58,500 | |
| Insurance expense | 2,600 | |
| Rent expense | 16,500 | |
| Freight-out | 4,300 | |
| Utilities expense | 8,700 | |
| | $476,200 | $476,200 |

Additional accounts maintained by the business include Wages Payable, Income Summary, Advertising Expense, Supplies Expense, and Depreciation Expense. Wheaton's accountant has derived the following data:

1 Advertising applicable to future periods: $3,600.
2 Supplies on hand: $1,600.
3 Depreciation on the equipment: $4,800.
4 Accrued wages: $3,100.
5 Ending inventory: $51,600.

Wheaton's capital account includes $4,000 of owner investments made during the year.

**Instructions**

a Complete a work sheet in good form for the Wheaton Company for the year ended December 31. The company uses the closing-entry method of accounting for inventory.

b Prepare a multiple-step income statement, statement of owner's equity, and a classified balance sheet in good form. The firm's selling activities account for 60% of the wage cost and 40% of insurance, rent, utilities, supplies, and depreciation expense.
c Record Wheaton's adjusting entries in the journal.
d Record Wheaton's closing entries in the journal.

**P5-B5** ***Income statement classification***
Home Entertainment distributes and sells video tapes to local retailers. The categories below were extracted from the company's multiple-step income statement.

1 Revenue
2 Cost of goods sold
3 Selling expenses
4 General & administrative expenses
5 Other revenue (expense)
6 Income taxes

The following accounts appear in the general ledger:

a Marketing expense
b Sales discounts
c Warehouse equipment
d Accounting fees
e Delivery expense
f Rental revenue (from a business that leases extra space in the parking lot)
g Office manager's salary
h Purchases returns
i Inventory (beginning)
j Loss from traffic accident
k Interest expense
l Prepaid advertising
m Travel expense (to visit local retailers)
n Transportation-in
o Ray Franklin, drawing
p Interest earned on short-term investments
q Sales
r Purchases
s Commissions paid

**Instructions**
Classify Home Entertainment's accounts as to their proper placement on the income statement. If any of the accounts do not appear on the income statement, determine whether they appear on the balance sheet or the statement of owner's equity.

**P5-B6** ***Income statement preparation***
Presented below is financial information for the Golf Equipment Corporation for the year ended December 31, 19XX.

| | |
|---|---|
| General & administrative expenses | |
| Executive salaries | $ 95,000 |
| Depreciation expense: building | 42,600 |
| Insurance expense | 3,900 |
| Merchandise inventory (beginning) | 61,800 |
| Interest revenue | 11,000 |
| Interest expense | 7,400 |
| Sales returns & allowances | 2,100 |
| Selling expenses | |
| Advertising | 16,800 |
| Sales salaries | 59,700 |
| Depreciation expense: building | 22,200 |
| Freight-out | 4,800 |
| Purchases | 350,700 |
| Loss on sale of warehouse equipment | 3,200 |
| Sales | 615,300 |
| Gain on sale of investments | 51,400 |
| Freight-in | 7,000 |

| | |
|---|---|
| Sales discounts | 18,500 |
| Purchases discounts | 21,300 |
| Purchases returns | 14,900 |
| Merchandise inventory (ending) | 56,000 |

The corporation is subject to a tax rate of 40%.

**Instructions**

a Prepare a multiple-step income statement for 19XX.

b Explain what you would have done differently if instruction (a) had called for the preparation of a single-step income statement. Would there be any benefit of employing the single-step approach from a financial statement user's viewpoint?

***P5-B7** ***Work sheet, adjusting entries, closing entries (adjusting entry method)***
Refer to Problem 5-B3.

**Instructions**

**Complete the requirements as stated on page 191. Assume, however, that Party Supply uses the adjusting entry method for handling end-of-period inventory rather than the closing entry method.**

***P5-B8** ***Work sheet, financial statements, and closing entries (adjusting entry method)***
Refer to Problem 5-B4.

**Instructions**

**Complete the requirements as stated on pages 191 and 192. Assume, however, that Wheaton Company uses the adjusting entry method of accounting for inventory rather than the closing entry method.**

## Beyond the Basics

**BB5-1** ***Journal entries and income computations***
Tubb's Tile Company (TTC) is a wholesale distributor of marble and tile. For the year just ended the firm reported gross sales of $630,000. Twenty percent of the sales were for cash; the remainder were on account. Credit sales were subject to terms of 1/10, n/30. Customers settled account balances that totaled $410,000 and took advantage of 40% of the discounts related to these balances. Sales returns amounted to $17,000, with TTC issuing cash refunds of $2,500. The returns all occurred before the discount period had expired.

Purchases on account during the past 12 months amounted to $316,600, including $4,400 of office equipment and $3,400 of warehouse supplies. When computing the total purchases figure, TTC office personnel included the actual list price of merchandise acquired from Ohio Marble Company. The list price was $10,000, subject to a 40% trade discount. Net payments to suppliers on account were $221,300; available cash discounts on the invoices paid amounted to $1,760. Unfortunately, $1,430 of these purchases discounts were lost because of a very tight cash position.

Freight charges incurred by TTC on incoming shipments of merchandise totaled $6,700. Charges amounting to $3,100 were originally prepaid by suppliers; the remainder, along with $2,700 of freight expense on outgoing shipments, was remitted directly to Move-On Trucking Lines.

The firm uses the gross method of accounting for purchases. A periodic inventory system is employed.

**Instructions**

a Prepare journal entries that reflect the preceding data.
b Compute (1) net sales, (2) cost of goods sold, and (3) gross profit. The beginning inventory on January 1 totaled $37,400; the ending inventory was $48,300.

**BB5-2** ***Analysis of merchandising data and activity***

As part of a class project for an accounting course, Paul Davis was asked to evaluate selected income and inventory data of two companies: LaStone and Q-Mart. LaStone operates a chain of jewelry stores in upscale shopping malls throughout the country. Q-Mart, on the other hand, has five discount department stores in California and Oregon. Selected data (in thousands of dollars) from the companies' financial statements follow.

| | *LaStone* | *Q-Mart* |
|---|---|---|
| Net sales | $3,000 | $6,400 |
| Net purchases | 1,400 | 3,800 |
| Beginning inventory | 400 | 900 |
| Ending inventory | 600 | 700 |

Both LaStone and Q-Mart employ a natural business year for reporting purposes, with the year-end occurring at the slowest point in the business cycle.

Davis recently completed a finance course where his instructor talked about gross profit and the ability of a firm to manage its inventories. The instructor noted that some companies sell goods more rapidly than others and are better able to generate cash and avoid inventory financing costs than their competitors.

**Instructions**

Assume the role of Paul Davis and answer the following:

a Which of the two firms would probably generate a higher gross profit for each dollar of merchandise sold? Briefly explain the rationale behind your answer.
b Determine whether your answer in part (a) was correct or incorrect by calculating gross profit for the two companies and then expressing gross profit as a percentage of net sales. Round computations to one decimal place.
c Picture the movement of goods through the average LaStone and Q-Mart stores. Which of the two entities would probably move merchandise more quickly? Why?
d Analyze the preceding data and computations. Explain how it is possible for companies that sell high profit items and those that sell low profit items to have roughly the same rate of bottom-line income (net income ÷ net sales) for a reporting period.
e Given these firms' business cycles, would the natural business year most likely end on November 30, December 31, or January 31? Briefly explain.

## Answers to Chapter Quiz

**1** d

**2** b

**3** c ($1,700 + $2,900 − $2,000)

**4** c ($8,000 − ($8,000 × 0.02) + $200)

**5** a

CHAPTER 6

# Information-Processing Systems and Internal Control

## Learning Objectives

After reading this chapter you should:

1 Understand the nature of internal control along with various internal control procedures.

2 Understand how special journals are used in an accounting system.

3 Be familiar with the relationship between control accounts and subsidiary ledgers.

4 Be familiar with the interaction between accounting and computers.

The creation and flow of information concerns many individuals engaged in day-to-day business operations. Large volumes of data must be processed into information that is usable by management and other readers of financial statements. From the material presented in the first five chapters of this text, you may think the generation of information is a relatively straightforward and simple operation. Unfortunately, many problems can arise. Managers frequently complain that (1) they lack the necessary information to properly perform their duties and (2) reports arrive too late to be useful. Furthermore, some employees are so overwhelmed with computer printouts that there is not enough time in a working day to study all the facts that flow across their desks.

The network that processes transactions and ultimately produces financial statements and other reports is known as an **accounting information system.** Such systems generate information from *data* (i.e., a variety of facts, figures, and/or transactions) for use in reporting, planning, controlling, and decision-making activities. In other words, data serve as the raw material for determining the period's income, the ending accounts receivable balance, the total cash inflows related to a proposed investment, and other key measures needed to evaluate an entity and its associated components (activities, products, and so forth).

Accounting information systems range from the simple to the sophisticated; many are computerized, others are not. No matter what the form, a properly designed system should contain an adequate degree of internal control.

## Internal Control

Perhaps the best way to introduce the concept of internal control is to cite a nearly 20-year-old report on the financial health of the Long Island Railroad, a railroad well known to those who live in and around New York City.[1] The report noted that the commuter line was losing revenue and operating in an unproductive manner largely because of a weak accounting system—so weak that the carrier was criticized as being less well managed than the average household. To become more specific:

- Cash balances had not been compared with bank statements for nearly a year, permitting an erroneous statement of cash position.
- Time sheets failed to reflect workers who arrived late and left early.
- Large amounts due the railroad hadn't been billed.
- Approximately 20,000 blank payroll checks were found in an unsecured vault; signed payroll checks were left lying on desks unprotected.
- A study of the number of tickets sold versus the number of passengers riding the trains showed an average of 670,000 free rides a month during a seven-month period.

Although the preceding situation may seem unthinkable and perhaps even laughable, similar occurrences are repeated on a daily basis in many businesses throughout the country.

[1] See "Long Island Railroad Is Said to be Losing Revenue Due to 'Weak' Accounting System," *The Wall Street Journal,* February 18, 1971, p. 10.

OBJECTIVE 1
Understand the nature of internal control along with various internal control procedures.

Accountants recognize that the design of a perfect system is an impossibility, as errors and inefficiencies will almost always occur when transactions are processed. A limited number of accidental errors are expected and tolerated; conversely, intentional errors via employee sabotage, fraud, and/or embezzlement are unacceptable. To minimize the probability of error occurrence and improve the credibility of financial statements and reports, features known as internal controls are built into accounting systems. We can define **internal control** to be the various measures adopted by an organization to safeguard company assets, check the reliability and accuracy of accounting information, ensure compliance with management policies, and evaluate operating performance and efficiency.

## The Internal Control Structure

The control structure (i.e., framework) of a business is dependent on several factors, including the accounting system itself, the control environment, and various control procedures.[2] Let us focus on the latter two elements for a moment.

A company's control environment represents the combined effect of many factors that relate to the implementation and evaluation of specified firm policies. For example, the environment is influenced by anything from sound personnel practices that enable a business to attract, motivate, and compensate competent personnel, to what may be viewed as the most crucial link in setting the overall control "tone" of the entity: management's philosophy and operating style. Is management prone to take and monitor business risks? What is the company's attitude toward financial reporting? Do executives exercise care in daily operations and in meeting budget and income goals? These issues tend to reflect the overall emphasis and importance of control within the business, as top management attitudes are often adopted and reflected at lower levels of the organizational structure.

In addition to creating a suitable control environment, a business must also establish various control procedures to ensure that company goals will be achieved. These procedures are integrated into both the control environment and accounting systems and generally include the following:

### Limited Access to Assets

The safeguarding of assets is a stated objective of internal control. One way to achieve this objective is by **limiting the access to assets** to only a few authorized personnel. Limited access may take different forms. For example, customers normally are not permitted in the back of a store to roam freely through the merchandise awaiting sale. This area is reserved for employees only. Furthermore, access to a company's mainframe computer and valuable processing time and data files is usually gained only after a secret password is entered into a computer terminal. The password is known by a select few. And, finally, when many retail establishments close for business at the end of the day, the cash that has been collected is often counted in a locked room. All of these procedures are designed to ensure that assets are adequately protected from theft and unauthorized use.

---

[2] Much of this discussion is based on "Consideration of the Internal Control Structure in a Financial Statement Audit," *Statement on Auditing Standards No. 55* (New York: American Institute of Certified Public Accountants, Inc., 1988).

## Separation of Duties

Many different functions (duties) performed within a company pertain to the firm's financial activities. These duties are frequently categorized into the following broad classes:

- Transaction authorization
- Transaction recording
- Asset custody

To explain, someone must first authorize a transaction. Later the transaction must be entered in the accounting records. And finally, because virtually all transactions immediately or eventually affect an asset, an entity must control and closely monitor its valuable resources.

To achieve the stated objectives of internal control, a business must provide for an adequate **separation of duties.** Incompatible duties, namely, authorization, recording, and custody, must be performed by different employees within an organization. Such separation helps to detect errors, since different personnel will be handling different aspects of the same transaction. In effect, then, the employees will be checking each other's work, and the likelihood that an error will proceed through a system from beginning to end is reduced.

Aside from assisting in error detection, separation of authorization, recording, and custody also makes fraud and embezzlement more difficult. As an example, suppose Rhonda Martin and Joe Harrison are both employed at the same firm. Martin physically handles the company's cash receipts, while Harrison maintains the Cash account in the accounting records. An adequate separation of duties is present in this case because physical control over the asset (i.e., custody) is segregated from transaction record keeping. Imagine, however, what could happen if Harrison was laid off and Martin, in addition to her present job, also assumed Joe's duties. If she desired, Martin could easily steal funds from the company and then adjust the accounting records to conceal the embezzlement. Two incompatible functions have been combined, opening the door for a variety of creative schemes.

Martin would have been less inclined to embezzle in the original situation, because Harrison would be maintaining an independent record of all transactions related to Cash and, in effect, monitoring Rhonda's actions. Of course, even if duties were separated in the appropriate manner, the theft would have still been possible had both employees conspired with one another to defraud the company.

## Accountability Procedures

A business can adopt different measures to achieve financial accountability. These measures, known as **accountability procedures,** may help to pinpoint responsibility within an organization, protect the assets, or detect errors. The measures vary and depend on the size and nature of a firm. Common accountability procedures include duty authorization, prenumbered documents, and verification of records.

***Duty Authorization*** Pinpointing responsibility is essential in medium and large organizations. In small businesses, many of the accounting and financial activities are handled by the owner/manager. In larger entities, because there are too many tasks for one individual to perform, the accounting duties are divided among the various employees. Each employee is authorized to perform certain functions and, as a result, is held responsible or accountable for those functions.

Frequently, the actions taken by personnel result in some form of documentation to provide the necessary basis for accountability. Did you ever observe, for example, that store clerks often initial customer checks, sales invoices, and other similar documents? These procedures assist management in pinpointing responsibility and are especially helpful should a question or problem arise. Management can quickly determine the employee involved and then take any necessary corrective action.

***Prenumbered Documents*** Important forms such as checks, sales invoices, and purchase orders are usually serially prenumbered and subsequently accounted for. This practice permits the discovery of missing documents by detecting a break in the numbering scheme. An investigation can then commence to locate the source of the problem.

***Verification of Records*** Another widely used accountability procedure is verification of company records by comparison with company assets. For example:

- At the end of the day a sales-entry terminal is emptied, and the cash collected is compared against the terminal's tape.
- At the end of a month a business compares the amount of cash in its checkbook against a statement issued by the bank.
- At the end of the annual reporting period, a firm counts inventory and compares the actual hand count against a perpetual book count.

If the comparisons do not agree, suspicions may be raised regarding errors in the recording process or possible theft.

## Independent Review

Personnel changes, the introduction of certain "shortcuts" by employees to improve job efficiency, and other similar occurrences may result in established procedures not being followed. In view of this situation, businesses should continually evaluate their accounting controls to determine if the controls are functioning as originally intended. Such evaluations are commonly made by internal auditors, who are far removed from daily operations and activities so that an independent review may be rendered.

Large companies also have a thorough examination (i.e., an audit) performed by an external CPA firm. Keep in mind that the transactions processed through a system affect an entity's financial statements. Because the external CPA must express an opinion about the fairness of the statements, an evaluation is needed of the internal controls in operation.

The results of the external CPA's examination are delivered to management for use within the firm. Given the consequences of weak control systems and the reliance placed on financial statements by various user groups, management sometimes comments publicly, in a general sense, about the organization's internal control practices. As an example, the following paragraphs were excerpted from a recent annual report of Scott Paper Company:

> . . . the Company maintains a system of internal accounting controls which is designed to provide what are believed to be reasonable assurances that assets are safeguarded, transactions are executed in accordance with the Company's authorization and financial records are reliable as a basis for preparation of financial statements. The Company is

> continually modifying its system of internal accounting controls in response to changes in business conditions and operations. Support for this system is provided by the Company's internal auditors through their periodic audits of Scott's operations throughout the world. . . .
>
> The Company's Board of Directors has had an Audit Committee composed solely of outside directors since 1969. This Committee reviews the Company's accounting controls and policies as well as its practices in financial reporting to shareholders and the public. It meets on a timely basis with the internal auditors, the independent accountants and Company management to review their work and to ensure that each is properly fulfilling its responsibilities. In addition, the internal auditors and independent accountants each meet periodically with the Committee, without Company management present, to discuss the results of their audit work and related matters.

### Costs and Benefits

Any business can design a system with elaborate controls, but exactly how far should companies go? Should a small firm hire several additional employees just to maintain an adequate separation of duties? Should a company perform a thorough background check and take extra security precautions for an employee who, on a part-time basis, issues cash refunds to customers? For many organizations these and related questions are difficult to answer.

When designing and installing specific internal controls, the accountant must treat each business individually, because no two entities are alike. The accountant must study the errors that can occur and the probability of occurrence. Once the probability is determined, controls must be selected for which the *benefits of use exceed the costs of implementation and operation.* If this practice is followed, an organization will have a positive and financially beneficial approach to internal control.

### Foreign Corrupt Practices Act

During the mid-1970s the American public began to question the ethical conduct of U.S. businesses engaged in international trade. The public was shocked to learn that corporations had paid hundreds of millions of dollars in bribes and questionable payments to foreign firms, governments, and political officials. In response to this situation, Congress enacted the **Foreign Corrupt Practices Act (FCPA),** which outlaws these payments and makes them a criminal offense. It is important to note that the act's provisions apply to all U.S. publicly owned companies, even those that conduct business solely within this country's boundaries.

The FCPA has had a significant impact on accountants. Many of the questionable payments involved falsifying accounting records or maintaining secret funds that were not carried on an entity's books. Occasionally, these practices were conducted without the knowledge of top management. To help curtail such actions, the FCPA requires that large businesses develop and maintain an effective system of internal control and keep detailed accounting records. In most organizations, these requirements have been practiced for many years; the FCPA, however, now makes their intentional absence a violation of the law.

## Special Journals

Having introduced the concept of internal control, we can now begin a study of processing systems. In Chapter 2, we noted that businesses record transactions in a general journal and then post to accounts in the general ledger. The processing was viewed as orderly and appeared to be efficient. Overall, this type of system provides a company with some basic information-generating capability and is best used when the volume of transactions is low.

A step above the preceding system is one that employs **special journals,** or journals that handle specialized (specific) types of high-frequency transactions. A review of many companies' business operations will often find that approximately 90% of the accompanying transactions fall into one of four categories. Hence, the following special journals are normally encountered:

OBJECTIVE 2
Understand how special journals are used in an accounting system.

| *Journal* | *Transactions Contained* |
|---|---|
| Sales journal | Sales of merchandise on account |
| Purchases journal | Purchases of merchandise on account |
| Cash receipts journal | Receipts of cash |
| Cash payments journal | Payments of cash |

Naturally, not all transactions and events will fit into the classifications just cited. Consider, for example, the need to record sales returns and allowances, purchases returns and allowances, adjusting entries, and closing entries. These and other similar items are therefore recorded in the general journal, which assumes a new role. Rather than being used to handle all business activity, the general journal is now employed *solely* for miscellaneous transactions and events (namely, those not accommodated in special journals).

**▶ TIPS & TECHNIQUES**

When first exposed to the operation of a special journal system, some students attempt to record a company's entire set of transactions in the general journal and also in the special journals just mentioned. This procedure is incorrect. A given transaction is entered in a special journal *or* the general journal, not both.

Companies that use special journals tend to receive two distinct benefits. First, firms are able to spread their work load, since each journal can be maintained by a different employee. All credit sales can be accounted for by one person, all cash receipts by another, and so on. Second, special journals significantly reduce the amount of posting necessary to process transactions—an important consideration, especially in high-volume environments where this type of processing system is found.

The bookkeeping efficiency associated with special journals will be illustrated shortly. Before doing so, however, we must first explore the concept of subsidiary ledgers and control accounts.

## Subsidiary Ledgers and Control Accounts

OBJECTIVE 3
Be familiar with the relationship between control accounts and subsidiary ledgers.

Earlier in the text the general ledger was defined to contain the various accounts that appear on a company's financial statements. Frequently, it is necessary to divide the balances that appear in several of these accounts into further detail. Common examples are shown in the table that follows.

| *General Ledger Account* | *Subdivided by* |
|---|---|
| Accounts Receivable | Customer |
| Accounts Payable | Creditor |
| Merchandise Inventory | Individual inventory items |
| Sales | Product line and/or territory |

A business must keep track of the amounts due from each customer, the balances owed to individual suppliers, and other specific information. Separate accounts are therefore established for each of these subdivisions. These accounts are collectively known as a **subsidiary ledger—**a group of lower level accounts that comprise a general ledger account. The general ledger account that is composed of subsidiary ledger accounts is, in turn, known as a **control account.**

If all accounting procedures are properly followed, the balance in a control account should equal the sum of the individual account balances contained within its subsidiary ledger. Thus, if Woodcraft Company lists $10,000 of accounts receivable on its May 31 balance sheet, the subsidiary ledger should contain customer accounts whose balances total $10,000. The equality between a subsidiary ledger and control account is checked on a periodic basis, often monthly, when a supporting schedule is prepared. The schedule is simply a listing of each account in the subsidiary ledger along with the related balance. Woodcraft's schedule of accounts receivable and the preceding relationships are shown in Exhibit 6-1.

## Sales Journal

The **sales journal** is employed to record sales of merchandise on account. We illustrate the journal's use by examining various transactions of Stereo Unlimited, a wholesale distributor of stereo equipment, records and tapes, and miscellaneous accessories. The firm had the following credit sales during January:

**Exhibit 6-1**
**Subsidiary Ledger/Control Account Relationships**

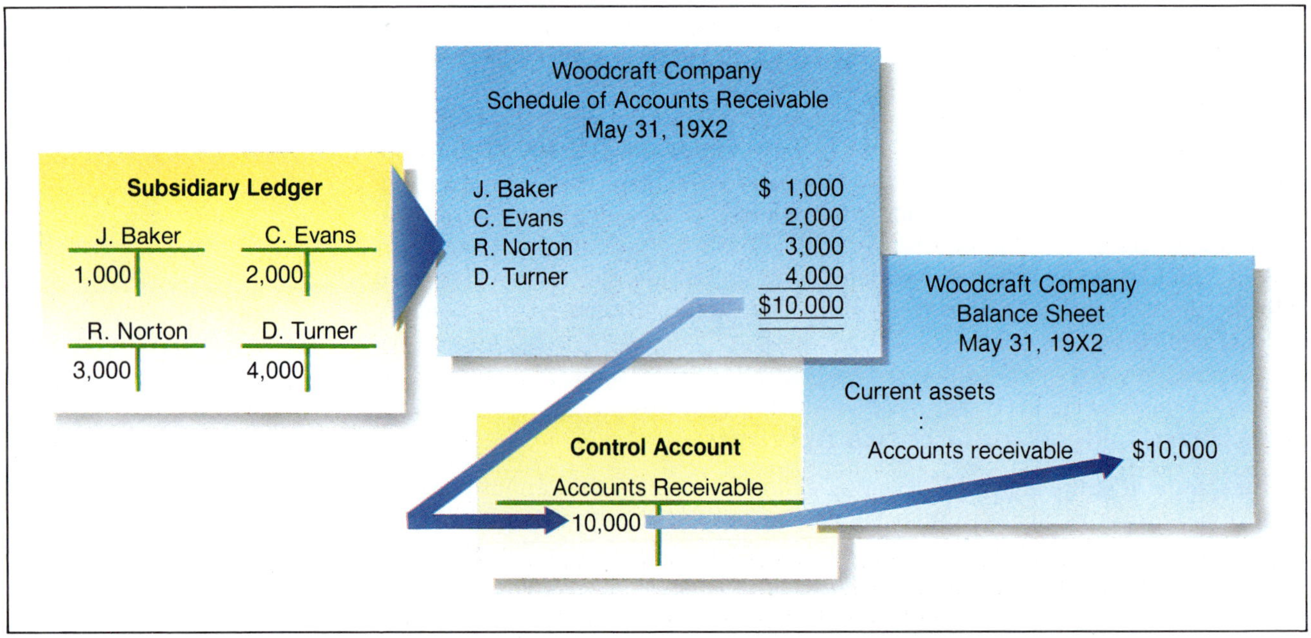

Jan. 4 Sold $1,350 of stereo equipment on account (invoice no. 101) to House of Music.

12 Opened an account for the Sound Center and sold $400 of records and tapes on account (invoice no. 102).

18 Sold $150 of stereo accessories on account (invoice no. 103) to Treetops Lounge.

25 Sold $1,200 of stereo equipment and $200 of records and tapes on account (invoice no. 104) to Walton's Music Store.

Stereo Unlimited's sales journal is shown in Exhibit 6-2. The entries are taken from the data that appear on each sales invoice. Notice that only one line is necessary to record an individual transaction and the usual debit/credit format is absent. Furthermore, journal entry explanations are no longer needed because all transactions are of the same type: a sale of merchandise on account.

To understand the journal's operation, let us keep our objectives in mind. The customer accounts in the subsidiary ledger must be updated to reflect the added amounts due the firm. Furthermore, the Accounts Receivable and Sales accounts must both be increased, the former to achieve the required control account/subsidiary ledger equality and the latter because the company has generated revenues from each of the four transactions. The preceding objectives are carried out through the posting process, which is illustrated in the exhibit.

## Posting the Sales Journal

Exhibit 6-2 reveals that individual sales are posted daily to the appropriate customer's account in the subsidiary ledger. Daily posting is necessary to keep up-to-date balances, which are helpful in both credit decisions and in responding to customer queries. To signify completion of this process and to provide an *audit trail* (i.e., a means to trace and access accounting information), one enters the notation S1 (sales journal, page 1) as a reference in the customer's account. Finally, a check mark is placed in the sales journal to indicate that the transaction was transferred to the subsidiary ledger.[3] These procedures are repeated until all transactions are posted.

Next, the control account is updated to maintain the necessary equality. Because the only type of transaction recorded in the sales journal is a sale of merchandise on account, the total of the amount column is posted periodically (often monthly) as a debit to Accounts Receivable control and a credit to Sales. The notation S1 is then entered in these accounts in the general ledger. To finish the process, the numbers of the accounts to which the $3,300 was posted, 110 and 410, are written beneath the total.

A review of these procedures will find that the four transactions were transferred to the proper accounts by a total of six postings: Accounts Receivable control, Sales, and four subsidiary accounts. If Stereo Unlimited failed to employ a special journal system and instead used a general journal to record all of its transactions, the number of postings would increase considerably. Four separate journal entries would be constructed, each one containing a debit to Accounts Receivable control and a credit to Sales. Further, the individual transaction amounts would have to be charged to customer accounts in the subsidiary ledger, creating a total of 12 separate postings. As you can well imagine, the bookkeeping would become over-

[3] Check marks are used because of the absence of account numbers in the subsidiary ledger. Companies that follow this practice arrange customer and creditor accounts alphabetically, thereby allowing for growth (or contraction) without having to modify numbering schemes.

**Exhibit 6-2**
**Sales Journal and Related Postings**

**Sales Journal**

Page 1

| Date | Customer | Invoice No. | Post Ref | Amount |
|---|---|---|---|---|
| 19XX | | | | |
| Jan. 4 | House of Music | 101 | ✓ | 1,350 |
| 12 | Sound Center | 102 | ✓ | 400 |
| 18 | Treetops Lounge | 103 | ✓ | 150 |
| 25 | Walton's Music Store | 104 | ✓ | 1,400 |
| | | | | 3,300 |
| | | | | (110/410) |

Total is posted monthly to general ledger accounts

Individual amounts are posted daily to customer accounts in the subsidiary ledger

**General Ledger**

Accounts Receivable — Account No. 110

| Date | Ref | Debit | Credit | Balance |
|---|---|---|---|---|
| 19XX | | | | |
| Jan. 31 | S1 | 3,300 | | 3,300 |

Sales — Account No. 410

| Date | Ref | Debit | Credit | Balance |
|---|---|---|---|---|
| 19XX | | | | |
| Jan. 31 | S1 | | 3,300 | 3,300 |

**Accounts Receivable Subsidiary Ledger**

House of Music

| Date | Ref | Debit | Credit | Balance |
|---|---|---|---|---|
| 19XX | | | | |
| Jan. 4 | S1 | 1,350 | | 1,350 |

Sound Center

| Date | Ref | Debit | Credit | Balance |
|---|---|---|---|---|
| 19XX | | | | |
| Jan. 12 | S1 | 400 | | 400 |

Treetops Lounge

| Date | Ref | Debit | Credit | Balance |
|---|---|---|---|---|
| 19XX | | | | |
| Jan. 18 | S1 | 150 | | 150 |

Walton's Music Store

| Date | Ref | Debit | Credit | Balance |
|---|---|---|---|---|
| 19XX | | | | |
| Jan. 25 | S1 | 1,400 | | 1,400 |

whelming as activity increases. Thankfully, the efficiency provided by a series of special journals is dramatic, particularly for firms that do not use computers.

### Journal Variations

The journals illustrated in this chapter are general models that can be altered to meet the needs of individual businesses. For example, if a company were charging its customers for sales taxes, an additional column could be added in the sales journal to record the taxes payable to the government. Or if management desired to report sales by product line, a minor design change would allow a firm to generate the necessary information. An expanded journal for Stereo Unlimited, for instance, might contain the following amount columns: Accounts Receivable debit, Stereo Equipment Sales credit, Record and Tape Sales credit, and Accessories Sales credit.

A number of variations in journal design are possible. Generally speaking, separate amount columns are established when (1) more detailed accounting information is desired, as in the preceding case, or (2) transactions occur on a highly repetitive basis. These design "rules" will become more apparent in later sections of the chapter.

## Purchases Journal

The procedures associated with the sales journal closely parallel those employed with the purchases journal. The **purchases journal** is used to record only one type of transaction: purchases of merchandise on account. Other types of acquisitions are recorded elsewhere. For example, a cash acquisition of merchandise would be entered in the cash payments journal, whereas a purchase of equipment on account would be placed in the general journal.

Every purchase of merchandise on account requires a debit to Purchases and a credit to Accounts Payable. In addition, because a business needs detailed information regarding the amounts owed to each supplier, a separate subsidiary ledger must be established. The sum of the individual creditor accounts in the subsidiary ledger must again equal the balance in the general ledger control account—Accounts Payable in this case.

Stereo Unlimited's purchases journal and related postings appear in Exhibit 6-3. Individual amounts for purchases are credited daily to suppliers' accounts in the subsidiary ledger, because the balances owed have increased. Once again, completion of posting is denoted by placing a check mark in the journal. The journal's total is then posted at the end of the month as a debit to Purchases and a credit to Accounts Payable control. The P1 references in the ledger accounts indicate that the entries were transferred from page 1 of the purchases journal.

Overall, you should observe two important similarities in the operation of the sales and purchases journals, namely:

- Individual transaction amounts that affect subsidiary ledgers are posted daily to the appropriate subsidiary ledger accounts.
- Totals that affect control accounts are posted monthly to the general ledger.

## Cash Receipts Journal

A company receives cash from many different sources, including cash sales, customer payments on account, the sale of old equipment, and bank loans. The possibilities are numerous. The **cash receipts journal** must therefore have multi-

**Purchases Journal**

Page 1

| Date | Supplier | Invoice Information | | | Post Ref | Amount |
|---|---|---|---|---|---|---|
| | | Date | No. | Terms | | |
| 19XX | | | | | | |
| Jan. 3 | Able Electronics | Jan. 3 | 1721 | — | ✓ | 2,100 |
| 8 | Columbia Records | 7 | 1777 | 2/10, n/30 | ✓ | 750 |
| 16 | Pioneer Associates | 16 | AF471 | — | ✓ | 420 |
| 26 | Sony Corp. | 26 | 9576 | 3/10, n/30 | ✓ | 2,060 |
| | | | | | | 5,330 |
| | | | | | | (501/201) |

Total is posted monthly to general ledger accounts

Individual amounts are posted daily to creditor accounts in the subsidiary ledger

**General Ledger**

Accounts Payable — Account No. 201

| Date | Ref | Debit | Credit | Balance |
|---|---|---|---|---|
| 19XX | | | | |
| Jan. 31 | P1 | | 5,330 | 5,330 |

Purchases — Account No. 501

| Date | Ref | Debit | Credit | Balance |
|---|---|---|---|---|
| 19XX | | | | |
| Jan. 31 | P1 | 5,330 | | 5,330 |

**Accounts Payable Subsidiary Ledger**

Able Electronics

| Date | Ref | Debit | Credit | Balance |
|---|---|---|---|---|
| 19XX | | | | |
| Jan. 3 | P1 | | 2,100 | 2,100 |

Columbia Records

| Date | Ref | Debit | Credit | Balance |
|---|---|---|---|---|
| 19XX | | | | |
| Jan. 8 | P1 | | 750 | 750 |

Pioneer Associates

| Date | Ref | Debit | Credit | Balance |
|---|---|---|---|---|
| 19XX | | | | |
| Jan. 16 | P1 | | 420 | 420 |

Sony Corp.

| Date | Ref | Debit | Credit | Balance |
|---|---|---|---|---|
| 19XX | | | | |
| Jan. 26 | P1 | | 2,060 | 2,060 |

**Exhibit 6-3**
**Purchases Journal and Related Postings**

ple amount columns since all cash receipts are recorded here. Normally, separate columns are established for transactions that occur on a frequent basis.

Stereo Unlimited had the following cash receipts during January:

Jan. 2 Received $2,000 from Patricia Monroe, owner of Stereo Unlimited, as an investment in the business.
9 Sold $650 of stereo equipment and $150 of tapes for cash to Central Stereo.
13 Received a check on account from the House of Music for the sale on January 4, minus the correct discount.
17 Received loan proceeds of $4,800 from California Trust Company to acquire several new display cases.
22 Sold $100 of records and $100 of accessories to Burrows Music Company for cash.
28 Received a $280 check on account from the Sound Center in partial payment of the sale made on January 12.

Proper recording of these transactions is shown in Exhibit 6-4. Assume all credit sales were subject to terms of 2/10, n/30.

## Operation of the Cash Receipts Journal

Transactions are entered in the cash receipts journal in accordance with accounting's normal debit/credit rules. To illustrate, examine the receipt on account from the Sound Center on January 28. An entry for $280 is placed in both the Cash debit column and the Accounts Receivable credit column. The Sound Center appears in the Account space because the firm's subsidiary ledger account must be updated.

Transactions that do not arise often are recorded in the Sundry or miscellaneous column. On January 2, for example, Stereo Unlimited received $2,000 from Patricia Monroe as an investment in the firm. The receipt requires a debit to Cash. Because owner investments are infrequent, the company has not established a separate Capital column. Instead, $2,000 is placed in Sundry and Patricia Monroe, Capital, is entered in the Account space.

Note that the Account space is left blank for cash sales. Stereo Unlimited, like many other businesses, makes no attempt to gather the names of cash customers. An explanation of the transaction may be entered if desired (e.g., Daily Cash Sales).

## Posting the Cash Receipts Journal

Individual amounts that appear in the Accounts Receivable and Sundry columns are posted throughout the month. Collections from credit customers are generally posted daily to the subsidiary ledger in an effort to maintain up-to-date account balances; entries in the Sundry column are transferred as they occur to minimize work during the hectic end of the period. As a result of this latter procedure, respective credits of $2,000 and $4,800 were posted to Patricia Monroe, Capital (account no. 301) and Loans Payable (account no. 210) in the general ledger. Entries in these accounts and others show a reference of CR1, indicating the amounts originated on page 1 of the cash receipts journal.

Upon conclusion of monthly activity, column totals are transferred to their respective ledger accounts. Before this process is performed, however, the equality

**Exhibit 6-4**
**Cash Receipts Journal and Related Postings**

**Cash Receipts Journal** — Page 1

| Date | Account | Post Ref | Cash Debit | Sales Discounts Debit | Accounts Receivable Credit | Sales Credit | Sundry Accounts Credit or (Debit) |
|---|---|---|---|---|---|---|---|
| 19XX | | | | | | | |
| Jan. 2 | Patricia Monroe, Capital | 301 | 2,000 | | | | 2,000 |
| 9 | — | | 800 | | | 800 | |
| 13 | House of Music | ✓ | 1,323 | 27 | 1,350 | | |
| 17 | Loans Payable | 210 | 4,800 | | | | 4,800 |
| 22 | — | | 200 | | | 200 | |
| 28 | Sound Center | ✓ | 280 | | 280 | | |
| | | | 9,403 | 27 | 1,630 | 1,000 | 6,800 |
| | | | (101) | (413) | (110) | (410) | (X) |

Totals, except Sundry, are posted monthly to general ledger accounts

Individual amounts are posted daily to general ledger accounts

Individual amounts are posted daily to customer accounts in the subsidiary ledger

**General Ledger**

Cash — Account No. 101

| Date | Ref | Debit | Credit | Balance |
|---|---|---|---|---|
| 19XX | | | | |
| Jan. 31 | CR1 | 9,403 | | 9,403 |

Accounts Receivable — Account No. 110

| Date | Ref | Debit | Credit | Balance |
|---|---|---|---|---|
| 19XX | | | | |
| Jan. 31 | S1 | 3,300 | | 3,300 |
| 31 | CR1 | | 1,630 | 1,670 |

Loans Payable — Account No. 210

| Date | Ref | Debit | Credit | Balance |
|---|---|---|---|---|
| 19XX | | | | |
| Jan. 17 | CR1 | | 4,800 | 4,800 |

Patricia Monroe, Capital — Account No. 301

| Date | Ref | Debit | Credit | Balance |
|---|---|---|---|---|
| 19XX | | | | |
| Jan. 2 | CR1 | | 2,000 | 2,000 |

Sales — Account No. 410

| Date | Ref | Debit | Credit | Balance |
|---|---|---|---|---|
| 19XX | | | | |
| Jan. 31 | S1 | | 3,300 | 3,300 |
| 31 | CR1 | | 1,000 | 4,300 |

Sales Discounts — Account No. 413

| Date | Ref | Debit | Credit | Balance |
|---|---|---|---|---|
| 19XX | | | | |
| Jan. 31 | CR1 | 27 | | 27 |

**Accounts Receivable Subsidiary Ledger**

House of Music

| Date | Ref | Debit | Credit | Balance |
|---|---|---|---|---|
| 19XX | | | | |
| Jan. 4 | S1 | 1,350 | | 1,350 |
| 13 | CR1 | | 1,350 | — |

Sound Center

| Date | Ref | Debit | Credit | Balance |
|---|---|---|---|---|
| 19XX | | | | |
| Jan. 12 | S1 | 400 | | 400 |
| 28 | CR1 | | 280 | 120 |

of debits and credits must be evaluated. In the case of Stereo Unlimited, the required equality is maintained:

| ***Debits*** | | ***Credits*** | |
|---|---|---|---|
| Cash | $9,403 | Accounts receivable | $1,630 |
| Sales discounts | 27 | Sales | 1,000 |
| | $9,430 | Sundry accounts | 6,800 |
| | | | $9,430 |

All column totals are posted, with one exception: Sundry. As the X in Exhibit 6-4 indicates, the total of the Sundry column is not posted, because its components ($2,000 and $4,800) have already been transferred to the proper accounts. The $6,800 total is generated only for use in determining whether total debits are equal to total credits.

## Cash Payments Journal

The **cash payments journal** is used to record virtually all cash disbursements that are made by a business.[4] Because cash outlays are made for many different purposes, the journal utilized for their recording must be multicolumn in format. Separate columns are again established when the same type of transaction occurs frequently or when more detailed accounting information is desired.

Stereo Unlimited's cash disbursements during January were as follows:

Jan. 4 Paid January rent of $750 to Kraft Management by issuing check no. 101.

11 Issued check no. 102 for $100 to Central Stereo for the return of stereo equipment sold for cash on January 9.

14 Paid invoice no. 1777, dated January 7, of Columbia Records by issuing check no. 103. The invoice totaled $750 and was subject to terms of 2/10, n/30.

19 Paid $650 of sales commissions to John Harrison by issuing check no. 104.

27 Issued check no. 105 to Able Electronics for $2,100, in payment of the purchase made on January 3.

These transactions are recorded in the cash payments journal that appears in Exhibit 6-5.

Observe that the journal possesses a Cash credit column since each payment reduces the company's cash balance. Furthermore, because the firm acquires its merchandise on credit, columns for Accounts Payable and Purchases Discounts are needed. Finally, a Sundry column is used to record disbursements that are made for other purposes. The journal has one additional feature: a check number column. All significant cash disbursements are made by check for reasons of safety and accountability. The check's number is entered in the journal to facilitate the audit trail (i.e., tracing) process.

[4] A minor exception occurs with small miscellaneous payments that are made from a petty cash system. The operation of a petty cash system is discussed in Chapter 7.

**Cash Payments Journal**

Page 1

| Date | Check No. | Payee | Account | Post Ref | Cash Credit | Purchases Discounts Credit | Accounts Payable Debit | Sundry Accounts Debit or (Credit) |
|---|---|---|---|---|---|---|---|---|
| 19XX | | | | | | | | |
| Jan. 4 | 101 | Kraft Management | Rent Expense | 530 | 750 | | | 750 |
| 11 | 102 | Central Stereo | Sales Returns & Allowances | 414 | 100 | | | 100 |
| 14 | 103 | Columbia Records | | ✓ | 735 | 15 | 750 | |
| 19 | 104 | John Harrison | Sales Commissions | 540 | 650 | | | 650 |
| 27 | 105 | Able Electronics | | ✓ | 2,100 | | 2,100 | |
| | | | | | 4,335 | 15 | 2,850 | 1,500 |
| | | | | | (101) | (504) | (201) | (X) |

Totals, except Sundry, are posted monthly to general ledger accounts

Individual amounts are posted daily to general ledger accounts

Individual amounts are posted daily to creditor accounts in the subsidiary ledger

**General Ledger**

Cash — Account No. 101

| Date | Ref | Debit | Credit | Balance |
|---|---|---|---|---|
| 19XX | | | | |
| Jan. 31 | CR1 | 9,403 | | 9,403 |
| 31 | CP1 | | 4,335 | 5,068 |

Accounts Payable — Account No. 201

| Date | Ref | Debit | Credit | Balance |
|---|---|---|---|---|
| 19XX | | | | |
| Jan. 31 | P1 | | 5,330 | 5,330 |
| 31 | CP1 | 2,850 | | 2,480 |

Sales Returns & Allowances — Account No. 414

| Date | Ref | Debit | Credit | Balance |
|---|---|---|---|---|
| 19XX | | | | |
| Jan. 11 | CP1 | 100 | | 100 |

Purchases Discounts — Account No. 504

| Date | Ref | Debit | Credit | Balance |
|---|---|---|---|---|
| 19XX | | | | |
| Jan. 31 | CP1 | | 15 | 15 |

Rent Expense — Account No. 530

| Date | Ref | Debit | Credit | Balance |
|---|---|---|---|---|
| 19XX | | | | |
| Jan. 4 | CP1 | 750 | | 750 |

Sales Commissions — Account No. 540

| Date | Ref | Debit | Credit | Balance |
|---|---|---|---|---|
| 19XX | | | | |
| Jan. 19 | CP1 | 650 | | 650 |

**Accounts Payable Subsidiary Ledger**

Able Electronics

| Date | Ref | Debit | Credit | Balance |
|---|---|---|---|---|
| 19XX | | | | |
| Jan. 3 | P1 | | 2,100 | 2,100 |
| 27 | CP1 | 2,100 | | — |

Columbia Records

| Date | Ref | Debit | Credit | Balance |
|---|---|---|---|---|
| 19XX | | | | |
| Jan. 8 | P1 | | 750 | 750 |
| 14 | CP1 | 750 | | — |

**Exhibit 6-5**
**Cash Payments Journal and Related Postings**

### Posting the Cash Payments Journal

Posting the cash payments journal is very similar to posting the cash receipts journal. Both journals are multicolumn in format, both have a Sundry column to record miscellaneous transactions, and both deal with a control account/subsidiary ledger arrangement. Throughout the month, individual amounts in the Sundry column are posted to the proper accounts in the general ledger (e.g., Rent Expense, Sales Returns & Allowances, and Sales Commissions). Similarly, entries in the Accounts Payable debit column are transferred daily to the Accounts Payable subsidiary ledger. At the end of the month the columns are totaled, and the equality of debits and credits is checked. Then all column totals are posted to the general ledger, with the exception of Sundry. As before, individual elements of the Sundry column have already been transferred. The entries referenced by CP1 have come from the cash payments journal, page 1.

## General Journal

Earlier in the chapter we noted that a business will have a number of transactions that cannot be accommodated in its special journals. Consider, for example, the journals that have been designed for Stereo Unlimited. Suppose that on January 19, the firm bought a piece of display equipment on account from Store Outfitters for $2,600. Because the purchases journal contains only purchases of merchandise, this acquisition must be recorded elsewhere, specifically, in the general journal. The general journal is used to record transactions that cannot be placed in special journals (e.g., miscellaneous transactions, adjusting entries, and closing entries). The necessary entry follows.

**General Journal**

Page 1

| | | | | |
|---|---|---|---|---|
| 19XX | | | | |
| Jan. 19 | Display Equipment | 130 | 2,600 | |
| | Accounts Payable: Store Outfitters | 201/✓ | | 2,600 |
| | Purchased equipment on account | | | |

As the posting references indicate, the transaction was transferred to the Display Equipment account and the Accounts Payable control account in the general ledger. In addition, Store Outfitters was credited in the Accounts Payable subsidiary ledger. The effect of the latter two postings can be seen by viewing the accounts depicted on page 212.

## Several Final Comments

Once all postings are completed, a general ledger trial balance is constructed as the first step in summarizing the period's activity. The necessary procedures are identical to those discussed in Chapter 2 and are not repeated here. In addition to preparing a trial balance, the subsidiary ledger/control account equality must be checked. The basic technique was introduced in Exhibit 6-1; it is shown for Stereo Unlimited's Accounts Payable account in Exhibit 6-6.

**Exhibit 6-6**
**Accounts Payable Relationships for Stereo Unlimited**

**Accounts Payable Subsidiary Ledger**

Pioneer Associates

| Date | Ref | Debit | Credit | Balance |
|---|---|---|---|---|
| 19XX | | | | |
| Jan. 16 | P1 | | 420 | 420 |

Sony Corp.

| Date | Ref | Debit | Credit | Balance |
|---|---|---|---|---|
| 19XX | | | | |
| Jan. 26 | P1 | | 2,060 | 2,060 |

Store Outfitters

| Date | Ref | Debit | Credit | Balance |
|---|---|---|---|---|
| 19XX | | | | |
| Jan. 19 | J1 | | 2,600 | 2,600 |

**STEREO UNLIMITED**
**Schedule of Accounts Payable**
**January 31, 19XX**

| | |
|---|---|
| Pioneer Associates | $ 420 |
| Sony Corp. | 2,060 |
| Store Outfitters | 2,600 |
| | $5,080 |

**Control Account**

Accounts Payable — Account No. 201

| Date | Ref | Debit | Credit | Balance |
|---|---|---|---|---|
| 19XX | | | | |
| Jan. 19 | J1 | | 2,600 | 2,600 |
| 31 | P1 | | 5,330 | 7,930 |
| 31 | CP1 | 2,850 | | 5,080 |

*Note:* The general journal transaction on January 19 is shown in the Accounts Payable control account here but not in the control account that appears in Exhibit 6-5. This situation arises because the transaction had not yet been introduced in the discussion, making inclusion in the earlier presentation inappropriate.

To conclude, be aware that the transaction-recording and posting processes illustrated in the previous pages are performed by bookkeepers, not accountants. The accountant, however, is often requested to audit the output of information systems, review internal controls, and design new systems for clients. He or she must therefore possess a fundamental knowledge of how transactions are processed into the dollar amounts that appear on both the trial balance and the financial statements.

## Computers in Accounting

OBJECTIVE 4
Be familiar with the interaction between accounting and computers.

The special journals just introduced greatly reduce the amount of posting required to maintain a set of accounting records. Nevertheless, these journals (and manual systems in general) lack the efficiency needed for use in higher-volume transaction-processing environments. In such situations, most companies have found that computers are the answer to a variety of record-keeping problems. Computers can process data more quickly and at a lower error rate than office personnel using manual accounting systems. Stated simply, electrical circuits and microchips do not become bored, fatigued, or emotional—real pluses when it comes to productivity.

With improved efficiency via electronics comes a lower cost per transaction processed. Costs have declined in recent years to the extent that computers are affordable by even the smallest of companies. Hardware and software that provide adequate data processing capability can now be purchased for considerably less than the annual salary and fringe benefit outlays for one bookkeeper. Much of this affordability can be attributed to an increase in the use of small computers (commonly known as *micros*), which have minimal installation and programming costs. Prewritten, or canned, programs are available for all aspects of a company's accounting activities, including payroll, billing, and inventory control. Consequently, a business that uses a microcomputer need not add a data processing specialist to its staff.

## Microcomputer Accounting Systems

Computerized accounting systems tend to parallel manual accounting systems in terms of function and objectives. Both types of systems process transactions, maintain ledger accounts, and produce financial statements and other reports for management's use. This is where the similarity ends, however, as the system's form, organization, and procedures differ greatly. An entity's manual journals and ledgers are replaced by computer files that are kept on a disk.[5] Posting is automated, and the closing process is often performed by pressing a single key on the computer's keyboard. Furthermore, many computerized systems have built-in controls to examine data validity before transactions are accepted as input. A transaction in which debits do not equal credits, for instance, would be rejected by the system.

The typical microcomputer accounting system consists of a series of integrated modules that are accessed by using a menu. A **menu** is a listing on a computer screen of the various program options available to a user. The user scans the listing and then chooses the desired option by entering a corresponding reference number on the computer's keyboard. A typical menu might appear as shown in Exhibit 6-7. Once a particular option is selected, a different menu will appear. The new menu will pertain to the selected alternative (e.g., the accounts receivable module) and will require the user to once again input a desired choice, this time for the module in question.

### Processing Modules

The screen display in Exhibit 6-7 is tied to the accounting system depicted in Exhibit 6-8. Observe how the system is composed of various modules and processing applications that are logically linked together with one another. In addition, notice the high degree of component interaction. Information flow between the component parts of a computer-based system is needed so that financial statements and other reports of an integrative nature can be produced.

An in-depth probe of Exhibit 6-8 is more clearly suited for an advanced accounting course. However, a brief overview of several key modules will show how computer-based systems differ operationally from manual systems. We have selected the general ledger, accounts receivable, and inventory management modules for further study.

[5] Accounting data are stored in computers by using records and files. A *record* stores information about one employee, one inventory item, one account, and so forth. A *file*, on the other hand, is a group of records. For instance, all customer records taken collectively comprise the accounts receivable file.

**Exhibit 6-7**
**Accounting System Menu**

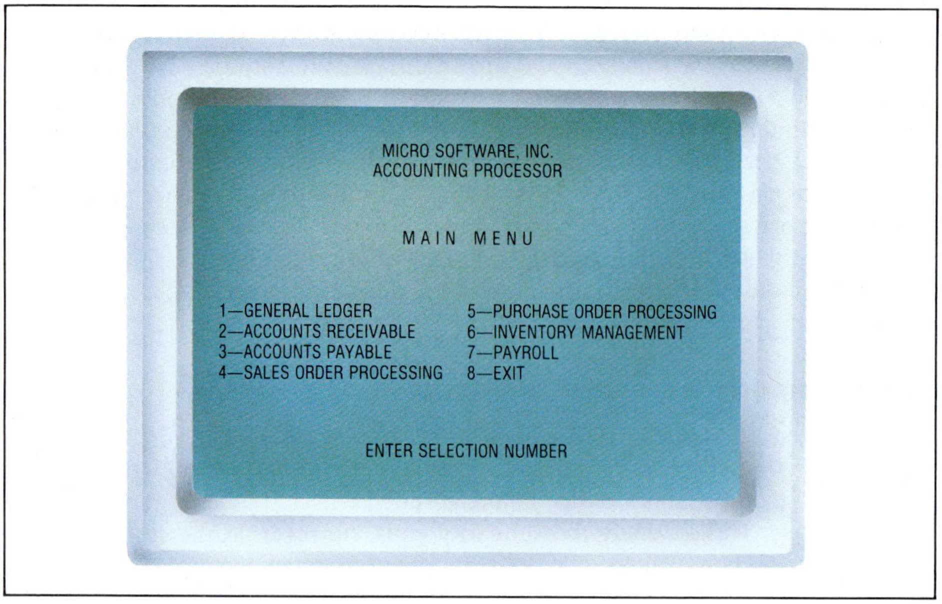


The *general ledger module* houses a company's accounts and the balances contained therein. All miscellaneous journal entries that are normally made in a general journal are recorded through use of this module. In addition, the general ledger package handles the construction and printing of an entity's financial statements.

The *accounts receivable module* is used to keep track of customer account balances and, in effect, contains the company's accounts receivable subsidiary ledger. The

**Exhibit 6-8**
**A Typical Accounting System**

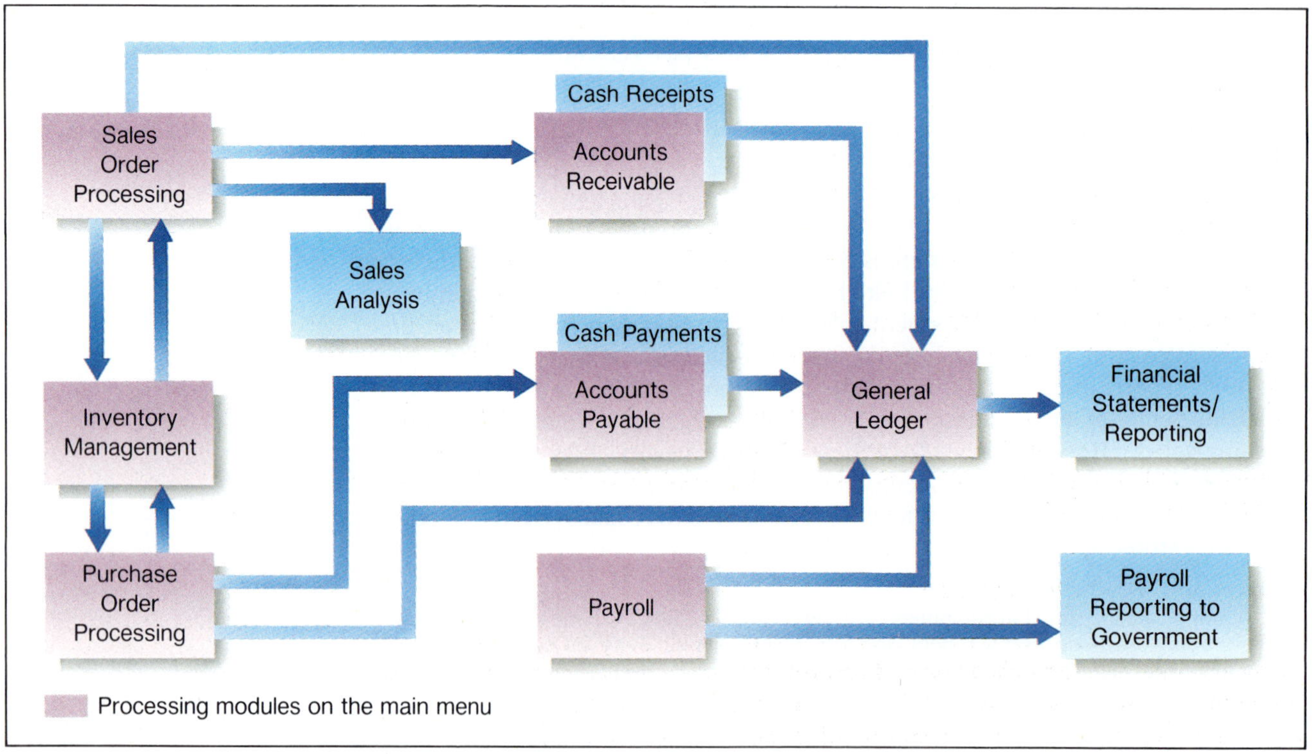

accompanying software is not only capable of determining balances due but can also analyze a firm's past collection experience and provide information concerning how long a particular account has been outstanding. Receipts from customers on account are entered into the system by using this module. Although a cash receipts journal is typically produced, the journal's format is somewhat different than that shown earlier in the chapter. Because this module handles only customer collections on account, other business receipts (e.g., cash sales) are recorded elsewhere, namely, by using the general ledger package.

Finally, the *inventory management module* focuses primarily on inventory control and item availability. This module accepts as input the various merchandise purchases of the firm. The goods on hand are updated, not only by purchases transactions but by sales transactions (via the sales order processing module) as well. Put together, the purchases and sales applications permit a business to maintain a perpetual inventory system and to closely monitor stock levels. These procedures lead to better inventory control and generally result in companies' experiencing few out-of-stock situations. A variety of key data are available from this module including reorder points (i.e., the level of units at which a new order should be placed) and end-of-period inventory quantities.

## Other Microcomputer Applications

Although this chapter has focused on transaction processing systems, be aware that microcomputers are used in many other accounting applications. Micros are used by CPA firms to process income tax returns. In addition, through the use of special telephone hook-ups, computers can be linked to distant data bases to allow the accountant to quickly search thousands of court cases and tax laws. Such capability aids in the performance of tax research. Turning to the audit field, microcomputers are employed in numerous statistical sampling applications when examining the transactions and accounts that serve as the basis for a company's financial statements.

A recent innovation that has become extremely popular is the **electronic spreadsheet.** The spreadsheet is, in effect, a computerized work sheet—a series of columns and rows that are filled with report headings, financial data, and computational formulas by the user. Spreadsheets are used to generate various types of reports (e.g., budgets and depreciation schedules) and are especially helpful in performing "what if" analysis.

Suppose, for instance, that a manager is studying an investment opportunity by using a certain set of assumptions such as projected levels of sales, expenses, cash inflows and outflows, and income tax rates. The manager may desire to study the proposal under a different set of conditions. If paper, pencil, and a calculator were the only tools available, the revised computations would take many hours to perform. By the touch of only a few computer keys, however, the essential calculations are automatically refigured. Much of the computational drudgery is therefore removed from the process, allowing more time for analysis and further "what if" scenarios.

## Computer Problems/Fraud

They improve productivity, reduce data processing costs, and provide timely information for management planning and control. Yet computers are not without their problems. Often, particularly with large-scale systems, considerable time will pass before an organization experiences the full benefits of computer implementation.

## HIGHLIGHT

# Computer Crime: The Wave of the Future

The introduction of fast, inexpensive microcomputers is one of the most important phenomena of our time. Along with giving managers instant access to information and making their jobs easier, the micro has made it relatively simple for a skilled bandit or dishonest employee to obtain confidential data—or millions of dollars—from unwitting companies, banks, and government agencies. Says a white-collar crime specialist with a large public accounting firm, "Business, industry, and government don't have any idea what's going on—they've just seen the tip of the iceberg. More and more people are learning how to get around the controls . . . as more people are computer-literate and have more opportunities, computer crime will increase."

Little wonder. Equipped with a PC, a modem, a telephone, and a few passwords, a computer hacker can electronically transfer millions of dollars in less than a second—and then program the computer to hide the tracks. [1] There are as many ways to make dishonest use of computing power as there are data processing applications. A study of recently prosecuted computer crimes, for example, found that cases ranged from a department store keyboard operator who changed delivery addresses so that thousands of dollars in merchandise was transported to accomplices, to a Colorado district attorney who was convicted for having records of his speeding tickets erased in order to reduce his auto insurance rates.

According to the same study, programmers, students, and input clerks were nabbed for offenses more often than any other occupations. Another study, which polled 785 major corporations, reported the typical computer criminal as a bright, highly qualified person who is a current or former employee and "who has discovered, sometimes by intent but more often by accident, a flaw in the computer security control system." This flaw, the criminal believes, can be exploited with minimal risk. Interestingly, the second study notes that half of the criminals caught by the corporations didn't even work in computer operations. [2]

One facet of computer crime is financial fraud, which often occurs when the top management of a troubled or startup company decides to "create" false assets and earnings to lure (and please) investors. In the notorious Equity Funding case, for instance, officials falsified 60,000 of the company's 97,000 insurance policies. They assigned a secret code to all fake policies, which forced the computer to skip those policies for billing purposes. When the federal investigators asked to audit the appropriate computer files, the company said they weren't immediately available, then forged hard-copy files complete with health reports, contracts, and supporting documents. The fraud ultimately cost investors $1 billion. [3]

To close, we cite the comments of a computer security manager, who notes: "While business people tend to get excited after a widely publicized incident . . . and talk about measures to protect themselves, most of them let the matter slide and consequently remain vulnerable." Adds the president of an agency that specializes in white-collar crime, "Unfortunately, we are usually not brought in to take preventive measures. We're called after the crime has been committed. And by then, of course, it's too late." [4]

SOURCES: Adapted from "'Star Wars' Crime: New Threat to Corporate Security," *Dun's Business Month*, June, 1986, pp. 85, 88 [4]; "Two Studies Attempt to Characterize Nature and Extent of Computer Crime," *PC Week*, June 3, 1986, pp. 107, 108 [2]; and "White-Collar Crime: The Threat from Within," *Management Review*, January, 1986, pp. 22–32 [1, 3]. The second article is reprinted from *PC Week*, copyright © 1986 Ziff Communications Company; the third article is reprinted by permission of the publisher, from *Management Review*, © 1986 American Management Association, New York. All rights reserved.

Occasionally the benefits never materialize. Both Trans World Airlines and United Airlines, for instance, scrapped their early reservations and ticketing systems after investing years of effort and millions of dollars. In the United case alone, $39 million was spent before management decided to abandon the project.

The possibility of fraud is another basic problem associated with computerized systems. **Computer fraud,** which involves the use of computers to aid in and conduct a fraud or embezzlement, seems to be occurring with increasing frequency and may involve significant sums of money. One study of past computer frauds, for instance, found that the *average* loss in cases dealing with corporate accounting amounted to approximately $621,000! Despite intensive research, though, relatively little is known about computer crime. Often, for fear of embarrassment and bad publicity, knowledge of computer-related incidents remains solely within the company involved. Furthermore, only a small portion of computer crime is discovered—and that is generally found by luck or accident.

As computer use expands and our society becomes more computer literate, the auditor will definitely play a more involved role in the prevention of computer crime. The cause of computer misuse is often a lack of adequate internal control in an entity's data processing network. As discussed earlier in the chapter, the auditor must examine an organization's accounting system and related controls to express an opinion on the fairness of the financial statements. No doubt the production of these statements will be increasingly influenced by electronics and state-of-the-art technology.

## Chapter Review

### Learning Objectives—The Key Points

**1 Understand the nature of internal control along with various internal control procedures.** Internal controls are various measures that help to safeguard a company's assets, check the reliability and accuracy of the accounting information produced, ensure compliance with management policies, and evaluate operating performance and efficiency. Such controls may take many different forms, including the limiting of access to assets to a few authorized personnel, maintaining an adequate separation of duties, implementing systems of authorization and approval, having prenumbered documents, and performing verifications of company records.

**2 Understand how special journals are used in an accounting system.** Special journals allow a firm to reduce the amount of bookkeeping associated with transaction processing and also enable the work load to be divided among several employees. Four special journals and the transactions contained therein are

- Sales—Sales of merchandise on account
- Purchases—Purchases of merchandise on account
- Cash receipts—Receipts of cash from various sources
- Cash payments—Payments of cash for various items

In addition to the preceding journals, a general journal is used to record miscellaneous transactions and events.

**3 Be familiar with the relationship between control accounts and subsidiary ledgers.** Control accounts appear on the financial statements and are comprised of various lower level accounts. The "lower level accounts," when taken collectively, make up the subsidiary ledger. As an example, the Accounts Receivable control account on the balance sheet is supported by customer accounts contained in the subsidiary ledger. At the end of a reporting period, the balance in the control account must equal the sum of the balances in the subsidiary ledger.

**4 Be familiar with the interaction between accounting and computers.** Computers are playing an increasingly important role in accounting, primarily because they are more efficient and cost effective than manual systems. Menu-driven microcomputer accounting systems enable a business to have adequate data processing capability without having the expense of a staff programmer. Furthermore, micros have provided managers with the ability to improve planning, control, and decision making via the use of electronic spreadsheets. Computers, however, have created several problems, including computer fraud (i.e., the use of computers to aid in and conduct a fraud or embezzlement).

## Chapter Quiz

The five questions that follow relate to several issues raised in the chapter. Test your knowledge of the issues by selecting the best answer. (The answers appear on p. 235.)

**1** Which of the following is not consistent with a strong system of internal control?
- a Transaction record keeping and asset custody are handled by the same employee.
- b The accounting records are audited at year-end by an external CPA.
- c At the end of the day the cash collected is compared with the tape produced by the sales-entry terminal.
- d A company's computer facility has a restricted, keycard employee entry system.

**2** Which of the following statements concerning special journals is true?
- a A company that uses special journals can split its transaction processing work load among several employees.
- b The number of postings to the general ledger is reduced.
- c A company that uses special journals has no need for a general journal.
- d Both (a) and (b) are true.

**3** The Accounts Receivable control account:
- a is found in the subsidiary ledger.
- b is found in the general ledger.
- c never appears on the balance sheet.
- d is updated daily by transactions that are posted from the sales journal.

**4** The total of the purchases journal at the end of the month is posted as:
- a a debit to Purchases and a credit to the Accounts Payable subsidiary ledger.
- b a debit to Purchases and a credit to the Accounts Payable control account.
- c a debit to the Accounts Payable subsidiary ledger and a credit to Purchases.
- d a debit to the Accounts Payable control account and a credit to Purchases.

**5** A computerized accounting system:
- a eliminates the need for internal controls.
- b is appropriate only if a company has a large, mainframe computer.
- c tends to reduce transaction processing costs in high volume situations.
- d often gives rise to a spreadsheet, which is a listing of program options available to a user.

## Summary Problem

Your friend is a candidate for an office position at PC Stores. To qualify for the job, each candidate must successfully pass an examination that covers basic accounting and bookkeeping procedures. To prepare for the upcoming ordeal, all candidates were given a copy of last year's questions. Several of these questions follow.

**1** PC Stores uses a set of journals (sales, purchases, cash receipts, cash payments, and general) to record daily activity. In which journal would the following transactions and events be found?
  a Received $600 from the sale of old equipment used in the business.
  b Purchased a $75 calculator (to be used in the office) for cash.
  c Recorded the adjusting entry for supplies consumed during the month.
  d Recorded daily cash sales of $900.
  e Acquired $400 of merchandise on account from BMI, Inc.

**2** PC Stores normally posts the total of its purchases journal on a weekly basis. To what accounts should this total be posted?

**3** Assume that a firm began operations on January 1 of the current year. Sales for the year just ended totaled $50,000, of which 30% were for cash. Credit customers paid 80% of their balances due.
  a Compute the balance in the Accounts Receivable control account at the end of the period.
  b Compute the total of all account balances in the Accounts Receivable subsidiary ledger at the end of the period.
  c Suppose that on December 29, the bookkeeper failed to record a $500 sale of merchandise on account to Alice White. Will the Accounts Receivable control account still be in agreement with the subsidiary ledger? Briefly explain.

**4** Corey Lassetter is in charge of maintaining PC's inventory records. Because of a personnel shortage, the warehouse manager would like to use Corey on a part-time basis to fill orders. Comment on the advisability of putting Corey to work in the warehouse.

**Instructions**

In an effort to be well prepared for the examination, your friend has requested help in answering last year's questions. Draft a response to each of the questions listed.

**Solution**

**1** a Cash receipts
  b Cash payments
  c General
  d Cash receipts
  e Purchases

**2** The total should be posted as a debit to Purchases and a credit to Accounts Payable.

**3** a

| | |
|---|---|
| Beginning balance, Jan. 1 | $ — |
| Add: Credit sales ($50,000 × 0.70) | 35,000 |
| | $35,000 |
| Deduct: Customer payments ($35,000 × 0.80) | 28,000 |
| Ending balance, Dec. 31 | $ 7,000 |

  b The account balances should total to $7,000.
  c Yes. A failure to record the sale means that the total posted to the Accounts Receivable control account was understated by $500. Further, the bookkeeper failed to update White's account in the subsidiary ledger. Although both the control account and subsidiary ledger are understated, their balances will still be in agreement.

**4** Corey should not be allowed to work in the warehouse. Because of his office position, Corey would have access to both the accounting records and inventory, thereby combining the record-keeping and custody functions. This combination leads to an improper separation of duties and weak internal control.

## Questions

**Q6-1** Briefly explain the meaning of internal control.

**Q6-2** In general, which accounting functions should be separated because of a lack of compatibility?

**Q6-3** What benefits are provided by an adequate separation of duties?

**Q6-4** What is the purpose behind the serial prenumbering of important documents?

**Q6-5** List several common procedures that are performed to help ensure that company accounting records are in agreement with company assets.

**Q6-6** What is the purpose of the independent review, as performed by an external CPA?

**Q6-7** What ultimate guideline should be used to decide the specific controls to build into a system?

**Q6-8** Should a company that operates solely within the United States be concerned about the Foreign Corrupt Practices Act? Why?

**Q6-9** Beach Wear is contemplating the implementation of a new accounting system that employs special journals. Can the company totally abandon its general journal, which it has used for many years? Why?

**Q6-10** Why are special journals employed in an accounting system?

**Q6-11** Explain and briefly illustrate the interrelationships between control accounts and subsidiary ledger accounts.

**Q6-12** When special journals are designed, what rule should be followed if a business has a high frequency of the same type of transaction?

**Q6-13** Perkins Company recorded and posted the following sales return in its general journal:

| Date | Accounts | Post Ref | Debit | Credit |
|---|---|---|---|---|
| May 16 | Sales Returns & Allowances | 415 | 125 | |
| | Accounts Receivable: Sue Hall | 110/ | | 125 |

Observe the posting reference column. Which items (journals, ledgers, accounts, and so on) will not be in balance with one another? Why? Briefly describe the procedure performed to detect this type of error.

**Q6-14** What are some of the similarities and differences between manual accounting systems and computerized accounting systems?

**Q6-15** Briefly list some possible uses of electronic spreadsheets.

## Exercises

**E6-1** ***Internal control weaknesses***

The Riverdale Company has just acquired a $95,000 computer to perform various accounting functions. The computer has been placed near the firm's receptionist for "showcasing" to company visitors. All of the computer's programs and files of data are stored in a central office supply closet, which is frequented daily by many employees. Numerous business forms such as blank checks and purchase orders are stored there as well. Bill Alpert is the only employee authorized to operate the computer. For amusement during lulls in the working day, Alpert purchased a program that permitted him to play several arcade-type games. He had such a good time that he gave his friends the computer's password so that they, too, could participate. Comment on any control weaknesses in Riverdale's computer operation.

**E6-2** ***Internal control weaknesses***

Multiple Charities conducts a large door-to-door fund-raising campaign each year to assist local charitable organizations. Contributions in the form of cash and checks are received by volunteer workers who, in turn, issue an official Multiple Charities' receipt. The fund-raising campaign lasts one week.

This year the officers of Theta Theta Beta fraternity have pledged the services of the entire membership to canvass the homes in Mountain Way, a small college town located approximately 100 miles from the headquarters of Multiple Charities. On Thursday afternoon of the campaign, the brothers of Theta Theta Beta ran out of official Multiple Charities' receipts. Because it was too late to obtain an additional supply, the fraternity's treasurer designed the following form and had it printed on the chapter's copying machine. The form would be given to each contributor.

***Multiple Charities***

*Date* ____________

*Contributor* ____________

*Amount Received* ____________

***Theta Theta Beta***

After dinner on Thursday, each member grabbed a handful of the forms for use in Friday's collections. Discuss this system in terms of internal control. Does the system ensure that all contributions collected by Theta Theta Beta will be submitted to Multiple Charities? Why?

**E6-3** ***Separation of duties***

An important facet of internal control is separation of duties.

a Briefly explain what is meant in accounting by "an adequate separation of duties."

b Determine whether an adequate separation of duties is present in the following cases. If the separation is adequate, label it as such. If it is inadequate, briefly state why.

(1) The warehouse foreman updates the accounting records for merchandise received.

(2) An employee who handles customer receipts also proves the equality of the balance in the Cash account with the cash balance as reported by the bank (i.e., prepares a bank reconciliation).

(3) An employee who approves customer credit also supervises the payment of supplier invoices.

**E6-4** ***Special journal selection and use***

Austin Office Supply employs the following journals:

- Sales
- Purchases
- Cash receipts
- Cash payments
- General

All journals are similar in format to those illustrated in this chapter. The following transactions and events occurred during February:

a Acquired merchandise on account from Texas Wholesalers.
b Sold merchandise to various customers for cash.
c Wrote check no. 118 in settlement of a past-due account payable.
d Acquired a new display counter on account for use in the store.
e Granted a cash refund to an irate customer for defective merchandise.
f Sold two new calculators on account to Tripro Auto Parts.
g Adjusted the Prepaid Advertising account to reflect February's advertising expense.
h Received $900 on account from Harris Enterprises, a customer.
i Returned merchandise acquired in error from Dean, Inc., Austin's chief supplier. Dean has agreed to reduce Austin's account.

Indicate the journal in which each of the preceding transactions and events would be recorded.

**E6-5** ***Operation of a special journal system***

Yum Yum Yogurt operates 10 frozen yogurt stores in Florida. The company uses special journals for sales, purchases, cash receipts, and cash payments, and a general journal. All are similar in format to those illustrated in this chapter. You have been requested to answer the following questions for an office clerk:

a In which journal would a store's daily cash sales be recorded?
b To which subsidiary ledger are the individual amounts in the purchases journal posted? How frequently should these amounts be posted?
c To which account is the total of the sales journal debited at the end of the month? To which account is the total credited?
d Where is the total of the Sundry column of the cash receipts journal posted at month-end?
e By month-end, which of the company's journals would probably contain the fewest transactions and events? Why?

**E6-6** ***Introduction to special journals***

Peartree Computing had the following credit sales during March 19X6:

| | | |
|---|---|---|
| Mar. | 6 | Sold $1,800 of computer equipment on account to Burger City. |
| | 16 | Sold $2,900 of computer equipment on account to Dave's Automotive. |
| | 24 | Sold $550 of computer equipment on account to Dallas Wallpaper. |

The March 1 balance in Accounts Receivable was $300, which arose from a sale to Dave's Automotive on February 22. There were no receipts on account from customers during February or March.

a Record Peartree's March transactions in a journal similar to that shown in Exhibit 6-2.
b Open T-accounts for Accounts Receivable (no. 110), Sales (no. 400), and the firm's customers. Post the sales journal and show how the accounts would appear as of March 31. Assume that credit sales transactions were posted from page 6 of the journal in February and page 7 in March.
c Prepare a schedule of accounts receivable as of March 31.
d What is the balance in the Accounts Receivable control account on March 31?

**E6-7** ***Special journal error***

Huntington Company uses a single-column purchases journal similar to that illustrated in this chapter. During June all transactions were recorded correctly, but the bookkeeper accidentally overadded the total purchases by $200. Assume all postings were made to the proper accounts.

a Will the trial balance remain in balance? Why?
b Will the Accounts Payable control account equal the sum of the balances in the subsidiary ledger? Why?
c If your answer to part (b) is no, is the control account or the subsidiary ledger smaller?

**E6-8** ***Overview of special journals, control accounts, and subsidiary ledgers***
Evaluate the comments that follow as being True or False. If the comment is false, briefly explain why.
a Sales of merchandise on account and for cash are recorded in the sales journal and the general journal, respectively.
b Individual transaction amounts in the purchases journal are posted on a daily basis to the Accounts Payable control account.
c The total of the sales journal is posted at the end of the month as a debit to the Accounts Receivable subsidiary ledger and a credit to Sales.
d A subsidiary ledger is nothing more than a detailed breakdown of a general ledger control account.
e The total of the Sundry column in the cash receipts journal is posted at month-end to the Sundry account in the general ledger.

**E6-9** ***Special journal/control account operation***
Summit Supply uses special journals similar to those illustrated in this chapter, along with a general journal to record miscellaneous transactions. On January 1 of the current year, the firm's Accounts Receivable and Accounts Payable control accounts revealed balances of $83,500 and $65,700, respectively.

The following information was obtained from a review of the journals on January 31:

| *Journal* | *Information* |
|---|---|
| Sales | Total transactions, $24,300 |
| Purchases | Total transactions, $19,900 |
| Cash receipts | Collections from customers on account, $23,100 |
| | Discounts taken by customers for prompt payment, $900 |
| Cash payments | Payments to suppliers on account, $30,200 |
| | Discounts taken on supplier invoices, $500 |
| General | Purchases of machinery on account, $5,700 |
| | Customer returns on account, $400 |

a Compute the balance in the Accounts Receivable control account on January 31 after all postings are made.
b Compute the balance in the Accounts Payable control account on January 31 after all postings are made. Assume that Summit uses the gross method of recording purchases.

**E6-10** ***Overview of microcomputers***
Western Art Works uses special journals. The company has grown over the years and Western is finding that the increase in volume is taxing the capacity of its system. Patricia Green, the firm's CPA, has recommended the acquisition of a microcomputer to ease the record-keeping burden.
a What benefits might Western experience by acquiring a microcomputer?
b Green told management that aside from processing daily transactions, the computer could also be used in conjunction with an electronic spreadsheet. Briefly explain what a spreadsheet is and how it can be used by managers.

# Problems

## Series A

**P6-A1** ***Internal control evaluation***

Assume that at a recent luncheon meeting, you overheard the following comments made by a group of executives sitting at the next table:

a There's no reason why a person who handles cash payments cannot also maintain the purchases journal and the Accounts Payable subsidiary ledger.

b We have many internal control procedures and can therefore overlook top management's carefree attitude and sometimes irresponsible decision making.

c The design of a perfect internal control system that detects and prevents all dishonest employee actions is really possible. Top management just won't pay for it.

d Dave handles both the Accounts Receivable *and* the Accounts Payable subsidiary ledgers.

e Every week, our store managers compare the cash collected against computer runs from the sales-entry terminal.

f We save money each year by handling the evaluation of internal control ourselves. The company's internal audit department is efficient and highly competent.

g Granted, separation of duties does help to make embezzlement more difficult. I don't believe, however, that it reduces the chance for the introduction of accidental errors when processing data.

### Instructions

Evaluate each of the preceding statements in terms of adequacy and/or understanding of internal control. If internal control is either lacking or misunderstood, briefly tell why.

**P6-A2** ***Internal control weaknesses***

The Reno Wildcats, a minor league baseball team, play at Wildcat Stadium and attract approximately 2,500 people per game. The stadium is small and antiquated, having only one entrance, one ticket booth, and no turnstiles.

All tickets are sold on the day of a game; there are no season ticket holders. Fans buy either bleacher seats for $3 or reserved seats for $4. All tickets are serially prenumbered and are sold by two cashiers located in a ticket booth outside the stadium's entrance. On entering the stadium, a fan must give a ticket to a ticket taker, who tears it in half. Half the ticket is returned to the customer to save as a rain check; the other half is tossed into a cardboard box. An exception to this procedure occurs when the Wildcats have special promotion nights (e.g., bat night). Admission for most of the attendees on these occasions is via a discount coupon in the local newspapers. In this case the coupon is shown at the ticket booth and cash is collected; however, no ticket is issued. The coupon is later surrendered and placed in the box with the ticket stubs.

The ticket operation is closed at the beginning of the fifth inning and the contents of the cardboard box are thrown in the trash. One of the cashiers (the team's bookkeeper) counts the cash, enters the game's revenues in the accounting records, and places the receipts in his desk to await deposit the next day at the bank. The bookkeeper is known for his accuracy and attention to detail. At the end of the baseball season, for example, he performs a thorough review (i.e., audit) of the team's records to ensure that all gate receipts have been properly accounted for.

### Instructions

Identify the control weaknesses in the Wildcats' system. Explain why the items cited are weaknesses.

**P6-A3** ***Understanding a special journal system***

Connor Medical Company furnishes medical supplies and equipment to local doctors and hospitals. The firm maintains a sales journal, purchases journal, cash receipts journal, cash payments journal, and a general journal. Further, the bookkeeper has established subsidiary ledgers for both accounts receivable and accounts payable.

The following transactions occurred during a recent month:

1 Sold $4,800 of medical supplies on account to Bay Hospital.
2 Received $2,100 on account from Dr. Roy Cohen.
3 Acquired $6,000 of diagnostic equipment on account from Webb Manufacturing.
4 Paid $900 of salaries to Beth Knight.
5 Borrowed $3,000 from the Society Bank.
6 Made $1,900 of cash sales to various customers.
7 Paid Webb Manufacturing for the acquisition described in (3), minus a 2% discount.
8 Received $15,000 from Al Connor as an additional investment in the business.
9 Acquired $2,700 of new office furniture on account from Office Interiors for use in the business.
10 Granted a $250 cash refund to Dr. Dan Smith for the return of defective medical supplies.

**Instructions**

Analyze the preceding transactions and determine:

A—The journal in which the transaction would be recorded.
B—Whether the transaction requires an immediate posting to a subsidiary ledger account.
C—Whether the transaction requires an immediate posting to a control account.
D—Whether the transaction requires an immediate posting to an account in the general ledger.

"Immediate" means that the posting occurs during the month as opposed to at month-end (e.g., as part of a total). Also, for items B, C, and D, if appropriate, indicate the name of the account. The first transaction is done as an example.

| | *(A) Journal* | *(B) Subsidiary Ledger Account* | *(C) Control Account* | *(D) General Ledger Account* |
|---|---|---|---|---|
| 1 | Sales | Yes, Bay Hospital | No | No |
| 2 | | | | |
| etc. | | | | |

**P6-A4** ***Detection of processing errors***

The Perez Company uses special journals to record sales, purchases, cash receipts, and cash payments. Perez also employs a general journal to record miscellaneous transactions and adjusting and closing entries. During March the following errors were made:

a A cash receipt on account from Joe Ellis was accidentally posted to Jay Elia's account in the Accounts Receivable subsidiary ledger.
b A clerk who also served as a part-time bookkeeper kept the cash received from a $100 cash sale and made no entry for the sale in the accounting records.
c The total of the purchases journal was accidentally underadded by $1,000.
d The $150 total of the Sales Discounts column in the cash receipts journal was posted to the Sales Discounts account as $1,500.
e A $600 sale on account to Jerry Avery was both entered in the sales journal and posted to Avery's account as $500.

f A cash receipt on account from Sue Cepeda was properly recorded in the cash receipts journal. The bookkeeper neglected to post the payment to Cepeda's account in the Accounts Receivable subsidiary ledger.

**Instructions**

State how each error is likely to be discovered. If discovery is unlikely, tell why.

**P6-A5** ***Special journals, transaction processing, and schedules***

Bryson Stamp and Coin began operations on May 1. A partial listing of its accounts (and account numbers) follows.

| | | | |
|---|---|---|---|
| Cash | 101 | Sales returns | 420 |
| Accounts receivable | 110 | Purchases | 510 |
| Merchandise inventory | 120 | Purchases returns | 520 |
| Prepaid insurance | 130 | Purchases discounts | 530 |
| Store equipment | 140 | Rent expense | 610 |
| Accounts payable | 210 | Salaries expense | 620 |
| Loan payable | 220 | Utilities expense | 630 |
| Ed Bryson, capital | 310 | Interest expense | 640 |
| Sales | 410 | | |

The company uses special journals to record sales, purchases, cash receipts, and cash payments, and a general journal for miscellaneous transactions and events. All journals are similar in format to those shown in this chapter.

Merchandise is purchased from wholesale distributors and agencies such as the U.S. Mint and the Postal Service. Wholesale distributors grant terms of 3/10, n/30; agencies require cash with the order. Bryson uses a periodic inventory system. The transactions for May follow.

May 1 Obtained $10,000 of financing from a $6,000 investment by Bryson and a $4,000 bank loan.
2 Purchased $6,500 of merchandise on account from the El Diego Stamp Company (invoice no. 1786 dated May 2).
3 Paid the first month's store rent of $700; issued check no. 101 to Plaza Way Shopping Center.
5 Purchased $400 of recent issues from the U.S. Postal Service; issued check no. 102.
6 Purchased a one-year inventory insurance policy from Balley Insurance. The yearly premium of $500 is due in 15 days.
8 Purchased several store counters on account from Deaton Office Equipment for $1,600.
12 Sold $250 of stamps on account to Del Aaron (invoice no. 1000).
13 Paid the balance owed to El Diego Stamp Company; issued check no. 103.
14 Cash sales for the week ended May 14 amounted to $1,050.
15 Purchased $1,700 of merchandise on account from Mar Vista Wholesalers (invoice no. 384 dated May 15).
17 Sold $450 of stamps and $150 of coins on account to Robert Barnhard (invoice no. 1001).
19 Issued check no. 104 to Balley Insurance in payment of the insurance policy purchased on May 6.
20 Because of a purchasing error, Bryson returned $300 of the merchandise acquired on May 15 from Mar Vista Wholesalers.
21 Received the amount due from Del Aaron.
21 Cash sales for the week ended May 21 amounted to $1,450.
22 Robert Barnhard returned $50 of stamps purchased on May 17. He also paid his remaining balance.

23 Paid the amount due to Mar Vista Wholesalers; issued check no. 105.
25 Paid $120 to California Edison for utilities; issued check no. 106.
28 Cash sales for the week ended May 28 amounted to $1,100.
29 Purchased $1,500 of merchandise on account from El Diego Stamp Company (invoice no. 1804 dated May 29).
30 Paid the first installment due on the May 1 loan. Issued check no. 107 to American Trust for $400, of which $80 is interest.
31 Paid Deaton Office Equipment for the purchase of May 8; issued check no. 108.
31 Sold $900 of coins on account to Wilbur Burns (invoice no. 1002).

**Instructions**

a Record the transactions in the correct journals. Post the proper individual amounts and general journal entries daily; at the end of the month post the appropriate totals.
b Prepare a trial balance of the general ledger accounts, a schedule of accounts receivable, and a schedule of accounts payable.

**P6-A6** ***Special journals, transaction processing, and schedules***
Midtown Camera Distributors is a small proprietorship located in South Carolina. A recent review of the accounting records disclosed that Evertson Photo owes the firm $2,600 from a purchase of merchandise on November 28. Further, Midtown owes $3,700 to Tokyo Camera Works (a supplier) for a transaction on November 29. All credit sales and merchandise acquisitions are subject to terms of 2/10, n/30. The following transactions took place during December:

Dec. 2 Received a $5,000 cash investment from the owner, Diane Pettit.
3 Sold $500 of merchandise on account to Duke's Camera Shop (invoice no. 642).
5 Purchased $2,900 of merchandise on account from Polaroid Corporation (invoice no. 6847 dated December 5).
6 Paid the proper amount due Tokyo Camera Works for the purchase on November 29; issued check no. 4305.
7 Cash sales for the week amounted to $2,330.
9 Issued check no. 4306 for $520 to Smith and Son Printers for brochures to be used in January's advertising program.
12 Duke's Camera Shop paid the proper amount due in settlement of its account balance.
14 Cash sales for the week totaled $3,230.
14 Issued check no. 4307 to Polaroid Corporation in payment of the purchase on December 5.
15 Issued check no. 4308 to Susan Woodard in payment of her $1,800 salary.
17 Sold $2,200 of cameras and $650 of accessories on account to Dave's Studio (invoice no. 643).
19 Received $225 for consulting services rendered to a suburban newspaper's photography staff.
21 Cash sales for the week amounted to $1,120.
22 Sold a $580 camera on account to Hawthorne Photo Supply (invoice no. 644).
23 Purchased $1,950 of merchandise on account from Tokyo Camera Works (invoice no. 8041 dated December 23).
24 Hawthorne Photo Supply returned the camera purchased on December 22 and its account was adjusted.
24 Paid $85 for utilities to South Carolina Power and Light; issued check no. 4309.

26 Received a $50 check from Smith and Son Printers. An accompanying note stated that Midtown's bill for the printing job on December 9 had been computed incorrectly.

28 Sold a $620 camera on account to Hay Photography (invoice no. 645).

29 Cash sales for the week totaled $910.

30 Purchased a used delivery van from Savings National for $6,000; paid $2,000 down and secured a short-term loan for the remaining balance. Issued check no. 4310.

Midtown employs single-column sales and purchases journals and multicolumn cash receipts and payments journals similar to those illustrated in this chapter. In addition, a general journal is used for miscellaneous transactions. The general ledger revealed the following balances on November 30:

| | | | |
|---|---|---|---|
| Cash (110) | $ 14,700 | Sales discounts (420) | $ 2,200 |
| Accounts receivable (120) | 2,600 | Sales returns (430) | 3,700 |
| Inventory (130) | 56,700 | Miscellaneous revenue (450) | — |
| Prepaid advertising (140) | 1,600 | Purchases (510) | 98,500 |
| Delivery van (150) | — | Purchases discounts (520) | 1,600 |
| Accounts payable (210) | 3,700 | Wage expense (530) | 24,400 |
| Loan payable (220) | — | Travel expense (540) | 3,200 |
| Diane Pettit, capital (310) | 85,300 | Rent expense (550) | 11,500 |
| Diane Pettit, drawing (320) | 15,000 | Utilities expense (560) | 3,100 |
| Sales (410) | 146,600 | | |

**Instructions**

a Open Midtown's accounts in the general ledger and the Accounts Receivable and Accounts Payable subsidiary ledgers. *Note:* This step is not necessary if you are using the preprinted working papers that accompany the text.

b Record the December transactions in the correct journals. Post the proper individual amounts and general journal entries daily; at the end of the month post the appropriate totals. All terms of sale are strictly followed.

c Prepare a trial balance of the general ledger accounts, a schedule of accounts receivable, and a schedule of accounts payable as of December 31.

## Series B

**P6-B1** ***Internal control evaluation***

Assume that at a recent luncheon meeting, you overheard the following comments made by a group of executives sitting at the next table. From the tone of the conversation you have determined that the executives are directors of the Drake County Stadium.

a The staff person who handles the Accounts Payable subsidiary ledger also maintains the cash payments journal.

b Our recent cost-cutting moves have improved profitability. Patrons now pay the appropriate amounts to the cashier, who grants direct entry into the stadium. The elimination of ticket takers (and tickets) has led to reduced lines and faster admittance.

c Personally, I don't agree with the county's policy of having Coopers and Young, the local CPA firm, perform an annual review of our accounting procedures. Susan Randolph at the county office has been helping us for years; she thoroughly knows and understands our system and operating problems.

d Michael Dalby, our treasurer, has just been given new responsibilities. He now handles and deposits cash receipts, issues checks, and maintains the cash payments journal.

e It is essential that our new data processing system provide for an adequate audit trail (i.e., the ability to trace and access accounting information). Although the benefits of doing so are marginal at best, we will be in compliance with the provisions of the Drake County systems handbook.

f Office employees should continue to initial the important documents and contracts that they have reviewed, prior to submission to the accounting and legal departments.

g To further consolidate operations, we should combine the positions of supplies receiving clerk and supplies accounting clerk. Greater efficiency should result.

**Instructions**

Evaluate each of the preceding statements in terms of adequacy and/or understanding of internal control. If internal control is either lacking or misunderstood, briefly tell why.

**P6-B2** ***Internal control weaknesses***

The Whitehall Company, a small distributor of dental products, has been in business for four months. The firm's accounting system was designed by Buck Whitehall, the owner, and operates in the following manner. All sales are made on account. Each morning, sales invoices are typed, recorded in the sales journal, and posted to the Accounts Receivable subsidiary ledger by Betty Clark. Clark has been with Whitehall since the company opened. She had several courses in high school bookkeeping and is presently working to earn money for her college education. Because the company is new and has a relatively low sales volume, Betty serves as a general secretary and receptionist for the majority of the day. Between greeting customers and answering the phone, Betty opens the mail, which often contains customer payments on account. Because of the long distance to the bank, she accumulates the payments during the week and hides them in an envelope buried at the bottom of a desk drawer. Betty carefully records these transactions in the journal and updates customers' accounts in the subsidiary ledger.

At the end of each month Betty prepares a schedule of accounts receivable so that Whitehall can follow up on slow-paying accounts. In addition, she bills customers and performs a bank reconciliation. The bank reconciliation compares the firm's general ledger cash balance with the cash balance as reported by the bank.

Whitehall is very pleased with Clark's performance. Betty is quiet and efficient and has not missed a day of work since the company opened. Betty, too, is quite pleased. On her $300 weekly salary she has been able to open a savings account for her education, rent a very nice apartment, and make a substantial down payment on a Nissan 300ZX.

**Instructions**

Identify the internal control weaknesses in Whitehall's system. Explain why the items cited are weaknesses.

**P6-B3** ***Understanding a special journal system***

Reese Athletics Company furnishes athletic supplies and equipment to local retailers and schools. The firm maintains a sales journal, purchases journal, cash receipts journal, cash payments journal, and a general journal. Further, the bookkeeper has established subsidiary ledgers for both accounts receivable and accounts payable.

The following transactions occurred during a recent month:

1 Sold $2,600 of athletic supplies on account to Plano High School.

2 Processed a $5,000 cash withdrawal from the business for Vicki Reese, the owner.

3 Paid $6,800 on account to Wilson Sporting Goods, a supplier. The discount period had lapsed.

4 Acquired $9,800 of merchandise on account from NIKE, Inc.

5 Received $4,500 on account, net of the proper discount, from the Lakeside School District.

6 Paid $2,000 to acquire inventory at a competitor's going-out-of-business sale.
7 Acquired $2,900 of computing equipment on account from Dr. Computer for use in the business.
8 Returned $800 of defective merchandise acquired on account from Ball Four. Ball Four has agreed to reduce Reese's account.
9 Paid P&T Management $1,500 for the month's rent.
10 Made $3,700 of cash sales to various customers.

**Instructions**

Analyze the preceding transactions and determine:

A—The journal in which the transaction would be recorded.
B—Whether the transaction requires an immediate posting to a subsidiary ledger account.
C—Whether the transaction requires an immediate posting to a control account.
D—Whether the transaction requires an immediate posting to an account in the general ledger.

"Immediate" means that the posting occurs during the month as opposed to at month-end (e.g., as part of a total). Also, for items B, C, and D, if appropriate, indicate the name of the account. The first transaction is done as an example.

| | *(A) Journal* | *(B) Subsidiary Ledger Account* | *(C) Control Account* | *(D) General Ledger Account* |
|---|---|---|---|---|
| 1 | Sales | Yes, Plano High | No | No |
| 2 | | | | |
| etc. | | | | |

**P6-B4** ***Detection of processing errors***

The Hartman Company uses special journals to record sales, purchases, cash receipts, and cash payments. Hartman also employs a general journal to record miscellaneous transactions and adjusting and closing entries. During August the following errors were made:

a The correct total of the single-column sales journal, $7,510, was posted to the Sales account in the general ledger as $5,710. The debit to Accounts Receivable was posted correctly.
b The total of the single-column sales journal was accidentally overadded by $10.
c A cash receipt on account from Norman Dresser was entered in the general journal.
d A sale on account to Bob Smith was accidentally posted to Bill Smith's account in the Accounts Receivable subsidiary ledger.
e A purchase of merchandise on account from Modern Equipment Sales was not entered in the accounting records.
f A cash payment on account to Hardware Wholesalers was properly recorded in the cash payments journal. The bookkeeper neglected to post the disbursement to Hardware Wholesalers' account in the Accounts Payable subsidiary ledger.

**Instructions**

State how each error is likely to be discovered. If discovery is unlikely, tell why.

**P6-B5** ***Special journals, transaction processing, and schedules***

Casual Wear began business on July 1. Selected accounts (and account numbers) follow.

| Account | No. | Account | No. |
|---|---|---|---|
| Cash | 100 | Sales returns | 401 |
| Accounts receivable | 110 | Purchases | 510 |
| Merchandise inventory | 120 | Purchases returns | 511 |
| Prepaid advertising | 130 | Purchases discounts | 512 |
| Office equipment | 140 | Rent expense | 610 |
| Accounts payable | 200 | Salaries expense | 620 |
| Loan payable | 210 | Utilities expense | 630 |
| Tina Sharp, capital | 300 | Interest expense | 640 |
| Sales | 400 | | |

The company uses special journals for sales, purchases, cash receipts, and cash payments, and a general journal to record miscellaneous transactions and events. The journals are similar in format to those illustrated in this chapter.

All merchandise is purchased on account, subject to terms of 2/10, n/30. Casual Wear uses a periodic inventory system. The transactions of July follow.

July 1 Secured $30,000 of financing from a $20,000 investment by the owner and a $10,000 bank loan.
1 Paid the first month's rent to Vantage Management; issued check no. 100 for $1,600.
2 Purchased $13,000 of merchandise on account from Jeans, Inc. (invoice no. 4421 dated July 2).
3 Purchased $3,000 of office equipment on account from Bronco Office Supply.
3 Paid $800 for five months of advertising in *Clothing Weekly;* issued check no. 101.
5 Sold $7,000 of goods on account to the Denver Woman (invoice no. 2000)
7 Purchased $9,500 of merchandise on account from New York Fashions (invoice no. 2487 dated July 7).
10 Paid the balance owed to Jeans, Inc.; issued check no. 102.
11 Returned $900 of the merchandise purchased on July 7 from New York Fashions.
13 Sold $3,700 of goods on account to Nan's (invoice no. 2001).
14 Cash sales for the week ended July 14 amounted to $1,230.
15 Paid the amount owed to Bronco Office Supply; issued check no. 103.
16 Paid the proper amount owed to New York Fashions from the transactions of July 7 and July 11; issued check no. 104.
19 Purchased $6,600 of goods on account from Seaside Creations (invoice no. 1824 dated July 19).
21 Cash sales for the week ended July 21 amounted to $2,300.
24 Paid $520 to Colorado Light & Power for July utilities; issued check no. 105.
26 Sold $5,800 of goods on account to the Wild One (invoice no. 2002).
27 Received the amount due from the Denver Woman.
28 Cash sales for the week ended July 28 amounted to $1,300.
29 Accepted a $600 return of goods on account from the Wild One. The goods were shipped in error on July 26.
29 Paid salaries of $3,300; issued check no. 106.
30 Obtained a $500 cash refund from Bronco Office Supply for the return of unneeded office equipment that was acquired on July 3.
31 Paid the first installment on the July 1 loan. Issued check no. 107 to Mountain Trust for $700, of which $150 is interest.

**Instructions**

a Record the transactions in the correct journals. Post the proper individual amounts and general journal entries daily; at the end of the month post the appropriate totals.

b Prepare a trial balance of the general ledger accounts, a schedule of accounts receivable, and a schedule of accounts payable.

**P6-B6** ***Special journals, transaction processing, and schedules***

The Wheeling Appliance Company is a small appliance store whose fiscal year runs from July 1 through June 30. Credit sales and merchandise purchases are subject to terms of 2/10, n/30. The general ledger contained the following balances on May 31 (account numbers appear in parentheses):

| | | | |
|---|---|---|---|
| Cash (101) | $ 6,000 | Sales returns (403) | $ 1,000 |
| Accounts receivable (110) | 1,100 | Miscellaneous revenue (450) | — |
| Inventory (120) | 22,000 | Purchases (501) | 46,200 |
| Prepaid insurance (130) | 160 | Purchases discounts (502) | 500 |
| Accounts payable (201) | 1,300 | Salaries expense (510) | 18,900 |
| Mike Ryan, capital (301) | 39,000 | Advertising expense (520) | 440 |
| Mike Ryan, drawing (302) | 12,600 | Utilities expense (530) | 400 |
| Sales (401) | 73,500 | Rent expense (540) | 4,700 |
| Sales discounts (402) | 800 | | |

The Accounts Receivable subsidiary ledger showed that Hal Jamison, a builder, purchased $1,100 of appliances on May 28. The Accounts Payable ledger revealed that Wheeling owes $1,300 to Metro Distributors for a purchase on May 27. The following transactions took place during June:

| | | |
|---|---|---|
| June | 2 | Sold an $800 television on account to Starbright TV (invoice no. 548). |
| | 3 | Hal Jamison paid the proper amount due in settlement of his account balance. |
| | 4 | Paid the proper amount due to Metro Distributors for the purchase on May 27; issued check no. 1252. |
| | 7 | Purchased $3,000 of merchandise on account from Vista Distribution Corporation (invoice no. 4706 dated June 7). |
| | 7 | Cash sales for the week amounted to $1,500. |
| | 10 | Starbright TV paid the proper amount due in settlement of its account balance. |
| | 10 | Issued check no. 1253 for $400 to Midtown Printers for brochures announcing Wheeling's June sale. |
| | 14 | Cash sales for the week totaled $1,000. |
| | 14 | Issued check no. 1254 to Vista Distribution Corporation in payment of the purchase on June 7. |
| | 15 | Issued check no. 1255 to Butch Graybark in payment of his $1,300 salary. |
| | 18 | Received $175 for consulting services rendered to the builder of a new apartment complex. |
| | 20 | Sold a $400 television and a $200 dryer on account to Walt's Home Center (invoice no. 549). |
| | 21 | Sold a $400 washing machine on account to Ken Perry (invoice no. 550). |
| | 21 | Cash sales for the week amounted to $600. |
| | 24 | Purchased $800 of appliances on account from Metro Distributors (invoice no. 1555 dated June 23). |
| | 24 | Ken Perry returned the washing machine purchased on June 21 and his account was adjusted. |

24 Paid $500 to Atlas Insurance for an insurance policy covering the next fiscal year; issued check no. 1256.
25 Received a $60 check from Midtown Printers. An accompanying note stated that Wheeling's bill for the printing job on June 10 had been computed incorrectly.
26 Sold a $600 television on account to Maxwell Stereo and TV (invoice no. 551).
28 Cash sales for the week amounted to $1,000.

Wheeling employs sales, purchases, cash receipts, and cash payments journals similar to those illustrated in this chapter. In addition, a general journal is used for miscellaneous transactions.

**Instructions**

a Open Wheeling's accounts in the general ledger and the Accounts Receivable and Accounts Payable subsidiary ledgers. *Note:* This step is not necessary if you are using the preprinted working papers that accompany the text.
b Record the transactions in the correct journals. Post the proper individual amounts and general journal entries daily; at the end of the month post the appropriate totals. All terms of sale are strictly followed.
c Prepare a trial balance of the general ledger accounts, a schedule of accounts receivable, and a schedule of accounts payable as of June 30.

## Beyond the Basics

**BB6-1** ***Understanding a special journal system***
London Club uses special journals to record sales, purchases, cash receipts, and cash payments, and a general journal for miscellaneous transactions and events. All journals are similar in format to those shown in this chapter. The company has experienced bad luck in recent months by hiring two incompetent bookkeepers in succession. London Club's office manager has therefore constructed the following examination problem, to be used as a screening device in the hiring process.

Review the accompanying data of a hypothetical business:

| Accounts Receivable | | | | | Account No. 110 |
|---|---|---|---|---|---|
| Date | Explanation | Post Ref | Debit | Credit | Balance |
| 19X2 | | | | | |
| May 1 | Balance | | | | 10,500 |
| 12 | | J4 | | 700 | 9,800 |
| 31 | | S9 | 23,800 | | 33,600 |
| 31 | | CR11 | | 26,400 | 7,200 |

| Ricki Jeffcote (a customer) | | | | | |
|---|---|---|---|---|---|
| Date | Explanation | Post Ref | Debit | Credit | Balance |
| 19X2 | | | | | |
| May 1 | Balance | | | | 2,300 |
| 4 | | S9 | 500 | | 2,800 |
| 10 | | CR11 | | 1,600 | 1,200 |
| 12 | | J4 | | 700 | 500 |
| 21 | | S9 | 900 | | 1,400 |

Column totals from the May cash receipts journal:

| | |
|---|---|
| Cash debit | $66,000 |
| Sales discounts debit | 300 |
| Accounts receivable credit | 26,400 |
| Sales credit | 15,900 |
| Sundry credit | 24,000* |

* Consists of credits to Laura Fields, Capital, and Loans Payable for $14,000 and $10,000, respectively.

All transactions have been recorded correctly, and there are no errors in postings or posting references. Consider the statements that follow:

_____ a Ricki Jeffcote purchased $1,400 of merchandise on account in May.
_____ b Credit sales for the month totaled $25,200 ($23,800 + $500 + $900).
_____ c Cash received from customers on account amounted to $26,400.
_____ d The schedule of accounts receivable will reveal that customers (other than Jeffcote) owe $5,800 as of May 31.
_____ e Tony Stockton, a customer, returned $300 of merchandise on May 28.
_____ f Credits of $24,000 were posted to the Sundry account in the general ledger during May.
_____ g The May 31 balance sheet will reveal $7,200 of Accounts Receivable; the income statement for May should disclose total (i.e., gross) sales of $39,700.

**Instructions**

As a candidate for the bookkeeping position at London Club, you are to respond to the preceding statements by using a code of T—True, F—False, or N—Not enough information to answer. For those statements that are answered F or N, present a brief explanation of the rationale behind your response.

**BB6-2** ***Accounting systems design***

Big Valley Electronics is an aggressive retailer of electronic equipment. The company sells four general categories of merchandise: televisions, radios, stereo equipment, and video cassette recorders. Seventy percent of Big Valley's sales are for cash; the remainder are on account, with no sales discounts offered. Because of the amount of bookkeeping required, management makes no attempt to divide revenues (and figure profitability) by product line.

All purchases of merchandise are on account, with most payments being made within the discount period offered by suppliers. Big Valley has only a few purchases returns each year, but a large number of sales returns. The company uses a manual accounting system.

**Instructions**

a What journals would you expect to find in use at Big Valley?
b What column headings are you likely to encounter in each of the journals cited in part (a)?
c What subsidiary ledgers would you expect to find in use at Big Valley?
d The company is considering the conversion of its manual system to an in-house microcomputer system. To assist management in its evaluation process, prepare a list of factors that should be considered before a decision is made.

## Answers to Chapter Quiz

**1** a
**2** d
**3** b
**4** b
**5** c

# Cash and Short-Term Investments

CHAPTER 7

## Learning Objectives

After reading this chapter you should:

**1** Understand the composition of cash and how cash is presented on a balance sheet.

**2** Understand cash management and be familiar with controls and procedures related to cash receipts and disbursements.

**3** Be able to reconcile a bank account.

**4** Be familiar with the operation of a petty cash system.

**5** Be familiar with the operation of a voucher system.

**6** Understand the proper accounting treatments for short-term investments, including the lower-of-cost-or-market method.

Financial statements provide a variety of information for decision making. The balance sheet, for example, discloses important relationships between the resources owned by a business and the amounts owed to creditors. Two balance sheet accounts of key interest to a number of parties are *cash* and *short-term investments.*

Cash and short-term investments are the most liquid of the current assets. Lenders, creditors, and prospective suppliers therefore study the amounts of these assets in comparison with current liabilities when judging a firm's debt-paying ability. Investors review the cash and short-term investments of a business to gauge the funds available for dividend distributions as well as for medium- and long-term projects that are important to future profitability. Even employees are interested in cash and short-term investments, because salary increases are sometimes tied to the funds available and the balances in these two accounts. It is imperative, then, that cash and short-term investments be properly accounted for and presented in the financial statements.

## Cash

**OBJECTIVE 1**
**Understand the composition of cash and how cash is presented on a balance sheet.**

The items reported in the Cash account on the balance sheet must be (1) acceptable to a bank for deposit and (2) free from restriction for use in satisfying current debts. **Cash** therefore includes *coins, currency, funds on deposit with a bank (checking accounts and savings accounts), checks, and money orders.* The following items are not considered to be cash for accounting purposes: certificates of deposit, postdated checks, IOUs, travel advances, and postage stamps.

1 *Certificates of deposit*—Sometimes called CDs, these are securities issued by banks that allow the investment of cash for short periods of time (six months, one year, and so forth). CDs pay a guaranteed interest rate and often contain penalty provisions should the purchaser decide to convert the securities to cash before their due date. Certificates of deposit are not considered to be cash but instead are classified as short-term investments.

2 *Postdated checks*—Postdated checks are checks that become payable on a date subsequent to the issue date. For example, suppose Buck Company issued a check to Foy Company on April 15. Buck dated the check April 22, because it lacked sufficient funds on the date of issuance. Since Foy cannot cash or deposit the check until the 22nd, the postdated check is not classified as cash. Postdated checks are receivables until the date they can be deposited.

3 *IOUs*—IOUs are written acknowledgments of debts; these items are not negotiable and usually cannot be used to pay off liabilities. IOUs are therefore considered to be receivables until the time of collection.

4 *Travel advances*—These amounts have been given to employees to cover out-of-pocket expenses incurred on business trips. The employees must either provide receipts for monies spent or return any unspent funds. As a result, travel advances are normally disclosed as receivables on the balance sheet.

5 *Postage stamps*—Postage stamps are usually classified as supplies or prepaid expenses.

### Balance Sheet Presentation

The Cash account is listed on the balance sheet in the current asset section. For concise reporting, all cash items are normally combined and presented as a single figure.

As we noted earlier, the amount reported for cash must be available for use in satisfying current debts. Sometimes, businesses establish restricted funds to accumulate cash for specific purposes. As an example, a special fund may be established to repay money borrowed (often termed a *sinking fund*) or to expand a manufacturing plant. These funds should not be classified as current assets on the balance sheet because they are not available to settle current obligations. Likewise, amounts held in foreign banks should not be reported as current assets if governmental regulations restrict the transfer of funds out of the foreign country.

During the past few years, some banks have required that a portion of any amount lent to customers remain on deposit in the bank for the duration of the loan period. These required deposits are termed **compensating balances.** The existence of compensating balances should be fully disclosed so that financial statement users are made aware of restrictions on funds availability.

## Cash Management

OBJECTIVE 2
**Understand cash management and be familiar with controls and procedures related to cash receipts and disbursements.**

Effective cash management is important to the success of any company. Care must be taken to ensure that sufficient cash is available to meet current obligations but that unnecessarily large cash balances do not remain in checking accounts. Such balances typically earn little or no interest and therefore represent a loss of earnings potential. In view of this situation, excess funds should be invested in short-term securities to earn higher rates of return or be used for new programs and projects.

The amount of cash necessary to meet current obligations varies among businesses. Consider the information that appeared in recent financial statements of Caesars World, The Toro Company, and Ralston Purina, as presented in Exhibit 7-1.

Caesars World's major line of business is the operation of gaming casinos and resorts, requiring significant cash balances to support daily activities. This situation is reflected by the fact that cash and short-term investments (i.e., securities easily converted into cash should the need arise) constitute in excess of 67% of total current assets. For The Toro Company and Ralston Purina it is an entirely different story. These firms stock inventories for production and sale and must carry large amounts of customer receivables. As a result, both these companies have lower cash balances as a percentage of total current assets and also a lower percentage of short-term investments.

**Exhibit 7-1**
**Current Asset Composition of Caesars World, The Toro Company, and Ralston Purina (in thousands)**

| | *Caesars World* | | *The Toro Company* | | *Ralston Purina* | |
|---|---|---|---|---|---|---|
| | *$* | *%** | *$* | *%** | *$* | *%** |
| Cash | $ 26,581 | 9.4% | $ 11,954 | 6.5% | $ 23,800 | 1.4% |
| Short-term investments | 165,157 | 58.3 | — | — | 337,100 | 19.9 |
| Receivables | 53,962 | 19.1 | 63,998 | 34.9 | 526,900 | 31.1 |
| Inventories | 9,491 | 3.4 | 99,337 | 54.2 | 559,900 | 33.0 |
| Prepaid expenses & other | 27,860 | 9.8 | 8,110 | 4.4 | 246,800 | 14.6 |
| | $283,051 | 100.0% | $183,399 | 100.0% | $1,694,500 | 100.0% |

* Percentages calculated by the authors.

HIGHLIGHT

# Borrowing Less and Investing More

Accelerate the inflows and delay the outflows. These are the keys to effective cash management. At the most basic level, virtually all businesses are involved with converting customer orders into cash in the bank. Glitches can occur at any point in the process; but the firm that bills promptly, collects aggressively, and makes maximum use of other people's money comes out ahead. This is an economic fact of life. [1]

An increasing number of companies use cash management procedures to reduce necessary borrowings and increase the amount of funds available for investment. Some of these procedures are basic, such as careful granting of credit and the use of cash discounts. Others are not and are possible only through the use of high-tech computer wizardry.

For instance, some companies that operate on an international basis constantly move money electronically from bank to bank and from country to country. This practice allows the transfer of surplus funds from one division to another where, perhaps, money can be invested at higher rates. Or perhaps the funds may be allocated to cash-poor business units, thereby reducing overall company borrowing costs. Such practices may be very beneficial. As one treasurer puts it, "Idle balances are extremely expensive. For instance, in Spain [interest] rates have been as high as 25%. Since our goal is to raise financing at the lowest cost, the easiest method to do this is just to use our own funds better." Money transfer practices would also be very helpful in Argentina, where borrowing rates recently averaged a staggering 330% per year! [2]

Another technique involves the use of a controlled disbursements account. Such a system monitors check clearances and notifies a firm of the dollar volume of checks that are expected to clear specific banks on any given day, at any given hour. Money to cover the checks is then forwarded from the firm's main bank, allowing businesses to keep their money invested until the very last minute to yield maximum returns. [3]

Becoming a bit more basic, many companies simply study mail delivery patterns and take advantage of those patterns when sending out checks. The U.S. Postal Service moves mail more efficiently to some areas than to others. By comparing postmark dates and receipt dates on incoming mail, an entity may find that it is able to cover checks later for some destinations than for others, even if mailing dates are identical.

Further, companies can use geographically dispersed bank accounts to maximize the so-called bank float (i.e., the period of time it takes for checks to travel through the Federal Reserve System's clearinghouse function). Thus, checks to a New Jersey supplier may be written by using a California bank account, and vice versa. The use of multiple accounts in different parts of the country may prove quite beneficial, letting businesses use their hard-earned funds for longer periods of time. Be aware, however, that various pilot programs in the banking system are presently aiming to reduce check clearance time.

Other simple techniques include not paying any bills early—not by a day, not by an hour. Liability due dates may be switched, with insurance premiums being paid at the end of the quarter instead of monthly, payroll being disbursed semimonthly instead of weekly, and so forth. [4] By doing so, companies can stretch their dollars and promote effective cash management practices, which often spell the difference between business success or ultimate failure.

SOURCES: Adapted from "Managing Your Company's Cash," *Nation's Business*, November, 1986, pp. 52–54 [1, 4]; "Managing Your Cash Around the World," *Management Review*, June, 1986, pp. 32–36 [2]; and "Making the Most of the Cash on Hand," *Business Week*, November 3, 1986, pp. 112–113 [3]. The first article is reprinted by permission of *Nation's Business*, November, 1986. 

## Cash Planning

The management of cash is subdivided into cash planning and cash control. **Cash planning systems** consist of those procedures adopted to ensure that adequate funds are available to meet normal business obligations and that any excess cash is invested. A major component of cash planning systems is the **cash budget**—an overall plan of activity that depicts cash inflows and outflows for a stated period of time. The cash budget is a very useful tool in the management of any organization, because it pinpoints when cash surpluses and shortages will occur. Predicting surpluses and shortages before they take place enables a business to analyze potential high-return investments and low-cost sources of funds and thereby improve investment and financing decisions.

## Cash Control

**Cash control systems** are the procedures adopted to safeguard an organization's funds. These systems establish adequate internal control over cash. Recall that internal control aids a company in safeguarding its assets, checking the reliability and accuracy of accounting information, promoting operational efficiency, and encouraging adherence to prescribed managerial policies. A strong cash control system is essential, because employees and others regard cash as a very desirable asset. In addition, cash is difficult to trace because it has no readily identifiable means to establish ownership. Although currency does have serial numbers, companies make no attempt to record these numbers in view of the overwhelming amount of bookkeeping that would be required.

***Internal Control for Cash*** The internal control system for cash is based on the general internal control features discussed in Chapter 6. An organization should limit the access to cash to a few authorized personnel only. Furthermore, incompatible duties such as the authorization of cash transactions, the entry of cash transactions in the accounting records, and the custody of cash should be separated. Finally, the following accountability procedures should be implemented: prenumbered checks, verification of invoices prior to payment, and verification of the cash balance as reported in the general ledger. These general control features become apparent when studying typical accounting procedures for cash receipts and cash disbursements.

***Receipts from Cash Sales*** The control of cash receipts attempts to ensure that all cash inflows are safeguarded from the time they are received by a company until the time of deposit in a bank account. A major source of cash inflows for many firms is cash sales. Control over cash sales is facilitated by the use of a cash register or a point-of-sale terminal (i.e., an electronic data entry station that is linked to a computer). Such devices require a salesperson to record each sale in full view of the customer and to provide the customer with a receipt. As the clerk enters the transaction information, the sale is simultaneously recorded on a paper tape. At the end of the business day a store manager compares the cash collected with the total cash sales listed on the tape. The tapes are then forwarded to the accounting department and entered in the company records. The cash is kept in a vault until deposited in the bank or picked up by an armored car service such as Brink's or Loomis.

Cash sale transactions often give rise to errors. Upon conclusion of business activity, for example, the actual cash on hand may differ slightly from the total indicated sales. If these errors are frequent, significant in amount, or traceable to the same employee, personnel adjustments may be necessary.

The accounting treatment for cash excesses and deficiencies is relatively simple. To illustrate, assume that cash sales for the Eldridge Shop on July 7 amounted to $1,247. However, cash in the register was only $1,237. The following entry is necessary:

| | | |
|---|---|---|
| Cash | 1,237 | |
| Cash Short & Over | 10 | |
| Sales | | 1,247 |
| To record cash sales and cash shortage | | |

In contrast to the preceding entry, the Cash Short & Over account would be credited when cash in the register exceeds the amount of cash sales. At the end of a reporting period, the net balance in Cash Short & Over is calculated. A net debit balance would be disclosed on the income statement with other miscellaneous expenses of the business, while a net credit balance is treated as miscellaneous revenue.

***Receipts from Customers on Account*** Many organizations generate large inflows of cash from customer payments on account. These inflows usually arrive in the mail, requiring a careful separation of duties. The following procedures are normally employed:

**1** The daily counting of cash receipts is assigned to one person or, in large businesses, to a group of specific personnel. The personnel open the mail, prepare a list of checks received, and forward the list to the accounting department.

**2** The checks are forwarded to a cashier, who prepares a deposit slip and deposits all receipts intact on a *daily* basis. Daily deposits prevent bills from being paid out of current receipts; they also minimize the amount of cash left on the premises at the end of the business day, thus reducing the possibility of large losses from theft. A duplicate deposit slip is then sent to the accounting department.

**3** The accounting department compares the list of cash receipts with the deposit slip and enters the daily mail-in receipts in the accounting records. Naturally, any discrepancies between the deposit slip and the list of receipts require investigation.

***Cash Disbursements*** The control over disbursements includes procedures that will allow only authorized payments for actual company expenditures. A cash disbursements system with proper internal control should include the following features:

**1** All significant disbursements are made by check so that a record (i.e., written evidence) exists for expenditures.

**2** Periodic comparisons are made of an organization's Cash account in the general ledger with the cash balance as reported by the bank.

**3** Certain small payments are made by using a *petty cash system.* (The operation of a petty cash system will be explained later in this chapter.)

**4** Before a disbursement is made from a company's checking account or petty cash system, the expenditure is verified and approved. Verification may take the form of examining purchase orders, invoices, and receiving reports.

These procedures, like so many others, are aided by a proper separation of duties. For example, the person signing the checks should not be the same individual who prepares the checks. In addition, the comparison of a company's general ledger cash balance with the cash balance as reported by the bank (record-keeping function) should not be performed by an employee who handles cash (custody function). Separation of duties helps in the detection of errors and also makes theft or fraud more difficult.

## Bank Reconciliations

As previously noted, adequate internal control requires the use of checks for significant cash payments. Canceled checks and their endorsements furnish written evidence that payments have been made. In addition, checking accounts provide security and safety for the large cash balances that many businesses must carry.

As you can well imagine, a company will have many cash receipts and disbursements during a given accounting period. Because of the high frequency of transactions and the potential for error, it is necessary to periodically examine the accuracy of the cash balance in the general ledger (or your checkbook). This process, called a **bank reconciliation,** is based on the Cash account and a document called a **bank statement.**

**OBJECTIVE 3**
**Be able to reconcile a bank account.**

***Bank Statements Versus Cash Accounts*** Businesses and individuals receive monthly bank statements for every checking account they maintain. An example of a bank statement appears in Exhibit 7-2. Bank statements summarize the activity in a checking account and report the ending monthly balance. It is important to understand that although the Cash account of a depositor (such as Johnson Manufacturing) is an asset, the depositor's account is carried on the bank's records as a *liability.* Consequently, checks and other debits by the bank *reduce* Johnson's account, while deposits and other credits *increase* the account.

At the end of a month the bank statement cash balance and the company's cash records will normally not agree. A major reason for this discrepancy is the timing differences associated with the use of a checking account. Timing differences result in an item being recorded on the depositor's books or the bank's books, but not both, in a given accounting period. Some of these timing differences arise from the operations of the Postal Service and the Federal Reserve System, as noted in the highlight on page 240.

Common examples of timing differences include the following:

1. Items reflected on company records but not yet reported on the bank statement, such as:
   a. **Deposits in transit**—receipts entered in a firm's accounts but not yet processed by the bank. This situation often occurs when deposits are mailed. Deposits in transit are determined by comparing deposits that appear on the bank statement with deposits as reported in an organization's Cash account.
   b. **Outstanding checks**—checks written but not yet processed by the bank. Outstanding checks are determined by comparing checks reported on the bank statement against checks written on the company's records.
2. Items reported on the bank statement but not yet entered in company records, such as:
   a. **Nonsufficient funds (NSF) checks**—customer checks returned because of a lack of funds. NSF checks are frequently reported on the bank statement via a debit memo notation, because the bank has reduced the depositor's account.

**Exhibit 7-2**
**Bank Statement**

FIRST CITY BANK TRUST
101 North James Ave.
Chicago, Illinois 60638

JOHNSON MANUFACTURING CORPORATION
1800 SOUTH MAIN
CHICAGO, ILLINOIS 60634

| *Account No.* | *Page No.* |
|---|---|
| 0008564201 | 1 |

Statement Period

| *From* | *To* |
|---|---|
| 7/31/XX | 8/31/XX |

| Deposits/Credits | | | Checks/Debits | | | Balance | |
|---|---|---|---|---|---|---|---|
| *Date* | *Amount* | | *No.* | *Date* | *Amount* | *Date* | *Amount* |
| 8/03 | 3,984.40 | | 606 | 8/01 | 1,250.40 | 8/01 | 18,257.10 |
| 8/05 | 3,150.43 | | 620 | 8/02 | 940.20 | 8/02 | 17,316.90 |
| 8/06 | 2,897.04 | | 624 | 8/05 | 1,960.85 | 8/03 | 21,301.30 |
| 8/07 | 4,925.75 | | 625 | 8/04 | 2,640.00 | 8/04 | 18,661.30 |
| 8/09 | 5,242.70 | | 626 | 8/08 | 375.00 | 8/05 | 19,850.88 |
| 8/13 | 4,600.80 | NC | 627 | 8/08 | 675.18 | 8/06 | 22,747.92 |
| 8/13 | 75.00 | IC | 628 | 8/11 | 540.20 | 8/07 | 27,673.67 |
| 8/20 | 4,167.10 | | 629 | 8/13 | 728.40 | 8/08 | 26,623.49 |
| 8/22 | 5,145.18 | | 630 | 8/12 | 139.50 | 8/09 | 31,866.19 |
| 8/27 | 4,752.30 | | 631 | 8/17 | 650.53 | 8/11 | 31,325.99 |
| 8/30 | 3,237.80 | | 632 | 8/17 | 437.29 | 8/12 | 31,058.59 |
| | | | 633 | 8/20 | 2,147.90 | 8/13 | 35,005.99 |
| | | | 634 | 8/23 | 989.05 | 8/17 | 33,918.17 |
| | | | 635 | 8/22 | 12,785.50 | 8/20 | 35,937.37 |
| | | | 636 | 8/27 | 10,640.90 | 8/22 | 28,297.05 |
| | | | 637 | 8/28 | 2,470.80 | 8/23 | 27,308.00 |
| | | | 639 | 8/30 | 740.15 | 8/27 | 21,419.40 |
| | | | DM | 8/12 | 127.90 | 8/28 | 18,948.60 |
| | | | SC | 8/31 | 20.00 | 8/30 | 21,446.25 |
| | | | | | | 8/31 | 21,426.25 |

| Beginning Balance | Deposits/Credits | | Checks/Debits | | Ending Balance |
|---|---|---|---|---|---|
| | *No.* | *Amount* | *No.* | *Amount* | |
| 19,507.50 | 11 | 42,178.50 | 19 | 40,259.75 | 21,426.25 |

*Code Explanation:* CM *Credit Memo* IC *Interest Collection* SC *Service Charge*
DM *Debit Memo* NC *Note Collection*

b Bank service charges for account processing.

c Notes receivable[1] and interest collected by the bank. The collection of a note and interest is sometimes reported with a credit memo notation because of the increase in the depositor's account balance.

d Interest earned on the account.

In addition to timing differences, errors may cause a discrepancy between the bank statement balance and company accounting records. Errors are possible by either the company or the bank and must be corrected as quickly as possible.

***The Reconciliation Process*** Several different types of reconciliations can be prepared. The most commonly encountered form results in determining the amount of

[1] A note is a written promise by an individual or company to pay a given sum of money on a specific date. Notes will be studied in detail later in the text.

**Exhibit 7-3**
**Illustrative Bank Reconciliation**

| | |
|---|---|
| Ending balance per bank statement | $XXX |
| Add: Receipts entered on company records but not reported on the bank statement | XXX |
| | $XXX |
| Deduct: Disbursements entered on company records but not reported on the bank statement | XXX |
| Adjusted cash balance: bank | $XXX |
| Ending balance per company records | $XXX |
| Add: Receipts reported on the bank statement but not entered on company records | XXX |
| | $XXX |
| Deduct: Disbursements reported on the bank statement but not entered on company records | XXX |
| Adjusted cash balance: company records | $XXX |

**These amounts must agree**

cash a company has control over and reports on its balance sheet at the end of the accounting period. An example appears in Exhibit 7-3.

The exhibit reveals the thrust of a reconciliation. That is, we strive to isolate specific items that cause a difference between the depositor's records and the bank statement balance. The accountant considers these items and adjusts one cash balance or the other to bring both balances into agreement.

If the balances do not agree and the reconciling items are deemed correct, there is an excellent chance that a record-keeping error has been made. Errors must be identified and then added or subtracted on the reconciliation to arrive at the corrected cash balance. For example, if a check written by a firm for $94.50 was incorrectly entered in the accounting records as $49.50, the accounting records will be overstated by $45.00 ($94.50 − $49.50). This amount ($45) should therefore be deducted from the ending cash balance per company records, since the company's books are in error. The bank, of course, will deduct the correct amount of the transaction ($94.50) when the check is received for payment. The reconciliation, then, not only highlights timing differences but also identifies errors made by either the bank or the depositor.

Most bank reconciliations contain adjustments to both the ending cash balance per bank statement and the ending balance per company records. After the reconciliation is completed, *general journal entries must be prepared for adjustments made to company records.* These adjustments are necessary to update the Cash account (and others) for corrections of company errors and information already processed by the bank.

### TIPS & TECHNIQUES

It is important to note that no journal entries are needed for adjustments made to the ending bank statement balance. These adjustments reflect items that have already been recorded in a company's accounts; thus, no further updating is necessary. Should the reconciliation process discover that the *bank statement balance* is in error, the problem is corrected by a visit, letter, or telephone call to a bank employee.

***An Example*** Exhibit 7-4 contains summarized data and the bank reconciliation of Johnson Manufacturing Corporation for the month ended August 31, 19XX. It is helpful if you refer back to Johnson's bank statement (see Exhibit 7-2), which serves as the source for much of the information presented.

**Exhibit 7-4**
**Data and Bank Reconciliation of Johnson Manufacturing Corporation**

***Data***

a Cash balance per bank statement, $21,426.25.
b Cash balance per company records, $17,473.35.
c A customer's check for $127.90 was returned because of insufficient funds.
d A customer's note receivable for $4,600.80 plus $75.00 of interest was collected by the bank and reported on the August bank statement.
e A deposit for $1,430.00, mailed to the bank on August 30, did not appear on the bank statement.
f Monthly bank service charge, $20.00.
g Customers' checks totaling $420.00 were on hand awaiting deposit.
h The following checks written by Johnson were outstanding at the end of the month:

| | |
|---|---|
| No. 638 | $410.00 |
| No. 640 | 320.00 |
| No. 641 | 240.00 |
| No. 642 | 323.00 |

i Check no. 627, written for $675.18, was erroneously entered as $657.18 in the company's records. The check involved a payment to a supplier on account.

**JOHNSON MANUFACTURING CORPORATION**
**Bank Reconciliation**
**August 31, 19XX**

| | | |
|---|---|---|
| Ending balance per bank statement | | $21,426.25 |
| Add: Deposit in transit | $1,430.00 | |
| Checks on hand | 420.00 | 1,850.00 |
| | | $23,276.25 |
| Deduct: Outstanding checks | | |
| No. 638 | $ 410.00 | |
| No. 640 | 320.00 | |
| No. 641 | 240.00 | |
| No. 642 | 323.00 | 1,293.00 |
| Adjusted cash balance: bank | | $21,983.25 |
| Ending balance per company records | | $17,473.35 |
| Add: Note receivable collected by bank | $4,600.80 | |
| Interest on note | 75.00 | 4,675.80 |
| | | $22,149.15 |
| Deduct: NSF check | $ 127.90 | |
| Monthly service charge | 20.00 | |
| Error in recording check no. 627 | 18.00 | 165.90 |
| Adjusted cash balance: company records | | $21,983.25 |

The reconciliation reveals two increases to the bank statement cash balance: (1) the deposit that was mailed prior to month-end but not reported by the bank and (2) the checks that were recorded by Johnson and are awaiting deposit. Johnson had control over each of these items as of August 31, and they should be included in the ending cash balance. The decrease to the bank statement cash balance was caused by checks Johnson had written that had not yet cleared the bank. The bank will receive these checks shortly, and the funds will then be deducted from the firm's account.

The increase to company records arose from the note receivable and interest, both of which appear on the bank statement. These funds are now on deposit in Johnson's bank account and must therefore be entered in the company's records. The deductions for the NSF check and service charge are also caused by items on the bank statement but not as yet in the firm's ledger. The error in recording check no. 627 was discovered during the reconciliation. The correct amount of the check was deducted by the bank, thereby requiring an adjustment to Johnson's records to bring them into agreement with those of First City.

On completion of the reconciliation, journal entries are needed for all items that affect company records. The following entries will be made on August 31:

| | Debit | Credit |
|---|---|---|
| Cash | 4,675.80 | |
| Notes Receivable | | 4,600.80 |
| Interest Revenue | | 75.00 |
| Note and interest collected by bank | | |
| | | |
| Accounts Receivable | 127.90 | |
| Miscellaneous Expense | 20.00 | |
| Accounts Payable | 18.00 | |
| Cash | | 165.90 |
| NSF check, bank service charge, and error in recording check no. 627 | | |

The first entry reflects the increase in cash caused by the collection of the note and $75.00 of interest. The second entry combines the company's three cash reductions. The NSF check is debited to Accounts Receivable because Johnson still has a claim against the customer for $127.90. The bank service charge is recorded as a miscellaneous expense. Finally, the error in recording check no. 627 was found to involve a payment on account; thus, Accounts Payable must be debited. These entries allow Johnson's records to reflect the true amount of cash held by the firm (see the accompanying T-account).

| Cash | | | |
|---|---|---|---|
| 8/31 | 17,473.35 | 8/31 | 165.90 |
| 8/31 | 4,675.80 | | |
| (21,983.25) | **22,149.15** | | |

## Petty Cash

**OBJECTIVE 4**
**Be familiar with the operation of a petty cash system.**

Another important element in the control of cash is a **petty cash system.** Under such a system, a fund is established for use in making small payments, especially those that are impractical or uneconomical to make by check. Examples of such payments include those for minor items like coffee and other miscellaneous office needs.

A petty cash fund is created by cashing a check drawn on the company's regular checking account. The proceeds from the check are then placed in a petty cash box that is controlled by an individual known as the fund custodian. The custodian supervises the fund and is held accountable for any discrepancies. The petty cash fund is established at a sufficient amount to cover payments for a short period of time (e.g., several weeks). Assuming this amount is $200, the necessary journal entry is as follows:

| | | |
|---|---|---|
| Petty Cash | 200 | |
| Cash | | 200 |
| To establish petty cash fund | | |

***Making Disbursements from the Fund*** As payments are made from the fund, the custodian completes a form known as a petty cash voucher (see Exhibit 7-5). Each voucher indicates the amount paid, the purpose of the expenditure, the date of the expenditure, and the individual receiving the money. Along with invoices and receipts, petty cash vouchers are used as evidence of disbursements.

The completed voucher is placed in the petty cash box by the custodian. Although a payment has been made, no journal entry is recorded at this time. Preparing a formal journal entry for each disbursement would give rise to considerable bookkeeping work and posting, all for relatively small amounts. At all times the following relationship should be true:

| | |
|---|---|
| Cash remaining in the fund | $XXX |
| Plus: Petty cash vouchers | XXX |
| Original amount of the fund | $ 200 |

***Replenishing the Petty Cash Fund*** The petty cash fund is replenished when the amount of cash in the fund becomes low. For instance, assume that a count of the petty cash on hand totaled $32.40. Vouchers revealed that the following expenses had been incurred: postage, $27.50; office supplies, $50.80; transportation, $73.40; and coffee, $15.90. The journal entry to record replenishment is as follows:

| | | |
|---|---|---|
| Postage Expense | 27.50 | |
| Office Supplies Expense | 50.80 | |
| Transportation Expense | 73.40 | |
| Miscellaneous Expense | 15.90 | |
| Cash | | 167.60 |
| To replenish petty cash fund | | |

Notice that the credit is to the Cash account and not Petty Cash. Although disbursements have been made from the petty cash box, the fund is restocked by writing a

**Exhibit 7-5**
**Petty Cash Voucher**

***Petty Cash Voucher No.*** ________

| | |
|---|---|
| *Date* ________ | *Payee* ________ |
| *Explanation* ________ | *Account* ________ |
| ________ | *Amount $* ________ |
| ________ | *Approved* ________ |
| | *Received Payment* ________ |

check for $167.60 on the company's regular checking account. Thus, payment (and replenishment) is really from Cash.

In addition to being restocked when the fund is low, petty cash is also replenished at the end of each accounting period. This procedure is necessary because no formal journal entries have been recorded for individual fund disbursements. Replenishment requires a journal entry, thereby ensuring that expenditures are charged to the period in which they arose.

***Errors in the Petty Cash Fund*** Occasionally, the sum of the petty cash vouchers and cash in the fund will not equal the original fund balance. This discrepancy usually occurs because of errors made by the fund custodian, some errors in the company's favor and some against. In such cases, the Cash Short & Over account is employed. Cash Short & Over is debited to record a shortage or credited to recognize an overage at the time the fund is replenished.

## Voucher System

**OBJECTIVE 5**
**Be familiar with the operation of a voucher system.**

Bank reconciliations and petty cash funds are two elements of a cash control system. A third element is a **voucher system,** which provides an alternative to the purchases and cash payments journals discussed in Chapter 6. Such a system improves control over all disbursements made by check. Every payment must be approved by a supervisor or officer of the company, with approval based on a review of a transaction's supporting documents. Improper disbursements of cash, whether intentional or unintentional, are therefore eliminated (or reduced). Further, as you will soon see, a voucher system enforces an adequate separation of duties.

A voucher system operates in the following manner:

1 An internal company document called a **voucher** is prepared for each invoice or expenditure that requires a cash disbursement.[2] Vouchers are prenumbered, summarize the details of the payment, and have supporting evidence such as invoices and paid receipts attached. An example of a voucher appears in Exhibit 7-6.

2 The voucher is examined for accuracy, approved, and then recorded in a **voucher register.** The voucher register is a multicolumn journal that is somewhat similar to an all-encompassing purchases journal. All vouchers are credited to a current liability account entitled Vouchers Payable (see Exhibit 7-7).

3 Vouchers are then filed in an unpaid voucher file by payment date. When the payment date arrives, the voucher is sent to the individual responsible for authorizing disbursements. Payment of the voucher is approved, and the paperwork is forwarded to the accounting department.

4 The voucher is paid by issuing a check. Each check is recorded in the **check register,** which is virtually identical to the cash payments journal. The check register has a debit column for Vouchers Payable and a credit column for Cash. Additionally, there is a credit column for Purchases Discounts. As each voucher is paid, the check number and the date paid are recorded in both the check

[2] Exceptions are disbursements made from a petty cash fund. As shown on page 248, the accounting forms used in a petty cash system are also called vouchers; however, they are less involved and unrelated to those described here.

**Exhibit 7-6**
**Voucher (as used in a voucher system)**

Voucher No. 415

Date: March 1, 19XX    Payee: Franklin Company
1420 West State St.
Chicago, Illinois 60603

| ITEM | AMOUNT |
|---|---|
| Merchandise (2/10, n/30) | $500.00 |

| Account Debited | Amount | Approval | |
|---|---|---|---|
| Purchases | | Acct Dept | J.L. |
| Office Supplies | | Controller | Dave S. |
| | | Payment | PAID |
| | | Date Paid | 3/10/XX |
| | | Check No. | 391 |

register and the voucher register, the latter as a means of cross-referencing. Exhibit 7-8 contains a check register.

**5** All paid vouchers are marked "paid" and filed in a paid voucher file.

At the end of the month all column totals in the voucher register and check register are totaled to determine whether debits equal credits. The column totals, with the exception of Sundry, are then posted to the general ledger in a manner similar to the methods discussed earlier in the text for special journals.

Finally, a listing of unpaid vouchers is prepared and totaled. The listing, similar to a schedule of accounts payable (see Chapter 6), is compared against the balance in the Vouchers Payable account. In this particular case, the total of unpaid vouchers no. 418 and no. 419 ($150 + $180 = $330) coincides with the Vouchers Payable balance ($1,605 − $1,275 = $330). It is apparent that the unpaid vouchers support the Vouchers Payable control account, and that equality between these items must be maintained.

***The Voucher System and Internal Control*** In reviewing the operation of the voucher system, it is important to observe the related procedures for authorization and approval. Such procedures assist an organization in safeguarding assets and detecting various errors in transaction processing.

The voucher system is also compatible with implementing an adequate separation of duties. Specifically, the person responsible for preparing vouchers and posting the voucher register does not have access to the funds of the business. Another individual (or department) actually prepares the checks and posts the check register. By following these practices, the recording of an expenditure and the related payable is segregated from the necessary accounting for cash. No single person or department can therefore process a transaction through the system from beginning to end. Consistent with the practices of authorization and accountability, an adequate separation of duties assists in error detection and makes fraudulent schemes more difficult to undertake.

As a final step to strengthen internal control within the voucher system, an independent review is generally performed. The review is conducted to assess

**Exhibit 7-7**
**Voucher Register**

| Date | Voucher No. | Payee | Check No. | Date Paid | Vouchers Payable Credit | Purchases Debit | Office Supplies Debit | Sundry Accounts Debit | Post Ref | Sundry Accounts Amount |
|---|---|---|---|---|---|---|---|---|---|---|
| Mar. 1 | 415 | Franklin Co. | 391 | Mar. 10 | 500 | 500 | | | | |
| 8 | 416 | Timely Supply | 392 | Mar. 18 | 125 | | 125 | | | |
| 12 | 417 | Wheatly Corp. | 393 | Mar. 22 | 650 | 650 | | | | |
| 21 | 418 | WPED Radio | | | 150 | | | Adv Exp | 525 | 150 |
| 25 | 419 | Timely Supply | | | 180 | | 180 | | | |
| | | | | | 1,605 | 1,150 | 305 | | | 150 |
| | | | | | (201) | (501) | (130) | | | (X) |

**Exhibit 7-8**
**Check Register**

| Date | Payee | Check No. | Voucher No. | Vouchers Payable Debit | Purchases Discounts Credit | Cash Credit |
|---|---|---|---|---|---|---|
| Mar. 10 | Franklin Co. | 391 | 415 | 500 | 10 | 490 |
| 18 | Timely Supply | 392 | 416 | 125 | | 125 |
| 22 | Wheatly Corp. | 393 | 417 | 650 | | 650 |
| | | | | 1,275 | 10 | 1,265 |
| | | | | (201) | (502) | (101) |

whether all vouchers recorded in the voucher register have been properly paid. A further objective is to determine if any checks in the check register were issued in the absence of an approved voucher.

## Short-Term Investments

Without question, cash is a key asset to an entity's survival. A company may possess numerous valuable resources, but without funds to meet employee payrolls and demands for payment from important suppliers, the eventual outcome may be bankruptcy. Maintaining an abundance of cash may therefore appear to be a sensible policy; normally, however, such action is not prudent and could actually cause an otherwise successful business to operate at a loss.

Effective cash management dictates that cash balances in excess of planned minimum levels be used to acquire securities that provide a return to the investor. Many companies therefore purchase **short-term investments** (sometimes called marketable securities), which include shares of capital stock of corporations, certificates of deposit, Treasury bills, and bonds. *Treasury bills* are U.S. government obligations that pay a fixed amount of money to the purchaser after a specified number of days has elapsed (usually 91 or 182). In contrast, *bonds* are securities issued by corporations and governmental units (e.g., municipalities) when such entities desire to borrow large sums of money. With the exception of capital stock, which generates a dividend for the investor, CDs, Treasury bills, and bonds are all interest bearing.

The short-term investments acquired by an organization are reported as current assets on the balance sheet if they are (1) readily salable and (2) intended to be converted into cash within the operating cycle or one year, whichever is longer. The key element in this reporting test is *managerial intent.* If management intends to convert a short-term investment into cash whenever the firm is in need of funds, the security is classified as a current asset.[3] Securities purchased with longer-term goals in mind, such as management control or affiliation, are disclosed as long-term investments.

OBJECTIVE 6
Understand the proper accounting treatments for short-term investments, including the lower-of-cost-or-market method.

### Recording Initial Cost and Changes in Value

All short-term investments are recorded initially at their acquisition price plus any other costs related to the transaction (e.g., brokerage fees). To illustrate the proper accounting, we will assume that Phillip Corporation purchased 200 shares of Allegro Corporation capital stock at $42 per share (for a total of $8,400). Brokerage fees of $50 were incurred on the purchase. This transaction would be recorded as follows:

| | | |
|---|---|---|
| Short-term Investments in Stock | 8,450 | |
| Cash | | 8,450 |
| Purchased 200 shares of Allegro Corporation stock | | |

Unlike the value of most other assets, the value of many short-term investments fluctuates continuously and can often be determined on a daily basis. Changes in the value of such investments (caused by the economy, investor expectations,

[3] In practice, the "intent" guideline has created problems for auditors. Intentions, of course, can change from one period to the next. Furthermore, intentions may be somewhat subjective and are rarely documented in company records.

earnings reports, and other factors) are readily obtainable from *The Wall Street Journal* or the business section of major metropolitan newspapers. In light of these characteristics, two alternative methods have been used to account for short-term investments: historical cost and lower of cost or market.

## Historical-Cost Method

The **historical-cost method** is typically employed for short-term debt investments, such as those in bonds. Under this approach, investments are reported on the balance sheet at acquisition (historical) cost until the time of sale. Accordingly, changes in value are ignored while the securities are being held, except perhaps for disclosure in the footnotes to the financial statements. Any revenue from the securities (e.g., interest) is recorded as it is earned by the investor.

In recent years, some companies have abandoned historical cost in favor of lower of cost or market (to be discussed next), which *must* be used for other specified types of securities. This switch simplifies the record-keeping process by achieving consistency in accounting treatments for the various classes of investments that may be acquired.

## Lower-of-Cost-or-Market Method

With the **lower-of-cost-or-market method,** valuation changes related to certain securities (e.g., shares of capital stock) are recognized and entered in the accounting records. Decreases in the market value of such securities are accounted for as losses, while recoveries in these market value declines are reported as revenue. Recoveries, however, are limited to the amount of previously recorded losses.[4]

The application of the lower-of-cost-or-market method is straightforward. The carrying value of the investment portfolio is the lower of its *aggregate* cost or market value on each balance sheet date. That is, the total cost and total market value of a firm's short-term investments are compared, and the *lower* figure is used for financial statement purposes.

To illustrate use of the lower-of-cost-or-market method for stock investments, assume that Carr Corporation acquired the following securities on January 1, 19X1:

| *Number of Shares* | *Corporation* | *Cost per Share* | *Total Cost* |
|---|---|---|---|
| 200 shares | Rolph Corporation | $ 50 | $10,000 |
| 400 shares | Dana, Inc. | 100 | 40,000 |
| 300 shares | Borg Corporation | 75 | 22,500 |
| | | | $72,500 |

The following journal entry is made to record these acquisitions:

| | | |
|---|---|---|
| Short-term Investments in Stock | 72,500 | |
| Cash | | 72,500 |
| Purchased Rolph, Dana, and Borg stock | | |

[4] "Accounting for Certain Marketable Equity Securities," *Statement of Financial Accounting Standards No. 12* (Stamford, Conn.: Financial Accounting Standards Board, 1975).

During 19X1, dividends of $4,500 were received. Dividends are revenue to the recipient and are recorded as follows:

| | | |
|---|---|---|
| Cash | 4,500 | |
| Dividend Revenue | | 4,500 |
| To record dividends received | | |

***Declines in Market Value*** On December 31, 19X1, the market value per share of Carr's three securities was Rolph, $48; Dana, $98; and Borg, $76. The accompanying table is used to summarize this information.

| ***Security*** | ***Cost*** | ***Market**** |
|---|---|---|
| Rolph Corporation (200 shares) | $10,000 | $ 9,600 |
| Dana, Inc. (400 shares) | 40,000 | 39,200 |
| Borg Corporation (300 shares) | 22,500 | 22,800 |
| | $72,500 | $71,600 |

* Number of shares multiplied by market value per share.

The table reveals that the portfolio's total market value is $900 less than cost ($72,500 − $71,600). The entry needed to record this decline in value is as follows:

| | | |
|---|---|---|
| Unrealized Loss on Short-term Investments | 900 | |
| Allowance for Decline in Market Value of Short-term Investments | | 900 |
| To record decline in market value | | |

As we noted earlier, decreases in the market value of short-term investments are accounted for as losses. The loss, known as an *unrealized loss,* appears on the income statement under the other expense classification.[5] Rather than credit the Short-term Investments account directly, one establishes an Allowance account. The Allowance for Decline in Market Value, a contra asset, is deducted from Short-term Investments on the balance sheet as follows:

| | |
|---|---|
| Current assets | |
| Short-term investments in stock | $72,500 |
| Less: Allowance for decline in market value of short-term investments | 900 |
| Short-term investments at the lower of cost or market | $71,600 |

Notice how the balance sheet discloses more information by using a separate valuation account.

***Recording Recoveries*** Continuing the previous example, assume it is one year later (19X2) and that dividends of $4,800 were received. The proper entry is

| | | |
|---|---|---|
| Cash | 4,800 | |
| Dividend Revenue | | 4,800 |
| To record dividends received | | |

Now suppose that on December 31, 19X2, the market values per share were Rolph, $49; Dana, $99; and Borg, $76. This information is summarized in the accompanying table.

[5] In most cases, gains and losses are said to be *realized* at the time of sale. Because Carr still owns the securities, the loss is labeled "unrealized."

| *Security* | *Cost* | *Market** |
|---|---|---|
| Rolph Corporation (200 shares) | $10,000 | $ 9,800 |
| Dana, Inc. (400 shares) | 40,000 | 39,600 |
| Borg Corporation (300 shares) | 22,500 | 22,800 |
| | $72,500 | $72,200 |

* Number of shares multiplied by market value per share.

The entry to record the recovery in market value of the portfolio from $71,600 (on December 31, 19X1) to $72,200 (on December 31, 19X2) is shown below.

| | | |
|---|---|---|
| Allowance for Decline in Market Value of Short-term Investments | 600 | |
| Recovery in Value of Short-term Investments | | 600 |
| To record recovery in market value | | |

In the second and all subsequent years, losses and loss recoveries are determined by comparing the required balance in the Allowance account at the end of the year with the account's balance on the last previous balance sheet date. The previous amount in the Allowance for Decline account was $900. As of December 31, 19X2, however, the market value of the portfolio is only $300 below cost ($72,500 − $72,200), which means that only a $300 balance is needed. Thus, Carr must debit the Allowance for $600 to achieve the desired result. The $600 figure represents a recovery or increase in value and is treated as revenue by the company.

The preceding events are shown in Carr's comparative financial statements for 19X1 and 19X2, which appear in Exhibit 7-9. Observe that if the stocks recover the remaining $300 to their original cost ($72,500), the valuation allowance would be eliminated. If the stocks continue to increase in value above $72,500, the additional increase is ignored. The lower-of-cost-or-market method would again value the securities at the lower figure, which is now the portfolio's cost.

**Exhibit 7-9**
**Comparative Financial Statements of Carr Corporation**

| | *19X2* | *19X1* |
|---|---|---|
| ***Balance Sheet*** | | |
| Current assets | | |
| Short-term investments in stock | $72,500 | $72,500 |
| Less: Allowance for decline in market value of short-term investments | 300 | 900 |
| Short-term investments at the lower of cost or market | $72,200 | $71,600 |
| ***Income Statement*** | | |
| Other revenue | | |
| Dividend revenue | $ 4,800 | $ 4,500 |
| Recovery in value of short-term investments | 600 | |
| Other expense | | |
| Unrealized loss on short-term investments | | 900 |

> **TIPS & TECHNIQUES**
>
> Recall that recoveries in portfolio value are limited to the amount of previously recorded losses. Thus, a company that recognized a $10,000 unrealized loss is limited to $10,000 of recoveries if and when the portfolio's value rebounds. If a business were allowed recoveries in excess of losses, the value of the securities in the accounting records would exceed the original outlay made at acquisition.

***Justification for Lower of Cost or Market*** The lower-of-cost-or-market method is justified by the accounting convention of **conservatism,** which holds that accounting practices be employed that are least likely to overstate assets and/or net income. The use of conservatism in financial reporting became popular many years ago, primarily because of support from bankers and other lenders. These individuals review balance sheets when making loan decisions and carefully study a firm's assets and the accompanying valuations. Should assets pledged as loan security (i.e., collateral) be overvalued, the lending institution could suffer extensive losses if the borrower failed to repay the debt and the assets were seized.

A review of the discussion on the preceding pages will show the conservatism associated with lower of cost or market. When a portfolio's aggregate market value is below cost, for example, a loss is recognized for the difference. Such recognition reduces net income, and the associated Allowance account lowers the securities' balance sheet valuation to market. In contrast, the practice of ignoring increases in market value *above* cost is justified because cost will produce the lower figure for both firm assets and earnings.

## Chapter Review

### Learning Objectives—The Key Points

**1 Understand the composition of cash and how cash is presented on a balance sheet.** Cash includes those items that are acceptable to a bank for deposit and free from restriction for use in satisfying current debts. Specific items included in cash, which is listed in the current asset section of the balance sheet, are coins, currency, funds on deposit with a bank in checking and savings accounts, checks, and money orders.

**2 Understand cash management and be familiar with controls and procedures related to cash receipts and disbursements.** Cash management involves programs to ensure that sufficient cash is available to meet current obligations and that any excess funds are invested. Such programs, which include both cash planning and cash control, help to guard against a loss of earnings for the firm. Cash control systems are adopted to safeguard an entity's funds and involve such features as using a cash register, making daily deposits, having an adequate separation of duties, making all significant disbursements by check, and preparing a bank reconciliation.

**3 Be able to reconcile a bank account.** A bank reconciliation involves an examination of the accuracy of the cash balance in the general ledger. Items are recognized that cause a difference between the depositor's records and the bank statement. Such items properly on the bank statement but not as yet on company records require a journal entry on the depositor's books. The resultant figure from this process is the amount of cash that a company has control over and reports on its balance sheet.

**4 Be familiar with the operation of a petty cash system.** A petty cash system for small payments is established by writing a check on a company's regular checking account. As payments are made from the fund, petty cash vouchers are prepared to document each disbursement. When the fund becomes low it is replenished, and a journal entry is made to record the disbursements that have occurred. The fund is also replenished at the end of the accounting period.

**5 Be familiar with the operation of a voucher system.** The voucher system is a system for controlling all disbursements made by check. The system begins with the preparation of a voucher for each invoice or expenditure that requires a disbursement. After it has been examined for accuracy and approved, the voucher is recorded in a voucher register and placed in an unpaid voucher file. When the payment date arrives, the voucher is settled by writing a check. The check is recorded in the check register, the voucher is marked "paid," and the voucher is placed in a paid voucher file.

**6 Understand the proper accounting treatments for short-term investments, including the lower-of-cost-or-market method.** Short-term investments are securities that are both readily salable and intended to be converted into cash within the operating cycle or one year, whichever is longer. Debt securities are often accounted for by using the historical-cost method, which ignores changes in the market value of securities while the securities are being held. In contrast, stock investments are accounted for by using lower of cost or market. With this approach, decreases in the aggregate market value of the investment portfolio are accounted for as losses, whereas recoveries in the portfolio's market value are reported as revenue. Recoveries, however, are limited to the amount of previously reported losses.

## Chapter Quiz

The five questions that follow relate to several issues raised in the chapter. Test your knowledge of the issues by selecting the best answer. (The answers appear on p. 271.)

**1** Liberty had a $10,000 balance in its checking account, $15,000 in certificates of deposit, $600 of postdated checks, $200 of employee IOUs, and $900 of cash on hand in the office safe. Further, the company had given out $500 of travel advances. The proper amount of cash to report on Liberty's balance sheet is:
a $10,900.
b $11,500.
c $25,900.
d $27,200.

**2** When preparing a bank reconciliation, deposits in transit are:
a added to the balance per company records.
b subtracted from the balance per company records.
c added to the balance per bank.
d subtracted from the balance per bank.

**3** Soccer, Inc., established a $200 petty cash fund. Five weeks later, the following was found in the petty cash box:

| | |
|---|---|
| Receipts for coffee and tea | $36 |
| Receipts for office supplies | 94 |
| Receipts for postage | ? |
| Coins and currency | 58 |

If the journal entry to replenish the fund contained a $2 debit to the Cash Short & Over account, the receipts for postage must have amounted to:
a $6.
b $10.
c $14.
d none of these.

4 Which of the following statements about a voucher system is true?
  a The Vouchers Payable account balance is a liability.
  b Unpaid vouchers are recorded in the voucher register at the end of the accounting period.
  c Each voucher is initially recorded in the check register.
  d A general journal entry is prepared for each voucher that has been paid during the period.

5 Berry's beginning-of-year portfolio of short-term stock investments had an aggregate cost and market value of $80,000 and $75,800, respectively. The portfolio's market value subsequently increased to $84,000 by year-end. For the current reporting period Berry should disclose:
  a an unrealized loss of $4,200.
  b a recovery in value of $4,000.
  c a recovery in value of $4,200.
  d a recovery in value of $8,200.

## Summary Problem

The Donnell Company recently hired Steve Hampton to fill a staff accounting position. On August 1, Hampton established a $400 petty cash fund. The count of petty cash on August 31 indicated that $92.30 remained in the fund. Petty cash vouchers disclosed that the following expenses were incurred during the month:

| | |
|---|---|
| Postage expense | $137.40 |
| Office supplies expense | 102.78 |
| Miscellaneous selling expenses | 65.52 |

Additionally, the following information concerning Donnell's checking account is available:

| | |
|---|---|
| Balance per bank statement | $1,671.32 |
| Balance per company records | 1,419.99 |
| Bank service charge | 22.00 |
| Outstanding checks | 318.46 |
| Undeposited receipts | 208.70 |
| Note and interest collected by the bank but not yet entered in the accounting records (note, $175.00; interest, $7.00) | 182.00 |
| NSF check returned by the bank with the bank statement | 18.43 |

**Instructions**

**a** Prepare the August 1 entry to establish the petty cash fund and the August 31 entry for replenishment.

**b** Prepare the August bank reconciliation for the firm's checking account. Assume the balance per company records has already been reduced for the petty cash replenishment.

**c** Prepare the necessary journal entries related to the bank reconciliation.

**Solution**

| | | | | |
|---|---|---|---|---|
| **a** Aug. | 1 | Petty Cash | 400.00 | |
| | | Cash | | 400.00 |
| | | To establish petty cash fund | | |
| | 31 | Postage Expense | 137.40 | |
| | | Office Supplies Expense | 102.78 | |
| | | Miscellaneous Selling Expenses | 65.52 | |
| | | Cash Short & Over* | 2.00 | |
| | | Cash | | 307.70 |
| | | To replenish petty cash fund | | |

| | | |
|---|---|---|
| * Original fund | | $400.00 |
| Less: Vouchers ($137.40 + $102.78 + $65.52) | $305.70 | |
| Cash in fund | 92.30 | 398.00 |
| Shortage | | $ 2.00 |

**b**

**DONNELL COMPANY**
**Bank Reconciliation**
**August 31, 19XX**

| | | |
|---|---|---|
| Ending balance per bank statement | | $1,671.32 |
| Add: Undeposited receipts | $208.70 | |
| Deduct: Outstanding checks | 318.46 | (109.76) |
| Adjusted cash balance: bank | | $1,561.56 |
| Ending balance per company records | | $1,419.99 |
| Add: Note collection | $175.00 | |
| Interest collection | 7.00 | 182.00 |
| | | $1,601.99 |
| Deduct: Bank service charge | $ 22.00 | |
| NSF check | 18.43 | 40.43 |
| Adjusted cash balance: company records | | $1,561.56 |

**c** All adjustments to company records require entries.

| | | | |
|---|---|---|---|
| Aug. 31 | Cash | 182.00 | |
| | Notes Receivable | | 175.00 |
| | Interest Revenue | | 7.00 |
| | Note and interest collected by the bank | | |
| 31 | Miscellaneous Expense | 22.00 | |
| | Accounts Receivable | 18.43 | |
| | Cash | | 40.43 |
| | Bank service charge and NSF check | | |

## Questions

**Q7-1** What items are normally included in the Cash account on the balance sheet?

**Q7-2** Define each of the following items and describe how they are classified on the balance sheet:
a Certificate of deposit
b Postdated check
c IOU
d Travel advance

**Q7-3** What is cash management? Briefly discuss the planning and control aspects of an effective cash management system.

**Q7-4** What general control features should be built into a cash control system?

**Q7-5** How is the Cash Short & Over account classified in the financial statements?

**Q7-6** Why should cash receipts be deposited daily?

**Q7-7** What is a bank reconciliation?

**Q7-8** What is the effect of a bank credit memo on a depositor's account balance?

**Q7-9** What are the reasons for the discrepancy between the cash balance reported on the bank statement and the cash balance in the accounting records?

**Q7-10** Which adjustments on a bank reconciliation require general journal entries in the accounting records?

**Q7-11** Briefly discuss the purpose of a petty cash system.

**Q7-12** Are journal entries made for individual disbursements from a petty cash system? Explain.

**Q7-13** When is a petty cash fund replenished?

**Q7-14** What is the purpose of a voucher system? What two journals are used to record transactions in a voucher system?

**Q7-15** Briefly discuss how a voucher system results in improved internal control.

**Q7-16** What are short-term investments? Why do companies make short-term investments?

**Q7-17** Briefly discuss the criteria that must be met to classify a short-term investment as a current asset.

**Q7-18** Describe two methods that are used to account for short-term investments. When is each method used?

**Q7-19** Briefly discuss the accounting convention of conservatism, including a short description of the relationship between conservatism and the lower-of-cost-or-market method.

## Exercises

**E7-1** ***Internal control: Procedures and weaknesses***

Dottie Lynn owns a women's apparel shop. Sales clerks record customer sales on various cash registers that are located throughout the store. Each clerk is trained to operate the registers and can use any of them. Unfortunately, the registers were manufactured many years ago and lack a salesperson identification key.

Customers who return goods are entitled to receive an immediate cash refund, which can be disbursed by any employee from any register. Returned goods are then reshelved by the same employee who issues the cash. At the end of the day a sales clerk compares the amount of cash collected with the total cash sales as reported by the register tape. The tapes are forwarded to the firm's bookkeeper, and Dottie stops by the bank each evening to deposit the day's receipts.

a What internal control procedures are present in this situation?

b What control weaknesses do you believe exist? How would you recommend strengthening Dottie's internal control procedures?

**E7-2** ***Internal control: Procedures and weaknesses***

Consider the following independent cases:

a A cashier stole $150 from a manufacturing business and made the following journal entry in the accounting records:

| | | |
|---|---|---|
| Miscellaneous Expense | 150 | |
| Cash | | 150 |

b Art's Market lost $12,800 (three days' cash receipts) in a robbery early Thursday morning.

c Disbursements at the alcohol rehabilitation center are made by check. To facilitate payments being made when the director is out of town, five blank, signed checks are kept in the secretary's desk.

For each of the foregoing cases, indicate any apparent internal control weakness and suggest procedures that may prevent the irregularity.

**E7-3** ***Bank reconciliations: Missing amounts***

The following independent cases relate to bank reconciliations. Compute the missing amounts, assuming that no other reconciling items exist.

| | *Case A* | *Case B* | *Case C* |
|---|---|---|---|
| Balance per bank | $6,000 | $4,000 | $ ? |
| Outstanding checks | 500 | 2,100 | 1,400 |
| Deposits in transit | 2,000 | ? | 1,000 |
| Balance per company records | ? | 8,000 | 450 |

**E7-4** ***Items on a bank reconciliation***

You are preparing the March bank reconciliation for Newark Enterprises. Identify the proper placement of items (a)–(f) on the reconciliation by using the following code:

1—An addition to the balance per bank as of March 31.
2—A deduction from the balance per bank as of March 31.
3—An addition to the balance per company records as of March 31.
4—A deduction from the balance per company records as of March 31.

_____ a A customer's NSF check.
_____ b Deposit in transit.
_____ c A note collected by the bank.
_____ d Newark's check no. 100 for $200, recorded in the checkbook as $20.
_____ e A $90 check from a customer, recorded by Newark's bookkeeper as $9.
_____ f An outstanding check.

**E7-5** ***Bank reconciliation and entries***

The following information was taken from the accounting records of Palo Pinto Company for the month of November:

| | |
|---|---|
| Balance per bank | $3,555.90 |
| Balance per company records | 2,230.20 |
| Note collected by the bank on November 19 | 600.00 |
| Interest on the preceding note | 60.00 |
| Deposit in transit | 954.15 |
| Outstanding checks | 2,197.80 |
| NSF check returned by the bank with the bank statement | 547.95 |
| Bank service charge for November | 30.00 |

a Prepare Palo Pinto's November bank reconciliation.
b Prepare any necessary journal entries for Palo Pinto.

**E7-6** ***Accounting for cash***

Evaluate the comments that follow as being True or False. If the comment is false, briefly explain why.

a A petty cash fund should be replenished at the conclusion of an accounting period.
b A journal entry is needed in a company's accounting records to record both a bank service charge and the firm's outstanding checks.
c As shown on May's bank statement, the Nebraska National Bank incorrectly deducted $200 from the account of Kay's Auto Parts. In doing its bank reconciliation, Kay's should deduct $200 from the accounting records so the adjusted cash balance (company records) will equal the adjusted cash balance (bank).
d Customer checks, money orders, and certificates of deposit are properly classified as cash on the balance sheet.
e To achieve strong internal control, a store cashier should have access to a company's accounting records for cash.

**E7-7** ***Petty cash fund***

The Rosewood Company instituted a petty cash system on June 1 to allow for the payment of small expenditures. The information that follows has come to your attention.

June 1 The fund was established at $150.
30 Cash in the fund had been reduced to $19.11. The petty cash vouchers were sorted into the following expense categories and the fund was replenished:

| | |
|---|---|
| Office supplies | $ 69.30 |
| Postage | 48.10 |
| Miscellaneous | 13.49 |
| | $130.89 |

a Prepare the journal entry necessary to record the establishment of the fund on June 1.
b Prepare the journal entry necessary to record replenishment of the fund on June 30.

**E7-8** ***Voucher system***
Saturn Cleaning Products uses a voucher system. Selected transactions from March follow.

Mar. 2 Prepared voucher no. 1001 for a $450 electric bill received from Valley Utilities.
13 Prepared voucher no. 1002 for $2,500, payable to Tacoma Wholesale for merchandise purchases (terms 3/10, n/30).
18 Issued check no. 100 in payment of voucher no. 1001.
21 Prepared voucher no. 1003 to establish a $35 petty cash fund.
22 Issued check no. 101 in payment of voucher no. 1002.

a Record the preceding transactions in general journal form. Assume that all terms of sale are strictly followed.
b In which register would Saturn record the transactions of March 2, 13, and 21?
c In which register would Saturn record the transactions of March 18 and 22?

**E7-9** ***Short-term investments: Acquisition and valuation***
On June 30, Trophy Company purchased the following short-term investments:

| | |
|---|---|
| Span-America | 200 shares at $40 per share |
| Quest Enterprises | 300 shares at $15 per share |

On December 31, the following market value information concerning the two short-term investments is available:

| ***Security*** | ***Market Value per Share*** |
|---|---|
| Span-America | $31 |
| Quest Enterprises | 20 |

a Prepare the journal entry to record the acquisition of Trophy's short-term investments.
b Prepare the journal entry to record the change in market value of the short-term investments.

**E7-10** ***Valuation and disclosure of short-term investments***
Xenon Company, formed during 19X1, invests excess cash in stocks of utility companies. The stocks are readily salable and management intends to sell the stocks whenever the firm is in need of cash. The accompanying table gives the cost and year-end market values of Xenon's short-term investments for 19X1 and 19X2.

| | *19X1* | *19X2* |
|---|---|---|
| Cost | $45,000 | $45,000 |
| Market value | 41,000 | 57,000 |

a Present Xenon's journal entries in 19X1 and 19X2 to value the short-term securities at the lower of cost or market.
b Show how the securities would appear on Xenon's 19X1 and 19X2 balance sheets.

## Problems

### Series A

**P7-A1** ***Cash on the balance sheet***
The following information has been gathered from the records of Bermuda Corporation as of December 31:

| | |
|---|---|
| Certificate of deposit | $15,000 |
| Reconciled balance in Center Bank checking account | 1,275 |
| Cash on hand | 4,210 |
| Employee's IOU | 345 |
| Balance in Metropolitan Trust savings account | 20,100 |
| Petty cash fund | 200 |
| Reconciled balance in American Bank checking account | 6,500 |
| Money orders on hand | 400 |
| Customer's postdated check | 560 |
| Postage stamps on hand | 75 |

**Instructions**

a Compute the total cash balance to be reported as a current asset on the December 31 balance sheet.
b Describe the balance sheet treatment of the items not included in the cash balance computed in part (a).

**P7-A2** ***Bank reconciliation and entries***
The March 31 bank statement for B&J Company disclosed a balance of $10,997.60. On this date the Cash account in B&J's general ledger totaled $3,742.20. The following information has come to your attention:
1 Deposit in transit on March 31, $1,400.
2 A note receivable of $10,000 and interest of $100 were collected by the bank but not as yet recorded in the accounts.
3 Outstanding checks were: No. 1624, $1,058; no. 1629, $547; no. 1632, $715; and no. 1633, $1,407.
4 Cash receipts of $2,561 for March 20 were recorded on the books and deposited at the bank. (B&J has a duplicate of the deposit slip.) The bank accidentally recorded the deposit in the account of B&T Company.
5 French's NSF check was returned with the bank statement, $1,681.60.
6 Bank service charge, $29.
7 A check on account from Gary Rubin for $2,011.70 was entered in the accounts as $2,911.70.

**Instructions**

a Prepare a bank reconciliation for B&J.
b Prepare the journal entries necessary for B&J as of March 31.
c Determine the cash balance that B&J would disclose on its March 31 balance sheet.

**P7-A3** ***Bank reconciliation from bank statement***

The Whitlow Corporation received the accompanying bank statement for September from First City Bank & Trust.

FIRST CITY BANK & TRUST

WHITLOW CORPORATION — SEPTEMBER BANK STATEMENT

| Deposits/Credits | | Checks/Debits | | | Balance | |
|---|---|---|---|---|---|---|
| *Date* | *Amount* | *No.* | *Date* | *Amount* | *Date* | *Amount* |
| | | | | | 9/01 | 10,480 |
| 9/02 | 150 | 911 | 9/02 | 740 | 9/02 | 9,890 |
| 9/15 | 2,350 | 912 | 9/04 | 325 | 9/03 | 9,490 |
| 9/22 | 1,820 | 913 | 9/03 | 400 | 9/04 | 9,165 |
| 9/27 | 740 CM | 915 | 9/06 | 380 | 9/06 | 8,785 |
| 9/28 | 2,570 | 916 | 9/08 | 500 | 9/08 | 8,285 |
| | | 917 | 9/12 | 480 | 9/12 | 6,965 |
| | | 918 | 9/12 | 200 | 9/15 | 9,315 |
| | | 919 | 9/12 | 640 | 9/18 | 9,105 |
| | | 920 | 9/18 | 210 | 9/21 | 8,320 |
| | | 921 | 9/21 | 370 | 9/22 | 8,690 |
| | | 922 | 9/22 | 610 | 9/25 | 7,970 |
| | | 923 | 9/22 | 840 | 9/26 | 7,670 |
| | | 924 | 9/26 | 300 | 9/27 | 8,190 |
| | | 925 | 9/27 | 220 | 9/28 | 10,280 |
| | | 926 | 9/25 | 720 | 9/30 | 9,750 |
| | | 927 | 9/28 | 480 | | |
| | | 929 | 9/30 | 515 | | |
| | | NSF | 9/21 | 415 | | |
| | | SC | 9/30 | 15 | | |

CM *Credit Memo* NSF *NSF Check* SC *Service Charge*

The credit memo represents the collection of a $700 note receivable plus $40 interest. Whitlow's cash receipts and disbursements records for September disclose the following:

| ***Deposits*** | | ***Checks Written*** | | | |
|---|---|---|---|---|---|
| 9/14 | $2,350 | no. 915 | $380 | no. 923 | $ 840 |
| 9/20 | 1,820 | 916 | 500 | 924 | 300 |
| 9/27 | 2,570 | 917 | 480 | 925 | 220 |
| 9/30 | 1,580 | 918 | 200 | 926 | 720 |
| | $8,320 | 919 | 640 | 928 | 180 |
| | | 920 | 210 | 929 | 515 |
| | | 921 | 370 | 930 | 720 |
| | | 922 | 610 | 931 | 510 |
| | | | | 932 | 460 |
| | | | | | $7,855 |

An examination of the August reconciliation revealed a deposit in transit on August 31 of $150. The following checks were listed as outstanding: No. 890, $615; no. 911, $740; no. 912, $325; and no. 913, $400.

**Instructions**

a Assuming a cash balance per company records on September 30 of $9,015, prepare Whitlow's bank reconciliation for September. Assume that any errors detected during the reconciliation process are the fault of Whitlow's bookkeeper.
b Prepare the necessary journal entries for Whitlow as of September 30.

**P7-A4** ***Petty cash fund***

United Enterprises operates a petty cash fund for small expenditures. The following information relates to August:

Aug. 1 Established the petty cash fund for $150.

12 Replenished the fund. The following items were found in the petty cash box:

| | |
|---|---|
| Vouchers for postage | $32 |
| Vouchers for supplies | 41 |
| Vouchers for miscellaneous expenses | 29 |
| Coins and currency | 48 |

22 Replenished the fund. The following items were found in the petty cash box:

| | |
|---|---|
| Vouchers for postage | $50 |
| Vouchers for supplies | 49 |
| Vouchers for miscellaneous expenses | 37 |
| Coins and currency | 10 |

31 Replenished the fund. The following items were found in the petty cash box:

| | |
|---|---|
| Vouchers for postage | $43 |
| Vouchers for supplies | 36 |
| Vouchers for miscellaneous expenses | 11 |
| Voucher stating: I owe the fund $10. Signed: Ronald Hargis (an employee) | |
| Coins and currency | 52 |

**Instructions**

a Record the necessary journal entries on August 1, 12, 22, and 31.
b Explain the probable reasoning behind the fund replenishment on August 31 despite the presence of $52 cash in the petty cash box.

**P7-A5** ***Voucher system***

The Memphis Import Company, which uses a voucher system to control cash payments, had the following transactions during August:

Aug. 4 Purchased $900 of merchandise on account from Acapulco, Inc., terms 2/10, n/30.
9 Purchased a $5,000 office computer on account from MC Computers.
10 Purchased $490 of office supplies on account from the Discount Supply Company.
13 Paid the proper amount to Acapulco, Inc.
19 Purchased $1,500 of merchandise on account from Tampico Co., terms 2/10, n/30.
21 Issued a check for $5,000 to MC Computers in payment of the purchase on August 9.
24 Paid the proper amount due to Discount Supply Company.
30 Acquired a used delivery truck for $2,000 from Budget Truck Sales; agreed to pay the amount due in three working days.

Memphis Import uses a voucher register and check register similar in format to those illustrated in this chapter. Assume that there is no balance in the Vouchers Payable account as of August 1.

**Instructions**

a Record the appropriate transactions in the voucher register and/or the check register. Begin with voucher no. 678 and check no. 651.
b Total the voucher register and check register at the end of the month.
c Compute the balance in the Vouchers Payable account as of August 31.
d Compute the total of unpaid vouchers as of August 31. If all procedures are properly followed, what should the total of the unpaid vouchers be?

**P7-A6** ***Short-term investments; lower of cost or market***

In the summer of 19X8, Poznan Company acquired the following short-term stock investments:

| | | |
|---|---|---|
| July | 15 | Purchased 900 shares of Diamond Co., for $4,450 plus $50 of brokerage fees. |
| | 18 | Purchased 500 shares of Blue, Inc., for $29,500 plus $500 of brokerage fees. |
| Aug. | 1 | Purchased 700 shares of Flame Co., for $48,000 plus $1,000 of brokerage fees. |

Dividends received during 19X8 and 19X8 year-end market values follow.

| | *Per Share* | |
|---|---|---|
| *Corporation* | *Dividends Received* | *Market Value* |
| Diamond | $0.50 | $ 4.50 |
| Blue | 3.00 | 61.00 |
| Flame | 2.00 | 68.00 |

**Instructions**

a Prepare journal entries to record the purchase of Poznan's short-term investments.
b Prepare a journal entry to record the dividends received in 19X8.
c Prepare a journal entry to properly value the securities as of December 31, 19X8.
d Show how Poznan's short-term investments would be disclosed on the December 31, 19X8, balance sheet.
e Suppose that the market price of the Flame stock advanced to $74 per share by the end of 19X9 while the other market values remained unchanged. Given this situation:
   (1) Prepare a journal entry to properly value the securities as of December 31, 19X9.
   (2) Indicate how the short-term investments would be reported on the company's 19X9 balance sheet.

## Series B

**P7-B1** ***Cash on the balance sheet***

The following information has been gathered from the records of Tyson Supply:

| | |
|---|---|
| Customer's postdated check | $ 900 |
| Reconciled balance in Pacific Bank checking account | 8,040 |
| Petty cash fund | 350 |

| | |
|---|---|
| Investment in Treasury bills | 40,000 |
| Certificate of deposit | 20,000 |
| Savings account balance at Meridian Federal | 2,115 |
| Postage stamps on hand | 50 |
| Employee IOU | 250 |
| Cash on hand | 975 |

**Instructions**

a Compute the total cash balance to be reported as a current asset on the December 31 balance sheet.

b Describe the balance sheet treatment of the items not included in the cash balance computed in part (a).

**P7-B2** ***Bank reconciliation and entries***

The December 31 bank statement of Eason Company disclosed a balance of $8,400.50. On this same date the Cash account in the general ledger indicated a balance of $4,375.75. The following information has come to your attention:

1 A deposit of $903.88, mailed by Eason on December 28, was entered in the accounting records on December 29 but was not received by the bank until January 3.

2 Outstanding checks on December 31 totaled $1,400.23, computed as follows:

| | |
|---|---|
| Checks written in November | $ 801.00 |
| Checks written in December | 599.23 |
| | $1,400.23 |

3 A customer's NSF check for $325 was returned with the bank statement.

4 Eason's check no. 888 for a $9,000 machinery acquisition was entered in the accounts as $9,900.

5 Bank service charge, $25.60.

6 A note receivable of $2,950 and interest of $54 were collected by the bank but not as yet recorded in the accounts.

7 A $25 debit memo, representing a check printing charge, appeared on the bank statement.

**Instructions**

a Prepare a bank reconciliation for Eason Company.

b Prepare the journal entries necessary for Eason as of December 31.

c Determine the cash balance that Eason would disclose on the December 31 balance sheet.

**P7-B3** ***Bank reconciliation from bank statement***

The Union Company is in the process of reconciling its bank account with Metropolitan Bank and Trust for May. Union's bank statement follows.

| METROPOLITAN BANK AND TRUST | | | | | | |
|---|---|---|---|---|---|---|
| UNION COMPANY | | | | | MAY BANK STATEMENT | |
| Deposits/Credits | | Checks/Debits | | | Balance | |
| *Date* | *Amount* | *No.* | *Date* | *Amount* | *Date* | *Amount* |
| | | | | | 5/01 | 8,440 |
| 5/02 | 400 | 384 | 5/02 | 725 | 5/02 | 6,175 |
| 5/07 | 625 | 406 | 5/02 | 1,080 | 5/05 | 5,675 |
| 5/11 | 370 | 407 | 5/02 | 860 | 5/07 | 5,990 |
| 5/16 | 1,150 | 408 | 5/05 | 500 | 5/08 | 5,300 |
| 5/19 | 2,340 | 409 | 5/08 | 690 | 5/11 | 5,180 |
| 5/27 | 850 CM | 410 | 5/07 | 310 | 5/12 | 4,750 |
| | | 412 | 5/12 | 430 | 5/14 | 4,240 |
| | | 413 | 5/11 | 490 | 5/16 | 5,280 |
| | | 415 | 5/16 | 110 | 5/19 | 7,620 |
| | | 416 | 5/20 | 665 | 5/20 | 6,955 |
| | | 417 | 5/24 | 1,210 | 5/24 | 5,745 |
| | | 421 | 5/27 | 800 | 5/27 | 5,795 |
| | | NSF | 5/14 | 510 | 5/31 | 5,785 |
| | | SC | 5/31 | 10 | | |

CM *Credit Memo* NSF *NSF Check* SC *Service Charge*

The credit memo represents the collection of an $830 note receivable plus $20 interest. Union's cash receipts and disbursements records for May are as follows:

| ***Deposits*** | | ***Checks Written*** | | | |
|---|---|---|---|---|---|
| 5/6 | $ 625 | no. 408 | $500 | no. 417 | $1,210 |
| 5/10 | 370 | 409 | 690 | 418 | 120 |
| 5/15 | 1,150 | 410 | 310 | 419 | 555 |
| 5/18 | 3,240 | 411 | Void | 420 | 440 |
| 5/31 | 780 | 412 | 430 | 421 | 800 |
| | $6,165 | 413 | 490 | 422 | 80 |
| | | 414 | Void | 423 | 90 |
| | | 415 | 110 | 424 | 100 |
| | | 416 | 665 | 425 | 200 |
| | | | | | $6,790 |

An examination of the April reconciliation revealed a deposit in transit on April 30 of $400. The following checks were listed as outstanding: No. 384, $725; no. 395, $600; no. 406, $1,080; and no. 407, $860.

**Instructions**

a Assuming a cash balance per company records on May 31 of $4,950, prepare Union's bank reconciliation for May. Assume that any errors detected during the reconciliation process are the fault of Union's bookkeeper.

b Prepare the necessary journal entries for Union as of May 31.

**P7-B4** ***Petty cash fund***

Mt. Vernon Corporation operates a petty cash fund for small expenditures. The information that follows relates to July.

July 1 Established the petty cash fund for $300.

8 Replenished the fund. The following items were found in the petty cash box:

| | |
|---|---|
| Vouchers for postage | $ 40 |
| Vouchers for store supplies | 115 |
| Vouchers for miscellaneous expenses | 85 |
| Coins and currency | 60 |

17 Replenished the fund. The following items were found in the petty cash box:

| | |
|---|---|
| Vouchers for postage | $155 |
| Vouchers for store supplies | 30 |
| Vouchers for miscellaneous expenses | 33 |
| Coins and currency | 85 |

31 Replenished the fund. The following items were found in the petty cash box:

| | |
|---|---|
| Vouchers for postage | $ 34 |
| Vouchers for store supplies | 165 |
| Vouchers for miscellaneous expenses | 24 |
| Voucher stating: I owe the fund $25. Signed: A. Baxter (an employee) | |
| Coins and currency | 50 |

**Instructions**

a Record the necessary journal entries on July 1, 8, 17, and 31.

b It is now December 14. Heather Collins, an auditor for Mt. Vernon, believes the petty cash custodian has been stealing from the fund for the past several months. Collins told the custodian that a detailed examination of the fund would be performed on December 15 and that "everything had better be in order." Do you see any problems in Heather's informing the custodian of the upcoming audit? Explain.

**P7-B5** ***Voucher system***

The O'Toole Company, which uses a voucher system to control cash payments, had the following transactions during April:

Apr. 3 Purchased $800 of merchandise on account from Morisson Corporation, terms 3/10, n/30.

7 Purchased $300 of office supplies on account from the Larkin Supply Company.

12 Paid the proper amount due to Morisson Corporation.

14 Purchased office equipment on account for $1,200 from the Otis Desk Company.

18 Purchased $900 of merchandise on account from Upton, Incorporated, terms 2/10, n/eom.

24 Paid the amount due to Larkin Supply Company.

25 Purchased $700 of merchandise on account from Lewis Company.

26 Paid the amount due to Upton, Incorporated.

29 Prepared a $650 voucher for the April electric bill from Atlantic Power.

O'Toole uses a voucher register and check register similar in format to those illustrated in this chapter. Assume that there is no balance in the Vouchers Payable account as of April 1.

**Instructions**

a Record the appropriate transactions in the voucher register and/or the check register. Begin with voucher no. 741 and check no. 732.
b Total the voucher register and check register at the end of the month.
c Compute the balance in the Vouchers Payable account as of April 30.
d Compute the total of unpaid vouchers as of April 30. If all procedures are properly followed, what should the total of the unpaid vouchers be?

**P7-B6** ***Short-term investments; lower of cost or market***
Drexel Company acquired the following short-term stock investments during 19X3:

June 14 Purchased 800 shares of Merriam Co., for $6,320 plus $80 of brokerage fees.
18 Purchased 100 shares of Tipp, Inc., for $4,800 plus $200 of brokerage fees.
Aug. 1 Purchased 7,000 shares of Tokay Co., for $55,500 plus $1,500 of brokerage fees.

Dividends received during 19X3 and 19X3 year-end market values follow.

| | *Per Share* | |
|---|---|---|
| *Corporation* | *Dividends Received* | *Market Value* |
| Merriam | $0.75 | $ 7.50 |
| Tipp | 3.00 | 61.00 |
| Tokay | 0.10 | 6.00 |

**Instructions**

a Prepare journal entries to record the purchase of Drexel's short-term investments.
b Prepare a journal entry to record the dividends received in 19X3.
c Prepare a journal entry to properly value the securities as of December 31, 19X3.
d Show how Drexel's short-term investments would be disclosed on the December 31, 19X3, balance sheet.
e Suppose that the market price of the Tokay stock advanced to $9 per share by the end of 19X4 while the other market values remained unchanged. Given this situation:
(1) Prepare a journal entry to properly value the securities as of December 31, 19X4.
(2) Indicate how the short-term investments would be reported on the company's 19X4 balance sheet.

## Beyond the Basics

**BB7-1** ***Internal control and cash shortages***
Frank Evans is employed as a sales clerk by the Bedford Variety Store. He is a close friend of Ned Fong, the store's bookkeeper. Evans is experiencing some personal financial problems and Fong has agreed to employ him a few extra hours each week to assist in the bookkeeping department. During the last two weeks of June, Fong was on vacation. The following information pertains to June 20.

Evans checked out the firm's point-of-sale computer terminal at the end of the day. The terminal's tape revealed total sales of $373: cash, $128; credit, $245. The items that follow were contained in the terminal's drawer.

| | |
|---|---|
| Change fund at all times | $ 50 |
| Cash collections | 125 |

The cash collections included two checks:

| *Check Date* | *Customer* | *Amount* |
|---|---|---|
| June 20 | Nancy Jordan | $40 |
| June 24 | Sam May | 30 |

Evans helped satisfy his financial problems by stealing $20 from the day's receipts.

**Instructions**

a Present the journal entry that should have been made when checking out the terminal on June 20. *Hint:* Disregard the theft.
b What must Evans do to the accounting records to conceal his theft?
c Are there any apparent violations of internal control at the Bedford Variety Store? Explain.

**BB7-2** ***Valuation of short-term investments, conservatism***
The data that follow pertain to the short-term stock investments of five different companies.

| *Firm* | *Cost of Securities* | *Market Value of Securities* | *Balance in Allowance* |
|---|---|---|---|
| Ace, Inc. | $36,900 | $34,200 | $ — |
| Baxter, Inc. | 45,200 | 53,500 | — |
| City Cleaning | 18,500 | 13,600 | 2,900 |
| Dakota Mining | 25,800 | 26,500 | 1,800 |
| Eastern Corp. | 33,400 | 32,600 | 3,000 |

The "Balance in Allowance" column reflects the balance in the Allowance for Decline in Market Value of Short-term Investments account prior to any necessary adjusting entries on December 31, 19X2.

**Instructions**

a Study the data presented and prepare the adjusting entries needed to properly value the securities at the lower of cost or market on December 31, 19X2.
b Show how these securities would appear on the December 31, 19X2, balance sheet for each of the firms.
c Generally speaking, is the lower-of-cost-or-market method consistent or inconsistent with the accounting convention of conservatism? Explain your answer by relating the proper accounting treatment for the securities investments of Ace, Inc., and Dakota Mining.

## Answers to Chapter Quiz

**1** a ($10,000 + $900)

**2** c

**3** b ($200 − $36 − $94 − $2 − $58)

**4** a

**5** c ($80,000 − $75,800)

# Receivables

CHAPTER 8

## Learning Objectives

After reading this chapter you should:

1 Understand the distinction between trade and nontrade receivables.

2 Be able to account for uncollectible accounts by using both the direct write-off and the allowance methods.

3 Understand the difference between the income statement and balance sheet approaches to estimating bad debts.

4 Be able to account for credit card sales.

5 Be able to account for notes receivable, including the related interest computation and discounted and dishonored obligations.

The extension of credit has been a significant factor behind economic growth in the United States. The purchase of goods and services on an installment plan, by the use of in-house charge accounts, or through bank cards such as Visa and MasterCard is a way of life for today's average business or consumer.

Businesses extend credit in order to increase sales. Frequently, however, firms concentrate on this objective and lose sight of the costs related to the credit-granting decision. Credit sales often create the need for a credit department to (1) investigate customer credit ratings, (2) approve the extension of credit, and (3) attempt to collect delinquent accounts.

Furthermore, a company must wait to receive any monies due, and despite the offer of a cash discount, many customers still fail to settle their balances within requested time limits. Consequently, businesses must often sell short-term investments and secure bank loans to obtain needed operating funds. The former action may result in the loss of future interest or dividends, while the latter will give rise to interest costs.

Another cost related to credit sales is the result of nonpayment by customers. Firms rarely collect all their accounts receivable because customers go bankrupt, leave town, and so on. This cost, known as *bad debts expense,* can be especially high for an entity that has tried to increase sales by being very liberal in granting credit. Although some marginal customers may be profitable, the end result is normally increased costs and a lack of collection by the firm.

### Receivables

OBJECTIVE 1
Understand the distinction between trade and nontrade receivables.

Credit sales and other transactions give rise to receivables. **Receivables** represent a variety of claims against customers and others that arise from the operation of a business enterprise. Receivables are reported on the balance sheet as either current or noncurrent assets until they are ultimately collected. Those amounts expected to be collected within one year or the operating cycle, whichever is longer, are classified as current assets; all other receivables are classified as noncurrent.

Receivables are subdivided into two categories: trade and nontrade. The majority of receivables are **trade receivables,** which result from the sale of products or services to customers. Trade receivables consist of accounts receivable and notes receivable. In contrast, **nontrade receivables** arise from other transactions and events and include accrued receivables, advances to employees, and deposits with utilities.

In this chapter we will concentrate on the accounting issues associated with current trade receivables. Accounting for other types of receivables is discussed elsewhere in the text.

## Accounts Receivable

**Accounts receivable** represent the amounts due an entity from credit sales of goods and services. As the figures in Exhibit 8-1 indicate, accounts receivable can be a substantial percentage of total assets for many firms.

Given the magnitude of accounts receivable, proper valuation and presentation on the balance sheet are essential. In Chapter 5 we discussed a number of items related to this important asset, including trade discounts, sales discounts, and sales returns and allowances. We will now focus on one additional accounting issue: uncollectible accounts.

| | Borden, Inc. | Compaq Computer | NIKE, Inc. | Texas Instruments |
|---|---|---|---|---|
| Net accounts receivable | $ 883,924 | $ 428,338 | $258,393 | $ 942,100 |
| Total assets | 4,440,326 | 1,589,997 | 709,095 | 4,427,500 |
| Net accounts receivable as a percentage of total assets | 19.9% | 26.9% | 36.4% | 21.3% |

**Exhibit 8-1**
**Accounts Receivable for Various Firms (000 Omitted)**

Despite the use of credit standards, some uncollectible accounts (i.e., **bad debts**) almost always arise. Uncollectible accounts have both income statement and balance sheet implications for businesses. On the income statement, for example, an "adequate" amount for bad debts expense should be matched against (deducted from) the sales revenues generated. The objective is to derive a fair measurement of net income. Turning to the balance sheet, the Accounts Receivable account should be reduced to reflect the amounts that a firm has a reasonable expectation of collecting. This latter procedure is an application of conservatism in financial reporting, which permits asset write-downs when related valuations have been diminished or impaired.

There are two methods of accounting for uncollectible accounts: the direct write-off method and the allowance method.

## Direct Write-off Method

OBJECTIVE 2
Be able to account for uncollectible accounts by using both the direct write-off and the allowance methods.

Under the **direct write-off method,** bad debts are recognized when the actual loss is confirmed. That is, when a customer account is deemed uncollectible, the account is written off as an expense of the current accounting period. To illustrate, assume that Bill McCracken owes the Warren Company $875. After repeated collection efforts, Warren has just learned that McCracken has filed for bankruptcy. The Warren Company would make the following entry:

| | | |
|---|---|---|
| Bad Debts Expense | 875 | |
| Accounts Receivable: Bill McCracken | | 875 |
| To write off uncollectible account | | |

The direct write-off method of accounting for bad debts is simple and has the advantage of reporting actual losses rather than estimates. There are several deficiencies with this approach, however. Frequently, a customer's account is not deemed uncollectible until long after a sale has been made. The direct write-off method could therefore result in the recognition of sales revenue in one period and the expense related to that revenue in a later period. Thus, an improper matching of revenues and expenses would take place. Furthermore, because the write-off may occur in the future, Accounts Receivable is sometimes overstated at the end of the year of sale. In view of these problems, the direct write-off approach is most often used by businesses that experience relatively low levels of uncollectibles.

## Allowance Method

The **allowance method** overcomes the objections to the direct write-off method by associating the revenue and expense in the same accounting period. Correct matching is achieved through the use of *estimates* of bad debts expense. Reasonable estimates can normally be obtained by studying a firm's past experience with uncollectible accounts and making adjustments for current economic conditions and credit standards.

When the estimate of bad debts is determined, a journal entry is recorded at the end of the accounting period in the form of an adjustment. The entry involves a debit to Bad Debts Expense and a credit to an account entitled Allowance for Bad Debts.[1] Because credit policy is typically a management decision, Bad Debts Expense is normally reported on the income statement as an administrative operating expense. In contrast, the Allowance for Bad Debts is a contra asset that is offset against Accounts Receivable on the balance sheet, as follows (amounts are assumed):

| | | |
|---|---|---|
| Current assets | | |
| Accounts receivable | $19,000 | |
| Less: Allowance for bad debts | 2,600 | $16,400 |

Offsetting the Allowance in this manner informs financial statement users of the expected **net realizable value** ($16,400), or the amount of cash expected from the collection of present customer balances. The use of this separate valuation account is required because the specific uncollectible customer accounts are unknown when the financial statements are prepared. As a result, we cannot credit individual subsidiary accounts (and the Accounts Receivable control account) at the time of bad debt estimation.

Bad debts expense can be estimated by observing historical relationships between the actual bad debts incurred and (1) sales or (2) accounts receivable. These relationships may be summarized as follows:

**1** Relationship to sales (income statement approach)
   a Percentage of sales
   b Percentage of credit sales

**2** Relationship to accounts receivable (balance sheet approach)
   a Percentage of outstanding accounts receivable
   b Aging of accounts receivable

OBJECTIVE 3
Understand the difference between the income statement and balance sheet approaches to estimating bad debts.

## Relationship to Sales: Income Statement Approach

Estimating bad debts on the basis of sales results in matching current revenues with the costs incurred in producing those revenues. Stated differently, the sales that ultimately give rise to the uncollectibles are used as the basis for the period's expense. Because of its matching emphasis, this method is commonly referred to as the **income statement approach.**

The estimate of bad debts expense may be computed on total sales or credit sales. Total sales can be used when there is a fairly stable relationship between cash and credit sales from one period to the next. If this relationship varies substantially, the use of total sales may not be appropriate. Generally speaking, most accountants favor estimation of bad debts on the basis of credit sales only—a more rational approach because bad debts are not incurred on cash collections. To illustrate the income statement approach, assume that Lukin Company's sales on account for the

[1] The Allowance account is sometimes called the Allowance for Doubtful Accounts or the Allowance for Uncollectible Accounts.

current year total $500,000 and that bad debts have historically amounted to 3% of credit sales. The following adjusting entry for $15,000 ($500,000 × 0.03) would be made:

| | | |
|---|---|---|
| Bad Debts Expense | 15,000 | |
| Allowance for Bad Debts | | 15,000 |
| Adjusting entry | | |

## Relationship to Accounts Receivable: Balance Sheet Approach

Bad debts may also be estimated on the basis of accounts receivable. This method, known as the **balance sheet approach,** focuses on reporting accounts receivable at net realizable value. When using the balance sheet method, we must therefore consider the previous balance in the Allowance for Bad Debts account. For example, assume Galaxy Electronics has determined that bad debts normally amount to 3% of the year-end accounts receivable balance. The company's accounting records at the end of the year, prior to the adjustment for bad debts, disclose the following information:

| | |
|---|---|
| Accounts receivable | $600,000 |
| Allowance for bad debts | 2,800 (credit balance) |

Collections from customer accounts are expected to total $582,000 [$600,000 − ($600,000 × 0.03)], thereby requiring an $18,000 balance in the Allowance for Bad Debts ($600,000 − $582,000). Because $2,800 is presently in the account, an additional $15,200 ($18,000 − $2,800) must be entered to achieve the desired result. The following adjusting entry is needed:

| | | |
|---|---|---|
| Bad Debts Expense | 15,200 | |
| Allowance for Bad Debts | | 15,200 |
| Adjusting entry | | |

The effect of this entry is shown in the accompanying T-accounts:

| ***Bad Debts Expense*** | |
|---|---|
| Adj 15,200 | |

| ***Allowance for Bad Debts*** | | |
|---|---|---|
| | Balance | 2,800 |
| | Adj | 15,200 |
| | | **18,000** |

The resulting balance sheet presentation of Galaxy's accounts receivable appears below.

| | | |
|---|---|---|
| Current assets | | |
| Accounts receivable | $600,000 | |
| Less: Allowance for bad debts | 18,000 | $582,000 |

Occasionally, the Allowance for Bad Debts account may possess a debit balance.[2] Suppose, for instance, that Galaxy's Allowance account had a $3,000 *debit* balance prior to the adjustment. As shown by the number scale in Exhibit 8-2, a $21,000 adjusting entry would be necessary.

[2] The situations that cause a debit balance are discussed later in the chapter.

**Exhibit 8-2**
**Allowance for Bad Debts: Galaxy Electronics**

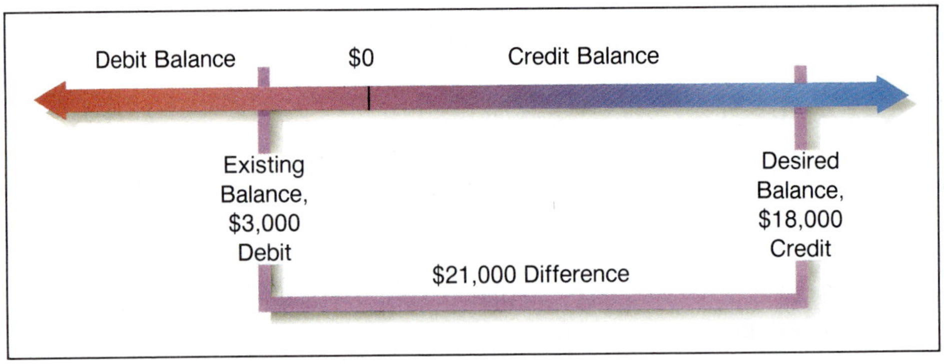


The $21,000 credit to the Allowance, when combined with the $3,000 debit balance, yields the desired $18,000 outcome.

> **TIPS & TECHNIQUES**
>
> The reported amount of bad debts expense is the focal point of the income statement approach; in contrast, the computation of net realizable value (i.e., accounts receivable valuation) is the thrust of the balance sheet method. Given the manner in which the Allowance for Bad Debts account is used to calculate net realizable value, the Allowance's balance must be considered in the adjustment process if the balance sheet approach is employed.

***Aging of Accounts Receivable*** Estimating bad debts as a flat percentage of outstanding accounts receivable ignores the due date of the many individual accounts that compose the total balance. The length of time a specific account has been outstanding is an important factor when assessing the probability of future collection. That is, a company is more likely to collect an account that is 30 days old than to collect one that is 180 days old. To overcome this problem, accountants have developed a more sophisticated approach to estimate bad debts. This method, termed **aging accounts receivable,** categorizes individual accounts according to the length of time outstanding. A historically developed bad debts percentage is then applied to each age category to determine the estimate.

The aging process not only furnishes information for the bad debt estimate but also serves as a useful management tool. The analysis of individual accounts provides insight regarding the success or failure of a firm's credit and collection efforts. Furthermore, close monitoring of specific customer activity will determine if any changes in a customer's credit rating are necessary.

To illustrate estimation by the aging process, examine Exhibit 8-3, which contains information from the records of the Livingston Corporation. The aging of individual customer accounts indicates that the Allowance for Bad Debts must contain a balance of $9,395 on December 31, 19XX.

As before, the previous balance in the Allowance account is considered when formulating the adjusting entry. If a review of Livingston's ledger revealed a credit balance of $2,200, then $7,195 ($9,395 − $2,200) would be needed to bring the Allowance up to the required figure. The following entry is necessary:

| | | |
|---|---|---|
| Bad Debts Expense | 7,195 | |
| Allowance for Bad Debts | | 7,195 |
| Adjusting entry | | |

**Exhibit 8-3**
**Aging Schedule**

**LIVINGSTON CORPORATION**
**Aging Schedule of Accounts Receivable**
**December 31, 19XX**

| | | *Length of Time Outstanding* | | | | |
|---|---|---|---|---|---|---|
| *Customer* | *Balance, 12/31/XX* | *Under 31 Days* | *31–60 Days* | *61–90 Days* | *91–120 Days* | *Over 120 Days* |
| Clark, Inc. | $ 15,000 | | | $6,000 | $5,000 | $4,000 |
| Gibbs Manufacturing | 36,000 | $31,000 | $ 5,000 | | | |
| Madden Co. | 19,500 | 15,000 | 4,500 | | | |
| Nunley Co. | 18,700 | 9,000 | 5,000 | 3,000 | 1,700 | |
| Patrick Corporation | 27,500 | 15,500 | 12,000 | | | |
| Total | $116,700 | $70,500 | $26,500 | $9,000 | $6,700 | $4,000 |

*Estimated Uncollectibles*

| *Age* | *Account Balances (from Above)* | × | *Estimated % Uncollectible* | = | *Estimated Amount of Uncollectibles* |
|---|---|---|---|---|---|
| Under 31 days | $ 70,500 | | 3% | | $2,115 |
| 31–60 days | 26,500 | | 7 | | 1,855 |
| 61–90 days | 9,000 | | 12 | | 1,080 |
| 91–120 days | 6,700 | | 35 | | 2,345 |
| Over 120 days | 4,000 | | 50 | | 2,000 |
| | $116,700 | | | | $9,395 |

In general, accountants favor the income statement approach over the balance sheet method. Their preference arises because of the emphasis on the matching of expenses and revenues and the reliance that financial statement users place on reported net income.

## Writing Off Uncollectible Accounts

Under the allowance method, individual accounts are written off when they are deemed uncollectible by debiting Allowance for Bad Debts and crediting Accounts Receivable. Note that Bad Debts Expense is not charged again at the time of write-off; to do so would result in double counting.

In view of this treatment, the write-off of an uncollectible account does not affect the net realizable value of the accounts receivable balance. As an example, consider the following information that appeared on Harvey Company's December 31, 19X1, balance sheet:

| | | |
|---|---|---|
| Current assets | | |
| Accounts receivable | $140,000 | |
| Less: Allowance for bad debts | 6,780 | $133,220 |

Assume that on January 18, 19X2, J. Waldrup's $425 balance is judged uncollectible. Thus, the entry that follows is made.

| | | |
|---|---|---|
| Allowance for Bad Debts | 425 | |
| Accounts Receivable: J. Waldrup | | 425 |
| To write off uncollectible account | | |

The write-off will not have any effect on the net accounts receivable balance because the entry reduces both the Allowance for Bad Debts and Accounts Receivable by the same amount. This result is shown below.

| | *Before* | *Write-off* | *After* |
|---|---|---|---|
| Accounts receivable | $140,000 | −$425 | $139,575 |
| Less: Allowance for bad debts | 6,780 | −425 | 6,355 |
| | $133,220 | | $133,220 |

The process of writing off an uncollectible account places debits in the Allowance for Bad Debts and may result in a debit balance at the end of the reporting period. This situation usually arises when a firm's estimate of expense (a credit in the Allowance account) is lower than its actual write-off experience. The debit balance is easily corrected by increasing the percentages used in the estimation process.

## Collection of an Account Previously Written Off

Occasionally, a customer whose account has been previously written off will pay the amount owed. In such cases the customer's receivable is first reestablished in the accounting records; the payment is then recorded. Continuing the previous example, assume J. Waldrup now pays $225 of his $425 balance. The following journal entries are needed:

| | | |
|---|---|---|
| Accounts Receivable: J. Waldrup | 225 | |
| Allowance for Bad Debts | | 225 |
| To reinstate account | | |
| Cash | 225 | |
| Accounts Receivable: J. Waldrup | | 225 |
| To record collection on account | | |

Observe that the reinstatement entry simply reverses the entry that was made for the write-off. If collection of the entire $425 is likely, Waldrup's account would be reestablished for the full amount.

Notice that the net effect on the Accounts Receivable account is zero, because it is debited and credited for the same figure. Yet, this two-entry procedure is preferred over one that results in a single debit to Cash and a credit to Allowance for Bad Debts. Why? By going back and reinstating the customer's account on the books, we are showing that an attempt has been made to pay the balance due. This action and information could be useful to management in future credit-granting decisions.

## Insights into Business Operations

A study of bad debt disclosures will reveal various insights about business activities. For instance, the allowance for bad debts as a percentage of ending accounts receivable varies significantly by company. This variation is caused, in part, by the type of product being sold, customer payment habits, and a firm's credit policy. A review of recent corporate annual reports found, for example, that The Coca-Cola Company has recorded an allowance of about $2 per $100 of accounts receivable;

Midway Airlines about $5 per $100 of accounts receivable; Reebok International about $6; and The New York Times Company, which, in addition to publishing its flagship newspaper, is also involved with other newspapers, periodicals, broadcasting, and forest products, about $12 per $100.

## Credit Card Sales

**OBJECTIVE 4**
**Be able to account for credit card sales.**

Many retailers and service establishments have found that maintaining credit departments, billing customers, and collecting accounts are costly and time-consuming processes. As a result, a large number of firms have stopped carrying their own accounts in favor of credit cards such as American Express, Visa, and MasterCard. A merchant's acceptance of these well-known cards usually offers the benefit of increased sales. In addition, the seller assumes little or no risk. If a customer does not pay his or her bill, the credit card issuer suffers the loss.

When a sale is made on one of the foregoing or similar cards, the purchaser signs a multipart form, which includes a credit card draft. The draft authorizes the credit card company to pay the seller, which it generally does shortly after the sale is made. The merchant, then, experiences faster cash inflows and need no longer wait 30 or more days for customers to settle their obligations. The credit card company later bills the customer for the amount of the purchase.

The drafts just discussed are submitted to credit card companies, such as American Express or Diners Club, or to banks in the case of Visa and MasterCard. In either situation sellers do not receive the full amount of the draft because a service charge is assessed. This charge is usually a percentage of each sale and, in essence, is a fee for the use of a credit department and customer billing services. The service charge varies and is partially determined by the seller's annual volume of credit card transactions.

When sales are made on bank cards, the merchant submits the drafts along with daily cash receipts to the bank. The bank increases the seller's account; the service charge is automatically deducted and often appears on the bank statement along with other account service charges. In view of this treatment, the credit card sale made on a bank card is really a cash sale.

If the transaction is on a nonbank card, the merchant normally mails the drafts to the credit card company.[3] Because reimbursement is not instantaneous, an account receivable is established for the amount of the sale. As an example, assume that Jacobs Jewelry sold $2,000 of merchandise on Charge-It, a nonbank credit card, giving rise to the following entry:

| | | |
|---|---|---|
| Accounts Receivable: Charge-It | 2,000 | |
| Sales | | 2,000 |
| To record credit card sale | | |

If the service fee charged by the card company is 5%, Jacobs would update the accounting records in the following manner when the receivable from Charge-It is collected:

| | | |
|---|---|---|
| Cash | 1,900 | |
| Credit Card Expense | 100 | |
| Accounts Receivable: Charge-It | | 2,000 |
| To record collection on account from credit card company | | |

[3] Credit card companies often allow merchants other alternatives, for instance, the direct deposit of drafts at designated banks. A higher service charge is usually assessed if this option is selected.

## HIGHLIGHT

# Bonnie and Clyde: A Bigger Payoff With Credit Cards

Bonnie and Clyde, the notorious bank robbers, probably lived too early. In their day posses followed in hot pursuit, shooting hot lead. Today, smart crooks are using plastic to steal more in a week than Bonnie and Clyde ever dreamed possible. Credit card fraud cost financial institutions about $700 million in a recent year, far exceeding amounts lost to currency counterfeiting. That's a sobering thought for a society intent upon replacing cash with credit.

As a result of growing credit card scams, Congress has assigned the Secret Service to police such fraud. Not a moment too soon, either. In an extremely successful credit card bust, the Service raided two New York City print shops and bagged 100,000 near-perfect Visas and MasterCards. Had those cards made it into circulation, the Service figures $500 million in fraud would have been committed.

How do these fraud artists work? In several ways and not always mysteriously. There is the case of Arturo Hoyo, who pleaded guilty of bilking American Express for $500,000. Hoyo simply placed an advertisement in *The Wall Street Journal*, offering brand name television/stereo equipment for $289.95. His ad listed a Miami toll-free number for American Express cardholders. "I got 600 calls a day," beams Hoyo. "What a great newspaper that is." Hoyo charged cardholders for equipment he never shipped and was paid promptly by the company on the basis of the fraudulent sales slips. By the time his charges began appearing on American Express bills and customers complained, Hoyo had folded his tent and moved on—complete with a new alias and corporate identity.

The ease with which these scams can be pulled off is sometimes frightening. In one instance, a company purchased at least 100,000 cardholder names and account numbers from such unsuspecting organizations as Neiman-Marcus and the American Automobile Association, sometimes paying as little as 6 cents apiece! Consumers, trusting these entities with their card numbers, never knew they were being sold out. In another case, reporters/researchers from *Forbes*, which published this article, had no trouble securing needed data and supplies. One enterprising individual snared a bag of Avis trash during a morning jog through Manhattan. Sure enough, the bag was filled with rental agreements imprinted with American Express, Visa, and MasterCards, plus all the driver's license data required for a counterfeit. And it took only three phone calls to find white vinyl sheet and laminating material suitable for producing credit cards.

Companies are becoming wise to such moves and are improving their controls. Software is now in use that spots unusual activity in merchant accounts. Card designs and lettering are more complicated. Some have holograms, which are difficult, though not impossible, to counterfeit. In all likelihood the next step forward will be cards with microchips.

The crooks, though, will find a way. Recall that Bonnie and Clyde were put to death in a well-known shootout. However, bank robbing and other scams didn't stop the day that the famous bloodbath took place.

SOURCE: Adapted from "How the Smart Crooks Use Plastic," *Forbes*, September 9, 1985, pp. 88–91, 94–95. Reprinted by permission of *Forbes* magazine, © Forbes Inc., 1985.

## Installment Receivables

A review of the balance sheets of many large retail businesses will disclose the presence of various types of accounts receivable. One type, known as an **installment receivable,** arises when customers purchase goods on a deferred payment plan. These plans are commonly used to finance a variety of costly acquisitions, such as large appliances and furniture.

An installment receivable is initially established in the accounting records at the sale price of the merchandise sold. Slowly the receivable is reduced, as the buyer makes specified, uniform payments over a predetermined number of months. Each payment collected by the firm consists of not only a reduction in the amount owed, but also an interest charge for use of the seller's funds.

The specific details of deferred payment plans are clearly beyond the scope of this text. It is important to note, however, that although many installment receivables will be collected several years into the future, these amounts are often classified as current assets. Such treatment is justified if the receivables arise from normal business activity and are therefore settled within the operating cycle of the company.

## Notes Receivable

The financial statements of many entities often reveal an asset entitled notes receivable. **Notes receivable** (sometimes called promissory notes) are written promises from clients or customers to pay a definite amount of money on a specific future date. These instruments are used in extending credit to customers and to lengthen the repayment period of outstanding accounts receivable. Notes are popular in some industries and seldom encountered in others. Exhibit 8-4 illustrates a typical promissory note.

In this particular case Precision Equipment is the **maker** of the note, namely, the person or firm that promises to pay the stipulated amount. Forseth Company is the **payee,** or the party to be paid. The stated amount (face value) of the note, $6,000, is termed the **principal.** Finally, February 9 is the **maturity date,** or the date that the note becomes due. The maturity date is computed as follows:

| | | |
|---|---|---|
| Term of note | | 60 days |
| Days outstanding in | | |
| December (31 − 11) | 20 | |
| January | 31 | 51 |
| Days outstanding in February until maturity | | 9 |

**Exhibit 8-4**
**Promissory Note**

$6,000    Boise, Idaho    December 11, 19X1

Sixty days after date we promise to

pay to the order of Forseth Company

Six thousand and no/100 ---------- dollars

for value received, with interest of 12%

payable at First City Bank

Due February 9, 19X2    Michelle McGregor

Precision Equipment Co.

Had the term of the note been two months (as opposed to 60 days), the maturity date would have been February 11, which is two months from the time of issue.

### The Nature of Interest

**Interest** is the charge imposed on the borrower of funds. The note in Exhibit 8-4 indicates that Precision Equipment owes Forseth $6,000; however, the amount is not due until February 9, 19X2. In return for this temporary extension of credit, Forseth has become entitled to interest at a rate of 12%. Does this mean that Precision will have to pay the principal plus an additional $720 ($6,000 × 0.12)? The answer is no.

Interest rates are normally quoted on an annual basis. As a result, the term of the note would have to be extended from 60 days to a full year in order for the charge to total $720. To compute interest for a given period, the following formula is needed:

$$\text{Interest} = \text{Principal} \times \text{Rate} \times \text{Time}$$

This formula mathematically expresses the intuitive feeling that interest depends on a financial agreement's rate, amount, and duration.

To fully understand the preceding computation, it is important to know that the definition of principal is expanded somewhat to be more than just the face value of a note. Principal, as used here, is the amount on which interest is figured and may be the balance of an account receivable (in the case of finance charges), the outstanding balance of a loan, or the amount on deposit in a savings account.

Further, the formula's time element can be expressed in either days or months. In our example, for instance, interest would be calculated as follows:

$$\$6{,}000 \times 0.12 \times \tfrac{60}{360} = \$120$$

In most applications and for ease of computation, a year is considered to have 360 days.[4] Because the 12% rate covers an annual time frame, a factor of $\frac{60}{360}$ is appropriate.

Had the term of the note been three months, a factor of $\frac{3}{12}$ would have been employed, to yield interest charges of $180:

$$\$6{,}000 \times 0.12 \times \tfrac{3}{12} = \$180$$

### Accounting for Notes and Interest

> OBJECTIVE 5
> Be able to account for notes receivable, including the related interest computation and discounted and dishonored obligations.

Notes receivable are initially entered in the accounting records at face value, requiring a debit to the Notes Receivable account. Because the note is owned by the payee firm, the associated interest is revenue. Interest revenue is recorded as it is received and as a year-end adjustment if the reporting period ends prior to the maturity date.

To illustrate, we will continue the Forseth Company example. The note in question was received on December 11, 19X1, from Precision Equipment, which desired to extend the repayment period of a previous purchase on account. Forseth would record the note as follows:

| | | | |
|---|---|---|---|
| Dec. 11 | Notes Receivable | 6,000 | |
| | Accounts Receivable: Precision Equipment | | 6,000 |
| | Received note in settlement of account balance | | |

[4] Federal agencies and some lenders use a 365-day year.

Precision has agreed to pay $6,120 on February 9: $6,000 principal plus $120 of interest ($6,000 × 0.12 × $\frac{60}{360}$). The amount due on the maturity date, principal plus interest, is commonly referred to as the **maturity value.**

Assume that December 31, 19X1, is the end of Forseth's accounting period. Although no interest has been received as of this date, 20 days' worth has been earned. Therefore, accrued interest revenue of $40 ($6,000 × 0.12 × $\frac{20}{360}$) is recorded by the following adjusting entry:

| | | | |
|---|---|---|---|
| Dec. 31 | Interest Receivable | 40 | |
| | Interest Revenue | | 40 |
| | Adjusting entry | | |

Also on December 31 closing entries would be recorded. The interest T-accounts, after closing, would appear as follows:

**Interest Receivable**

| | | |
|---|---|---|
| 12/31 | 40 | |

**Interest Revenue**

| | | | |
|---|---|---|---|
| 12/31 Closing | 40 | 12/31 | 40 |

On February 9, 19X2, when Precision Equipment pays the note, Forseth will make the entry that is shown below.

| | | | |
|---|---|---|---|
| Feb. 9 | Cash | 6,120 | |
| | Interest Receivable | | 40 |
| | Interest Revenue | | 80 |
| | Notes Receivable | | 6,000 |
| | Collected note and interest from Precision Equipment | | |

To explain, the receipt of the maturity value calls for a debit to Cash for $6,120 and a credit to Notes Receivable for the original amount of the obligation ($6,000). One-third of the interest of $120 is located in the Interest Receivable account; thus, Interest Receivable must be credited for $40. The remaining $80, which has been earned during 19X2, is revenue. Observe how the adjusting entry effectively splits the interest: $40 of revenue in 19X1 (20 days) and $80 of revenue in 19X2 (40 days).

## Discounting Notes Receivable

Companies frequently find that unexpected conditions dictate the need for additional cash on a short-term basis. One of the many ways to satisfy this need involves the payee's discounting a note receivable at the bank. **Discounting** allows the payee to generate cash at the time of discounting rather than wait until the note comes due and is paid by the maker. The maker is notified to pay the bank directly on the note's maturity date, but the payee usually guarantees payment should the maker default. Consequently, during the period from the discount date to the maturity date, the note represents a **contingent (possible) liability** to the payee. Such amounts are disclosed in the footnotes to the financial statements, as opposed to the liability section of the balance sheet, because a *definite* obligation does not exist.

Since the maker is not obligated to pay the bank until maturity, the bank, in effect, is lending the discounting firm a sum of money. As in all loans, interest is charged. In this case, however, the interest is called a *discount* and is determined by the discount percentage (interest rate) assessed by the bank. At the time a note is discounted, the payee records the proceeds received and nets the discount against any interest revenue to be earned on the note. The entries to record the receipt, discounting, and collection of a note receivable are illustrated in the following example.

On March 10, the Kyle Corporation received a $20,000, 90-day note from Walt Dailey, a customer, in settlement of his overdue account balance. The note carried a 10% interest rate. On April 9, 30 days later, Kyle discounted the note at the bank at a 12% discount rate. The entries below are necessary to record these transactions.

| | | | |
|---|---|---|---|
| Mar. 10 | Notes Receivable | 20,000 | |
| | Accounts Receivable: Walt Dailey | | 20,000 |
| | Received note in settlement of account balance | | |
| Apr. 9 | Cash | 20,090 | |
| | Interest Revenue | | 90 |
| | Notes Receivable | | 20,000 |
| | Proceeds from Dailey's discounted note | | |

The calculation of the cash proceeds from the bank is as follows:

| | |
|---|---|
| Face amount of note | $20,000 |
| Add: Interest revenue ($20,000 × 0.10 × $\frac{90}{360}$) | 500 |
| Maturity value | $20,500 |
| Deduct: Discount ($20,500 × 0.12 × $\frac{60}{360}$) | 410 |
| Proceeds | $20,090 |

The discount is based on the maturity value of $20,500, which is the value of the note to the bank. The bank subtracts the discount from the maturity value to determine the cash proceeds. Observe that the bank's discount calculation ($410) is dependent on the number of days the money will be advanced to Kyle. Because Kyle held the 90-day note for 30 days, the bank expects to be repaid in 60 days. Finally, notice that Kyle collected $20,090 for a $20,000 receivable, requiring the recognition of interest revenue of $90. If the proceeds had been less than $20,000, the firm would have incurred interest expense. The deciding factors behind the generation of interest revenue or interest expense are the interest rate on the note, the bank's discount rate, and the holding periods involved.

If a balance sheet is prepared prior to the note's maturity date (June 8), Kyle will construct a footnote to the financial statements similar to the following:

> Note E: Contingencies
>
> On April 30, 19XX, the company was contingently liable for a discounted note receivable having a maturity value of $20,500.

The footnote is needed until June 8, at which time Dailey will either pay the bank (and thereby clear Kyle) or default.

## Dishonoring a Note

In the event that Dailey fails to settle his obligation ($20,500), the note is said to be **dishonored.** Kyle must now pay this amount to the bank because of the contin-

> **▶ TIPS & TECHNIQUES**
>
> The formulas that follow serve to summarize many of the computations related to discounted notes receivable.
>
> Interest = Principal × Rate × Note Term*
>
> Maturity Value = Principal + Interest
>
> Discount = Maturity Value × Discount Rate × Time Note is Held by Bank*
>
> Proceeds = Maturity Value − Discount
>
> If the proceeds exceed the note's face value, interest revenue is generated. Conversely, the opposite situation (proceeds less than face value) gives rise to interest expense.
>
> * Expressed as a fraction of 360 days or, if appropriate, 12 months.

gent liability; furthermore, the company might be assessed a service charge (termed a **protest fee**). The required accounting is shown by continuing our illustration.

Assume that on June 8 the bank notified Kyle that Dailey had defaulted and also levied a $25 protest fee. Kyle paid the amount due ($20,500 + $25 = $20,525) and recorded the following entry:

| | | | |
|---|---|---|---|
| June 8 | Accounts Receivable: Walt Dailey | 20,525 | |
| | Cash | | 20,525 |
| | To record payment to the bank from note default by Walt Dailey | | |

Notice that the protest fee is not considered an expense. Rather, the total amount disbursed is charged to Accounts Receivable in hopes of future collection. If collection attempts fail, the account will be written off as a bad debt, using procedures discussed earlier in the chapter.

## Notes Not Yet Discounted

Our example of a dishonored note focused on an obligation that had been previously discounted at the bank. It is possible, of course, that a note is dishonored at maturity while still in the possession of the payee. If Kyle Corporation had held Dailey's note until maturity, the following journal entry would have been recorded:

| | | | |
|---|---|---|---|
| June 8 | Accounts Receivable: Walt Dailey | 20,500 | |
| | Notes Receivable | | 20,000 |
| | Interest Revenue | | 500 |
| | To record dishonored note by Walt Dailey | | |

Observe that the obligation's face value is transferred out of Notes Receivable and into Accounts Receivable. This procedure leaves only nonmaturing obligations in the Notes Receivable account and generates a record in the Accounts Receivable subsidiary ledger that Dailey has defaulted. Such information may be useful in future credit-granting decisions.

Furthermore, the entry reveals that any interest that has been earned is (1) recognized as revenue and (2) added to the amount due from the maker. Although this latter procedure may seem bizarre in view of the default, be aware that the payee has a valid claim against the maker not only for the face value of the note but for the interest as well.

## Chapter Review

### Learning Objectives—The Key Points

**1 Understand the distinction between trade and nontrade receivables.** Trade receivables result from the sale of products or services to customers and consist of accounts receivable and notes receivable. In contrast, nontrade receivables arise from other transactions and events and include accrued receivables, advances to employees, and deposits with utilities.

**2 Be able to account for uncollectible accounts by using both the direct write-off and the allowance methods.** Under the direct write-off method, bad debts are recognized when the actual loss is confirmed. Use of this approach may result in a mismatch of revenue and expense on the income statement and overstated receivables on the balance sheet. With the allowance method, improved matching and receivables valuation are achieved through the use of bad debt estimates in the adjusting process. The proper adjusting entry involves a debit to Bad Debts Expense and a credit to Allowance for Bad Debts. The latter account is a contra asset that appears on the balance sheet as a deduction from Accounts Receivable.

**3 Understand the difference between the income statement and balance sheet approaches to estimating bad debts.** The income statement approach to estimation involves bad debt estimates that are calculated on the basis of sales. This procedure results in matching current revenues with the costs incurred in producing those revenues. Alternatively, under the balance sheet approach, bad debts are estimated on the basis of accounts receivable, sometimes by using the aging process. This method focuses on reporting accounts receivable at net realizable value, thereby requiring that the existing balance in the Allowance for Bad Debts account be considered when constructing the adjusting entry.

**4 Be able to account for credit card sales.** Credit card sales made on bank cards (e.g., Visa and MasterCard) are similar to cash sales. Drafts deposited at the bank are credited to the depositor's account, with an appropriate service charge often appearing on the month-end bank statement. For sales on nonbank cards such as American Express, the seller normally mails the drafts to the credit card company and records a receivable for the amount due. The receivable is eliminated upon receipt of funds from the credit card company, at which time the card company's service charge is recorded as an expense.

**5 Be able to account for notes receivable, including the related interest computation and discounted and dishonored obligations.** Notes receivable are written promises from clients or customers to pay a definite amount of money on a specific date. Such obligations are recorded at face value and normally bear interest, a charge for the use of borrowed funds. Interest is computed by using the following formula: interest = principal × rate × time.

The payee may discount the note at a bank to obtain needed funds, a process that creates a contingent liability. Should the maker fail to pay the bank on the scheduled date, the payee must settle the maker's obligation. The note is said to be dishonored (i.e., not paid at maturity), giving rise to a debit to Accounts Receivable in hopes of future collection. Such a procedure is necessary for dishonored notes that have been previously discounted as well as for those that are held by a business until maturity.

## Chapter Quiz

The five questions that follow relate to several issues raised in the chapter. Test your knowledge of the issues by selecting the best answer. (The answers appear on p. 301.)

**1** The following information is available for Hardy Company:

| | |
|---|---|
| Credit sales during 19X8 | $100,000 |
| Allowance for Bad Debts, 1/1/X8 | 2,000 (credit) |
| Accounts written off during 19X8 | 4,500 |

Hardy estimated that bad debts would amount to 5% of credit sales. What amount should Hardy record as bad debts expense for the year ended December 31, 19X8?

a $3,000.
b $4,500.
c $5,000.
d $7,000.

**2** An aging schedule indicated that Murphy had $12,500 of uncollectible accounts. Yet, the adjusting entry for bad debts expense was prepared for only $6,000. This situation arose because:

a there was a $6,500 debit balance in the Allowance for Bad Debts account prior to adjustment.
b there was a $6,500 credit balance in the Allowance for Bad Debts account prior to adjustment.
c the Bad Debts Expense account had an existing balance of $6,500.
d $6,500 of uncollectible accounts were written off during the accounting period.

**3** The write-off of a bad debt by a business that uses the allowance method:

a increases the Allowance for Bad Debts.
b decreases the net realizable value of Accounts Receivable.
c has no effect on the net realizable value of Accounts Receivable.
d increases Bad Debts Expense.

**4** On November 1, 19X6, Trendy Company received a $24,000, 3-month, 10% note receivable. How much interest revenue should be reported in 19X6 from this note assuming that Trendy closes its books on December 31, 19X6?

a $200.
b $400.
c $600.
d $2,400.

**5** When a note receivable is discounted at a bank:

a the maker receives the maturity value of the note.
b the payee receives the face value of the note.
c the payee has a contingent liability to the bank.
d the bank has a contingent liability to the payee.

## Summary Problem

The Shank Company's balance sheet revealed the following information as of January 1:

| | | |
|---|---|---|
| Accounts receivable | $75,800 | |
| Less: Allowance for bad debts | 6,500 | $69,300 |

The following transactions took place during the first quarter of the year:

| | | |
|---|---|---|
| Jan. | 2 | Received a $4,000, 60-day, 12% note from T. Abernathy in settlement of his account balance. |
| | 18 | Wrote off the $1,300 balance owed by Magna Company as uncollectible. |

| | | |
|---|---|---|
| Feb. | 11 | Discounted Abernathy's note at the bank at a 15% discount rate. |
| | 17 | Received $180 from Pat Young. Young's account had been written off as uncollectible in the previous year. |
| Mar. | 4 | Received notification from the bank that Abernathy's note had been dishonored. Paid the bank the proper amount due, plus a $15 protest fee. |

Shank's credit sales for the first quarter totaled $142,000.

**Instructions**

**a** Prepare journal entries for the transactions from January 2 through March 4.

**b** Prepare the journal entry on March 31 to adjust the Allowance account, assuming bad debts are estimated at 3% of credit sales.

**Solution**

| | | | | | |
|---|---|---|---|---|---|
| **a** | Jan. | 2 | Notes Receivable | 4,000 | |
| | | | Accounts Receivable: T. Abernathy | | 4,000 |
| | | | Received note in settlement of account balance | | |
| | | 18 | Allowance for Bad Debts | 1,300 | |
| | | | Accounts Receivable: Magna Company | | 1,300 |
| | | | To write off uncollectible account | | |
| | Feb. | 11 | Cash | 4,046 | |
| | | | Interest Revenue | | 46 |
| | | | Notes Receivable | | 4,000 |
| | | | Discounted note of T. Abernathy | | |

Calculations:

| | |
|---|---|
| Face amount of note | $4,000 |
| Add: Interest revenue ($\$4{,}000 \times 0.12 \times \frac{60}{360}$) | 80 |
| Maturity value | $4,080 |
| Deduct: Discount ($\$4{,}080 \times 0.15 \times \frac{20}{360}$) | 34 |
| Proceeds | $4,046 |

| | | | | | |
|---|---|---|---|---|---|
| | | 17 | Accounts Receivable: Pat Young | 180 | |
| | | | Allowance for Bad Debts | | 180 |
| | | | To reinstate account | | |
| | | | Cash | 180 | |
| | | | Accounts Receivable: Pat Young | | 180 |
| | | | To record collection on account | | |
| | Mar. | 4 | Accounts Receivable: T. Abernathy | 4,095 | |
| | | | Cash | | 4,095 |
| | | | To record payment to the bank from note default of T. Abernathy | | |
| **b** | Mar. | 31 | Bad Debts Expense | 4,260 | |
| | | | Allowance for Bad Debts | | 4,260 |
| | | | Adjusting entry ($\$142{,}000 \times 0.03$) | | |

## Questions

**Q8-1** Distinguish between trade and nontrade receivables. Give three examples of the latter.

**Q8-2** Explain why uncollectible accounts have both income statement and balance sheet implications for accountants.

**Q8-3** Explain how the doctrine of conservatism relates to accounting for uncollectible accounts.

**Q8-4** Briefly describe the two methods that can be used to record losses from bad debts.

**Q8-5** Discuss some possible deficiencies with the direct write-off method of uncollectible accounts.

**Q8-6** Define the term "net realizable value" as it relates to accounts receivable.

**Q8-7** Briefly describe the two general approaches that may be used for the estimation of bad debts.

**Q8-8** Discuss the advantages of aging schedules over the use of a flat percentage of accounts receivable for estimates of uncollectible accounts.

**Q8-9** The Howard Corporation uses the allowance method of accounting for bad debts. What is the impact, if any, on bad debts expense of the write-off of an uncollectible customer account?

**Q8-10** The York Company has written off the $375 balance of Dick Peterson as uncollectible. The merchandise purchased by Peterson originally cost York $250. If Peterson later pays his account, determine the additional revenue that York would generate. York uses the allowance method of accounting for bad debts.

**Q8-11** Why do companies accept credit cards such as Visa and American Express?

**Q8-12** Discuss the accounting procedures required for sales of merchandise made on nonbank credit cards in those situations where drafts are mailed to the credit card company.

**Q8-13** In which section of a balance sheet are installment receivables often disclosed?

**Q8-14** What is a note receivable?

**Q8-15** What is the interest computation formula? Why is the inclusion of a time factor necessary?

**Q8-16** What is the purpose behind the discounting of a note receivable?

**Q8-17** Where does the payee's contingent liability appear in the financial statements when a note receivable has been discounted at a bank?

**Q8-18** Artivo Company recently paid a $20 protest fee to the bank, which relates to a customer's dishonored note. The bookkeeper charged the payment to Protest Fee Expense. Is this treatment correct? Why?

**Q8-19** Why is Accounts Receivable increased for both the principal and interest earned when a nondiscounted note receivable is dishonored?

## Exercises

**E8-1** ***Direct write-off method***

Harrisburg Company, which began business in early 19X7, reported $40,000 of accounts receivable on the December 31, 19X7, balance sheet. Included in this amount was a $550 claim against Tom Mattingly from a sale made in July. On January 4, 19X8, the company learned that Mattingly had filed for personal bankruptcy. Harrisburg uses the direct write-off method to account for bad debts.

a Prepare the journal entry needed to write off Mattingly's account.

b Comment on the ability of the direct write-off method to value receivables on the year-end balance sheet.

**E8-2** ***Allowance method: Estimation and balance sheet disclosure***

The following preadjusted information for the Minoso Company is available on December 31:

| | | |
|---|---|---|
| Cash sales | $105,000 | |
| Credit sales | 195,000 | |
| Total sales | | $300,000 |
| Accounts receivable | | 92,600 |
| Allowance for bad debts | | 5,300 (credit balance) |

a Prepare the journal entries necessary to record Minoso's bad debt expense under each of the following assumptions:
   (1) Bad debts are estimated to be 3% of sales.
   (2) Bad debts are estimated to be 5% of credit sales.
   (3) Bad debts are estimated to be 8% of accounts receivable.

b How would Minoso's accounts receivable appear on the December 31 balance sheet under assumption (2) of part (a)?

c How would Minoso's accounts receivable appear on the December 31 balance sheet under assumption (3) of part (a)?

**E8-3** ***Bad debt estimation: Balance sheet approach***

Folsom Company has gathered the following information to estimate bad debts by the use of an aging schedule:

| *Age of Receivable* | *Amount* | *Estimated Percentage Uncollectible* |
|---|---|---|
| Under 31 days | $300,000 | 2% |
| 31–60 days | 140,000 | 8 |
| 61–90 days | 60,000 | 30 |
| 91–120 days | 30,000 | 40 |
| Over 120 days | 8,000 | 70 |
| | $538,000 | |

a Determine the estimated amount of uncollectible accounts.

b Prepare the journal entry to record bad debts expense, assuming the previous Allowance for Bad Debts account balance was
   (1) $7,400 (credit).
   (2) $2,900 (debit).

c Assume that the proper adjusting entry has been made in case (1) of part (b). Present the correct balance sheet disclosure of Folsom's receivables.

**E8-4** ***Allowance method: Account write-off and collection***

On January 2, Maher Company has the following information available concerning its accounts receivable balance:

| | |
|---|---|
| Accounts receivable | $192,500 |
| Less: Allowance for bad debts | 7,800 |
| | $184,700 |

During January, Maher learned that J. Smitham, a customer, was unable to pay his balance of $2,500. The account was written off the accounting records on January 31. Later, on February 18, Maher received a $2,500 check from Smitham.

a Prepare Maher's journal entries to record (1) the write-off of the Smitham account and (2) the payment by Smitham.

b What is the impact of the transactions in part (a) on the net realizable value of Maher's accounts receivable?

**E8-5** ***Allowance method: Analysis of account write-off***

The Syracuse Company, which uses the allowance method of accounting for bad debts, has just written off the $640 balance of Providence Company as uncollectible. Determine the impact of the write-off (increase, decrease, or no effect) on each of the following:

a Bad debts expense
b Net income
c Accounts receivable
d Allowance for bad debts
e Net realizable value of accounts receivable

**E8-6** ***Credit card sales***

Compton Sales Company sold $8,400 of merchandise during August on Charge All, a national credit card. Charge All's collection fee is 4%.

a Prepare the journal entries required by Compton to record (1) credit card sales and (2) subsequent reimbursement from Charge All. Assume Charge All is not a bank card and that credit card drafts are mailed to Charge All.
b Discuss several of the benefits and problems of accepting credit cards.

**E8-7** ***Notes receivable and interest: Basic computations***

The following notes receivable were held by Rizzuto, Inc.:

| *Date of Note* | *Principal* | *Interest Rate* | *Term* |
|---|---|---|---|
| April 3 | $ 3,000 | 10% | 2 months |
| June 21 | 10,000 | 12 | 90 days |

a Determine the maturity date for each of the notes.
b Determine the interest earned on each of the notes if the notes are held until maturity.
c Assume that Rizzuto's fiscal year ends on June 30. Calculate the amount of accrued interest receivable that the company would disclose on its June 30 balance sheet.

**E8-8** ***Journal entries for notes receivable***

The Watson Company received a $6,000, 90-day, 12% note from Carla London on November 11, 19X1. London had previously purchased merchandise from Watson and wished to extend the repayment date of the receivable. Prepare the journal entries required by Watson to record the following:

a The receipt of the note from London.
b Accrued interest on December 31, 19X1, the end of Watson's accounting year.
c The payment of the note by London on February 9, 19X2.

**E8-9** ***Journal entries for discounting***

On May 1 of the current year, Sax Company accepted a $15,000, 60-day, 12% note on account from Royal Corporation. On June 9, Sax discounted the note at the First Street Bank at a 14% discount rate.

a Prepare the appropriate journal entry to record the receipt of the note on May 1.
b Prepare the appropriate journal entry to record the discounting on June 9.
c On June 30, Sax received notification that Royal had dishonored the note. Prepare the appropriate journal entry for Sax, assuming a protest fee of $20.

**E8-10** ***Accrued interest; dishonored notes***

The Nugget Company sells used cars. Greg Schulte, a customer, purchased a $5,000 automobile on November 1, 19X1. He paid $200 as a down payment and signed an

18%, 90-day note for the remaining balance. Prepare Nugget's journal entries to record the following:

a The sale on November 1, 19X1.

b Accrued interest on December 31, 19X1, the end of Nugget's accounting period.

c Schulte's failure to pay at maturity on January 30, 19X2.

**E8-11** ***Overview of notes receivable***

Evaluate the comments that follow as being True or False. If the comment is false, briefly explain why.

a Fred James gave Nancy Foster a 60-day note receivable. Foster is deemed the payee in this situation.

b A $30,000 note having a maturity value of $32,600 was discounted at a bank, with the proceeds amounting to $31,800. The maker should record $800 of interest expense on the transaction.

c A note's payee is contingently liable if the note is discounted at a bank. The maker, on the other hand, is absolutely liable.

d Protest fees are normally charged to Accounts Receivable by the paying firm.

e A note receivable of Mark Cooke that is held by Joe Swindell falls due on August 29. If the note is dishonored, Swindell should charge both the interest earned over the note's term and the note's maturity value to Accounts Receivable in hopes of future collection.

# Problems

## Series A

**P8-A1** ***Direct write-off and allowance methods; matching***

The December 31, 19X2, year-end trial balance of Targa Company revealed the following account information:

| | *Debits* | *Credits* |
|---|---|---|
| Accounts receivable | $252,000 | |
| Allowance for bad debts | | $ 3,000 |
| Sales | | 855,000 |
| Sales returns & allowances | 12,900 | |
| Sales discounts | 8,100 | |

**Instructions**

a Determine the adjusting entry for bad debts under each of the following conditions:

(1) An aging schedule indicates that $12,420 of accounts receivable will be uncollectible.

(2) Uncollectible accounts are estimated at 2% of net sales.

b On January 19, 19X3, Targa learned that House Company, a customer, had declared bankruptcy. Present the proper entry to write off House's $950 balance.

c Repeat the requirement in part (b), using the direct write-off method.

d In light of the House bankruptcy, examine the allowance and direct write-off methods in terms of their ability to properly match revenues and expenses.

**P8-A2** ***Allowance method: Income statement and balance sheet approaches***

Huffy Company reported accounts receivable of $500,000 and an allowance for bad debts of $20,000 (credit) on the December 31, 19X4, balance sheet. The data that follow pertain to 19X5 activities and operations.

| | |
|---|---:|
| Sales on account | $7,000,000 |
| Sales returns & allowances | 400,000 |
| Sales discounts | 210,000 |
| Cash collections from credit customers | 6,000,000 |
| Uncollectible accounts written off | 19,000 |
| Collections on accounts that were previously written off | 2,500 |

**Instructions**

a Prepare summary journal entries to record the sales- and receivables-related transactions from 19X5.

b Prepare the December 31, 19X5, adjusting entry for uncollectible accounts assuming that bad debts are estimated to be 1% of net credit sales.

c Prepare the December 31, 19X5, adjusting entry for uncollectible accounts assuming that bad debts are estimated at ½ of 1% of year-end accounts receivable.

d Compute the amount of the adjusting entry in part (c) assuming that $34,000 of accounts were written off, rather than $19,000, in 19X5.

**P8-A3** ***Allowance method; analysis of receivables***

A review of the accounting records of Ontario, Inc., on December 31, 19XX, disclosed balances in Accounts Receivable and the Allowance for Bad Debts of $600,000 and $32,000 (credit), respectively. Both balances were prior to any year-end adjusting entries. Management has decided to estimate uncollectible accounts on the basis of the following aging schedule:

| *Days Account Outstanding* | *Amount* | *Probability of Collection* |
|---|---:|---:|
| Less than 31 days | $375,000 | .97 |
| From 31–60 days | 95,000 | .80 |
| From 61–90 days | 50,000 | .70 |
| From 91–120 days | 40,000 | .60 |
| From 121–150 days | 25,000 | .50 |
| Over 150 days | 15,000 | .10 |

Sales for 19XX totaled $1.9 million, of which 30% were for cash. Customers paid a total of $1,218,000 on account. Finally, during the past 12 months, management wrote off $16,000 of accounts as uncollectible.

**Instructions**

a Compute the net realizable value of Ontario's accounts receivable on January 1, 19XX.

b Present the necessary journal entry on December 31, 19XX, to record the firm's bad debt expense.

c Show how accounts receivable would be presented on the December 31, 19XX, balance sheet.

**P8-A4** ***Journal entries for accounts and notes receivable***

The following selected transactions and events pertain to the Schaeffer Corporation for the last quarter of the year:

| | | |
|---|---|---|
| Oct. | 4 | Sold merchandise on account to J. R. Konrath. Konrath issued a $7,500, 60-day, 12% note in settlement of her account. |
| | 15 | Wrote off the $1,900 balance owed by Sanford Company as uncollectible. |
| | 24 | Discounted Konrath's note at the bank; discount rate 14%. |

Nov. 9 Received $480 in final settlement of Bill Stewart's $1,500 account balance. Stewart's account had been written off as uncollectible in the previous year.

16 Received a 30-day, 12%, $800 note from Doug Campbell in settlement of his past-due account balance.

Dec. 4 Received notification from the bank that Konrath had paid her note.

16 Campbell dishonored his note of November 16 but promised to pay the proper amount due within five days. Schaeffer has agreed not to charge any additional interest.

19 Campell paid his account balance in full.

31 Recorded the necessary adjusting entry for bad debts. On September 30, Schaeffer reported a $6,200 credit balance in the Allowance for Bad Debts account.

On December 31 the Accounts Receivable account contained a balance of $74,900.

**Instructions**

a Record the quarter's transactions and events in general journal form, assuming that Schaeffer uses the allowance method of accounting for bad debts. An aging schedule indicates that $5,800 of accounts receivable will be uncollectible.

b Compute the net realizable value of accounts receivable on December 31.

c Suppose Schaeffer used the income statement approach for estimating bad debts. Two percent of the total sales of $290,000 are anticipated to be uncollectible. Would you have done anything differently on December 31? Explain.

**P8-A5** ***Journal entries for notes***

The following information was taken from the records of the Lima Company:

Mar. 8 Sold merchandise to R. Porter; accepted an $18,000, 10%, 120-day note.

Apr. 7 Discounted Porter's note at the bank at a 12% discount rate.

27 Received a $12,000, 10%, 90-day note from S. Taylor, a customer, in settlement of his account balance.

May 27 Discounted Taylor's note at the bank at a discount rate of 14%.

July 7 Received notification from the bank that Porter had paid her note.

26 Received notification from the bank that Taylor had defaulted on his note; paid the amount due plus a protest fee of $20. Lima informed Taylor that 15% annual interest would be charged on the face amount of the note, the interest, and the protest fee.

Aug. 10 Received the proper amount due from Taylor, including interest.

16 Received a 12%, 60-day, $30,000 note from Forge Manufacturing, a customer, in settlement of its past-due account.

Oct. 15 Forge Manufacturing paid the proper amount due on the note of August 16.

**Instructions**

a Assuming Lima's year ends on December 31, prepare journal entries to record the transactions.

b If Lima's year ends on August 31, present the necessary adjusting entry on August 31 for accrued interest. Also, present the proper entry for the receipt of cash on October 15.

## Series B

**P8-B1** ***Direct write-off and allowance methods; matching***

The December 31, 19X3, year-end trial balance of Yelland Company revealed the account information that follows.

| | *Debits* | *Credits* |
|---|---|---|
| Accounts receivable | $90,000 | |
| Allowance for bad debts | | $ 2,500 |
| Sales | | 410,000 |
| Sales returns | 10,000 | |
| Sales discounts | 8,000 | |

**Instructions**

a Determine the adjusting entry for bad debts under each of the following conditions:
   (1) Uncollectible accounts are estimated at 1% of net sales.
   (2) An aging schedule indicates that $12,050 of accounts receivable will be uncollectible.

b On January 13, 19X4, Yelland learned that Kaiser Distributors, a customer, had gone bankrupt. Present the proper entry to write off Kaiser's $480 balance.

c Repeat the requirement in part (b), using the direct write-off method.

d Compare the allowance and direct write-off methods by:
   (1) Determining the impact on net income of the Kaiser write-off.
   (2) Examining the methods' ability to match revenues and expenses.

**P8-B2** ***Allowance method: Income statement and balance sheet approaches***
Tempe Company reported accounts receivable of $300,000 and an allowance for bad debts of $31,000 (credit) on the December 31, 19X2, balance sheet. The following data pertain to 19X3 activities and operations:

| | |
|---|---|
| Sales on account | $2,000,000 |
| Cash collections from credit customers | 1,600,000 |
| Sales discounts | 50,000 |
| Sales returns & allowances | 100,000 |
| Uncollectible accounts written off | 29,000 |
| Collections on accounts that were previously written off | 2,700 |

**Instructions**

a Prepare summary journal entries to record the sales- and receivables-related transactions from 19X3.

b Prepare the December 31, 19X3, adjusting entry for uncollectible accounts assuming that bad debts are estimated to be 2% of net credit sales.

c Prepare the December 31, 19X3, adjusting entry for uncollectible accounts assuming that bad debts are estimated at 1% of year-end accounts receivable.

d Compute the amount of the adjusting entry in part (c) assuming that $46,000 of accounts were written off, rather than $29,000, in 19X3.

**P8-B3** ***Allowance method; analysis of receivables***
A review of the accounting records of Metal, Inc., on December 31, 19XX, disclosed balances in Accounts Receivable and the Allowance for Bad Debts of $530,000 and $25,000 (credit), respectively. Both balances were prior to any year-end adjusting entries. Management has decided to estimate uncollectible accounts on the basis of the aging schedule that follows.

| *Days Account Outstanding* | *Amount* | *Probability of Collection* |
|---|---|---|
| Less than 16 days | $300,000 | .98 |
| From 16–30 days | 100,000 | .90 |
| From 31–45 days | 50,000 | .80 |
| From 46–60 days | 30,000 | .70 |
| From 61–75 days | 10,000 | .60 |
| Over 75 days | 40,000 | .10 |

Sales for 19XX totaled $3 million, of which 40% were for cash. Customers paid a total of $1,650,000 on account. Finally, during the past 12 months, management wrote off $55,000 of accounts as uncollectible.

**Instructions**

a Compute the net realizable value of Metal's accounts receivable on January 1, 19XX.
b Present the necessary journal entry on December 31, 19XX, to record the firm's bad debt expense.
c Show how accounts receivable would be presented on the December 31, 19XX, balance sheet.

**P8-B4** ***Journal entries for accounts and notes receivable***

The following selected transactions and events pertain to the McHale Company for the last quarter of the year:

| | | |
|---|---|---|
| Oct. | 9 | Sold merchandise to Dan Owen. Owen issued a $15,000, 60-day, 14% note in settlement of his account. |
| | 24 | Discounted Owen's note at the bank; discount rate 16%. |
| | 29 | Wrote off the $4,200 balance owed by Worth Company as uncollectible. |
| Nov. | 21 | Received a 30-day, 12%, $2,000 note from Cindy Raymond in settlement of her past-due account balance. |
| | 28 | Received $1,500 in final settlement of Doug Light's $2,400 account balance. Light's account had been written off as uncollectible in the previous year. |
| Dec. | 9 | Received notification from the bank that Owen had paid his note. |
| | 21 | Raymond dishonored her note of November 21 but agreed to pay the proper amount due within five days. Management has agreed not to charge any additional interest. |
| | 26 | Raymond paid her account balance in full. |
| | 31 | Recorded the necessary adjusting entry for bad debts. On September 30, McHale reported an $8,200 credit balance in the Allowance for Bad Debts account. |

The Accounts Receivable account contained a balance of $92,100 on December 31.

**Instructions**

a Record the quarter's transactions and events in general journal form, assuming that McHale uses the allowance method of accounting for bad debts. An aging schedule indicates that $8,300 of accounts receivable will be uncollectible.
b Compute the net realizable value of accounts receivable.
c Assume that financial statements were prepared at the end of October for purposes of obtaining a bank loan. Indicate how Owen's discounted note would be reported to the loan officer.

**P8-B5** ***Journal entries for notes***

The following information was taken from the records of the Richardson Wholesale Company:

| | | |
|---|---|---|
| Jan. | 19 | Received a $4,000, 10%, 90-day note from Tom Warren, a customer, in settlement of his account balance. |
| Feb. | 18 | Sold merchandise to Julie Bradford, Inc.; accepted a $6,000, 10%, 120-day note. |
| Mar. | 20 | Discounted both notes at the bank at a discount rate of 12%. |
| Apr. | 20 | Received notification from the bank that Warren had paid his note. |
| June | 18 | Received notification from the bank that Bradford had defaulted on its note; paid the amount due plus a $25 protest fee. Richardson informed Bradford that 12% annual interest would be charged on the face amount of the note, the interest, and the protest fee. |
| July | 19 | Received a 12%, 60-day, $40,000 note from Kramer, Inc., for the sale of a parcel of land. |
| | 28 | Received the proper amount due from Bradford, including interest. |
| Sept. | 17 | Kramer, Inc., paid the proper amount due on the note of July 19. |

**Instructions**

a Assuming Richardson's year ends on December 31, prepare the necessary journal entries to record the transactions.

b If Richardson's year ends on July 31, present the necessary adjusting entry on July 31 for accrued interest. Also, present the proper entry for the receipt of cash on September 17.

## Beyond the Basics

**BB8-1** ***Allowance method and errors***

A newly hired bookkeeper recently reported an $88,000 balance in the Accounts Receivable control account of Starr Manufacturing Company. An aging schedule revealed the following:

| *Age* | *Amount* | *Percentage Uncollectible* |
|---|---|---|
| Current | $40,000 | 1% |
| 31–60 days | 20,000 | 5 |
| 61–90 days | 14,000 | 10 |
| 91–120 days | 9,000 | 30 |
| Over 120 days | 5,000 | 60 |
| | $88,000 | |

A detailed investigation of the bookkeeper's work discovered three items:

1 Hill Manufacturing, a customer, has entered bankruptcy proceedings. Hill has owed Starr $3,000 for the past five months; management feels there is no hope of collection.

2 An analysis of accounts in the 31–60 day category discovered the four outstanding balances that follow, all of which were verified as being correct.

| | |
|---|---|
| Baker Concrete, Inc. | $13,500 |
| Haxton Distributors | 2,000 |
| New Jersey Builders | 4,900 |
| ToyotaTown | 4,600 |

3 Joe Kline's $4,000 account balance (91–120 day category) had been written off as uncollectible on October 19 by the following journal entry:

| | | |
|---|---|---|
| Allowance for Bad Debts | 4,000 | |
| Bad Debts Expense: Joe Kline | | 4,000 |
| To write off uncollectible account | | |

The December 31 balance before adjustment in the Allowance for Bad Debts account was $2,550 (credit).

**Instructions**

a Determine the proper accounting treatment for the account of Hill Manufacturing. Be specific.

b Was the write-off on October 19 handled correctly? If not, how would you correct the error if the books are not as yet closed?

c Determine the adjusting entry for bad debts that should be made on December 31. Assume proper handling of all preceding items.

**BB8-2** ***Analysis of the impact of receivables transactions***

Selected transactions and events of the World of Music for 19X1 follow. The firm uses the allowance method when accounting for bad debts.

| | |
|---|---|
| Jan. 4 | Collected an account receivable from Roger Donovan. |
| Mar. 8 | Wrote off the delinquent account of James North. |
| Apr. 15 | Received full payment from Susan Baxter, whose account was written off eight months ago. |
| May 22 | Received a 30-day, 12% note on account from Tony Perotti. |
| June 21 | Received the proper amount due from Tony Perotti in settlement of his note issued on May 22. |
| July 5 | Performed the necessary record keeping for the note of Gary Fields, which was dishonored after being held for six months. |
| Aug. 20 | Discounted a note received one month ago from the Sound Store. Proceeds received from the bank were in excess of the note's face value. |
| Oct. 20 | Learned that the Sound Store had settled its obligation with the bank for the note discounted on August 20. |
| Dec. 31 | Recorded the necessary adjusting entry to estimate uncollectible accounts for the year. The company prepares an aging schedule when analyzing accounts receivable. |

**Instructions**

Using the accompanying chart, determine the effect of each of the preceding transactions and events on bad debts expense, net income, accounts receivable, the allowance for bad debts, and net realizable value of accounts receivable. Use the following notation: I = increase, D = decrease, and NE = no effect. The transaction (i.e., entry) on January 4 is shown as an example.

| *Date* | *Bad Debts Expense* | *Net Income* | *Accounts Receivable* | *Allowance for Bad Debts* | *Net Realizable Value* |
|---|---|---|---|---|---|
| Jan. 4 | NE | NE | D | NE | D |

## Answers to Chapter Quiz

**1** c

**2** b (\$6,500 credit + \$6,000 credit = \$12,500)

**3** c

**4** b (\$24,000 × 0.10 × $\frac{2}{12}$)

**5** c

# Inventory

CHAPTER 9

## Learning Objectives

After reading this chapter you should:

1 Understand the ownership issues related to goods in transit and goods on consignment.

2 Understand the effects of inventory errors on financial statements.

3 Be familiar with the specific identification, FIFO, LIFO, and weighted-average inventory methods.

4 Understand the factors that are considered when selecting an inventory method and the effects of such a selection on financial statements.

5 Be familiar with the lower-of-cost-or-market rule of inventory valuation.

6 Understand the importance of inventory estimates and be able to formulate estimates by using the gross profit and retail methods.

7 Understand the differences between the periodic and perpetual inventory systems.

In Chapter 5 we noted that inventory is a concern for both the finance and marketing functions within a business. Finance desires to reduce the amount of funds committed to the inventory investment, while marketing wants to avoid out-of-stock situations that could result in lost sales and lost customers. The accountant also has a keen interest in inventory. Excessive inventory investments, lost sales, and lost customers all affect net income. Furthermore, for many firms, especially those engaged in merchandising activities, inventories represent the largest asset on the balance sheet. These goods ultimately become a significant element on the income statement in the form of cost of goods sold.

The possession of inventory gives rise to various issues that the accountant must resolve. For example, consider Margo's Dress Shop, which overstocked a particular dress style eight months ago. Because of rapid changes in the fashion world, these dresses are now worth only a fraction of their original cost. Should Margo's continue to carry this inventory in the accounting records at original cost, or should the goods be marked down to reflect a loss in value? Focusing on another issue, we turn to the Fast-Mix Concrete Company. Throughout the year Fast-Mix has been purchasing large quantities of sand, stone, and limestone at rapidly changing prices. Each product is piled in huge mounds near the company's production facility. If Fast-Mix used 10 tons of stone on a given day, how can the firm determine its cost? All the stone purchases have been mixed together and it has been impossible to mark or associate each ton with its acquisition cost. Should Fast-Mix use the most recent cost, the oldest cost, or an average cost? The company's selection will have a definite impact on profitability.

These questions and a number of other issues related to inventory must be addressed by accountants. This chapter focuses on inventory accounting, emphasizing the valuation of inventory on the balance sheet and the determination of cost of goods sold for the income statement.

## What is Inventory?

When discussing merchandising businesses, we defined **inventory** as goods acquired for resale to customers. Although this definition is satisfactory for the retailer and wholesaler, it must be expanded for the manufacturer. The manufacturer, of course, does not acquire goods for resale—it makes them. Inventories, therefore, are said to include the following:

1 *Raw materials*—items to be processed into salable products.

2 *Work in process*—goods started but not as yet completed.

3 *Finished goods*—goods completed and awaiting sale.

Since inventories are used or sold and converted into cash within the operating cycle, they are reported as current assets on the balance sheet. Inventory is usually listed immediately following accounts receivable because, in comparison with amounts due from customers, it is one step further removed from cash in terms of liquidity.

### Ownership Problems

In Chapter 1, assets were defined as the economic resources owned by a firm that benefit future time periods. Let us concentrate on ownership for a moment. When the ownership of merchandise transfers to a company, the merchandise should be included as part of that company's inventory and reported on the firm's balance sheet. This principle is followed even though a business may lack physical possession of the units at the end of the reporting period—a situation that often arises with goods in transit and goods on consignment.

## Goods in Transit

**Goods in transit** between the buyer and seller belong to the party that holds legal ownership (title) of the goods. Legal ownership, in turn, is dependent on freight terms, namely, F.O.B. shipping point and F.O.B. destination. Recall from Chapter 5 that the F.O.B. point indicates the location where the seller's responsibility for shipping ceases. As a logical extension, the F.O.B. point also indicates where (or when) legal title to the goods is transferred from the seller to the buyer. Under F.O.B. shipping point, for example, title transfers to the purchaser when the goods are shipped; conversely, under F.O.B. destination, title passes when the goods arrive at their destination (e.g., the buyer's warehouse).

OBJECTIVE 1
Understand the ownership issues related to goods in transit and goods on consignment.

When title passes, the seller should record a sale and the buyer should record a purchase. Accordingly, inventories should be respectively reduced and increased at this time, even though the goods may still be on hand or in transit. To illustrate, suppose a company buys $10,000 of merchandise, F.O.B. shipping point, on December 29. The goods are shipped on December 30 and are in transit at the end of the purchaser's accounting year. Despite this fact, the buyer should enter a purchase in the records and include the goods in the ending inventory count because title has passed.

To simplify bookkeeping *during the year,* many companies operate on a receipt and shipment basis. Specifically, purchases are recorded upon receipt regardless of the F.O.B. point, and sales are recognized upon shipment. If year-end in-transit shipments are significant, firms should examine their records and make appropriate account adjustments so that all merchandise owned is properly reflected in the ending inventory balance. Incorrect accounting for sales and purchases will influence inventory and often affect cost of goods sold, net income, owner's equity, accounts receivable, and accounts payable.

## Goods on Consignment

Some companies transfer merchandise to sales agents (to sell to potential buyers) without transferring ownership. This process is known as **consignment.** If the products on consignment are sold, the agent receives a commission. If the merchandise is not sold, the goods are returned to the supplying company (i.e., the consignor). It is important to note that the consignor retains title to the transferred merchandise even though the goods are possessed by the sales agent. Consigned goods are therefore reported as part of the consignor's inventory until the time of sale and should not appear in the Inventory account of the agent.

## Taking a Physical Inventory

We have determined the goods that should be reported as an asset on the balance sheet. It now becomes necessary to hand count these goods at the conclusion of the reporting period to derive the correct ending inventory figure. This procedure is needed because the Inventory account under a *periodic* system has not been debited or credited to reflect the individual purchases and sales made by the business. As a result, the account's year-end balance fails to reflect the cost of goods owned by the firm. The necessary information to update Inventory is not found in the formal accounting records, but is obtained by reviewing goods in transit and counting merchandise on hand and stored in warehouses.

This process, known as **taking a physical inventory,** may involve much more than "counting." For example, many small items (such as nuts and bolts) may need to be weighed. Other products, such as the amount of oil in a storage tank, must be measured. In addition, an inventory counter must determine whether the goods appearing to be in the warehouse are actually there. To explain, suppose an inventory counter observes a stack of cartons 10 across by 10 deep by 15 high. A quick conclusion at the end of a long day might be that the firm has 1,500 (10 × 10 × 15) cartons on hand. A potential problem could exist, however: the middle of the stack might be hollow or less than 15 cartons high. Or some of the cartons may be empty. Indeed, a careful look at the inventory is required to avoid a serious misstatement. Proper inventory counts are so important that items may be counted and checked a second time to verify the accuracy of the original figure.

The inventory count, although costly and time-consuming, strengthens the credibility of the inventory figure reported on the year-end balance sheet. Even so, a physical count of inventory (and its observance by an outside independent auditor) has not always been a required practice. It took a massive fraud case to induce change. The 1937 financial statements of McKesson Corporation (formerly McKesson & Robbins), were found to contain significant amounts of fictitious inventories—all related to a fraud that had been perpetrated by the president and his brothers over a period of 12 years. The fraud was finally uncovered when an accounting executive of the company went to a warehouse to check some reported inventory and found none in existence. As an outcome of this case, generally accepted auditing standards now require the observation of physical inventory counts by audit personnel, as well as other procedures that help to avoid misstatements of assets in the financial statements.

## Effects of Inventory Errors on Financial Statements

OBJECTIVE 2
**Understand the effects of inventory errors on financial statements.**

Many errors are possible in the inventory-counting process. Inventory items may be counted incorrectly, completely omitted in the counting process, and sometimes counted twice. Furthermore, in the computation of total inventory cost, mathematical errors can be made when multiplying the number of units owned by the cost per unit. Unfortunately, these errors are carried forward to the financial statements. Incorrect inventory determination can result in incorrect current asset valuation, net income, and owner's equity.

To understand the effect of inventory errors we will study The Backert Company, which accidentally excluded $2,000 of goods on display in its showroom from the ending inventory count. The firm's income statement appears in Exhibit 9-1. The figures on the left are based on the correct ending inventory valuation of $34,000. In contrast, the figures on the right omit the display merchandise and use an ending inventory of $32,000.

Because of the understated ending inventory, Backert is subtracting a number that is too small from goods available for sale. The resulting cost of goods sold is therefore overstated and produces a depressed net income figure. Regrettably, the problem does not stop here. Remember that net income increases owner's equity. Thus, ending owner's equity, which appears on both the statement of owner's equity and the balance sheet, is understated as well. The balance sheet will balance,

HIGHLIGHT

# An Inventoryless Inventory System

For many firms, particularly manufacturers, inventories represent a sizable portion of total assets. Companies generally strive to operate with as little inventory as possible to free up funds. Instead of having money tied up in goods that are sitting in a warehouse, managers would rather invest their hard-earned dollars in other, more profitable projects or perhaps in other areas of the business.

From Toyota, the Japanese automaker, has come a relatively new approach called just-in-time (JIT) inventory management. JIT has probably received more attention in a short period of time than any other manufacturing technique. In the simplest of terms it involves the philosophy that all inventories are undesirable and should be eliminated or minimized. [1] Rather than have backup goods for insurance against unexpected shortages and delays—just in case of this or just in case of that—firms using JIT produce and deliver goods just in time to be sold. Additionally, purchased materials are acquired just in time to enter manufacturing activities. Given this philosophy, having backup inventory is normally viewed as evidence of poor planning and control. [2]

When implementing a JIT system, a firm needs just-in-time purchasing and just-in-time production. Focusing on the former, an overview of traditional purchasing activities would find that companies have historically selected suppliers on the basis of cost. With JIT, teamwork, trust, confidence, cooperation, and joint commitment are frequently considered more important and may justify paying a few extra cents per unit. So that materials can be put immediately into production when needed, just-in-time requires dependable suppliers who deliver on a timely basis. Deliveries are small and are often made daily; just as important, the goods must be free of defects. In a JIT system, one batch of late or defective raw material can stop an entire assembly line.

Consider Firestone and General Motors (GM) as evidence of the supplier/purchaser relationships that must develop. The latter company is a recent convert to JIT. Information about GM's tire requirements is transmitted via an on-line computer system to Firestone's transportation department and manufacturing plants. Each delivery from Firestone contains the exact quantity and size required by GM's assembly line for a specified six-hour period. The deliveries are then made at a specific loading dock by truck, near the assembly line where the tires will be used. As a consequence, GM has almost eliminated its need to carry a tire inventory to meet production requirements.

Truckers have also gotten into the act in assisting the auto maker. One transportation firm, for example, receives 128 different parts in trailerload batches from a Delco (GM) Division plant in Dayton, Ohio. Standardized containers are then prepared, with the parts arranged in the exact sequence needed by the assembly line. The containers are delivered to two General Motors' plants in Lansing, Michigan, four times each day. This procedure has helped reduce the auto plants' minimum inventory requirements to a four-hour supply of these parts. [3]

Close coordination and an attention for detail are the keys to success. Because of the timing involved (i.e., raw materials acquired just in time to enter production, and goods produced just in time to be sold), normal inefficiencies of manufacturing cannot be tolerated. As one purchasing manager explains, "We understand how difficult it is to produce perfect parts and . . . we will accept a few rejects from our suppliers. We insist only that our suppliers first separate their bad parts from their good ones and ship them to us separately." The purchasing manager was only kidding—at least we think he was. [4]

SOURCES: Adapted from "Just-in-Time: An Inventory System Whose Time Has Come," *Management Accounting*, December, 1985, pp. 36–39, 42–44 [1, 3]; "Trends in Manufacturing," *Cost Accounting, Robotics, and the New Manufacturing Environment*, Management Accounting Section of the American Accounting Association, 1987; and "What's Your Excuse for not Using JIT?," *Harvard Business Review*, March/April, 1986, pp. 38–39, 42, 46, 50, 52, and 54 [2, 4]. The first article is reprinted by permission of the National Association of Accountants, Montvale, NJ. 

**Exhibit 9-1**

| THE BACKERT COMPANY<br>Income Statement<br>For the Year Ended December 31, 19X1 | | | | |
|---|---|---|---|---|
| | *Correct Ending Inventory of $34,000* | | *Incorrect Ending Inventory of $32,000* | |
| Net sales | | $80,000 | | $80,000 |
| Cost of goods sold | | | | |
| Beginning inventory | $26,000 | | $26,000 | |
| Add: Net purchases | 59,000 | | 59,000 | |
| Goods available for sale | $85,000 | | $85,000 | |
| Less: Ending inventory | 34,000 | | 32,000 | |
| Cost of goods sold | | 51,000 | | 53,000 |
| Gross profit | | $29,000 | | $27,000 |
| Operating expenses | | 20,000 | | 20,000 |
| Net income | | $ 9,000 | | $ 7,000 |

however, because of a $2,000 understatement of inventory in the current assets section. The effects of the display merchandise error are summarized as follows:

| | |
|---|---|
| ***Income Statement*** | |
| Cost of goods sold | Overstated |
| Gross profit | Understated |
| Net income | Understated |
| ***Statement of Owner's Equity*** | |
| Ending owner's equity | Understated |
| ***Balance Sheet*** | |
| Ending owner's equity | Understated |
| Total current assets | Understated |

The results of an overstatement of ending inventory are the opposite of those just described. We recommend that you not attempt to memorize this material, as inventory errors can become quite complex. Instead, understand how to trace an error through the system and analyze its impact.

### Counterbalancing Errors

Inventory errors have counterbalancing effects; that is, errors causing an overstatement of net income in one year create an understatement in the following year and vice versa. This situation arises because the ending inventory from one period becomes the beginning inventory of the next. As an example, assume that the goods on display in Backert's showroom were subsequently sold and that company personnel correctly costed the 19X2 ending inventory at $41,000. Backert's $2,000 inventory error from 19X1 is carried forward as a $2,000 understatement of the 19X2 beginning inventory. The impact on the 19X2 income statement is shown in Exhibit 9-2.

Observe that the understated beginning inventory reduces goods available for sale. The ending inventory is not affected by the earlier error because the $41,000 figure is derived by a separate physical count and valuation. Overall, then, cost of goods sold is understated, which produces an overstated gross profit and net income. The $2,000 depression of net income in 19X1 is therefore counterbalanced by a $2,000 overstatement in 19X2. Although the 19X2 income statement is in error, the ending owner's equity is correct. This outcome is shown as follows:

| | *Using Correct 19X1 and 19X2 Net Income* | *Using Incorrect 19X1 and 19X2 Net Income* |
|---|---|---|
| Beginning owner's equity, Jan. 1, 19X1 (assumed) | $50,000 | $50,000 |
| + 19X1 net income | 9,000 | 7,000 |
| + 19X2 net income | 11,000 | 13,000 |
| Ending owner's equity, Dec. 31, 19X2 | $70,000 | $70,000 |

Because the initial error has been counterbalanced, you might argue that the error is of little importance. Remember, however, that net income influences financial decision making. Financial statements are used by many different groups; errors, of course, could distort trends in the data that are used for evaluation.

**Exhibit 9-2**

**THE BACKERT COMPANY**
**Income Statement**
**For the Year Ended December 31, 19X2**

| | *Correct Beginning Inventory of $34,000* | | *Incorrect Beginning Inventory of $32,000* | |
|---|---|---|---|---|
| Net sales | | $97,000 | | $97,000 |
| Cost of goods sold | | | | |
| Beginning inventory | $ 34,000 | | $ 32,000 | |
| Add: Net purchases | 71,000 | | 71,000 | |
| Goods available for sale | $105,000 | | $103,000 | |
| Less: Ending inventory (correct) | 41,000 | | 41,000 | |
| Cost of goods sold | | 64,000 | | 62,000 |
| Gross profit | | $33,000 | | $35,000 |
| Operating expenses | | 22,000 | | 22,000 |
| Net income | | $11,000 | | $13,000 |

## Inventory Valuation and Income Measurement

As we have just shown, inventory affects both the balance sheet and the income statement. Ending inventory valuation and the determination of cost of goods sold are probably the two most significant inventory problems faced by accountants. If a firm purchased all of its merchandise at the same price throughout the year, there would be little difficulty. Ending inventory could be determined by multiplying the ending quantity of merchandise owned by the unit cost. The resulting amount would then be subtracted from goods available for sale to generate cost of goods sold.

Purchase prices, however, rarely remain constant during an accounting period. Further complicating matters, we are often unable to attach the price paid for an item to the item itself. Picture the concrete company cited at the beginning of this chapter or a business that deals in large quantities of liquids. The goods are all mixed together, and if different prices are paid, accounting becomes a problem.

### Matching: The Key Objective

Throughout a reporting period a business has a "pool" of inventory costs to account for. This "pool" consists of the beginning inventory cost plus the cost of merchandise acquired for resale.[1] In more familiar terms, the pool is equivalent to goods available for sale. By the end of the period, many of the items available for sale have been sold, while others remain on hand. Thus, goods available for sale must be divided between cost of goods sold and ending inventory, as shown in Exhibit 9-3.

We will soon see that several different methods can be used to allocate inventory costs between the income statement and the balance sheet. Often a given method favors one financial statement or the other, but not both. In keeping with the income statement's growth in importance, *a major objective of inventory accounting is to associate or match the costs of the items sold against the sales revenues generated.* Balance sheet valuation, then, may be looked on as a residual. That is, after assign-

**Exhibit 9-3**
**Allocation of Inventory Cost Between the Income Statement and the Balance Sheet**

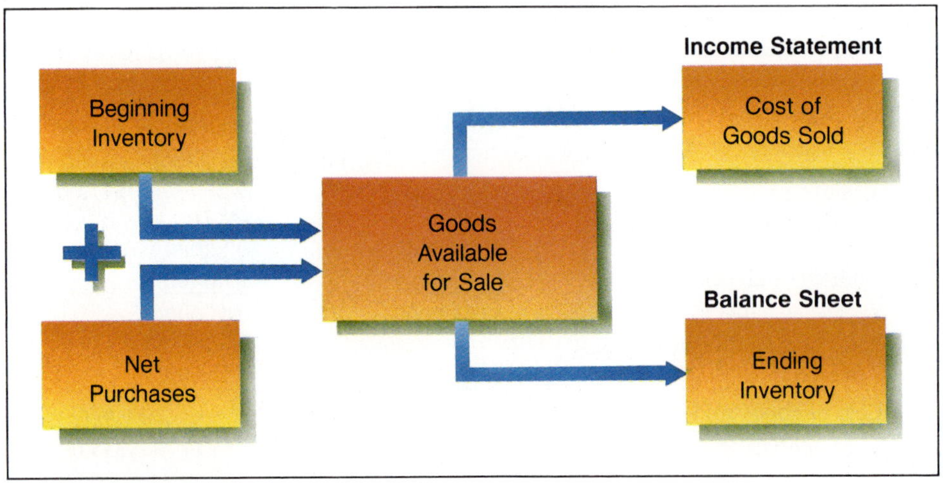


[1] For a manufacturer the cost of merchandise acquired for resale would be replaced by the cost of goods manufactured.

ment of costs to the income statement, those costs that remain are carried as inventory on the balance sheet.

## Cost Determination

The computation of an inventory item's cost is the starting point for inventory valuation and figuring cost of goods sold. The recorded cost of inventory incorporates all expenditures related to acquisition, such as the purchase price of the merchandise (minus any discounts), transportation charges incurred by the purchaser, and insurance costs incurred on the merchandise while in transit.

Once the preceding expenditures are determined, the unit cost of each inventory item can be calculated. The purchase price of inventory is easily associated with specific items, but it is frequently difficult to compute unit amounts for transportation, insurance, and discounts. Keep in mind that transportation and insurance are often incurred on shipments that consist of a variety of different goods. Similarly, the purchase discount on a single invoice may relate to numerous products. How, then, should these cost elements be handled?

When discounts, transportation, and insurance are traceable to a particular inventory item (i.e., the ideal situation), the cost of that item is computed accordingly. For example, suppose Virginia Company had the following costs for part no. 1088:

| | |
|---|---|
| Purchase price: 500 units @ $10 | $5,000 |
| Add: Transportation charges | 350 |
| | $5,350 |
| Less: Purchases discounts | 100 |
| Total cost | $5,250 |

Cost per unit: $5,250 ÷ 500 units = $10.50

It is assumed that (1) these costs relate *strictly* to part no. 1088 and (2) there is no beginning inventory. If 400 units were sold during the year, Virginia's inventory pool would be divided as shown in Exhibit 9-4.

If discounts, transportation, and other acquisition costs are significant in amount and cannot be traced to specific inventory items, some form of equitable proration is necessary between the total ending inventory and cost of goods sold.

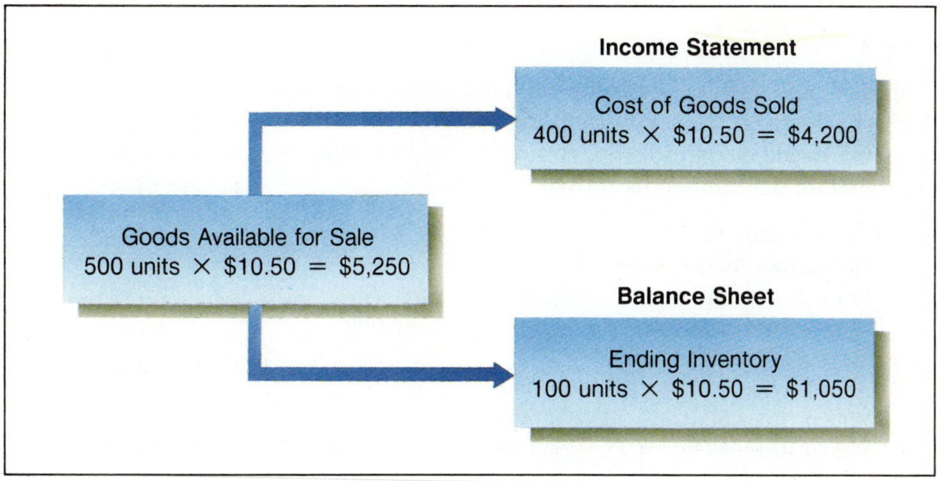


**Exhibit 9-4**
**Allocation of Virginia Company's Inventory Pool**

The lack of such proration could result in a serious misstatement on both the balance sheet and the income statement. In many cases, however, discounts and transportation charges are fairly small in relation to an item's purchase price. As a matter of expediency, no proration is attempted, and the Purchases Discounts and Freight-in accounts are entered in their entirety on the income statement. This latter approach was illustrated earlier in the text (see Chapter 5).

## Costing Methods

Once the unit cost of each inventory item is determined, a firm can begin the necessary assignment to cost of goods sold and ending inventory. The following sections describe four acceptable methods for performing this process.

### Specific Identification

OBJECTIVE 3
**Be familiar with the specific identification, FIFO, LIFO, and weighted-average inventory methods.**

The **specific identification method** requires a business to identify each unit of merchandise with the unit's cost and retain that identification until the inventory is sold. Tags or stickers that reveal a stock number are often attached to the inventory item; the stock number, in turn, is listed in the accounting records along with the item's cost. You may have noticed, for example, that at many new car dealerships, each car has a number on the windshield or side window. That number references the net invoice cost of the vehicle in the dealer's records.

To illustrate the procedures associated with specific identification, we will focus on the January operations of Unique Creations, a seller of expensive watches and bracelets. Assume the company has the following data:

| | *Stock Number* | *Cost* |
|---|---|---|
| Inventory, Jan. 1 | | |
| Watch | 4618 | $ 6,000 |
| Bracelet | 3207 | 11,000 |
| January purchases | | |
| Watch | 4623 | 7,500 |
| Watch | 4624 | 8,100 |
| Bracelet | 3210 | 14,000 |
| Bracelet | 3211 | 18,000 |
| | | $64,600 |

A physical inventory of the goods on hand on January 31 revealed that three items were still in stock: the watch from the beginning of the year and the two bracelets acquired during the month. The company's ending inventory and cost of goods sold are therefore determined as shown.

| | | |
|---|---|---|
| Inventory, Jan. 31 | | |
| Watch (no. 4618) | $ 6,000 | |
| Bracelet (no. 3210) | 14,000 | |
| Bracelet (no. 3211) | 18,000 | $38,000 |
| Cost of good sold | | |
| Bracelet (no. 3207) | $11,000 | |
| Watch (no. 4623) | 7,500 | |
| Watch (no. 4624) | 8,100 | 26,600 |
| | | $64,600 |

The specific identification method offers the advantage of matching the actual cost of the units sold against sales revenues; however, most companies find that the accompanying operating costs are excessive. For example, the physical tagging or coding of individual units of merchandise is impractical, if not impossible, in those situations where sales volume is high and a company's inventory consists of many (e.g., thousands of) different items. Specific identification is most feasible when sales volume is low and the cost of individual units is high. This method might therefore be used to account for jewelry, automobiles, valuable antiques, or yachts.

## Cost Flow Assumptions

When specific identification is not employed, the accountant must make an assumption regarding the movement of costs through a firm's accounting system. This **cost flow assumption** pertains strictly to the *flow of cost* in the accounts and has no direct relationship to the actual *physical flow of goods*. For example, picture a company that strives to sell the oldest merchandise first because of a threat of obsolescence or spoilage. It is very possible that this same business will cost these goods at the most recent costs experienced or perhaps even an average cost.

Cost flow assumptions are used to derive computations for cost of goods sold on the income statement and ending inventory valuation on the balance sheet. The selection of an assumption is based on several different factors that will be discussed shortly. At this point, however, we wish to introduce the three most widely used cost flow assumptions in accounting: first-in, first-out (FIFO); last-in, first-out (LIFO); and weighted average.

### A General Introduction to FIFO and LIFO

To introduce the FIFO and LIFO cost flow assumptions, it is helpful to visualize a chronological listing of units and their related costs. For example, a company may have an inventory of goods on hand at the beginning of the reporting period. Then, throughout the period, additional goods are acquired by purchases from the firm's suppliers. As depicted in the middle block of Exhibit 9-5, the costs that pertain to a given inventory item can be subdivided into older costs (i.e., the beginning inventory and older purchases) and recent costs (more recent purchases). Collectively, the graphic's vertical height represents goods available for sale.

As discussed earlier in the chapter, a company's goods available for sale figure is allocated between cost of goods sold and ending inventory. This allocation may be performed in several different ways. One such approach, known as **first-in, first-out (FIFO),** is based on the premise that costs should be matched against revenues in the order that the costs were incurred. In other words, the oldest costs (i.e., those that were "first-in") are matched against revenues first, then the next oldest costs as the firm works forward in time, and so forth. This matching takes place in the form of cost of goods sold on the income statement. The block on the left reveals this process and shows that a company's more current costs wind up in ending inventory on the balance sheet.

The process is reversed under another acceptable approach, the **last-in, first-out (LIFO)** method. Under this procedure, costs are matched against revenues in the *reverse* order of incurrence. That is, the most recent costs incurred (i.e., the "last-in") are the first to be charged to cost of goods sold, then the next most recent, and so on. By viewing the exhibit's right-hand block you will see that a user must go backward in time. The recent cost layers are eventually exhausted, meaning that older costs are then allocated to inventory.

**Exhibit 9-5**
**A Graphical Overview of FIFO and LIFO**

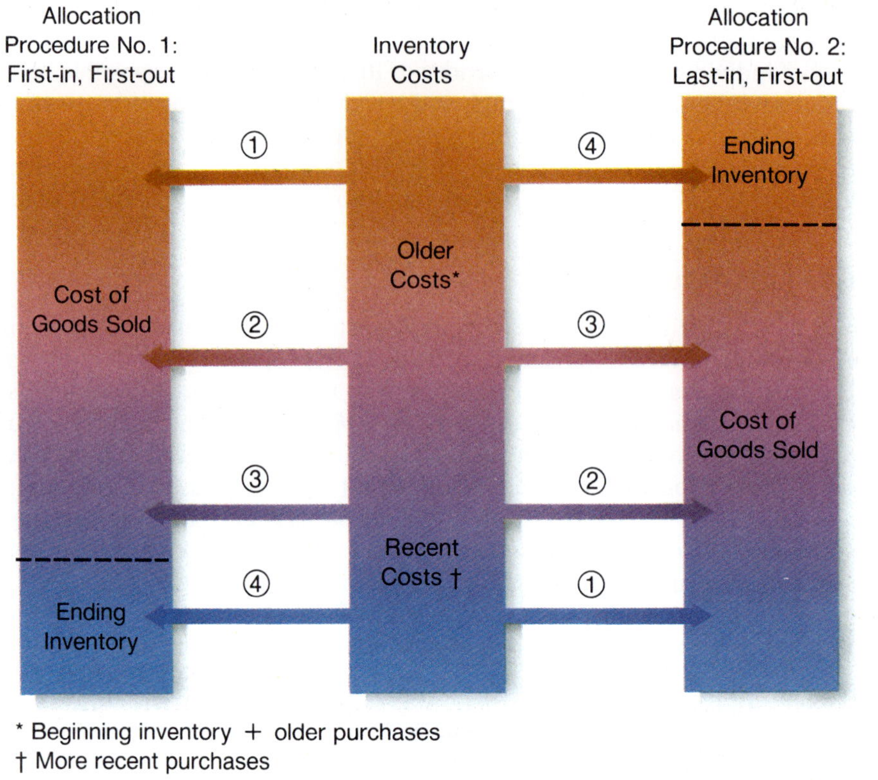


## First-in, First-out Calculations

To illustrate the calculations related to FIFO (and the other cost flow assumptions as well), we introduce the following data of the Tracy Company:

| | *Number of Units* | × *Cost per Unit* | = *Total Cost* |
|---|---|---|---|
| Beginning inventory | 3,000 | $3.00 | $ 9,000 |
| Purchase (Feb. 28) | 4,000 | 3.10 | 12,400 |
| Purchase (May 15) | 5,000 | 3.23 | 16,150 |
| Purchase (Aug. 1) | 1,000 | 3.50 | 3,500 |
| Purchase (Oct. 31) | 3,000 | 3.65 | 10,950 |
| Goods available for sale | 16,000 | | $52,000 |

During the year Tracy sold 11,800 units, leaving 4,200 units (16,000 −11,800) in inventory.

The FIFO computations are most easily understood if we begin with the firm's inventory valuation, which must consist of recent purchases. The 4,200-unit ending inventory is costed in the following manner:

| | | |
|---|---|---|
| Most recent purchase (Oct. 31) | 3,000 units × $3.65 = | $10,950 |
| Next most recent purchase (Aug. 1) | 1,000 units × $3.50 = | 3,500 |
| Next most recent purchase (May 15) | 200 units × $3.23 = | 646 |
| Ending inventory | 4,200 units | $15,096 |

Observe that only 200 units from the May 15 purchase are needed to complete the accounting for the goods that remain from the May acquisition. The other 4,800 units (5,000 − 200) are no longer on hand.

The cost of the 11,800 units sold may now be calculated by using two different approaches. First, we can focus on the flow of the older (i.e., "first-in") costs to the income statement, as shown below.

| | | |
|---|---|---|
| Beginning inventory | 3,000 units × $3.00 = | $ 9,000 |
| Oldest purchase (Feb. 28) | 4,000 units × $3.10 = | 12,400 |
| Next oldest purchase (May 15) | 4,800 units × $3.23 = | 15,504 |
| Cost of goods sold | 11,800 units | $36,904 |

Alternatively, the company's ending inventory can be subtracted from goods available for sale:

| | |
|---|---|
| Goods available for sale (see original data) | $52,000 |
| Less: Ending inventory | 15,096 |
| Cost of goods sold | $36,904 |

## Last-in, First-out Calculations

Recall that under this method, the cost of older purchases is assigned to ending inventory. As the figures that follow indicate, the LIFO flow assumption produces a $12,720 inventory valuation for Tracy Company's 4,200 units on hand.

| | | |
|---|---|---|
| Beginning inventory | 3,000 units × $3.00 = | $ 9,000 |
| Oldest purchase (Feb. 28) | 1,200 units × $3.10 = | 3,720 |
| Ending inventory | 4,200 units | $12,720 |

Although the firm purchased 4,000 units on February 28, the cost of only 1,200 of these units is needed for inclusion in the ending inventory.

The cost of goods sold is $39,280:

| | |
|---|---|
| Goods available for sale (see original data) | $52,000 |
| Less: Ending inventory | 12,720 |
| Cost of goods sold | $39,280 |

## Weighted Average

Another inventory approach, the **weighted-average method,** recognizes that there are both high and low costs during an accounting period. Rather than focus on the time when costs are incurred (i.e., currently or in the past), an average cost is calculated by weighting (multiplying) the cost per unit with the number of units purchased. Referring to page 314, observe that the outcome of this process results in $52,000—the cost of goods available for sale. The weighted average unit cost can now be computed as shown below.

Cost of Goods Available for Sale ÷ Units Available for Sale

$52,000 ÷ 16,000 = $3.25

The unit cost of $3.25 is applied to the ending inventory, as follows:

4,200 units × $3.25 = $13,650

**Exhibit 9-6**
**Alternative Inventory Costing Methods for Tracy Company**

| | *FIFO* | *LIFO* | *Weighted Average* |
|---|---|---|---|
| Sales | $125,000 | $125,000 | $125,000 |
| Cost of goods sold | | | |
| Beginning inventory | $ 9,000 | $ 9,000 | $ 9,000 |
| Add: Purchases* | 43,000 | 43,000 | 43,000 |
| Goods available for sale | $ 52,000 | $ 52,000 | $ 52,000 |
| Less: Ending inventory | 15,096 | 12,720 | 13,650 |
| Cost of goods sold | $ 36,904 | $ 39,280 | $ 38,350 |
| Gross profit | $ 88,096 | $ 85,720 | $ 86,650 |
| Expenses | 60,000 | 60,000 | 60,000 |
| Net income | $ 28,096 | $ 25,720 | $ 26,650 |

* Purchases are computed by subtracting Tracy's beginning inventory from the cost of goods available for sale: $52,000 − $9,000 = $43,000.

Cost of goods sold is computed in the same manner as before; that is:

| | |
|---|---|
| Goods available for sale | $52,000 |
| Less: Ending inventory | 13,650 |
| Cost of goods sold | $38,350 |

The weighted-average method is, in effect, a compromise between FIFO and LIFO. Those who favor the weighted-average method base their argument on the belief that all goods available for sale in a period should reflect the same unit cost.

## Comparison and Evaluation of Alternative Inventory Valuation Methods

The effects of using a particular cost flow assumption are summarized in Exhibit 9-6. The exhibit is based on the assumptions that sales and expenses were $125,000 and $60,000, respectively.

As you can see, each of the three methods results in reporting a different net income and ending inventory valuation. The magnitude of the differences depends on the number of units acquired and sold during the year and the extent of price changes. In light of the historical trend in purchase prices, it is possible that Tracy was experiencing an inflationary economy.

Because the last-in, first-out method charges recent (higher) costs to cost of goods sold, LIFO will usually report the lowest net income in a period of rising prices. In contrast, FIFO will report a larger net income. The results, of course, are reversed in a period of falling prices. Weighted average is a compromise between FIFO and LIFO and normally yields results somewhere between these two approaches.

All three assumptions are acceptable accounting alternatives, and each is used extensively. A survey of large corporations revealed the data that follow.[2]

[2] *Accounting Trends & Techniques: 1988* (New York: American Institute of Certified Public Accountants, Inc., 1988), p. 110.

| Method | Percentage of Use |
|---|---|
| FIFO | 37.4% |
| LIFO | 37.3 |
| Average | 20.6 |
| Other | 4.7 |

## Which Method Should Be Selected?

OBJECTIVE 4
**Understand the factors that are considered when selecting an inventory method and the effects of such a selection on financial statements.**

It would be nice to generalize and state that, in certain situations, a firm should always use FIFO or LIFO or one of the other inventory valuation methods. Unfortunately, we cannot. No one approach best meets the needs and peculiarities of all businesses. Management considers several factors when selecting an inventory method, including income taxes and their related cash outlays, and financial statement presentation.

***Income Taxes*** In the past 15 to 20 years, LIFO has gained popularity because of overall rising prices in our economy. As just discussed, LIFO will produce lower net incomes and, thus, lower income tax payments for its users in an inflationary climate.[3] Lower taxes result in more cash available for investment purposes.

The amount of cash is dependent on several variables, such as the rate of inflation and applicable tax rates, and can be especially significant for companies that carry large amounts of inventory. As evidence, we offer the data that appear in Exhibit 9-7, which show estimated cash savings from using LIFO (as opposed to FIFO) for valuation of goods.

***Financial Statement Presentation*** The resulting financial statements must also be considered when selecting an inventory method. For example, the use of LIFO over long periods of time can generate a somewhat meaningless ending inventory figure on the balance sheet. Remember that the oldest costs are used as the basis for inventory valuation; consequently, units may be carried at costs incurred many years ago. In contrast, FIFO values the ending inventory at an amount close to the cost of replacement.

While producing a reasonable balance sheet valuation, FIFO frequently results in a mismatch of revenue and expense on the income statement. Cost of goods sold

| *Corporation* | *Inventory Using LIFO (in millions)* | *Inventory Using FIFO (in millions)* | *Estimated Cash Savings* (in millions)* |
|---|---|---|---|
| Johnson & Johnson | $1,273.0 | $ 1,385.0 | $ 38.1 |
| Sears, Roebuck & Co. | 3,715.5 | 4,459.1 | 252.8 |
| Kimberly-Clark | 566.5 | 713.2 | 49.9 |
| General Motors | 7,984.3 | 10,509.6 | 858.6 |

* Cash savings are calculated as the excess of FIFO inventory over LIFO inventory, multiplied by the 34% corporate income tax rate in effect at the time of this writing.

**Exhibit 9-7**
**Estimated Cash Savings from LIFO**

[3] According to current tax regulations, companies that use LIFO for tax purposes must also utilize LIFO for financial reporting.

is determined by using older costs; revenues, on the other hand, are based on selling prices that were charged to customers during the current accounting period. The use of old costs and fairly current prices generally raises questions about the meaningfulness of the net income figure. The mechanics of LIFO tend to overcome this problem by charging an entity's most recent costs against sales. A better match is produced, leading many accountants to say that LIFO is superior to FIFO from an income measurement viewpoint.

When choosing an inventory valuation method, management must keep in mind that the income statement and balance sheet have somewhat different purposes. On the income statement, cost of goods sold should reflect a fair measure of inventory cost to be matched against revenue. The balance sheet's ending inventory valuation, on the other hand, should be consistent with the definition of a current asset and reflect the amount of resources available to meet current obligations. In sum, asset valuation and income determination are not always compatible and often result in compromises to arrive at an acceptable reporting of financial position and profitability.

### Consistency in Method Application

The inventory method ultimately selected should be used consistently from one year to the next. Such a practice helps to produce financial statements that can be compared over time and is very useful when assessing trends and performing other types of analysis. Consistency should *not* be interpreted to mean that a business can never change inventory valuation methods. A change can and should be made when it is beneficial in terms of measuring economic activity, for instance, to achieve a better matching of revenues and expenses. If a change is made, the impact should be fully disclosed in the footnotes that accompany the financial statements.

## Lower of Cost or Market

**OBJECTIVE 5**
**Be familiar with the lower-of-cost-or-market rule of inventory valuation.**

Although inventories are generally valued at cost, circumstances sometimes arise where departures from cost are appropriate. As an example, assume that Art Nesbit, a loan officer at the First National Bank, is examining the financial statements of Tuttle Company for purposes of granting a loan. Nesbit's primary concern is Tuttle's ability to meet loan payments as the payments come due. Nesbit is also interested in the value of certain assets that might be pledged as collateral on the loan. The following disclosure appears on Tuttle's balance sheet:

Inventories: at cost $84,000

Nesbit knows that accounting is based on the principle of historical cost and that several cost assignment methods are available for inventory valuation. Because Tuttle's inventory levels and purchase prices have been relatively stable, the assignment method is not an issue. Nesbit's major worry is: Can the bank get $84,000 for the inventory if Tuttle defaults on the loan? Nesbit might have some difficulty with the $84,000 figure if he knew that Tuttle's merchandise had suffered considerable smoke damage from a fire; consisted of numerous perishable goods with a six-month shelf life that were acquired 10 months ago; and was heavily loaded with fad products that are no longer popular.

Inventories are susceptible to damage, spoilage, and obsolescence. Over time the utility or usefulness of many goods declines, and a business may have to drop its selling price to ensure disposal. To achieve a better valuation of these inventory items, accountants turn to the **lower-of-cost-or-market rule.** The use of lower of cost or market is justified when the market potential for a particular product has been significantly reduced.

## Measuring the Decline in Value

The decline in value of an inventory item is measured by the difference between its cost and market value. Cost is determined by any one of the previously discussed methods: specific identification, FIFO, LIFO, or weighted average. **Market value** is defined as replacement cost, or the cost that would be incurred to reproduce or repurchase the item. In the case of damaged goods, market value is the amount obtainable from disposal.

To illustrate lower of cost or market, assume Tuttle stocks an electronic component that cost $170 when purchased several months ago. Because of rapidly advancing technology, the component can now be replaced for $155. Tuttle has therefore suffered a $15 decline in value on this inventory item. To value the component at the *lower* of cost or market, we would compare $170 (original cost) with $155 (market value) and choose $155 (the lower).

There are two exceptions to the replacement cost definition of market value. First, market value cannot be greater than **net realizable value,** which is an item's selling price minus completion and disposal costs. For example, assume Tuttle carries an inventory item that originally cost $12; replacement cost is now $11.25 because of obsolescence. If Tuttle can realize only $10 by selling the item and if there are no completion and disposal costs, the true decline in value is $2 ($12 − $10). Thus, the item would be carried at $10, not the higher replacement cost of $11.25.

The second exception is that market value cannot be less than net realizable value minus a normal profit margin. For instance, suppose a business stocks an item that originally cost $250 but can now be replaced for $200. Assume that the firm can sell this item for $300, which allows for recovery of a normal profit margin of 20%. Apparently, the "value" of this item is really $240 [$300 − 0.20 ($300)]. Carrying the inventory at the lower replacement cost of $200 would understate asset valuation on the balance sheet.

## Application of the Lower-of-Cost-or-Market Rule

The lower-of-cost-or-market rule may be applied to each individual item in inventory. To illustrate, suppose Tuttle's inventory consisted of the following:

| | | *(2) Per Unit* | | *(1) × (2) Total Inventory* | | |
|---|---|---|---|---|---|---|
| *Item No.* | *(1) Quantity* | *Cost* | *Market* | *Cost* | *Market* | *Lower of Cost or Market* |
| 101 | 1,000 | $ 12 | $ 10 | $12,000 | $10,000 | $10,000 |
| 102 | 500 | 20 | 23 | 10,000 | 11,500 | 10,000 |
| 103 | 3,000 | 15 | 16 | 45,000 | 48,000 | 45,000 |
| 104 | 100 | 170 | 155 | 17,000 | 15,500 | 15,500 |
| | | | | $84,000 | $85,000 | $80,500 |

The proper inventory valuation of $80,500 (right-hand column) is obtained by taking the lower of the cost and the market figures for each inventory item. Be aware, however, that other application methods are also acceptable. For example, rather than evaluate each individual item, one can analyze the inventory as a whole. If Tuttle followed this latter approach, the inventory would be valued at $84,000. This figure is obtained by comparing the inventory's total cost ($84,000) with the total market value ($85,000) and selecting the lower amount. Turning to a third method, significant inventory subclasses can be defined, with the lower-of-cost-or-market rule applied to each subclass. Of the three possibilities, the individual item approach results in the lowest and most conservative inventory valuation.

Once the proper valuation is determined, the accounting records must be updated. If Tuttle analyzes its four inventory items individually, a $3,500 reduction in value ($84,000 vs. $80,500) is recognized. This reduction in value is a loss and is entered in the accounts as follows:

| | | |
|---|---|---|
| Loss Due to Decline in Inventory Value | 3,500 | |
| Inventory | | 3,500 |
| To reduce inventory to lower of cost or market | | |

The Inventory account now contains the lower-of-cost-or-market valuation of $80,500 and is reported as such on the balance sheet. Furthermore, Tuttle's net income is reduced by the loss.

## Inventory Estimates

OBJECTIVE 6
Understand the importance of inventory estimates and be able to formulate estimates by using the gross profit and retail methods.

Earlier in the chapter, we noted that taking a physical inventory is a costly and time-consuming process. A physical count is mandatory, however, for determining the inventory balance that is reported in the year-end financial statements. There are numerous situations in business where an inventory valuation is needed and management desires to avoid a physical count. For these situations (and others), several inventory estimation procedures have been developed. These procedures allow the preparation of interim financial statements for periods between physical counts. In addition, the procedures allow businesses to estimate the goods on hand when physical counts are not possible. Such would be the case with disasters like tornadoes or fires, where inventories are destroyed or heavily damaged and estimates are needed for insurance claims. Estimation techniques, if they are reasonable, also permit an entity to determine the accuracy of an actual hand count. A comparison of the hand count with the estimate could reveal gross errors in the counting and valuation processes. Two widely used estimation techniques are the gross profit method and the retail method.

### Gross Profit Method

The **gross profit method** estimates inventory on the basis of a company's gross profit rate, that is, gross profit expressed as a percentage of net sales. The rate, which is the key to the entire process, is developed from past transactions and adjusted for any known changes in the entity's recent profit experience. Once the rate is established, gross profit for the period can be determined by applying the rate to the current period's sales. Given this computation, we can then calculate current cost of goods sold and the estimated ending inventory.

To illustrate, assume that Henderson Supply desires to prepare financial statements for August without taking a physical inventory. The information that follows is available for the period ended August 31.

| | |
|---|---|
| Net sales | $80,000 |
| Beginning inventory, Jan. 1 | 10,000 |
| Net purchases | 40,000 |
| Estimated gross profit percentage | 60% |

Because gross profit is estimated at 60% of net sales, current gross profit is $48,000 ($80,000 × 0.60). Cost of goods sold for August therefore amounts to $32,000 ($80,000 − $48,000), and the ending inventory is found by the following computation:

| | | |
|---|---|---|
| Net sales | | $80,000 |
| Cost of goods sold | | |
| Beginning inventory | $10,000 | |
| Add: Net purchases | 40,000 | |
| Goods available for sale | $50,000 | |
| Less: Ending inventory | ? | |
| Cost of goods sold | | 32,000 |
| Gross profit | | $48,000 |

The August 31 inventory is estimated at $18,000 ($50,000 − $32,000).

## Retail Method

Both department and discount stores carry a variety of different items that are tagged or marked with retail selling prices. Suppose it is the end of an accounting period and a department store takes a count of the inventory on hand. To determine the "value" of the goods, one need only multiply the quantities found by their readily identifiable retail prices. Unfortunately, the resulting figures cannot be used in the financial statements, which carry inventories at cost or at the lower of cost or market, not selling prices. An inventory valued at retail could be converted to cost by inspecting numerous individual paid invoices and other records. This task is a rather formidable one, however, for businesses that carry large product lines. Alternatively, the retail method of inventory valuation can be employed.

The **retail method** is widely used by merchandising firms to value and/or estimate ending inventory. The method's thrust is to first determine the ending inventory at retail prices. This amount is subsequently converted to cost on the basis of the percentage relationship between the cost and retail valuations of goods available for sale. As you will now see, the following information must be accumulated in the accounting records to perform the necessary computations:

1 The beginning inventory valued at both cost and retail amounts

2 Net purchases priced at both cost and retail

3 Net sales for the period

To illustrate the retail method, suppose Boulder Sales Organization desires an inventory estimate as of March 31 in order to compute quarterly income. The required calculations appear at the top of the next page.

Observe that net sales are subtracted from goods available for sale to yield an ending inventory at retail of $180,000.[4] To convert this figure to cost, Boulder has

[4] Frequently, additional factors (such as markups and markdowns to original selling prices) are considered when computing the ending inventory at retail.

| | Cost | Retail |
|---|---|---|
| Beginning inventory, Jan. 1 | $ 60,000 | $ 88,000 |
| Net purchases, Jan. through Mar. | 293,600 | 432,000 |
| Goods available for sale | $353,600 | $520,000 |
| Ratio of cost to retail prices<br>$353,600 ÷ $520,000 = 68% | | |
| Less: Net sales | | 340,000 |
| Estimated ending inventory at retail | | $180,000 |
| Estimated ending inventory at cost ($180,000 × 0.68) | | $122,400 |

computed a cost-to-retail ratio of 68%, indicating $0.68 of inventory cost for every $1.00 of retail valuation. As a result, the $180,000 estimated ending inventory is multiplied by the 68% ratio to arrive at the $122,400 cost-based valuation.

In this example the retail method was used to obtain an interim estimate of inventory. This same method can also be employed to study a company's experience with theft and shoplifting. For instance, assume the figures in the Boulder illustration relate to a full calendar year. A physical count on December 31 has revealed an inventory of $171,000 at retail prices. Thus, Boulder has a $9,000 shortage at retail ($180,000 − $171,000), which cost the firm $6,120 ($9,000 × 0.68).

## Periodic and Perpetual Inventory Systems

OBJECTIVE 7
Understand the differences between the periodic and perpetual inventory systems.

Throughout this chapter and in earlier chapters, we have emphasized the **periodic inventory system.** Recall that under a periodic system, merchandise purchases are recorded in the Purchases account and sales are credited to the Sales account. These procedures result in a constant balance in Inventory throughout the year. The periodic system is frequently employed by businesses because of its minimal record-keeping requirements and is especially attractive for companies that (1) sell slow-moving products, (2) carry a large variety of low-cost inventory items, and (3) use manual accounting systems.

Two significant problems associated with a periodic system make it undesirable for many organizations. First, a business has no record of the number of units in stock at any given time. Remember, no entries are made to the Inventory account for acquisitions and sales. This lack of information could lead to stockouts and poor customer service. The second problem lies in the calculation of cost of goods sold. To explain, we present the following computations (the amounts are assumed):

| Cost of goods sold | |
|---|---|
| Beginning inventory | $19,000 |
| Add: Net purchases | 47,000 |
| Goods available for sale | $66,000 |
| Less: Ending inventory | 24,000 |
| Cost of goods sold | $42,000 |

By subtracting the $24,000 ending inventory per the physical count, we are assuming that $42,000 of goods were sold. This assumption could be erroneous, however, because theft or errors may have occurred. Unfortunately, there is no basis for comparison, as the periodic system does not monitor the amount of inventory that *should be* on hand.

## Perpetual Systems

The preceding problems are overcome by using a **perpetual inventory system.** A perpetual system maintains a continuous record of the inflows and outflows of merchandise, resulting in a running count of the goods on hand. By maintaining records in this manner, a company can readily answer the questions of its salespeople and customers concerning item availability. In addition, a perpetual system leads to improved inventory control. By knowing the number of units that are supposed to be on hand, a business can reorder in sufficient time to avoid stockouts. Furthermore, the extent of any theft or errors can be determined by comparing the inventory records against a physical count. We stress that although a firm has a record of the number of units in stock, a physical inventory is still necessary to verify the books at the end of the accounting period.

Perpetual systems are being used by an increasing number of businesses, primarily because of computers and state-of-the-art information systems. Computers can perform the related record keeping in a matter of seconds, and many companies have found that on-line terminals allow inventory records to be updated as each sale (and purchase) is made. Key product data are entered into the computer when goods are sold or acquired, often by using bar codes or code numbers and a scanning device. The process is extremely efficient, providing management with important inventory information on an economical basis.

## Illustration of a Perpetual System

We will illustrate the operation of a perpetual inventory system by focusing on the FIFO cost flow assumption, as discussed earlier in the chapter. Assume the following data were taken from the records of Bankston Company and pertain to part no. 1058:

Beginning inventory: 3,000 units @ $5.00

| *Purchases on Account* | | | *Sales on Account* | | |
|---|---|---|---|---|---|
| 3/10 | 2,000 units @ $6.25 = | $12,500 | 3/13 | 2,600 units @ $9 = | $23,400 |
| 3/19 | 1,600 units @ $6.50 = | 10,400 | 3/22 | 2,300 units @ $9 = | 20,700 |
| | 3,600 | $22,900 | | 4,900 | $44,100 |

Because the perpetual system closely monitors inventory levels, subsidiary records are normally established for each item stocked. The subsidiary record for part no. 1058 appears in Exhibit 9-8.

A careful study of this record shows that the purchase on March 10 gives rise to two different cost layers: 3,000 units at $5 and 2,000 units at $6.25. Because the unit costs differ, the layers are maintained separately and listed chronologically. The sale on March 13 reduces the inventory by 2,600 units. Although the units were sold for $9 each, they must be removed from the inventory records at cost. With FIFO, the sale is costed at the oldest purchase price of $5 (i.e., the "first-in"), leaving 400 units from the beginning layer (3,000 − 2,600) plus 2,000 units from the purchase of March 10 on hand. The sale of 2,300 units on March 22 is handled in a similar fashion. The oldest costs (the remaining 400 units from the first layer plus 1,900 units from the second layer) become the cost of goods sold.

**Exhibit 9-8**
**Perpetual Inventory Record: FIFO**

PERPETUAL INVENTORY RECORD

*Part No.* 1058 *Reorder Point* 2,500 units

| Date | Purchases | Sales | Balance |
|---|---|---|---|
| 3/1 | | | 3,000 @ $5.00 |
| 3/10 | 2,000 @ $6.25 | | 3,000 @ $5.00<br>2,000 @ $6.25 |
| 3/13 | | 2,600 @ $5.00 | 400 @ $5.00<br>2,000 @ $6.25 |
| 3/19 | 1,600 @ $6.50 | | 400 @ $5.00<br>2,000 @ $6.25<br>1,600 @ $6.50 |
| 3/22 | | 400 @ $5.00<br>1,900 @ $6.25 | 100 @ $6.25<br>1,600 @ $6.50 |
| | | | |

The Bankston illustration shows that cost of goods sold is computed when each sale occurs; in contrast, under a periodic system, the calculation is made at the end of the accounting period. Despite the procedural difference, perpetual and periodic systems will yield identical results when FIFO is used. Put simply, no matter when cost of goods sold is determined, this key income statement component will always consist of the same (i.e., the earliest) inventory charges.

Our example has focused on the FIFO cost flow assumption. The LIFO and average costing methods may be employed as well; related computations and procedures are shown in an appendix to this chapter.

## General Ledger Updating

Recall the control account/subsidiary ledger relationship that was discussed in Chapter 6. Because Bankston has been increasing and decreasing its subsidiary records for part no. 1058, the firm must also enter the purchases and sales in the general ledger control account (Inventory) to preserve the necessary equality. The transactions on March 10 and 13 are recorded as follows:

| | | | |
|---|---|---|---|
| Mar. 10 | Inventory | 12,500 | |
| | Accounts Payable | | 12,500 |
| | Purchased 2,000 units at $6.25 | | |
| 13 | Cost of Goods Sold | 13,000 | |
| | Inventory | | 13,000 |
| | Sold 2,600 units having a cost of $5 per unit | | |
| 13 | Accounts Receivable | 23,400 | |
| | Sales | | 23,400 |
| | Sold 2,600 units at a selling price of $9 per unit | | |

Observe that both the purchase and the sale are recorded in the Inventory account; the Purchases account is no longer used. Furthermore, notice that a sale now requires two entries. The first entry on March 13 reduces Inventory and recognizes the cost of the units sold (via a debit to a new account entitled Cost of Goods Sold); the second entry is needed to record the appropriate sales revenue. With the use of entries such as these throughout the period, both Cost of Goods Sold and Inventory are updated continuously.

**TIPS & TECHNIQUES**

Avoid the common mistake of making an entry on March 13 similar to the following: Debit Accounts Receivable, $23,400; Credit Inventory, $13,000; Credit Profit on Sale, $10,400. There is no account entitled Profit on Sale. The income on this transaction is derived by subtracting Cost of Goods Sold from Sales and would be disclosed on the income statement in the familiar format of:

| | |
|---|---|
| Sales | $23,400 |
| Less: Cost of goods sold | 13,000 |
| Gross profit | $10,400 |

As you can see, the operation of a perpetual inventory system entails considerable record keeping. Consequently, some businesses modify the procedures just illustrated. A number of firms keep their subsidiary records in units only; that is, dollars are ignored. At the end of the accounting period, inventory valuation and cost of goods sold are computed by using the periodic method. By following these procedures, businesses are taking advantage of the benefits associated with both systems: the reduced record keeping of a periodic system and the perpetual system's improved inventory control.

## APPENDIX LIFO and Average Costing Under a Perpetual Inventory System

The example just concluded was based on a FIFO cost flow assumption. Perpetual inventory systems may also be used in conjunction with both LIFO and average costing. These methods will now be shown, with inventory data from Bankston Company once again serving as the basis for our illustrations. The data are repeated here for your convenience.

Beginning inventory: 3,000 units @ $5.00

| *Purchases on Account* | | | *Sales on Account* | | |
|---|---|---|---|---|---|
| 3/10 | 2,000 units @ $6.25 = | $12,500 | 3/13 | 2,600 units @ $9 = | $23,400 |
| 3/19 | 1,600 units @ $6.50 = | 10,400 | 3/22 | 2,300 units @ $9 = | 20,700 |
| | 3,600 | $22,900 | | 4,900 | $44,100 |

### LIFO

With a LIFO perpetual system, cost of goods sold is figured by using the most recent costs experienced. For instance, in Bankston's case, the company has two layers of goods available for sale after the acquisition on March 10: 3,000 units at $5 and 2,000 units at $6.25 (see Exhibit 9-9). Assume it is now March 13 and the firm employs a LIFO inventory system. The cost of the 2,600-unit sale would be determined by first using the most recent cost layer (i.e., the "last-in"), which is the purchase from three days earlier. Bankston must then cut into its older goods to account for the remaining 600 units, leaving 2,400 units (3,000 − 600) at $5 in stock.

The sale on March 22 would be treated in an identical manner. The firm's goods available for sale are now 2,400 units at $5 plus the acquisition on March 19 (1,600 units at $6.50). The 2,300-unit sale would again be costed at the most recent costs experienced, namely, 1,600 units at $6.50 plus 700 units from the older layer at $5. Bankston's ending inventory is therefore 1,700 units (2,400 − 700) at $5.

Normally, because of the timing of the charges to cost of goods sold, the results obtained with a LIFO perpetual system will differ from those that occur under a periodic system. With the perpetual approach, the most recent costs *at the time of each sale* are evaluated and transferred to the income statement. When a periodic system is employed, however, the transfer process begins with the most recent costs incurred *during the period,* namely, after all purchases have been made.

### Moving Average

The average cost approach when used with a perpetual system is often called **moving average.** With this method, a new average unit cost is computed each time that inventory is purchased. This amount is later employed to determine cost of goods sold and ending inventory valuations.

Continuing the Bankston Company example, the firm's acquisition on March 10 will produce the following results:

| | | |
|---|---|---|
| Inventory on 3/1: | 3,000 units at $5.00 = | $15,000 |
| Purchase on 3/10: | 2,000 units at $6.25 = | 12,500 |
| | 5,000 | $27,500 |

Average cost per unit: $27,500 ÷ 5,000 units = $5.50

**Exhibit 9-9**
**Perpetual Inventory Record: LIFO**

PERPETUAL INVENTORY RECORD

*Part No.* 1058 *Reorder Point* 2,500 units

| Date | Purchases | Sales | Balance |
|---|---|---|---|
| 3/1 | | | 3,000 @ $5.00 |
| 3/10 | 2,000 @ $6.25 | | 3,000 @ $5.00<br>2,000 @ $6.25 |
| 3/13 | | 2,000 @ $6.25<br>600 @ $5.00 | 2,400 @ $5.00 |
| 3/19 | 1,600 @ $6.50 | | 2,400 @ $5.00<br>1,600 @ $6.50 |
| 3/22 | | 1,600 @ $6.50<br>700 @ $5.00 | 1,700 @ $5.00 |

Thus, when 2,600 units are sold on March 13, cost of goods sold will amount to \$14,300 (2,600 units × \$5.50) and 2,400 units (5,000 − 2,600) will be left in inventory. These latter goods will be assigned a cost of \$5.50 as well, yielding an inventory valuation of \$13,200 (2,400 units × \$5.50).

A new average cost will be calculated on March 19 because of the purchase of 1,600 units:

| | | |
|---|---|---|
| Inventory on 3/13: | 2,400 units at \$5.50 = | \$13,200 |
| Purchase on 3/19: | 1,600 units at \$6.50 = | 10,400 |
| | 4,000 | \$23,600 |

Average cost per unit: \$23,600 ÷ 4,000 units = \$5.90

To complete the example, the sale on March 22 would be costed at \$13,570 (2,300 units × \$5.90), while the month-end inventory of 1,700 units (4,000 − 2,300) would total \$10,030 (1,700 units × \$5.90).

When using the average costing approach, the difference between the perpetual and periodic systems lies in the frequency of computation. Average unit costs are calculated after each purchase in the perpetual system; in contrast, under the periodic approach, a single average cost is derived upon conclusion of the accounting period. In view of the nature of the computation, ending inventory and cost of goods sold will differ between the two methods.

## Chapter Review

### Learning Objectives—The Key Points

**1 Understand the ownership issues related to goods in transit and goods on consignment.** Inventory ownership is dependent on possession of legal title to the goods, which, in turn, is dependent on freight terms. Under F.O.B. shipping point, title passes to the purchaser when goods are shipped. In contrast, under F.O.B. destination, title will pass when merchandise arrives at its destination. With consignment sales, merchandise transferred to sales agents is considered part of the consignor's inventory until sold even though the goods are not in the consignor's possession.

**2 Understand the effects of inventory errors on financial statements.** An inaccurate inventory figure results in an incorrect income statement, statement of owner's equity, and balance sheet. For example, if the ending inventory is understated, cost of goods sold will be overstated and net income will be understated. This, in turn, produces understated amounts for both ending owner's equity and inventory. Inventory errors are counterbalanced over a two-year period because the ending inventory of one year becomes the beginning inventory of the next.

**3 Be familiar with the specific identification, FIFO, LIFO, and weighted-average inventory methods.** The specific identification method results in associating the cost of the units with the units themselves, often via code numbers and stickers. This method has limited applications, thereby requiring most businesses to adopt a cost flow assumption. With the FIFO (first-in, first-out) assumption, costs are matched against revenues in the order that the costs were incurred. Thus, cost of goods sold is comprised of older costs (i.e., the "first-in"), whereas ending inventory is composed of the most recent purchase prices experienced by the firm. In contrast, the LIFO (last-in, first-out) method results in recent costs being transferred to the income statement for cost-of-goods-sold determination. Older costs therefore remain in inventory. Finally, with the weighted-average method, an average cost is calculated by dividing the cost of goods available for sale by the number of units available for sale. The unit cost is then used to compute both cost of goods sold and ending inventory.

**4 Understand the factors that are considered when selecting an inventory method and the effects of such a selection on financial statements.** Income taxes are an important consideration for many businesses. Because LIFO produces lower net income and lower income tax payments than FIFO in periods of inflation, the LIFO method has gained in popularity in the past 15 to 20 years.

These flow assumptions also have different effects on the financial statements. For example, FIFO's use of the oldest costs in cost-of-goods-sold calculations produces a poor match of costs and revenues on the income statement. However, the balance sheet valuation is improved because inventories consist of fairly recent costs. The LIFO method would produce effects opposite of those just described.

**5 Be familiar with the lower-of-cost-or-market rule of inventory valuation.** The lower-of-cost-or-market rule permits the write-down of inventories to market if the goods' value has been reduced because of damage, spoilage, or obsolescence. Market is generally defined as replacement cost, or the cost that would be incurred to reproduce or repurchase the item. Write-downs entail the recognition of a loss, which lowers net income, and a reduction in the recorded cost of inventory. This procedure, which produces conservative asset valuations and income figures, can be applied to individual inventory items, to subclasses of similar items, or to the inventory as a whole.

**6 Understand the importance of inventory estimates and be able to formulate estimates by using the gross profit and retail methods.** Inventory estimates facilitate the issuance of interim financial statements, the filing of insurance claims in cases of disaster, and the determination of reasonableness of actual physical counts. With the gross profit method, inventory is estimated on the basis of a company's gross profit rate. An estimated gross profit figure is derived for use in computing cost of goods sold. Then, cost of goods sold is subtracted from goods available for sale to arrive at the estimate of inventory. In contrast, with the retail method, ending inventory is first calculated at retail prices. This figure is subsequently converted to cost on the basis of the percentage relationship between the cost and retail valuations of goods available for sale (i.e., the cost-to-retail ratio).

**7 Understand the differences between the periodic and perpetual inventory systems.** With a periodic inventory system, a continual record of merchandise on hand is not maintained. The inventory at the end of the period and the related cost-of-goods-sold figure are determined on the basis of a physical count. The perpetual system, on the other hand, keeps a running record of merchandise inflows and outflows. Thus, the Inventory account is increased for acquisitions and decreased for sales. Cost of goods sold is also maintained on a continual basis, being increased when each sale occurs. The perpetual system results in improved managerial control and may be used in conjunction with a FIFO, LIFO, and average cost flow assumption.

## Chapter Quiz

The five questions that follow relate to several issues raised in the chapter. Test your knowledge of the issues by selecting the best answer. (The answers appear on p. 342.)

**1** Because of a mathematical error, the 19X8 ending inventory included goods at a \$170 figure that had actually cost \$710. As a result of this error:
- a net income for 19X8 is overstated.
- b net income for 19X8 is understated.
- c operating expenses for 19X8 are understated.
- d total liabilities at the end of 19X8 are overstated.

**2** The inventory cost flow assumption in which the oldest costs incurred become part of cost of goods sold when units are sold is:
- a LIFO.
- b FIFO.
- c weighted average.
- d retail.

**3** The LIFO inventory valuation method:
a is acceptable only if a company sells its newest goods first.
b will result in higher income levels than FIFO in periods of rising prices.
c will result in a match of fairly current inventory costs against recent selling prices on the income statement.
d cannot be used with a periodic inventory system.

**4** Stanley Company sells two different products. The following information is available at year-end:

| *Inventory Item* | *Units* | *Cost Per Unit* | *Market Value Per Unit* |
|---|---|---|---|
| A | 100 | $4 | $6 |
| B | 200 | 5 | 3 |

Applying the lower-of-cost-or-market rule to each item, Stanley's ending inventory balance would be:
a $1,000. c $1,400.
b $1,200. d some other amount.

**5** Which of the following accounting systems maintains a running (continuous) record of merchandising purchases and sales by inventory item?
a Perpetual. c Periodic.
b Gross profit. d Retail.

## Summary Problem

Tiger Company sells a single product and uses a periodic inventory system. The following information was extracted from the accounting records:

| | *Purchases* | *Sales* |
|---|---|---|
| Feb. | 800 units @ $4.75 | 1,500 units @ $ 8.50 |
| June | 600 units @ $5.50 | 500 units @ $10.00 |
| Oct. | 900 units @ $6.00 | |

The firm's beginning inventory on January 1 totaled 200 units and cost $800.

### Instructions

Compute Tiger's ending inventory, cost of goods sold, and gross profit, using the following inventory valuation methods: (1) FIFO; (2) LIFO; (3) weighted average.

### Solution

Sales

| | |
|---|---|
| 1,500 units @ $ 8.50 = | $12,750 |
| 500 units @ $10.00 = | 5,000 |
| 2,000 units | $17,750 |

Goods available for sale

| | | |
|---|---|---|
| Beginning inventory | 200 units @ $4.00 = | $ 800 |
| Feb. purchase | 800 units @ $4.75 = | 3,800 |
| June purchase | 600 units @ $5.50 = | 3,300 |
| Oct. purchase | 900 units @ $6.00 = | 5,400 |
| | 2,500 units | $13,300 |

Ending inventory

| | |
|---|---|
| Goods available for sale | 2,500 units |
| Less: Sales | 2,000 units |
| Ending inventory | 500 units |

FIFO ending inventory consists of the most recent costs; therefore:

500 units @ \$6.00 = \$3,000

LIFO ending inventory consists of the oldest costs; therefore:

| | |
|---|---|
| 200 units @ \$4.00 = | \$ 800 |
| 300 units @ \$4.75 = | 1,425 |
| | \$2,225 |

Weighted average ending inventory

\$13,300 ÷ 2,500 units = \$5.32 per unit

500 units × \$5.32 = \$2,660

| | *FIFO* | *LIFO* | *Weighted Average* |
|---|---|---|---|
| Sales | \$17,750 | \$17,750 | \$17,750 |
| Less: Cost of goods sold | | | |
| Beginning inventory | \$ 800 | \$ 800 | \$ 800 |
| Add: Purchases* | 12,500 | 12,500 | 12,500 |
| Goods available for sale | \$13,300 | \$13,300 | \$13,300 |
| Less: Ending inventory | 3,000 | 2,225 | 2,660 |
| Cost of goods sold | \$10,300 | \$11,075 | \$10,640 |
| Gross profit | \$ 7,450 | \$ 6,675 | \$ 7,110 |

* Goods available for sale minus the beginning inventory.

## Questions

**Q9-1** What items are reported as inventory for (a) merchandising and (b) manufacturing companies?

**Q9-2** The Potter Company purchased the following merchandise on December 28:

| *Supplier* | *Terms* | *Amount* |
|---|---|---|
| Pax Company | F.O.B. destination | \$1,800 |
| James Manufacturing | F.O.B. shipping point | 2,500 |

Both purchases were shipped December 30, but neither had been received by December 31. Should the purchases be included in Potter's December 31 ending inventory? Explain.

**Q9-3** What are goods on consignment? Who has title to goods on consignment?

**Q9-4** Why is it necessary to take a physical count of inventory at the end of each accounting period?

**Q9-5** The Wood Company made the following mathematical error in determining the cost of its April 30 ending inventory:

| *Item No.* | *Quantity* | *Cost per Unit* | *Total Cost* |
|---|---|---|---|
| S775 | 150 | $34 | $3,100 |

Determine the effect of the error on the following:
a Cost of goods sold for the year ended April 30
b Operating expenses for the year ended April 30
c Net income for the year ended April 30
d Owner's equity as of April 30
e Total current assets as of April 30

**Q9-6** At the end of an accounting period, goods available for sale is segregated into two different costs. What are these two costs? Explain which of the costs is given primary emphasis by accountants.

**Q9-7** Why is the specific identification method of inventory valuation used infrequently?

**Q9-8** Discuss the difference between the physical flow of goods and a cost flow assumption.

**Q9-9** Why has LIFO gained in popularity in recent years?

**Q9-10** In a period of rising prices, which inventory valuation method (LIFO or FIFO) tends to result in the following?
a Highest cost of goods sold
b Lowest inventory valuation
c Highest income taxes

**Q9-11** Are businesses permitted to arbitrarily change inventory valuation methods from one year to the next? Briefly explain.

**Q9-12** What is meant by the term "market" as used in the phrase "lower of cost or market"?

**Q9-13** Why do businesses need to estimate their inventory balances?

**Q9-14** Discuss the advantages of a perpetual inventory system when compared with a periodic system. Does the perpetual system have any limitations?

**Q9-15** Why are two journal entries required to record a sale under a perpetual inventory system?

***Q9-16** Will the ending inventory figure computed by using a weighted-average periodic system normally agree with that calculated under a moving-average perpetual system? Why?

## Exercises

**E9-1** ***Inventory errors and income measurement***

The income statements of Keagle Company for 19X3 and 19X4 follow.

* An asterisk preceding an item indicates that the material is covered in an appendix to this chapter.

| | 19X3 | 19X4 |
|---|---|---|
| Sales | $100,000 | $109,000 |
| Cost of goods sold | 62,000 | 74,000 |
| Gross profit | $ 38,000 | $ 35,000 |
| Expenses | 26,000 | 22,000 |
| Net income | $ 12,000 | $ 13,000 |

A recent review of the accounting records discovered that the 19X3 ending inventory had been understated by $4,000.

a Prepare corrected 19X3 and 19X4 income statements.

b What is the effect of the error on ending owner's equity for 19X3 and 19X4?

**E9-2** ***Specific identification method***

Boston Galleries uses the specific identification method for inventory valuation. Inventory information for several oil paintings follows.

| | | | Painting | Cost |
|---|---|---|---|---|
| Jan. | 2 | Beginning inventory | Woods | $11,000 |
| Apr. | 19 | Purchase | Sunset | 21,800 |
| June | 7 | Purchase | Earth | 31,200 |
| Dec. | 16 | Purchase | Moon | 4,000 |

Woods and Moon were sold during the year for a total of $35,000. Determine the firm's:

a Cost of goods sold.

b Gross profit.

c Ending inventory.

**E9-3** ***Inventory valuation methods: Basic computations***

The following information is available for the Remington Company for the month of April:

| | | | |
|---|---|---|---|
| Apr. | 1 | Beginning inventory | 600 units @ $3.00 |
| | 7 | Purchase | 1,000 units @ $3.10 |
| | 17 | Purchase | 2,000 units @ $3.50 |
| | 24 | Purchase | 400 units @ $4.25 |

On April 30, 800 units were unsold and remained in inventory. The firm uses a periodic inventory system.

Compute the ending inventory balance under each of the following valuation methods:

a First-in, first-out

b Last-in, first-out

c Weighted average

**E9-4** ***Inventory valuation methods: Basic computations***

The January 1 beginning inventory of the Metric Company consisted of 400 units at a unit cost of $16. During the first quarter, Metric purchased 1,000 units at $18 and then 600 units at $20. Sales during the first quarter were 850 units at $28 per unit. The firm uses a periodic inventory system.

Determine the ending inventory and cost of goods sold under each of the following inventory valuation methods:

a FIFO

b LIFO

c Weighted average

**E9-5** ***Analysis of LIFO vs. FIFO***

Indicate whether LIFO or FIFO best describes each of the following:

a Gives highest profits when prices fall.

b Yields lowest income taxes when prices rise.

c Generates an ending inventory valuation that somewhat approximates replacement cost.

d Matches recent costs against current selling prices on the income statement.

e Comes closest to approximating the physical flow of goods of a fruit and vegetable dealer.

f Results in lowest cost of goods sold in inflationary periods.

**E9-6** ***Lower-of-cost-or-market rule***

The Springfield Company sells five different products. The following information is available on December 31:

| *Inventory Item* | *Units* | *Cost per Unit* | *Market Value per Unit* |
|---|---|---|---|
| A | 700 | $3.00 | $3.20 |
| B | 1,100 | 6.00 | 5.70 |
| C | 1,400 | 8.00 | 9.00 |
| D | 800 | 7.00 | 7.50 |
| E | 2,600 | 2.00 | 1.60 |

a Apply the lower-of-cost-or-market rule to each inventory item and determine Springfield's ending inventory balance.

b Prepare the required journal entry to reduce the inventory to the lower of cost or market.

**E9-7** ***Overview of inventory ownership and costing***

Evaluate the comments that follow as being True or False. If the comment is false, briefly explain why.

a Franco purchased goods from Wholesale Supply on December 28. Although the merchandise was still in transit on December 31, Franco should nevertheless report these goods on its year-end balance sheet as an asset if the goods were sent F.O.B. shipping point.

b If a company sells its oldest goods first, the firm must use the FIFO method of inventory valuation.

c LIFO normally results in fairly current inventory costs being reported on the income statement as cost of goods sold.

d Under a weighted-average (periodic) inventory system, all goods sold during a period are costed at the same unit cost.

e Data on Olympia's inventory follow.

| *Item* | *Total Cost* | *Total Market* |
|---|---|---|
| A | $15,900 | $11,900 |
| B | 20,600 | 24,600 |

Olympia values its inventory on an item-by-item basis in accordance with rules stipulated by the accounting profession. Because the $4,000 loss suffered on item A is precisely offset by a $4,000 gain on item B, the company need not adjust its Inventory account at the end of the period.

**E9-8** ***Gross profit method and casualty loss***

Metro Insurance Company is reviewing a claim from Electronic Hobbies (EH), a long-time client. EH experienced an inventory loss on May 5, when a tornado struck its warehouse. The information that follows is available.

| | |
|---|---|
| Inventory, Jan. 1 | $ 62,000 |
| Purchases, Jan. 1–May 5 | 104,000 |
| Sales, Jan. 1–May 5 | 180,000 |
| Claim request | 47,500 |
| Estimated gross profit rate | 35% |

By using the gross profit method, evaluate the reasonableness of EH's insurance claim.

**E9-9** ***Retail inventory method***
Hunt & Fish, a sporting goods store, uses the retail method of inventory valuation. The following information is available on December 31:

| | *Cost* | *Retail* |
|---|---|---|
| Inventory, Jan. 1 | $140,000 | $235,000 |
| Purchases, Jan.–Dec. | 382,000 | 635,000 |
| Sales, Jan.–Dec. | | 527,740 |
| Returns & allowances | | |
| Sales | | 24,000 |
| Purchases | 12,000 | 20,000 |

Estimate the cost of the store's December 31 ending inventory.

**E9-10** ***Perpetual inventory systems: FIFO***
Alabama Industries had a beginning inventory on January 1 of 2,000 units that cost $6 each. Purchases and sales throughout the year were as follows:

| *Purchases* | | *Sales* | |
|---|---|---|---|
| Apr. 3 | 3,000 units at $8.00 | Apr. 9 | 3,500 units at $10.00 |
| Oct. 4 | 4,000 units at $8.85 | Dec. 3 | 3,000 units at $11.00 |

The company uses a perpetual inventory system. Calculate the ending inventory valuation by using the FIFO cost flow assumption.

**E9-11** ***Journal entries for periodic and perpetual inventory systems***
Barto's, a well-known men's shop, had the following transactions during May:

| | |
|---|---|
| Purchases on account | |
| 100 shirts @ $15 | $1,500 |
| Sales on account | |
| 60 of the above shirts | 1,380 |
| Returns on account | |
| 15 of the above unsold shirts | |

a Record the preceding transactions by using a periodic inventory system.
b Record the preceding transactions by using a perpetual inventory system.

***E9-12** ***Perpetual inventory systems: LIFO and moving average***
Refer to the beginning inventory, purchases, and sales data of Alabama Industries in Exercise 9-10. Assuming use of a perpetual inventory system, calculate the company's ending inventory valuation under the following cost flow assumptions:
a LIFO
b Moving average

## Problems

### Series A

**P9-A1** ***Inventory errors***

The income statements of Diamond Company for the years ended December 31, 19X1, and 19X2 follow.

| | *19X1* | | *19X2* | |
|---|---|---|---|---|
| Net sales | | $440,000 | | $483,000 |
| Cost of goods sold | | | | |
| Beginning inventory | $ 95,000 | | $109,000 | |
| Add: Net purchases | 380,000 | | 404,000 | |
| Goods available for sale | $475,000 | | $513,000 | |
| Less: Ending inventory | 109,000 | | 127,000 | |
| Cost of goods sold | | 366,000 | | 386,000 |
| Gross profit | | $ 74,000 | | $ 97,000 |
| Operating expenses | | 58,000 | | 67,000 |
| Net income | | $ 16,000 | | $ 30,000 |

Diamond uses a periodic inventory system. A detailed review of the accounting records revealed the following errors:

1 A review of 19X1 purchase invoices revealed that a clerk had incorrectly recorded a $12,600 purchase as $1,260.

2 A $4,800 purchase was made on December 30, 19X2, terms F.O.B. shipping point. The invoice was not recorded in 19X2 nor were the goods included in the 19X2 ending physical inventory count. Both the goods and invoice were received in early 19X3, with the invoice being recorded at that time.

3 Goods costing $3,000 were accidentally excluded from the 19X1 ending physical inventory count. These goods were sold during 19X2, and all aspects of the sale were properly recorded.

**Instructions**

a Prepare corrected income statements for 19X1 and 19X2.

b Determine the impact of the preceding errors on the December 31, 19X2, owner's equity balance.

**P9-A2** ***Inventory valuation methods: Basic computations***

Palo Alto Sales Company began business on January 1. Purchases of merchandise during the year were as follows:

| | | |
|---|---|---|
| Jan. | 2 | 500 units @ $1.98 |
| Feb. | 6 | 800 units @ $2.10 |
| May | 9 | 2,200 units @ $2.40 |
| Aug. | 22 | 3,500 units @ $2.50 |
| Oct. | 14 | 2,500 units @ $2.60 |
| Dec. | 2 | 3,000 units @ $2.60 |

During the year, 11,000 units were sold: 4,000 units were sold for $4.00 per unit; the remainder were sold for $4.20 per unit. The firm uses a periodic inventory system.

**Instructions**

Determine Palo Alto's ending inventory balance, cost of goods sold, and gross profit under each of the following inventory valuation methods:

a First-in, first-out
b Last-in, first-out
c Weighted average

**P9-A3** ***FIFO; lower of cost or market***

On January 2 of the current year, Jim Bryan became manager of a newly opened branch store of Tire City. Bryan made the following purchases during the first month of operation:

| | |
|---|---|
| 13-inch Tires | |
| Jan. 2 | 1,100 units @ $37 |
| 28 | 480 units @ $42 |
| 14-inch Tires | |
| Jan. 2 | 420 units @ $43 |
| 14 | 360 units @ $49 |
| 27 | 80 units @ $53 |
| 15-inch Tires | |
| Jan. 2 | 600 units @ $45 |

An end-of-month physical inventory count revealed that the branch had 430 of the 13-inch tires, 123 of the 14-inch tires, and 570 of the 15-inch tires in stock. Total sales for January amounted to $142,100; expenses (excluding cost of goods sold) were $45,800.

The company uses the FIFO inventory valuation method in conjunction with a periodic inventory system.

**Instructions**

a Compute the branch's ending inventory, cost of goods sold, and net income for the first month of operation.
b Assume that the manufacturer of the 14-inch tires recently announced a price decrease to $48. Determine the impact of the announcement on the branch's ending inventory valuation.
c Prepare the journal entry necessary to value the company's inventory at the lower of cost or market.

**P9-A4** ***Gross profit method and fire loss***

On January 28, 19X4, a fire heavily damaged the office and warehouse of Sunset Products. The following information has been obtained:

1 Sunset's condensed income statement for the year ended December 31, 19X3, is as follows:

| | | |
|---|---|---|
| Sales | | $500,000 |
| Cost of goods sold | | |
| Beginning inventory | $195,000 | |
| Add: Net purchases | 325,000 | |
| Goods available for sale | $520,000 | |
| Less: Ending inventory | 290,000 | |
| Cost of goods sold | | 230,000 |
| Gross profit | | $270,000 |
| Expenses | | 209,600 |
| Net income | | $ 60,400 |

2 Net sales and net purchases made during the first 28 days of January were $38,000 and $19,900, respectively.
3 Purchases entered in the accounting records but still in transit as of January 28 amounted to $1,700.

Sunset's insurance company agreed to reimburse the firm for the fire loss on the basis of an estimate of inventory by using the gross profit method. The gross profit rate will be derived by examining last year's operating results.

**Instructions**

a Determine the cost of inventory on hand on January 28.
b Taking your answer in part (a) into consideration, assume that goods were recovered and sold to a salvage firm for $6,000. Compute Sunset's total fire loss.
c In addition to computing fire losses, are there other possible uses of the gross profit method? Explain.

**P9-A5 *Retail method and inventory shrinkage***

Express, a clothing store, uses the retail method of inventory valuation. A review of the company's accounting records disclosed the following information for the year ended December 31:

| | | | |
|---|---|---|---|
| Inventory, Jan. 1 | | Purchasing Activity | |
| Cost | $ 55,700 | Purchases | |
| Retail | 85,000 | Cost | $177,650 |
| Sales | 295,000 | Retail | 276,800 |
| Sales returns | 6,400 | Returns | |
| | | Cost | 3,900 |
| | | Retail | 8,800 |

**Instructions**

a Using the retail method, estimate the cost of the company's inventory on December 31.
b If the firm's physical count on December 31 revealed an ending inventory at retail of $60,000, compute the cost of inventory shrinkage.

**P9-A6 *Perpetual inventory systems: FIFO***

The McGeorge Company carries parts that are in high demand by the automotive industry. Given the competitive nature of its business, McGeorge uses a perpetual inventory system. The following information pertains to a particular exhaust component:

June 1 Beginning inventory: 800 units @ $14

| *Purchases* | | *Sales* | |
|---|---|---|---|
| June 10 | 1,000 units @ $15.50 | June 7 | 300 units @ $22 |
| 17 | 600 units @ $16.10 | 12 | 400 units @ $23 |
| 20 | 1,000 units @ $16.25 | 14 | 600 units @ $23 |
| | | 19 | 800 units @ $24 |
| | | 28 | 900 units @ $24 |

**Instructions**

a Using a format similar to that of Exhibit 9-8, prepare a perpetual inventory record for the exhaust component. McGeorge uses the FIFO method of inventory valuation.
b Prepare summary journal entries to record total purchases and sales.
c Why do you think McGeorge implemented a perpetual inventory system rather than a periodic system?

***P9-A7** ***Perpetual inventory systems: LIFO and moving average***
Refer to the beginning inventory, purchases, and sales data of the McGeorge Company in Problem 9-A6.

**Instructions**

a Assuming use of a LIFO cost flow assumption, prepare a perpetual inventory record for the exhaust component by using a format similar to that shown in Exhibit 9-9.
b Assuming use of the moving average method, determine the cost of the June 30 ending inventory and also the cost of goods sold during June.

## Series B

**P9-B1** ***Inventory errors***
The income statements of Maxum Company for the years ended December 31, 19X4, and 19X5 follow.

| | *19X4* | | *19X5* | |
|---|---|---|---|---|
| Net sales | | $820,000 | | $840,000 |
| Cost of goods sold | | | | |
| Beginning inventory | $245,000 | | $315,000 | |
| Add: Net purchases | 710,000 | | 680,000 | |
| Goods available for sale | $955,000 | | $995,000 | |
| Less: Ending inventory | 315,000 | | 340,000 | |
| Cost of goods sold | | 640,000 | | 655,000 |
| Gross profit | | $180,000 | | $185,000 |
| Operating expenses | | 126,000 | | 140,000 |
| Net income | | $ 54,000 | | $ 45,000 |

Maxum uses a periodic inventory system. A detailed review of the accounting records revealed the following errors:

1 Because of a clerical error, 60 units of merchandise in the 19X5 ending inventory count were costed at $540 per unit rather than the correct amount of $54 per unit.
2 A $5,000 merchandise purchase on December 31, 19X4, terms F.O.B. destination, was included in the 19X4 ending physical inventory count even though the goods had not yet been received. An investigation revealed that the invoice was recorded when the goods arrived on January 4, 19X5.
3 An examination of 19X4 purchasing activity revealed that a $26,000 acquisition of land had been incorrectly charged to the Purchases account.

**Instructions**

a Prepare corrected income statements for 19X4 and 19X5.
b Determine the impact of the preceding errors on the December 31, 19X5, owner's equity balance.

**P9-B2** ***Inventory valuation methods: Basic computations***
The Branch Company sells a single product. The following information is available for the month of April:

| | | | |
|---|---|---|---|
| Apr. | 1 | Beginning inventory | 600 units @ $5.95 |
| | 9 | Purchase | 800 units @ $6.00 |
| | 16 | Purchase | 700 units @ $6.10 |
| | 22 | Purchase | 500 units @ $6.20 |
| | 29 | Purchase | 400 units @ $6.25 |

During April, 1,900 units were sold at $10 per unit. The firm uses a periodic inventory system.

**Instructions**

Determine Branch's ending inventory balance, cost of goods sold, and gross profit under each of the following inventory valuation methods:

a First-in, first-out
b Last-in, first-out
c Weighted average

**P9-B3** ***FIFO; lower of cost or market***

On March 2 of the current year, Glen Riley became manager of a newly opened branch store of the Tall Pine Nursery. Riley made the following purchases during the first month of operation:

| | |
|---|---|
| Spruce trees | |
| Mar. 2 | 105 trees @ $30 |
| 16 | 155 trees @ $40 |
| Elm trees | |
| Mar. 2 | 130 trees @ $10 |
| 18 | 70 trees @ $15 |
| 29 | 30 trees @ $18 |
| Maple trees | |
| Mar. 2 | 40 trees @ $50 |

An end-of-month physical inventory count revealed that the nursery had 75 spruce trees, 58 elm trees, and 38 maple trees in stock. Total sales for March amounted to $14,500; expenses (excluding cost of goods sold) were $3,100.

The company uses the FIFO inventory valuation method in conjunction with a periodic inventory system.

**Instructions**

a Compute the nursery's ending inventory, cost of goods sold, and net income for the first month of operation.
b Assume that the grower of the elm trees recently announced a price decrease to $14.50. Determine the impact of the announcement on the nursery's ending inventory valuation.
c Prepare the journal entry necessary to value the company's inventory at the lower of cost or market.

**P9-B4** ***Gross profit method and tornado damage***

On March 19, 19X2, a tornado heavily damaged the office and warehouse of Wingtip Distributors. The following information has been obtained:

1 Wingtip's condensed income statement for the year ended December 31, 19X1, is as follows:

| | | |
|---|---|---|
| Net sales | | $640,000 |
| Cost of goods sold | | |
| Beginning inventory | $115,900 | |
| Add: Net purchases | 301,600 | |
| Goods available for sale | $417,500 | |
| Less: Ending inventory | 148,700 | |
| Cost of goods sold | | 268,800 |
| Gross profit | | $371,200 |
| Operating expenses | | 234,500 |
| Net incomc | | $136,700 |

2 Net sales and net purchases made through March 19 were $122,000 and $36,900, respectively.
3 Purchases entered in the accounting records but still in transit as of March 19 amounted to $4,200.

Wingtip's insurance company agreed to reimburse the firm for the tornado loss on the basis of an estimate of inventory by using the gross profit method. The gross profit rate will be derived by examining last year's operating results.

**Instructions**

a Determine the cost of inventory on hand on March 19.
b Taking your answer in part (a) into consideration, assume that goods were recovered and sold to a salvage firm for $14,300. Compute Wingtip's total loss from the tornado.
c Suppose the company's inventory consisted of many different product lines with widely varying profit margins. What should Wingtip do to improve the accuracy of the inventory estimate?

**P9-B5** ***Retail method and inventory shrinkage***

TJ's, a sporting goods store, uses the retail method of inventory valuation. A review of the company's accounting records disclosed the following information for the year ended December 31:

| | | | |
|---|---|---|---|
| Inventory, Jan. 1 | | Purchasing Activity | |
| Cost | $ 79,300 | Purchases | |
| Retail | 128,900 | Cost | $296,600 |
| Sales | 432,000 | Retail | 498,100 |
| Sales returns | 17,600 | Returns | |
| | | Cost | 7,200 |
| | | Retail | 12,500 |

**Instructions**

a Using the retail method, estimate the cost of the company's inventory on December 31.
b If the firm's physical count on December 31 revealed an ending inventory at retail of $185,500, compute the cost of inventory shrinkage.

**P9-B6** ***Perpetual inventory systems: FIFO***

The Schaber Company carries parts that are used in emergency medical situations. Given the critical nature of its business, Schaber uses a perpetual inventory system. The following information pertains to a particular heart monitor:

May 1 Beginning inventory: 100 units @ $6,800

| *Purchases* | | *Sales* | |
|---|---|---|---|
| May 3 | 50 units @ $7,100 | May 7 | 30 units @ $11,400 |
| 18 | 75 units @ $7,200 | 14 | 70 units @ $11,400 |
| 25 | 40 units @ $7,250 | 20 | 55 units @ $11,600 |
| | | 24 | 25 units @ $11,600 |
| | | 29 | 20 units @ $11,700 |

**Instructions**

a Using a format similar to that of Exhibit 9-8, prepare a perpetual inventory record for the heart monitor. Schaber uses the FIFO method of inventory valuation.

b Prepare summary journal entries to record total purchases and sales.

c Assume that Schaber had used a periodic inventory system rather than a perpetual inventory system. Would the company's cost of goods sold and ending inventory differ from the amounts computed in part (a)? Why?

***P9-B7** ***Perpetual inventory systems: LIFO and moving average***

Refer to the beginning inventory, purchases, and sales data of the Schaber Company in Problem 9-B6.

**Instructions**

a Assuming use of a LIFO cost flow assumption, prepare a perpetual inventory record for the heart monitor by using a format similar to that shown in Exhibit 9-9.

b Assuming use of the moving average method, determine the cost of the May 31 ending inventory and also the cost of goods sold during May.

## Beyond the Basics

**BB9-1** ***An in-depth probe of LIFO***

The Biscayne Company, a newly organized Florida corporation, is composed of two divisions: Parts Manufacturing and Motor Car Sales. Both divisions presently use the LIFO method of inventory valuation. Because business is slumping, the controller has begun an in-depth review of operations.

The Parts Manufacturing division has experienced skyrocketing raw materials costs and labor difficulties. Two strikes by machinists and assemblers have been especially severe, causing Biscayne to close its plant for the past three months. Fortunately, existing finished goods inventories have been large enough to fill incoming sales orders.

The Motor Car Sales division has been hit with a sharp decline in sales, and the controller is contemplating a change from LIFO to FIFO. The year-end inventory under the LIFO method is anticipated to be $20 million. If FIFO is used, the ending inventory balance would increase to $28 million.

**Instructions**

a As the Parts Manufacturing division cuts deeper and deeper into finished goods inventory, which costs (high or low) will be charged to cost of goods sold?

b Given your answer in part (a), determine the effect of the strike on earnings and the related tax payments.

c Assuming the Motor Car Sales division is subject to an income tax rate of 40%, determine the effect on net income of the shift from LIFO to FIFO.

d Present a detailed analysis to Biscayne's president regarding the advantages and disadvantages of making the shift.

**BB9-2** ***Retail method; inventory shortage***

The Body Hanger, a clothes store that specializes in high fashion fad merchandise, is located at a regional shopping mall. Sales over the past few years have averaged approximately $120,000 per month, with merchandise priced consistently at 250% of cost.

Lynn Landau was recently hired as a special marketing consultant in an effort to boost sales. Landau immediately recommended that the single entry door, which was constantly tended by a fancily attired doorman, be replaced with an "open wall" concept. The new concept would allow patrons to enter and exit along the entire front of the store. The data that follow relate to the three-month period following the implementation of the "open wall" design.

| | *Month 1* | *Month 2* | *Month 3* |
|---|---|---|---|
| Purchases (at cost) | $ 70,000 | $ 91,000 | $ 65,000 |
| Purchases returns (at cost) | 3,000 | — | 5,000 |
| Sales | 160,000 | 210,000 | 190,000 |
| Sales returns | 5,000 | 10,000 | 25,000 |

The cost of inventory on hand at the beginning of month 1 was $150,000.

**Instructions**

a Using the retail method, estimate the cost of the store's ending inventory for each of the three months.

b Using your answers from part (a), calculate The Body Hanger's gross profit for each of the three months. Comment on the success or failure of the "open wall" concept.

c A physical inventory count at the end of the third month revealed an actual ending inventory of only $90,000 (at cost). Explain a probable cause of this situation, and reevaluate Landau's recommendation in terms of being either a financial success or an economic disaster. Show appropriate calculations.

## Answers to Chapter Quiz

**1** b

**2** b

**3** c

**4** a ($400 for A + $600 for B)

**5** a

# Property, Plant, and Equipment: Acquisition and Depreciation

CHAPTER 10

## Learning Objectives

After reading this chapter you should:

1 Be able to differentiate between capital and revenue expenditures.

2 Be able to account for cash and lump-sum purchases of property, plant, and equipment.

3 Understand the meaning of "depreciation" as the term is used by accountants.

4 Understand the factors that affect the determination of service life.

5 Be able to compute depreciation by using the straight-line, units-of-output, declining balance, and sum-of-the-years'-digits methods.

6 Understand the financial reporting issues related to the various depreciation methods.

7 Be able to revise a depreciation rate.

8 Have a general understanding of depreciation and the tax laws.

Many organizations invest large amounts of money in assets that are used to manufacture products or provide services. Chrysler Corporation, for example, recently reported an investment in such assets of over $10 billion, AT&T reported $41 billion, and IBM reported $45 billion. Assets with long lives acquired for use in business operations are termed **property, plant, and equipment** and include land, buildings, vehicles, office equipment, machinery, store equipment, and furniture and fixtures. This asset category is sometimes referred to as plant and equipment, plant assets, or fixed assets. Property, plant, and equipment is the most descriptive of these titles, however, and has gained the widest acceptance among accountants for the presentation of productive and service capacity on the balance sheet.

Long-lived assets must be currently used in a business to be classified as part of property, plant, and equipment. Idle buildings and machinery, and land held for speculation or for future expansion are therefore excluded from this important asset category. These and similar items are classified as long-term investments or other assets.

Assets that appear under the property, plant, and equipment caption may be viewed as long-term prepaid expenses, because their acquisition entails an advance payment for years of future service. To explain, a firm that prepays rent for several months into the next accounting period will record a prepaid expense on its balance sheet. If that same firm purchases a building, it has, in essence, prepaid for the future services the building is expected to render.

Like prepaid expenses, items of property, plant, and equipment can provide benefits for only a certain period of time and are said to possess a limited service life. (An exception is land, which provides services indefinitely.) As a result, then, just as prepaid expenses become expenses when consumed, the amounts paid for plant and equipment are gradually charged to depreciation as the assets are used in operations.

Our discussion of long-lived assets in this chapter and Chapter 11 will focus on the following key issues, which are depicted in Exhibit 10-1:

1. Measurement of asset cost (Chapter 10)
2. Allocation of asset cost to the accounting periods benefited (Chapter 10)
3. Accounting for expenditures that occur after asset acquisition, such as repairs and improvements (Chapter 11)
4. Recording disposals of plant and equipment in the accounts (Chapter 11)

## Determining the Cost of Property, Plant, and Equipment

OBJECTIVE 1
Be able to differentiate between capital and revenue expenditures.

The cost of property, plant, and equipment includes acquisition or construction expenditures (and related amounts) required to ready the assets for business use. For the purchase of equipment such expenditures include the invoice price of the equipment, freight charges incurred by the buyer, insurance on the equipment while in transit, and installation costs such as special electrical wiring and initial testing. The cost of land includes the purchase price; attorney's fees; commissions to a real estate broker; recording fees with the city or county; surveying costs; costs to clear, drain, and grade the land; and the assumption of any mortgages or delinquent property taxes. Thus, if a company purchased a parcel of land by paying $45,000 cash and assuming $5,000 of delinquent property taxes and a $55,000 mortgage, the land is recorded at a cost of $105,000.

The rationale for the preceding accounting treatment is clear. To charge costs related to asset acquisition as an expense of the acquisition period would result in a

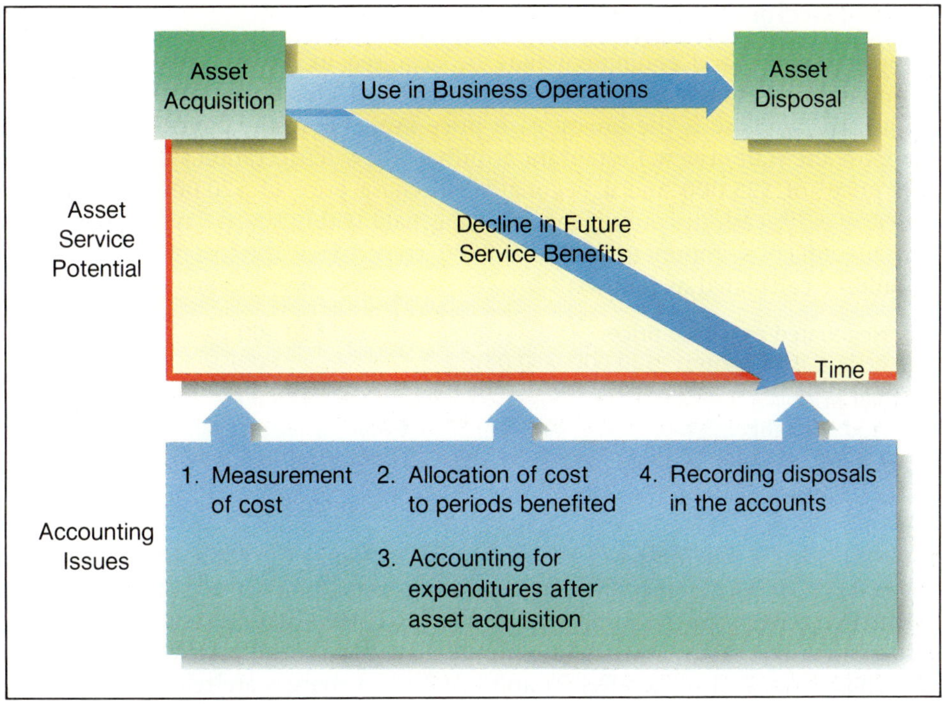


**Exhibit 10-1**
**Issues Related to Long-Lived Assets**

mismatch of revenues and expenses. Property, plant, and equipment will serve a business for many years, and incidental expenditures like freight, installation, and broker's fees are necessary for acquisition and subsequent asset use to occur. In effect, then, these items provide long-run benefits and should be shown on the balance sheet as part of an asset's cost. Such amounts are commonly known as **capital expenditures.**

Expenditures related to asset acquisition and preparation that fail to provide future economic benefits are expenses. For example, if a piece of equipment was damaged while being installed, the repair costs would not be added to the cost of the equipment. Instead, the repairs are treated as an expense of the current accounting period. Likewise, if a newly purchased machine was being delivered on the buyer's truck and the truck was involved in a traffic accident, the cost of fixing the truck, any damages paid to other parties in the accident, and any fines levied on the driver are not charged to the Machinery account. These outlays are not "ordinary and necessary" to place the machine in a position ready to serve the purchaser and are therefore expensed. Expenditures that fail to provide benefits to future periods are commonly known as **revenue expenditures.**

A cost that we failed to cite in the preceding discussion is interest. Stated simply, the proper accounting treatment is dependent on the method of asset acquisition. As a general rule, interest costs incurred to finance the *purchase* of property, plant, and equipment are written off as expense. In contrast, interest charges related to financing the *construction* of plant and equipment for a company's own use are capitalized (i.e., added to the cost of the asset). These latter charges must be incurred during the construction period and be significant in amount to qualify for this special treatment.[1]

[1] "Capitalization of Interest Costs," *Statement of Financial Accounting Standards No. 34* (Stamford, Conn.: Financial Accounting Standards Board, 1979).

## Cash Purchase

> OBJECTIVE 2
> Be able to account for cash and lump-sum purchases of property, plant, and equipment.

Property, plant, and equipment may be acquired in a variety of ways, with a commonly encountered method being the **cash purchase.** The recorded asset cost in a cash purchase is the lowest cash price available to the buyer. For example, suppose the Harborview Restaurant acquired a new refrigeration system that has a list price[2] of $25,000 and a negotiated purchase price of $20,000. The seller is offering a 5% cash discount if the invoice is paid within seven days. If freight and installation costs amount to $400 and $900, respectively, the cost of the equipment would be calculated as follows:

| | | |
|---|---|---|
| Negotiated purchase price | | $20,000 |
| Less: Cash discount ($20,000 × 0.05) | | (1,000) |
| Net price | | $19,000 |
| Add: Freight | $400 | |
| Installation | 900 | 1,300 |
| Acquisition cost | | $20,300 |

The list price is not relevant; it is used only as a guide in establishing the actual amount of the sale by the seller. In a discount store, for instance, you will find that virtually all items can be purchased at a cost well below their stated (and usually crossed out) list price. When determining the cost of the equipment, the negotiated purchase price and related freight and installation charges are relevant; so, too, is the offer of the cash discount.

If Harborview issued a check for $20,300, the refrigeration system would be entered in the Kitchen Equipment account for that amount. If the company could not take advantage of the discount because of a lack of funds, the Kitchen Equipment account would still be debited for $20,300. The $1,000 discount lost is treated as a financing expense (namely, interest) of the current accounting period. The necessary journal entry for the second situation follows.

| | | |
|---|---|---|
| Kitchen Equipment | 20,300 | |
| Interest Expense | 1,000 | |
| Cash | | 21,300 |
| To record acquisition of refrigeration system; discount missed | | |

## Lump-Sum Purchase

Frequently, a business will purchase a number of assets together for a single amount. For example, the acquisition of developed property will often include such assets as land, buildings, parking lots, fences, and lawn sprinkler systems. Transactions of this type are termed **lump-sum purchases.** The cost of a lump-sum purchase must be apportioned among the various assets acquired for reporting and depreciation purposes. These assets generally benefit a business for different periods of time, thereby requiring different depreciation rates.

Appraisals are often used to aid in the apportionment. To illustrate, assume that Hartley Development Company purchased a building, land improvements (e.g., parking lots and lawn sprinkler systems), and land for $40 million cash. The assets' appraisal values along with the necessary cost apportionment follow.

[2] The list price is sometimes referred to as the manufacturer's suggested retail price.

| | *Appraisal Value* | *Percentage of Total Appraisal Value* | *Recorded Cost* |
|---|---|---|---|
| Building | $25,000,000 | 50% | $20,000,000 |
| Land improvements | 5,000,000 | 10 | 4,000,000 |
| Land | 20,000,000 | 40 | 16,000,000 |
| Total | $50,000,000 | 100% | $40,000,000 |

The acquisition cost is apportioned on the basis of an individual asset's appraised value relative to the appraised value of the entire purchase. For example, because the building is 50% of the property's total value ($25,000,000 ÷ $50,000,000), the cost of the building is established at $20,000,000 ($40,000,000 × 0.50). The recorded amounts for land improvements and land are determined in the same manner. The journal entry to record the purchase is therefore as follows:

| | | |
|---|---|---|
| Building | 20,000,000 | |
| Land Improvements | 4,000,000 | |
| Land | 16,000,000 | |
| Cash | | 40,000,000 |
| To record acquisition of developed property | | |

Notice that a distinction is made between land and *land improvements.* It is necessary to establish separate accounts for these assets, because a parcel of land has an indefinite life whereas land improvements do not. As a result, land improvements are depreciated over the number of periods they render benefits or service to a business.

Companies sometimes acquire developed property and subsequently undertake a demolition program, thereby paving the way for new construction. In these instances the entire purchase price is debited to the Land account, along with the costs of removing the old buildings and improvements. Conversely, any proceeds received from selling materials that are salvaged from the demolition process are credited to Land.

## Small Items of Property, Plant, and Equipment

Businesses purchase many long-lived items (e.g., tape dispensers, pencil sharpeners, and office clocks) that technically should be classified as property, plant, and equipment. Because of their insignificant purchase price, however, these items are not established as assets in the accounting records. Instead, such amounts are normally treated as revenue expenditures and written off as expenses in the period of acquisition. This procedure reduces paperwork costs and avoids depreciating small items over long periods of time. Imagine the record keeping associated with depreciating a $5 wastepaper basket over a 10-year life. Virtually all accountants would agree that the $0.50 annual write-off is hardly worth the effort.

In an attempt to avoid an in-depth analysis of its many expenditures, a business will typically make the expense versus capitalize decision by using a pre-established minimum dollar cutoff. If, for example, a firm sets a $100 cutoff, all expenditures of $100 or less would automatically be deemed too small to be recorded as part of property, plant, and equipment. Such amounts would therefore be expensed immediately. On the other hand, outlays that exceed $100 would be considered significant and thus treated as assets, to be written off gradually as benefits are received.[3]

### Cost/Benefit and Materiality

The determination of whether an outlay should be expensed or carried as an asset is a matter of professional judgment. When evaluating the possible treatments, the accountant must assess the magnitude and importance of the item in question. An alternative should be selected only after careful consideration of two factors: cost/benefit and materiality. More specifically, the expense of developing exact accounting information must be studied relative to the benefits of added precision. If the cost of a company's efforts exceed the benefits that financial statement users will receive, the extra precision is deemed wasteful and should not be attempted.

This cost/benefit theme is consistent with the concept of **materiality,** which refers to the significance of a particular item or transaction. If judged to be immaterial, an item or transaction would likely have no influence on the decisions made by informed financial statement users. In such cases, theory would take a back seat to practice, and the accountant would handle the item in the most expedient manner possible. Thus, for items of $100 or less in the preceding example, an immediate write-off is preferred rather than a prolonged allocation to the periods of benefit.

## Depreciation

OBJECTIVE 3
Understand the meaning of "depreciation" as the term is used by accountants.

As we previously noted, all items of property, plant, and equipment (except land) have limited lives and render services over several accounting periods. These services often result in the production of revenues for the firm. Proper accounting therefore requires that a portion of the cost of long-lived assets be written off each year to expense, to be matched against revenues on the income statement. Stated differently, because revenues are generated in each year of asset use, it is only correct that each year's income absorb the costs of producing that revenue.

The process used to allocate the cost of long-lived assets to the accounting periods benefited is known as **depreciation.** Be aware, however, that other definitions of depreciation are commonly encountered. For example, you may have heard new car owners mention the "depreciation" they have suffered since their purchase. To this group depreciation represents a decrease in value, specifically, the difference between the amount paid for the car and the vehicle's present resale value. Accountants make no attempt to integrate information into the accounts about the ever-changing market values of property, plant, and equipment. Instead, assets classified in this category are maintained in the accounting records at cost. For depreciable assets this cost is subsequently allocated as expense to the years receiving service or benefits. In accounting, then, *depreciation is a process of allocation, not valuation.*

### Determining Service Life

Before an asset's cost is allocated among the periods benefited, a service life must be estimated. **Service life,** sometimes called economic or useful life, is the period of

[3] Cutoff limits typically vary from firm to firm and are often dependent on company size. A large expenditure for Joe's Auto Repair, for instance, could be an insignificant amount to Exxon Corporation.

time that depreciable assets provide service to a business. It is important to understand that an asset's service life is frequently different from its physical life. That is, an asset may have physical existence long after its useful life to a business has concluded. Witness, for example, the abandoned equipment behind many manufacturing plants and the numerous railroad tracks that are no longer used by their owners.

When determining an asset's service life, we must consider three factors: physical deterioration, obsolescence, and inadequacy.

### Physical Deterioration

**OBJECTIVE 4**
**Understand the factors that affect the determination of service life.**

The physical deterioration of an asset, sometimes termed "wear and tear," is caused by use in the normal course of business. Repair and maintenance may prolong an asset's service life, but at some point the asset usually requires replacement because it has become worn out. Physical deterioration normally establishes the maximum limit for the estimate of service life.

### Obsolescence

Obsolescence is a technological factor relating to being out of date. New technology frequently shortens the service life of assets well before their physical life is over. Businesses that use obsolete machines, for example, cannot compete effectively with companies that use modern, more efficient equipment.

Obsolescence has been a significant factor in shortening the service life of computers. Recent advances in engineering have been dramatic. Businesses that purchased a computer three to five years ago are finding faster, more versatile models are now available, making their equipment out of date and less desirable.

### Inadequacy

Business growth may cause certain items of depreciable property, plant, and equipment to become inadequate in their service capabilities. Plants may become unable to keep pace with demand, trucks may become too small, and equipment may become too slow. When assets are inadequate to meet the competitive needs of a company, their service lives have ended. Like obsolescence, inadequacy is an economic (as opposed to physical) determinant of service life.

### Relative Significance of the Three Factors

All three of the preceding factors should be considered when estimating service life. It is conceivable, of course, that one factor may be more important than the others for certain assets. Consider, for example, a small commuter airline that desires to expand and begin service to large metropolitan areas. The airline may find that the service life of its flight equipment is determined primarily by the factor of inadequacy. On the other hand, a high-precision manufacturer that uses advanced electronics may view obsolescence as the most important determinant of service life for much of its equipment.

In other business situations all of the factors may be equally important for a particular depreciable asset. In these cases the estimation of service life becomes more difficult. Companies having no experience with a particular type of asset may seek guidance from their accountants, engineers, trade associations, or the asset's seller.

## HIGHLIGHT

# Depreciation: Is Nothing Sacred?

At an office of the Roman Catholic diocese in Brooklyn, New York, Monsignor Austin Bennett was going about his spiritual and worldly chores. He was helping minority-group students get room to study at the diocese's 22 schools. He was helping priests take care of their aging parents. And he was helping a custodian from Central America get documents to apply for U.S. citizenship. Then he wrote a nasty letter to the Financial Accounting Standards Board (FASB).

Why was this friendly, pipe-smoking individual launching verbal barbs against the chief rule-making body for accountants? "Because the board is . . . causing more trouble for American churches than all the sinners in their congregations." Msgr. Bennett, accounting practices chairman of the U.S. Catholic Conference, was referring to a then proposed, now enacted ruling that forces churches to depreciate their houses of worship and monuments. The churches, which have always been exempt from this accounting procedure, will naturally find their income reduced because of the added expense.

A reduced level of income could be important since many religious institutions, particularly big ones, issue audited financial statements to substantiate their financial health to suppliers, bank lenders, and parishioners. "Our cathedrals last for centuries and often gain in value with age," Msgr. Bennett asserts. "But they don't last forever," counters a project manager at the FASB. "The Parthenon may still be there, but its roof has fallen in. Physical assets that are exhaustible should be depreciated."

The period that preceded the FASB's decision brought forth some interesting (and heated) debate. "Depreciating cathedrals and churches is stupid," said a well-known professor emeritus at the Harvard Business School and expert on accounting for nonprofit groups. "It would be like trying to compare the cost per soul saved among churches." And a retired Treasury Department official added, "Depreciating churches would be like depreciating the Pyramids and the Sphinx of Egypt, and the Sistine Chapel at the Vatican." Figuring such depreciation would be "the acme of futility."

The ungodly flap over depreciation began several years ago when the accounting profession sought uniformity among nonprofit organizations, as some organizations depreciated their assets whereas others did not. Religious institutions generally argued against depreciation. Notes the FASB's director of accounting standards, "Basically they told us that the structures have been here long before us and would be here long after we're gone. It made sense."

After some debate on the matter, the FASB ruled in favor of depreciation. The board stressed that cathedrals are used up not only by wear and tear but also by the continuous destructive effects of pollutants, vibrations, and so forth. As an FASB spokesman succintly observes, "Church properties can wear out; therefore, they should be depreciated. I can see quibbling about the Pyramids, because their [service] life is so long that the costs per year would be immaterial. But not most churches. Even St. Patrick's Cathedral in Manhattan has parts that must be replaced and other parts that can be salvaged." A "maverick" pastor from Baltimore agrees; he accepts depreciation because he likes challenges. However, as Msgr. Bennett maintains, "[The pastor] is entitled to his opinion, but he speaks only for himself. He has no official accounting status in the Catholic Church."

SOURCES: Adapted from "Is Nothing Sacred? Churches Fight Plan to Alter Accounting," *The Wall Street Journal*, April 16, 1987, pp. 1, 20; and "Recognition of Depreciation by Not-for-Profit Organizations," *Statement of Financial Accounting Standards No. 93* (Stamford, Conn.: Financial Accounting Standards Board, 1987). 

## Methods of Depreciation

There are several acceptable methods for computing depreciation. The four methods used most often are straight-line, units-of-output, declining balance, and sum-of-the-years'-digits. Exhibit 10-2 discloses the variation in depreciation policies of several large businesses.

### Straight-Line Method

Largely because of its simplicity, the **straight-line method** is the most popular way to compute depreciation. Under this approach, the cost of a depreciable asset, minus residual value, is allocated equally over the estimated service life. The **residual value** (sometimes called salvage value) is the amount a business expects to receive upon disposal of an asset at the end of the asset's life. Given the nature of the allocation, the straight-line method is best applied to assets that provide constant, uniform service to an entity.

OBJECTIVE 5
Be able to compute depreciation by using the straight-line, units-of-output, declining balance, and sum-of-the-years'-digits methods.

To illustrate the straight-line method, assume WBBB-TV bought a new television camera for $30,000. The camera has an estimated residual value of $3,000 and an estimated service life of five years. The annual depreciation expense is computed as follows:

$$\frac{\text{Cost} - \text{Residual Value}}{\text{Service Life in Years}} = \frac{\$30{,}000 - \$3{,}000}{5 \text{ years}}$$

$$= \$5{,}400 \text{ annual depreciation}$$

The deduction of the $3,000 residual value from the asset's cost of $30,000 yields a $27,000 **depreciable base**—the total amount that will be written off to depreciation expense over the asset's life.

**Exhibit 10-2**
**Comparison of Depreciation Policies**

| *Company* | *Depreciation Policy* |
|---|---|
| Eastman Kodak Company | Calculated generally by accelerated methods for assets in the United States and by the straight-line method for assets outside the United States. |
| Budget Rent a Car | Computed by using the straight-line method. Vehicles are depreciated at rates ranging from 1.5% to 3.5% per month, depending on vehicle type. |
| Mobil Corporation | Computed on a straight-line basis over the useful lives of the various classes of properties or, where appropriate for producing properties, on a unit-of-production basis by individual fields. |
| Zenith Electronics | Straight-line method for additions of plant and equipment with useful lives of eight years or more; accelerated methods for substantially all other plant and equipment items, including shorter-lived high-technology equipment that may be subject to rapid economic obsolescence. |

The journal entries to record depreciation for the first two years of the camera's life follow.

| *Year 1* | | |
|---|---|---|
| Depreciation Expense: Broadcasting Equipment | 5,400 | |
| Accumulated Depreciation: Broadcasting Equipment | | 5,400 |
| To record annual depreciation expense | | |

| *Year 2* | | |
|---|---|---|
| Depreciation Expense: Broadcasting Equipment | 5,400 | |
| Accumulated Depreciation: Broadcasting Equipment | | 5,400 |
| To record annual depreciation expense | | |

These entries reflect a very common practice: the creation of separate accounts for each major group of depreciable assets (e.g., buildings, office equipment, furniture and fixtures, and so forth). Such breakdowns are helpful for internal management analysis as well as for external financial reporting.

In view of the preceding data, WBBB's income statement would reveal annual depreciation expense of $5,400. The firm's balance sheet would disclose the following:

| | *Year 1* | *Year 2* |
|---|---|---|
| Property, plant, & equipment | | |
| Broadcasting equipment | $30,000 | $30,000 |
| Less: Accumulated depreciation | 5,400 | 10,800 |
| | $24,600 | $19,200 |

These figures show that accumulated depreciation increases by $5,400 during each year of service life. Recall that the cost of an asset, minus accumulated depreciation, is termed **book value.** As the accompanying schedule illustrates, book value decreases each year and equals the residual value ($3,000) at the end of the camera's life. The asset is said to be fully depreciated at this point and no further depreciation is recorded.

| *Year* | *Depreciation Expense* | *Accumulated Depreciation* | *Book Value* |
|---|---|---|---|
| | | | $30,000 |
| 1 | $5,400 | $ 5,400 | 24,600 |
| 2 | 5,400 | 10,800 | 19,200 |
| 3 | 5,400 | 16,200 | 13,800 |
| 4 | 5,400 | 21,600 | 8,400 |
| 5 | 5,400 | 27,000 | 3,000 |

Businesses that use the straight-line method often convert their service lives to percentages. For example, annual depreciation on an asset having a 50-year service life would be 2% of the depreciable base, because the fraction $\frac{1}{50}$ is equal to 2%. Similarly, an asset with a 10-year service life is depreciated at a rate of $\frac{1}{10}$, or 10%, per year.

**TIPS & TECHNIQUES**

Be aware that a fully depreciated asset may continue to be used in business activities. Put simply, a company will not dispose of dependable equipment and buildings just because the estimated service life has come to an end. The use of such assets beyond their estimated lives may actually boost earnings, as the revenues generated are not decreased by any depreciation expense. Remember, once an asset is fully depreciated, no further write-offs can be taken.

***Partial Periods*** In the preceding example we assumed the camera was acquired on January 1. If the purchase was made later in the year, WBBB would record a prorated percentage of the annual depreciation charge. Assuming acquisition on May 1, depreciation for the first year would be \$3,600 (\$5,400 × $\frac{8}{12}$), because the asset provided services for only eight months. The remaining depreciation expense would then be \$5,400 for Years 2, 3, 4, and 5 and \$1,800 (\$5,400 × $\frac{4}{12}$) for the first four months of Year 6. As before, depreciation totals \$27,000 and is recorded over five years of service.

Asset purchases do not always take place on the first day of the month. Most companies have established their own practices for recording depreciation in this situation. For example, when a depreciable asset is acquired during the first 15 days of a month, the purchase is often handled as if it occurred on the first day of the month. If the asset is acquired in the last half of a month, the transaction is treated as occurring on the first day of the following month, and the depreciation computation commences at this time. Other companies record one-half of the first full year's depreciation in the year of acquisition regardless of the date of purchase. Such an approach simplifies the depreciation computation because acquisition dates are ignored. These and other similar practices are acceptable as long as they are followed consistently.

## Units-of-Output Method

The **units-of-output method,** sometimes called the units-of-production or activity method, can be employed when an asset's service life is expressible in terms of output (such as miles, hours, or number of times used). Under this approach the asset's cost, minus residual value, is divided by the total estimated output during the service life. This computation generates the depreciation rate. Annual depreciation expense is then calculated by multiplying the depreciation rate by the yearly output. To illustrate, assume a large corporation purchased a business jet for \$4 million that has a residual value of \$1.5 million. The service life is estimated to be 10,000 flying hours. The depreciation rate is calculated as follows:

$$\frac{\text{Cost} - \text{Residual Value}}{\text{Service Life in Output}} = \frac{\$4{,}000{,}000 - \$1{,}500{,}000}{10{,}000 \text{ flying hours}}$$

$$= \$250 \text{ per flying hour}$$

If the jet was used for 500 hours during the year, depreciation expense would total \$125,000 (\$250 × 500).

The units-of-output method is used when (1) the service capacity of an asset can be reasonably estimated and (2) there is a direct relationship between an asset's use and its decline in service potential. Assets that meet these two criteria include cars, trucks, and machines. In situations where the amount of an asset's output varies considerably from period to period, the units-of-output method achieves a better allocation of cost than do the straight-line or other depreciation approaches. For example, in years of great activity, more of an asset's cost would be depreciated and matched against revenues; in years of low activity, less depreciation expense is recorded. In contrast, the straight-line method produces a constant depreciation charge regardless of the services provided.

## Accelerated Depreciation Methods

The two remaining depreciation methods are declining balance and sum-of-the-years'-digits. Both approaches speed up the recognition of expense and are appropriately termed **accelerated depreciation methods.** As you will soon see, relatively large amounts of depreciation are generated in the early years of asset use and small amounts in later years.

There are a variety of reasons why businesses may prefer to use an accelerated depreciation method. First, companies recognize that the services provided by many assets tend to decline over time. For example, consider the transportation services provided by a new car versus those of a less dependable older model. Or note the quality of machining obtained from a new high-precision drill press versus that from an older press with less accurate tolerances. If the services provided are actually greater in the earlier years of asset use, a proper matching of revenues and expenses dictates a gradual reduction in depreciation charges over an asset's lifetime.

Another reason for using an accelerated depreciation method is that repair and maintenance costs normally increase as an asset grows older. When combined with a decreasing amount of depreciation from an accelerated method, the total amount of yearly expense is leveled. The end result for assets that furnish uniform service is a better match of expense against revenue than would be possible by the straight-line technique.

***Declining Balance Method*** The **declining balance method** involves applying a fixed depreciation rate to the remaining book value of an asset. The rate employed is a multiple of that calculated under the straight-line method. For instance, if a company is computing depreciation by utilizing the popular **double-declining balance** approach, the rate used is twice the straight-line rate. Additionally, any residual value is ignored in the depreciation calculation, thereby permitting even greater expense in the early years of asset use. Consistent with the other approaches presented, however, an asset's book value *cannot* be reduced below the estimated residual value.

Applying the double-declining balance method to the television camera example cited earlier (cost, \$30,000; residual value, \$3,000; service life, five years), we obtain the accompanying depreciation schedule.

| *Year* | *Depreciation Expense* | *Accumulated Depreciation* | *Book Value* |
|---|---|---|---|
| | | | \$30,000 |
| 1 | \$12,000 (\$30,000 × 40%) | \$12,000 | 18,000 |
| 2 | 7,200 (\$18,000 × 40%) | 19,200 | 10,800 |
| 3 | 4,320 (\$10,800 × 40%) | 23,520 | 6,480 |
| 4 | 2,592 (\$6,480 × 40%) | 26,112 | 3,888 |
| 5 | 888 (\$3,888 − \$3,000) | 27,000 | 3,000 |

To explain, with the five-year service life, the straight-line depreciation rate is $\frac{1}{5}$, or 20%, per year. The double-declining balance rate, therefore, is 40% (2 × 20%). Depreciation expense in the first year is 40% times the $30,000 book value, or $12,000. The journal entry to record depreciation at the end of the year places $12,000 in the Accumulated Depreciation account, thus reducing the camera's book value to $18,000. Depreciation in the second year falls to $7,200, that is, book value of $18,000 × 40%. In the same manner, the third year's depreciation is $4,320 ($10,800 × 40%), and the fourth year's is $2,592 ($6,480 × 40%). The last year of service life is handled differently. If we continued with the same approach, depreciation expense in the fifth year would be $1,555 ($3,888 × 40%). However, the camera's book value would be reduced to $2,333 ($3,888 − $1,555), which is below the $3,000 estimated residual value. Thus, depreciation expense in Year 5 amounts to only $888 ($3,888 − $3,000).

If the television camera had been purchased on September 1, depreciation expense would be computed for only four months in Year 1 and would total $4,000 [($30,000 × 40%) × $\frac{4}{12}$]. The necessary procedures for all future periods are similar to those shown in the earlier illustration. For example, because book value at the beginning of Year 2 would be $26,000 ($30,000 − $4,000), depreciation expense for the second year is $10,400 ($26,000 × 40%).

### ▶ TIPS & TECHNIQUES

Be extremely careful to ignore residual value in the computation of *yearly* depreciation expense under the double-declining balance method. As the name of this approach implies, depreciation is calculated on a declining base (i.e., book value). Book value is derived by subtracting a growing, accumulated depreciation figure from asset cost. In contrast, residual value is considered *only* when deriving an asset's minimum book value (and, thus, total allowable depreciation write-offs over a service life).

***Sum-of-the-Years'-Digits Method*** Similar to the double-declining balance method, the **sum-of-the-years'-digits method** also produces more depreciation expense in the early years of asset use. Under this approach a successively lower depreciation rate is applied each year to a constant depreciable base (cost minus residual value). The rate, which is really a fraction, is derived by setting the numerator equal to the remaining years of life at the beginning of the period; the denominator, in turn, equals the total of the service years. In the case of the television camera, which has a five-year life, the denominator would always equal 15 (5 + 4 + 3 + 2 + 1 = 15). Similarly, for assets having a four-year life, the denominator would be 10 (4 + 3 + 2 + 1 = 10).[4] Continuing the camera example, the numera-

[4] The denominator can be easily calculated by the following formula:

$$D = \frac{n(n + 1)}{2}$$

where $D$ equals the denominator and $n$ equals the number of service years. For example, the denominator of an asset having a 10-year service life would be computed as

$$D = \frac{10(10 + 1)}{2} = \frac{110}{2} = 55$$

tor for the first year is 5 because five years of service life remain; then 4 for the second year, and so forth. WBBB's depreciation schedule using the sum-of-the-years'-digits method follows.

| *Year* | *Depreciation Expense* | *Accumulated Depreciation* | *Book Value* |
|---|---|---|---|
| | | | $30,000 |
| 1 | $9,000 ($27,000 × $\frac{5}{15}$) | $ 9,000 | 21,000 |
| 2 | 7,200 ($27,000 × $\frac{4}{15}$) | 16,200 | 13,800 |
| 3 | 5,400 ($27,000 × $\frac{3}{15}$) | 21,600 | 8,400 |
| 4 | 3,600 ($27,000 × $\frac{2}{15}$) | 25,200 | 4,800 |
| 5 | 1,800 ($27,000 × $\frac{1}{15}$) | 27,000 | 3,000 |

For assets acquired during the year, the allocation of cost over the service life is more complex. The key to understanding the necessary procedures is to recognize that each fraction ($\frac{5}{15}$, $\frac{4}{15}$, $\frac{3}{15}$, and so on) must be employed for 12 months no matter when the asset is acquired. For example, if the camera was purchased on April 1 and used for nine months, the $\frac{5}{15}$ rate would be applied for the remainder of Year 1, producing depreciation expense of $6,750 [($27,000 × $\frac{5}{15}$) × $\frac{9}{12}$]. Depreciation expense for the second year totals $7,650 and is computed by using the $\frac{5}{15}$ rate for three months and the $\frac{4}{15}$ rate for nine months; specifically,

OBJECTIVE 6
Understand the financial reporting issues related to the various depreciation methods.

$$\begin{aligned} \$27{,}000 \times \tfrac{5}{15} \times \tfrac{3}{12} &= \$2{,}250 \\ 27{,}000 \times \tfrac{4}{15} \times \tfrac{9}{12} &= \underline{\phantom{\$}5{,}400} \\ &\phantom{=} \underline{\underline{\$7{,}650}} \end{aligned}$$

This process is subsequently continued into Year 6.

## Selection of a Depreciation Method

Exhibit 10-3 shows the annual depreciation expense for the three depreciation methods used with the television camera: straight-line, double-declining balance, and sum-of-the-years'-digits. The units-of-output method is disregarded here because the camera's service capacity in units could not be reasonably estimated.

By summing the annual charges from the preceding schedules, you will see that the same total amount is ultimately written off by all of the methods, namely, cost minus residual value. However, as the exhibit so clearly reveals, the amounts and patterns of the yearly allocations differ markedly. The straight-line approach produces lower depreciation expense in the early years of an asset's life than either of the accelerated methods. The gap among these methods tends to decrease as time passes, with a reversal occurring in Year 3. That is, the $5,400 straight-line expense figure actually exceeds the charges obtained with double-declining balance or sum-of-the-years'-digits in later years of use.

Exhibit 10-3 also reveals the movement of book value over time. Although the book value figures under the various approaches decline at differing rates, the end result is the same: the amount ultimately left on the accounting records is residual value ($3,000).

Which method, then, should be selected? The answer to this question depends on a number of factors, including usage patterns, the generation of operating efficiencies, obsolescence, and the timing of repair costs. Conceptually, the method chosen should be the one that best parallels the services delivered (or benefits

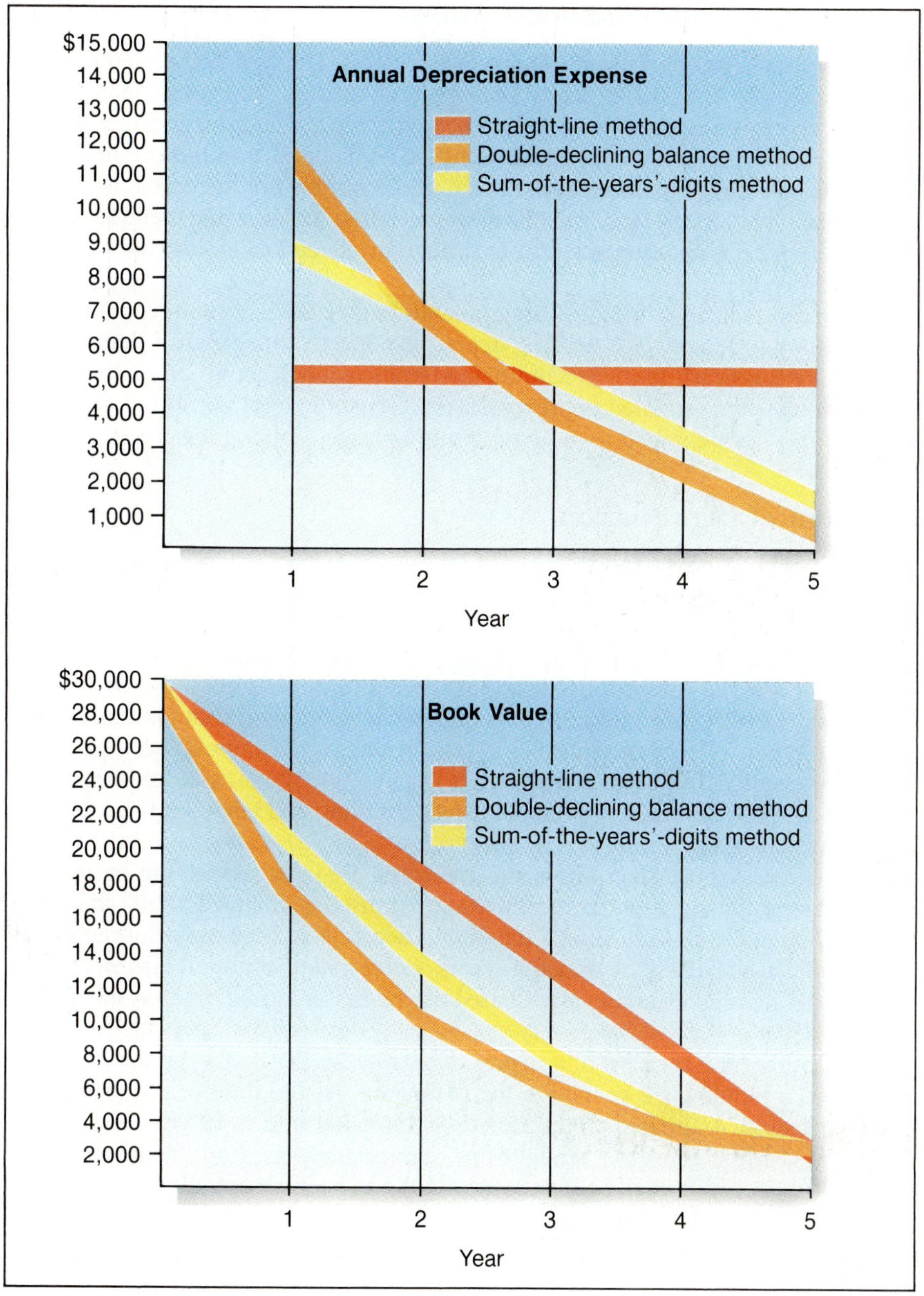


**Exhibit 10-3**
**A Graphical Overview of Depreciation Methods**

provided) by an asset. Such a selection is consistent with proper matching of revenues and expenses. Because the pattern of service is sometimes difficult to measure, however, practice often differs from theory. Recent surveys of reporting practices have shown the straight-line method to be the most popular approach. Companies that use this method often do so because of the constant nature of the depreciation charge—an element that helps to portray financial stability and smooth earnings over time.

## Depreciation: Two Common Fallacies

There are two common fallacies about depreciation. The first is that depreciation generates funds. This belief arises because, unlike most expenses, depreciation involves no cash payment; thus, many people assume that a business is "saving money." We could make depreciation entries all day and through the night and still not have a nickel for our efforts. The Cash account is not increased, nor is any current liability reduced by our debits to Depreciation Expense and credits to Accumulated Depreciation. Depreciation is simply an allocation of cost over an estimated service life.

The second fallacy is that the Accumulated Depreciation account contains cash that will be used to replace existing depreciable assets at the end of their service lives. There is no cash in the Accumulated Depreciation account; all cash is in the Cash account. Accumulated depreciation represents the total portion of an asset's cost that has been charged to expense, nothing more, nothing less.

## Revisions of Depreciation

OBJECTIVE 7
Be able to revise a depreciation rate.

The calculation of depreciation depends on two estimates: service life and residual value. Estimates, of course, are subject to change and are often incorrect. As an example, unanticipated suburban growth and new developments on the outskirts of town may shorten the service life of buildings located in older, central-city areas. Equipment may be useful for fewer years owing to new technology. Or residual values may need revision because of economic developments that take place after an asset has been placed in service. Such occurrences are commonplace. USAir, for instance, recently conducted a study of its Boeing 737-300 aircraft and decided to increase the residual value of each plane by $4 million and lengthen the useful life from 17 to 20 years.

When new information alters the estimates used for service life or residual value, the yearly depreciation computation must be changed. This change is achieved by allocating the asset's remaining depreciable base over the remaining service life. Corrections of previous years' depreciation amounts are *not* made, because the original estimates were based on the best information available at that time.

To illustrate the revision of a depreciation rate, suppose that Patriot Company purchased a building 10 years ago for $5 million. At the time of acquisition the building had an estimated $1 million residual value and a 40-year service life. Assuming Patriot uses the straight-line depreciation method, depreciation of $100,000 [($5,000,000 − $1,000,000) ÷ 40] has been recorded annually for 10 years. The Accumulated Depreciation account as a result presently totals $1 million. Because of altered traffic patterns, management now anticipates a remaining service life of only 20 years. Beginning with the current accounting period, the revised depreciation expense will be $150,000 per year, computed as follows:

| | |
|---|---|
| Building cost | $5,000,000 |
| Less: Residual value | 1,000,000 |
| Original depreciable base | $4,000,000 |
| Less: Depreciation already taken | 1,000,000 |
| Remaining depreciable base | $3,000,000 |
| Remaining life | 20 years |
| Revised depreciation per year | $3,000,000 ÷ 20 = $150,000 |

If the remaining service life had been extended to 50 years, annual depreciation expense would have decreased to $60,000 ($3,000,000 ÷ 50).

## Depreciation and the Tax Laws

**OBJECTIVE 8**
**Have a general understanding of depreciation and the tax laws.**

Businesses are entitled to a depreciation deduction when computing the amount of income taxes owed to the federal government. Such a deduction reduces a company's taxable income and associated income tax payments, thereby leaving more cash available for purposes of investment.

The tax laws that pertain to depreciation have changed over the years, with significant change occurring in the last decade. Not too long ago, for example, the U.S. Congress enacted a new **Accelerated Cost Recovery System (ACRS)** that allowed for a more rapid write-off of asset cost than was previously possible. The system's provisions were subsequently fine-tuned by the Tax Reform Act of 1986, to become what is known as Modified ACRS or MACRS. More than likely this legislation will change further as our federal deficit and trade imbalance come under increased scrutiny in Washington. The MACRS provisions are acceptable for income tax purposes only; they are not in accord with generally accepted accounting principles and should not be used for financial reporting purposes.[5]

The Modified Accelerated Cost Recovery System allows companies to depreciate assets over specified predetermined "recovery periods" when computing taxable income. These recovery periods are three, five, seven, or 10 years, among others, and depend on the asset in question. For example, automobiles and light-duty trucks have a five-year recovery period (i.e., are said to be "five-year property"), while most machinery, equipment, and furniture are written off over seven years. In general, the recovery period of an asset is shorter than the service life estimate, thereby permitting a business to reap quicker tax savings.

MACRS also speeds up the process of cost recovery by using rates that reflect a specialized accelerated depreciation method, namely, a form of declining balance. The rates in effect at the time of this writing for selected property classes are reproduced in Exhibit 10-4.

The exhibit reveals that "three-year property" is really written off over a four-year period, "five-year property" over a six-year period, and so forth. This apparent inconsistency is caused by the so-called *half-year convention,* which allows businesses to calculate (and deduct) a half year's depreciation in the year of asset acquisition regardless of the specific date of purchase. Given this feature, the cost of, say, three-year property is recovered by using the half-year convention for the first year and full depreciation allowances in Years 2 and 3. Then, any remaining balance is written off in the fourth year.

### An Illustration

To illustrate use of MACRS, assume that Gooden & Company purchased a $30,000 light-duty truck on August 1. The vehicle is expected to have a $3,000 residual

---

[5] To achieve consistency between a company's tax return and its income statement, many small businesses use Modified ACRS for both tax *and* financial reporting. Although theoretically deficient, this practice is followed when cost recovery amounts are relatively insignificant and do not vary greatly from those computed under conventional depreciation methods.

**Exhibit 10-4**
**Depreciation Rates for Federal Income Tax Purposes**

| | Property Class | | |
|---|---|---|---|
| ***Year*** | ***3-Year*** | ***5-Year*** | ***7-Year*** |
| 1 | 33.3% | 20.0% | 14.3% |
| 2 | 44.4 | 32.0 | 24.5 |
| 3 | 14.8 | 19.2 | 17.5 |
| 4 | 7.5 | 11.5 | 12.5 |
| 5 | | 11.5 | 8.9 |
| 6 | | 5.8 | 8.9 |
| 7 | | | 8.9 |
| 8 | | | 4.5 |
| | 100.0% | 100.0% | 100.0% |

Note: These rates may change when applied to certain automobiles and other items specified in the Internal Revenue Code.

value at the end of its eight-year service life. Light-duty trucks are classified as five-year property, resulting in the following figures:

| *Year* | *Depreciation Expense/ Cost Recovery* | *Accumulated Depreciation* | *Book Value* |
|---|---|---|---|
| | | | $30,000 |
| 1 | $6,000 ($30,000 × 0.200) | $ 6,000 | 24,000 |
| 2 | 9,600 ($30,000 × 0.320) | 15,600 | 14,400 |
| 3 | 5,760 ($30,000 × 0.192) | 21,360 | 8,640 |
| 4 | 3,450 ($30,000 × 0.115) | 24,810 | 5,190 |
| 5 | 3,450 ($30,000 × 0.115) | 28,260 | 1,740 |
| 6 | 1,740 ($30,000 × 0.058) | 30,000 | — |

Observe that residual value is ignored in MACRS computations and that the half-year convention is automatically reflected in the rates that were presented (i.e., there is no need to multiply the Year 1 calculation by 1/2).

## Chapter Review

### Learning Objectives—The Key Points

**1 Be able to differentiate between capital and revenue expenditures.** Capital expenditures are costs that benefit future accounting periods. Such items, which are shown on the balance sheet as part of an asset's cost, include acquisition expenditures and related amounts needed to ready the asset for business use (e.g., freight, insurance while in transit, and installation). In contrast, revenue expenditures fail to provide future economic benefits and are expensed when incurred. A typical example of a revenue expenditure is the cost incurred to repair a damaged asset, assuming the damage occurred during installation.

**2 Be able to account for cash and lump-sum purchases of property, plant, and equipment.** Cash purchases of property, plant, and equipment are recorded at the lowest cash price offered to the buyer. Any discounts lost are therefore charged to Interest Expense.

Lump-sum purchases involve the acquisition of several assets for a single price. For reporting and depreciation purposes, the amount paid (or to be paid) must be allocated among the various assets acquired. The necessary apportionment is generally made on the basis of an individual asset's appraised value relative to the appraised value of the entire purchase.

**3 Understand the meaning of "depreciation" as the term is used by accountants.** Accountants define depreciation as the allocation of cost of long-lived assets over an estimated service life. Because depreciation makes no attempt to reflect market values in a company's accounting records, it is said to be a process of allocation, not valuation.

**4 Understand the factors that affect the determination of service life.** The factors of physical deterioration, obsolescence, and inadequacy must be considered when estimating an asset's service life. Physical deterioration, often called "wear and tear," is caused by asset use and usually sets the maximum limit for the estimate of service life. Obsolescence, a technological factor relating to being out of date, often shortens the service life of an asset to be less than its physical life. Finally, inadequacy relates to an asset's inability to meet expected service needs in a competitive environment.

**5 Be able to compute depreciation by using the straight-line, units-of-output, declining balance, and sum-of-the-years'-digits methods.** With the popular straight-line method, an equal amount of an asset's depreciable base (cost minus residual value) is allocated to each accounting period. In contrast, with the units-of-output method, the depreciation write-off is based on asset use. A depreciation rate is first calculated by dividing the depreciable base by the total estimated output during the service life. The rate is then multiplied by the yearly usage to arrive at depreciation expense.

The two remaining methods, declining balance and sum-of-the-years'-digits, are accelerated methods, which generate more depreciation in the early years of an asset's life and less in later years. With declining balance, a fixed depreciation rate (twice the straight-line rate with double declining balance) is applied each year to a declining book value. In contrast, the sum-of-the-years'-digits approach uses successively lower rates (fractions) and a constant base (cost minus residual value).

**6 Understand the financial reporting issues related to the various depreciation methods.** The depreciation method selected affects business income. Conceptually, the method chosen should be the one that best parallels the services delivered or benefits provided by an asset, thereby achieving a proper matching of revenues and expenses. Practically, however, many firms use the straight-line method to help portray financial stability and smooth earnings over time.

**7 Be able to revise a depreciation rate.** Companies often find that original estimates of service life and/or residual value are incorrect and in need of revision. When this situation occurs, the new estimates are used to determine depreciation expense. Such changes require the remaining depreciable base be spread over the new estimate of remaining service life, with no corrections made to prior years' depreciation amounts.

**8 Have a general understanding of depreciation and the tax laws.** Depreciation is a deductible expense on a company's federal income tax return. Businesses generally employ the Modified Accelerated Cost Recovery System (MACRS) for tax purposes, which gives rise to quicker tax savings from shortened asset recovery periods and a specialized accelerated write-off. Quicker tax savings are attractive to an entity because of available investment opportunities.

## Chapter Quiz

The five questions that follow relate to several issues raised in the chapter. Test your knowledge of the issues by selecting the best answer. (The answers appear on p. 372.)

**1** A company financed a land purchase by paying $120,000 cash and assuming a $100,000 mortgage payable. County fees to record the transfer of the land to the buyer totaled $150. Costs to clear the land of rocks and trees amounted to $850. The recorded cost of the land is:

a $120,000.
b $220,000.
c $220,850.
d $221,000.

**2** Depreciation is:

a a system of cost allocation, not valuation.
b a system of valuation.
c recorded in an effort to reduce assets to their fair market value.
d based on an asset's cost and residual value, but not service life.

**3** A machine was purchased four years ago for $45,000, has an accumulated depreciation balance of $8,000, and a residual value of $5,000. Assuming that the straight-line method of depreciation was used, the machine's estimated service life:

a is 4 years.
b is 8 years.
c is 20 years.
d cannot be determined from the above facts.

**4** Tiger Lines purchased and began depreciating a new truck on April 1, 19X4. The truck cost $60,000, had a five-year service life, and a $12,000 residual value. Assuming use of the double-declining balance method, what is the *19X5* depreciation expense?

a $13,440.
b $14,400.
c $16,800.
d $18,000.

**5** Revising a depreciation rate because of a change in a service life estimate:

a requires the correction of prior years' financial statements.
b involves allocating the remaining depreciable base over the new service life.
c requires that sufficient cash be available in the Accumulated Depreciation account to replace the asset at the end of the new service life.
d is permitted only if the service life is shortened.

## Summary Problem

On January 1, 19X1, Hardy Company acquired an automatic can labeler for $63,000, which included shipping charges of $1,000. The machine has an estimated service life of five years (or 30,000 hours of operation) and a residual value of $6,000. Insurance on the machine while in transit was $300; insurance against fire and water damage for one year amounted to $500. Finally, installation costs were $2,000 and test runs totaled $700.

During the five years of use (19X1–19X5), the machine was operated for 6,300, 6,000, 5,800, 5,700, and 6,200 hours, respectively.

### Instructions

**a** Compute the machine's cost.

**b** Rounding final calculations to the nearest dollar, compute yearly depreciation expense by using each of the following methods: (1) straight-line; (2) units-of-output; (3) double-declining balance; and (4) sum-of-the-years'-digits.

**c** Explain why plant assets are depreciated as opposed to being expensed entirely in the year of acquisition.

### Solution

| **a** | |
|---|---|
| Purchase price (including shipping) | $63,000 |
| Insurance in transit | 300 |
| Installation | 2,000 |
| Test runs | 700 |
| Total cost | $66,000 |

**b** (1) Straight-line:

$$\frac{\text{Cost} - \text{Residual Value}}{\text{Service Life in Years}} = \text{Annual Depreciation}$$

$$\frac{\$66{,}000 - \$6{,}000}{5 \text{ years}} = \$12{,}000 \text{ per year}$$

(2) Units-of-output:

$$\frac{\text{Cost} - \text{Residual Value}}{\text{Service Life in Output}} = \text{Depreciation per Unit of Output}$$

$$\frac{\$66{,}000 - \$6{,}000}{30{,}000 \text{ hours}} = \$2.00 \text{ per hour}$$

| *Year* | *Hours of Operation* | × | *Depreciation per Hour* | = | *Depreciation Expense* |
|---|---|---|---|---|---|
| 19X1 | 6,300 | | $2.00 | | $12,600 |
| 19X2 | 6,000 | | 2.00 | | 12,000 |
| 19X3 | 5,800 | | 2.00 | | 11,600 |
| 19X4 | 5,700 | | 2.00 | | 11,400 |
| 19X5 | 6,200 | | 2.00 | | 12,400 |

(3) Double-declining balance:

5-year life = $\frac{1}{5}$ = 20%; 20% × 2 = 40% depreciation rate

| *Year* | *Depreciation Expense* | *Accumulated Depreciation* | *Book Value* |
|---|---|---|---|
| | | | $66,000 |
| 19X1 | $26,400 ($66,000 × 40%) | $26,400 | 39,600 |
| 19X2 | 15,840 ($39,600 × 40%) | 42,240 | 23,760 |
| 19X3 | 9,504 ($23,760 × 40%) | 51,744 | 14,256 |
| 19X4 | 5,702 ($14,256 × 40%) | 57,446 | 8,554 |
| 19X5 | 2,554 ($8,554 − $6,000)* | 60,000 | 6,000 |

* $8,554 × 40% would reduce the book value below residual value.

(4) Sum-of-the-years'-digits:

| *Year* | *Depreciation Expense* |
|---|---|
| 19X1 | $20,000 ($60,000 × $\frac{5}{15}$) |
| 19X2 | 16,000 ($60,000 × $\frac{4}{15}$) |
| 19X3 | 12,000 ($60,000 × $\frac{3}{15}$) |
| 19X4 | 8,000 ($60,000 × $\frac{2}{15}$) |
| 19X5 | 4,000 ($60,000 × $\frac{1}{15}$) |

**c** Plant assets have long lives and have years of future service potential. Expensing the entire cost when acquired would result in a mismatch of revenues and expenses on the income statement.

## Questions

**Q10-1** Do all items of property, plant, and equipment have a limited life? Explain.

**Q10-2** How is the acquisition cost of a machine determined? Which of the following items are included in the cost of an asset: purchase price, freight charges, cost of installation, medical costs of injured installer, special electrical wiring?

**Q10-3** What is the difference between a capital expenditure and a revenue expenditure?

**Q10-4** Explain the proper treatment of interest costs related to the purchase of a new automobile.

**Q10-5** Which price is used to record the acquisition cost of equipment: list price, negotiated price, or negotiated price minus available cash discount?

**Q10-6** How should the cost of property, plant, and equipment acquired in a lump-sum purchase be apportioned to the individual assets? Why is such a division necessary?

**Q10-7** Briefly discuss the concept of materiality.

**Q10-8** What does the term "depreciation" mean in accounting? Is the term used differently by others? Explain.

**Q10-9** How is the service life of depreciable plant and equipment determined? Discuss the factors of physical deterioration, obsolescence, and inadequacy in the establishment of service lives.

**Q10-10** Define the term "depreciable base."

**Q10-11** Describe how the straight-line method of depreciation differs from the units-of-output method.

**Q10-12** Is the units-of-output method of depreciation more appropriate to use for some items of plant and equipment than for others? Why?

**Q10-13** Briefly explain the concept of accelerated depreciation.

**Q10-14** What does the balance in the Accumulated Depreciation account represent? How much of the balance represents cash?

**Q10-15** How does a change in the estimated remaining service life of a piece of equipment affect past and future depreciation amounts?

**Q10-16** What is the Modified Accelerated Cost Recovery System (MACRS)? Can MACRS be used for financial reporting? Briefly discuss.

**Q10-17** What is meant by the term "recovery period," as related to the Modified Accelerated Cost Recovery System?

## Exercises

**E10-1** ***Determining acquisition cost***

City Express, a metropolitan transportation company, purchased several new buses at an invoice price of $500,000. The buses had a list price of $550,000. By taking advantage of a cash discount, City paid the seller $460,000. Costs of $12,000 were incurred in transporting the buses to City, and insurance charges during transportation were $650. Specially trained mechanics who tested the buses were paid $250; initial test runs around the area cost another $400. On the basis of requests from the mechanics, special safety devices were installed at a cost of $800. Finally, annual bus registration fees amounted to $120.

a Compute the acquisition cost of the buses.
b Prepare journal entries for all preceding expenditures.

**E10-2** ***Capital versus revenue expenditures***

Consider the following costs:

a Cost of initial testing of new machinery
b Cost of a paper stapler purchased for office use
c Interest charges on the purchase of new office equipment
d Plant remodeling cost related to installation of new machinery
e Architect's fee on new building
f Surveying costs of newly acquired land

g Salary of building security guard
h Initial paving of parking lot for employees
i Attorney's fee related to newly acquired land

Identify each of the costs as either a capital expenditure or a revenue expenditure.

**E10-3** ***Lump-sum purchase***

Nile agreed to purchase the property of Crescent for $50 million cash. Included in the purchase were the following assets:

| *Asset* | *Appraised Value* |
|---|---|
| Building | $15,000,000 |
| Equipment | 12,000,000 |
| Furniture | 3,000,000 |
| Land | 24,000,000 |
| Land improvements | 6,000,000 |

a Allocate the purchase price of $50 million among the various assets acquired.
b Prepare a journal entry for the acquisition.

**E10-4** ***Asset acquisition and straight-line depreciation***

A machine was purchased on October 1, 19X1, at a cost of $8,000. Installation charges were $600 and freight was $400. The machine has a residual value of $1,200, a service life of five years, and a physical life of eight years.

a Assuming all expenditures were for cash, record the necessary journal entry to enter the machine in the accounting records.
b Record the entry for straight-line depreciation at the end of 19X1.
c How would the machine and its related depreciation account appear on a balance sheet as of December 31, 19X2? Use proper amounts.

**E10-5** ***Depreciation methods***

Betsy Ross Enterprises purchased a delivery van for $30,000 on January 1, 19X7. The van was estimated to have a service life of five years and a residual value of $6,000. The company is planning to drive the van 20,000 miles annually.

Compute depreciation expense for *19X8* by using each of the following methods:

a Units-of-output, assuming 17,000 miles were driven during 19X8
b Straight-line
c Sum-of-the-years'-digits
d Double-declining balance

**E10-6** ***Depreciation computations***

Alpha Alpha Alpha, a college fraternity, purchased a new heavy-duty washing machine on January 1, 19X3. The machine cost $1,000, had an estimated residual value of $100, and an estimated service life of four years (1,800 washing cycles). Calculate the following:

a The machine's book value on December 31, 19X5, assuming use of the straight-line depreciation method.
b Depreciation expense for 19X4, assuming use of the units-of-output depreciation method. Actual washing cycles in 19X4 totaled 500.
c Accumulated depreciation on December 31, 19X5, assuming use of the double-declining balance depreciation method.
d Depreciation expense in 19X4 and 19X5, assuming use of the sum-of-the-years'-digits depreciation method.

**E10-7** ***Accelerated depreciation; partial periods***

Stemmons Enterprises purchased a special device on April 1, 19X1, that will be depreciated over a service life of five years. The device cost $30,000 and has a $9,000 estimated residual value.

a Calculate depreciation expense for the year ended December 31, 19X1, by using the sum-of-the-years'-digits and double-declining balance methods.
b Compute the firm's 19X2 depreciation expense by using the sum-of-the-years'-digits and double-declining balance methods.

**E10-8** ***Depreciation concepts***
Evaluate the comments that follow as being True or False. If the comment is false, briefly explain why.
a Depreciation is recorded over the years so that a company's asset valuations are reduced to reflect lower market values.
b A depreciable asset's cost, minus accumulated depreciation, equals book value.
c An asset's depreciable base and book value are identical at the end of the asset's service life.
d A company that uses accelerated depreciation will find that depreciation write-offs speed up, with increased amounts occurring in the later years of an asset's service life.
e Straight-line depreciation is probably the most popular accelerated depreciation method used by businesses.

**E10-9** ***Revisions of depreciation***
MJD, a health care company, holds clinics on how to treat heart attack victims. One year ago the firm bought a $20,000 supply of lifelike rubber bodies for seminar use. At the time of acquisition the service life and residual value were estimated to be five years and $500, respectively. These estimates now need revision.

Calculate yearly depreciation expense with the straight-line method under the following conditions:
a MJD now estimates that total service life (including earlier years of use) will be eight years and the residual value will be $700.
b MJD now estimates that the remaining time of use will be three years, with an $1,100 residual value.

**E10-10** ***Modified Accelerated Cost Recovery System***
Lynch, Inc., acquired $100,000 of three-year property on January 1, 19X1. The property has a $10,000 residual value at the end of its service life.
a Compute the company's depreciation expense (i.e., cost recovery) for 19X1 through 19X4, assuming use of the Modified Accelerated Cost Recovery System.
b Repeat part (a), assuming the property was acquired on August 1, 19X1, rather than January 1, 19X1.
c Consider your answers in part (a). Would these amounts be more likely to appear on Lynch's tax return or in the company's financial statements? Briefly explain, assuming that Lynch is a large corporation.

## Problems

### Series A

**P10-A1** ***Cost treatment***
Consider the following costs of Damon Company:
1 Cost of grading land prior to construction
2 Cost of material used during trial runs of new machinery
3 Delinquent property taxes on newly acquired land
4 Damage to equipment, which occurred during installation
5 Fine for fire code violation in building
6 Freight charges on newly acquired equipment
7 Cost of parking lot constructed on property
8 Cost of three wastebaskets purchased for office use

9 Cost of clearing land prior to construction
10 Cost of purchasing used equipment
11 Interest incurred to purchase machinery on credit
12 Current property taxes on land and building
13 Attorney's fees for land and building purchase
14 Construction costs of fence at company headquarters
15 Construction costs of new building
16 Cost of sprinkling system for landscaping

**Instructions**

a Identify each of the costs as a capital expenditure or a revenue expenditure.
b For the capital expenditures only, indicate which asset account(s) should be increased.

**P10-A2** ***Allocation of costs to plant asset accounts; lump-sum purchase***
The following transactions relate to the Henley Company for 19X2:

| | |
|---|---|
| Jan. 7 | Acquired a parcel of land by paying $200,000 cash to the seller, securing a $350,000 mortgage payable, and paying $20,000 to Harris County for delinquent property taxes. |
| Feb. 14 | Acquired a 50-year old historic building for $950,000. The building had cost the seller only $200,000 several years ago. |
| Mar. 10 | Purchased new equipment for $14,000 cash. Freight charges amounted to $200, special noise reduction paneling placed around the equipment cost $400, and test runs totaled $850. |
| Apr. 15 | Paid $40,000 to SRO Asphalt Company to pave a new customer parking lot. |
| May 1 | Incurred $25,000 of interest on monies borrowed to finance the historic building acquisition on February 14. |
| June 9 | Purchased several small electric drills for $80, plus 5% state sales tax. |
| July 10 | Acquired a one-year fire insurance policy on the historic building for $33,000. |
| Aug. 27 | Planted shrubs and trees at the historic building for $12,000. |
| Sept. 4 | Acquired equipment having a list price of $24,000 and a negotiated price of $22,000. A 3% cash discount was offered if the invoice was settled in 10 days. Because of a clerical oversight, settlement was delayed until October. |
| Oct. 19 | Purchased developed property from U-2 Company for $4 million. On the date of acquisition the appraised value of the property totaled $5 million, subdivided as follows: land, $3.7 million; land improvements, $200,000; and building, $1.1 million. |

**Instructions**

Assign appropriate costs to the Land, Land Improvements, Buildings, and Equipment accounts by using the format that follows. Obtain year-end totals. If a cost is not charged to the preceding accounts, indicate how the expenditure should be treated.

| *Date* | *Land* | *Land Improvements* | *Buildings* | *Equipment* |
|---|---|---|---|---|
| | $ | $ | $ | $ |

**P10-A3** ***Depreciation computations***

Eastgate Company purchased a specialized piece of machinery for $40,000 on January 1, 19X1. At the time of acquisition, the machine was estimated to have a service life of five years (10,000 operating hours) and a residual value of $4,000.

During the five years of operation (19X1–19X5), the machine was used for 2,300, 2,100, 1,700, 2,000, and 1,900 hours, respectively.

**Instructions**

a Compute depreciation for 19X1–19X5 by using the (1) straight-line method, (2) units-of-output method, (3) double-declining balance method, and (4) sum-of-the-years'-digits method.

b Determine the impact of using the double-declining balance method as compared to the straight-line method on company income for the two-year period 19X1–19X2.

c Briefly describe what you would have done differently in part (a) if Eastgate, in addition to the $40,000 outlay, had to pay $1,500 for the machine's installation, $800 for freight, and $300 to repair damage that occurred while the machine was being unloaded from the carrier's truck.

**P10-A4** ***Depreciation calculations, partial periods***

Empire Treats, Inc., a food wholesaler, operates three delivery vehicles in central Kansas. Data on the vehicles follow.

| *Vehicle* | *Date Acquired* | *Cost* | *Residual Value* | *Service Life (Years)* | *Depreciation Method* |
|---|---|---|---|---|---|
| 2-ton Chevrolet | 8/31/X2 | $21,000 | $ — | 7 | Straight-line |
| 2-ton Dodge | 5/1/X1 | 15,000 | 1,000 | 5 | Double-declining balance |
| 2-ton Ford | 1/31/X1 | 22,000 | 4,000 | 4 | Sum-of-the-years'-digits |

**Instructions**

a Calculate depreciation expense for the 12-month period ended December 31, 19X3.

b Compute the December 31, 19X3, accumulated depreciation and book value of each vehicle.

**P10-A5** ***Depreciation methods, changes in rates, partial periods***

Walnut Company purchased a corporate jet for $22.5 million on May 1, 19X1. The jet had an estimated residual value of 30% of cost and a 10-year (50,000-flying-hour) service life. On January 1, 19X2, the service life was extended to recognize 12 years (or 60,000 flying hours) of remaining service from that date. Flying hours during 19X1 and the first quarter of 19X2 totaled 4,200 and 1,600, respectively. Accumulated depreciation accounts based on the straight-line, units-of-output, double-declining balance, and sum-of-the-years'-digits depreciation methods follow.

a

| *Accumulated Depreciation* | |
|---|---|
| | 12/31/X1 ? |
| | 3/31/X2 532,343 |

b

| *Accumulated Depreciation* | |
|---|---|
| | 12/31/X1 ? |
| | 3/31/X2 384,720 |

c

| *Accumulated Depreciation* | |
|---|---|
| | 12/31/X1 ? |
| | 3/31/X2 306,250 |

d

| *Accumulated Depreciation* | |
|---|---|
| | 12/31/X1 ? |
| | 3/31/X2 812,500 |

**Instructions**

Determine which Accumulated Depreciation account corresponds to each of the depreciation methods. Walnut rounds final depreciation computations to the nearest dollar.

## Series B

**P10-B1** ***Cost treatment***

Consider the following costs of the United Company:

1 Cost of three antique works of art for the company's new building
2 Purchase price of the land and building
3 Cost of outside lighting fixtures on the new building's grounds
4 Cost of initial test runs of new equipment
5 Interest incurred to purchase equipment on credit
6 Traffic fines paid by United for a driver who was delivering equipment to the new building
7 Cost of grading land prior to construction
8 Current property taxes on the land and building
9 Party costs to celebrate the opening of United's new building
10 Installation costs of new machinery
11 Cost of newly installed security fences that surround the parking lot
12 Cost of delinquent property taxes assumed when purchasing land
13 The current month's premium for building fire and liability insurance
14 Significant overhaul costs related to acquisition of used machinery; needed to ready the machinery for its intended use
15 Attorney's fees related to land acquisition
16 Real estate commissions related to land acquisition

**Instructions**

a Identify each of the costs as a capital expenditure or a revenue expenditure.
b For the capital expenditures only, indicate which asset account(s) should be increased.

**P10-B2** ***Allocation of costs to plant asset accounts; lump-sum purchase***

The following transactions relate to the Post Oak Company for 19X5:

| | | |
|---|---|---|
| Jan. | 10 | Purchased new machinery for $12,000 cash. Freight charges amounted to $600, special electrical wiring cost $4,000, and test runs totaled $800. |
| Feb. | 19 | Purchased developed property from Baxter Company for $1 million. On the date of acquisition the appraised value of the property totaled $1.5 million, subdivided as follows: land, $750,000; land improvements, $60,000; and building, $690,000. |
| Mar. | 21 | Acquired a 40-year old apartment building for $1.3 million. The building had cost the seller only $400,000 several years ago. |
| Apr. | 3 | Installed $12,000 of security fencing around the apartment. |
| May | 14 | Acquired a one-year fire insurance policy on the apartment building for $7,000. |
| June | 16 | Paid $50,000 to the Advance Paving Company to construct a parking lot for the apartment tenants. |
| July | 8 | Incurred $11,000 of interest on monies borrowed to finance the apartment building acquisition on March 21. |
| Aug. | 9 | Acquired a parcel of land by securing a $290,000 mortgage payable and paying $10,000 of delinquent property taxes to Duval County. |
| Sept. | 15 | Purchased several smoke detectors for the apartment from a mail order firm. The detectors cost $64, plus a $6 shipping fee. |
| Oct. | 30 | Acquired equipment having a list price of $33,000 and a negotiated price of $27,000. A 4% cash discount was offered if the invoice was |

settled in 10 days. Because of a clerical oversight, settlement was delayed until December.

**Instructions**

Assign appropriate costs to the Land, Land Improvements, Buildings, and Equipment accounts by using the format that follows. Obtain year-end totals. If a cost is not charged to the preceding accounts, indicate how the expenditure should be treated.

| *Date* | *Land* | *Land Improvements* | *Buildings* | *Equipment* |
|---|---|---|---|---|
| | $ | $ | $ | $ |

**P10-B3** ***Depreciation computations***

Asian Imports purchased a specialized piece of machinery for $50,000 on January 1, 19X3. At the time of acquisition, the machine was estimated to have a service life of five years (25,000 operating hours) and a residual value of $5,000. During the five years of operations (19X3–19X7), the machine was used for 5,100, 4,800, 3,200, 6,000, and 5,900 hours, respectively.

**Instructions**

a Compute depreciation for 19X3–19X7 by using the (1) straight-line method, (2) units-of-output method, (3) double-declining balance method, and (4) sum-of-the-years'-digits method.

b Determine the impact of using the sum-of-the-years'-digits method as compared to the straight-line method on asset valuation for the two-year period 19X3–19X4.

c Briefly describe what you would have done differently in part (a) if Asian Imports had paid $47,800 for the machinery rather than $50,000. In addition, assume that the company incurred $800 of freight charges, $1,400 for machine set-up and testing, and $300 for insurance during the first year of use.

**P10-B4** ***Depreciation calculations, partial periods***

Allied Company, a frozen food wholesaler, has three freezers in its warehouse in southern Montana. Data on the freezers follow.

| *Freezer* | *Date Acquired* | *Cost* | *Residual Value* | *Service Life (Years)* | *Depreciation Method* |
|---|---|---|---|---|---|
| Armstrong no. 13 | 2/28/X1 | $26,000 | $2,000 | 5 | Straight-line |
| Modern no. 79 | 10/1/X1 | 44,000 | 2,000 | 6 | Sum-of-the-years'-digits |
| Arctic B-46 | 5/1/X2 | 45,000 | — | 10 | Double-declining balance |

**Instructions**

a Calculate depreciation expense for the 12-month period ended December 31, 19X3.

b Compute the December 31, 19X3, accumulated depreciation and book value of each freezer.

**P10-B5** ***Depreciation methods, changes in rates, partial periods***

Ridgemar, Inc., purchased a bus for $200,000 on April 1, 19X1. The bus had a residual value of $50,000 and a 10-year (150,000-mile) service life. On January 1, 19X2, the service life was decreased to recognize eight years (or 120,000 miles) of remaining service from that date. Miles driven during 19X1 and the first quarter of 19X2 totaled 16,400 and 4,700, respectively. Accumulated Depreciation accounts based on the straight-line, units-of-output, double-declining balance, and sum-of-the-years'-digits depreciation methods follow.

a

| *Accumulated Depreciation* | | |
|---|---|---|
| | 12/31/X1 | ? |
| | 3/31/X2 | 4,336 |

b

| *Accumulated Depreciation* | | |
|---|---|---|
| | 12/31/X1 | ? |
| | 3/31/X2 | 10,625 |

c

| *Accumulated Depreciation* | | |
|---|---|---|
| | 12/31/X1 | ? |
| | 3/31/X2 | 5,233 |

d

| *Accumulated Depreciation* | | |
|---|---|---|
| | 12/31/X1 | ? |
| | 3/31/X2 | 7,197 |

**Instructions**

Determine which Accumulated Depreciation account corresponds to each of the depreciation methods. Ridgemar rounds final depreciation computations to the nearest dollar.

## Beyond the Basics

**BB10-1** ***Acquisition cost, lump-sum purchase, correction of errors***

Monrovia Company purchased a small farm on April 1, 19X1, with the intentio converting it to a go-cart track. Monrovia agreed to pay $300,000 over the next six months and to assume the remaining mortgage on the property of $200,000. These costs, together with other transactions related to the conversion, are presented in the Property account.

| *Property* | | | | | |
|---|---|---|---|---|---|
| 4/1 | Purchase price | 500,000 | 12/31 | Accumulated depreciation (estimate) | 6,000 |
| 4/10 | Land title | 1,000 | | | |
| 4/12 | Survey costs | 4,000 | | | |
| 4/15 | Land grading and draining | 15,000 | | | |
| 4/30 | One-year fire insurance policy on buildings | 3,000 | | | |
| 5/1 | Material and labor cost to refurbish buildings | 20,000 | | | |
| 5/2 | Advertising costs for grand opening | 3,000 | | | |
| 10/1 | Current year's property taxes on land | 9,000 | | | |

The property acquired included land (appraised value $450,000), buildings (appraised value $90,000), and equipment (appraised value $60,000). The go-cart track opened on May 1, 19X1.

**Instructions**

a List the errors made by Monrovia in accounting for the purchase and related costs.

b Prepare a schedule that shows how the original lump-sum purchase of property, plant, and equipment should have been handled.

c Prepare a journal entry on December 31, 19X1, that closes out the Property account and allocates the amounts therein to Land, Buildings, Equipment, Accumulated Depreciation, and other appropriate accounts. Assume the buildings and equipment have respective service lives of 20 years and 10 years from the grand opening. The straight-line method of depreciation is used; no residual value is anticipated.

d Present the property, plant, and equipment section of Monrovia's balance sheet as of December 31, 19X1.

## Answers to Chapter Quiz

**1** d ($120,000 + $100,000 + $150 + $850)

**2** a

**3** c [$8,000 ÷ 4 years = $2,000 per year; ($45,000 − $5,000) ÷ $2,000 = 20 years]

**4** c [5-year life = 20% per year; 20% × 2 = 40%; $60,000 × 40% × 9/12 = $18,000; ($60,000 − $18,000) × 40% = $16,800]

**5** b

CHAPTER 11

# Property, Plant, and Equipment/ Natural Resources/ Intangibles

## Learning Objectives

After reading this chapter you should:

1 Be familiar with the accounting for property, plant, and equipment costs incurred after asset acquisition.

2 Be able to record gains and losses on the disposal of property, plant, and equipment.

3 Be able to account for exchanges and trade-ins for financial accounting and tax purposes.

4 Understand the use of subsidiary ledgers for property, plant, and equipment.

5 Know how to account for natural resources and depletion.

6 Recognize the various types of intangible assets and their legal lives and understand the amortization process.

This chapter continues our discussion of long-lived assets. We will study several additional issues related to property, plant, and equipment and examine two other types of assets that provide long-term benefits to their owners: natural resources and intangibles.

## Plant and Equipment Costs Subsequent to Asset Acquisition

OBJECTIVE 1
Be familiar with the accounting for property, plant, and equipment costs incurred after asset acquisition.

The costs related to fixed assets often do not stop at acquisition. Many expenditures are made after buildings, machines, and various pieces of equipment have started to serve a business. For example, repairs are performed, new features are added to improve efficiency, major overhauls are undertaken, and parts are replaced.

The accountant must determine how to record these items. Whether they are added to the depreciable base of the asset or written off as expenses may have a significant impact on reported profitability for the period. If the costs are treated as *capital expenditures* (i.e., costs that benefit future periods) and debited to property, plant, and equipment accounts, current net income is not directly lowered. However, the long-lived asset now has a larger depreciable base, which results in greater depreciation expense in the years to come. Alternatively, if these costs are treated as *revenue expenditures* and expensed when incurred, profit is affected immediately.

Property, plant, and equipment costs incurred after asset acquisition should be added to an asset's depreciable base if *future economic benefits result from the expenditure.* Future economic benefits occur under the following conditions:

**1** The service life of an asset is prolonged.

**2** The quantity of services expected from an asset has increased.

**3** The quality of services expected from an asset has improved.

Expenditures that do not fulfill at least one of these criteria are treated as revenue expenditures and written off as expenses of the current period. We will now examine the application of these rules to several commonly encountered items.

### Repairs

Amounts spent to maintain the normal operating condition of an asset are termed **repairs.** Repairs include regular maintenance, minor parts replacement, painting, cleaning, and inspection. Repairs do not increase the future service potential of an asset; rather, such amounts assist in attaining the original service life estimate and anticipated operating efficiency. As a consequence, repair costs are debited to the Repairs Expense account when incurred.

### Additions

**Additions** are items that will provide future benefits and be affixed to existing assets. Examples of additions include the placement of air conditioning in a building or vehicle and the construction of a new wing on a building. The cost of an addition is a capital expenditure and is therefore recorded in a property, plant, or equipment account (i.e., capitalized). Generally, the cost is entered in the same account as the original asset to simplify record keeping.

### Betterments

**Betterments,** sometimes called improvements or extraordinary repairs, are expenditures that improve or increase the future service potential of an asset. Occasionally, a betterment occurs by replacing a major part of an existing asset with a similar but superior component, for example, the installation of (1) a new, more efficient heating/cooling system in a building and (2) a new engine in a vehicle. In other cases the betterment may involve an extraordinary repair such as a major overhaul. Extraordinary repairs generally extend the service life of an asset beyond the original estimate.

Often the difference between extraordinary repairs and ordinary repairs and maintenance is not readily evident; yet the accountant must properly distinguish between these two items, because their accounting treatment differs. Ordinary repairs, as we noted earlier, are expenses. In contrast, expenditures that prolong an asset's life are capitalized in the following manner.

Assume the Simmons Company acquired a freezer on January 1, 19X1, for $20,000. The freezer had an estimated service life of five years, with no residual value. Simmons has depreciated the asset for four years by using the straight-line method, resulting in the following balance sheet disclosure as of December 31, 19X4:

| | | |
|---|---|---|
| Freezer | $20,000 | |
| Less: Accumulated depreciation | 16,000 | $4,000 |

On January 1, 19X5, a new motor costing $1,000 was installed, which extended the freezer's service life by one year. The cost of the new motor is *not* recorded in the Freezer account. Rather $1,000 is debited to Accumulated Depreciation in the manner shown.

| | | |
|---|---|---|
| Accumulated Depreciation: Freezer | 1,000 | |
| Cash | | 1,000 |
| To record cost of new motor | | |

This journal entry reduces the balance in the Accumulated Depreciation account to $15,000 ($16,000 − $1,000). The freezer's new book value of $5,000 ($20,000 − $15,000) will be depreciated over the remaining two years of service life at the rate of $2,500 ($5,000 ÷ 2) per year. Upon conclusion of the six-year life, then, depreciation expense will total $21,000, which equals the original cost of the freezer plus the $1,000 motor.

Notice that the debit to Accumulated Depreciation increases the asset's book value, as would a debit to the Freezer account. We follow the former approach for expenditures that prolong an asset's life to, in effect, reclaim (reduce) some past depreciation—an appropriate procedure in view of the service life extension.

## Assessments

Property owners are often assessed for improvements such as new streets, curbs, sidewalks, streetlights, and sewers. These improvements are made for the benefit of the property owners and other residents of the municipality. **Assessments** are normally added to the Land account, because projects such as those just cited are relatively permanent and are maintained and upgraded by the municipality.

### TIPS & TECHNIQUES

The proper treatment of costs incurred after asset acquisition is sometimes confusing. The generalized chart that appears on page 376 may prove helpful when analyzing a transaction and determining its correct handling in the accounting records.

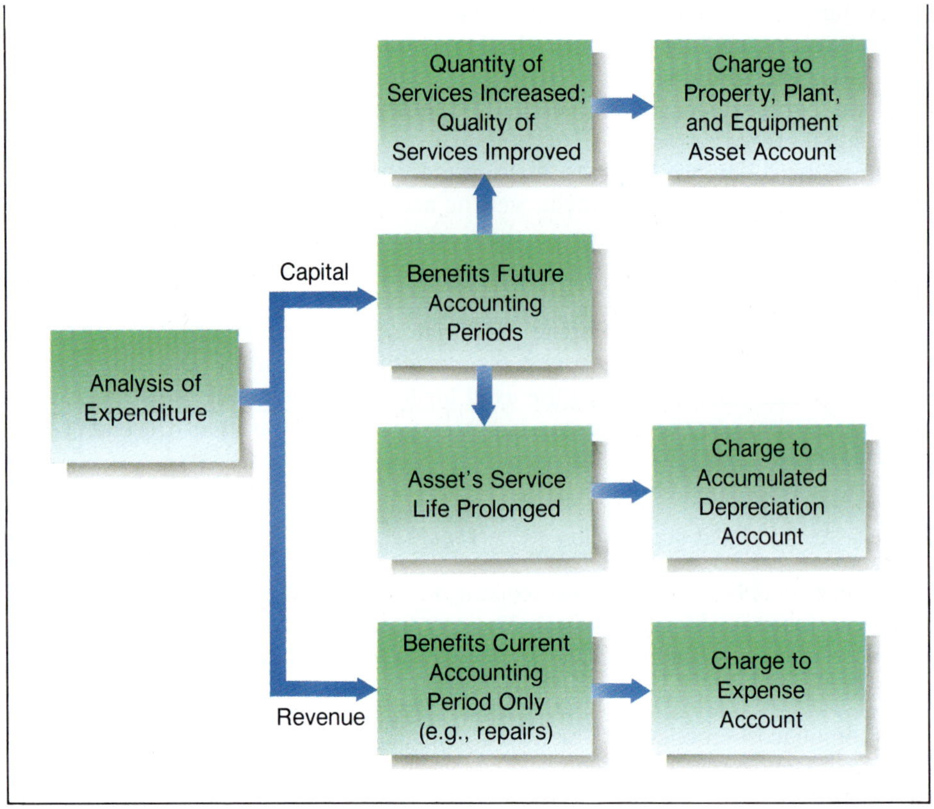


## Disposals of Property, Plant, and Equipment

OBJECTIVE 2
Be able to record gains and losses on the disposal of property, plant, and equipment.

Items of property, plant, and equipment are acquired by a firm to render benefits for a number of years. Eventually these assets will be retired from use by being discarded, sold, or exchanged. When a company disposes of a depreciable asset, depreciation must be taken up to the date of disposal to ensure a proper matching of expenses and revenues.

To illustrate, suppose that Bennigan Company acquired a machine on January 1, 19X1, at a cost of $15,000. The machine has a residual value of $1,000 and is being depreciated over a seven-year life by the straight-line method. As of December 31, 19X2, the machine would appear in the accounting records as follows:

| ***Machinery*** | | | |
|---|---|---|---|
| 1/1/X1 | 15,000 | | |

| ***Accumulated Depreciation: Machinery*** | | | |
|---|---|---|---|
| | | 12/31/X1 | 2,000 |
| | | 12/31/X2 | 2,000 |

Assume that Bennigan discarded the machine on October 1, 19X3. Because depreciation was last recorded on December 31, 19X2, nine months of additional depreciation must be taken. Thus, $1,500 ($\$2,000 \times \frac{9}{12}$) is entered in the accounts by means of the entry that follows.

| | | | |
|---|---|---|---|
| Oct. 1 | Depreciation Expense: Machinery | 1,500 | |
| | Accumulated Depreciation: Machinery | | 1,500 |
| | To record nine months' depreciation | | |

## Removal of Assets from the Accounts

Once depreciation is brought up to date, any account balances associated with the machine must be removed from the books. This step is accomplished by debiting the Accumulated Depreciation account for the total depreciation taken to the date of disposal and then crediting the asset account for the asset's original cost. For Bennigan's machine the necessary journal entry is as follows:

| | | | |
|---|---|---|---|
| Oct. 1 | Loss on Disposal of Property, Plant, & Equipment | 9,500 | |
| | Accumulated Depreciation: Machinery | 5,500 | |
| | Machinery | | 15,000 |
| | To record discarded machine | | |

To explain, recall that an asset's cost, minus accumulated depreciation, represents *book value,* which is the "value" of the asset in the accounting records. Because Bennigan received nothing for a machine having a $9,500 book value ($15,000 − $5,500), a $9,500 loss is incurred.

## Sale of Depreciable Assets

In addition to being discarded or abandoned, depreciable assets can also be sold. To properly account for the transaction, the proceeds received upon sale must be compared against book value. If the amount received is greater than the asset's book value, a gain results; if the proceeds are less than book value, a loss arises. For example, assume that an executive desk was acquired for $2,000. Over the years, depreciation in the amount of $1,200 has been recorded. The asset's book value of $800 ($2,000 − $1,200) appears in the accounts as follows:

| ***Office Furniture*** | |
|---|---|
| 2,000 | |

| ***Accumulated Depreciation: Office Furniture*** | |
|---|---|
| | 1,200 |

If the desk is sold for an amount equal to its book value, the sale would be recorded in the following manner:

| | | |
|---|---|---|
| Cash | 800 | |
| Accumulated Depreciation: Office Furniture | 1,200 | |
| Office Furniture | | 2,000 |
| To record furniture sold at a price equal to book value | | |

No gain or loss results; furniture with a book value of $800 is replaced by $800 cash.

If the desk is sold for $500 because of a low demand for used office furniture, a loss occurs. The entry to record this transaction would be as shown:

**Exhibit 11-3**
**Trademarks and Symbols**

UPS and UPS in shield design are registered trademarks of United Parcel Service of America, Inc. Used with permission. The Campbell Soup logo is reprinted with permission of Campbell Soup Company. The MasterCard logo is a registered trademark of MasterCard International Incorporated. The Domino's Pizza logo is reprinted with permission of Domino's Pizza.

of the same name and may be rather substantial. For example, Safeway Stores, the Oakland-based supermarket operator, recently reported leasehold improvements of $691 million. Leasehold improvements normally become the property of the lessor at the end of the lease period. As such, the amounts expended are written off to expense over the remaining life of the lease or the life of the improvement, whichever is shorter.

## Goodwill

The term "goodwill" means different things to different people. A business often refers to the customer goodwill that flows from an excellent reputation, superior products, and prime location. A large corporation may claim it is furthering community goodwill by sponsoring a Little League baseball team and a series of concerts open to the public. Do the foregoing types of goodwill have any value to a business? Of course they do. However, placing a dollar value on such attributes is exceedingly difficult. These items involve considerable personal opinion and cannot be measured objectively. If the owners and managers of a business were permitted to arbitrarily place a value on such goodwill for entry into the accounting records, the resulting financial statements could seriously misrepresent the entity's financial position.

As a result, generally accepted accounting principles allow only the recording of "purchased" goodwill. For example, suppose that Diamond Computers, owner of a chain of computer stores throughout the country, purchased a local retailer (Valley

## HIGHLIGHT

# Beretta the Gun Versus Beretta the Car

Does the name Beretta ring a bell? It should. It's the name of a famous brand of Italian guns favored by the fictional master-spy James Bond. But apparently the people who name the cars at General Motors didn't think of that when they chose Beretta as the name for a new compact car introduced in early 1987. The makers of Beretta, the gun, have therefore filed a suit against the maker of Beretta, the car, for $250 million in damages in a trademark infringement suit. The gun maker said that GM's use of the Beretta name on a line of compact cars "is an [intentional insult] not only to the Beretta corporation, but also to the Beretta family."

The lawsuit is the culmination of a dispute that began building when Beretta, the gun makers, found out about GM's Beretta from the auto maker's advertising. "We were most concerned about what the lawyers call dilution," said a spokesman. "When people heard of our firearms, they'd start to think of autos."

Normally, manufacturers take great pains to be sure that names chosen for new products aren't encumbered by patent or trademark protection. But the gun maker said GM offered no explanation to Beretta of why the Beretta name didn't ring an alarm bell, despite the fact that it's been a registered trademark in the U.S. since 1954. The Beretta family has been making guns and marketing them under the family name since 1526. "I don't recall we ever received any kind of logic as to why they (GM) used the name," the gun maker noted.

GM said in a statement that Beretta's suit has "no basis," because "there is no likelihood of confusion" between the GM car and Beretta products. The auto maker conceded that "the GM employee who selected the Beretta name was unaware of the existence of the Beretta gun company," but added that in the U.S., "it's not uncommon that vehicle models and firearms have the same names, such as Colt and Marlin." Like Colt (horse) and Marlin (fish), Beretta also has an alternate meaning that is not the subject of a trademark: Roman Catholic cardinals and bishops wear caps called berettas, or birettas.

But Beretta isn't accepting any excuses. The gun maker is demanding that GM compensate it for any profits gained from using its name and for infringing on its trademark. Beretta is also demanding that GM stop using the name on its cars. The final demand, if granted by the court, could hurt GM almost as much as handing over $250 million. The Beretta is, at the time of the suit, one of the hottest-selling passenger cars in the U.S. Whether GM will fight to hang onto the name—and the value that it now has for GM's business—remains to be seen. One thing is certain, though. If it weren't for a trademark and the accompanying rights, life would definitely be more interesting. Imagine the possibilities . . .

Authors' update: As the text goes to press, we have just learned of a settlement in the trademark suit. The chairman of the firearms manufacturer accepted a $500,000 donation from General Motors, to be used as a contribution toward cancer research by the Beretta Foundation for Cancer Research and Treatment. Concurrently, the gun company granted General Motors rights to use the Beretta name and trademark for the popular automobile. Symbolizing the agreement, chief executives of the two firms exchanged gifts: a Chevrolet Beretta GTU coupe, and a Beretta hunting rifle and shotgun.

SOURCE: Adapted from "Beretta, the Maker of Guns, Sues GM Over Its Beretta Car," *The Wall Street Journal*, July 20, 1988, p. 28. Reprinted by permission of *The Wall Street Journal*, 

Computer) on October 1 for $500,000 cash. The current value of Valley's assets and liabilities on the date of acquisition were as follows:

| | |
|---|---|
| Building | $150,000 |
| Store fixtures | 30,000 |
| Inventory | 300,000 |
| Prepaid expenses | 10,000 |
| Bank loan | (90,000) |
| | $400,000 |

Why did Diamond pay $500,000 when the individual assets, minus liabilities, were worth only $400,000? In all likelihood, Diamond's management was impressed with the financial history of Valley and anticipated that Valley's earnings record would continue into the future. To an accountant, the $100,000 difference between the purchase price of the business and the current value of the assets and liabilities acquired is an intangible known as **goodwill.**

The existence of goodwill is normally evidenced by a company's ability to earn a higher rate of income than other businesses in the same field of endeavor. Stated differently, goodwill occurs when the value of the company *as an operating entity* exceeds the value of its individual components (*measurable assets and liabilities*). The entity's resources, including the special attributes of reputation, favorable location, and skillful management, have all been working together to increase the value of the business in the eyes of the purchaser—an increase that is over and above the current value of the resources acquired and liabilities assumed. Generally, the individual impact of each of the preceding factors is not readily identifiable, and the purchaser is paying a lump-sum for their collective benefits.

## Accounting for Goodwill

The proper accounting for goodwill is demonstrated by continuing the previous example. It is important to recognize that although Valley developed the goodwill, disclosure by management on Valley's financial statements is inappropriate because of the measurement difficulties cited earlier. Diamond, on the other hand, paid $100,000 for this intangible in a valid business transaction and can record the following journal entry:

| | | |
|---|---|---|
| Building | 150,000 | |
| Store Fixtures | 30,000 | |
| Inventory | 300,000 | |
| Prepaid Expenses | 10,000 | |
| Goodwill | 100,000 | |
| Loan Payable | | 90,000 |
| Cash | | 500,000 |
| Acquired the assets and liabilities of Valley Computer | | |

Observe the manner in which the current value of the assets and liabilities acquired becomes the cost to Diamond. If Valley lacked the ability to achieve above-average earnings because of a marginal location or other factors, Diamond would have probably paid less than $500,000. If, for example, the agreed-upon purchase price was $400,000, Diamond would have bought only the separate assets, minus liabilities; nothing would have been paid for the unique features of the business.

### Guidelines to Determine Goodwill

Calculating the amount *paid* for goodwill in the purchase of a business is fairly straightforward, as was observed in the preceding example. Determining how much a purchaser *should be willing to pay* is another matter. Several techniques have been proposed for estimating goodwill. Among these are the following:

- Multiply sales during the last 12 months by a stipulated percentage.
- Multiply earnings during the last 12 months by a stipulated percentage.
- Multiply the amount by which earnings exceed an industry norm by a stipulated percentage.

Bear in mind that these techniques are merely estimation tools. The exact amount of goodwill is based on the actual selling price of the business, as determined by the buyer and the seller. The preceding tools are just that—tools—and cannot take the place of sound business logic and intelligent financial negotiation.

## Amortization of Intangibles

Earlier in the text we discussed the topic of depreciation—a process by which the cost of plant and equipment is allocated to expense over an estimated service life. This same process is applied to intangible assets; the name is changed, however, and it is known as **amortization.** The entry to record the periodic amortization of an intangible is a debit to Amortization Expense and a credit to the intangible asset account. This treatment differs slightly from the depreciation entry, where the credit involves the contra asset Accumulated Depreciation. An Accumulated Amortization account is seldom used.

### Amortization Procedures

The most troublesome issue in amortization is estimating the intangible's service life. Imagine the difficulty of determining when a food trademark, the unique flavor of a soft drink, or an ice cream franchise would have no future economic value to their owners.

As previously noted, many intangibles have specified legal lives, for instance, 17 years for a patent and the life of the creator plus 50 years for a copyright. Despite the legal life, the service life of an intangible may be considerably shorter. For example, although the inventor of a new electronic device can obtain exclusive manufacturing and sales rights for 17 years through a patent, the patent may be useful for only five years because of intense competition and rapid technological developments in the electronics industry. Accordingly, the patent should be written off over a five-year period. In general, an intangible should be amortized over the shorter of its legal life or service life; however, in no event should the amortization period exceed 40 years.[2] This latter rule is especially applicable to goodwill and other intangibles that provide seemingly unlimited benefits to their owners.

Because it is difficult to measure changes in the yearly benefits provided by intangibles, most companies use the straight-line method of amortization. Similar to straight-line depreciation, an equal amount of expense is recorded each period. Several examples of intangible assets and related amortization practices appear in Exhibit 11-4.

---

[2] "Intangible Assets," *Opinions of the Accounting Principles Board No. 17* (New York: American Institute of Certified Public Accountants, 1970), paragraph 29.

**Exhibit 11-4**
**Intangible Assets and Amortization Practices**

| *Company* | *Intangible* | *Amortization Policy* |
|---|---|---|
| A&W Brands, Inc. | Secret flavor formulas | Amortized on a straight-line basis over 37 to 40 years. |
| McDonald's Corporation | Franchise rights reacquired from franchisees and affiliates | Amortized by the straight-line method, principally over 20 years. |
| Turner Broadcasting System, Inc. (Atlanta Braves) | Player contracts | Amortized and expensed as earned over the contracted service period. |
| The Walt Disney Company | Rights to the name, likeness, and portrait of Walt Disney | Amortized over 40 years. |

### An Example

To illustrate the amortization of an intangible asset, assume Kelley Corporation purchased a patent from an inventor for $720,000 on July 1, Year 6. The patent was originally granted to the inventor on January 1, Year 1; will provide benefits to Kelley until December 31, Year 13; and has no residual value. The entries to record the purchase on July 1 and amortization on December 31, Year 6, follow.

| | | | |
|---|---|---|---|
| July 1 | Patents | 720,000 | |
| | Cash | | 720,000 |
| | To record purchase of patent | | |
| Dec. 31 | Amortization Expense: Patents | 48,000 | |
| | Patents | | 48,000 |
| | To record six months of amortization expense | | |

Although the patent has a 17-year legal life, the service life to Kelley is only 90 months (July 1, Year 6 through December 31, Year 13). Because monthly amortization equals $8,000 ($720,000 ÷ 90), amortization of $48,000 is recorded. The Patents account would appear on the firm's December 31, Year 6, balance sheet at $672,000 ($720,000 − $48,000).

Kelley would continue to amortize the patent at the $8,000 monthly rate. Should the service life change, the rate is revised by following procedures similar to those shown for depreciation and depletion; specifically, the remaining unamortized cost, minus any residual value, is spread over the remaining service life.

## Chapter Review

### Learning Objectives—The Key Points

**1 Be familiar with the accounting for property, plant, and equipment costs incurred after asset acquisition.** Expenditures incurred after items of property, plant, and equipment are placed in service often prolong an asset's life, increase the quantity of services provided by an asset, or improve service quality. Such expenditures (e.g., additions and betterments) provide future benefits and should be capitalized in the accounts. If an expenditure does not meet at least one of the preceding criteria, it is expensed. A typical expense would be ordinary repairs and maintenance, which are incurred to maintain the normal operating condition of the asset.

**2 Be able to record gains and losses on the disposal of property, plant, and equipment.** When an asset is discarded or sold, depreciation must be updated to the date of disposal and the asset's cost and accompanying accumulated depreciation must be removed from the accounting records. Gains and losses are recognized by comparing the asset's book value with the proceeds received. A gain arises when the proceeds received exceed book value; a loss occurs in the opposite situation.

**3 Be able to account for exchanges and trade-ins for financial accounting and tax purposes.** When similar assets are exchanged or traded, gains and losses are derived by comparing book value against the old asset's fair market value. When fair value exceeds book value, an apparent gain results. However, the gain is not recognized, and the new asset is recorded at the book value of the old asset plus any cash paid or to be paid. In cases where the fair value of the asset given up is less than book value, a loss is recognized and the new asset is recorded at its invoice price. For federal tax purposes, neither gains nor losses are recorded on such transactions.

**4 Understand the use of subsidiary ledgers for property, plant, and equipment.** Businesses usually maintain separate asset and accumulated depreciation control accounts for each major category of property, plant, and equipment. These control accounts are linked to subsidiary ledgers that keep track of the details on the individual assets owned (e.g., cost, service life, location, where acquired, and so forth)—a procedure that helps to improve asset management and control. At the end of the accounting period, the balances in the control accounts should equal the sum of the balances in the subsidiary ledgers.

**5 Know how to account for natural resources and depletion.** Natural resources, such as oil and gas and mineral deposits, provide long-term benefits until they are totally consumed through extraction. Such assets are entered in the accounting records at cost, which includes amounts expended for exploration and development. Depletion involves the allocation of this cost to the resources extracted during the period. It is calculated by dividing cost, minus residual value, by the total estimated units in the resource deposit. This computation yields depletion per unit of output, which is multiplied by the number of units extracted to arrive at the depletion charge.

**6 Recognize the various types of intangible assets and their legal lives and understand the amortization process.** Long-term assets that lack physical existence and contribute to the earnings capability of a company are called intangibles. Examples of intangibles and accompanying legal lives are patents (17 years), copyrights (life of the creator plus 50 years), franchises, trademarks (10 years, with renewals possible), leasehold improvements, and goodwill. An intangible is gradually expensed via amortization over its legal life or service life, whichever is shorter. In no case may the amortization period exceed 40 years.

## Chapter Quiz

The five questions that follow relate to several issues raised in the chapter. Test your knowledge of the issues by selecting the best answer. (The answers appear on p. 403.)

1 Gamble, Inc., installed a heater in one of its earth moving vehicles at a cost of $1,200. The vehicle did not previously have a heater. Gamble should account for this cost:
  a as an intangible asset.
  b by reducing the Earth Moving Equipment account.
  c by reducing the Accumulated Depreciation account associated with the vehicle.
  d by increasing the book value of the vehicle.

**2** Gains and losses on the sale of a depreciable asset are determined by comparing:
a book value and the proceeds received.
b book value and the asset's cost.
c the proceeds received and the asset's cost.
d book value and the Accumulated Depreciation account.

**3** Solo Company spent $10 million to develop a mine having an estimated four million ounces of silver. During 19X7, 50,000 ounces were mined and processed; 5,000 ounces were sold at $8 per ounce. The 19X7 depletion *expense* is:
a $2.50 c $112,500.
b $12,500. d $125,000.

**4** On January 1, 19X1, Betty Ross purchased a patent for $102,000. The patent had an original legal life of 17 years at the date of issuance; only six of the 17 years remained when acquired. The expected service life to Ross is two years. The 19X1 amortization expense is:
a $6,000. c $51,000.
b $17,000. d $102,000.

**5** Goodwill:
a is an intangible asset that need not be amortized.
b is recorded by the seller of a business prior to the sale transaction.
c is an intangible asset that must be amortized over a period of 40 years or more.
d may be recorded by the buyer of a business when the acquisition is completed.

## Questions

**Q11-1** What factors should be considered to determine whether costs incurred after the acquisition of property, plant, and equipment are treated as capital expenditures or as revenue expenditures?

**Q11-2** Discuss the accounting treatment normally given to the following:
a Repairs
b Additions
c Betterments
d Assessments

**Q11-3** Why is it necessary to update the depreciation accounts when depreciable assets are sold, discarded, or exchanged?

**Q11-4** How is a gain or loss on the sale of an asset calculated?

**Q11-5** How are gains and losses on the exchange of similar items of property, plant, and equipment handled for financial reporting purposes? For federal income tax purposes?

**Q11-6** Why are control accounts and subsidiary ledgers used to account for property, plant, and equipment? What information does the subsidiary ledger provide?

**Q11-7** Why should an inventory of property, plant, and equipment be periodically taken and compared with the subsidiary ledger records?

**Q11-8** What costs are commonly capitalized in a natural resource account?

**Q11-9** Define "depletion."

**Q11-10** Explain how a portion of the depletion charge can be included in the current asset section of the balance sheet.

**Q11-11** How should a company determine the service life of a company-owned railroad track that is adjacent to a coal mine? Explain which depreciation method may be most appropriate for the railroad track.

**Q11-12** Discuss the treatment of research and development costs that are incurred in the development of a patent.

**Q11-13** What is a leasehold improvement?

**Q11-14** Define "goodwill" and explain how the cost of goodwill is determined.

**Q11-15** How is the amortization period of an intangible determined?

## Exercises

**E11-1** ***Costs incurred after asset acquisition***

The following expenditures were incurred by the Sanchez Company. Determine whether each item is a capital or a revenue expenditure.

a Spent $18,000 to equip the office building with energy-saving solar screens.
b Adjusted the brakes in three trucks, $150.
c Installed wind deflectors costing $8,000 on 10 trucks to improve fuel efficiency.
d Installed a new motor in truck no. 741, $6,700.
e Fixed the glove compartment in truck no. 744 at a cost of $15.
f Installed office partitions in facilities that the company is leasing from Midwest Property Management, $3,500.

**E11-2** ***Accounting for betterments***

Al's Bookstore purchased a building several years ago for $500,000. Straight-line depreciation has been used, assuming a residual value of $50,000 and a service life of 30 years. On June 30, 19XX, the end of Al's fiscal year, the building had a book value of $380,000. On July 1, 19XX, betterments (extraordinary repairs) were made to the building at a cost of $86,000. The betterments were expected to extend the service life of the building by four years, resulting in a remaining service life of 26 years.

a Compute the balance in the Accumulated Depreciation account on June 30, 19XX.
b To what account should the betterments be debited? Why?
c Compute the book value of the building after the betterments have been recorded.
d Calculate depreciation expense for the current and future fiscal years, assuming no change in the estimated residual value.

**E11-3** ***Journal entries for costs incurred after asset acquisition***

Coolidge Company had the following transactions:

a Paid $34,200 for a major overhaul of the firm's overhead conveyor system. The overhaul is expected to extend the system's life by five years.
b Paid $1,000 to install an extra gasoline tank on a heavy-duty truck.
c Paid $105 to have a microcomputer repaired.
d Paid $2,400 to the City of Townsend. The payment covered an assessment to have curbs installed on Coolidge's property.

Prepare the journal entries necessary to record the preceding transactions.

**E11-4** ***Asset disposals***

Lincoln Company purchased a truck on January 1, 19X3. The truck cost $90,000, had a service life of eight years, and had an estimated residual value of $30,000. Lincoln uses the straight-line method of depreciation. Consider the following *independent* cases:

a If Lincoln sold the truck on April 1, 19X6, for $58,000, compute the gain or loss on the sale.
b Assume that Lincoln's driver demolished the truck on July 1, 19X8. The company carries no insurance. If depreciation was last recorded on December 31,

19X7, prepare the necessary entries to (1) update depreciation and (2) remove the truck from the accounts.

**E11-5** ***Accounting for a trade-in***

Ryan purchased a sorting machine on January 1, 19X1, for $2,400. The machine had an estimated service life of five years and no residual value. On April 1, 19X4, Ryan acquired a new sorter. The invoice price of the new machine was $4,000, service life was estimated to be 10 years, and no residual value was anticipated. Ryan received a $1,200 trade-in allowance, which was equal to the old sorter's fair value, and paid the balance due in cash. Depreciation was last recorded on December 31, 19X3, by use of the straight-line method.

a Prepare Ryan's journal entry(ies) to record the trade-in.

b Repeat part (a), assuming the life of the old sorter was eight years (instead of five years).

**E11-6** ***Accounting for disposals and exchanges***

Evaluate the comments that follow as being True or False. If the comment is false, briefly explain why.

a Losses on the exchange of similar assets are recognized for financial reporting purposes.

b When a depreciable asset is sold, a gain results when the cash received exceeds the asset's book value.

c Financial accounting and tax accounting parallel each other when handling gains and losses related to exchanges of similar assets.

d A dealer's trade-in allowance is normally used for financial accounting purposes when valuing an asset surrendered in an exchange transaction.

e An exchange of similar assets has occurred and must be entered in the accounting records. If the old asset's book value is less than fair market value, the newly acquired asset is recorded at the invoice price.

**E11-7** ***Depletion***

Case Company recently incurred the following costs in developing a mine site:

| | |
|---|---:|
| Mine development | $6,400,000 |
| Rights | 300,000 |
| Exploration | 1,800,000 |
| | $8,500,000 |

The mine is expected to contain five million tons of ore. Case extracted and sold 410,000 tons during the first year of operation.

a Present the necessary journal entry to record depletion.

b Show the proper disclosure of the mining property upon conclusion of the first year of operation.

c What would you have done differently in part (a) if Case had extracted 410,000 tons but sold only 360,000? Be specific.

**E11-8** ***Depletion; revision of rates***

Kentucky Mining Company purchased a coal mine for $6.5 million in 19X1. An estimated 500,000 recoverable tons of coal existed in the mine at the time of purchase. Tons of coal mined and sold from 19X1–19X3 were as follows:

| | |
|---|---|
| 19X1 | 150,000 tons |
| 19X2 | 100,000 tons |
| 19X3 | 200,000 tons |

a Calculate depletion expense for 19X1, 19X2, and 19X3.

b Compute the book value of the mine at the end of 19X3.

c If a geologist retained by the company determined that 325,000 recoverable tons of coal remained in the mine at the beginning of 19X4, calculate the new depletion rate for 19X4 and future years.

**E11-9** ***Acquisition and amortization of intangibles***

On September 1, 19X1, Delta Company paid cash to acquire a patent for $100,000, a copyright for $75,000, a trademark for $42,000, and a franchise for $4,000. The patent expires in 19X9 but is expected to produce benefits for only five more years. The copyright has a service life of 10 years, and the trademark has an unlimited service life. The franchise allows Delta to be the exclusive sales agent for a new product for one year.

a Record the necessary journal entry for the acquisition of the intangibles on September 1, 19X1.

b Record amortization of the intangibles at the end of the company's fiscal year on August 31, 19X2.

**E11-10** ***Goodwill***

Rebecca Sprague is negotiating to buy the Lodi Crushers Football Club. The following information was extracted from the club's recent balance sheet:

| | |
|---|---|
| Cash | $ — |
| Accounts receivable | 19,000 |
| Prepaid expenses | 8,000 |
| Practice field | 25,000 |
| Equipment (net) | 7,000 |
| Franchise—Nebraska League | 10,000 |
| Accounts payable | 12,000 |
| Salaries payable | 53,000 |

Current values of the practice field and equipment are $35,000 and $3,000, respectively.

a If Sprague assumed the Crushers' liabilities and purchased the team for $22,000 cash, how much did she pay for goodwill?

b Prepare Sprague's entry to record the purchase of the team.

## Problems

### Series A

**P11-A1** ***Costs incurred after purchase; disposals***

Indiana Company had the following transactions and events during the year ended December 31, 19X2:

1 The company's land was assessed $6,000 because the city plans to install water and sewer lines to the property. The assessment was paid on January 1.

2 Sold office equipment on January 1 for $4,000 cash. The equipment cost $16,500 and had a book value of $6,100 as of December 31, 19X1.

3 On January 2, the company paid $24,000 for a new roof on its building. The new roof will extend the building's service life from an original estimate of 35 years to a total life of 40 years. The building originally cost $800,000, has a residual value of $100,000, and had accumulated depreciation at the beginning of 19X2 of $400,000. Straight-line depreciation is being used.

4 Repaired truck no. 131 on June 1 for $150. The accounting records revealed that the truck initially cost $21,000 and had accumulated depreciation at the beginning of 19X2 of $4,200. Depreciation is based on a five-year service life and zero residual value. The straight-line depreciation method has been used.

5 Added an air-conditioning unit to truck no. 131 on July 1. The unit cost $1,400, has no estimated residual value, and will be depreciated by the straight-line

method. The air conditioner will provide benefits to the company over the remaining life of the truck.

6 Discarded some old machinery on November 30 at the local landfill. Subsidiary records showed that the machinery cost $4,150 and had accumulated depreciation of $3,400 at the beginning of the year. The machinery had been fully depreciated down to a residual value of $750 by the double-declining balance method.

**Instructions**

a Prepare journal entries to record Indiana's transactions and events. Depreciation was last recorded on December 31, 19X1.

b Determine depreciation expense for the year ended December 31, 19X2, for the building and truck no. 131.

**P11-A2** ***Journal entries for disposals and exchanges***

Metro Transit purchased a specialized van on January 1, 19X1, to transport handicapped persons around the city. The van cost $40,000, had an estimated service life of seven years, and a residual value of $5,000. The company uses the straight-line depreciation method, with depreciation last recorded on December 31, 19X3.

**Instructions**

a The van was sold for cash on April 1, 19X4. Prepare the required journal entry to update depreciation and then record the sale, assuming a sales price of:
(1) $30,700.
(2) $17,500.

b Independent of part (a), assume the van was exchanged on January 1, 19X4, for a similar van having a $30,000 invoice price. Prepare the required journal entry to record the exchange if the old van had a fair market value of:
(1) $26,000 and Metro gave the dealer $4,000 cash.
(2) $22,000 and Metro gave the dealer $8,000 cash.

c Referring to cases (1) and (2) of part (b), will the new van have the same recorded cost for both financial reporting and federal income tax purposes? Briefly explain.

**P11-A3** ***Disposals and exchanges; analysis***

Third Avenue Manufacturing disposed of five assets during the 19X2 fiscal year. Information pertaining to these assets follows.

| *Asset* | *Cost* | *Accumulated Depreciation* | *Cash Received (Paid)* | *Fair Market Value on Date of Disposal* |
|---|---|---|---|---|
| Furniture | $ 2,800 | $ 2,600 | $ — | $ — |
| Computer | 10,400 | 7,100 | 3,800 | 3,800 |
| Truck | 15,500 | 6,800 | (7,800) | 9,300 |
| Building | 86,700 | 15,400 | 95,000 | 95,000 |
| Machine | 37,500 | 22,800 | (18,000) | 14,000 |

A review of the accounting records revealed the following additional information:

- *Furniture*—The furniture was discarded at a local landfill.
- *Computer*—The computer was sold to Micromatic Systems, one of Third Avenue's suppliers.
- *Truck*—The truck was exchanged for a new truck that had an invoice price of $17,100.
- *Building*—The building was destroyed by fire; insurance proceeds, which were based on market value, amounted to $95,000.

- *Machine*—The company acquired a new machine having a $42,000 invoice price. The machinery dealer took Third Avenue's old machine in trade along with $18,000 cash and a $10,000 note payable.

The company's accountant is in the process of computing net income for 19X2. She has determined that income before any gains and losses from asset disposals amounts to $34,800.

**Instructions**

a Compute Third Avenue's income after considering gains and losses on the five asset disposals.

b Suppose (1) the machine's fair market value amounted to $15,100 rather than $14,000 and (2) the invoice price of the new machine was $43,100. In view of this new data, will your answer in part (a) increase or decrease? By how much?

**P11-A4** ***Depletion and natural resources***

The Aztec Mining Company purchased a tract of land, together with mineral rights, for $155,000. After incurring exploration costs of $125,000 and legal fees of $20,000, Aztec learned that 140,000 tons of high-grade ore could be extracted from the site. The company estimates that production will be 20,000 tons each year. The mining site is anticipated to have a residual value of $20,000 since the land can be used for farming after all mining operations have ceased.

Aztec plans to construct the necessary mining structures (buildings, sheds, and bunkhouses) on the site for $154,000. According to the contractor, the structures will have a life of 20 years, with no residual value; they will be abandoned when production ceases. Finally, machinery and equipment must be acquired that costs $100,000, has a life of 10 years, and has a residual value of $10,000. All equipment will be moved to other company properties after the mine site is closed.

**Instructions**

a Determine the company's depletion and depreciation expense for each year the mine is anticipated to operate. Aztec will depreciate the structures by the units-of-output method and the machinery and equipment by the straight-line method.

b Assume that during the first year, 18,000 tons of ore were extracted from the mine. If sales were only 12,000 tons, calculate the total depletion charge and explain how it is treated in the financial statements.

c Assume that the following production has been attained: Year 1, 18,000 tons; Year 2, 18,000 tons; Year 3, 25,000 tons; Year 4, 15,000 tons; and Year 5, 30,000 tons. According to a new report received from the company geologist, 100,000 tons of ore remain in the mine at the start of Year 6. Calculate the depletion charge per ton on future production.

**P11-A5** ***Intangibles: Acquisition cost and amortization***

Selected 19X1 transactions of the El Paso Company follow.

Jan. 1 Acquired a patent to a new type of sprayer that was developed in the company's research laboratory. Paid $50,000 of related costs, as follows: legal and filing fees, $3,400; research and development expenditures, $46,600. The patent has an estimated service life equal to its legal life.

Apr. 1 Purchased the patent rights for $24,000 to a product known as Wham. The patent has a remaining legal life of eight years and should provide benefits to El Paso for three years.

July 1 Redecorated facilities that the company is leasing from Senator Enterprises. El Paso's lease expires on July 1, 19X5; redecorating costs amounted to $30,000.

Sept. 1 Acquired the copyright to a play from the estate of the play's author for $7,800 cash. The author died 30 years ago; El Paso should receive benefits from the copyright for a five-year period.

Oct. 1 Acquired a perpetual franchise to promote cellular telephones in exchange for a $32,000 note payable. Similar franchises are currently selling for $100,000.

Dec. 1 Registered a new trademark with the federal government; paid legal, filing, and design costs amounting to $48,000.

**Instructions**

a Prepare journal entries to record the preceding transactions.
b Compute El Paso's amortization expense for the year ended December 31, 19X1.
c Prepare a compound (combined) entry to amortize the intangibles for *19X2*.

**P11-A6** ***Goodwill***

After two years of negotiating between the owners, Haswell Enterprises agreed to purchase Estronia Company for $200,000. Key balance sheet data of Estronia on November 1, 19XX, the date of acquisition, follow.

| | |
|---|---|
| Cash | $ 45,000 |
| Accounts receivable | 26,400 |
| Inventories | 82,000 |
| Prepaid expenses | 800 |
| Land | 80,000 |
| Building | 100,000 |
| Equipment | 20,000 |
| Franchise | 800 |
| Accounts payable | 61,000 |
| Salaries payable | 32,000 |
| Mortgage payable | 43,000 |

A probe of Estronia's records revealed the following:

1 The books were last closed on May 1, 19XX, the end of the company's accounting year. No adjustments have been made since that time.
2 The inventories include $18,000 of goods that are obsolete and will be given away to charity.
3 The receivables are overstated by $4,000.
4 Prepaid expenses of $600 have expired.
5 Current market values of property, plant, and equipment are as follows:

| | |
|---|---|
| Land | $100,000 |
| Building | 85,000 |
| Equipment | 10,000 |

6 The franchise will render no future benefits to Haswell.
7 Salaries payable are understated by $5,000 because of a clerical error.

**Instructions**

a Calculate the amount Haswell paid for goodwill in the acquisition of Estronia.
b Prepare Haswell's journal entry to record the purchase of Estronia. Haswell paid $65,000 cash and issued a short-term note payable for the remaining balance.
c Generally speaking, what gives rise to goodwill?

## Series B

**P11-B1** ***Cost incurred after purchase; disposals***

Centerline Company had the following transactions and events during the year ended December 31, 19X4:

1 Discarded office furniture on January 1 at the local landfill. Subsidiary records showed that the furniture cost $400 and had accumulated depreciation of $350 at the end of 19X3. The furniture has been fully depreciated down to a residual value of $50 by the double-declining balance method.
2 On January 1, the company paid $46,000 for a new roof on its building. The new roof will extend the building's service life from an original estimate of 25 years to a total life of 30 years. The building originally cost $800,000, has a residual value of $300,000, and had accumulated depreciation at the end of 19X3 of $200,000. Straight-line depreciation is being used.
3 Sold store equipment on January 1 for $4,000 cash. The equipment cost $12,000 and had a book value of $5,000 as of December 31, 19X3.
4 Received a $6,480 land assessment because the city plans to install water and sewer lines to the property. The assessment was paid on March 1.
5 Repaired truck no. 10 on March 1 for $75. The accounting records revealed that the truck initially cost $28,000 and had accumulated depreciation at the beginning of 19X4 of $7,000. Depreciation is based on a four-year service life and zero residual value. The straight-line depreciation method has been used.
6 Added a radio unit to truck no. 10 on July 1. The unit cost $600, has no estimated residual value, and will be depreciated by the straight-line method. The radio will provide benefits to the company over the remaining life of the truck.

**Instructions**

a Prepare journal entries to record Centerline's transactions and events. Depreciation was last recorded on December 31, 19X3.
b Determine depreciation expense for the year ended December 31, 19X4, for the building and truck no. 10.

**P11-B2** ***Journal entries for disposals and exchanges***
New York Law purchased a specialized computer on January 1, 19X1, to handle its law office needs. The computer cost $32,000, had an estimated service life of five years, and a residual value of $4,000. The practice uses the straight-line depreciation method, with depreciation last recorded on December 31, 19X2.

**Instructions**

a The computer was sold for cash on October 1, 19X3. Prepare the required journal entry to update depreciation and then record the sale, assuming a sales price of:
(1) $10,400.
(2) $19,800.
b Independent of part (a), assume the computer was exchanged on January 1, 19X3, for a similar computer having a $45,000 invoice price. Prepare the required journal entry to record the exchange if the old computer had a fair market value of:
(1) $9,000 and New York Law gave the dealer $36,000 cash.
(2) $24,000 and New York Law gave the dealer $21,000 cash.
c Referring to cases (1) and (2) of part (b), will the new computer have the same recorded cost for both financial reporting and federal income tax purposes? Briefly explain.

**P11-B3** ***Disposals and exchanges; analysis***
Ocean Enterprises, Inc., disposed of five assets during the 19X7 fiscal year. Information pertaining to these assets follows.

| Asset | Cost | Accumulated Depreciation | Cash Received (Paid) | Fair Market Value on Date of Disposal |
|---|---|---|---|---|
| Freezer | $ 5,000 | $ 3,600 | $ 1,200 | $ 1,200 |
| Furniture | 4,000 | 4,000 | — | — |
| Auto | 21,000 | 9,000 | (8,200) | 8,100 |
| Building | 99,000 | 38,000 | 77,000 | 77,000 |
| Machine | 75,000 | 46,600 | (36,000) | 30,000 |

A review of the accounting records revealed the following additional information:

- *Freezer*—The freezer was sold to Romar Manufacturing, one of Ocean's customers.
- *Furniture*—The furniture was donated to an American Veterans group.
- *Auto*—The auto was exchanged for a new auto that had an invoice price of $16,300.
- *Building*—The building was destroyed by an earthquake; insurance proceeds, which were based on market value, amounted to $77,000.
- *Machine*—The company acquired a new machine having an $84,000 invoice price. The machinery dealer took Ocean's old machine in trade along with $36,000 cash and an $18,000 note payable.

The company's accountant is in the process of computing net income for 19X7. He has determined that income before any gains and losses from asset disposals amounts to $70,000.

**Instructions**

a Compute Ocean's income after considering gains and losses on the five asset disposals.

b Suppose (1) the auto's fair market value amounted to $13,000 rather than $8,100 and (2) the invoice price of the new auto was $21,200. In view of this new data, will your answer in part (a) increase or decrease? By how much?

**P11-B4** ***Depletion and natural resources***

The Creekside Coal Company purchased a tract of land, together with mineral rights, for $825,000. After incurring exploration costs of $675,000 and legal fees of $150,000, Creekside learned that 2.2 million tons of coal could be extracted from the site. The company estimates that production will be 200,000 tons during the first year and 125,000 tons each year thereafter. The mining site is estimated to have a residual value of $330,000.

Creekside plans to construct the necessary mining structures (buildings, sheds, and so on) on the site for $770,000. According to the contractor, the structures have a life of 20 years, with no residual value. The company does not intend to move the structures when production ceases. Finally, machinery and equipment must be acquired that costs $880,000, has a life of 20 years, and has a residual value of $20,000. The equipment will be moved to other company properties after the mine site is closed.

**Instructions**

a Determine the company's depletion and depreciation expense for each year the mine is anticipated to operate. Creekside will depreciate the structures by the units-of-output method and the machinery and equipment by the straight-line method.

b Assume that during the first year, 180,000 tons of coal were extracted from the mine. If sales were only 160,000 tons, calculate the total depletion charge and explain how it is treated in the financial statements.

c Assume that the following production has been attained: Year 1, 180,000 tons; Year 2, 170,000 tons; Year 3, 150,000 tons; Year 4, 110,000 tons; and Year 5, 90,000 tons. According to a new report received from the company geologist, one million tons of coal remain in the mine at the start of Year 6. Calculate the depletion charge per ton on future production.

**P11-B5** ***Intangibles: Acquisition cost and amortization***

Selected 19X3 transactions of the San Jose Company follow.

Jan. 1 Purchased the patent rights for $12,000 for a product known as Servo. The patent has a remaining legal life of 10 years and should provide benefits to San Jose for two years.

Apr. 1 Acquired a patent to a new type of boxing glove that was developed in the company's research department. Paid $86,700 of related costs, as follows: legal and filing fees, $1,700; research and development expenditures, $85,000. The patent has an estimated service life equal to its legal life.

July 1 Installed wall partitions in a facility that the company is leasing from Iowa Enterprises. San Jose's lease expires on December 31, 19X6; the partitions cost $14,000.

Aug. 1 Acquired a perpetual franchise to promote sporting events within a 100-mile radius of the city in exchange for a $4,800 note payable. Similar franchises are currently selling for $9,000.

Sept. 1 Acquired the copyright to a play from the estate of the play's author for $3,600 cash. The author died 10 years ago; San Jose should receive benefits from the copyright for a three-year period.

Oct. 1 Registered a new trademark with the federal government; paid legal, filing, and design costs amounting to $10,000.

**Instructions**

a Prepare journal entries to record the preceding transactions.

b Compute San Jose's amortization expense for the year ended December 31, 19X3.

c Prepare a compound (combined) entry to amortize the intangibles for *19X4*.

**P11-B6** ***Goodwill***

After three years of negotiating between the owners, Michael English agreed to purchase Sports Gear for $40,000. Key balance sheet data of Sports Gear on December 1, 19XX, the date of acquisition, follow.

| | |
|---|---|
| Cash | $ 3,000 |
| Accounts receivable | 38,000 |
| Inventories | 10,000 |
| Prepaid expenses | 1,000 |
| Building | 60,000 |
| Equipment | 11,000 |
| Patent | 40,000 |
| Accounts payable | 17,000 |
| Bank loan payable | 55,000 |

A probe of Sports Gear's records revealed the following:

1 The books were last closed on June 30, 19XX, the end of the company's accounting year. No adjustments have been made since that time.

2 The inventories include $2,000 of products that are defective and must be discarded.

3 Prepaid expenses of $500 have expired.

4 Current market values of the building and equipment are: building, $28,000; equipment, $4,000.
5 The patent, purchased four years ago, is related to a new type of stop watch. The patent's remaining legal life is 10 years; English believes it is worthless.
6 Accounts payable is overstated by $900 because of a clerical error.

**Instructions**

a Calculate the amount English paid for goodwill in the acquisition of Sports Gear.
b Prepare English's journal entry to record the purchase of Sports Gear. Assume that English paid $10,000 cash and issued a short-term note payable for the remaining balance.
c Should the goodwill be amortized? Why?

## Beyond the Basics

**BB11-1** ***Property, plant, and equipment errors***
Ace Compressor depreciates machinery by the straight-line method. The following information was found in the accounting records pertaining to machine T607:

*Machinery—T607*

| Debit | | Credit | |
|---|---|---|---|
| 19XX | | 19XX | |
| 1/3 Purchase | 50,000 | 10/2 Proceeds from sale | 41,300 |
| 1/5 Installation | 3,000 | | |
| 7/4 Miscellaneous repairs | 2,000 | | |

Machine T607 had an estimated service life of five years and a $10,000 residual value. The machine was sold for $41,300 on October 2, 19XX, because of a consolidation of operations. The following entry was made:

| | | |
|---|---|---|
| Cash | 41,300 | |
| Machinery | | 41,300 |
| Disposal of machine T607 | | |

**Instructions**

a Present all necessary journal entries to correct the accounts as of December 31, 19XX. Assume the books have not been closed.
b Discuss the impact on the financial statements, both current and future, of the incorrect capitalization of a revenue expenditure.

**BB11-2** ***Patent accounting; loan decision***
Dudley Finfrock is the assistant vice-president for commercial lending of the Maplewood National Bank. He has recently been approached by two aggressive companies for business loans. Both companies are engaged in high-technology product development and sales, but each company has used a different approach to achieve its ultimate profit objective.

Linden Electronics is run by two ex-employees of Woodhaven Semiconductor: Judy Brown and Stan Hall. Brown has an orientation toward research; Hall's specialty is sales. With an initial capital of $150,000 the two partners have developed many valuable products. Over $80,000 has been spent on research and development, and from this effort three patents have been obtained. (Legal costs and filing fees connected with the patents were negligible because Linden's attorney is a family relative.) Advertising and sales promotion costs have consumed the remaining funds.

Rabway Electronics is also managed by two bright entrepreneurs: Harry Scott and Jack Monroe. Scott and Monroe were finance majors at the local university and possess minimal knowledge of electronics and sales. To establish a viable company, Rabway acquired existing patents from a California firm for $100,000. To generate sales, Scott and Monroe also purchased a franchise for $40,000 to sell a product similar to their own. In this manner the two products could be marketed together. Finally, Rabway spent $10,000 for legal fees related to the patents and franchise.

In the first few years of business Linden operated at a net loss, while Rabway has generated impressive profits. A comparison of the financial statements and other operating information revealed that sales and production costs of the two companies were virtually identical. In addition, their products were very similar.

**Instructions**

a Explain the probable cause behind Linden's net losses and Rabway's profits.
b If you were in Dudley's position, would you grant a loan to either of the firms? What factors should be considered?

## Answers to Chapter Quiz

**1** d

**2** a

**3** b ($10 million ÷ 4 million ounces = $2.50 per ounce; 5,000 ounces × $2.50 = $12,500)

**4** c ($102,000 ÷ 2 years = $51,000)

**5** d

# Current Liabilities and Payroll

CHAPTER 12

## Learning Objectives

After reading this chapter you should:

1 Be familiar with the occurrence of and accounting for typical current liabilities of a business.

2 Understand how the accounting treatment of notes payable differs when interest is included in the face value of a note and when interest is recorded separately.

3 Recognize contingent liabilities and discern when they should be recorded in the accounts and when footnote disclosure is appropriate.

4 Understand accounting for warranty costs.

5 Be familiar with payroll accounting and the treatment of payroll taxes.

The five preceding chapters have presented various valuation and income determination issues related to current and long-term assets. We now turn our attention to another important element of the fundamental accounting equation: liabilities. **Liabilities** are obligations that (1) have arisen from past transactions or events and (2) are payable in cash, other assets, or services. The measurement and disclosure of liabilities in the financial statements are extremely important, because future cash outlays or services are involved. Many suppliers, for example, refuse to grant credit to businesses that have high levels of liabilities for fear of nonpayment. Similarly, most investors shy away from companies heavily burdened by debt because of the risk involved. Substantial debt payments are often accompanied by large outlays for interest, thus reducing an investor's chance of receiving dividends. Adding to this problem is the fact that the firm's cash position may be extremely weak in periods of a softening economy.

Be aware that a *commitment* for goods and services is not recognized in the accounting records as a liability. For instance, Ford Motor may sign a three-year labor contract with its hourly personnel. The contract represents a mutual agreement for a future transaction: wages will be paid at the time a service is provided. Note that upon contract signing, Ford's assets have not changed nor does the company owe specific resources to its employees. Consistent with the definition of a liability—an obligation that arises from *past* transactions or events—the contract is not entered into the accounts and fails to appear on the balance sheet of the entity. Such amounts are sometimes disclosed in the footnotes that accompany the financial statements.

Earlier in the text we noted that liabilities are classified as either current or long-term, depending on the due date (or dates). We will discuss current liabilities in this chapter and long-term obligations in Chapter 17.

## Current Liabilities

OBJECTIVE 1
Be familiar with the occurrence of and accounting for typical current liabilities of a business.

**Current liabilities** are debts or obligations that will be paid within one year or the operating cycle, whichever is longer. Payment of current liabilities involves the use of current assets (usually cash) or, on occasion, the creation of another current liability. For example, an account payable could be settled by issuing a short-term interest-bearing note to the creditor.

Current liabilities are reported on the balance sheet at the amount necessary to settle the obligation. Naturally, it is imperative that all debts and obligations be disclosed. The failure to record a current liability not only understates total liabilities but affects assets or expenses as well. Because management may deliberately try to boost net income by hiding unpaid bills, accountants must take great care in their recognition of an entity's short-term debts.

Typical current liabilities include the following:

1. Accounts payable
2. Prepayments (advances) by customers
3. Amounts collected for and payable to third parties
4. The portion of long-term debt due within one year or the operating cycle, whichever is longer
5. Accrued liabilities for expenses incurred but not yet paid
6. Notes payable to banks and other parties
7. Contingent liabilities

HIGHLIGHT

# Freebies Create a Growing Liability

Question: What do the white sandy beaches of Hawaii, the Eiffel Tower in Paris, and San Francisco cable cars have in common? Give up? A careful study will reveal that each is a popular "must see" when it comes to tourists and their vacations. All are also helping to create an increasing liability for airlines.

Early in the 1980s, most large air carriers established frequent-flier programs to help attract the business traveler as a steady customer. Such programs keep track of the miles flown by each member, occasionally doubling or tripling the miles on a flight when certain conditions are met. When a stipulated number of miles have been accumulated, the frequent flier is eligible for a host of awards that range from free trips to discounts on hotels and rental cars. [1]

The awards were insignificant to the airlines when the programs first started, but time and "mileage maniacs" have brought change. Mileage maniacs are people who literally plan their lives to win awards. One such individual, Howard Landau, a tire dealer from New Jersey, is addicted to squeezing the most miles out of the cheapest flights possible. Landau notes, "It has become an obsession, a compulsion, with me. I live, eat, and breathe the United Airlines Mileage Plus Program." So much so that he recently set up a cross-country trip that will net him 32,000 miles in three days. He will make 10 stops and pay a total of $368 for his tickets. Landau has racked up in excess of 200,000 miles, though he has actually flown only 50,551. [2]

Currently, frequent-flier programs are so popular that airlines owe passengers about 25 billion miles of free travel. This amounts to an industry-wide liability of about $500 million, based on the current redemption rates of 30% of all miles flown. If all miles earned were cashed in, it would cost the airlines $1.7 billion. The airlines, however, see a much smaller liability—not the "value" of the tickets but rather the $8 cost to feed and transport a passenger in an otherwise empty seat. Further, the airlines record a liability only when a passenger has flown enough miles (30,000 to 50,000) to claim a free ticket.

The accounting profession is concerned about this, as evidenced by the issuance of suggested guidelines to be followed when accounting for and measuring this gigantic giveaway to attract loyal clientele. Observes the head of the task force to draft the guidelines, "You can no longer say that the revenue process is substantially complete when the ticket is sold. Passengers are purchasing tickets with the expectation of a free flight, and [airlines] have to account for that liability." [3]

Figures such as those just cited are not surprising; they, in turn, have prompted the airlines to limit awards or to offer incentives for program participants to redeem awards in off-peak periods. Nevertheless, ask almost any airline marketing executive and he or she will generally agree that frequent-flier programs are a bonanza. Free trips to exotic locations cannot be beat as an incentive to attract the business traveler, who is often forced to travel on a full fare, nondiscounted ticket. The jury is still out, however, for the airlines' finance and accounting departments.

SOURCES: Adapted from "Accounting for an Albatross," *Forbes*, June 13, 1988, p. 62 [3]; "Frequent-Flier Plans Become Obsessions," *The Wall Street Journal*, September 6, 1988, p. 31 [2]; and "New Airline Figures Show Unused Awards Mounting," *The Wall Street Journal*, July 15, 1987, p. 25 [1]. The first article listed is reprinted by permission of *Forbes* magazine, © Forbes Inc., 1988.

## Accounts Payable

**Accounts payable,** sometimes called *trade accounts payable,* represent amounts owed to suppliers for the purchase of goods or services. The creation and control of these short-term obligations were discussed in Chapters 5 and 6.

Most accounting systems are capable of recording trade payables when goods and services are acquired or rendered. More often than not, however, the payable is recorded when an invoice is received from the supplier. Unfortunately, delays, timing differences, and errors frequently permeate the process. For example, the invoice may sit in an in-basket for a few days awaiting processing. Or goods purchased under terms of F.O.B. shipping point may still be in transit at the end of the period. Although the goods legally belong to the purchaser because of the passage of title, the liability (and inventory) may be erroneously overlooked. After all, there would be no paperwork documenting the goods' arrival at the warehouse, and there is a strong possibility that the purchaser has yet to be invoiced. Because of these and other problems, the accountant must pay particular attention to transactions that occur at the beginning and end of an accounting period. By so doing, the purchases of goods and services (and their associated liabilities) will be correctly entered in the records.

## Prepayments (Advances) by Customers

Businesses often receive **prepayments,** or advances, from customers. Insurance companies collect premiums; publishers sell magazine subscriptions; stores issue gift certificates; and transportation firms sell tickets and tokens before their service is delivered. These amounts, frequently termed *unearned revenues* or *deferred revenues,* represent liabilities to the recipient because goods or services are owed in return. You were originally introduced to unearned revenues in Chapter 3 and may find a review of this earlier material helpful.

The balance sheet should report the amount of goods and services owed as of the statement's date. As the obligations are settled, the prepayments are reduced and increased revenues are reported on the income statement. Prepayments for most businesses are relatively modest in amount. A review of recent corporate annual reports found several exceptions (and some sizable ones!), as shown in Exhibit 12-1.

**Exhibit 12-1**
**Examples of Customer Prepayments**

| *Organization* | *Prepayment Form* | *Amount (in Thousands)* | *Percentage of Total Current Liabilities* |
|---|---|---|---|
| Sears, Roebuck and Co. | Unearned maintenance agreement income | $930,400 | 9.4% |
| Unisys Corporation | Customers' deposits and prepayments | 308,700 | 9.0 |
| Delta Air Lines | Advance ticket sales | 504,083 | 36.2 |
| Carnival Cruise Lines | Cruise deposits | 69,438 | 31.4 |

## Collections for Third Parties

In the normal course of business, organizations often collect money from customers and employees that is payable to others. Retailers, for instance, accumulate sales tax from customers when goods are sold. Subsequently, the monies collected are remitted to the proper governmental authority. Similarly, companies sometimes become involved in United Way or disaster relief activities, receiving funds that are ultimately disbursed to various social service agencies. And, as presented later in this chapter, payroll deductions are customarily made from employee wages for taxes and other items, which must be forwarded to third parties.

Collections for third parties, such as those just mentioned, are recognized as current liabilities until cash is disbursed to the proper authority. To illustrate the necessary accounting, assume that Yorktown Candle Shoppe sells $1,000 of merchandise on account in a state having a 5% sales tax. The entry to record the sale follows.

| | | |
|---|---|---|
| Accounts Receivable | 1,050 | |
| Sales | | 1,000 |
| Sales Taxes Payable | | 50 |
| To record sale and related sales tax | | |

A liability of $50 ($1,000 × 0.05) is established for the sales tax, which Yorktown now owes to the state treasury. When the tax is remitted, Sales Taxes Payable will be debited and Cash will be credited. The liability is thus eliminated. Other third-party collections are handled in a similar manner.

## Current Portion of Long-term Debt

As we noted, long-term liabilities will be discussed at length in a later chapter. At this point, however, it is important to understand that the portion of long-term debt due within one year or the normal operating cycle, whichever is longer, is reported as a current liability. For example, suppose that a company borrowed $200,000 via a long-term loan. If $30,000 is payable within the next 12 months, the appropriate balance sheet disclosure would be as follows:

| | | |
|---|---|---|
| Current liabilities | | |
| Current portion of long-term debt | | $ 30,000 |
| | | |
| Long-term liabilities | | |
| Loan payable | $200,000 | |
| Less: Balance due currently | 30,000 | 170,000 |

Treatment as a current liability presumes that the short-term portion will be liquidated by the use of current assets or by the creation of other current liabilities. If not, such amounts remain classified as long-term liabilities until paid or refinanced.

## Accrued Liabilities

**Accrued liabilities,** often called accrued expenses, were also introduced in Chapter 3. Under the accrual basis of accounting, expenses are matched against revenues in the period when incurred. This practice generally results in the recognition of some unpaid expenses and calls for the placement of accrued liabilities on the balance sheet. Examples of accrued liabilities include salaries and wages, vacation pay, income taxes (both federal and state), local property taxes, and interest. To demonstrate the required accounting, we now present illustrations that relate to salaries and vacation pay.

### Accrued Salaries

Accrued salaries and wages result when a reporting period ends in the midst of a payroll period. For example, suppose that Rosenthal Company has a five-day workweek and all employees are paid on Friday. Also assume that the end of the annual accounting period, November 30, falls on Thursday. Although employees will not be compensated until December 1, Rosenthal must accrue payroll expense on November 30 for the work performed from Monday through Thursday. In so doing, revenue and expense for the period just ended will be correctly matched and current liabilities will be properly recorded. If salaries total $10,500 per day, the adjusting entry is as follows:

| | | |
|---|---|---|
| Salaries Expense | 42,000 | |
| Salaries Payable | | 42,000 |
| To accrue four days of salaries at $10,500 per day* | | |

* Payroll taxes should also be accrued at this time.

### Accrued Vacation Pay

Many businesses provide paid vacations for their employees. By working 50 weeks throughout the year, for instance, a worker may earn two weeks of paid time-off. From the employer's viewpoint, such fringe benefit plans increase the total cost of employee service—in this particular case by 4% of wage cost (2 ÷ 50).

Proper accounting treatment requires that the cost of (and obligation for) paid vacations be spread over the entire year so that each reporting period receives an equal share of expense. Imagine the total compensation expense of July and August for many companies if this practice were not followed. The popularity of summer vacations could very well result in depressed earnings for the third calendar quarter. Because the paid time-off is earned by employees working *throughout the year,* such amounts should be accrued as services are performed.

To illustrate, assume that Prestonwood Company has a two-week paid vacation plan and monthly salaries of $90,000. In view of personnel turnover, the firm estimates that only 60% of the employees will be entitled to this fringe benefit. Prestonwood's monthly vacation pay accrual will amount to $2,160 ($90,000 × 0.04 × 0.60) and is recorded by the following journal entry:

| | | |
|---|---|---|
| Vacation Pay Expense | 2,160 | |
| Accrued Vacation Pay | | 2,160 |
| To record estimated vacation pay expense | | |

The Accrued Vacation Pay account is disclosed in the current liability section of the balance sheet and is reduced when actual vacations are taken. For example, assume that Prestonwood now disburses $400 to an employee during her paid time-off. The disbursement is recorded as a debit to Accrued Vacation Pay and a credit to Cash.

## Notes Payable

Short-term notes have many uses in the business world. Notes payable are often employed to finance purchases of merchandise, equipment, real estate, and other similar assets. In addition, notes can be used to secure short-term borrowings from banks. General Mills, for instance, recently reported notes payable to banks of $85 million on its year-end balance sheet. Such temporary use of bank credit for periods of less than one year is commonplace and serves as a vital source of funds for many businesses.

Notes payable are also issued at the request of creditors when a firm (or individual) is past due in the payment of an account payable. The note is simply substituted for the account payable on the books of the issuing entity. A creditor prefers a note to a delinquent open account; should the issuer fail to pay the debt on schedule, a signed note provides better security if legal remedies are necessary.

## Accounting for Notes Payable

**OBJECTIVE 2**
**Understand how the accounting treatment of notes payable differs when interest is included in the face value of a note and when interest is recorded separately.**

To illustrate the proper accounting for notes payable, assume that Corsica Trading Corporation borrowed $80,000 from the Mercantile National Bank on June 3 by signing the obligation shown in Exhibit 12-2. The journal entry to record the receipt of funds and issuance of the note follows.

| | | |
|---|---|---|
| Cash | 80,000 | |
| Notes Payable | | 80,000 |
| To record note payable to bank; 180 days at 15% | | |

Observe that the face value of the note is equal to the amount borrowed and that no interest expense is recorded on the date of issue. Interest will be incurred on a daily basis over the term of the loan.

Next, assume that Corsica's fiscal year ends on October 31. Because the note was issued on June 3 and does not mature until November 30, total interest expense must be apportioned between two accounting periods. As of October 31, the obligation has been outstanding for 150 days, requiring the following adjusting entry:

| | | |
|---|---|---|
| Interest Expense | 5,000 | |
| Interest Payable | | 5,000 |
| To accrue interest for 150 days: $\$80{,}000 \times 0.15 \times \frac{150}{360}$ | | |

Corsica's balance sheet disclosure would therefore appear as shown below.

| | | |
|---|---|---|
| Current liabilities | | |
| Notes payable | $80,000 | |
| Interest payable | 5,000 | $85,000 |

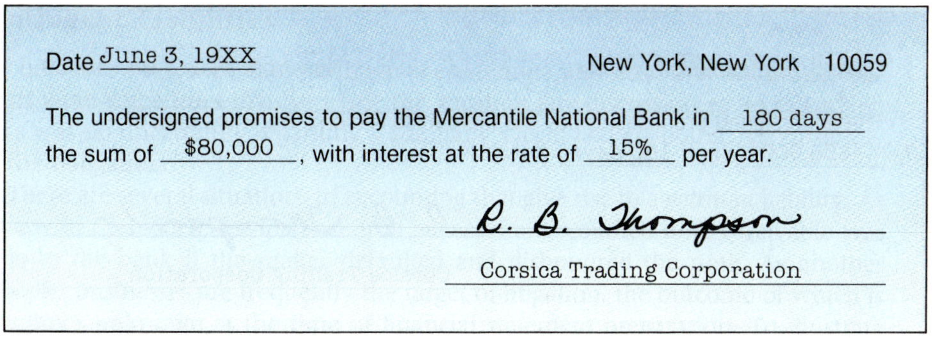
Date June 3, 19XX New York, New York 10059

The undersigned promises to pay the Mercantile National Bank in 180 days the sum of $80,000, with interest at the rate of 15% per year.

R. B. Thompson

Corsica Trading Corporation

**Exhibit 12-2**
**Example of Note Payable**

## Social Security Taxes (FICA)

The **Federal Insurance Contributions Act (FICA),** commonly called Social Security, provides retirement, financial, and medical benefits to the aged, disabled, widows, and orphans. Employers are required to withhold a portion of each employee's gross earnings to help fund these programs. Additionally, the employer must match the employee's contribution. As an example, assume that Kathy Durham earns \$24,000 and that all of the earnings are subject to FICA taxes of 7.5%. Durham will have \$1,800 (\$24,000 × 0.075) withheld from her paychecks. A total of \$3,600 will ultimately be remitted to the government, composed of Durham's contribution and a matching amount by her employer (\$1,800 × 2 = \$3,600).

In recent years both the amount of earnings subject to FICA tax (termed the FICA base) and the tax rate have increased dramatically. At the inception of Social Security in 1937, for example, the first \$3,000 of earnings was taxed at a rate of 1%, resulting in a maximum employee contribution of \$30. At the time of this writing, the \$30 amount had grown to \$3,604.80.

Changes in both the FICA base and tax rate have been made over the years to meet increased operating costs of the Social Security system. These changes, however, do not alter the fundamental accounting treatment for this tax. Illustrations throughout the remainder of the chapter will use an assumed rate of 7.5% for both the employee and the employer, computed on an earnings base of \$45,000.

## Federal, State, and City Income Taxes

Employers must also withhold a portion of an employee's gross earnings to satisfy federal income tax laws and the laws of many states and local municipalities. These **income tax withholdings** are later submitted to the appropriate governmental authorities in payment of the employee's tax liability. Because of the nature of the system, income taxes are actually remitted on a pay-as-you-go basis.

The amount withheld for federal income taxes is based on employee earnings, frequency of pay, marital status, and the number of **withholding allowances** claimed. The allowances are reported to an employer at the time of hire on a Form W-4 (Withholding Allowance Certificate) and depend on various factors, including marital status and number of children.

In an effort to secure operating revenues, many state and local governmental units have enacted laws that tax an employee's gross earnings. The amounts withheld for state and local income taxes vary widely but are often a stipulated percentage of gross pay.

## Other Deductions

In addition to required Social Security and income tax withholdings, many employees voluntarily authorize other deductions from their paychecks. Common examples of such deductions include payments for insurance programs (life, medical, dental) and U.S. savings bonds, contributions to a pension plan, union dues, and charitable contributions.

## Calculation of Take-Home Pay

To illustrate the computation of net or take-home pay, we will focus on Tony Disano, a married employee of Trimble Services who earns a weekly salary of \$1,100. The information that follows is available.

1 According to his W-4 form, Disano is claiming three withholding allowances.
2 Ohio, the state of employment, has a 2% income tax (assumed).
3 FICA taxes are 7.5% on a base of $45,000. Tony's year-to-date earnings before considering the present payroll period amount to $44,000.
4 Disano has authorized a $40 deduction for medical insurance and a $10 contribution to the United Way.

Disano's take-home pay for the current week is calculated as follows:

| | | |
|---|---|---|
| Gross earnings | | $1,100 |
| Less deductions | | |
| Federal income tax | $187 | |
| State income tax ($1,100 × 0.02) | 22 | |
| FICA taxes | 75 | |
| Medical insurance | 40 | |
| United Way contribution | 10 | 334 |
| Net pay | | $ 766 |

The federal income tax withholding amount is based on tables provided by the government. To determine the appropriate withholding, Disano's employer would refer to the table for married persons who are paid on a weekly basis. Trimble would then locate (or in many cases, figure) the amount that corresponds to three allowances and earnings of $1,100. Using tables in effect at the time of this writing, Disano's federal income tax withholding amounts to $187.

Turning to FICA, employees are subject to a 7.5% tax computed on a base of $45,000. According to the data presented, Disano has year-to-date earnings of $44,000. Thus, when his current week's salary of $1,100 is considered, the maximum taxable base will be exceeded. For this reason only $1,000 ($45,000 − $44,000) of the current earnings is subject to FICA taxation, and Trimble will deduct $75 ($1,000 × 0.075) from Disano's gross pay.

## Payroll Recording and Record Keeping

At the end of each payroll period the gross earnings, deductions, and net pay of all employees are entered in a **payroll register,** a journal-like device used to record a company's salary and wage data. The top part of Exhibit 12-5 contains the payroll register of Trimble Services (see pages 420–421).

Observe the manner in which Tony Disano's previously illustrated net pay computation occupies one line of the register. Also note that each employee's gross pay is classified as sales salaries expense or office salaries expense, depending on the type of work performed. Based on data in the register, the following entry is needed to record Trimble's payroll for the last week of the year:

| | | |
|---|---|---|
| Sales Salaries Expense | 1,840.00 | |
| Office Salaries Expense | 1,385.00 | |
| Employees' Federal Income Taxes Payable | | 458.00 |
| Employees' State Income Taxes Payable | | 64.50 |
| FICA Taxes Payable | | 234.38 |
| Employees' Insurance Program Payable | | 125.00 |
| Savings Bonds Payable | | 15.00 |
| United Way Contributions Payable | | 50.00 |
| Salaries Payable | | 2,278.12 |
| To record payroll and withholdings | | |

**Exhibit 12-5 Payroll Record Keeping**

*Payroll Register*

| Name | Sales or Office | Total Hours | Earnings: Regular | Earnings: Overtime | Earnings: Total | Federal Income Tax | State Income Tax |
|---|---|---|---|---|---|---|---|
| Al Baker | Sales | 40 | 320.00 | | 320.00 | 46.00 | 6.40 |
| Tony Disano | Office | - | 1,100.00 | | 1,100.00 | 187.00 | 22.00 |
| Sue Kennedy | Sales | 40 | 720.00 | | 720.00 | 77.00 | 14.40 |
| Pete Roe | Sales | - | 800.00 | | 800.00 | 114.00 | 16.00 |
| Alice Yurkow | Office | 45 | 240.00 | 45.00 | 285.00 | 34.00 | 5.70 |
| | | | 3,180.00 | 45.00 | 3,225.00 | 458.00 | 64.50 |

*Employee Earnings Record*

Name Tony J. Disano

Address 79 Flora Street

Cleveland, Ohio 44106

Position Office/Data Processing Manager

Social Security Number 579-89-1111

Single ____ Married x

Withholding Allowances 3

| Period Ending | Total Hours | Earnings: Regular | Earnings: Overtime | Earnings: Total | Earnings: Cumulative | Federal Income Tax |
|---|---|---|---|---|---|---|
| 12/7 | | 1,100.00 | | 1,100.00 | 41,800.00 | 187.00 |
| 12/14 | | 1,100.00 | | 1,100.00 | 42,900.00 | 187.00 |
| 12/21 | | 1,100.00 | | 1,100.00 | 44,000.00 | 187.00 |
| 12/28 | | 1,100.00 | | 1,100.00 | 45,100.00 | 187.00 |
| | | 45,100.00 | | 45,100.00 | | 7,667.00 |

1 Control number — OMB No. 1545-0008

2 Employer's name, address, and ZIP code: Trimble Services, Inc., 805 Tuck Place, Cleveland, Ohio 44108

3 Employer's identification number: 59-1411366

4 Employer's state I.D. number: 35-11486

5 Statutory employee / Deceased / Pension plan / Legal rep / 942 emp / Subtotal / Deferred compensation / Void

6 Allocated tips

7 Advance EIC payment

8 Employee's social security number: 579-89-1111

9 Federal income tax withheld: 7,667.00

10 Wages, tips, other compensation: 45,100.00

11 Social security tax withheld: 3,375.00

12 Employee's name, address, and ZIP code: Tony Disano, 79 Flora Street, Cleveland, Ohio 44106

13 Social security wages: 45,000.00

14 Social security tips

16 Insurance--1,640.00

17 State income tax: 902.00

18 State wages, tips, etc.: 45,100.00

19 Name of state: Ohio

20 Local income tax

21 Local wages, tips, etc.

22 Name of locality

Form W-2 Wage and Tax Statement 19X8

This information is being furnished to the Internal Revenue Service.

Copy B To be filed with employee's FEDERAL tax return

Dept. of the Treasury—IRS

| Deductions | | | | Payment | | Distribution | |
|---|---|---|---|---|---|---|---|
| FICA Tax | Insurance | Other | Total Deductions | Net Earnings | Check No. | Sales Salaries Expense | Office Salaries Expense |
| 24.00 | 15.00 | SB 10.00 | 101.40 | 218.60 | 1089 | 320.00 | |
| 75.00 | 40.00 | UW 10.00 | 334.00 | 766.00 | 1090 | | 1,100.00 |
| 54.00 | 35.00 | UW 20.00 | 200.40 | 519.60 | 1091 | 720.00 | |
| 60.00 | 25.00 | UW 20.00 | 235.00 | 565.00 | 1092 | 800.00 | |
| 21.38 | 10.00 | SB 5.00 | 76.08 | 208.92 | 1093 | | 285.00 |
| 234.38 | 125.00 | 65.00 | 946.88 | 2,278.12 | | 1,840.00 | 1,385.00 |

SB = *Savings Bonds*  UW = *United Way*

*Pay* $1,100 *per* — *Hour* ____ *Week* x — *Two Weeks* ____ *Month* ____

*Employee Number* 2

*Date of Birth* 5/14/XX

*Date Hired* 3/20/X8

*Date Terminated* ____

| Deductions | | | | | Payment | |
|---|---|---|---|---|---|---|
| State Income Tax | FICA Tax | Insurance | Other | Total Deductions | Net Earnings | Check No. |
| 22.00 | 82.50 | 40.00 | | 331.50 | 768.50 | 1003 |
| 22.00 | 82.50 | 40.00 | | 331.50 | 768.50 | 1030 |
| 22.00 | 82.50 | 40.00 | | 331.50 | 768.50 | 1056 |
| 22.00 | 75.00 | 40.00 | UW 10.00 | 334.00 | 766.00 | 1090 |
| 902.00 | 3,375.00 | 1,640.00 | 10.00 | 13,594.00 | 31,506.00 | |

The credit to Salaries Payable represents the net amount that will be disbursed to personnel on payday. (Generally, several days elapse between the end of the payroll period and payday to allow a company ample time to accumulate information and prepare checks.) Finally, the withholdings are current liabilities because the amounts are owed to various authorities (e.g., the federal government, the United Way, and so forth) and must be paid within a relatively short period of time. At the time of settlement, the proper payable is debited and Cash is credited.

### Employee Records

Shortly after the conclusion of a calendar year, an employer must furnish an accounting to each employee of the gross wages and salaries earned and the taxes withheld. Individual employee records are therefore a necessity. These records not only provide the basis for determining the preceding amounts but also assist in the computation of FICA and other taxes. For example, a cumulative earnings column (see Tony Disano's earnings record in Exhibit 12-5) will signal to Trimble Services that the $45,000 FICA taxable base is exceeded in the last pay period of the year.

The employer provides the required information to the employee on a **Wage and Tax Statement,** more commonly known as a **W-2** (also shown in Exhibit 12-5). Upon receipt, an employee can proceed with completion of the various tax forms that are filed with the Internal Revenue Service and state and local taxing authorities.

## Payroll Taxes of the Employer

Thus far, our discussion of taxes has focused on the employee. Employers are also subject to payroll taxes, specifically FICA, federal unemployment, and state unemployment.

### FICA Tax

The most significant payroll tax levied on the employer is FICA. As we noted earlier, employers must match the contributions of their employees to the Social Security program. Consequently, FICA tax rates on the employee and the employer are identical.

### Federal Unemployment Tax

Another tax on the employer requires payments under the **Federal Unemployment Tax Act (FUTA).** FUTA is a joint program between the federal government and the various states to financially assist the unemployed. Taxes collected are not distributed directly to those out of work; instead, the funds are used to support the administrative costs of state unemployment programs.

FUTA taxes are levied only on employers. At the time this text was written, the tax was 6.2% of the first $7,000 paid to each employee. Employers, however, can receive a credit of up to 5.4% for amounts remitted to state unemployment funds. Accordingly, many states have set a rate of at least 5.4% for their own programs, resulting in a *net* FUTA cost of 0.8% (6.2% − 5.4%) on a $7,000 earnings base.

### State Unemployment Taxes

**State unemployment taxes,** the amounts collected and then paid to those out of work, are disbursed through the various state programs. As we just noted, many states have implemented a tax rate of at least 5.4%, also computed on an employee's first $7,000 of gross pay. Normally, however, a merit reduction is granted to businesses with good labor records. This practice makes sense economically because these firms have a low number of layoffs and terminations, thereby avoiding large payments for unemployment compensation. Employers receiving merit reductions can still obtain a credit for federal purposes of up to 5.4%.

### Recording the Employer's Taxes

The entry to record the payroll taxes levied on an employer is made at the same time payroll is recorded. To illustrate the necessary accounting, we will continue the Trimble Services example. Study the payroll register that appears in Exhibit 12-5, along with the following assumptions:

1 Only Tony Disano has exceeded the FICA base of $45,000. Recall that only $1,000 of Tony's current gross earnings ($1,100) were taxed at the 7.5% rate.

2 Federal and state unemployment tax rates are 0.6% and 5.4%, respectively, of an employee's first $7,000 of gross earnings. All employees except Pete Roe, a new hire, have earned more than $7,000 for the year.

The payroll tax obligation, an expense, is recorded as follows:

| | | |
|---|---|---|
| Payroll Tax Expense | 282.38 | |
| FICA Taxes Payable | | 234.38* |
| Federal Unemployment Taxes Payable | | 4.80† |
| State Unemployment Taxes Payable | | 43.20† |
| To record employer's payroll taxes | | |

* All gross earnings are subject to FICA taxes except for $100 of Disano's salary ($1,100 − $1,000). Thus, FICA taxes are based on $3,125 ($3,225 − $100).

† Unemployment taxes are calculated only on Roe's salary because all other employees are over the limit. Federal: $800 × 0.006 = $4.80; state: $800 × 0.054 = $43.20.

Observe how Trimble's FICA tax expense is identical to the FICA taxes withheld from employee earnings. The liabilities will eventually be removed from the accounting records upon remittance to the proper authority.

## Chapter Review

### Learning Objectives—The Key Points

**1 Be familiar with the occurrence of and accounting for typical current liabilities of a business.** Current liabilities are debts or obligations that will be paid within one year or the operating cycle, whichever is longer. The settlement of current liabilities normally involves the use of current assets (e.g., cash) or the creation of other current liabilities (e.g., a note payable is used to settle an account payable). Examples of current liabilities include accounts payable, notes payable, the current portion of long-term debt, and accrued liabilities for expenses incurred but not yet paid.

**2 Understand how the accounting treatment of notes payable differs when interest is included in the face value of a note and when interest is recorded separately.** When interest is included in a note's face value, the difference between the note's proceeds and face value is recorded in a contra liability account, Discount on Notes Payable. At the end of each accounting period, this account is amortized (reduced) by the process of recognizing interest expense. In contrast, if interest is stated separately, no Discount account is established. Instead, interest is recorded at the end of the period by a debit to Interest Expense and, if unpaid, a credit to Interest Payable.

**3 Recognize contingent liabilities and discern when they should be recorded in the accounts and when footnote disclosure is appropriate.** A contingent liability is a potential liability that may become a definite obligation or be eliminated entirely as the result of a future event. An example is a lawsuit. Contingencies should be recorded in the accounts when it is probable that the future event will occur *and* the amount of the liability can be reasonably estimated. If only one of these guidelines is met, footnote disclosure is appropriate.

**4 Understand accounting for warranty costs.** Warranties are promises made by sellers and manufacturers to correct defects in product quality. Because warranties help to promote the sale of such products, an estimated service cost should be matched against sales revenues when the revenues are generated. This procedure, in turn, establishes a liability in the accounting records. The liability is reduced, perhaps several periods later, when the warranties are honored.

**5 Be familiar with payroll accounting and the treatment of payroll taxes.** Businesses must maintain detailed payroll records on their employees, keeping track of gross earnings and various payroll deductions (e.g., FICA tax, federal and state income tax withholdings, medical insurance, and pension plan contributions). The amounts deducted from employee paychecks are liabilities until paid to the appropriate authorities. A firm must also consider and record the following payroll taxes, which are levied on the employer: FICA, federal unemployment, and state unemployment.

## Chapter Quiz

The five questions that follow relate to several issues raised in the chapter. Test your knowledge of the issues by selecting the best answer. (The answers appear on p. 437.)

**1** Which of the following comments is false? Current liabilities:
- a include prepayments (advances) by customers.
- b will be settled within one year or the operating cycle, whichever is longer.
- c must be settled by using cash.
- d arise from past transactions and events.

**2** The Discount on Notes Payable account:
- a usually has a credit balance.
- b is associated with a note payable when interest is included in the obligation's face value.
- c represents future interest revenue on the note payable.
- d is used for notes payable when interest is not included in the obligation's face value.

**3** A balance in the Estimated Liability for Warranties account at year-end indicates:
- a that the accounting records have not been closed.
- b that the accounting records have not been adjusted.
- c the amount incurred during the year to service outstanding warranty agreements.
- d future amounts expected to be incurred when honoring outstanding warranty agreements.

**4** Assume that Robert Conrad, a technical engineer, worked 45 hours last week. He is paid $28 per hour, with hours in excess of 40 being compensated at one and one-half times the regular rate. Income tax withholdings amounted to $270; his medical insurance deduction was $30. The FICA tax rate is 7.5% on the first $45,000 earned; cumulative earnings before considering the above data totaled $44,202. Conrad's take-home pay is:
a $930.25.
b $970.15.
c $1,103.85.
d some amount other than those listed above.

**5** The FICA tax for social security is levied on:
a employees only.
b employers only.
c both employees and employers.
d either the employee or the employer depending on the number of withholding allowances claimed by the employee.

## Summary Problem

The following transactions took place in July and pertain to Meadowlands Corporation:

1 Two notes were issued during the month to raise needed cash. On July 1, a 3-month, 12%, $5,000 note was issued to the First National Bank. The company also executed a 60-day, $3,000 note on July 17 to the Second National Bank. Interest of $80 is included in the face value of the latter obligation.

2 The company recorded its payroll on July 31. Total salaries amounted to $30,000; 80% pertain to the sales staff and 20% to office personnel. FICA taxes are 7.5% on a base of $45,000 for each employee. All employees are under the base except for Mike Dixon, who earned $9,000 during the month. Additional data follow.

| | |
|---|---|
| Federal income taxes withheld | $3,850 |
| State income taxes withheld | 300 |
| Insurance program withholdings | 680 |

Meadowlands has a fiscal year-end of August 31.

### Instructions

**a** Prepare entries on July 1 and July 17 to record issuance of the notes.

**b** Prepare an entry on July 31 to record the company's payroll.

**c** Prepare an entry on July 31 to record the company's payroll taxes. Assume the state and federal unemployment tax rates are 5.4% and 0.6%, respectively. Thirty percent of the gross earnings are subject to unemployment taxes.

**d** Prepare the journal entries required on August 31 to accrue interest on each of the two notes.

### Solution

| | | | | |
|---|---|---|---|---|
| **a** July | 1 | Cash | 5,000 | |
| | | Notes Payable | | 5,000 |
| | | To record note payable to bank; 3 months at 12% | | |
| | 17 | Cash | 2,920 | |
| | | Discount on Notes Payable | 80 | |
| | | Notes Payable | | 3,000 |
| | | To record note payable to bank; 60 days until maturity | | |

| | | | Debit | Credit |
|---|---|---|---|---|
| **b** | July 31 | Sales Salaries Expense | 24,000* | |
| | | Office Salaries Expense | 6,000* | |
| | | FICA Taxes Payable | | 1,575† |
| | | Employees' Federal Income Taxes Payable | | 3,850 |
| | | Employees' State Income Taxes Payable | | 300 |
| | | Employees' Insurance Program Payable | | 680 |
| | | Salaries Payable | | 23,595 |
| | | To record payroll and withholdings | | |

* $30,000 × 0.8 = $24,000; $30,000 × 0.2 = $6,000.
† ($30,000 − $9,000) × 0.075 = $1,575.

| | | | Debit | Credit |
|---|---|---|---|---|
| **c** | July 31 | Payroll Tax Expense | 2,115 | |
| | | FICA Taxes Payable | | 1,575* |
| | | State Unemployment Taxes Payable | | 486† |
| | | Federal Unemployment Taxes Payable | | 54‡ |
| | | To record employer's payroll taxes | | |

* ($30,000 − $9,000) × 0.075 = $1,575.
† $30,000 × 0.3 = $9,000; $9,000 × 0.054 = $486.
‡ $30,000 × 0.3 = $9,000; $9,000 × 0.006 = $54.

| | | | Debit | Credit |
|---|---|---|---|---|
| **d** | Aug. 31 | Interest Expense | 100 | |
| | | Interest Payable | | 100 |
| | | To accrue interest for two months: $\$5,000 \times 0.12 \times \frac{2}{12}$ | | |
| | 31 | Interest Expense | 60 | |
| | | Discount on Notes Payable | | 60 |
| | | To accrue interest for 45 days and amortize the discount: $\$80 \times \frac{45}{60}$ | | |

## Questions

**Q12-1** Is a commitment for future goods and services entered in the accounting records as a liability? Explain.

**Q12-2** Define the term "current liability" and present six examples.

**Q12-3** Why are customer prepayments classified as liabilities?

**Q12-4** Present three different situations where a business collects monies from customers and employees and reports such amounts as current liabilities.

**Q12-5** Briefly discuss the correct treatment of vacation pay in the accounting records.

**Q12-6** Discuss several common uses of notes payable.

**Q12-7** What does the Discount on Notes Payable account represent?

**Q12-8** Does discount amortization increase or decrease a company's reported interest expense for the year?

**Q12-9** How does a contingent liability differ from an absolute liability? Present three examples of contingent liabilities.

**Q12-10** What guidelines must be met in order for a contingent liability to be recorded in the accounts?

**Q12-11** Why is a warranty considered a contingent liability?

**Q12-12** Are internal control procedures important in the area of payroll? Why?

**Q12-13** Differentiate between "employees" and "independent contractors." For which group must detailed payroll records be kept?

**Q12-14** What is the purpose of requiring businesses to withhold income taxes (federal, state, and local) from employee wages? How are these withholdings treated in the accounting records of the employer?

**Q12-15** Discuss the interrelationships between the payroll register, employee earnings record, and Form W-2.

**Q12-16** Which payroll taxes are incurred by an employer? How are these taxes treated in the accounting records?

**Q12-17** Do most state unemployment programs grant merit reductions to businesses? What is the purpose behind merit reductions?

## Exercises

**E12-1** ***Prepayments by customers***

Down-Under Tours sells prepaid package tours of Australia. The following information pertains to 19X1:

| *Tour* | *Number of Tours Sold* | *Selling Price per Tour* |
|---|---|---|
| Perth | 400 | $3,000 |
| Brisbane | 200 | 3,400 |
| Sydney | 800 | 4,000 |

Seventy percent of the tours sold were used during the year; the remainder will be used early in 19X2.

a Prepare journal entries in 19X1 to record (1) the sale of the tour packages and (2) the tours used during the year.

b Present proper disclosure of the unused tour packages on Down-Under's 19X1 year-end balance sheet.

**E12-2** ***Accrued liability; current portion of long-term debt***

On July 1, 19X1, Hall Company borrowed $225,000 via a long-term loan. Terms of the loan require that Hall pay interest and $75,000 of principal on July 1, 19X2, 19X3, and 19X4. The unpaid balance of the loan accrues interest at the rate of 10% per year. Hall has a December 31 year-end.

a Compute Hall's accrued interest as of December 31, 19X1.

b Present the appropriate balance sheet disclosure for the accrued interest and the current and long-term portion of the outstanding debt as of December 31, 19X1.

c Repeat parts (a) and (b) using a date of December 31, 19X2, rather than December 31, 19X1. Assume that Hall is in compliance with the terms of the loan agreement.

**E12-3** ***Accrued vacation pay***

Don Pedro Mexican Restaurants, Inc., has a two-week paid vacation plan. Monthly salaries and wages average $400,000. Because of high turnover, the firm estimates that only 30% of the employees will qualify for the fringe benefit.

a Briefly explain the proper accounting treatment for the vacation pay.

b Prepare the journal entry for March that reflects the proper treatment.

c Prepare a journal entry to record the disbursement of $7,500 to employees who took their vacations in August.

**E12-4** ***Notes payable***

Dillon Transportation Corporation purchased storage containers from Dobbs Equipment Manufacturing on October 1, 19X1, for $800,000. Dillon paid Dobbs $400,000 cash and signed a $400,000, 12%, 6-month note for the balance. Prepare journal entries for Dillon Transportation to record the following:

a The purchase of the storage containers on October 1, 19X1

b Accrued interest for the fiscal year ended November 30, 19X1

c The payment of the note and interest on March 31, 19X2

**E12-5** ***Notes payable; discount amortization***

Morgantown Foods purchased four delivery trucks from Metro Truck Sales on October 1, 19X1, for $240,000. Morgantown signed a 9-month note for $261,000; interest is included in the note's face value. Prepare journal entries for Morgantown Foods to record the following:

a The purchase of the trucks on October 1, 19X1

b Accrued interest for the year ended December 31, 19X1

c The note payment and discount amortization on July 1, 19X2

**E12-6** ***Warranty costs***

KMS sells sophisticated scientific instruments to fusion research laboratories. All instruments have a one-year warranty. The company estimates that 5% of the 1,200 units sold during 19X8 will require rework or replacement, at an estimated cost of $150 per unit.

a Is a warranty an example of an absolute liability or a contingent liability? Briefly discuss.

b Prepare the required journal entry to record warranty costs for 19X8.

c Present the necessary balance sheet disclosure on December 31, 19X8, if 35 instruments were returned for servicing during 19X8. Assume that the actual rework cost per unit conformed to original expectations.

**E12-7** ***Payroll accounting***

Evaluate the comments that follow as being True or False. If the comment is false, briefly explain why.

a FICA taxes are levied on the total wages of an employee.

b Employers must match the amount of FICA taxes withheld from employee wages.

c State unemployment taxes are paid by both employees and employers.

d Take-home pay and gross pay are different terms for the same concept.

e Federal and state income tax withholdings are current liabilities of the employer until remitted to governmental authorities.

**E12-8** ***Payroll accounting***

The payroll register of Westchester Company for the month of March contained the following information:

| | |
|---|---|
| Office salaries | $22,500 |
| Sales salaries | 16,500 |

Payroll deductions were made for FICA taxes at the rate of 7.5% of total earnings, federal income taxes of $3,950, state income taxes of 3% of gross earnings, and dental insurance of $420.

a Prepare the necessary entry to record Westchester's March payroll.

b Record the company's payroll tax expense. Assume that unemployment taxes are 6.0% of the first $7,000 paid to each employee (5.4% for state unemployment and 0.6% for federal unemployment). All employees have earned less than $7,000 for the year.

**E12-9** ***Payroll accounting***

The following payroll information relates to Warner Company for the month of July:

| | |
|---|---|
| Total (gross) employee earnings | $150,000 |
| Earnings in excess of FICA base earnings | 18,000 |
| Earnings in excess of unemployment base earnings | 94,000 |
| Federal income taxes withheld | 14,500 |
| State income taxes withheld | 3,000 |
| Employee deductions for medical insurance | 2,200 |

The FICA tax rate is 7.5% on the first $45,000 earned per employee. The state and federal unemployment tax rates are 5.4% and 0.6%, respectively, on the first $7,000 earned per employee.

a Compute the employees' total take-home pay.
b Compute Warner's total payroll-related expenses.
c Assuming a stable work force, is total take-home pay likely to increase, decrease, or remain the same in September? Briefly explain.

**E12-10** ***Payroll: Computations and analysis***

Al Busby and John Moore work part-time for the Fast Freight Company as technical specialists. Busby earns $18 per hour; Moore is paid a salary of $34,800. Both men worked 1,400 hours during the year. FICA taxes are 7.5% of an employee's first $45,000 of gross earnings; unemployment taxes are computed on each employee's earnings up to $7,000. The state unemployment rate is only 4.6% because of a merit reduction, and the federal unemployment tax rate is 0.6%.

a Calculate the company's annual payroll tax expense for Busby and Moore.
b What is the total annual cost of having Busby and Moore on the payroll?
c Would your answer to part (b) be different if Moore decided to work full-time for $60,000 per year and Busby was laid off? Explain, assuming no change in the unemployment tax rates.

# Problems

## Series A

**P12-A1** ***Current liabilities: Recognition and valuation***

The seven transactions and events that follow relate to the 19X2 operations of Blue Giant Products.

1 On February 1, the company signed a one-year contract with the food processors union, agreeing to a 6% wage increase for all employees. The cost of the wage increase is estimated to be $100,000 per month.
2 A customer slipped on a soft drink that he had spilled while walking through a Blue Giant store. The customer injured his back and has filed a $50,000 damage suit against the company. Blue Giant attorneys feel the suit is uncalled for and without merit.
3 Blue Giant purchased merchandise on October 15 for $4,000; terms 5/15, n/60. The company overlooked the discount and intends to pay the supplier in January 19X3.
4 Equipment that cost $12,000 was acquired on November 1 by issuing a three-month, 10%, $12,000 note payable.
5 Office furniture that cost $4,000 was purchased on December 1, with Blue Giant signing a $4,240, 12-month note payable. Interest is included in the note's face value.
6 Cash receipts from December merchandise sales totaled $318,000. The $318,000 figure includes a 6% state sales tax.
7 On the last day of 19X2, the company borrowed $1 million from the Monticello Bank. The loan's principal is due in 10 equal annual installments of $100,000 each, with each installment payable on December 31. The loan has a 9% interest rate.

### Instructions

a Indicate which of the seven transactions and events would appear in the current liability section of the firm's December 31, 19X2, balance sheet.
b Show how the items in part (a) would be disclosed. Use proper dollar amounts.
c Indicate how the transactions and events that are not current liabilities would be handled for accounting purposes.

**P12-A2** ***Current liabilities: Entries and disclosure***

A review of selected financial activities of Asbury Company during 19XX disclosed the following:

| | | |
|---|---|---|
| Mar. | 1 | Purchased $6,000 of office furniture on account from the Fenton Company, terms 2/10, n/45. |
| | 3 | Received $1,000 cash from the employees to forward to the Earthquake Relief Fund. The cash will be remitted in several days. |
| | 5 | The Asbury Company has agreed to match the employee contributions to the Earthquake Fund; issued check no. 658 to cover the donations of both parties. |
| | 7 | Bought $18,000 of store equipment; signed an $18,800 note payable due in 120 days. |
| | 10 | Established a warranty liability for the Mop-o-Matic, a new product. Sales are expected to total 1,000 units during the month. Past experience with similar products indicates that 3% of the units will require replacement, with warranty costs averaging $8 per unit. |
| | 16 | Borrowed $20,000 from the Bank of Asbury by signing a 60-day, 12% note payable. Interest and principal are due at maturity. |
| | 31 | Accrued two days of wage expense; daily payroll amounts to $3,700. |
| | 31 | Accrued vacation pay amounting to 7% of March's $81,000 wage expense. |
| | 31 | Replaced 24 Mop-o-Matics during the month at a total cost of $192. |

**Instructions**

a Prepare journal entries to record the preceding transactions and events.
b Determine accrued interest as of March 31, 19XX, and prepare the necessary adjusting entry(ies).
c Prepare the current liability section of Asbury Company's March 31, 19XX, balance sheet.

**P12-A3** ***Notes payable***

The Blue Smoke Company was involved in the following transactions during the fiscal year ended September 30:

| | | |
|---|---|---|
| June | 2 | Issued a $65,000 note to Euless Office Supply for the purchase of $65,000 of office furniture. The note is due in 180 days and carries a 12% interest rate. |
| July | 14 | Borrowed $100,000 from the Second National Bank by signing a 90-day note for $103,000. |
| Aug. | 1 | Issued a $40,000 note to Al Kinder in settlement of an overdue account payable of the same amount. The note is due in 30 days and carries an 18% interest rate. |
| | 15 | Purchased merchandise from San Diego Industries in the amount of $18,000. Blue Smoke issued a 30-day, 15% note in settlement of the balance owed. |
| | 31 | The note to Kinder was due today, but Blue Smoke was unable to make payment. Management authorized the issuance of a new 30-day, 18% note for $40,600, the maturity value of the original obligation. |
| Sept. | 14 | The note to San Diego Industries was paid in full. |
| | 30 | The new note to Al Kinder was paid in full. |

**Instructions**

a Prepare journal entries to record the transactions.
b Prepare adjusting entries on September 30 to record accrued interest.

c Prepare the current liability section of Blue Smoke's balance sheet as of September 30. Assume the Accounts Payable account totals $321,700 on this date.

**P12-A4** ***Payroll journal entries***

Upscale Shoppers incurred wages and salaries of $300,000 during November, 30% of which relate to office personnel and the remainder to sales personnel. FICA taxes are 7.5% on a base of $45,000 for each employee. All employees are under the $45,000 base except for Susan Hatfield, who earned $7,000 during the month. Federal income taxes withheld amounted to $75,900 and state income taxes withheld totaled $9,000. Other deductions from payroll were authorized for pensions (2% of gross earnings), insurance (1% of gross earnings), and United Way contributions (0.5% of gross earnings).

**Instructions**

a Prepare the journal entry to record the payroll.

b Prepare a journal entry to record Upscale's payroll taxes and other related payroll costs. Assume that state unemployment tax is 4.0% because of a merit reduction, and that federal unemployment tax is 0.6%. Twenty percent of the gross earnings are subject to unemployment taxes. Also, Upscale matches employee contributions to the United Way and insurance programs. These amounts will be remitted to the proper authorities on December 15.

c Compute total payroll expense for November.

**P12-A5** ***Payroll register and entries***

The China Shop has three hourly employees and two salaried employees. Payroll data for the month of November follow.

| *Employee* | *Hours Reg* | *Hours OT** | *Pay Rate* | *Gross Pay for Month* | *Federal Income Tax Withheld* | *Compensation through Oct. 31* |
|---|---|---|---|---|---|---|
| David | 160 | | $5/hr | $ 800 | $ 165 | $ 1,600 |
| Larimore | 160 | 20 | $6/hr | 1,140 | 195 | 6,200 |
| Markoff | 160 | 10 | $4/hr | 700 | 100 | 7,500 |
| Ramon | | | $2,000/mo | 2,000 | 220 | 20,000 |
| Wykovich | | | $5,000/mo | 5,000 | 1,030 | 43,000 |
| | | | | $9,640 | $1,710 | |

* Overtime hours are compensated at 150% of the regular hourly rate.

Other information is as follows:

1 FICA taxes are 7.5% on a base of $45,000 for each employee.

2 Unemployment taxes are based on the first $7,000 of an employee's earnings. The state and federal rates are 5.4% and 0.6%, respectively.

3 Deductions are made for life and medical insurance (5% of gross earnings) and for contributions to the United Way (1% of gross earnings). The company matches United Way donations.

4 Ramon and Wykovich perform administrative work; other employees are involved with sales.

**Instructions**

a Prepare a payroll register for the month of November. Use the column headings that follow and round to the nearest cent.

| | | Deductions | | | | |
|---|---|---|---|---|---|---|
| Employee | Gross Pay | Federal Income Tax | FICA Tax | Insurance | United Way | Net Pay |

b Prepare the necessary journal entry to record the payroll.
c Record the employer's payroll taxes and United Way contribution. The United Way contribution will be remitted on December 15.

**P12-A6** ***Wage and tax statement; payroll taxes***
Space Age, Inc., began operation at the beginning of 19X1. The company hired its current staff of seven employees throughout the year. No employees quit or were fired during 19X1, and there were no changes in salary amounts.

Space Age disburses its payroll at the end of each month and deducts withholdings for federal income tax, state income tax (4% of gross earnings), and FICA taxes. The FICA tax is 7.5% on the first $45,000 earned. Pertinent employee data follow.

| Employee | Date Hired | Monthly Salary | Monthly Federal Income Taxes Withheld |
|---|---|---|---|
| Battle | Jan. 1 | $4,000 | $ 650 |
| Kemper | Feb. 1 | 4,200 | 825 |
| Pierce | Mar. 1 | 6,000 | 1,090 |
| Reeves | Sept. 1 | 5,000 | 750 |
| Smith | Sept. 1 | 3,600 | 450 |
| Walsh | Nov. 1 | 1,000 | 120 |
| Wyatt | Dec. 1 | 2,400 | 300 |

**Instructions**

a Complete the following table with the amounts to be reported on each employee's W-2 form (Wage and Tax Statement) for the year:

| | | Income Taxes Withheld | | | |
|---|---|---|---|---|---|
| Employee | Gross Earnings | Federal | State | Earnings Subject to FICA Taxes | FICA Taxes Withheld |

b Calculate Space Age's 19X1 payroll tax expense for:
(1) FICA taxes.
(2) Federal unemployment tax, which is 0.6% of the first $7,000 of an employee's gross earnings.
(3) State unemployment tax, which is 3% of the first $7,000 of an employee's gross earnings.

c If tax rates remain constant and all current employees work throughout *19X2* at the same monthly salary amounts, by how much will total payroll taxes increase in the forthcoming year?

## Series B

**P12-B1** ***Current liabilities: Recognition and valuation***
The seven transactions and events that follow relate to the 19X7 operations of Sussex Company.

1 During the Easter season, the company sold 400 $25 gift certificates to customers. By December 31, 275 certificates had been redeemed for merchandise.
2 Equipment that cost $40,000 was acquired on May 1 by signing a 12-month, 12% note payable for $40,000.
3 The company introduced a new product on July 1; sales totaled 500,000 units through the remainder of the year. Each unit carried a 12-month warranty. Sussex estimated that defective units would amount to 2% of sales, with the cost of each unit's replacement averaging $15. During 19X7, 6,000 units were returned and replaced at a cost of $90,000.
4 A $10,000 computer system was purchased on October 1 by signing a nine-month note payable for $10,900. Interest is included in the note's face value.
5 On November 1, the company signed a contract to purchase $360,000 of spare parts from Central Supply during the next 24 months. The contract called for prices that are 15% below those of Arrow Wholesale, Sussex's present supplier.
6 Accrued salaries payable at year-end total $45,000. This amount was paid on January 3, 19X8.
7 Federal income taxes withheld from employees' paychecks during December totaled $13,000. The withholdings must be remitted to tax authorities by February 1, 19X8.

**Instructions**

a Indicate which of the seven transactions and events would appear in the current liability section of the firm's December 31, 19X7, balance sheet.
b Show how the items in part (a) would be disclosed. Use proper dollar amounts.
c Indicate how the transactions and events that are not current liabilities would be handled for accounting purposes.

**P12-B2** ***Current liabilities: Entries and disclosure***

A review of selected financial activities of Angelo's during 19XX disclosed the following:

Dec. 1 Borrowed $20,000 from the First City Bank by signing a 3-month, 15% note payable. Interest and principal are due at maturity.
10 Established a warranty liability for the XY-80, a new product. Sales are expected to total 1,000 units during the month. Past experience with similar products indicates that 2% of the units will require repair, with warranty costs averaging $27 per unit.
20 Received $175 cash from the employees to forward to the Children's Christmas Fund. The cash will be remitted in several days.
24 Angelo's has agreed to match the employee contributions to the Children's Christmas Fund; issued check no. 178 to cover the donations of both parties.
26 Purchased $16,000 of merchandise on account from Oregon Company, terms 2/10, n/30.
26 Borrowed $5,000 from the First City Bank; signed a $5,120 note payable due in 60 days.
31 Repaired six XY-80s during the month at a total cost of $162.
31 Accrued three days of salaries at a total cost of $1,400.
31 Accrued vacation pay amounting to 6% of December's $36,000 total wage and salary expense.

**Instructions**

a Prepare journal entries to record the preceding transactions and events.
b Determine accrued interest as of December 31, 19XX, and prepare the necessary adjusting entry(ies).
c Prepare the current liability section of Angelo's December 31, 19XX, balance sheet.

**P12-B3** *Notes payable*

Red Bank Enterprises was involved in the following transactions during the fiscal year ended October 31:

| | | |
|---|---|---|
| Aug. | 2 | Borrowed $75,000 from the Bank of Kingsville by signing a 120-day note for $79,000. |
| | 20 | Issued a $40,000 note to Harris Motors for the purchase of a $40,000 delivery truck. The note is due in 180 days and carries a 12% interest rate. |
| Sept. | 10 | Purchased merchandise from Paris Enterprises in the amount of $15,000. Issued a 30-day, 12% note in settlement of the balance owed. |
| | 11 | Issued a $60,000 note to Datatex Equipment in settlement of an overdue account payable of the same amount. The note is due in 30 days and carries a 14% interest rate. |
| Oct. | 10 | The note to Paris Enterprises was paid in full. |
| | 11 | The note to Datatex Equipment was due today, but insufficient funds were available for payment. Management authorized the issuance of a new 20-day, 18% note for $60,700, the maturity value of the original obligation. |
| | 31 | The new note to Datatex Equipment was paid in full. |

**Instructions**

a Prepare journal entries to record the transactions.

b Prepare adjusting entries on October 31 to record accrued interest.

c Prepare the current liability section of Red Bank's balance sheet as of October 31. Assume the Accounts Payable account totals $203,600 on this date.

**P12-B4** *Payroll journal entries*

Griffith Distributors incurred salaries and wages of $155,000 during September, 60% of which relate to sales personnel and 40% to office personnel. FICA taxes are 7.5% on a base of $45,000 for each employee. All employees are under the $45,000 base except for Jeff Salem, who earned $6,000 during the month. Additional data follow.

| | |
|---|---|
| Federal income taxes withheld | $26,100 |
| State income taxes withheld | 4,450 |
| City income taxes withheld | 1,550 |

Other deductions from payroll were authorized for pensions (3% of gross earnings), insurance (2% of gross earnings), and charitable contributions (0.2% of gross earnings).

**Instructions**

a Prepare the journal entry to record the payroll.

b Prepare a journal entry to record Griffith's payroll taxes and other related payroll costs. Assume that state unemployment tax is 4% because of a merit reduction and that federal unemployment tax is 0.6%. Thirty percent of the gross earnings are subject to unemployment taxes. Also, Griffith matches employees' deductions for pensions and insurance. Employee and employer contributions for pensions and insurance will be remitted to the James Insurance Agency on October 10.

c Compute the total payroll expense for September.

**P12-B5** *Payroll register and entries*

Holland Company has three hourly employees and two salaried employees. Payroll data for the month of October follow.

| Employee | Hours Reg | Hours OT* | Pay Rate | Gross Pay for Month | Federal Income Tax Withheld | Compensation through Sept. 30 |
|---|---|---|---|---|---|---|
| Baker | 160 | 10 | $6/hr | $1,050 | $ 180 | $ 6,300 |
| Chang | 100 | | $7/hr | 700 | 120 | 3,600 |
| Mintz | 160 | 20 | $8/hr | 1,520 | 290 | 11,900 |
| Sawyer | | | $1,800/mo | 1,800 | 335 | 16,200 |
| West | | | $4,800/mo | 4,800 | 700 | 43,200 |
| | | | | $9,870 | $1,625 | |

* Overtime hours are compensated at 150% of the regular hourly rate.

Other information is as follows:

1 FICA taxes are 7.5% on a base of $45,000 for each employee.

2 Unemployment taxes are based on the first $7,000 of an employee's earnings. The state and federal rates are 5.4% and 0.6%, respectively.

3 Deductions are made for life and medical insurance (6% of gross earnings) and for contributions to the United Way (1% of gross earnings). The company matches United Way donations.

4 Sawyer and West perform administrative work; other employees are involved with sales.

**Instructions**

a Prepare a payroll register for the month of October. Use the following column headings and round to the nearest cent:

| | | Deductions | | | | |
|---|---|---|---|---|---|---|
| Employee | Gross Pay | Federal Income Tax | FICA Tax | Insurance | United Way | Net Pay |

b Prepare the necessary journal entry to record the payroll.

c Record the employer's payroll taxes and United Way contribution. The United Way contribution will be remitted on November 10.

**P12-B6** ***Wage and tax statement; payroll taxes***

LaserTech, Inc., began operation at the beginning of 19X4. The company hired its current staff of seven employees throughout the year. No employees quit or were fired during 19X4, and there were no changes in salary amounts.

LaserTech disburses its payroll at the end of each month and deducts withholdings for federal income tax, state income tax (3% of gross earnings), and FICA taxes. The FICA tax is 7.5% on the first $45,000 earned. Pertinent employee data follow.

| Employee | Date Hired | Monthly Salary | Monthly Federal Income Taxes Withheld |
|---|---|---|---|
| Cohen | Jan. 1 | $4,300 | $ 900 |
| Davis | Mar. 1 | 1,200 | 125 |
| Eaton | Apr. 1 | 5,800 | 1,050 |
| Jetson | May 1 | 3,000 | 550 |
| Lowry | Aug. 1 | 3,600 | 650 |
| Paul | Oct. 1 | 1,400 | 155 |
| Simon | Dec. 1 | 3,600 | 600 |

**Instructions**

a Complete the following table with the amounts to be reported on each employee's W-2 form (Wage and Tax Statement) for the year:

| | | *Income Taxes Withheld* | | | |
|---|---|---|---|---|---|
| *Employee* | *Gross Earnings* | *Federal* | *State* | *Earnings Subject to FICA Taxes* | *FICA Taxes Withheld* |

b Calculate LaserTech's 19X4 payroll tax expense for:
  (1) FICA taxes.
  (2) Federal unemployment tax, which is 0.6% of the first $7,000 of an employee's gross earnings.
  (3) State unemployment tax, which is 4% of the first $7,000 of an employee's gross earnings.

c Assume that tax rates remain constant and all current employees work throughout *19X5* at the same monthly salary amounts. Will LaserTech's total payroll tax expense increase or decrease in the forthcoming year? By how much?

## Beyond the Basics

**BB12-1** ***Current liabilities and errors***

Preliminary figures of Clifton Company revealed the following liabilities as of December 31, 19X1:

| | | |
|---|---|---|
| Current liabilities | | |
| Accounts payable | $123,000 | |
| Notes payable | 60,000 | $183,000 |
| Long-term liabilities | | |
| Loan payable | | 210,000 |

The following information has come to your attention:

1 Notes payable include an eight-month, $50,000 obligation issued on August 1 to the Second National Bank. Clifton received proceeds of $46,800.
2 No accrued interest has been recorded. Excluding the Second National note, accrued interest amounted to $5,100.
3 The long-term loan was due in five equal annual installments, the first to be paid on March 13, 19X2.
4 Clifton rented some unused warehouse space on December 1 to Sherman Corporation. Sherman prepaid six months' rent and Clifton made the following entry:

| | | |
|---|---|---|
| Cash | 4,800 | |
| Rent Revenue | | 4,800 |

No adjusting entry has been recorded.

Assume that net income for 19X1 amounted to $80,000 before considering these items. The books have not been closed.

**Instructions**

a Determine the correct net income for 19X1.
b Prepare the liability section of Clifton's December 31 balance sheet in good form.

**BB12-2** ***Contingent liabilities***

Consider the following independent cases:

1 From January through August of the current year, Western Manufacturing worked on and completed a defense contract for the U.S. Air Force. Western has been reimbursed for its costs plus a profit margin, the costs determined by following Defense Department guidelines. On December 28, Western was informed by government auditors that the firm had computed its costs incorrectly. The Air Force has requested a $74,000 reimbursement. Conversations with Western's cost accounting department revealed that the Air Force's claim was both accurate and correct.

2 Chase Corporation offers a one-year warranty on its sole product. The probable warranty claims from a given level of sales can be determined on the basis of past experience.

3 On December 15, an explosion occurred at the Vesper Glue Company. Ten people were injured, and five houses located near Vesper's manufacturing facility were severely damaged. Although no lawsuits had been filed by the end of the year, management anticipates future court appearances and several out-of-court settlements. The company was uninsured for the casualty.

4 Washington Company has always had an excellent reputation for product quality. Management was therefore shocked to learn that a governmental agency was investigating one of the firm's products for safety violations. Although the investigation has just commenced, Washington's legal counsel said there was "a very remote chance of a product recall."

5 Bonanza, Inc., was sued in February for discriminatory hiring practices. Bonanza's lawyers noted that the plaintiffs had a strong case and would likely win the suit. Although the suit was for $100,000, it would probably be settled for $40,000.

**Instructions**

a Discuss the accounting treatment for contingent liabilities.

b Indicate and discuss how each of the five cases would be treated in the financial statements. Assume each company's year ends on December 31. Present journal entries when appropriate.

## Answers to Chapter Quiz

**1** c

**2** b

**3** d

**4** b [(40 hours × $28) + (5 hours × $42) = $1,330; ($45,000 − $44,202) × 0.075 = $59.85; $1,330.00 − $59.85 − $270.00 − $30.00 = $970.15]

**5** c

# The Foundation of Financial Accounting and Reporting

CHAPTER 13

## Learning Objectives

After reading this chapter you should:

1 Be familiar with the objectives of financial reporting.

2 Be aware of the desirable characteristics of accounting information: relevancy, reliability, comparability, and understandability.

3 Understand generally accepted accounting principles and the roles of various bodies, specifically the Securities and Exchange Commission and the Financial Accounting Standards Board, in the development process.

4 Be familiar with the assumptions, concepts, and modifying conventions that underlie financial accounting and reporting.

5 Understand the revenue realization principle and be able to apply the percentage-of-completion and installment methods.

6 Understand the impact of inflation on financial statements.

Not too long ago the chairman of Price Waterhouse, one of this country's largest public accounting firms, made the following observations about the accounting profession:

> The public accounting profession is faced with an important challenge—the need to strengthen public confidence in its effectiveness. The Securities and Exchange Commission, Congress, the courts, and the public have focused on recent business collapses, deficient financial reporting and other aspects of corporate disclosure. Congressional investigators ask repeatedly: Where were the auditors? And, for the second time in 10 years, the system is being questioned.
>
> Recent business failures have affected shareholders, depositors and others engaged in transactions with failed banks, savings and loan associations, and government securities dealers. The failures have been caused by fraudulent activities, changed economic conditions, poor management or a combination of these. In the public's judgment the auditors should have detected the fraud or recognized that failure was imminent and taken steps to ensure that the public was warned on a timely basis . . .
>
> . . . the accounting profession occupies a privileged position in our society. When we are perceived to be meeting our responsibilities and fulfilling our prescribed role, no other profession or occupation enjoys a higher level of public confidence. That confidence is immeasurably valuable and eminently worth preserving and nurturing.[1]

These comments reveal that accounting and its financial reporting function have been the subject of some significant criticism over the years. Perhaps the criticism has been well deserved; perhaps not.

Previous chapters of this text have focused on specific practices used to record business transactions and disclose financial affairs. In this chapter we wish to present a broad overview of financial accounting by defining the objectives of financial reporting and the characteristics of accounting information. Our emphasis, however, will be on the assumptions and concepts that serve as the underlying foundation for the balance sheet, income statement, and statement of owner's equity, namely, generally accepted accounting principles. The presentation concludes with a look at the impact of inflation on income measurement.

## Objectives of Financial Reporting

**OBJECTIVE 1**
**Be familiar with the objectives of financial reporting.**

What are the goals of financial accounting and reporting? How can these goals best be attained? Since the mid-1970s the accounting profession has devoted considerable effort to a conceptual framework project aimed at discovering the answers to these questions. This project has resulted in a series of pronouncements that are expected to provide the necessary structure and direction for the development of improved measurement and disclosure practices.

The first of these pronouncements identified several objectives of financial reporting.[2] The objectives stipulated that the reporting function should generate information that is helpful:

1 To present and potential investors, creditors, and other users in making various types of decisions.

[1] Joseph E. Connor, "Enhancing Public Confidence in the Accounting Profession," *Journal of Accountancy,* July 1986, p. 76. Reprinted with permission from *Journal of Accountancy,* Copyright © 1986 by American Institute of Certified Public Accountants, Inc. Opinions of the authors are their own and do not necessarily reflect policies of the Institute.

[2] See "Objectives of Financial Reporting by Business Enterprises," *Statement of Financial Accounting Concepts No. 1* (Stamford, Conn.: Financial Accounting Standards Board, November 1978).

2 In assessing the amounts, timing, and uncertainty of an organization's cash inflows and outflows.

3 In studying an enterprise's resources, the claims to those resources by creditors and owners, and any related changes in either of the foregoing during an accounting period.

4 In examining an enterprise's financial performance, namely, measures of earnings and its components.

These goals relate to the information needs of various groups of financial statement users. Creditors, stockholders, analysts, and others utilize accounting data for a variety of reasons. Creditors, for example, assess an enterprise's debt-paying ability, while stockholders have an obvious concern about corporate earnings and the probability of future dividend distributions. Given this variety, financial statements must be *general-purpose* in orientation and be useful in satisfying different needs of different parties. Unbiased determination and communication of economic information is therefore of utmost importance.

## Characteristics of Financial Information

**OBJECTIVE 2**
**Be aware of the desirable characteristics of accounting information: relevancy, reliability, comparability, and understandability.**

Having established the objectives of financial reporting, the profession then studied desirable characteristics of accounting information.[3] As explained throughout the text, firms are often given a choice among various accounting policies. Using specified or unspecified criteria, a business must somehow make a decision concerning the best policy to implement in a specific set of circumstances. Presumably, the selected alternative would be the one that generates the most useful financial information. To judge usefulness, the profession noted that information should possess the following characteristics:

- Relevancy
- Reliability
- Comparability
- Understandability

Sometimes, as we will now see, these characteristics may conflict with one another.

### Relevancy

Information is deemed relevant if it influences the actions of a decision maker. On the surface the concept of relevancy is simple: only produce information that can be actively employed by financial statement users. A deeper probe, however, reveals several practical problems. As noted earlier, different users have different needs. Obviously, a given set of financial statements cannot satisfy *all* needs of *all* interested parties; thus, some compromise is necessary. In addition, if the relevancy concept is implemented in the strictest sense, businesses would have to abandon the traditional cost basis of accounting. To illustrate, consider a company that purchased a parcel of land many years ago for $40,000. If the land is now worth $500,000, the company's balance sheet would continue to reveal a valuation of $40,000. Unfortunately, the latter figure (i.e., cost) is totally irrelevant for a deci-

[3] See "Qualitative Characteristics of Accounting Information," *Statement of Financial Accounting Concepts No. 2* (Stamford, Conn.: Financial Accounting Standards Board, May 1980).

sion maker who is attempting to evaluate the current worth of the entity. This particular problem has prompted accountants to study alternative means of asset valuation and is explored further in a later section of this chapter.

## Reliability

Financial information must be reliable; specifically, the information must accurately depict the conditions it purports to represent. If net income is a reliable figure, for instance, it must truly represent a summary of an enterprise's profit-generating activities. Similarly, the accounts payable figure reported on a balance sheet must represent the summation of trade creditor claims against the entity.

Reliability is influenced by a number of factors, one of which is bias. A measure may represent what it is supposed to, but determination of that measure may be biased. For example, suppose a company that uses LIFO for valuation of inventory and cost of goods sold is operating in a highly inflationary economy. Assume that management has decided to curtail purchasing activities during the last few months of the accounting period to conserve cash. As a result of this action, inventory levels will decline and, given the nature of the last-in, first-out system, units that are sold currently will be costed at older (and cheaper) prices. Cost of goods sold will therefore be lower than that computed under the firm's prior (i.e., regular) purchasing program. Overall higher earnings are reported along with a reliable but possibly biased measure of performance. Cost of goods sold is reliable in that it represents the cost of the units sold; however, the measure may be biased by showing significantly lower costs, caused perhaps by a purposeful manipulation of buying habits and, thus, earnings.

Bias usually benefits certain groups at the expense of others and could erode the public's confidence in financial reporting. Accounting information must be neutral ". . . and report economic activity as faithfully as possible, without coloring the image it communicates for the purpose of influencing behavior in *some particular direction.*"[4] In so doing, accounting and financial reporting are enhanced, thereby increasing their usefulness to parties with widely varying interests.

## Comparability

The usefulness of accounting information is enhanced if a company's financial statements are comparable with statements of other enterprises and with those of the same company at different points in time. Comparability among entities is difficult because of the variety of accounting methods found in practice—a situation that is not likely to change.

Comparability of a *single firm's* statements through time is achieved by use of the same accounting methods from one period to the next. This practice offers the advantage of better performance evaluation. Imagine the difficulty, for example, of assessing income trends if a company indiscriminately switched depreciation methods during each financial reporting period. Indeed, an analyst would have trouble determining whether variations in earnings are caused by changes in the entity's activities and efficiency or by changes in its accounting methods. Our discussion here has been intentionally brief; comparability of financial statements over time is discussed further in this chapter under the heading of "Consistency Principle."

---

[4] Ibid., paragraph 100.

### Understandability

To achieve any degree of usefulness, financial information must be understandable. Often, as is true in many technical disciplines, terminology and jargon can be extremely troublesome. Consider, for instance, the following satirical interaction between Leonard (a stockholder) and President Jones at an annual stockholders' meeting:

> Leonard motioned for the floor and stood up. "You commented previously that total sales increased. Will you comment on our apparent decrease in earnings?"
>
> "Perhaps I should have pointed out," replied President Jones, "that our figures from year to year reflect changes in accounting. For example, we have used LIFO and FIFO. Our depreciation policy is flexible. There is the question of reporting [earnings] per share on the total amount of shares outstanding, the average amount, or the fully converted amount. Our figures also take into account pooling of interest of our latest acquisition. This is a company making a patented banana slicer suitable for any household. Thus it fits nicely into our banana sales. Let me also point out that our final bottom-line figures are reduced by some write-offs. In addition, we have written off some prepaid costs that we know we will incur in coming years. As a result, we had no taxable income this year. We were fortunate in being able to fund some of our short-term borrowings but at an increased interest cost. These and other such adjustments are included in the footnotes to our annual report."[5]

Many people feel that this parody, written nearly 20 years ago, accurately reflects the present state of affairs in financial reporting. Economic activities have become so complex that down-to-earth explanations in everyday terms are a near impossibility.

The accounting profession services individuals with varied business and educational backgrounds. Contrary to the impression one may receive when reviewing a firm's financial statements or a company's annual report, accountants do not strive for a presentation geared especially for bankers, financial analysts, and other long-term veterans of the business world. Our goal is to produce information that is "comprehensible to those who have a *reasonable* understanding of business and economic activities and are willing to study the information with *reasonable* diligence"[6] (emphasis added).

## The Foundation of Accounting

Suppose you are pursuing the study of accounting at a university located in the heart of a major metropolitan area. You are living at home in a nice suburb and must drive 12 miles twice each week to attend class. Assume it is common knowledge that the local police department is lax in its enforcement of driving regulations. Speeding, running red lights, tailgating, and other offenses are common occurrences. Given the goings-on around you, your trip to campus would surely be an "exciting" experience. Different drivers doing their own thing results in a hectic, if not chaotic, commuting environment.

Much of the same would undoubtedly be said about financial reporting if each company could summarize business activity in its own unique way. Picture the plight of an investor who is attempting to evaluate performance of two different

[5] Gerald M. Loeb, "Peter and Leonard Attend an Annual Meeting," *Financial Analysts Journal*, May–June 1971, p. 30. Reprinted with permission of *Financial Analysts Journal*.

[6] "Objectives of Financial Reporting by Business Enterprises," op. cit., paragraph 34.

entities whose profitability is measured by two widely divergent sets of rules. The investor's task would be formidable, to say the least.

## Generally Accepted Accounting Principles (GAAP)

> OBJECTIVE 3
> Understand generally accepted accounting principles and the roles of various bodies, specifically the Securities and Exchange Commission and the Financial Accounting Standards Board, in the development process.

To bring order to the accounting and reporting process, the accounting profession has developed an underlying foundation for measuring and disclosing the results of business transactions and events. The foundation is a set of assumptions, concepts, standards, and procedures collectively known as **generally accepted accounting principles (GAAP).** The establishment of GAAP does not mean that all organizations report and measure financial activity in the same manner. Witness, for example, the accounting alternatives available for bad debt estimates, depreciation computations, and inventory valuation. Each business is somewhat unique, and thus a rigid set of measurement and reporting techniques is not feasible. In view of this fact, the accounting profession has formulated a generalized framework (i.e., ground rules) within which some diversity is possible.

Accounting principles differ dramatically from principles in such fields as chemistry and physics. Principles (or laws) relating to the sciences generally arise after repeated experiments and observations hold that a certain phenomenon is true. For example, by performing extensive research in their laboratories, scientists have learned that the speed of light is 186,000 miles per second and that each molecule of water consists of two atoms of hydrogen and one atom of oxygen. Unlike scientific law, accounting principles are not discovered; instead, the principles are formulated to enhance the objectives of financial reporting cited earlier. To illustrate, in an effort to inform statement readers about a company's financial position, the profession requires the presentation of a balance sheet. This means of disclosure cannot be scientifically proven as being right or wrong; it is, however, the generally accepted procedure for reporting the assets, liabilities, and owner's equity of a business enterprise.

### The Development of GAAP

For the most part, generally accepted accounting principles are an outgrowth of the profession's efforts during the past 60 years. The accounting profession made very little progress toward the establishment of principles and practices until the late 1920s and early 1930s. As with many developments in this country, a disaster provided the stimulus to get the ball rolling and headed in the right direction. Both the stock market crash of 1929 and the accompanying depression dictated a need for improvements in financial measurement and reporting. In many cases the financial statements of this period failed to disclose the correct financial position and profitability of an entity. Numerous businesses overstated net income along with their financial well-being. Because of this situation, efforts were made to protect investors and establish a generalized set of accounting principles.

***The Securities and Exchange Commission*** Given a widespread belief in the 1930s that government should play an increased role in the regulation of business, Congress passed several acts pertaining to the preparation of financial statements for publicly held corporations. The **Securities and Exchange Commission (SEC)** was given the power to administer these acts and to prescribe accounting principles and reporting practices for companies that issue publicly traded securities. Although the SEC has the authority for ultimately deciding what constitutes GAAP, most of the SEC's power has been informally delegated to other rule-making bodies of the accounting profession. The SEC has primarily served in an advisory role in the development of newly proposed accounting standards and has been especially active in promoting the disclosure of added information for financial statement users.

***The American Institute of Certified Public Accountants and the Accounting Principles Board*** Several years after the SEC came into existence, the **American Institute of Certified Public Accountants (AICPA),** a national association of licensed CPAs, began to publish bulletins on suggested accounting practices and rules through its newly organized Committee on Accounting Procedure (CAP). CAP had no authority to enforce its pronouncements and met with some criticism over the years.

In 1959, the AICPA formed a new policymaking body called the **Accounting Principles Board (APB)** to advance the development of generally accepted financial reporting practices. The APB studied different problem areas and issued rulings (termed *Opinions of the Accounting Principles Board*) on suggested treatment of various topics. Unlike CAP, which could advise and not enforce, the AICPA and the APB collectively declared that departures from the *Opinions* (i.e., GAAP) must be detailed and explained in a company's published financial statements. In view of this ruling, most companies follow GAAP when measuring and disclosing business activity. This practice avoids negative criticism of the firm by creditors and stockholders and, at the same time, reduces the possibility of lawsuits that sometimes arise from ill-advised reporting techniques.

In the late 1960s and early 1970s disagreement once again arose concerning the development of accounting principles. The work of the APB was branded as ineffective, primarily because of the following factors:

**1** Members of the Accounting Principles Board were part-time, unpaid volunteers. Thus, policies were formulated by professionals who could not devote their full attention to the issues at hand.

**2** Board members maintained relationships with their accounting firms and clients, and may have inadvertently compromised their position and vote for fear of injuring clientele.

The AICPA reacted to this criticism by performing a thorough study of the APB's operation and policymaking procedures. In the early 1970s the APB was abolished and replaced by the Financial Accounting Standards Board, a body independent of the AICPA. Although the APB and the Committee on Accounting Procedure are no longer in operation, their pronouncements are still in force and considered GAAP unless specifically amended or superseded by newer rulings.

***The Financial Accounting Standards Board*** The **Financial Accounting Standards Board (FASB)** is the private-sector organization presently in charge of formulating standards of financial reporting in the United States. Rulings of the board are GAAP and are called *Statements of Financial Accounting Standards* as opposed to *Opinions.*

Aside from its independence from the AICPA, the FASB differs from the APB in three major respects. First, members of the FASB serve on a full-time basis and must sever all ties with their previous employers. Member independence is therefore increased since the chance for employer or client influence is reduced (and probably eliminated). Second, FASB members are well paid for their efforts. At the time of this writing, their annual salaries were as follows: chairman, $330,000; board members, $265,000. The final difference between the FASB and APB deals with representation. Recognizing that accounting has far-reaching effects, the FASB has a broader-based membership, with backgrounds in public accounting as well as industry, government, academia, and the securities markets. This last characteristic enables the board to better serve the public interest.

During its existence the FASB has been relatively active. However, there is criticism that the board moves too slowly on certain critical financial reporting issues, fails to field test its proposals, and overlooks the cost of policy implementation. Some individuals in the financial community feel the FASB should be overhauled.

***Other Influential Bodies*** In addition to the SEC and the FASB, many other groups influence the establishment of generally accepted accounting principles. There are various accounting organizations, such as the *American Accounting Association (AAA)* and the *National Association of Accountants (NAA)*. The AAA is comprised primarily of educators; in contrast, most of the NAA's members are employed in business as cost and managerial accountants. These organizations play no official role in the development of accounting standards; however, they regularly communicate their position on numerous matters to the profession's policymaking bodies. The *Internal Revenue Service (IRS)*, which administers the tax laws passed by Congress, also has some impact on the development process. Although most tax regulations do not directly affect financial reporting, businesses often simplify matters by using specified tax practices for both the filing of tax returns with the government *and* the preparation of financial statements.

Add to the foregoing organizations various professional and trade associations; public accounting and business firms; and bankers, analysts, and other financial statement users. The net result is the formula for how generally accepted accounting principles (standards) are developed in this country. The overall process is depicted in Exhibit 13-1.

**Exhibit 13-1**
**The Development of Financial Accounting Standards**

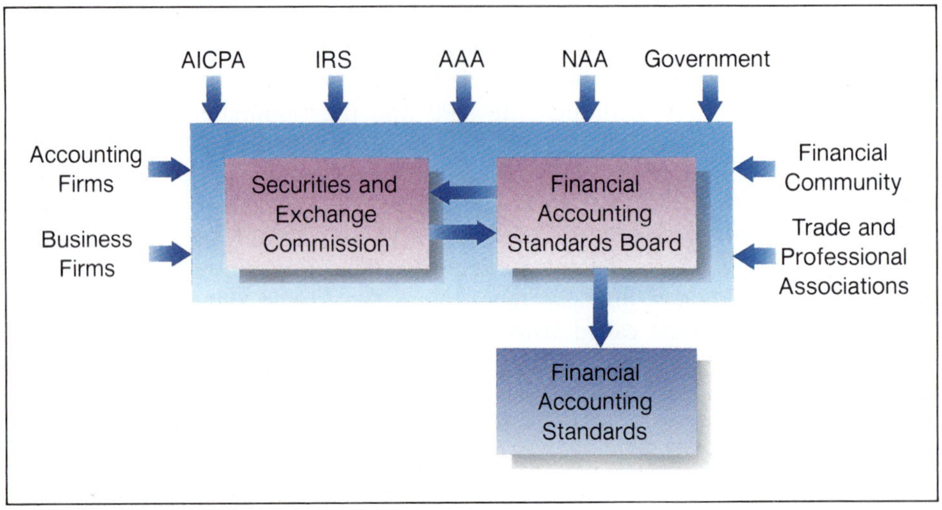

## Specific Principles and Assumptions

OBJECTIVE 4
**Be familiar with the assumptions, concepts, and modifying conventions that underlie financial accounting and reporting.**

APB *Opinions* and FASB *Statements* stipulate the proper accounting treatments that are afforded to a number of different topical areas. Throughout the first 12 chapters of this text, you were exposed to the following pronouncements, among others:

| *Pronouncement* | *Topic* |
|---|---|
| APB Opinion No. 17 | Intangible assets |
| FASB Statement No. 2 | Accounting for research and development costs |
| FASB Statement No. 5 | Accounting for contingencies |
| FASB Statement No. 12 | Short-term investments |
| FASB Statement No. 34 | Capitalization of interest cost |

Although the *Opinions* and *Statements* are considered GAAP by the accounting profession and the financial community, these pronouncements are not, in a true sense, "principles." Instead, they are rulings that pertain to accounting practice. Underlying accounting practice is a set of assumptions, concepts, and modifying conventions that form the basis for the FASB's work. These items will be discussed in the following sections.

### Entity Assumption

Recall from Chapter 1 that financial reporting is based on the entity assumption. An **entity** is an economic unit organized to pursue business activity. Examples of entities include corporations, individuals, clubs, governmental units, and a host of other organizations. It is important to note that each entity has its own assets, liabilities, revenues, and expenses and must be accounted for accordingly. In effect, the entity is a boundary for reporting, namely, a unit that is separate and distinct both from its owners and from other operations.

The absence of the entity assumption would make a mockery of the accounting process. To illustrate, assume that Jeremy Carson, a well-to-do engineer, organized a small company to conduct research in the solar energy field. If Carson's individual transactions were merged with those of the business, the company's balance sheet would include Carson's own clothing, his residence, his automobile, and other assets and liabilities that pertain solely to his personal well-being. Similarly, the income statement would combine business transactions with personal revenues and expenses. In sum, the financial statements of the business would fail to reflect the energy company's proper financial position and operating performance.

To correctly assess the outcome of economic activity, each entity must maintain separate accounting records and prepare separate sets of financial statements. That is, owner and business transactions must be segregated, along with the transactions of other independent economic units.

### Going-Concern Assumption

A key assumption in accounting is that a business will continue to operate for an indefinite period of time unless there is substantial evidence to the contrary. Stated differently, the business is presumed to be a **going concern.** Even though all entities do not survive, the going-concern assumption is valid in the majority of cases and forms the basis for many accounting procedures encountered in practice.

For example, if we contemplated business termination in the near future, assets such as property, plant, and equipment and prepaid expenses would be more properly expensed upon acquisition because of a low probability of receiving benefits beyond the current reporting period. The going-concern assumption also provides some justification for the use of an accounting system based on historical cost. Should a company plan to terminate operations in the near term, asset valuation on the balance sheet could properly take the form of liquidation (sale) prices because of the assets' impending disposal.

## Periodicity Assumption

Although a business is assumed to conduct operations for long periods of time, investors, creditors, governmental authorities, and other financial statement users cannot wait forever to analyze performance. Initially introduced in Chapter 3, the **periodicity assumption** holds that for reporting purposes, an entity's life can be divided into discrete time periods such as months, quarters, or years. As a result of this assumption, the accountant must assign business transactions to specific reporting periods. In many cases this task presents no special problems. For example, a check written on March 1 in payment of March rent is easily traced to March.

Difficulty arises, however, when dealing with expenditures that span several accounting periods. To illustrate, consider the cost of a long-lived machine. If a company desires to produce a yearly income statement, the machine's cost must be allocated to the period in question via depreciation expense. As you saw in Chapter 10, depreciation can be computed and allocated by several acceptable methods, each producing different results. Most accountants recognize that cost allocations normally result in arbitrary measures of performance and can diminish the usefulness of financial statements. Aside from depreciation, the periodicity assumption also forms the basis for amortization and the adjusting process at the conclusion of an accounting period.

## Monetary Unit Assumption

All countries have a unit of exchange. In the United States it is the dollar; in Mexico it is the peso; and in Japan it is the yen. Business organizations adopt the national currency of their home country to quantify financial activity. Accounting therefore assumes that an entity's transactions can be expressed in terms of a common measuring unit, namely, money. If all organizations in a given country use the same measure, or **monetary unit,** extensive comparative analysis is possible by financial statement users.

Financial reporting in the United States is based on the premise that the dollar is a stable evaluation unit, thereby permitting dollars of different years to be combined in the financial statements. When computing the balance in a company's Land account, for instance, land transactions of the 1990s are mixed with transactions that occurred in prior years. This calculation is reasonable provided that the dollar is, in fact, stable. Historically, accounting policymakers have taken the position that fluctuations in the value of the dollar are small and can be ignored.

Is this a valid position, however? Consider the dollar in comparison with other units of measure, say square feet. If you were to measure the area of the room you are presently in today, next year, and five years from now, an accurate measurement would undoubtedly yield the same result each time. In contrast, consider the amount of goods and services you could purchase for $50 over the same time period. In all likelihood the goods and services acquired would decline each year due to rising prices and a reduction in the dollar's purchasing power. Because of this behavior (i.e., instability), especially in periods of high inflation, some accountants contend that transactions occurring today cannot be combined with those of earlier periods. The net result would be the combination of dollars of different purchasing powers and, hence, misleading financial statements. The impact of inflation on financial reporting will be explored shortly.

## Historical-Cost Principle

Accountants have been faced with many problems over the years. One of the most troublesome (and debated) issues has been the financial statement valuation of goods, services, and resources acquired in business transactions. As noted in Chapter 1, accounting is based on the **historical-cost principle.** That is, acquisitions of the preceding items are recorded in the accounts at cost, with cost defined as the exchange or transaction price.

The use of historical cost has received mixed reviews. In its favor, historical cost is objective and definite. To explain, the use of cost and exchange prices gives rise to objective valuations created by negotiation between two *independent* parties—a buyer and a seller. Also on the favorable end of the spectrum, cost can be verified via canceled checks, contracts, invoices, and other similar documents.

Critics of historical cost note that employment of the cost basis *subsequent to asset acquisition* produces out-of-date asset valuations and distorted income figures. The latter arise because of cost-based depreciation and amortization computations. Critics therefore contend that fair market values should be integrated in the financial statements. This practice, while having obvious benefits, does have an inherent problem. Assume, for instance, that five accountants are trying to compute the fair market value ("current worth") of an old manufacturing plant. The "current worth" would probably be influenced by a number of factors that are difficult to quantify, such as the plant's physical condition, its location, and the general state of the real estate market. Even competent appraisal services that specialize in this type of work would have differing ideas, culminating in dissimilar (and subjective) estimates. Subjectivity, of course, would erode the public's confidence in a company's financial statements.

## Objectivity Principle

The thrust of the objectivity principle has been discussed in preceding sections of this chapter. Simply stated, the **objectivity principle** requires that accounting information be free from bias and verifiable by an independent party (such as an external auditor). The resulting financial statements will therefore reflect a fair and neutral view of an organization's business affairs.

Although a high degree of objectivity is desirable, it is difficult to eliminate all personal opinion and judgment from accounting measurement. Consider the accounting procedures related to depreciable assets, for example. Although the cost of a long-lived asset can be determined objectively, estimates are needed when computing service life and residual value, and personal opinion is used when selecting a depreciation method. Naturally, variations in any of the preceding factors will produce different effects on net income and asset valuations. As long as the estimates and related decisions are reasonable, made by a competent party, and verifiable, the objectivity principle is considered to have been implemented to the greatest extent possible.

## Revenue Realization Principle

**OBJECTIVE 5**
**Understand the revenue realization principle and be able to apply the percentage-of-completion and installment methods.**

The generation of revenue in our economy takes many different forms. Hospitals, for instance, earn revenues by rendering health care services; professional sports clubs sell tickets and broadcasting rights; department stores sell merchandise; and construction companies build roads, homes, office complexes, and a host of other items. Although our list of revenue-generating activities is far from complete, a question arises as to when these enterprises should recognize revenue in their accounting records. Theoretically, revenue generation is a continuous process for most firms. Practically, however, revenue is said to be *realized* (earned) when both of the following conditions are satisfied:

1 The earnings process is complete or virtually complete.
2 The amount of revenue can be objectively measured.

For most businesses these two tests are met when merchandise is sold or when services are rendered. In either case the transaction and earnings process is complete at this point, and the revenue is measurable on the basis of the exchange price between the buyer and the seller.

Although the time of sale (or rendering of services) is the general rule for recognizing revenue, realization is sometimes advanced or delayed, as depicted in the time line shown in Exhibit 13-2.

***Revenue Recognized During Production*** Many companies engage in construction projects that take several years to complete, such as ships, shopping malls, and dams. Because these firms generate revenues by building, it may be more appropriate to enter revenue in the accounting records over a project's life instead of waiting until the venture is completed (i.e., the point of sale). Accordingly, a method of revenue recognition termed **percentage of completion (POC)** may be used. Under the POC method, profit is allocated to each accounting period on the basis of progress toward project completion. Completion is usually judged by comparing the current period's construction costs with the total expected costs over the project's life.

As an example, assume that Brennan Construction signed a $44 million contract to build a shopping mall over the next three years. Brennan's accounting department has estimated total construction costs at $40 million, resulting in a $4

**Exhibit 13-2**
**Revenue Recognition Time Line**

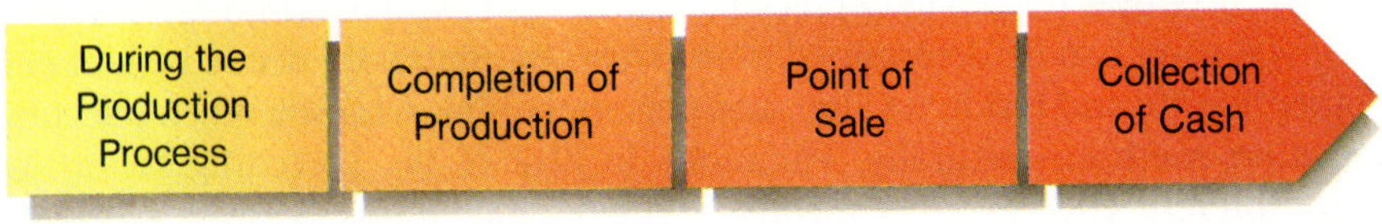

HIGHLIGHT

# Claiming Tomorrow's Profits Today

Not too long ago, Jiffy Lube International, a Baltimore-based franchiser of quick-oil-change centers, was ordered by the Securities and Exchange Commission to change its accounting. The surprise order resulted in a staggering earnings hit for the first quarter of Jiffy's fiscal year: net income of $95,000, less than 25% of what Jiffy would have reported. Why the SEC order? Because the commission said Jiffy was claiming income it hadn't yet earned.

Over the past two years, the SEC has made similar charges against about half a dozen other fast-growing startups in the franchise field. Among them: Moto Photo, Inc., Swensen's Inc., and Le Peep Restaurants, Inc. The accounting issue involves the tricky problem of revenue recognition from the sale of so-called area development rights. These are contracts sold by the company granting a developer the exclusive right to open franchises in a particular territory. In return, the developer traditionally pays the company a nonrefundable fee up front.

For years some franchisers have been reporting these upfront fees as current income. But the SEC argues that the increasing complexity of the contracts no longer makes doing so permissible. These days, area developers are often required to open a certain number of stores within a set time period. In some cases, the franchiser also agrees to provide training and advertising support services to the developer. By imposing such conditions on the agreement, the SEC notes, the franchiser changes the nature of the fee paid in the deal.

The SEC's position is based on two long-held accounting principles: Revenue must be earned in order to be recognized; and costs must be matched with revenues as they are earned. Says a professor of accounting at the University of Pennsylvania: "If some effort or sacrifice isn't put forth, then the revenue hasn't been earned." The SEC claims that in the case of area development fees, companies have not truly earned the revenues until the franchise units are open and operating. Moreover, the SEC argues that franchise companies sometimes use area development fees to meet the costs of servicing the developer; therefore, this income should not be recognized until the costs are incurred as well.

Franchisers complain that the SEC's position will particularly hurt startup companies, which depend on area development agreements to attract sophisticated entrepreneurs to their businesses, as well as to provide them with much-needed cash. "In the long run, this could have a major financial impact," says the counsel for the International Franchise Association. That way overstates the case according to some. After all, fee income will still be realized—just not up front all at once. In fact, the SEC's position may well have a favorable long-term effect in preventing small franchisers from trying to grow too quickly.

SOURCE: Adapted from "Claiming Tomorrow's Profits Today," *Forbes*, October 17, 1988, p. 78. Reprinted by permission of *Forbes* magazine, © Forbes Inc., 1988.

million profit for the company. The following schedule shows the actual costs incurred along with the annual profit recognized:

| *Year* | *(A) Actual Costs Incurred* | *(B) Percentage of Work Completed (A ÷ $40,000,000)* | *(C) Profit Recognized ($4,000,000 × B)* |
|---|---|---|---|
| 1 | $10,000,000 | 25% | $1,000,000 |
| 2 | 24,000,000 | 60 | 2,400,000 |
| 3 | 6,300,000 | Remainder | 300,000* |
| | $40,300,000 | | $3,700,000 |

* Remaining amount needed to yield total income of $3.7 million.

For the first two years the percentage of work completed is derived by dividing the actual costs incurred by the $40 million total project cost. The resulting percentage is then multiplied by the $4 million estimated profit to compute annual income. Year 3, the last year of construction, is handled in a different fashion. Total construction costs amount to $40.3 million, generating an overall contract profit of $3.7 million ($44,000,000 − $40,300,000). Since profit of $3.4 million has already been recognized ($1,000,000 + $2,400,000), Brennan can realize only $300,000 in Year 3.

Because of the objectivity principle, the POC method is used only when a business has the ability to make reasonably dependable estimates of contract revenues, contract costs, and the extent of progress toward completion. In those instances where substantial uncertainty surrounds the estimation process, other procedures are followed.

### TIPS & TECHNIQUES

Percentage of completion can be employed for either all or part of a company's operation. Westinghouse Electric, for instance, noted the following in a recent annual report:

> Sales are recorded primarily as products are shipped and services are rendered. The percentage-of-completion method of accounting is used for nuclear steam supply system orders with delivery schedules generally in excess of five years and for certain construction projects where this method of accounting is consistent with industry practices.

***Revenue Recognized Upon Completion of Production*** In some situations revenue is recognized at the end of production. For example, assume that Brennan Construction had great difficulty in determining total contract costs. Because the related percentage calculations would be somewhat questionable, it is more appropriate to recognize the entire profit ($3.7 million) at the time of project completion, when all facts are known.

Another case in which recognition occurs upon completion of production is in selected, well-developed markets such as certain farm products and precious metals. For instance, a farmer may face a situation in which the sale and price of his crop are reasonably assured and no significant delivery costs are involved. Revenue in this situation can be recognized upon harvest, as the earnings process is complete and the amount of revenue can be objectively measured.

***Revenue Recognized at the Time of Receipt*** As we noted in Chapter 3, many professionals (e.g., lawyers, dentists, and architects) use a form of cash basis accounting for their practices. Under the cash basis, revenue is realized at the time cash is collected from customers and clients. Probably because of the method's simplicity and its acceptance by the Internal Revenue Service, cash basis accounting is widely used by individuals and small businesses. The cash basis is not in accord with GAAP, however, because revenue realization is delayed beyond the point where the earnings process is complete.[7] The cash basis is appropriate in those few instances when revenues cannot be correctly determined at the time of sale, specifically, when collectibility of customer accounts is in serious doubt. This situation sometimes arises with installment sales made to individuals who have no (or poor) credit histories.

Installment sales occur in the retail field, especially home furnishings and appliances, where payments are spread over several years. Revenues can be recognized by using a variation of the cash basis called the **installment method.** Sellers that use the installment method allocate a sale's profit to different accounting periods based on the amount of cash received from customers. For example, suppose that on September 1, Beachwood Kitchens sold $1,500 of new appliances to Joyce Chambers, who has no credit history and has been employed for only two weeks. Chambers paid $300 down and agreed to remit the balance owed via 24 end-of-month installments of $50 each.[8] If the appliances cost Beachwood $900, the company has generated a $600 profit, or a 40% return on sales ($600 ÷ $1,500 = 40%). Because each dollar collected from Chambers represents a 40% profit, the company's recognition schedule would appear as follows:

| *Year* | *Cash Collected* | | *Profit Percentage* | | *Profit Recognized* |
|---|---|---|---|---|---|
| 1 | $ 500* | × | 40% | = | $200 |
| 2 | 600† | × | 40 | = | 240 |
| 3 | 400‡ | × | 40 | = | 160 |
| | $1,500 | | | | $600 |

* $300 down payment + four monthly installments of $50 each.
† Twelve monthly installments of $50 each.
‡ Eight monthly installments of $50 each.

Similar to the cash basis, the installment method does not conform to GAAP unless, as noted earlier, considerable uncertainty surrounds collectibility of the receivable. With certain restrictions and conditions, the installment method is acceptable by the IRS and affords users the advantage of postponing income taxes. Postponement arises because revenues are not taxed until cash is received.

[7] Most professional practices do not issue "published financial statements," or statements to owners (i.e., stockholders) that have been audited by a CPA. "Unpublished" statements need not be prepared in accordance with GAAP.

[8] To simplify matters we will ignore interest.

### Matching Principle

Like revenue realization, the **matching principle** is another important consideration in the determination of accounting income. Originally discussed in Chapter 3, this principle holds that all costs and expenses associated with the production of revenue be recognized when the revenue is recognized. Stated differently, expenses should be matched against and deducted from the revenues they helped to create.

The matching principle is the underlying reason behind the adjusting process. Consider, for example, the accounting treatment for depreciable assets. At the end of a reporting period, depreciation expense is recorded in the accounts via an adjustment. Why? Long-term assets such as plant and equipment generate revenues (or benefits) for prolonged periods of time. Thus, a *portion* of the assets' cost (i.e., depreciation expense) is written off each period and matched against the revenues created by the assets' use. Notice that only part of the cost is currently expensed; the remainder will be written off in future periods against the future revenues generated.

### Consistency Principle

Financial statements are frequently compared over periods of time to examine trends, assess growth patterns, and so forth. To enhance these studies, accountants have implemented the principle of **consistency,** which holds that entities employ the same accounting practices in each reporting period. Picture the difficulties that would result if a company switched back and forth between LIFO and FIFO and other measurement techniques at will. Indeed, such a practice would create havoc for financial statement users who, in many cases, would be forced to compare the noncomparable.

It is important to note that consistency does not completely prohibit change. Changes in the methods of recording and reporting business transactions are allowable whenever the end result is a better or more fair presentation of economic activity. When such changes occur, the reason for the change and the impact on net income must be disclosed in the financial statements.

### Disclosure Principle

So that investors, creditors, and analysts are not misled, a set of financial statements includes much more than just account balances. An entity must provide a complete reporting **(disclosure)** of all facts important enough to influence the judgment of an informed user of financial information. Just what an "informed user" really means is, itself, open to debate; however, accountants have agreed that disclosure should include the following items as a minimum:

1 A summary of the significant accounting policies used in statement preparation.
2 Principles and practices peculiar to the industry in which the entity operates, along with departures from GAAP.
3 Changes in accounting policies and the resultant impact on net income.
4 Impending lawsuits and contingencies.
5 Significant events that occurred subsequent to the accounting period being reported but prior to issuance of the financial statements, for example, major casualties such as fires and tornadoes.
6 Significant transactions that took place during the period, such as business acquisitions and mergers.

Disclosure often takes the form of parenthetical comments within the body of the statements and separate footnotes. A complete set of footnotes can be observed in the financial statements that appear in Appendix B at the end of the text.

## Materiality

There are many instances in accounting where theory gives way to expediency, especially when dealing with very small amounts or transactions. To illustrate, suppose a company recently acquired five pencil sharpeners for $75. If the principles and practices introduced in the preceding pages are followed to the letter, the sharpeners would be entered in the accounts as long-term assets and depreciated over their lifetime. Assuming a 10-year life, annual straight-line depreciation would amount to $7.50, a pittance for almost any organization. To avoid the administrative problems and costs of keeping track of these items over the next 10 years, most companies would expense the entire $75 immediately at the time of acquisition.

This accounting treatment is justified for two reasons. First, the transaction is very small; and second, it will probably have a minimal impact on the financial statements. This example has focused on the concept of materiality. **Materiality** dictates that the accountant must judge the impact and importance of each transaction (or event) to determine the proper treatment in the accounting records and the resultant financial statements. In general, an amount is said to be material if knowledge of it would influence the decisions of an informed financial statement user.

Materiality is a relative concept and is often judged by using comparative analysis. For example, a potential expense item could be compared against some type of dollar limit. If the item exceeds the limit, it is deemed material; if under the limit, the item is considered immaterial and would be expensed. The dollar limit and exactly what is material varies from company to company: what is immaterial for Shell Oil might be very significant to Joe's Garage. There is no guideline stating that 10% is always material or that any expenditure over $500 is always significant. Again, materiality is a relative concept.

## Conservatism

An accountant is faced with a number of different decisions in attempting to measure and report the financial affairs of an enterprise. Frequently, the "proper" decision is difficult to determine. After exercising sound judgment and considering the objectives of financial reporting, other accounting principles, and industry practices, the accountant often turns to the doctrine of conservatism. **Conservatism** stipulates that when alternative accounting valuations and measurements are possible, the one selected should be that which is least likely to overstate assets and/or net income.

Over the years conservative financial statements have found favor with statement users. Conservatism allows users to downplay the impact of overly optimistic company managements who may be inclined to record revenue in the accounts before the revenue is realized, capitalize items that should be expensed, and follow other similar practices, many of which tend to improve reported financial position and profitability. Overly optimistic financial statements could mask impending losses and mislead users.

The application of conservatism in accounting becomes evident when studying the lower-of-cost-or-market method for valuing short-term investments. For instance, suppose Remy Company purchased $15,000 of stock on October 1, to be held as a short-term investment. Assume that on December 31, the end of the firm's accounting period, the investment was worth $22,000. If this is the only security held by Remy, the $7,000 increase in value would be ignored when preparing the financial statements. Conservatism says to disregard increases in value while holding the stock; consistent with revenue realization, gains (i.e., profits) will be recognized upon sale. Interestingly, however, if the value of the securities had fallen by $7,000, a write down below cost and the recording of a loss are justified. Why? The result is a lower, more conservative asset valuation and a reduced net income.

## Accounting for Inflation

OBJECTIVE 6
**Understand the impact of inflation on financial statements.**

As you know, the United States has experienced periodic rounds of inflation. **Inflation** is a rise in the general price level that causes a decline in the purchasing power of the dollar. Stated simply, a dollar will not buy as much today as it did several years ago. Just as you are affected by inflation in steadily rising prices for food, entertainment, transportation, and tuition, businesses, too, have similar problems. Many profitable companies have experienced difficulty obtaining sufficient funds to purchase inventories and property, plant, and equipment.

On numerous occasions throughout the text, we have stressed that financial statements are an outgrowth of the historical-cost principle. These statements are also based on the *monetary unit assumption,* which holds that the dollar is a stable evaluation unit. As noted earlier in the chapter, the stability of the dollar and the meaningfulness of historical-cost statements are often questioned during periods of moderate and high inflation (see pp. 448–449). Businesses, for example, will raise selling prices to help offset price increases from their suppliers. Yet the costs that are matched against sales on the income statement are frequently those incurred many years earlier, with a primary example being depreciation on low-cost, aged machinery. The result is a questionable net income figure, which may lead owners or management to make incorrect decisions.

This problem and several others have prompted accountants to study and develop financial reporting models other than historical cost. Two of the more prominent models are constant purchasing power accounting and current cost accounting.

### Constant Purchasing Power Accounting

Under **constant purchasing power accounting,** historical-cost data are adjusted for changes in the value (purchasing power) of the dollar by using a general price level index. To explain, the federal government monitors price changes in our economy by sampling various goods and services. The goods and services (often called a *market basket*) are priced at different points in time to determine how much such amounts have risen or fallen. The outcome is an index, with one of the most popular being the consumer price index (CPI).

The CPI measures retail price changes of a variety of items (e.g., food, clothing, shelter, transportation, and so forth) throughout the country. For comparative purposes, the 1982–1984 prices of these items were assigned an index number of 100. In subsequent years the index number is revised to correspond with the percentage increase or decrease in the price of the market basket. By June 1989, for example, the index had risen to 124.1, which meant it cost $124.10 in 1989 to purchase goods that sold for $100.00 in 1982–1984.

With the constant purchasing power approach, a general price level index is applied to account balances to adjust for transactions that occur at different times and, thus, different price levels. In this manner financial information becomes more meaningful, because it is presented in terms of dollars that have identical purchasing power. Consider, for instance, a company that acquired equipment in 1960, 1970, and 1980. The addition of purchase prices generates total equipment cost; yet the true meaning of the total is questionable. Dollars spent in 1980 are not equivalent to dollars spent in 1970 or 1960 because of changes in purchasing power. In effect, calculations such as the foregoing are dealing with apples and oranges, that is, dollars of a differing size.

The constant purchasing power approach recognizes this problem and converts historical cost into constant dollars by means of the following formula:

$$\text{Historical Cost} \times \frac{\text{Index Converting To}}{\text{Index Converting From}} = \text{Restated Amount}$$

As an example, suppose Oliva Corporation acquired a machine on December 31, 19X1, for $50,000. Assume the following price indices:

| | |
|---|---|
| December 31, 19X1 | 100 |
| December 31, 19X2 | 120 |
| December 31, 19X3 | 130 |
| 19X3 average index | 125 |

Prices increased by 20% (120 − 100) from 19X1 to 19X2. The cost of Oliva's asset is therefore reported on the December 31, 19X2, constant purchasing power balance sheet as $60,000 ($50,000 × 120/100). Stated differently, Oliva would need 60,000 19X2 dollars to possess the same purchasing power as the 50,000 19X1 dollars.

Notice that our illustration employed an end-of-year price index. Frequently, a business will have many transactions that occur uniformly throughout the year. Typical examples of such transactions include sales, merchandise purchases, and the incurrence of operating expenses. These items are more appropriately adjusted by using an average price index. If Oliva's 19X3 sales totaled $200,000, the company's constant purchasing power income statement for the year ended December 31, 19X3, would report sales of $208,000 ($200,000 × 130/125). Again the same technique of adjusting is employed: index converting to divided by index converting from.

## Monetary and Nonmonetary Items

When constant purchasing power financial statements are prepared, it is necessary to distinguish between monetary and nonmonetary items. **Monetary items** consist of cash and contractual claims to receive or pay a fixed amount of cash in the future. Monetary items include **monetary assets** (such as cash, accounts receivable, and notes receivable) and **monetary liabilities** (e.g., accounts payable, notes payable, and salaries payable). By their very nature, monetary assets and liabilities are (1) already expressed in terms of current dollars and (2) fixed by contractual obligation. For instance, accounts receivable represent a right to collect a stated number of dollars in the future, irrespective of the purchasing power of those dollars. Similarly, accounts payable are extinguished by the disbursement of an agreed-on dollar outlay, regardless of the price level that exists at the time of payment.

The remaining items on the balance sheet are **nonmonetary.** The number of dollars that a nonmonetary item commands can change over time. For example, you have probably observed an overall increase in the prices of land, homes, and automobiles during the past few years. These items do not represent a claim to a "fixed" amount of cash and therefore tend to increase in price as the purchasing power of the dollar declines. Other nonmonetary items include inventory, equipment, obligations under warranties, and owner's equity.

### Purchasing Power Gains and Losses

The distinction between monetary and nonmonetary items is important. The analysis of *monetary* items during an accounting period will indicate whether a company has experienced a **purchasing power gain or loss.** In periods of inflation the holders of monetary assets suffer a purchasing power loss. To illustrate, suppose that at the beginning of a period with an annual inflation rate of 15%, you put $100 cash in a cookie jar to save for emergencies. Because of rising prices, goods that cost $100 when the funds were put aside will cost $115 at the end of the year. Thus, a $15 purchasing power loss is incurred.

In contrast, the holders of monetary liabilities experience purchasing power gains during inflationary periods, because obligations are repaid with dollars of a lower value. For instance, assume that a friend borrowed $500 from you and paid it back one year later without interest. If the annual inflation rate was 10%, your friend has generated a purchasing power gain of $50. Specifically, he or she received $500 of purchasing power at the time of the loan. At the end of the year the number of dollars representing the same purchasing power had risen to $550 ($500 × 1.10); yet only $500 must be repaid. Your friend's purchasing power gain is your purchasing power loss.

Given this reality, businesses generally have few reservations about going into debt during periods of inflation. By so doing, they generate a favorable monetary liability position and maximize purchasing power gains. Because debt normally bears an interest cost and obligates an entity to periodic principal payments, a debt financing philosophy should be pursued with caution and conservatism. Finally, note that nonmonetary items do not create purchasing power gains or losses, since such items are not claims to or against specific sums of money.

## Current Cost Accounting

The general price level index used in the constant purchasing power approach is, as its name implies, general. That is, a variety of goods and services are considered in the index's computation. If all prices behaved in the same manner as the index, there would be few problems. Normally, however, there is considerable variation. In a given year the prices of certain items may soar while others either remain the same or decline. In the past decade, for example, housing and energy costs increased considerably. During the same years the cost of many electronic products (e.g., computers, calculators, and home appliances) actually decreased because of technological advances.

An alternative measurement and reporting model is termed **current cost accounting.** This approach recognizes price changes in the individual assets owned by an enterprise and restates each asset separately in terms of its current worth.

Although "worth" may be defined in various ways, a very popular approach uses **current cost,** or the present cost of replacing an asset with a similar asset in similar condition. For example, the current cost of a company's 1988 delivery truck would be computed as the present retail selling price for a similar truck with approximately the same mileage.

Unfortunately, the computation of current cost is not always straightforward. Although manufacturers' price lists and appraisal values (in the case of real estate) are helpful, complications may be encountered. Sometimes, used asset markets do not exist. Furthermore, existing assets are often difficult to value, especially if the assets are antiquated and newer, more advanced technology is available. Factors such as these must be addressed when applying the current cost approach; yet the related problems are not easily overcome.

### Holding Gains and Losses

When current cost accounting is used, a business will normally experience **holding gains** or **holding losses.** To illustrate, assume that Flame Company purchased 5,000 units of inventory on November 15 at $2 per unit. By December 31, the end of Flame's accounting period, the current cost of the goods had increased to $2.50, for a total of $12,500 (5,000 units × $2.50). Current cost financial statements would disclose the inventory at $12,500 along with a $2,500 gain [5,000 units × ($2.50 − $2.00)]. This gain is termed a *holding gain* because it relates to an increase in asset value during the period the inventory was held by the firm. If the goods had declined in value, a *holding loss* would have occurred.

There are two types of holding gains and losses: unrealized and realized. **Unrealized gains and losses** relate to assets that are still owned at the end of the accounting period and are typified by the $2,500 gain in the Flame illustration. Be aware, however, that if the company had sold some of its units, the computation would change.

For instance, assume that inventory cost peaked at $2.50 immediately after the purchase on November 15. If 2,000 units were later sold at $8 each, the firm would *realize* a $1,000 holding gain. To explain, **realized holding gains and losses** are calculated on the basis of assets sold or consumed. As before, Flame must compute the difference between acquisition cost ($2.00) and current cost ($2.50). The business will therefore report a $1,000 realized holding gain (2,000 units × $0.50) on its current cost income statement. Flame will also show a $1,500 unrealized gain relating to the 3,000 units that remain in ending inventory (3,000 units × $0.50 = $1,500).

## The FASB and Inflation

For a brief period of time during the early and mid-1980s, the Financial Accounting Standards Board required that large publicly held companies disclose certain inflation-adjusted information.[9] This reporting requirement was issued as part of an *experiment,* with the FASB making clear that changes were not to be made in the

[9] See "Financial Reporting and Changing Prices," *Statement of Financial Accounting Standards No. 33* (Stamford, Conn.: Financial Accounting Standards Board, 1979); and "Financial Reporting and Changing Prices: Elimination of Certain Disclosures," *Statement of Financial Accounting Standards No. 82* (Stamford, Conn.: Financial Accounting Standards Board, 1984).

financial statements themselves. In other words, accounting records and reports of financial position and profitability would continue to be based on the historical-cost principle. The selected inflation-adjusted information was to be reported on a supplementary basis only (and was typically included in the footnotes to the financial statements).

In 1986, the FASB made such disclosures voluntary.[10] This decision was brought about by several factors, including business complaints that the required information was too expensive to produce and could be misinterpreted by users, a lowering of inflation rates, and a diminished interest by the SEC in such revelations. As a result of the FASB's action, few companies are choosing to participate in this disclosure exercise.

The authors doubt that inflation accounting is a dead issue. There is a virtual certainty that debate on the two approaches discussed will continue. If moderate or double-digit inflation returns, we expect that the lessons learned from the Board's experiment will serve as a starting point for the development of a new reporting standard.

## Chapter Review

### Learning Objectives—The Key Points

**1 Be familiar with the objectives of financial reporting.** The financial reporting function should generate information that is useful (1) to a wide variety of users who must make various types of decisions, (2) in assessing future cash flows, (3) in studying a firm's financial position and any related changes during the accounting period, and (4) in examining an entity's financial performance (i.e., earnings). Above all, the information conveyed should be general purpose and unbiased in its orientation.

**2 Be aware of the desirable characteristics of accounting information: relevancy, reliability, comparability, and understandability.** Relevancy relates to the influence of information on the actions of a decision maker. That is, information would be deemed relevant if it influences the actions of an investor, creditor, or other financial statement user. Reliability, on the other hand, refers to the ability of information to accurately depict the conditions it is supposed to represent. To be reliable and to instill public confidence in the information being reported, an entity's disclosures must be free from bias. Comparability refers to making a company's financial statements comparable with the statements of other firms and with those of the same firm at different points in time. Finally, understandability involves making a company's financial statements comprehensible to those who have a reasonable understanding of business activities and are willing to study the information with reasonable diligence.

**3 Understand generally accepted accounting principles and the roles of various bodies, specifically the Securities and Exchange Commission and the Financial Accounting Standards Board, in the development process.** The foundation of accounting and reporting is a set of assumptions, concepts, standards, and procedures known as generally accepted accounting principles (GAAP). In the 1930s, the Securities and Exchange Commission was given the power to prescribe accounting principles and practices for publicly held corporations. Since its beginning, however, the SEC has elected to delegate authority to rule-making bodies of the accounting profession. The current private-sector

[10] "Financial Reporting and Changing Prices," *Statement of Financial Accounting Standards No. 89* (Stamford, Conn.: Financial Accounting Standards Board, 1986).

group in charge of formulating GAAP is the Financial Accounting Standards Board. Although other groups influence the development of GAAP, financial reporting is largely the result of FASB and SEC interaction.

**4 Be familiar with the assumptions, concepts, and modifying conventions that underlie financial accounting and reporting.** Twelve fundamental concepts form the basis for financial accounting. A short description of each follows.

- *Entity assumption*—an assumption that a business is viewed as a unit separate and apart from its owners and other firms.
- *Going-concern assumption*—the belief that a business will continue to operate for an indefinite period of time unless there is substantial evidence to the contrary.
- *Periodicity assumption*—a financial reporting assumption; holds that an entity's life can be divided into discrete time periods.
- *Monetary unit assumption*—the ideas that (1) an entity's transactions and events can be expressed in terms of a common measuring unit (i.e., the dollar) and (2) the dollar's purchasing power is stable.
- *Historical-cost principle*—the principle of recording goods, resources, and services at cost, with cost defined as the exchange or transaction price.
- *Objectivity principle*—the requirement that accounting information be definite, verifiable, and free from bias.
- *Revenue realization*—the basis that allows companies to enter revenue in the accounting records when earned, which is generally when goods are sold or when services are rendered.
- *Matching principle*—the principle that expenses should be recognized in the same period as the revenues that they helped to produce.
- *Consistency principle*—the idea that businesses employ the same accounting practices in each reporting period to improve comparability of financial statements.
- *Disclosure principle*—the requirement that an entity provide a complete reporting of all facts important enough to influence the judgment of an informed user of financial information.
- *Materiality*—a concept dictating that an accountant judge the impact and importance of each transaction and event to determine its proper handling in the accounting records. Minor items are treated in the most expedient manner possible.
- *Conservatism*—a doctrine that when alternative valuations and measurements are possible, the alternative selected should be the one that is least likely to overstate assets and/or net income.

**5 Understand the revenue realization principle and be able to apply the percentage-of-completion and installment methods.** Revenue is said to be realized when (1) the earnings process is complete or virtually complete and (2) the amount of revenue can be objectively measured. Most revenues are realized when merchandise is sold or services are rendered. However, when the earnings process is spread over several accounting periods, the percentage of completion (POC) and installment methods may be used.

POC is often employed to account for long-term construction contracts. Profit is recognized on the basis of progress toward project completion, which is frequently determined by relating the amount of cost incurred to the total cost to be incurred. Another approach, the installment method, is used in retail environments when collectibility of cash is in doubt. With this method, profit is allocated to different accounting periods on the basis of cash received from customers.

**6 Understand the impact of inflation on financial statements.** Inflation is a rise in the general price level that causes a decline in the purchasing power of the dollar. Two approaches to prepare inflation-adjusted financial information are constant purchasing power accounting and current cost accounting. Under constant purchasing power, historical cost amounts are restated via a price level index conversion formula. Only nonmonetary items (i.e., items other than cash and contractual obligations to receive or pay a fixed amount of cash in the future) are restated. With current cost accounting, changes in the value of specific assets are recognized. Also with this method, gains and losses associated with holding assets during an inflationary period are taken into account. The FASB has experimented with inflation-adjusted supplemental disclosures, and such disclosures are now voluntary.

## Chapter Quiz

The five questions that follow relate to several issues raised in the chapter. Test your knowledge of the issues by selecting the best answer. (The answers appear on p. 477.)

**1** If financial statements are prepared so that creditors benefit at the expense of other user groups, the financial statements are not:
a understandable.
b reliable.
c relevant.
d comparable.

**2** Generally accepted accounting principles:
a vary from state to state.
b dictate that all large companies use the exact same accounting practices.
c are presently established by the Accounting Principles Society of America.
d are established by the Financial Accounting Standards Board.

**3** Which assumption or principle holds that financial statements should be verifiable by an independent party?
a Periodicity.
b Matching.
c Consistency.
d Objectivity.

**4** Kent signed a $20 million contract to construct a four-mile road over a two-year period. It is estimated that total costs for the road will be $18 million, producing a $2 million profit. Three miles of the road were completed during Year 1 at a cost of $13.5 million. Kent recognized $1.5 million in profit by following the percentage-of-completion method. If the road was finished in Year 2 at an additional cost of $4.2 million, how much profit should be recognized in Year 2?
a $0.
b $500,000.
c $800,000.
d $2,300,000.

**5** The preparation and presentation of inflation-adjusted financial information is currently:
a mandatory for large companies.
b mandatory for companies that follow generally accepted accounting principles.
c voluntary for all firms that follow generally accepted accounting principles.
d required of companies that use the monetary unit assumption in the measurement of financial affairs.

## Questions

**Q13-1** Financial reporting attempts to generate information that is helpful in assessing the amounts, timing, and uncertainty of an organization's cash inflows and outflows. Briefly discuss why creditors would be interested in this information.

**Q13-2** Briefly explain why accountants prepare general-purpose financial statements.

**Q13-3** Bearing in mind that accounting information should be relevant, discuss a possible problem of using financial statements that are based on historical cost.

**Q13-4** Briefly discuss the need for an underlying foundation of financial reporting, namely, generally accepted accounting principles.

**Q13-5** Which organization has ultimate authority over the reporting practices of most large corporations? Explain.

**Q13-6** Discuss the basic differences between the APB and the FASB.

**Q13-7** Define the entity assumption and discuss its need in financial reporting.

**Q13-8** The going-concern assumption forms the basis for many of the accounting practices illustrated in this text. Define the going-concern assumption and list several of these practices.

**Q13-9** Discuss the basic problem that underlies the monetary unit assumption.

**Q13-10** Briefly define the historical-cost principle. Why is cost preferred for asset valuations?

**Q13-11** Revenue is said to be realized when two tests are met. What are these two tests and when are they met by most businesses?

**Q13-12** Present an example of when it is permissible to recognize revenue during the production process.

**Q13-13** Present an example of when it is permissible to recognize revenue at the time of receipt.

**Q13-14** Metro Delivery was founded in 19X1 and implemented a straight-line depreciation policy for its truck fleet.

a Should Metro use straight-line depreciation in 19X2 and 19X3? Why? Discuss from the viewpoint of a statement user.

b *Must* Metro use straight-line depreciation in 19X2 and 19X3? Explain.

**Q13-15** Discuss materiality. How is the materiality of a particular item often determined?

**Q13-16** Lionel Johnson, staff accountant for Martin Machinery, is attempting to compute the company's purchasing power gain or loss. Discuss the meaning of a purchasing power gain or loss, and determine whether Johnson would be more interested in monetary or nonmonetary items in completing his assignment. Explain your answer.

**Q13-17** From a purchasing power viewpoint, is it better to hold monetary assets or monetary liabilities during a period of inflation? Why?

**Q13-18** Discuss the meaning of unrealized and realized holding gains.

**Q13-19** Is the disclosure of inflation-adjusted financial information mandatory or voluntary?

## Exercises

**E13-1** ***Knowledge of GAAP***

Evaluate the comments that follow as being True or False. If the comment is false, briefly explain why.

a The entity assumption holds that a business unit may not arbitrarily change its accounting practices from one year to the next.

b Expenses incurred in the generation of revenue should be recognized in the same accounting period that the revenue is recognized.

c According to conservatism, small expenditures for assets are expensed as incurred rather than capitalized.

d The going-concern assumption dictates that financial statements be prepared both quarterly and annually to report financial position and profitability.

e Increases in the value of assets above cost are ignored in a company's accounting records.

**E13-2** ***Analysis of GAAP***

Twenty years ago, the president of Samson Company began a policy of investing excess company funds in classic cars. Total investments over the years have amounted to $102,000. The company is now in need of a bank loan to finance an equipment modernization program. To impress the banker, the president proposed valuing the cars on the company's balance sheet at $157,500—the current fair market value.

a According to GAAP, at what amount should the cars be valued? Why?

b Which of the two preceding amounts is consistent with the principle of objectivity and the doctrine of conservatism? Explain.

c Which of the two amounts is more relevant to the banker? Explain.

**E13-3** ***Revenue realization; percentage of completion***

Stoneridge Construction recently signed a $90 million contract to build a new office and shopping complex. Management has estimated total construction costs at $82 million and feels the project can be completed within three years. Assume costs were actually incurred as follows: Year 1, $16.4 million; Year 2, $53.3 million; and Year 3, $13.1 million.

Prepare a schedule that discloses the annual profit recognized during the three-year period. Stoneridge uses the percentage-of-completion method of revenue realization.

**E13-4** ***Revenue realization; installment method***

Atherton Appliance uses the installment method of revenue realization. On May 19, 19X1, the company sold $2,000 of appliances on account to John Spagnola. Spagnola paid $500 down and agreed to remit the balance owed via 20 monthly installments of $75 each. The first installment was due on June 1. Assume the appliances cost Atherton $1,600; disregard interest considerations.

a Prepare a schedule that discloses the yearly profit realized on the sale to Spagnola. Atherton's accounting year ends on December 31.

b Briefly explain the installment method's conformity (or lack thereof) to GAAP.

**E13-5** ***Revenue realization***

Consider the following transactions and events, which occurred during 19X3:

1 Eagle Corporation rendered services on account amounting to $34,600. Of this total, clients had paid $27,900 by year-end.

2 Johnson Publishing received $72 on May 5 for a two-year subscription of *The Modern Accountant,* a monthly publication. The subscription began with the magazine's June issue.

3 Crown Construction uses the percentage-of-completion method to recognize revenue. On January 2, the company signed a $70 million long-term contract to build a new manufacturing plant. Total costs were expected to be $64 million. Crown incurred $16 million of construction expenditures during 19X3 related to this project.

4 Ontario Furnishings sold $350,000 of goods on installment contracts at an average gross profit rate of 30%. Outstanding customer balances on these contracts by year-end amounted to $305,000.

All four companies follow generally accepted accounting principles and have a December 31 year-end. In the case of Ontario Furnishings, assume that the installment method is permissible because collectibility of customer receivables is in doubt.

a Determine the amount of revenue that Eagle Corporation and Johnson Publishing would recognize during 19X3.

b Determine the amount of profit that Crown Construction and Ontario Furnishings would recognize during 19X3.

**E13-6** ***Analysis of GAAP***

Jody Vogel and Kaye Lewis are accountants for Bright Beverage and Bottling Corporation. Bright recently completed a special promotion in which customers won cash prizes based on amounts printed on the underside of bottle caps. Vogel believes that the cost of the promotional activities should be recorded as an asset. He feels that the campaign attracted new customers who will continue to buy Bright products long into the future. Lewis, on the other hand, feels that future benefits are uncertain; therefore the promotional costs should be expensed immediately. Robert Williams, chief financial officer for Bright, was asked to express an opinion on the matter. He said that either method would be acceptable because of the dollar amounts involved.

Briefly discuss the positions of Vogel, Lewis, and Williams. Be sure to introduce the appropriate assumptions, principles, and modifying conventions that form the basis of each employee's suggested treatment.

**E13-7** ***Conservatism***

The president of Diaz Corporation believes that financial statements should present a conservative picture of an entity's financial position and profitability. Accordingly, the company's accountant did the following:

1 A $10,000 major overhaul on machinery was expensed when incurred. The overhaul was expected to extend the life of the machinery by three years.
2 Obsolete inventory in the amount of $5,000 was written off as a loss.
3 Diaz recently received a $30,000 offer to sell one of its buildings, which had a book value of $33,000. The accountant therefore recorded a $3,000 loss even though the offer was ultimately rejected.
4 The company had properly recorded the receipt of $7,000 of unearned revenue related to service contracts sold throughout the year. Although $2,500 of services had been rendered, the accountant continued to show a $7,000 liability on the balance sheet.

a Briefly explain what is meant by "conservative" financial statements.
b Determine if conservatism was properly applied with items (1)–(4). If an improper application has occurred, explain why and cite other generally accepted accounting principles if appropriate.

**E13-8** ***Purchasing power gains and losses***

Trout Company has the following accounts, among others, in its general ledger: Cash; Notes Receivable; Inventory; Accounts Payable; Sarah Trout, Capital.

a Which of the accounts would be needed in computing the net purchasing power gain or loss?
b Which of the accounts would probably fluctuate with changes in the purchasing power of the dollar?

**E13-9** ***Inflation disclosures***

Sergio Valdez, president of Caribbean Company, is concerned about the reaction of a local banker to the firm's financial statements. Total assets amount to $14 million as of December 31, 19XX, whereas company losses for the year just ended (19XX) equal $2 million. Valdez is questioning how the company can issue financial statements that "don't tell the truth." The assets are currently worth $17 million, resulting in an extra $3 million of earnings. In view of this situation, the company's accountant has been directed to value the assets at $17 million on the balance sheet and to prepare an income statement that reveals a $1 million profit. The "fictitious figures" ($14 million and $2 million) would not be disclosed.

Before the financial statements can be released to the banker, Caribbean must secure the services of a CPA firm to conduct an audit. What will the auditors likely say about Valdez's directive to the company's accountant?

## Problems

### Series A

**P13-A1** ***Analysis of GAAP and transactions***

You are the chief accountant of Westside Tool & Die, Inc. The president of the firm, Jim Norton, having graduated from college over 20 years ago, has decided to update himself in the area of financial reporting. After completing several weeks of an accounting course at a local university, Norton became involved in a heated debate with Joan Mencer, one of your staff members. The following topics were discussed:

a Three years ago the company acquired a patent from an inventor for $52,000. The current book value is $40,000 as a result of amortization. A recent appraisal indicated that the patent is worth $115,000. Norton believes that the balance sheet should contain the current valuation of $115,000; Mencer, on the other hand, favors $40,000.

b Westside recently acquired a sophisticated computer system for $240,000. Following Norton's suggestion, all system expenditures costing less than $100 were expensed. Such expenditures totaled $4,000. Mencer felt that these outlays should be capitalized in the Computer Equipment account because they render long-term benefits.

c Norton had company personnel design and build a security gate for his vacation home. He claimed that no entry is needed on the company's books because the personnel didn't have to work overtime on the project. Mencer believes that the $11,000 cost should be recorded as follows:

| | | |
|---|---|---|
| Miscellaneous Expense | 11,000 | |
| Cash, Supplies, and so on | | 11,000 |

d The company was having an exceptionally poor fourth quarter. Norton instructed the plant's accountant to omit the quarterly adjusting entry for truck depreciation in an effort to boost net income. Mencer was opposed to this treatment for reasons not stated.

e Westside sold a large machine on the installment basis to the Brazilian Air Force at a profit of $4 million. Norton wants to recognize the profit in the year of sale, even though no cash has yet to be received. Mencer prefers to recognize profit as the Air Force settles its obligation, because Brazil has had great difficulty in paying its international debt.

f The company has been sued for $1 million on a sex discrimination charge by a former secretary. Consultation with Westside's attorney indicates that the secretary has a very strong case. Norton wants to indicate the possibility of a lawsuit in the footnotes to the financial statements. Mencer claims that a footnote is unnecessary because the case has not yet been decided.

Assume that prior to considering any of these items, Westside had tentatively figured 19XX net income at $800,000.

**Instructions**

Decide who, if anyone, is correct in each of the disagreements and state the logic for your answer. Cite GAAP when appropriate. In some cases more than one principle may apply.

**P13-A2** ***Analysis of GAAP and transactions; financial statement impact***

You are reviewing the accounting records of Reno Enterprises for the current year ended December 31. The information that follows has come to your attention.

1 On December 9, the company determined that a $5,000 uninsured theft of cash had occurred. The accounts have yet to be adjusted for the amount of the theft.
2 The company, which uses the accrual basis of accounting, failed to record $1,400 of wage expense. Payment will take place in the next reporting period.
3 Inventories costing $15,600 had a year-end fair market value of $21,700. Accordingly, Reno's bookkeeper made the following adjustment in the accounting records:

| | | |
|---|---|---|
| Inventories | 6,100 | |
| Income from Appreciation | | 6,100 |

4 Import duties of $1,200 relating to the purchase of equipment on December 29 were improperly expensed when incurred.
5 On October 1, Reno purchased $120,000 of equipment at a going-out-of-business sale. The equipment, which normally sold for $150,000, was recorded as follows:

| | | |
|---|---|---|
| Equipment | 150,000 | |
| Cash | | 120,000 |
| Gain on Bargain Purchase | | 30,000 |

Reno expects to use the equipment for 10 years and employs the straight-line method of depreciation.
6 The company's financial statements for the current year revealed the following information:

| | |
|---|---|
| Net loss | $ (2,000) |
| Assets | 195,000 |
| Liabilities | 120,000 |
| Owner's equity | 75,000 |

**Instructions**

a Set up a four-column schedule with the following headings: net income (loss), assets, liabilities, and owner's equity. By adjusting the company's reported balances, compute corrected financial statement totals using the information presented in items (1)–(5).
b For items (2)–(5) only, determine if any generally accepted accounting principles have been violated. Briefly explain your answer.

**P13-A3** ***GAAP: Multiple-choice questions***

The following multiple-choice questions relate to GAAP. Select the best answer.

1 Which of the following concepts states that accounting information should be neutral (i.e., free from bias)?
a Matching.
b Objectivity.
c Periodicity.
d Monetary unit.
e None of the above.

2 Howard Corporation recently recorded the following entry to reflect increased values of its real estate holdings:

| | | |
|---|---|---|
| Land | 70,000 | |
| Buildings | 340,000 | |
| Income from Appreciation | | 410,000 |

Howard Corporation:
a Has followed GAAP.
b Has violated the historical-cost principle.
c Has violated the revenue realization principle.
d Has followed conservative accounting practices.
e Has done more than one of the above, namely, ____, ____.

3 The principle of consistency requires that:
  a Entities within the same industry use the same accounting practices.
  b Entities implement accounting practices that result in a consistent rate of return.
  c Entities employ the same accounting practices from one period to the next.
  d Companies that have several divisions employ the same accounting practices for all divisions.
  e More than one of the above is correct, namely, ____, ____.

4 The use of accelerated depreciation recognizes that assets often provide decreasing benefits over their service lives. The accounting assumption or principle most relevant to this situation is:
  a The entity assumption.
  b The objectivity principle.
  c The matching principle.
  d The monetary unit assumption.
  e None of the above.

5 The entity assumption:
  a Applies only to corporations.
  b Requires the allocation of cost among various periods of benefit.
  c Suggests that companies follow conservative accounting practices and disclose such practices in the financial statements.
  d Requires the separation of personal transactions of the owners from the affairs of the business.
  e Is described by none of the above.

6 Which of the following statements regarding revenue realization is false?
  a Most businesses recognize revenue at the time of sale or when services are rendered.
  b The installment method of revenue recognition is normally in accordance with GAAP.
  c Revenue should be recognized when the earnings process is complete or virtually complete.
  d The percentage-of-completion method postpones revenue recognition on a construction project until such time that title to the property passes to the buyer.
  e More than one of the above is false, namely, ____, ____.

7 A company is considering the implementation of equally acceptable accounting practices. Which accounting principle or assumption should govern the selection decision?
  a Historical cost.
  b Full disclosure.
  c Periodicity.
  d Conservatism.
  e None of the above.

8 Farmer Corporation, with total assets of $175,000, has a policy of immediately expensing all items of plant and equipment that cost less than $75. In view of this policy, we can say that Farmer is:
  a Correctly following the doctrine of materiality.
  b Incorrectly following the doctrine of materiality.
  c Technically in violation of the matching principle.
  d Not in violation of the matching principle.
  e Doing more than one of the above, namely, ____, ____.

**P13-A4** ***Revenue realization: Percentage-of-completion and installment methods***

Ace Building, Inc., recently signed a long-term contract for the construction of town homes throughout Florida for $40 million. Ace's accounting department has estimated total construction costs of $32 million. The contract stipulated a $2 million payment to Ace upon contract signing and periodic payments throughout the project's three-year life. Additional information follows.

| | *19X5* | *19X6* | *19X7* |
|---|---|---|---|
| Cash collected | $11,500,000* | $15,800,000 | $12,700,000 |
| Actual costs incurred | 11,840,000 | 11,200,000 | 9,750,000 |

* Includes the $2 million payment upon signing.

The project was completed on December 24, 19X7.

In a separate transaction, the company sold a parcel of land to Retirement World for $12 million. Ace originally paid $8.4 million for the parcel. Terms of sale required a 25% down payment on October 1, 19X5, by Retirement World and 24 equal monthly payments beginning on November 1, 19X5.

**Instructions**

a Calculate the total profit that Ace has earned on the town home project.

b Ace will use the percentage-of-completion method to account for the town home project. Prepare a schedule that reveals the profit earned in 19X5, 19X6, and 19X7.

c Ace will use the installment method to account for the land sale. Prepare a schedule that reveals the profit earned in 19X5, 19X6, and 19X7.

**P13-A5** ***Matching principle, income statement construction***

On January 1 of the current year, Ron Tracy opened a furniture repair business. The first year's income statement, prepared by using the cash basis of accounting, follows.

**TRACY'S REPAIR SHOP**
**Income Statement**
**For the Year Ended December 31, 19XX**

| | | |
|---|---|---|
| Cash receipts | | |
| Cash sales | $30,000 | |
| Receipts from customers on account | 3,500 | |
| Interest on savings account | 300 | |
| Total receipts | | $33,800 |
| Cash disbursements | | |
| Owner withdrawals | $ 3,600 | |
| Employee wages | 13,000 | |
| Supplies | 4,200 | |
| Delivery van | 12,400 | |
| Insurance | 200 | |
| Utilities | 700 | |
| Rent | 2,500 | |
| Total disbursements | | 36,600 |
| Net income (loss) | | $ (2,800) |

The following information was obtained from a review of the company's records:

1 Customers still owe $2,900 for repair services performed. Tracy believes that bad debts will total 3% of credit sales; to date, however, no accounts have been written off as uncollectible.

2 Tracy owes his sole employee $570 for services rendered during the last two weeks of the year.
3 As of December 31, Tracy owed various vendors $1,500 for purchases of supplies. An inventory count on this date revealed $1,100 of supplies remained on hand.
4 The delivery van was acquired on March 1 and was expected to have a service life of five years. The $12,400 figure on the income statement includes $400 of minor repairs performed on various dates subsequent to acquisition.
5 Insurance outlays include prepayments of $75.
6 On December 31, Tracy owed DCI, Inc., $100 for 19XX shop rental charges.

Tracy recently learned from one of his customers, a CPA, that the cash basis improperly matches expenses against related revenues.

**Instructions**

a Using the matching principle along with other generally accepted accounting principles, prepare an income statement that better reflects financial performance. Assume use of straight-line depreciation for the van.
b As shown in the income statement, Tracy deducted the entire cost of the delivery van in the year of acquisition. Explain how this accounting treatment violates the matching principle.

**P13-A6** ***Inflation-adjusted financial information***

This problem consists of two unrelated questions that pertain to inflation accounting.

**Part I** The Nottingham Company reported the following income statement data for 19X6:

| | |
|---|---|
| Sales | $450,000 |
| Cost of goods sold | 312,000 |
| Operating expenses | |
| Cash expenses | 92,400 |
| Depreciation | 25,500 |

The general price level index at the beginning of the year was 110. During the year the index averaged 120 and stood at 130 by December 31, 19X6. All sales, purchases, and cash expenses occurred evenly throughout 19X6. Depreciation relates to equipment that was acquired when the price index was 85.

**Instructions**

a Compute the net income (loss) figure that would appear on the 19X6 income statement.
b Convert sales, cost of goods sold, cash expenses, and depreciation to end-of-year 19X6 dollars by using the constant purchasing power approach.
c Assuming no purchasing power gains and losses, compute the company's 19X6 net income (loss) when adjusted for inflation.

**Part II** On October 9, Saratoga purchased 7,000 electronic components at $6 per unit. Shortly thereafter, because of technological advances, the same component could be purchased for $4.75. On December 31, the end of the firm's accounting period, 400 components remained in inventory.

**Instructions**

By using current cost accounting, compute Saratoga's:
a Realized holding loss.
b Unrealized holding loss.
c Ending inventory valuation.

## Series B

**P13-B1** ***Analysis of GAAP and transactions***

You are the chief accountant of Atlanta Stereo & TV. The owner of the firm, Gene Cummings, having graduated from college several years ago, has decided to update himself in the area of financial reporting. After completing several weeks of accounting at a local university, Cummings became involved in a heated debate with Al Warren, one of your staff members. The following topics were discussed:

a In reviewing the inventory records, Warren found that LIFO was used to account for stereos and FIFO was used for all other merchandise. Warren maintains that this procedure violates generally accepted accounting principles. Cummings, on the other hand, has no objections to the firm's inventory costing techniques.

b In December 19X1, the company spent $50,000 for 25 vacation tours to Hawaii. The tours will be awarded to salespeople who produce the highest first quarter sales in 19X2. The following entry was made:

| | | |
|---|---|---|
| Marketing Expense | 50,000 | |
| Cash | | 50,000 |

Warren claims the entry is satisfactory. Cummings disagrees, claiming there is no justification for reducing 19X1 income.

c On May 13, Atlanta sold $3,200 of merchandise on account to Jerry Burns, a valued customer. Warren favors a journal entry on May 13 that reflects $3,200 of sales; in contrast, Cummings feels the sale should be recorded when cash is received by the firm.

d Atlanta recently completed and occupied a new office building. Following Warren's suggestion, all items of office equipment having a unit cost of less than $100 were expensed. The equipment had an average life of five years and a total cost of $34,000. Cummings is opposed to this accounting treatment for reasons not stated.

e Two years ago Atlanta acquired a building complex (including land) for $550,000. The current book value is $470,000. A recent appraisal indicated that the land and building are worth $120,000 and $600,000, respectively. Cummings favored the following balance sheet presentation:

| | |
|---|---|
| Building and land | $470,000 |

The presentation favored by Warren was: Land, $120,000; Building, $600,000.

f A bid was received to build a loading platform for $4,700. Feeling that the amount was too high, warehouse employees built their own platform for $3,000. Warren feels the platform should be recorded in the accounts at $3,000; Cummings favors the following entry:

| | | |
|---|---|---|
| Loading Platform | 4,700 | |
| Cash, Supplies, and so on | | 3,000 |
| Construction Gain | | 1,700 |

Assume that prior to considering any of these items, Atlanta had tentatively figured 19X1 net income at $234,000.

### Instructions

Decide who, if anyone, is correct in each of the disagreements and state the logic for your answer. Cite GAAP when appropriate. In some cases more than one principle may apply.

**P13-B2** ***Analysis of GAAP and transactions; financial statement impact***

You are reviewing the accounting records of Yost Merchandising, a sole proprietorship, for the current year ended December 31. The following information has come to your attention:

1 The company, which uses the accrual basis of accounting, failed to record $8,000 of interest revenue. Collection will take place in the next reporting period.

2 Frank Yost, the owner, purchased a new car solely for personal use and had the bookkeeper record the following entry:

| | | |
|---|---|---|
| Delivery Equipment | 17,000 | |
| Cash | | 17,000 |

Depreciation pertaining to the car of $4,000 was recorded on December 31.

3 Freight charges of $2,500 relating to the purchase of equipment on December 28 were expensed when incurred.

4 Inventories that cost $9,000 had a year-end fair market value of $10,100. Accordingly, the company's accountant made the following entry:

| | | |
|---|---|---|
| Inventories | 1,100 | |
| Gain from Appreciation | | 1,100 |

5 On December 30, the company determined that a $6,200 embezzlement of cash had recently occurred. The accounts have yet to be adjusted for the amount of the theft.

6 Yost's financial statements for the current year revealed the following information:

| | |
|---|---|
| Net income | $ 32,400 |
| Assets | 100,000 |
| Liabilities | 60,000 |
| Owner's equity | 40,000 |

**Instructions**

a Set up a four-column schedule with the following headings: net income, assets, liabilities, and owner's equity. By adjusting Yost's reported balances, compute corrected financial statement totals using the information presented in items (1)–(5).

b For items (1)–(4) only, determine if any generally accepted accounting principles have been violated. Briefly explain your answer.

**P13-B3** ***GAAP: Multiple-choice questions***

The following multiple-choice questions relate to GAAP. Select the best answer.

1 Which of the following assumptions and concepts is most subject to question and why?
   a Going concern, because many companies go bankrupt each year.
   b Monetary unit, because the dollar is not a stable measuring unit.
   c Periodicity, because companies present annual and interim financial reports.
   d Entity assumption, because companies acquire other companies on a regular basis.
   e Objectivity, because increased use of computerized accounting systems makes data verification more difficult.

2 Hamilton Company uses straight-line depreciation for one group of its assets and accelerated depreciation for another group. Hamilton:
   a Is probably using this procedure to improve matching of revenue and expense.
   b Is in violation of the consistency principle.
   c Is following the principle of revenue recognition.
   d Is being extremely conservative in the disclosure of its asset investment.
   e More than one of the above is true, namely, _____, _____.

3 Which of the following statements is false?
  a Objectivity strives to eliminate bias in a company's financial statements.
  b Conservatism encourages optimism in the preparation of financial statements.
  c Disclosure assists a user in a more complete understanding of financial statements.
  d Materiality is concerned with relative dollar amounts.
  e The entity assumption requires separation of personal activity from business activity in the transaction recording process.

4 Which of the following is an application of conservatism in accounting?
  a Use of the lower-of-cost-or-market method for inventory valuation.
  b Overestimation of revenues when constructing a budgeted income statement.
  c Use of FIFO to determine cost of goods sold in a period of rising prices.
  d Overestimation of cash balances when preparing a budgeted balance sheet.
  e Ignoring a potential liability for product warranties when preparing the financial statements.

5 A company that has $12 billion of assets is permitted to "lump" $600 million of miscellaneous assets together on its balance sheet because of:
  a Periodicity.
  b Objectivity.
  c Conservatism.
  d Materiality.
  e None of the above.

6 Of the five choices that follow, which one gives rise to the worst match of revenue and expense on the income statement?
  a Use of the percentage-of-completion method, which recognizes revenue over time.
  b Use of bad debt expense estimates in the form of a year-end adjusting entry.
  c Use of accelerated depreciation for an asset that renders declining benefits over time.
  d Use of straight-line depreciation for an asset that renders uniform benefits over time.
  e Write off of a cost in the current period that is expected to provide future revenues for a firm.

7 Revenue recognition:
  a Generally occurs when cash is received.
  b Occurs for most companies when goods are sold or when services are rendered.
  c May occur over time by use of the installment basis when collectibility of receivables is virtually assured.
  d Occurs when the earnings process is complete and an exchange has taken place.
  e More than one of the above is true, namely, _____, _____.

8 Although challenged frequently, the historical-cost principle is still widely supported for financial reporting because historical cost:
  a Is an objectively determinable amount.
  b Is a good measure of current value for a going concern.
  c Facilitates the calculation of economic income.
  d Results in the lowest income tax accruals.
  e Facilitates comparisons between years.

**P13-B4** ***Revenue realization: Percentage-of-completion and installment methods***
Bennett Developers recently signed a long-term contract for the construction of apartments throughout New Mexico for $40 million. Bennett's accounting depart-

ment has estimated total construction costs of $38 million. The contract stipulated a $900,000 payment to Bennett upon contract signing and periodic payments throughout the project's three-year life. Additional information follows.

| | *19X1* | *19X2* | *19X3* |
|---|---|---|---|
| Cash collected | $12,000,000* | $18,000,000 | $10,000,000 |
| Actual costs incurred | 9,500,000 | 22,800,000 | 5,900,000 |

* Includes the $900,000 payment upon signing.

The project was completed on December 28, 19X3.

In a separate transaction, the company sold a parcel of land to Recreational Housing for $5 million. Bennett originally paid $4.2 million for the parcel. Terms of sale required a 30% down payment on December 1, 19X1, by Recreational Housing and 20 equal monthly payments beginning on January 1, 19X2.

**Instructions**

a Calculate the total profit that Bennett has earned on the apartment project.

b Bennett will use the percentage-of-completion method to account for the apartment project. Prepare a schedule that reveals the profit earned in 19X1, 19X2, and 19X3.

c Bennett will use the installment method to account for the land sale. Prepare a schedule that reveals the profit earned in 19X1, 19X2, and 19X3.

**P13-B5** ***Matching principle, income statement construction***

On January 1 of the current year, Bill Moritz opened an appliance repair business. The first year's income statement, prepared by using the cash basis of accounting, follows.

**MORITZ'S REPAIR SHOP**
**Income Statement**
**For the Year Ended December 31, 19XX**

| | | |
|---|---|---|
| Cash receipts | | |
| Owner investments | $ 3,000 | |
| Cash sales | 21,000 | |
| Receipts from customers on account | 8,500 | |
| Interest on savings account | 100 | |
| Total receipts | | $32,600 |
| Cash disbursements | | |
| Wages paid to helper | $14,200 | |
| Supplies | 4,400 | |
| Delivery van | 6,400 | |
| Advertising | 1,200 | |
| Utilities | 900 | |
| Rent | 2,400 | |
| Total disbursements | | 29,500 |
| Net income | | $ 3,100 |

The following information was obtained from a review of the company's records:

1 Customers still owe $3,800 for repair services performed. Moritz believes that

bad debts will total 4% of credit sales; to date, however, no accounts have been written off as uncollectible.

2 Moritz owes his helper $370 for services rendered during the last two weeks of the year.
3 As of December 31, Moritz owed various vendors $1,900 for purchases of supplies. An inventory count on this date revealed $2,800 of supplies remained on hand.
4 The delivery van was acquired on April 1 and was expected to have a service life of five years. The $6,400 figure on the income statement includes $400 of minor repairs performed on various dates subsequent to acquisition.
5 Advertising outlays include prepayments of $150.
6 On December 31, Moritz owed New Hampshire Power & Light $100.

Moritz recently learned from one of his customers, a CPA, that the cash basis improperly matches expenses against related revenues.

**Instructions**

a Prepare a brief explanation of the matching principle.
b Using the matching principle along with other generally accepted accounting principles, prepare an income statement that better reflects financial performance. Assume use of straight-line depreciation for the van.

**P13-B6** ***Inflation-adjusted financial information***

This problem consists of two unrelated questions that pertain to inflation accounting.

**Part I** On April 6, TriStar purchased 5,000 radio speakers for $26 per unit. Shortly thereafter, because of an industry-wide shortage, the same speaker could be purchased for $32.50. TriStar sold 2,000 of these speakers throughout the year.

**Instructions**

By using current cost accounting, compute TriStar's:
a Realized holding gain.
b Unrealized holding gain.
c Ending inventory valuation.

**Part II** The Metro Company reported the following income statement data for 19X5:

| | |
|---|---|
| Sales | $528,000 |
| Cost of goods sold | 429,000 |
| Operating expenses | |
| Cash expenses | 88,000 |
| Depreciation | 50,000 |

The general price level index at the beginning of the year was 150. During the year the index averaged 165 and stood at 180 by December 31, 19X5. All sales, purchases, and cash expenses occurred evenly throughout 19X5. Depreciation relates to equipment that was acquired when the price index was 120.

**Instructions**

a Compute the net income (loss) figure that would appear on the 19X5 income statement.
b Convert sales, cost of goods sold, cash expenses, and depreciation to end-of-year 19X5 dollars by using the constant purchasing power approach.
c Assuming no purchasing power gains and losses, compute the company's 19X5 net income (loss) when adjusted for inflation.

## Beyond the Basics

**BB13-1** ***Analysis of GAAP***

Lambert Corporation, a manufacturer of mobile homes, has experienced substantial operating losses in recent years and is in dire financial trouble. As a result, the firm's creditors have become concerned and are now refusing to lend additional funds. To help determine what corrective actions are necessary, management has retained the services of an independent consultant. The consultant's report follows.

*To the Directors of Lambert Corporation:*

*I have reviewed the financial position of Lambert Corporation. In short, Lambert qualifies as the typical going concern, as it may soon go out of business. I feel that the changes described in the following paragraphs are needed.*

*First, the firm must adopt different accounting procedures. For example, I strongly believe that revenue realization should occur at the start of production when the earnings process is complete. I was shocked to learn that your accountants wait until the point of sale; this clearly explains the recent operating losses. My recommendation will bring your policies in line with those of other companies for which I do consulting work. The change to a comparable reporting practice will mean that the firm is following GAAP, specifically, the principle of consistency.*

*Next, management needs to borrow funds to meet current operating expenses. These funds can be obtained by borrowing against certain assets. Before approaching another banker, however, I would recommend that you first increase the carrying amount of specified assets (e.g., land and buildings) on the balance sheet to reflect current market values. This practice is acceptable because costs have risen over the years. Also, I suggest that you list on the balance sheet certain personal assets of the corporation's directors.*

*Finally, the fears of your creditors are well understood. Bear in mind, however, that the creditors are not accounting experts and, as such, are not expected to read and understand financial statements. Perhaps they think you are burying something in the footnotes. Henceforth, I would recommend that Lambert comply with disclosure rules. These rules require that a firm fully reveal all pertinent financial facts directly on the face of the balance sheet and the income statement.*

*In review, your problems are accounting related. I trust my recommendations will assist the company and will help return it to profitable operations. If I may be of further assistance, please do not hesitate to call.*

*Very truly,*

*Arthur Cannon*
*Consultant*

**Instructions**

a Identify the various accounting assumptions, principles, concepts, and conventions that Arthur Cannon alluded to in his report.

b Discuss how Cannon misused each of the items identified in requirement (a).

**BB13-2** ***Revenue realization***

Exacto Tools, Inc., manufactures various types of equipment used in the aerospace industry. On March 1, 19X1, the firm began to produce a new electrostatic injector.

Demand was very strong, far exceeding the company's annual manufacturing capacity. The injector has a selling price of $300,000 and costs $240,000 to produce. The following information pertains to the year ended December 31, 19X1:

- Twenty-five units were manufactured and sold, with customers paying the total amount due on 19 of the units by December 31. A 30% down payment was received on the other six injectors.
- Nine units were still in production by the end of the year. Two of these injectors were judged to be 70% complete by Exacto's engineers; the other seven units were 60% complete. Manufacturing costs are incurred evenly throughout production. Sales contracts had been signed on these units by December 31.

**Instructions**

a Determine the total profit to be recognized by December 31 if Exacto uses the installment method of revenue realization.

b Repeat part (a), assuming that Exacto realizes profit upon completion of production.

c Repeat part (a), assuming use of the percentage-of-completion method of revenue realization.

## Answers to Chapter Quiz

**1** b

**2** d

**3** d

**4** c ($20.0 million − $13.5 million − $4.2 million = $2.3 million total profit; $2.3 million − $1.5 million = $800,000)

**5** c

# Partnerships

CHAPTER 14

## Learning Objectives

After reading this chapter you should:

1 Understand the distinctive features of a partnership.

2 Be able to account for partnership formation and income distribution, including situations that give rise to an earnings deficiency.

3 Understand the accounting that is necessary for partner admissions and partner withdrawals.

4 Be familiar with the accounting procedures required for partnership liquidations.

Through the first thirteen chapters of this text we have focused on the sole proprietorship to illustrate financial reporting and measurement practices. We now turn our attention to another popular entity form: the partnership. The Uniform Partnership Act, adopted by most states to govern this form of organization, defines a **partnership** as "an association of two or more persons to carry on, as co-owners, a business for profit." Partnerships are an attractive type of entity for small emerging companies, which often need more talent, experience, and capital than a single owner can provide.

Most partnerships have fewer than five owners; others, however, are quite large. Ernst & Young, for example, an international public accounting firm, recently reported having 6,075 partners and offices in over 100 countries. The partnership form of organization is commonly encountered in professional practices such as accounting, law, medicine, and dentistry. Furthermore, it is popular among small retail establishments, manufacturers, home builders, and service businesses.

## Characteristics of a Partnership

OBJECTIVE 1
Understand the distinctive features of a partnership.

Partnerships possess several distinctive features that have important implications for accountants. These features are discussed in the following sections.

### Ease of Formation

A partnership is easily created by a voluntary agreement between two or more people. Although the agreement may be oral and finalized by a handshake, good business practice dictates the creation of a formal written "contract" between the parties involved.

This document is commonly known as the **articles of partnership.** Generally speaking, the articles detail the rights, responsibilities, and duties of the partners. In addition, specific policies are normally stated with regard to partner investments and withdrawals, the division of net income (and net loss), the admission of new partners, the withdrawal of partners, and procedures to be followed in the event of partner disputes or a partner's death.

### Unlimited Liability

Consistent with the financial reporting principles discussed in the previous chapter, a partnership is viewed as an *accounting entity* that is separate and distinct from its owners. Consequently, personal economic activities of the partners (e.g., the acquisition of household furniture, the payment of a weekly grocery bill) are not combined with the transactions of the business. In contrast, the partnership is not a separate *legal entity* and as such, has no legal status under common law.

Because of this latter feature, each owner is held personally liable (i.e., has **unlimited liability**) for the debts of the enterprise. Thus, if a partnership experiences cash flow problems and becomes unable to pay its bills, the partners are required to surrender personal assets to help settle the firm's obligations.

### Mutual Agency

Partnerships have **mutual agency;** that is, each partner acts as an agent of the partnership in business transactions. As a result, the partnership is bound to the commitments and obligations made by any partner on behalf of the firm. For this

HIGHLIGHT

# A Handshake Cost Me $15,000

Partnerships are founded on the basis of a common understanding and common goals. Because such entities involve several parties, future problems can arise unless a partner relationship is initially established with some built-in safeguards. As one young physician learned, no matter how impressive your prospective partner, never enter into a professional association without a written contract. He now tells his story.

. . . After finishing my medical training in the Midwest, I visited relatives in a large city on the West Coast. . . . By chance, I learned there was an opening for a general practitioner at a clinic in the city. I promptly went around and introduced myself to the owner, a physician I'll call Brown.

As it turned out, Brown also came from the Midwest; he even knew doctors with whom I'd trained. So I felt comfortable with him, despite the difference in our ages. . . . I was impressed with him and also by his clinic, which was started fifteen years earlier. The clinic was large and well-equipped. The staff was large, too—an administrator, a chief nurse, three other nurses, two receptionists, a secretary, a billing clerk, an insurance clerk, and a laboratory technician.

Surprisingly, Brown was the only physician. An associate had left a short time before for unspecified reasons, and Brown was anxious to find a replacement. He asked me if I would like the position. Brown's faith in me was flattering and the terms of the offer were generous. The starting salary was $40,000, with an increase of $10,000 after six months if all went well. There'd also be a bonus of $5,000 for good performance, two weeks' vacation after one year, and health and malpractice insurance at no cost. Eventually, I could become a partner.

I felt as though I'd tumbled into a gold mine, and quickly accepted. I never thought to ask for a written agreement. Over time, however, several practice-related matters began to disturb me. I also became upset by Brown's continued unwillingness to provide a written agreement covering our arrangement. From time to time I brought up the subject, but his responses were always evasive: "If we like each other, there's no need for a contract . . . If you're fair with me, I'll be fair with you. Let's wait and see. . . . After you're here long enough, we'll consider something on a permanent basis." Sometimes when I asked, I was referred to Lyle, the clinic administrator.

One night, Brown died. Shortly thereafter, Lyle vanished, apparently frightened off by an attorney/accountant team who'd moved in to audit the practice. There were many indications that Lyle had embezzled a whopping amount of money. One day when the lawyer, accountant, and Mrs. Brown were together in my office, I brought up the subject of my verbal agreement with Brown and asked that it be put in writing.

They all glanced at each other, then the lawyer told me, "We have no record of that—only your word." "Mrs. Brown knows of the agreement; she can vouch for me," I said. But she didn't. She looked me straight in the eye and said, "I don't know what you're talking about. Why are you making up such a story while I'm still in mourning?" . . .

The lawyer then asked me how much money I thought I was owed. I said at least $15,000—the promised bonus and the raise that never came through, plus vacation pay and past-due salary. After a brief conference they agreed to pay me only the $5,000 bonus. Shortly afterward the check bounced, and I learned that Brown's practice had been sold to an outside hospital group. Unfortunately, I didn't have sufficient funds to pursue litigation. . . . The lack of written agreement was certainly a costly lesson.

SOURCE: Excerpted from "A Handshake Cost Me $15,000," *Medical Economics*, June 27, 1983, pp. 68–73. Copyright © 1983 and published by Medical Economics Company, Inc., at Oradell, NJ 07649.

reason partners must be selected with great care, as irresponsible personnel could create a difficult working environment and spell financial disaster.

### Co-ownership of Property and Income

According to the Uniform Partnership Act, partners are really the co-owners of an enterprise. Consequently, if a partner invests a building in the firm, no personal rights to the building are retained; the asset becomes jointly owned by all partners. Similarly, the partnership's net income belongs to all of the partners and can be divided among them in any agreed-upon manner.

### Limited Life

Unless there is an agreement to the contrary, the death, bankruptcy, retirement, incapacity, or withdrawal of a partner ends the partnership. Other events that call for termination include accomplishment of the firm's objective and the admission of new partners. When a partnership's life has ended, the business is **dissolved.** Dissolution does not necessarily mean that operations cease and the remaining assets are sold. Rather, if the surviving partners agree, activities can continue uninterrupted by the formation of a new entity.

### An Overview: Advantages and Disadvantages of Partnerships

There are several advantages to the partnership form of organization. Initially, there is the obvious opportunity to combine persons who possess capital and/or specialized skills to start and operate a business. Furthermore, in comparison with corporations, partnerships have more operating flexibility because of fewer reporting requirements and less governmental regulation. Many decisions that require formal (and time-consuming) actions by stockholders and corporate management can often be settled quickly among the partnership's members.

As for disadvantages, the features of mutual agency, limited life, and unlimited liability sometimes present problems. Unlimited liability is especially an obstacle when trying to raise substantial amounts of additional capital. Most people who invest in stocks and other alternatives (e.g., stamps, coins, art, or gold) are willing to incur a loss. However, because personal assets such as a home and a car may be exposed to a partnership's creditors, many investors tend to shy away from this entity form. The risk is simply too great.

One additional factor should be considered when evaluating the partnership: income taxes. A business that operates as a partnership does not pay income taxes. Instead, the firm's net income (or net loss) is allocated to the partners, and the partners pay income taxes personally on their share. This treatment is in contrast to that afforded corporations. A corporation is a taxable entity and the shareholders are taxed only on the amount of dividends received.[1] In view of these facts, partners who have personal tax rates lower than corporate rates often benefit from the partnership form of organization; those with higher rates, on the other hand, lose out. Because the tax aspect may be either pro or con, effective tax planning is mandatory when considering the proper entity form for a new business.

---

[1] Should the shareholders sell their stock, income tax is levied on any gains that arise.

Partnership accounting does not differ significantly from that described earlier in the text for sole proprietorships. Transactions unique to partnerships arise only in the area of owner's equity and relate to business formation, income distribution, admittance and withdrawal of partners, and liquidation. To handle the necessary record keeping, separate capital and drawing accounts are maintained for each owner.

## Partnership Accounting

### Partnership Formation and Owner Investments

OBJECTIVE 2
Be able to account for partnership formation and income distribution, including situations that give rise to an earnings deficiency.

Accounting for a partnership commences when owners (i.e., partners) invest their personal assets into the firm. Investments in a partnership may take the form of cash, noncash assets such as land or buildings, and even an entire operating business. To illustrate the proper record keeping, suppose that Steve Leake and Dotty Mueller, both CPAs, decided to form a partnership on January 1, 19X1. Leake invested $15,000 cash; Mueller invested her existing accounting practice. According to the December 31 balance sheet from the preceding year, the practice had the following assets and liabilities:

| | | |
|---|---|---|
| Assets | | |
| Cash | | $ 3,000 |
| Accounts receivable | $4,000 | |
| Less: Allowance for bad debts | 500 | 3,500 |
| Supplies | | 1,000 |
| Equipment | $5,000 | |
| Less: Accumulated depreciation | 1,200 | 3,800 |
| Total assets | | $11,300 |
| Liabilities | | |
| Accounts payable | | $ 2,500 |

As of January 1, 19X1, the equipment had a fair market value of $6,000. The necessary journal entries to record the partners' investments follow.

| | | |
|---|---|---|
| Cash | 15,000 | |
| Leake, Capital | | 15,000 |
| To record investment by Leake in the partnership of Leake and Mueller | | |
| | | |
| Cash | 3,000 | |
| Accounts Receivable | 4,000 | |
| Supplies | 1,000 | |
| Equipment | 6,000 | |
| Allowance for Bad Debts | | 500 |
| Accounts Payable | | 2,500 |
| Mueller, Capital | | 11,000* |
| To record investment by Mueller in the partnership of Leake and Mueller | | |

* The capital account is credited for the net assets (total assets minus total liabilities) contributed by Mueller.

Observe that the Equipment account is debited for $6,000 and *not* the book value of $3,800. Noncash assets are entered in the new records at fair market value—the actual acquisition cost to the partnership. A failure to use fair market value would improperly ignore prior increases in asset valuation. To explain, suppose the equipment was recorded at its $3,800 book value and immediately sold by the partnership for $6,000. The $2,200 gain would be shared by both partners, which is unfair to Mueller. The increase in valuation occurred while the asset was in her possession; therefore she should receive full and proper credit for her investment. The use of book value in this case would significantly understate Mueller's capital account on the books of the new entity.

## Partnership Earnings: Nature and Distribution

Similar to the measurement practices followed by other companies, partnership earnings represent the excess of revenues over expenses for a given period of time. A partnership's expenses are the costs incurred in producing revenue. As in a proprietorship, these costs result from transactions between the entity and the various external organizations (and individuals) with which the entity conducts business.

Because a partnership lacks separate legal status, custom and law dictate that partners cannot establish employee-type relationships with their own firms. This practice is akin to denying an individual the right to enter into an agreement with himself or herself and means that partners are owners and *not* employees. Consequently, any amounts disbursed as remuneration for services rendered are considered withdrawals of capital as opposed to expenses of the period.

Treatment as an expense would destroy net income as a measure of the enterprise's earnings ability, because an owner would be in a position to set his or her own compensation level and could greatly influence the reported profit figure. Generally accepted accounting practice holds that the partner/manager strives to improve the overall financial well-being of the business and is not just working to earn a weekly paycheck. A similar philosophy is followed when a partner invests personal assets (e.g., cash) into a partnership: any interest paid on such amounts is not considered an expense. As a result of the preceding treatment, partnership earnings are said to include three components: (1) compensation for the services rendered by a partner, (2) interest for the use of a partner's invested capital, and (3) a "pure" economic profit (i.e., reward) for the risks associated with operating a business.

Earnings (or losses) can be split among the partners in numerous ways. Most partnership contracts are quite specific on this matter and are structured to recognize partner variations in terms of service and/or capital contributions provided. For example, if one partner works countless hours on behalf of the firm while another devotes only a few evenings each week, this fact is typically reflected in the profit- and loss-sharing agreement. If no provisions are stated, profits and losses are divided equally.

### Recognition of Services

A study of many partnerships will often reveal considerable differences among the partners in the form of service. Some partners have been with the business for many years; others are relative newcomers. One partner may have an outstanding reputation for some type of specialty interest, say, open-heart surgery; others, possibly, do not. Variations in these factors, business contacts, and time devoted to the firm are often recognized in the form of salary differentials. Assume, for example, that Leake and Mueller's articles of partnership provide for monthly salary allowances of $1,000 and $1,200, respectively, with any remaining net income to be divided equally. If 19X1 net income amounted to $38,000, the following division would be made:

| | *Leake* | *Mueller* | *Total* |
|---|---|---|---|
| Division of net income | | | |
| Salary | | | |
| Leake ($1,000 × 12 months) | $12,000 | | $26,400 |
| Mueller ($1,200 × 12 months) | | $14,400 | |
| Remainder of $11,600 ($38,000 − $26,400) divided equally | 5,800 | 5,800 | 11,600 |
| | $17,800 | $20,200 | $38,000 |

Once determined, net income is transferred to the capital accounts by the following closing entry:

| | | |
|---|---|---|
| Income Summary | 38,000 | |
| Leake, Capital | | 17,800 |
| Mueller, Capital | | 20,200 |
| To record the division of net income | | |

Observe the similarity between this entry and the entry to close the Income Summary account for a sole proprietorship (see p. 124).

We again stress that partners are owners and *not* employees. Thus, **salary allowances** are not business expenses; rather, these amounts are considered only in the division of net income. Partners often withdraw their salaries throughout the year; if and when a withdrawal is made, entries are recorded in the drawing accounts. To illustrate the proper accounting, assume that Leake and Mueller have each withdrawn their salary allowances along with an additional $800. End-of-period balances in the partners' drawing accounts will total $12,800 ($12,000 + $800) and $15,200 ($14,400 + $800), respectively. The impact of these events is shown on the firm's statement of partners' (i.e., owners') equity, which appears in Exhibit 14-1.

**Exhibit 14-1**
**Statement of Partners' Equity**

**LEAKE AND MUELLER, CPAs**
**Statement of Partners' Equity**
**For the Year Ended December 31, 19X1**

| | *Leake* | *Mueller* | *Total* |
|---|---|---|---|
| Investment, Jan. 1 | $15,000 | $11,000 | $26,000 |
| Add: Net income | 17,800 | 20,200 | 38,000 |
| Subtotal | $32,800 | $31,200 | $64,000 |
| Deduct | | | |
| Drawings: salary | $12,000 | $14,400 | $26,400 |
| Drawings: other | 800 | 800 | 1,600 |
| Total | $12,800 | $15,200 | $28,000 |
| Ending balance, Dec. 31 | $20,000 | $16,000 | $36,000 |

The statement's bottom line is eventually carried forward to the practice's December 31 balance sheet in the following manner (liability total is assumed):

| ⋮ | | |
|---|---|---|
| Total liabilities | | $58,500 |
| Partners' equity | | |
| Steve Leake, capital | $20,000 | |
| Dotty Mueller, capital | 16,000 | 36,000 |
| Total liabilities & partners' equity | | $94,500 |

As a final step, the drawing accounts would be closed to the partners' capital accounts:

| | | |
|---|---|---|
| Leake, Capital | 12,800 | |
| Mueller, Capital | 15,200 | |
| Leake, Drawing | | 12,800 |
| Mueller, Drawing | | 15,200 |
| To close partners' drawing accounts | | |

By tracing through the entries presented, observe that the capital accounts were credited for the initial investment at the time of formation and later for each partner's share of net income. The entry to close the drawing accounts will therefore reduce Leake, Capital, and Mueller, Capital, to the balances reported on the partners' equity statement.

## Recognition of Invested Capital

Total invested capital is a major factor in the success of businesses that carry inventory or that have substantial equipment needs. Thus, partnership agreements often consider differences in the amount of capital contributed by individual partners. Recognition is particularly prevalent for firms that have "silent" partners, or partners who provide substantial financial support but do not become involved in daily management activities.

Several methods are commonly employed that focus on the amount of a partner's capital contribution. For example, an entity's income (or loss) may be distributed by using a ratio of the beginning-of-period capital balances. If partner A's capital account contains, say, $120,000 on January 1 and B's contains $80,000, the total owners' equity of the firm, $200,000, forms the basis for the proper allocation. In this particular case, any earnings (or losses) generated would be divided in a 60 : 40 ratio (A: $120,000 ÷ $200,000 = 60%; B: $80,000 ÷ $200,000 = 40%).

A careful study of this procedure could prompt a partner to withdraw vast sums of cash for personal use shortly after the period begins and then to make appropriate reinvestments late in the year, just prior to calculation of the allocation base for the next accounting period. Although the partner may personally profit from this practice, the business could experience a capital shortage. To discourage large withdrawals and at the same time promote capital retention, partnership agreements sometimes call for the ratio to be calculated on the basis of *average* account balances. This latter approach relies on a month-by-month analysis of a partner's invested capital and results in the computation of a "weighted average" balance for use in the allocation procedure.

The amount of a partner's invested capital can also be recognized by use of an **interest allowance,** computed on either the beginning or average balance in the capital account. The interest allowance is similar to the salary allowance discussed earlier; specifically, it is employed only in the division of net income (or loss) and is not an expense of the partnership.

To illustrate the accounting that accompanies an interest allowance, we will continue the Leake and Mueller example. Assume that the partnership agreement now contains the following provisions:

1 Monthly salaries of $1,000 and $1,200 to Leake and Mueller, respectively
2 Interest of 15% to both partners, computed on the basis of their beginning capital balances
3 Any remaining income (or loss) to be divided equally

It is one year later and 19X2 net income totals $42,000. The proper division between Leake and Mueller follows.

| | *Leake* | *Mueller* | *Total* |
|---|---|---|---|
| Division of net income | | | |
| Salary | | | |
| Leake ($1,000 × 12 months) | $12,000 | | $26,400 |
| Mueller ($1,200 × 12 months) | | $14,400 | |
| Interest* | | | |
| Leake ($20,000 × 0.15) | 3,000 | | 5,400 |
| Mueller ($16,000 × 0.15) | | 2,400 | |
| | $15,000 | $16,800 | $31,800 |
| Remainder of $10,200 ($42,000 − $31,800) divided equally | 5,100 | 5,100 | 10,200 |
| | $20,100 | $21,900 | $42,000 |

* Interest is computed on the January 1, 19X2 (i.e., December 31, 19X1), capital balances. These balances are taken from the statement of partners' equity that appears in Exhibit 14-1.

The journal entry to close the accounting records requires a debit to Income Summary for $42,000 and a credit to Leake, Capital, and Mueller, Capital, for $20,100 and $21,900, respectively.

## Earnings Deficiency

In the previous examples, salary and interest allowances were less than the total earnings of the firm. Naturally, it is possible for a partnership to incur a net loss or have insufficient income to cover the allowances. In these cases an **earnings deficiency** arises. Unless provisions are made to the contrary, the partnership agreement is still followed; that is, authorized salary and interest allowances continue to be recognized. Because of insufficient earnings, however, a deficiency is allocated to the partners in the same ratio as that for profits and losses. Leake and Mueller, for example, would share the deficiency equally.

To focus on the related procedures, suppose that Leake and Mueller's partnership agreement continues to stipulate respective monthly salaries of $1,000 and $1,200 and interest allowances of 15%. Now, however, assume that 19X2 net income amounted to only $20,000. The proper allocation follows.

| | Leake | Mueller | Total |
|---|---|---|---|
| Division of net income | | | |
| Salary | $12,000 | $14,400 | $ 26,400 |
| Interest | 3,000 | 2,400 | 5,400 |
| | $15,000 | $16,800 | $ 31,800 |
| Deficiency of $11,800 ($31,800 − $20,000) divided equally | (5,900) | (5,900) | (11,800) |
| | $ 9,100 | $10,900 | $ 20,000 |

The required closing entry is similar to those shown previously: Income Summary is debited for $20,000, with corresponding credits of $9,100 to Leake, Capital, and $10,900 to Mueller, Capital.

## Admission of a New Partner

**OBJECTIVE 3**
**Understand the accounting that is necessary for partner admissions and partner withdrawals.**

The Leake and Mueller partnership was a new entity formed with investments from both Steve Leake and Dotty Mueller. Observe that Leake did not invest in Mueller's accounting practice; instead, a new business was established. Frequently, individuals are admitted to existing partnerships either by (1) purchasing an interest from one or more of the present partners or (2) making an investment directly in the firm. The method of entry depends on several factors. For example, interests are often purchased when existing partners wish to decrease their involvement in daily activities because of goals that have changed, illness, or retirement. Investments directly in the business, on the other hand, sometimes occur when firms are growing and have a need for additional capital.

### Purchase of an Interest

When an entering partner purchases an interest from a present partner, the assets and liabilities of the firm remain constant. To illustrate, assume that Leake and Mueller have capital balances of $20,000 and $16,000, respectively. After lengthy negotiation both partners have agreed to sell 40% of their respective interests in the business to Ann Colby, a CPA. Colby will pay Leake and Mueller $15,000 each. The effect of the transaction, shown pictorially in Exhibit 14-2, gives rise to the journal entry that follows.

| | | |
|---|---|---|
| Leake, Capital | 8,000 | |
| Mueller, Capital | 6,400 | |
| Colby, Capital | | 14,400 |
| To record the transfer of 40% of present capital balances to Colby | | |

Notice that the price paid by Colby is in excess of the interest acquired from each partner. This situation arises from the negotiation process and is a personal matter among the parties involved. The cash goes to Leake and Mueller personally and all that is needed on the firm's records is a transfer of ownership (i.e., capital balances).

### Investment in the Firm

In addition to purchasing an interest from existing partners, an incoming partner may invest directly in the business. In this case the new partner makes payment to

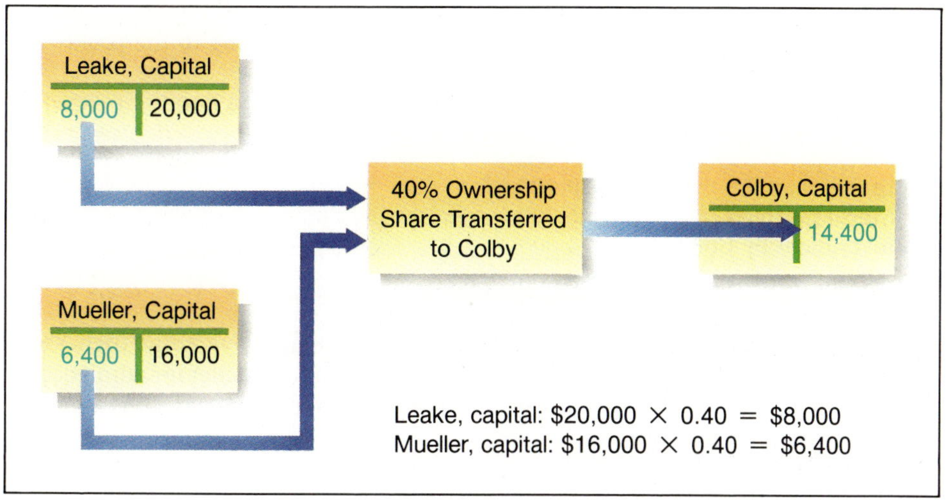


**Exhibit 14-2**
**Purchase of a Partnership Interest**

the partnership, and total firm assets increase. If the partnership assets and liabilities are valued correctly, the entering partner's investment will be equal to the negotiated percentage of the new entity's total capital. To explain, we will again assume Leake and Mueller have respective capital balances of $20,000 and $16,000. Suppose that both partners have agreed to grant Colby a one-third interest in the business for a cash investment of $18,000. Colby's investment will bring total firm capital to $54,000:

| | |
|---|---|
| Leake, capital | $20,000 |
| Mueller, capital | 16,000 |
| Investment by Colby | 18,000 |
| Total | $54,000 |

Observe that the $18,000 investment represents one-third of the owners' equity of the new partnership ($54,000 × $\frac{1}{3}$ = $18,000). Colby paid nothing extra to gain a one-third interest; nothing extra was given to her to provide the cash inflow. The necessary journal entry is therefore as follows:

| | | |
|---|---|---|
| Cash | 18,000 | |
| Colby, Capital | | 18,000 |
| To record the admission of Colby to the partnership | | |

**TIPS & TECHNIQUES**

Many students mistakenly believe that a new partner who acquires a specified partnership interest, say, one-third, is automatically entitled to the same share of the entity's earnings. As noted earlier, income-sharing agreements often contain interest and salary allowances that consider unique attributes of the partners. The division of net income (or loss) is subject to negotiation among the owners and may therefore be quite different from the partners' percentage ownership interests.

***Bonus to Existing Partners*** If the prospect of joining a partnership is especially appealing because of past earnings records and other favorable factors, an incoming partner may be required to pay a bonus to the existing owners. Any bonuses paid are allocated to the present partners' capital accounts according to the profit- and loss-sharing ratio in the partnership agreement.

For instance, assume that Colby was required to invest $24,000 for a one-third interest in the firm. Total capital would amount to $60,000:

| | |
|---|---|
| Leake, capital | $20,000 |
| Mueller, capital | 16,000 |
| Investment by Colby | 24,000 |
| Total | $60,000 |

Colby's interest would therefore be $20,000 ($60,000 × $\frac{1}{3}$). Apparently, then, she is paying a $4,000 bonus ($24,000 − $20,000) to Leake and Mueller for admission. If profits and losses are shared equally, the bonus is split 50 : 50 and the required journal entry is as follows:

| | | |
|---|---|---|
| Cash | 24,000 | |
| Leake, Capital | | 2,000 |
| Mueller, Capital | | 2,000 |
| Colby, Capital | | 20,000 |
| To record the investment of Colby and bonus to existing partners | | |

***Bonus to New Partner*** Occasionally, an organization is anxious to attract a new partner who possesses specialized skills, significant capital, or unique managerial ability. In these instances the existing owners may grant the incoming partner a larger business interest than is justified by the amount of the investment. In essence, a bonus is being given to the newcomer.

For example, assume that Colby was required to invest only $9,000 for her one-third interest. As the following figures show, total capital after admission would amount to $45,000:

| | |
|---|---|
| Leake, capital | $20,000 |
| Mueller, capital | 16,000 |
| Investment by Colby | 9,000 |
| Total | $45,000 |

Because a one-third interest has been granted, Colby, Capital, must contain a balance of $15,000 ($45,000 × $\frac{1}{3}$) after the transaction. She has therefore received a $6,000 bonus over and above her $9,000 investment—namely, a bonus provided by Leake and Mueller. Given the source of the bonus and the fact that profits and losses are shared equally, $3,000 reductions in each of the existing capital accounts are needed to properly reflect Colby's equity interest:

| | | |
|---|---|---|
| Cash | 9,000 | |
| Leake, Capital | 3,000 | |
| Mueller, Capital | 3,000 | |
| Colby, Capital | | 15,000 |
| To record the investment of Colby and bonus to new partner | | |

## Withdrawal of a Partner

Aside from admission, the composition of a partnership will also change when an owner withdraws or retires from the firm. The exiting owner's business interest may be purchased by the remaining partners or even an outsider (if the other partners approve). In both cases the assets and liabilities of the firm remain unchanged because the exchange of interests is strictly a personal matter among the parties involved. However, a journal entry is needed to eliminate the withdrawing partner's capital balance and to record an increase in the capital account(s) of the purchaser(s). The required entry parallels that shown on page 488 for the admission of a new partner who purchases an interest from a present owner.

## Purchase by the Partnership

Rather than sell to other individuals, the withdrawing party may agree to sell his or her interest to the partnership. In this situation, company assets will be used for payment. Quite often, the articles of partnership will specify the procedures to follow and the price to be paid for a withdrawing owner's interest. The price can vary widely and may be equal to, less than, or greater than the partner's capital balance. The first case is the simplest and requires a debit to the appropriate partner's capital account and a credit to Cash. The other situations are more complex and are discussed in the following sections.

***Payment Less than the Capital Balance*** A partnership may pay less than the capital balance of the exiting owner if past operations have been relatively unsuccessful or if the firm has an extremely weak cash position. In addition, this situation sometimes arises if friction has developed between the partner leaving and those remaining in the business. Because the exiting partner is willing to accept an amount less than that appearing in the accounting records, a bonus is actually being paid to the remaining owners. The bonus is split among these individuals according to the firm's profit- and loss-sharing ratio.

To illustrate, we will continue the Leake-Mueller-Colby partnership example. Assume that (1) the partners have present capital balances of $20,000, $16,000, and $18,000, respectively, and (2) all profits and losses are divided equally. Mueller has decided to withdraw from the firm and has agreed to accept $10,000 for her interest. The following entry is necessary:

| | | |
|---|---|---|
| Mueller, Capital | 16,000 | |
| Leake, Capital | | 3,000 |
| Colby, Capital | | 3,000 |
| Cash | | 10,000 |
| To record the purchase of Mueller's interest by the partnership | | |

Observe that Leake and Colby have "profited" from Mueller's settlement. The elimination of a $16,000 capital balance for only $10,000 benefits the business by $6,000, which is split equally among the on-going owners.

***Payment Greater than the Capital Balance*** Negotiations between the firm and an exiting partner sometimes result in a settlement price in excess of the partner's capital balance. Frequently, the agreed-upon price is considerably greater. Keep in mind that accounting records are based on historical cost; thus, increases in the market values of company assets have been ignored. Historical-cost valuations, coupled with the fact that the partnership may have substantial earnings potential, could result in a somewhat unrealistic (i.e., low) capital balance. If the outcome of negotiation involves a payment in excess of the withdrawing partner's equity, the capital balances of the on-going partners are reduced according to the profit- and loss-sharing ratio. In this situation, a bonus is being paid to the exiting owner.

For example, assume the present respective capital balances of Leake, Mueller, and Colby are $20,000, $16,000, and $18,000. Mueller has decided to leave the business and the firm has agreed to pay $30,000 for her interest. If net income is divided equally, Mueller's withdrawal and payment of her $14,000 bonus ($30,000 − $16,000) would be recorded as follows:

| | | |
|---|---|---|
| Mueller, Capital | 16,000 | |
| Leake, Capital | 7,000 | |
| Colby, Capital | 7,000 | |
| Cash | | 30,000 |
| To record the purchase of Mueller's interest by the partnership | | |

In this case the bonus is charged against the capital accounts of Leake and Colby. Stated differently, the firm (i.e., the remaining owners) must "foot the bill" for the payout to Mueller over and above her capital interest.

The accounting for partner withdrawals and admissions is summarized in Exhibit 14-3. By following the color coding scheme, you can clearly see that accounting for withdrawals closely parallels that for admissions.

## Death of a Partner

The death of a partnership member automatically ends the legal life of a partnership. At this point, the firm's obligation to the estate of the deceased owner must be

**Exhibit 14-3**
**Accounting for Partner Admissions and Withdrawals**

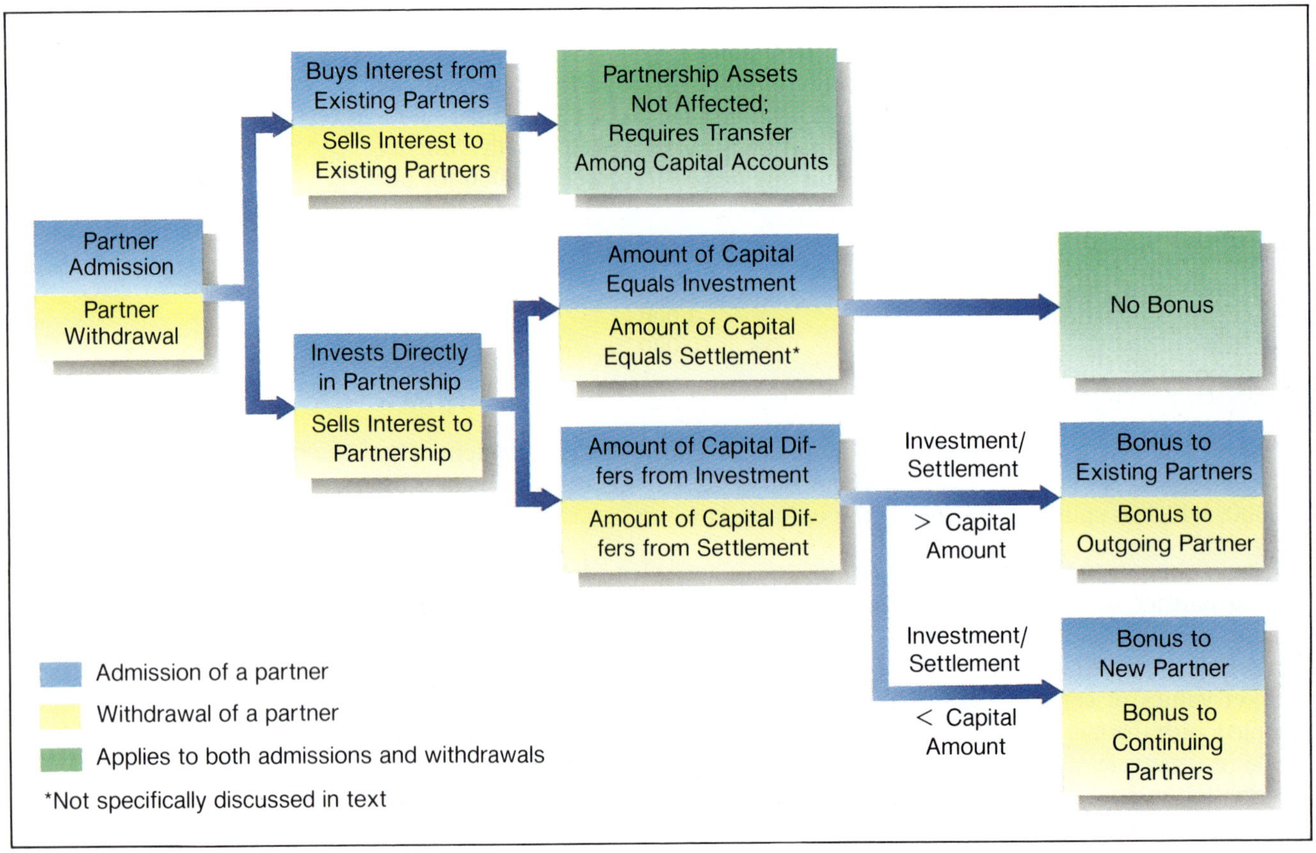

determined. It is therefore necessary to compute income (or loss) from the beginning of the current accounting period to the date of death so that a proper share can be included in the deceased partner's capital account.

The articles of partnership typically state the procedures to be followed in the event of an owner's death, including how assets are to be valued and when payment should be made to the estate. Often, insurance policies are carried on all partners, with the firm named as beneficiary. This practice ensures that adequate cash is available at the time of death and that requirements of the partnership agreement can be satisfied by the business.

## Liquidation of a Partnership

OBJECTIVE 4
Be familiar with the accounting procedures required for partnership liquidations.

Earlier in the chapter we noted that a partnership is dissolved when a new partner is admitted to the firm or an existing partner withdraws from the business. Although dissolution has occurred, the partnership's activities may continue if the remaining partners agree to form a new entity.

If this course of action is undesirable or if the entity has experienced significant financial problems (e.g., sizable losses), it may be in the partners' best interests to cease operations. The process of terminating a partnership and discontinuing business activities is known as **liquidation.** In the usual case, liquidation involves three steps:

1 The noncash assets are sold for cash.
2 The amounts due creditors (i.e., liabilities) are paid.
3 Any cash that remains is distributed to the partners.

These transactions and events normally occur over a period of time and in piecemeal fashion. For simplicity, our illustrative example will assume that all noncash assets are sold for a single, lump-sum amount and all liabilities are settled at the same time. Because liquidations can be complex and are covered in advanced accounting courses, only a basic overview is presented in this text.

### Sale of Noncash Assets at a Loss

We begin our discussion by focusing on a situation where the noncash assets are sold at a loss. Assume that the partnership of Leake, Mueller, and Colby has decided to suspend operations. The firm's balance sheet prior to liquidation follows.

| Assets | | Liabilities & partners' equity | |
|---|---|---|---|
| Cash | $ 60,000 | Accounts payable | $ 15,000 |
| Noncash assets | 50,000 | Leake, capital | 43,000 |
| | $110,000 | Mueller, capital | 40,000 |
| | | Colby, capital | 12,000 |
| | | | $110,000 |

Suppose the noncash assets are sold for $32,000, which results in an $18,000 loss ($50,000 − $32,000) for the firm. Such gains and losses are absorbed by the partners in the profit- and loss-sharing ratio as stipulated in the articles of partnership. If the ratio calls for an equal division, the journal entry to record the asset sale would be as follows:

| | | |
|---|---|---|
| Cash | 32,000 | |
| Leake, Capital | 6,000 | |
| Mueller, Capital | 6,000 | |
| Colby, Capital | 6,000 | |
| Noncash Assets | | 50,000 |
| To record the sale of noncash assets | | |

Notice that the loss is charged directly to the owners' capital accounts, resulting in the following balances:[2]

| | Cash | + Noncash Assets | = Accounts Payable | + Leake, Capital | + Mueller, Capital | + Colby, Capital |
|---|---|---|---|---|---|---|
| Prior to asset sale | $60,000 | $50,000 | $15,000 | $43,000 | $40,000 | $12,000 |
| Asset sale | +32,000 | −50,000 | | −6,000 | −6,000 | −6,000 |
| | $92,000 | $ — | $15,000 | $37,000 | $34,000 | $ 6,000 |

Once the assets are sold, the liabilities are paid. Any cash that remains is then distributed to Leake, Mueller, and Colby *in an amount equal to their capital balances.* The necessary journal entries are:

| | | |
|---|---|---|
| Accounts Payable | 15,000 | |
| Cash | | 15,000 |
| To record payment of liabilities | | |
| Leake, Capital | 37,000 | |
| Mueller, Capital | 34,000 | |
| Colby, Capital | 6,000 | |
| Cash | | 77,000 |
| To record cash distributions to partners | | |

**TIPS & TECHNIQUES**

Notice that the profit- and loss-sharing ratio is used in the division of liquidation gains and losses, *not* in the allocation of assets among the owners. The ratio's name indicates its purpose. The distribution of assets at liquidation is really the opposite of what occurs when partners invest directly into the firm at the time of business formation. Neither situation is dependent on or influenced by the income-sharing agreement.

***Creation of a Capital Deficiency*** In the previous example, each partner's capital account was of sufficient size to absorb the $6,000 share of the loss. Suppose, however, that the noncash assets are sold for only $8,000. In this case a $42,000 loss arises ($50,000 − $8,000), which reduces each of the capital balances by $14,000 ($42,000 ÷ 3). After the liabilities are paid, $53,000 cash remains in the business, and Colby's capital account contains a $2,000 debit balance. These figures are shown in the accompanying chart.

[2] An alternative treatment calls for an $18,000 debit to a separate Loss on Sale of Assets account. The Loss account's balance is then allocated equally to the partners, producing the same $6,000 reductions as those just shown.

| | Cash | + Noncash Assets | = Accounts Payable | + Leake, Capital | + Mueller, Capital | + Colby, Capital |
|---|---|---|---|---|---|---|
| Prior to asset sale | $60,000 | $50,000 | $15,000 | $43,000 | $40,000 | $12,000 |
| Asset sale | +8,000 | −50,000 | | −14,000 | −14,000 | −14,000 |
| | $68,000 | $ — | $15,000 | $29,000 | $26,000 | $ (2,000) |
| Payment of liabilities | −15,000 | | −15,000 | | | |
| | $53,000 | $ — | $ — | $29,000 | $26,000 | $ (2,000) |

The $2,000 debit balance is commonly referred to as a **capital deficiency.** Just as Leake and Mueller have respective claims against the partnership of $29,000 and $26,000, the partnership has a $2,000 claim against Colby. Notice that until the deficiency is settled, insufficient cash is available for disbursement to the owners who possess credit balances. Colby would therefore be requested to remit $2,000 to the firm.

***Removal of a Capital Deficiency*** If Colby settles her $2,000 obligation, the deficiency is removed from the accounting records. As a result of this receipt, the partnership's cash would increase to $55,000 and thus allow a distribution of $29,000 to Leake and $26,000 to Mueller. The required journal entries follow.

| | | |
|---|---|---|
| Cash | 2,000 | |
| Colby, Capital | | 2,000 |
| To record receipt of cash from Colby to settle deficiency | | |

| | | |
|---|---|---|
| Leake, Capital | 29,000 | |
| Mueller, Capital | 26,000 | |
| Cash | | 55,000 |
| To record cash distributions to partners | | |

On the other hand, if Colby is unable or unwilling to pay, the $2,000 deficiency is charged against the other partners according to the profit- and loss-sharing ratio. Leake and Mueller would therefore absorb $1,000 each to allow the closing of the partnership's books.[3] The following entry is needed:

| | | |
|---|---|---|
| Leake, Capital | 1,000 | |
| Mueller, Capital | 1,000 | |
| Colby, Capital | | 2,000 |
| To distribute capital deficiency and close Colby's capital account | | |

The cash balance of $53,000 would then be distributed, with $28,000 going to Leake and $25,000 to Mueller.

| | | |
|---|---|---|
| Leake, Capital | 28,000 | |
| Mueller, Capital | 25,000 | |
| Cash | | 53,000 |
| To record cash distributions to partners | | |

[3] In the event of an unequal profit- and loss-sharing ratio, similar procedures would continue to be followed. Suppose, for example, that partners A, B, and C share income in a ratio of 50 : 40 : 10, respectively. If C has an $18,000 capital deficiency, the deficiency would be split between A and B in the following manner: A, 50/90 × $18,000 = $10,000; B, 40/90 × $18,000 = $8,000.

Colby's inability to pay the $2,000 capital deficiency does not relieve her liability to Leake and Mueller. If the latter two individuals desire, legal action could be initiated to obtain the amount due. Bear in mind that with unlimited liability, a deficient partner's personal assets can be taken and sold by the court to raise the necessary funds.

### Sale of Noncash Assets at a Gain

The primary focus in our liquidation example has been the sale of assets at a loss, primarily because of the unique accounting problems associated with a capital deficiency. Noncash assets can, of course, be sold at a gain. If, for example, the partnership's noncash assets of $50,000 were sold for $71,000, a $21,000 gain would arise. Assuming that profits and losses continue to be shared equally, Leake, Mueller, and Colby would each pick up $7,000 ($21,000 ÷ 3) of gain. The required journal entry would thus contain credits of $7,000 to each partner's capital account to reflect the increase in equity from the transaction. The remaining journal entries for settlement of liabilities and the partners' cash distributions parallel those shown earlier.

## Chapter Review

### Learning Objectives—The Key Points

**1 Understand the distinctive features of a partnership.** A partnership is a business owned by two or more persons. This popular organizational form is a separate accounting entity but is not a separate legal and tax entity. Partnerships are easy to establish, with any property invested in the business (and subsequent income earned) being jointly owned by the partners. Partners have unlimited liability for the debts of the firm and are bound by the commitments and obligations made by the other owners (i.e., mutual agency). Further, unless otherwise agreed on, a partnership is dissolved by the withdrawal of a partner or the admission of new partners.

**2 Be able to account for partnership formation and income distribution, including situations that give rise to an earnings deficiency.** Accounting for partnerships begins when the owners invest their personal assets into the firm. Noncash investments are recorded at fair market value, and both noncash and cash investments are entered in the proper partner's capital account.

Any net income or net loss of the business is divided among the partners according to the partnership agreement. If no provisions are stated, profits and losses are shared equally. In the income allocation process, recognition may be given for services provided to the business (via salary allowances) and/or for capital provided (via interest allowances). Such allowances must be considered regardless of the firm's earnings. If insufficient income is available to cover the allowances, an earnings deficiency arises, with the deficiency being allocated to the partners in the profit- and loss-sharing ratio.

**3 Understand the accounting that is necessary for partner admissions and partner withdrawals.** When an entering partner purchases an interest from an existing partner, no change in partnership assets occurs. However, the capital accounts must be updated to reflect the transfer of equity interests among the owners. In another type of transaction, an entering partner may make an investment directly in the firm. Company assets increase and the new partner must be given credit in the accounting records for the amount invested (or some multiple thereof). If the amount invested is greater than the capital balance awarded, a bonus is being given to the existing partners. Should the situation be reversed, the present partners are providing a bonus to the incoming owner. Bonuses are divided among the partners according to the firm's profit- and loss-sharing ratio.

Partner withdrawals are accounted for in a manner similar to that of partner admittances. The withdrawing partner may sell his or her interest to the continuing partners or to the partnership itself. In the latter case, the exiting owner's capital balance is compared against the amount of cash settlement to determine whether any bonuses are involved. Once again, bonuses may be provided either by or to the ongoing partners.

**4 Be familiar with the accounting procedures required for partnership liquidations.** The liquidation of a partnership involves three steps: sale of noncash assets, payment of creditors, and distribution of remaining cash to the partners in the amount of the partners' capital balances. When selling the noncash assets, a gain or loss may arise. Such gains and losses are allocated among the partners according to the profit- and loss-sharing ratio.

The allocation of losses may cause a capital deficiency (i.e., debit balance) in a partner's capital account. When the deficiency is settled, adequate cash will then exist to pay partners who possess credit balances. If the deficiency is not settled, it is allocated among the "nondeficient" partners consistent with the profit- and loss-sharing ratio.

## Chapter Quiz

The five questions that follow relate to several issues raised in the chapter. Test your knowledge of the issues by selecting the best answer. (The answers appear on p. 510.)

**1** Which of the following statements about partnerships is true?
- a A partnership has an unlimited life.
- b A partnership pays income taxes on its earnings.
- c Partners have unlimited liability for the debts of the firm.
- d Partners who invest assets in a partnership retain sole ownership rights to the assets until it is evident that the business will be successful.

**2** Land invested in a partnership by a partner should be recorded in the partnership's accounting records at:
- a the investing partner's acquisition cost.
- b the book value on the investing partner's accounting records.
- c the land's fair market value at the time of investment.
- d the land's expected selling price on the date of disposal.

**3** Rome and Athens formed a partnership by investing $30,000 and $60,000, respectively. The following terms regarding the division of income were agreed on: (1) Rome is to receive a salary allowance of $10,000; (2) both partners are entitled to a 10% interest allowance, computed on the original capital investments. Any remaining amounts are to be split equally. How would net income of $15,000 be divided?
- a Rome, $6,000; Athens, $9,000.
- b Rome, $7,500; Athens, $7,500.
- c Rome, $11,000; Athens, $4,000.
- d Rome, $13,000; Athens, $6,000.

**4** The law firm of Lincoln, Stein, and Dyke is organized as a partnership. The partners' capital balances are $100,000, $200,000, and $150,000, respectively. Lincoln is leaving the firm for health reasons and is being paid $127,000 by the partnership for her interest. Assume that all profits and losses are divided equally. As a result of this withdrawal, Stein's capital balance will:
- a remain at $200,000.
- b increase to $213,500.
- c decrease to $191,000.
- d decrease to $186,500.

**5** The Uncle Otto partnership is being liquidated. The firm's balance sheet follows.

| | |
|---|---|
| Assets | |
| Noncash assets | $108,000 |
| Partners' equity | |
| Allen, capital | $ 60,000 |
| Tyler, capital | 41,000 |
| Flynn, capital | 7,000 |
| | $108,000 |

If the noncash assets are sold for $38,000 and profits and losses are divided in a 4 : 2 : 1 ratio, how much cash will be distributed to Allen? Assume that any capital deficiencies are not paid by the deficient partner.

a $18,000.
b $18,500.
c $20,000.
d $60,000.

## Questions

**Q14-1** What are the articles of partnership?

**Q14-2** Describe "mutual agency" and "unlimited liability" as related to partnerships. How do these features influence the selection of partners?

**Q14-3** A partnership is said to have a limited life. Does the death of a partner terminate business operations? Explain.

**Q14-4** Briefly discuss the advantages and disadvantages of the partnership form of organization.

**Q14-5** Akers and Howard are discussing the formation of a partnership. Howard will invest a computer system that originally cost $24,000. If the system has a $15,000 fair market value at the time of investment, what amount will be recorded in Howard's capital account? Why?

**Q14-6** Discuss the accounting treatment of salary allowances that are provided to partners. Are the allowances considered an expense? Why?

**Q14-7** What are the three components of partnership earnings?

**Q14-8** What problem could arise if a partnership's earnings are allocated to partners by using a ratio computed on the basis of beginning-of-period capital balances? How can this problem be resolved?

**Q14-9** What is an earnings deficiency? How is such a deficiency resolved?

**Q14-10** Baker has a $24,000 capital interest in the ABC partnership and is entitled to one-third of all profits and losses. Assume Baker sells her entire interest to Doane for $60,000.
a What amount will be recorded in Doane's account on the partnership's books?
b How much cash will be received by the business?

**Q14-11** Suppose James is withdrawing from the JKL partnership. Why might James be willing to settle for less than the balance in her capital account? How would this difference be recorded?

**Q14-12** Briefly distinguish between partnership dissolution and partnership liquidation.

**Q14-13** Name the three steps that are performed in a partnership liquidation.

**Q14-14** How are liquidation gains and losses divided among a firm's partners? Assuming no capital deficiency, how is any remaining cash divided among the partners?

**Q14-15** Capital deficiencies sometimes occur during the liquidation of a partnership. What is a "capital deficiency" and how is it treated for accounting purposes?

## Exercises

**E14-1** ***Partner investments; journal entries***

Jeff Duggan and Lisa Brown recently formed a partnership. Duggan invested $22,000 cash, and Brown contributed assets from a business that she had operated over the past three years. More specifically, she contributed $1,500 cash, $6,000 of accounts receivable, $16,200 of inventory, and $21,900 of machinery. These amounts were extracted from the firm's balance sheet, which also revealed a $900 allowance for bad debts and $7,200 of accumulated depreciation.

Duggan and Brown agreed that the bad debt allowance should be increased by $700. In addition, the partners determined that the inventory and machinery had respective fair market values on the date of partnership formation of $25,000 and $23,500.

Prepare the necessary journal entries to record the investments of Duggan and Brown.

**E14-2** ***Income distribution: Different arrangements***

Frank, Gatti, and Hogan recently invested $30,000 each and formed the Apex partnership. During the first year of operation, the business generated a net income of $39,000. Determine the proper division of income among the partners for the following independent cases:

a Income is divided on the basis of a ratio of the beginning capital investments.

b Partners are allowed 12% interest on their investments; the remaining profits and losses are allocated on a 6 : 1 : 3 basis.

c Frank and Hogan each receive salary allowances of $24,000 per year; the remaining profits and losses are shared equally.

**E14-3** ***Income distribution among partners***

Paul, Quick, and Rogers recently invested $20,000 each and formed the PQR partnership. The articles of partnership contained the following stipulations:

1 Partners are allowed 15% interest on investments.

2 Paul and Quick each have salary allowances of $15,000.

3 Remaining profits and losses are shared equally among the three partners.

Determine the proper division of net income (or net loss) among Paul, Quick, and Rogers for the following independent cases:

a Net income of $60,000

b Net income of $33,000

c Net loss of $3,000

**E14-4** ***Statement of partners' equity***

Patrick Newton and Debbie Stevens are partners in Soup & Such, a small restaurant. Terms of the partnership agreement call for respective monthly salaries of $900 and $1,200, with any remaining profits and losses to be divided equally. The restaurant generated net income of $26,800 during the year. Other information follows.

| | *Newton* | *Stevens* |
|---|---|---|
| Beginning capital balance | $24,300 | $36,800 |
| Withdrawals during the year | 15,600 | 20,400 |

Prepare a statement of partners' equity for the year ended December 31.

**E14-5** ***Partner admission; journal entries***

Dawson and Beach are partners in a toy business and have capital balances of \$126,000 and \$144,000, respectively. Net income (or net loss) is shared equally. Prepare journal entries to record the admission of a new partner, Berg, assuming each of the following independent situations:

a Berg invests \$67,500 and receives a 20% interest in the new partnership.

b Berg invests \$40,000 in the partnership for a 15% interest. Is a bonus being awarded to Dawson and Beach or to Berg?

c Berg invests \$100,000 in the partnership for a 25% interest. Is a bonus being awarded to Dawson and Beach or to Berg?

**E14-6** ***Partner withdrawal; journal entries***

Keystone, Nesbitt, and Sunshine are partners in a machinery business. On January 1 of the current year the capital balances of the three partners were \$10,000, \$20,000, and \$30,000, respectively. All profits and losses are shared equally. Prepare journal entries to record the withdrawal of Nesbitt from the partnership for each of the following independent situations:

a Acosta purchased Nesbitt's interest for \$24,500; the purchase was approved by the other partners.

b The partnership purchased Nesbitt's interest for \$28,000. Will total partnership capital increase or decrease?

c The partnership purchased Nesbitt's interest for \$15,000. Will total partnership capital increase or decrease?

**E14-7** ***Partnership liquidation; no capital deficiency***

Paul, Potts, and Prater formed a partnership in 19X1 to practice law. On September 5, 19X7, the partners decided to liquidate. The firm's balance sheet follows.

**PAUL, POTTS, AND PRATER**
**Balance Sheet**
**September 5, 19X7**

| | |
|---|---|
| Assets | |
| Cash | \$ 40,000 |
| Noncash assets | 100,000 |
| | \$140,000 |
| Liabilities & partners' equity | |
| Payables | \$ 12,000 |
| Paul, capital | 48,000 |
| Potts, capital | 45,000 |
| Prater, capital | 35,000 |
| | \$140,000 |

Assume that profits and losses are divided equally. Prepare journal entries to record (1) the sale of noncash assets, (2) payment of the liabilities, and (3) cash distributions to the partners for the following independent situations:

a The noncash assets are sold for \$82,000, all creditors are paid, and all cash is distributed.

b The noncash assets are sold for \$112,000, all creditors are paid, and all cash is distributed.

**E14-8** ***Partnership liquidation***

The JKL partnership is about to liquidate. The company's accountant has prepared the following tabulation:

| *Cash* | + | *Noncash Assets* | = | *Accounts Payable* | + | *Jacobs, Capital* | + | *Key, Capital* | + | *Landon, Capital* |
|---|---|---|---|---|---|---|---|---|---|---|
| $60,000 | | $250,000 | | $25,000 | | $80,000 | | $170,000 | | $35,000 |

Assume the partners share profits and losses equally and if a capital deficiency arises, none of it is paid by the deficient partner. The noncash assets will be sold for $100,000.

a Determine whether the JKL partnership will experience a gain or a loss on the sale of noncash assets. How much of this gain or loss is allocated to each partner?

b Does a capital deficiency arise in this situation? Explain.

c By using the preceding tabulation, show the asset sale, the payment of accounts payable, and the final cash distribution to the partners.

**E14-9** ***Analysis of partnership liquidation***

The Davis-Edwards-Felix partnership recently liquidated. Noncash assets were sold for $96,000, and all creditors have been paid. Partners shared profits and losses as follows: Davis, 20%; Edwards, 30%; Felix, 50%. Balances in each partner's capital account before and after the asset sale follow.

| | *Davis* | *Edwards* | *Felix* |
|---|---|---|---|
| Before assets were sold | $30,000 | $ 2,000 | $27,000 |
| After assets were sold | 22,400 | (9,400) | 8,000 |

a Determine the book value of the assets that were sold.

b Calculate the amount of cash on hand at the present time. Assume Edwards has not yet settled his capital deficiency.

**E14-10** ***Partnership concepts***

Evaluate the comments that follow as being True or False. If the comment is false, briefly explain why.

a In the absence of a formal profit- and loss-sharing agreement, all profits and losses are divided equally among the partners.

b Salary and interest allowances are normal expenses of a partnership.

c An earnings deficiency is allocated to a firm's partners in accordance with the profit- and loss-sharing agreement.

d In partnership liquidations, cash is distributed to partners in accordance with the profit- and loss-sharing agreement.

e Jones invested $50,000 in the Smith/Sampson/Black partnership and was given a $42,000 capital interest in return. As a result of this transaction, the balance in Smith's capital account will increase because a bonus is being given to the existing partners.

## Problems

### Series A

**P14-A1** ***Investment by partners; financial statements***

On July 5, 19XX, Able, Garcia, and Smyth agreed to form a partnership to distribute auto products. Able invested cash of $42,000 and a vehicle that originally cost

$28,000. The vehicle's fair market value at the time of investment was $20,000. Garcia contributed the following items from his existing business:

| | *Recorded Value* | *Fair Market Value* |
|---|---|---|
| Accounts receivable | $41,000 | $41,000 |
| Allowance for bad debts | (4,000) | (7,000) |
| Merchandise inventory | 45,000 | 51,000 |
| Delivery equipment (net) | 18,500 | 26,500 |
| Accounts payable | 13,500 | 13,500 |

Finally, Smyth contributed short-term marketable securities consisting of 500 shares of VBG, Inc., capital stock (cost per share, $120; market value per share, $150).

**Instructions**

a Prepare journal entries to record the investments of Able, Garcia, and Smyth in the partnership.

b Prepare a classified balance sheet for the partnership immediately after the investments.

c Assume that net income of $54,000 was generated through the end of 19XX. Cash withdrawals of $24,000 were made by Able, $31,000 by Garcia, and $44,000 by Smyth. If the partners divide all profits and losses equally, prepare the December 31, 19XX, statement of partners' equity for the firm.

**P14-A2** ***Income distribution; statement of partners' equity***

Johnson, Kenyon, and Rambo are partners in a bookkeeping service. The partners' beginning and average capital balances for 19XX follow.

| | *Beginning* | *Average* |
|---|---|---|
| Johnson | $85,000 | $90,000 |
| Kenyon | 40,000 | 40,000 |
| Rambo | 65,000 | 75,000 |

Investments during the year amounted to $10,000 for Johnson and $20,000 for Rambo. Net income totaled $36,000.

**Instructions**

a Prepare a schedule to show the distribution of net income among the partners for each of the following independent cases:

(1) The partners are granted a 12% interest allowance on beginning capital and share any remaining income equally.

(2) Johnson, Kenyon, and Rambo are granted a 12% interest allowance on average capital and respectively share any remaining income on a 5 : 3 : 2 basis.

(3) Each partner is granted both a 10% interest allowance on average capital and a monthly salary allowance of $1,100. Johnson, Kenyon, and Rambo respectively share remaining profits or losses on a 4 : 4 : 2 basis.

b Focusing on case (1) in part (a), assume that the interest allowances were withdrawn during the year along with other amounts as follows: Johnson, $4,000; Kenyon, $3,500; and Rambo, $7,800. All withdrawals were recorded in the partners' drawing accounts. Prepare the statement of partners' equity for the year ended December 31, 19XX.

**P14-A3** ***Income distribution; journal entries***

Jackson, Hudson, and Rice invested $70,000 each at the beginning of 19X2 and formed a partnership to operate a restaurant. The articles of partnership contained the following provisions:

1 Partners are granted 20% interest on their beginning investments.
2 Hudson will receive an annual salary allowance of $10,000; Rice's annual salary allowance is $40,000.
3 Remaining profits and losses are shared on a 4 : 4 : 2 basis among the partners.

Jackson and Rice withdrew their interest allowances during 19X2 along with an additional $12,000 and $20,000, respectively. Hudson had no withdrawals.

**Instructions**

a Determine the proper division of net income (or net loss) among Jackson, Hudson, and Rice for the following independent cases:
   (1) Net income of $100,000.
   (2) Net income of $70,000.
   (3) Net loss of $60,000.
b For part (a1), prepare journal entries to record (1) the transfer of net income to the capital accounts and (2) the closing of the drawing accounts.
c For part (a1), present the proper disclosure of partners' equity on the firm's December 31, 19X2, balance sheet.

**P14-A4** ***Admission to a partnership***

Harvard, Issel, and Lear operate a partnership to perform medical research. A review of the firm's articles of partnership found no provisions for interest and salary allowances. Further study of this document and the accounting records disclosed the following information:

| | *Capital Balance, December 31, 19X5* | *Share of Profits and Losses* |
|---|---|---|
| Kenneth Harvard | $50,000 | 20% |
| Robin Issel | 80,000 | 55 |
| Daniel Lear | 20,000 | 25 |

Assume that Gary Ogden will be admitted to the partnership on January 1, 19X6, and the partnership agreement will be redrawn.

**Instructions**

a Prepare journal entries to record the admittance of Ogden under each of the following independent cases:
   (1) Issel sells 15% of her interest to Ogden for $12,000.
   (2) Ogden invests $50,000 in the partnership and receives a 25% interest in the firm.
   (3) Ogden invests $80,000 in the partnership and receives a 30% interest in the firm.
   (4) Harvard gives 10% of his capital interest to Ogden, who is a close family relative.
   (5) Lear sells 75% of his interest to Ogden for $28,000.
   (6) Ogden invests $60,000 in the partnership and receives a 35% interest in the firm.
b Focus on part (a3) for a moment. Briefly discuss several possible reasons that might explain why Ogden was willing to invest $80,000 in exchange for a 30% interest in the firm.

**P14-A5** ***Partner withdrawal; journal entries***

The Chen family has operated a business called Dockside Imports for many years. The capital balances of the partners on December 31, 19X8, were: Dorothy Chen, $320,000; Robert Chen, $400,000; and Tina Chen, $180,000.

The first eight months of 19X9 generated favorable financial results, with the following figures being reported: sales, $5 million; cost of goods sold, $3.64 million; and operating expenses, $860,000. On the basis of these results, the partners anticipated that the business would be profitable for the tenth straight year. The partnership agreement stipulates that Dorothy, Robert, and Tina share profits (and losses) on a 3 : 6 : 1 basis, respectively.

On September 1, 19X9, because of serious health problems, Tina requested permission for an immediate withdrawal from the partnership. Because the Chens are a very close-knit family, Dorothy and Robert approved the request with absolutely no hesitation.

**Instructions**

a Update the partners' capital accounts through August 31 for the appropriate share of income or loss and then prepare journal entries to record the withdrawal of Tina under the following independent cases:
   (1) Per stipulations in the articles of partnership, Tina sells her interest to the partnership at an amount equal to the balance in her capital account.
   (2) Tina sells her interest to the partnership for $120,000 cash and a $20,000 note.
   (3) Tina sells 40% of her interest to each of the two remaining partners for $125,000 (for a total of $250,000).
   (4) Tina sells her interest to a new partner, Louise Wong, for $600,000.
   (5) Tina sells her interest to the partnership in exchange for a $500,000 note, to be paid in ten annual installments of $50,000 each.

b Compute the total partners' equity of the firm after Tina sells her interest in case (2) of part (a).

c Considering all facts presented in the problem's narrative, is case (2) of part (a) likely to occur? Briefly explain.

**P14-A6** ***Partnership liquidation***

Coe, Dodd, and Eaton operate a repair business as a partnership and share net income (and net losses) in a 3 : 4 : 3 ratio, respectively. Because the business was not as successful as planned, the partners decided to liquidate. A post-closing trial balance disclosed the following account balances as of December 31, 19X1:

**COE, DODD, AND EATON**
**Post-Closing Trial Balance**
**December 31, 19X1**

| | | |
|---|---|---|
| Cash | $ 40,000 | |
| Inventory | 31,000 | |
| Equipment (net) | 60,000 | |
| Accounts payable | | $ 11,000 |
| Salaries payable | | 1,000 |
| Coe, capital | | 23,100 |
| Dodd, capital | | 58,000 |
| Eaton, capital | | 37,900 |
| | $131,000 | $131,000 |

### Instructions

a Prepare journal entries to record the sale of the noncash assets and payment of the liabilities assuming the noncash assets are sold for:
  (1) $141,000.
  (2) $7,000.

b Assume that case (2) of part (a) actually occurred.
  (1) Determine the partnership's cash balance after the liabilities are settled.
  (2) Assume that any partner with a capital deficiency is able to pay the balance due the partnership. Present journal entries to record the receipt of cash from the deficient partner and distribute the firm's ending cash balance.
  (3) Assume that any partner with a capital deficiency is unable to pay the balance due the partnership. Prepare journal entries to allocate the deficiency to the remaining partners and distribute the firm's ending cash balance.

## Series B

### P14-B1 *Investment by partners; financial statements*

On August 8, 19XX, Lancer, Mix, and Norton formed a partnership to distribute computer supplies. Lancer invested cash of $85,000 and a delivery van that originally cost $7,500. The vehicle's fair market value at the time of investment was $5,000. Mix contributed short-term marketable securities consisting of 1,000 shares of U.S. Paper capital stock (cost per share, $40; market value per share, $70). Finally, Norton contributed the following items from his existing business:

| | *Recorded Value* | *Fair Market Value* |
|---|---|---|
| Accounts receivable | $32,000 | $32,000 |
| Allowance for bad debts | (2,000) | (6,000) |
| Computer supplies inventory | 51,000 | 57,000 |
| Warehouse equipment (net) | 0* | 7,000 |
| Accounts payable | 10,500 | 10,500 |

* Fully depreciated.

### Instructions

a Prepare journal entries to record the investments of Lancer, Mix, and Norton in the partnership.

b Prepare a classified balance sheet for the partnership immediately after the investments.

c Assume that net income of $72,600 was generated through the end of 19XX. Cash withdrawals of $25,000 were made by Lancer, $30,000 by Mix, and $45,000 by Norton. If the partners divide all profits and losses equally, prepare the December 31, 19XX, statement of partners' equity for the firm.

### P14-B2 *Income distribution; statement of partners' equity*

Nolan, Epstein, and Tyree are partners in a bowling franchise. Investments during the year amounted to $10,000 for Nolan and $20,000 for Tyree. Net income totaled $64,000. The partners' beginning and average capital balances for 19XX follow.

| | *Beginning* | *Average* |
|---|---|---|
| Nolan | $40,000 | $45,000 |
| Epstein | 25,000 | 25,000 |
| Tyree | 5,000 | 15,000 |

**Instructions**

a Prepare a schedule to show the distribution of net income among the partners for each of the following independent cases:
  (1) The partners are granted a 10% interest allowance on average capital and share any remaining income equally.
  (2) Nolan, Epstein, and Tyree are granted a 12% interest allowance on beginning capital and respectively share any remaining income on a 3 : 2 : 5 basis.
  (3) Each partner is granted a 12% interest allowance on average capital; Nolan and Epstein have respective monthly salary allowances of $3,000 and $1,800. Nolan, Epstein, and Tyree respectively share any remaining profits or losses on a 5 : 3 : 2 basis.

b Focusing on case (2) in part (a), assume that the interest allowances were withdrawn during the year along with other amounts as follows: Nolan, $7,000; Epstein, $10,000; and Tyree, $2,500. All withdrawals were recorded in the partners' drawing accounts. Prepare the statement of partners' equity for the year ended December 31, 19XX.

**P14-B3** ***Income distribution; journal entries***

Lemont, Whittaker, and Wiley invested $20,000 each on January 1, 19X4, and formed a partnership to operate a car dealership. The articles of partnership contained the following provisions:

1 Partners are granted 10% interest on their beginning investments.
2 Lemont will receive a monthly salary allowance of $1,000.
3 Remaining profits and losses are shared on a 5 : 3 : 2 basis among the partners.

Whittaker and Wiley withdrew their interest allowances during 19X4 along with an additional $3,000 and $15,000, respectively. Lemont withdrew 80% of her salary allowance.

**Instructions**

a Determine the proper division of 19X4 net income (or net loss) among Lemont, Whittaker, and Wiley for the following independent cases:
  (1) Net income of $50,000.
  (2) Net income of $5,000.
  (3) Net loss of $20,000.

b For part (a2), prepare journal entries to record (1) the transfer of net income to the capital accounts and (2) the closing of the drawing accounts.

c For part (a2), present the proper disclosure of partners' equity on the firm's December 31, 19X4, balance sheet.

**P14-B4** ***Admission to a partnership***

Mantle, Maris, and Berra operate a partnership to render financial planning services. A review of the firm's articles of partnership found no provisions for interest and salary allowances. Further study of this document and the accounting records disclosed the following information:

| | *Capital Balance, December 31, 19X3* | *Share of Profits and Losses* |
|---|---|---|
| Henry Mantle | $90,000 | 30% |
| Cheryl Maris | 70,000 | 45 |
| Thomas Berra | 40,000 | 25 |

Assume that Terri Richardson will be admitted to the partnership on January 1, 19X4, and the partnership agreement will be redrawn.

### Instructions

a Prepare journal entries to record the admittance of Richardson under each of the following independent cases:
   (1) Richardson invests $100,000 in the partnership and receives a one-third interest in the firm.
   (2) Because of increasing friction between Maris and Berra, Maris sells 80% of her interest to Richardson for $30,000.
   (3) Richardson invests $80,000 in the partnership and receives a 40% interest in the firm.
   (4) Mantle gives 20% of his capital interest to Richardson, who is his niece.
   (5) Richardson invests $50,000 in the partnership and receives a 15% interest in the firm.
   (6) Richardson purchases 60% of Berra's interest directly from Berra for $24,000.

b Focus on part (a3) for a moment. Briefly discuss several possible reasons that might explain why Richardson received a 40% interest in the firm for her $80,000 investment.

## P14-B5 *Partner withdrawal; journal entries*

Fertig, Marino, and Piper have operated a business called the Pike Street Market for many years. The capital balances of the partners on December 31, 19X1, were: Fertig, $250,000; Marino, $300,000; and Piper, $75,000.

The first nine months of 19X2 generated favorable financial results, with the following figures being reported: sales, $1 million; cost of goods sold, $575,000; and operating expenses, $325,000. The partners were hopeful that the year's final quarter would be profitable, so that a net income would be reported for the fifteenth straight year. The partnership agreement stipulates that Fertig, Marino, and Piper share profits (and losses) on a 4 : 4 : 2 basis, respectively.

On October 1, 19X2, because of marital problems and an impending divorce settlement, Marino requested permission for an immediate withdrawal from the partnership. Although they were sorry to see him go, Fertig and Piper approved Marino's request.

### Instructions

a Update the partners' capital accounts through September 30 for the appropriate share of income or loss and then prepare journal entries to record the withdrawal of Marino under the following independent cases:
   (1) Marino sells his interest to a new partner, Diaz, for $760,000.
   (2) Marino sells 50% of his interest to each of the two remaining partners for $300,000 (for a total of $600,000).
   (3) Per stipulations in the articles of partnership, Marino sells his interest to the partnership at an amount equal to the balance in his capital account.
   (4) Marino sells his interest to the partnership for $460,000.
   (5) Marino sells his interest to the partnership in exchange for a $190,000 note due in 10 months.

b Compute the total partners' equity of the firm after Marino sells his interest in case (4) of part (a).

c Why is a bonus sometimes paid to a withdrawing partner?

## P14-B6 *Partnership liquidation*

Manny, Moe, and Abe operate a delivery business as a partnership and share net income (and net losses) in a 5 : 3 : 2 ratio, respectively. Because the business was not as successful as planned, the partners decided to liquidate. A post-closing trial balance disclosed the following account balances as of December 31, 19X3:

**MANNY, MOE, AND ABE**
**Post-Closing Trial Balance**
**December 31, 19X3**

| | | |
|---|---|---|
| Cash | $ 38,000 | |
| Short-term investments | 3,000 | |
| Delivery equipment (net) | 64,000 | |
| Accounts payable | | $ 1,800 |
| Utilities payable | | 200 |
| Manny, capital | | 35,000 |
| Moe, capital | | 60,000 |
| Abe, capital | | 8,000 |
| | $105,000 | $105,000 |

**Instructions**

a Prepare journal entries to record the sale of the noncash assets and payment of the liabilities assuming the noncash assets are sold for:
   (1) $14,000.
   (2) $98,000.

b Assume that case (1) of part (a) actually occurred.
   (1) Determine the partnership's cash balance after the liabilities are settled.
   (2) Assume that any partner with a capital deficiency is unable to pay the balance due the partnership. Prepare journal entries to allocate the deficiency to the remaining partners and distribute the firm's ending cash balance.
   (3) Assume that any partner with a capital deficiency is able to pay the balance due the partnership. Present journal entries to record the receipt of cash from the deficient partner and distribute the firm's ending cash balance.

## Beyond the Basics

**BB14-1** ***Partnership features***

Knapp, Shingler, and Smith, three dentists from Indianapolis, recently attended a convention of the National Dental Association. There they heard a speaker who talked about the formation of successful dental partnerships. An excerpt from the speaker's presentation follows.

> Several guidelines should be considered when entering this entity form. First, prospective partners must be compatible; they need the ability to exchange and discuss business and/or professional viewpoints freely. Second, the partnership should provide the anticipated return (i.e., profit) on investment for all parties. Third, prospective partners should be willing to share in the decision making. Finally, all partners must contribute with equal capacity, unless differences are known and accepted in advance. Quite simply, effort and commitment that differs from that originally anticipated is the biggest disrupter of partnerships.

Smith came away impressed and approached Knapp and Shingler about merging their respective practices, forming a partnership, and building suitable professional space.

Knapp is 57 years old, married, with two grown children. Shingler is 33, married, with four young children. Smith is 29, twice divorced, and has no offspring. Knapp and Shingler have conservative life-styles; Smith could be characterized as a jet-setter. The three doctors are respected by their patients. Knapp and Shingler are active in community affairs and the local dental society.

Selected data from the three practices during the past 12 months follow.

| | *Knapp* | *Shingler* | *Smith* |
|---|---|---|---|
| Billings for services | $240,000 | $180,000 | $100,000 |
| Collections | 235,000 | 160,000 | 75,000 |
| Office expenses | 90,000 | 130,000 | 50,000 |
| Dental assistants | 4 | 6 | 1 |
| Hours worked per week | 40 | 50 | 28 |

In forming the partnership, each dentist would contribute $50,000. Knapp would write a check for the entire amount, while Shingler would invest $25,000 cash and sign a note for the remaining balance. Smith, on the other hand, is presently strapped for cash and would have to borrow his total contribution from a local bank.

**Instructions**

a Analyze the data presented and discuss the possible reasons why Knapp, Shingler, and Smith are considering a partnership.
b Are the guidelines for a successful partnership present in this proposed merger? Briefly explain.
c Should written articles of partnership be prepared for the practice? If "yes," list several items to be included in the agreement.
d Recommend a method to divide the practice's profit (or loss).
e Briefly assess the likelihood that the proposed partnership will survive on a long-term basis.

**BB14-2** ***Partnership accounting: A comprehensive overview***

The Pathway partnership was organized on June 2, 19XX, to operate a computer consulting and repair service. Dave Jones invested $5,000 cash and equipment (original cost: $13,000) that had a fair market value of $11,000. Tim Perini invested equipment valued at $20,000 and supplies worth $7,000. Perini still owed $8,000 on the equipment; the partnership assumed the obligation, an account payable. On June 4, 19XX, the partners invited Dr. Matt Zajack, a former university professor, to join the firm. Zajack was given a 25% interest in the business in exchange for a token cash investment of $1,000.

The articles of partnership granted the following monthly salary allowances: Jones, $500; Perini, $750; and Zajack, $1,500. Any remaining profits (or losses) are to be divided equally. In an effort to conserve cash, no withdrawals were made during June; however, on July 31, each partner withdrew two months' salary. Earnings for the period June 2–July 31 totaled $17,800.

Jones decided to withdraw from the partnership on August 1 because of personal problems; the business agreed to purchase his interest for a lump-sum amount of $25,000. A new partnership agreement was assembled that retained the salary allowances for Perini and Zajack and stipulated the equal division of remaining income (or loss).

Because of intense competition, earnings for the two-month period ended September 30 amounted to only $300. Neither partner withdrew salary allowances for August or September.

In view of the entity's operating environment and increased personality clashes between Zajack and Perini, the partners decided to liquidate. The account balances that follow existed on October 3.

| | |
|---|---:|
| Cash | $ 5,200 |
| Noncash assets (total) | 43,400 |
| Accounts payable | 17,000 |
| Notes payable | 8,000 |

The noncash assets were sold for $20,000 and the liabilities were paid. Any remaining cash was distributed to the partners. Should a capital deficiency arise, assume that none of it is paid by the deficient partner.

**Instructions**

Prepare all journal entries needed to record the preceding transactions and events, including the division of earnings on July 31 and September 30. Assume that Pathway closes its books on these dates.

## Answers to Chapter Quiz

**1** c

**2** c

**3** c [Rome: $10,000 + ($30,000 × 0.10) = $13,000; Athens: $60,000 × 0.10 = $6,000; deficiency of $4,000 (($13,000 + $6,000) − $15,000) shared equally). Thus, Rome: $13,000 − $2,000 = $11,000; Athens: $6,000 − $2,000 = $4,000.]

**4** d ($127,000 − $100,000 = $27,000 bonus paid by continuing partners, to be shared equally; $200,000 − $13,500 = $186,500)

**5** a [$108,000 − $38,000 = $70,000 loss; Allen's share: $70,000 × $\frac{4}{7}$ = $40,000; Flynn's share: $70,000 × $\frac{1}{7}$ = $10,000, causing a $3,000 capital deficiency ($7,000 − $10,000); Allen's share of deficiency: $3,000 × $\frac{4}{6}$ = $2,000; cash distribution: $60,000 − $40,000 − $2,000 = $18,000]

# Introduction to Corporations

CHAPTER 15

## Learning Objectives

After reading this chapter you should:

1. Be familiar with the features, advantages, and disadvantages of a corporate entity.
2. Understand the difference between common and preferred stock.
3. Be able to account for dividends associated with preferred stock.
4. Be familiar with the concepts of and accounting treatments for par, no-par, and stated-value stock, and stock subscriptions.
5. Be familiar with the stockholders' equity section of a corporate balance sheet.
6. Understand the computation and meaning of book value per share.

Economic activity in the United States is conducted via three forms of business organization: sole proprietorships, partnerships, and corporations. Although the vast majority of companies operate as either proprietorships or partnerships, the bulk of private sector receipts and earnings are generated by corporations. These facts become apparent after studying the data that appear in Exhibit 15-1.

Perhaps the most obvious conclusion to be drawn from these figures is that corporations engage in financial activities on a much larger scale than the other entity types. Given that 19.4% of the firms produce 90.2% of this country's business receipts, the corporate form of organization clearly dominates our economy in monetary terms.

This chapter introduces accounting considerations unique to corporations and expands upon the material presented earlier in the text. Our focus will be on issues that relate to owners' (in this case, *stockholders'*) equity—the major area of difference among the three popular enterprise alternatives.

## The Nature of Corporations

OBJECTIVE 1
Be familiar with the features, advantages, and disadvantages of a corporate entity.

In the early 1800s, Supreme Court Justice Marshall defined a **corporation** as "an artificial being, invisible, intangible, and existing only in contemplation of the law." Consistent with this definition, the corporation is viewed as a legal entity having an existence separate and distinct from its owners. Corporations may therefore buy and sell property in their own names. Additionally, corporations can enter into contracts, defend themselves in court, and transact business in the same manner as a person would.

### Corporate Form of Organization: Advantages

The corporate form of organization is often considered preferable to both a sole proprietorship and a partnership for conducting business affairs. This preference arises for the following reasons.

#### Transferability of Ownership

Recall from our previous discussions that a corporation is divided into transferable units of ownership called **shares of stock.** These shares are readily transferable

**Exhibit 15-1**
**A Comparison of Alternative Forms of Business Organization**

| | | | *Business Receipts** | | *Net Income** | |
|---|---|---|---|---|---|---|
| *Entity Form* | *Number of Firms* | *Percent of Total* | *$* | *Percent of Total* | *$* | *Percent of Total* |
| Sole proprietorship† | 11,929,000 | 70.5% | $ 540 | 5.8% | $ 79 | 25.5% |
| Partnership | 1,714,000 | 10.1 | 368 | 4.0 | (9) | (2.9) |
| Corporation | 3,277,000 | 19.4 | 8,398 | 90.2 | 240 | 77.4 |
| | 16,920,000 | 100.0% | $9,306 | 100.0% | $310 | 100.0% |

* Dollar amounts are in billions.
† Figures are for nonfarm proprietorships only.
SOURCE: U.S. Bureau of the Census, *Statistical Abstract of the United States, 1989* (Washington, D.C., Government Printing Office, 1989), p. 516.

from one investor to another without affecting corporate operations. Frequently, the transfer occurs in an organized market such as the New York Stock Exchange, a mechanism where the stocks of roughly 2,000 businesses can be bought or sold. With the possible exception of family-owned entities or corporations owned by a few persons (termed **closely held corporations**), the acquisition and sale of stock are routine matters and do not require the approval of other owners.

### Perpetual Existence

Because a transfer of ownership does not affect business operations, a corporation is said to have a continuous, or perpetual, existence. Contrast this feature with that of a partnership where, unless so stated in the partnership agreement, a change in ownership terminates the entity's life. Since it is not unusual for millions of shares to change hands on a single day, perpetual existence is needed to ensure continuity of financial activities and the achievement of company objectives.

### Limited Liability of Stockholders

The owners of a corporation are termed its **stockholders.** Because of the corporation's separate legal existence, stockholders have *limited liability;* that is, the most they can lose is the amount of their investment. Creditors of the firm have a claim against the entity's assets only; the personal assets of the owners cannot be used to satisfy corporate debts. Recall that this feature does not apply to partnerships (and sole proprietorships also), where each owner may be held liable for the debts of the business.

### Ease of Raising Capital

Limited liability tends to make the corporation an attractive alternative for investors. This feature, coupled with the fact that ownership is divided into many units, provides a corporation with ready access to additional capital funds. The need for and the ability to raise substantial amounts of capital have prompted virtually all large businesses to adopt the corporate form of organization.

## Corporate Form of Organization: Disadvantages

Although the corporation offers many advantages, several disadvantages must be considered.

### Double Taxation

As noted in Chapter 14, partnerships are not taxable entities; instead, an owner is taxed personally on his or her share of the earnings. This same feature also applies to proprietorships. Corporations, on the other hand, are required to pay income taxes. The taxes are heavy and often amount to approximately 40% of taxable net income after both federal and state obligations are considered. In addition, any earnings distributed as dividends are income to the recipient stockholders and are subject to personal income tax. Thus, the same earnings can be taxed twice. The taxing of income to the corporation and the subsequent taxing of dividends to the stockholder is commonly termed **double taxation.**

HIGHLIGHT

## Public! Private! Public! Private!

Want to raise a lot of money to finance a brand new company? Many businesses will assume the corporate form of organization and sell stock to the general public. Virtually all large entities follow this route to generate capital for growth and expansion. Interestingly, though, not all business giants are publicly held.

Consider the other side of corporate America—the private or closely held firms. You know about them; common examples (and rank among the largest private companies) follow. [1]

| ***Company*** | ***Rank*** |
|---|---|
| Safeway Stores | 4 |
| United Parcel Service | 5 |
| Trans World Airlines | 16 |
| Hallmark Cards | 46 |
| Estée Lauder | 72 |
| Reader's Digest Association | 75 |
| Duracell | 95 |
| Avis | 123 |
| E & J Gallo Winery | 131 |
| Domino's Pizza | 161 |
| United Van Lines | 240 |

Some private businesses grew big without ever tapping the public equity market. Mars, the immensely successful maker of Milky Way candy bars and M&Ms, is in that category. Others are employee-owned. Still others were public until the recent craze of leveraged buyouts. Firms in the latter group include Levi Strauss, Uniroyal, and R.H. Macy & Co. [2]

What is a leveraged buyout, you say? Sometimes known as an LBO, it is a business transaction in which top management buys out the public shareholders and finances the deal by borrowing money against the company's assets or future earnings. Bought-out shareholders get fat premiums, often more than 50% over their shares' current value in the marketplace. Furthermore, executives get new incentive to manage efficiently—they now own the company—and a shot at becoming very, very rich. The disadvantage: a large amount of debt and huge outlays for interest expense. [3]

So why go private? What motivates management to load debt on the company just to take it out of public hands? Often, it's not one reason but many. The time, cost, and hassles of dealing with inquisitive shareholders and Wall Street analysts are frequently cited. That kind of scrutiny can pressure management into short-term strategies just to pacify this constituency. As one consultant notes, "Owners of private companies have the luxury of not having to live in a fishbowl." [4]

But others say that the real motives behind most LBOs are primarily economic. A finance professor at the University of Pennsylvania's Wharton School observes, "It's not so much getting out of the public eye but an economic decision. Let's say a company can be bought for $100. [In an LBO] you can borrow $99 of that and put up $1 of your own money. Hopefully, earnings are sufficient to pay the debt in five years. You end up owning the company by using other people's money." [5]

Sounds good, but not everybody wins. Although shareholders and management benefit, rank and file employees of firms face uncertainty and even layoffs, as the newly burdened firm seeks to cut expenses and sell assets in order to pay its debt. In a classic case, Dr Pepper went private in a $640 million LBO, financed with $610 million of debt. Quite a load, obviously. To raise cash the company sold off its Canada Dry operation and reduced its work force from about 4,000 to 500. These transactions enabled the firm to reduce borrowings by $490 million to help lighten the burden. [6]

Whether they went private via the LBO or had very few shares to begin with, the private companies are an important force in our economy. These firms have forsaken life in the fast lane; yet many are alive and well and extremely successful in their fields of endeavor.

SOURCES: Adapted from "Behind the Paper Curtain," *Forbes*, November 18, 1985, pp. 128–130 [2, 4]; "The 400 Largest Private Companies in the U.S.," *Forbes*, December 12, 1988, pp. 180–207 [1]; "'Going Private' is Popular Route for Public Companies, *Dallas Times Herald*, October 23, 1985, pp. B1, B7 [5]; and "Leveraged Buyouts: Height of Financial Fashion," *Dallas Times Herald*, November 10, 1985, pp. E1, E3 [3, 6], reprinted courtesy of the *Dallas Times Herald*.

### Heavy Regulation

In comparison with sole proprietorships and partnerships, corporations are subject to heavier governmental regulation. Most corporations that sell their stock to the general public (termed **publicly held corporations**) must follow the financial reporting regulations of the Securities and Exchange Commission (SEC). Corporate entities are also subject to widely varying state laws. Furthermore, depending on the activities in which it is involved, a corporation may come under the scrutiny of specialized agencies. Examples of such agencies include the Interstate Commerce Commission, the Nuclear Regulatory Commission, and the Federal Deposit Insurance Corporation.

## Organization of a Corporation

A corporation is created by obtaining a **charter** from one of the states. The charter is granted after the appropriate state department reviews and approves an application for incorporation. The charter specifies, among other things, the firm's business purpose, its organizational structure, and the types and amounts of stock that can be issued.

After the entity is created, a stockholders' meeting is usually held to adopt the bylaws that govern the conduct of business activities and also to elect the *board of directors.* The board of directors is entrusted with wide-ranging powers and serves to protect the basic interests of stockholders. In fulfilling its duties and obligations, the board will usually meet several times each year to discuss and evaluate various matters, for example, corporate policy, general business affairs, the declaration of dividends, major contract decisions, and the hiring and remuneration of officers.

Corporate officers manage the company and oversee daily activities. Executives typically included in this select group are a president, several vice-presidents, a secretary, and a treasurer. The president is the chief executive of the company and has final authority (subject to review by the board of directors) for most major decisions. Numerous vice-presidents normally assist the president; these individuals usually specialize in a significant functional area such as marketing, finance, production, personnel, and so on. The secretary is charged with maintaining minutes for meetings of directors and stockholders. The secretary may also become involved in various other legal and contractual matters that affect the corporation.

The treasurer is the custodian of corporate funds and must oversee cash position, monitor cash inflows and outflows, and review major financing activities. Given the nature of the related duties, the treasurer and the controller often report to the vice-president—finance. The **controller** is the chief accounting officer of the firm and is responsible for internal and external reporting. More specifically, the controller oversees the company's internal control system; supplies management with information needed for planning, control, and decision making; and is held accountable for generating financial statements and the various reports that are filed with regulatory agencies (such as the Securities and Exchange Commission). Exhibit 15-2 illustrates the typical upper-level organizational structure of a medium-size corporate entity.

Naturally, in smaller corporations, several of these functions may be combined. For instance, the treasurer and the vice-president of finance may be the same individual. Furthermore, it is not uncommon in many family-run businesses for a husband/wife team to comprise both top management *and* the board of directors.

**Exhibit 15-2**
**Corporate Organizational Structure**

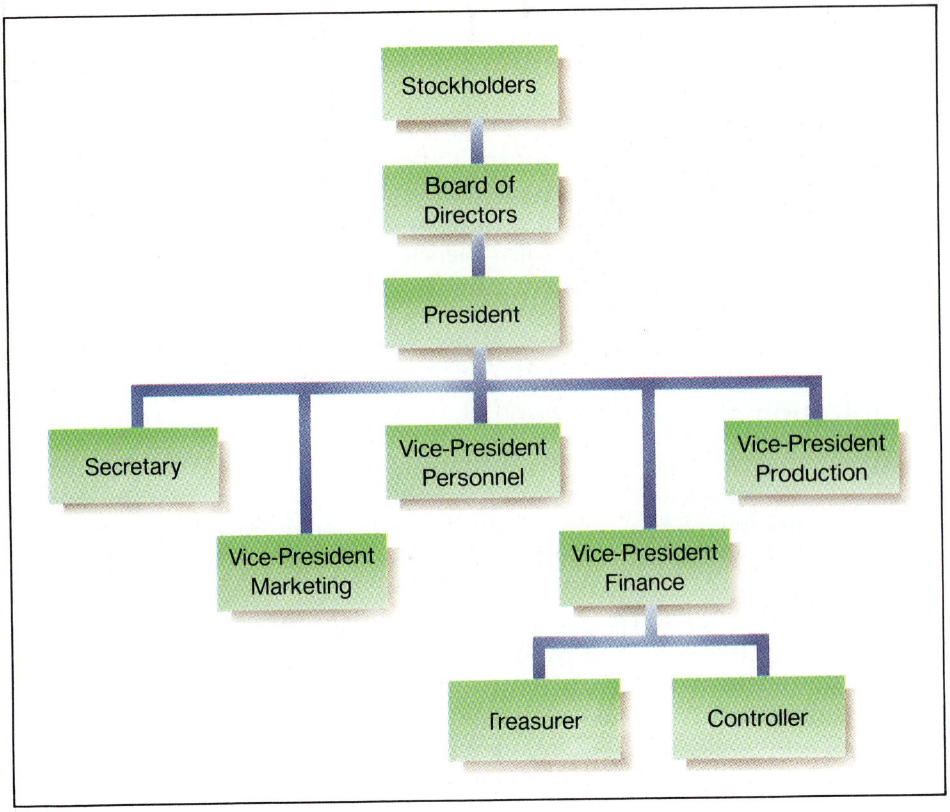


## Organization Costs

Forming a corporation is more involved and costly than forming a sole proprietorship or partnership. In addition to state incorporation fees, there are legal costs connected with preparing the application for incorporation, expenses incurred by the founders, and numerous other outlays.[1] These one-time expenditures are debited to an account entitled Organization Costs, which is disclosed on the balance sheet as either an intangible asset or an "other asset."

Treatment as an asset is justified because such costs contribute to corporate formation; thus, the benefits derived extend over a number of years. Normally, however, the number of years is unknown, since most corporations have an indefinite life. Recall from Chapter 11 that intangible assets with seemingly unlimited lives are amortized over a period not to exceed 40 years. Most firms amortize organization costs over five years, which is the minimum period allowable under existing income tax regulations. Businesses are permitted to follow this practice because organization costs are small in relation to total assets, and the effect of the associated amortization charges on net income is typically insignificant.

[1] A study of small businesses found that the typical cost of a $10 million initial public stock offering amounted to $1,182,000. See "Special Report: Small Business," *The Wall Street Journal*, May 15, 1987, p. 13D.

## Common Stock

OBJECTIVE 2
Understand the difference between common and preferred stock.

The corporate charter specifies the types and number of shares of capital stock that a corporation is permitted to issue. Normally, the charter allows for the issuance of more shares than are currently needed. This practice saves the time and expense of seeking repeated approvals from stockholders and state authorities for additional stock issues at a later date. The number of shares allowed by the charter is termed the **authorized stock.**

Many corporations issue different classes of stock to permit flexibility in raising capital and to appeal to various types of investors. The stock classes are usually characterized by having distinctive rights and privileges. All corporations issue **common stock**—an ownership interest that controls the board of directors (and thus corporate management) by exercising voting rights. Common stockholders are often rewarded with increased stock values when net income rises and, conversely, with decreased values when profitability falls. Overall, then, it is the common stockholder who reaps the benefits of corporate success and pays the price of business failure.

Evidence of corporate ownership is provided by a legal document known as a *stock certificate.* An example of such a certificate for the common shares of American Telephone and Telegraph (AT&T) is shown in Exhibit 15-3.

### Rights of Common Stockholders

The owners of common stock typically have the following rights:

**1** To share in any dividend distributions that may be declared by the board of directors.

**Exhibit 15-3**
**Stock Certificate**

2 To subscribe to any additional common stock issued by the corporation (known as the **preemptive right**). Existing stockholders are given the opportunity to maintain their respective interests in a corporate entity by acquiring additional shares on a pro rata basis. A stockholder who owns 15% of a corporation's common stock is therefore allowed to purchase 15% of any new shares issued before those shares are offered to other investors.

   The preemptive right is not a hard and steadfast rule. For example, stockholders have sometimes waived the preemptive right, thereby permitting the issuance of large blocks of stock to be used in acquiring other businesses. In other situations, certain states have allowed the issuance of shares with no preemptive rights attached.

3 To share in the final disposition of assets if the corporation is liquidated. At the end of a corporation's life its assets are sold, and the cash generated is used to settle the claims of creditors. Any remaining cash (or assets) is shared proportionately by the common stockholders on the basis of the number of shares owned.

4 To elect the board of directors and to vote on other important corporate issues. Common stockholders are frequently asked to consider such matters as proposed mergers; the selection of independent auditors; changes in corporate bylaws and management pension programs; and the types and amounts of stock that can be issued.

The preceding rights apply to most common stockholders, not all. Sometimes, different classes of common stock are issued with rights other than those described. The Adolph Coors Company, for instance, perhaps best known for its brewing operation, has Class A and Class B common stock. Class A stock has voting rights and is retained by the Coors family; Class B stock is nonvoting and has been issued to the general public.

## Preferred Stock: Nature and Characteristics

Rather than have multiple classes of common stock, some corporations have achieved differentiation by issuing **preferred stock.** As its name implies, preferred stock has several preferential rights; in comparison with common stock, however, other rights are given up in return.[2] Normally, preferred stock appeals to investors who want a safe investment with a steady dividend. Why? The reasons become apparent in the upcoming sections where we discuss characteristics of most preferred stocks.

### No Voting Rights

Preferred stockholders generally have no vote in corporate affairs. Exceptions are made, however, by special contracts or by state law. In some cases voting privileges are awarded after certain conditions have been met, such as the absence of dividends for a specified period of time.

[2] Similar to common shares, corporations may issue various classes of preferred stock. In what might be an extreme case, Pacific Gas & Electric (a San Francisco–based public utility) has 21 different types of preferred shares, each with its own features and rights.

## Dividend Preference

**OBJECTIVE 3**
**Be able to account for dividends associated with preferred stock.**

Voting rights are often forfeited in exchange for a preference in dividend distributions. Specifically, preferred stockholders are entitled to receive dividends before any distributions are made to common stockholders. In most instances, however, the owners of preferred shares receive only a stipulated amount per share regardless of the profitability of the firm. This situation arises because preferred dividends are expressed either on a per-year basis or as a percentage of par value. (Par value refers to the face value of a share of stock and is discussed later in the chapter.) A 10% preferred stock with a $25 par value, for example, has a dividend of $2.50 per year.

Although many businesses take pride in their dividend records, keep in mind that dividend distributions are not mandatory but are subject to the discretion of the board of directors. Consequently, when a company's cash position is weak or when earnings are marginal, dividends may not be disbursed. For this reason most preferred stocks are **cumulative.** That is, the rights to preferred dividends that are omitted in a given year accumulate, with the amounts said to be **in arrears.** Dividends in arrears must be paid before any subsequent dividends can be declared and paid on a corporation's common stock.

To illustrate, suppose Flora, Inc., has 20,000 shares of 10%, $5 par, cumulative preferred stock and 50,000 shares of $1 par common. Dividend distributions for the past four years are listed in the second column of the following table. Because the annual preferred dividend requirement is $10,000 (20,000 shares × $5 × 0.10), the dividends would be divided between preferred and common shareholders as shown.

| | | | | *Dividends Distributed* | |
|---|---|---|---|---|---|
| *Year* | *Total Dividends Distributed* | *Annual Preferred Requirement* | *Dividends in Arrears* | *Preferred* | *Common* |
| 1 | $27,000 | $10,000 | $ — | $10,000 | $17,000 |
| 2 | 6,000 | 10,000 | 4,000 | 6,000 | — |
| 3 | 3,000 | 10,000 | 11,000 | 3,000 | — |
| 4 | 25,000 | 10,000 | — | 21,000 | 4,000 |

Observe that distributions in Year 2 amounted to only $6,000. Since preferred stockholders are entitled to receive $10,000, dividends are $4,000 in arrears. All $6,000 thus goes to the preferred stockholders because of their right to receive dividends before any distributions to common. In Year 3, Flora failed to cover the annual preferred requirement by $7,000 ($10,000 − $3,000), raising arrearages to $11,000. Preferred again gets the entire distribution, in this instance $3,000. Finally, the dividends in Year 4 were sufficient to meet not only the annual requirement but also the arrearage. Common stockholders therefore receive the remaining $4,000 ($25,000 − $10,000 − $11,000).

Dividends in arrears are not a liability because they have never been declared by the board of directors. Such amounts are typically disclosed in the footnotes to the financial statements. Although we have emphasized the cumulative feature, realize that some preferred stock is noncumulative; that is, unpaid dividends do not accumulate and are lost. Because noncumulative preferred stock lacks investor appeal, it is not frequently encountered in practice.

## Participation Feature

The preceding example showed that once preferred stockholders received the $10,000 annual distribution (plus arrearages), any remaining dividends were given to holders of common shares. Some preferred stock is entitled to yet additional amounts by **participating** ratably with common in any excess dividends that may be declared. Extra dividends are paid only after three conditions are met: (1) appropriate arrearages have been settled; (2) the annual preferred requirement is satisfied; and (3) common shareholders have been given a "matching" amount on their stock.

To illustrate, assume that a corporation has $200,000 of cumulative, participating, 10% preferred stock and $300,000 of common stock. Dividends are $8,000 in arrears at the start of 19X6. If the board of directors authorizes distributions during 19X6 that total $61,000, the dividends would be split as follows:

| | *Preferred* | *Common* |
|---|---|---|
| Dividends in arrears | $ 8,000 | |
| 19X6 preferred dividend ($200,000 × 0.10) | 20,000 | |
| 10% "matching" dividend on common stock ($300,000 × 0.10) | | $30,000 |
| Excess allocated proportionately | | |
| Preferred: $3,000 × 0.40* | 1,200 | |
| Common: $3,000 × 0.60† | | 1,800 |
| Total distribution | $29,200 | $31,800 |

* $200,000 ÷ ($200,000 + $300,000) = 40%
† $300,000 ÷ ($200,000 + $300,000) = 60%

The matching common dividend is the same 10% as that given to preferred shareholders; however, the distribution is figured on the common stock of $300,000. Once this amount is allocated, the $3,000 remainder ($61,000 − $8,000 − $20,000 − $30,000) is split proportionately on the basis of preferred and common equity. Preferred and common equity total $500,000, with preferred representing 40% and common representing 60%.

## Asset Preference upon Liquidation

Most preferred stock has a preference over common stock in the event of corporate liquidation. After creditor claims are settled, preferred stockholders are entitled to their share of the remaining assets, prior to any distributions to the holders of common (i.e., the residual owners).

## Callable

Many preferred stock issues are **callable,** which means the issuing corporation retains the right to reacquire (call) the stock at a preset price. To make this feature somewhat attractive to investors, the call price is generally set slightly above the original issue price.

The call feature allows a corporation to raise capital from a stock issuance and then cancel the stock and return the investors' funds. Such actions may be desirable when the cash is no longer needed or the stock becomes financially burdensome. The latter situation will arise if the preferred stock is issued when interest (and dividend) rates are high. Should the rates drop suddenly, the stock can be called and replaced with cheaper financing.

### Convertible

Some preferred stock is **convertible** into common stock at the option of the stockholder. Conversion is normally in a stipulated exchange ratio; for example, one share of preferred may be convertible into five shares of common. Convertible preferred is appealing to both investors and the issuing company. From the investors' viewpoint, there is a strong likelihood of a regular, assured dividend on the preferred stock. Furthermore, should the corporation's common stock rise in value, investors have the privilege of conversion and can thereby increase the worth of their holdings. From the company's point of view, a smaller dividend can normally be paid because of the conversion feature's attractiveness to investors.

## Par-Value Stock

**OBJECTIVE 4**
**Be familiar with the concepts of and accounting treatments for par, no-par, and stated-value stock, and stock subscriptions.**

The common and preferred classifications are based on the rights afforded to the respective groups of stockholders. Stocks can also be categorized as par value or no-par value. **Par-value stock** has a fixed dollar amount per share specified by the corporate charter. The amount varies among businesses and is sometimes influenced by state laws that tax the par value of shares issued.

The significance of par value is that it represents the **legal capital** per share of stock. Total legal capital, obtained by multiplying the par value per share times the number of shares issued, denotes the minimum amount of owners' equity that must be maintained for protection of the creditors. To explain, recall that stockholders have limited liability and cannot be held personally liable for corporate obligations. In an effort to provide some protection to the creditors, state laws thus require a minimum permanent investment from the owners to help settle claims on company assets. Dividend declarations that reduce total stockholders' equity below legal capital are therefore not permitted.

### Issuing Par-Value Stock

If a corporation is large or is attempting to sell a substantial amount of stock, the services of an investment banking firm will normally be used. Typical investment bankers include Shearson Lehman Hutton Inc., and Merrill Lynch, Pierce, Fenner & Smith Inc. The investment banker, often referred to as an *underwriter,* has the responsibility of selling the stock, at a set price, to the public. Underwriters charge a commission for their services and often advertise stock issuances in newspapers and business periodicals. The sale of stock is typically made on the basis of a **prospectus,** a document required by the SEC that contains information about the corporation's products, management, and financial affairs.

### Issue Price

Stocks may be issued at, above, or below par value, given the arbitrary manner in which par is determined. The latter issuances are seldom encountered and are actually illegal in many states. Why? Although the sale proceeds are less than par, the stock is still considered fully paid. However, the stockholder is held contingently liable to the corporation's creditors for the difference between the sale price and the par amount specified in the firm's charter. Should corporate assets be insufficient to settle creditor claims if operations cease, the original stockholders may be called upon to furnish additional cash. To avoid this situation, virtually all corporations issue stock at or above par.

The issue price for new stock is determined by the corporation along with an underwriter or financial advisers. The following factors are considered: past, present, and future corporate earnings; financial position; expected dividend rates; market position of the company's products and services; current state of the investment market; and recent prices of competitors' stock.

Once stock is issued, its **market price** (the price at which a share can be bought or sold) continually changes. The changes reflect investor evaluation of the corporation's progress and prospects. If growth prospects are evident, the price of the shares should rise; if the future looks bleak, the price should fall. Note that if a corporation sells its stock at $5 and the market price later jumps to $35, the firm receives no benefits from the increase in value. The appreciation goes to the stockholders. Of course, if more investment capital is needed, the entity may issue additional shares at or near the existing market price, in this case $35.

## Accounting for Par-Value Stock

The issuance of par-value stock may require entries in more than one owners' equity account. Specifically, an amount equal to the par value of the shares issued is placed in a capital stock account, either Common Stock or Preferred Stock. Then, if the stock is issued at a price greater than par, the difference between the issue price and par is recorded in an account entitled Paid-in Capital in Excess of Par Value. To state this important allocation differently, the funds received from investors are recorded as legal capital (the par value) and as additional paid-in capital (amounts received in excess of par).

To illustrate the proper accounting, assume McCord Corporation is authorized to issue 50,000 shares of $5 par, 8% cumulative preferred stock and 20,000 shares of $10 par common. Further assume that the corporation has issued 30,000 shares of preferred at par and 10,000 shares of common at $18. The required journal entries follow.

| | | |
|---|---|---|
| Cash | 150,000 | |
| Preferred Stock | | 150,000 |
| To record issuance of 30,000 shares of $5 par, 8% preferred at $5 per share | | |

| | | |
|---|---|---|
| Cash | 180,000 | |
| Common Stock | | 100,000 |
| Paid-in Capital in Excess of Par Value | | 80,000 |
| To record issuance of 10,000 shares of $10 par common at $18 per share | | |

Observe that in both cases the par value of the issued shares was placed in a capital stock account. In addition, note that the $80,000 paid in excess of par was recorded separately. When stock is issued at a price above par, the difference between the issue price and the par value is often called a **premium.** Alternatively, then, an account termed Premium on Common Stock could have been credited for $80,000.

**TIPS & TECHNIQUES**

Realize that the preceding entries are made *only* at the time of stock issuance. Daily stock transactions of investors (e.g., purchases and sales) normally involve shares that have been previously issued, with no additional cash being received by the corporation. In these instances the corporation does not record a formal journal entry; all that is needed is an updating of the list of stockholders.

## Balance Sheet Presentation

**OBJECTIVE 5**
**Be familiar with the stockholders' equity section of a corporate balance sheet.**

The owners' (stockholders') equity section of McCord's balance sheet would appear as shown in Exhibit 15-4. Notice how the balance sheet discloses the two major sources of corporate equity: stockholder investments **(paid-in capital)** and **retained earnings.** Retained earnings represents capital generated from profitable operations that is kept in the business; an in-depth discussion will be presented in Chapter 16. At this point assume the account's $240,000 balance was obtained from McCord's general ledger.

Exhibit 15-4 reveals two other important points. First, considerable detail is required in terms of disclosure. The features of the various stock issues are described along with the number of shares authorized by the corporate charter, issued by the firm, and held by the stockholders (termed **outstanding shares**).[3] Second, note that the $80,000 paid by stockholders in excess of par value is considered neither revenue nor profit. It is merely additional invested capital that is shown separately from the capital stock accounts.

Our illustration has focused on the issuance of stock at par and in excess of par. Should stock be issued below par, the difference between par and the issue price (i.e., a **discount**) is debited to an account entitled Discount on Capital Stock. The discount account is subtracted from the capital stock accounts when determining total paid-in capital.

**Exhibit 15 4**
**Stockholders' Equity of McCord Corporation**

| *Stockholders' Equity* | | |
|---|---|---|
| Capital stock | | |
| Cumulative 8% preferred stock, $5 par, 50,000 shares authorized, 30,000 shares issued and outstanding | $150,000 | |
| Common stock, $10 par, 20,000 shares authorized, 10,000 shares issued and outstanding | 100,000 | $250,000 |
| Paid-in capital in excess of par value: common | | 80,000 |
| Total paid-in capital | | $330,000 |
| Retained earnings | | 240,000 |
| Total stockholders' equity | | $570,000 |

[3] The number of shares issued and the number of shares outstanding can differ. This situation will also be shown in Chapter 16.

## No-Par Stock

In the early days of corporations, the issuance of par-value stock sometimes misled investors. Par value was occasionally equated with the "true" worth of the stock, that is, market value. This factor, coupled with the contingent liability problem should issuance take place at a discount, prompted many corporations to consider **no-par stock.** Because the par-value concept is absent, no premium or discount is recorded at the time of issue; instead, the entire proceeds are credited to a capital stock account. For instance, assume Canton Corporation is authorized to issue 20,000 shares of no-par common stock. If 10,000 shares are issued at $18 per share, the required journal entry would be as follows:

| | | |
|---|---|---|
| Cash | 180,000 | |
| Common Stock | | 180,000 |
| To record issuance of 10,000 shares of no-par common at $18 per share | | |

This example has deliberately used the same numbers as the McCord Corporation illustration on page 522. Notice that both issues of common stock generated identical proceeds: $180,000. With no-par stock, however, total invested capital is recorded in one equity account rather than two.

### Stated-Value Stock

Although most states permit the issuance of no-par stock, some states require corporations to set a minimum issue price. This price, known as the stock's **stated value,** allows for protection of the creditors in terms of legal capital. In essence, then, stated value can be likened to par value.

Because of the similarity, accounting for stated-value stock closely parallels that for par-value stock. To illustrate, we will continue the Canton Corporation example. Assume that to comply with state law, Canton's board of directors has assigned a $10 stated value to each share. The issuance of 10,000 shares at $18 per share would now be recorded as follows:

| | | |
|---|---|---|
| Cash | 180,000 | |
| Common Stock | | 100,000 |
| Paid-in Capital in Excess of Stated Value | | 80,000 |
| To record issuance of 10,000 shares of no-par common (stated value, $10) at $18 per share | | |

The stated value of the issued stock is entered in the Common Stock account. Any added amount is then recorded as Paid-in Capital in Excess of Stated Value, which is similar to additional paid-in capital received on par-value shares.

## Stock Subscriptions

Rather than use the services of an underwriter, small corporations occasionally sell stock directly to investors on a **subscription** basis. Investors agree to purchase the stock at a given price, with payment taking place on a specific future date or via installments. After the subscriber pays in full, the shares of stock are issued.

For example, assume investors subscribed to 1,000 shares of Glover Corporation $5 par common stock at $22 per share. The journal entry that follows would be made.

| | | |
|---|---|---|
| Subscriptions Receivable: Common Stock | 22,000 | |
| Common Stock Subscribed | | 5,000 |
| Paid-in Capital in Excess of Par Value | | 17,000 |
| To record subscriptions to 1,000 shares of $5 par common at $22 per share | | |

Subscriptions Receivable is established to indicate that $22,000 will be forthcoming from investors. This account is similar to other receivables and normally appears as a current asset on the balance sheet. Common Stock Subscribed is a temporary paid-in capital account that is credited for the par value of the shares subscribed (1,000 shares × $5). Observe that at this point it would be incorrect to credit Common Stock, because the shares have not yet been issued. Finally, the $17,000 premium is placed in the Paid-in Capital in Excess of Par Value account.

Next, assume investors subscribing to 750 shares paid in full. Glover would therefore issue the stock and record the following entries:

| | | |
|---|---|---|
| Cash | 16,500 | |
| Subscriptions Receivable: Common Stock | | 16,500 |
| To record collections from subscribers of 750 shares (750 × $22 = $16,500) | | |

| | | |
|---|---|---|
| Common Stock Subscribed | 3,750 | |
| Common Stock | | 3,750 |
| To record issuance of 750 shares under subscription agreements | | |

The first entry is similar to that made to record other receipts of cash on account. The second entry removes $3,750 (750 shares × $5 par) from Common Stock Subscribed and recognizes the issuance of common shares. Consistent with previous illustrations, the capital stock account is again carried at par value.

Should subscribers to the remaining 250 shares now pay 40% of their balances due, no additional shares would be issued. Issuances occur only when full payment is made; consequently, the required journal entry would be:

| | | |
|---|---|---|
| Cash | 2,200 | |
| Subscriptions Receivable: Common Stock | | 2,200 |
| To record partial payment on subscriptions for 250 shares (250 shares × $22 × 0.40) | | |

## Issuing Stock for Assets Other than Cash

Thus far we have concentrated on stock issues that generate cash. The cash, in turn, was used for the purchase of assets, payment of expenses, and other similar purposes. Frequently, corporations issue stock in direct exchange for land, buildings, and even other businesses. In addition, stock is sometimes used to settle claims of attorneys and other professionals for services rendered, particularly at the time of corporate formation, when cash balances may be low.

The issuance of shares for noncash assets or services creates a valuation problem. Specifically, at what value should the transaction be recorded? The general rule is that the assets or services acquired are recorded at their fair market value or the fair market value of the stock, whichever is more clearly discernible. If the corporation's shares are actively traded on one of the stock exchanges, determination of the stock's market value is a relatively simple matter. *The Wall Street Journal* and the financial pages of most metropolitan newspapers will provide the necessary information. When stock is not actively traded, as in a closely held corporation, an appraisal of the asset's (or service's) market value may be more appropriate.

To illustrate the proper accounting treatment, assume Fuqua Industries is a small family-run business located in Wyoming. Fuqua's attorney has agreed to accept 40 shares of $5 par common for $850 of legal work performed in organizing the corporation. The required journal entry follows.

| | | |
|---|---|---|
| Organization Costs | 850 | |
| Common Stock | | 200 |
| Paid-in Capital in Excess of Par Value | | 650 |
| To record issuance of common stock in exchange for legal services | | |

Because Fuqua's stock is not actively traded, the $850 billing is more clearly determinable as the market value of the transaction.

## Corporate Equity: A Comprehensive Illustration

The stockholders' equity section in Exhibit 15-5 brings together several of the concepts discussed in the chapter. Notice that preferred stock is presented first, followed by common stock. Next, additional paid-in capital is disclosed to complete total equity contributed by stockholders. The final element is retained earnings. Although variations in terminology and presentation exist in practice, the exhibit is representative and should convey the message that corporate equity is more complex than equity of both sole proprietorships and partnerships.

**Exhibit 15-5**
**Corporate Equity**

***Stockholders' Equity***

| | | |
|---|---|---|
| Capital stock | | |
| Cumulative 9% preferred stock, $10 par, 30,000 shares authorized, 20,000 shares issued and outstanding | | $200,000 |
| Common stock, no-par, $5 stated value, 15,000 shares authorized, 10,000 shares issued and outstanding | $ 50,000 | |
| Common stock subscribed, no-par, $5 stated value, 2,000 shares | 10,000 | 60,000 |
| Total capital stock | | $260,000 |
| Additional paid-in capital | | |
| Paid-in capital in excess of par value: preferred | $120,000 | |
| Paid-in capital in excess of stated value: common | 48,000 | 168,000 |
| Total paid-in capital | | $428,000 |
| Retained earnings | | 150,000 |
| Total stockholders' equity | | $578,000 |

## Book Value Per Share

**OBJECTIVE 6**
**Understand the computation and meaning of book value per share.**

Owners, creditors, and analysts use a variety of measures to assess corporate performance and financial position. One of these measures is **book value per share,** or the amount of stockholders' equity allocable to an individual share of stock. Stated differently, book value represents a corporation's net assets (total assets minus total liabilities) expressed on a per-share basis.

The calculation of book value depends on the classes of stock outstanding. If a corporation has only common stock, book value is computed by dividing total stockholders' equity by the number of common shares outstanding at the end of the accounting period. For example, assume Ranger Corporation has the following stockholders' equity on August 31, the end of the firm's fiscal year:

***Stockholders' Equity***

| | |
|---|---:|
| Common stock, \$1 par value, 100,000 shares authorized, 50,000 shares issued and outstanding | \$ 50,000 |
| Paid-in capital in excess of par value | 350,000 |
| Retained earnings | 600,000 |
| Total stockholders' equity | \$1,000,000 |

The book value per share is therefore \$20 (\$1,000,000 ÷ 50,000 shares).

### An Example with Two Classes of Stock

If a corporation has two classes of stock (e.g., common and preferred), total stockholders' equity must be allocated between the respective ownership interests. The allocation is achieved by first assigning the call value (sometimes referred to as the *redemption or liquidating value*) of the preferred stock plus any dividends in arrears[4] as preferred equity. The sum of these two items is next subtracted from total stockholders' equity to generate equity attributable to the common shareholders. The book value per common and preferred shares can then be determined by dividing the equity relating to the two stock classes by their respective outstanding shares.

To illustrate the necessary accounting, we will focus on the stockholders' equity section of Orleans, Inc. (see Exhibit 15-6). Further information reveals that dividends on the preferred stock are \$4,000 in arrears.

The allocation of Orleans' stockholders' equity follows.

| | | |
|---|---:|---:|
| Total stockholders' equity | | \$870,000 |
| Allocated to preferred stock | | |
| Call value: 400 shares × \$110 | \$44,000 | |
| Dividends in arrears | 4,000 | 48,000 |
| Allocated to common stock | | \$822,000 |

[4] Dividends in arrears apply solely to cumulative preferred stock.

**Exhibit 15-6**
**Stockholders' Equity of Orleans, Inc.**

| *Stockholders' Equity* | | |
|---|---|---|
| Preferred stock, $100 par value, 5% cumulative, callable at $110, 1,000 shares authorized, 400 shares issued and outstanding | $ 40,000 | |
| Common stock, $1 par value, 100,000 shares authorized, 30,000 shares issued and outstanding | 30,000 | $ 70,000 |
| Additional paid-in capital | | |
| Paid-in capital in excess of par: preferred | $ 5,000 | |
| Paid-in capital in excess of par: common | 200,000 | 205,000 |
| Total paid-in capital | | $275,000 |
| Retained earnings | | 595,000 |
| Total stockholders' equity | | $870,000 |

Observe that the $5,000 paid-in capital in excess of par on the preferred stock is not allocated to preferred equity. This amount will not be returned to the preferred shareholders should their stock be called.

The book value per share for each class of stock can now be calculated in the following manner:

Preferred stock: $48,000 ÷ 400 shares = $120.00 per share

Common stock: $822,000 ÷ 30,000 shares = $27.40 per share

## Meaning of Book Value

Book value is equivalent to a corporation's net assets per share of stock. Some stockholders therefore believe that should the corporation terminate operations and liquidate, they would receive an amount equal to the book value per share. Rarely, however, does this belief become reality. When an entity liquidates, the assets are usually sold at a price far different from their valuation on a balance sheet. Remember, the balance sheet is cost-based and ignores increases in valuation that arise from inflation. Furthermore, because the corporation is selling out, the amounts received for certain assets may be only a small percentage of their original cost. Added to this is the fact that liabilities are often settled at less than the amount owed. These events alter corporate equity and the amounts disbursed to stockholders upon liquidation.

The importance of book value arises from its inclusion in many legal contracts. In a small corporation, for instance, stockholders may agree to sell their holdings to the other owners at the book value per share existing on specified future dates. Or banks may lend funds to a corporation, subject to the maintenance of a minimum book value. Under no circumstances should book value per share be equated with a stock's market value, as these two measures normally differ. Consider, for example, the following figures, which were in existence at the time this text was written:

| *Corporation* | *Book Value per Share* | *Market Value per Share* |
|---|---|---|
| Chase Manhattan Corp. | $40.55 | $28.63 |
| Chevron Corp. | 43.23 | 45.75 |
| Marriott Corp. | 1.76 | 31.63 |
| Paine Webber Group | 24.87 | 16.13 |
| Sony Corp. | 20.64 | 51.00 |
| TGI Friday's | 8.87 | 12.88 |

Book value, a measure based on historical cost, is just one of the many factors investors use in studying the appropriateness of a stock's market price.

## Chapter Review

### Learning Objectives—The Key Points

**1 Be familiar with the features, advantages, and disadvantages of a corporate entity.** The corporate form of organization has several key features, which often make it preferable for conducting business affairs. Shares of ownership are easily transferred and regardless of any change in ownership, the corporation has a continuous existence. In addition, the stockholders have limited liability, which serves to protect the assets of the owners from use in satisfying corporate obligations. Finally, because of limited liability and the fact that ownership is divided into many shares, capital is more easily raised by corporations than by the other forms of business organization.

Two disadvantages of corporations are double taxation and heavy regulation. Double taxation is the taxing of income to the corporation and the subsequent taxing of dividends to stockholders.

**2 Understand the difference between common and preferred stock.** Common stock represents an ownership interest that controls the board of directors via the voting process. In addition, common stockholders have the rights to (1) share in dividend distributions, (2) subscribe to any additional common stock that is issued by the company (i.e., the preemptive right), and (3) share in the final disposition of assets in the event of liquidation.

In contrast, preferred stock is an ownership interest that has certain preferential rights over those associated with common stock; however, to obtain these rights, others (e.g., voting) are given up in return. Preferred stockholders are entitled to receive dividends before any distributions are made to common stockholders. Furthermore, most preferred stock has preference over common stock in asset distributions should corporate liquidation occur.

**3 Be able to account for dividends associated with preferred stock.** Preferred stockholders are entitled to receive dividends each period. If the stock is cumulative, any preferred dividends omitted in a given year accumulate and must be paid before future dividends are declared and paid on common shares. Such accumulated amounts are said to be in arrears and are disclosed in the footnotes to the financial statements. If the preferred stock is participating, preferred stockholders may receive dividends in excess of the amounts the corporation is required to distribute.

**4 Be familiar with the concepts of and accounting treatments for par, no-par, and stated-value stock, and stock subscriptions.** A corporation's stock may be characterized as having a par value or no par value. Par value is an amount specified in the corporate charter; it represents the firm's legal capital (a minimum permanent investment) per share. When par-value stock is sold, an amount equal to the par value of the issuance is placed in a capital stock account. Any receipts in excess of par are recorded in Paid-in Capital in Excess of Par Value. When no-par stock is issued, the entire proceeds are credited to a capital stock account. No-par stock may have a stated value assigned by the board of directors, which, in effect, serves to establish a minimum issue price. Accounting for stated-value stock is similar to that for par-value stock.

Small corporations sometimes sell stock directly to investors on a subscription basis. When subscriptions are received, credit entries are made to the Common Stock Subscribed account for the par or stated value of the shares and to Paid-in Capital in Excess of Par (or Stated) Value for any excess. When the stock is issued to investors, the Common Stock Subscribed account is debited and Common Stock is credited.

**5 Be familiar with the stockholders' equity section of a corporate balance sheet.** Stockholders' equity has three sections. The first, called capital stock, discloses the Preferred Stock, Common Stock, and Stock Subscribed accounts. The additional paid-in capital section appears next and contains the accounts for any amounts paid in excess of par or stated value. The final section is for retained earnings.

**6 Understand the computation and meaning of book value per share.** Book value per share is the amount of stockholders' equity allocable to an individual share of stock. If a corporation has both preferred and common stock, book value is calculated for both classes. To compute book value for preferred shares, the total of the shares' call (i.e., redemption) value, plus any dividends in arrears if the stock is cumulative, is divided by preferred shares outstanding. The book value of common stock is total stockholders' equity, minus the preferred equity just described, divided by the common shares outstanding. Although book value is not equivalent to the value of stock in the marketplace, it is nonetheless an important element in many legal contracts.

## Chapter Quiz

The five questions that follow relate to several issues raised in the chapter. Test your knowledge of the issues by selecting the best answer. (The answers appear on p. 540.)

**1** Which of the following statements is false?
- a All corporations issue preferred stock.
- b Stockholders have limited liability.
- c Corporate earnings are subject to double taxation.
- d Corporations face heavier governmental regulation than sole proprietorships.

**2** Which of the following rights do not apply to common stockholders?
- a The right to share in dividends if declared by the board of directors.
- b The pre-emptive right.
- c The right to vote on changes in a corporation's bylaws.
- d The right to receive dividends that are in arrears.

**3** Fenton Corporation is authorized to issue 10,000 shares of $5 par-value common stock. If 60% of these shares are issued at $20, what amount should be credited to the Common Stock account?
- a $30,000.
- b $50,000.
- c $90,000.
- d $120,000.

**4** Equador's balance sheet revealed the following accounts:

| | |
|---|---|
| Notes payable | $150,000 |
| Preferred stock | 100,000 |
| Common stock | 200,000 |
| Paid-in capital in excess of par: preferred | 10,000 |
| Paid-in capital in excess of par: common | 95,000 |
| Retained earnings | 400,000 |

The total amount invested by stockholders and the total stockholders' equity are:

| | *Invested by Stockholders* | *Total Stockholders' Equity* |
|---|---|---|
| a | $105,000 | $955,000 |
| b | 305,000 | 805,000 |
| c | 405,000 | 805,000 |
| d | 555,000 | 955,000 |

**5** Bright Eyes, Inc., has outstanding 100,000 shares of $5 par-value common stock and 10,000 shares of $100 par-value preferred stock. The preferred stock is cumulative and has a call price of $115 per share. If there are no dividends in arrears and total stockholders' equity amounts to $4,000,000, what is the book value per share of the common stock?

a $2.85.
b $5.00.
c $28.50.
d $30.00.

## Questions

**Q15-1** What is a corporation? Discuss the advantages of the corporate form of organization.

**Q15-2** Briefly explain the disadvantages of the corporate form of organization.

**Q15-3** Discuss the duties and responsibilities of the directors of a corporation. How do directors gain their authority?

**Q15-4** Describe a typical corporation's leadership structure.

**Q15-5** List the rights typically possessed by common stockholders.

**Q15-6** Briefly explain the dividend preference associated with preferred stock.

**Q15-7** How does cumulative preferred stock differ from noncumulative preferred stock?

**Q15-8** Are dividends in arrears on cumulative preferred stock a liability? Explain.

**Q15-9** What is "participating preferred stock"?

**Q15-10** What is "callable preferred stock"? Why do corporations issue such stock?

**Q15-11** Discuss the meaning of "legal capital."

**Q15-12** Why is stock rarely issued below par value?

**Q15-13** Discuss the impact of par value in determining the market price of a new stock issue.

**Q15-14** Discuss the process of selling par-value stock on a subscription basis.

**Q15-15** When stock is issued in exchange for services or noncash assets, at what amount should the transaction be recorded?

**Q15-16** Define book value per share. Describe how book value per common share is calculated when a corporation has both common and preferred stock outstanding.

**Q15-17** Integrity Machining's common stock has a book value per share of $20. Will the stock's market price be less than, equal to, or greater than $20 per share? Briefly discuss.

## Exercises

**E15-1** ***Stockholders' equity concepts***

Evaluate the comments that follow as being True or False. If the comment is false, briefly explain why.

a Corporations are subject to double taxation. Thus, a 40% tax rate on income becomes an effective tax rate of 80% to the corporation.
b Common stockholders are likely to be rewarded with increases in the market value of their shares as a corporation becomes more profitable.
c Most preferred stockholders are entitled to a fixed dividend amount each year.
d Par value virtually always coincides with a stock's original issue price.
e Par-value stock is generally worth more than no-par stock.

**E15-2** ***Preferred stock dividends***

The following information was extracted from the balance sheet of the Bluebonnet Corporation:

| | |
|---|---|
| Capital stock | |
| Cumulative, nonparticipating 11% preferred stock, $50 par, 3,000 shares authorized, 2,000 shares issued and outstanding | $100,000 |
| Common stock, $10 par, 20,000 shares authorized, 15,000 shares issued and outstanding | 150,000 |
| Total capital stock | $250,000 |

Dividends declared during the past four years were: 19X3, $20,000; 19X4, $4,000; 19X5, $12,000; and 19X6, $19,000.

a Calculate the dividends paid to preferred stockholders and to common stockholders during each of the four years.
b Repeat requirement (a), assuming the preferred stock is noncumulative.

**E15-3** ***Issuance of stock***

Prepare journal entries to record the issuance of 100,000 shares of common stock at $20 per share for each of the following independent cases:

a Jackson Corporation has common stock with a par value of $1 per share.
b Royal Corporation has no-par common with a stated value of $5 per share.
c French Corporation has no-par common; no stated value has been assigned.

**E15-4** ***Issuance of stock; organization costs***

The Snowbound Corporation was incorporated in July. The firm's charter authorized the sale of 200,000 shares of $10 par-value common stock. The following transactions occurred during the year:

| | | |
|---|---|---|
| July | 1 | Sold 45,000 shares of common stock to investors for $18 per share. Cash was collected and the shares were issued. |
| | 7 | Issued 600 shares to Sharon Dale, attorney-at-law, for services rendered during the corporation's organizational phase. Dale charged $12,600 for her work. |
| Aug. | 11 | Sold 20,000 shares to investors for $22 per share. Cash was collected and the shares were issued. |
| Dec. | 14 | Issued 30,000 shares to the MJB Company for land valued at $900,000. |

Prepare journal entries to record each of the transactions.

**E15-5** ***Stock subscriptions; journal entries***

Investors recently subscribed to 5,000 shares of B&J Travel's $1 par-value common stock at $10 per share. During the year, the company received 80% of the balances due, which resulted in the issuance of 4,000 shares of stock.

a Prepare journal entries to record:
   (1) The subscriptions to investors.
   (2) The receipt of cash from subscribers.
   (3) The issuance of shares.

b Determine the year-end balance in the Common Stock Subscribed account.
c Determine the year-end balance in the Common Stock Subscriptions Receivable account.

**E15-6** ***Stock subscriptions; analysis***

During 19X1, investors subscribed to 5,000 shares of Gates Corporation $1 par-value common stock at $4 per share. The firm's December 31, 19X1, balance sheet revealed the following accounts:

| | |
|---|---|
| Common stock subscriptions receivable | $9,000 |
| Common stock subscribed | 2,600 |

a Present the journal entry recorded by Gates when the original subscriptions were made.
b Determine the amount of cash received from subscribers.
c Determine the number of subscribed shares issued by the company.

**E15-7** ***Analysis of stockholders' equity***

The stockholders' equity sections of Discount Mart at the end of 19X2 and 19X1 follow.

| | *19X2* | *19X1* |
|---|---|---|
| Preferred stock, $100 par value, 12% | $1,000,000 | $ 600,000 |
| Common stock, $20 par value | 2,000,000 | 1,800,000 |
| Paid-in capital in excess of par value | | |
| Preferred | 16,000 | — |
| Common | 4,350,000 | 3,750,000 |
| Retained earnings | 80,000 | 180,000 |
| Total stockholders' equity | $7,446,000 | $6,330,000 |

a How many shares of preferred stock were issued during 19X2? At what price were the shares issued?
b How many shares of common stock were issued during 19X2? At what price were the shares issued?
c Did Discount Mart's total legal capital increase or decrease during 19X2? By what amount?
d Did Discount Mart's total paid-in capital increase or decrease during 19X2? By what amount?

**E15-8** ***Preparation of stockholders' equity section***

The accounts and balances that follow were extracted from the adjusted trial balance of Grove Park Enterprises:

| | |
|---|---|
| Common stock, $5 par value | $ ? |
| Paid-in capital in excess of par value: common | 90,000 |
| Common stock subscribed | 6,000 |
| Preferred stock, $2 par value | ? |
| Paid-in capital in excess of par value: preferred | 66,000 |
| Retained earnings | 74,000 |

A review of the corporate charter revealed that Grove Park was authorized to issue 100,000 shares of common stock and 80,000 shares of 10% cumulative preferred stock. The number of shares issued and outstanding were: common, 10,000; preferred, 15,000.

Prepare Grove Park's stockholders' equity section in good form.

**E15-9** ***Preparation of stockholders' equity section***

The following data relate to LeMaster Corporation as of December 31, 19XX, the close of the current accounting period:

- *Preferred stock*—The company has 1,000 shares of $50 par-value cumulative preferred stock authorized. The stock pays a 10% dividend; to date, 400 shares have been issued at $55 per share.
- *Common stock*—A total of 25,000 shares of $1 stated value common stock is authorized. To date, 10,000 shares have been issued at $10 per share and an additional 3,000 shares have been subscribed to at $15 per share.

Assuming a retained earnings balance of $177,000, prepare the stockholders' equity section of LeMaster's December 31,19XX, balance sheet.

**E15-10** ***Book value per share***

Orange Corporation has the following stockholders' equity:

| | |
|---|---|
| Common stock, $2 par value | $200,000 |
| Paid-in capital in excess of par value: common | 350,000 |
| Retained earnings | 250,000 |
| | $800,000 |

a Determine Orange's book value per share.

b Assume that Orange also has a preferred stock issue of 1,000 shares ($100 par value; $125 call price) that generated the firm $100,000 upon issuance. Compute the book value per share of both the preferred and the common stock. There are no dividends in arrears.

## Problems

### Series A

**P15-A1** ***Preferred stock dividends***

The annual dividends declared by the board of directors of A-1 Engine Parts, Inc., for 19X2 through 19X6 follow.

| *Year* | *Total Dividends* | *Preferred Dividends* | *Common Dividends* |
|---|---|---|---|
| 19X2 | $ 40,000 | | |
| 19X3 | 80,000 | | |
| 19X4 | 55,000 | | |
| 19X5 | 194,000 | | |
| 19X6 | 480,000 | | |

The company has had two classes of capital stock outstanding since 19X1: preferred stock and common stock. The preferred issue is comprised of 5,000 shares of cumulative, nonparticipating, 12%, $100 par-value stock. There are also 500,000 shares of $2 par-value common. There were no dividends in arrears at the beginning of 19X2.

**Instructions**

a Determine the dividends distributed in each of the years to preferred stockholders and to common stockholders.

b Repeat part (a) assuming the preferred stock is cumulative and participating.

c Where in the financial statements are dividends in arrears disclosed?

**P15-A2** ***Issuance of stock***

Ventures, Inc., was formed on January 1 to invest in artwork. The company is authorized to issue 10,000 shares of $1 par-value common stock and 1,000 shares of 10%, $50 par-value cumulative preferred stock. The following selected transactions occurred during the first quarter of operation:

| | | |
|---|---|---|
| Jan. | 3 | Sold 5,000 shares of common stock to the corporation's founders at $30 per share. |
| | 19 | Sold 600 shares of preferred stock at $58 per share. |
| Feb. | 4 | Issued 100 common shares to an attorney for $3,300 of legal work related to corporate start-up and formation. |
| | 11 | Issued 2,000 shares of common stock to Pierre LaTour in exchange for a painting appraised at $75,000. The art originally cost LaTour $30,000. |

**Instructions**

a Prepare journal entries to record the company's transactions.

b Prepare the stockholders' equity section of the firm's March 31 balance sheet. The Retained Earnings balance on this date totals $41,000.

c The president of Ventures believes that organization costs should be expensed immediately. Briefly explain why the president's view is incorrect.

**P15-A3** ***Preparation of stockholders' equity section***

Barney's corporate charter authorized the issuance of 100,000 shares of $100 par, 12%, cumulative, nonparticipating preferred stock and 1 million shares of no-par common. The board of directors has assigned a $5-per-share stated value to the common stock. Through December 31 of the current year the firm has issued 25,000 of the preferred shares, generating $3 million cash. In addition, common shares were issued as follows:

- Five hundred thousand shares were sold to investors at $8 per share.
- Four hundred thousand shares were exchanged for buildings and equipment having a fair market value of $3.1 million and $450,000, respectively.

Dividends on the preferred stock were $150,000 in arrears at the beginning of the current year. Dividend distributions in the past 12 months have amounted to $500,000.

On December 17, Barney's finance department learned that one of the initial corporate investors sold his entire holding of 3,900 common shares to Harold Lundgen for $22 per share. The investor originally paid $8 per share.

**Instructions**

Prepare Barney's stockholders' equity section as of December 31 of the current year along with any appropriate footnotes. Assume the Retained Earnings balance on this date totals $1,430,000.

**P15-A4** ***Stock subscriptions***

The Juarez Corporation is authorized to issue 30,000 shares of no-par common stock that have a stated value of $1 per share. The following transactions occurred during the year:

| | | |
|---|---|---|
| Apr. | 1 | The company issued 1,000 shares to the corporation's founders for $6,000. Cash was received and the stock certificates were issued. |
| May | 1 | The company received subscription contracts for 7,500 shares at $8 per share. No cash was collected at this time. |
| June | 1 | Thirty percent of the amounts due under the subscription contracts were received. No shares were issued at this time. |
| July | 1 | Forty percent of the total subscription amount was received from |

subscribers. Three thousand shares were now fully paid and the certificates were issued.

Aug. 1 The final 30% of the total subscription amount was received and the appropriate certificates were issued.

**Instructions**

a Prepare journal entries to record the preceding transactions.
b Prepare the stockholders' equity section of Juarez's balance sheet as of July 31. Retained earnings on this date amounted to $14,400.
c Prepare the stockholders' equity section of Juarez's balance sheet as of August 31. Retained earnings on this date amounted to $16,300.
d Determine the impact of the issuance of previously subscribed shares on (1) total common stock as reported on the balance sheet and (2) total current assets.

**P15-A5** ***Analysis of stockholders' equity accounts***

The following accounts appear on the balance sheet of Las Vegas, Inc.:

| | |
|---|---|
| Preferred stock, $100 par value | $ 80,000 |
| Paid-in capital in excess of par value: preferred | 12,800 |
| Common stock, $5 stated value | 375,000 |
| Paid-in capital in excess of stated value: common | 675,000 |
| Subscriptions receivable: common stock | 60,000 |
| Common stock subscribed | 10,000 |
| Notes payable | 320,000 |
| Retained earnings | 215,000 |

**Instructions**

a How many shares of preferred stock and common stock have been issued?
b What was the average issue price of the preferred stock?
c How much remains to be paid on the common stock subscriptions?
d How many shares of common stock have been subscribed but not yet issued?
e Compute the total amount of legal capital. *Note:* Consider common stock subscribed as part of legal capital.
f Compute the total paid-in capital.
g Which accounts, if any, would be ignored in computing total stockholders' equity?

**P15-A6** ***Book value per share***

The stockholders' equity section of Quarry, Inc., revealed the following information on January 1, 19XX:

| | |
|---|---|
| Preferred stock, $100 par value, 9% cumulative, callable at $108 | $ 100,000 |
| Common stock, $3 par value | 300,000 |
| Paid-in capital in excess of par value: preferred | 12,000 |
| Paid-in capital in excess of par value: common | 1,200,000 |
| Retained earnings | 188,000 |
| Total stockholders' equity | $1,800,000 |

Dividends in arrears on the preferred stock totaled $18,000 at the beginning of 19XX.

**Instructions**

a Calculate the book value per share of both the preferred stock and the common stock on January 1.
b Calculate the book value per common share immediately after each of the following transactions and events. Consider each item independently.

(1) An additional 10,000 shares of common stock were sold to the public for $24 per share.
(2) The Retained Earnings account contained a balance of $1,138,000 on December 31, 19XX; no preferred dividends had been paid during the year.

c Explain the meaning of book value per share to one of Quarry's stockholders. Assume the stockholder has a weak accounting background.

## Series B

**P15-B1** ***Preferred stock dividends***

The annual dividends declared by the board of directors of Arizona Mechanical for 19X4 through 19X8 follow.

| *Year* | *Total Dividends* | *Preferred Dividends* | *Common Dividends* |
|---|---|---|---|
| 19X4 | $300,000 | | |
| 19X5 | 100,000 | | |
| 19X6 | 50,000 | | |
| 19X7 | 353,000 | | |
| 19X8 | 360,000 | | |

The company has had two classes of capital stock outstanding since 19X3: preferred stock and common stock. The preferred issue is comprised of 200,000 shares of cumulative, participating, 8%, $5 par-value stock. There are also 3,000,000 shares of $1 par-value common. There were no dividends in arrears at the beginning of 19X4.

**Instructions**

a Determine the dividends distributed in each of the years to preferred stockholders and to common stockholders.

b Repeat part (a) assuming the preferred stock is cumulative and nonparticipating.

c Given a choice, would a common stockholder desire that Arizona Mechanical's preferred stock be noncumulative, nonparticipating or cumulative, participating? Briefly explain.

**P15-B2** ***Issuance of stock***

Music Land, Inc., was formed on January 1, 19X3. The company is authorized to issue 20,000 shares of $2 par-value common stock and 10,000 shares of 12%, $100 par-value cumulative preferred stock. The following selected transactions occurred during the first year of operation:

| | | |
|---|---|---|
| Jan. | 2 | Sold 10,000 shares of common stock to the corporation's founders at $40 per share. |
| | 6 | Issued 100 common shares to an attorney for $4,200 of legal work related to corporate start-up and formation. |
| Apr. | 15 | Sold 6,000 shares of preferred stock at $110 per share. |
| Nov. | 24 | Issued 3,000 shares of common stock to Marcus Investment Company in exchange for a parcel of land appraised at $140,000. The land originally cost Marcus $65,000. |

**Instructions**

a Prepare journal entries to record the company's transactions.

b Prepare the stockholders' equity section of Music Land's December 31 balance sheet. The Retained Earnings balance at year-end is $90,000.

c What would you have done differently on January 6 if Music Land's common stock was no-par value with a $2 stated value?

**P15-B3** ***Preparation of stockholders' equity section***

Gordon's corporate charter authorized the issuance of 5,000 shares of $100 par, 10%, cumulative, nonparticipating preferred stock and 100,000 shares of no-par common. The board of directors has assigned a $2-per-share stated value to the common stock. Through December 31 of the current year the firm has issued 2,000 of the preferred shares, generating $206,000 cash. In addition, common shares were issued as follows:

- Three thousand shares were sold to investors at $30 per share.
- One thousand shares were exchanged for land and buildings having a fair market value of $20,000 and $28,000, respectively.

Dividends on the preferred stock were $22,000 in arrears at the beginning of the current year. Dividend distributions in the past 12 months have amounted to $67,500.

On December 6, Gordon's finance department learned that one of the initial investors in the corporation sold his entire holding of 600 common shares to Vernon Lewis for $54 per share. The investor originally paid $30 per share.

**Instructions**

Prepare Gordon's stockholders' equity section as of December 31 of the current year along with any appropriate footnotes. Assume the Retained Earnings balance on this date totals $217,300.

**P15-B4** ***Stock subscriptions***

The Radford Corporation is authorized to issue 100,000 shares of $1 par-value common stock. The following transactions occurred during the year:

| | |
|---|---|
| Mar. 14 | The company issued 25,000 shares to the corporation's founders for $200,000. Cash was received and the stock certificates were issued. |
| Apr. 17 | The company received subscription contracts for 7,000 shares at $9 per share. No cash was collected at this time. |
| May 17 | Forty percent of the amounts due under the subscription contracts were received. No shares were issued at this time. |
| June 17 | Twenty-five percent of the total subscription amount was received from subscribers. Four thousand shares were now fully paid and the certificates were issued. |
| July 17 | The final 35% of the total subscription amount was received and the appropriate certificates were issued. |

**Instructions**

a Prepare journal entries to record the preceding transactions.
b Prepare the stockholders' equity section of Radford's balance sheet as of June 30. Retained earnings on this date amounted to $47,800.
c Prepare the stockholders' equity section of Radford's balance sheet as of July 31. Retained earnings on this date amounted to $52,600.
d Determine the impact of the issuance of previously subscribed shares on (1) total retained earnings and (2) total paid-in capital.

**P15-B5** ***Analysis of stockholders' equity accounts***

The following accounts appear on the balance sheet of the Austin Corporation:

| | |
|---|---:|
| Preferred stock, $5 par value | $105,000 |
| Paid-in capital in excess of par value: preferred | 189,000 |
| Common stock, $10 par value | 270,000 |
| Paid-in capital in excess of par value: common | 216,000 |
| Common stock subscribed | 3,500 |

| | |
|---|---|
| Retained earnings | 576,800 |
| Notes payable | 59,600 |
| Subscriptions receivable: common stock | 7,400 |

**Instructions**

a How many shares of preferred stock and common stock have been issued?
b What was the average issue price of the preferred stock?
c How many shares of common stock have been subscribed but not yet issued?
d How much remains to be paid on the common stock subscriptions?
e Compute the total amount of legal capital. *Note:* Consider common stock subscribed as part of legal capital.
f Compute the total paid-in capital.
g Compute the total stockholders' equity.

**P15-B6** ***Book value per share***

The stockholders' equity section of Camping Haven, Inc., revealed the following information on January 1, 19XX:

| | |
|---|---|
| Preferred stock, $100 par value, 10% cumulative, callable at $105 | $ 200,000 |
| Common stock, $2 par value | 600,000 |
| Paid-in capital in excess of par value: preferred | 10,000 |
| Paid-in capital in excess of par value: common | 1,400,000 |
| Retained earnings | 990,000 |
| Total stockholders' equity | $3,200,000 |

Dividends in arrears on the preferred stock totaled $20,000 at the beginning of 19XX.

**Instructions**

a Calculate the book value per share of both the preferred stock and the common stock on January 1.
b Calculate the book value per common share immediately after each of the following transactions and events. Consider each item independently.
   (1) An additional 20,000 shares of common stock were sold to the public at $10.70 per share.
   (2) The Retained Earnings account contained a balance on December 31, 19XX, of $1,055,000; preferred dividends totaling $15,000 had been paid during the year.
c Does book value per share indicate the amount stockholders would receive if a corporation sold its assets, paid its bills, and liquidated? Explain.

## Beyond the Basics

**BB15-1** ***Financing alternatives***

Jim Seagram is the manager of a local sporting goods store. Recently, during some spare time, he invented a device called Ski-Matic, which allows users to improve their skiing skills and balance. Seagram has approached Professor Pujak at the local university's school of business to assist him in developing a budget for mass production of the device. Pujak believes that $400,000 in capital will be needed to establish manufacturing facilities, commence production, and effectively advertise the product. Pujak is excited about the project and is willing to invest $10,000 for a share of the company. Because Seagram can invest only $20,000, considerable outside funding is necessary.

There are three options open to Seagram to finance his venture. First, he could establish a partnership and solicit investments. Second, he could incorporate and try to sell common stock to the public. Finally, he could incorporate and (1) sell 12% preferred stock to outside investors and (2) issue common stock to both himself and Pujak.

**Instructions**

a Discuss several advantages and disadvantages of each of the three financing alternatives. Disregard income tax considerations.

b Which alternative would appear to have the best chance of success in raising capital? Explain your answer.

c Assuming that Ski-Matic was a tremendous success, which alternative would most likely be in the best interests of Seagram? Explain your answer.

**BB15-2** ***Unlimited and limited liability; owner and creditor perspectives***

Winter Wonderland, a small partnership, reported the following balance sheet data at the end of the current year:

| | | |
|---|---|---|
| Assets | | $80,000 |
| Liabilities | $25,000 | |
| Owners' equity | 55,000 | $80,000 |

**Instructions**

a Briefly discuss the meaning of unlimited liability from a partner's point of view.

b Assume that the partners plan to withdraw $54,500 of assets. What would be your reaction as a creditor if the firm was in serious financial difficulty and, prior to settling creditor obligations, expected to sell remaining assets for only 60% of book (carrying) value? Consider the unlimited liability characteristic in drafting your response.

c Briefly discuss the meaning of limited liability from a stockholder's point of view. Is limited liability an advantage or disadvantage of being a stockholder?

d Given the same facts as in part (b), namely, withdrawals of $54,500 and a 60% liquidation value, would your response as a creditor change if Winter Wonderland was a small, closely held corporation rather than a partnership? Explain.

## Answers to Chapter Quiz

**1** a

**2** d

**3** a (6,000 shares × $5 per share)

**4** c (Invested by stockholders: $100,000 + $200,000 + $10,000 + $95,000 = $405,000; Total stockholders' equity: $405,000 + $400,000 = $805,000)

**5** c (10,000 shares × $115 = $1,150,000; $4,000,000 − $1,150,000 = $2,850,000; $2,850,000 ÷ 100,000 shares = $28.50)

CHAPTER 16

# Corporations: Additional Equity Issues and Income Reporting

## Learning Objectives

After reading this chapter you should:

1. Understand what treasury stock is and how to account for its acquisition and reissuance.
2. Understand the distinctions among cash dividends, property dividends, stock dividends, and stock splits.
3. Be familiar with prior period adjustments and appropriations of retained earnings.
4. Be familiar with discontinued operations, extraordinary items, accounting changes, and intraperiod tax allocation.
5. Have a basic knowledge of earnings per share.

In the preceding chapter we discussed various topics that pertain to the corporate form of business organization. The discussion included the advantages and disadvantages of this popular entity form, the computation of book value per share, and the proper accounting treatment for preferred and common stock issuances. This chapter continues our presentation of corporate equity. Specifically, we will focus on the reacquisition of stock by corporations, retained earnings, dividends and stock splits, and corporate reporting of income and earnings per share.

Much of the material contained within these pages is particularly important to present and potential investors—some of the key users of financial statements. Newspapers, for example, consistently publish articles with headlines similar to the following:

- General United's Earnings per Share Falls 15%
- Largent Corporation Has 3-for-2 Stock Split
- Garrett, Inc., Declares 10% Stock Dividend

The investing public must have a fundamental understanding of these events to correctly determine the impact on both corporate financial affairs and, more important, investment holdings. Although your present financial position may not permit "wheeling and dealing" in the stock market, the future often brings change. Our goal is to provide you with an introduction to the topics noted in the first paragraph so that some analysis of corporate equity and profitability is possible.

## Treasury Stock

OBJECTIVE 1
Understand what treasury stock is and how to account for its acquisition and reissuance.

Corporations frequently find it advantageous to reacquire shares of their own stock. These shares, which are commonly reissued at a later date, are termed **treasury stock.** Treasury stock is purchased for a variety of reasons. Some corporations have reacquired their own shares for use in company retirement and employee stock purchase programs. Other companies have purchased treasury stock to rid themselves of a particular stockholder or group of stockholders. For instance, large corporate entities sometimes purchase the interests of very small investors (e.g., those owning 10 shares or less) to save the costs of mailing annual reports, processing minute dividend checks, and so forth. Treasury stock is also acquired for use in future acquisitions of other companies, to guard against hostile takeovers by other firms, and for investment purposes. Corporations that purchase treasury shares for the last reason do so when the market price is depressed, hoping to achieve an attractive return on their invested funds.[1] Finally, some businesses have secured treasury holdings in an attempt to boost the *earnings per share of common stock*—a measure widely used to judge the operating success of an entity.

Whatever the purpose, the acquisition of treasury stock is commonplace. A review of recent annual reports disclosed the treasury stock holdings that appear in Exhibit 16-1.

Corporate action to purchase treasury stock reduces the number of shares outstanding; however, the number of shares issued is unaffected. Issued shares can be reduced only if they are formally retired and canceled by the corporation. Because treasury stock is no longer outstanding, it is not entitled to voting privileges or any cash dividends declared by the board of directors.

[1] Many companies took advantage of Black Monday to increase their treasury holdings. Black Monday was that frightful day in 1987 when the stock market crashed and the Dow Jones Industrial Average plunged 508 points, nearly 23% of its total "value."

**Exhibit 16-1**
**Treasury Stock Holdings**

| *Corporation* | *Number of Treasury Shares* | *Percent of Total Shares Issued* | *Acquisition Cost of Treasury Shares* |
|---|---|---|---|
| Alberto-Culver | 3,155,348 | 19.5% | $ 29,325,128 |
| Bassett Furniture | 1,256,409 | 13.1 | 27,068,811 |
| Borden, Inc. | 27,082,089 | 26.8 | 503,836,000 |
| H. J. Heinz | 16,081,931 | 11.2 | 547,738,000 |
| Polaroid Corporation | 3,792,600 | 5.0 | 46,900,000 |

*Note:* All citations refer to common stock only.

## Acquisitions of Treasury Stock

The most common treatment for treasury stock acquisitions requires a debit to a Treasury Stock account. Thus, if Hunt Corporation purchased 5,000 shares of its $10 par-value common stock at $70 per share, the journal entry would be as follows:

| | | |
|---|---|---|
| Treasury Stock | 350,000 | |
| Cash | | 350,000 |
| To record the purchase of 5,000 shares of treasury stock at $70 per share | | |

Treasury stock is *not* regarded as an asset, even if the shares are purchased for investment purposes. In plain and simple terms, a corporation cannot own part of itself. The acquisition of treasury stock really involves a reduction in stockholders' equity, because funds are being returned to the selling stockholders. To illustrate, assume Hunt had authorization to issue 15,000 shares of $10 par-value common stock. Further, assume that all of the shares were issued at $90 per share and that retained earnings amounts to $440,000. After the acquisition of the 5,000 treasury shares, the firm's stockholders' equity section would appear as follows:

***Stockholders' Equity***

| | |
|---|---|
| Common stock, $10 par value, 15,000 shares authorized and issued, 10,000 shares outstanding | $ 150,000 |
| Paid-in capital in excess of par value | 1,200,000 |
| Total paid-in capital | $1,350,000 |
| Retained earnings | 440,000 |
| | $1,790,000 |
| Deduct: Treasury stock (5,000 shares) at cost | 350,000 |
| Total stockholders' equity | $1,440,000 |

Observe that the Common Stock and Paid-in Capital in Excess of Par Value accounts are not reduced by the treasury stock purchase. However, the cost of the 5,000 shares is deducted later in the stockholders' equity section. Finally, note that the number of shares issued and the number outstanding now differ because of the shares held "in the treasury."

## Reissuance of Treasury Stock

At the time of reissuance the Treasury Stock account is credited for the acquisition cost of the reissued shares. If the reissue price exceeds the acquisition cost, the difference is recorded as additional paid-in capital. For example, assume Hunt now sells 1,000 of the treasury shares for $79 per share. The necessary journal entry follows.

| | | |
|---|---|---|
| Cash | 79,000 | |
| Treasury Stock | | 70,000 |
| Paid-in Capital from Treasury Stock | | 9,000 |
| To record sale of 1,000 shares of treasury stock at $79 per share | | |

The $70,000 credit to the Treasury Stock account is based on the $70-per-share acquisition cost. It is important to note that the $9,000 excess over cost is not a gain to be reported on the income statement. As shown throughout the text, gains and losses arise from the sale of goods and services and from other earnings activities. Conversely, transactions that involve the issuance (or reissuance) of capital stock are equity transactions and affect paid-in capital. In Hunt's case, investors were willing to pay $79,000 for shares that had an original acquisition cost of $70,000; thus, paid-in capital must increase by $9,000. The increase is recorded in a separate account entitled Paid-in Capital from Treasury Stock.

The stockholders' equity section immediately after the reissuance would appear as follows:

***Stockholders' Equity***

| | | |
|---|---|---|
| Capital stock | | |
| Common stock, $10 par value, 15,000 shares authorized and issued, 11,000 shares outstanding | | $ 150,000 |
| Additional paid-in capital | | |
| Paid-in capital in excess of par value | $1,200,000 | |
| Paid-in capital from treasury stock | 9,000 | 1,209,000 |
| Total paid-in capital | | $1,359,000 |
| Retained earnings | | 440,000 |
| | | $1,799,000 |
| Deduct: Treasury stock (4,000 shares) at cost | | 280,000 |
| Total stockholders' equity | | $1,519,000 |

Total stockholders' equity has increased by $79,000 ($1,519,000 vs. $1,440,000), reflecting the amount of funds generated from the treasury stock sale.

### Reissuance Below Cost

Treasury shares can also be reissued at or below cost. We will now illustrate the latter case because of the complexities involved. Just as reissuance above cost gave rise to additional paid-in capital, reissuance below cost calls for a reduction of paid-in capital. For example, assume Hunt sells an additional 2,000 treasury shares. This time, however, the selling price is only $66 per share. The journal entry to record the sale is:

| | | |
|---|---|---|
| Cash | 132,000 | |
| Paid-in Capital from Treasury Stock | 8,000 | |
| Treasury Stock | | 140,000 |
| To record sale of 2,000 shares of treasury stock at $66 per share | | |

As before, Treasury Stock is credited for the cost of the reissued shares, in this case $140,000 (2,000 shares × $70). Because the sale has generated proceeds of only $132,000, paid-in capital must be reduced by $8,000 ($140,000 − $132,000). In effect, the reduction is a cancellation of paid-in capital from earlier treasury stock sales, thereby requiring a debit to the Paid-in Capital from Treasury Stock account for $8,000.

If this account's balance is insufficient to absorb the entire (or any of the) reduction, the remaining debit is entered in the Retained Earnings account. To illustrate, if the 2,000 shares were sold for $128,000, paid-in capital should be reduced by $12,000 ($140,000 − $128,000). As shown in the stockholders' equity section from the previous illustration, however, Paid-in Capital from Treasury Stock has a balance of only $9,000. Consequently, the required journal entry would debit this account for $9,000 and charge the remaining $3,000 against Retained Earnings.

## Retained Earnings

We now turn our attention to the last major element of stockholders' equity: retained earnings. As defined in Chapter 15, **retained earnings** represents the portion of stockholders' equity that has been generated by profitable operations and kept in the business. At the conclusion of the reporting period, a corporation's net income is transferred to the Retained Earnings account as part of the closing process. More specifically, the following journal entry is needed (amount is assumed):

| | | |
|---|---|---|
| Income Summary | 150,000 | |
| Retained Earnings | | 150,000 |
| To close net income to Retained Earnings | | |

Because of this treatment, the Retained Earnings account will normally possess a credit balance. On occasion, though, a debit ("negative") balance may arise, which is commonly referred to as a **deficit.** Deficits are usually caused when firms operate at a loss for a number of years or have a sizable loss in one period that wipes out years of profitability.

### Dividends

OBJECTIVE 2
Understand the distinctions among cash dividends, property dividends, stock dividends, and stock splits.

A number of items affect the retained earnings balance throughout the year, including dividends. **Dividends** represent a distribution of corporate earnings to stockholders and may be in the form of cash, property, or additional shares of stock.

Many corporate entities attempt to attract investors by establishing a consistent dividend policy; in contrast, numerous businesses pay no dividends or severely restrict distributions. Many of these latter firms are referred to as *growth companies* because they are continually reinvesting profits in expansionary projects to achieve even greater income levels. Investors in growth companies expect to realize a return on investment by selling their shares at a substantial gain.

Occasionally, in addition to a corporation's regular dividend, a special (extra) dividend is distributed. The special dividend usually results from a corporation having an especially profitable year; its labeling as "special" implies no commitment to an increased payout in the future.

## Dividend Dates

There are three important dates connected with dividend distributions.

1 **Date of declaration**—All dividends must be declared (approved) by the board of directors. The declaration date is the date when the dividend is formally approved and the corporation becomes legally liable for payment.
2 **Date of record**—The stockholders of a corporate entity constantly change. To determine who will receive the dividend, the corporation establishes a record date. All stockholders as of the date of record are entitled to the declared dividend even if they dispose of their holdings prior to the dividend's distribution. As a result, stock sold between the record date and the date of distribution is sold without the current dividend rights attached, that is, *ex-dividend.* The record date follows the date of declaration by a few weeks, thereby allowing the completion of any stock transactions that may be in process.
3 **Date of payment**—As specified in the dividend declaration, the date of payment is the date when the dividend will be issued to the stockholders. Generally, the date of payment is several weeks after the record date.

## Cash Dividends

Most dividends are paid in cash. To distribute a cash dividend, companies must satisfy two conditions. First, an entity must have an adequate cash balance. A lack of funds or an extremely tight cash position can force a corporation's board of directors to reduce or omit a payout. Such distribution decisions must be done with great care, because dividends are often a key element in an investor's expected return from holding stock. The market price of stock has been known to drop dramatically when a dividend declaration was less than anticipated.

The second condition for a dividend requires an adequate balance in the Retained Earnings account. Keep in mind that dividends are distributions of earnings; total corporate profits must therefore be sufficient to *support* amounts given to stockholders. Remember, though, that dividends are not *paid* with earnings; payments take place with cash.

It is, of course, entirely possible for a company to be both profit-rich and cash-poor. As an example, consider recent data extracted from the financial statements of Maytag Corporation, the well-known appliance manufacturer. The company had an ending retained earnings balance of $641 million and a cash balance of only $11 million. Although the firm has been profitable over the years and has generated sizable earnings, its cash balance would permit only a much smaller distribution of funds to stockholders.

***Accounting for Cash Dividends*** To illustrate the necessary accounting for cash dividends, assume Dale Corporation has 100,000 shares of common stock outstanding. On July 15, the board of directors declared a $0.25 quarterly dividend to stockholders of record on August 7. The dividend will be distributed on September 1. The proper journal entries follow.

| | | | | |
|---|---|---|---|---|
| July | 15 | Retained Earnings | 25,000 | |
| | | Dividends Payable | | 25,000 |
| | | To record declaration of cash dividend of $0.25 per share | | |
| Aug. | 7 | No entry required | | |
| Sept. | 1 | Dividends Payable | 25,000 | |
| | | Cash | | 25,000 |
| | | To record payment of dividend declared on July 15 | | |

Observe that the cash dividend is based on the number of shares outstanding. If Dale had originally issued 100,000 shares and then reacquired 10,000 as treasury stock, the board of directors would have declared a quarterly dividend of $22,500 (90,000 shares × $0.25). Should a balance sheet be prepared after the date of declaration but prior to the date of payment, Dividends Payable would be disclosed as a current liability.

Some corporations follow an alternative recording practice on the declaration date. Rather than reduce Retained Earnings directly, the debit is recorded in a temporary account called Dividends. The Dividends account is then closed to Retained Earnings at the end of the accounting period.

### Property Dividends

Sometimes a corporation will distribute assets other than cash as dividends. These distributions, known as **property dividends,** allow a business to conserve funds while providing stockholders with a return on their investment. Property dividends have been paid in the form of merchandise, real estate, and investments in the stock of other companies and have occasionally bordered on the imaginative and bizarre. A mining company, for example, once paid dividends to shareholders by distributing gold and silver.

### Stock Dividends

Many corporations distribute additional shares of their own stock as dividends. The distribution, referred to as a **stock dividend,** most frequently involves the issuance of common shares to existing common stockholders. Additional shares are issued in proportion to stockholders' present ownership in the firm. For example, suppose Ellen Bagley owns 20,000 shares of a cosmetics company that she founded several years ago. Assuming a total of 100,000 shares are outstanding, Bagley has a 20% ownership interest. If the board of directors declares a 10% stock dividend, an additional 10,000 shares (100,000 shares × 0.10) will be issued to stockholders. Bagley is entitled to 20% of the distribution, which results in the following figures:

| | *Before Stock Dividend* | *10% Stock Dividend* | *After Stock Dividend* |
|---|---|---|---|
| Corporate shares | 100,000 | 10,000 | 110,000 |
| Ellen Bagley's shares | 20,000 | 2,000 | 22,000 |
| Ownership interest | 20% | 20% | 20% |

As you can see, a stockholder's percentage ownership remains the same. Furthermore, the corporation's assets and liabilities are unaffected because they are not

Large stock dividends, namely, those in excess of 20–25%, are a different matter. Because of a substantial increase in the number of shares outstanding, the market price per share will drop significantly. For example, if a firm doubles the outstanding shares by a 100% stock dividend, the market price should fall by about 50%. Large stock dividends are therefore afforded different accounting treatment from that of small stock dividends. Rather than value the distribution at fair market value, the Retained Earnings account is debited for the par or stated value of the dividend, with a corresponding credit to Stock Dividend Distributable. This treatment is a logical outgrowth of accounting for stock splits, the next topic for discussion. As we will now see, large stock dividends are similar to stock splits.

### Stock Splits

Most publicly held corporations are interested in maintaining the marketability of their stock. Frequently, when a share's market price rises substantially, many small investors look for other investment alternatives. Stated simply, investors prefer to purchase round lots of stock (i.e., 100-share multiples) to take advantage of lower commission rates from brokers. Because a high-priced stock would place the round lot beyond the reach of those individuals with limited funds, corporations often attempt to reduce the market price per share.

One way to accomplish a reduction in market price is by the issuance of a large stock dividend; another way is a stock split. A **stock split** involves increasing the number of shares outstanding and, at the same time, reducing the stock's par or stated value per share. For example, assume a corporation has 200,000 shares of $10 par-value stock outstanding, which is currently selling for $80 per share. The company wants to reduce the market price to $20 per share and, accordingly, a 4-for-1 stock split is approved by the board of directors.

This action results in a reduction of par value from $10 to $2.50 ($10 ÷ 4) and an increase in the number of outstanding shares from 200,000 to 800,000 (200,000 × 4). Total corporate equity thus remains unchanged. A stockholder who owned 200 shares prior to the split will possess 800 shares after the split. Observe that the stockholder is no better off, since the total market value of his or her shares remains at $16,000: 200 shares × $80 versus 800 shares × $20. The stockholder's position is improved only if the market value of the stock subsequently increases.

Because a stock split does not change the balance in any of the corporation's accounts, no formal entry is required. However, a memorandum should be recorded in the journal to note that a stock split has occurred. The memorandum should reveal that (1) the number of shares issued and outstanding has increased and (2) the par or stated value per share has been reduced. The accounting treatment for stock splits therefore differs from that of large stock dividends, the latter of which requires a transfer from Retained Earnings to capital stock accounts. The reason for the differing treatments is that although both splits and dividends increase the number of shares, stock dividends do not affect a share's par or stated value. An entry is therefore needed to record the increased amount of legal capital caused by the distribution.

## Other Items That Affect Retained Earnings

Although our presentation has concentrated on dividends, other items affect retained earnings as well. As we noted earlier in the chapter, for example, the reissuance of treasury stock at a price below cost may give rise to a reduction in retained earnings. Retained earnings are also influenced by prior period adjustments and appropriations.

## Prior Period Adjustments

**OBJECTIVE 3**
**Be familiar with prior period adjustments and appropriations of retained earnings.**

Accountants, like other professionals, are not perfect. Even with a strong system of internal control, significant errors sometimes enter the financial records. Most are detected soon after occurrence; some, however, may go unnoticed for several years. Examples of such errors include mathematical mistakes, oversights, and the use of unacceptable principles and methods.

Errors that affect the net income of previous periods are corrected by the use of **prior period adjustments.** To illustrate the proper accounting treatment, assume Mercer Corporation overlooked several pieces of equipment in 19X1 and thereby understated depreciation expense by $10,000. If the error is not discovered until a subsequent reporting period, say 19X2, the prior period adjustment to correct the records would be as follows:

| | | |
|---|---|---|
| Retained Earnings | 10,000 | |
| Accumulated Depreciation: Equipment | | 10,000 |
| To correct the 19X1 understatement of depreciation expense | | |

Correcting 19X1 depreciation expense directly is not possible because the year's revenue and expense accounts have been closed. The understated expense overstated net income, which in turn overstated the balance in the Retained Earnings account at the end of the period. Retained Earnings is therefore debited to record the necessary reduction.

Prior period adjustments are reported as an adjustment to the Retained Earnings balance at the beginning of the year in which the correction is made, 19X2 in Mercer's case. The adjustment is shown on a net-of-tax basis and is disclosed on the statement of retained earnings. (Both net-of-tax reporting and the appropriate method of disclosure will be discussed shortly.)

## Appropriations of Retained Earnings

Corporations occasionally transfer part of their retained earnings balances into separate accounts termed **appropriations.** The purpose of this practice is to inform financial statement readers that a portion of retained earnings is unavailable for dividend distributions. Appropriations may be made by the board of directors for such items as plant expansion, replacement of existing machinery and equipment, or a possible assessment of additional federal income taxes. In some cases an appropriation may be required because of contractual or legal restrictions. For example, many states require a retained earnings appropriation equal to the cost of any treasury stock held by the entity.

Appropriations are sometimes handled by formal journal entries in the accounting records. For instance, assume Husky Corporation appropriated one-third of its $150,000 retained earnings balance for future plant expansion. The necessary journal entry follows.

| | | |
|---|---|---|
| Retained Earnings | 50,000 | |
| Retained Earnings Appropriated for Plant Expansion | | 50,000 |
| To record retained earnings appropriation | | |

The stockholders' equity section of the balance sheet would reveal the following:

| Retained earnings | |
|---|---|
| Appropriated for plant expansion | $ 50,000 |
| Unappropriated | 100,000 |
| Total | $150,000 |

Observe the appropriation has no effect on total retained earnings; it does, however, accomplish its sole objective—that of restricting the earnings available for dividends. When the restriction is no longer needed, Husky will debit the appropriation and credit Retained Earnings.

> **TIPS & TECHNIQUES**
>
> The use of an appropriation does *not* mean that cash has been set aside for the stated purpose. As evidence, examine Husky's journal entry and notice the absence of a credit to the Cash account. To accumulate the necessary funds, corporations often establish special asset accounts to which deposits are made (and invested). When needed, funds are then disbursed from these accounts for the intended objective. The appropriation *by itself* is not sufficient to restrict cash; a separate management action is needed.

Rather than use a journal entry approach, an increasing number of corporations disclose retained earnings restrictions (and others) in the footnotes that accompany the financial statements. As an example, American Greetings, noted for its cards and other consumer products (Strawberry Shortcake and the Care Bears) recently reported a retained earnings balance of $424 million, along with the following:

> Provisions of certain loan agreements contain restrictions of the payment of cash dividends, under the most restrictive of which, retained earnings of approximately [$18.5 million] are available for the payment of dividends at [the end of the current fiscal year].

### Statement of Retained Earnings

Changes in the Retained Earnings account are often disclosed on a separate financial report known as the **statement of retained earnings,** as illustrated in Exhibit 16-2. The form of the retained earnings statement varies widely. Some corporations divide their statements into appropriated and unappropriated sections, disclosing increases and decreases that occurred during the year. Other corporations construct a combined statement of income and retained earnings, thereby doing away with a separately prepared income statement. The combined statement has received mixed reviews from accountants. The major advantage is that all items affecting retained earnings are disclosed in a single report and are less apt to be overlooked by statement users. However, many accountants assert that the combined approach downplays the importance of earnings by burying net income in the midst of other, less important financial data.[3]

[3] Yet another approach involves preparation of a statement of stockholders' equity. This statement reveals changes in all the stockholders' equity components of an entity, including retained earnings.

**Exhibit 16-2**
**Statement of Retained Earnings**

**DONLEY CORPORATION**
**Statement of Retained Earnings**
**For the Year Ended December 31, 19X2**

| | | |
|---|---|---|
| Retained earnings, 12/31/X1 (as reported) | | $ 80,000 |
| Less: Correction of prior period inventory error (net of $6,000 tax) | | 9,000 |
| Retained earnings, 12/31/X1 (restated) | | $ 71,000 |
| Add: Net income | | 100,000 |
| | | $171,000 |
| Less: Cash dividends on preferred stock | $15,000 | |
| Stock dividends on common stock | 45,000 | 60,000 |
| Retained earnings, 12/31/X2 (note A) | | $111,000 |

*Note A:* The company has various debt agreements restricting the amount of retained earnings that can be used for dividend distributions. As of December 31, 19X2, income retained in the business of $74,000 was free of such restrictions.

## Corporate Income Reporting

Investors are extremely interested in the periodic net income earned by corporations. Net income provides the basis for dividend distributions and greatly influences the market price of a corporation's common stock. Because of these factors, the income statement must provide adequate disclosure of earnings activities and be constructed in a format that is useful and informative to investors and other users.

To achieve these goals, the accounting profession has stipulated the segregation of ordinary business income from income caused by unusual and uncommon transactions and events. Why? Imagine the difficulty in evaluating corporate earnings if ordinary business transactions—such as buying and selling merchandise, renting equipment, and paying wages—were mixed together with the results of major catastrophes and other nonrecurring events. A high or low net income figure could be interpreted as being typical, even though it was caused by one-time and unusual happenings.

Current accounting practice dictates separate disclosure for the results of continuing operations (a very useful figure for prediction of future earnings), followed by the results of discontinued operations, extraordinary items, and the financial effects of changes in accounting principle. Because of their unique nature, we will now explore the latter three topical areas.

### Discontinued Operations

**OBJECTIVE 4**
**Be familiar with discontinued operations, extraordinary items, accounting changes, and intraperiod tax allocation.**

Many corporations are involved in diverse types of business activities. Consider American Brands, for instance, which produces a variety of well-known consumer goods. The firm is involved in such areas as hardware (Master Lock), tobacco products (Pall Mall and Lucky Strike), golf and leisure products (Titleist), distilled beverages (Jim Beam bourbon), optical goods, office products, and life insurance. It is apparent that American Brands, like many other entities, conducts operations

HIGHLIGHT

# Crystal-Ball Income Reporting

Several years back shareholder Steven Goldman filed a class-action lawsuit against a company called Sykes Datatronics, Inc., charging it with forecasting improved earnings when actually its profits were about to turn down. The Second U.S. Circuit Court of Appeals refused to dismiss the case, noting that Goldman and his co-plaintiffs deserved their day in court.

Not too long ago, Control Data Corporation canceled a $300 million stock and note offering at the last moment because loss projections had worsened since forecasts were circulated to the public. Had the offering gone through, Control Data would have been exposed to potential lawsuits of the kind Sykes encountered. The Securities & Exchange Commission (SEC) had nothing to say on the matter, as usual.

The reason? Since 1979 the SEC has been trying to expand corporate reporting, encouraging companies to make public their forecasts of sales, earnings, and business conditions that most of them prepare internally anyway. To motivate corporations to stick their necks out, the commission came up with "safe harbor" rules: As long as companies make their forecasts in good faith, have a reasonable basis for believing them, and disclose the underlying assumptions, they won't be held liable by the commission if the predictions turn out to be wrong.

So why don't most companies publicize their forecasts of income? For a good reason: The judicial system is much less forgiving than the SEC. It's true that the commission's safe harbor rules could provide the basis for a legal defense. But the expense of lengthy litigation might drive a vulnerable company under even if it were ultimately vindicated. Most class-action suits are expensive to defend; an inaccurate-forecast suit is even worse. It's so broad that a company can find itself defending every fact and assumption it has ever made about its business. Notes a prominent lawyer, "It questions everything you've been doing. All the pieces of paper you've been generating are open for discovery. This can just be crippling."

Further complicating the problem, a company can also be sued over nonofficial statements—those made at shareholder meetings, in company press releases, or in answer to reporters' questions. Ronald Palamara, then chief executive officer of a computer service and software company, found this out the hard way. In an interview in *The Wall Street Journal*, he said he felt "comfortable" with analysts' estimates of $1 per share earnings for the fiscal year ended June 30. Three weeks later the company said it expected a loss for the fourth quarter, and eventually turned in a loss for the year of almost $4 million.

Did Palamara make a forecast in commenting on the forecasts of others? A group of his company's stockholders thought so. They brought a class-action suit, citing that interview and other instances of false and misleading statements. The shareholders won, and the company and its auditors settled the case for $4.5 million in cash and securities.

Where was the SEC's safe harbor? Nowhere, as it turns out. The American Institute of Certified Public Accountants, a national association of CPAs, recently issued guidelines for forecasting, to be followed by those firms that feel compelled to go out on a limb. It appears, though, as the examples cited imply, that crystal-ball income reporting can be a risky business. Perhaps a more conservative route is to avoid the future tense and focus on the past. That is, after all, the essence of financial accounting: a factual reporting of what has happened, not what will.

SOURCE: Adapted from "Damned if You Do . . . ," *Forbes*, October 21, 1985, p. 98. Reprinted by permission of *Forbes* magazine, © Forbes Inc., 1985.

in several distinct business segments. A **segment** is defined as a component of a company whose activities represent a major line of business or class of customer.[4] Normally, the assets and operating results of a given segment are clearly distinguishable from the other assets and operations of the firm.

Often, after an in-depth review of corporate activity and profitability, an entity will decide to dispose of one or more of its segments. A disposal usually results from inadequate earnings or disappointing expectations about the segment's future. Sometimes, however, a segment is sold not because of weak financial performance but because the company desires to concentrate in other activities.

When a segment is sold, abandoned, or otherwise disposed of, its operations are said to be **discontinued.** The results of discontinued operations are disclosed in a separate category on the income statement immediately after income from continuing operations. Specifically, the operating results of the disposed segment (i.e., revenues minus cost of goods sold and expenses) along with any gain or loss on the disposal must be shown net-of-tax.

To illustrate the proper accounting treatment, we will focus on Quality Products, Inc., a company that produces bakery goods and soft drinks. In addition, the firm operates a chain of movie theaters and golf courses throughout the country. Recently, in a downsizing effort, Quality sold its beverage segment (Hi-Pro Fruit Drinks) and generated a substantial profit on the transaction. A condensed income statement is presented in Exhibit 16-3.

As you can see by analyzing the data, the disposed properties significantly boosted Quality's "bottom-line" earnings. Note also that the bulk of earnings from

**Exhibit 16-3**
**Disclosure of Discontinued Operations**

**QUALITY PRODUCTS, INC.**
**Income Statement**
**For the Year Ended December 31, 19X2**

| | | |
|---|---|---|
| Sales | | $920,000 |
| Cost of goods sold | | 640,000 |
| Gross profit | | $280,000 |
| Operating expenses | | 170,000 |
| Income from continuing operations before tax | | $110,000 |
| Income tax on continuing operations | | 35,000 |
| Income from continuing operations | | $ 65,000 |
| Discontinued operations | | |
| Income from discontinued operations, net-of-tax | $ 1,500 | |
| Gain on disposal of Hi-Pro Division, net-of-tax | 35,500 | 37,000 |
| Net income | | $102,000 |

[4] "Reporting the Results of Operations," *Opinions of the Accounting Principles Board No. 30* (New York: American Institute of Certified Public Accountants, 1973), paragraph 13.

discontinued operations came from the sale of Hi-Pro's assets and facilities, not from operating activities. It should now be apparent that separate disclosure of discontinued operations in this manner helps financial statement users better assess the future of an entity's ongoing business affairs.

## Extraordinary Items

Corporate income statements disclose earnings from all types of business endeavors. Occasionally, sizable gains and losses arise from transactions and events that are clearly different from the usual affairs of the firm. Such occurrences, known as **extraordinary items,** are afforded special accounting treatment.

To achieve uniformity in reporting, the accounting profession has stipulated that extraordinary items be *unusual in nature* and *occur infrequently.*[5] Note that *both* criteria must be satisfied. A transaction or event is considered unusual if it has a high degree of abnormality and is unrelated to the ordinary and typical activities of the entity. To judge whether the "unusual" criterion is met, one must consider a company's scope of operation, lines of business, operating policies, and environment. The environment includes such factors as industry characteristics, geographical location of facilities and activities, and the extent of governmental regulation. Turning to the second criterion, an event or transaction of a type not reasonably expected to recur in the foreseeable future is considered to occur infrequently. Past experience and the environment in which a business operates are primary considerations.

### Applying the Guidelines

Occurrences that meet the two criteria are rare. Examples *may* include major casualties such as earthquakes, floods, and hurricanes; a seizure of assets by a foreign government; and the financial effects caused by a prohibition under a newly enacted law or regulation. From a practical point of view, it is difficult to generalize whether a particular happening is always extraordinary. As the following illustration shows, each case must be evaluated on its own merits.

Suppose a business is located in a low-lying area that is prone to flooding once every four or five years. If a heavy rainstorm and its flood waters cause considerable damage to the firm's inventory, the loss is not considered extraordinary because it fails the infrequency-of-occurrence criterion. That is, on the basis of past history, another flood will probably occur in the foreseeable future. Changing the example slightly, suppose the flood loss is caused by a dam that breaks in a nearby valley. The break is highly unusual and, once repaired, not likely to happen again. Because both tests are met, this flood loss is labeled extraordinary.

The following specific items are not considered extraordinary by the accounting profession:[6]

1 Write-down or write-off of receivables, inventories, and intangible assets.

2 Gains and losses from the sale or abandonment of property, plant, and equipment used in a business.

3 Effects of a strike, including those against competitors and major suppliers.

---

[5] Ibid., paragraph 20.

[6] Ibid., paragraph 23.

Such items, if material, are normally presented among nonoperating (other) revenues and expenses.

### Disclosure of Extraordinary Items

Extraordinary items are disclosed in a separate section of the income statement immediately following discontinued operations. If a company has no discontinued operations, extraordinary items are presented after earnings from continuing activities. Again, a net-of-tax amount must be shown.

## Changes in Accounting Principle

Recall that accountants follow the consistency principle when preparing financial statements. Consistency requires that the same valuation methods be employed from one period to the next. Occasionally, a company may decide an alternative reporting practice is more appropriate than the method currently in use. For example, in view of changing business conditions, an entity may now find an accelerated depreciation method (e.g., double-declining balance) to be preferable to the straight-line approach, or the weighted-average inventory valuation technique to be more proper when compared with FIFO. The preceding examples illustrate a **change in accounting principle,** namely, a switch from one generally accepted accounting principle to another. To avoid deteriorating the comparability of financial statements over time, such changes should be made infrequently and only when the newly implemented practice will result in improved financial reporting.

When a company changes its reporting methods and practices, it must compute the cumulative effect of such changes. The **cumulative effect** is the difference in the total net income reported in prior years and the income that would have been reported over the same period had the new practice been in use. For example, assume that Addison Corporation has decided to switch depreciation methods, from straight-line to double-declining balance. A review of the accounting records reveals that total aftertax income would have been $50,000 less had the accelerated method been employed in earlier years. The $50,000 figure (i.e., the cumulative effect of the change in accounting principle) is reported on the income statement of the period of change as a reduction in earnings. The reduction is presented at the bottom of the statement, after any discontinued operations or extraordinary items, and is labeled as follows: "Cumulative effect on prior years of a change in accounting principle, net-of-tax."

A corporation's annual report to shareholders normally includes financial statements from prior periods, thereby allowing the shareholder to perform various types of comparative studies. These statements *are not recast* to reflect the change in principle; however, additional supplemental disclosure is required to show recomputed amounts for selected items "as if" the new principle had been in use.[7] Details of this supplemental disclosure (and the accompanying footnote) are usually covered in advanced accounting courses.

## Intraperiod Tax Allocation

Examine the income statement of Bridgeport Corporation, which is presented in Exhibit 16-4. Observe how the statement is consistent with the special income

[7]A few accounting changes have been pinpointed by the profession as requiring a restatement of the financial statements of prior periods.

**Exhibit 16-4 Intraperiod Tax Allocation and Corporate Income Reporting**

**BRIDGEPORT CORPORATION**
**Income Statement**
**For the Year Ended December 31, 19XX**

| | | | |
|---|---|---|---|
| | Sales | | $2,000,000 |
| | Cost of goods sold | | 1,200,000 |
| | Gross profit | | $ 800,000 |
| | Operating expenses | | |
| | Selling | $ 280,000 | |
| | Administrative | 170,000 | 450,000 |
| | Income from operations | | $ 350,000 |
| ① | Other revenue (expense) | | |
| | Loss on sale of machinery | | (50,000) |
| ② | Income from continuing operations before tax | | $ 300,000 |
| | Income tax on continuing operations | | 120,000 |
| | Income from continuing operations | | $ 180,000 |
| ③ | Discontinued operations | | |
| | Earnings from Sunrise Division operations, less applicable taxes ($110,000 − $44,000) | $ 66,000 | |
| | Loss on disposal of Sunrise facilities, less tax savings ($250,000 − $100,000) | (150,000) | (84,000) |
| | Income before extraordinary item | | $ 96,000 |
| ④ | Extraordinary item | | |
| | Flood loss, less tax savings ($60,000 − $24,000) | | (36,000) |
| ⑤ | Cumulative effect on prior years of a change in accounting principle, less applicable taxes ($25,000 − $10,000) | | 15,000 |
| | Net income | | $ 75,000 |

KEY

① *Other revenue (expense)*: Before-tax gains, losses, revenues, and expenses that arise from transactions and events not directly related to ordinary business activities (see Chapter 5).

② *Income from continuing operations:* Net-of-tax reporting for the income generated from ongoing activities of the entity.

③ *Discontinued operations:* Net-of-tax reporting for a discontinued segment of the business. The segment's operating results and any gains or losses on the disposal of the segment are disclosed separately.

④ *Extraordinary items:* Net-of-tax reporting for gains/losses that arise from unusual and infrequent transactions and events.

⑤ *Cumulative effect of a change in accounting principle:* Net-of-tax reporting for the impact on prior years' income of a change in reporting practices.

reporting categories discussed earlier in the chapter. In addition, notice the treatment of Bridgeport's tax expense as it relates to these elements. The company is following a practice known as **intraperiod tax allocation,** which relates (i.e., matches) income taxes to the various elements that contribute to the firm's tax bill. Such items include continuing operations, discontinued operations, extraordinary items, changes in accounting principle, and prior period adjustments.[8]

[8] Prior period adjustments and the related tax impact are shown on the statement of retained earnings (see Exhibit 16-2).

To expand, a careful review of Bridgeport's disclosures will find the company is subject to a 40% income tax rate. Items that raise net income result in a 40% tax expense; items that reduce net income generate a 40% tax savings. From the information presented in Exhibit 16-4, Bridgeport's net tax expense totals $50,000:

| | |
|---|---|
| Tax on continuing operations | $ 120,000 |
| Tax on Sunrise Division operations | 44,000 |
| Tax savings on disposal of Sunrise facilities | (100,000) |
| Tax savings on flood loss | (24,000) |
| Tax on change in accounting principle | 10,000 |
| Net tax expense | $ 50,000 |

Without intraperiod allocation, the tax expense would appear as a single line item on the income statement, as shown below.

Income tax expense $50,000

Such a presentation is deficient, especially for the uninformed financial statement user. The presentation fails to show that the company had two significant tax-saving items during the period: the loss on the disposal of Sunrise facilities and the flood loss. Further, the $50,000 expense amount could be construed as being "typical," even though only one of the contributing factors (the continuing operations) is likely to recur in the future. Most accountants agree that intraperiod tax allocation results in improved disclosure, which is less apt to mislead statement readers.

**TIPS & TECHNIQUES**

Students often have trouble remembering the proper sequence of disclosures on the bottom portion of a comprehensive income statement. The acronym O-DEC is helpful to overcome the problem. *O* stands for *other revenue and expense*, which is really part of income from continuing operations. Thus, there is a hyphen for separation from the other three components. *D* represents *discontinued operations; E* stands for *extraordinary items;* and C symbolizes a *change in accounting principle.*

## Earnings Per Share

OBJECTIVE 5
Have a basic knowledge of earnings per share.

The income statement provides considerable insight into the profitability of corporate activities. Rather than take the time to study all of the statement's intricacies, investors frequently rely on a single computation called **earnings per share (EPS)** of common stock. Earnings per share is similar to the won-loss percentage of a sports club at the end of the season. Specifically, it represents a summary of all items that affect profitability. Earnings-per-share data are widely disseminated in the financial press and must be disclosed on the face of the income statement. No other ratio is afforded such prominence.

Earnings per share is often analyzed to assess future prospects for corporate income and dividends. If current earnings are favorable and the financial outlook is bright, investors are usually willing to pay a higher price to acquire shares of the corporation's common stock. Generally stated, a higher EPS will result in a higher market price.

To study the relationship between market price and earnings per share, investors and financial analysts often use a popular measure called the **price-earnings (P/E) ratio.** The ratio is computed by dividing the market price of a share of common stock by the annual earnings per share. Price-earnings ratios can vary considerably. For example, at the time this text is being written, the P/E ratios of Hilton Hotels and LA Gear are 35 and 14, respectively. By showing a willingness to pay more for each dollar of reported earnings, investors must feel Hilton's financial future will be more prosperous than that of the popular shoe manufacturer.

Because of the widespread use of the earnings per share measure, numerous computational and disclosure rules have been established to achieve reporting uniformity throughout the financial community.[9] Our discussion will concentrate on the basics only, because the specific rules are technical and complex. Like several other topics presented in this chapter, earnings per share is typically covered in depth in an advanced accounting course.

Two preliminary steps are needed to figure the earnings per share of common stock: (1) determine the weighted-average number of shares outstanding and (2) compute the earnings available to common stockholders.

### Weighted-Average Shares Outstanding

The computation of earnings per share begins with an assessment of the number of common shares outstanding. In some firms the number of common shares remains constant during the accounting period. For many corporations, however, outstanding shares will change because of new stock issues, the purchase of treasury stock, and other similar transactions. In these situations earnings per share is based on a weighted average. The weighted average is calculated by multiplying the number of common shares outstanding by the fraction of the year the shares are in the hands of stockholders.

To illustrate, assume that Briarwood Manufacturing had 60,000 common shares outstanding at the beginning of the year. On September 1, an additional 15,000 shares were issued. The weighted-average number of shares would be computed as follows:

| *Outstanding Shares* | | *Fraction of Year Outstanding* | | *Weighted Average* |
|---|---|---|---|---|
| 60,000 | × | $\frac{8}{12}$ | = | 40,000 |
| 75,000 | × | $\frac{4}{12}$ | = | 25,000 |
| | | | | 65,000 |

The weighted average represents the number of equivalent shares that have been outstanding for the entire year. That is, the initial 60,000 shares were outstanding for 12 months. In contrast, the 15,000-share issuance has been outstanding for only four months, which is equivalent to 5,000 shares for the entire year ($15,000 \times \frac{4}{12} = 5,000$). Thus, Briarwood's weighted-average total is 65,000 ($60,000 + 5,000$). The weighting procedure is necessary because the capital provided by the new stock has helped generate earnings for only a fraction of the accounting period.

[9] See "Earnings Per Share," *Opinions of the Accounting Principles Board No. 15* (New York: American Institute of Certified Public Accountants, 1969).

### Earnings Available to Common Stockholders

Keep in mind that our goal is to derive the earnings per share of *common stock.* For corporations that have only common shares outstanding, all reported earnings are allocated to the common stockholders. If some preferred stock is outstanding, however, a different procedure is followed. Preferred stock is a *senior security,* so called because of its preferential treatment in dividend distributions and corporate liquidations. As a result, dividend claims of preferred stockholders must be deducted from net income to arrive at the earnings allocable to common shares.

For example, assume that Briarwood had issued 5,000 shares of $100 par-value, 10% preferred stock in addition to the common shares described earlier. If net income for the year amounted to $180,000, the earnings available to common stockholders would total $130,000:

| | |
|---|---|
| Net income | $180,000 |
| Less: Dividends on preferred stock (5,000 shares × $100 × 0.10) | 50,000 |
| Earnings available to common stockholders | $130,000 |

Earnings per share of common stock can now be computed as follows:

$$\text{Earnings Per Share} = \frac{\text{Earnings Available to Common Stockholders}}{\text{Weighted-Average Common Shares Outstanding}}$$

$$\text{EPS} = \frac{\$130{,}000}{65{,}000}$$

$$\text{EPS} = \underline{\underline{\$2.00}}$$

### Primary Versus Fully Diluted Earnings Per Share

As we noted in the previous chapter, many preferred stocks are convertible into common shares. If these or other types of convertible securities are ultimately exchanged for common stock, the number of common shares will increase and earnings per share will be reduced (i.e., *diluted*). To inform common stockholders of the potential dilution, businesses must disclose additional EPS information. Specifically, corporations with potentially dilutive securities must report both **primary earnings per share** and **fully diluted earnings per share.**

Primary earnings per share is calculated by ignoring the dilutive effect of convertible securities.[10] Fully diluted EPS, on the other hand, is based on the *assumption* that all dilutive securities were converted into common shares at the beginning of the accounting period. If the securities were issued during the current reporting period, conversion is assumed as of the date of issuance. Note that the conversion is merely an assumption. The intention is to show how earnings per share would be affected *if* common stock was issued to satisfy all existing dilutive commitments.

To illustrate the required computations and disclosure, we will continue the Briarwood Manufacturing example, with one modification. Assume that each of the firm's preferred shares is convertible into seven common shares at the option of the preferred stockholder. If we assume conversion at the beginning of the current period, then

[10] If convertible securities (and others) meet certain tests, the securities are considered as being equivalent to common stock and enter into primary-earnings-per-share calculations. These tests are beyond the scope of this text and will be ignored.

- No dividends would have been paid on the preferred stock.
- An additional 35,000 shares of common stock (5,000 preferred shares × 7) would be outstanding.

Briarwood's required earnings-per-share calculations are as follows:

| | *Primary** | *Fully Diluted* |
|---|---|---|
| Net income | $180,000 | $180,000 |
| Less: Dividends on convertible preferred stock (5,000 shares × $100 × 0.10) | 50,000 | — |
| Earnings available to common stockholders | $130,000 ÷ | $180,000 ÷ |
| Weighted-average common shares outstanding | | |
| For primary earnings per share | 65,000 | |
| For fully diluted earnings per share (65,000 shares + 35,000 shares from assumed conversion) | | 100,000 |
| Earnings per share | $2.00 | $1.80 |

* This is the same computation that appeared on page 561.

### EPS Disclosure

The reporting of earnings per share parallels the information shown on the income statement. Thus, if a corporation has discontinued operations, extraordinary items, or a cumulative effect from a change in accounting principle, per-share data for these elements are disclosed. Most financial analysts feel that by presenting such disclosures, a clearer picture of financial performance is made available for evaluation purposes. A sample presentation of per-share data for Midway Corporation, which has potentially dilutive securities, follows.

| | |
|---|---|
| Income from continuing operations | $100,000 |
| Income from discontinued operations (net-of-tax) | 50,000 |
| Income before extraordinary item | $150,000 |
| Extraordinary loss (net-of-tax) | (10,000) |
| Net income | $140,000 |

| | *Primary* | *Fully Diluted* |
|---|---|---|
| Earnings per share | | |
| Income from continuing operations | $ 1.00 | $ 0.50 |
| Income from discontinued operations | 0.50 | 0.25 |
| Extraordinary loss | (0.10) | (0.05) |
| Net income | $ 1.40 | $ 0.70 |

## Chapter Review

### Learning Objectives—The Key Points

**1 Understand what treasury stock is and how to account for its acquisition and reissuance.** Treasury stock represents shares of stock that have been reacquired by the issuing corporation. The shares' cost is charged to the Treasury Stock account at the time of

## Questions

**Q16-1** What is treasury stock? Why do corporations purchase treasury stock?

**Q16-2** Should purchased treasury stock be disclosed as an asset? Why?

**Q16-3** Explain how the Retained Earnings account can have a debit balance.

**Q16-4** Does a corporation become legally liable for dividend distributions on the date of declaration or the date of record?

**Q16-5** What two conditions must be satisfied to declare and distribute a cash dividend?

**Q16-6** The XYZ Corporation has an extremely tight cash position and wishes to distribute a dividend to its stockholders. Suggest several courses of action that XYZ might follow.

**Q16-7** Discuss the effect of a stock dividend on (1) a stockholder's percentage ownership position and (2) total stockholders' equity of the issuing corporation.

**Q16-8** Differentiate between a small and a large stock dividend. Are both of these dividends accounted for in the same manner? Explain.

**Q16-9** Differentiate between a large stock dividend and a stock split.

**Q16-10** What is a prior period adjustment? Explain the proper accounting and reporting treatment for prior period adjustments.

**Q16-11** What is the purpose of an appropriation of retained earnings? How are appropriations disclosed in the financial statements?

**Q16-12** Why should a corporation segregate ordinary business income from income caused by unusual and infrequent transactions and events?

**Q16-13** How are the financial results of discontinued operations disclosed on the income statement?

**Q16-14** What two criteria must be satisfied for an event or transaction to be classified as an extraordinary item? Discuss each of the criteria and present three examples of possible extraordinary items.

**Q16-15** Explain the proper treatment for a change in accounting principle.

**Q16-16** Briefly discuss the practice of intraperiod tax allocation. Explain what the practice is and why it is used.

**Q16-17** Why do stockholders closely monitor an entity's earnings per share?

**Q16-18** Is the earnings-per-share calculation based on shares outstanding at the beginning of the year or the end of the year, or on a weighted-average of the shares outstanding during the year?

**Q16-19** Differentiate between primary and fully diluted earnings per share.

## Exercises

**E16-1** ***Treasury stock transactions***

Kansas Corporation reacquired 15,000 shares of its common stock ($5 par value) on January 19 for $30 per share. These shares were subsequently sold as follows:

Mar. 10 2,000 shares at $45 per share
Aug. 16 4,000 shares at $30 per share
Nov. 29 4,000 shares at $23 per share

Prepare all necessary journal entries for Kansas Corporation.

**E16-2** ***Journal entries for dividends and stock splits***

Hayward Corporation has the following stockholders' equity on January 1, 19X3:

| | |
|---|---|
| Common stock, $10 par value | $200,000 |
| Paid-in capital in excess of par value | 375,000 |
| Retained earnings | 180,000 |
| Total stockholders' equity | $755,000 |

Prepare journal entries, if needed, for each of the following transactions and events. Consider each item independently.

a Declared a $0.30-per-share cash dividend, to be distributed in the next accounting period.

b Declared a 5% stock dividend; market value at the time of declaration was $24 per share. The dividend will be distributed in the next accounting period.

c Paid a $5,500 cash dividend that was declared in 19X2.

d Authorized a 4-for-1 stock split.

**E16-3** ***Preparation of stockholders' equity section***

MBM Corporation had the following equity accounts at the beginning of the year:

| | |
|---|---|
| Common stock, $10 par | $200,000 |
| Paid-in capital in excess of par value | 100,000 |
| Retained earnings | 500,000 |
| Total stockholders' equity | $800,000 |

The following events took place during the current year:

| | | |
|---|---|---|
| Feb. | 24 | Declared a $2 dividend per share. |
| May | 10 | Announced a 2-for-1 stock split. |
| Sept. | 18 | Declared and issued a 10% stock dividend; market value at the time of declaration was $12 per share. |
| Dec. | 30 | Reacquired 500 shares of common (treasury) stock at $18 per share. |

Assuming net income of $92,000, prepare an updated stockholders' equity section for MBM at the end of the year, after the accounting records have been closed.

**E16-4** ***Statement of retained earnings***

Cary Corporation had an ending retained earnings balance on December 31, 19X2, of $4.8 million. The following information pertains to 19X3:

a Cash dividends of $300,000 were declared and paid to common stockholders.

b A 3% stock dividend was declared and distributed on December 31. The stock's fair market value at the time of declaration was $20 per share; 150,000 shares were outstanding.

c Income was $600,000 before tax.

d An error was discovered on March 17 that occurred in 19X1 and understated before-tax income of that year by $40,000.

e Cary is subject to a 40% income tax rate.

Prepare the corporation's 19X3 statement of retained earnings.

**E16-5** ***Discontinued operations***

The following information pertains to Stovall Corporation for the year ended December 31, 19XX:

| | |
|---|---|
| Sales | $1,000,000 |
| Cost of goods sold | 600,000 |
| Selling expenses | 150,000 |
| Administrative expenses | 200,000 |

In 19XX, Stovall disposed of its retail division. The retail division generated 20% of the firm's total sales and accounted for 25% and 30% of total cost of goods sold and operating expenses, respectively. The division was sold at a before-tax gain of $25,000. Prepare Stovall's 19XX income statement, assuming a 40% tax rate.

**E16-6** ***Abbreviated income statement***

LBO, Inc., had income from operations of $180,000 for the year ended December 31, 19X5. A review of the accounting records disclosed the following:

| | |
|---|---|
| Gain on sale of building | $60,000 |
| Dividends | 10,000 |
| Extraordinary loss | 40,000 |
| Prior period adjustment from an understatement of advertising expense | 25,000 |

LBO is subject to a 40% income tax rate.

a Which of the preceding items would not appear on the company's income statement? Where would these items be disclosed?

b Prepare an abbreviated income statement for LBO, beginning with income from operations. Use good form; disregard earnings-per-share data.

**E16-7** ***Extraordinary items***

Which of the following events and transactions would be accounted for as an extraordinary item of Gavin Corporation? Discuss the reasoning behind your answers.

a The company experienced a devastating flood in its southern warehouse. Flood damage in the area occurs approximately once every six years.

b The company experienced an unusually long strike at one of its plants, causing the plant to lose $150,000.

c The company sold its midwestern division to another corporation and realized a sizable gain on the sale.

d The company had to write off its entire inventory of toys because the toys failed to meet an obscure federal safety standard.

e The company experienced an unusual loss from hailstorm damage in the Central American division. Hailstorm damage in this location is rare.

**E16-8** ***Equity issues and income reporting***

Evaluate the comments that follow as being True or False. If the comment is false, briefly explain why.

a A purchase of treasury stock reduces the stockholders' equity of the acquiring company.

b An appropriation of retained earnings reduces a company's total retained earnings balance.

c The issuance of a previously-declared 3,000-share stock dividend causes a reduction in the Retained Earnings account.

d If certain criteria are met, extraordinary gains and losses may be disclosed on the statement of retained earnings.

e Gains and losses from discontinued operations should be disclosed on the income statement on a net-of-tax basis.

**E16-9** ***Weighted-average shares outstanding***

Autorama, Inc., began the year with 80,000 common shares outstanding. On April 1, 28,000 newly issued shares were sold to the public for $45 per share. On August 1, the company reacquired 6,000 shares (i.e., treasury stock), which were subsequently reissued two months later. Calculate the weighted-average shares outstanding during the year.

**E16-10** ***Basic earnings-per-share computation***

Tabor Corporation reported after-tax net income for the current year of $235,000. The company had 10,000 common shares outstanding on January 1 and issued another 10,000 shares on July 1. Preferred dividends of $10,000 were paid during the year. Compute Tabor's earnings per share of common stock.

**E16-11** ***Primary and fully diluted earnings per share***

Truman, Inc., had the following stock outstanding throughout the year:

| | |
|---|---|
| Common stock, $1 par, 500,000 shares | $ 500,000 |
| 8% preferred stock, $100 par, 10,000 shares | 1,000,000 |

Each share of preferred is convertible into 30 shares of common stock. Net income for the year totaled $400,000.

a Compute primary earnings per share.

b Compute fully diluted earnings per share.

**E16-12** ***Corporate income reporting***

The following item appeared under the heading of Business Briefs in a recent edition of the *California Tribune:*

**SEA BREEZE REPORTS 152% RISE IN EARNINGS PER SHARE**

Los Angeles—David Anthony, chairman and chief executive officer of Sea Breeze, a nationwide retailer of swimwear, today announced a 152% rise in earnings per share. The company reported earnings per share of $2.90 for the year ended September 30, 19X2, which compares favorably with $1.15 per share for 19X1.

Assume that you attended the stockholders' meeting where the announcement was made. The data that follow were distributed to all attendees.

| | *Fiscal Year Ended* | |
|---|---|---|
| | ***9/30/X2*** | ***9/30/X1*** |
| Earnings per common share | | |
| Continuing retail operations | $ 2.84 | $ 2.42 |
| Discontinued operations | 0.14 | (1.27) |
| Extraordinary item | (0.08) | — |
| Net income | $ 2.90 | $ 1.15 |

Evaluate the *Tribune's* reporting of Sea Breeze's earnings.

## Problems

### Series A

**P16-A1** ***Accounting for treasury stock, cash dividends, and stock splits***

Quizmaster, Inc., had the following stockholders' equity on January 1, 19X5:

| | |
|---|---|
| Common stock, $2 par value, 600,000 shares authorized, 100,000 shares issued and outstanding | $200,000 |
| Paid-in capital in excess of par value | 345,000 |
| Retained earnings | 190,000 |
| Total stockholders' equity | $735,000 |

The following transactions and events occurred during the year:

| | |
|---|---|
| Jan. 19 | Approved a 4-for-1 stock split. |
| Feb. 20 | Declared a cash dividend of $0.15 per share. |
| Mar. 7 | Reacquired 24,000 common shares for $168,000, to be held as treasury stock. |
| 20 | Distributed the dividend that was declared on February 20. |
| June 24 | Sold 5,000 of the treasury shares for $50,000. |
| Oct. 31 | Sold 8,000 of the treasury shares for $48,000. |
| Dec. 15 | Declared a special cash dividend of $0.20 per share. |

**Instructions**

a Prepare the journal entries needed to record Quizmaster's transactions and events.

b Prepare the company's stockholders' equity section as of December 31, 19X5. Net income for the year amounted to $85,700.

**P16-A2** ***Equity transactions: Journal entries and stockholders' equity section***

An examination of the ledger of Dugan Enterprises revealed the following accounts on January 1:

| | |
|---|---|
| Common stock, $1 par, 50,000 shares authorized, 30,000 shares issued, 29,500 shares outstanding | $ 30,000 |
| Paid-in capital in excess of par value | 270,000 |
| Appropriation for plant expansion | 150,000 |
| Appropriation for treasury stock | 6,000 |
| Retained earnings (unappropriated) | 214,500 |
| Treasury stock, 500 shares at cost | 6,000 |

The following transactions and events occurred during the year:

| | | |
|---|---|---|
| Jan. | 7 | Declared a $0.20 dividend per share to stockholders of record on January 23. The dividend will be distributed on February 8. |
| Feb. | 3 | Increased the appropriation for plant expansion by $25,000. |
| | 8 | Paid the dividend declared on January 7. |
| Apr. | 15 | Sold 300 shares of treasury stock for $4,500 and reduced the treasury stock appropriation by $3,600. |
| June | 30 | Declared a 10% stock dividend on the shares outstanding, to stockholders of record on July 15. The dividend will be distributed on August 15. Fair market value on the date of declaration was $14 per share. |
| Aug. | 15 | Issued the stock dividend declared on June 30. |
| Dec. | 31 | Net income for the year amounted to $98,000. Closed the Income Summary account to Retained Earnings. |

**Instructions**

a Prepare journal entries to record Dugan's transactions and events.

b Prepare the stockholders' equity section of Dugan's December 31 balance sheet.

**P16-A3** ***Statement of retained earnings and stockholders' equity section***

Pismo Beach, Inc., had the following paid-in capital on January 1, 19X4:

| | |
|---|---|
| Common stock, $1 par, 80,000 shares authorized, 50,000 shares issued and outstanding | $ 50,000 |
| Paid-in capital in excess of par value | 540,000 |

On December 31, 19X4, prior to the accounting records being closed, the Retained Earnings account contained the following entries:

***Retained Earnings***

| | | | | | |
|---|---|---|---|---|---|
| 1/15 | Stock dividend | 55,000 | 1/1 | Balance | 400,000 |
| 12/31 | Cash dividend | 25,900 | 6/4 | Correction of error | 36,000 |

A review of the accounting records disclosed that:

1 The $36,000 error correction is net of $24,000 of tax and relates to 19X3 advertising expense.

2 A 10% stock dividend was declared on January 15 when the market price was $11 per share. The dividend was distributed one month later.
3 Eight thousand treasury shares were reacquired beginning in April at a total cost of $72,000. Sixty percent of these shares were subsequently sold for $57,000.
4 19X4 net income amounted to $90,400.

**Instructions**

a Prepare a statement of retained earnings for the year ended December 31, 19X4.
b Prepare the stockholders' equity section of the company's December 31, 19X4, balance sheet.

**P16-A4** ***Corporate financial reporting***
Champion, Inc., has requested your advice concerning the proper accounting treatment for each of the following events and transactions, which occurred during 19XX:

1 On October 15, Champion sold stock of Wiser Corporation at a $30,000 loss. The Wiser stock was acquired as an investment several years earlier. Champion regularly engages in such investment activity.
2 The company has used the double-declining balance depreciation method on all items of plant and equipment. At the beginning of 19XX, management decided to change to the straight-line approach and calculated that prior years' depreciation expense would have been $150,000 lower had the new method been employed.
3 The company disposed of its oil drilling segment in July. The sale of the division resulted in a $750,000 loss. From January 1, 19XX, through the date of sale, however, the segment had generated $200,000 of income from operations.
4 One of the company's warehouses received $300,000 of damage in April when a truck hauling nuclear waste crashed into the structure. Champion's insurance does not cover this type of damage, and the trucking company responsible has filed for bankruptcy.

Champion, Inc., is subject to a 40% income tax rate and had 10,000 shares of common stock outstanding throughout 19XX. The firm's accountant has correctly computed 19XX income from operations at $880,000. Assume that all dollar amounts cited in items (1)–(4) are before tax.

**Instructions**

a Discuss the proper accounting treatment for the transactions and events described in items (1)–(4).
b Prepare the lower portion of the company's income statement (starting with income from operations) for the year ended December 31, 19XX. Include appropriate earnings-per-share information.

**P16-A5** ***Corporate income reporting***
Astro, Inc., operates a chain of bodybuilding centers and driving schools. The driving schools have been marginally profitable and were discontinued in May 19X3. The data that follow pertain to the 19X3 fiscal year.

| | *Bodybuilding Centers* | *Driving Schools* |
|---|---|---|
| Sales | $5,000,000 | $3,400,000 |
| Operating expenses | 3,200,000 | 3,150,000 |
| Loss on disposal of driving school assets | | (400,000) |
| Gain on sale of building | 300,000 | |
| Extraordinary flood loss | (100,000) | |
| Change in accounting principle | 70,000 | |

The change in accounting principle resulted from a switch in depreciation methods for the bodybuilding centers. The cumulative effect of the switch will cause a $70,000 hike in earnings.

Astro had 100,000 shares of no-par common stock outstanding throughout 19X3. Dividends of $20,000 were declared and paid on these shares in October. The company is subject to a 40% income tax rate; all amounts presented in the problem are expressed on a before-tax basis.

**Instructions**

Prepare Astro's 19X3 income statement for the year ended November 30. Use good form and be sure to disclose the company's earnings per share.

**P16-A6** ***Earnings per share***

The following information was extracted from the records of Bonneville, Inc.:

1 Preferred stock, 10%, $100 par value, 10,000 shares outstanding during the entire year. Each share is convertible into 12½ shares of common stock.

2 Common stock, $1 par value, 300,000 shares outstanding at the beginning of the year. Additional shares were sold as follows:

| | |
|---|---|
| May 1 | 100,000 shares |
| Aug. 1 | 200,000 shares |
| Oct. 1 | 200,000 shares |

3 Net income for the year, $1 million.

**Instructions**

a Calculate primary earnings per share.

b Calculate fully diluted earnings per share.

c A stockholder believes that the fully diluted computation should be based on 925,000 shares outstanding, calculated as follows:

| | |
|---|---|
| Original issuance | 300,000 |
| Additional common shares sold | 500,000 |
| Actual shares issued to stockholders from preferred conversion | 125,000 |
| | 925,000 |

The stockholder has made two errors. Identify and briefly discuss each error.

## Series B

**P16-B1** ***Accounting for treasury stock, cash dividends, and stock splits***

You Fix It, Inc., had the following stockholders' equity on January 1, 19X8:

| | |
|---|---|
| Common stock, $5 par value, 400,000 shares authorized, 70,000 shares issued and outstanding | $350,000 |
| Paid-in capital in excess of par value | 185,000 |
| Retained earnings | 360,000 |
| Total stockholders' equity | $895,000 |

The following transactions and events occurred during the year:

| | |
|---|---|
| Jan. 11 | Approved a 2-for-1 stock split. |
| Feb. 23 | Reacquired 10,000 common shares for $220,000, to be held as treasury stock. |
| July 6 | Declared a cash dividend of $0.80 per share. |
| 13 | Sold 3,000 of the treasury shares for $87,000. |
| Aug. 5 | Distributed the dividend that was declared on July 6. |

Nov. 22 Declared a special cash dividend of $1 per share.
Dec. 15 Sold 6,000 of the treasury shares for $114,000.

**Instructions**

a Prepare the journal entries needed to record You Fix It's transactions and events.
b Prepare the company's stockholders' equity section as of December 31, 19X8. Net income for the year amounted to $112,800.

**P16-B2** ***Equity transactions: Journal entries and stockholders' equity section***
An examination of the ledger of London Enterprises revealed the following accounts on January 1:

| | |
|---|---|
| Common stock, $10 par, 50,000 shares authorized, 30,000 shares issued, 28,000 shares outstanding | $300,000 |
| Paid-in capital in excess of par value | 90,000 |
| Appropriation for equipment acquisitions | 70,000 |
| Appropriation for treasury stock | 25,000 |
| Retained earnings (unappropriated) | 145,000 |
| Treasury stock, 2,000 shares at cost | 25,000 |

The following transactions and events occurred during the year:

| | |
|---|---|
| Feb. 1 | Increased the appropriation for equipment acquisitions by $15,000. |
| Mar. 14 | Declared a 4% stock dividend on the shares outstanding, to stockholders of record on March 28. The dividend will be distributed on April 14. Fair market value on the date of declaration was $15 per share. |
| Apr. 3 | Sold 1,500 shares of treasury stock for $21,000 and reduced the treasury stock appropriation by $18,750. |
| 14 | Issued the stock dividend declared on March 14. |
| Oct. 9 | Declared a $0.65 dividend per share to stockholders of record on October 23. The dividend will be distributed on November 9. |
| Nov. 9 | Paid the dividend declared on October 9. |
| Dec. 31 | Net income for the year amounted to $105,000. Closed the Income Summary account to Retained Earnings. |

**Instructions**

a Prepare journal entries to record London's transactions and events.
b Prepare the stockholders' equity section of London's December 31 balance sheet.

**P16-B3** ***Statement of retained earnings and stockholders' equity section***
Roadside Equipment had the following paid-in capital on January 1, 19X2:

| | |
|---|---|
| Common stock, $5 par, 150,000 shares authorized, 20,000 shares issued and outstanding | $100,000 |
| Paid-in capital in excess of par value | 370,000 |

On December 31, 19X2, prior to the accounting records being closed, the Retained Earnings account contained the following entries:

***Retained Earnings***

| | | | | | |
|---|---|---|---|---|---|
| 2/18 | Stock dividend | 120,000 | 1/1 | Balance | 290,000 |
| 5/14 | Correction of error | 48,000 | | | |
| 12/31 | Cash dividend | 52,000 | | | |

A review of the accounting records disclosed that:

1 A 15% stock dividend was declared on February 18 when the market price was $40 per share. The dividend was distributed one month later.
2 The $48,000 error correction is net of $32,000 of tax and relates to 19X1 sales revenue.
3 Four thousand treasury shares were reacquired beginning in May at a total cost of $140,000. Seventy percent of these shares were subsequently sold for $121,000.
4 19X2 net income amounted to $110,700.

**Instructions**

a Prepare a statement of retained earnings for the year ended December 31, 19X2.
b Prepare the stockholders' equity section of the company's December 31, 19X2, balance sheet.

**P16-B4** ***Corporate financial reporting***

Fidelity Corporation has requested your advice concerning the proper accounting treatment for each of the following events and transactions, which occurred during 19XX:

1 One of the company's distribution centers received $400,000 of damage in July when a satellite fell from outer space and crashed into the building. Fidelity's insurance does not cover the damage and the foreign government that owned the satellite refuses to accept responsibility.
2 The company disposed of its leisure goods segment in October. The sale of the division resulted in a $1.3 million gain. From January 1, 19XX, through the date of sale, however, the segment lost $500,000 from operations.
3 On March 3, Fidelity sold stock of Simon Corporation at a $50,000 gain. The Simon stock was acquired as an investment several years earlier. Fidelity regularly engages in such investment activity.
4 The company has used the straight-line depreciation method on all items of plant and equipment. At the beginning of 19XX, management decided to change to the sum-of-the-years'-digits approach and calculated that prior years' depreciation expense would have been $200,000 greater had the accelerated method been employed.

Fidelity Corporation is subject to a 40% income tax rate and had 100,000 shares of common stock outstanding throughout 19XX. The firm's accountant has correctly computed 19XX income from operations at $6.5 million. Assume that all dollar amounts cited in items (1)–(4) are before tax.

**Instructions**

a Discuss the proper accounting treatment for the transactions and events described in items (1)–(4).
b Prepare the lower portion of the company's income statement (starting with income from operations) for the year ended December 31, 19XX. Include appropriate earnings-per-share information.

**P16-B5** ***Corporate income reporting***

Sarasota, Inc., operates a chain of fast food restaurants and health food stores. The health food stores have been marginally profitable and were discontinued in February 19X1. The data that follow pertain to the 19X1 fiscal year.

| | *Fast Food Restaurants* | *Health Food Stores* |
|---|---|---|
| Sales | $10,000,000 | $2,000,000 |
| Operating expenses | 7,000,000 | 2,150,000 |
| Gain on disposal of health food store assets | | 130,000 |
| Gain on sale of equipment | 60,000 | |
| Extraordinary loss from hurricane | (300,000) | |
| Change in accounting principle | (100,000) | |

The change in accounting principle resulted from a switch in inventory valuation methods for the fast food restaurants. The cumulative effect of the switch will cause a $100,000 decrease in earnings.

Sarasota had 100,000 shares of no-par common stock outstanding throughout 19X1. Dividends of $50,000 were declared and paid on these shares in July. The company is subject to a 40% income tax rate; all amounts presented in the problem are expressed on a before-tax basis.

**Instructions**

Prepare Sarasota's 19X1 income statement for the year ended October 31. Use good form and be sure to disclose the company's earnings per share.

**P16-B6** ***Earnings per share***

The following information was extracted from the records of Haxton, Inc.:

1 Preferred stock, 8%, $100 par value, 100,000 shares outstanding during the entire year. Each share is convertible into three shares of common stock.

2 Common stock, $10 par value, 500,000 shares outstanding at the beginning of the year. Additional shares were sold as follows:

| | |
|---|---|
| Apr. 1 | 100,000 shares |
| Aug. 1 | 300,000 shares |
| Oct. 1 | 100,000 shares |

3 Net income for the year, $3.7 million.

**Instructions**

a Calculate primary earnings per share.

b Calculate fully diluted earnings per share.

c Explain the purpose behind the fully-diluted-earnings-per-share presentation on the income statement.

## Beyond the Basics

**BB16-1** ***Analysis of equity transactions***

Pacific Rim, Inc., had the following transactions and events during the year:

| | |
|---|---|
| Jan. 13 | Purchased 500 shares of treasury stock for $30 per share. |
| Feb. 18 | Sold 200 shares of the treasury stock purchased on January 13. The selling price was $36 per share. |
| Mar. 23 | Appropriated retained earnings for plant expansion. |
| Apr. 19 | Declared a cash dividend. |
| May 19 | Distributed the April 19 dividend. |
| Aug. 7 | Authorized a 4-for-1 stock split. |
| Nov. 10 | Declared a 15% stock dividend. |
| Dec. 10 | Distributed the November 10 dividend. |

**Instructions**

Using the accompanying chart, determine the effect of each of Pacific Rim's transactions and events on total assets, total liabilities, total ending retained earnings, and total stockholders' equity. Use the following notation: I = increase, D = decrease, and NE = no effect. The January 13 transaction is done as an example.

| *Transaction Date* | *Total Assets* | *Total Liabilities* | *Total Ending Retained Earnings* | *Total Stockholders' Equity* |
|---|---|---|---|---|
| Jan. 13 | D | NE | NE | D |

**BB16-2** ***Analysis of stock dividends and splits***

This problem consists of two unrelated questions that pertain to stock dividends and stock splits.

**Part I**

Evaluate the following statements for the management of Dakota, Inc., and decide whether the statements apply to:

1 Stock dividends only
2 Stock splits only
3 Both stock dividends and stock splits
4 Neither stock dividends nor stock splits

_____ a The par or stated value of the stock is changed.
_____ b Total stockholders' equity remains unchanged.
_____ c The distribution is considered an expense of the issuing corporation.
_____ d There is a transfer from Retained Earnings to capital stock accounts.
_____ e The distribution results in income upon receipt by the stockholder.
_____ f The distribution results in a larger percentage of corporate ownership for an individual stockholder.

**Part II**

On December 31, 19X1, Dakota, Inc., had the following stockholders' equity section:

| | |
|---|---|
| Common stock, $100 par | $2,000,000 |
| Paid-in capital in excess of par value | 400,000 |
| Retained earnings | 1,900,000 |
| Total stockholders' equity | $4,300,000 |

Net income of $340,000 was generated during 19X2. Four independent stockholders' equity sections for Dakota as of December 31, 19X2, follow. The sections differ because of various transactions that occurred during the year. Fair market value of the common stock when each transaction occurred was $120 per share. By using the following code, indicate the type of transaction that took place.

1 Small stock dividend
2 Large stock dividend
3 Stock split
4 None of the above

| | A | B | C | D |
|---|---|---|---|---|
| Shares outstanding | 21,000 | 40,000 | 26,000 | 20,000 |
| Common stock | $2,100,000 | $2,000,000 | $2,600,000 | $2,000,000 |
| Paid-in capital in excess of par value | 420,000 | 400,000 | 400,000 | 400,000 |
| Retained earnings | 2,120,000 | 2,240,000 | 1,640,000 | 2,240,000 |
| Transaction type | ______ | ______ | ______ | ______ |

**BB16-3** ***Comprehensive stockholders' equity: Analysis and presentation***

On January 1 of the current year Bowen Enterprises reported a retained earnings balance of $4,565,000. The following information has been obtained from a review of the company's records:

1 On April 9, Bowen declared a cash dividend of $0.90 per share.
2 Stockholders' equity as of September 30 follows.

| | |
|---|---|
| Common stock, $5 par, 4,000,000 shares authorized | $3,000,000 |
| Paid-in capital in excess of par value | 1,900,000 |
| Retained earnings | 4,850,000 |
| | $9,750,000 |

3 On November 9, Bowen reacquired 30,000 shares of its own stock for $408,000. Twenty thousand of these shares were reissued on December 21 at $15 per share.
4 Another cash dividend of $0.90 per share was declared on December 23.
5 Net income for the fourth quarter of the year amounted to $380,000.

**Instructions**

a Compute Bowen's total net income for the current year.
b Compute the number of shares outstanding as of December 31.
c Determine the balance in the Retained Earnings account as of December 31.
d Prepare the stockholders' equity section of Bowen's December 31 balance sheet in good form. Bowen is required to restrict retained earnings for treasury stock purchases and discloses such restrictions in the footnotes to the financial statements.

## Answers to Chapter Quiz

**1** b

**2** a

**3** d (The $16,000 decrease to Retained Earnings is offset by a $4,000 increase to Stock Dividend Distributable and a $12,000 increase to Paid-in Capital in Excess of Par Value.)

**4** d

**5** b

# Long-Term Liabilities

CHAPTER 17

## Learning Objectives

After reading this chapter you should:

1 Be familiar with the basic differences between bondholders and stockholders.

2 Be aware of the different types of bonds that may be issued.

3 Be able to account for bond issues, including those issued between interest dates.

4 Understand the distinction between contract and effective interest rates, and premiums and discounts.

5 Be familiar with the concept of present value.

6 Understand the need for amortization and the differences between the straight-line and effective-interest methods.

7 Be able to account for bond retirements and convertible bonds.

8 Be able to account for mortgage notes.

9 Understand the basic accounting issues related to leases and deferred taxes.

Businesses constantly need funds to finance their diverse activities. As we have shown in earlier chapters, funds may be obtained from different sources. For example, short-term projects and investments in current assets (e.g., inventory buildups) are typically financed by short-term credit such as accounts payable and by the cash generated from profitable operations. These funding sources are not always adequate or satisfactory, however. Long-term projects such as an expansion of facilities or the addition of a new product line dictate the need for a more permanent source of capital. Imagine the difficulty of financing a new office complex with liabilities that would have to be renewed every three months. Indeed, the prospect of resecuring the necessary credit four times a year for the next 30 or 40 years is unappealing.

Generally speaking, long-term investments are financed by long-term capital. Examples of long-term capital include capital stock and numerous types of debt, such as bonds and notes. Bonds and notes are commonly encountered in practice and can vary in importance as a source of asset funding (see Exhibit 17-1).

This chapter explores long-term liabilities, with a concentration on bonds. Other long-term liabilities, specifically, mortgages, leases, and deferred taxes, will be considered as well.

## Bonds

Suppose an automobile manufacturer has decided to build a new plant to produce subcompacts. The plant's construction cost might be more than a single lender is capable of supplying. The manufacturer therefore has two basic financing alternatives available: the issuance of additional shares of stock or the issuance of bonds. **Bonds** enable a borrower to split a large loan into many small divisible units. Each of these units (known as a bond) is essentially a note payable, that is, a written promise to pay a sum of money on a specified future date. Like capital stock, bonds are issued through an underwriter to the investing public. Once outstanding, they can be bought and sold on organized securities exchanges and are thus easily transferable.

OBJECTIVE 1
Be familiar with the basic differences between bondholders and stockholders.

Although stocks and bonds may seem somewhat similar, their holders have distinctly different rights. Stockholders are the owners of a corporation; bondholders, on the other hand, are creditors whose claims are classified as long-term debt on the balance sheet. To protect the bondholders' interests, the issuing firm usually appoints a *trustee*. The trustee, often a large bank, plays the role of a third party to

**Exhibit 17-1**
**Bonds and Notes as a Source of Funding**

| *Corporation* | *Bonds and Notes Outstanding (000 Omitted)* | *Net Long-Term Assets (000 Omitted)* | *Bonds and Notes as a Percentage of Net Long-Term Assets* |
|---|---|---|---|
| H&R Block, Inc. | $ 4,689 | $ 230,918 | 2.0% |
| The Clorox Company | 29,190 | 651,649 | 4.5 |
| Rubbermaid Incorporated | 39,023 | 374,219 | 10.4 |
| Monsanto Company | 1,408,000 | 5,364,000 | 26.2 |
| Gerber Products | 146,982 | 360,854 | 40.7 |
| Capital Cities/ABC | 1,693,543 | 3,717,122 | 45.6 |
| Eastman Kodak | 7,779,000 | 14,280,000 | 54.5 |

monitor the issuer's adherence to stated terms of the bonds. For example, bond issues frequently permit dividends to stockholders only if certain working capital levels are maintained. If bond provisions are violated, the trustee may initiate appropriate action, such as lawsuits or perhaps the seizure and foreclosure of any property pledged as collateral on the bond issue. The provisions of a bond issue are normally stipulated in an accompanying document called a **bond indenture.**

Exhibit 17-2 summarizes two further differences between bondholders and stockholders based on the creditor/owner relationship.

## Financing with Bonds and Stock

Many factors must be evaluated when deciding whether to finance with bonds or stock. One of the most important considerations is that bond interest is deductible for federal income tax purposes, whereas dividends are not. To illustrate the tax effects of a financing decision, assume Greenlaw Corporation currently has 200,000 shares of common stock outstanding and must raise $2 million for modernization of plant and equipment. Two alternatives are being reviewed: (1) issue 100,000 additional shares of stock at $20 per share or (2) issue 12%, 20-year bonds. Management estimates that the company will have annual earnings of $800,000 before deducting bond interest and income taxes. The following figures show net income along with earnings per share (EPS) data for both options:

| | *Issue Shares of Stock* | *Issue 12% Bonds* |
|---|---|---|
| Total financing needed | $2,000,000 | $2,000,000 |
| Earnings before interest and taxes | $ 800,000 | $ 800,000 |
| Less: Bond interest ($2,000,000 × 0.12) | — | 240,000 |
| Earnings before income taxes | $ 800,000 | $ 560,000 |
| Less: Income taxes at 40% | 320,000 | 224,000 |
| Net income | $ 480,000 | $ 336,000 |
| Common shares outstanding | 300,000 | 200,000 |
| Earnings per share of stock | $1.60 | $1.68 |

**Exhibit 17-2**
**Differences Between Bondholders and Stockholders**

| | *Bondholders (Creditors)* | *Stockholders (Owners)* |
|---|---|---|
| Claim on income | Bondholders receive interest and have a yearly fixed claim on income. Interest must be paid regardless of the level of earnings. | Stockholders are paid dividends subject to income levels and the discretion of the corporate directors. |
| Claim in liquidation | Bondholders have a prior claim on assets in the event of bankruptcy. | Stockholders have a residual claim on business assets. Should bankruptcy occur, the owners receive proceeds from asset liquidation only after the amounts due creditors have been settled. |

Observe that Greenlaw will report higher income if common stock is issued ($480,000 vs. $336,000) since no interest is incurred. However, earnings per share will be lower (i.e., diluted) because of the additional 100,000 shares outstanding. In this particular case the stockholders would probably prefer the use of debt financing. Why? An attractive EPS figure will frequently increase the value of an investor's shares in the marketplace.

If earnings fall substantially, the bonds can take their toll. Assume the same facts as before except that projected earnings before interest and taxes now amount to only $400,000. Earnings per share figures would appear as follows:

| | *Issue Shares of Stock* | *Issue 12% Bonds* |
|---|---|---|
| Total financing needed | $2,000,000 | $2,000,000 |
| Earnings before interest and taxes | $ 400,000 | $ 400,000 |
| Less: Bond interest ($2,000,000 × 0.12) | — | 240,000 |
| Earnings before income taxes | $ 400,000 | $ 160,000 |
| Less: Income taxes at 40% | 160,000 | 64,000 |
| Net income | $ 240,000 | $ 96,000 |
| Common shares outstanding | 300,000 | 200,000 |
| Earnings per share of stock | $0.80 | $0.48 |

EPS is now more attractive with stock financing because of the bonds' large interest charge in relation to total earnings. By extending this example, we would see that businesses with high debt levels in weak or recessionary economies are prone to poor financial performance and perhaps bankruptcy. Simply stated, interest and principal payments must be made whether or not customers are coming in the front door. Both debt and equity financing are considered further in Chapter 20.

## Types of Bonds

OBJECTIVE 2
Be aware of the different types of bonds that may be issued.

Bonds are issued by corporations, the federal government, states, school districts, and local municipalities. These entities have varying financial needs, and the bonds the entities issue appeal to different types of investors. As a result, many types of bonds are used in the fund-raising process. Consider, for example, the recent long-term liability disclosure of AMR Corporation, parent company of American Airlines (see Exhibit 17-3).

Although this illustration is somewhat technical, the following discussion should help to clarify the firm's balance sheet presentation.

### Secured and Debenture Bonds

Many bonds are **secured;** that is, specific assets have been pledged as security for the bondholders should the issuing company fail to meet its obligations under the indenture agreement. Virtually any type of property can be pledged. As an example, mortgage bonds are generally secured by property, plant, and equipment; collateral trust bonds by negotiable securities; and so forth.

In contrast to secured bonds, **debenture bonds** have no assets pledged as security. The marketability of debenture bonds is therefore based on the general credit of the issuing company. To sell debentures, the issuer must have a long

**Exhibit 17-3**
**Long-term Liability Disclosure of AMR Corporation (in millions)**

| | | |
|---|---|---|
| Long-term debt* | | |
| Senior debt | | |
| $4\frac{1}{4}$%–15.63% promissory notes due through 2025 | $489.6 | |
| 8.95%–$10\frac{1}{8}$% equipment trust certificates due through 1998 | 148.7 | |
| Floating rate notes due through 2024 | 111.3 | |
| $8\frac{5}{8}$% debentures due 2017 | 98.1 | |
| 9% debentures due 2016 | 96.8 | |
| Other | 67.2 | $1,011.7 |
| Subordinated debentures | | |
| Various issues | | 194.8 |
| Long-term debt, less current maturities | | $1,206.5 |

* Various details have been omitted by the authors for the sake of brevity.

period of substantial earnings as well as favorable prospects for future income and solvency. Many corporations have issued *subordinated* debentures. Should liquidation occur, the holders of subordinated bonds are paid only if sufficient assets remain after settling the claims of other designated creditors (as specified in the indenture agreement).

## Registered and Coupon Bonds

Bonds can also be classified by the manner in which the related interest is disbursed. Most of the bonds issued in recent years have been **registered bonds;** that is, the issuing firm maintains a record of the purchaser's name and address. At the time interest is paid, the disbursing company simply mails a check to the bond's registered owner. Naturally, when a change in ownership occurs, the issuing company must be notified so that interest can be paid to the proper party.

Interest payments on **coupon bonds** are handled in a different fashion. Coupon bonds have small detachable coupons that are made payable to the bearer and that correspond to each interest period. When one of the coupons falls due, it is detached by the bondholder and deposited at a bank for collection. By shifting the responsibility for collection to the bondholder and the bank, the issuing company need not maintain an up-to-date list of bond owners.

## Other Bond Classifications

Many bond issues have a single maturity date for the entire issue. With **serial bonds,** however, bondholders are repaid in periodic installments over a number of years. For example, a company could issue $20 million of bonds in 19X1 that begin to mature in 19X6 at the rate of $4 million per year. This staggering of maturity dates allows investors (i.e., lenders) to select bonds that satisfy their cash flow needs.

Companies often create a special fund to repay a bond issue. Cash is set aside each year and invested in income-producing securities. The periodic cash deposits plus the investment income are then used for repayment. Funds of this type are commonly termed **sinking funds** and, appropriately, the bonds are sometimes called **sinking-fund debentures.** Sinking funds will be discussed later in this chapter.

Some bonds are **convertible** into shares of common stock at the option of the bondholder. The conversion feature allows a creditor to exchange a security with fixed interest receipts for one whose increase in value will be substantial should the issuing company enjoy high levels of profitability. Convertible bonds are also discussed later in the chapter.

Finally, many bonds are **callable** at the option of the issuing firm. Callable bonds permit the issuer to repay bondholders prior to the specified maturity date, a feature that is often exercised if funds become available at lower interest rates. In return for this feature, the issuer compensates the bondholder by setting a call price that normally exceeds the bonds' face value.

## Accounting for Bond Issues

OBJECTIVE 3
Be able to account for bond issues, including those issued between interest dates.

Accounting for bonds can be quite complex; no doubt you will see why as we proceed through the chapter. For this reason we will start with a very basic illustration, with modifications (and realism) being added along the way. Before doing so, however, two simple facts regarding bonds must be explained. First, all bonds have a *face value*—a set amount to be repaid on the bond's maturity date. The face value is usually $1,000 or some multiple thereof. Second, bonds can be issued at any price; the price, in turn, is normally expressed as a percentage of face value. For example, a $1,000 bond issued at 97 will cost the buyer $970.

Given this information, assume that on January 1, Tyler Corporation issued $500,000 of 10-year, 12% bonds at 100. Interest is payable semiannually on January 1 and July 1. The entry to record the issuance follows.

| | | | |
|---|---|---|---|
| Jan. 1 | Cash | 500,000 | |
| | Bonds Payable | | 500,000 |
| | To record issuance of 10-year, 12% bonds | | |

The Bonds Payable account is classified in the long-term liability section of the balance sheet until one year prior to the maturity date. At that time the bonds become a current liability and are disclosed accordingly. An exception to this treatment occurs when bonds will be retired by using a sinking fund, which is a noncurrent asset. Bonds retired by the use of noncurrent assets continue to be classified as long-term liabilities until the date of maturity.

The first semiannual interest date is July 1. Interest of $30,000 ($\$500,000 \times 0.12 \times \frac{6}{12}$) will be disbursed to bondholders and is recorded as follows:

| | | | |
|---|---|---|---|
| July 1 | Bond Interest Expense | 30,000 | |
| | Cash | | 30,000 |
| | To record semiannual interest on bonds | | |

Upon maturity Tyler must repay the $500,000 it has borrowed. The entry to record the cash outlay and bond retirement is:

| | | | |
|---|---|---|---|
| ***(Year of Retirement)*** | | | |
| Jan. 1 | Bonds Payable | 500,000 | |
| | Cash | | 500,000 |
| | To record retirement of bonds | | |

### Bonds Issued Between Interest Payment Dates

The interest payment dates associated with a bond are printed on the face of the bond certificate. Bonds, however, can be issued at any time and issuance between interest dates is a frequent occurrence. To simplify record keeping, it is common practice to collect from the bond's purchaser any interest that has accumulated since the last interest date. The issuing firm can then pay a full period's interest to the bondholder on the next semiannual disbursement date without having to keep track of the date of sale. As we will now show, the interest that has been collected is later returned to the investor.

Continuing the Tyler Corporation example, we assume the same facts as before except that the bonds are issued on May 1, four months after the printed interest date. The entry to record the issuance follows.

| | | | |
|---|---|---|---|
| May 1 | Cash | 520,000 | |
| | Bonds Payable | | 500,000 |
| | Bond Interest Payable | | 20,000 |
| | To record issuance of bonds plus collection of 4 months' accrued interest | | |

Tyler has received $520,000: the $500,000 issue price plus $20,000 of interest, which has accumulated from January 1 through April 30 ($500,000 × 0.12 × $\frac{4}{12}$). The interest is recorded as a current liability because it is owed to the bondholders and will be returned on the first subsequent interest date.

When semiannual interest is paid two months later on July 1, Tyler will record the following entry:

| | | | |
|---|---|---|---|
| July 1 | Bond Interest Payable | 20,000 | |
| | Bond Interest Expense | 10,000 | |
| | Cash | | 30,000 |
| | To record semiannual interest payment | | |

Although six months' interest is being paid, remember that the company received four months' accrued interest on May 1. Thus, Tyler's actual expense is for May and June only and amounts to $10,000 ($500,000 × 0.12 × $\frac{2}{12}$).

## Factors that Affect Issue Prices

**OBJECTIVE 4**
**Understand the distinction between contract and effective interest rates, and premiums and discounts.**

Suppose a large corporation is in the process of issuing bonds that bear a 10% interest rate. In addition to receiving approval from the firm's directors, the corporation must (1) obtain permission from the SEC, (2) have the bond certificates printed, and (3) have the bond issue publicized. All of these procedures take time. Given the dynamic nature of our economy, the original 10% interest rate may or may not be attractive to investors by the time the bonds are actually issued. Investors may therefore be willing to pay more or less than face value to secure a particular holding.

To illustrate, assume the going rate of interest is presently 11%. The corporation attempting to market the 10% bond issue mentioned previously may encounter some difficulty, because investors can obtain higher yields elsewhere. To make the bonds more attractive, the corporation could sell the issue for less than face value. In this manner a bondholder would still receive 10% interest as printed on the certificate (often called the nominal or **contract interest rate**); however, by lending the corporation a smaller amount, the investor's actual yield is increased. For example, if a $1,000 bond was issued at 91, the corporation cited would pay

$100 of interest ($1,000 × 0.10) for the use of $910. Thus, the actual or **effective interest rate** is greater than 10%. In conclusion, bonds are frequently issued below face value when their contract interest rate is less than the interest rate prevailing at the time of sale.

Interest rates are but one factor affecting the issue price. Consider, for instance, bond issues of companies with poor earnings records. Suppose that an entity with a history of losses issued 11% bonds at a time when the going rate of interest was 11%. Many investors might possibly be reluctant to purchase these bonds because of the firm's financial difficulties. Bondholders, of course, are concerned about timely interest receipts and the retirement of debt on the scheduled maturity date. As in the previous example, a drop in the issue price may be needed to make the bonds an attractive investment. When bonds are sold at less than face value, the difference between the issue price and face value is commonly referred to as a **discount.**

Naturally, the opposite situation can occur, with issuance at a price in excess of face value. If, for example, a company attempted to sell a 13% bond issue when the prevailing interest rate was 11%, demand could be overwhelming. Investors might be willing to pay more than face value to obtain the 13% receipts, thus depressing the actual, or yield rate. In this particular case the difference between the issue price and face value is called a **premium.**

## Present Value

OBJECTIVE 5
Be familiar with the concept of present value.

The amount an investor is willing to pay for a bond is determined by three items: (1) the cash inflows connected with the bond issue, (2) the timing of the cash inflows, and (3) the rate of return acceptable to the investor. To explain, there are two cash inflows related to a bond investment: periodic interest receipts and the return of principal on the maturity date. Interest, of course, is a primary consideration; if the receipts are unattractive, the investor will turn elsewhere to find more profitable opportunities.

The timing of these cash flows is also of importance. After an initial outlay, investors prefer a rapid inflow of funds so that reinvestment and other projects can be pursued. Dollars received soon after an investment is made are therefore looked upon more favorably than inflows that occur in later periods. Finally, all investors seek a return on their precious funds. The return they desire is dependent on a number of factors, one of which is risk. Different investments have different risk levels. Consider, for example, the purchase of a certificate of deposit at a bank (a safe investment) versus the acquisition of a racehorse, which could produce large profits or large losses. Investors generally require higher rates of return as their exposure to risk increases.

A tool known as **present value** integrates cash flows, their timing, and the rate of return to determine quantitatively the amount an investor is willing to pay for a bond—or for that matter any investment. An introduction to present value appears in the Appendix to this chapter; a more detailed discussion is contained in Chapter 28.

## Bonds Issued at a Discount

To illustrate the necessary accounting for bonds issued at a discount, assume Homestead Corporation sold $200,000 of 4-year, 9% bonds on January 1. The company received only $193,537 because the going rate of interest in the marketplace was in excess of 9%. The entry that follows is needed to record the bond issue.

| | | | |
|---|---|---|---|
| Jan. 1 | Cash | 193,537 | |
| | Discount on Bonds Payable | 6,463 | |
| | Bonds Payable | | 200,000 |
| | To record issuance of 4-year, 9% bonds | | |

The bonds would appear on Homestead's balance sheet as follows:

| | | |
|---|---|---|
| Long-term liabilities | | |
| Bonds payable | $200,000 | |
| Less: Discount on bonds payable | 6,463 | $193,537 |

By deducting the Discount on Bonds Payable account from the bonds' face value, Homestead's net liability becomes $193,537—the amount borrowed on January 1. Stated differently, the bonds are shown at their **carrying value,** or face value minus the unamortized discount.[1]

## Meaning of a Bond Discount

OBJECTIVE 6
Understand the need for amortization and the differences between the straight-line and effective-interest methods.

As we discussed in Chapter 12, a discount represents future interest expense. This idea is best understood by examining the cash flows related to the bond issue:

| | | |
|---|---|---|
| Cash to be paid | | |
| Interest payments over 4 years ($200,000 × 0.09 × 4) | $ 72,000 | |
| Face value at maturity | 200,000 | $272,000 |
| Cash received | | 193,537 |
| Total cost of borrowing | | $ 78,463 |

Although Homestead is required to pay $72,000 of interest per the bond indenture, issuance at a discount has raised the cost of borrowing by $6,463 ($78,463 − $72,000). Not by accident, this increase corresponds with the balance in the Discount account as of January 1.

To reflect the higher borrowing cost, the discount must be periodically transferred to interest expense over the bond issue's life. This process, commonly known as *discount amortization,* is performed by using the straight-line method or the effective interest method.

## Discount Amortization: Straight-Line Method

Under **straight-line amortization,** an equal amount of discount is allocated to each interest period. If we assume Homestead pays interest semiannually on June 30 and December 31, the discount will be amortized over 8 installments (4 years × 2 interest periods per year) of $808 each ($6,463 ÷ 8). The following entries are therefore necessary on each interest date:

| | | |
|---|---|---|
| Bond Interest Expense | 9,000 | |
| Cash | | 9,000 |
| To record semiannual interest payment: $200,000 × 0.09 × $\frac{6}{12}$ | | |
| | | |
| Bond Interest Expense | 808 | |
| Discount on Bonds Payable | | 808 |
| To record semiannual discount amortization | | |

[1] Carrying value is defined differently for bonds issued in excess of face value. This definition will be presented shortly.

The two entries show that Homestead's interest expense is determined by the semiannual contractual payment of $9,000 and by amortization of the discount. Interest therefore amounts to $9,808 and grows to $78,464 ($9,808 × 8 periods) over the life of the bond issue. Notice that aside from a $1 rounding error, this figure agrees with the total borrowing cost computed in the preceding discussion.

In addition to affecting Interest Expense, the amortization entry also reduces the Discount account and forces an increase in bond carrying value. For example, Homestead's balance sheet disclosure on June 30 (six months after issuance) would be as follows:

| | | |
|---|---|---|
| Long-term liabilities | | |
| Bonds payable | $200,000 | |
| Less: Discount on bonds payable | 5,655* | $194,345 |

* $6,463 − $808.

By the time the maturity date is reached, the balance in Discount on Bonds Payable will be zero, which results in a $200,000 net liability.

Amortization procedures vary somewhat in practice. Many companies record amortization at the end of the accounting period rather than on each interest payment date. Furthermore, rather than have separate journal entries to record discount amortization and the payment of interest, some businesses use a compound (combined) entry. Homestead's entries on June 30, for instance, could have been recorded as follows:

| | | |
|---|---|---|
| Bond Interest Expense | 9,808 | |
| Discount on Bonds Payable | | 808 |
| Cash | | 9,000 |
| To record semiannual interest payment and discount amortization | | |

## Discount Amortization: Effective-Interest Method

Despite its widespread use and popularity, the straight-line amortization of bond discount has a conceptual flaw. Straight-line amortization recognizes an equal amount of interest expense each period. At the same time, however, the bond carrying value (i.e., the net amount owed) is growing. Many accountants object to the straight-line method because of this apparent inconsistency. That is, if increasing amounts are owed, the amount of interest expense recorded each period should increase throughout the bond issue's life.

The preceding problem can be overcome by using the **effective-interest method** of amortization. With this approach, interest expense is calculated as a constant *percentage* of bond carrying value; thus, increasing carrying values are matched by increasing amounts of expense. Consistent with the method's name, the related computations are derived by using a bond's effective interest rate, not the contract rate. According to a ruling issued by the accounting profession, the effective-interest method must be utilized when it produces results that differ significantly from the straight-line approach.[2] Often, however, the two methods generate similar outcomes within a given reporting period.

[2] See "Interest on Receivables and Payables," *Opinions of the Accounting Principles Board No. 21* (New York: American Institute of Certified Public Accountants, 1971).

To illustrate discount amortization with the effective-interest method, we will use the same facts we employed in the previous example; our initial approach, however, will be from a slightly different perspective. The facts are as follows:

- A $200,000, 4-year, 9% bond issue.
- Semiannual interest payments on June 30 and December 31.
- Proceeds amounting to $193,537, resulting in a 10% effective interest rate.[3]

Recall that (1) the amount an individual or firm is willing to pay for an investment is termed present value and (2) *present value is in part dependent on the rate of return acceptable to the investor* (10% in this case). Now, assume that you recently inherited $193,537 from a wealthy relative. After lengthy negotiation you have agreed to open a savings account at a local bank and leave the money on deposit for the next four years. The bank will pay you $9,000 at the end of each six-month period and will return $200,000 upon conclusion of the fourth year. Assuming the $9,000 is withdrawn semiannually, the savings account would appear as follows for the first year:

| | *First 6-Month Period* | | *Second 6-Month Period* | |
|---|---|---|---|---|
| Beginning balance | $193,537 | | $194,214 | |
| Add: Interest at 5%* | 9,677 | | 9,711 | |
| | $203,214 | +$677 | $203,925 | +$711 |
| Less: Semiannual cash withdrawal | 9,000 | | 9,000 | |
| Ending balance | $194,214 | | $194,925 | |

* 10% annual rate ÷ 2 semiannual interest periods.

Observe that the account's balance is rising each period. Furthermore, notice that the increase is equal to the difference between the semiannual interest of 5% and the cash withdrawal. By changing our perspective, we could say that the balance in the savings account corresponds to the carrying value of the bond issue. The increase in carrying value is caused by discount amortization, which, during the first six months outstanding, amounted to $677. These facts are reflected in the discount amortization schedule that appears in Exhibit 17-4. A review of the exhibit reveals that interest expense and discount amortization rise each period, a direct result of applying a constant interest rate against a growing bond carrying value.

The journal entries for the effective-interest method are the same as those noted earlier for straight-line amortization; naturally, however, the amounts differ. Using information presented in the amortization table, the entries at the end of the first semiannual interest period would be as follows:

| | | |
|---|---|---|
| Bond Interest Expense | 9,000 | |
| Cash | | 9,000 |
| To record semiannual interest payment | | |
| Bond Interest Expense | 677 | |
| Discount on Bonds Payable | | 677 |
| To record semiannual discount amortization | | |

[3] The relationship between bond prices and the effective interest rate becomes apparent after studying the Appendix to this chapter.

| Semiannual Interest Period | (A) Effective Semiannual Interest Expense (5% × Carrying Value) | (B) Semiannual Interest Payment ($4\frac{1}{2}$% × Face Value) | (C) Discount Amortization (A − B) | (D) Bond Discount Balance | (E) End-of-Period Bond Carrying Value (Face Value − D) |
|---|---|---|---|---|---|
| Issue date | | | | $6,463 | $193,537 |
| 1 | $9,677 | $9,000 | $677 | 5,786 | 194,214 |
| 2 | 9,711 | 9,000 | 711 | 5,075 | 194,925 |
| 3 | 9,746 | 9,000 | 746 | 4,329 | 195,671 |
| 4 | 9,784 | 9,000 | 784 | 3,545 | 196,455 |
| 5 | 9,823 | 9,000 | 823 | 2,722 | 197,278 |
| 6 | 9,864 | 9,000 | 864 | 1,858 | 198,142 |
| 7 | 9,907 | 9,000 | 907 | 951 | 199,049 |
| 8 | 9,951* | 9,000 | 951 | — | 200,000 |

* Difference due to rounding.

**Exhibit 17-4**
**Discount Amortization Schedule**

## Bonds Issued at a Premium

Bonds are sold at a premium when their contract interest rate exceeds the prevailing market rate for bonds of a similar grade. In this particular case, investors are willing to pay more than face value to obtain the higher interest receipts. To illustrate the proper accounting, we will again use the Homestead Corporation example, with one modification. Assume the $200,000, 9% bond issue is now sold for $206,733. The entry to record the bond issue is:

| | | | |
|---|---|---|---|
| Jan. 1 | Cash | 206,733 | |
| | Premium on Bonds Payable | | 6,733 |
| | Bonds Payable | | 200,000 |
| | To record issuance of 4-year, 9% bonds | | |

If Homestead were to prepare a balance sheet on January 1, the bonds would be disclosed as follows:

| | | |
|---|---|---|
| Long-term liabilities | | |
| Bonds payable | $200,000 | |
| Add: Premium on bonds payable | 6,733 | $206,733 |

The bond carrying value of $206,733 is Homestead's net liability and is calculated by adding the premium to the bonds' face value. Since only $200,000 will be repaid at maturity (per the bond indenture), the carrying value must be reduced over the life of the issue. The necessary reduction is achieved through the amortization process discussed earlier.

### Meaning of a Bond Premium

The meaning of a bond premium is best explained by examining the cash inflows and outflows related to the company's issue.

> **TIPS & TECHNIQUES**
>
> The thrust of premium and discount amortization is perhaps best explained by means of the following diagram:
>
> 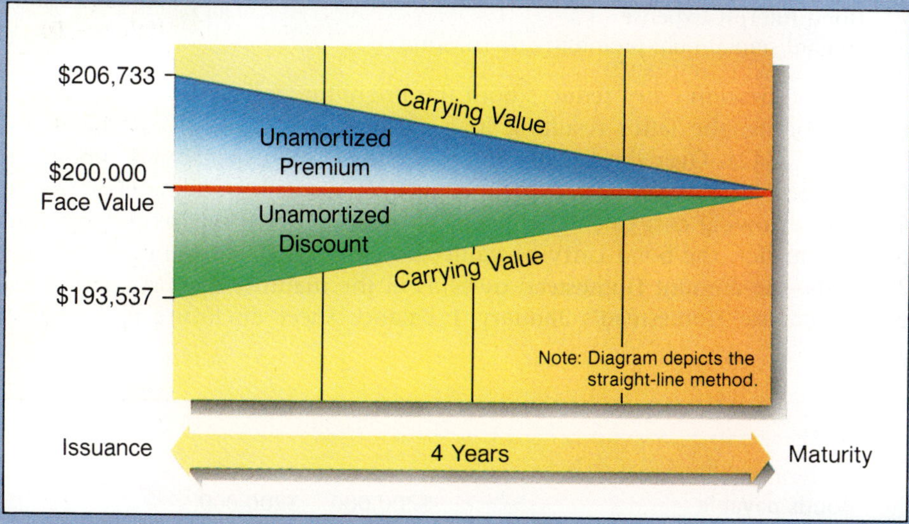
> 
>
> Each year, a selected amount of premium or discount is written off to interest expense. The write off of discount raises bond carrying value; in contrast, premium amortization produces a carrying-value reduction. In both cases, by the end of four years, carrying value reaches $200,000—the bonds' face value and the company's payoff at maturity.

| | | |
|---|---|---|
| Cash to be paid | | |
| Interest payments over 4 years ($200,000 × 0.09 × 4) | $ 72,000 | |
| Face value at maturity | 200,000 | $272,000 |
| Cash received | | 206,733 |
| Total cost of borrowing | | $ 65,267 |

Notice that Homestead's cash payments for interest amount to $72,000; however, the total cost of borrowing is only $65,267. It is apparent, then, that a premium represents a payment by bondholders that reduces the issuing firm's interest expense, in this instance by $6,733 ($72,000 − $65,267). Observe that the reduction equals the balance in the Premium account on January 1. At this point we can conclude that a premium is the opposite of a discount, given the premium's effect on interest expense and its disclosure on the balance sheet (i.e., an addition to Bonds Payable as opposed to a reduction).

## Premium Amortization

A bond premium can also be amortized by either the straight-line or effective-interest methods. If straight-line amortization is used, $842 of premium ($6,733 ÷ 8) will be written off during each semiannual interest period. The entries that follow are therefore required on June 30 and each subsequent interest date.

| | | |
|---|---|---|
| Bond Interest Expense | 9,000 | |
| Cash | | 9,000 |
| To record semiannual interest payment: $200,000 × 0.09 × $\frac{6}{12}$ | | |
| Premium on Bonds Payable | 842 | |
| Bond Interest Expense | | 842 |
| To record semiannual premium amortization | | |

The amortization entry reduces both the Premium and the Bond Interest Expense accounts, the latter resulting in a six-month borrowing cost of $8,158 ($9,000 − $842). Over the life of the bond issue, total expense will amount to $65,264 ($8,158 × 8 periods), which, except for a small rounding error, agrees with the borrowing cost calculated earlier. Finally, observe that as the premium becomes smaller, the bond carrying value decreases and will eventually become $200,000—the amount Homestead owes as of the maturity date. As partial evidence, compare Homestead's January 1 balance sheet disclosure with that of June 30:

| | *Jan. 1* | *June 30* |
|---|---|---|
| Long-term liabilities | | |
| Bonds payable | $200,000 | $200,000 |
| Add: Premium on bonds payable | 6,733 | 5,891* |
| | $206,733 | $205,891 |

* $6,733 − $842.

We turn now to the effective-interest method. Applying a constant percentage against a declining carrying value yields decreasing amounts of interest expense each period. For instance, suppose the bond issue's proceeds of $206,733 came about because investors were willing to accept an 8% effective interest rate. Returning to our earlier method of explanation, assume that you have agreed to open a $206,733 savings account in exchange for a $9,000 payment at the end of each six-month period. The savings account would appear as follows for the first year:

| | *First 6-Month Period* | | *Second 6-Month Period* | |
|---|---|---|---|---|
| Beginning balance | $206,733 | | $206,002 | |
| Add: Interest at 4%* | 8,269 | | 8,240 | |
| | $215,002 | −$731 | $214,242 | −$760 |
| Less: Semiannual cash withdrawal | 9,000 | | 9,000 | |
| Ending balance | $206,002 | | $205,242 | |

* 8% annual rate ÷ 2 semiannual interest periods.

The savings account's balance, which corresponds to the bond carrying value, declines each period because the 4% interest is less than the $9,000 cash withdrawal. The difference between these two amounts is equivalent to the premium amortization of the bond issuer. Homestead's premium amortization schedule is shown in Exhibit 17-5.

| Semiannual Interest Period | (A) Effective Semiannual Interest Expense (4% × Carrying Value) | (B) Semiannual Interest Payment ($4\frac{1}{2}$% × Face Value) | (C) Premium Amortization (B − A) | (D) Bond Premium Balance | (E) End-of-Period Bond Carrying Value (Face Value + D) |
|---|---|---|---|---|---|
| Issue date | | | | $6,733 | $206,733 |
| 1 | $8,269 | $9,000 | $731 | 6,002 | 206,002 |
| 2 | 8,240 | 9,000 | 760 | 5,242 | 205,242 |
| 3 | 8,210 | 9,000 | 790 | 4,452 | 204,452 |
| 4 | 8,178 | 9,000 | 822 | 3,630 | 203,630 |
| 5 | 8,145 | 9,000 | 855 | 2,775 | 202,775 |
| 6 | 8,111 | 9,000 | 889 | 1,886 | 201,886 |
| 7 | 8,075 | 9,000 | 925 | 961 | 200,961 |
| 8 | 8,039* | 9,000 | 961 | — | 200,000 |

* Difference due to rounding.

**Exhibit 17-5**
**Premium Amortization Schedule**

## Year-End Interest Accruals

In previous examples we assumed that one of the semiannual interest dates coincided with the end of the issuer's fiscal year. When this situation does not occur, it is necessary to accrue interest from the last payment date until the end of the reporting period. Because premiums and discounts affect interest expense, amortization must be recorded as well.

To illustrate the required procedures, we will use data from the preceding example in which Homestead issued its bonds at a premium. Recalling that the interest payment dates were June 30 and December 31, assume the company's fiscal year now ends on August 31. Prior to preparing the financial statements, the following adjusting entries are needed:

| | | | |
|---|---|---|---|
| Aug. 31 | Bond Interest Expense | 3,000 | |
| | Bond Interest Payable | | 3,000 |
| | To accrue interest expense for 2 months | | |

| | | *Straight-Line* | | *Effective-Interest* | |
|---|---|---|---|---|---|
| Aug. 31 | Premium on Bonds Payable | 281 | | 253 | |
| | Bond Interest Expense | | 281 | | 253 |
| | To amortize bond premium for 2 months | | | | |

The first entry recognizes the company's contractual obligation to disburse $9,000 of interest for each six-month period the bonds are outstanding. Because bondholders were last paid on June 30, Homestead has incurred and owes interest of $3,000 ($9,000 × $\frac{2}{6}$). Turning to the second entry, the Bond Interest Expense account must be credited to reduce Homestead's borrowing cost for the months of

July and August. Semiannual amortization under the straight-line method amounted to $842 (see p. 591); thus, $281 ($842 × $\frac{2}{6}$) of amortization must be recorded. If the effective-interest method is used, the computation is slightly more complex. According to information that appears in Exhibit 17-5, Homestead would have recorded $731 of premium amortization upon conclusion of the first semiannual interest period and $760 at the end of the second period. Because two months of the second period have now passed, year-end amortization amounts to $253 ($760 × $\frac{2}{6}$).

On December 31, the next interest payment date, two entries are again necessary:

| | | | |
|---|---|---|---|
| Dec. 31 | Bond Interest Payable | 3,000 | |
| | Bond Interest Expense | 6,000 | |
| | Cash | | 9,000 |
| | To record semiannual interest payment | | |

| | | *Straight-Line* | | *Effective-Interest* | |
|---|---|---|---|---|---|
| Dec. 31 | Premium on Bonds Payable | 561 | | 507 | |
| | Bond Interest Expense | | 561 | | 507 |
| | To amortize bond premium for 4 months | | | | |

The first entry records the semiannual interest payment and another four months of interest expense (September 1–December 31). The Bond Interest Payable account is debited to eliminate the two months of interest owed as of August 31. The second entry records premium amortization as follows: straight-line, $561 ($842 × $\frac{4}{6}$); effective-interest, $507 ($760 × $\frac{4}{6}$). Similar procedures are then followed in later reporting periods. Had the bonds been issued at a discount, the amortization entry would have required a debit to Bond Interest Expense and a credit to Discount on Bonds Payable.

## Bond Retirement

> OBJECTIVE 7
> Be able to account for bond retirements and convertible bonds.

Bonds are sold under the money and credit conditions that prevail at the time of issue. Frequently, in order to raise the necessary funds, the issuing company must incur high effective interest rates and make promises to bondholders that inhibit future financing flexibility. Examples of such promises include restrictions on dividend payments and the maintenance of a certain working capital position (current assets minus current liabilities).

Most companies protect themselves and take advantage of changing market conditions (and possible lower interest rates) by including a call provision on bond issues. Such a provision allows issuers to reacquire the bonds at a stipulated percentage of face value. Bonds may be called and be replaced by an issue that carries a lower interest rate (known as **bond refunding**) or be retired and canceled (known as **bond retirement**). In either case, any difference between the bond carrying value and the call price is treated as a gain or a loss in the year when the call occurs.[4]

[4] Sizable gains and losses that result from the extinguishment of debt are reported on the income statement as an extraordinary item. This special disclosure treatment arose from market conditions that existed in the early 1970s, allowing companies to realize significant gains (sometimes amounting to millions of dollars) on the early retirement of debt.

To illustrate the proper accounting, assume Troup Manufacturing retired a $400,000, 8% bond issue that had an unamortized premium balance of $16,000. If the bonds were called at 106 on one of the semiannual interest dates,[5] Troup would record the following entry:

| | | |
|---|---|---|
| Bonds Payable | 400,000 | |
| Premium on Bonds Payable | 16,000 | |
| Loss on Bond Retirement | 8,000 | |
| Cash | | 424,000 |
| To record retirement of bond issue at 106 | | |

The retirement calls for the removal of the bonds from the accounting records at their current carrying value ($416,000); thus, Bonds Payable and Premium on Bonds Payable are both debited. The loss arose because the amount paid was greater than the carrying value; had the opposite situation occurred, a gain would have been generated. Overall, the required accounting treatment is similar to that for the retirement and sale of a depreciable asset. Recall that depreciation expense is first updated. Next, the asset's book value is removed from the records via both the asset and accumulated depreciation accounts. As a final step, a gain or loss on disposal is computed by comparing book value with the sale proceeds.

## Convertible Bonds

Earlier in the chapter we noted that some bonds can be converted into shares of common stock at the option of the bondholder. Because of the conversion feature, the value of the bond will usually rise as the market value (i.e., price) of the issuing company's stock increases. Even if the market price of the stock remains static or drops, the bondholder will continue to receive periodic interest payments, as well as the bond's face value on the maturity date. Conversion is therefore a desirable feature for an investor—and also for the issuing company. The company benefits because investors are willing to accept lower interest rates in exchange for the conversion privilege. Furthermore, upon conversion, the company issues shares at a preset exchange price—a price per share that is typically higher than the stock's market price at the time the bond was issued.

If bonds are converted, the carrying value of the bonds must be transferred to the common stock accounts. For example, assume Maynard Corporation has the following convertible bond issue outstanding:

| | | |
|---|---|---|
| Long-term liabilities | | |
| Bonds payable | $80,000 | |
| Less: Discount on bonds payable | 4,000 | $76,000 |

Each $1,000 bond may be converted into 40 shares of $20 par-value common stock. If all of the bonds are converted, the following entry is needed:

| | | |
|---|---|---|
| Bonds Payable | 80,000 | |
| Discount on Bonds Payable | | 4,000 |
| Common Stock | | 64,000 |
| Paid-in Capital in Excess of Par Value | | 12,000 |
| To record bond conversion into 3,200 shares of common stock (80 bonds × 40 shares per bond) | | |

[5] Prior to recording the retirement, journal entries are needed to update related interest payments and premium (or discount) amortization.

In accordance with proper equity accounting, the Common Stock account is credited for the par value of the shares issued (3,200 shares × $20 par = $64,000). Given this treatment, the $12,000 difference between the carrying value ($76,000) and par value ($64,000) is recorded as paid-in capital in excess of par value. Observe that no gain or loss is recognized; the reason is that no earnings activity has occurred. The transaction is a simple exchange of long-term debt for shares of common stock.

### Bond Sinking Funds

In an effort to further protect the bondholders, companies are sometimes required to make periodic deposits to a special fund that is used for retiring the bonds at maturity. The fund, commonly called a **bond sinking fund,** is normally under the supervision of a trustee. The trustee is permitted to invest the company's deposits in income-producing securities. If all goes according to plan, the cash deposits plus the investment income should be sufficient to pay the bondholders the proper amount due. Any cash deficiencies would be supplemented by additional deposits; in contrast, excess cash is returned by the trustee to the contributing company.

The cash and securities in a sinking fund are restricted solely for use in bond retirement and cannot be used to meet current expenses or pay current liabilities. Sinking funds, therefore, are not current assets; instead, such amounts are disclosed in the long-term investments section of the balance sheet.

## Other Long-term Obligations

In addition to bonds, other types of long-term obligations are frequently encountered in practice. These obligations include mortgage notes, leases, and deferred income taxes.

### Mortgage Notes

OBJECTIVE 8
Be able to account for mortgage notes.

**Mortgage notes** are often used to finance the purchase of real estate. To secure the necessary funding, borrowers agree to pledge certain assets as collateral (security) for the note. Should the borrower fail to meet required payments or other specified conditions, the lender may foreclose on the assets pledged.

Mortgage notes are normally paid in monthly installments, with each installment representing both interest and partial payment on the note's principal. Although the total monthly payment usually remains constant, the allocation between interest and principal will differ each period. Virtually all mortgage obligations, as well as other long-term loans, require that interest be computed on the basis of the unpaid principal. Thus, each successive monthly payment contains a declining interest charge because of the decreasing note balance. For example, assume that an entity secured a 12%, $200,000 mortgage on August 1. Based on monthly payments of $3,500, the allocation between interest and principal for payments of September through December would be as follows:

| Payment Date | (A) Monthly Payment | (B) Monthly Interest (1% of Unpaid Note Balance)* | (C) Reduction in Principal (A − B) | (D) Unpaid Note Balance (Previous Balance − C) |
|---|---|---|---|---|
| Issuance date | | | | $200,000 |
| Sept. 1 | $3,500 | $2,000 | $1,500 | 198,500 |
| Oct. 1 | 3,500 | 1,985 | 1,515 | 196,985 |
| Nov. 1 | 3,500 | 1,970 | 1,530 | 195,455 |
| Dec. 1 | 3,500 | 1,955 | 1,545 | 193,910 |

* 12% annual rate ÷ 12 one-month interest periods. All figures are rounded to the nearest dollar.

These data are then entered in the accounting records via formal journal entries. To illustrate, the entry needed on September 1 is:

| | | | |
|---|---|---|---|
| Sept. 1 | Interest Expense | 2,000 | |
| | Mortgage Note Payable | 1,500 | |
| | Cash | | 3,500 |
| | To record monthly payment of interest and reduction in principal of note | | |

## Leases

OBJECTIVE 9
Understand the basic accounting issues related to leases and deferred taxes.

Businesses are faced with several options when acquiring the services of long-term assets. There is, of course, the outright purchase. Another possibility that has become extremely popular in recent years is some form of lease agreement. A **lease** is an arrangement that allows one party, the *lessee,* to use the assets of another party, the *lessor,* for a stated period of time. Leases are available for a variety of different items including automobiles, airplanes, office equipment, and machinery.

Leasing has grown in significance even though in the long run it is usually more expensive than purchasing. Some of the advantages of leasing from the lessee's viewpoint are

**1** Lease payments are generally 100% tax deductible in the year the amounts are paid.

**2** A lease arrangement usually permits 100% financing; that is, no down payment may be necessary.

**3** The risk of obsolescence on the leased asset rests with the lessor.

### Operating Leases Versus Capital Leases

There are two general categories of leases: operating and capital. Under an **operating lease,** the lessee obtains the right to use leased property for a limited period of time and treats amounts paid under the agreement as expense. The lessor, in turn, recognizes amounts received as revenue and retains the leased asset on its balance sheet. The contract signed by a person who rents a car for a day, a week, or some other short period of time is an example of an operating lease.

In contrast, many lease agreements provide usage rights for nearly the entire service life of the leased asset. Such agreements frequently contain a provision for the lessee to acquire the property at a bargain purchase price upon conclusion of the contract term. Leases that meet these or other specific criteria are known as

**capital leases.**[6] A careful study of a capital lease reveals the lessee is really acquiring an asset through an installment purchase plan. Yet prior to the mid-1970s, long-term lessees were not required to disclose the asset and obligation for future lease payments (a liability) on their balance sheets. This practice gave rise to the term *off balance-sheet financing.* Under current regulations, however, the lessee must now record both the assets leased under a capital lease agreement and the liability to the lessor.

### Accounting for Capital Leases

Although the details of accounting for capital leases are quite complex, you already have a frame of reference to understand the necessary fundamentals. We have indicated that a capital lease is similar to an installment purchase, with the lessee recording the asset leased (i.e., "purchased"), along with the related obligation to the lessor. Subsequent to this initial recording, the lessee will depreciate the asset by using one of the depreciation methods discussed earlier in the text (straight-line, sum-of-the-years'-digits, and so forth). Turning to the liability, the required accounting tends to resemble the accounting for a mortgage note. Each lease payment is allocated between principal and interest; furthermore, the interest is calculated as a percentage of the outstanding balance due the lessor. Each successive payment therefore involves a decreasing amount of interest expense and an increasing reduction of principal.

The following excerpt from a recent annual report of Scott Paper Company provides a representative example of the disclosure that is typically given to capital leases.

> A capital lease transfers substantially all of the benefits and risks of ownership of the leased property to the Company. On the Company's consolidated balance sheet the following amounts of capitalized leases are included in plant assets and the related obligations are included in debt:

| | ***(Millions)*** |
|---|---|
| Plant assets under capital leases | $ 51.4 |
| Accumulated depreciation | (22.7) |
| Net capital leases | $ 28.7 |
| Current lease obligations | $ 4.6 |
| Long-term lease obligations | 21.5 |
| Capital lease obligations | $ 26.1 |

> All other leases are accounted for as operating expenses. . . .

## Liabilities for Federal Income Taxes

Corporations in this country are subject to the federal income tax laws enacted by Congress. As a result, these businesses must report the amount of income subject to taxation, along with the related tax obligation, to the Internal Revenue Service. Taxes must also be disclosed on the income statement because such amounts affect profitability. In the attempt to satisfy the government and, at the same time, stock-

[6] See "Accounting for Leases," *Statement of Financial Accounting Standards No. 13* (Stamford, Conn.: Financial Accounting Standards Board, 1976).

holders, creditors, and managers, a reporting problem typically arises—one that has an impact on the liability section of corporate balance sheets.

Financial statements are not governed by tax law; rather, they are based on generally accepted accounting principles (GAAP). The income statement, for example, strives to present a fair picture of operating results by a proper matching of revenues and expenses. Because of differences between GAAP and income tax regulations, there is often a difference between pretax income as reported in the financial statements (called **pretax financial income**) and income reportable to the IRS (known as **taxable income**). In view of this situation, the *taxes paid* (or *due*) to the government may not be an appropriate measure of a company's *tax expense* for a given accounting period.

## Differences Between Taxable Income and Financial Income

Variations between taxable income and pretax financial income arise from several different factors. Consider, for instance, that some business transactions and events have no tax consequences.[7] To illustrate, the payment of traffic fines is an expense to be presented on the income statement. Yet such amounts are not deductible for federal income tax purposes and are therefore ignored in the computation of a company's taxable income.

In addition, there are so-called **temporary differences.** These items result when revenues and expenses are recognized in different accounting periods for income tax and financial reporting purposes. As an example, property management companies often receive advance rental payments from tenants. For tax purposes, these amounts are generally included in taxable income immediately upon receipt. In contrast, for accounting purposes, the rentals are reported on the balance sheet as a liability, with revenues recognized in future periods as the facilities are occupied (and services provided). Focusing on another situation, items of plant and equipment may be depreciated over different lives for tax and financial reporting purposes. Often, given the features of the Modified Accelerated Cost Recovery System, a shorter life is used for reporting to the IRS. Such a practice allows a taxpayer a faster recovery of investment dollars from quicker tax savings.

## Deferred Income Taxes

The temporary differences just discussed (and others) cause financial income and taxable income figures to differ in future years. To illustrate the reporting issues, assume Dinah, Inc., had previously experienced temporary differences that are expected to cause taxable income to be greater than financial income by $30,000 annually for the next three years, 19X2–19X4. Further assume that Dinah is subject to a 40% tax rate. In view of these facts, the firm would report a $36,000 deferred tax liability on December 31, 19X1, computed as follows:

| *Year* | *Taxable Difference* | × | *Tax Rate* | = | *Deferred Tax Liability* |
|---|---|---|---|---|---|
| 19X2 | $30,000 | | 40% | | $12,000 |
| 19X3 | 30,000 | | 40% | | 12,000 |
| 19X4 | 30,000 | | 40% | | 12,000 |
| Total | | | | | $36,000 |

[7] See "Accounting for Income Taxes," *Statement of Financial Accounting Standards No. 96* (Stamford, Conn.: Financial Accounting Standards Board, 1987).

## HIGHLIGHT

# The Case of the Missing Liability

Bonds, mortgages, lease obligations, and deferred taxes are all prominently displayed in the long-term liability section of the balance sheets of corporate America. Missing for most firms, however, is another long-term obligation—one that could run as high as $3 *trillion* for U.S. businesses. We're talking about post-retirement healthcare benefits. "It's a bit of a bombshell sitting there that could have a very significant impact on corporate values," notes the president of the nonprofit Employee Benefit Research Institute. "Very, very few companies that promise these benefits have really looked beyond the tips of their noses on liabilities inherent in the promise." [1]

A little history should provide more insight about the issue. A report from the Institute states that 76% of the full-time health plan participants in medium-sized and large organizations have healthcare coverage that continues after early retirement; 90% have coverage that continues after age 65. Further, virtually all firms expense such costs as they pay the premiums or claims—that is, they use the pay-as-you-go (cash basis) of accounting. The problem? Huge liabilities that a company has committed itself to and owe never pop up on the balance sheet.

One of the underlying reasons for this treatment has been that of measurement. Most post-retirement plans don't set a limit on healthcare benefits. No matter how serious the illness is or how long it lasts, the benefits will continue to flow, and coverage may also apply to the spouse and other dependents. Further, the level of utilization of healthcare benefits is hard to predict. The U.S. population is aging and living longer; aging people require more medical treatment. Therefore, an increase in utilization is inevitable. Also, new illnesses that cause unexpected changes in utilization can occur—such as Legionnaire's Disease and AIDS.

So what does the accounting profession propose for these significant employee commitments? As we go to press, there is sentiment that accruals would solve much of the problem. Consistent with the matching principle, a company would record an expense during the period of employment, which is when the future obligation really arises. At the same time an expense is entered in the accounting records, a liability is created for disclosure on the balance sheet. [2]

The impact of such a procedure could be staggering. A recent study by an actuarial consulting firm estimates that the average accrued cost for companies that provide such benefits will be $2,000 *annually* per current employee. Based on profits reported by the 500 largest U.S. industrial corporations, subtracting the expense would reduce profits by 14% for companies at the top of the list and even create losses for some businesses. The study estimates average income reductions of 30% to 60%. [3] Mature industries with many retirees would be particularly affected. Some steel companies, for example, average two retired workers for every active employee. Also hard hit would be firms that compete with foreign businesses whose governments provide healthcare or where employer-provided benefits are not customary. [4]

Fortunately, the FASB realizes the enormous pressure that accrual accounting would create on America's finances. For this reason, a spokesperson says, such a change would be phased in over a period of years. "We have this tremendous . . . obligation right now," she said. "To put that on the balance sheet would be just onerous. We recognize that." [5]

SOURCES: Adapted from "The Big Unfunded Liability: Postretirement Healthcare Benefits," *Journal of Accountancy,* November 1988, pp. 28–39 [2, 4]; "Health Costs Haunting Firms," *San Francisco Chronicle,* November 26, 1988, p. B2 [5]; and "New Accounting Regulations Might Affect Companies' Health," *Fort Worth Star-Telegram,* November 13, 1987, section 2, p. 3 [1, 3]. 

To explain, the amount of tax to be paid to the government is based on taxable income, whereas the amount of tax expense on the income statement is computed by using financial income. Because taxable income is expected to exceed financial income over the next three years, the firm anticipates owing additional monies to the government—amounts in excess of those reported as tax expense. Hence, an account called Deferred Income Tax Liability would have a $36,000 balance at the end of *19X1*. The deferred tax liability would be shown on a classified balance sheet in two categories. The amount related to 19X2, $12,000, would appear in the statement's current liability section; the remaining $24,000 (related to 19X3 and 19X4) would be disclosed as a long-term obligation.

The use of temporary differences to defer large amounts of income tax is a very popular business practice that results in substantial benefits. Consider, for instance, that Squibb Corporation, the giant drug producer, recently reported a long-term deferred tax liability of over $76 million, or approximately 32.8% of total long-term debt. Such postponements enable the company to retain cash, which can then be used to cover operating expenses or for reinvestment in the firm.

## APPENDIX Present Value

As we noted in the body of this chapter, investors use the concept of present value to determine the amount they are willing to pay for a bond issue. To illustrate present value, assume that today is January 1 and you have $1,000 to invest. After studying various alternatives, you have narrowed the field to investments A and B. The investments each promise a $100 cash inflow during the next 12 months; however, as the following schedule shows, the timing differs.

| | *A* | *B* |
|---|---|---|
| Cash outlay required on Jan. 1 | $1,000 | $1,000 |
| Forecasted cash inflows | | |
| Mar. 31 | $ 25 | |
| June 30 | 25 | |
| Sept. 30 | 25 | |
| Dec. 31 | 25 | $100 |
| | $100 | $100 |

Although A and B both yield a 10% rate of return ($100 ÷ $1,000), most people would select investment A for two reasons. First, the future is generally unpredictable and full of uncertainty. Thus, all other things being equal, a more rapid recovery of investment dollars helps to reduce the risk associated with an outlay. The dollars are in hand and the investor becomes less concerned about events that may stop or inhibit the generation of returns. Investment A is also preferred for another reason. Money has a *time value;* specifically, a dollar today is worth more than a dollar in the future. Dollars received early in the year or in the early years of a long-lived project can be reinvested to generate additional earnings. The inflows associated with investment A can, therefore, be put to work; nothing, however, can be done with the $100 from investment B until December 31.

Present value recognizes the time value of money and weights cash flows occurring in earlier periods more heavily than those that take place further in the future. Before we proceed, we must first examine a concept with which most of you are familiar—compound interest.

## Compound Interest and Present Value

Earlier in the text we introduced the computation of simple interest with the following formula:

$$\text{Interest} = \text{Principal} \times \text{Rate} \times \text{Time}$$

Notice that interest is calculated on principal only. In contrast, **compound interest** is computed on principal *and* on previously computed interest as well. To illustrate the related calculations, assume you deposited \$100 in a savings account that pays 10% interest. If interest is compounded annually, the deposit will grow to \$121 by the end of two years.

| | *Year 1* | *Year 2* |
|---|---|---|
| Beginning of year | \$100 | \$110 |
| Add: 10% interest | 10 | 11* |
| End of year | \$110 | \$121 |

* \$110 × 0.10.

The preceding concept is sometimes referred to as **future value,** because it reflects the amount to which an outlay will grow by the conclusion of a designated time period.

Approaching the same example from a slightly different perspective, suppose you are willing to accept a 10% return on your money. If an investment opportunity is available that promises a \$110 cash inflow at the end of one year, how much would you be willing to invest today to obtain that inflow? We hope you answered \$100. Why? If you invest \$100 today at a 10% interest rate, the investment will grow to the \$110 you can receive. The \$100 is termed the investment's **present value,** or the amount an investor is willing to pay to obtain a specified cash flow (\$110) on a future date (one year from now) at a given rate of return (10%).

Observe that the preceding question could have been phrased as follows: Given a 10% rate of return, how much would you be willing to invest today to receive \$121 at the end of two years? As before, the answer is \$100.

## Relationship Between Compound Interest and Present Value

By using a factor of $(1 + r)^n$, where r is equal to the interest rate per period and n equals the number of periods, we can illustrate the relationship between present value and compound interest (i.e., future value). For compound interest the calculations are as follows:

| *Original Amount* → | | | *End of Year 1* → | | | *End of Year 2* |
|---|---|---|---|---|---|---|
| \$100 | × $(1.10)^1$ | = | \$110 | × $(1.10)^1$ | = | \$121 |

Alternatively, the same results could have been achieved by the following computation:

$$\$100 \times (1.10)^2 = \$121$$

In either case a present amount is compounded at a 10% interest rate and extended two years into the future.

For present value the situation is reversed—a future amount is *discounted* and brought back to today. This process is diagrammed below.

| *End of Year 2* | → | *End of Year 1* | → | *Original Amount* |
|---|---|---|---|---|
| \$121 | $\times \frac{1}{(1.10)^1} =$ | \$110 | $\times \frac{1}{(1.10)^1} =$ | \$100 |

In a manner similar to compound interest, discounting could have been illustrated as follows:

$$\$121 \times \frac{1}{(1.10)^2} = \$100$$

Fortunately, there are tables available to simplify present value calculations. See Table 1 in Appendix C at the end of the text, which is the present value of \$1 at various interest rates and for various time periods. The use of the table may be shown with the example just cited. Observe that the 10% column and 2-period row reveals a factor of 0.82645, which is the present value of \$1 received in two years at a 10% interest rate. Because we desire to find the present value of \$121 and not \$1, the following multiplication is necessary:

| *Cash Flow* | | *Present Value Factor* | | *Present Value* |
|---|---|---|---|---|
| \$121 | × | 0.82645 | = | \$100 |

## Multiple Cash Flows and Annuities

Most investment opportunities are accompanied by cash flows that occur over a time span of several years. Consider, for instance, the following schedule of discounted cash flows that has been constructed for a planned investment of Westcott Enterprises. The schedule is based on a 10% interest rate.

| *Year* | *Cash Flow* | | *Present Value Factor* | | *Present Value* |
|---|---|---|---|---|---|
| 1 | \$2,000 | × | 0.90909 | = | \$1,818 |
| 2 | 2,000 | × | 0.82645 | = | 1,653 |
| 3 | 2,000 | × | 0.75132 | = | 1,503 |
| 4 | 2,000 | × | 0.68301 | = | 1,366 |
| 5 | 2,000 | × | 0.62092 | = | 1,242 |
| Total present value | | | | | \$7,582 |

Although more cash flows are involved, we continue to multiply monetary amounts by present value factors extracted from Table 1. These factors reveal the time value of money, with the \$2,000 inflow that occurs in Year 1 having a greater present value (i.e., "worth") to Westcott than the inflow that occurs in Year 5 (\$1,818 vs. \$1,242). The figures indicate a total present value of \$7,582—the maximum amount the firm can afford to pay to acquire this investment and still generate a 10% return on its funds.

As you may have gathered, present value computations can become rather tedious. The Westcott illustration dealt with five cash flows; the calculations would indeed be more burdensome in a longer term, more realistic investment, say 10 years, with different inflows and outflows occurring within a single period. Fortunately, two shortcuts are available to minimize the procedural difficulties.

Notice that in each year the present value factor is multiplied by a $2,000 monetary amount. The calculations would have required less work had the annual cash flow been multiplied by the summation of the individual factors (0.90909 + 0.82645 + 0.75132 + 0.68301 + 0.62092 = 3.79079). As the following figures show, the same result is achieved: $2,000 × 3.79079 = $7,582.

Another possibility is to recognize that this example has focused on the concept of an **annuity**—a series of equal cash receipts or disbursements over a number of years. To further simplify the process, the individual present value factors from Table 1 are often combined to produce an annuity table (see Table 2 in Appendix C). The factor in Table 2 for a $1 annuity to be received in each of the next five years, discounted at 10%, is 3.79079. Thus, the following calculation becomes appropriate:

| *Cash Flow* | | *Present Value Factor* | | *Present Value* |
|---|---|---|---|---|
| $2,000 | × | 3.79079 | = | $7,582 |

## Periods of Less Than One Year

Virtually all of our illustrations have focused on annual cash flows. Cash flows may occur more frequently; for example, bond interest is often paid on a semiannual basis, quarterly interest is added to savings accounts, and so forth. The tables included at the end of the text can continue to be used when this situation arises; however, a slight modification is necessary.

The time that elapses between the cash flows under evaluation is termed the **interest period.** It is imperative that *the percentage rate employed correspond with the interest period in question.* For instance, consider a company that desires a 12% return via $50,000 annual cash flows in each of the next eight years. In this particular case the tables may be used as illustrated in earlier examples, giving rise to a factor from the 12% column and the 8-period row. Suppose, however, that the cash flows will now be $25,000 on a semiannual basis. The semiannual flows occur every 6 months, giving rise to 2 interest periods per year and a total of 16 over the project's life. The 12% annual rate must be halved to 6% to become aligned with the 6-month period. Thus, the proper factor is found at the intersection of the 6% column and the 16-period row.

The procedures just shown may be used not only with more frequent cash flows but also with more frequent compounding. For instance, if 8% interest is compounded quarterly over the next 3 years, there would be 12 interest periods (4 periods × 3 years) of 2% each.

## Present Value and Bond Prices

The present value concepts discussed in this appendix are frequently used to determine bond issue prices. The issue price is calculated by figuring the present value of the cash flows related to the bonds, namely interest payments and the return of principal to the bondholders. As an example, assume Franklin Corporation plans to issue $500,000 of 10-year, 10% bonds. Interest of $25,000 will be payable semiannually on June 30 and December 31 ($500,000 × 0.10 × $\frac{6}{12}$ = $25,000). If the going rate of interest in the economy is also 10%, the issuance price would be computed as follows:

| | |
|---|---|
| Present value of interest payments: $25,000 × 12.46221* | $311,555 |
| Present value of principal payment: $500,000 × 0.37689† | 188,445 |
| Total present value (anticipated issue price) | $500,000 |

* Table 2, 5%, 20 periods.
† Table 1, 5%, 20 periods.

Notice how the present value coincides with the face value of the bonds. The reason is because Franklin's bonds pay interest equal to the prevailing market rate; thus, investors are willing to pay 100% of face value for bond acquisitions.

Modifying the illustration, suppose the annual interest rate for other similar bond issues is now 12%. Franklin's bonds, however, continue to pay 10% (i.e., $25,000 interest for each six-month period). By using factors for the prevailing 12% rate,[8] the present value becomes $442,648:

| | |
|---|---|
| Present value of interest payments: $25,000 × 11.46992* | $286,748 |
| Present value of principal payment: $500,000 × 0.31180† | 155,900 |
| Total present value (anticipated issue price) | $442,648 |

* Table 2, 6%, 20 periods.
† Table 1, 6%, 20 periods.

The bonds will be issued at a discount because investors can obtain a 12% return elsewhere. By receiving less than face value and still paying the same 10% contract interest, the effective rate is increased. Franklin's bonds have now become competitive for the limited funds of the investing public.

## Chapter Review

### Learning Objectives—The Key Points

**1 Be familiar with the basic differences between bondholders and stockholders.** Stockholders are the owners of a corporation. As such, they may receive dividends, subject to funds availability and the discretion of corporate directors. In the event of liquidation, stockholders are entitled to asset proceeds only if monies are available after paying all other claims. Bondholders, on the other hand, are creditors who are entitled to regular interest payments regardless of income levels. Furthermore, creditors have a claim against assets (before stockholders) if a business were to liquidate.

**2 Be aware of the different types of bonds that may be issued.** The chart that follows summarizes key characteristics of the bonds discussed in this chapter.

| Type of Bond | Distinguishing Characteristics |
|---|---|
| Secured | Has specific assets pledged as security for the bondholders. |
| Debenture | Issued on the general credit of the corporation. |

[8] The prevailing rate is used in present value calculations because it is the lowest rate of return an investor is willing to accept.

| Type of Bond | Distinguishing Characteristics |
|---|---|
| Registered | Issuing company maintains a record of bond purchasers and mails interest directly to bond owners. |
| Coupon | Has small detachable coupons that are used for interest collection. |
| Serial | Issue has staggered maturity dates. |
| Sinking-fund debenture | Is repaid by using proceeds from a special fund called a sinking fund. |
| Convertible | Can be converted into common stock at the option of the bondholder. |
| Callable | Can be reacquired by the issuing firm prior to maturity. |

**3 Be able to account for bond issues, including those issued between interest dates.** Bonds are recorded at their original issue price, along with any interest that has accrued since the last interest payment date. The first interest disbursement will include interest expense from the issue date to the payment date, plus a return of any accrued interest received when the obligations were sold. Periodic interest expense should be increased for amortization of discount and decreased for amortization of premium.

**4 Understand the distinction between contract and effective interest rates, and premiums and discounts.** The issue price of a bond is affected by the interest rate printed on the bond (the contract interest rate) relative to the going market rate for obligations of a similar grade. In general, if a bond has a contract rate that is less than the market rate, it will sell below face value (i.e., at a discount). The opposite case will give rise to a premium. The discount or premium causes the actual interest rate, known as the effective rate, to differ from the contract rate. Discounts raise the actual yield rate above the contract rate, and premiums have the opposite impact. Bond prices are also affected by the issuer's financial condition.

**5 Be familiar with the concept of present value.** Present value represents the amount an investor is willing to pay to secure a stream of future cash flows at a given rate of return. The cash flows related to a bond issue are the periodic interest receipts and the return of principal. These amounts are multiplied by the appropriate factors, which are available in table form and based on the number of periods and the effective interest rate, to derive the issue price. The periodic receipts of interest often represent an annuity, or a series of equal cash flows.

**6 Understand the need for amortization and the differences between the straight-line and effective-interest methods.** Discounts and premiums must be amortized over a bond issue's life to reflect differences between the contract interest cost and the effective interest cost. The straight-line method assigns a constant dollar amount of amortization to each period. In contrast, the theoretically preferred effective-interest method assigns sufficient amortization to each period so that interest expense is a constant percentage of bond carrying value.

**7 Be able to account for bond retirements and convertible bonds.** When bonds are retired, interest and amortization should be updated and the related unamortized premium or discount removed from the accounting records. The difference between the bond carrying value and the amount paid to retire the bonds results in a gain or a loss. Convertible bond accounting involves removing the bonds and any related premium or discount from the books. Furthermore, common stock and additional paid-in capital equal to the bond carrying value are recorded, and no gain or loss is recognized.

**8 Be able to account for mortgage notes.** Mortgage notes are long-term liabilities used to purchase real estate. Mortgages are typically paid in equal monthly installments, with each payment representing both interest and a reduction of the note's principal. Interest is computed on the basis of the unpaid note balance, a declining amount each month. As such, each successive payment consists of a decreasing interest component and a greater amount to apply toward principal.

**9 Understand the basic accounting issues related to leases and deferred taxes.** A lease is an agreement that allows one party, the lessee, to use the assets of another party, the lessor, for a stated period of time. With an operating lease, the lessee obtains the right to use leased property for a limited time period and treats amounts paid to the lessor as an expense. The lessor recognizes the monies received as revenue and retains the leased asset on its balance sheet. Alternatively, capital leases are structured so that the lessee is really acquiring an asset through an installment purchase. In this case the lessee records the leased asset in its accounting records, along with the accompanying liability to the lessor.

Income reported in the financial statements is based on generally accepted accounting principles, whereas income reported to the government (namely, the Internal Revenue Service) is based on tax regulations. Differences between pretax financial income and taxable income are common, often arising from so-called temporary differences. These items result when revenues and expenses are recognized in different periods for income tax and financial reporting purposes. When temporary differences have occurred and are expected to cause future taxable income to be greater than financial income, a Deferred Income Tax Liability account is established to reflect the future taxes due the government.

## Chapter Quiz

The five questions that follow relate to several issues raised in the chapter. Test your knowledge of the issues by selecting the best answer. (The answers appear on p. 620.)

**1** When the interest payment dates of a bond are June 1 and December 1, and a bond issue is sold on August 1, the amount of cash received by the issuer upon sale will be:
a increased by the accrued interest from August 1 to December 1.
b increased by the accrued interest from June 1 to August 1.
c decreased by the accrued interest from August 1 to December 1.
d decreased by the accrued interest from June 1 to August 1.

**2** Bonds payable are sold at 98 when there is a difference between the:
a issue date and maturity date.
b contract interest rate and effective interest rate.
c carrying value and maturity value.
d face value and maturity value.

**3** Bonds payable sold at 104 should be disclosed on the balance sheet at their face value:
a plus any unamortized discount.
b plus any unamortized premium.
c minus any unamortized discount.
d minus any unamortized premium.

**4** On June 1, 19X7, Denver, Inc., issued $100,000 of 10%, 5-year debenture bonds at 105. The bonds were dated June 1, 19X7; the company uses the straight-line amortization method. If the bonds are called and retired at 105 on June 1, 19X9, the company would experience:
a a loss of $2,000.
b a gain of $2,000.
c a loss of $3,000.
d neither a gain nor a loss.

**5** Sampson recently purchased land secured by an interest-bearing mortgage note that requires 120 monthly payments of $500, for a total of $60,000. Which of the following best describes the note's principal?
a Less than $60,000.
b More than $60,000.
c Exactly $60,000.
d Cannot be determined from the above facts.

## Summary Problem

On January 1, 19X1, Kristopher Corporation issued $100,000 of 8%, 10-year bonds for $87,538. The bonds were priced to generate an effective yield of 10% to investors, are dated January 1, 19X1, and pay semiannual interest on June 30 and December 31. On April 1, 19X2, the entire bond issue was called at 103 plus accrued interest. Kristopher uses the straight-line method of amortization and rounds all computations to the nearest dollar.

### Instructions

**a** Prepare journal entries to record (1) the bond issuance on January 1, 19X1, and (2) the semiannual interest payment and discount amortization on June 30, 19X1, and December 31, 19X1. Note: Combine the interest payment and amortization into a single entry (see p. 588).

**b** Compute total bond interest expense for 19X1.

**c** Present the proper disclosure of the bond issue on Kristopher's December 31, 19X1, balance sheet.

**d** Prepare journal entries to record the bond retirement on April 1, 19X2. *Hint*: Examine when amortization was last recorded.

**e** Compute the discount amortization to be recorded on June 30, 19X1, and December 31, 19X1, if Kristopher had used the effective-interest method rather than the straight-line method.

### Solution

**a**

| Date | Account | Debit | Credit |
|---|---|---|---|
| Jan. 1 | Cash | 87,538 | |
| | Discount on Bonds Payable | 12,462 | |
| | Bonds Payable | | 100,000 |
| | To record issuance of bonds | | |
| June 30 | Bond Interest Expense | 4,623 | |
| | Discount on Bonds Payable | | 623 |
| | Cash | | 4,000 |
| | To record semiannual interest payment and amortization | | |
| Dec. 31 | Bond Interest Expense | 4,623 | |
| | Discount on Bonds Payable | | 623 |
| | Cash | | 4,000 |
| | To record semiannual interest payment and amortization | | |
| | Calculations: See part (b) | | |

**b**

| | |
|---|---|
| Cash payment for interest each 6 months ($100,000 × 0.08 × $\frac{6}{12}$) | $4,000 |
| Straight-line discount amortization each 6 months [($12,462 ÷ 10 years) × $\frac{6}{12}$] | 623 |
| Total bond interest expense | $4,623 |
| Number of 6-month periods | ×2 |
| Bond interest expense for 19X1 | $9,246 |

**c**

| | | |
|---|---|---|
| Long-term liabilities | | |
| Bonds payable | $100,000 | |
| Less: Discount on bonds payable | 11,216* | $88,784 |

* $12,462 − $623 − $623

| | | | |
|---|---|---|---|
| **d** Apr. 1 | Bond Interest Expense | 312 | |
| | Discount on Bonds Payable | | 312 |
| | To amortize bond discount for 3 months: ($12,462 ÷ 10 years) × $\frac{3}{12}$ | | |
| | Bonds Payable | 100,000 | |
| | Bond Interest Expense | 2,000 | |
| | Loss on Bond Retirement | 13,904 | |
| | Discount on Bonds Payable | | 10,904 |
| | Cash | | 105,000 |
| | To record retirement of bond issue at 103 plus accrued interest | | |

Calculations:

| | |
|---|---|
| Cash payment | |
| Accrued interest ($100,000 × 0.08 × $\frac{3}{12}$) | $ 2,000 |
| Bond acquisition ($100,000 × 1.03) | 103,000 |
| | $105,000 |
| Loss on retirement | |
| Bonds payable | $100,000 |
| Less: Unamortized discount on 4/1/X2 ($11,216 − $312) | 10,904 |
| Bond carrying value | $ 89,096 |
| Less: Call price ($100,000 × 1.03) | 103,000 |
| Loss on bond retirement | $ 13,904 |

**e**

| *Semiannual Interest Period* | *(A) Effective Semiannual Interest Expense (5% × Carrying Value)* | *(B) Semiannual Interest Payment (4% × Face Value)* | *(C) Discount Amortization (A − B)* | *(D) Bond Discount Balance* | *(E) End-of-Period Bond Carrying Value (Face Value − D)* |
|---|---|---|---|---|---|
| Issue date | | | | $12,462 | $87,538 |
| 6/30/X1 | $4,377 | $4,000 | $377 | 12,085 | 87,915 |
| 12/31/X1 | 4,396 | 4,000 | 396 | 11,689 | 88,311 |

## Questions

**Q17-1** Are bonds normally used to meet current obligations and pay operating expenses? Explain.

**Q17-2** Differentiate between the rights of stockholders and those of bondholders.

**Q17-3** A company is considering the issuance of either additional common stock or bonds to finance a plant expansion. Explain how earnings per share could benefit under the bond alternative despite the presence of additional interest expense on the income statement.

**Q17-4** Differentiate between registered and coupon bonds.

**Q17-5** Jupiter Corporation is issuing bonds that have an individual face value of $500. If the bonds are sold at 104, will Jupiter receive $104 for each bond? Explain.

**Q17-6** How is interest handled on bonds that are issued between interest payment dates? Explain the purpose behind this accounting treatment.

**Q17-7** Bates, Inc., recently issued $400,000 of 10% bonds at 102.
- a Were the bonds sold at a discount or at a premium?
- b In all likelihood, was the prevailing rate of interest in the marketplace for similar bonds equal to, greater than, or less than 10%?
- c Is the effective interest rate equal to, greater than, or less than the contract interest rate?

**Q17-8** What is meant by the term "bond carrying value"? Will carrying value increase or decrease over the life of a bond issue when bonds are issued at a discount?

**Q17-9** Differentiate between a bond discount and a bond premium.

**Q17-10** Differentiate between straight-line and effective-interest amortization. Which method is preferred? Why?

**Q17-11** How does bond retirement differ from bond refunding?

**Q17-12** What is a bond sinking fund? Where is a sinking fund disclosed on the balance sheet?

**Q17-13** Explain how a typical mortgage note payment is allocated between principal and interest.

**Q17-14** A student once commented, "All leases are fundamentally alike, with amounts paid by the lessee recorded as an expense of the period." Evaluate the student's remark.

**Q17-15** For a given accounting period, does pretax financial income normally differ from taxable income? Why?

***Q17-16** What is meant by the term "future value"?

***Q17-17** Explain the concept of present value to someone with a limited business background.

***Q17-18** Explain the relationship between compound interest and present value.

***Q17-19** What is an annuity?

## Exercises

**E17-1** ***Bonds issued between interest dates***

Sage Corporation issued $500,000 of 12% bonds on May 1, 19X1, at 100 plus accrued interest. The bonds are dated January 1, 19X1, and pay interest each June 30 and December 31.
- a Prepare journal entries to record (1) bond issuance on May 1, 19X1; (2) the first interest payment on June 30, 19X1; and (3) the second interest payment on December 31, 19X1.
- b Compute Sage's 19X1 bond interest expense.

**E17-2** ***Overview of bonds***

Evaluate the comments that follow as being True or False. If the comment is false, briefly explain why.
- a When bonds are issued at a discount, the proceeds received exceed the bonds' face value.
- b The effective interest rate is lower than the contract interest rate for bonds that are issued at a premium.
- c For bonds that are sold at a discount, carrying value is lower than face value.
- d Premium amortization results in a company's interest expense being less than interest paid.

* An asterisk preceding an item indicates that the material is covered in the Appendix to this chapter.

e The journal entry to amortize a discount involves a debit to Discount on Bonds Payable.

**E17-3** ***Bond discount; straight-line amortization***

Monroe Company issued $300,000 of 8% bonds on January 1, 19X1, for $282,000. The bonds are due on December 31, 19X6, and pay interest semiannually on June 30 and December 31.

a Prepare the required journal entry to record bond issuance on January 1, 19X1.
b Prepare entries to record the interest payment and discount amortization on June 30 and December 31, 19X1. Monroe uses the straight-line method of amortization.
c Compute 19X1 bond interest expense.
d Present the proper disclosure of the bond issue on Monroe's December 31, 19X1, balance sheet.

**E17-4** ***Bond premium; straight-line amortization***

Castillo Company issued $200,000 of 10%, 4-year bonds on January 1, 19X1, for $216,000. The bonds pay interest semiannually on June 30 and December 31.

a Prepare the required journal entry to record bond issuance on January 1, 19X1.
b Prepare entries to record the interest payment and premium amortization on June 30 and December 31, 19X1. Castillo uses the straight-line method of amortization.
c Compute 19X1 bond interest expense.
d Present the proper disclosure of the bond issue on Castillo's December 31, 19X1, balance sheet.

**E17-5** ***Bond discount; effective-interest amortization***

The Eagle Corporation issued $400,000 of 8% bonds for $382,056 on January 1, 19X1. The bonds pay interest semiannually on June 30 and December 31 and were priced to yield an effective interest rate of 9%.

a Prepare the required journal entry to record bond issuance on January 1.
b Prepare entries to record the interest payment and discount amortization on June 30 and December 31, 19X1. Eagle uses the effective-interest method of amortization; round to the nearest dollar.
c Compute 19X1 bond interest expense.
d Present the proper disclosure of the bond issue on Eagle's December 31, 19X1, balance sheet

**E17-6** ***Bond premium; effective-interest amortization***

The Purcell Corporation issued $500,000 of 5-year, 10% bonds for $519,783 on January 1, 19X2. The bonds pay interest semiannually on June 30 and December 31 and were priced to yield an effective interest rate of 9%.

a Prepare the required journal entry to record bond issuance on January 1.
b Prepare entries to record the interest payment and premium amortization on June 30 and December 31, 19X2. Purcell uses the effective-interest method of amortization; round to the nearest dollar.
c Compute 19X2 bond interest expense.
d Present the proper disclosure of the bond issue on Purcell's December 31, 19X2, balance sheet.

**E17-7** ***Bond retirement***

The Mumphrey Corporation issued $500,000 of 10% bonds at 98 on January 1, 19X1. Interest is paid semiannually on June 30 and December 31. The bonds have a 10-year life from the date of issuance; Mumphrey uses the straight-line method of amortization. On July 1, 19X5, the bonds were called at 106 and retired.

a Compute the amount of unamortized discount as of the call date.
b Present the entry necessary on July 1, 19X5.
c Discuss possible reasons why Mumphrey exercised the call provision.

**E17-8** ***Convertible bonds***

On January 1, Howard Corporation issued $500,000 of convertible bonds. Each $1,000 bond is convertible into 20 shares of Howard's $2 par-value common stock. All of the bonds were converted exactly four years after issue, when the unamortized bond discount stood at $7,400.

a Prepare the journal entry necessary to record the bond conversion.

b Explain why convertible bonds are attractive for (1) an investor and (2) the issuing company.

**E17-9** ***Mortgage notes***

On June 1 of the current year Leonard Company acquired a building complex for $2 million, which included $500,000 of land. Leonard paid $400,000 down and secured a long-term mortgage note for the remaining balance. The note carried a 12% interest rate, which is computed on the unpaid balance at the beginning of each month. Leonard will repay the note in monthly installments of $19,000, with the first installment due on July 1.

a Prepare the journal entry to record Leonard's purchase on June 1.

b Prepare the journal entry to record Leonard's first payment on July 1.

c Compute the company's interest expense for the current fiscal year ended August 31. Round to the nearest dollar.

**E17-10** ***Leases and lease accounting***

Henry Company, a small family-owned corporation, is studying the possibility of signing a long-term lease for two new delivery vehicles. Walter Henry, the company's president, is skeptical of leasing and has always believed in the outright purchase of needed property, plant, and equipment.

a Discuss the advantages of leasing from Henry's viewpoint.

b Discuss the basic difference between an operating lease and a capital lease.

c Would Henry's lease probably be accounted for as an operating lease or as a capital lease? Why?

d Discuss the balance sheet impact, if any, of Henry's lease.

**E17-11** ***Income taxes; temporary differences***

Gemstar Homes, Inc., recently completed financial projections for the next four years, 19X2–19X5. Taxable income is expected to exceed financial income because of past temporary differences, as follows: 19X2, $80,000; 19X3, $70,000; 19X4, $50,000; and 19X5, $90,000. Assume that Gemstar will be subject to a 40% income tax rate.

a Prepare computations that indicate the amount of deferred income taxes to report at the end of *19X1*.

b On what financial statement and in which section would the amount of deferred taxes typically appear?

***E17-12** ***Time value of money and present value***

Stephanie Rogers requires a 14% rate of return on all investments. She is considering an investment that will provide the following cash inflows:

| *At the End of Year* | *Cash Inflow* | |
|---|---|---|
| 1 | $15,000 | $30,000 |
| 2 | 15,000 | |
| 3 | 16,000 | $30,000 |
| 4 | 14,000 | |
| | $60,000 | |

a Observe how the investment results in two cash inflows of $30,000, each of which is spread over two years. Which of the $30,000 inflows would be more attractive to Rogers? Explain your answer.

b By using present value, compute the maximum amount that Rogers should be willing to pay for this investment. Round to the nearest dollar.

***E17-13** ***Present value computations***

Rounding to the nearest dollar, determine the present value of the following cash flows:

a Annual receipts of $24,000 for the next 6 years, discounted at a rate of 14%.

b Receipts of $3,000 every 6 months for 5 years, discounted at a rate of 12%.

c Payments of $60,000 for the next 8 years, followed by payments of $40,000 for 2 years. All cash flows are discounted at a rate of 10%.

***E17-14** ***Bond pricing***

Thunder Manufacturing is considering the issuance of $800,000 of 5-year bonds that have a 14% contract interest rate. The bonds pay interest semiannually on June 30 and December 31. Assume a prevailing interest rate of 12% for similar bonds.

a Determine whether the bonds will be issued at a premium or a discount. Explain your answer. *Hint:* No computations are necessary.

b Determine the anticipated proceeds (i.e., present value) of the bond issue. Round your calculations to the nearest dollar.

## Problems

### Series A

**P17-A1** ***Bonds: Balance sheet presentation and analysis***

The following account balances were extracted from the general ledger of Richmond Corporation on January 1, 19XX:

| | |
|---|---|
| 12% secured bonds | $200,000 |
| 9% debenture bonds | 100,000 |
| Premium on secured bonds | 1,000 |
| Discount on debenture bonds | 3,000 |

Monthly amortization of premium and discount amounts to $20 and $50, respectively.

**Instructions**

a A study of the company's accounts reveals the presence of both secured bonds and debenture bonds. All other things being equal, would an investor prefer secured bonds or debenture bonds? Briefly explain.

b Determine the company's net bond liability to investors on January 1, 19XX.

c Prepare the proper balance sheet disclosure for the bond issues outstanding as of December 31, 19XX.

d Explain the necessity of discount and premium amortization.

e Which of the two bond issues (secured or debenture) has a contract interest rate that is less than the effective rate? Briefly explain.

**P17-A2** ***Bond computations: Straight-line amortization***

The Sobol Corporation issued $800,000 of 12% bonds on April 1, 19X1. The bonds pay interest on April 1 and October 1 and mature in 10 years. Assume the independent cases that follow.

- *Case A*—The bonds are issued at 100.
- *Case B*—The bonds are issued at 97.
- *Case C*—The bonds are issued at 106.

Sobol uses the straight-line method of amortization.

**Instructions**

Complete the following table:

| | *Case A* | *Case B* | *Case C* |
|---|---|---|---|
| a Cash inflow on the issuance date | ____ | ____ | ____ |
| b Total cash outflow through maturity | ____ | ____ | ____ |
| c Total borrowing cost over the life of the bond issue | ____ | ____ | ____ |
| d Interest expense for the year ended December 31, 19X1 | ____ | ____ | ____ |
| e Amortization for the year ended December 31, 19X1 | ____ | ____ | ____ |
| f Unamortized premium as of December 31, 19X1 | ____ | ____ | ____ |
| g Unamortized discount as of December 31, 19X1 | ____ | ____ | ____ |
| h Bond carrying value as of December 31, 19X1 | ____ | ____ | ____ |

**P17-A3** ***Bonds: Journal entries, issuance through retirement***

On March 1, 19X3, Trans International, Inc., issued $600,000 of 10%, 10-year bonds for $606,545 plus accrued interest. The bonds are dated February 1, 19X3, and pay semiannual interest on February 1 and August 1.

On April 1, 19X4, the entire bond issue was called at 103 plus accrued interest. Trans International uses the straight-line method of amortization and will amortize the premium over the 119 months the bonds are outstanding.

**Instructions**

a Prepare journal entries to record (1) the bond issuance on March 1, 19X3; (2) the semiannual interest payment and premium amortization on August 1, 19X3; and (3) accrued interest and premium amortization on December 31, 19X3.

b Compute total bond interest expense for 19X3.

c Present the proper disclosure of the bond issue on Trans International's December 31, 19X3, balance sheet.

d Prepare journal entries to record the semiannual interest payment and premium amortization on February 1, 19X4.

e Prepare journal entries to record the bond retirement on April 1, 19X4. *Hint:* Examine when amortization was last recorded.

**P17-A4** ***Amortization analysis and journal entries***

The schedule that follows reflects Burk Corporation's issuance of three-year bonds on January 1, 19X1, and the subsequent interest amounts.

| Date | *Interest Expense* | *Interest Paid* | *Amount Unamortized* | *Carrying Value* |
|---|---|---|---|---|
| 1/1/X1 | | | $6,000 | $ 94,000 |
| 6/30/X1 | $6,500 | $5,500 | 5,000 | 95,000 |
| 12/31/X1 | 6,500 | 5,500 | 4,000 | 96,000 |
| 6/30/X2 | 6,500 | 5,500 | 3,000 | 97,000 |
| 12/31/X2 | 6,500 | 5,500 | 2,000 | 98,000 |
| 6/30/X3 | 6,500 | 5,500 | 1,000 | 99,000 |
| 12/31/X3 | 6,500 | 5,500 | — | 100,000 |

**Instructions**

a Determine whether the bonds were issued at a premium or at a discount. Explain your answer.
b Did Burk Corporation use the straight-line or effective-interest amortization method? Explain your answer.
c What is the annual contract interest rate on the bonds?
d Present the journal entry to record bond issuance on January 1, 19X1. The bonds are dated January 1, 19X1.
e Present the journal entries required on June 30, 19X1.

**P17-A5** ***Bonds: Effective-interest discount amortization***

Morris Manufacturing issued $100,000 of 4-year, 11% bonds on January 1, 19X2. The bonds pay interest semiannually on June 30 and December 31 and were priced to generate an effective yield of 12% to investors. The bonds were sold for $96,895.

**Instructions**

a Prepare the journal entry necessary on January 1 to record issuance of the bonds.
b Assuming that Morris uses the effective-interest method of amortization, prepare the following:
   (1) A discount amortization schedule similar in format to Exhibit 17-4. Round calculations to the nearest dollar.
   (2) Compound journal entries to record semiannual interest payments and discount amortization for the first year the bonds are outstanding.
c Present the proper disclosure of the company's bonds on the December 31, *19X3*, balance sheet.

**P17-A6** ***Accounting for mortgage notes***

Martinez Corporation is purchasing a tract of land located near a new airport. The agreed-on purchase price is $2.4 million; Martinez will pay $400,000 down and the present owner will finance the balance by accepting a mortgage note.

The present owner has indicated that the mortgage note will carry a 12% interest rate (computed on the unpaid balance) and may be executed for either a two- or a four-year period. Regardless of the term, payments will occur in one lump sum at the end of each year and will be as follows:

| *Term of Note* | *Annual Payment* |
|---|---|
| 2 years | $1,183,396 |
| 4 years | 658,469 |

Martinez expects that the sale will be finalized (and the note executed) on January 1, 19X1.

### Instructions

a For the two-year mortgage note, prepare a table that reflects the allocation of each payment between principal and interest. Use the following column headings and round to the nearest dollar:

| *Payment Date* | *Annual Payment* | *Annual Interest* | *Reduction in Principal* | *Unpaid Note Balance* |
|---|---|---|---|---|

b Repeat part (a) for the four-year mortgage note.

c Examine the mortgage note tables and comment on why the four-year payment amount is more than 50% of the two-year payment amount.

## Series B

**P17-B1** ***Bonds: Balance sheet presentation and analysis***

The following account balances were extracted from the general ledger of Drexel Corporation on January 1, 19XX:

| | |
|---|---|
| 10% secured bonds | $100,000 |
| 11% debenture bonds | 50,000 |
| Discount on secured bonds | 3,000 |
| Premium on debenture bonds | 1,000 |

Monthly amortization of discount and premium amounts to $100 and $40, respectively.

### Instructions

a Differentiate between secured bonds and debenture bonds.

b Determine the company's net bond liability to investors on January 1, 19XX.

c Prepare the proper balance sheet disclosure for the bond issues outstanding as of December 31, 19XX.

d Explain the necessity of discount and premium amortization.

e Offer a probable explanation why one bond issue sold at a premium and the other at a discount.

**P17-B2** ***Bond computations: Straight-line amortization***

The Pardee Corporation issued $600,000 of 10% bonds on May 1, 19X3. The bonds pay interest on May 1 and November 1 and mature in eight years. Assume the following independent cases:

- *Case A*—The bonds are issued at 100.
- *Case B*—The bonds are issued at 104.
- *Case C*—The bonds are issued at 98.

Pardee uses the straight-line method of amortization.

### Instructions

Complete the table that follows.

| | Case A | Case B | Case C |
|---|---|---|---|
| a Cash inflow on the issuance date | _____ | _____ | _____ |
| b Total cash outflow through maturity | _____ | _____ | _____ |
| c Total borrowing cost over the life of the bond issue | _____ | _____ | _____ |
| d Amortization for the year ended December 31, 19X3 | _____ | _____ | _____ |
| e Interest expense for the year ended December 31, 19X3 | _____ | _____ | _____ |
| f Unamortized discount as of December 31, 19X3 | _____ | _____ | _____ |
| g Unamortized premium as of December 31, 19X3 | _____ | _____ | _____ |
| h Bond carrying value as of December 31, 19X3 | _____ | _____ | _____ |

**P17-B3** ***Bonds: Journal entries, issuance through retirement***

On May 1, 19X1, American Housing Corporation issued $300,000 of 12%, 5-year bonds for $294,200 plus accrued interest. The bonds are dated March 1, 19X1, and pay semiannual interest on March 1 and September 1.

On July 1, 19X2, the entire bond issue was called at 101 plus accrued interest. American uses the straight-line method of amortization and will amortize the discount over the 58 months the bonds are outstanding.

**Instructions**

a Prepare journal entries to record (1) the bond issuance on May 1, 19X1; (2) the semiannual interest payment and discount amortization on September 1, 19X1; and (3) accrued interest and discount amortization on December 31, 19X1.
b Compute total bond interest expense for 19X1.
c Present the proper disclosure of the bond issue on American's December 31, 19X1, balance sheet.
d Prepare journal entries to record the semiannual interest payment and discount amortization on March 1, 19X2.
e Prepare journal entries to record the bond retirement on July 1, 19X2. *Hint:* Examine when amortization was last recorded.

**P17-B4** ***Amortization analysis and journal entries***

The following schedule reflects Zeta Corporation's issuance of three-year bonds on January 1, 19X5, and the subsequent interest amounts:

| Date | *Interest Expense* | *Interest Paid* | *Amount Unamortized* | *Carrying Value* |
|---|---|---|---|---|
| 1/1/X5 | | | $10,152 | $210,152 |
| 6/30/X5 | $10,508 | $12,000 | 8,660 | 208,660 |
| 12/31/X5 | 10,433 | 12,000 | 7,093 | 207,093 |
| 6/30/X6 | 10,355 | 12,000 | 5,448 | 205,448 |
| 12/31/X6 | 10,272 | 12,000 | 3,720 | 203,720 |
| 6/30/X7 | 10,186 | 12,000 | 1,906 | 201,906 |
| 12/31/X7 | 10,094* | 12,000 | — | 200,000 |

* Difference due to rounding.

### Instructions

a Did Zeta Corporation use the straight-line or effective-interest amortization method? Explain your answer.
b Determine whether the bonds were issued at a premium or at a discount. Explain your answer.
c What is the annual contract interest rate on the bonds?
d Present the journal entry to record bond issuance on January 1, 19X5. The bonds are dated January 1, 19X5.
e Present the journal entries required on June 30, 19X6.

**P17-B5** ***Bonds: Effective-interest premium amortization***

Far East Electronics issued $800,000 of 4-year, 11% bonds on January 1, 19X4. The bonds pay interest semiannually on June 30 and December 31 and were priced to generate an effective yield of 10% to investors. The bonds were sold for $825,853.

### Instructions

a Prepare the journal entry necessary on January 1 to record issuance of the bonds.
b Assuming that Far East uses the effective-interest method of amortization, prepare the following:
  (1) A premium amortization schedule similar in format to Exhibit 17-5. Round calculations to the nearest dollar.
  (2) Compound journal entries to record semiannual interest payments and premium amortization for the first year the bonds are outstanding.
c Present the proper disclosure of the company's bonds on the December 31, *19X6*, balance sheet.

**P17-B6** ***Accounting for mortgage notes***

Trask Broadcasting is purchasing a tract of land located near a busy freeway. The agreed-on purchase price is $1,250,000; Trask will pay $250,000 down and the present owner will finance the balance by accepting a mortgage note.

The present owner has indicated that the mortgage note will carry a 10% interest rate (computed on the unpaid balance) and may be executed for either a three- or a six-year period. Regardless of the term, payments will occur in one lump sum at the end of each year and will be as follows:

| *Term of Note* | *Annual Payment* |
|---|---|
| 3 years | $402,115 |
| 6 years | 229,607 |

Trask expects that the sale will be finalized (and the note executed) on January 1, 19X3.

### Instructions

a For the three-year mortgage note, prepare a table that reflects the allocation of each payment between principal and interest. Use the following column headings and round to the nearest dollar:

| *Payment Date* | *Annual Payment* | *Annual Interest* | *Reduction in Principal* | *Unpaid Note Balance* |
|---|---|---|---|---|

b Repeat part (a) for the six-year mortgage note.
c Comment on the differences, if any, between the two notes in terms of
  (1) Total interest incurred.
  (2) The allocation of yearly payments between principal and interest.

## Beyond the Basics

**BB17-1** ***Bond financing versus stock financing***

LaRue, Inc., operates a chain of upscale clothing stores throughout the country. A recent balance sheet of the firm revealed $200,000 of 8% bonds payable and $400,000 of common stock. A proposed modernization program requires that the company raise $300,000 of new financing. Two alternatives are being considered: (1) issue 10% bonds or (2) issue 10,000 additional shares of common stock, increasing the total number of shares in the hands of stockholders to 30,000.

LaRue has been marginally profitable over the last few years, generating income significantly below that of other firms in the same line of business. Fortunately, the company has been able to avoid operating at a loss. Inventories, receivables, and payables balances are at all-time highs; cash balances, on the other hand, are at dangerously low levels.

**Instructions**

a Suppose you are a stockholder of LaRue. Do you see any possible problems of financing the modernization program with bonds? Explain.

b Suppose the company is leaning toward selection of the bond alternative. Given the present state of affairs, would the issuance of debenture bonds or secured bonds be more appropriate? Why?

c Assume that LaRue is subject to a 40% income tax rate. Calculate earnings-per-share figures for the two alternatives if management expects earnings before interest and taxes of:

(1) $50,000.

(2) $120,000.

d Briefly explain the results of your computations in part (c).

**BB17-2** ***Bonds: Multiple-choice questions***

The following multiple-choice questions relate to bonds. Select the best answer.

1 Montgomery Company plans to issue bonds that have a contract interest rate of 9%. If the prevailing interest rate for bonds of a similar grade is 10%, one could expect that:

a The bonds are not an attractive investment.

b The bonds will be sold at face value.

c The bonds will be sold at a premium.

d The bonds will be sold at a discount.

2 McNeil Corporation neglected to amortize $900 of bond premium during the current year. This error would:

a Understate total liabilities at the end of the current year.

b Overstate total liabilities at the end of the current year.

c Understate the current year's net income.

d Overstate the current year's net income.

e Result in more than one of the above, namely, _____, _____.

3 Korta, Inc., issued $500,000 of 10%, 10-year bonds on January 1, 19X1, at 96. The bonds are dated January 1 and pay interest semiannually on June 30 and December 31. Which of the following is correct, assuming use of straight-line amortization?

| | *Cash Paid for Interest in 19X1* | *19X1 Interest Expense* |
|---|---|---|
| a | $48,000 | $50,000 |
| b | 50,000 | 48,000 |
| c | 52,000 | 50,000 |
| d | 50,000 | 52,000 |
| e | 50,000 | 50,000 |

4 Tapper and Romo issued $400,000 of 12%, 10-year bonds and received proceeds of $415,000. The bonds were dated August 1, 19X1, and were sold on August 1. Assuming the company records straight-line amortization at the close of its fiscal year on October 31, the 19X1 amortization entry would include a credit to:
a Discount on Bonds Payable for $375.
b Interest Expense for $375.
c Premium on Bonds Payable for $375.
d Interest Expense for $1,500.
e None of the above.

5 On June 1, 19X1, Rankin Manufacturing issued $600,000 of 10-year, 8% bonds at 104. Interest is payable semiannually on June 1 and December 1. On June 1, 19X8, 40% of the bonds were called at 106 and retired. Assuming use of straight-line amortization, Rankin would realize:
a A loss of $7,200.
b A gain of $7,200.
c A gain of $11,520.
d A loss of $11,520.
e None of the above.

6 The balance sheet of Trend Setters, Inc., revealed the following convertible bond disclosure on April 1, 19X1:

| | |
|---|---|
| Bonds payable | $200,000 |
| Less: Discount on bonds payable | 6,490 |
| | $193,510 |

On April 1, 19X2, 60% of these bonds were converted into 5,000 shares of $5 par-value common stock. If the discount is being amortized over 118 months, the firm's gain or loss on the conversion would amount to:
a $0.
b A loss of $91,106.
c A loss of $91,502.
d None of the above.

## Answers to Chapter Quiz

**1** b

**2** b

**3** b

**4** a (Carrying value on June 1, 19X9, is $103,000: $100,000 + $3,000 unamortized premium; $105,000 payment − $103,000 carrying value = $2,000 loss)

**5** a

# Long-Term Investments

CHAPTER 18

## Learning Objectives

After reading this chapter you should:

1 Understand how to account for investments in bonds.

2 Understand accounting for stock investments with the lower-of-cost-or-market and the equity methods.

3 Be familiar with parent/subsidiary relationships.

4 Understand the reason for consolidated financial statements, including the concepts of intercompany transactions and elimination entries.

5 Be able to prepare consolidated financial statements immediately after acquisition.

6 Understand how to account for minority interests.

7 Be able to account for subsidiaries acquired at a cost in excess of book value.

8 Understand the differences between purchase and pooling-of-interests accounting.

Investments in assets are a fact of life for all businesses. Companies that sell merchandise or render services must invest vast sums of money for needed inventories, machinery, equipment, and facilities. Frequently, when sufficient funds are available, a business will purchase the securities of other entities. As we saw in Chapter 7, for example, excess funds are commonly used to acquire various short-term investments. Recall that short-term investments are both *readily salable* and *intended to be converted into cash* within the current operating cycle or one year, whichever is longer.

Investments in securities that do not meet these criteria are classified as noncurrent (long-term) assets on the balance sheet. Long-term securities investments are made for a variety of reasons. Many companies desire the dividend or interest income associated with the securities. Furthermore, businesses often seek to obtain a sufficient number of shares to substantially influence or control the operations of other entities. This practice is followed by firms that want to expand activities in existing markets, diversify by adding new product lines, or ensure a steady source of raw materials and supplies. The preceding points are illustrated in Exhibit 18-1, which lists several corporations along with selected controlled subsidiaries.

This chapter focuses on long-term investments in corporate securities—both bonds and stocks. As you will see, accounting for stock acquisitions can become quite complicated because proper record keeping depends on the percentage of shares owned.

## Investments in Bonds

OBJECTIVE 1
Understand how to account for investments in bonds.

In Chapter 17 we discussed bonds from the viewpoint of the issuing corporation. We now turn our attention to bond accounting by investors. The major issues involved are recording the initial investment, treatment of interest and the related amortization of bond discount or premium, and the sale of bonds before maturity. The following sections will show that bond accounting for the investor is very similar to that practiced by the issuer.

**Exhibit 18-1**
**Corporations and Selected Subsidiaries**

| *Corporation* | *Primary Area of Identity* | *Subsidiaries* |
|---|---|---|
| General Electric | Appliances, aerospace, and lighting | National Broadcasting Company (NBC) |
| General Mills | Food products | Red Lobster Restaurants<br>Olive Garden Restaurants |
| Greyhound Corporation | Intercity bus transportation | Dial Corporation<br>Dobbs House Restaurants<br>Motor Coach Industries (bus manufacturer) |
| Philip Morris Companies | Tobacco products | General Foods (Post, Jell-O, Oscar Mayer)<br>Miller Brewing Company |
| Quaker Oats | Food products | Fisher-Price (toy manufacturer) |

## Recording the Initial Investment

Bond investments are initially entered in the accounts at cost, that is, the purchase price plus brokerage fees and any other costs related to acquisition. The amount paid for a bond depends on the market price that exists on the date of purchase. A bond's market price is influenced by a number of different factors, including the cash flows associated with the bond issue, the timing of the cash flows, and the rate of return acceptable to the investor.

In addition to the purchase price and other incidental costs, bond investors may be required to pay accrued interest. Recall that the issuing corporation disburses a full period's interest on each interest payment date, regardless of the period of time a bond is held by an investor. As a result of this practice, the purchaser must pay for any interest that has accumulated up to the date of acquisition. To illustrate, assume Foxmire Corporation purchased $300,000 of Harkness Corporation 10-year bonds on March 1, 19X1. Additional facts that relate to Foxmire's investment follow.

- Date of bonds: January 1, 19X1
- Contract interest rate: 8%
- Interest payment dates: June 30 and December 31
- Purchase price: $262,991 plus accrued interest

The journal entry to record the bond purchase is:

| | | | |
|---|---|---|---|
| Mar. 1 | Investment in Bonds | 262,991 | |
| | Bond Interest Receivable | 4,000 | |
| | Cash | | 266,991 |
| | To record investment in Harkness bonds | | |

Consistent with the proper accounting treatment for all assets, the Investment in Bonds account is established at cost. Although the bonds were acquired at an amount different from their face value, a separate discount (or premium) account is not used. Instead, the discount (or premium) is commingled with the investment and will be amortized over the remaining life of the bond issue. Finally, observe that Foxmire paid $4,000 for accrued interest for the two months that have passed since January 1 ($\$300,000 \times 0.08 \times \frac{2}{12} = \$4,000$). The Bond Interest Receivable account is debited, because Foxmire expects to collect the interest from Harkness at a later date.

## Bond Interest Revenue

The periodic interest receipts normally represent the primary source of revenue related to a bond investment. Continuing our previous example, suppose it is now June 30 and Foxmire receives the first semiannual interest payment of $12,000 ($\$300,000 \times 0.08 \times \frac{6}{12}$). Because two months of this interest ($4,000) was recorded as Bond Interest Receivable on March 1, the following entry is necessary:

| | | | |
|---|---|---|---|
| June 30 | Cash | 12,000 | |
| | Bond Interest Receivable | | 4,000 |
| | Bond Interest Revenue | | 8,000 |
| | To record the receipt of semiannual interest | | |

The $8,000 credit shows that Foxmire has earned interest for only four months (March 1–June 30)—the length of time the company has owned the securities.

Assuming a calendar year reporting period, future interest receipts would be recorded in their entirety in the Bond Interest Revenue account.

## Bond Discounts

As we illustrated in Chapter 17, bond discounts and premiums respectively increase and decrease the interest expense incurred by the issuing corporation. Similarly, discounts and premiums also affect the interest earned by the investor. In Foxmire's case, for example, the bonds were acquired below their $300,000 face value, thus giving rise to a $37,009 discount ($300,000 − $262,991). As the following computations show, the discount raises the firm's investment income above the total interest collected during the life of the bond issue:

| | | |
|---|---|---|
| Cash to be received | | |
| Interest receipts over 10 years ($300,000 × 0.08 × 10 years) | $240,000 | |
| Face value at maturity | 300,000 | $540,000 |
| Cash paid for investment | | |
| Purchase price | $262,991 | |
| Accrued interest | 4,000 | 266,991 |
| Income from investment | | $273,009 |

The $273,009 of investment income is deemed interest because it is generated on money that has been lent to Harkness.

***Discount Amortization*** In addition to the cash interest received, Foxmire must gradually recognize income from the discount. This income can be derived by using the effective-interest amortization process described earlier in the text.[1] The proper accounting procedures are slightly different, however, because of the manner in which the discount was initially recorded.

Under the effective-interest method, the amount of amortization to recognize each period is determined by a two-step process:

**1** Multiply the bonds' carrying value by the effective interest rate to figure total interest revenue.

**2** Compute amortization as the difference between the amount of interest revenue calculated in Step 1 and the cash received for interest.

In the Foxmire illustration, for instance, the bonds have an initial carrying value of $262,991. Although this amount was given as part of the example's original data on page 623, it would actually be derived by discounting the future cash flows related to the bond issue. Assume for the sake of simplicity that the discounting process generated an effective yield to investors of 10%. In view of this new information, we can now compute the amortization to be recorded on June 30—the first semiannual interest date.

Observe that four months have passed since Foxmire's acquisition on March 1. Total interest revenue for this period, Step 1 of the process, is $8,766 ($262,991 ×

[1] The straight-line amortization method is also acceptable if the results obtained do not differ significantly from those achieved with the effective-interest method. The latter approach is conceptually superior and will be utilized throughout the chapter.

$0.10 \times \frac{4}{12}$). During this same period, the company's *net* cash flow from interest amounted to $8,000:

| | |
|---|---|
| Receipts on June 30 | $12,000 |
| Less: Accrued interest paid to Harkness on March 1 | 4,000 |
| Net cash flow from interest | $ 8,000 |

As described in Step 2, the amortization to be recorded is thus $766 ($8,766 − $8,000), giving rise to the following journal entry:

| | | | |
|---|---|---|---|
| June 30 | Investment in Bonds | 766 | |
| | Bond Interest Revenue | | 766 |
| | To record discount amortization | | |

The entry's credit is logical because, as shown earlier, a discount increases investment income above the cash amounts received for interest. The debit to Investment in Bonds is not as easily understood. Keep in mind that Foxmire's discount is included in the Investment account. *For illustrative purposes only,* assume that the discount had been recorded separately. The amortization entry on June 30 would therefore have had the following impact:

| *Account* | *As of Acquisition* | *Amortization* | *As of June 30* |
|---|---|---|---|
| Investment in bonds | $300,000 | $ — | $300,000 |
| Less: Discount on bond investment | 37,009 | 766 | 36,243 |
| | $262,991 | $766 | $263,757 |

The net result is a $766 rise in the investment's carrying value. To enter this increase in the accounting records, the amortization entry must appropriately debit the Investment in Bonds account.

Continuing the example, the interest revenue to recognize on December 31, the next semiannual interest date, will be $13,188 ($263,757 $\times$ 0.10 $\times \frac{6}{12}$). Because the semiannual cash receipt from Harkness will again amount to $12,000 ($300,000 $\times$ 0.08 $\times \frac{6}{12}$), the proper amortization figure is $1,188 ($13,188 − $12,000). The amortization process will continue over the life of the bond issue, with the carrying value increasing to $300,000 on the bonds' scheduled maturity date. More detailed illustrations of effective-interest amortization (as related to bonds payable) can be found in Chapter 17.

## Premium Amortization

Although our example has focused on the acquisition of bonds at a discount, similar procedures are followed for bonds purchased at a price in excess of face value, that is, at a premium. The investment is still entered in the accounting records at cost. However, a premium has the opposite effect of a discount and reduces interest income over the life of the issue. The premium must therefore be amortized by means of this entry:

| | | |
|---|---|---|
| Bond Interest Revenue | XXX | |
| Investment in Bonds | | XXX |
| To record premium amortization | | |

The debit records the reduction in interest revenue, while the credit lowers the Investment in Bonds account. Eventually, the Investment account will equal the face value of the bonds acquired.

The amortization computations are obtained by using the two-step process described earlier for bonds acquired at a discount. In Step 2, however, the cash received from interest will now exceed the interest revenue figure. In view of this situation, the difference between these two amounts (i.e., the period's amortization) is subtracted from bond carrying value rather than added.

### Sale of Bonds Before Maturity

Because of other investment opportunities or perhaps favorable conditions in the bond market, long-term bond investments are often sold prior to their scheduled maturity date. When the sale occurs, it is necessary to update amortization to the date of disposal. This procedure is required to ensure that the correct amount of interest revenue has been recorded and also to determine the investment's carrying value as of the sale date.

To focus on the required accounting, let us return to the Foxmire Corporation example. Suppose that Foxmire sold its investment in Harkness bonds on August 31, 19X3. Recall that the company amortizes the discount on each semiannual interest date, resulting in a carrying value of $268,877 on June 30, 19X3. We will assume that all journal entries through June 30 have been properly prepared.

Because two months have passed since amortization was last recorded, Foxmire must update the accounts in the following manner:

| | | | |
|---|---|---|---|
| Aug. 31 | Investment in Bonds | 481 | |
| | Bond Interest Revenue | | 481 |
| | To record two months of discount amortization [($268,877 × 0.10 × $\frac{2}{12}$) − ($300,000 × 0.08 × $\frac{2}{12}$)] | | |

The entry causes an increase in the investment's carrying value to $269,358 ($268,877 + $481).

If the bonds were sold at 102 plus accrued interest, the following entry would be needed to record the sale and eliminate the investment from the books:

| | | | |
|---|---|---|---|
| Aug. 31 | Cash | 310,000 | |
| | Investment in Bonds | | 269,358 |
| | Bond Interest Revenue | | 4,000 |
| | Gain on Sale of Bonds | | 36,642 |
| | To record sale of bond investment | | |

Foxmire has generated $310,000 of cash from the transaction, composed of a $306,000 sale price ($300,000 × 1.02) and $4,000 of accrued interest ($300,000 × 0.08 × $\frac{2}{12}$). The gain arises because the bonds' selling price exceeds the investment's carrying value ($269,358); had the situation been reversed, a loss would have been recorded.

## Investments in Stock

In addition to purchasing bonds, companies can also invest in the capital stock of other entities. Like bonds, stock investments are initially entered in the accounts at cost, namely, the purchase price plus any other necessary expenditures related to acquisition (e.g., brokers' fees). Subsequent to the initial recording, the accounting treatment to be used depends on the degree of control that can be exerted over the company whose shares were acquired (known as the **investee**). Generally speaking, the degree of control is influenced by the percentage of the investee's common stock owned by the investor.

Three accounting/reporting methods have been developed: (1) lower of cost or market, (2) equity, and (3) consolidated financial statements. The use of these methods is summarized in Exhibit 18-2.[2] The underlying details of the exhibit, along with the meaning of influence and control, will become apparent in the upcoming presentation.

**OBJECTIVE 2**
**Understand accounting for stock investments with the lower-of-cost-or-market and the equity methods.**

## Lower-of-Cost-or-Market Method

The **lower-of-cost-or-market method** is used to account for long-term stock acquisitions of investors who are unable to exercise significant influence over the investee corporation. The ability to exert influence over an entity may take several different forms, including ownership of a sizable percentage of the investee's outstanding common shares, representation on the investee's board of directors, participation in policymaking processes, interchange of managerial personnel, and technological dependency. In many instances the determination of whether an investor can influence an investee is not always clear. To provide some uniformity in practice, the accounting profession has recommended that "an investment of less than 20% of the voting stock of an investee should lead to a presumption that an investor does not have the ability to exercise significant influence unless such ability can be demonstrated."[3]

Under the lower-of-cost-or-market method, stock investments are initially entered in the accounting records at cost. Any dividends received from the investment during the reporting period are recorded as revenue. Furthermore, changes in the value of the securities (subject to certain limits) are recognized and recorded in the accounts by comparing an investment portfolio's aggregate market value against its cost. If this cost-versus-market comparison sounds familiar, the technique is similar to that discussed earlier in the text for short-term investments. Should you need a refresher, refer to Chapter 7.

To illustrate the lower-of-cost-or-market method, assume the following information relates to Savko Company:

- On January 1, Savko purchased 15,000 common shares of Fresno Manufacturing Corporation at $30 per share. Fresno has 150,000 shares of common stock outstanding.

| *Percentage of Investee Corporation Owned* | *Presumed Degree of Influence Over Investee* | *Accounting/Reporting Method* |
|---|---|---|
| Less than 20% | No significant influence | Lower of cost or market |
| From 20% to 50% | Significant influence | Equity |
| Greater than 50% | Controlling interest | Consolidated statements |

**Exhibit 18-2**
**Use of Accounting/Reporting Methods**

[2] See "The Equity Method of Accounting for Investments in Common Stock," *Opinions of the Accounting Principles Board No. 18* (New York: American Institute of Certified Public Accountants, 1971).

[3] Ibid., paragraph 17.

- During the year Fresno reported net income of $290,000 and paid $120,000 of dividends.
- On December 31, the close of Savko's accounting year, Fresno's common stock had a market value of $27 per share.

Given that Savko owns 10% of Fresno (15,000 shares ÷ 150,000 shares), the following entries are necessary to record the previously mentioned transactions and events:

***Investment by Savko***

| | | |
|---|---|---|
| Investment in Fresno Manufacturing | 450,000 | |
| Cash | | 450,000 |
| To record the acquisition of 15,000 shares of Fresno at $30 per share | | |

***Announcement of Fresno's earnings of $290,000***

No entry required

***Receipt of cash dividends***

| | | |
|---|---|---|
| Cash | 12,000 | |
| Dividend Revenue | | 12,000 |
| To record the receipt of 10% of Fresno's dividends | | |

***Valuation at lower of cost or market on December 31****

| | | |
|---|---|---|
| Unrealized Loss on Long-term Investments† | 45,000 | |
| Allowance for Decline in Market Value of Long-term Investments | | 45,000 |
| To reduce the investment in Fresno to market value: ($30 − $27) × 15,000 shares | | |

* For simplicity we will assume that Fresno is the only long-term investment owned by Savko.

† According to a ruling of the Financial Accounting Standards Board, unrealized gains and losses on *long-term* investments are not included in the current year's net income. Unrealized losses related to such investments are shown on the balance sheet as a reduction of stockholders' equity.

On the basis of these entries, Savko's investment would appear as follows on the year-end balance sheet:

| | | |
|---|---|---|
| Long-term investments | | |
| Investment in Fresno Manufacturing | $450,000 | |
| Less: Allowance for decline in market value of long-term investments | 45,000 | $405,000 |

## Equity Method

When a company acquires a substantial percentage (20% or more) of the voting shares of a corporation, the acquiring firm normally gains the ability to significantly influence both the financial and the operating policies of the investee. In such instances, unless there is evidence to the contrary, a material economic relationship is formed between the investor and investee and the **equity method** of accounting must be used.

Under the equity method, long-term investments in common stock are initially recorded at acquisition cost. The Investment account is then increased or decreased to reflect changes in the retained earnings of the investee. Specifically, the Investment account is increased for the investor's share of reported investee net income and decreased for the investor's share of any investee net losses or dividends. The "investor's share" is based on the percentage of voting stock owned; the income, loss, and dividend amounts relate strictly to periods after the stock is acquired. Realize that *the equity method focuses principally on changes in the investee's retained earnings, not changes in the market value of the investee's shares.*

To illustrate the equity method, we will use the same facts as in the previous example. Assume, however, that Savko purchased 45,000 shares of Fresno, resulting in a 30% ownership interest (45,000 shares ÷ 150,000 shares). Savko will use the equity method, which requires the following entries:

***Investment by Savko***

| | | |
|---|---|---|
| Investment in Fresno Manufacturing | 1,350,000 | |
| Cash | | 1,350,000 |
| To record the acquisition of 45,000 shares of Fresno at $30 per share | | |

***Announcement of Fresno's earnings of $290,000***

| | | |
|---|---|---|
| Investment in Fresno Manufacturing | 87,000 | |
| Investment Revenue | | 87,000 |
| To record 30% share of Fresno's earnings: $290,000 × 0.30 = $87,000 | | |

***Receipt of cash dividends***

| | | |
|---|---|---|
| Cash | 36,000 | |
| Investment in Fresno Manufacturing | | 36,000 |
| To record the receipt of cash dividends: $120,000 × 0.30 = $36,000 | | |

***Valuation at lower of cost or market on December 31***

No entry required

On the basis of these entries, Savko's investment would be reported on the year-end balance sheet at $1,401,000, as shown by the following T-account:

| *Investment in Fresno Manufacturing* | | | |
|---|---|---|---|
| Initial investment | 1,350,000 | Share of dividends | 36,000 |
| Share of income | 87,000 | | |
| (1,401,000) | **1,437,000** | | |

Observe that the $51,000 increase in the investment's carrying value (after the initial acquisition) corresponds to 30% of the increase in Fresno's Retained Earnings account [($290,000 net income − $120,000 dividends) × 0.30 = $51,000]. Also notice that Savko did not recognize any revenue at the time the dividend was received. Although this procedure may seem illogical, bear in mind that (1) dividends represent a distribution of earnings and (2) Savko has already recognized $87,000 of Fresno's net income. If the dividends were recorded as additional revenue, they would be double-counted. Appropriately, then, the Investment account is reduced because the dividend has decreased Savko's share of Fresno's net worth (i.e., retained earnings).

## Rationale for the Equity Method

As we have shown on numerous occasions throughout this text, financial statements are used by a number of different parties (e.g., owners, managers, and creditors, to name just a few). To meet the varied needs of these groups, the statements must be objective and neutral. Should bias be present, some users may benefit at the expense of others. For example, if management can manipulate revenue recognition to show higher earnings, creditors and investors may make incorrect decisions regarding the financial health and well-being of the enterprise. It is in this light that the equity method was developed.

Suppose for a moment that a company owned 40% of an investee corporation. Also assume that the investor company was experiencing abnormally low earnings, while the investee was extremely profitable. The investor, with significant influence over operations because of its ownership position, could convince the investee to distribute unusually large amounts of dividends. Had the equity method not been developed, the investor would report the dividends as revenue and thereby manipulate (i.e., control) its own profit. In situations where the ownership interest is 20% or more, the equity method presents a better picture of financial performance because such distributions do not affect investor earnings. Instead, these amounts are treated as a reduction in the Investment account.

## Controlling Investments

OBJECTIVE 3
Be familiar with parent/subsidiary relationships.

Thus far we have studied the prescribed accounting practices for companies that have minimal effect (i.e., less than 20% ownership) and those that have significant influence (i.e., from 20% to 50% ownership) on their investee corporations. We now turn our attention to a control type of relationship, that is, possession of more than 50% of the common shares outstanding. By exercising the voting rights connected with these shares, the investor can elect the board of directors of the investee corporation and thereby control the latter's policies and activities.

### Legal Versus Economic Entities

Given the relationship between the majority owner (termed the **parent**) and its majority-owned companies (termed **subsidiaries**), a question arises concerning the definition of the entity. For example, if Company A owns more than 50% of Companies B, C, and D, are four separate business units involved or is there just one large interwoven operation? To explore this issue more fully, we must become more specific. In our example we have four separate companies that operate as individual **legal entities**—units authorized by the relevant governmental authorities to conduct business. These firms engage in their own activities and prepare separate sets of financial statements. In reality, however, Companies B, C, and D are affiliated with Company A and together form a single **economic entity.** The relationship between the legal and the economic unit is shown in Exhibit 18-3.

The economic entity is assembled to pursue the objectives of operational efficiency and profit. As we noted earlier in the chapter, for example, many companies have controlling interests in other corporations to ensure themselves of a steady source of raw materials and supplies. General Motors, for instance, owns a firm engaged in providing financial services to customers and dealers (General Motors Acceptance Corporation). As another example, Southland Corporation, operator of the 7-Eleven convenience stores, has created various food processing and distribution firms.

General Motors and Southland are just two of the many organizations that have decided to operate separate subsidiaries rather than merge all activities into a single massive legal entity. The reasons behind this practice often include a savings in

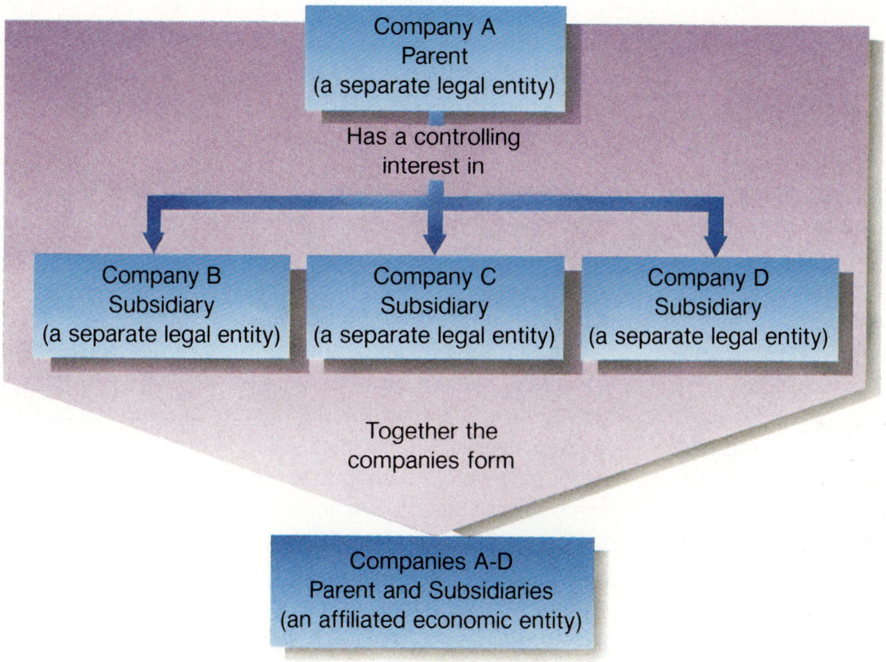


**Exhibit 18-3**
**Legal Versus Economic Entity**

income taxes, conformity with governmental regulation, and a reduction of risk. To explain the risk factor, should a particular subsidiary encounter financial difficulties, the separate entity could be sold or liquidated without having a significant impact on the other companies in the corporate group.

## Consolidated Financial Statements

OBJECTIVE 4
Understand the reason for consolidated financial statements, including the concepts of intercompany transactions and elimination entries.

Because of their separate legal status, a parent and its subsidiaries maintain individual accounting records and prepare separate sets of financial statements. Normally, however, the operating performance and financial position of the single economic entity are collectively reported to stockholders and other user groups via consolidated financial statements.

**Consolidated financial statements** present a combined picture of the parent and its controlled subsidiaries, as if only one company existed. On a consolidated balance sheet, for instance, the Cash account shows the total cash owned by the entire affiliated group; Accounts Payable reveals the total amounts owed to suppliers, and so forth. This same collective process applies to a consolidated income statement; for example, the balance in the Sales account represents the total sales revenues earned by a parent and its subsidiary firms.

Consolidated statements disclose the financial activities of the total enterprise, specifically, the activities that are under the parent's control. Furthermore, the statements provide more insight than could be gained by examining the separate statements of the various individual legal entities. Representative consolidated statements appear at the end of this text in Appendix B.

HIGHLIGHT

# Control-Type Investments and a People Problem

Companies seek controlling interests in other businesses for a variety of reasons. Millions of dollars are normally involved in merger activities, so it is only after a thorough financial analysis that the decision is made to acquire another entity. What looks good on paper, though, often turns out to be a disaster. How can it miss, especially when the transaction is characterized by synergy—the perfect meshing of two distinct enterprises to create a more competitive force in the marketplace?

A Massachusetts-based consultant figures at least 75% of all corporate marriages fail to fulfill desired objectives. "There've been a lot of bum deals . . . ," he says. In fact, during the last few years the number of split-ups resulting from poor matches have been rising steadily, about 37% annually. Although there are many reasons for merger failure, an important one is people. Stated simply, there is often a mass exodus of top executives and personnel after the papers are signed.

All too often, the acquiring companies fail to realize the importance of personnel as an asset. United Technologies learned the hard way when the firm paid generously to buy out semiconductor pioneer Mostek. United found that it had taken over a company deprived of its finest intellectual properties—the founding engineers and executives. They had left in a flurry for new and exciting ventures. Such occurrences are typical, especially in high-tech enterprises, which are commonly created and built by entrepreneurial-minded management teams. When such companies are acquired by larger corporations, the management teams tend to leave en masse. And with them goes much of the value of the company they built.

Management turnover is a chronic problem that plagues acquisitions. Notes a spokesman for a leading New York executive recruiting firm, "Executives have less incentive to stay around these days. Why shouldn't they take advantage of increasingly generous severance packages and bail out?" Interestingly, the recruiting firm studied companies that were among the largest 150 corporate acquisitions during a recent period and found that within three years after the transaction took place, 75% of the managers had left their jobs.

Part of the reason for such turnover is that sometimes, corporate cultures just don't mix. When high-tech defense contractor LTV snapped up a number of steel plants, its white-collar work force found itself in a culture warp. "Suddenly we were lumped in with big labor interests in some remote steel towns in Pennsylvania and Alabama," says one LTV engineer. "There was no way we could relate to them nor they to us." A side note: Largely because of these steel acquisitions, although other factors were certainly involved, LTV was forced to file for bankruptcy.

In sum, when one company seeks a controlling interest in another firm, a definite people problem does arise. As the following statistics show, we cannot just concentrate on the accounting and financial aspects of the combination. We must also consider the human aspect; without highly motivated executives and the proper management team in place, a corporate marriage will simply not survive.

**THE MERGER AFTERMATH: AN EXECUTIVE VIEWPOINT**

| | ***Executives Who Left*** | ***Executives Who Stayed*** |
|---|---|---|
| Acquisition described as: | | |
| Friendly takeover | 33% | 70% |
| Hostile takeover | 55 | 25 |
| Other | 12 | 5 |
| Mergers appeared to: | | |
| Create executive jobs | 3 | 5 |
| Eliminate executive jobs | 97 | 95 |

SOURCE: Adapted from "Megamerger Aftermath: Great Expectations Turn Up Short," Dallas, Inc., section of the *Dallas Times Herald*, May 19–25, 1986, pp. 12–13. 

## Intercompany Transactions

Companies within an affiliated group frequently have transactions with one another. Parent firms often purchase materials and supplies from their subsidiaries. In addition, a parent will commonly lend money to a subsidiary to help finance operations or capital improvement programs. Such transactions, referred to as **intercompany transactions,** present no special accounting problems for the individual entities involved. When consolidated financial statements are prepared, however, it is an entirely different story.

As an example, assume Parent Company owns a controlling interest of Sub Company. Sub is in need of funds and borrows $100,000 from Parent by signing a note payable. The transaction would appear on the balance sheets of both enterprises in the following manner:

| PARENT COMPANY Balance Sheet | |
|---|---|
| Assets | |
| Notes receivable | $100,000 |

| SUB COMPANY Balance Sheet | |
|---|---|
| Liabilities | |
| Notes payable | $100,000 |

Suppose that a consolidated balance sheet of the two companies is now desired. If the two balance sheets were merely added together to reflect the financial position of the combined entity, the results would be misleading. Put simply, the combined entity would report that it expects to both receive and pay $100,000 in the near future. Actually, this disclosure is incorrect because the $100,000 represents an expected transfer of cash from Sub to Parent, both of which are in the same economic unit.

**TIPS & TECHNIQUES**

Expanding further on our illustration, we emphasize that the combined unit does not have a claim on an outside party, nor does the unit owe an outsider. To properly reflect the impact of this transaction on the Parent/Sub affiliation, neither the note receivable nor the note payable should appear on the companies' consolidated balance sheet.

## Work Sheet and Eliminations

When constructing the consolidated financial statements, the accountant first prepares a formal work sheet to combine the account balances of the parent and its subsidiary companies. Although the amounts are merged on the work sheet, combined accounting records are *not* established in a ledger.

As we will soon illustrate, most work sheets have two columns that are used for eliminations. **Eliminations** are required for intercompany items contained in the records of the parent and subsidiaries that do not appear in the consolidated financial statements, for example, the note receivable and note payable cited earlier. The elimination is performed by making an entry on the work sheet that debits intercompany credit balances and credits intercompany debit balances. To illustrate, the elimination entry that follows is needed for the $100,000 note.

| | | |
|---|---|---|
| Notes Payable (Sub) | 100,000 | |
| Notes Receivable (Parent) | | 100,000 |
| To eliminate intercompany receivable and payable | | |

We stress that eliminations are made on the work sheet only; they are *never* entered in the accounts of either a parent or its subsidiaries. Entries into the accounts would formally (and erroneously) cancel the transactions between the companies.

## Consolidation upon Acquisition

OBJECTIVE 5
Be able to prepare consolidated financial statements immediately after acquisition.

To demonstrate the consolidation process, consider the balance sheets of Engle Corporation and Grant, Inc., that appear in Exhibit 18-4. On January 1, 19X2, Engle acquired 100% of Grant's outstanding stock from existing shareholders for $175,000—the stock's book value. Engle will record the acquisition as follows:

| | | | |
|---|---|---|---|
| Jan. 1 | Investment in Grant | 175,000 | |
| | Cash | | 175,000 |
| | To record the acquisition of 100% of Grant, Inc. | | |

The only effect of this transaction on Engle's accounting records is the exchange of one asset, Cash, for another (Investment in Grant, Inc.). The Investment account is established in Engle's ledger and will be maintained under the equity method of accounting, as described in an earlier section of this chapter.[4] Grant's books are unaffected, because the exchange of outstanding shares among stockholders has no impact on the issuing firm. The balance sheets of the two companies immediately after the acquisition appear in the first two columns of the work sheet contained in Exhibit 18-5.

**Exhibit 18-4**
**Balance Sheets of Engle Corporation and Grant, Inc. (as of December 31, 19X1)**

| | *Engle* | *Grant* |
|---|---|---|
| Cash | $ 400,000 | $ 25,000 |
| Accounts receivable (net) | 600,000 | 30,000 |
| Inventories | 800,000 | 40,000 |
| Property, plant, & equipment (net) | 1,500,000 | 230,000 |
| Total assets | $3,300,000 | $325,000 |
| Accounts payable | $ 300,000 | $ 60,000 |
| Bonds payable | 1,300,000 | 90,000 |
| Common stock | 1,000,000 | 100,000 |
| Retained earnings | 700,000 | 75,000 |
| Total liabilities & stockholders' equity | $3,300,000 | $325,000 |

[4] When consolidated financial statements are prepared, the parent may employ an alternative practice (called the cost method) to maintain the Investment in Subsidiary Company account. Because the same consolidated results can be derived from either approach, we will assume use of the equity method to simplify our discussion.

**ENGLE AND GRANT**
**Consolidated Balance Sheet Work Sheet**
**January 1, 19X2**

| Account | Engle | Grant | Intercompany Eliminations | | Consolidated Balance Sheet |
|---|---|---|---|---|---|
| | | | Debit | Credit | |
| Cash | 225,000* | 25,000 | | | 250,000 |
| Accounts receivable (net) | 600,000 | 30,000 | | | 630,000 |
| Inventories | 800,000 | 40,000 | | | 840,000 |
| Investment in Grant | 175,000 | | | (a) 175,000 | |
| Property, plant, & equipment (net) | 1,500,000 | 230,000 | | | 1,730,000 |
| | 3,300,000 | 325,000 | | | 3,450,000 |
| Accounts payable | 300,000 | 60,000 | | | 360,000 |
| Bonds payable | 1,300,000 | 90,000 | | | 1,390,000 |
| Common stock: Engle | 1,000,000 | | | | 1,000,000 |
| Common stock: Grant | | 100,000 | (a) 100,000 | | |
| Retained earnings: Engle | 700,000 | | | | 700,000 |
| Retained earnings: Grant | | 75,000 | (a) 75,000 | | |
| | 3,300,000 | 325,000 | 175,000 | 175,000 | 3,450,000 |

* $400,000 original balance minus $175,000 acquisition cost.

**Exhibit 18-5**

***The Investment Elimination*** As Exhibit 18-5 reveals, an intercompany transaction must be eliminated in order to prepare the consolidated balance sheet. The color numbers in the first two columns show that the $175,000 investment by Engle (a 100% ownership interest) is represented by Grant's stockholders' equity accounts of Common Stock ($100,000) and Retained Earnings ($75,000). Stated differently, since Engle owns 100% of Grant, all common stock financing of the combined entity is provided by Engle's shareholders. Thus, if the stockholders' equity accounts of the parent and subsidiary were simply combined on a consolidated statement, the financing provided by Engle's investors and operations (i.e., retained earnings) would be overstated. For these reasons the Investment account must be eliminated (via a credit because it has a debit balance), along with Grant's Common Stock and Retained Earnings accounts (via debits because they possess credit balances).

The result is a consolidated balance sheet—the combination of Engle and Grant's individual balance sheets minus the elimination. The information that appears in the right-hand column of the work sheet is recast as shown in Exhibit 18-6. The consolidated financial statement reveals that the combined entity has $3.45 million of assets, owes $1.75 million to outside creditors, and has $1.7 million of stockholders' equity, the last amount being provided solely by Engle Corporation.

Exhibit 18-6

**ENGLE AND GRANT**
**Consolidated Balance Sheet**
**January 1, 19X2**

| *Assets* | | |
|---|---|---|
| Current assets | | |
| Cash | | $ 250,000 |
| Accounts receivable (net) | | 630,000 |
| Inventories | | 840,000 |
| Total current assets | | $1,720,000 |
| Property, plant, & equipment (net) | | 1,730,000 |
| Total assets | | $3,450,000 |
| ***Liabilities & Stockholders' Equity*** | | |
| Current liabilities | | |
| Accounts payable | | $ 360,000 |
| Long-term liabilities | | |
| Bonds payable | | 1,390,000 |
| Total liabilities | | $1,750,000 |
| Stockholders' equity | | |
| Common stock | $1,000,000 | |
| Retained earnings | 700,000 | |
| Total stockholders' equity | | 1,700,000 |
| Total liabilities & stockholders' equity | | $3,450,000 |

## Minority Interest

OBJECTIVE 6
Understand how to account for minority interests.

To obtain control of a subsidiary, the parent need not acquire a 100% ownership interest as in the previous example. Acquisitions of more than 50% but less than 100% of the outstanding voting stock of other corporations are frequent in occurrence. In such cases the parent company is said to obtain a majority interest, while the other owners of the subsidiary have a **minority interest.**

To illustrate the proper accounting for a minority interest, we will modify the Engle/Grant example. Recall that Grant had $100,000 of common stock and $75,000 of retained earnings as of December 31, 19X1. Assume now that Engle purchases an 80% interest in Grant for $140,000, the purchase price corresponding to the book value of Grant's stock ($175,000 × 0.80 = $140,000). Engle will record the acquisition by the following entry:

| | | Debit | Credit |
|---|---|---|---|
| Jan. 1 | Investment in Grant | 140,000 | |
| | Cash | | 140,000 |
| | To record the acquisition of 80% of Grant, Inc. | | |

The companies' ownership position is shown in Exhibit 18-7. Since Engle owns 80% of Grant, 80% of the subsidiary's common stock and retained earnings balances are eliminated when consolidated financial statements are prepared. The remaining 20% of Grant's ownership represents the minority interest and is listed as such on the consolidated balance sheet (see Exhibit 18-8).

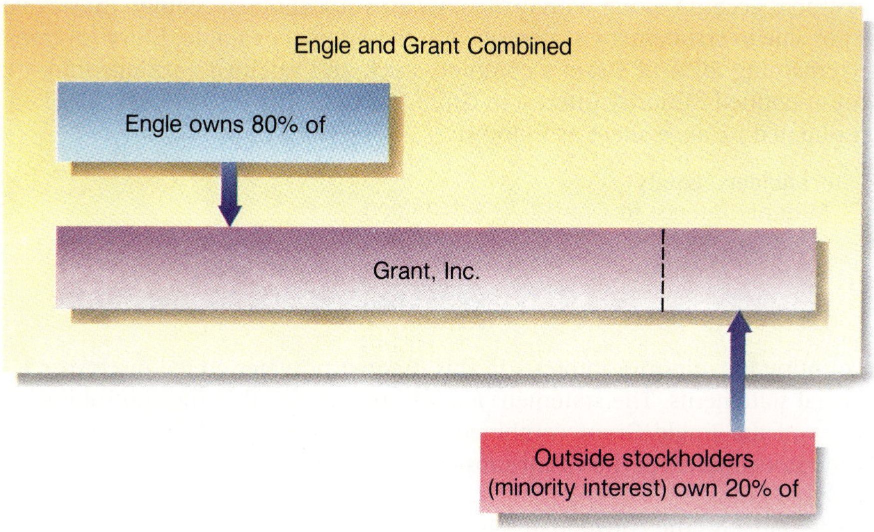


**Exhibit 18-7**
**Illustration of Minority Interest**

**Exhibit 18-8**

**ENGLE AND GRANT**
**Consolidated Balance Sheet Work Sheet**
**January 1, 19X2**

| Account | Engle | Grant | Intercompany Eliminations Debit | Intercompany Eliminations Credit | Consolidated Balance Sheet |
|---|---|---|---|---|---|
| Cash | 260,000* | 25,000 | | | 285,000 |
| Accounts receivable (net) | 600,000 | 30,000 | | | 630,000 |
| Inventories | 800,000 | 40,000 | | | 840,000 |
| Investment in Grant | 140,000 | | | (a) 140,000 | |
| Property, plant, & equipment (net) | 1,500,000 | 230,000 | | | 1,730,000 |
| | 3,300,000 | 325,000 | | | 3,485,000 |
| Accounts payable | 300,000 | 60,000 | | | 360,000 |
| Bonds payable | 1,300,000 | 90,000 | | | 1,390,000 |
| Common stock: Engle | 1,000,000 | | | | 1,000,000 |
| Common stock: Grant | | 100,000 | (a) 80,000<br>(b) 20,000 | | |
| Retained earnings: Engle | 700,000 | | | | 700,000 |
| Retained earnings: Grant | | 75,000 | (a) 60,000<br>(b) 15,000 | | |
| Minority interest in Grant | | | | (b) 35,000 | 35,000 |
| | 3,300,000 | 325,000 | 175,000 | 175,000 | 3,485,000 |

* $400,000 original balance minus $140,000 acquisition cost.

The work sheet contains two elimination entries. Entry (*a*) eliminates Engle's investment account along with 80% of Grant's stockholders' equity, thus avoiding the possible overstatement as described in the original example. Entry (*b*) transfers the remaining 20% of Grant's common stock and retained earnings into a new account entitled Minority Interest in Grant. The minority interest is reported on the consolidated balance sheet as follows:

| Stockholders' equity | |
|---|---|
| Minority interest in Grant | $ 35,000 |
| Common stock | 1,000,000 |
| Retained earnings | 700,000 |
| | $1,735,000 |

Accounting for minority interests in this manner provides added disclosure in the financial statements. The statement reader can now see that the controlling stockholders of the Engle/Grant combined entity have equity of $1.7 million, while outside stockholders of the Grant subsidiary have equity (i.e., claims against Grant) of only $35,000.

Alternatively, the consolidated balance sheets of some corporations report the minority interest between the liability and stockholders' equity sections. Companies that follow this practice are stressing the limited role of the minority interest in ownership affairs.

## Acquisition of Subsidiary at More or Less than Book Value

**OBJECTIVE 7**
**Be able to account for subsidiaries acquired at a cost in excess of book value.**

In all of our illustrations thus far, we have assumed the amount paid by the parent was equal to the book value of the ownership interest acquired. In the preceding example, for instance, Engle paid $140,000 to purchase 80% of Grant's $175,000 stockholders' equity ($175,000 × 0.80 = $140,000). Normally, the acquisition cost of a subsidiary does not coincide with the subsidiary's book value.

Remember from Chapter 15 that book value represents a company's net assets (assets minus liabilities) and is calculated on figures extracted from the balance sheet—a cost-based financial statement. Given the impact of inflation in our economy, asset valuations and book value are frequently understated and do not reflect current market values. Adding to this problem, an ongoing business often has a number of "unrecorded assets" that a purchaser is willing to pay for and acquire. As an example, a corporation's established reputation among clientele, its ability to earn greater-than-normal profits, and the company's top management team all enable a buyer to begin operations in a favorable position. Finally, a business may have something of vital interest to a purchaser such as valuable patents or established product markets. Collectively, the foregoing factors all contribute to the fact that subsidiaries are often acquired at a price in excess of book value. Sometimes, the difference between cost and book value is substantial. Caesars World, for example, reports a cost nearly $44 million in excess of book amounts on the purchase of its Caesars Palace hotel operation in Las Vegas.

***An Example*** To illustrate the necessary accounting in this type of situation, assume Stafford Corporation acquired a 100% controlling interest in Trout, Inc., for $260,000 on December 31, 19XX. The balance sheets of both companies immediately *after* the acquisition are shown in Exhibit 18-9.

Stafford has paid $260,000 for a company having a book value (i.e., stockholders' equity) of $200,000. Why? Assume that during negotiations for the acquisi-

**Exhibit 18-9**
**Balance Sheets of Stafford Corporation and Trout, Inc. (as of December 31, 19XX)**

| | *Stafford* | *Trout* |
|---|---|---|
| Cash and other assets | $ 90,000 | $ 70,000 |
| Property, plant, & equipment (net) | 140,000 | 180,000 |
| Investment in Trout | 260,000 | — |
| Total assets | $490,000 | $250,000 |
| Accounts payable | $ 60,000 | $ 50,000 |
| Common stock | 250,000 | 160,000 |
| Retained earnings | 180,000 | 40,000 |
| Total liabilities & stockholders' equity | $490,000 | $250,000 |

tion, Stafford's management found that Trout's property, plant, and equipment was undervalued by $35,000. In addition, Stafford was willing to pay an extra $25,000 because of favorable forecasts of Trout's future earnings and Trout's leadership position in its field of operation. To summarize, the $260,000 investment is represented by the following:

| | |
|---|---|
| 100% ownership interest | |
| Common stock: Trout | $160,000 |
| Retained earnings: Trout | 40,000 |
| Increase in property, plant, & equipment (net) | 35,000 |
| Favorable earnings prospects, reputation, and so on | 25,000 |
| | $260,000 |

In the preparation of a consolidated balance sheet, the following work sheet elimination entry is needed:

| | | |
|---|---|---|
| Common Stock: Trout | 160,000 | |
| Retained Earnings: Trout | 40,000 | |
| Property, Plant, & Equipment | 35,000 | |
| Goodwill | 25,000 | |
| Investment in Trout | | 260,000 |
| To eliminate Trout's stockholders' equity accounts against the Investment account and to revalue the assets acquired | | |

The entry first offsets the stockholders' equity accounts of Trout against Stafford's $260,000 investment. Furthermore, since Stafford paid an additional $35,000 to acquire the subsidiary's plant and equipment, the Property, Plant, & Equipment account is debited to reflect the increased cost. Finally, favorable earnings prospects, reputation, good management, and other similar factors collectively give rise to the intangible asset *goodwill,* requiring a $25,000 debit to that account. The preceding treatment is in accordance with a ruling of the accounting profession, which states that "the excess of the cost of the acquired company over the sum of the amounts assigned to identifiable assets acquired less liabilities assumed should be recorded as goodwill."[5] Rather than debit Goodwill, a firm will some-

[5] "Accounting for Business Combinations," *Opinions of the Accounting Principles Board No. 16* (New York: American Institute of Certified Public Accountants, 1970), paragraph 87.

times use a more descriptive account title such as Excess of Cost over Book Value in Subsidiary.

The net result of the elimination is the consolidated balance sheet that appears in Exhibit 18-10.

***Book Value in Excess of Cost*** Our example has focused on the case of when a parent pays more than the book value of the subsidiary acquired. The opposite situation, book value greater than cost, is not encountered as frequently in practice. The necessary accounting treatment is somewhat similar to that just illustrated. Because of added complexities, however, discussion of the required procedures is appropriately postponed to advanced-level courses.

## Consolidated Income Statement

A consolidated income statement is prepared in much the same fashion as a consolidated balance sheet. Revenue and expense accounts of the parent and subsidiaries are combined, and intercompany transactions are eliminated. The eliminations allow statement users to analyze the consolidated entity's profit- (or loss-) generating activities with outsiders as opposed to those activities that occur solely within the affiliated company network.

As an example, consider a corporation that is engaged in the manufacture and sale of motion picture films. The corporation has established two separate entities: production and marketing. Production sells its entire output to marketing, which, in turn, distributes the films to movie theaters and other outside establishments. It is apparent that marketing is the true generator of sales revenues for the corpora-

**Exhibit 18-10**

**STAFFORD AND TROUT**
**Consolidated Balance Sheet**
**December 31, 19XX**

| | | |
|---|---|---|
| ***Assets*** | | |
| Cash and other assets | | $160,000 |
| Property, plant, & equipment (net) | | 355,000* |
| Goodwill | | 25,000 |
| Total assets | | $540,000 |
| ***Liabilities & Stockholders' Equity*** | | |
| Current liabilities | | |
| Accounts payable | | $110,000 |
| Stockholders' equity | | |
| Common stock | $250,000 | |
| Retained earnings | 180,000 | |
| Total stockholders' equity | | 430,000 |
| Total liabilities & stockholders' equity | | $540,000 |

* $140,000 + $180,000 + $35,000 = $355,000.

tion, with production's revenues being strictly intercompany. Unless an elimination entry is made in the preparation of the consolidated income statement, the combination of the two Sales accounts would present an incorrect picture of corporate revenues and net income.

Two typical transactions that require an elimination entry are intercompany sales and interest on loans (or other obligations) between the parent and the subsidiary. When analyzing these transactions, keep in mind that a sale by one affiliate is represented by a purchase or, if the merchandise is sold, by cost of goods sold on another affiliate's records. Similarly, interest revenue for one member of the consolidated entity becomes interest expense for another. The necessary eliminations that underlie the preparation of a consolidated income statement can become quite complicated and are clearly beyond the scope of this text.

## Stock Investments: A Brief Overview

Although our presentation of long-term stock investments has focused on basic concepts only, you may have found this material to be somewhat detailed and complex. In an effort to briefly summarize the foregoing pages, we will study Moore Enterprises, which owns stock in several different companies. These companies and the percentage of shares owned are: A, 15%; B, 30%; C, 60%; and D, 100%. From the preceding data, you are to determine:

1 The method used to account for each investee company (i.e., lower-of-cost-or-market or equity), and
2 Whether the investee's operations should be consolidated with those of Moore.

The answers appear in the tabulation that follows; however, make an honest attempt at deriving the solutions before viewing the proper responses.

| *Company* | *Method Used to Account for Investee* | *Consolidated with Moore?* |
|---|---|---|
| A | Lower of cost or market* | No, lack of control |
| B | Equity | No, lack of control |
| C | Equity† | Yes, possess control |
| D | Equity† | Yes, possess control |

* Less than 20% ownership.
† See footnote 4 on page 634.

The next part of the review is more difficult. Determine the proper disclosure of each investee on Moore's balance sheet. Keep in mind that in some cases the financial activities of the investee have been consolidated with those of Moore; in other cases they have not. The correct responses appear in Exhibit 18-11.

## An Addendum: Purchase Versus Pooling of Interests

OBJECTIVE 8
Understand the differences between purchase and pooling-of-interests accounting.

In all of our illustrations the subsidiary ownership interest has been obtained for cash. When acquisitions are complex, the payment of cash is sometimes supplemented with notes payable and even shares of stock of the acquiring company. The form of the transaction is important when determining the proper accounting treatment. Most business combinations are treated as if a **purchase** has occurred. That is, (1) a parent has purchased an interest in a subsidiary by obtaining shares of

**Exhibit 18-11 Disclosure of Moore Investees**

| *Company* | | | |
|---|---|---|---|
| A | Investment in A | $XXX | |
| | Less: Allowance for decline in market value | XXX | $XXX |
| B | Investment in B | | $XXX |
| C | Minority interest in C | | $XXX |
| | The Investment account has been eliminated against 60% of the subsidiary's stockholders' equity. The remaining 40% is replaced with a Minority Interest account.* | | |
| D | ——— | | $— |
| | The Investment account has been eliminated along with 100% of the subsidiary's stockholders' equity; no minority interest exists.* | | |

* Subsidiary asset and liability accounts would be combined with Moore's assets and liabilities.

the subsidiary's stock, and (2) the subsidiary's stockholders have terminated their investment by selling their shares to the parent.

Although the foregoing may appear clear-cut, an accounting problem arises when one company exchanges its own common stock to acquire virtually all the outstanding voting shares of another firm. Specifically, has a purchase (and accompanying sale by the subsidiary's stockholders) really taken place? After all, most of the subsidiary's stockholders now own shares in the parent corporation. In effect, only an *exchange* of shares has occurred, and one could correctly conclude that the two companies have simply combined themselves to operate as a single economic entity. When this type of exchange transaction arises and certain other criteria are met, the combination of the two entities is deemed a **pooling of interests.**

As we noted in Chapter 15, the issuance of stock to acquire noncash assets dictates that the transaction be entered in the accounts at fair market value. In a pooling, however, no purchase or sale is said to occur. The Investment account is therefore debited for the book value of the net assets (assets minus liabilities) obtained. This treatment results in the assets and liabilities of the subsidiary being carried forward to the combined corporation, with no change in valuation.

## Pooling and Reported Earnings

In comparison with the purchase method, business combinations that qualify as a pooling of interests usually result in higher consolidated earnings from book value valuations and the policy of absorbing a subsidiary's earnings for the entire year. To explain the former, specific assets obtained in a business combination that is accounted for as a *purchase* are assigned a cost equal to their fair market value on the date of acquisition.[6] This practice typically results in increased valuations from inflation and will cause larger depreciation deductions and reduced earnings figures. Additionally, the purchase method frequently gives rise to goodwill because of an investment's cost exceeding the fair value of the ownership interest acquired.

[6] Ibid., paragraph 47.

In accordance with proper accounting for intangible assets, the goodwill must be amortized, thereby lowering net income even further. Neither of these situations would occur under a pooling because, again, assets are not revalued. Consequently, market valuations and goodwill would not be reflected in the accounts.

Turning to the second issue (i.e., absorption of a subsidiary's earnings for the entire year), suppose that Apex Company obtained a 100% interest in Belmont Company on October 1, 19X1. If the acquisition is deemed a purchase, Apex would consolidate Belmont's earnings from October 1 onward. As with any type of purchase, benefits accrue from the date of acquisition into the future. If the transaction is considered a pooling, however, the two companies' figures are simply merged together. Apex is permitted to absorb Belmont's earnings for all of 19X1, even though a combined relationship did not exist for the entire period. Assuming that Belmont was a profitable entity, Apex would report greater net income under the pooling-of-interests method.

## Chapter Review

### Learning Objectives—The Key Points

**1 Understand how to account for investments in bonds.** Bond investments are recorded at their purchase price plus any costs incidental to the acquisition (e.g., brokerage fees). Additionally, a bond investor will pay for any accrued interest as of the date of purchase, with such amounts being recorded in the Bond Interest Receivable account. On the next interest payment date, the investor will receive a full period's interest regardless of how long the investment has been held.

The amount of bond interest revenue is respectively increased or decreased by the periodic amortization of discounts and premiums. The discount or premium should be amortized by the effective-interest method, which basically involves two steps. Interest revenue is first calculated by multiplying the carrying value by the effective interest rate. The amortization amount is then computed as the difference between interest revenue and the cash received for interest.

When bond investments are sold, the amortization process is updated to the date of disposal. The bonds are removed from the accounts and the sale proceeds and any accrued interest are recorded. Finally, the difference between the updated carrying value and the selling price is recognized as a gain or a loss on the transaction.

**2 Understand accounting for stock investments with the lower-of-cost-or-market and the equity methods.** Stock investments are accounted for by either the lower-of-cost-or-market method or the equity method. The lower-of-cost-or-market approach is used when the investor lacks the ability to exercise significant influence over the investee (typically less than 20% ownership). Under this method, the investment is recorded in the accounts at cost, and any dividends received are recognized as revenue. Should the market value of the shares fall below cost, an unrealized loss is entered in the accounting records.

The equity method is used when the investor has the ability to exercise significant influence over an investee (typically 20% or more ownership). With this approach, the Investment account is increased for the investor's pro rata share of investee net income, and decreased for any dividends received and net losses incurred. The Investment account therefore increases and decreases with changes in the retained earnings of the investee corporation.

**3 Be familiar with parent/subsidiary relationships.** When one company acquires a controlling interest (over 50% ownership) in another business, a parent/subsidiary relationship is created. The acquiring company becomes the parent, and the acquired company is the subsidiary. Although the companies remain separate legal entities and maintain separate accounting records, the firms have (in substance) become a single affiliated economic unit.

**4 Understand the reason for consolidated financial statements, including the concepts of intercompany transactions and elimination entries.** Consolidated financial statements are prepared because the parent and subsidiary represent a single economic unit. As such, transactions among the affiliated firms (i.e., intercompany transactions) must be eliminated on the work sheet when consolidated statements are constructed. A failure to do so would result in misleading reports of financial position and profitability, because the entity would be reporting both transactions it has with outside businesses and also with itself.

**5 Be able to prepare consolidated financial statements immediately after acquisition.** Consolidated financial statements are often prepared by first constructing a work sheet. The work sheet is used to combine assets, liabilities, and stockholders' equity of the parent and its subsidiaries. Prior to these amounts being merged, a set of columns is used to record the elimination of intercompany transactions (e.g., intercompany investments/equity, payables/receivables, and so forth). After all appropriate eliminations are made, the columns are summed across the work sheet to arrive at the amounts to be disclosed in the consolidated financial statements.

**6 Understand how to account for minority interests.** A minority interest is created in the consolidation process when a parent owns less than 100% of a controlled subsidiary. The portion of subsidiary equity owned by outsiders is not eliminated against the parent's investment but instead is transferred to a Minority Interest account. Such amounts appear on the consolidated balance sheet, often being disclosed in the stockholders' equity section.

**7 Be able to account for subsidiaries acquired at a cost in excess of book value.** When a subsidiary is acquired at more than book value, the excess is attributable to undervalued assets and/or goodwill. To consolidate, the elimination entry involves a credit to the Investment account and debits to the equity accounts of the subsidiary. Because the credit is greater than the debits, additional debits must be recorded on the books. These amounts will increase specific assets that are undervalued and, when appropriate, record goodwill.

**8 Understand the differences between purchase and pooling-of-interests accounting.** Purchase accounting presumes that one entity has clearly acquired another firm. As such, the transaction is based on the fair value of the assets and liabilities involved, and earnings are combined only from the date of acquisition.

When common stock is exchanged for substantially all of the common stock of another entity, a pooling of interests has occurred. Pooling-of-interests accounting is applicable if the companies have merely combined their resources and neither company has clearly bought the other. In this instance the book values of recorded assets and liabilities are combined, and no revaluation of assets occurs as with a purchase. In addition, the subsidiary's earnings are absorbed for the entire year as if the previously separate companies were one entity throughout the period.

## Chapter Quiz

The five questions that follow relate to several issues raised in the chapter. Test your knowledge of the issues by selecting the best answer. (The answers appear on p. 658.)

**1** Tobias purchased $400,000 of Sanborn Co., bonds at 104, plus accrued interest of $8,000. Brokerage fees amounted to $2,000. As a result of this purchase, Tobias should increase the Investment in Bonds account by:

a $402,000. c $418,000.
b $410,000. d $426,000.

**2** When the percentage ownership of an investee corporation is less than 20% of the outstanding voting stock and no significant investor influence is present, the accounting method to be used is:

a consolidated financial statements.
b lower of cost or market.
c equity.
d pooling of interests.

**3** On January 1, 19X2, Hansen paid $2 million to acquire 40% of TYG Corporation's common stock. Hansen exercises significant influence over TYG via membership on the latter firm's board of directors. During 19X2, TYG distributed total dividends of $125,000 and reported $600,000 of net income. The carrying value of Hansen's investment on December 31, 19X2, should be:
a $2,000,000.
b $2,190,000.
c $2,475,000.
d $2,600,000.

**4** Which of the following statements concerning consolidated financial statements is true?
a Elimination entries should be recorded in the accounting records of the parent.
b Elimination entries should be recorded in the accounting records of subsidiary companies.
c Elimination entries should be recorded in the accounting records of both the parent and its subsidiary companies.
d Elimination entries should be recorded only on the consolidated work sheet.

**5** On a consolidated balance sheet for a parent company and a 60% owned subsidiary, the total stockholders' equity will typically equal:
a the parent's stockholders' equity.
b the parent's stockholders' equity plus the minority interest.
c the parent's stockholders' equity minus the minority interest.
d the subsidiary's stockholders' equity.

## Questions

**Q18-1** Why do companies make long-term securities investments?

**Q18-2** What is the proper accounting treatment for brokers' fees incurred on the purchase of corporate securities?

**Q18-3** Putnam Company must pay $6,000 of accrued interest to acquire $100,000 of Zimmer Corporation bonds. If the bonds are purchased at 98, should Putnam debit the Investment in Bonds account for $104,000 ($98,000 + $6,000)? Explain.

**Q18-4** Explain when the straight-line amortization method is an acceptable substitute for effective-interest amortization.

**Q18-5** What steps are performed when computing effective-interest amortization?

**Q18-6** Garcia Corporation recently amortized $3,000 of discount on a bond investment. Determine the impact of the amortization entry on the following:
a Interest revenue for the year
b Interest received from the bond issuer
c The bond investment's carrying value

**Q18-7** Discuss the differences between the lower-of-cost-or-market and equity methods when accounting for an investor's share of investee dividends and net income.

**Q18-8** Benjamin, Inc., owns 30% of Baugh Corporation. During the current year Baugh paid dividends totaling $40,000. Discuss (a) the proper treatment of the dividends on Benjamin's records and (b) the underlying reason behind that treatment.

**Q18-9** Discuss the rationale that underlies the equity method of accounting.

**Q18-10** Distinguish between a legal entity and an economic entity.

**Q18-11** Why are elimination entries needed in the preparation of consolidated financial statements? Where are the eliminations recorded?

**Q18-12** Explain why the acquisition cost of a subsidiary seldom agrees with the subsidiary's book value.

**Q18-13** Suggest several reasons why earnings tend to be higher for a business combination that is treated as a pooling of interests as opposed to a purchase.

## Exercises

**E18-1** ***Straightforward bond investment; no amortization***

Freeman Corporation acquired $200,000 of 9% bonds on May 1 at 100% of face value, plus accrued interest. The bonds are dated January 1 and pay interest each June 30 and December 31.

a Prepare journal entries to record (1) the bond acquisition on May 1; (2) the receipt of interest on June 30; and (3) the receipt of interest on December 31.

b Compute Freeman's total interest revenue for the year ended December 31.

**E18-2** ***Bond investments; effective-interest amortization***

Ohio Investing purchased $800,000 of 10% bonds on January 1, 19XX, for $708,237. The bonds have a 10-year life, pay semiannual interest each June 30 and December 31, and were priced to generate a 12% effective interest rate.

a Prepare Ohio's journal entry to record the bond purchase on January 1.

b Prepare entries to record the interest receipt and discount amortization on June 30 and December 31, 19XX. Ohio uses the effective-interest method of amortization; round calculations to the nearest dollar.

c Compute total interest revenue for 19XX.

d Present the proper disclosure of the bond investment on Ohio's December 31, 19XX, balance sheet.

**E18-3** ***Effective-interest amortization of bond discount and premium***

On January 1, 19X2, Hopkins Company purchased two different bond issues to be held as long-term investments. The following information is available:

| *Bond Issue* | *Face Value* | *Contract Interest Rate (%)* | *Effective Interest Rate (%)* | *Purchase Price* |
|---|---|---|---|---|
| 1 | $100,000 | 8% | 10% | $ 87,538 |
| 2 | 100,000 | 7 | 6 | 107,439 |

All bonds pay interest on June 30 and December 31. Hopkins uses the effective-interest method of amortization.

a Compute the total interest *received* during 19X2.

b Compute amortization to be recorded during 19X2. Round calculations to the nearest dollar.

c Determine the amount of bond interest revenue to be reported on the firm's 19X2 income statement.

**E18-4** ***Sale of bond investment***

The Wizard Corporation purchased $500,000 of 9% bonds for $470,776 on January 1, 19X1. The bonds were dated January 1, 19X1, were scheduled to mature on December 31, 19X9, and had an effective yield to investors of 10%. Interest is paid semiannually on June 30 and December 31. On October 1, 19X3, Wizard sold the bonds at 103 plus accrued interest.

a Assume that the investment's carrying value stands at $476,517 as of June 30, 19X3. Using effective-interest amortization and rounding computations to the nearest dollar, determine the carrying value as of October 1, 19X3.

b Prepare the journal entries necessary on October 1, 19X3.

**E18-5** ***Basic accounting for stock investment***

On January 1 of the current year, Hagan Company acquired 10,000 shares of Atlantic Corporation's common stock at $10 per share. The following information has come to your attention:

1 During the current year Atlantic generated net income of $240,000 and paid dividends totaling $72,000.
2 The year-end market price of Atlantic's common stock was $9.25 per share.
3 Hagan has no other long-term investments.

Assume that Atlantic has 100,000 shares of common stock outstanding.

a Determine which method (lower-of-cost-or-market or equity) should be used to account for Hagan's investment.
b Present all appropriate journal entries for Hagan Company.
c Compute the year-end carrying value of Hagan's investment.

**E18-6** ***Basic accounting for stock investment***

On January 1 of the current year, Marietta Company acquired 7,000 common shares of Kenyon, Inc., at $40 per share. The following information has come to your attention:

1 During the current year Kenyon generated net income of $30,000 and paid dividends totaling $24,000.
2 The year-end market price of Kenyon's common stock was $38 per share.
3 Marietta has no other long-term investments.

Assume that Kenyon has 20,000 shares of common stock outstanding.

a Determine which method (lower-of-cost-or-market or equity) should be used to account for Marietta's investment.
b Present all appropriate journal entries for Marietta Company.
c Compute the year-end carrying value of Marietta's investment.

**E18-7** ***Lower-of-cost-or-market and equity methods***

On January 1, 19X3, Davidson Enterprises purchased 10,000 common shares of Keystone, Inc., and 30,000 common shares of Software, Inc. The acquisitions cost $57,500 and $240,000, respectively. Information about these two firms follows.

| | *Keystone, Inc.* | *Software, Inc.* |
|---|---|---|
| Common shares outstanding | 40,000 | 300,000 |
| 19X3 net income | $72,000 | $190,000 |
| 19X3 dividends | $20,000 | $ 60,000 |
| 19X3 year-end market value per share | $5 | $7 |

a Determine whether the investments in Keystone and Software should be accounted for by using the lower-of-cost-or-market method or the equity method. Explain the rationale behind your answer.
b Present the proper disclosure of Davidson's long-term stock investments on the December 31, 19X3, balance sheet.
c Compute the total investment revenue and dividend revenue that Davidson would report on its 19X3 income statement.

**E18-8** ***Straightforward consolidation; minority interest***

On June 30, Park Company acquired 80% of the outstanding common shares of Santo Corporation for $400,000. The condensed balance sheets of the two companies immediately after the acquisition follow.

| | *Park* | *Santo* |
|---|---|---|
| Cash | $ 120,000 | $ 80,000 |
| Other assets | 980,000 | 520,000 |
| Investment in Santo | 400,000 | — |
| | $1,500,000 | $600,000 |
| Liabilities | $ 700,000 | $100,000 |
| Common stock | 340,000 | 200,000 |
| Retained earnings | 460,000 | 300,000 |
| | $1,500,000 | $600,000 |

a Prepare any necessary elimination entries.
b Prepare a consolidated balance sheet for the two companies immediately after the acquisition. A work sheet is not required.

**E18-9** ***Overview of consolidation concepts***

On December 31, NBA Company acquired a key competitor by purchasing 90% of CBA Corporation's outstanding common stock for $2,700,000. CBA's year-end balance sheet disclosed the following information:

| | |
|---|---|
| Assets | $3,300,000 |
| Liabilities | 300,000 |
| Common stock ($10 par) | 2,250,000 |
| Retained earnings | 750,000 |

In negotiating the acquisition, management determined that the amounts appearing on CBA's balance sheet approximated current market values.
a Should consolidated financial statements be prepared in this situation? Why?
b Calculate the difference, if any, between acquisition cost and the book value of the subsidiary interest purchased.
c Calculate the minority interest and explain what the minority interest represents.

**E18-10** ***Elimination entries***

Perryton Corporation acquired 100% of the outstanding common shares of Shannon Corporation for $218,000. On the date of acquisition, Shannon's balance sheet revealed the following information:

| | |
|---|---|
| Cash and other current assets | $ 45,000 |
| Property, plant, & equipment (net) | 270,000 |
| | $315,000 |
| Accounts payable | $ 17,000 |
| Notes payable | 100,000 |
| Common stock | 50,000 |
| Retained earnings | 148,000 |
| | $315,000 |

Additional information is as follows:
1 The fair market value of the property, plant, and equipment on the acquisition date totaled $275,000.
2 Shannon is expected to have higher-than-normal earnings in the next few years, a fact Perryton considered when negotiating the $218,000 acquisition price.
3 Two months ago Shannon signed a note payable to Perryton for $14,000. The note is still outstanding.

a The $14,000 note payable requires an elimination entry. Present the entry in general journal form and explain the implications of *not* making the elimination when preparing the consolidated financial statements.
b Prepare any other elimination entries that are necessary to consolidate the two companies' balance sheets.
c Discuss why a parent may be willing to pay an amount that differs from book value in the acquisition of a subsidiary.

**E18-11** ***Overview of stock investments***
Evaluate the comments that follow as being True or False. If the comment is false, briefly explain why.
a When an investment is accounted for by using the equity method, an allowance account is needed to reduce the investment to market value.
b Dividends received are treated as revenue under the equity method.
c When financial statements of a parent are consolidated with those of a 60% owned subsidiary, the Investment account is offset against the minority interest of the investee.
d CyberTech has 50,000 common shares outstanding. If Ross owns 4,500 of these shares, Ross should use the lower-of-cost-or-market method to account for its investment.
e Only in rare cases are subsidiaries acquired at a cost in excess of book value.

**E18-12** ***Purchase versus pooling-of-interests accounting***
In December 19XX, Petro Company issued 20,000 shares of $10 par-value common stock in exchange for 95% of the outstanding common stock of Moustafa Corporation.
a Should this business combination be accounted for as a purchase or as a pooling of interests? Why?
b Briefly explain the differences between a purchase and a pooling of interests in terms of (1) substance of the transaction and (2) probable effect on reported earnings.

## Problems

### Series A

**P18-A1** ***Bond investment computations***
Boston Graphics purchased $400,000 of 9% bonds on June 1, 19X1. The bonds pay interest on June 1 and December 1 and mature in five years. Assume the following independent cases:

- *Case A*—The bonds are purchased for $355,838, representing a 12% effective yield to investors.
- *Case B*—The bonds are purchased for $416,220, representing an 8% effective yield to investors.

Boston uses the effective-interest method of amortization and has an accounting period that ends on December 31.

**Instructions**
Complete the following table, rounding all computations to the nearest dollar.

| | Case A | Case B |
|---|---|---|
| a Cash outflow for acquisition on June 1, 19X1 | ______ | ______ |
| b Total cash inflow through maturity (interest plus principal) | ______ | ______ |
| c Total investment income over the life of the bond issue | ______ | ______ |
| d Interest received in 19X1 | ______ | ______ |
| e Amortization to be recorded in 19X1 | ______ | ______ |
| f Total interest revenue for 19X1 | ______ | ______ |
| g Investment carrying valuc as of December 31, 19X1 | ______ | ______ |

**P18-A2** ***Bond entries: Acquisition through sale, bond discounts***

On January 1, 19X1, Wilson Corporation purchased $900,000 of 9%, 10-year bonds for $843,921. The bonds are dated January 1, 19X1, and pay semiannual interest on June 30 and December 31. On March 1, 19X2, Wilson sold 70% of the bonds at 102 plus accrued interest. The company uses effective-interest amortization and rounds all computations to the nearest dollar. The effective interest rate is 10%.

**Instructions**

a Prepare journal entries to record the following:
   (1) The bond investment on January 1, 19X1.
   (2) The semiannual interest receipt and discount amortization on June 30, 19X1, and December 31, 19X1.

b Compute total bond interest revenue for 19X1.

c Present the proper disclosure of the bond investment on Wilson's December 31, 19X1, balance sheet.

d Prepare entries to record the bond sale on March 1, 19X2. *Hint:* Examine when amortization was last recorded.

**P18-A3** ***Lower-of-cost-or-market and equity methods***

The Sargent Corporation recently acquired a long-term investment in Worley, Inc. Worley has 50,000 shares of $10 par-value common stock outstanding. The following information is available:

| | | |
|---|---|---|
| Jan. | 1 | Purchased 5,000 shares of Worley common stock at $15 per share. |
| Dec. | 31 | Received a copy of Worley's income statement that disclosed net income of $40,000. |
| | 31 | Worley declared and paid a cash dividend of $0.50 per share. |
| | 31 | The market price of Worley's stock was $14 per share. |

**Instructions**

a Which accounting method should Sargent use for its long-term investment in Worley, Inc.? Why should this method be used?

b Present Sargent's required journal entries.

c Present the proper disclosure of the Investment account on Sargent's December 31 balance sheet.

d Repeat requirements (a), (b), and (c), assuming that Sargent had purchased 20,000 shares of Worley's stock at $15 per share.

**P18-A4** ***Long-term stock investment concepts***

Presley Corporation, a distributor of music memorabilia, has long-term investments in different companies. The companies and percentage of voting stock owned are: A, 60%; B, 5%; C, 40%; and D, 100%. To prepare for the annual stockholders' meeting, Presley's president has asked for a "crash course" in accounting for such investments.

**Instructions**

a Complete the following table:

| | *Company* | | | |
|---|---|---|---|---|
| | ***A*** | ***B*** | ***C*** | ***D*** |
| (1) Does Presley have a controlling interest in the company? | ____ | ____ | ____ | ____ |
| (2) What method should Presley use to account for the investment (lower-of-cost-or-market or equity)? | ____ | ____ | ____ | ____ |
| (3) Are declines in the company's market value per share recognized in Presley's financial statements? | ____ | ____ | ____ | ____ |
| (4) Would a share of the company's earnings be reflected in Presley's financial statements? | ____ | ____ | ____ | ____ |
| (5) Would Presley recognize a share of the company's dividends as revenue? | ____ | ____ | ____ | ____ |
| (6) Should the company's financial statements be consolidated with those of Presley? | ____ | ____ | ____ | ____ |
| (7) For those companies that are consolidated, does a minority interest appear in the consolidated financial statements? | ____ | ____ | ____ | ____ |

b Explain to Presley's president the basic differences between a parent, a subsidiary, and an investee.

**P18-A5** ***Straightforward consolidation; minority interest***

For the past few years Omega Company and Stanford, Inc., have been friendly business rivals. Although the companies are not affiliated, Omega has borrowed money from Stanford and vice versa. Part of this friendliness stems from the fact that the presidents of the two firms are sisters.

On December 31 of the current year, Omega acquired a 60% interest in Stanford for $84,000 cash. The balance sheets of the two companies *prior to the acquisition* follow.

**OMEGA COMPANY**

| | |
|---|---|
| Cash | $180,000 |
| Note receivable from Stanford | 70,000 |
| Other assets | 200,000 |
| Total assets | $450,000 |
| Current liabilities | $ 80,000 |
| Note payable to Stanford | 30,000 |
| Common stock | 150,000 |
| Retained earnings | 190,000 |
| Total liabilities & stockholders' equity | $450,000 |

**STANFORD, INC.**

| | |
|---|---|
| Cash | $ 50,000 |
| Note receivable from Omega | 30,000 |
| Other assets | 220,000 |
| Total assets | $300,000 |
| Current liabilities | $ 90,000 |
| Note payable to Omega | 70,000 |
| Common stock | 100,000 |
| Retained earnings | 40,000 |
| Total liabilities & stockholders' equity | $300,000 |

Instructions

a Present Omega's journal entry to record the acquisition of Stanford.
b Prepare a consolidated work sheet similar in form to that illustrated in the text.
c Prepare a formal consolidated balance sheet for the combined entity.

**P18-A6** ***Straightforward consolidation; cost in excess of book value***

On December 31, 19X4, Sharp Oil Corporation acquired 100% of the outstanding stock of Val Verde Drilling Company for $650,000. Balance sheet information for the two companies immediately after the acquisition follows.

| | ***Sharp*** | ***Val Verde*** |
|---|---|---|
| Cash | $ 98,300 | $ 41,500 |
| Accounts receivable (net) | 112,500 | 57,600 |
| Inventories | 317,600 | 191,400 |
| Investment in Val Verde | 650,000 | — |
| Land | 60,000 | 12,750 |
| Property, plant, & equipment (net) | 566,100 | 306,950 |
| Receivable from Val Verde | 20,000 | — |
| | $1,824,500 | $610,200 |

| | | |
|---|---|---|
| Accounts payable | $ 142,000 | $ 49,400 |
| Taxes payable | 39,700 | 13,800 |
| Bonds payable | 500,000 | — |
| Payable to Sharp Oil | — | 20,000 |
| Common stock ($5 par) | 800,000 | — |
| Common stock ($10 par) | — | 400,000 |
| Retained earnings | 342,800 | 127,000 |
| | $1,824,500 | $610,200 |

With the exception of land, the fair market value of Val Verde's assets and liabilities corresponded to the book value amounts as of the acquisition date. A recent appraisal indicated Val Verde's land was worth $65,000.

**Instructions**

a Prepare a consolidated work sheet similar in format to that illustrated in the chapter.

b Prepare a formal consolidated balance sheet.

## Series B

**P18-B1** ***Bond investment computations***

Productivity, Inc., purchased $600,000 of 12% bonds on March 1, 19X2. The bonds pay interest on March 1 and September 1 and mature in four years. Assume the following independent cases:

- *Case A*—The bonds are purchased for $638,780, representing a 10% yield to investors.
- *Case B*—The bonds are purchased for $531,041, representing a 16% yield to investors.

Productivity uses the effective-interest method of amortization and has an accounting period that ends on December 31.

**Instructions**

Complete the following table, rounding all computations to the nearest dollar.

| | *Case A* | *Case B* |
|---|---|---|
| a Cash outflow for acquisition on March 1, 19X2 | ______ | ______ |
| b Total cash inflow through maturity (interest plus principal) | ______ | ______ |
| c Total investment income over the life of the bond issue | ______ | ______ |
| d Interest received in 19X2 | ______ | ______ |
| e Amortization to be recorded in 19X2 | ______ | ______ |
| f Total interest revenue for 19X2 | ______ | ______ |
| g Investment carrying value as of December 31, 19X2 | ______ | ______ |

**P18-B2** ***Bond entries: Acquisition through sale, bond premiums***

On January 1, 19X3, Miller Corporation purchased $600,000 of 13%, 10-year bonds for $634,407. The bonds are dated January 1, 19X3, and pay semiannual interest on June 30 and December 31. On May 1, 19X4, Miller sold 40% of the bonds at 101 plus accrued interest. The company uses effective-interest amortization and rounds all computations to the nearest dollar. The effective interest rate is 12%.

**Instructions**

a Prepare journal entries to record the following:
   (1) The bond investment on January 1, 19X3.
   (2) The semiannual interest receipt and premium amortization on June 30, 19X3, and December 31, 19X3.

b Compute total bond interest revenue for 19X3.

c Present the proper disclosure of the bond investment on Miller's December 31, 19X3, balance sheet.

d Prepare entries to record the bond sale on May 1, 19X4. *Hint:* Examine when amortization was last recorded.

**P18-B3** ***Lower-of-cost-or-market and equity methods***

Birmingham Corporation recently acquired a long-term investment in Ambrose, Inc. Ambrose has 40,000 shares of $2 par-value common stock outstanding. The following information is available:

| | | |
|---|---|---|
| Jan. | 1 | Purchased 10,000 shares of Ambrose common stock at $20 per share. |
| Dec. | 31 | Ambrose declared and paid a cash dividend of $0.60 per share. |
| | 31 | Received a copy of Ambrose's income statement that disclosed net income of $42,000. |
| | 31 | The market price of Ambrose's stock was $17 per share. |

**Instructions**

a Which accounting method should Birmingham use for its long-term investment in Ambrose, Inc.? Why should this method be used?

b Present Birmingham's required journal entries.

c Present the proper disclosure of the Investment account on Birmingham's December 31 balance sheet.

d Repeat requirements (a), (b), and (c), assuming that Birmingham had purchased 3,000 shares of Ambrose's stock at $20 per share.

**P18-B4** ***Long-term stock investment concepts***

Surf Corporation, a manufacturer of automotive equipment, has long-term investments in different companies. The companies and percentage of voting stock owned are: A, 80%; B, 30%; C, 100%; and D, 10%. To prepare for the annual stockholders' meeting, Surf's president has asked for a "crash course" in accounting for such investments.

**Instructions**

a Complete the table that follows.

| | Company | | | |
|---|---|---|---|---|
| | A | B | C | D |
| (1) Does Surf have a controlling interest in the company? | ____ | ____ | ____ | ____ |
| (2) What method should Surf use to account for the investment (lower-of-cost-or-market or equity)? | ____ | ____ | ____ | ____ |
| (3) Should the company's financial statements be consolidated with those of Surf? | ____ | ____ | ____ | ____ |
| (4) For those companies that are consolidated, does a minority interest appear in the consolidated financial statements? | ____ | ____ | ____ | ____ |
| (5) Are declines in the company's market value per share recognized in Surf's financial statements? | ____ | ____ | ____ | ____ |
| (6) Would a share of the company's earnings be reflected in Surf's financial statements? | ____ | ____ | ____ | ____ |
| (7) Would Surf recognize a share of the company's dividends as revenue? | ____ | ____ | ____ | ____ |

b Explain to Surf's president the basic differences between the lower-of-cost-or-market method and the equity method.

**P18-B5** ***Straightforward consolidation; minority interest***

For the past few years Lincoln Company and Summit, Inc., have been friendly business rivals. Although the companies are not affiliated, Lincoln has borrowed money from Summit and vice versa. Part of this friendliness stems from the fact that the presidents of the two firms are brothers.

On December 31 of the current year, Lincoln acquired a 75% interest in Summit for $180,000 cash. The balance sheets of the two companies *prior to the acquisition* follow.

| LINCOLN COMPANY | |
|---|---|
| Cash | $370,000 |
| Note receivable from Summit | 40,000 |
| Other assets | 290,000 |
| Total assets | $700,000 |
| Current liabilities | $ 80,000 |
| Note payable to Summit | 50,000 |
| Common stock | 250,000 |
| Retained earnings | 320,000 |
| Total liabilities & stockholders' equity | $700,000 |

| SUMMIT, INC. | |
|---|---|
| Cash | $ 65,000 |
| Note receivable from Lincoln | 50,000 |
| Other assets | 190,000 |
| Total assets | $305,000 |
| Current liabilities | $ 25,000 |
| Note payable to Lincoln | 40,000 |
| Common stock | 70,000 |
| Retained earnings | 170,000 |
| Total liabilities & stockholders' equity | $305,000 |

**Instructions**

a Present Lincoln's journal entry to record the acquisition of Summit.
b Prepare a consolidated work sheet similar in form to that illustrated in the text.
c Prepare a formal consolidated balance sheet for the combined entity.

**P18-B6** ***Straightforward consolidation; cost in excess of book value***
On December 31, 19X1, Harris Corporation acquired 100% of the outstanding stock of Redford Company for $350,000. Balance sheet information for the two companies immediately after the acquisition follows.

| | *Harris* | *Redford* |
|---|---|---|
| Cash | $ 73,300 | $ 41,500 |
| Accounts receivable (net) | 128,700 | 56,000 |
| Inventories | 269,600 | 182,300 |
| Investment in Redford | 350,000 | — |
| Land | 60,000 | 57,000 |
| Equipment (net) | 166,100 | 36,000 |
| Receivable from Redford | 50,000 | — |
| | $1,097,700 | $372,800 |
| Accounts payable | $ 39,600 | $ 29,500 |
| Salaries payable | 1,700 | 8,300 |
| Loan payable | 80,000 | — |
| Payable to Harris | — | 50,000 |
| Common stock ($1 par) | 460,000 | — |
| Common stock ($5 par) | — | 100,000 |
| Retained earnings | 516,400 | 185,000 |
| | $1,097,700 | $372,800 |

With the exception of equipment, the fair market value of Redford's assets and liabilities corresponded to the book value amounts as of the acquisition date. A recent appraisal indicated Redford's equipment was worth $61,000.

**Instructions**

a Prepare a consolidated work sheet similar in format to that illustrated in the chapter.
b Prepare a formal consolidated balance sheet.

## Beyond the Basics

**BB18-1** ***Understanding consolidated statements***

Payton, Inc., has two subsidiaries, Atlas Manufacturing and Miami Glass Corporation, and possesses 80% and 100% of the respective firms' outstanding voting shares. A review of the companies' consolidated balance sheet revealed the following selected information:

| | |
|---|---|
| Assets | |
| Investment in Atlas Manufacturing | $ — |
| Investment in Miami Glass | — |
| Excess of cost over book value in subsidiary investment | 45,000 |
| Liabilities | |
| Loans payable | 85,000 |
| Stockholders' equity | |
| Minority interest | 65,000 |
| Common stock | 150,000 |
| Paid-in capital in excess of par value | 50,000 |
| Retained earnings | 215,000 |

**Instructions**

One of Payton's stockholders has been reviewing the consolidated statements and has come to you with the following questions. Prepare appropriate answers, explaining any necessary assumptions.

a Payton has two long-term investments. Why do both Investment accounts contain zero balances?

b What gives rise to an excess of cost over book value?

c What is meant by the Minority Interest account and to which subsidiary does it relate?

d A leading financial publication recently contained an article regarding a $750,000 loan from Payton to Atlas; yet the loan was not disclosed on the consolidated balance sheet? Why?

**BB18-2** ***Analysis of consolidated statements***

Power Craft Enterprises and Singer Steel Corporation recently completed a business combination. Terms of the combination required that Power Craft receive common shares of Singer Steel in exchange for a lump-sum cash payment. The following schedule includes information about the separate and consolidated balance sheets of the two companies immediately after acquisition:

| *Account* | *Power Craft* | *Singer Steel* | *Consol-idated* |
|---|---|---|---|
| Cash | $ 37,000 | $ 11,000 | $ 48,000 |
| Notes receivable | 12,000 | 9,000 | 14,000 |
| Inventories | 24,000 | 23,000 | 47,000 |
| Investment in Singer Steel | 75,000 | — | — |
| Property, plant, & equipment (net) | 87,000 | 96,000 | 183,000 |
| Total assets | $235,000 | $139,000 | $292,000 |
| Accounts payable | $ 6,000 | $ 30,000 | $ 36,000 |
| Notes payable | 19,000 | 9,000 | 21,000 |
| Common stock: Power Craft | 38,000 | — | 38,000 |
| Common stock: Singer Steel | — | 40,000 | — |
| Retained earnings: Power Craft | 172,000 | — | 172,000 |
| Retained earnings: Singer Steel | — | 60,000 | — |
| Minority interest in Singer Steel | — | — | 25,000 |
| Total liabilities & stockholders' equity | $235,000 | $139,000 | $292,000 |

**Instructions**

a What percentage of the outstanding shares of Singer Steel are held by Power Craft?

b Should Power Craft's acquisition of Singer Steel be accounted for as a purchase or as a pooling of interests? Briefly explain.

c Briefly discuss the absence of goodwill on the consolidated balance sheet.

d Singer Steel held a $2,000 note receivable from Power Craft. Did Power Craft hold any notes receivable from Singer Steel? If so, how much?

e Would Power Craft stockholders be entitled to any dividends that are declared by Singer's board of directors? Briefly explain.

## Answers to Chapter Quiz

**1** c [($400,000 × 1.04) + $2,000]

**2** b

**3** b [$2,000,000 + ($600,000 × 0.40) − ($125,000 × 0.40)]

**4** d

**5** b

# Statement of Cash Flows

CHAPTER 19

## Learning Objectives

After reading this chapter you should:

1 Understand the purpose of the statement of cash flows.

2 Be able to distinguish among operating, investing, and financing activities.

3 Understand the proper accounting treatment for significant noncash investing/financing transactions.

4 Be familiar with the direct and indirect methods of computing cash flows from operating activities.

5 Be able to prepare a statement of cash flows.

OBJECTIVE 1
Understand the purpose of the statement of cash flows.

Most accountants will agree that the income statement and the balance sheet disclose valuable information to investors, creditors, managers, and a host of other parties. The income statement, for example, focuses on the results of operations and reveals an entity's revenues and expenses for a given accounting period. The balance sheet, on the other hand, discloses information concerning the economic resources, financial obligations, and owners' equity of a company at a specific point in time.

One of the purposes of financial statements is to assist users in making predictions about an entity's future cash inflows and outflows. Users can predict the future only if they have a sufficient information base; unfortunately, the income statement and balance sheet alone are not capable of providing this base. The accounting profession therefore requires another report to improve financial disclosures of business enterprises. This report is the **statement of cash flows,** which reveals the cash flows generated or consumed by a firm's operating, investing, and financing activities. The information contained on the statement is helpful in answering questions such as the following:

- Did an entity fund its activities from operations? From bank loans? From stockholder investments?
- Were the funds obtained by an organization used to expand facilities? Reduce outstanding debt? Replace aging plant and equipment?
- Were the dividends paid greater than the funds provided by business operations?
- Why did net income differ from the firm's cash receipts and disbursements?

Questions similar to the foregoing are routinely asked by creditors, stockholders, and financial analysts. By collecting information on how funds are generated and used in an organization, the statement of cash flows provides insight that is not afforded by other financial disclosures and reports.

## Statement Format

OBJECTIVE 2
Be able to distinguish among operating, investing, and financing activities.

The statement of cash flows has undergone considerable change in recent years. For a long period of time, companies revealed inflows and outflows of funds on a report known as the *statement of changes in financial position.* Businesses could employ differing definitions of funds and had few set rules to follow when presenting such information to external statement users. Because of this situation, a great deal of difficulty arose when analysts compared the reports of different companies.

The Financial Accounting Standards Board studied the problem and decided that clearer definitional and presentation guidelines were necessary.[1] The outcome of the Board's work is the statement shown in Exhibit 19-1. As you can see, businesses must disclose the cash flows that arise from three broad categories: operating activities, investing activities, and financing activities. In addition, organizations are required to reveal significant *noncash* investing/financing transactions. For Matrix Corporation, the firm was able to produce net cash inflows from operating activities and financing activities of $70,000 and $4,000, respectively. Investing transactions, on the other hand, were a cash drain, resulting in a $15,000 excess of disbursements over receipts. We will now discuss each of the statement's major sections in detail.

[1] See "Statement of Cash Flows," *Statement of Financial Accounting Standards No. 95* (Stamford, Conn.: Financial Accounting Standards Board, 1987).

| MATRIX CORPORATION<br>Statement of Cash Flows<br>For the Year Ended December 31, 19XX | |
|---|---|
| Cash flows from operating activities | |
| Details | |
| Net cash provided (used) by operating activities | $ 70,000 |
| Cash flows from investing activities | |
| Details | |
| Net cash provided (used) by investing activities | (15,000) |
| Cash flows from financing activities | |
| Details | |
| Net cash provided (used) by financing activities | 4,000 |
| Net increase (decrease) in cash | $ 59,000 |
| Cash balance, January 1, 19XX | 31,000 |
| Cash balance, December 31, 19XX | $ 90,000 |
| Schedule of noncash investing/financing activities | |
| Details | $ 12,000 |

**Exhibit 19-1**
**Example of a Statement of Cash Flows**

## Operating Activities

Generally speaking, **operating activities** give rise to transactions and events that enter into net income computations. Picture, for instance, the production and sale of goods and services—the major source of earnings for most large businesses. The cash flows related to these activities, such as receipts from customers, and payments for inventory, employee salaries and wages, taxes, interest, and other normal business expenses are classified as operating cash flows. Receipts of both loan interest and dividends also qualify for inclusion in this category. A review of *Statement No. 95* will find that the FASB defined operating activities in a "catch-all" sense, namely, to include all transactions and events not otherwise classified as investing or financing items.

## Investing Activities

**Investing activities,** or those that involve investment of an entity's resources, constitute the next major type of activity for a business. Companies acquire the securities (e.g., bonds and shares of stock) of other firms and purchase long-term assets such as property, plant, and equipment. In addition, an entity (e.g., a financial institution) may make a loan to another organization. All of these transactions arise from a company's investing activities and result in a cash outflow during the period.

In a similar but opposite manner, these activities frequently generate cash inflows. The stock and bond investments and long-term productive resources may be sold, and loans may be paid off by the collection of principal from the borrower. Needless to say, investing activities may take many different forms and consume and generate substantial amounts of cash. We will now take a closer look at several of these items.

### Purchase of Long-Term Assets

When long-term assets such as land, buildings, equipment, and stock investments are acquired, cash will decrease by the amount of funds disbursed. For example, if a business purchases $50,000 of equipment for cash, the outflow would represent a $50,000 investing activity.

### Sale of Long-Term Assets

Businesses may obtain cash by selling the assets just noted. For instance, suppose that a company sold a parcel of land that originally cost $100,000 for $180,000 cash. The transaction produces an $80,000 gain, which would be entered in the accounting records as follows:

| | | |
|---|---|---|
| Cash | 180,000 | |
| Land | | 100,000 |
| Gain on Sale of Land | | 80,000 |
| To record sale of land at a gain | | |

Because Cash increased by $180,000, the transaction generates a $180,000 inflow of funds from an investment-related activity. The amount of cash inflow is reflected by the debit to Cash, no matter whether the disposal produces a gain or a loss.[2]

### Loan Generation and Subsequent Collection

Companies lend money to other business entities and expect to be repaid. These actions constitute investing activities for the *lending* firm, with loans made being reported as cash outflows in the statement's investment section. Similarly, when the principal of a loan is repaid, the investing-activities section will disclose a cash inflow. This latter procedure is followed because the funds related to the loan's principal are being "disinvested" and are no longer producing any interest revenue for the firm. As noted, any interest revenue that has been generated is considered when figuring the cash flows from *operating* activities.

## Financing Activities

Companies need funds for a variety of business purposes. These funds are often obtained from different sources such as the issuance of capital stock, bonds, and mortgage notes, and various types of loan agreements. **Financing activities** are those activities that supply a firm with funds from either the firm's owners or creditors. The items just cited (stock, bonds, and so forth) all provide an entity with cash inflows and normally commit the entity to specific cash outflows (e.g., dividends and the repayment of principal). These latter items are also considered to arise from financing activities, as are cash outflows for treasury stock acquisitions. Two exceptions to financing cash flows are trade payables and interest, both of which are related to the operating activities of the business.

[2] Proper treatment of gains and losses will be shown shortly.

The reporting of cash flows associated with financing activities parallels that just shown for investing activities. For example, if a corporation obtained $1 million via the sale of bonds or the issuance of common stock, the corporation's financing section would reveal an inflow of $1 million. In a similar but opposite fashion, the acquisition of $250,000 of treasury stock would be disclosed as a $250,000 financing outflow.

Exhibit 19-2 summarizes an entity's various cash flow activities and presents examples of typical inflows and outflows for the operating, investing, and financing categories. The movement of cash within these three spheres of business activity is shown pictorially in Exhibit 19-3.

## Investing and Financing Transactions that Do Not Affect Cash

OBJECTIVE 3
Understand the proper accounting treatment for significant noncash investing/financing transactions.

Several significant investing and financing transactions affect the financial position of a business but do not affect cash. For example, a building may be acquired by securing a long-term loan such as a mortgage payable. Or land may be obtained in exchange for preferred stock. Neither transaction involves an immediate receipt or disbursement of cash; nonetheless, the financial position of the enterprise has changed through the increases in assets, liabilities, and stockholders' equity. Because a statement of cash flows would be incomplete if significant investing and financing transactions were omitted, the accounting profession requires that such transactions be reported even though no receipts and payments are involved.

**Exhibit 19-2**
**An Overview of Operating, Investing, and Financing Activities**

### Operating Activities

- *General thrust*—Activities primarily related to the production and sale of goods and services, and that enter into the determination of income for the firm
- *Typical cash inflows*—Receipts from customers, loan interest, dividends
- *Typical cash outflows*—Payments for inventory, employee salaries and wages, taxes, interest, and other normal business expenses

### Investing Activities

- *General thrust*—Activities that involve investment of a company's resources
- *Typical cash inflows*—Receipts from the sale of stocks and bonds of other firms, and from the disposal of long-term productive resources such as land, buildings, and equipment; the receipt of loan principal from borrowers
- *Typical cash outflows*—Payments made to acquire long-term assets or the securities of other firms; loans made by the entity to other businesses

### Financing Activities

- *General thrust*—Activities that provide a business with resources from either its owners or creditors
- *Typical cash inflows*—Receipts from stock and bond issuances, proceeds from mortgage notes and loans
- *Typical cash outflows*—Payments of loan principal to creditors, acquisitions of treasury stock, and dividend distributions

**Exhibit 19-3**
**Cash Movement within a Business**

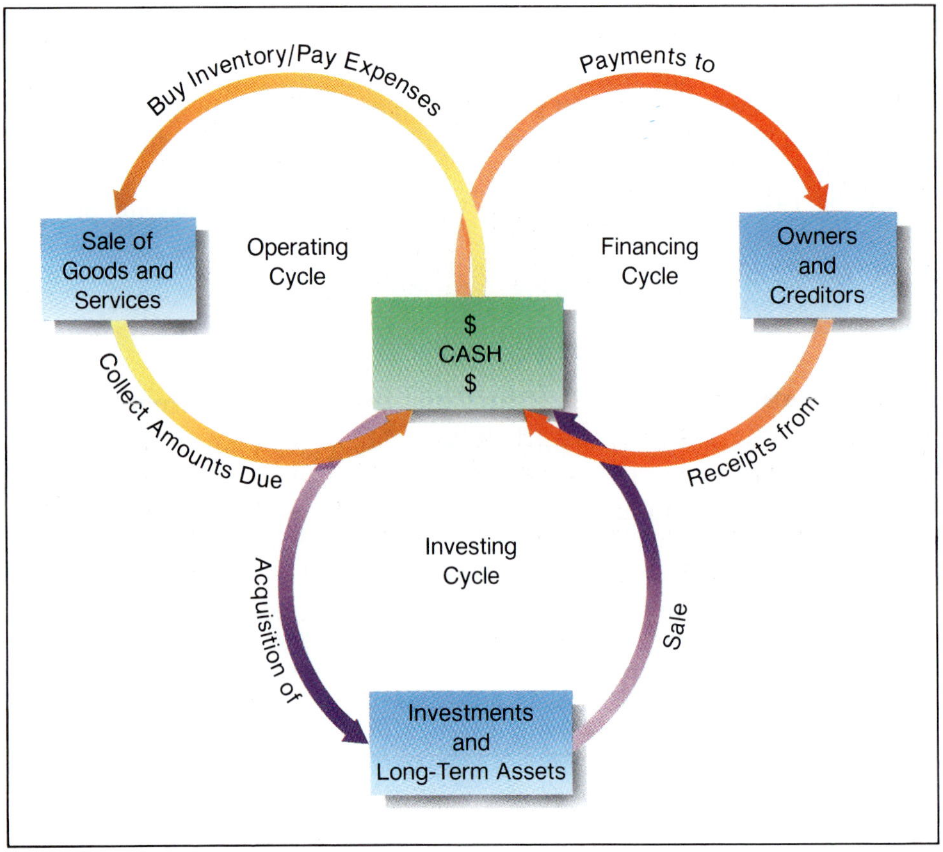


Noncash transactions are disclosed on the statement as a separate noncash investing/financing activity. To illustrate, assume $10 million of common stock is exchanged for a building of the same value. The event would be separately reported as a $10 million noncash transaction, appropriately labeled as Common Stock Issued for Building. In essence, one could visualize that common stock is issued for cash (a financing inflow), and the cash is simultaneously disbursed to acquire the asset (an investing outflow). We emphasize that this scenario is mentioned merely to assist your understanding of the exchange. Keep in mind that no cash was ever involved.

## A Further Probe of Operating Activities

Before we can illustrate the procedures needed to prepare the statement of cash flows, it is necessary to further study the area of operating activities. Recall that transactions and events related to operating activities affect a firm's net income. Also recall from earlier chapters that most large companies, to be in accord with generally accepted accounting principles, compute net income by using the accrual basis of accounting. Under the accrual basis, revenues are recognized when goods and services are sold or rendered, and expenses are recognized when incurred.

Because of the focus on amounts *earned* and *incurred,* the resulting net income figure likely includes revenues not yet collected from customers and expenses not yet paid to creditors. Sales, of course, may be made in one period and collected in another. In addition, expenses such as taxes, salaries, and interest are often accrued at the end of one period, with payment occurring in the future. As a consequence of these "timing" differences, the accrual-based net income figure must be adjusted in the statement-preparation process to achieve our objective: a focus on the entity's operating cash flows. The required adjustments basically involve a conversion to the cash basis of accounting, thereby allowing a business to report the revenues *received* and the expenses *paid.*

The conversion may be accomplished by two different approaches: the direct method and the indirect method. Both approaches are acceptable for purposes of external financial reporting; however, use of the direct method is encouraged by the FASB.

## The Direct Method

OBJECTIVE 4
Be familiar with the direct and indirect methods of computing cash flows from operating activities.

Under the **direct method,** individual items on the income statement are translated from the accrual basis to the cash basis of accounting. Sales, for example, is adjusted to reflect the actual cash inflows remitted by customers, while cost of goods sold and expenses are converted to show the amounts disbursed to suppliers, employees, and so forth. The result of this translation process follows.

| | | |
|---|---|---|
| Cash received from customers | | $XX,XXX |
| Less cash payments for: | | |
| Purchases of merchandise | $XX,XXX | |
| Selling & administrative expenses | XX,XXX | |
| Interest | XX,XXX | |
| Income taxes | XX,XXX | XX,XXX |
| Net cash provided (used) by operating activities | | $XX,XXX |

To illustrate the necessary procedures, we will utilize selected data of the Powell Corporation (see Exhibit 19-4).

Exhibit 19-4
Powell Corporation Data

**POWELL CORPORATION**
**Income Statement**
**For the Year Ended December 31, 19X2**

| | | |
|---|---|---|
| Sales | | $3,000,000 |
| Cost of goods sold | | 1,200,000 |
| Gross profit | | $1,800,000 |
| Expenses | | |
| Selling & administrative | $1,455,000 | |
| Building depreciation | 25,000 | |
| Equipment depreciation | 70,000 | 1,550,000 |
| | | $ 250,000 |
| Other revenue (expense) | | |
| Interest expense | $ (200,000) | |
| Loss on sale of equipment | (5,000) | |
| Gain on sale of long-term investments | 15,000 | (190,000) |
| Income before income taxes | | $ 60,000 |
| Income taxes | | 20,000 |
| Net income | | $ 40,000 |

**Exhibit 19-4 (continued)**

| *Account* | *Dec. 31, 19X2* | *Dec. 31, 19X1* | *Increase (Decrease)* |
|---|---|---|---|
| Accounts receivable (net) | $400,000 | $375,000 | $ 25,000 |
| Merchandise inventory | 425,000 | 450,000 | (25,000) |
| Prepaid selling expenses | 5,000 | 4,000 | 1,000 |
| Accounts payable | 470,000 | 340,000 | 130,000 |
| Income taxes payable | 40,000 | 39,000 | 1,000 |

## Cash Received from Customers

Most companies extend credit to their customers. Because of both credit sales and the accompanying possibility of bad debts, accrual-based sales revenues generally do not coincide with cash collections. In Powell's case, for instance, Accounts Receivable rose by $25,000 during the year. This increase indicates that revenues have been earned; however, certain customers have yet to settle their balances with the firm.

The data that follow are based on the figures shown in Exhibit 19-4.

| ***Accounts Receivable*** | | | |
|---|---|---|---|
| 12/31/X1 | 375,000 | Collections | ? |
| Sales | 3,000,000 | | |
| | **3,375,000** | | |
| **400,000** | | | |

To derive the ending balance of $400,000, it is apparent that Powell collected $2,975,000 ($3,375,000 − $400,000) from clientele. The conversion of accrual-based sales revenues to cash collections may therefore be generalized via the following formula:

$$\text{Cash Received from Customers} = \text{Sales} \begin{cases} + \text{ Decrease in Accounts Receivable} \\ - \text{ Increase in Accounts Receivable} \end{cases}$$

$2,975,000 = $3,000,000 − $25,000

## Cash Payments for Merchandise

The computation of cash outlays for merchandise is slightly more complex than the calculation just illustrated. The starting point is the cost-of-goods-sold figure on the income statement. Complications arise, however, since goods acquired during the period may still be in inventory or, conversely, goods purchased in previous periods may have been sold during 19X2. Furthermore, it is likely that cash payments to suppliers will differ from the total cost of merchandise acquired because of purchases made on credit. In view of this situation, changes in *both* the Merchandise Inventory and Accounts Payable accounts must be taken into consideration.

Data for Powell Corporation reveal a $25,000 decrease in inventory, meaning the company disposed of merchandise that was acquired prior to 19X2. The firm's cost of goods sold will therefore exceed the cost of goods purchased during the year. As the figures that follow indicate, 19X2 purchases amounted to $1,175,000.

***Merchandise Inventory***

| | | | |
|---|---|---|---|
| 12/31/X1 | 450,000 | Cost of goods sold | 1,200,000 |
| Purchases | ? | | |
| 425,000 | | | |

Let X = purchases
$450,000 + X − $1,200,000 = $425,000
X = $1,175,000

The next issue is: Did Powell pay for all of these goods during the period? This question can be answered by examining the amounts owed to suppliers.[3]

***Accounts Payable***

| | | | |
|---|---|---|---|
| Payments | ? | 12/31/X1 | 340,000 |
| | | Purchases | 1,175,000 |
| | | | **1,515,000** |
| | | | 470,000 |

The T-account shows that the $470,000 owed as of December 31, 19X2, arises only if 19X2 payments totaled $1,045,000 ($1,515,000 − $470,000). Alternatively, we can arrive at the same conclusion by analyzing the change in Accounts Payable. For example, the $130,000 rise in the account ($470,000 − $340,000) means that some goods acquired in 19X2 were not paid for by year-end. Cash payments to suppliers were therefore less than the cost of merchandise purchased, with total disbursements amounting to $1,045,000 ($1,175,000 − $130,000).

The preceding computations are summarized in the formula that follows.

$$\text{Cash Payments for Merchandise} = \text{Cost of Goods Sold} \begin{cases} + \text{ Increase in Inventory} \\ - \text{ Decrease in Inventory} \end{cases} \begin{cases} + \text{ Decrease in Accounts Payable} \\ - \text{ Increase in Accounts Payable} \end{cases}$$

$1,045,000 = $1,200,000 − $25,000 − $130,000

## Cash Payments for Selling and Administrative Expenses

There is a strong likelihood that selling and administrative expenses as reported on the income statement will not equal cash payments for services acquired. Several factors serve to cause a difference between these two amounts, including prepaid expenses. Recall that companies frequently pay for items in advance (e.g., insurance, rent, and advertising), with the amounts expended being written off to expense upon consumption. As a result of this accounting treatment, a rising balance of prepaid expenses indicates that the cost of prepaid items acquired during the year exceeded the cost of those consumed. Thus, cash outflows would exceed the amounts expensed.

[3] We are assuming that all accounts payable are related to purchases of merchandise.

An examination of Powell's prepaid expenses revealed a $1,000 increase during 19X2. Given that the company reported $1,455,000 of selling and administrative expenses on its accrual-based income statement, cash payments must have amounted to $1,456,000 ($1,455,000 + $1,000). The following formula may be used in the conversion process:[4]

$$\text{Cash Payments for Selling \& Administrative Expenses} = \text{Selling \& Administrative Expenses} \begin{cases} + \text{ Increases in Prepaid Expenses} \\ - \text{ Decreases in Prepaid Expenses} \end{cases}$$

## Cash Payments for Interest and Income Taxes

The final items to consider are interest and income taxes. For most businesses, the related cash outflows seldom coincide with the amount of expense incurred. Interest and taxes are often accrued at the end of one period, with payment taking place on some future date. For example, a review of Powell's data reveals a $1,000 increase in the Income Taxes Payable account, meaning that some reported expense has yet to be paid to taxing authorities. Cash payments for taxes will therefore be less than the accrual-based expense figure. An appropriate formula to use is:

$$\text{Cash Payments for Income Taxes} = \text{Income Tax Expense} \begin{cases} + \text{ Decrease in Income Taxes Payable} \\ - \text{ Increase in Income Taxes Payable} \end{cases}$$

The computation for Powell reveals that $19,000 was disbursed during the period:

$$\$19{,}000 = \$20{,}000 - \$1{,}000$$

A similar procedure is followed to derive interest payments. Because of the absence of an Interest Payable account, the company's expense as disclosed on the income statement ($200,000) equals the funds remitted to lenders.

## The Need for Flexibility

Our examples of prepaid expenses and accruals dealt with selling and administrative items and income taxes, respectively. Be aware that businesses often accrue amounts in the selling and administrative category (e.g., wages), and those same businesses may prepay income taxes and/or interest. The proper accounting treatment in such cases parallels that illustrated earlier. That is, the appropriate prepaid items would be handled with income tax and interest computations (increases being added and decreases subtracted). Also, relevant accruals such as Wages Payable would be merged with selling and administrative expenses, resulting in the following formula:

$$\text{Cash Payments for Selling \& Administrative Expenses} = \text{Selling \& Administrative Expenses} \begin{cases} + \text{ Increases in Prepaid Expenses} \\ - \text{ Decreases in Prepaid Expenses} \end{cases} \begin{cases} + \text{ Decreases in Accrued Liabilities} \\ - \text{ Increases in Accrued Liabilities} \end{cases}$$

[4] This formula and the next one are sometimes modified; see the discussion entitled "The Need for Flexibility" that appears later on this page.

## An Overview

The calculations in the preceding sections can be summarized to show that operating activities generated a net cash inflow of $255,000:

| | | |
|---|---|---|
| Cash received from customers | | $2,975,000 |
| Less cash payments for: | | |
| Purchases of merchandise | $1,045,000 | |
| Selling & administrative expenses | 1,456,000 | |
| Interest | 200,000 | |
| Income taxes | 19,000 | 2,720,000 |
| Net cash provided by operating activities | | $ 255,000 |

This information is eventually combined with the results of financing and investing activities to form the statement of cash flows. The necessary procedures will be shown shortly.

Our discussion of the mechanics related to the direct method is now complete. A careful review of the data in Exhibit 19-4 will reveal that we failed to analyze several items on Powell's income statement, namely, depreciation expense, the loss on the sale of equipment, and the gain from the sale of long-term investments. The reasons will become clear in the next sections.

## Noncash Expenses

Companies normally incur certain *noncash* expenses in the generation of revenue. To illustrate, let us consider depreciation of plant and equipment and amortization of intangibles. The proper journal entries for these items follow.

***Depreciation***

| | | |
|---|---|---|
| Depreciation Expense | XXX | |
| Accumulated Depreciation | | XXX |

***Amortization***

| | | |
|---|---|---|
| Amortization Expense | XXX | |
| Patent, Copyright, etc. | | XXX |

It is evident that cash is not affected by these entries. Because the focus of the direct method is to derive cash flows from operating activities, items such as depreciation and amortization expense can be disregarded in the conversion process.

## Nonoperating Gains and Losses

From time to time a business will generate gains and losses from nonoperating transactions. Common examples are those that arise from bond retirements (a financing activity) and sales of property, plant, and equipment (an investing activity). Regardless of the nature of the underlying transaction, all gains and losses are included in the calculation of net income and shown on the income statement.

On a statement of cash flows, however, the *cash flow effects* of such gains and losses are reflected in a company's financing and investing disclosures. As evidence, the illustration on page 662 gives rise to a $180,000 inflow from an investing activity, which includes the $80,000 gain on the transaction. This illustration shows that when deriving *operating* cash flows with the direct method, any gains or losses related to financing and investing activities should be ignored. Such a procedure is needed to avoid a double-counting.

## The Indirect Method

A company's cash flow from operating activities may be computed by using an alternative approach to that just presented. Under the **indirect method,** operating cash flows are calculated by starting with accrual-basis net income as reported on the income statement. This figure is then converted to the cash basis by adding and subtracting certain amounts. Stated differently, rather than adjust the *individual* income-statement items (sales, cost of goods sold, interest expense, and so forth) to reflect receipts and disbursements, the conversion is done indirectly through bottom-line income.

The conversion process requires the accountant once again to address the issues of noncash expenses, gains and losses on nonoperating transactions, and changes in the balances of selected accounts (e.g., Accounts Receivable and Merchandise Inventory). As we will see, these items are now considered from a slightly different perspective.

### Noncash Expenses; Nonoperating Gains and Losses

Under the direct method, noncash expenses such as depreciation and amortization were ignored when deriving cash flows from operating activities. Keep in mind that with the *indirect* method, the starting point is net income. Depreciation and amortization, of course, are deducted from revenues in computing this figure. Because these expenses cause a decrease in profitability without an accompanying reduction in cash, they must be added back to net income to arrive at an entity's operating cash flows. In Powell's case, the $40,000 net income figure would be increased by the depreciation write-offs of $25,000 and $70,000 as the first step in computing the proper cash flow number.

Similar procedures are followed for gains and losses from nonoperating activities, which are also considered in the calculation of net income. As noted earlier, the cash flow effects of such transactions are reflected in the financing and investing disclosures of a firm. Accordingly, the computation of net cash flows from *operating* activities requires that such amounts be "backed out" of accrual income when performing the conversion process. To the extent that net income includes nonoperating gains, these gains must be subtracted to arrive at cash flows from operating activities; conversely, losses must be added.

### Current Assets and Current Liabilities

As a final step, changes in certain account balances must be studied to determine uncollected revenues, unpaid purchases, interest and income taxes incurred but not yet disbursed, and so forth. The accounts are the same as those utilized with the direct method, namely, the current assets and current liabilities of Powell Corporation that appear in Exhibit 19-4.

When using the indirect method the accountant is making additions to and subtractions from net income rather than adjusting individual income-statement components. With one exception, the rules concerning the treatment of increases and decreases in account balances are identical to those shown on the preceding pages. Powell, for instance, subtracted its $25,000 increase in Accounts Receivable from sales when converting the accrual-based figure to cash received from customers (see p. 666). The same effect is achieved under the indirect method, but now the increase is subtracted from net income. Had there been a decrease in the accounts receivable balance, the decrease would have been added to net income.

The exception just noted relates to components that are deducted from revenues in the determination of net income, namely, cost of goods sold, selling and administrative expenses, interest expense, and income tax expense. Rules for the addition and subtraction of current assets and current liabilities connected with these items are the opposite of those presented earlier. For example, Powell's $1,000 increase in the Income Taxes Payable account means reported expense exceeded disbursements to taxing authorities. A larger expense amount translates into less income than cash flow, calling for an *addition* to net income when converting to the cash basis. Generally stated, decreases in current assets and increases in current liabilities are added to accrual-based net income in the conversion process, while increases in current assets and decreases in current liabilities are subtracted.

These addition and subtraction rules apply only to current assets and current liabilities that are related to operations. Consider that certain short-term obligations (e.g., notes payable and notes receivable) are often created in borrowing transactions, which are *financing* activities. Placement of such items in the operating section of the cash flows statement is therefore not appropriate.

The procedures required by the indirect method are summarized in Exhibit 19-5. Application of these rules to the Powell Corporation data yields a net cash flow from operating activities of $255,000—the same result as that achieved under the direct approach. The outcome is identical; only the methodology differs.

## Preparation of a Statement of Cash Flows

**OBJECTIVE 5**
**Be able to prepare a statement of cash flows.**

Having introduced you to the various sections of the statement of cash flows, we now turn our attention to the procedures required for preparation. The information needed to construct the statement comes from a variety of sources: the income statement, statement of retained earnings, comparative balance sheets, and ledger accounts. To illustrate the necessary procedures, we will continue the Powell Corporation example (see Exhibit 19-6 for additional data). As you study this material, proceed slowly and keep the previous discussion in mind.

### Step 1: Analyze the Cash Account

Because the statement will concentrate on the inflows and outflows of cash, the first step is to determine the change in Powell's Cash account. According to the comparative balance sheets, the company's cash increased by $50,000 during 19X2. The increase, which represents the bottom-line amount to be explained on the statement of cash flows, is caused by the firm's operating, investing, and financing activities.

### Step 2: Determine Net Cash Flow from Operating Activities

Step 2, which is the focal point of the direct and indirect methods, has already been performed. Observe that the account balance changes introduced earlier for current assets and current liabilities (Accounts Receivable, Merchandise Inventory, Prepaid Selling Expenses, Accounts Payable, and Income Taxes Payable) are now reflected

**Exhibit 19-5**
**Computing the Cash Flow from Operating Activities: Indirect Approach**

| | *Adjustment Needed to Accrual-Basis Income* |
|---|---|
| Net income, accrual basis | $XX,XXX |
| Add (deduct) items to convert net income to a cash basis | |
| Noncash expenses (e.g., depreciation, amortization) | Add |
| Gains/losses related to nonoperating activities | |
| Gains | Deduct |
| Losses | Add |
| Current assets related to operating activities | |
| Increase in account balance | Deduct |
| Decrease in account balance | Add |
| Current liabilities related to operating activities | |
| Increase in account balance | Add |
| Decrease in account balance | Deduct |
| Net cash provided (used) by operating activities | $XX,XXX |

***For Powell Corporation***

| | | |
|---|---|---|
| Cash flows from operating activities | | |
| Net income | | $ 40,000 |
| Add (deduct) items to convert net income to a cash basis | | |
| Building depreciation expense | $ 25,000 | |
| Equipment depreciation expense | 70,000 | |
| Loss on sale of equipment | 5,000 | |
| Gain on sale of long-term investments | (15,000) | |
| Increase in accounts receivable (net) | (25,000) | |
| Decrease in merchandise inventory | 25,000 | |
| Increase in prepaid selling expenses | (1,000) | |
| Increase in accounts payable | 130,000 | |
| Increase in income taxes payable | 1,000 | 215,000 |
| Net cash provided by operating activities | | $255,000 |

in the firm's comparative balance sheets. A careful study of the balance sheets, however, will find two current accounts—Cash and Notes Payable—that were ignored in the initial presentation (Exhibit 19-4). Cash was omitted because our objective was to show how changes in other current accounts affected the cash generated from operations. Similarly, Notes Payable was disregarded because the obligations arose from borrowing transactions (i.e., *financing* activities) conducted with First Pacific Trust. Remember, the current assets and current liabilities used with the direct and indirect conversion methods must pertain to operations.

## Step 3: Analyze Remaining Balance Sheet Accounts

The third step is to analyze the remaining balance-sheet accounts to determine the effect, if any, of a company's investing and financing activities. We begin with an evaluation of Land.

## HIGHLIGHT

# Let the Cash Flow

The statement of cash flows has evolved from a supplementary academic exercise into a report that is considered to be a primary financial statement. As recently as 30 years ago, few companies monitored cash flows very closely even though accounting educators urged them to do so. Why the fuss over inflows and outflows? In plain and simple terms, all companies move on cash, not income. You can't pay creditors with profits; they accept cash. You can't pay employees with earnings, only cash. And when someone asks if a firm has been making money, all they probably want to know is whether the company has any cash left over to show for its efforts.

A finance professor at the University of Southern California notes that the preceding comments may sound extreme. However, he observes that time and time again managers complain, "If I'm making such big profits, why don't I have any money?" It doesn't matter whether the industry is high tech or low, smokestack or service. In the end an entity must have enough money to pay its obligations or its survival will be threatened. [1] Although they have since reorganized and continue to operate, many companies (including Chrysler) have learned this lesson the hard way.

To the surprise of many, businesses can have cash flow problems not only when sales are low but also when demand is strong. To illustrate the phenomenon of going broke while making a profit, we will focus on the Pure Spring Water Co., which began operations in May with $30,000 cash. [2] The firm expects to find customers for its bottled water products who are willing to pay $25 per month. Customers are billed when serviced and settle their accounts in the following month. Pure Spring pays its supplier $15 per customer upon pick-up of the bottled goods.

---

The company serviced 400 customers in May. Customer billings totaled $10,000 (400 × $25); the supplier was paid $6,000 (400 × $15). No receivables were collected.

May 31: Cash, $24,000 Receivables, $10,000
Net income, $4,000

---

Sales tripled during June, with the firm servicing 1,200 customers. Pure Spring paid its supplier $18,000 (1,200 × $15) and billed customers $30,000 (1,200 × $25) for water sold. The company collected May's receivables of $10,000.

June 30: Cash, $16,000 Receivables, $30,000
Net income, $12,000

---

During July, sales once again skyrocketed. Sales and billings amounting to $75,000 were made to 3,000 customers (3,000 × $25 = $75,000). Pure Spring paid the supplier $45,000 (3,000 × $15) and collected $30,000 from June's receivables.

July 31: Cash, $1,000 Receivables, $75,000
Net income, $30,000

---

A heat wave struck and temperatures soared in August. The firm serviced 6,000 customers and billed $150,000 for water sold. July's receivables of $75,000 were collected, and Pure Spring wrote a $90,000 check (6,000 × $15) to cover the cost of its purchases. The check was paid by the bank, but only after the bank president was assured that the rapidly-growing water company would "clean up its act."

August 31: Cash, $(14,000) Receivables, $150,000
Net income, $60,000

---

Pure Spring's dilemma (along with those of much less successful entities) would have been highlighted in the operating activities section of the statement of cash flows. In general, the statement of cash flows signals effective implementation of a company's cash management strategies or, conversely, forthcoming problems.

SOURCES: Adapted from "How to Go Broke . . . While Making a Profit," *Business Week*, April 28, 1956, pp. 46–47 [2]; and "When is There Cash in Cash Flow?", *Harvard Business Review*, March/April 1987, pp. 38–39, 42–43, 46, 48–49 [1].

**Exhibit 19-6**
**Powell Corporation Financial Information**

**POWELL CORPORATION**
**Comparative Balance Sheets**
**December 31, 19X2 and 19X1**

| | *19X2* | *19X1* | *Increase (Decrease)* |
|---|---|---|---|
| ***Assets*** | | | |
| Current assets | | | |
| Cash | $ 100,000 | $ 50,000 | $ 50,000 |
| Accounts receivable (net) | 400,000 | 375,000 | 25,000 |
| Merchandise inventory | 425,000 | 450,000 | (25,000) |
| Prepaid selling expenses | 5,000 | 4,000 | 1,000 |
| Total current assets | $ 930,000 | $ 879,000 | $ 51,000 |
| Property, plant, & equipment | | | |
| Land | $ 200,000 | $ 115,000 | $ 85,000 |
| Buildings | 1,450,000 | 1,250,000 | 200,000 |
| Accumulated depreciation: buildings | (50,000) | (25,000) | (25,000) |
| Equipment | 725,000 | 800,000 | (75,000) |
| Accumulated depreciation: equipment | (250,000) | (260,000) | 10,000 |
| Total property, plant, & equipment | $2,075,000 | $1,880,000 | $ 195,000 |
| Other assets | | | |
| Long-term investments | $ 880,000 | $1,000,000 | $(120,000) |
| Total assets | $3,885,000 | $3,759,000 | $ 126,000 |
| ***Liabilities & Stockholders' Equity*** | | | |
| Current liabilities | | | |
| Accounts payable | $ 470,000 | $ 340,000 | $ 130,000 |
| Notes payable* | — | 300,000 | (300,000) |
| Income taxes payable | 40,000 | 39,000 | 1,000 |
| Total current liabilities | $ 510,000 | $ 679,000 | $(169,000) |
| Long-term liabilities | | | |
| Bonds payable | $2,070,000 | $2,000,000 | $ 70,000 |
| Stockholders' equity | | | |
| Common stock, par value $1 | $ 195,000 | $ 130,000 | $ 65,000 |
| Paid-in capital in excess of par | 635,000 | 500,000 | 135,000 |
| Retained earnings | 475,000 | 450,000 | 25,000 |
| Total stockholders' equity | $1,305,000 | $1,080,000 | $ 225,000 |
| Total liabilities & stockholders' equity | $3,885,000 | $3,759,000 | $ 126,000 |

* Owed to First Pacific Trust for monies borrowed in late 19X1.

**Exhibit 19-6 (continued)**

**POWELL CORPORATION**
**Statement of Retained Earnings**
**For the Year Ended December 31, 19X2**

| | |
|---|---|
| Retained earnings, 1/1/X2 | $450,000 |
| Add: Net income | 40,000 |
| | $490,000 |
| Less: Cash dividend | 15,000 |
| Retained earnings, 12/31/X2 | $475,000 |

## Land

The Land account increased by $85,000 during the year. An analysis of the ledger account revealed that land was purchased for cash on October 19.

***Land***

| Date | Description | Debit | Credit |
|---|---|---|---|
| 1/1/X2 | Balance | 115,000 | |
| 10/19/X2 | Purchased land for cash | 85,000 | |
| | | **200,000** | |

The increase in this asset results from an $85,000 use of cash and would be reported in the statement of cash flows as an investing activity, as follows:

| | |
|---|---|
| Cash flows from investing activities | |
| Purchase of land | $(85,000) |

## Buildings

Continuing down the balance sheet, the next account, Buildings, increased $200,000, from $1.25 million to $1.45 million. An examination of the ledger account revealed that a building was acquired on the last day of the year in exchange for 65,000 shares of the company's $1 par-value common stock.

***Buildings***

| Date | Description | Debit | Credit |
|---|---|---|---|
| 1/1/X2 | Balance | 1,250,000 | |
| 12/31/X2 | Acquired building; issued common stock | 200,000 | |
| | | **1,450,000** | |

Although the acquisition does not involve cash, the financial position of Powell Corporation has been significantly affected. Recall from our earlier discussion that such exchange transactions are reported on the statement of cash flows as a noncash investing/financing activity. Therefore, the building acquisition is disclosed in a separate schedule in the manner shown.

| Schedule of noncash investing/financing activities | |
|---|---|
| Common stock issued for building | $200,000 |

## Accumulated Depreciation: Buildings

The Accumulated Depreciation: Buildings account increased by $25,000 during 19X2 because of annual depreciation expense (see the income statement in Exhibit 19-4).

| *Accumulated Depreciation: Buildings* | | | |
|---|---|---|---|
| | 1/1/X2 | Balance | 25,000 |
| | 12/31/X2 | Adjusting entry: annual depreciation | 25,000 |
| | | | **50,000** |

The proper treatment of this expense was considered previously in the computation of net cash flows from operating activities and need not be addressed again.

## Equipment and Accumulated Depreciation: Equipment

Powell's Equipment balance decreased by $75,000 during the year, perhaps because of a discard or a sale. A probe of the general ledger revealed that two transactions actually occurred.

May 1 Sold $100,000 of equipment for cash.
Nov. 1 Purchased $25,000 of equipment for cash.

| *Equipment* | | | | | |
|---|---|---|---|---|---|
| 1/1/X2 | Balance | 800,000 | 5/1/X2 | Disposal for cash | 100,000 |
| 11/1/X2 | Purchase for cash | 25,000 | | | |
| | (725,000) | **825,000** | | | |

As you can see, an overreliance on ending account balances could result in a failure to detect all changes in cash. In this case, for instance, Powell had a receipt and a disbursement of cash that require separate disclosure. Offsetting or netting is really inappropriate.

Continuing our examination of these two transactions, the Accumulated Depreciation: Equipment account reveals that (1) depreciation associated with the disposal totaled $80,000 and (2) 19X2 depreciation expense amounted to $70,000.

| Accumulated Depreciation: Equipment | | | | | |
|---|---|---|---|---|---|
| 5/1/X2 | Disposal | 80,000 | 1/1/X2 | Balance | 260,000 |
| | | | 12/31/X2 | Adjusting entry: annual depreciation | 70,000 |
| | | | | 250,000 | 330,000 |

From an analysis of both ledger accounts we can determine that the equipment sold on May 1 had a $20,000 book value (cost of $100,000 minus accumulated depreciation of $80,000). Furthermore, the income statement reported a $5,000 loss from equipment sales, meaning that Powell must have received cash proceeds of $15,000 on the disposal. The necessary calculations are:

| | |
|---|---|
| Equipment cost | $100,000 |
| Accumulated depreciation | 80,000 |
| Book value | $ 20,000 |
| Proceeds from disposal | 15,000 |
| Loss | $ 5,000 |

The purchase and sale of equipment arose from investment-related activities and are disclosed on the statement of cash flows, as follows:

| | |
|---|---|
| Cash flows from investing activities | |
| Purchase of equipment | $(25,000) |
| Proceeds from disposal of equipment | 15,000 |

The proper treatment of equipment depreciation expense and the loss was discussed in the section that pertained to operating cash flows and is not repeated here.

## Long-Term Investments

The comparative balance sheets indicate that the Long-term Investments account decreased from $1 million to $880,000 during the year. The ledger account appears as shown:

| Long-term Investments | | | | | |
|---|---|---|---|---|---|
| 1/1/X2 | Balance | 1,000,000 | 4/15/X2 | Sold securities for cash | 120,000 |
| | 880,000 | | | | |

Powell's management reports that the securities were sold for $135,000, thus generating the $15,000 gain that appears on the income statement (see Exhibit 19-4). The gain was handled previously when computing the net cash flow from operating activities. The $135,000 inflow, on the other hand, would be disclosed in the investing-activities section as follows:

| Cash flows from investing activities | |
|---|---|
| Proceeds from sale of long-term investments | $135,000 |

## Notes Payable

The next balance-sheet account to be considered is Notes Payable.

**Notes Payable**

| | | | | | |
|---|---|---|---|---|---|
| 8/15/X2 | Paid to First Pacific Trust | 300,000 | 1/1/X2 | Balance | 300,000 |
| | | | | -0- | |

As stated in Exhibit 19-6, the balance in this account arose from a borrowing transaction with First Pacific Trust. The $300,000 debt reduction during 19X2 was caused by repayment of the note's principal and is therefore considered a financing activity of the firm. The proper presentation on the statement of cash flows is

| Cash flows from financing activities | |
|---|---|
| Payment to settle short-term note | $(300,000) |

## Bonds Payable

A review of the ledger showed that Powell had issued $70,000 of bonds on February 14.

**Bonds Payable**

| | | | | | |
|---|---|---|---|---|---|
| | | | 1/1/X2 | Balance | 2,000,000 |
| | | | 2/14/X2 | Issued bonds at face for cash | 70,000 |
| | | | | | **2,070,000** |

The issuance is disclosed in the financing-activities section of the statement of cash flows in the following manner:

| Cash flows from financing activities | |
|---|---|
| Proceeds from bond issue | $70,000 |

## Common Stock and Paid-in Capital in Excess of Par

During 19X2, the Common Stock and Paid-in Capital in Excess of Par accounts increased by $65,000 and $135,000, respectively. These hikes were caused by the issuance of 65,000 shares of $1 par-value stock in exchange for a $200,000 building (see p. 675) and appear in the ledger as shown:

| *Common Stock, Par Value $1* | | | |
|---|---|---|---|
| | 1/1/X2 | Balance | 130,000 |
| | 12/31/X2 | Issued 65,000 shares for building | 65,000 |
| | | | **195,000** |

| *Paid-in Capital in Excess of Par* | | | |
|---|---|---|---|
| | 1/1/X2 | Balance | 500,000 |
| | 12/31/X2 | Issued 65,000 shares for building | 135,000 |
| | | | **635,000** |

Proper disclosure of the December 31 issuance on the statement of cash flows was illustrated earlier when the Buildings account was discussed. Observe that *for statement presentation purposes,* it is not necessary to subdivide the $200,000 into the individual amounts that were credited to Common Stock and Paid-in Capital in Excess of Par. Such a breakdown would have minimal value to financial statement users.

## Retained Earnings

The final account on Powell's comparative balance sheet is Retained Earnings, which increased by $25,000 during 19X2. As reported on the statement of retained earnings (see Exhibit 19-6), this increase was the result of $40,000 of net income and a $15,000 cash dividend. The Retained Earnings account therefore appears as follows:

| *Retained Earnings* | | | | | |
|---|---|---|---|---|---|
| 4/30/X2 | Cash dividend | 15,000 | 1/1/X2 | Balance | 450,000 |
| | | | 12/31/X2 | Net income (via closing) | 40,000 |
| | | | | (475,000) | **490,000** |

Net income was previously considered when computing cash flow from operating activities. The dividend distribution, a financing transaction, is reported in the following manner:

| Cash flows from financing activities | |
|---|---|
| Dividend paid | $(15,000) |

## Step 4: Financial Statement Preparation

Once the changes in all balance-sheet accounts have been determined and analyzed, the formal financial statement is prepared. The statement of cash flows for

Powell Corporation appears in Exhibit 19-7 (direct method) and Exhibit 19-8 (indirect method). Observe that the statement is merely the summation of the operating activities discussion (direct, p. 669; indirect, Exhibit 19-5) and the individual investing, financing, and noncash investing/financing activities (noted in shaded blocks) from Step 3. The combined inflows and outflows under both methods produce a $50,000 increase in cash, which agrees with the company's comparative balance-sheet presentation.

## ▶ TIPS & TECHNIQUES

A review of Exhibits 19-7 and 19-8 will reveal identical investing and financing disclosures; only the operating sections differ. The direct approach is said to be more useful to lenders, who desire information on specific inflows and outflows when judging a company's ability to repay debt. However, many people find the indirect approach easier to understand, because most businesses have used this means of disclosure in the past. In sum, neither method is clearly superior, and the method selected for reporting is a matter of personal preference.

**Exhibit 19-7**
**Statement of Cash Flows: Direct Approach**

**POWELL CORPORATION**
**Statement of Cash Flows—Direct Approach**
**For the Year Ended December 31, 19X2**

| | | |
|---|---|---|
| Cash flows from operating activities | | |
| Cash received from customers | | $2,975,000 |
| Less cash payments for: | | |
| Purchases of merchandise | $1,045,000 | |
| Selling & administrative expenses | 1,456,000 | |
| Interest | 200,000 | |
| Income taxes | 19,000 | 2,720,000 |
| Net cash provided by operating activities | | $ 255,000 |
| Cash flows from investing activities | | |
| Purchase of land | $ (85,000) | |
| Purchase of equipment | (25,000) | |
| Proceeds from disposal of equipment | 15,000 | |
| Proceeds from sale of long-term investments | 135,000 | |
| Net cash provided by investing activities | | 40,000 |
| Cash flows from financing activities | | |
| Payment to settle short-term note | $ (300,000) | |
| Proceeds from bond issue | 70,000 | |
| Dividend paid | (15,000) | |
| Net cash used by financing activities | | (245,000) |
| Net increase (decrease) in cash | | $ 50,000 |
| Cash balance, January 1, 19X2 | | 50,000 |
| Cash balance, December 31, 19X2 | | $ 100,000 |
| Schedule of noncash investing/financing activities | | |
| Common stock issued for building | | $ 200,000 |

**Exhibit 19-8**
**Statement of Cash Flows: Indirect Approach**

**POWELL CORPORATION**
**Statement of Cash Flows—Indirect Approach**
**For the Year Ended December 31, 19X2**

| | | |
|---|---|---|
| Cash flows from operating activities | | |
| Net income | | $ 40,000 |
| Add (deduct) items to convert net income to a cash basis | | |
| Building depreciation expense | $ 25,000 | |
| Equipment depreciation expense | 70,000 | |
| Loss on sale of equipment | 5,000 | |
| Gain on sale of long-term investments | (15,000) | |
| Increase in accounts receivable (net) | (25,000) | |
| Decrease in merchandise inventory | 25,000 | |
| Increase in prepaid selling expenses | (1,000) | |
| Increase in accounts payable | 130,000 | |
| Increase in income taxes payable | 1,000 | 215,000 |
| Net cash provided by operating activities | | $ 255,000 |
| Cash flows from investing activities | | |
| Purchase of land | $ (85,000) | |
| Purchase of equipment | (25,000) | |
| Proceeds from disposal of equipment | 15,000 | |
| Proceeds from sale of long-term investments | 135,000 | |
| Net cash provided by investing activities | | 40,000 |
| Cash flows from financing activities | | |
| Payment to settle short-term note | $(300,000) | |
| Proceeds from bond issue | 70,000 | |
| Dividend paid | (15,000) | |
| Net cash used by financing activities | | (245,000) |
| Net increase (decrease) in cash | | $ 50,000 |
| Cash balance, January 1, 19X2 | | 50,000 |
| Cash balance, December 31, 19X2 | | $ 100,000 |
| Schedule of noncash investing/financing activities | | |
| Common stock issued for building | | $ 200,000 |

## APPENDIX Work Sheet for Preparing a Statement of Cash Flows—Indirect Approach

Some accountants use a work sheet when constructing the statement of cash flows. A work sheet provides more structure and helps to ensure that no accounts are accidentally overlooked in the statement preparation process. Whether or not a work sheet is generated, the end result is the same: a financial report that reveals an entity's operating, investing, and financing activities.

To illustrate a work sheet for the indirect method of statement presentation, we will utilize data introduced earlier in the chapter that relate to Powell Corporation. It is helpful to review Exhibits 19-4 and 19-6 at this time.

**Exhibit 19-9**
**Cash Flow Work Sheet—Indirect Approach**

**POWELL CORPORATION**
**Work Sheet for Statement of Cash Flows—Indirect Approach**
**For the Year Ended December 31, 19X2**

| | *Account Balances, 12/31/X1* | *Analysis of Transactions for 19X2* | | | | *Account Balances, 12/31/X2* |
|---|---|---|---|---|---|---|
| | | *Debit* | | *Credit* | | |
| ***Debits*** | | | | | | |
| Cash | 50,000 | (*x*) | 50,000 | | | 100,000 |
| Accounts receivable (net) | 375,000 | (*d*) | 25,000 | | | 400,000 |
| Merchandise inventory | 450,000 | | | (*e*) | 25,000 | 425,000 |
| Prepaid selling expenses | 4,000 | (*f*) | 1,000 | | | 5,000 |
| Land | 115,000 | (*i*) | 85,000 | | | 200,000 |
| Buildings | 1,250,000 | (*j**) | 200,000 | | | 1,450,000 |
| Equipment | 800,000 | (*k*) | 25,000 | (*l*) | 100,000 | 725,000 |
| Long-term investments | 1,000,000 | | | (*m*) | 120,000 | 880,000 |
| | 4,044,000 | | | | | 4,185,000 |
| ***Credits*** | | | | | | |
| Accumulated depreciation: buildings | 25,000 | | | (*b*) | 25,000 | 50,000 |
| Accumulated depreciation: equipment | 260,000 | (*l*) | 80,000 | (*c*) | 70,000 | 250,000 |
| Accounts payable | 340,000 | | | (*g*) | 130,000 | 470,000 |
| Notes payable | 300,000 | (*n*) | 300,000 | | | — |
| Income taxes payable | 39,000 | | | (*h*) | 1,000 | 40,000 |
| Bonds payable | 2,000,000 | | | (*o*) | 70,000 | 2,070,000 |
| Common stock | 130,000 | | | (*j*) | 65,000 | 195,000 |
| Paid-in capital in excess of par | 500,000 | | | (*j*) | 135,000 | 635,000 |
| Retained earnings | 450,000 | (*p*) | 15,000 | (*a*) | 40,000 | 475,000 |
| | 4,044,000 | | | | | 4,185,000 |

| | | | | | |
|---|---|---|---|---|---|
| Operating activities | | | | | |
| Net income | | (*a*) | 40,000 | | |
| Building depreciation expense | | (*b*) | 25,000 | | |
| Equipment depreciation expense | | (*c*) | 70,000 | | |
| Increase in accounts receivable | | | | (*d*) | 25,000 |
| Decrease in merchandise inventory | | (*e*) | 25,000 | | |
| Increase in prepaid selling expenses | | | | (*f*) | 1,000 |
| Increase in accounts payable | | (*g*) | 130,000 | | |
| Increase in income taxes payable | | (*h*) | 1,000 | | |
| Loss on sale of equipment | | (*l*) | 5,000 | | |
| Gain on sale of long-term investments | | | | (*m*) | 15,000 |
| Investing activities | | | | | |
| Purchase of land | | | | (*i*) | 85,000 |
| Purchase of equipment | | | | (*k*) | 25,000 |
| Proceeds from disposal of equipment | | (*l*) | 15,000 | | |
| Proceeds from sale of long-term investments | | (*m*) | 135,000 | | |
| Financing activities | | | | | |
| Payment to settle short-term note | | | | (*n*) | 300,000 |
| Proceeds from bond issue | | (*o*) | 70,000 | | |
| Dividends paid | | | | (*p*) | 15,000 |
| Noncash activities | | | | | |
| Common stock issued for building | | (*j*) | 200,000 | (*j**) | 200,000 |
| | | | 1,497,000 | | 1,447,000 |
| Increase in cash | | | | (*x*) | 50,000 |
| | | | 1,497,000 | | 1,497,000 |

Construction of a work sheet requires performance of the five steps that follow.

- *Step 1*—Enter the beginning and ending account balances of all balance sheet items (see Exhibit 19-9). All accounts with debit balances are listed first, followed by those with credit balances. This procedure results in the accumulated depreciation accounts being listed together with liabilities and the components of stockholders' equity.
- *Step 2*—Obtain the total of the debits and credits, both at the beginning and end of the year, to assure that the required equality is maintained on the two dates.
- *Step 3*—Insert the headings "Operating Activities," "Investing Activities," "Financing Activities," and "Noncash Activities" on the work sheet where shown. Leave sufficient space so that a number of items may eventually be recorded.
- *Step 4*—Make entries in the Analysis columns of the work sheet to account for (1) changes in the noncash accounts during the reporting period *and* (2) the accompanying inflows and outflows of cash. These entries are used for work sheet preparation purposes only; they are never recorded in the general journal. The entries may be made in any order; our sequence will parallel Exhibit 19-5 and the discussion on pages 675–679.

  (*a*) *Generated net income of $40,000 during the year.* Profitable operations represent a source of cash for a firm. The analysis entry recognizes this fact by establishing a line entitled "Net Income" in the Operating Activities section. In addition, Retained Earnings is increased (credited) for $40,000 to reflect that income is closed to this account at the end of the reporting period.

  (*b*) *Building depreciation expense of $25,000.* Depreciation must be added back to net income to arrive at cash flows from operating activities. Recall that although depreciation is deducted from revenues to determine an entity's earnings, no cash is consumed. The required entry in the Analysis columns involves a credit to Accumulated Depreciation: Buildings and an offsetting debit to Building Depreciation Expense, immediately below Powell's net income figure.

  (*c*) *Equipment depreciation expense of $70,000.* This amount is treated in similar fashion to that cited in item (*b*).

  (*d*) *Increase in accounts receivable, $25,000.* As noted earlier in the chapter, changes in both current assets and current liabilities related to operations must be considered when deriving the cash flow from operating activities. Decreases in current assets and increases in current liabilities are added to net income to convert to a cash-basis figure, while increases in current assets and decreases in current liabilities are subtracted. The analysis entry reflects the rise in accounts receivable via a $25,000 debit to that account. Further, a credit appears in the Operating Activities section to produce a subtraction from net income, the net income amount having been entered earlier as a debit.

  The following require similar entries on the work sheet to compute the net cash flow from operating activities:

  (*e*) *Decrease in merchandise inventory, $25,000.*
  (*f*) *Increase in prepaid selling expenses, $1,000.*
  (*g*) *Increase in accounts payable, $130,000.*
  (*h*) *Increase in income taxes payable, $1,000.*

  As shown in Exhibit 19-5, two additional items were considered in the operating cash-flow computation: a $5,000 loss on the sale of equipment and a $15,000 gain from the sale of long-term investments. Discussion of these items will be presented shortly.

(*i*) *Purchased land for $85,000 cash.* This transaction required the use of cash and also resulted in an $85,000 increase to the Land account. The necessary entry is therefore a debit to Land, with an offsetting credit to establish a line for Purchase of Land in the Investing Activities section.

(*j*) *Acquired a $200,000 building in exchange for 65,000 shares of $1 par-value common stock.* This exchange transaction involves three accounts and is disclosed as a noncash activity. First, the Common Stock and Paid-in Capital in Excess of Par Value accounts are respectively credited for $65,000 and $135,000 to reflect the issuance of additional shares, with a $200,000 debit then being made to the line "Common Stock Issued for Building." Next, the Buildings account is debited (see *j**) to record the acquisition, and a credit is entered on the same line as that just noted: "Common Stock Issued for Building."

(*k*) *Purchased $25,000 of equipment for cash.* This acquisition resulted in a cash outflow and also a $25,000 increase in the Equipment account. The analysis entry requires a debit to Equipment; in addition, a corresponding credit is needed in the Investing Activities section to establish the Purchase of Equipment line item.

(*l*) *Disposed of $100,000 of equipment for cash; incurred a $5,000 loss.* The underlying details of this transaction are shown on page 677. The required work sheet entry involves recognition of $15,000 cash proceeds, along with reductions in Equipment ($100,000) and Accumulated Depreciation: Equipment ($80,000). The $5,000 loss is recorded via a debit and is added to net income to arrive at cash flows from operations.

(*m*) *Sold $120,000 of long-term investments for $135,000; generated a $15,000 gain.* This transaction requires a reduction (i.e., credit) in the Long-term Investments account for $120,000, and the establishment of a $135,000 receipt of cash in the Investing Activities section (via a corresponding debit). Furthermore, because the $15,000 gain is already included in net income, it must be subtracted when computing cash flows from operating activities to avoid a double-counting. The gain is therefore set out (via a credit) in the Operating Activities section to yield the desired result.

(*n*) *Paid a short-term note payable, $300,000.* This financing activity resulted in a cash outflow during the period. The necessary entry is reflected by a debit to the Notes Payable account and a credit to the line entitled "Payment to Settle Short-term Note."

(*o*) *Issued $70,000 of bonds payable at face value.* The issuance increases cash via a financing activity. The work sheet entry recognizes this fact and also increases (credits) the Bonds Payable account to reflect the rise in Powell's liabilities.

(*p*) *Paid cash dividends, $15,000.* Powell paid $15,000 of dividends during 19X2. The analysis entry therefore involves a $15,000 debit to Retained Earnings to record the appropriate reduction. In addition, a $15,000 credit is made in the Financing Activities section to establish a line item for the payment.

- *Step 5*—Compute the difference between the beginning and ending cash balances, and place the difference (labeled *x*) on the Cash line in the Analysis columns. Increases are entered in the debit column and decreases in the credit column. Next, total the Analysis columns and place the amount labeled *x* at the bottom of the work sheet for balancing purposes. The document is now complete and can be used to prepare the formal statement of cash flows. (Compare the bottom of the work sheet with the statement that appears in Exhibit 19-8.)

## Chapter Review

### Learning Objectives—The Key Points

**1 Understand the purpose of the statement of cash flows.** The statement of cash flows is designed to provide information about the nature and sources of an entity's cash inflows and outflows. These items are categorized into operating, investing, and financing classifications. Overall, this important report lends insight into a company's need for external financing and the firm's ability to generate future cash flows, meet obligations, and pay dividends.

**2 Be able to distinguish among operating, investing, and financing activities.** Operating activities give rise to transactions and events that enter into the determination of net income. The FASB defines these activities to include all transactions and events that are not otherwise classified in the investing or financing categories. Examples include receipts from customers, normal business expenses, and receipts of dividends and loan interest. In contrast, investing activities involve the investment of a firm's resources. Typical examples of such transactions are the acquisition and sale of both productive assets (e.g., property, plant, and equipment) and securities of other firms. Finally, financing activities provide a business with resources from either its owners or its creditors. Common financing transactions include the issuance and retirement of stock and debt.

**3 Understand the proper accounting treatment for significant noncash investing/financing activities.** Noncash investing and financing transactions (e.g., the issuance of stock for land) are reported separately on the statement of cash flows. The purpose of this disclosure is to reveal the impact of such transactions on a company's financial position, even though no direct receipt or disbursement of cash has occurred.

**4 Be familiar with the direct and indirect methods of computing cash flows from operating activities.** Under the direct method, individual income statement items are converted from the accrual basis of accounting to the cash basis of accounting. For instance, to translate sales revenues into the amount of cash received from customers, decreases in accounts receivable are added to sales and increases are subtracted. To determine cash payments for merchandise, it is necessary to adjust an entity's cost of goods sold for changes in merchandise inventory (increases are added and decreases are subtracted) and accounts payable (decreases are added and increases are subtracted).

The indirect method, on the other hand, begins with the net income figure, adds back noncash expenses (e.g., depreciation and amortization), and adjusts for gains and losses on nonoperating transactions. In addition, changes in current assets and current liabilities related to operations are added to or subtracted from net income. Decreases in current assets and increases in current liabilities are added to net income, while increases in current assets and decreases in current liabilities are subtracted.

**5 Be able to prepare a statement of cash flows.** The statement of cash flows may be prepared by using either the direct method or the indirect method, although the former approach is encouraged by the Financial Accounting Standards Board. The direct method begins with a presentation of cash receipts and disbursements for specific operating items (including interest and taxes) to arrive at cash flows from operating activities. Cash flows from investing and financing activities are reported next, followed by a schedule of noncash investing/financing transactions.

The indirect method begins with a reconciliation of net income to cash flows from operations and then presents cash flows from investing and financing activities. The statement concludes with the same schedule of noncash investing/financing transactions.

## Chapter Quiz

The five questions that follow relate to several issues raised in the chapter. Test your knowledge of the issues by selecting the best answer. (The answers appear on p. 707.)

**1** Which of the following is a financing activity?
a Purchase of office equipment.
b Payment of dividends.
c Receipt of dividends.
d Sale of merchandise inventory on account.

**2** When preparing a statement of cash flows, the direct method is often used in calculating the cash flows from:
a operating, investing, and financing activities.
b investing and financing activities.
c operating and investing activities.
d operating activities only.

**3** When converting accrual-based net income to the cash basis with the indirect method, which of the following items is added in the operating activities section of the cash-flow statement?
a Dividends paid.
b Cash dividends received.
c Loss on the sale of land.
d Gain on the sale of land.

**4** Phillips Corporation's net cash flow provided by investing activities totaled $100,000 for the year. Dividends paid amounted to $5,000, payments to retire outstanding loans were $40,000, depreciation expense on buildings was $15,000, and new equipment acquired cost $30,000. If the company sold land for cash, the proceeds from the sale must have been:
a $10,000.
b $25,000.
c $100,000.
d $130,000.

**5** The balance of Ebony's Machinery account decreased by $50,000 during the year. Machinery that cost $80,000 was discarded at a local landfill; additional equipment of $130,000 was purchased via the issuance of common stock. In view of these transactions, an examination of the company's cash flows from investing activities will show:
a a $130,000 outflow for the machinery purchase.
b a $130,000 outflow for the machinery purchase and an $80,000 inflow from disposal.
c a $130,000 outflow for the machinery purchase and an $80,000 loss.
d nothing.

## Summary Problem

Colwell Corporation had the balance sheets that appear on the top of the next page.

| | Dec. 31, 19X2 | Dec. 31, 19X1 |
|---|---|---|
| ***Assets*** | | |
| Cash | $ 59,000 | $ 87,000 |
| Accounts receivable (net) | 189,000 | 223,000 |
| Inventory | 65,000 | 45,000 |
| Prepaid selling expenses | 15,000 | 12,000 |
| Land | 150,000 | 120,000 |
| Equipment | 125,000 | 150,000 |
| Accumulated depreciation: equipment | (85,000) | (75,000) |
| Buildings | 280,000 | 200,000 |
| Accumulated depreciation: buildings | (85,000) | (70,000) |
| Patents (net of amortization) | 24,000 | 27,000 |
| Total assets | $737,000 | $719,000 |
| ***Liabilities & Stockholders' Equity*** | | |
| Accounts payable | $ 88,000 | $120,000 |
| Notes payable | 160,000 | 90,000 |
| Income taxes payable | 60,000 | 70,000 |
| Bonds payable | 100,000 | 150,000 |
| Common stock, $10 par | 210,000 | 180,000 |
| Additional paid-in capital | 50,000 | 50,000 |
| Retained earnings | 69,000 | 59,000 |
| Total liabilities & stockholders' equity | $737,000 | $719,000 |

The following additional information was extracted from the accounting records:

1 Three thousand shares of common stock were issued for land having a fair market value of $30,000.
2 Equipment having a book value of $13,000 (cost, $25,000; accumulated depreciation, $12,000) was sold for $20,000 cash, producing a $7,000 gain.
3 A building was constructed for $80,000 cash.
4 The notes payable relate to various borrowing agreements signed with Fairfax Savings Bank.
5 Long-term bonds of $50,000 were retired; no gain or loss was incurred.
6 Cash dividends of $10,000 were declared and paid during 19X2.
7 The 19X2 income statement revealed the data shown:

| | |
|---|---|
| Sales | $1,450,000 |
| Cost of goods sold | 835,000 |
| Selling and administrative expenses | 510,000 |
| Equipment depreciation expense | 22,000 |
| Building depreciation expense | 15,000 |
| Patent amortization expense | 3,000 |
| Interest expense | 32,000 |
| Income tax expense | 20,000 |
| Net income | 20,000 |

**Instructions**

**a** Prepare a statement of cash flows for the year ended December 31, 19X2. Use the direct method.

**b** Prepare a statement of cash flows for the year ended December 31, 19X2. Use the indirect method.

**Solution**

**a**

**COLWELL CORPORATION**
**Statement of Cash Flows**
**For the Year Ended December 31, 19X2**

| | | |
|---|---|---|
| Cash flows from operating activities | | |
| Cash received from customers | | $1,484,000* |
| Less cash payments for: | | |
| Purchases of merchandise | $887,000† | |
| Selling & administrative expenses | 513,000‡ | |
| Interest | 32,000 | |
| Income taxes | 30,000• | 1,462,000 |
| Net cash provided by operating activities | | $ 22,000 |
| Cash flows from investing activities | | |
| Proceeds from sale of equipment | $ 20,000 | |
| Payment for building construction | (80,000) | |
| Net cash used by investing activities | | (60,000) |
| Cash flows from financing activities | | |
| Proceeds from issuance of notes payable | $ 70,000 | |
| Payment to retire bonds payable | (50,000) | |
| Payment of cash dividends | (10,000) | |
| Net cash provided by financing activities | | 10,000 |
| Net increase (decrease) in cash | | $ (28,000) |
| Cash balance, January 1, 19X2 | | 87,000 |
| Cash balance, December 31, 19X2 | | $ 59,000 |
| Schedule of noncash investing/financing activities | | |
| Common stock issued for land | | $ 30,000 |

* Sales ($1,450,000) + decrease in accounts receivable ($34,000).
† Cost of goods sold ($835,000) + increase in inventory ($20,000) + decrease in accounts payable ($32,000).
‡ Selling and administrative expenses ($510,000) + increase in prepaid selling expenses ($3,000).
• Income tax expense ($20,000) + decrease in income taxes payable ($10,000).

**b**

| COLWELL CORPORATION<br>Statement of Cash Flows<br>For the Year Ended December 31, 19X2 | | |
|---|---|---|
| Cash flows from operating activities | | |
| Net income | | $ 20,000 |
| Add (deduct) items to convert net income to a cash basis | | |
| Equipment depreciation expense | $ 22,000 | |
| Building depreciation expense | 15,000 | |
| Patent amortization expense | 3,000 | |
| Gain on sale of equipment | (7,000) | |
| Decrease in accounts receivable (net) | 34,000 | |
| Increase in inventory | (20,000) | |
| Increase in prepaid selling expenses | (3,000) | |
| Decrease in accounts payable | (32,000) | |
| Decrease in income taxes payable | (10,000) | 2,000 |
| Net cash provided by operating activities | | $ 22,000 |
| Cash flows from investing activities | | |
| Proceeds from sale of equipment | $ 20,000 | |
| Payment for building construction | (80,000) | |
| Net cash used by investing activities | | (60,000) |
| Cash flows from financing activities | | |
| Proceeds from issuance of notes payable | $ 70,000 | |
| Payment to retire bonds payable | (50,000) | |
| Payment of cash dividends | (10,000) | |
| Net cash provided by financing activities | | 10,000 |
| Net increase (decrease) in cash | | $(28,000) |
| Cash balance, January 1, 19X2 | | 87,000 |
| Cash balance, December 31, 19X2 | | $ 59,000 |
| Schedule of noncash investing/financing activities | | |
| Common stock issued for land | | $ 30,000 |

## Questions

**Q19-1** What information does the statement of cash flows disclose? Give several examples.

**Q19-2** Describe the nature of operating activities, including specific examples of operating cash inflows and outflows.

**Q19-3** Define investing activities, citing several examples of typical investing inflows and outflows.

**Q19-4** List five types of financing activities. Which of these cause cash inflows and which cause cash outflows?

**Q19-5** Why are noncash transactions, such as the exchange of common stock for a building, included on a statement of cash flows? How are these noncash transactions disclosed?

**Q19-6** Sonny Parker purchased a television station for $500,000. He paid $100,000 cash and signed a long-term note payable for $400,000. How would the transaction be shown on a statement of cash flows?

**Q19-7** Differentiate between the direct and indirect methods of preparing the statement of cash flows.

**Q19-8** Both the direct and indirect methods of reporting are permitted when preparing the statement of cash flows. Which of the two approaches is encouraged by the Financial Accounting Standards Board?

**Q19-9** Deck-the-Halls, Inc., reported $24,000 of customer receivables at the beginning of the year and balances totaling $29,000 at the end of the year. If sales amounted to $384,000, compute the amount of customer collections to report on the statement of cash flows, prepared by using the direct approach.

**Q19-10** Is net income normally equal to cash provided by operating activities? Why?

**Q19-11** Items such as depreciation expense reduce net income without an accompanying decrease in cash. Under the indirect method, how are these and similar items treated when determining the cash provided from operating activities?

**Q19-12** Meridian Corporation recently sold some equipment, generating a $6,000 loss on one transaction and a $5,000 gain on another. How are these items treated when computing the net cash flow from operating activities? Assume use of the indirect method.

## Exercises

**E19-1** ***Classification of activities***

The Reed Company had the following transactions and events during the year:

a Sold equipment having a book value of $32,000 for $28,000 cash.
b Purchased vehicles that cost $60,000 by issuing a long-term note payable of $60,000.
c Borrowed $40,000 from the First National Bank.
d Declared and paid a cash dividend of $0.50 per share on 25,000 common shares.
e Sold long-term investments that cost $85,000 for $95,000 cash.
f Generated $75,000 of cash sales to customers.

Consider each of these items independently. Determine whether the item arises from an operating, investing, financing, or noncash investing/financing activity.

**E19-2** ***Direct calculation of operating cash flows***

Selected balance sheet accounts of Mission Company at the end of 19X1 and 19X2 follow.

| | *Dec. 31, 19X2* | *Dec. 31, 19X1* |
|---|---|---|
| Accounts receivable | $ 40,000 | $ 38,000 |
| Inventory | 107,000 | 120,000 |
| Accounts payable (suppliers of merchandise) | 140,000 | 100,000 |
| Interest payable | 26,000 | 29,000 |

Mission makes all sales and purchases on account and employs the accrual basis of accounting. The firm's 19X2 income statement revealed sales, cost of goods sold, and interest expense of $350,000, $200,000, and $33,000, respectively.

Determine the following, assuming the company plans to prepare a statement of cash flows by using the direct method:

a Cash collections from customers
b Merchandise purchases for the year
c Cash paid to suppliers of merchandise
d Interest paid during the year

**E19-3** ***Calculations related to operating cash flows***

Auto Security reported the following selected accrual-basis information for the year ended December 31, 19X2:

| | |
|---|---|
| Sales | $900,000 |
| Cost of goods sold | 300,000 |
| Selling & administrative expenses | 140,000 |
| Income tax expense | 170,000 |

The company also reported cash receipts and disbursements as follows:

| | |
|---|---|
| Cash received from customers | $925,000 |
| Cash payments for: | |
| Purchases of merchandise | 310,000 |
| Selling & administrative expenses | 120,000 |
| Income taxes | 184,000 |

All purchases of merchandise were for cash; there were no prepaid items at the beginning or end of 19X2. Determine whether the following account balances increased or decreased during 19X2, and be sure to indicate the dollar amount of the change.

a Accounts Receivable
b Merchandise Inventory
c Accounts Payable (related to selling & administrative expenses)
d Income Taxes Payable

**E19-4** ***Indirect calculation of operating cash flows***

Video Corporation's balance sheet revealed the following account balance information:

| *Account* | *Dec. 31, 19X6* | *Dec. 31, 19X5* |
|---|---|---|
| Accounts receivable | $52,000 | $57,000 |
| Merchandise inventory | 75,000 | 68,000 |
| Accounts payable | 21,000 | 19,500 |

The accrual-basis net income was $107,000. In computing net income, the company recorded $12,600 of depreciation expense; there were no gains or losses from investing and financing activities.

On the basis of the preceding information, calculate Video's cash flows from operating activities by using the indirect method.

**E19-5** ***Indirect calculation of operating cash flows***

Specialty Services, Inc., reported a net income of $110,000 for the year just ended, which includes an $18,000 gain on the sale of long-term investments. The following data were obtained from comparative balance sheets:

| | *Oct. 31, 19X2* | *Oct. 31, 19X1* |
|---|---|---|
| Trade accounts receivable | $245,000 | $203,000 |
| Merchandise inventory | 230,000 | 308,000 |
| Accumulated depreciation: equipment | 120,000 | 65,000 |
| Accounts payable | 190,000 | 124,000 |
| Accrued liabilities | 38,000 | 73,000 |

There were no purchases or disposals of equipment during the year. The long-term investment had a carrying (book) value of $77,000 and was sold for cash on June 15.

On the basis of the preceding information, determine the cash provided by operating activities from November 1, 19X1, through October 31, 19X2. The firm uses the indirect method of statement preparation.

**E19-6** ***Overview of direct and indirect methods***

Evaluate the comments that follow as being True or False. If the comment is false, briefly explain why.

a Both the direct and indirect methods will produce the same cash flow from operating activities.

b Depreciation expense is added back to net income when using the indirect method.

c One of the advantages of using the direct method rather than the indirect method is that larger cash flows from financing activities will be reported.

d The cash paid to suppliers is normally disclosed on the statement of cash flows when the indirect method of statement preparation is employed.

e The dollar change in the Merchandise Inventory account appears on the statement of cash flows only when the direct method of statement preparation is used.

**E19-7** ***Statement preparation: Direct method***

The comparative balance sheets of Village Company follow.

**VILLAGE COMPANY**
**Comparative Balance Sheets**
**December 31, 19X2 and 19X1**

| | *Dec. 31, 19X2* | *Dec. 31, 19X1* |
|---|---|---|
| Cash | $ 5,000 | $ 7,000 |
| Accounts receivable (net) | 12,000 | 18,000 |
| Merchandise inventory | 35,000 | 28,000 |
| Property, plant, & equipment | 40,000 | 30,000 |
| Less: Accumulated depreciation | (17,000) | (10,000) |
| Total assets | $ 75,000 | $ 73,000 |
| Accounts payable* | $ 25,000 | $ 21,000 |
| Income taxes payable | 4,000 | 1,000 |
| Common stock | 24,000 | 24,000 |
| Retained earnings | 22,000 | 27,000 |
| Total liabilities & stockholders' equity | $ 75,000 | $ 73,000 |

* Relate to purchases of merchandise.

The firm's accrual-basis income statement revealed the following data: sales, $120,000; cost of goods sold, $80,000; selling and administrative expenses, $25,000; depreciation expense, $7,000; and income taxes, $3,000. (There was no interest expense.) Dividends declared and paid during 19X2 totaled $10,000. Finally, Village purchased $10,000 of equipment for cash on August 14.

a Determine the increase or decrease in cash during 19X2.

b Prepare a statement of cash flows by using the direct method.

**E19-8** ***Statement preparation: Indirect method***

Refer to the data presented in Exercise 19-7 that pertain to Village Company.

a Determine the increase or decrease in cash during 19X2.

b Prepare a statement of cash flows by using the indirect method.

**E19-9** ***Equipment transaction and cash flow reporting***

The property, plant, and equipment section of Carswell Company's comparative balance sheet follows.

| | *Dec. 31, 19X2* | *Dec. 31, 19X1* |
|---|---|---|
| Property, plant, & equipment | | |
| Land | $ 150,000 | $ 150,000 |
| Equipment | 850,000 | 680,000 |
| Less: Accumulated depreciation | (270,000) | (295,000) |

New equipment purchased during 19X2 totaled $300,000. The 19X2 income statement disclosed equipment depreciation expense of $50,000 and a $12,000 gain on the sale of equipment.

a Determine the cost and accumulated depreciation of the equipment sold during 19X2.

b Determine the selling price of the equipment sold.

c Show how the sale of equipment would appear on a statement of cash flows prepared by using the indirect method.

**E19-10** ***Evaluation of cash flows***

The following statement of cash flows was prepared for Yellowstone Company:

**YELLOWSTONE COMPANY**
**Statement of Cash Flows**
**For the Year Ended December 31, 19X2**

| | | |
|---|---|---|
| Cash flows from operating activities | | |
| Cash received from customers | | $240,000 |
| Less cash payments for: | | |
| Purchases of merchandise | $180,000 | |
| Selling & administrative expenses | 75,000 | |
| Interest | 20,000 | 275,000 |
| Net cash used by operating activities | | $ (35,000) |
| Cash flows from investing activities | | |
| Sale of equipment | $ 20,000 | |
| Sale of vehicles | 10,000 | |
| Sale of long-term investments | 40,000 | |
| Net cash provided by investing activities | | 70,000 |
| Cash flows from financing activities | | |
| Retirement of long-term debt | | (50,000) |
| Net increase (decrease) in cash | | $ (15,000) |
| Cash balance, January 1, 19X2 | | 54,000 |
| Cash balance, December 31, 19X2 | | $ 39,000 |

Evaluate the nature of the decrease in cash. Does your analysis indicate any potential problems for Yellowstone?

**E19-11** ***Evaluation of cash flows***

Summaries of the cash flow statements issued by Halper, Porter, and Bryan follow.

| | *Halper* | *Porter* | *Bryan* |
|---|---|---|---|
| Cash flows provided by operating activities | $ 9,000 | $63,000 | $ 6,700 |
| Cash flows provided by investing activities | 2,200 | 4,900 | 56,200 |
| Cash flows provided by financing activities | 67,300 | 10,600 | 15,600 |
| Total | $78,500 | $78,500 | $78,500 |

A review of the companies' statements found that Halper issued $70,000 of bonds during the period; Bryan, on the other hand, sold a parcel of land for $65,000.

Focusing solely on the facts presented, assume that Halper, Porter, and Bryan have approached you for a line of credit to buy merchandise from your store. Which of the three companies would you likely favor? Briefly explain.

## Problems

### Series A

**P19-A1** ***Transaction analysis: Operating, investing, and financing activities***

The management of Maui Corporation desires to know the nature of each of the following transactions and events:

1 Collected cash from customers for cash sales.
2 Purchased a short-term investment for cash.
3 Secured a mortgage note to finance the acquisition of a building.
4 Issued 10-year bonds for cash.
5 Paid a short-term nonoperating note.
6 Sold equipment having a book value of $30,000 for $30,000 cash.
7 Sold a parcel of land at cost; received a long-term note.
8 Received dividends on a long-term stock investment.
9 Paid income taxes.
10 Issued preferred stock in exchange for a valuable patent.
11 Reacquired treasury stock for cash.
12 Paid previously declared cash dividends.

**Instructions**

a Briefly explain the difference between investing and financing activities and noncash investing/financing activities.

b Design a sheet of paper with the following columnar headings: operating activity, investing activity, financing activity, and noncash investing/financing activity. Classify the 12 transactions listed by using these headings. For all classifications except noncash investing/financing, indicate whether the transaction causes a cash inflow (+) or a cash outflow (−).

**P19-A2** ***Operating activities: Direct and indirect methods***

The information that follows was taken from the financial statements of Eye Care, Inc.

| | Dec. 31, 19X2 | Dec. 31, 19X1 |
|---|---|---|
| Balance sheet accounts | | |
| Accounts receivable (net) | $ 49,700 | $ 54,300 |
| Inventory | 88,500 | 68,600 |
| Supplies | 4,600 | 3,900 |
| Accounts payable (relate to merchandise purchases) | 61,800 | 59,700 |
| Interest payable | 6,200 | 7,300 |
| Mortgage payable (long-term) | 158,000 | 168,000 |
| 19X2 income statement data | | |
| Sales | $1,200,000 | |
| Sales returns & allowances | 15,000 | |
| Cost of goods sold | 800,000 | |
| Selling & administrative expenses | 60,000 | |
| Depreciation expense | 40,000 | |
| Interest expense | 20,000 | |
| Loss on sale of equipment | 45,000 | |
| Income tax expense | 75,000 | |

**Instructions**

a Prepare the operating activities section of the statement of cash flows by using the direct method.

b Prepare the operating activities section of the statement of cash flows by using the indirect method.

**P19-A3** ***Investing and financing activities***

The following information was extracted from the financial statements and accounting records of Public Storage Company:

Income statement for 19X5
  Gain on sale of machinery: $4,000
  Loss from fire in building: $14,000

Comparative balance sheets, 12/31/X5 and 12/31/X4
  Machinery: Decreased by $13,000*
  Buildings: Increased by $300,000*
  Common stock: Increased by $180,000
  Paid-in capital in excess of par: Increased by $135,000

Additional information
  Public Storage received $7,000 from machinery sales (machinery cost, $40,000; accumulated depreciation, $37,000). New machines were purchased during 19X5 for cash.
  Buildings having a cost of $400,000 were acquired in May, one for $140,000 cash and the other in exchange for 50,000 shares of the company's $3 par-value stock, which were valued at $260,000. The firm received $45,000 of insurance proceeds in February when a fire destroyed one of its facilities. Accumulated depreciation on the facility totaled $41,000.
  Ten thousand shares of common stock were sold to the public for cash.

* These amounts are before any deductions for accumulated depreciation.

**Instructions**

a Prepare the investing and financing sections of the company's statement of cash flows.

b Prepare the disclosure of the company's noncash investing/financing transactions that would appear on a statement of cash flows.

**P19-A4** ***Statement of cash flows: Direct method***

The Omaha Bullets, Inc., a minor league baseball team, is having great difficulty paying its bills. Management cannot understand how the firm can generate net income and continually be short of cash. The balance sheet accounts of the Bullets follow.

| | *Sept. 30, 19X2* | *Oct. 1, 19X1* |
|---|---|---|
| Cash | $ — | $ 25,000 |
| Receivable from major league affiliate | 400,000 | 634,000 |
| Concessions inventory | 134,000 | 79,000 |
| Prepaid selling expenses | 25,700 | 19,000 |
| Ball park stands and structures | 792,600 | 748,600 |
| Accumulated depreciation: ball park | 442,000 | 400,000 |
| Other fixed assets | 130,000 | 108,400 |
| Accumulated depreciation: other fixed assets | 85,000 | 80,000 |
| Accounts payable (for concessions) | 29,000 | 50,800 |
| Salaries payable | 46,000 | 54,000 |
| Bonuses payable | 51,200 | 176,500 |
| Accrued taxes payable | 16,000 | 14,000 |
| Federal income taxes payable | — | 129,000 |
| Common stock | 600,000 | 580,000 |
| Retained earnings | 213,100 | 129,700 |

Other data are as follows:

1 Net income was $100,000. Dividends declared and paid totaled $16,600.
2 The accrual-basis income statement revealed revenues from admissions, concessions, and the major league affiliate that totaled $4,350,000. Other key figures are cost of concessions sold, $950,000; selling and administrative expenses, $3,179,000; depreciation expense, $47,000; income tax expense, $74,000; and interest expense, $0.
3 The Accrued Taxes Payable account is used for various taxes that are treated as selling and administrative expenses.
4 No disposals of ball park stands, structures, or other fixed assets occurred during the year.
5 In February, the Bullets acquired a new scoreboard and other fixed assets for cash.
6 Additional common stock was sold on May 15 for $20,000 cash.

**Instructions**

a Prepare a statement of cash flows for the year ended September 30, 19X2, by using the direct method.
b Prepare a brief evaluation of the Bullets' existing cash problem.

**P19-A5** ***Cash flow information: Direct and indirect methods***

The 19X8 accrual-basis income statement of Underwater Gear, Inc., follows.

| UNDERWATER GEAR, INC.<br>Income Statement<br>For the Year Ended December 31, 19X8 | | |
|---|---|---|
| Sales | | $1,985,000 |
| Less: Cost of goods sold | | 960,000 |
| Gross profit | | $1,025,000 |
| Less: Selling & administrative expenses | $720,000 | |
| Depreciation expense | 10,000 | |
| Interest expense | 19,000 | 749,000 |
| | | $ 276,000 |
| Add: Gain on sale of long-term investments | | 7,000 |
| Income before taxes | | $ 283,000 |
| Income taxes | | 72,000 |
| Net income | | $ 211,000 |

Balance sheets for 19X7 and 19X8 contained the following accounts:

| | *Dec. 31, 19X8* | *Dec. 31, 19X7* |
|---|---|---|
| ***Assets*** | | |
| Cash | $ 50,000 | $207,000 |
| Accounts receivable (net) | 420,000 | 230,000 |
| Merchandise inventory | 350,000 | 180,000 |
| Store equipment (net) | 95,000 | 80,000 |
| Long-term investments | — | 8,000 |
| Total assets | $915,000 | $705,000 |
| ***Liabilities & Stockholders' Equity*** | | |
| Accounts payable | $208,000 | $190,000 |
| Bonds payable | 200,000 | 214,000 |
| Common stock, $5 par value | 129,000 | 120,000 |
| Paid-in capital in excess of par value | 106,000 | 79,000 |
| Retained earnings | 272,000 | 102,000 |
| Total liabilities & stockholders' equity | $915,000 | $705,000 |

Other data are:

1 Common stock (1,800 shares) was sold in February 19X8 at $20 per share.
2 Store equipment having a cost of $20,000 and accumulated depreciation of $18,000 was sold for $2,000 cash. Other store equipment was purchased for cash.
3 Long-term investments that cost $8,000 were recently sold for $15,000 cash.
4 The company retired $14,000 of bonds during the year; no gain or loss was incurred.
5 Dividends of $41,000 were declared and paid in December 19X8.
6 Changes in the Accounts Receivable and Accounts Payable accounts were caused by sales and purchases of merchandise, respectively.

**Instructions**

a Prepare the disclosure that would appear for cash flows from operating activities on the company's formal statement of cash flows, assuming use of:
   (1) The direct method.
   (2) The indirect method.

b Prepare the company's financial statement disclosure of cash flows from investing activities and cash flows from financing activities.

**P19-A6** ***Statement of cash flows: Indirect method***
Comparative balance sheets of Ski Warehouse, Inc., appear as follows:

**SKI WAREHOUSE, INC.**
**Comparative Balance Sheets**
**October 31, 19X5 and 19X4**

| | 19X5 | | 19X4 | |
|---|---|---|---|---|
| ***Assets*** | | | | |
| Current assets | | | | |
| Cash | | $ 427,000 | | $ 130,000 |
| Short-term investments | | 105,000 | | 205,000 |
| Accounts receivable (net) | | 195,000 | | 377,000 |
| Merchandise inventory | | 1,100,000 | | 918,000 |
| Total current assets | | $1,827,000 | | $1,630,000 |
| Property, plant, & equipment | | | | |
| Land | | $ 17,000 | | $ 20,000 |
| Equipment | $500,000 | | $300,000 | |
| Less: Accumulated depreciation | 97,000 | 403,000 | 80,000 | 220,000 |
| Total property, plant, & equipment | | $ 420,000 | | $ 240,000 |
| Intangible assets | | | | |
| Copyrights (cost of $19,000 less amortization) | | 7,000 | | 8,000 |
| Total assets | | $2,254,000 | | $1,878,000 |
| ***Liabilities & Stockholders' Equity*** | | | | |
| Current liabilities | | | | |
| Accounts payable (for merchandise) | | $ 600,000 | | $ 732,000 |
| Accrued liabilities | | 150,000 | | 15,000 |
| Income taxes payable | | 280,000 | | 120,000 |
| Total current liabilities | | $1,030,000 | | $ 867,000 |
| Long-term liabilities | | | | |
| Bonds payable | | 650,000 | | 900,000 |
| Stockholders' equity | | | | |
| Common stock | $300,000 | | $100,000 | |
| Retained earnings | 274,000 | 574,000 | 11,000 | 111,000 |
| Total liabilities & stockholders' equity | | $2,254,000 | | $1,878,000 |

Additional information:

a The company retired $250,000 of bonds during the year and sold $100,000 of short-term investments. No gain or loss was incurred on either transaction.

b Common stock of $200,000 was issued at par value to acquire equipment.

c The 19X5 accrual basis income statement revealed net income of $263,000, along with the following: sales, $946,000; cost of goods sold, $419,700; selling and administrative expenses, $97,800; depreciation and amortization expense, $18,000; interest expense, $74,000; gain on the sale of land, $5,000; and income tax expense, $78,500.

d No dividends were paid during the year.

**Instructions**

Prepare a statement of cash flows by using the indirect method.

***P19-A7** ***Work sheet: Statement of cash flows***

Refer to the data in Problem 19-A6 that pertain to Ski Warehouse, Inc.

**Instructions**

a Prepare a work sheet similar in format to that shown in Exhibit 19-9.

b Prepare a formal statement of cash flows by using the indirect method.

## Series B

**P19-B1** ***Transaction analysis: Operating, investing, and financing activities***

The management of St. Thomas Corporation desires to know the nature of each of the following transactions and events:

1 Issued common stock for cash.
2 Issued preferred stock in exchange for a parcel of land and a building.
3 Paid employee salaries.
4 Called and retired $200,000 of bonds.
5 Borrowed money by signing a note payable due in three years.
6 Purchased merchandise for cash.
7 Received interest on an outstanding loan.
8 Purchased new equipment for cash.
9 Reduced the balance of a long-term nonoperating note payable by issuing common stock.
10 Sold land for cash.
11 Paid dividends to stockholders.
12 Received cash from customers on account.

**Instructions**

a Briefly explain the difference between operating, investing, and financing activities.

b Design a sheet of paper with the following columnar headings: operating activity, investing activity, financing activity, and noncash investing/financing activity. Classify the 12 transactions listed by using these headings. For all classifications except noncash investing/financing, indicate whether the transaction causes a cash inflow (+) or a cash outflow (−).

**P19-B2** ***Operating activities: Direct and indirect methods***

The 19X5 income statement of Office Products, Inc., follows.

* An asterisk preceding an item indicates that the material is covered in an appendix to this chapter.

**OFFICE PRODUCTS, INC.**
**Income Statement**
**For the Year Ended December 31, 19X5**

| | | |
|---|---|---|
| Net sales | | $980,000 |
| Cost of goods sold | | |
| Beginning inventory | $235,000 | |
| Net purchases | 720,000 | |
| Goods available for sale | $955,000 | |
| Less: Ending inventory | 260,000 | |
| Cost of goods sold | | 695,000 |
| Gross profit | | $285,000 |
| Expenses | | |
| Selling & administrative | $149,000 | |
| Depreciation | 54,000 | 203,000 |
| | | $ 82,000 |
| Other revenue (expense) | | |
| Interest expense | $ (18,000) | |
| Gain on sale of equipment | 26,000 | 8,000 |
| Income before income taxes | | $ 90,000 |
| Income taxes | | 27,000 |
| Net income | | $ 63,000 |

The following additional information was obtained from the general ledger and management personnel:

1 Accounts payable related to the purchases of merchandise decreased during 19X5 by $32,800. In contrast, accounts receivable increased by $23,700.
2 Prepaid expenses and wages payable increased throughout 19X5 by $2,400 and $5,600, respectively.
3 The balance in the Income Taxes Payable account on January 1 was $4,900; the December 31 balance was $4,100.
4 The company financed a $78,000 equipment purchase by signing a note payable that is due in 19X8.

**Instructions**

a Prepare the operating activities section of the statement of cash flows by using the direct method.
b Prepare the operating activities section of the statement of cash flows by using the indirect method.

**P19-B3** ***Investing and financing activities***

The following information was extracted from the financial statements and accounting records of Ace Lanes:

Comparative balance sheets, 12/31/X3 and 12/31/X2
Bowling equipment: Increased by $7,000*
Buildings: Increased by $500,000*
Long-term note payable: Increased by $286,000
Common stock: Increased by $150,000
Paid-in capital in excess of par: Increased by $200,000

Income statement for 19X3
  Gain on sale of bowling equipment: $66,000
  Loss from flood in building: $50,000

Additional information
  The company received cash from sales of bowling equipment (equipment cost, $120,000; accumulated depreciation, $30,000). New equipment was purchased and paid for in June.
  Buildings having a cost of $750,000 were acquired in May, one for cash and the other in exchange for a $300,000 long-term note payable.
  Ace received $60,000 of insurance proceeds in February when a flood destroyed one of its facilities. Accumulated depreciation on the facility totaled $140,000.
  A review of the general ledger found that 75,000 shares of $2 par-value common stock were sold to the public, generating proceeds of $350,000. Furthermore, Ace was found to be in compliance with the payment schedule established for the long-term note payable.

* These amounts are before any deductions for accumulated depreciation.

**Instructions**

a Prepare the investing and financing sections of the company's statement of cash flows.

b Prepare the disclosure of the company's noncash investing/financing transactions that would appear on a statement of cash flows.

**P19-B4** ***Statement of cash flows: Direct method***

Luther Jones, manager of Supreme Corporation, is disturbed about the size of the firm's ending cash balance. The balance sheet accounts for Supreme follow.

| | *Dec. 31, 19X6* | *Jan. 1, 19X6* |
|---|---|---|
| Cash | $ 25 | $15,500 |
| Accounts receivable | 64,500 | 32,000 |
| Merchandise inventory | 23,500 | 10,500 |
| Prepaid rent | 2,540 | 1,750 |
| Equipment | 20,000 | 16,500 |
| Accumulated depreciation: equipment | 14,750 | 12,000 |
| Vans | 18,500 | 18,500 |
| Accumulated depreciation: vans | 12,500 | 10,000 |
| Goodwill | 5,500 | 6,000 |
| Accounts payable (for merchandise) | 17,500 | 11,500 |
| Federal income taxes payable | 650 | 900 |
| Current portion of long-term van notes | 2,000 | 2,000 |
| Notes payable on vans (long-term) | 4,000 | 6,000 |
| Common stock | 50,000 | 50,000 |
| Retained earnings | 33,165 | 8,350 |

Other data are as follows:

1 The accrual-basis income statement revealed net income of $30,000, composed of the following: sales revenues, $246,000; cost of goods sold, $160,000; selling and administrative expenses, $40,000; depreciation expense, $5,250; amortization expense, $500; income tax expense, $9,450; and interest expense, $800.

2 Cash dividends were declared and paid in June.

3 No disposals or sales of equipment took place; however, Supreme purchased new machinery for cash in August.

**Instructions**

a Prepare a statement of cash flows for the year ended December 31, 19X6, by using the direct method.

b Prepare a brief evaluation of Supreme's current cash dilemma.

**P19-B5** ***Cash flow information: Direct and indirect methods***

The 19X2 accrual-basis income statement of Restaurant Outfitters, Inc., follows.

**RESTAURANT OUTFITTERS, INC.**
**Income Statement**
**For the Year Ended December 31, 19X2**

| | | |
|---|---|---|
| Sales | | $490,000 |
| Less: Cost of goods sold | | 210,000 |
| Gross profit | | $280,000 |
| Less: Selling & administrative expenses | $195,000 | |
| Depreciation expense | 15,000 | |
| Interest expense | 1,000 | 211,000 |
| | | $ 69,000 |
| Less: Loss on sale of machinery | | 3,000 |
| Income before taxes | | $ 66,000 |
| Less: Income tax expense | | 22,000 |
| Net income | | $ 44,000 |

Balance sheets for 19X1 and 19X2 contained the following accounts:

| | Dec. 31, 19X2 | Dec. 31, 19X1 |
|---|---|---|
| ***Assets*** | | |
| Cash | $ 5,000 | $ 45,000 |
| Accounts receivable (net) | 52,000 | 37,000 |
| Inventory | 41,000 | 25,000 |
| Machinery (net) | 60,000 | 60,000 |
| Total assets | $158,000 | $167,000 |
| ***Liabilities & Stockholders' Equity*** | | |
| Accounts payable | $ 27,000 | $ 64,000 |
| Long-term note payable | 5,000 | 20,000 |
| Common stock, $5 par value | 5,000 | 4,000 |
| Paid-in capital in excess of par value | 20,000 | 16,000 |
| Retained earnings | 101,000 | 63,000 |
| Total liabilities & stockholders' equity | $158,000 | $167,000 |

Other data are:

1 Common stock (200 shares) was sold for $25 per share in the middle of 19X2.
2 Dividends of $6 per share were declared and paid in late 19X2.
3 Machinery that cost $20,000, having a book value of $13,000, was sold for $10,000 cash. New machinery was purchased for $28,000 cash.
4 Changes in the Accounts Receivable and Accounts Payable accounts were caused by sales and purchases of merchandise, respectively.
5 The note payable relates to a borrowing transaction.

**Instructions**

a Prepare the disclosure that would appear for cash flows from operating activities on the company's formal statement of cash flows, assuming use of:
  (1) The direct method.
  (2) The indirect method.
b Prepare the company's financial statement disclosure of cash flows from investing activities and cash flows from financing activities.

**P19-B6** ***Statement of cash flows: Indirect method***

Comparative balance sheets of Goodrich Company appear on the next page.

**GOODRICH COMPANY**
**Comparative Balance Sheets**
**December 31, 19X2 and 19X1**

| | 19X2 | | 19X1 | |
|---|---|---|---|---|
| *Assets* | | | | |
| Current assets | | | | |
| Cash | | $ 15,000 | | $ 45,000 |
| Accounts receivable (net) | | 100,000 | | 115,000 |
| Inventory | | 485,000 | | 400,000 |
| Total current assets | | $600,000 | | $560,000 |
| Property, plant, & equipment | | | | |
| Land | | $ 12,000 | | $ 9,000 |
| Machinery | $ 90,000 | | $ 70,000 | |
| Less: Accumulated depreciation | 24,000 | 66,000 | 14,000 | 56,000 |
| Total property, plant, & equipment | | $ 78,000 | | $ 65,000 |
| Intangible assets | | | | |
| Patents (cost of $10,000 less amortization) | | 3,000 | | 4,000 |
| Total assets | | $681,000 | | $629,000 |
| *Liabilities & Stockholders' Equity* | | | | |
| Current liabilities | | | | |
| Accounts payable (for merchandise) | | $390,000 | | $370,000 |
| Income taxes payable | | 10,000 | | 8,000 |
| Total current liabilities | | $400,000 | | $378,000 |
| Long-term liabilities | | | | |
| Mortgage payable | | 6,000 | | 7,000 |
| Stockholders' equity | | | | |
| Common stock | $200,000 | | $180,000 | |
| Retained earnings | 75,000 | 275,000 | 64,000 | 244,000 |
| Total liabilities & stockholders' equity | | $681,000 | | $629,000 |

Additional information:

a No dividends were declared or paid during 19X2.

b The 19X2 accrual-basis income statement revealed net income of $11,000 along with the following: sales, $647,000; cost of goods sold, $579,000; selling and administrative expenses, $40,300; depreciation and amortization expense, $11,000; interest expense, $700; and income tax expense, $5,000.

c Common stock of $20,000 was issued at par value to acquire machinery on February 4.

d Land was purchased for cash on May 10.

e Goodrich paid $1,000 on the mortgage note during the year.

**Instructions**

Prepare a statement of cash flows by using the indirect method.

***P19-B7** ***Work sheet: Statement of cash flows***
Refer to the data in Problem 19-B6 that pertain to Goodrich Company.

**Instructions**

a Prepare a work sheet similar in format to that shown in Exhibit 19-9.
b Prepare a formal statement of cash flows by using the indirect method.

## Beyond the Basics

**BB19-1** ***Balance sheet preparation from cash flow information***
Anderson Corporation reported the following balance-sheet information as of January 1, 19X1:

| | | | |
|---|---|---|---|
| Cash | $ 10,000 | Accounts payable | $12,000 |
| Accounts receivable | 24,000 | Interest payable | 5,000 |
| Inventory | 37,000 | Bonds payable | 70,000 |
| Equipment | 119,000 | Common stock | 50,000 |
| Accumulated depreciation | (39,000) | Retained earnings | 14,000 |

The company's statement of cash flows for the year ended December 31, 19X1, follows.

**ANDERSON CORPORATION**
**Statement of Cash Flows**
**For the Year Ended December 31, 19X1**

| | | |
|---|---|---|
| Cash flows from operating activities | | |
| Cash received from customers | | $174,000 |
| Less cash payments for: | | |
| Purchases of merchandise | $ 57,000 | |
| Selling & administrative expenses | 41,000 | |
| Interest | 9,000 | |
| Income taxes | 18,000 | 125,000 |
| Net cash provided by operating activities | | $ 49,000 |
| Cash flows from investing activities | | |
| Purchase of land | | (20,000) |
| Cash flows from financing activities | | |
| Payment to retire bonds | $(20,000) | |
| Dividends paid | (7,000) | |
| Net cash used by financing activities | | (27,000) |
| Net increase (decrease) in cash | | $ 2,000 |
| Cash balance, January 1, 19X1 | | 10,000 |
| Cash balance, December 31, 19X1 | | $ 12,000 |

The company's income statement disclosed that $45,000 of net income had been generated during 19X1. Depreciation expense amounted to $6,000. A review of the general ledger revealed the following changes in account balances during the year:

| | |
|---|---|
| Accounts receivable, increase | $10,000 |
| Inventory, decrease | 7,000 |
| Accounts payable,* increase | 4,000 |
| Interest payable, decrease | 3,000 |

* Relate to purchases of merchandise.

**Instructions**

Prepare a balance sheet for Anderson Corporation as of December 31, 19X1.

## Answers to Chapter Quiz

**1** b

**2** d

**3** c

**4** d (Proceeds − $30,000 = $100,000; proceeds = $130,000)

**5** d

# Financial Statements: Analysis and Further Disclosures

CHAPTER 20

## Learning Objectives

After reading this chapter you should:

**1** Be familiar with the advantages and problems of financial statement analysis.

**2** Be able to perform a horizontal analysis of comparative financial statements.

**3** Be able to perform a vertical analysis and understand the associated benefits of common-size statements.

**4** Be familiar with ratio analysis.

**5** Have a basic knowledge of financial statement footnotes.

**6** Have a general familiarity with several of the basic issues of international accounting.

OBJECTIVE 1
Be familiar with the advantages and problems of financial statement analysis.

Financial statements and accompanying footnotes provide a wealth of information. Upon receipt, users will typically analyze this information to study factors that are of interest to them, for example, a company's debt-paying ability and operating efficiency. It is important to understand that the *individual* dollar amounts reported in the financial statements are very inadequate when it comes to judging performance. To illustrate, The Kroger Co. (a large supermarket operator) recently reported an ending cash and short-term investment balance of $211 million and net income in excess of $34 million. When interpreted in isolation, these amounts are surely impressive. Most readers will agree, however, that perspectives might change upon learning that current liabilities totaled $2.165 billion and net income represented a mere 0.18¢ of every sales dollar. Hopefully, you can see that a clearer picture of performance results by establishing and analyzing certain financial statement relationships.

## Words of Caution

Before proceeding with our discussion, we offer several words of caution. First, financial statement analysis employs many different tools (e.g., ratios, trend studies) to furnish information about operating activity. These tools must be used judiciously. The tools are not ends in themselves; rather, they are measures to be examined in conjunction with other, more subjective factors such as the state of the economy, industry outlooks, and management quality. Statement analysis is most effective when evaluation techniques are coupled with good judgment and decision-making experience.

### Comparative Standards

A second caution concerns comparative standards. When performing analysis work, accountants, creditors, stockholders, and others continually seek comparative standards against which to judge an entity's present financial relationships. Standards commonly employed include past performance of the entity and performance of other firms in the same industry.

Relating the current data of a company with data of preceding years provides insight for determining whether financial relationships are improving or deteriorating. Unfortunately, single-company comparisons do not provide a sufficiently broad basis for evaluation. For example, if a candy manufacturer incurred a net loss of $200,000 in 19X1 and a net loss of only $50,000 in 19X2, the firm has shown considerable improvement. However, if the manufacturer remains the only unprofitable candy producer in the country, the earnings records of both years can be viewed as being unfavorable.

The use of an external standard (or yardstick) frequently overcomes the limitations of single-company studies. That is, an entity's financial performance can be compared with the performance of a similar company or the average of several companies in the same industry (called *industry norms*). Extreme care is necessary when using these comparisons, however, to make certain they are both valid and reasonable.

Consider, for instance, an evaluation of the profitability and financial position of IBM and Unisys Corporation, two computer manufacturers. IBM uses the weighted-average method for inventory valuation; in contrast, Unisys uses the first-in, first-out method. Such a difference, as well as variations in other accounting practices, may hamper comparisons.

Additionally, many businesses today are diversified and cannot be neatly classified by industry lines. As an example, suppose that we desire to analyze Anheuser-Busch. The Adolph Coors Company would appear to be a natural comparison for our study. Upon examination, however, we would soon find that the two firms have many significant operational differences. In addition to making various brands of beer, Anheuser-Busch produces bakery goods and Eagle snack foods, operates amusement parks, is involved with residential and commercial real estate development, owns the St. Louis Cardinals baseball club, and furnishes railroad transportation services. Coors, noted primarily for its brewing operation, also sells oil and natural gas and is an industry leader in technical ceramics. As you can well imagine, a comparison of the *overall* financial statements of the two organizations would not be very meaningful.

Some analysis may be possible, however, by examining selected figures from the brewing *segments* of both companies as reported in the footnotes to the financial statements. Such reporting is required of companies that meet certain criteria and are involved in more than one business activity. Segment reporting is discussed in more depth later in the chapter.

## Tools of Analysis

Three tools are frequently used to evaluate financial statements: horizontal analysis, vertical analysis, and ratio analysis. To illustrate these tools, we will focus on a set of two-year comparative financial statements of the Handy Corporation. In addition, we will integrate other analyses that are of special interest to particular statement users.

### Horizontal Analysis

**OBJECTIVE 2**
**Be able to perform a horizontal analysis of comparative financial statements.**

The calculation of dollar and percentage changes for corresponding items in comparative financial statements is termed **horizontal analysis.** In such an analysis the earlier period is established as a base against which the later period is compared. As an example, the percentage change in the Cash account is computed by dividing the account's change between the two periods (say 19X2 and 19X1) by the Cash balance of the base period (19X1). A complete horizontal analysis of the financial statements of Handy Corporation is presented in Exhibit 20-1.

Focusing on the income statement, the horizontal analysis reveals that the sizable increase in net income was mainly due to a $4 million rise in sales (11.1%) coupled with reductions in cost of goods sold ($2 million; 8.3%), administrative expenses ($650,000; 16.3%), and interest expense ($150,000; 18.8%). These reductions, however, were offset by increases in selling expenses and income taxes, the former causing an overall hike in operating expenses of $550,000, or 6.3%.

Overall, horizontal analysis provides information about the magnitude, direction, and relative importance of changes in individual and aggregate financial statement items. Such information is useful in assessing whether an enterprise has become stronger or weaker over a period of time and whether improvements are needed in particular areas.

**Exhibit 20-1**
**Horizontal Analysis of Comparative Financial Statements**

**HANDY CORPORATION**
**Comparative Income Statements**
**For the Years Ended December 31, 19X2 and 19X1**

| | *19X2* | *19X1* | *Increase (Decrease)* | *Percentage Change from 19X1* |
|---|---|---|---|---|
| Net sales | $40,000,000 | $36,000,000 | $ 4,000,000 | 11.1% |
| Cost of goods sold | 22,000,000 | 24,000,000 | (2,000,000) | (8.3) |
| Gross profit | $18,000,000 | $12,000,000 | $ 6,000,000 | 50.0 |
| Operating expenses | | | | |
| Selling | $ 6,000,000 | $ 4,800,000 | $ 1,200,000 | 25.0 |
| Administrative | 3,350,000 | 4,000,000 | (650,000) | (16.3) |
| Total operating expenses | $ 9,350,000 | $ 8,800,000 | $ 550,000 | 6.3 |
| Operating income | $ 8,650,000 | $ 3,200,000 | $ 5,450,000 | 170.3 |
| Interest expense | 650,000 | 800,000 | (150,000) | (18.8) |
| Income before income taxes | $ 8,000,000 | $ 2,400,000 | $ 5,600,000 | 233.3 |
| Income taxes, 40% | 3,200,000 | 960,000 | 2,240,000 | 233.3 |
| Net income | $ 4,800,000 | $ 1,440,000 | $ 3,360,000 | 233.3 |
| Earnings per share* | $2.38 | $0.70 | $1.68 | 240.0 |

* Calculated as $\frac{\text{Net Income} - \text{Preferred Dividends}}{\text{Common Shares Outstanding}}$

**HANDY CORPORATION**
**Comparative Statements of Retained Earnings**
**For the Years Ended December 31, 19X2 and 19X1**

| | *19X2* | *19X1* | *Increase (Decrease)* | *Percentage Change from 19X1* |
|---|---|---|---|---|
| Balance, Jan. 1 | $ 5,900,000 | $5,500,000 | $ 400,000 | 7.3% |
| Net income | 4,800,000 | 1,440,000 | 3,360,000 | 233.3 |
| Total | $10,700,000 | $6,940,000 | $3,760,000 | 54.2 |
| Less: Dividends | | | | |
| Common | $ 2,000,000 | $1,000,000 | $1,000,000 | 100.0 |
| Preferred | 40,000 | 40,000 | — | — |
| Total dividends | $ 2,040,000 | $1,040,000 | $1,000,000 | 96.2 |
| Balance, Dec. 31 | $ 8,660,000 | $5,900,000 | $2,760,000 | 46.8 |

**Exhibit 20-1 (continued)**

**HANDY CORPORATION**
**Comparative Balance Sheets**
**December 31, 19X2 and 19X1**

| | *19X2* | *19X1* | *Increase (Decrease)* | *Percentage Change from 19X1* |
|---|---|---|---|---|
| ***Assets*** | | | | |
| Current assets | $ 8,000,000 | $ 7,000,000 | $ 1,000,000 | 14.3% |
| Plant & equipment (net) | 12,200,000 | 11,500,000 | 700,000 | 6.1 |
| Intangibles (net) | 1,000,000 | 1,200,000 | (200,000) | (16.7) |
| Other assets | 410,000 | 550,000 | (140,000) | (25.5) |
| Total assets | $21,610,000 | $20,250,000 | $ 1,360,000 | 6.7 |
| ***Liabilities & Stockholders' Equity*** | | | | |
| Liabilities | | | | |
| Current liabilities | $ 3,500,000 | $ 3,400,000 | $ 100,000 | 2.9 |
| Long-term liabilities | 6,500,000 | 8,000,000 | (1,500,000) | (18.8) |
| Total liabilities | $10,000,000 | $11,400,000 | $(1,400,000) | (12.3) |
| Stockholders' equity | | | | |
| 10% preferred stock, $10 par value | $ 400,000 | $ 400,000 | $ — | — |
| Common stock, $1 par value | 2,000,000 | 2,000,000 | — | — |
| Paid-in capital, common stock | 550,000 | 550,000 | — | — |
| Retained earnings | 8,660,000 | 5,900,000 | 2,760,000 | 46.8 |
| Total stockholders' equity | $11,610,000 | $ 8,850,000 | $ 2,760,000 | 31.2 |
| Total liabilities & stockholders' equity | $21,610,000 | $20,250,000 | $ 1,360,000 | 6.7 |

## Vertical Analysis

OBJECTIVE 3
Be able to perform a vertical analysis and understand the associated benefits of common-size statements.

Important changes and trends can also be studied by using vertical analysis. With **vertical analysis,** each figure on a financial statement is related to a relevant total and stated as a percentage of that total. Examine Exhibit 20-2, which contains a vertical analysis of Handy's income statements. Observe how each item is expressed as a percentage of net sales. The analysis reveals that 12¢ of every sales dollar remained as profit in 19X2, up from 4¢ in 19X1.

**Exhibit 20-2**
**Vertical Analysis of Income Statements**

**HANDY CORPORATION**
**Comparative Income Statements**
**For the Years Ended December 31, 19X2 and 19X1**

| | *19X2* | | *19X1* | |
|---|---|---|---|---|
| | *$* | *Percent* | *$* | *Percent* |
| Net sales | $40,000,000 | 100.0% | $36,000,000 | 100.0% |
| Cost of goods sold | 22,000,000 | 55.0 | 24,000,000 | 66.7 |
| Gross profit | $18,000,000 | 45.0 | $12,000,000 | 33.3 |
| Operating expenses | | | | |
| Selling | $ 6,000,000 | 15.0 | $ 4,800,000 | 13.3 |
| Administrative | 3,350,000 | 8.4 | 4,000,000 | 11.1 |
| Total operating expenses | $ 9,350,000 | 23.4 | $ 8,800,000 | 24.4 |
| Operating income | $ 8,650,000 | 21.6 | $ 3,200,000 | 8.9 |
| Interest expense | 650,000 | 1.6 | 800,000 | 2.2 |
| Income before income taxes | $ 8,000,000 | 20.0 | $ 2,400,000 | 6.7 |
| Income taxes, 40% | 3,200,000 | 8.0 | 960,000 | 2.7 |
| Net income | $ 4,800,000 | 12.0% | $ 1,440,000 | 4.0% |

Switching to the balance sheet, individual assets are stated as a percentage of total assets, and each of the liability and stockholders' equity accounts is expressed in relation to the total of liabilities plus stockholders' equity. As an example, a vertical analysis of Handy's assets follows.

| | *19X2* | | *19X1* | |
|---|---|---|---|---|
| | *$* | *Percent* | *$* | *Percent* |
| *Assets* | | | | |
| Current assets | $ 8,000,000 | 37.0% | $ 7,000,000 | 34.6% |
| Plant & equipment (net) | 12,200,000 | 56.5 | 11,500,000 | 56.8 |
| Intangibles (net) | 1,000,000 | 4.6 | 1,200,000 | 5.9 |
| Other assets | 410,000 | 1.9 | 550,000 | 2.7 |
| Total assets | $21,610,000 | 100.0% | $20,250,000 | 100.0% |

The figures show that despite a $1.36 million increase in total assets, the individual components remained relatively stable. The largest change is noted for current assets, which, in terms of total assets, increased by 2.4% (37.0% − 34.6%).

## Common-Size Financial Statements

One of the basic benefits of vertical analysis is the final product: **common-size financial statements.** That is, with all items stated on some common ground (e.g., percentages), users can evaluate financial statements in relative terms and not be concerned about differences in absolute size. This benefit becomes especially helpful when comparing one company against another company or industry norms. Consider, for example, recent abbreviated income statements (in thousands) of NIKE, Inc., and Reebok International Ltd., well-known producers of athletic footwear and other goods:

| | *NIKE, Inc.* | | *Reebok International* | |
|---|---|---|---|---|
| | *$* | *Percent* | *$* | *Percent* |
| Net sales | $1,203,440 | 100.0% | $1,785,935 | 100.0% |
| Cost of goods sold | 803,380 | 66.8 | 1,122,226 | 62.8 |
| Gross profit | $ 400,060 | 33.2% | $ 663,709 | 37.2% |
| Operating expenses & income taxes | 298,365 | 24.8 | 526,707 | 29.5 |
| Net income | $ 101,695 | 8.4% | $ 137,002 | 7.7% |

Reebok's sales were nearly 48% in excess of those of NIKE, thus producing larger dollar figures for both cost of goods sold and operating expenses and income taxes. In addition, a higher profit was generated. However, when percentages are considered, NIKE was actually more profitable, having 8.4¢ of every sales dollar left as income (in comparison with 7.7¢ for its competitor).

## Ratio Analysis

A third method of financial statement evaluation is **ratio analysis.** Ratios are employed to study liquidity, activity, profitability, and coverage of obligations. Although any number of ratios can be constructed and presented, our discussion will focus only on those that are commonly encountered and widely used by statement analysts.

OBJECTIVE 4
**Be familiar with ratio analysis.**

It is important to note that a ratio is merely a mathematical expression of relationships. In essence, one could view a ratio as being similar to a thermometer, that is, a gauge of performance. For example, suppose you are ill, you take your temperature, and the thermometer reads 102.6 degrees. The obvious conclusion? Something is wrong with your body. In no way, however, can the thermometer indicate whether you have the flu, an infected ear, or mononucleosis. The thermometer simply indicates that something is amiss and serves as a starting point for further investigation. Similarly, a ratio presents information regarding a single financial relationship; it cannot tell the complete story.

### Liquidity Ratios

**Liquidity ratios** measure the ability of a business to meet current debts as the obligations come due. Appropriately, short-term creditors have great interest in the liquidity ratios of their clients and customers, both present and potential. Weak ratios sometimes indicate a high probability of nonpayment. In addition to short-term creditors, management and stockholders are also interested in liquidity ratios, especially those of their own firm. The inability to meet current obligations taints a company's reputation, reduces its credit rating, and generally means an increase in future borrowing costs.

***Current Ratio*** The most widely used measure of liquidity is the **current ratio,** which relates total current assets to total current liabilities. The computation of the current ratio for Handy Corporation, based on figures presented in Exhibit 20-1, follows.

$$\text{Current Ratio} = \frac{\text{Current Assets}}{\text{Current Liabilities}}$$

**19X2**

$$\frac{\$8,000,000}{\$3,500,000} = 2.29$$

**19X1**

$$\frac{\$7,000,000}{\$3,400,000} = 2.06$$

Handy's ratios show that at the end of 19X2 the company had $2.29 of current assets for every $1.00 of current liabilities. Thus, an improvement is noted from the firm's position at the end of 19X1.

Although the ratio has increased, is Handy really "better off"? This is actually a difficult question to answer, especially when the following factors are considered. Observe that the current ratio uses a numerator of *total* current assets. Given the nature of the computation, all current assets are therefore treated equally, with a disregard for composition and individual component liquidities. One hundred dollars of cash, for example, is obviously more useful in satisfying existing obligations than $100 of unsold inventory. Because both amounts are treated in the same manner when deriving the ratio, knowledge of Handy's asset composition is needed to determine whether debt-paying ability has really improved.

To further complicate the picture, the current ratio can be manipulated by management. A business can deliberately improve its current ratio by paying short-term obligations at or near the end of the accounting period. Although current assets and current liabilities will both decline by the same amount, the ratio actually increases. For example, if a firm with current assets of $100,000 and current liabilities of $50,000 voluntarily paid a $10,000 account payable, the current ratio would improve from 2 to 2.25 ($90,000 ÷ $40,000). The practice of intentionally increasing a ratio to improve financial appearance is commonly known as *window dressing.*

Given these problems, the current ratio (and others) must be used with great care. The general rule employed by bankers and other creditors is that the current ratio should be at least 2. Be aware, however, that ratios tend to vary by type of business. For instance, the median current ratio is 0.7 for restaurants, 1.2 for wholesalers of dairy products, and 2.1 for footwear manufacturers.[1] Such variations are caused by differences in operating practices. Companies in some industries carry high levels of inventories and receivables to serve their customers. Also, certain industries tend to rely more heavily on trade accounts payable than others. Consequently, the general rule of 2 is just as its name implies—general. There are, as always, many exceptions.

***Quick Ratio*** The **quick ratio** is another measure of short-term, debt-paying ability. Rather than rely on total current assets for comparison with current liabilities, the quick ratio excludes merchandise inventory and prepaid expenses from the

[1] The industry figures used in this chapter are taken from *'88 Annual Statement Studies* (Philadelphia: Robert Morris Associates, 1988).

asset base. Inventory is not an immediate source of cash because months may pass until the time of sale, and prepaid expenses are consumed in operations. Thus, the current assets that remain—cash, short-term investments, and accounts receivable—represent a ready or "nearly ready" source of cash to satisfy the claims of creditors. In comparison with the current ratio, the quick ratio represents a more stringent test of debt-paying ability.

Handy's individual current assets appear below.

| | *19X2* | *19X1* |
|---|---|---|
| Current assets | | |
| Cash | $1,000,000 | $ 400,000 |
| Short-term investments | 1,000,000 | 1,000,000 |
| Accounts receivable (net) | 2,000,000 | 1,500,000 |
| Merchandise inventory | 3,900,000 | 4,000,000 |
| Prepaid expenses | 100,000 | 100,000 |
| | $8,000,000 | $7,000,000 |

The company's quick ratio is therefore computed as follows:

$$\text{Quick Ratio} = \frac{\text{Cash} + \text{Short-Term Investments} + \text{Accounts Receivable}}{\text{Current Liabilities}}$$

**19X2**

$$\frac{\$1,000,000 + \$1,000,000 + \$2,000,000}{\$3,500,000} = 1.14$$

**19X1**

$$\frac{\$400,000 + \$1,000,000 + \$1,500,000}{\$3,400,000} = 0.85$$

Many analysts feel that a quick ratio of 1 is satisfactory, with each dollar of short-term debt being backed by $1 of cash or near cash assets. Handy's ratio improved to meet this standard by the end of 19X2. Keep in mind that similar to the current ratio, this liquidity measure is subject to manipulation. Further note that the quick ratio will vary among industries; thus, the standard guideline of 1 should be used with caution.

## Activity Ratios

**Activity ratios,** often termed *turnover ratios,* are employed to analyze a firm's effectiveness in using specific resources. Managers, and to a lesser extent stockholders and short-term creditors, have a keen interest in these performance measures. The two most popular activity ratios are accounts receivable turnover and inventory turnover.

***Accounts Receivable Turnover*** **Accounts receivable turnover** shows the number of times each year a company's receivables turn into cash. As a result, this ratio provides some indication of the quality of both the receivables and a firm's collection efforts.

Accounts receivable turnover is computed by dividing net credit sales by the average accounts receivable during the year. Average receivables are calculated by summing the beginning and ending receivables and dividing by 2. Assuming that Handy Corporation's sales are all on account, the 19X2 turnover ratio would be computed as follows:

$$\text{Accounts Receivable Turnover} = \frac{\text{Net Credit Sales}}{\text{Average Accounts Receivable}}$$

$$= \frac{\$40{,}000{,}000}{\dfrac{\$1{,}500{,}000 + \$2{,}000{,}000}{2}}$$

$$= 22.86 \text{ times}$$

The fact that receivables turned over 22.86 times indicates an average collection period of about 16 days (365 days ÷ 22.86 times). To assess whether this result is satisfactory, additional information is needed with regard to Handy's credit terms. If the terms are n/30, then the company is doing an excellent job in granting credit and collecting the resulting accounts. If the terms are n/10, however, questions may surface concerning receivables management. Perhaps sales are being made to poor credit risks, or perhaps the company's collection efforts have been lax.

Like other ratios, receivables turnover and collection periods vary among businesses. This fact becomes apparent when studying the following figures:

| *Type of Business* | *Median Collection Period (Days)* |
|---|---|
| Radio and TV retailers | 9 |
| Grocery wholesalers | 21 |
| Sports and recreation clubs | 30 |
| Knitted goods manufacturers | 42 |
| Optical goods manufacturers | 54 |

As the collection period grows longer, more funds are tied up in receivables, thereby restricting the funds available for other investment opportunities.

***Inventory Turnover*** The **inventory turnover ratio** shows the number of times that a firm's inventory investment is turned into sales. Normally, high turnovers are indicative of sound inventory management, at least in terms of generating cash. To explain, inventory turnover is calculated by dividing cost of goods sold by the average inventory. Average inventory, in turn, is computed by adding the beginning and ending inventories and dividing by 2. As the average inventory grows, turnover will decrease unless there is a corresponding increase in sales and the accompanying cost of goods sold. Thus, a company that stocks a larger-than-normal inventory will have a lower turnover than another business that can generate the same sales with a lower merchandise investment.

As a result, it appears that organizations should maintain low inventories to achieve high turnovers. By doing so, firms minimize funds invested in excessive (and sometimes slow-moving) goods and reduce associated carrying costs (e.g., storage, insurance, taxes, obsolescence, and deterioration). This strategy may backfire, however, as low inventories frequently lead to stockouts, lost sales, and lost customers. Furthermore, quantity discounts and reduced freight rates may be unavailable because of insufficient purchasing activity. Inventory management is, indeed, a double-edged sword that requires close attention.

The 19X2 inventory turnover ratio for Handy Corporation is calculated as follows:

$$\text{Inventory Turnover Ratio} = \frac{\text{Cost of Goods Sold}}{\text{Average Inventory}}$$

$$= \frac{\$22{,}000{,}000}{\dfrac{\$4{,}000{,}000 + \$3{,}900{,}000}{2}}$$

$$= 5.57 \text{ times}$$

The ratio shows that the inventory turned 5.57 times, or approximately once every 66 days (365 days ÷ 5.57 times). To improve turnover, management could purchase more conservatively or stimulate sales from existing stock.

## Profitability Ratios

Ratios are also used to examine an organization's operating success (or lack thereof) during an accounting period. These measures, known as **profitability ratios,** are computed on the basis of sales or investment and are of special interest to management, stockholders, union officials and employees, and creditors.

***Profit Margin on Sales*** The ratio of net income to net sales (called the **profit margin on sales**) is a popular measure of profitability. Significant decreases in this ratio from year to year should be investigated; consistent deterioration may indicate a need for stringent cost control programs. As noted below, Handy's profit margin for 19X2 showed a great improvement over 19X1.

$$\text{Profit Margin on Sales} = \frac{\text{Net Income}}{\text{Net Sales}}$$

| **19X2** | **19X1** |
|---|---|
| $\dfrac{\$4{,}800{,}000}{\$40{,}000{,}000} = 12.0\%$ | $\dfrac{\$1{,}440{,}000}{\$36{,}000{,}000} = 4.0\%$ |

Profit margins can be computed separately, as shown, or be considered an outgrowth of vertical analysis (see Exhibit 20-2).

***Return on Assets*** The **return on assets,** often termed *return on investment* or *ROI,* measures profitability from a given level of asset investment. This ratio focuses on operations, specifically, the effectiveness of resources used in generating profit. Return on investment is typically calculated by dividing net income plus interest expense by the average total assets employed in business activity. The addition of interest expense produces a figure that represents earnings from operations, prior to any financing costs. Stated differently, we wish to focus on how well the asset investment was *used,* not on the related methods and costs of securing an entity's resources. The 19X2 return on assets for Handy Corporation is computed as follows:

$$\text{Return on Assets} = \frac{\text{Net Income} + \text{Interest Expense}}{\text{Average Assets}}$$

$$= \frac{\$4{,}800{,}000 + \$650{,}000}{\frac{\$20{,}250{,}000 + \$21{,}610{,}000}{2}}$$

$$= \frac{\$5{,}450{,}000}{\$20{,}930{,}000}$$

$$= 26.0\%$$

Handy's rate of return is quite high. For every \$1.00 of assets employed, the company has generated \$0.26 of income.

***Return on Common Stockholders' Equity*** Many corporations are heavily financed from investments made by common stockholders. A widely-used ratio, called **return on common stockholders' equity,** measures the profit generated on funds provided by these investors. This ratio is often calculated by dividing net income, minus preferred dividends, by the average common stockholders' equity. By subtracting preferred dividends, we derive the income that belongs to the common shareholders—the true residual owners of a corporation. Handy's 19X2 ratio is computed as follows:

$$\text{Return on Common Stockholders' Equity} = \frac{\text{Net Income} - \text{Preferred Dividends}}{\text{Average Common Stockholders' Equity}}$$

$$= \frac{\$4{,}800{,}000 - \$40{,}000}{\frac{\$8{,}450{,}000 + \$11{,}210{,}000}{2}}$$

$$= \frac{\$4{,}760{,}000}{\$9{,}830{,}000}$$

$$= 48.4\%$$

The common stockholders' equity figures are obtained from Exhibit 20-1 by taking total stockholders' equity and subtracting the \$400,000 of preferred stock outstanding.

Handy has earned over 48¢ for each dollar invested by common shareholders, which, like the return on assets discussed earlier, is quite impressive. Notice, however, that the return on common equity is much higher than the return on assets. The difference is caused by trading on the equity.

***Trading on the Equity*** **Trading on the equity,** sometimes called *leverage,* describes the process of securing funds at fixed interest and preferred dividend rates and then investing the funds to earn a return greater than their cost. To explain, Handy is earning 26.0% on its assets; yet a careful review of Exhibit 20-1 will find that the company is paying only 10% before tax for funds obtained via long-term debt (\$650,000 interest expense ÷ \$6,500,000 of long-term liabilities)[2] and a 10% dividend on outstanding preferred stock (\$40,000 ÷ \$400,000). The difference

[2] For purposes of simplicity we are assuming the interest pertains strictly to long-term obligations.

between the amounts earned and the amounts paid on such funds benefits the common stockholders and is reflected by the 48.4% return on their equity.

The company is said to be trading on the equity at a gain; that is, it has positive financial leverage. Naturally, the opposite case is possible. For instance, if the firm obtained funding at 10% but earned only 7% on investments, Handy would be trading on the equity at a loss. Net income suffers along with the payoff to the common stockholders.

***Other Profitability Ratios*** Several other profitability ratios were introduced earlier in the text. The calculation of **earnings per share** was discussed in Chapter 16 along with the **price-earnings ratio** (the current market price of a share of common stock divided by earnings per share).

An additional measure is the **dividend payout ratio,** which is used to study the percentage of earnings distributed to stockholders. The necessary computations involve dividing the annual cash dividend per share by earnings per share. A related ratio, the **dividend yield,** is the annual cash dividend per share divided by the current market price of the stock. This ratio provides insight to investors about the short-term rate of return (from dividends) on their invested funds.

**TIPS & TECHNIQUES**

The interpretation of a company's dividend yield must be done with great care. Many investors prefer to acquire stocks that have attractive yields because of the cash flow involved. Be cautioned, however, that the company now has less cash to invest in its own projects, perhaps restricting growth. Some investors will therefore focus on businesses that pay few, if any, dividends but that have high expansion potential accompanied by steadily rising stock prices.

## Coverage Ratios

**Coverage ratios** are computed to judge the solvency of an entity. These ratios are of primary importance to long-term creditors, who have an obvious concern regarding the receipt of interest and the repayment of amounts borrowed.

***Debt to Total Assets*** The **debt to total assets ratio** shows the percentage of total capital provided by the creditors of a business. Debt includes all obligations, both current and long-term. The debt to total assets ratios for Handy at the end of 19X2 and 19X1 follow.

$$\text{Debt to Total Assets} = \frac{\text{Total Debt}}{\text{Total Assets}}$$

| **19X2** | **19X1** |
|---|---|
| $\frac{\$10{,}000{,}000}{\$21{,}610{,}000} = 46.3\%$ | $\frac{\$11{,}400{,}000}{\$20{,}250{,}000} = 56.3\%$ |

As you can see, total liabilities outstanding declined by $1.4 million during 19X2. Furthermore, observe that debt declined in percentage terms as a means of financing Handy's asset investment. Apparently, the creditors are playing a reduced role (when compared with the owners) in terms of providing investment funds. This fact becomes evident when focusing on a *ratio of total debt to total stockholders' equity*. The debt to equity ratio for Handy at the end of 19X2 was 0.86 ($10,000,000 ÷ $11,610,000), down from 1.29 ($11,400,000 ÷ $8,850,000) upon conclusion of 19X1. A ratio of 1 signifies that the creditors and owners are furnishing equal amounts of funds for business activity.

The debt to total assets ratio is of interest to both creditors and stockholders. Creditors generally prefer a low ratio, indicating that a large percentage of asset financing is provided by the owners and/or operations. Low debt means low monthly outlays for principal and interest and, thus, a reduced risk of nonpayment should sales and earnings fall.

Stockholders, on the other hand, sometimes desire a high debt to total assets ratio. As shown earlier, the presence of debt in the capital structure can give rise to positive leverage and benefit the common stockholders. Increased debt normally increases leverage. However, too much debt may actually cause the reduction or elimination of common stock dividends in periods of slow business activity. Remember, interest payments must be met; in contrast, dividends to common stockholders are subject to the discretion of the board of directors. What we have are conflicting views. Generally, debt is acceptable if it is used in moderation. However, the "right" amount of debt varies among industries and is extremely difficult to determine.

***Times Interest Earned*** Although a company may be heavily financed by debt, it is possible that earnings are more than adequate to cover the required interest charges. If, however, interest coverage is marginal, the creditors' position may be threatened. Insight into the amount of protection that is afforded the long-term creditors is provided by a ratio called **times interest earned.**

The times interest earned ratio is computed by dividing income before taxes and interest by the interest charges themselves. Observe that income *before* taxes is used because interest, in part, determines tax expense. For Handy the number of times interest was earned improved significantly from 19X1 to 19X2. As the following calculations show, the more than threefold increase was caused by a combination of lower interest charges and higher earnings.

$$\text{Times Interest Earned} = \frac{\text{Income Before Income Taxes and Interest}}{\text{Interest Charges}}$$

| **19X2** | **19X1** |
|---|---|
| $\frac{\$8{,}650{,}000}{\$650{,}000} = 13.3$ | $\frac{\$3{,}200{,}000}{\$800{,}000} = 4$ |

## Ratio Analysis: A Concluding Comment

Ratio analysis is an extremely useful tool for assessing financial performance. Several studies have shown, for example, that specific ratio changes are oftentimes a predictor of bankruptcy. The ratios presented in these pages will, we hope, whet your appetite for a deeper investigation of financial statements. When used in conjunction with industry norms and data of other companies, a very powerful tool is at your disposal. Keep in mind, however, that ratios are not ends in themselves and cannot tell the complete story behind financial success or failure. They are merely a starting point for further analysis and questioning.

## Notes to Financial Statements

OBJECTIVE 5
Have a basic knowledge of financial statement footnotes.

A thorough analysis of a company's financial statements normally involves a look beyond the statements themselves. Because of added disclosure requirements of the accounting profession and a greater demand for details by statement users, much of the information needed to study an entity's financial relationships lies in a series of accompanying **footnotes.**[3]

These footnotes are quite varied, as each company has its own unique set of transactions, contracts, and circumstances. Normally, however, footnotes serve one of three basic functions by (1) summarizing significant accounting policies, (2) providing explanatory information, or (3) disclosing supplementary information.

### Summary of Significant Accounting Policies

Corporations that issue financial statements in accordance with GAAP must include a summary of significant accounting policies. This disclosure is important because of the many methods available to recognize revenues and expenses and to value assets. Statement users must be aware of the accounting practices employed by a business so that a sound evaluation can be made.

The summary is typically presented as the first footnote to the financial statements or in a separate section just before the footnotes. Within this section companies generally describe those principles and methods that have been selected for use from the available alternatives. In addition, disclosure is made of both unusual or creative applications of generally accepted accounting principles, and practices that are peculiar to the industry in which the business operates.

*Excerpts* from the summary of significant accounting policies for K mart Corporation appear in Exhibit 20-3. Here we learn, among other things, that the company uses the retail method of inventory valuation in conjunction with (primarily) a LIFO cost flow assumption. Furthermore, straight-line depreciation is employed for financial statement purposes, while accelerated methods are used when reporting income taxes to the government. In addition, store operating costs incurred prior to the opening of a new facility are expensed when incurred.

### Explanatory Information

Footnotes may also be used to expand on the information presented in the body of the financial statements. For example, the property, plant, and equipment owned by a firm is often disclosed via a single line-item on the balance sheet. To provide further information, a footnote may reveal the individual components (land, land improvements, buildings, machinery and equipment) and their related cost. Long-term liabilities are often treated in this manner, with a footnote used to furnish details on the types and amounts of debt owed by the business (e.g., installment notes, mortgage notes, bonds, and so forth).

### Supplementary Information

An increasing number of footnotes are devoted to fulfilling the requirements of the SEC and FASB for supplemental (additional) financial information. Such is the

[3] A complete set of footnotes to the financial statements of the Alberto-Culver Company appears in Appendix B at the end of the text.

**Exhibit 20-3**
**Notes to Consolidated Financial Statements**

**(A) Summary of Significant Accounting Policies**

*Fiscal Year:* The company's fiscal year ends on the last Wednesday in January. Fiscal years 1988, 1987 and 1986 consisted of 52 weeks and ended on January 25, 1989, January 27, 1988 and January 28, 1987, respectively.

*Inventories:* Merchandise inventories are valued at the lower of cost or market, using the retail method, on the last-in, first-out basis for substantially all domestic inventories and the first-in, first-out basis for the remainder.

*Depreciation:* The company computes depreciation on owned property principally on the straight-line method for financial statement purposes and on accelerated methods for income tax purposes. Most store properties are leased and improvements are amortized over the term of the lease but not more than 25 years. Other annual rates used in computing depreciation for financial statement purposes are 2% to 4% for buildings, 10% to 14% for store fixtures and 5% to 33% for other fixtures and equipment.

*Pre-Opening and Closing Costs:* The company follows the practice of treating store operating costs incurred prior to opening a new retail unit as current period expenses. When the decision to close a retail unit is made, the company provides for future net lease obligations, nonrecoverable investments in fixed assets, other expenses directly related to discontinuance of operations and estimated operating losses through expected closing dates.

case with *interim* (quarterly) financial data, which are disclosed as a supplemental footnote to the year-end statements. These data allow users to compare quarterly results and gain insights regarding the pattern of sales and earnings over the year. Disclosure in this manner is especially helpful in the evaluation of seasonal businesses, or those firms that generate the majority of their revenues in a relatively short period of time. A classic example of such a business would be a natural gas utility, whose peak activity occurs during the winter months.

## Segment Reporting

Another example of supplemental disclosure is **segment reporting,** which concerns the disclosure of selected financial information when a company is involved in several distinctly different business activities (e.g., soft drink bottling, small appliances, and movie theater operation). Per *Statement of Financial Accounting Standards No. 14,* such information is presented in the footnotes and serves to supplement that shown in the financial statements. This practice makes it more difficult for firms to "hide" segments that incur huge losses, produce substantial profits, or experience difficulty in generating sales.

To illustrate the concept of segment reporting, we will focus on the activities of Sara Lee Corporation. The company, whose major businesses are the manufacturing and marketing of consumer products, has three operating segments. The segments, along with selected subsidiaries, include packaged foods [Sara Lee Packaged Meats (Jimmy Dean, Hillshire Farm, Bryan Foods, Kahn's); Sara Lee Bakery]; foodservice; and packaged consumer products (Hanes, L'eggs, Coach Leatherware, Fuller Brush). Sara Lee's recent annual report revealed the following segment data (in millions):

| *Segment* | *Sales* | *Operating Income* | *Identifiable Assets* |
|---|---|---|---|
| Packaged foods | $5,255 | $366 | $2,354 |
| Foodservice | 2,607 | 61 | 247 |
| Packaged consumer products | 4,000 | 420 | 3,507 |

The company's disclosure shows some interesting results. The second largest segment, packaged consumer products, was Sara Lee's most profitable line of business. However, management had a far greater asset investment to work with to generate income. It appears that the other two segments, especially foodservice, used their assets more efficiently in profitable endeavors and produced higher returns (i.e., profits) per dollar invested. These facts become more evident in the chart that follows, which reveals the operating income on sales ratios and the return on assets.

| | *Operating Income on Sales Ratio* | | *Return on Assets* | |
|---|---|---|---|---|
| *Segment* | *Percent* | *Rank* | *Percent* | *Rank* |
| Packaged foods | 6.96% | 2 | 15.55% | 2 |
| Foodservice | 2.34 | 3 | 24.70 | 1 |
| Packaged consumer products | 10.50 | 1 | 11.98 | 3 |

## International Accounting

OBJECTIVE 6
Have a general familiarity with several of the basic issues of international accounting.

Today's communication and transportation technology has facilitated rapid business expansion, with numerous entities evolving into multinational concerns. As Exhibit 20-4 shows, large U.S.-based multinationals obtain a hefty share of their revenues and profit from foreign operations. (*Note:* Companies are ranked in terms of foreign revenue.)

An extensive level of international activity for today's business giants is not unusual. Put simply, there is a major desire to develop foreign trade by large American corporations, given the magnitude of world markets. As these firms are well aware, however, international trade is a two-way street. Witness popular consumer items in this country such as Nestlé chocolate, Shell Oil gasoline, Mercedes-Benz automobiles, and Corona beer, all of which are products of companies headquartered in foreign lands.

Within the environment of multinational expansion, international accounting considerations have begun to receive increased attention. Our discussion of international accounting is composed of four topics: uniformity of international accounting standards, accounting for foreign currency transactions, translation of foreign currency financial statements, and the disclosure of international financial affairs.

### Uniformity of International Accounting Standards

As noted several times in this text, a desirable characteristic of financial information is comparability among firms. We observed that differences in accounting methods sometimes make such comparisons difficult. These difficulties are compounded at

**Exhibit 20-4**
**Large U.S. Multinational Firms**

| *Rank* | *Company* | *Foreign Revenue as a Percentage of Total Revenue* | *Foreign Operating Profit as a Percentage of Total Operating Profit* |
|---|---|---|---|
| 1 | Exxon | 71.6% | 72.9% |
| 2 | Ford Motor | 45.3 | 43.1 |
| 3 | IBM | 57.6 | 74.1 |
| 4 | Mobil | 67.1 | 60.3 |
| 5 | General Motors | 24.2 | 63.2 |
| 11 | Procter & Gamble | 37.7 | 23.6 |
| 13 | Chase Manhattan | 49.2 | 32.0 |
| 22 | Goodyear | 43.8 | 40.9 |
| 35 | FW Woolworth | 43.3 | 31.6 |
| 53 | PepsiCo | 18.9 | 39.2 |

SOURCE: Adapted from "The 100 Largest U.S. Multinationals," *Forbes*, July 24, 1989, pp. 320–324.

the international level because of significant variations in economic systems and fundamental principles of measurement. For example, many countries require that financial accounting information be derived by the same techniques used to figure an entity's income tax liability. This situation is not true in the United States, where generally accepted accounting principles frequently produce earnings figures that differ greatly from data reported to taxing authorities. Other differences exist in the areas of inventory valuation, depreciation, consolidation of financial statements, inflation accounting, and goodwill amortization, to name just a few.

Because more businesses and investors are adopting a global perspective, there is an increasing need and demand for uniform international accounting standards. To meet this need, several private sector and governmental standard setting organizations have been established. Foremost among these groups are the International Accounting Standards Committee (IASC) and the International Federation of Accountants (IFAC).

The IASC membership consists of representatives from professional accounting societies of numerous countries. The U.S. representative to this organization is the American Institute of Certified Public Accountants. The IASC operates in a manner very similar to the Financial Accounting Standards Board (FASB) and issues standards that relate to specific financial reporting topics. Unlike the FASB, however, the IASC lacks authority to prescribe accounting rules, relying instead on members' attempts to have the standards adopted in their respective countries.

The IFAC is also comprised of representatives from professional accounting organizations throughout the world. Like the IASC, the IFAC's authority is self-imposed by the voluntary efforts of its membership. This body is primarily concerned with auditing and other professional matters, such as ethics and education.

The major goals of these organizations are to bring a degree of uniformity to international accounting standards and to develop and enhance a coordinated worldwide accounting profession. Realistically, achievement of these goals will be a long and difficult process. One should remember that the development of generally accepted accounting principles within even a single country (e.g., the United States) is usually represented by decades of evolution and debate.

## HIGHLIGHT

# International Business and H. J. Heinz

H. J. Heinz, whose major brands include Heinz ketchup, Ore-Ida frozen potatoes, 9 Lives cat food, Star-Kist tuna, and Weight Watchers, currently obtains about 35% of its total revenue from foreign operations. Eager to do even more business abroad, Heinz's president, Dr. Anthony J. F. O'Reilly, recently noted that his company is looking for new geography to provide growth opportunities in the 1990s. Before the Investment Analysts Society of Chicago, O'Reilly said,

> Four years ago at the annual meeting, I told shareholders that 85% of the world's population were not consumers, indeed had never heard of Heinz products. I pointed out that, despite the well-publicized financial problems of Third World countries, they would eventually evolve into new markets for convenience food products. We recognized geographical expansion as a promising direction that we intended to follow.
>
> I am happy to say that our pursuit of that objective has been fruitful. Through its Olivine Industries partnership with the Zimbabwean government in the making and marketing of soap, margarine, and cooking oil, Heinz has experienced profitable steady growth and expansion. Crop experimentation there holds promise of eventually opening up the Zimbabwean market to new Heinz food products . . . This success has now led us to neighboring Zambia, where we have been invited by the government to buy an interest in and operate a company similar to Olivine.
>
> In Asia, Heinz Japan Ltd., which began as a partnership in 1961, is now wholly-owned, making a profit, and generating its first substantial dividends . . . This year, Heinz Japan pushed imported Ore-Ida frozen potatoes into a #1 brand share position, while our patient and innovative Japanese management has established a thriving business in soups and sauces for the restaurant trade.
>
> Heinz Japan, once an isolated outpost of the company in the Pacific Basin, has been joined during the past three years by two additional, potentially important Heinz subsidiaries. We entered into an agreement . . . with Seoul Food, Ltd., in the rapidly expanding South Korean market to take a controlling share in a company that offers a wide range of food products similar to ours. . . .
>
> Perhaps the Far East development that offers the greatest promise as a profit center is the Heinz-UFE Ltd. partnership that we entered in 1984 in the People's Republic of China. Our factory in Guangdong Province was erected . . . in a record time. Today, it is in full operation and selling all of the dry baby food cereal it can produce. I think it is fair to say that this initial experiment on the Chinese mainland will lead to additional facilities in other provinces of that immense country, which welcomes 16 million new babies a year, as compared with three million in the U.S. In fact, we are in active negotiations to build a second plant shortly.
>
> Our success to date has caused us to intensify our exploration of other parts of the Orient and Africa. We are quite agreeable to participation in a wide range of business relationships, either alone or with all manner of partners. In a geopolitical sense, especially in Zimbabwe and China, where we have very satisfied governmental partners, we have contributed to a trend toward denationalization and a style of management that focuses on efficient, competitive satisfaction of consumer needs. These are policies that are seen as increasingly apolitical and represent, in our view, an important statement about American management practices and philosophies.

SOURCE: Remarks by Dr. Anthony J. F. O'Reilly before the Investment Analysts Society of Chicago, March 17, 1987, pp. 14–16. 

## Accounting for Foreign Currency Transactions

International trade is complicated by the various currencies that are used in the world's marketplace. Whenever an entity buys goods from a foreign supplier or sells goods to a foreign customer, the parties involved must agree on the currency to be used in settling the transaction. From the perspective of a U.S. company, if settlement will be made in U.S. dollars, then no unique measurement and reporting problems arise. In contrast, if settlement requires the use of a foreign currency, special accounting considerations are introduced. To appreciate these considerations, it is necessary to first have a basic understanding of *currency exchange rates.*

At any point in time, the currency of one country may be exchanged into the currency of another. The conversion is based on the **spot rate** in effect at the time of exchange. For example, the spot rate might indicate that a U.S. firm could purchase one Swiss franc for $0.70. Spot rates tend to fluctuate throughout a reporting period in response to changes in inflation, interest rates, and political climate.

The impact of currency exchange rates on a business that has foreign operations is easily seen by studying the situation faced by the Toronto Blue Jays, the American League baseball club.[4] During a recent season the club drew 2.5 million spectators, up 17% from the previous year, but still lost $1.1 million. Much of the trouble arose because approximately 75% of the Blue Jays' revenue (e.g., gate receipts, concessions, and local broadcasting rights) was generated in Canadian dollars, which at the time were worth about 73% of the U.S. counterpart. However, two-thirds of the team's expenses (e.g., travel, salaries, five U.S. farm teams, 30 U.S. talent scouts, and Florida training grounds) are paid in U.S. dollars. Says the team's vice president of finance, "The economic realities don't allow us to make money."

### Purchase Transactions

To illustrate accounting for foreign currency transactions, suppose that Jewelry Import (JI) of New York purchased watches from Alps Exporting of Switzerland. According to terms of the transaction, JI must pay 20,000 Swiss francs to the foreign firm in 60 days. If the spot rate at the time of purchase was $0.70 per franc, how should Jewelry Import enter the transaction in its accounts? Recording the transaction in francs would result in financial records that contain a hodgepodge of different currencies, making data summarization and financial statement preparation impossible. It is therefore necessary to enter the transaction in U.S. dollars even though ultimate settlement will be made in the Swiss currency. The entry needed on the date of purchase is as follows:

| | | |
|---|---|---|
| Purchases | 14,000 | |
| Accounts Payable | | 14,000 |
| Purchased merchandise on account | | |

Notice that the account payable is established at the number of U.S. dollars required to purchase 20,000 francs at $0.70 each.

Sixty days later, Jewelry Import will acquire the francs from a commercial bank at the spot rate in effect on that date. These francs will then be delivered to Alps Exporting in settlement of the transaction. Because exchange rates fluctuate daily, the spot rate will likely differ from the $0.70 rate that existed on the date of

[4] "The Blue Jay Blues," *Forbes,* November 18, 1985, p. 10.

purchase. Suppose, for example, that the spot rate has changed and stands at $0.68 on the date of settlement. When Jewelry Import purchases the Swiss currency, the firm will be required to pay only $13,600 (20,000 francs × $0.68). A journal entry to reflect the purchase of francs and the payment to Alps Exporting would be

| | | |
|---|---|---|
| Accounts Payable | 14,000 | |
| Exchange Gain | | 400 |
| Cash | | 13,600 |
| Acquired Swiss francs and paid related foreign currency payable | | |

This entry indicates that a liability originally established at $14,000 was settled by a cash outlay of only $13,600. The difference constitutes a foreign currency transaction exchange gain. Conversely, Jewelry Import would have suffered an exchange loss had the spot rate risen between the date of purchase and the date of payment.

## Sale Transactions

Similar accounting treatment applies to sales on account that will be settled in a foreign currency. Suppose, for example, that American Export sells goods to a British company. The terms of sale require the foreign firm to pay 1,000 British pounds in 90 days. If the spot rate on the date of sale is $1.80 per pound, the transaction would be recorded as follows:

| | | |
|---|---|---|
| Accounts Receivable | 1,800 | |
| Sales | | 1,800 |
| Sold merchandise on account | | |

Ninety days later, assume the spot rate stands at $1.75 and the purchaser delivers the British currency to American Export. If American Export immediately sells the pounds at a commercial bank for $1,750 (1,000 pounds × $1.75), the appropriate journal entry would be as shown.

| | | |
|---|---|---|
| Cash | 1,750 | |
| Exchange Loss | 50 | |
| Accounts Receivable | | 1,800 |
| Collected British pounds on account and converted to U.S. dollars | | |

The exchange loss reflects the fact that American Export agreed to accept 1,000 pounds and that the value of those pounds declined by $0.05 each. If the exchange rate had risen, a gain would have resulted.

## End-of-Period Adjustments

In each of the preceding illustrations, the exchange gains and losses were recorded upon settlement of the payable or receivable. Because financial statements are often prepared between the date of a transaction and the time of settlement, an end-of-period adjustment is required. Specifically, foreign currency payables and receivables must be adjusted to reflect their U.S. dollar amount as of the financial statement date. For instance, suppose that a U.S. company having a December 31 year-end purchased goods on December 1 and agreed to pay 1 million Japanese yen in 60 days. The spot rate was $0.0074 per yen on December 1, $0.0077 on December 31, and $0.0076 near the end of January when the payable was settled. The entries that follow would be needed.

| | | | | |
|---|---|---|---|---|
| Dec. | 1 | Purchases | 7,400 | |
| | | Accounts Payable | | 7,400 |
| | | Purchased merchandise on account | | |
| | 31 | Exchange Loss | 300 | |
| | | Accounts Payable | | 300 |
| | | Adjusted foreign currency payable to reflect spot rate | | |
| Jan. | 30 | Accounts Payable | 7,700 | |
| | | Exchange Gain | | 100 |
| | | Cash | | 7,600 |
| | | Acquired yen and paid related foreign currency payable | | |

Notice that on December 31 the payable is adjusted upward by $300 [($0.0077 − $0.0074) × 1,000,000 yen] and the related loss is recorded. On January 30, however, the firm needs only $7,600 to settle its debt. The $100 change from year-end is therefore reported as a gain. This accounting treatment reflects the impact of rate changes on income as the changes occur and also results in proper valuation of foreign currency payables and receivables.

## Translation of Foreign Currency Financial Statements

A third international accounting consideration pertains to the translation of financial statements of foreign affiliates. As pointed out in Chapter 18, one entity may acquire all or part of the outstanding common stock of another corporation (termed the *investee*) for the purpose of investment or control. When a U.S. corporation obtains a significant investment in a foreign business, an accounting problem arises: the foreign entity's financial statements will likely be prepared in a currency other than the U.S. dollar.

Because of this situation, it is necessary to translate the foreign affiliate's accounting data into U.S. currency so the economic affairs of the investor and investee companies can be consolidated (combined). This process involves multiplying the foreign corporation's account balances by various exchange rates and often results in a series of translation adjustments. These adjustments are afforded special treatment by the accounting profession. The details of this treatment, along with the procedures that underlie statement translation, are more appropriately covered in advanced courses (and texts).

## Disclosure of International Financial Affairs

The internationalization of business has led to increased financial statement disclosures, generally in the accompanying footnotes. Companies that meet certain guidelines must reveal specified segment information relative to their international operations. Such information is useful to investors and creditors who are sensitive to the unique risks associated with conducting business in foreign lands. For example, if an entity generates a large percentage of its sales and earnings in a country that has a past history of governmental takeovers, a potential (and somewhat pessimistic) investor might shy away from a long-term commitment of funds.

Typical corporate disclosures include sales, income, and identifiable assets, all categorized by major geographic area of operation. A sample presentation is shown in footnote 9 of Appendix B at the conclusion of the text.

## Chapter Review

### Learning Objectives—The Key Points

**1 Be familiar with the advantages and problems of financial statement analysis.** By establishing and studying certain financial relationships, financial statement analysis permits statement users to see a clearer picture of performance (e.g., the *relationship* between total current assets and total current liabilities, as opposed to a fragmented interpretation of amounts in isolation from one another). Problem areas to avoid include (1) failing to team the results of the analysis with subjective factors and sound judgment and (2) choosing an "incorrect" standard for comparison. The latter situation may arise when companies are selected that have widely varying activities and accounting policies from those of the business under study.

**2 Be able to perform a horizontal analysis of comparative financial statements.** Horizontal analysis provides information about the magnitude, direction, and relative importance of changes in individual and aggregate financial statement items. The process involves the calculation of dollar and percentage changes by establishing earlier period dollar amounts as a base against which later period amounts are compared.

**3 Be able to perform a vertical analysis and understand the associated benefits of common-size financial statements.** With vertical analysis, each figure on a financial statement is related to a relevant total and stated as a percentage of that total. On an income statement, for instance, each amount is expressed as a percentage of net sales. This type of analysis assists users when interpreting performance and is the basis for the preparation of common-size financial statements. Such statements focus on percentages, thereby allowing a valid comparison of companies that are vastly different in terms of size.

**4 Be familiar with ratio analysis.** Ratio analysis involves the mathematical expression of selected financial relationships. Liquidity ratios, for example, measure the ability of a business to meet current debts as the obligations come due. In contrast, activity ratios measure a firm's effectiveness in using specific resources (e.g., inventory). Profitability ratios are employed to assess an organization's operating success (or lack thereof) during an accounting period, and coverage ratios, such as times interest earned, are computed to measure the solvency of an entity. Thirteen ratios used daily in American business are discussed in the chapter and summarized in the table that follows.

| *Ratio* | *Method of Computation* | *Significance* |
|---|---|---|
| (1) Liquidity ratios | | |
| (a) Current ratio | $\frac{\text{Current assets}}{\text{Current liabilities}}$ | Measures ability to meet short-term debts |
| (b) Quick ratio | $\frac{\text{Cash + short-term investments + accounts receivable}}{\text{Current liabilities}}$ | Measures very short-term debt paying ability |
| (2) Activity ratios | | |
| (a) Accounts receivable turnover | $\frac{\text{Net credit sales}}{\text{Average accounts receivable}}$ | Provides insight into credit and collection policies |
| (b) Inventory turnover | $\frac{\text{Cost of goods sold}}{\text{Average inventory}}$ | Provides insight into inventory management policies |
| (3) Profitability ratios | | |
| (a) Profit margin on sales | $\frac{\text{Net income}}{\text{Net sales}}$ | Shows the net income generated from each sales dollar |

| Ratio | Method of Computation | Significance |
|---|---|---|
| (b) Return on assets | Net income + interest expense / Average assets | Indicates effectiveness of resources used in generating profit |
| (c) Return on common stockholders' equity | Net income − preferred dividends / Average common stockholders' equity | Reveals the earning rate of capital provided by common shareholders |
| (d) Earnings per share | See Chapter 16 | Measures the earnings applicable to a share of common stock |
| (e) Price-earnings ratio | Market price per share / Earnings per share | Shows the amount investors are willing to pay for each dollar of corporate earnings |
| (f) Dividend payout ratio | Cash dividend per share / Earnings per share | Reveals corporate policy regarding retention or distribution of earnings |
| (g) Dividend yield | Cash dividend per share / Market price per share | Indicates the investor's short-term rate of return from dividends |
| (4) Coverage ratios | | |
| (a) Debt to total assets | Total debt / Total assets | Shows the percentage of assets financed by long- and short-term borrowings |
| (b) Times interest earned | Income before income taxes and interest / Interest charges | Measures a firm's ability to cover and meet fixed interest charges |

**5 Have a basic knowledge of financial statement footnotes.** Footnotes are used to summarize accounting policies, present the underlying details of financial statement items (e.g., the composition of a company's investment in plant and equipment), and disclose supplemental data consistent with the rulings of the SEC and the FASB. Disclosures that fall in the last category include those for interim and segment data.

**6 Have a general familiarity with several of the basic issues of international accounting.** There are four basic issues related to international accounting. First, because of variations in economic systems and accounting principles, comparability and compatibility of financial information prepared in different countries is impaired. Several groups, however, are working to bring a degree of uniformity to international accounting standards. Foreign currency transactions are a second area of concern to accountants, as international trade occurs in various currencies. If settlement is to be made in a foreign currency, a gain or loss must be recorded if the exchange rate fluctuates between the transaction date and the date of settlement (or the end of the period). Two other areas of concern include the translation of a foreign affiliate's financial statements into U.S. dollars for purposes of consolidation and the segment disclosure of foreign operations.

## Chapter Quiz

The five questions that follow relate to several issues raised in the chapter. Test your knowledge of the issues by selecting the best answer. (The answers appear on p. 752.)

**1** Vertical analysis:
- a cannot be used to compare companies of different size.
- b provides information about the magnitude, direction, and relative importance of changes in individual financial statement items.
- c is needed to assess the coverage of obligations.
- d results in common-size financial statements.

**2** London Corporation paid $1,000 of accounts payable with cash on the last day of the month. The company had a current ratio of 4 before the disbursement. As a result of this payment, the current ratio will:
a increase.
b decrease.
c remain unchanged.
d fluctuate, but the direction of the change depends on unstated facts.

**3** Jedd, Inc., has obtained long-term debt at a 14% interest rate and is achieving a return on assets of 42%. These figures indicate that Jedd will have:
a a 28% increase in earnings per share.
b a 28% increase in the profit margin on sales.
c a return on common stockholders' equity of less than 14%.
d a return on common stockholders' equity of more than 14%.

**4** The following information relates to the North Airlines, Pencil, and Aluminum Siding Company:

| | *Sales* | *Operating Income* | *Identifiable Assets* |
|---|---|---|---|
| Airline | $4,000 | $ 20 | $2,000 |
| Pencils | 1,000 | 80 | 1,600 |
| Aluminum siding | 2,000 | 400 | 4,000 |

Which of the segments was least profitable in terms of dollar profit, profit margin on sales, and return on assets, respectively?
a Pencils, airline, aluminum siding.
b Airline, pencils, aluminum siding.
c Airline, airline, airline.
d Airline, airline, pencils.

**5** Tyson (USA) sold merchandise to a Hong Kong company for 100,000 Hong Kong dollars when the spot rate was $0.13 per U.S. dollar. At year-end, the spot rate was $0.15; by the date of settlement, it had risen to $0.16. Tyson would record the sale in its accounting records at:
a $13,000.
b $15,000.
c $16,000.
d some amount other than those above.

## Questions

**Q20-1** Why is financial information of a business often compared with the past performance of the same company and the performance of other companies? What difficulties exist in comparisons with other firms?

**Q20-2** Distinguish between horizontal analysis and vertical analysis. Which type of analysis results in common-size financial statements?

**Q20-3** A student once noted: "This ratio stuff is great. It's unbelievable how ratios can tell the complete story behind the problems of a business." Comment on the student's observation.

**Q20-4** Briefly describe the following types of ratios and identify the financial statement users most interested in each type.
a Liquidity ratios
b Activity ratios
c Profitability ratios
d Coverage ratios

**Q20-5** What is the current ratio? Present a short critique of this widely used financial measure.

**Q20-6** Why do many analysts prefer the quick ratio over the current ratio for judging debt-paying ability?

**Q20-7** What insight can be provided by the accounts receivable turnover ratio? The inventory turnover ratio?

**Q20-8** Discuss the differences between the return on assets and the return on common stockholders' equity.

**Q20-9** What does it mean to "trade on the equity"? How can such trading be successful? Unsuccessful?

**Q20-10** Briefly explain what types of information are typically disclosed by footnotes to the financial statements.

**Q20-11** Why are interim data useful to readers of financial statements?

**Q20-12** Have strides been made toward the uniformity of international accounting standards? Briefly discuss.

**Q20-13** How can companies experience gains and losses from foreign currency transactions?

**Q20-14** Why is the translation of foreign currency financial statements necessary?

## Exercises

**E20-1** ***Horizontal analysis***

The Mary Lynn Corporation has been operating for several years. Selected data from the 19X1 and 19X2 financial statements follow.

| | *19X2* | *19X1* |
|---|---:|---:|
| Current assets | $ 76,000 | $ 80,000 |
| Property, plant, & equipment (net) | 99,000 | 90,000 |
| Intangibles | 25,000 | 50,000 |
| Current liabilities | 40,800 | 48,000 |
| Long-term liabilities | 143,000 | 160,000 |
| Stockholders' equity | 16,200 | 12,000 |
| Net sales | 500,000 | 500,000 |
| Cost of goods sold | 332,500 | 350,000 |
| Operating expenses | 93,500 | 85,000 |

Prepare a horizontal analysis for 19X1 and 19X2. Briefly comment on the results of your work.

**E20-2** ***Vertical analysis***

Study the data that appear in Exercise 20-1 pertaining to the Mary Lynn Corporation. Prepare a vertical analysis for 19X1 and 19X2, and briefly evaluate the results of your work.

**E20-3** ***Liquidity ratios***

Edison, Stagg, and Thornton have the following financial information at the close of business on July 10:

| | *Edison* | *Stagg* | *Thornton* |
|---|---|---|---|
| Cash | $4,000 | $2,500 | $1,000 |
| Short-term investments | 3,000 | 2,500 | 2,000 |
| Accounts receivable | 2,000 | 2,500 | 3,000 |
| Inventory | 1,000 | 2,500 | 4,000 |
| Prepaid expenses | 800 | 800 | 800 |
| Accounts payable | 200 | 200 | 200 |
| Notes payable: short-term | 3,100 | 3,100 | 3,100 |
| Accrued payables | 300 | 300 | 300 |
| Long-term liabilities | 3,800 | 3,800 | 3,800 |

a Compute the current and quick ratios for each of the three companies. (Round calculations to two decimal places.) Which firm is the most liquid? Why?

b Suppose Thornton is using FIFO for inventory valuation and Edison is using LIFO. Comment on the comparability of information between these two companies.

c If all short-term notes payable are due on July 11 at 8 A.M., comment on each company's ability to settle its obligation in a timely manner.

**E20-4** ***Liquidity and activity ratios***

Evaluate the comments that follow as being True or False. If the comment is false, briefly explain why.

a The current ratio can be deliberately improved by performing a process known as window dressing.

b All other things being equal, a company normally prefers to have a high inventory turnover rather than a low inventory turnover.

c The basic difference between the current ratio and the quick ratio lies in the treatment of accounts receivable and prepaid expenses.

d The current ratio treats all current assets as being equally liquid.

e The sale of merchandise to businesses that have marginal credit ratings tends to improve a firm's accounts receivable turnover.

**E20-5** ***Activity ratios***

The president of Vonnie Summer, Inc., has furnished you with the following selected information.

| | *19X2* | *19X1* |
|---|---|---|
| Net sales | $48,008,000 | $54,863,000 |
| Cost of goods sold | 35,489,000 | 35,243,000 |
| Gross profit | $12,519,000 | $19,620,000 |
| Expenses | 12,867,000 | 13,658,000 |
| Income before taxes | $ (348,000) | $ 5,962,000 |
| Current assets | | |
| Cash | $ 782,000 | $ 1,286,000 |
| Short-term investments | 100,000 | 5,716,000 |
| Accounts receivable (net) | 9,390,000 | 11,727,000 |
| Inventories | 14,000,000 | 10,642,000 |
| Prepaid expenses | 486,000 | 373,000 |

The company is planning to borrow several million dollars for the purchase of inventory by securing a 180-day bank loan.

a Compute the accounts receivable and inventory turnover ratios for 19X2. Assume that all sales are on account, and round calculations to two decimal places.

b Study the ratios and comment on the ability of the company to repay a bank loan in 180 days.

**E20-6** ***Activity ratios***

The following information pertains to the Rockville Corporation:

| | |
|---|---|
| Ending accounts receivable | $ 340,000 |
| Ending inventory | 265,000 |
| Total sales | 2,000,000 |
| Customer collections on account | 1,560,000 |
| Purchases | 1,250,000 |
| Gross profit rate | 40% |
| Percent of credit sales to total sales | 80% |

a Compute the firm's accounts receivable turnover ratio.
b Compute the firm's inventory turnover ratio.

**E20-7** ***Profitability ratios***

Garden Spot, Inc., had the following selected data for 19X2:

| | |
|---|---|
| Net sales | $6,000,000 |
| Cost of goods sold | 3,600,000 |
| Operating expenses | 1,200,000 |
| Interest expense | 80,000 |
| Income tax expense | 360,000 |
| Cash dividends: common | 220,000 |
| Cash dividends: preferred | 60,000 |

In addition, the items that follow were extracted from the company's comparative balance sheets for the years ended December 31, 19X2 and December 31, 19X1.

| | *19X2* | *19X1* |
|---|---|---|
| Total assets | $5,538,000 | $5,448,000 |
| Total liabilities | 2,910,000 | 3,300,000 |
| Preferred stock | 600,000 | 600,000 |
| Common stock | 300,000 | 300,000 |
| Paid-in capital in excess of par: common | 48,000 | 48,000 |
| Retained earnings | 1,680,000 | 1,200,000 |

a Compute the 19X2 profit margin on sales and the rates of return on assets and common stockholders' equity, rounding calculations to two decimal places.
b Evaluate the firm's performance and its use of "trading on the equity" in light of the following industry norms:

| | |
|---|---|
| Profit margin on sales | 10% |
| Return on assets | 12 |
| Return on common stockholders' equity | 18 |

**E20-8** ***Coverage ratios***

Dresser, Inc., has the following financial information:

| | *19X6* | *19X5* |
|---|---|---|
| Current liabilities | $ 800,000 | $1,000,000 |
| Long-term liabilities | 2,000,000 | 1,800,000 |
| Common stock | 1,000,000 | 1,000,000 |
| Retained earnings | 4,200,000 | 3,200,000 |
| Total liabilities & stockholders' equity | $8,000,000 | $7,000,000 |

During 19X6, Dresser incurred interest expense and income taxes of $200,000 and $500,000, respectively. No dividends were paid during the year.

Compute the following ratios for 19X6, rounding calculations to two decimal places:

a Debt to total assets
b Debt to total ending stockholders' equity
c Times interest earned

**E20-9** ***Segment reporting***

U.S. Industries operates in three business segments: modular homes, household appliances, and decorating services. The following information (amounts are all in thousands) pertains to the year just ended:

| | *Modular Homes* | *Household Appliances* | *Decorating Services* |
|---|---|---|---|
| Sales | $18,900 | $24,700 | $7,200 |
| Operating income | 2,100 | 2,900 | 1,500 |

By analyzing the preceding data and, when appropriate, rounding computations to two decimal places, determine:

a The segment that contributes the greatest amount toward overall corporate profitability.
b The segment that contributes the smallest amount toward overall corporate revenue.
c The segment that has the largest amount of operating income per dollar of sales.

**E20-10** ***International accounting***

Midland Trading Corporation is a U.S. company that engages in numerous transactions involving foreign currencies. Three of the firm's transactions follow.

- *Transaction no. 1*—Purchased merchandise on account from Mizu Company of Japan, agreeing to pay $4,000 in 30 days. On the date of purchase the spot rate was $0.0070 per Japanese yen. On the settlement date the spot rate was $0.0066 per yen.
- *Transaction no. 2*—Purchased merchandise on account from Luxar Company of Switzerland, agreeing to pay 30,000 Swiss francs in 60 days. The spot rate was $0.73 per franc on the date of purchase and increased to $0.79 by the settlement date.
- *Transaction no. 3*—Sold merchandise on account to Downing Clothing Corporation of London, agreeing to accept 9,000 British pounds in 90 days. The spot rate was $1.78 per pound at the time of settlement, up from $1.68 on the sale date.

Prepare journal entries for Midland Trading Corporation to record each of these transactions and their related settlement. Disregard year-end financial statement adjustments.

**E20-11** ***International accounting***

On December 1, 19X1, a U.S. company having a December 31 year-end purchased goods on account from a Swiss supplier. Terms of the purchase required the U.S. company to deliver 200,000 Swiss francs to the supplier on January 15, 19X2. The spot rate for a Swiss franc fluctuated as follows:

| *Date* | *Spot Rate* |
|---|---|
| Dec. 1, 19X1 | $0.73 |
| Dec. 31, 19X1 | 0.70 |
| Jan. 15, 19X2 | 0.71 |

Prepare the three journal entries required by this transaction.

## Problems

### Series A

**P20-A1** ***Horizontal and vertical analysis***

The following financial statements pertain to Waterloo Corporation:

**WATERLOO CORPORATION**
**Comparative Balance Sheets**
**December 31, 19X5 and 19X4**

| | *19X5* | *19X4* |
|---|---|---|
| ***Assets*** | | |
| Current assets | | |
| Cash | $ 11,250 | $ 12,500 |
| Accounts receivable (net) | 18,500 | 25,000 |
| Inventories | 38,500 | 35,000 |
| Prepaid expenses | 3,750 | 3,750 |
| Total current assets | $ 72,000 | $ 76,250 |
| Property, plant, & equipment | | |
| Buildings (net) | $102,750 | $101,250 |
| Equipment (net) | 28,500 | 30,000 |
| Vehicles (net) | 32,000 | 40,000 |
| Total property, plant, & equipment | $163,250 | $171,250 |
| Trademarks (net) | $ 14,750 | $ 2,500 |
| Total assets | $250,000 | $250,000 |
| ***Liabilities & Stockholders' Equity*** | | |
| Current liabilities | | |
| Accounts payable | $ 49,000 | $ 70,000 |
| Notes payable | 13,500 | 40,000 |
| Federal taxes payable | 2,500 | 25,000 |
| Total current liabilities | $ 65,000 | $135,000 |
| Long-term debt | $ 50,000 | $ 25,000 |
| Total liabilities | $115,000 | $160,000 |
| Stockholders' equity | | |
| Common stock, $10 par | $ 25,000 | $ 25,000 |
| Retained earnings | 110,000 | 65,000 |
| Total stockholders' equity | $135,000 | $ 90,000 |
| Total liabilities & stockholders' equity | $250,000 | $250,000 |

**WATERLOO CORPORATION**
**Comparative Income Statements**
**For the Years Ended December 31, 19X5 and 19X4**

| | *19X5* | *19X4* |
|---|---|---|
| Net sales | $550,000 | $500,000 |
| Cost of goods sold | 330,000 | 250,000 |
| Gross profit | $220,000 | $250,000 |
| Operating expenses | 132,500 | 100,000 |
| Income before interest & taxes | $ 87,500 | $150,000 |
| Interest expense | 12,500 | 3,000 |
| Income before taxes | $ 75,000 | $147,000 |
| Income taxes | 30,000 | 58,800 |
| Net income | $ 45,000 | $ 88,200 |

**Instructions**

a Prepare a horizontal analysis of the balance sheet, showing dollar and percentage changes. Round all calculations in instructions (a) and (b) to two decimal places.

b Prepare a vertical analysis of the income statement by relating each item to net sales.

c Briefly comment on the results of your analysis.

**P20-A2** ***Ratio computation***

The financial statements of the Lone Pine Company follow.

**LONE PINE COMPANY**
**Comparative Balance Sheets**
**December 31, 19X2 and 19X1**
**($000 Omitted)**

| | *19X2* | *19X1* |
|---|---|---|
| ***Assets*** | | |
| Current assets | | |
| Cash & short-term investments | $ 400 | $ 600 |
| Accounts receivable (net) | 3,000 | 2,400 |
| Inventories | 2,000 | 2,200 |
| Total current assets | $5,400 | $5,200 |
| Property, plant, & equipment | | |
| Land | $1,700 | $ 600 |
| Buildings & equipment (net) | 1,500 | 1,000 |
| Total property, plant, & equipment | $3,200 | $1,600 |
| Total assets | $8,600 | $6,800 |
| ***Liabilities & Stockholders' Equity*** | | |
| Current liabilities | | |
| Accounts payable | $1,800 | $1,700 |
| Notes payable | 1,100 | 1,900 |
| Total current liabilities | $2,900 | $3,600 |
| Long-term liabilities | | |
| Bonds payable | 4,100 | 2,100 |
| Total liabilities | $7,000 | $5,700 |
| Stockholders' equity | | |
| Common stock | $ 200 | $ 200 |
| Retained earnings | 1,400 | 900 |
| Total stockholders' equity | $1,600 | $1,100 |
| Total liabilities & stockholders' equity | $8,600 | $6,800 |

**LONE PINE COMPANY**
**Statement of Income and Retained Earnings**
**For the Year Ended December 31, 19X2**
**($000 Omitted)**

| | | |
|---|---|---|
| Net sales* | | $36,000 |
| Less: Cost of goods sold | $20,000 | |
| Selling expenses | 6,000 | |
| Administrative expenses | 4,000 | |
| Interest expense | 400 | |
| Income taxes | 2,000 | 32,400 |
| Net income | | $ 3,600 |
| Retained earnings, Jan. 1 | | 900 |
| | | $ 4,500 |
| Cash dividends declared and paid | | 3,100 |
| Retained earnings, Dec. 31 | | $ 1,400 |

* All sales are on account.

**Instructions**

Compute the following items for the Lone Pine Company for 19X2, rounding all calculations to two decimal places when necessary:

a Quick ratio
b Current ratio
c Inventory turnover ratio
d Accounts receivable turnover ratio
e Return on assets
f Profit margin on sales
g Return on common stockholders' equity
h Debt to total assets
i Number of times interest is earned
j Dividend payout ratio

**P20-A3** ***Financial statement construction via ratios***
Incomplete financial statements of Image, Inc., are presented on the next page.

**IMAGE, INC.**
**Balance Sheet**
**December 31, 19X7**

| *Assets* | |
|---|---|
| Cash | $ 1,000,000 |
| Accounts receivable | ? |
| Inventory | ? |
| Property, plant, & equipment | ? |
| Total assets | $16,000,000 |
| ***Liabilities & Stockholders' Equity*** | |
| Accounts payable | $ 700,000 |
| Notes payable (short-term) | ? |
| Bonds payable | ? |
| Common stock | ? |
| Retained earnings | 1,500,000 |
| Total liabilities & stockholders' equity | $16,000,000 |

**IMAGE, INC.**
**Income Statement**
**For the Year Ended December 31, 19X7**

| | |
|---|---|
| Sales | $ ? |
| Cost of goods sold | 12,000,000 |
| Gross profit | $ ? |
| Operating expenses & interest | ? |
| Income before tax | $ ? |
| Income taxes, 35% | ? |
| Net income | $ ? |

Further information:

1 The accounts receivable turnover ratio is 10. Credit sales, which amount to 80% of total sales, are $20 million. The accounts receivable balance doubled during the year.
2 The inventory turnover ratio is 5. The beginning inventory was $3 million.
3 The current ratio is 2 : 1.
4 The debt to total assets ratio is 75%.
5 Operating expenses and interest total 40% of sales.

**Instructions**

Using the preceding data, complete the balance sheet and the income statement. Round computations to the nearest dollar.

**P20-A4** ***Effect of transactions and events on ratios***

Bullet, Inc., had the following ratios based on its 19X2 financial statements:

1 Current ratio: 1.5.
2 Quick ratio: 1.1.
3 Accounts receivable turnover: 10.3 times.
4 Inventory turnover: 12.5 times.
5 Total debt to total assets: 60%.
6 Times interest earned: 6.
7 Profit margin on sales: 5%.
8 Return on assets: 10%.
9 Return on common stockholders' equity: 28.2%.

During 19X3, the following selected transactions and events took place:

a Declared a cash dividend on common stock.
b Paid a previously declared cash dividend.
c Issued long-term bonds payable for cash. (*Note:* Disregard amortization and subsequent interest payments.)
d Sold common stock to the public for cash.
e Purchased merchandise inventory on account.
f Collected an account receivable.
g Recorded depreciation for the year.

**Instructions**

Consider items (a)–(g) individually. List the ratios affected by each transaction and event.

**P20-A5** ***Segment reporting and analysis***

The Walt Disney Company is a large Los Angeles-based entertainment corporation. The firm has three operating segments: theme parks and resorts, filmed entertainment, and consumer products. The following segment information (in millions) was obtained from a recent annual report:

| *Segment* | *Revenues* | *Operating Income* | *Identifiable Assets* |
|---|---|---|---|
| Theme parks and resorts | $1,834.2 | $548.9 | $2,291.3 |
| Filmed entertainment | 875.6 | 130.6 | 483.0 |
| Consumer products | 167.0 | 97.3 | 30.6 |

**Instructions**

a Relate operating income to identifiable assets and determine which segment was the least effective in terms of generating income from each dollar of asset investment.
b Relate operating income to revenues and determine which segment was least successful in terms of generating income from a given dollar of sales.
c Which of the segments was most successful in terms of generating revenues from each dollar of asset investment? Briefly explain and show related computations.
d Briefly discuss the benefits associated with the disclosure of segment information.

**P20-A6** ***International accounting***

Scorpio Enterprises is a U.S. company engaged in international trade. The business activity that follows occurred in 19XX.

| | | |
|---|---|---|
| Jan. | 9 | Sold merchandise on account to Peking Company of China, agreeing to accept 1 million yuan in 60 days. The current spot rate is $0.269 per yuan. |
| Feb. | 2 | Purchased merchandise on account from the TYT Company of Austria, agreeing to pay 100,000 schillings in 60 days. The spot rate is presently $0.078 per schilling. |
| Mar. | 10 | Settled the transaction of January 9. The spot rate was $0.22 per yuan. |
| Apr. | 2 | Settled the purchase of February 2. The spot rate was $0.085 per schilling. |
| | 18 | Purchased merchandise on account from Paris Products, agreeing to pay 500,000 French francs in 90 days. The spot rate on this date stood at $0.16 per franc. |
| May | 14 | Sold merchandise on account to Spanish Imports, agreeing to accept 3 million pesetas in 60 days. The current spot rate is $0.009 per peseta. |

**Instructions**

a Prepare journal entries to record the preceding transactions.

b Scorpio Enterprises ends its fiscal year on May 31. Prepare any adjusting entries that may be necessary to update the accounting records for exchange gains and losses. The spot rates for foreign currencies on this date are as follows:

| | |
|---|---|
| Austrian schilling | $0.09 |
| Chinese yuan | 0.23 |
| French franc | 0.15 |
| Spanish peseta | 0.011 |

## Series B

**P20-B1** ***Horizontal and vertical analysis***

The financial statements that follow pertain to Roseville Corporation.

**ROSEVILLE CORPORATION**
**Comparative Balance Sheets**
**December 31, 19X2 and 19X1**

| | *19X2* | *19X1* |
|---|---|---|
| ***Assets*** | | |
| Current assets | | |
| Cash | $ 5,000 | $ 20,000 |
| Short-term investments | — | 35,000 |
| Accounts receivable (net) | 250,000 | 50,000 |
| Inventories | 370,000 | 115,000 |
| Prepaid expenses | 15,000 | 10,000 |
| Total current assets | $ 640,000 | $ 230,000 |
| Property, plant, & equipment | | |
| Land | $ 45,000 | $ 15,000 |
| Buildings (net) | 440,000 | 450,000 |
| Equipment (net) | 250,000 | 200,000 |
| Vehicles (net) | 121,000 | 100,000 |
| Total property, plant, & equipment | $ 856,000 | $ 765,000 |
| Copyright (net) | $ 4,000 | $ 5,000 |
| Total assets | $1,500,000 | $1,000,000 |
| ***Liabilities & Stockholders' Equity*** | | |
| Current liabilities | | |
| Accounts payable | $ 300,000 | $ 140,000 |
| Salaries payable | 10,000 | 10,000 |
| Income taxes payable | 190,000 | 150,000 |
| Total current liabilities | $ 500,000 | $ 300,000 |
| Long-term debt | $ 400,000 | $ 400,000 |
| Total liabilities | $ 900,000 | $ 700,000 |
| Stockholders' equity | | |
| Common stock, $5 par | $ 200,000 | $ 50,000 |
| Retained earnings | 400,000 | 250,000 |
| Total stockholders' equity | $ 600,000 | $ 300,000 |
| Total liabilities & stockholders' equity | $1,500,000 | $1,000,000 |

**ROSEVILLE CORPORATION**
**Comparative Income Statements**
**For the Years Ended December 31, 19X2 and 19X1**

| | *19X2* | *19X1* |
|---|---|---|
| Net sales | $8,000,000 | $4,000,000 |
| Cost of goods sold | 4,500,000 | 2,500,000 |
| Gross profit | $3,500,000 | $1,500,000 |
| Operating expenses | 2,500,000 | 750,000 |
| Income before interest & taxes | $1,000,000 | $ 750,000 |
| Interest expense | 35,000 | 40,000 |
| Income before taxes | $ 965,000 | $ 710,000 |
| Income taxes | 386,000 | 284,000 |
| Net income | $ 579,000 | $ 426,000 |

**Instructions**

a Prepare a horizontal analysis of the income statement, showing dollar and percentage changes. Round all calculations in instructions (a) and (b) to two decimal places.

b Prepare a vertical analysis of the balance sheet, relating each asset to total assets and each liability and stockholders' equity account to the total of liabilities plus stockholders' equity.

c Briefly comment on the results of your analysis.

**P20-B2** ***Ratio computation***

The financial statements of the Greensboro Company follow.

**GREENSBORO COMPANY**
**Comparative Balance Sheets**
**December 31, 19X2 and 19X1**
**($000 Omitted)**

| | *19X2* | *19X1* |
|---|---|---|
| ***Assets*** | | |
| Current assets | | |
| Cash & short-term investments | $ 200 | $ 700 |
| Accounts receivable (net) | 2,400 | 3,000 |
| Inventories | 4,000 | 3,500 |
| Total current assets | $ 6,600 | $7,200 |
| Property, plant, & equipment | | |
| Land | $ 4,700 | $2,000 |
| Buildings & equipment (net) | 1,200 | 700 |
| Total property, plant, & equipment | $ 5,900 | $2,700 |
| Total assets | $12,500 | $9,900 |
| ***Liabilities & Stockholders' Equity*** | | |
| Current liabilities | | |
| Accounts payable | $ 3,000 | $1,500 |
| Notes payable | 2,000 | 2,400 |
| Total current liabilities | $ 5,000 | $3,900 |
| Long-term liabilities | | |
| Bonds payable | 2,000 | 2,000 |
| Total liabilities | $ 7,000 | $5,900 |
| Stockholders' equity | | |
| Common stock | $ 700 | $ 700 |
| Retained earnings | 4,800 | 3,300 |
| Total stockholders' equity | $ 5,500 | $4,000 |
| Total liabilities & stockholders' equity | $12,500 | $9,900 |

**GREENSBORO COMPANY**
**Statement of Income and Retained Earnings**
**For the Year Ended December 31, 19X2**
**($000 Omitted)**

| | | |
|---|---|---|
| Net sales* | | $40,000 |
| Less: Cost of goods sold | $30,000 | |
| Selling expenses | 2,000 | |
| Administrative expenses | 3,000 | |
| Interest expense | 400 | |
| Income taxes | 1,000 | 36,400 |
| Net income | | $ 3,600 |
| Retained earnings, Jan. 1 | | 3,300 |
| | | $ 6,900 |
| Cash dividends declared and paid | | 2,100 |
| Retained earnings, Dec. 31 | | $ 4,800 |

* All sales are on account.

**Instructions**

Compute the following items for the Greensboro Company for 19X2, rounding all calculations to two decimal places when necessary:

a Current ratio
b Quick ratio
c Accounts receivable turnover ratio
d Inventory turnover ratio
e Profit margin on sales
f Return on assets
g Return on common stockholders' equity
h Debt to total assets
i Dividend payout ratio
j Number of times interest is earned

**P20-B3** ***Financial statement construction via ratios***
Incomplete financial statements of Lock Box, Inc., are presented below.

**LOCK BOX, INC.**
**Income Statement**
**For the Year Ended December 31, 19X3**

| | |
|---|---|
| Sales | $ ? |
| Cost of goods sold | ? |
| Gross profit | $15,000,000 |
| Operating expenses & interest | ? |
| Income before tax | $ ? |
| Income taxes, 40% | ? |
| Net income | $ ? |

**LOCK BOX, INC.**
**Balance Sheet**
**December 31, 19X3**

| *Assets* | |
|---|---|
| Cash | $ ? |
| Accounts receivable | ? |
| Inventory | ? |
| Property, plant, & equipment | 8,000,000 |
| Total assets | $24,000,000 |
| ***Liabilities & Stockholders' Equity*** | |
| Accounts payable | $ ? |
| Notes payable (short-term) | 600,000 |
| Bonds payable | 4,600,000 |
| Common stock | 2,000,000 |
| Retained earnings | ? |
| Total liabilities & stockholders' equity | $24,000,000 |

Further information:

1 Cost of goods sold is 60% of sales. All sales are on account.
2 The company's beginning inventory is $5 million; inventory turnover is 4.
3 The debt to total assets ratio is 70%.
4 The profit margin on sales is 6%.
5 The firm's accounts receivable turnover is 5. Receivables increased by $400,000 during the year.

**Instructions**

Using the preceding data, complete the income statement and the balance sheet.

**P20-B4** ***Effect of transactions and events on ratios***

Puget, Inc., had the following ratios based on its 19X2 financial statements:

1 Current ratio: 3.0.
2 Quick ratio: 1.3.
3 Accounts receivable turnover: 15.0 times.
4 Inventory turnover: 10.0 times.
5 Total debt to total assets: 80%.
6 Times interest earned: 10.
7 Profit margin on sales: 12%.
8 Return on assets: 20%.
9 Return on common stockholders' equity: 30%.

During 19X3, the following selected transactions and events took place:

a Sold 14% preferred stock to the public for cash.
b Paid an account payable.
c Purchased short-term investments for cash.
d Sold merchandise inventory on account at a higher-than-normal markup.
e Recorded patent amortization for the year.
f Paid monthly interest expense to the bank.
g Purchased merchandise inventory for cash from a competitor who was going out of business.

### Instructions

Consider items (a)–(g) individually. List the ratios affected by each transaction and event.

**P20-B5** ***Segment reporting and analysis***

The Gillette Company is a large diversified firm headquartered in Boston, Mass. The company has five major operating segments. The segments, along with selected subsidiaries, include blades and razors, toiletries and cosmetics, writing instruments and office products (Paper Mate and Liquid Paper), Braun products (a West German manufacturer of small appliances), and other. The following segment information (in millions) was obtained from a recent annual report:

| *Segment* | *Revenues* | *Operating Income* | *Identifiable Assets* |
|---|---|---|---|
| Blades & razors | $1,030.6 | $326.8 | $738.4 |
| Toiletries & cosmetics | 926.0 | 94.8 | 561.4 |
| Writing instruments & office products | 320.0 | 32.6 | 299.1 |
| Braun products | 703.0 | 71.9 | 546.2 |
| Other | 187.2 | 8.7 | 286.0 |

### Instructions

a Relate operating income to revenues and determine which segment was most successful in terms of generating income from a given dollar of sales.

b Relate operating income to identifiable assets and determine which segment was the second most effective in terms of generating income from each dollar of asset investment.

c Assume that corporate management believes that for every dollar of asset investment, at least one dollar of sales revenue should be generated. Did any of the segments fail to meet this goal? Briefly explain and show related computations.

d Where is segment information typically disclosed?

**P20-B6** ***International accounting***

Gilroy Enterprises is a U.S. company engaged in international trade. The following business activity occurred in 19XX:

| | | |
|---|---|---|
| Jan. | 15 | Purchased merchandise on account from the Toronto Company of Canada, agreeing to pay 15,000 Canadian dollars in 60 days. The spot rate is presently $0.84 per Canadian dollar. |
| Feb. | 22 | Sold merchandise on account to an Israeli company, agreeing to accept 6 million shekels in 60 days. The current spot rate is $0.55 per shekel. |
| Mar. | 16 | Settled the purchase of January 15. The spot rate was $0.82 per Canadian dollar. |
| Apr. | 10 | Purchased merchandise on account from a Pakistani firm, agreeing to pay 1 million rupees in 90 days. The spot rate on this date stood at $0.057 per rupee. |
| | 17 | Settled the transaction of February 22. The spot rate was $0.59. |
| May | 1 | Sold merchandise on account to Swedish Imports, agreeing to accept 50,000 krona in 50 days. The current spot rate is $0.165 per krona. |

### Instructions

a Prepare journal entries to record the preceding transactions.

b Gilroy Enterprises ends its fiscal year on May 31. Prepare any adjusting entries that may be necessary to update the accounting records for exchange gains and losses. The spot rates for foreign currencies on this date are as follows:

| | |
|---|---|
| Canadian dollar | $0.92 |
| Israeli shekel | 0.58 |
| Pakistani rupee | 0.066 |
| Swedish krona | 0.18 |

## Beyond the Basics

**BB20-1** ***Ratio calculation and interpretation; turnover emphasis***

Holly Dixon and Robert Stafford are employed as student assistants of Dr. William Bennett, an accounting professor. Bennett has just received a telephone call concerning an out-of-town family emergency and has instructed Dixon to prepare a quiz for tomorrow's class. He noted, "The quiz should focus on turnover ratios and be somewhat challenging, even for my best students."

After working for several hours, Dixon has constructed the questions that follow.

### Question #1

The following data were extracted from Akron Corporation's 19X2 year-end financial statements:

| | |
|---|---|
| Current liabilities | $240,000 |
| Current ratio | 2.0 |
| Quick ratio | 1.5 |
| Gross profit percentage | 60% |
| Inventory turnover | 8 times |

Akron has no prepaid expenses and reported a 19X1 year-end inventory of $160,000. Compute net sales for 19X2.

### Question #2

Columbus Manufacturing has experienced relatively flat sales and income for the three-year period, 19X3–19X5. Selected data follow.

| | *19X5* | *19X4* | *19X3* |
|---|---|---|---|
| Current ratio | 2.48 | 2.43 | 2.30 |
| Quick ratio | 1.00 | 1.13 | 1.23 |
| Accounts receivable turnover | 6.10 | 7.48 | 8.66 |
| Inventory turnover | 2.98 | 3.87 | 4.38 |

Analyze the ratios and determine a possible factor that explains why the current ratio is increasing while the quick ratio is decreasing.

### Question #3

Dayton Company and Toledo Company began business on January 1, 19X1. Both firms had identical purchases and sales of inventory, as follows:

19X1 Purchase #1: 8,000 units at $10
Purchase #2: 5,000 units at $11
Sales: 10,000 units

19X2 Purchase #1: 7,000 units at $12
Purchase #2: 9,000 units at $13
Sales: 12,000 units

Dayton and Toledo use a periodic inventory system. Dayton employs a FIFO cost flow assumption and Toledo uses a LIFO flow assumption.

a Compute the 19X2 inventory turnover ratio for each firm.

b Explain one of the problems encountered when performing a comparative financial analysis among companies.

Holly Dixon has asked Robert Stafford to help her by constructing an answer key for the quiz.

**Instructions**

Assume the role of Robert Stafford and answer the questions that Dixon has prepared.

## Answers to Chapter Quiz

**1** d

**2** a

**3** d

**4** c

| *Segment* | *Dollar Profit* | *Profit Margin on Sales* | *Return on Assets* |
|---|---|---|---|
| Airline | $ 20 | $20 ÷ $4,000 = 0.5% | $20 ÷ $2,000 = 1% |
| Pencils | 80 | $80 ÷ $1,000 = 8.0% | $80 ÷ $1,600 = 5% |
| Aluminum siding | 400 | $400 ÷ $2,000 = 20.0% | $400 ÷ $4,000 = 10% |

**5** a

# Introduction to Managerial and Cost Accounting

CHAPTER 21

## Learning Objectives

After reading this chapter you should:

**1** Understand the distinction between financial and managerial accounting.

**2** Be able to describe planning, control, and decision-making applications of managerial accounting.

**3** Be familiar with the field of cost accounting, including its recent changes.

**4** Understand the meaning of direct materials, direct labor, and factory overhead.

**5** Understand the difference between product and period costs.

**6** Be familiar with the unique features of the manufacturing balance sheet and income statement.

**7** Understand variable and fixed cost behavior.

**8** (Appendix) Know how to prepare a work sheet and the related closing entries for a manufacturing concern.

As we move into Chapter 21, a look back at previous discussions reveals that many diverse topics have been presented. These topics have ranged in scope from earnings per share, to the valuation of inventory on the balance sheet, to the statement of cash flows. Although diversity appears to have been the theme, a substantial amount of this material does have some common ground. This common ground is known as financial accounting. A brief overview of financial accounting is helpful at this point because of the differences between it and the thrust of most of the text's remaining chapters—managerial accounting.

## Financial Accounting

OBJECTIVE 1
**Understand the distinction between financial and managerial accounting.**

**Financial accounting** is concerned primarily with external reporting, that is, reporting the results of economic activities to parties outside the firm. Interested recipients of financial accounting information include present and potential owners, suppliers, bankers, and bondholders. Owners and investors use this information in determining whether to buy, hold, or sell ownership interests (e.g., shares of stock). Suppliers, bankers, and bondholders will conduct business with an entity if repayment will be forthcoming. As a result, these latter groups find financial accounting information useful in deciding whether or not to extend credit. In general, by communicating such information as net income (income statement) and financial position (balance sheet), financial accounting strives to present a fair picture of the business in which the foregoing parties have an interest.

A probe of our earlier presentations will reveal several other distinguishing characteristics of financial accounting. For example, the financial statements that are constructed for external distribution tend to be highly aggregated, with a focus on disclosures for a company as a whole. Segmented reportings, although required in some instances, normally present minimal detail on the "parts" of a firm.

Further, the financial statements serve to summarize transactions and events that have already occurred. In other words, the focus is on past, historical data. The data are summarized and reported in conformity with generally accepted accounting principles (GAAP), which facilitates the comparison of widely varying businesses and operations by investors and analysts. In addition, the use of GAAP provides assurances to outsiders that an entity's financial disclosures are based on a set of common rules that have been accepted by the accounting profession. Such a practice avoids having to rely on an organization's unique measurement methods that may have been creatively formulated to inflate economic well-being.

Finally, much of financial accounting is mandatory, with a business having little or no say in the matter. The underlying reason is regulation—a fact of life in our society. Ranging in scope from the powerful Securities and Exchange Commission (SEC) to the departments that handle state sales tax collections, various agencies must determine whether a business has complied with the laws and mandates to which it is subject. Financial accounting and an historical record keeping system are a company's information source for satisfying the demands of these agencies (e.g., the issuance of financial statements to investors, the filing of a tax return with the Internal Revenue Service, and so forth).

## Managerial Accounting

Exhibit 21-1 summarizes the key issues just raised and shows that financial accounting can be contrasted with managerial accounting.

**Exhibit 21-1**
**Differences Between Financial and Managerial Accounting**

| *Issue* | *Financial Accounting* | *Managerial Accounting* |
|---|---|---|
| Users of information | External parties: stockholders, creditors, analysts, regulatory agencies | Internal parties: managers of the firm |
| Scope of reports | Highly aggregated | Focus on a firm's segments (e.g., products and departments); often cover a short period of time |
| Information reported | Past transactions and events | Both past and future items (e.g., costs, cash flows, and so forth) |
| Reporting standards | Based on generally accepted accounting principles (GAAP) | No constraining factors |
| Nature of reporting | Mandatory: reports must be filed consistent with regulatory agency requirements | Highly discretionary; considerable diversity among businesses and managers |

As its name implies, **managerial accounting** is oriented toward reporting the results of operations to managers and other interested parties within a business. Much of this information, unlike that produced via financial accounting, is often concerned with small segments of activity. For example, a company may construct a quarterly income statement for stockholders as part of its financial reporting requirements. Managers, however, generally need more detail to properly perform their duties. Thus, for internal use, profitability reports are often generated on a monthly basis and subdivided by divisions, departments, and products.

Given that many managers are involved with planning activities (to be discussed shortly), reports that are issued to executives frequently have a strong future orientation. Historical data are accumulated and reported, but only to the extent that such figures help to assess (1) conformity with current plans or (2) what the future will bring. In view of this situation, it is not uncommon for managerial reports to focus on *forthcoming* costs, revenues, cash flows, and resource needs—items that are ignored in financial accounting because of the emphasis on past transactions and events.

It is important to note that internal reports may be prepared by using an "anything goes" philosophy. GAAP, which apply to financial accounting only, need not be followed, thereby allowing a company to do whatever it pleases when reporting to in-house personnel (i.e., management). For example, if a business wanted to ignore depreciation on internally distributed financial statements, it could do so. Or if a company desired to write up inventory and short-term investments to reflect market values in excess of cost, that, too, would be permissible.[1]

[1] Although diversity is the rule, most firms have not strayed too far from the norm. A majority of businesses have implemented specific internal reporting practices and analysis methods that have been developed (fine tuned) over the years.

## A Cost/Benefit Theme

Accounting systems produce a wide assortment of information so that executives can manage a business. As an example, see Exhibit 21-2.

Given the absence of preestablished rules, much of the information generated for use within a firm is discretionary (optional). The information is produced because it is helpful to a manager when performing his or her duties. Varying responsibilities among managers, of course, create different information needs, and some of the needs are more important than others.

Because of limited resources, an organization normally cannot satisfy all the desires of its executives. As a result, a guideline must be established for the generation of discretionary information. A suggested approach employs **cost-benefit analysis,** with a manager comparing the cost of producing information against the benefits to be derived from the information's use. If the benefits exceed the costs, generation of the needed facts and figures is appropriate; if not, rejection is in order.

## Managerial Accounting Applications

OBJECTIVE 2
**Be able to describe planning, control, and decision-making applications of managerial accounting.**

There are three basic areas in which managerial accounting plays an important role. Consistent with the functions of management, these areas are planning, control, and decision making.

### Planning

Virtually every company is formed to achieve certain goals and objectives. The owners, for example, expect the firm to earn a profit and an adequate return on investment, while management strives to produce goods and services that are characterized by quality and dependability. Marketing and the sales force attempt to achieve a reasonable share of the market by attracting loyal customers.

An organization attains its objectives by planning. **Planning** involves the formulation of methods and strategies that implement a company's objectives in definite terms. As an example, consider the common business practice of establishing specified credit policies. These policies permit the generation of profitable sales volume without an abnormally high rate of uncollectible accounts, thereby providing a return to the owners. At the same time, if the entity's credit policies are

**Exhibit 21-2**
**Examples of Information Generated for Internal Use**

| *Company* | *Information Reported* |
|---|---|
| Hyatt Hotels | Construction cost per room at a planned facility |
| Kellogg Company | Cash outlay necessary to manufacture and introduce a new type of breakfast cereal |
| Toys "R" Us | Profit per square foot of selling space |
| United Airlines | Revenues generated and percentage of seats filled on flights from Chicago to Denver |
| MCI Communications | Uncollectible accounts experience with residential and commercial users |

consistent with the terms offered by competitors, an acceptable market share can be attained.[2]

Sometimes, the objectives of a business are in conflict with one another. For instance, suppose a company decided to enlarge its market share. To attract new customers, the firm might loosen its credit policy. Conceivably, an excessive concentration on obtaining market share could result in high levels of uncollectible accounts, thus undermining the objective of profitability. A business must continually evaluate its objectives and the policies implemented for their attainment. Although it is extremely difficult to eliminate all conflict, harmony and consistency (achieved via intensive planning) help an organization improve overall results.

Planning takes place in all facets of an organization. Often, plans are expressed quantitatively in formal reports known as **budgets,** which are generated for areas that management deems critical and in need of close monitoring and evaluation. Such areas include (but are not limited to) sales, production, capital expenditures, and cash flow. Even entire financial statements can be forecast. Although budgeting and forecasting are readily associated with managerial accounting, managerial accounting assists in other planning activities as well. This fact is noted in higher-level courses and in the study of other business disciplines such as quantitative methods, marketing, and finance.

## Control

The control function is an outgrowth of planning. No matter how extensively and effectively a business plans, unexpected events can occur. Furthermore, because plans merely reflect an organization's best guess about the future, prediction errors are common.

If management is to have insight regarding a company's progress toward its objectives, feedback is a necessity. Frequently, the feedback is in the form of a performance report (see Exhibit 21-3). The performance report pinpoints **variances,** or deviations from the budget. The individual in charge of Western Territory operations, for example, analyzes the variances, explains to management why August net income was $6,700 less than budget, and takes corrective action. Such action may be in the form of generating additional sales, cutting costs, or changing personnel.

Whatever the form, the common feature is **control,** which helps bring an organization back on target in terms of achieving the original plan. Control not only assists in eliminating deviations from budgets, but it also renders valuable perspectives for the next round of the planning process. By closely monitoring operations, managers generally obtain a better "feel" of the business, which, in turn, leads to more effective budgeting and policy formation. The relationship between planning and control is shown in Exhibit 21-4.

## Decision Making

Managerial accounting also plays an important role in **decision making.** Decision making can be viewed as an integral part of planning and control rather than as a separate, independent management function. The implementation of a successful

---

[2] Many other factors influence market share, such as price, advertising policies, and product quality.

**Exhibit 21-3**
**Performance Report**

**THORNDIKE ENTERPRISES**
**Western Territory Performance Report**
**For the Month Ended August 31, 19XX**

| | *Budget* | *Actual* | *Variance* | *Explanation* |
|---|---|---|---|---|
| Sales | $68,000 | $62,100 | $5,900U | |
| Cost of goods sold | 42,500 | 42,700 | 200U | |
| Gross profit | $25,500 | $19,400 | $6,100U | |
| Operating expenses | | | | |
| Salaries | $ 6,400 | $ 6,600 | $ 200U | |
| Fuel | 3,100 | 3,800 | 700U | |
| Advertising | 4,500 | 4,200 | 300F | |
| Rent | 2,000 | 2,000 | — | |
| Total expenses | $16,000 | $16,600 | $ 600U | |
| Net income | $ 9,500 | $ 2,800 | $6,700U | |

U = unfavorable; F = favorable

planning program, for example, requires that managers choose from among alternative objectives and policies. Similarly, the fine tuning and control of operations dictates that appropriate corrective action be selected and implemented.

The decision process has far-reaching effects and normally involves much more than just "number crunching." Many managers, especially those involved with accounting and finance, place considerable emphasis on net income, earnings per share, and cash flow, that is, various quantitative measures of performance. Often, important qualitative factors such as business ethics, corporate image, and employee morale are mistakenly disregarded.

To illustrate the importance of qualitative factors in decision making, assume that Frank Rosa is employed as a foreman by the Nicholson Manufacturing Company. Management has just decided to install some new machinery in Rosa's department. Although Rosa and his workers will be using the machines, they were not consulted in the selection process. Rosa has received minimal pay increases over the past few years, and with this latest incident, he has an extremely negative

**Exhibit 21-4**
**Planning and Control**

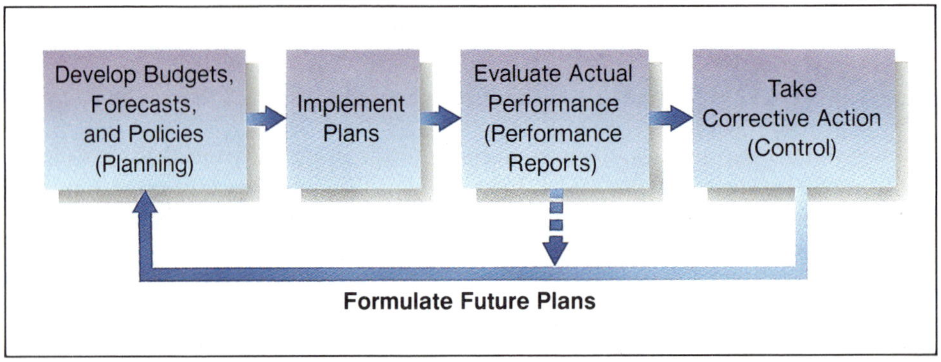

HIGHLIGHT

# The Grateful Dead: Planning + Control + Decision Making

More than any other rock musicians, San Francisco's Grateful Dead have consciously put the building of goodwill among their fans before immediate profitability. Partly as a result, fans, friends, and unscrupulous managers have stuck the band with overpriced equipment, traded freely on the group's trademarks and copyrights, and ripped them off in countless other ways. The Dead's rhythm guitarist reckons the band has piddled away anywhere from \$20 million to \$50 million over the years. Why put up with this?

The Grateful Dead are a business—a band with a plan, one with a knack for making good decisions. No group's fans are as loyal as the Dead's fans are. This is a major reason, in an industry where superstars become burned out within a few years, the Grateful Dead still sell out concerts after more than 20 years. The Dead, says a rock promoter, "are the closest thing to Living Theater, to the communal expression of breaking down the walls."

The fans, known as "Dead Heads," often congregate at concerts in such numbers that they've become a traveling sideshow. Dead Head vendors use card tables, car trunks, and backpacks to hawk shirts, jewelry, Dead books and newsletters, bootleg records and tapes, and food. On a good day, notes the group's merchandising manager, "we're losing \$200,000 in sales out there." But the band gets the money back in other ways. Those fans spend much of their parking lot earnings to buy tickets and gas to follow the band around. Inside the arenas, the Dead still sell perhaps 1,000 shirts per concert, at prices ranging from \$10 for last year's T-shirts to \$20 for a golf shirt.

Operating with a staff of about 35 from two offices, the band maintains a "Dead hotline" to update fans about band gossip, concert dates, and mail-order tickets. A separate line handles orders for Dead T-shirts and accessories. More than 50% of all tickets are sold directly by the band. That means the Dead needn't split much of their take with ticket brokers, who generally get \$1 or \$2 a ticket. The Dead's 10 phones handle 1,500 to 6,000 calls per day, and a computerized mailing list reaches 150,000.

Unlike other rock groups, the Grateful Dead permit fans to tape concerts from a special seating section. This has spawned dozens of unauthorized records, but it also gives fans a chance to relive their concert visions and freshens demand for the group. In two recent years alone, playing almost always to sold-out arenas and stadiums, the band has grossed more than \$20,000,000, according to a trade publication.

In tune with the times, the laid-back Dead recently reorganized its business operations, hiring a new accountant, linking to one another by Apple MacIntoshes, and holding board meetings every two weeks. The moves come as the Dead find themselves on the threshold of huge financial success—records, tapes, movies, and merchandise. "This will be a great year for us because we finally have the business together," says the drummer and chief financial officer. "We're a straight business now."

SOURCE: Adapted from "We're a Straight Business Now," *Forbes*, May 18, 1987, p. 43. Reprinted by permission of *Forbes* magazine, © Forbes Inc., 1987.

attitude about the company. His "I don't give a darn," or "who cares," outlook is reflected in his work and possibly in the work of his subordinates. Because negativism at the top of an enterprise tends to permeate lower levels of the organizational structure, Rosa's workers are probably disenchanted and could have low morale. Low morale often affects productivity, which, in turn, impacts profitability. In Nicholson's case it is apparent that employee morale and the involvement of users in the decision process (both qualitative considerations) are indeed important. Effective decision making requires an evaluation of qualitative factors in conjunction with the quantitative outcome.

## Cost Accounting

OBJECTIVE 3
**Be familiar with the field of cost accounting, including its recent changes.**

All businesses need an intimate knowledge of their costs to help ensure successful performance. As we progress through the study of managerial accounting, you will find that cost analysis can be somewhat troublesome. Some costs vary as activity changes, while other costs remain constant. Certain costs are relevant when evaluating a decision alternative; others can be ignored. Because of management's dependence on cost information, a brief introduction to cost accounting is a logical starting point for understanding the planning, control, and decision-making functions.

**Cost accounting** deals with the collection, assignment, and interpretation of cost. Cost data are captured by an organization's information system and then assigned to various business segments and activities. Examples of such segments include territories, departments, and products. Activities, on the other hand, may encompass the design of a new advertising campaign, the operation of a summer recreation program by a city, and the implementation of a new all-day ticket plan by an amusement park. The purpose of the assignment process is to answer the age-old question, "How much does it cost?" Once cost is determined, management can proceed with an analysis of the following:

- Anticipated cost for various planning needs.
- Budgeted versus actual cost for control and evaluation.
- Relevant costs of different alternatives for use in decision making.
- Costs of producing goods and services for use in pricing and inventory valuation.

### A Changing Face

The field of cost accounting has undergone three significant changes in recent years, all of which appear to be interrelated. Historically, cost accounting has had a heavy financial accounting orientation because of its use by manufacturers to determine production costs. The cost of goods produced influences inventory valuation on the balance sheet and cost of goods sold on the income statement. As we have just shown, however, cost accounting also provides information to management for planning, controlling, and decision making. Thus, cost accounting is now viewed as an integral part of both financial *and* managerial accounting. In many companies the managerial emphasis is growing because of business restructurings and mergers, expansion into international markets, and changing operating environments.

A second change is an expanding use of cost accounting by merchandising and service organizations. Operating efficiency is a goal of all entities; cost information is therefore a necessity. Retailers, wholesalers, lawyers, medical practices, governmental units, and other nonmanufacturers all use cost accounting. Although we will be stressing the manufacturer in forthcoming chapters, many of the concepts and practices presented are applicable to merchandising and service enterprises as well.

The third change in cost accounting is an increased interface of the cost department with the other functional areas within an entity. The marketing department, for example, uses cost information to assist in the determination of a competitive sales price and appropriate sales strategies. The research and development department analyzes costs in design and production decisions. Finally, the personnel department utilizes cost information to assure compliance with various federal laws and union contracts. In sum, the preceding examples represent a mere sampling of the many and varied applications of this powerful management tool.

## Manufacturing Organizations

To illustrate the basics of cost accounting, we turn our attention to manufacturers. Unlike the merchandising company, which purchases goods for resale, a manufacturer acquires raw materials and uses its plant, equipment, and employees to produce a finished product. Because of their production activities, accounting for manufacturers is more complex than accounting for service businesses and merchandisers. Realize, however, that like the other two types of organizations, the manufacturer also has sales, administrative, and financial reporting responsibilities. Consequently, manufacturers face many of the same measurement problems and use many of the same accounting practices as service and merchandising concerns.

## Manufacturing Costs

In order to produce finished goods from raw materials, a manufacturer incurs three types of costs: direct materials, direct labor, and factory overhead.

OBJECTIVE 4
Understand the meaning of direct materials, direct labor, and factory overhead.

### Direct Materials

**Direct materials** include all materials that (1) form an integral part of the finished product and (2) are easily traced to the finished product. Several examples of direct materials are major subassemblies such as the seat, back, and frame of a chair; the wheels of a bicycle; the electronic components in a calculator; and the sheet metal and glass in an automobile. Direct materials do not include minor items like glue, varnish, and nails. Although no one would dispute the importance of these latter items to a finished product, determining and tracing their cost to the units manufactured is troublesome (and expensive). Imagine, for example, the difficulty of calculating the cost of glue consumed in producing a single piece of wooden furniture. As a result of these problems and for purposes of expediency, minor materials are normally accounted for as **indirect materials** and treated as part of factory overhead.

### Direct Labor

**Direct labor** represents the gross wages of personnel who worked directly on the goods being produced. The wages of assembly-line workers and machine operators are included in this cost classification. A manufacturer employs many other personnel who indirectly contribute to the production of finished goods. Examples include maintenance workers, supervisors, plant guards, and storeroom personnel. Again, a traceability problem arises when attempting to charge the cost of these latter personnel to specific units manufactured. The wages of factory employees who fail to work directly on the product are therefore accounted for as **indirect labor** and treated as part of factory overhead.

### Factory Overhead

**Factory overhead,** sometimes called manufacturing burden, consists of all factory-related costs other than direct materials and direct labor. Included in this classification are indirect materials, indirect labor, factory and equipment depreciation, utilities, taxes, repairs, and maintenance. Observe that factory overhead includes costs that pertain solely to manufacturing activity. For example, depreciation on machinery used in production is properly considered part of overhead, while depreciation on cars used by the sales staff is not; the latter cost is a selling expense. Similarly, insurance on the factory facilities is overhead. Insurance on the corporate offices, however, is treated as an administrative expense. Frequently, costs incurred by an entity as a whole (e.g., utilities and general maintenance) must be allocated among factory overhead, selling expense, and administrative expense to ensure proper accounting. This allocation is necessary because, as we will soon illustrate, the accounting treatment of selling and administrative expenses is considerably different from that for overhead.

Like indirect materials and indirect labor, the other elements of factory overhead are extremely difficult to trace to specific units of production. Thus, accountants normally estimate the overhead that goes into each product as opposed to determining the actual cost incurred. Overhead is discussed in more detail in Chapter 22.

The three production cost elements are sometimes combined by accountants. **Prime cost** consists of costs easily traced to the finished product, that is, direct materials plus direct labor. **Conversion cost** is the cost to convert raw material into finished product, namely, direct labor plus factory overhead.

## Financial Statements of a Manufacturer

Direct materials, direct labor, and factory overhead eventually find their way to the financial statements. This process is easily understood if we first review the accounting practices of a merchandising concern. As a merchandising business acquires goods for resale, the costs incurred are inventoried on the balance sheet as an asset. Later, when sales are made, the inventory is taken off the balance sheet and transferred to the income statement in the form of cost of goods sold. The reason for this procedure is to match the cost of the items sold against related sales revenues.

Essentially the same practice is performed by the manufacturer. Rather than pay significant sums of money to acquire merchandise for resale, the manufacturer purchases direct materials, hires and compensates a labor force, and incurs factory overhead. These costs are all put "in process" and eventually result in the manufacture of finished product. At the end of the accounting period the finished goods still owned appear as inventory on the balance sheet, while the units sold are written off via cost of goods sold. This process is illustrated in Exhibit 21-5.

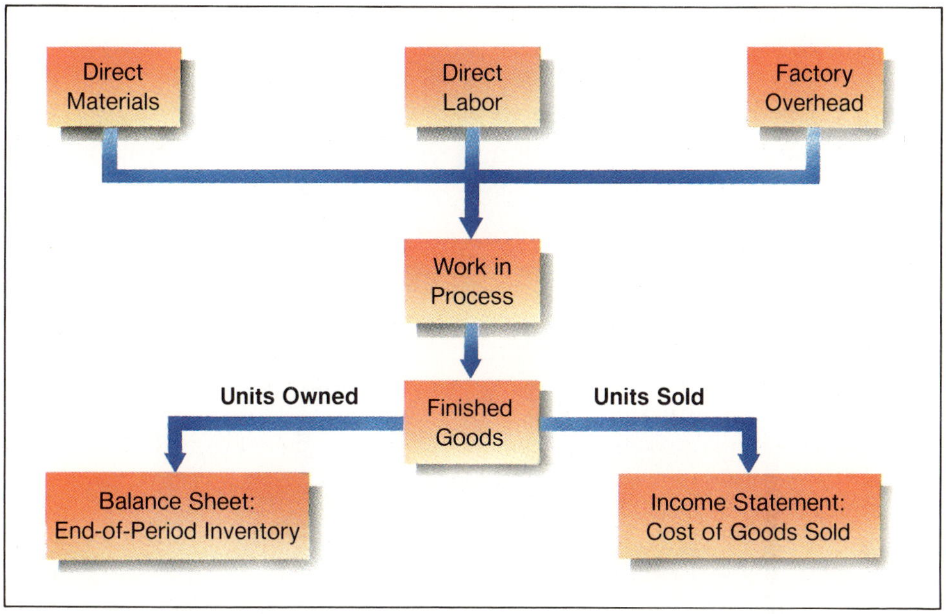


**Exhibit 21-5**
**The Manufacturing Process**

## Product and Period Costs

OBJECTIVE 5
Understand the difference between product and period costs.

The costs that go into inventory—direct materials, direct labor, and factory overhead—are termed **product costs.** These costs are attached to the units they helped to produce and are inventoried until the time of sale. This accounting treatment can be contrasted with that of **period costs**—noninventoriable costs that are deducted as expenses of the current reporting period. Such treatment is justified because no future benefits are said to result from the related expenditure. Period costs consist of selling and administrative expenses and include sales commissions, advertising, and management salaries.

To better illustrate the difference between product and period costs, assume that Conant Manufacturing Corporation began operations in 19X1. Building depreciation for the year amounted to $50,000; 50% relates to sales and administrative facilities and 50% to the factory. Of the total units produced, 80% were sold in 19X1 and 20% in 19X2. Assuming no ending work in process, Exhibit 21-6 depicts the timing of the 19X1 building depreciation on the related income statements.

To explain, the selling and administrative costs are expensed when incurred. In contrast, the factory (product) cost is attached to inventory. Because only 80% of the production is sold in 19X1, $20,000 ($25,000 × 0.80) of depreciation is initially written off through cost of goods sold; the $5,000 balance is included in the cost of inventory. When the units are sold in 19X2, the remaining factory depreciation is then released to the income statement. Overall it is a matter of timing. Period costs are expensed upon incurrence; product costs are written off when the related inventory is sold.

The correct determination of product and period costs is important since errors will likely affect net income and the reported inventory valuation. Unfortunately, however, the distinction between these two costs is not always clear. Consider, for example, the salary of the manufacturing vice-president. This individual spends considerable time overseeing production policies and problems. Should the salary be treated as part of factory overhead or as an administrative operating expense?

**Exhibit 21-6**
**Product and Period Cost Timing**

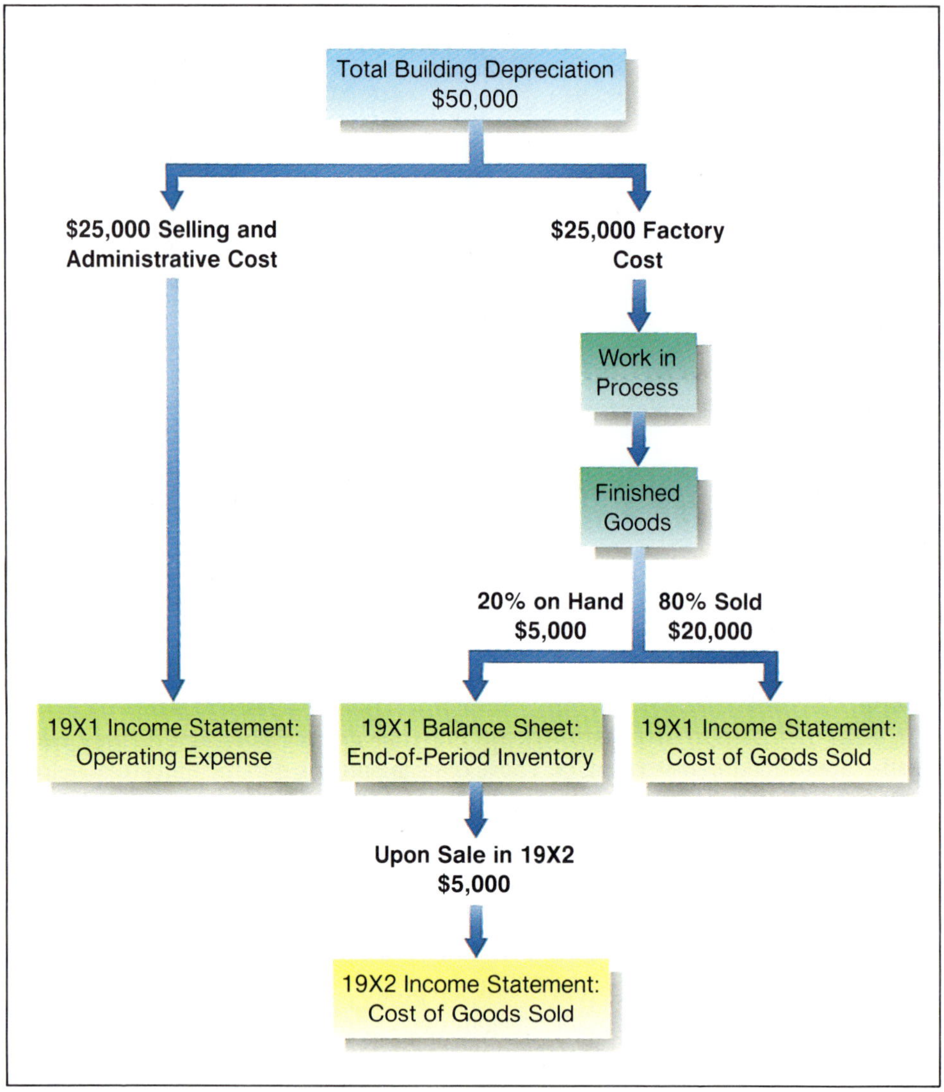


Perhaps the salary should be allocated between the two cost classifications on some equitable basis. If so, what basis should be used? Although most companies would treat the salary of the manufacturing vice-president as an administrative expense, issues like these are difficult to resolve. Businesses must therefore analyze each cost in depth, make an informed decision, and be consistent in their accounting treatment.

## Balance Sheet

OBJECTIVE 6
Be familiar with the unique features of the manufacturing balance sheet and income statement.

Now that you have a better grasp of production cost flows, we can examine the manufacturer's financial statements. The balance sheet of a manufacturer is identical to that of a merchandising concern, with one exception (see Exhibit 21-7). A merchandiser normally discloses one inventory account: Inventory or Merchandise Inventory. In contrast, businesses engaged in production activities usually establish three inventory accounts: Raw Materials, Work in Process, and Finished Goods.

**MERCHANDISING FIRM**

| | | |
|---|---|---|
| Current assets | | |
| Cash | | $ 15,000 |
| Accounts receivable | $64,000 | |
| Less: Allowance for bad debts | 4,000 | 60,000 |
| Inventory | | 190,000 |
| Prepaid expenses | | 6,000 |
| Total current assets | | $271,000 |

**MANUFACTURER**

| | | |
|---|---|---|
| Current assets | | |
| Cash | | $ 10,000 |
| Accounts receivable | $ 43,000 | |
| Less: Allowance for bad debts | 3,000 | 40,000 |
| Inventories | | |
| Finished goods | $115,000 | |
| Work in process | 51,000 | |
| Raw materials | 24,000 | 190,000 |
| Prepaid expenses | | 11,000 |
| Total current assets | | $251,000 |

**Exhibit 21-7**
**Merchandising and Manufacturing Balance Sheets**

**Raw Materials** includes the items to be processed into salable goods. **Work in Process** represents the cost of goods started but not completed by the end of the reporting period. The balance in this account is computed by totaling the direct material, direct labor, and factory overhead charges that pertain to the production in process. Finally, as its name implies, **Finished Goods** contains the cost of completed production that is owned by a firm.[3]

***Balance Sheets in Practice*** Although Raw Materials, Work in Process, and Finished Goods is the traditional split of inventory accounts, variations are frequently found in practice. For example, consider the disclosures in Exhibit 21-8, which appeared in recent corporate annual reports. These businesses have adapted the general model to meet their own needs. This practice is acceptable providing that it results in adequate disclosure and a fair measure of financial position.

## Income Statement

To illustrate the computation of net income for a manufacturer, assume that Golden, Inc., produces paint and various decorating supplies. Exhibit 21-9 contrasts Golden's income statement with that of Meadow Paint and Wallpaper, a retailer.

Notice that the two income statements are very similar. Meadow's cost of goods sold is computed on the basis of the firm's beginning and ending inventories and net purchases. Golden, on the other hand, does not acquire goods for resale; it makes them. Thus, the cost of goods manufactured replaces net purchases.

[3] Many companies have made a conscientious effort to reduce the balances in these accounts by adopting a **just-in-time** inventory system. A description of this system is found in the chapter highlight that appears on page 307.

**Exhibit 21-8**
**Inventory Disclosures (in thousands)**

***Apple Computer***

| | |
|---|---|
| Inventories | |
| Purchased parts | $160,599 |
| Work in process (including material held by subcontractors) | 56,639 |
| Finished goods | 244,232 |
| | $461,470 |

***Quaker State Corporation***

| | |
|---|---|
| Inventories | |
| Crude oil | $ 3,435 |
| Finished and in-process petroleum products | 35,511 |
| Coal | 1,897 |
| Other | 13,609 |
| | $ 54,452 |

***Scott Paper Company***

| | |
|---|---|
| Inventories | |
| Finished products | $180,200 |
| Work in process | 75,300 |
| Pulp, logs and pulpwood | 97,700 |
| Maintenance parts | 93,400 |
| Other materials and supplies | 75,600 |
| | $522,200 |

**TIPS & TECHNIQUES**

Observe that of the three inventory accounts carried by a manufacturer, only Finished Goods is used in the cost-of-goods-sold calculation. The rationale for this treatment is that a manufacturer's finished goods correspond to the merchandise inventory of a retailer (or wholesaler), with both inventory types being offered for sale. Raw Materials and Work in Process, of course, are not resold.

**Cost of goods manufactured** (see the supporting schedule in Exhibit 21-9) is derived by examining the three cost elements of a manufactured product. Direct materials used, direct labor, and factory overhead are summed to arrive at the total production costs for the period. Next, the beginning and ending work in process inventories are respectively added and subtracted to generate cost of goods manufactured. The reason for involving work in process can be described as follows. At the beginning of the accounting period Golden had $7,000 of goods in production. During the period $282,000 of manufacturing costs were incurred, yielding $289,000 ($7,000 + $282,000) of costs "in process." If $12,000 of production

**MEADOW PAINT AND WALLPAPER**
**(Merchandiser)**
**Income Statement**

| | | |
|---|---|---|
| Sales | | $224,000 |
| Cost of goods sold | | |
| Beginning inventory | $ 36,000 | |
| Net purchases | 161,000 | |
| Goods available for sale | $197,000 | |
| Less: Ending inventory | 55,000 | |
| Cost of goods sold | | 142,000 |
| Gross profit | | $ 82,000 |
| Operating expenses | | |
| Selling | $ 46,000 | |
| Administrative | 24,000 | 70,000 |
| Net income | | $ 12,000 |

**GOLDEN, INC.**
**(Manufacturer)**
**Income Statement**

| | | |
|---|---|---|
| Sales | | $356,000 |
| Cost of goods sold | | |
| Beginning finished goods inventory | $ 45,000 | |
| Cost of goods manufactured | 277,000 | |
| Goods available for sale | $322,000 | |
| Less: Ending finished goods inventory | 61,000 | |
| Cost of goods sold | | 261,000 |
| Gross profit | | $ 95,000 |
| Operating expenses | | |
| Selling | $ 58,000 | |
| Administrative | 29,000 | 87,000 |
| Net income | | $ 8,000 |

**GOLDEN, INC.**
**Schedule of Cost of Goods Manufactured**

| | | |
|---|---|---|
| Direct materials used | | |
| Beginning raw materials inventory | $ 21,000 | |
| Net purchases | 109,000 | |
| Direct materials available | $130,000 | |
| Less: Ending raw materials inventory | 28,000 | |
| Direct materials used | | $102,000 |
| Direct labor | | 79,000 |
| Factory overhead | | |
| Indirect materials used | $ 6,000 | |
| Indirect labor | 36,000 | |
| Utilities | 15,000 | |
| Depreciation: factory | 23,000 | |
| Taxes | 17,000 | |
| Insurance | 4,000 | 101,000 |
| Total manufacturing costs | | $282,000 |
| Add: Beginning work in process inventory | | 7,000 |
| | | $289,000 |
| Less: Ending work in process inventory | | 12,000 |
| Cost of goods manufactured | | $277,000 |

*Note:* This example assumes that the Raw Materials account contains direct materials only, with indirect materials being housed in a separate Factory Supplies account. Under an alternative procedure that is shown in the next chapter, the cost of both materials types may be entered in the same account.

**Exhibit 21-9**
**Income Statements of a Merchandising Firm and a Manufacturer**

remains in process at the end of the period, $277,000 ($289,000 − $12,000) of goods must have been completed. Stated differently, $277,000 represents the cost of goods manufactured. This amount is subsequently transferred to the income statement to compute cost of goods sold.

## Cost Behavior

OBJECTIVE 7
Understand variable and fixed cost behavior.

The manufacturing, selling, and administrative costs of an organization are not always presented in the traditional financial statement formats for purposes of planning and control. Frequently, costs are subdivided and studied in terms of their behavior. As noted earlier, some costs vary with changes in activity, while others remain constant. We will now overview variable and fixed cost behavior so that you better understand the subject matter that follows. An in-depth study of this topic appears in Chapter 25.

### Variable Costs

**Variable costs** vary in direct proportion to a change in an activity base. The activity base may be sales, production, miles driven, students in a university, hours of machine operation, or any other measure of volume. To illustrate the concept of a variable cost, assume the Green Company is a manufacturer of ball-point pens. The firm's top selling model, the Smoothwriter, requires $0.30 of direct materials. Green sells the Smoothwriter for $1.20 and pays its sales force a 5% commission. Two activity bases are involved in this example. The cost of direct materials used varies with production, and total commissions vary with the number of pens sold. This distinction is shown in the table that follows. Observe that a variable cost changes in total, but the cost per unit remains the same.

| *Direct Materials* | | | *Sales Commissions* | | |
|---|---|---|---|---|---|
| *Number of Pens Produced* | *Material Cost per Pen* | *Total Material Cost* | *Number of Pens Sold* | *Commission per Pen** | *Sales Commissions* |
| 50,000 | $0.30 | $15,000 | 45,000 | $0.06 | $2,700 |
| 60,000 | 0.30 | 18,000 | 55,000 | 0.06 | 3,300 |
| 70,000 | 0.30 | 21,000 | 65,000 | 0.06 | 3,900 |
| 80,000 | 0.30 | 24,000 | 75,000 | 0.06 | 4,500 |

* $1.20 × 0.05 = $0.06.

In addition to direct materials and sales commissions, other common examples of variable costs include direct labor, supplies, and fuel.

### Fixed Costs

Unlike variable costs, **fixed costs** remain constant in total when changes occur in the activity base. As a result of this behavior, the fixed cost *per unit* fluctuates. That is, an increase in activity will cause a given sum of dollars to be spread over a greater volume level, thereby causing a decrease in the per-unit figure. Naturally, opposite results will occur if activity falls. Typical fixed costs include management salaries, advertising, straight-line depreciation, rent, property taxes, and insurance.

Continuing the Green Company example, assume that the firm uses an $85,000 machine in its manufacturing activities. The machine has a $5,000 residual value and a five-year service life, generating annual straight-line depreciation of $16,000 [($85,000 − $5,000) ÷ 5]. On the basis of different production levels, the depreciation per pen will be as follows:

| *Annual Depreciation* | *Number of Pens Produced* | *Depreciation per Pen* |
|---|---|---|
| $16,000 | 50,000 | $0.32 |
| 16,000 | 60,000 | 0.267 |
| 16,000 | 70,000 | 0.229 |
| 16,000 | 80,000 | 0.20 |

From the preceding figures it is apparent that the fixed cost per unit (i.e., depreciation per pen) is relevant at one activity level and *only* one activity level. The multiplication of a $0.20-per-pen depreciation rate, for example, by production levels other than 80,000 fails to yield the total depreciation charge of $16,000. When dealing with fixed costs, it is usually safer to deal in terms of total costs as opposed to unit costs.

## APPENDIX Work Sheet and Closing Entries for a Manufacturer

Earlier in the text we presented a columnar form known as a work sheet. The work sheet was shown to be a useful tool in performing certain end-of-period procedures and served as an excellent springboard for the construction of the financial statements. Although our illustrations dealt with service businesses and merchandising concerns, the concepts presented can be used by a manufacturing firm as well.

### Work Sheet Preparation

OBJECTIVE 8
Know how to prepare a work sheet and the related closing entries for a manufacturing concern.

The next few pages illustrate the preparation of a manufacturing work sheet. The data for our example pertain to Golden, Inc., whose income statement and schedule of cost of goods manufactured appeared on page 767. For your convenience the cost-of-goods-manufactured schedule is reproduced in Exhibit 21-10. The work sheet that serves as the basis for this schedule is shown in Exhibit 21-11. A review of the work sheet will show that we have omitted the company's trial balance data and adjusting entries—a treatment justified because the required procedures are identical to those shown in Chapter 5 for a merchandising business.

Recall from our earlier presentations that amounts listed in the adjusted trial balance columns are extended to the proper financial statement section. Cash, an asset, is extended to the balance sheet debit column; Sales, a revenue account, is transferred to the income statement credit column; and so forth.

Further, observe the presence of two new columns on the manufacturer's work sheet (cost of goods manufactured) that were not on earlier versions of this document. Any amount that is needed to calculate the cost of goods completed during the period is extended to this section. Notice that balances in Raw Materials, Work in Process, Direct Labor, and Factory Insurance—for that matter, all amounts shown on Golden's cost of goods manufactured schedule—appear in the section's debit and credit columns.

**Exhibit 21-10**

| GOLDEN, INC.<br>Schedule of Cost of Goods Manufactured | | |
|---|---|---|
| Direct materials used | | |
| Beginning raw materials inventory | $ 21,000 | |
| Net purchases | 109,000 | |
| Direct materials available | $130,000 | |
| Less: Ending raw materials inventory | 28,000 | |
| Direct materials used | | $102,000 |
| Direct labor | | 79,000 |
| Factory overhead | | |
| Indirect materials used | $ 6,000 | |
| Indirect labor | 36,000 | |
| Utilities | 15,000 | |
| Depreciation: factory | 23,000 | |
| Taxes | 17,000 | |
| Insurance | 4,000 | 101,000 |
| Total manufacturing costs | | $282,000 |
| Add: Beginning work in process inventory | | 7,000 |
| | | $289,000 |
| Less: Ending work in process inventory | | 12,000 |
| Cost of goods manufactured | | $277,000 |

The difference between the column totals ($317,000 − $40,000 = $277,000) represents the cost of goods completed during the period. This amount is extended to the income statement debit column because of its use in computing cost of goods sold on the income statement.

## Treatment of Inventory Accounts

A review of the work sheet's construction will find the required procedures are very straightforward. A possible exception, however, may be the treatment of the three inventory accounts: Raw Materials, Work in Process, and Finished Goods. Special treatment is required because Golden, Inc., uses a periodic inventory system. Recall that under such a system, inventory accounts do not reflect the various inflows and outflows of goods that have occurred during the months of operating activity.[4] As a result, the accounts must be updated at the end of the period by physical counts, in this case of the raw materials, work in process, and finished goods still owned by the firm. In view of this situation, the following work-sheet procedures are performed.

Golden had a beginning finished goods inventory of $45,000. This amount is transferred to the income statement debit column for use in the cost-of-goods-sold

[4] The use of a perpetual inventory system, which maintains a continuous record of goods, is explored in Chapter 22.

**GOLDEN, INC.**
**Abbreviated Work Sheet**
**For the Year Ended December 31, 19XX**

| | *Adjusted Trial Balance* | | *Cost of Goods Manufactured* | | *Income Statement* | | *Balance Sheet* | |
|---|---|---|---|---|---|---|---|---|
| | *Debit* | *Credit* | *Debit* | *Credit* | *Debit* | *Credit* | *Debit* | *Credit* |
| Cash | 15,000 | | | | | | 15,000 | |
| Accounts receivable (net) | 24,000 | | | | | | 24,000 | |
| Inventories | | | | | | | | |
| Raw materials | 21,000 | | 21,000 | 28,000 | | | 28,000 | |
| Work in process | 7,000 | | 7,000 | 12,000 | | | 12,000 | |
| Finished goods | 45,000 | | | | 45,000 | 61,000 | 61,000 | |
| Prepaid insurance | 3,000 | | | | | | 3,000 | |
| Factory supplies | 18,000 | | | | | | 18,000 | |
| Factory | 414,000 | | | | | | 414,000 | |
| Accumulated depreciation: factory | | 102,000 | | | | | | 102,000 |
| Accounts payable | | 42,000 | | | | | | 42,000 |
| Taxes payable | | 9,000 | | | | | | 9,000 |
| Common stock | | 150,000 | | | | | | 150,000 |
| Retained earnings, Jan. 1 | | 264,000 | | | | | | 264,000 |
| Sales | | 356,000 | | | | 356,000 | | |
| Raw material purchases | 109,000 | | 109,000 | | | | | |
| Indirect materials used | 6,000 | | 6,000 | | | | | |
| Direct labor | 79,000 | | 79,000 | | | | | |
| Indirect labor | 36,000 | | 36,000 | | | | | |
| Factory utilities | 15,000 | | 15,000 | | | | | |
| Factory depreciation | 23,000 | | 23,000 | | | | | |
| Factory taxes | 17,000 | | 17,000 | | | | | |
| Factory insurance | 4,000 | | 4,000 | | | | | |
| Selling expenses | 58,000 | | | | 58,000 | | | |
| Administrative expenses | 29,000 | | | | 29,000 | | | |
| | 923,000 | 923,000 | 317,000 | 40,000 | | | | |
| Cost of goods manufactured | | | | 277,000 | 277,000 | | | |
| | | | 317,000 | 317,000 | 409,000 | 417,000 | 575,000 | 567,000 |
| Net income | | | | | 8,000 | | | 8,000 |
| | | | | | 417,000 | 417,000 | 575,000 | 575,000 |

**Exhibit 21-11**
**Manufacturing Work Sheet**

calculation. Because the ending finished goods ($61,000) must be both subtracted from goods available for sale and disclosed on the year-end balance sheet, it is entered in the income statement credit column and also the balance sheet debit column.

Somewhat different procedures are followed for the beginning balances in Raw Materials ($21,000) and Work in Process ($7,000). These amounts are needed to figure cost of goods manufactured; they are therefore transferred to the debit column of the work sheet's cost-of-goods-manufactured section. A review of the schedule in Exhibit 21-10 will find the ending balances in both these accounts are subtracted to compute the cost of goods completed; thus, $28,000 and $12,000 are entered in the section's credit column. Consistent with the treatment of the ending finished goods inventory, the $28,000 and $12,000 figures are also entered in the balance sheet debit column for reporting in the company's formal financial statements.

## The Closing Process

The closing process for a manufacturer parallels that of a merchandising business, with all temporary accounts being closed at the end of the reporting period. Such accounts include those listed in the work sheet's income statement section, along with the Dividends (or drawing) account. As part of this process, the Finished Goods account must be credited for $45,000 to reduce its balance to zero. This account is then debited for $61,000 to reflect the cost of completed goods owned by the firm at year-end. All of these procedures are performed by using the Income Summary account, as shown in Chapter 5.

The temporary manufacturing accounts must be closed in a similar manner. The related procedures reduce the account balances to zero so the accounts are ready to begin the cost accumulation process for the next reporting period. Also, the Raw Materials and Work in Process accounts must be updated to reflect the ending inventory balances. A review of the manufacturing work sheet will find *all the necessary figures for these tasks are contained in the cost-of-goods-manufactured section.* Rather than close the amounts through Income Summary, however, a new account entitled Manufacturing Summary is used.

### Closing Entries Illustrated

We begin our illustration of the required closing entries by closing the debit balances of Golden's manufacturing accounts to the Manufacturing Summary.

| | | | |
|---|---|---|---|
| Dec. 31 | Manufacturing Summary | 317,000 | |
| | Raw Materials | | 21,000 |
| | Work in Process | | 7,000 |
| | Raw Material Purchases | | 109,000 |
| | Indirect Materials Used | | 6,000 |
| | Direct Labor | | 79,000 |
| | Indirect Labor | | 36,000 |
| | Factory Utilities | | 15,000 |
| | Factory Depreciation | | 23,000 |
| | Factory Taxes | | 17,000 |
| | Factory Insurance | | 4,000 |
| | To remove beginning raw materials and work in process balances and close manufacturing accounts having debit balances | | |

Next, the company's December 31 physical counts of raw materials and work in process must be entered in the accounting records.

| | | | |
|---|---|---|---|
| Dec. 31 | Raw Materials | 28,000 | |
| | Work in Process | 12,000 | |
| | Manufacturing Summary | | 40,000 |
| | To record ending inventories of raw materials and work in process | | |

As shown by the T-account that follows, Manufacturing Summary contains a $277,000 balance. This amount represents Golden's cost of goods manufactured.

| *Manufacturing Summary* | | | |
|---|---|---|---|
| 12/31 | 317,000 | 12/31 | 40,000 |
| | 277,000 | | |

The Manufacturing Summary account is now closed to Income Summary because the balance affects net income (via the cost-of-goods-sold calculation). This step is performed at the same time that income statement debit account balances are closed and the balance in the Finished Goods account (i.e., the beginning inventory) is reduced to zero.

| | | | |
|---|---|---|---|
| Dec. 31 | Income Summary | 409,000 | |
| | Finished Goods | | 45,000 |
| | Selling Expenses | | 58,000 |
| | Administrative Expenses | | 29,000 |
| | Manufacturing Summary | | 277,000 |
| | To remove beginning finished goods balance, close income statement accounts having debit balances, and close the Manufacturing Summary | | |

To wrap-up the process, the ending inventory of completed goods is entered in the Finished Goods account, the income statement accounts with credit balances are reduced to zero, and the Income Summary balance is transferred to Retained Earnings. The two entries that follow are needed:

| | | | |
|---|---|---|---|
| Dec. 31 | Finished Goods | 61,000 | |
| | Sales | 356,000 | |
| | Income Summary | | 417,000 |
| | To record ending finished goods and close income statement accounts having credit balances | | |
| 31 | Income Summary | 8,000 | |
| | Retained Earnings | | 8,000 |
| | To close Income Summary: $417,000 − $409,000 = $8,000 | | |

## Chapter Review

### Learning Objectives—The Key Points

**1 Understand the distinction between financial and managerial accounting.** Financial accounting focuses on reporting financial position and the results of operations to external parties (i.e., those outside the organization). The information presented is highly aggregated and is really a summary of an entity's past transactions and events. Financial accounting disclosures are based on generally accepted accounting principles (GAAP) and, for the most part, are mandatory.

In contrast, managerial accounting is concerned with reporting to managers within a business. Both past and future data items are reported, normally for selected "parts" of the firm (e.g., divisions, products, and so forth). There are no rules and regulations that must be followed for internal reporting, with the result being a wide variety of reports and disclosures among businesses and managers. The decision to produce internal information is normally made on a cost-benefit basis.

**2 Be able to describe planning, control, and decision-making applications of managerial accounting.** Planning involves the study of an organization's objectives and the translation of those objectives into various methods, strategies, and programs. One form of planning is the creation of budgets. Control involves the monitoring of actual results in comparison with an entity's original plan. Feedback is provided via performance reports and variances, allowing a manager to focus on areas where corrective action may be needed. Finally, decision making requires the selection of a given alternative from a set of alternatives. If good decisions are to be made, a manager must consider both the quantitative outcome and the related qualitative factors.

**3 Be familiar with cost accounting, including its recent changes.** Cost accounting involves the collection, assignment, and interpretation of cost to answer an age-old question: "How much does it cost?" Costs may be compiled for anything from a product, to a department, to a program run by a city. Several recent changes have taken place in this field. Cost accounting's major focus over the years has been on inventory valuation; this has changed whereby cost information now plays a significant role in the planning, control, and decision-making activities of a firm. Further, cost information is being used more and more in the management of service businesses (as opposed to manufacturers), as well as by managers of a company's other functional areas (e.g., marketing).

**4 Understand the meaning of direct materials, direct labor, and factory overhead.** Direct materials, direct labor, and factory overhead are the three cost components of manufactured goods. Direct materials are those materials that form an integral part of the finished product and, at the same time, are easily traced to the product. Direct labor consists of the wages of those employees who work directly on the product (e.g., an assembly-line worker). Finally, factory overhead comprises all other factory costs such as indirect materials, indirect labor, and equipment depreciation. Unlike direct materials and direct labor, factory overhead is not easily traced to a manufactured good.

**5 Understand the difference between product and period costs.** Product costs are the costs incurred in manufacturing operations, namely, direct materials, direct labor, and factory overhead. These costs are inventoried until the manufactured good is sold, at which time the costs are transferred to cost of goods sold on the income statement. In contrast, period costs are unrelated to production operations. Such costs are expensed as incurred and include those generated by selling and administrative activities.

**6 Be familiar with the unique features of the manufacturing balance sheet and income statement.** The balance sheet of a manufacturer is characterized by the disclosure of three inventory accounts: Raw Materials, Work in Process, and Finished Goods. The manufacturing income statement is the same as that for a merchandising firm, with one exception: net purchases is replaced by an entity's cost of goods manufactured. Cost of goods manufactured is computed by summing the costs of direct materials used, direct labor, and factory overhead, and then adding the beginning work in process balance and subtracting the ending work in process.

**7 Understand variable and fixed cost behavior.** Variable costs are those that change in direct proportion to a change in an activity base (sales, production, and so on). Fixed costs, on the other hand, remain constant. Because of these behavior patterns, variable costs per unit remain constant and per-unit fixed costs fluctuate.

**8 (Appendix) Know how to prepare a work sheet and the related closing entries for a manufacturing concern.** The work sheet for a manufacturer parallels that for a merchandising business. However, a new section called Cost of Goods Manufactured is created to house all amounts that are needed in this important computation. The mathematical difference between the section's debit and credit columns represents cost of goods manufactured and is transferred to the income statement section for use in the cost-of-goods-sold calculation. At the end of the period the temporary manufacturing accounts are closed to the Manufacturing Summary account, which is later closed to Income Summary.

## Chapter Quiz

The five questions that follow relate to several issues raised in the chapter. Test your knowledge of the issues by selecting the best answer. (The answers appear on p. 789.)

**1** Managerial accounting:
- a focuses primarily on reporting to regulatory agencies.
- b is governed by generally accepted accounting principles.
- c is highly discretionary and varies greatly from business to business.
- d should be considered as a substitute for financial accounting.

**2** Which of the following items is properly classified as factory overhead?
- a Wages of a carpenter who builds fine wooden furniture.
- b The cost of sandpaper used in the production of furniture.
- c The cost of the plastic keys on a microcomputer's keyboard.
- d Depreciation on office equipment used at a company's corporate headquarters.

**3** Which of the following statements is correct?
- a Period costs are properly inventoried on the balance sheet.
- b Direct labor is a typical example of a period cost.
- c Product costs are expensed as incurred.
- d Direct material is a typical product cost.

**4** Cost of goods manufactured:
- a is added to the cost of the beginning finished goods inventory on the income statement.
- b includes selling and administrative expenses.
- c ignores the beginning and ending balances of the Work in Process account.
- d is normally disclosed on a company's balance sheet.

**5** Which of the following is an example of a variable cost?
- a Salary of a plant supervisor.
- b Advertising costs.
- c Direct materials.
- d Straight-line depreciation on a factory machine.

## Questions

**Q21-1** Briefly discuss several of the major features associated with financial accounting.

**Q21-2** Is managerial accounting concerned solely with the reporting of past transactions and events? Why?

**Q21-3** What agency, if any, establishes the "ground rules" for managerial accounting practices?

**Q21-4** How does a company ultimately decide whether to produce a discretionary report for a manager?

**Q21-5** The sales manager of Snyder Company desires to maximize the firm's market share and has proposed a loosening of credit terms. Discuss the conflict that might arise between the sales manager and the vice-president of finance.

**Q21-6** What is the purpose of issuing performance reports?

**Q21-7** In addition to the quantitative outcome, what other factors should be considered in the decision process? Why?

**Q21-8** Is cost accounting a part of financial accounting or managerial accounting? Explain.

**Q21-9** What are the three cost elements of a manufactured product?

**Q21-10** Why are indirect materials and indirect labor treated as part of factory overhead?

**Q21-11** Differentiate among direct materials, direct labor, and factory overhead in terms of cost traceability to the finished product.

**Q21-12** Dave Malloy, an engineer at Lexton Manufacturing, has just spent an exhausting weekend analyzing utility costs. Management desired to know the approximate percentage of electricity consumed by the company's (1) sales and administrative offices and (2) manufacturing plant. Dave mumbled under his breath, "Who cares? Utility cost is utility cost." Explain to Malloy why his analysis is needed.

**Q21-13** When does a product cost appear on a balance sheet? On an income statement?

**Q21-14** Discuss the balance sheet differences between a merchandiser and a manufacturer.

**Q21-15** Blakely Manufacturing and Diaz Wholesalers both employ a sales manager. Discuss the differences, if any, in the accounting treatment of the salaries of the two sales managers.

***Q21-16** What balance would normally appear in the Manufacturing Summary account before the account is closed to Income Summary?

## Exercises

**E21-1** ***Product costs and period costs***

The costs that follow were extracted from the accounting records of several different manufacturers:

1 Weekly wages of an equipment maintenance worker
2 Marketing costs of a soft drink bottler
3 Cost of sheet metal in a Honda automobile
4 Cost of president's subscription to *Fortune* magazine
5 Monthly operating costs of pollution control equipment
6 Weekly wages of a seamstress employed by a jeans maker
7 Cost of compact discs (CDs) for newly recorded releases of Rush, Billy Joel, and the Beach Boys

a Determine which of these costs are product costs and which are period costs.
b For the product costs only, determine those that are easily traced to the finished product and those that are not.

---

* An asterisk preceding an item indicates that the material is covered in the appendix to this chapter.

**E21-2** ***Overview of manufacturing costs***

Evaluate the comments that follow as being True or False. If the comment is false, briefly explain why.

a The cost of cement in a road-building project would typically be classified as direct material.

b Normally, conversion costs are easily traced to a finished product.

c The Finished Goods inventory account contains the period costs of a manufacturer.

d Direct materials used + direct labor + beginning work in process inventory − ending work in process inventory = cost of goods manufactured.

e Product costs appear as inventory on a balance sheet until such time that the related units are sold.

**E21-3** ***Definitions of manufacturing concepts***

Interstate Manufacturing produces brass fasteners and incurred the following costs for the year just ended:

| | |
|---|---|
| Materials and supplies | |
| Brass | $ 75,000 |
| Repair parts | 16,000 |
| Machine lubricants | 9,000 |
| Wages and salaries | |
| Machine operators | 128,000 |
| Production supervisors | 64,000 |
| Maintenance personnel | 41,000 |
| Other factory overhead | |
| Variable | 35,000 |
| Fixed | 46,000 |
| Sales commissions | 20,000 |

Compute:

a Total direct materials used

b Total direct labor

c Total prime cost

d Total conversion cost

**E21-4** ***Basic manufacturing computations***

Florida Manufacturing reported total manufacturing costs (direct materials used, direct labor, and factory overhead) of $326,000 for 19X7. Sales and operating expenses were $528,600 and $129,800, respectively. The following information appeared on company balance sheets:

| | *For the Year Ended* | |
|---|---|---|
| | ***12/31/X7*** | ***12/31/X6*** |
| Finished goods | $106,500 | $ 97,000 |
| Work in process | 162,400 | 178,500 |

Compute cost of goods manufactured, cost of goods sold, and net income for 19X7.

**E21-5** ***Schedule of cost of goods manufactured, income statement***

The following information was taken from the ledger of Jefferson Industries, Inc.:

| | | | |
|---|---|---|---|
| Direct labor | $ 85,000 | Administrative expenses | $59,000 |
| Selling expenses | 34,000 | Work in process | |
| Sales | 300,000 | Jan. 1 | 29,000 |
| Finished goods | | Dec. 31 | 21,000 |
| Jan. 1 | 115,000 | Direct material purchases | 88,000 |
| Dec. 31 | 131,000 | Depreciation: factory | 18,000 |
| Raw (direct) materials on hand | | Indirect materials used | 10,000 |
| | | Indirect labor | 24,000 |
| Jan. 1 | 31,000 | Factory taxes | 8,000 |
| Dec. 31 | 40,000 | Factory utilities | 11,000 |

Prepare the following:

a A schedule of cost of goods manufactured for the year ended December 31.
b An income statement for the year ended December 31.

**E21-6** ***Manufacturing cost errors***

A staff assistant of the Toronto Company recently computed the firm's cost of goods manufactured at $234,800. However, the following errors were noted in his work:

a Depreciation of $32,600 related to store equipment was included in factory overhead.
b The beginning work in process inventory was understated by $21,900.
c A $24,000 invoice for property taxes was charged as an operating expense of the current period. Management estimates that 60% of the invoice pertains to the manufacturing plant.
d Direct labor costs of $11,700 were accidentally accounted for as indirect labor.
e The total cost of direct materials used during the period was overstated by $38,900.

Determine the correct cost of goods manufactured.

**E21-7** ***Understanding cost behavior***

The planning department of Herzog Company has prepared budgets for three probable levels of operation for the upcoming year. Because of their significance, the following costs have been selected for study:

| | ***Level of Activity (Units)*** | | | | | |
|---|---|---|---|---|---|---|
| | ***10,000*** | | ***12,000*** | | ***15,000*** | |
| | ***Total*** | ***Per Unit*** | ***Total*** | ***Per Unit*** | ***Total*** | ***Per Unit*** |
| Direct materials | $ 90,000 | $ 9.00 | $108,000 | $ 9.00 | $135,000 | $ 9.00 |
| Direct labor | 120,000 | 12.00 | 144,000 | 12.00 | 180,000 | 12.00 |
| Advertising | 300,000 | 30.00 | 300,000 | 25.00 | 300,000 | 20.00 |
| Management salaries | 180,000 | 18.00 | 180,000 | 15.00 | 180,000 | 12.00 |
| | $690,000 | $69.00 | $732,000 | $61.00 | $795,000 | $53.00 |

Addressing his executive staff, Herzog's president commented: "It's imperative that we implement cost-cutting programs to reduce advertising and management salaries. As shown by the per-unit costs, these variable costs are destroying our profit margins. Our fixed costs of direct materials and direct labor (constant at $9.00 and $12.00 per unit, respectively) also need some improvement. I know our competitors are paying approximately $19.25 for these same two production factors."

Comment on the president's remarks.

**E21-8** ***Variable and fixed cost calculations***

Frontier Industries began operations on January 1 of the current year to produce a single product. Sales far exceeded expectations, with the firm disposing of all 50,000 units manufactured. The following unit costs were incurred:

| | |
|---|---|
| Direct material | $36 |
| Direct labor | 14 |
| Variable factory overhead | 6 |
| Fixed factory overhead | 20 |
| Variable selling costs | 4 |
| Fixed selling costs | 8 |

Management is expecting to produce and sell 58,000 units and 54,000 units, respectively, in the upcoming accounting period.

Compute the company's total expected production and selling costs. Assume that unit variable costs and total fixed costs are unchanged from the previous period.

***E21-9** ***Closing entries for a manufacturer***

Refer to the data in Exercise 21-5 that pertain to Jefferson Industries, Inc. Prepare the company's closing entries as of December 31.

## Problems

### Series A

**P21-A1** ***Cost classification***

E. Turner & Sons manufactures barbecue grills. For each of the following costs, determine cost behavior (variable or fixed) and whether the cost is a product or a period cost. If a product cost, identify the cost as direct materials (DM), direct labor (DL), or factory overhead (FOH). Item (a) is presented as an example.

| *Cost* | *Variable/Fixed* | *Product/Period* | *DM/DL/FOH* |
|---|---|---|---|
| a Property taxes on the factory | Fixed | Product | FOH |
| b Salary of the production supervisor | | | |
| c Freight costs on shipments to out-of-state customers | | | |
| d Wages of assembly personnel | | | |
| e Grill tops and frames | | | |
| f Straight-line depreciation on factory equipment | | | |
| g Paint used to touch up production scratches | | | |
| h Customer rebate offered on grill no. 301 | | | |

*(continued)*

| Cost | Variable/Fixed | Product/Period | DM/DL/FOH |
|---|---|---|---|
| i Heating costs for manufacturing facilities | ________ | ________ | ________ |
| j Wheels attached to portable models | ________ | ________ | ________ |
| k Fees paid for plant security | ________ | ________ | ________ |
| l Advertising costs for new product line | ________ | ________ | ________ |

**P21-A2** ***Straightforward manufacturing statements***

The following information was extracted from the accounting records of Olympic Company for the year just ended:

| | |
|---|---|
| Sales | $628,000 |
| Work in process, Jan. 1 | 56,700 |
| Advertising expense | 23,500 |
| Direct material purchases | 231,500 |
| Finished goods, Dec. 31 | 67,800 |
| Indirect materials used | 12,300 |
| Direct labor | 85,600 |
| Direct materials, Jan. 1 | 45,500 |
| Finished goods, Jan. 1 | 55,900 |
| Direct materials, Dec. 31 | 38,200 |
| Sales-staff salaries | 33,300 |
| Work in process, Dec. 31 | 47,400 |
| Indirect labor | 50,700 |

Utilities, taxes, insurance, and depreciation are incurred jointly by Olympic's manufacturing, sales, and administrative facilities. The costs were as follows:

| | |
|---|---|
| Utilities | $40,000 |
| Taxes | 25,000 |
| Insurance | 10,000 |
| Depreciation | 36,000 |

The first three costs are allocated proportionately on the basis of square feet occupied by the three functional areas. A review of the company's facilities revealed the following percentages would be appropriate: manufacturing, 50%; sales, 30%; and administrative, 20%. Depreciation is allocated 70%, 20%, and 10%, respectively.

**Instructions**

a Prepare a schedule of cost of goods manufactured in good form.
b Prepare an income statement in good form.

**P21-A3** ***Manufacturing accounting computations***

The following information was obtained from the records of Post Corporation for the current year ended December 31:

| | |
|---|---|
| Direct materials | |
| Beginning inventory | 1,600 units @ $8.30 |
| Purchase no. 1 | 2,300 units @ $8.30 |
| Purchase no. 2 | 1,000 units @ $8.30 |

| | | |
|---|---|---|
| Payroll costs | | |
| Direct labor | $59,700 | |
| Indirect labor | 30,000 | |
| Administrative salaries | 24,600 | |
| Sales salaries | 29,500 | |
| Other costs | | |
| Building depreciation (80% of the building is devoted to production activities, with the remainder split equally between sales and administration) | | $35,000 |
| Other factory costs | | 22,700 |
| Other selling expenses | | 9,100 |
| Other administrative expenses | | 15,800 |

Post's beginning work in process inventory totaled $8,900; the ending work in process was $10,100. During the accounting period the finished goods inventory declined from 2,100 units (cost: $206,400) to 1,650 units (cost: $178,800). The company produced 750 completed units, sold 1,200 completed units at $320 each, and consumed 3,500 units of direct materials.

**Instructions**

a Calculate the cost of the ending direct materials inventory.
b Compute Post's cost of goods manufactured.
c Compute the company's cost of goods sold.
d Determine net income for the year just ended.

**P21-A4** ***Error recognition and statement preparation***
Eltron Company manufactures fine wooden furniture. An income statement, prepared by a new employee, follows.

**ELTRON COMPANY**
**Income Statement**
**For the Year Ended December 31, 19X8**

| | | |
|---|---|---|
| Sales | | $680,000 |
| Cost of goods sold: | | |
| Lumber used | $110,000 | |
| Advertising | 42,000 | |
| Indirect labor | 46,000 | |
| Depreciation | 52,000 | |
| Marketing & administrative salaries | 100,000 | |
| Facility rent | 90,000 | |
| Purchases of lumber | 75,000 | |
| Direct labor | 180,000 | |
| Utilities | 28,000 | |
| Factory equipment | 30,000 | 753,000 |
| Net income (loss) | | $ (73,000) |

The company's president is very unhappy with Eltron's performance, as profitable operations have been the rule rather than the exception. Doris Wexler has been asked to review the accounting records to determine whether the income statement is correct. The information that follows has come to her attention.

1 Inventory data:

| | 1/1/X8 | 12/31/X8 |
|---|---|---|
| Lumber | $ 99,000 | $ 64,000 |
| Work in process | 129,000 | 147,000 |
| Finished goods | 256,000 | 288,000 |

2 Depreciation, rent, and utilities should be allocated to manufacturing and selling and administrative activities as follows:

| | *Manufacturing* | *Selling & Administrative* |
|---|---|---|
| Depreciation | 90% | 10% |
| Rent | — | 100% |
| Utilities | 60% | 40% |

3 The factory equipment was purchased on the last day of 19X8 and is expected to benefit the company for the next 10 years.

**Instructions**

Assume the role of Doris Wexler and:

a Prepare a schedule of cost of goods manufactured.

b Prepare a corrected income statement.

**P21-A5** ***Manufacturing statements and cost behavior***

The Willow Creek Company, a manufacturer of specialized calculators, began operations on January 1 of the current year. Each calculator requires the following variable costs:

| | |
|---|---|
| Direct materials | $12 |
| Direct labor | 5 |
| Variable factory overhead | 14 |
| | $31 |

The fixed costs incurred during the year are shown below.

| | |
|---|---|
| Factory overhead | $ 80,000 |
| Selling | 40,000 |
| Administrative | 120,000 |
| | $240,000 |

Production totaled 40,000 calculators, of which 38,000 were sold at $40 each. Assume no work in process. Willow Creek carries its finished goods inventory at the average unit cost of production.

**Instructions**

a Determine the cost of Willow Creek's ending finished goods inventory.

b Present Willow Creek's income statement for the current year ended December 31.

c Suppose Willow Creek reduced production to meet decreased demand. If the present cost behavior patterns continue, determine the effect of the new production policy on the manufactured cost per calculator. Explain the reasoning behind your answer.

***P21-A6** ***Work sheet preparation; closing entries***

The adjusted trial balance that follows pertains to Brooklyn Manufacturing as of December 31, 19X5:

| | | |
|---|---|---|
| Cash | $ 25,000 | |
| Accounts receivable (net) | 31,000 | |
| Raw materials | 34,000 | |
| Work in process | 59,000 | |
| Finished goods | 98,000 | |
| Factory supplies | 23,000 | |
| Building & equipment | 217,000 | |
| Accumulated depreciation: building & equipment | | $ 85,000 |
| Accounts payable | | 76,000 |
| Taxes payable | | 37,000 |
| Common stock | | 100,000 |
| Retained earnings | | 145,000 |
| Sales | | 550,000 |
| Raw material purchases | 125,000 | |
| Indirect materials used | 80,000 | |
| Direct labor | 100,000 | |
| Indirect labor | 45,000 | |
| Factory taxes | 15,000 | |
| Factory utilities | 19,000 | |
| Factory depreciation | 27,000 | |
| Selling expenses | 52,000 | |
| Administrative expenses | 43,000 | |
| | $993,000 | $993,000 |

Ending inventories, obtained by a physical count, were as follows: raw materials, $29,000; work in process, $62,000; and finished goods, $102,000.

**Instructions**

a Prepare a work sheet for the company as of December 31. Use the same format as that shown in Exhibit 21-11.

b Prepare the firm's closing entries.

c How much was Brooklyn's cost of goods manufactured? Where would this amount be disclosed in the company's formal financial statements?

## Series B

**P21-B1** ***Cost classification***

The Robin Hill Company manufactures corrugated cardboard boxes for industrial use. For each of the following costs, determine cost behavior (variable or fixed) and whether the cost is a product or a period cost. If a product cost, identify the cost as direct materials (DM), direct labor (DL), or factory overhead (FOH). Item (a) is presented as an example.

| *Cost* | *Variable/Fixed* | *Product/Period* | *DM/DL/FOH* |
|---|---|---|---|
| a Fire insurance on the factory | Fixed | Product | FOH |
| b Rolls of paper used in production | | | |

*(continued)*

| Cost | *Variable/Fixed* | *Product/Period* | *DM/DL/FOH* |
|---|---|---|---|
| c Ink consumed in printing operations | ________ | ________ | ________ |
| d Salary of the sales manager | ________ | ________ | ________ |
| e Wages paid to folding machine operators | ________ | ________ | ________ |
| f Auditor's fees | ________ | ________ | ________ |
| g Monthly salaries of inspection personnel | ________ | ________ | ________ |
| h Units-of-output depreciation on cutting machine | ________ | ________ | ________ |
| i Air-conditioning costs of executive offices | ________ | ________ | ________ |
| j Machine lubricant | ________ | ________ | ________ |
| k Machine repair costs | ________ | ________ | ________ |
| l Freight-out | ________ | ________ | ________ |

**P21-B2** ***Straightforward manufacturing statements***

The following information was extracted from the accounting records of Fitness Manufacturing for the year just ended:

| | |
|---|---|
| Work in process, Dec. 31 | $ 42,700 |
| Advertising expense | 19,300 |
| Direct materials, Jan. 1 | 55,400 |
| Finished goods, Dec. 31 | 79,600 |
| Sales | 570,500 |
| Indirect materials used | 18,000 |
| Direct material purchases | 188,900 |
| Finished goods, Jan. 1 | 68,500 |
| Direct materials, Dec. 31 | 70,100 |
| Sales commissions | 61,400 |
| Direct labor | 121,400 |
| Work in process, Jan. 1 | 44,700 |
| Indirect labor | 39,500 |

Utilities, taxes, insurance, and depreciation are incurred jointly by the company's manufacturing, sales, and administrative facilities. The costs were as follows:

| | |
|---|---|
| Utilities | $45,000 |
| Taxes | 27,000 |
| Insurance | 12,000 |
| Depreciation | 65,000 |

The first three costs are allocated proportionately on the basis of square feet occupied by the three functional areas. A review of the firm's facilities revealed the following percentages would be appropriate: manufacturing, 60%; sales, 25%; and administrative, 15%. Depreciation is allocated 75%, 20%, and 5%, respectively.

**Instructions**

a Prepare a schedule of cost of goods manufactured in good form.
b Prepare an income statement in good form.

**P21-B3** ***Manufacturing accounting computations***

The following information was obtained from the records of Metropolitan Corporation for the current year ended December 31:

| | | |
|---|---|---|
| Direct materials | | |
| Beginning inventory | 500 units @ $6.20 | |
| Purchase no. 1 | 1,100 units @ $6.20 | |
| Purchase no. 2 | 1,400 units @ $6.20 | |
| Payroll costs | | |
| Direct labor | $40,500 | |
| Indirect labor | 18,600 | |
| Administrative salaries | 83,600 | |
| Sales salaries | 38,200 | |
| Other costs | | |
| Building depreciation (70% of the building is devoted to production activities, with the remainder split equally between sales and administration) | | $30,000 |
| Other factory costs | | 5,900 |
| Other selling expenses | | 16,100 |
| Other administrative expenses | | 18,800 |

Metropolitan's beginning work in process inventory totaled $10,500; the ending work in process was $6,000. During the accounting period the finished goods inventory rose from 300 units (cost: $21,250) to 1,000 units (cost: $68,700). The company produced 1,500 completed units, sold 800 completed units at $280 each, and consumed 2,000 units of direct materials.

**Instructions**

a Calculate the cost of direct materials used during the accounting period.
b Compute Metropolitan's cost of goods manufactured.
c Compute the company's cost of goods sold.
d Determine net income for the year just ended.

**P21-B4** ***Error recognition and statement preparation***

Easy Step Company manufactures designer shoes. An income statement, prepared by a new employee, follows.

**EASY STEP COMPANY**
**Income Statement**
**For the Year Ended October 31, 19X6**

| | | |
|---|---|---|
| Sales | | $850,000 |
| Cost of goods sold: | | |
| Heat, light, & power | $ 40,000 | |
| Sales commissions | 52,000 | |
| Direct labor | 150,000 | |
| Depreciation | 90,000 | |
| Administrative salaries | 220,000 | |
| Bank loan proceeds | (35,000) | |
| Leather purchases | 165,000 | |
| Indirect materials used | 42,000 | |
| Indirect labor | 70,000 | |
| Expired insurance | 25,000 | 819,000 |
| Net income (loss) | | $ 31,000 |

The company's president is very pleased with Easy Step's performance, as net losses have been the rule rather than the exception. Ray French has been asked to review the accounting records to determine whether the income statement is, in fact, correct. The following information has come to his attention:

1 Inventory data:

| | *1/1/X6* | *12/31/X6* |
|---|---|---|
| Leather | $ 63,000 | $ 72,000 |
| Work in process | 115,000 | 93,000 |
| Finished goods | 224,000 | 191,000 |

2 Heat, light, and power, depreciation, and expired insurance should be allocated to manufacturing and selling and administrative activities as follows:

| | *Manufacturing* | *Selling & Administrative* |
|---|---|---|
| Heat, light, & power | 70% | 30% |
| Depreciation | 40% | 60% |
| Expired insurance | 80% | 20% |

3 The bank loan proceeds were secured on October 31, 19X6, to finance a forthcoming purchase of manufacturing equipment. The equipment has a 5-year service life.

**Instructions**

Assume the role of Ray French and:

a Prepare a schedule of cost of goods manufactured.

b Prepare a corrected income statement.

**P21-B5** ***Manufacturing statements and cost behavior***

Park Row, Inc., a manufacturer of decorative metal products, began operations on January 1 of the current year. One of its products, an entrance gate, requires the following variable costs:

| | |
|---|---|
| Direct materials | $30 |
| Direct labor | 24 |
| Variable factory overhead | 20 |
| | $74 |

The fixed costs incurred during the year are shown below.

| | |
|---|---|
| Factory overhead | $64,000 |
| Selling | 12,000 |
| Administrative | 20,000 |
| | $96,000 |

Production totaled 1,000 gates, of which 750 were sold at $200 each. Assume no work in process. Park Row carries its finished goods inventory at the average unit cost of production.

**Instructions**

a Determine the cost of Park Row's ending finished goods inventory.

b Present Park Row's income statement for the current year ended December 31.

c Suppose Park Row stepped up production to meet increased demand. If present cost behavior patterns continue, determine the effect of the new production policy on (1) the $74-per-unit variable cost and (2) the fixed cost per unit. Explain the reasoning behind your answer.

***P21-B6** ***Work sheet preparation; closing entries***

The adjusted trial balance that follows pertains to Sand Run Manufacturing as of May 31, 19X4:

| | | |
|---|---|---|
| Cash | $ 19,000 | |
| Accounts receivable (net) | 25,000 | |
| Raw materials | 30,000 | |
| Work in process | 71,000 | |
| Finished goods | 103,000 | |
| Factory supplies | 18,000 | |
| Plant & equipment | 195,000 | |
| Accumulated depreciation: plant & equipment | | $ 55,000 |
| Accounts payable | | 66,000 |
| Taxes payable | | 11,000 |
| Common stock | | 150,000 |
| Retained earnings | | 138,000 |
| Sales | | 506,000 |
| Raw material purchases | 111,000 | |
| Factory supplies used | 22,000 | |
| Direct labor | 145,000 | |
| Indirect labor | 35,000 | |
| Factory depreciation | 14,000 | |
| Factory taxes | 26,000 | |
| Factory utilities | 29,000 | |
| Selling expenses | 44,000 | |
| Administrative expenses | 39,000 | |
| | $926,000 | $926,000 |

Ending inventories, obtained by a physical count, were as follows: raw materials, $23,000; work in process, $72,000; and finished goods, $109,000.

**Instructions**

a Prepare a work sheet for the company as of May 31. Use the same format as that shown in Exhibit 21-11.
b Prepare the firm's closing entries.
c Compute Sand Run's cost of goods sold.

## Beyond the Basics

**BB21-1** ***Analysis of product cost error***

Mansfield, Inc., began to manufacture a new product in January 19X1. The following costs were incurred in the production of 15,000 units:

| | |
|---|---|
| Direct materials | $ 51,000 |
| Direct labor | 90,000 |
| Overhead | 31,500 |
| | $172,500 |

Demand was below expectations and by the end of 19X1 production was stopped. Mansfield sold 11,000 units in 19X1 and 3,000 units in 19X2. The firm's accountant recently discovered that Sales Salaries Expense was accidentally debited in 19X1 for $19,500 of wages paid to assembly-line workers.

**Instructions**

Assuming no work in process at the end of 19X1, determine the impact and amount of the error on the following:
a 19X1 ending finished goods inventory and net income
b 19X2 ending finished goods inventory and net income

**BB21-2** ***Estimate of ending inventories***

Midway Products, a manufacturer of painting equipment, suffered extensive damage at its main manufacturing plant on March 31 as a result of a fire. Fortunately, all raw materials inventories were stored in an adjacent warehouse. The following information has been gathered in an attempt to estimate the cost of the work in process and finished goods inventories destroyed:

| | |
|---|---|
| Goods available for sale on Mar. 31 | $220,000 |
| Direct labor | 70,000 |
| Sales through Mar. 31 | 280,000 |
| Work in process, Jan. 1 | 13,000 |
| Finished goods, Jan. 1 | 29,000 |
| Net income through Mar. 31 | 25,000 |

The company's accounting staff indicated that sales are usually made at a gross profit rate of 40%. Furthermore, the cost of direct materials consumed averages 30% of prime cost, and factory overhead amounts to 50% of total manufacturing costs incurred. Midway expects full reimbursement from its insurance company for any losses suffered.

**Instructions**

Estimate the work in process and finished goods inventories destroyed. *Hint:* Prepare a detailed schedule of cost of goods manufactured and an income statement for the quarter ended March 31.

## Answers to Chapter Quiz

**1** c

**2** b

**3** d

**4** a

**5** c

# Job Order Costing Systems

CHAPTER 22

## Learning Objectives

After reading this chapter you should:

1 Be familiar with the problem of determining the actual cost of a product or service.

2 Understand the use and operation of job order costing systems.

3 Be able to compute and use an overhead application rate.

4 Be able to account for over- or underapplied overhead at the end of the accounting period.

5 Understand the applicability of job costing systems in service organizations.

As shown in the previous chapter, cost accounting generates information that both meets the needs of management and satisfies external-reporting requirements. Specifically, cost information assists in planning, control, and decision making while, at the same time, providing a basis for inventory valuation and income measurement. In order to accomplish these tasks, an organization must be able to calculate (i.e., accumulate) the cost of its goods, services, and activities. This chapter introduces the topic of cost accumulation by focusing on job order costing systems, which are used by both manufacturing and service businesses.

## Cost Determination

OBJECTIVE 1
**Be familiar with the problem of determining the actual cost of a product or service.**

The determination of the "actual" cost of a good or service is extremely difficult. Several topics presented in earlier chapters of the text attest to this fact. In the area of inventory, for example, many people feel that the specific identification method is the most precise method of inventory costing. Recall that under specific identification the cost of the units is attached to the units themselves, leaving little doubt regarding the cost of units on hand, used, or sold. Despite this attribute, relatively few businesses use this costing method because of the many practical problems it presents. Instead, most firms turn to a cost flow *assumption* such as LIFO, FIFO, or weighted average. Although these assumptions are acceptable accounting alternatives, the inability to determine actual cost introduces imprecision into the costing process.

Further complicating cost determination are costs that are not easily traced to the finished product. As we noted in Chapter 21, factory overhead possesses this characteristic. Factory depreciation, utilities, plant security, and other comparable production costs are incurred by manufacturing activities as a whole, and identification with specific goods is very troublesome.

A similar traceability problem exists in many divisionalized organizations, where a given cost benefits several segments of activity. Picture Sears, Roebuck and Co., for example, which owns and operates the following subsidiaries:

| *Subsidiary* | *Area of Identity* |
|---|---|
| Allstate Insurance | Insurance |
| Dean Witter | Financial services |
| Coldwell Banker | Real estate |
| Discover Credit Corp. | Credit cards |

The president and others in the high-level corporate staff of Sears make decisions and handle operating matters that serve the entity as a whole. Significant difficulties arise, however, when attempting to trace the cost of broad corporate activities back to smaller segments, such as a new insurance program from Allstate or a real estate promotion from Coldwell Banker. The program and promotion have probably benefited from the actions of top management and should therefore absorb a portion of corporate cost. Yet, determining the proper cost that each activity should bear is a guess, at best.

Because a clear and definitive relationship between inputs (costs) and outputs (products and activities) is often lacking, cost determination frequently relies on estimates. Estimates, of course, are subjective and arbitrary. In sum, although the material presented in the forthcoming pages may appear very detailed and exacting, realize that the calculation of the actual cost of a process, good, or service on a timely basis is a near impossibility.

## Job Order Systems

**OBJECTIVE 2**
**Understand the use and operation of job order costing systems.**

Several different types of systems are available to an entity to accumulate costs. We now turn our attention to job order costing; another popular system, process cost accounting, is discussed in Chapter 23.

With a **job order system,** costs are gathered by job or order. Such systems are commonly used when cost accumulation by job is a fairly easy task, a situation that often arises when goods are made (1) upon the receipt of a customer order, (2) according to customer specifications, or (3) in separate batches. Custom-home builders, for example, frequently employ job systems because of the ease in tracing costs to specific building sites. Similarly, print shops use job systems to cost individual customer orders.

The costs of each job are accumulated on a separate **job cost sheet** (see Exhibit 22-1). Direct materials used and direct labor are identified with and charged to the specific job on which they were incurred. Since factory overhead is not easily traced to a manufactured product, individual jobs are charged with an estimated overhead cost.

The operation of a job cost system follows the flow of costs illustrated in Chapter 21. The three cost elements of direct materials, direct labor, and factory overhead are combined and put "in process" to manufacture products. Eventually, the work in process is completed. The completed goods that are sold are reported as cost of goods sold on the income statement; the unsold units are carried in the Finished Goods inventory account on the balance sheet. This process is shown in the top half of Exhibit 22-2.

**Exhibit 22-1**
**Job Cost Sheet**

JOB COST SHEET

*Manufactured for:* — *Job No.* ________

*Stock* ________ — *Date:*

*Customer* ________ — *Needed* ________

*Started* ________

*Completed* ________

*Product* ________ — *No. of Units* ________

| Direct Materials | | | Direct Labor | | | | Factory Overhead | |
|---|---|---|---|---|---|---|---|---|
| Date | Requisition No. | Amount | Date | Ticket No. | Hours | Amount | Date | Amount |
| | | | | | | | | |

Overhead Rate: ________

COST SUMMARY

*Direct materials* $ ________

*Direct labor* ________

*Factory overhead* ________

*Total cost* $ ________

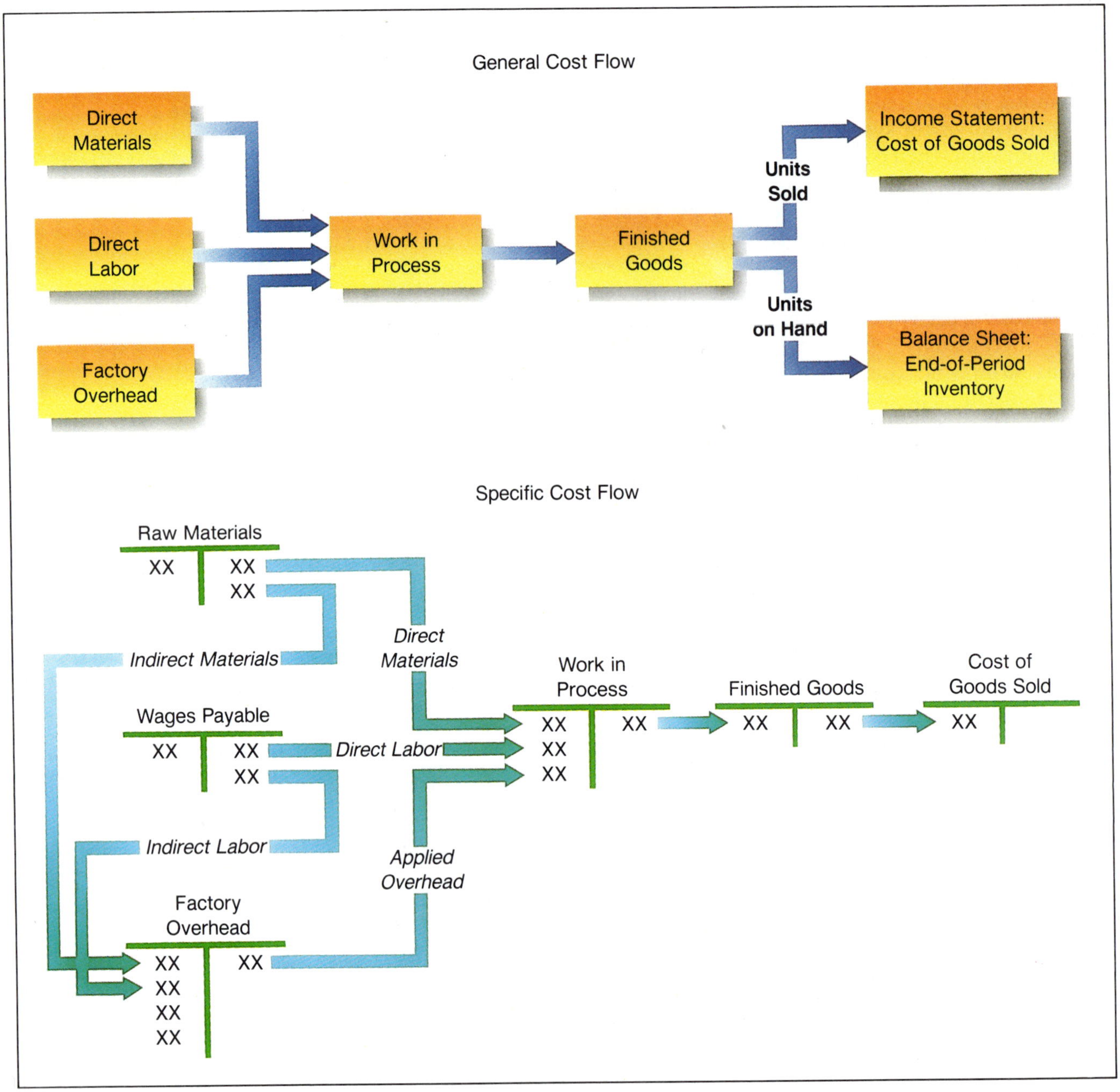


**Exhibit 22-2**
**Manufacturing Cost Flows**

## Perpetual Inventories

To handle the necessary record keeping, a manufacturing firm establishes various accounts and procedures that parallel the general cost flow (see the bottom half of Exhibit 22-2). Many manufacturers use perpetual inventory systems in which the Raw Materials, Work in Process, and Finished Goods accounts are continually updated during the period to reflect increases and decreases. Especially popular with those companies that have computerized their accounting records, perpetual systems improve managerial control and allow for more timely reporting of operating results and financial position. To illustrate use of a perpetual inventory system in conjunction with job order costing, we will explore the August transactions of Valley Manufacturing Corporation.

## Accounting for Materials

As noted in the previous chapter, the costs of direct and indirect materials owned may be housed together in a single Raw Materials inventory account. We will assume that this procedure is followed by Valley Manufacturing and all companies in our end-of-chapter exercises and problems. The following entry was therefore made when Valley purchased $80,000 of materials and factory supplies (i.e., indirect materials) on account:

| | | |
|---|---|---|
| Raw Materials | 80,000 | |
| Accounts Payable | | 80,000 |
| Purchased direct materials and factory supplies | | |

Materials are kept in a storeroom or warehouse and issued upon receipt of a **materials requisition.** As shown in Exhibit 22-3, $4,000 of materials have been issued for use on job no. 864. These materials are *direct materials* because they can be identified with a given job; as such, information that appears on the requisition is posted to the related cost sheet. The entry to record the issuance of direct materials to production is shown below.

| | | |
|---|---|---|
| Work in Process | 4,000 | |
| Raw Materials | | 4,000 |
| Issued direct materials for job no. 864 | | |

Indirect materials (e.g., sandpaper, lubricants, and so on) are not easily (or economically) traced to individual jobs; thus, no attempt is made to charge specific cost sheets. Instead, indirect materials consumed are treated as part of factory overhead. During August, Valley used $2,800 of miscellaneous factory supplies in manufacturing operations. The following entry is needed:

| | | |
|---|---|---|
| Factory Overhead | 2,800 | |
| Raw Materials | | 2,800 |
| Issued indirect materials | | |

The Factory Overhead account is debited to record *actual* overhead charges. The manner in which each job is charged with an *estimated* (*applied*) share of overhead will be illustrated shortly.

## Accounting for Labor

The accounting treatment for labor is very similar to that of materials. Factory labor costs are classified as either direct or indirect. Recall that direct labor, like direct materials, is easily identified with given jobs. Indirect labor, on the other hand, is not and is considered part of factory overhead.

Labor costs are accumulated by means of time tickets and labor summaries. Each day, each factory employee completes a **time ticket.** As shown in Exhibit 22-3, the time ticket gathers daily labor information and shows the specific job to

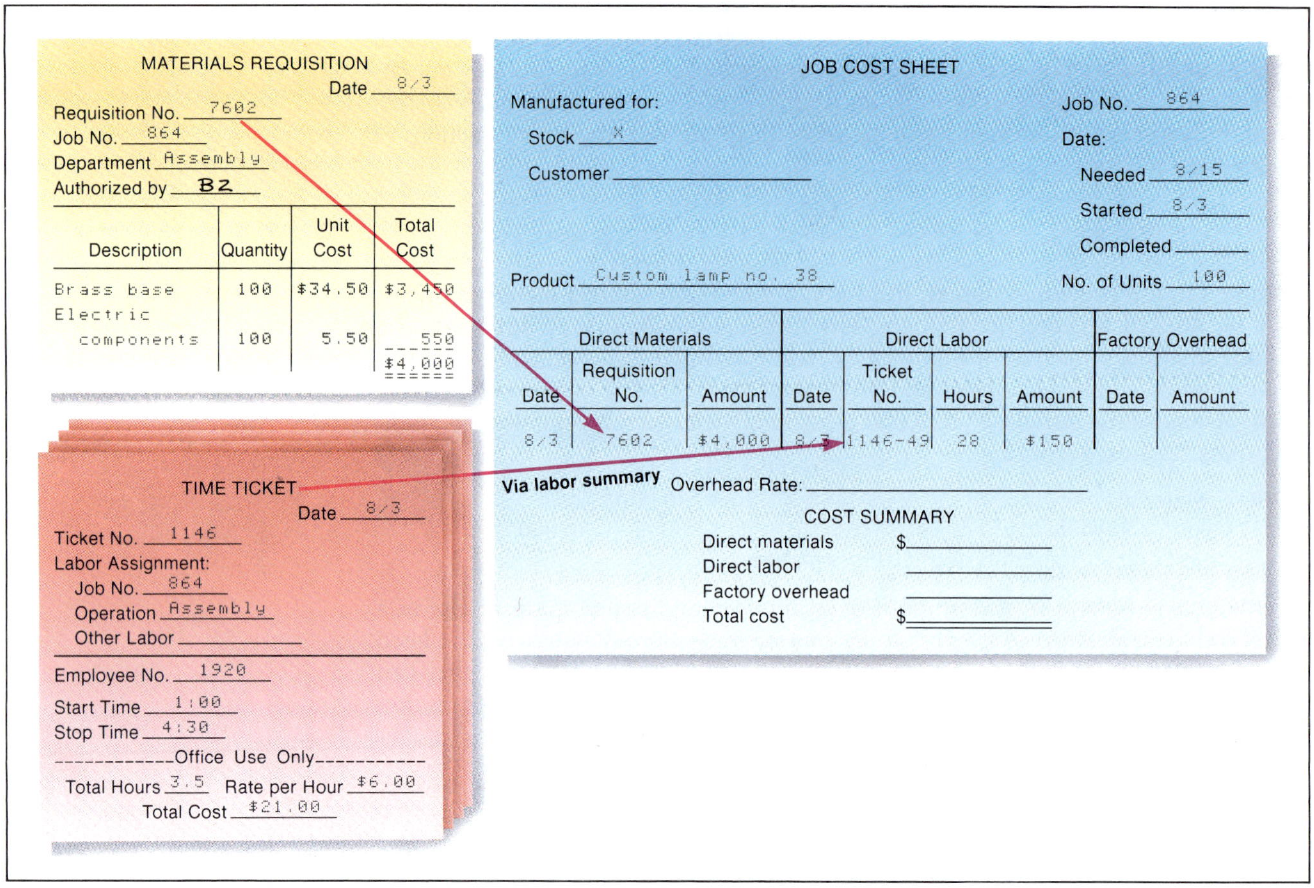


**Exhibit 22-3**
**Document Interrelationships in a Job Order System**

which the employee was assigned. If the employee was not working on a job, the type of indirect labor activity performed would be noted as "Other Labor." At the end of the day the time tickets are collected, sorted, and summarized in the form of a *labor summary,* which shows the total direct and indirect labor costs incurred. Direct labor costs are subdivided by job and then posted to job cost sheets.

The proper entry to record the direct labor on job no. 864 and the incurrence of $200 of indirect labor follows.[1]

| | | |
|---|---|---|
| Work in Process | 150 | |
| Factory Overhead | 200 | |
| Wages Payable | | 350 |
| To record direct and indirect labor | | |

Like the cost of direct materials, the cost of direct labor is charged to Work in Process to accumulate the cost of jobs in production. When the employees are paid, Wages Payable will be debited and Cash will be credited.

## Accounting for Overhead

Up to this point the computation of job cost has not been difficult, primarily because of the ease in tracing direct materials and direct labor to individual jobs.

[1] We are ignoring employee withholdings in this example.

We now turn our attention to the third and most complicated element of product cost: factory overhead.

Because of traceability and record-keeping problems, jobs are charged with an estimated (as opposed to actual) overhead cost. The use of estimated overhead charges is not only practical but also has two side benefits. First, total job cost can be figured at the time of job completion. Timely cost information is beneficial in setting prices for customers and in other routine operating decisions that are made by management.

Second, estimated overhead charges tend to smooth product costs over a period of time. Actual costs change each month, and in addition, volume fluctuates. The cost of production is therefore dependent on when manufacturing takes place. As an example, picture the highly seasonal business of a soft drink manufacturer. Fixed production costs remain relatively stable month after month; consequently, when volume peaks in the hot summer months, the actual manufacturing cost per bottle will decrease. This decrease results from spreading constant fixed costs over increased activity levels. In winter when production is lower, the cost per bottle will rise. In an effort to avoid fluctuating overhead charges, estimated rates are set and implemented for a certain period of time, often one year. This practice removes the cost "penalties" and "bonuses" of producing in December and July, respectively, because inventory is costed at the same amount no matter when manufacturing occurs.

OBJECTIVE 3
Be able to compute and use an overhead application rate.

***Overhead Application Rates*** The estimated overhead cost of a job or product is determined by using an **overhead application rate.** The application rate relates overhead to a specific application base and is computed as follows:

$$\frac{\text{Estimated Factory Overhead}}{\text{Estimated Application Base}} = \text{Overhead Application Rate}$$

To explain, product costs must be determined as accurately as possible. Therefore at the beginning of a reporting period, the accountant performs an in-depth study of factory overhead. The accountant is interested in learning how overhead behaves in relation to changes in various factors of production (e.g., direct labor hours, direct labor cost, or machine hours). If a strong correlation exists between factory overhead and, say, direct labor cost, a fairly accurate estimate of overhead can be developed by applying (measuring) overhead on the basis of the labor cost identified with the job or product. In a heavily automated situation where much of the overhead is caused by the operation of machines, machine hours may be appropriate for an application base. In other cases where manual labor predominates, direct labor hours may have a strong relation to overhead.

In general, we select an application base that (1) is inexpensive to compute, (2) is easily traced to the job or product, and (3) has a strong cause and effect relationship with overhead. The last guideline means that the application base should have a significant influence on the amount of overhead incurred, thereby helping to improve accuracy in the estimation process.

***Use of the Overhead Application Rate*** Once the application base is chosen, the overhead rate can be developed and used in product costing. The amount of overhead charged to an individual job is determined by multiplying the application rate by the amount of application base associated with that job. This process is best seen by using a numerical example.

Assume that Valley Manufacturing has chosen direct labor hours as an application base because of the company's heavy emphasis on manual assembly work. After a review of operations, Valley's accountant has predicted 40,000 direct labor hours of activity for the year. In addition, the following factory overhead estimates have been derived:

| | |
|---|---|
| Indirect materials used | $ 20,000 |
| Indirect labor | 140,000 |
| Utilities | 15,000 |
| Taxes | 30,000 |
| Insurance | 10,000 |
| Building depreciation | 40,000 |
| Equipment depreciation | 25,000 |
| Total estimated overhead | $280,000 |

The firm's overhead application rate of $7 per direct labor hour is computed as follows:

$$\frac{\text{Estimated Factory Overhead}}{\text{Estimated Application Base}} = \text{Overhead Application Rate}$$

$$\frac{\$280{,}000}{40{,}000 \text{ direct labor hours}} = \$7 \text{ per direct labor hour}$$

The $7 rate can now be applied to individual jobs to determine the estimated overhead cost. Examine Exhibit 22-4, which contains the completed cost sheet for job no. 864. Compare this exhibit with Exhibit 22-3, and notice that additional material costs (requisition no. 7638) and additional labor costs (tickets no. 1187–89 and no. 2010–11) have been incurred. On the basis of the total of 58 direct labor hours, Valley has applied or estimated an overhead cost of $406 (58 hours × $7).[2] The proper entry to record the applied overhead is:

| | | |
|---|---|---|
| Work in Process | 406 | |
| Factory Overhead | | 406 |
| To record applied overhead | | |

The Work in Process account is debited to add factory overhead to the other two costs of production: direct materials used and direct labor. As a result of the preced-

**▶ TIPS & TECHNIQUES**

Students sometimes reverse the computation of the application rate, dividing the estimated application base by estimated factory overhead. An easy way to remember the proper calculation is to picture the definition of the word "base," namely, the lowest layer or foundation. Translating, the *bottom* number in the formula serves as the *basis* on which a company desires to apply overhead to production.

[2] If desired, overhead could be applied daily as the number of direct labor hours becomes known. If a job is not completed by the end of the accounting period, overhead should be applied on the basis of the work performed to date to properly value the production in process.

JOB COST SHEET

*Manufactured for:* Job No. 864

*Stock* X

*Customer*

*Date:*

*Needed* 8/15

*Started* 8/3

*Completed* 8/5

*Product* Custom lamp no. 38

*No. of Units* 100

| Direct Materials | | | Direct Labor | | | | Factory Overhead | |
|---|---|---|---|---|---|---|---|---|
| Date | Requisition No. | Amount | Date | Ticket No. | Hours | Amount | Date | Amount |
| 8/3 | 7602 | $4,000 | 8/3 | 1146-49 | 28 | $150 | 8/5 | $406 |
| 8/5 | 7638 | 1,050 | 8/4 | 1187-89 | 20 | 120 | | |
| | | $5,050 | 8/5 | 2010-11 | 10 | 54 | | |
| | | | | | 58 | $324 | | |

Overhead Rate: $7 per direct labor hour

COST SUMMARY

| | |
|---|---|
| *Direct materials* | $ 5,050 |
| *Direct labor* | 324 |
| *Factory overhead* | 406 |
| *Total cost* | $ 5,780 |

**Exhibit 22-4**
**Completed Job Cost Sheet**

ing entry, Work in Process now contains all the costs that pertain to job no. 864. The credit to the Factory Overhead account takes an estimated portion of Valley's total overhead and applies it to specific jobs—a process that should become clearer after the next two sections.

***Actual Overhead*** The Factory Overhead account is used to accumulate both actual and applied overhead. As was shown earlier, for example, Factory Overhead is debited to record indirect materials used and indirect labor. Other actual overhead items are recorded in this account as well. To illustrate, assume that Valley Manufacturing experienced the following factory costs during August:

| | |
|---|---|
| Utilities | $ 1,300 |
| Taxes | 2,500 |
| Insurance | 900 |
| Building depreciation | 3,500 |
| Equipment depreciation | 2,200 |
| Total | $10,400 |

Further assume that payments for utilities and taxes are not due until September and that the insurance figure represents the expiration of a prepaid policy. Valley's required journal entry to record these overhead costs is:

| | | |
|---|---|---|
| Factory Overhead | 10,400 | |
| Accounts Payable | | 1,300 |
| Taxes Payable | | 2,500 |
| Prepaid Insurance | | 900 |
| Accumulated Depreciation: Building | | 3,500 |
| Accumulated Depreciation: Equipment | | 2,200 |
| To record actual overhead costs | | |

The entry's credits should be familiar; they are identical to those shown in the first part of the text. The expiration of a prepaid expense calls for a reduction in an asset account; recording depreciation generates a credit to Accumulated Depreciation; and so forth. The debit, however, is different. In earlier chapters all these costs were charged to expense accounts. Now, no expenses are involved and the costs are debited to Factory Overhead. Why? The change in procedure is caused by a change in business purpose. These costs are not expenses for a manufacturing entity; rather they are product costs, which must be attached to the units produced. This attachment takes place via the application of factory overhead discussed earlier.

Only *factory* costs are recorded in the overhead account. Selling and administrative costs such as advertising, managerial salaries, and sales commissions continue to be written off as expenses. Remember, these costs are period costs and, as such, never inventoried.

***Applied Overhead*** The accumulation of actual overhead throughout the period and the application of overhead to jobs force the Factory Overhead account to assume the following status:

| | *Factory Overhead* | | |
|---|---|---|---|
| Actual overhead costs are recorded by debits as incurred | XXX<br>XXX<br>XXX | XXX<br>XXX<br>XXX | Overhead is applied to jobs during the period via credits |

It should be apparent that the application process simply takes a "chunk" of overhead and attaches it to production. By the end of the reporting period, if all goes according to plan, overhead applied will equal total overhead incurred. This situation rarely occurs, however, and a later section of the chapter will show the proper accounting treatment for such cases.

## Accounting for the Completion and Sale of Manufactured Products

By viewing Exhibit 22-5, you can see the interrelationships among the journal entries illustrated in the preceding sections, the job cost sheet, and Valley's Work in Process account. In practice, separate entries would be made on August 3, 4, and 5 to record the individual transactions.

Upon completion, jobs are transferred to the finished goods warehouse to await sale. Paralleling this physical transfer, Valley would record the following entry to recognize the completion of production:

| | | |
|---|---|---|
| Finished Goods | 5,780 | |
| Work in Process | | 5,780 |
| Completed job no. 864 | | |

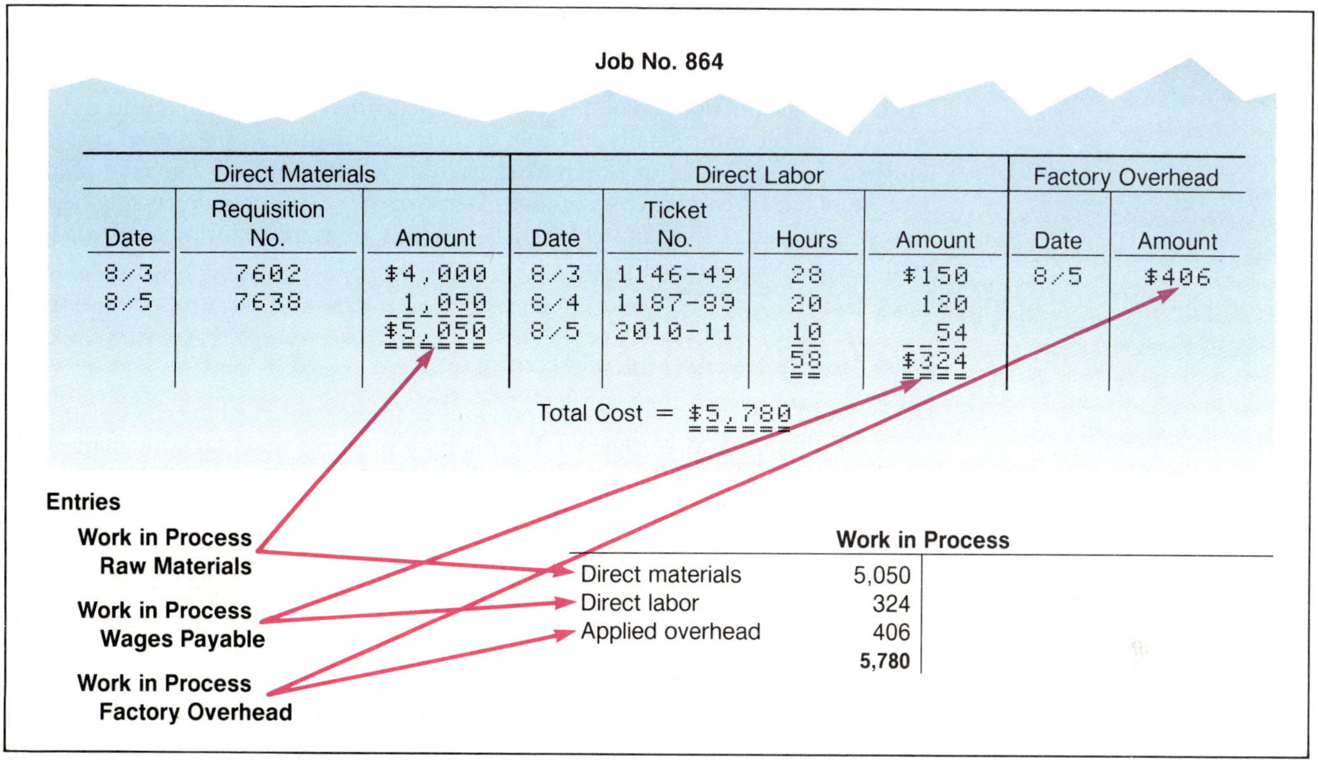


**Exhibit 22-5 Interrelationships Among Manufacturing Journal Entries, the Job Cost Sheet, and the Work in Process Account**

Eventually, the finished goods inventory will be sold. Suppose, for example, that 25 of the 100 lamps manufactured on job no. 864 are sold on account at $80 apiece. From information found on the job cost sheet, the cost per lamp is $57.80 ($5,780 ÷ 100 lamps). Thus, two entries are needed:

| | | |
|---|---|---|
| Cost of Goods Sold | 1,445 | |
| Finished Goods | | 1,445 |
| To record the cost of lamps sold | | |
| Accounts Receivable | 2,000 | |
| Sales | | 2,000 |
| To record sale on account | | |

The first entry transfers the production cost of the 25 lamps sold ($57.80 × 25 = $1,445) from Finished Goods to the Cost of Goods Sold account. The second entry places the sales revenues generated ($80 × 25 = $2,000) in the accounting records. As noted at the beginning of this example, Valley Manufacturing uses a perpetual inventory system. Should you need a review of inventory systems, we refer you to Chapter 9.

## A Recap

The sale of finished production completes the flow of manufacturing costs through the accounting system. Please reexamine the bottom half of Exhibit 22-2. Notice that material, labor, and overhead costs all begin in their own accounts. Indirect materials used and indirect labor are recognized as overhead and transferred to Factory Overhead to join other miscellaneous production costs. Direct materials used, direct labor, and factory overhead applied are then charged to Work in Process. As production is completed, manufacturing costs are debited to the Finished Goods account. Finally, the sale of inventory requires a transfer of cost from Finished Goods to Cost of Goods Sold. Although variations are found in practice because of added complexities of manufacturing (e.g., multiple processing departments), Exhibit 22-2 accurately depicts the flow of manufacturing costs for both small firms and industrial giants.

## Work in Process: A Control Account

The Work in Process account in the previous example contained the costs of job no. 864 until the job was completed. Normally, a business manufactures many jobs simultaneously and is unable to finish all production by the end of the accounting period. To handle the necessary record keeping, Work in Process assumes the role of a control account and is supported by individual job cost sheets.

To illustrate, assume that Avanti Corporation had job no. 614 in process on January 1. Information relating to job no. 614 follows.

| | |
|---|---|
| Direct materials used | $ 5,500 |
| Direct labor | 8,000 |
| Factory overhead applied, 150% of direct labor | 12,000 |
| | $25,500 |

Manufacturing activity that took place during the year is shown in Exhibit 22-6.

Avanti's Work in Process account and summary journal entries appear in Exhibit 22-7. Observe that the cost of completed jobs (no. 614 and no. 615) has been removed from Work in Process and transferred to Finished Goods. Jobs no. 616 and no. 617 are still in production; thus, the $89,000 ending Work in Process balance coincides with the total of these two jobs' cost sheets ($65,000 + $24,000 = $89,000). The Work in Process and job cost sheet relationship is an example of the control account/subsidiary ledger arrangement discussed in Chapter 6. Recall

**Exhibit 22-6**
**Avanti Corporation Manufacturing Activity**

| | *Job No. 614* | *Job No. 615* | *Job No. 616* | *Job No. 617* | *Total* |
|---|---|---|---|---|---|
| Direct materials used | $ — | $ 9,000 | $20,000 | $ 4,000 | $ 33,000 |
| Direct labor | 5,000 | 10,000 | 18,000 | 8,000 | 41,000 |
| Factory overhead applied, 150% of direct labor | 7,500 | 15,000 | 27,000 | 12,000 | 61,500 |
| Total | $12,500 | $34,000 | $65,000 | $24,000 | $135,500 |
| Job status, Dec. 31 | Completed | Completed and sold | In process | In process | |

**Exhibit 22-7**
**Work in Process Control Account of Avanti Corporation**

| *Work in Process* | | | |
|---|---|---|---|
| Beginning balance (no. 614) | 25,500 | Completed job (no. 614) | 38,000* |
| Direct materials | 33,000 | Completed job (no. 615) | 34,000 |
| Direct labor | 41,000 | | **72,000** |
| Overhead applied | 61,500 | | |
| (**89,000**) | **161,000** | | |

* $25,500 + $12,500 = $38,000.

***Entries***

| | | |
|---|---|---|
| Work in Process | 33,000 | |
| Raw Materials | | 33,000 |
| Work in Process | 41,000 | |
| Wages Payable | | 41,000 |
| Work in Process | 61,500 | |
| Factory Overhead | | 61,500 |

| *Cost Sheet—Job No. 616* | |
|---|---|
| Direct materials | $20,000 |
| Direct labor | 18,000 |
| Overhead applied | 27,000 |
| | $65,000 |

| *Cost Sheet—Job No. 617* | |
|---|---|
| Direct materials | $ 4,000 |
| Direct labor | 8,000 |
| Overhead applied | 12,000 |
| | $24,000 |

that a control account (Work in Process) appears in the general ledger and is composed of various lower-level accounts. The lower-level accounts (in this case, job cost sheets) that support a control account are collectively known as a subsidiary ledger.

## A Further Probe of Overhead

OBJECTIVE 4
Be able to account for over- or underapplied overhead at the end of the accounting period.

At the end of an accounting period it is unlikely that the overhead applied to production will equal the actual overhead incurred. The application rate that is used to charge overhead to jobs and products is based on two estimates: estimated overhead and an estimated application base. Unexpected price changes from suppliers, variations in production levels, and increases and decreases in plant efficiency all cause actual experience to differ from amounts originally forecast.

Overhead can be either overapplied or underapplied. If, for example, a company applied $74,000 of overhead but actually incurred $68,000, overhead is said to be **overapplied** by $6,000. If the situation was reversed, overhead would be **underapplied.** To examine the implications of over- and underapplication, we will continue the Avanti Corporation example.

Avanti has been applying overhead to jobs at the rate of 150% of direct labor cost. The rate was computed by taking the year's forecasted factory overhead and direct labor costs, $60,000 and $40,000, respectively, and performing the following calculation:

$$\text{Application Rate} = \frac{\text{Estimated Factory Overhead}}{\text{Estimated Application Base}} = \frac{\$60,000}{\$40,000} = 150\%$$

The 150% rate says that for every $1.00 of direct labor expected to be incurred, the firm anticipates $1.50 of factory overhead.

Throughout the accounting period Avanti applied $61,500 of overhead to jobs no. 614–617 (see Exhibit 22-6). If we assume that actual overhead incurred amounted to $65,000, overhead would be underapplied by $3,500:

| | |
|---|---|
| Actual overhead | $65,000 |
| Applied overhead | |
| Direct labor cost × 150% ($41,000 × 150%) | 61,500 |
| Underapplied overhead | $ 3,500 |

Exhibit 22-8 depicts the entire process in pictorial form.

## Effects of Over- and Underapplied Overhead

Avanti's underapplication means that insufficient overhead has been charged to the Work in Process account. Unfortunately, the problem does not stop here, because each job produced during the period has been costed incorrectly. From the job status that appears in Exhibit 22-6, jobs no. 616 and no. 617 are still in process (Work in Process), job no. 614 has been completed but is still on hand (Finished Goods), and job no. 615 has been sold (Cost of Goods Sold). Because of the understated application rate, the ending balances in these three accounts are un-

**Exhibit 22-8 Application of Factory Overhead for Avanti Corporation**

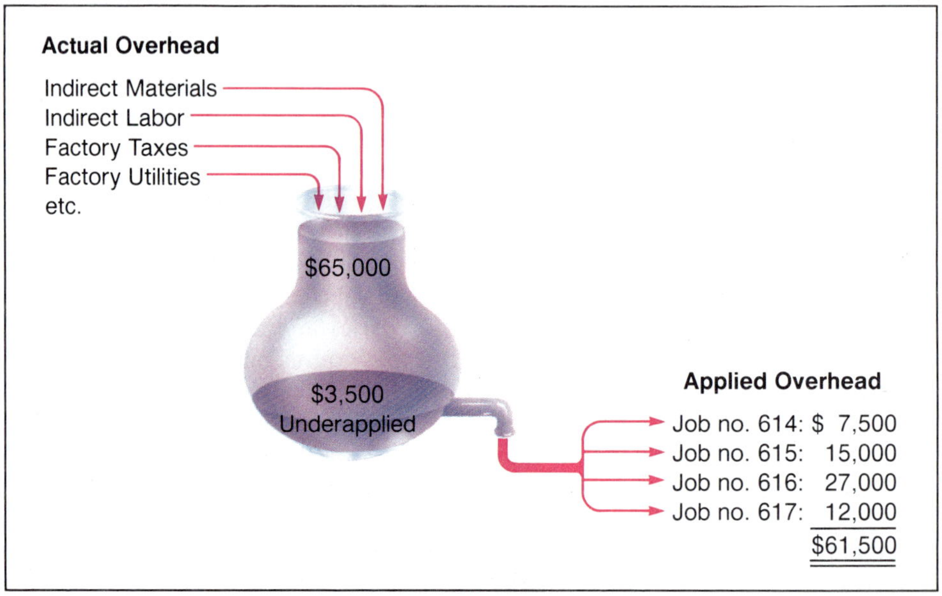

derstated as well. Thus, an adjusting entry is needed upon conclusion of the reporting period.

The adjusting entry first considers the status of the Factory Overhead account. In Avanti's case the account appears as follows:

| *Factory Overhead* | |
|---|---|
| Actual | Applied |
| 65,000 | 61,500 |

The overhead account must be closed so the company can start anew, accumulating costs for the next period's production activities. Thus, Factory Overhead is credited for $3,500. The $3,500 debit can either be (1) allocated to Work in Process, Finished Goods, and Cost of Goods Sold on some equitable basis or (2) charged entirely to Cost of Goods Sold.

The first approach, which raises each account's balance to counteract the understatement, is theoretically correct. However, because the balances in the three accounts cited consist of the costs of individual jobs, each job cost sheet must be adjusted as well. Avanti had only four jobs; in a more realistic environment, the amount of bookkeeping required could be overwhelming. Consequently, the allocation approach is only used when the amount of over- or underapplied overhead is so great that a lack of proration will result in misleading financial statements.

The second method, charging the entire $3,500 to Cost of Goods Sold, is the more popular approach. The necessary journal entry follows.

| | | |
|---|---|---|
| Cost of Goods Sold | 3,500 | |
| Factory Overhead | | 3,500 |
| To adjust cost of goods sold for underapplied overhead | | |

The entry raises Cost of Goods Sold to $37,500 ($34,000 from job no. 615 + $3,500), and this amount is reported on Avanti's income statement.

The procedures illustrated are reversed for overapplied overhead.

## The New Manufacturing Environment

Earlier in the chapter we noted that the application base selected should have a strong cause and effect relationship with overhead. Labor hours or labor cost may be appropriate in a setting where there is considerable manual assembly work to complete a product; hospital beds occupied may explain a large portion of the overhead incurred at a health care facility; a company's building maintenance costs may be tied to square footage; and so forth. These application bases are said to be **cost drivers,** or factors that cause specific costs to be incurred within an organization.

Companies naturally have a wide selection of application bases to choose from, with some bases being better than others. If an improper base is selected—one that fails to cause (i.e., drive) overhead costs—the outcome will be questionable overhead application rates. Such rates typically result in distorted product costs, inventory valuations, and income measurements, perhaps leading to erroneous decisions on the part of management.

Surveys of manufacturers' accounting practices have found (and continue to find) that direct labor is one of the most popular, if not *the* most popular, application base for factory overhead. This finding is interesting, especially when one considers the dramatic change in cost drivers over the years. Factory workers are continually being replaced by robots and computer-controlled machines, as companies strive to trim costs and improve product quality. As a result of heavily automated facilities, it is not uncommon for overhead (which includes equipment depreciation and operating costs) to account for more than half of all production costs. Direct labor, on the other hand, which may have comprised 40% of manufacturing costs as recently as 25 years ago, frequently amounts to no more than 5% today.[3]

The declining labor component, coupled with increasing overhead charges, has led some businesses to experience application rates in excess of 1,000% of direct labor. Although direct labor is an appropriate cost driver in some situations, it certainly is not in all. Many firms' cost accounting systems are obsolete and in need of change, especially in light of increased competition. Accurate cost information is often the deciding factor in gaining the strongly pursued and eagerly awaited competitive advantage.

## Job Costing: Service Applications

OBJECTIVE 5
Understand the applicability of job costing systems in service organizations.

Thus far, most of our discussion has dealt with a production-type setting, perhaps leaving you with the impression that job costing systems are used almost exclusively by manufacturing organizations. This is not the case, as cost accumulation by job is popular in the service sector of our economy as well. Such systems are used to determine the cost of:

- Servicing clients by accountants, financial planners, management consultants, architects, and lawyers.
- Providing patient care by hospitals.
- Implementing drug abuse programs by social service agencies.
- Beginning new flights to vacation resort areas by airlines.

In the preceding examples the "job" becomes the client, patient, program, and flight segment, respectively.

Job cost information is used in several of these cases for setting prices, which, of course, affect profitability. Even for those organizations that operate without a profit motive (e.g., colleges and universities, charitable organizations, and so forth), job cost input assists managers when planning, controlling operations, and allocating resources among competing programs.

### Direct and Indirect Costs

Job costing in service entities revolves around the proper handling of direct and indirect costs. **Direct costs,** or those easily traced to a job, are charged to the individual jobs that are worked on during the accounting period. In contrast, **indirect costs** (those not easily traced) are treated as general overhead and applied in the same manner as factory overhead for a manufacturer.[4]

[3] For an enlightening article on the new manufacturing technology, see "Accounting Bores You? Wake Up," *Fortune,* October 12, 1987, pp. 43–44, 48, 52–53.

[4] These definitions will be expanded somewhat in Chapter 27.

## HIGHLIGHT

# Flight Costing by Airlines

The accumulation of material, labor, and overhead charges by job is an important function for many companies engaged in manufacturing activities. The techniques illustrated in the text can, with some modification, be used by airlines in figuring the cost of given flight segments.

Stop to think about the various tasks that are performed to transport a paying passenger from city A to city B. A reservation must be made; tickets are produced; the plane is serviced; the flight is made; and baggage is handled. These are only a few of the necessary steps to successfully serve the public. Although service (as opposed to manufacturing) in orientation, an airline needs feedback regarding the profitability of its flight operations—not only in total but on specific flights as well. Enter job order costing, as shown by the following example. (*Note:* Numbers are assumed and estimates.)

Suppose an airline offers transcontinental service from New York to Los Angeles with a 70%-full Boeing 747. Flying time of approximately six hours is necessary to cover the 2,475 statute miles. How much does it cost to put the jumbo jet in the sky and complete the journey? The categories below provide some insight, with the breakdowns varying considerably from the material, labor, and overhead classifications of a manufacturer.

| | |
|---|---|
| Hourly related charges (cockpit and cabin crew, fuel, engine maintenance) | $21,500 |
| Departure related charges (airframe maintenance and servicing, ground facilities maintenance, landing fees, ticket collection) | 3,700 |
| Costs per passenger boarded (reservations and ticketing, baggage handling) | 2,100 |
| Costs per passenger mile (commissions to travel agents, food, passenger inconvenience cost—baggage loss, denied boarding compensation) | 7,500 |
| Costs per ton (cargo handling) | 700 |
| Cost per plane mile (general overhead) | 4,700 |
| Ownership cost per aircraft day (depreciation and hull insurance) | 3,500 |
| Total flight segment cost | $43,700 |

Costs are traced to specific flight segments (i.e., jobs). Interestingly, observe the variety of costing bases that are employed—flight hours, days, number of passengers, number of departures, and so forth. The various bases (cost drivers) are needed for accuracy and attempt to charge each flight with the approximate amount of cost incurred. Why, for example, would airlines charge some maintenance cost on the number of departures and other maintenance costs on time? A landing gear is employed during takeoff and arrival; wear and tear is totally unrelated to flight time. Engine use, on the other hand, obviously varies with aircraft utilization.

Job cost provides significant insights for management for purposes of planning, control, decision making, and evaluation of performance. The next time that airfares seem too high or that nonstop flights are unavailable to your destination, realize that cost data may be the underlying reason. The airline in question has probably gathered costs by flight and made a sound business decision on the basis of the facts presented.

*Authors' note:* Factors other than cost will influence airfares and schedules, for example, the level of competition, season, and time of day.

SOURCE: Adapted from information given to the authors by William Barzelay, Flight Department, American Airlines, Dallas–Fort Worth Airport, Texas.

A review of job costing systems and procedures over the years will find an increased attempt by service entities to have more of their costs fall in the direct category. This practice, which is now more easily accomplished because of computers and available software, helps satisfy client inquiries concerning fee composition. This is an important consideration, especially in a highly competitive business environment. Further, added accuracy in costing is generally achieved.

## An Illustration

Given the distinction between direct and indirect costs, we now focus on the operations of InfoNet, a consulting firm that specializes in the design of management information systems. A portion of InfoNet's budget for 19X3 follows.

| | | |
|---|---|---|
| Revenue from billings | | $10,500,000 |
| Less direct costs | | |
| Professional staff time | $4,000,000 | |
| Computer charges | 2,600,000 | |
| Long-distance charges | 350,000 | |
| Overnight delivery | 50,000 | 7,000,000 |
| | | $ 3,500,000 |
| Less indirect costs (rent, utilities, other nontraceable items) | | 2,100,000 |
| Operating income | | $ 1,400,000 |

The company's accountants and management feel that total direct costs is the most appropriate base to charge overhead (i.e., indirect costs) to client jobs. Accordingly, a 30% application rate was developed:

$$\text{Application Rate} = \frac{\text{Estimated Overhead}}{\text{Estimated Application Base}}$$

$$= \frac{\$2{,}100{,}000}{\$7{,}000{,}000}$$

$$= 30\%$$

In March, InfoNet completed a consulting job for Oregon Department Stores. The job cost sheet for this engagement is shown in Exhibit 22-9. Directly traceable costs total $30,000 and are charged to the Oregon engagement. In addition, $9,000 ($30,000 × 0.30) of overhead is applied to the job, bringing the total cost to $39,000.

## Client Billings

Notice that the last two lines of the client's cost sheet are left blank. If desired, InfoNet could compute a target income amount that management wishes to earn on each job. The target is set so the company can proceed toward attaining its overall operating income goal of $1,400,000. The job's income and costs are eventually combined to yield the amount that InfoNet must bill the client.

For example, InfoNet's original budget reveals estimated operating income and direct costs of $1,400,000 and $7,000,000, respectively. If each job is anticipated to produce the same rate of profit for the company, an income computation rate could

**Exhibit 22-9**
**Job Cost Sheet for a Service Business**

JOB COST SHEET

*Client* Oregon Department Stores
Portland, Oregon

*Job No.* 165

*Engagement* Design of marketing retrieval system

*Date:*
*Started* 1/10/X3
*Completed* 3/29/X3

| | |
|---|---|
| Direct costs: | |
| Professional staff time | $ 19,000 |
| Computer charges | 10,500 |
| Long-distance charges | 400 |
| Overnight delivery | 100 |
| Total | $ 30,000 |
| General overhead (30% of total direct costs) | 9,000 |
| Total cost of engagement | $ 39,000 |
| Target income (___% of total direct costs) | $ |
| Client billing | $ |

be developed in a manner similar to that shown for an overhead application rate, namely:

$$\text{Income Computation Rate} = \frac{\text{Estimated Income}}{\text{Estimated Application Base}}$$

$$= \frac{\$1{,}400{,}000}{\$7{,}000{,}000}$$

$$= 20\%$$

InfoNet desires that the Oregon job earn \$6,000 (\$30,000 × 0.20), meaning that the amount billed must equal \$45,000 (\$39,000 + \$6,000). Stated differently, if revenues from the job are \$45,000 and costs amount to \$39,000, the Oregon engagement will contribute \$6,000 toward InfoNet's 19X3 total operating income.

## Chapter Review

### Learning Objectives—The Key Points

**1 Be familiar with the problem of determining the actual cost of a product or service.** The actual cost of a good or service is usually very difficult to compute. Various estimates and assumptions are used in accounting, which introduces imprecision into the costing process. Further, many costs (e.g., factory overhead, corporate administration, and so forth) are not easily traced to finished products, departments, and divisions.

**2 Understand the use and operation of job order costing systems.** Job costing systems are used in environments where it is relatively easy to classify costs by job or order. This situation often arises when goods are manufactured upon the receipt of a customer's order, according to customer specifications, or in separate batches. The costs of direct materials used, direct labor, and factory overhead applied are all accumulated on a job cost sheet. These costs are charged to the Work in Process account. Upon job completion the costs are transferred to Finished Goods inventory and, at the time of sale, to Cost of Goods Sold.

**3 Be able to compute and use an overhead application rate.** Because of the difficulty and/or cost of tracing factory overhead to a manufactured product, it becomes necessary to apply (i.e., estimate) overhead for inventory costing purposes. An application rate is developed by dividing a company's estimated factory overhead by an estimated application base. The rate is then multiplied by the amount of the application base associated with the job in question. Overhead bases should be relatively inexpensive to compute, easily traced to the product, and have a strong bearing (i.e., be a cost driver) on the amount of overhead actually incurred.

**4 Be able to account for over- or underapplied overhead at the end of the accounting period.** Overhead is applied in the manner just described under learning objective no. 3. The required journal entry involves a debit to the Work in Process account and a credit to Factory Overhead. The Factory Overhead account is also used to accumulate (on the debit side) the actual overhead incurred by the company. At the end of the reporting period, the amount of over- or underapplication is computed as the difference between actual overhead and applied overhead. Over- or underapplied amounts are most commonly adjusted against the Cost of Goods Sold account or, if significant, allocated among Work in Process, Finished Goods, and Cost of Goods Sold.

**5 Understand the applicability of job costing in service organizations.** Job costing systems can be used by service enterprises to accumulate the costs of rendering a service. The "job" may consist of providing consulting services to a client, repair services to a customer, health care services to a patient, and so forth. Direct costs (those easily traced to a client job) are charged to the job cost sheet. Indirect costs, or those not easily traced, are treated as overhead and applied in a manner similar to that for factory overhead.

## Chapter Quiz

The five questions that follow relate to several issues raised in the chapter. Test your knowledge of the issues by selecting the best answer. (The answers appear on p. 826.)

**1** Which of the following businesses would be least likely to use a job costing system?
- a Automobile repair shop.
- b Custom home builder.
- c Crude oil refinery.
- d Motion picture producer.

**2** The journal entry to record the use of indirect materials in production activities is:
- a debit Work in Process; credit Raw Materials.
- b debit Factory Overhead; credit Raw Materials.
- c debit Raw Materials; credit Work in Process.
- d debit Work in Process; credit Factory Overhead.

**3** Direct materials, direct labor, and factory overhead applied are initially brought together in which of the following accounts?
- a Work in Process.
- b Finished Goods.
- c Cost of Goods Sold.
- d Income Summary.

**4** SRT, Inc., applies factory overhead on the basis of direct labor cost. The company's accountant has forecast $180,000 of factory overhead and $200,000 of direct labor for 19X5. Actual factory overhead and direct labor for 19X5 amounted to $185,000 and $210,000, respectively. Overhead for 19X5 is:
- a underapplied by $4,000.
- b underapplied by $9,000.
- c overapplied by $4,000.
- d overapplied by $9,000.

**5** In today's modern manufacturing environment, many companies:
  a are experiencing a decrease in overhead application rates.
  b are experiencing a decrease in factory overhead and an increase in direct labor cost.
  c can ignore cost drivers because of a recent pronouncement from the Financial Accounting Standards Board.
  d have a labor component that may be as low as 5% of total product cost.

## Summary Problem

Riverdale Manufacturing Company uses a job order system to accumulate production costs. The firm, which applies overhead on the basis of direct labor hours, derived the following estimates for 19X3 manufacturing activity:

- Estimated direct labor hours: 45,000
- Estimated factory overhead: $180,000

Selected data applicable to January 19X3 follow.

- January 1 balance of work in process: $19,000
- Direct materials used: $60,000
- Direct labor incurred (3,500 hours): $28,000
- Indirect materials used: $3,900
- Indirect labor incurred: $7,600
- Factory utilities: $1,000
- Equipment depreciation: $2,000
- Cost of goods completed: $94,500

### Instructions

**a** Determine Riverdale's overhead application rate.

**b** Calculate the amount of overhead applied to production during January.

**c** Present entries to record (1) direct materials used, (2) direct labor incurred, (3) factory overhead incurred, (4) factory overhead applied to production, and (5) cost of goods completed during the month.

**d** Determine the cost of the company's work in process inventory on January 31.

**e** Determine the amount of over- or underapplied overhead during January.

### Solution

**a** $$\text{Overhead Application Rate} = \frac{\text{Estimated Factory Overhead}}{\text{Estimated Application Base}} = \frac{\$180{,}000}{45{,}000 \text{ hours}} = \$4 \text{ per direct labor hour}$$

**b** Overhead applied: 3,500 hours × $4 = $14,000

**c**

| | | Debit | Credit |
|---|---|---|---|
| (1) | Work in Process | 60,000 | |
| | Raw Materials | | 60,000 |
| | Issued direct materials to production | | |
| (2) | Work in Process | 28,000 | |
| | Wages Payable | | 28,000 |
| | To record direct labor incurred | | |

| | | Debit | Credit |
|---|---|---|---|
| (3) | Factory Overhead | 14,500 | |
| | Raw Materials | | 3,900 |
| | Wages Payable | | 7,600 |
| | Accounts Payable | | 1,000 |
| | Accumulated Depreciation: Equipment | | 2,000 |
| | To record actual factory overhead costs | | |
| (4) | Work in Process | 14,000 | |
| | Factory Overhead | | 14,000 |
| | To record applied overhead [see part (b)] | | |
| (5) | Finished Goods | 94,500 | |
| | Work in Process | | 94,500 |
| | To transfer completed units to finished goods | | |

**d** Riverdale's ending work in process inventory is $26,500, as shown by the following T-account:

***Work in Process***

| | | | |
|---|---|---|---|
| Balance | 19,000 | (5) | 94,500 |
| (1) | 60,000 | | |
| (2) | 28,000 | | |
| (4) | 14,000 | | |
| | **121,000** | | |
| | **26,500** | | |

**e** Overhead is underapplied by $500.

| | |
|---|---|
| Overhead incurred | $14,500 |
| Overhead applied | 14,000 |
| Underapplied overhead | $ 500 |

## Questions

**Q22-1** Discuss the general features associated with a job order costing system. In what types of applications are job order systems used?

**Q22-2** What is the purpose of using job cost sheets?

**Q22-3** Explain how the flow of costs through an accounting system parallels the flow of goods and materials through a manufacturing plant.

**Q22-4** Contrast the proper accounting treatments of direct materials and indirect materials.

**Q22-5** How does the use of a predetermined overhead rate smooth product costs over a period of time?

**Q22-6** Explain how an overhead application rate is developed and used to apply overhead to specific jobs.

**Q22-7** List the characteristics of a good overhead application base.

**Q22-8** Ritten Company's factory depreciation for the year just ended totaled $40,000 and was recorded as follows:

| | | |
|---|---|---|
| Depreciation Expense | 40,000 | |
| Accumulated Depreciation: Factory | | 40,000 |

Comment on the appropriateness of the preceding journal entry.

**Q22-9** Discuss the relationship between the Work in Process account and individual job cost sheets.

**Q22-10** If overhead is overapplied, will the Factory Overhead account possess a debit or credit balance? What is the probable effect of the overapplication on the Work in Process balance (before adjustment) at the end of the accounting period?

**Q22-11** What is a cost driver?

**Q22-12** What is probably the most popular application base for overhead? Can this base be criticized in light of today's manufacturing environment? Briefly explain.

**Q22-13** List several possible applications of job costing systems by service enterprises.

**Q22-14** Distinguish between a direct cost and an indirect cost.

## Exercises

**E22-1** ***Manufacturing journal entries***

The following selected transactions and events occurred at Pipeline Manufacturing during March:

| | | |
|---|---|---|
| Mar. | 3 | Purchased $10,000 of direct materials and $7,300 of indirect materials on account from Sunbelt Distributors. |
| | 7 | Issued $3,100 of direct materials and $700 of indirect materials from the storeroom. |
| | 14 | Incurred $5,600 of direct labor and $3,400 of indirect labor. |
| | 17 | Recorded $1,300 of overhead incurred on account. |
| | 20 | Applied $2,800 of overhead to production. |
| | 23 | Noted that $6,200 of production had been completed. |
| | 26 | Sold goods on account at a profit of 30% of cost. The goods cost $5,000. |

Prepare journal entries to record the preceding transactions and events.

**E22-2** ***Cost flows and overhead application***

Cleveland Metals uses a job order cost system and applies factory overhead to production at a predetermined rate of 180% of direct labor cost. Data pertaining to recent operations follow.

- Job 636 was the only job in process on January 1 of the current year. The Work in Process account contained a $24,600 balance on this date.
- Jobs 637, 638, and 639 were started during January.
- Total direct material requisitions and direct labor incurred during January amounted to $89,200 and $114,500, respectively.
- The only job that remained in process on January 31 was job 638, with costs of $15,000 for direct materials and $20,000 for direct labor.

a Compute the total cost of the work in process inventory on January 31.

b Compute the cost of jobs completed during January, and present the proper journal entry to reflect job completion.

**E22-3** ***Job costing and overhead application***

Horizon Unlimited applies overhead on the basis of direct labor cost. In December 19X1, the company's cost accountant made the following predictions for 19X2 operations: direct labor cost, $450,000; factory overhead, $585,000.

Horizon worked on jobs no. 109 and no. 110 in January. The costs incurred and production status of these two jobs appear in the table that follows.

| | Job No. 109 | Job No. 110 |
|---|---|---|
| Direct materials | $17,000 | $23,000 |
| Direct labor | 12,000 | 15,000 |
| Production status | In process | In process |

By the end of 19X2, actual direct labor cost amounted to $440,000, and factory overhead incurred totaled $580,000. There was no work in process on January 1, 19X2.

Compute the following:

a Horizon's overhead application rate.

b The balance of the Work in Process account on January 31, 19X2.

c The amount of over- or underapplied overhead for 19X2. Be sure to indicate whether overhead was overapplied or underapplied.

**E22-4** ***Job costing and overhead application***

Oxford Enterprises uses a job costing system to accumulate manufacturing costs. Overhead is applied to products on the basis of machine hours in the machining department and direct labor cost in the assembly department. The following estimates pertain to 19X4:

| | Machining | Assembly |
|---|---|---|
| Machine hours | 40,000 | 5,000 |
| Direct labor cost | $270,000 | $800,000 |
| Factory overhead | 810,000 | 960,000 |

Job no. 328 was the only job in process at the end of 19X4. Its cost sheet revealed the data that follow.

| | Machining | Assembly |
|---|---|---|
| Machine hours | 100 | 10 |
| Direct labor cost | $1,100 | $3,500 |
| Direct materials cost | 1,900 | 3,400 |

a Compute Oxford's overhead application rates in the machining department and the assembly department.

b Calculate the total amount of overhead applied to job no. 328.

c Determine the total cost of job no. 328.

**E22-5** ***Overview of job costing and overhead application***

Evaluate the comments that follow as being True or False. If the comment is false, briefly explain why.

a A materials requisition forms the basis for the following journal entry: Debit Work in Process; Credit Raw Materials.

b The Work in Process account normally contains the following costs for the jobs in production at year-end: direct materials used, direct labor, and actual factory overhead.

c Direct labor cost is a good overhead application base to use if a company is highly automated.

d The amount of over- or underapplied overhead at year-end is normally closed to the Work in Process account.

e An overhead application rate is derived by the following computation: estimated factory overhead divided by an estimated application base.

**E22-6** ***Overhead identification and application***

Missouri City uses a predetermined factory overhead rate to apply overhead to jobs throughout the year. Overhead is applied by using a base of direct labor cost. The following information pertains to the current year:

| | |
|---|---:|
| Estimated direct labor cost for the year | $ 800,000 |
| Estimated total factory overhead for the year | 1,000,000 |
| Actual direct materials used | 550,000 |
| Actual direct labor cost for the year | 830,000 |
| Actual indirect materials used | 90,000 |
| Actual indirect labor incurred | 220,000 |
| Actual company administrative expenses | 190,000 |
| Actual factory depreciation | 140,000 |
| Actual factory utilities | 150,000 |
| Actual factory taxes | 70,000 |
| Other actual factory overhead costs | 350,000 |
| Actual selling costs | 40,000 |

a Determine the factory overhead application rate that was used during the year.
b Compute the amount of under- or overapplied overhead for the year. Be sure to label your answer as either underapplied or overapplied.

**E22-7** ***Overhead application: Working backward***

The Towson Manufacturing Corporation applies overhead on the basis of machine hours. The following divisional information is presented for your review:

| | *Division A* | *Division B* |
|---|---:|---:|
| Actual machine hours | 22,500 | ? |
| Estimated machine hours | 20,000 | ? |
| Overhead application rate | $4.50 | $5.00 |
| Actual overhead | $110,000 | ? |
| Estimated overhead | ? | $90,000 |
| Applied overhead | ? | $86,000 |
| Over- (under-) applied overhead | ? | $6,500 |

Find the unknowns for each of the divisions.

**E22-8** ***Direct costs and indirect costs***

Executive Airlines is studying whether to begin flight service from Chicago to St. Louis. Identify the following costs as a direct cost or an indirect cost of the Chicago/St. Louis flight segment, assuming the route would be serviced by aircraft that would continue to be flown throughout Executive's extensive route system:

a Passenger beverage service
b Airport landing fees
c Monthly engine maintenance service
d Fuel consumed
e Commissions paid to travel agents on tickets sold
f Salary of Executive's director of route planning

## Problems

### Series A

**P22-A1** ***Preparation of job cost sheet and journal entries***

Provo, Inc., manufactures items that are used in the electronics industry. The company, which uses a job costing system, has two departments: machining and finishing. The machining department applies overhead to products at the rate of $15 per machine hour; finishing, on the other hand, uses an application rate of 250% of direct labor cost.

On March 19, 19X3, Provo received an order from Sensormatic for 225 photons, model no. 116. Production began immediately, and the order (known as job no. 4155) was completed on March 31. Paperwork supporting the order revealed the following:

| *Document** | *Date* | *Department* | *Hours* | *Amount* |
|---|---|---|---|---|
| MR 1165 | 3/19 | Machining | — | $5,600 |
| MR 1169 | 3/21 | Machining | — | 3,500 |
| TT 1450-52 | 3/23 | Machining | 45 | 400 |
| MUR 46 | 3/23 | Machining | 105 | — |
| MR 4330 | 3/27 | Finishing | — | 700 |
| TT 1475-76 | 3/31 | Machining | 30 | 300 |
| MUR 47 | 3/31 | Machining | 50 | — |
| TT 6608-13 | 3/31 | Finishing | 200 | 2,000 |

* MR = materials requisition; TT = time ticket; MUR = machine usage report

Various factory supplies (cost = $12) were used in manufacturing the Sensormatic order. Provo accounts for such supplies as indirect materials.

**Instructions**

a Prepare a job cost sheet for the Sensormatic order as of March 31. Use the following column headings:

| | *Direct Materials* | | *Direct Labor* | | | *Machine Usage* | | *Factory Overhead* |
|---|---|---|---|---|---|---|---|---|
| *Date* | *Requisition* | *Amount* | *Ticket* | *Hours* | *Amount* | *Report* | *Hours* | *Amount* |

b Prepare journal entries to record (1) the issuance of direct materials, (2) direct labor incurred on the order, (3) the application of factory overhead, and (4) the issuance of factory supplies. All materials requisitions should be combined in one entry, all time tickets in another, and so forth.

c If company policy is to sell goods at a profit of 80% of total job cost, present the journal entries necessary to recognize completion and sale of the photons.

**P22-A2** ***Basic job order costing with journal entries***

Apache Manufacturing uses a job order system to accumulate production costs. On March 1, the only job in process was job no. 74. Its cost sheet appears as follows:

| | *Job No. 74* |
|---|---|
| Direct materials | $10,900 |
| Direct labor | 14,500 |
| Applied overhead | 13,050 |
| | $38,450 |

The following costs were incurred during March:

| | Job No. 74 | Job No. 75 | Job No. 76 | Job No. 77 | Total |
|---|---|---|---|---|---|
| Direct materials | $7,000 | $10,000 | $14,000 | $12,500 | $43,500 |
| Indirect materials | | | | | 5,100 |
| Direct labor | 5,000 | 12,000 | 8,000 | 16,000 | 41,000 |
| Indirect labor | | | | | 8,800 |
| | | | | | $98,400 |

Overhead is applied on the basis of direct labor cost. During March, jobs no. 74 and no. 76 were completed, job no. 74 was sold on account for $60,500, and miscellaneous overhead incurred amounted to $14,900.

**Instructions**

a Determine Apache's overhead application rate by analyzing job no. 74.

b Prepare journal entries for March to record the following. (*Note:* Prepare summary entries by combining individual job data.)
(1) The issuance of direct and indirect materials
(2) The direct and indirect labor incurred
(3) The miscellaneous overhead charges
(4) The application of overhead to production
(5) The completion of jobs no. 74 and no. 76
(6) The sale of job no. 74

**P22-A3** ***Computations using a job order system***

General Corporation employs a job order cost system. On May 1, the following balances were extracted from the general ledger:

| | |
|---|---|
| Work in process | $ 35,200 |
| Finished goods | 86,900 |
| Cost of goods sold | 128,700 |

Work in Process consisted of two jobs, no. 101 ($20,400) and no. 103 ($14,800). During May, direct materials requisitioned from the storeroom amounted to $96,500, and direct labor incurred totaled $114,500. These figures are subdivided as follows:

| Direct Materials | | Direct Labor | |
|---|---|---|---|
| Job No. | Amount | Job No. | Amount |
| 101 | $ 5,000 | 101 | $ 7,800 |
| 115 | 19,500 | 103 | 20,800 |
| 116 | 36,200 | 115 | 42,000 |
| Other | 35,800 | 116 | 18,000 |
| | $96,500 | Other | 25,900 |
| | | | $114,500 |

Job no. 115 was the only job in process at the end of the month. Job no. 101 and three other jobs (material cost, $21,000; labor cost, $17,400—the costs of job no. 101 are not included in these figures) were sold during May at a profit of 20% of cost.

General applies overhead daily at the rate of 150% of direct labor cost as labor summaries are posted to job orders. The firm's fiscal year ends May 31.

**Instructions**

a Compute the total overhead applied to production during May.
b Compute the cost of the ending work in process inventory.
c Compute the cost of jobs completed during May.
d Compute the cost of goods sold for the year ended May 31.

**P22-A4** ***Job order costing, overhead emphasis***

Madison Brothers uses a job order system to accumulate manufacturing costs. On December 31, 19X4, the work in process inventory consisted of job no. 176, costed as follows:

| | |
|---|---|
| Direct materials | $ 39,800 |
| Direct labor | 50,000 |
| Applied overhead | 60,000 |
| | $149,800 |

Because of changing plant conditions and labor markets, the cost accounting department calculated a new overhead application rate for use throughout 19X5. Estimated totals for direct labor cost and factory overhead for 19X5 amounted to $700,000 and $910,000, respectively. Actual results follow.

| | |
|---|---|
| Direct materials used | $ 822,500 |
| Direct labor | 710,000 |
| Indirect materials | 64,500 |
| Indirect labor | 461,900 |
| Factory depreciation | 122,700 |
| Factory insurance | 10,900 |
| Factory utilities | 238,600 |
| | $2,431,100 |

All jobs were completed and sold by December 31, 19X5, except for job no. 229, which contained direct material costs of $31,400 and direct labor charges of $42,800. This job was still in production and was anticipated to be completed in early January. The company charges any under- or overapplied overhead to Cost of Goods Sold.

**Instructions**

a Determine the 19X5 overhead application rate, using direct labor cost as the application base.
b Determine the total cost of the company's work in process inventory as of December 31, 19X5.
c Determine the amount of under- or overapplied overhead for the year. Be sure to indicate whether overhead was underapplied or overapplied.
d Compute the company's cost of goods sold. Madison Brothers had no finished goods inventory on January 1, 19X5.

**P22-A5** ***Flow of costs: Finding unknowns***

Selected ledger accounts for the year ended December 31, 19X4, for Ruffin Manufacturing follow.

| *Raw Materials* | | | |
|---|---|---|---|
| Balance, 1/1 | 19,000 | | 89,000 |
| | ? | | |

| Wages Payable | | | |
|---|---|---|---|
| | | | 58,000 |

| Factory Overhead | | | |
|---|---|---|---|
| Indirect materials | 7,000 | | ? |
| All other | 97,000 | | |

| Work in Process | | | |
|---|---|---|---|
| Balance, 1/1 | ? | | 240,000 |
| Direct materials | ? | | |
| Direct labor | 51,000 | | |
| Applied overhead | ? | | |

| Finished Goods | | | |
|---|---|---|---|
| Balance, 1/1 | 114,000 | | ? |

| Cost of Goods Sold | | | |
|---|---|---|---|
| | 296,000 | | |

A year-end count revealed ending raw materials and work in process inventories of $25,000 and $14,000, respectively. Ruffin uses an overhead application rate of 200% of direct labor cost.

### Instructions

a Compute the amount of indirect labor incurred in operations.
b Compute total direct materials used.
c Determine Ruffin's purchases of raw materials during the year.
d How much overhead was applied to production?
e Determine the cost of the ending finished goods inventory.
f Compute the cost of the beginning work in process inventory.

**P22-A6** ***Job costing in a service business***

Datanet, Inc., renders consulting services in the computer and information systems field. To determine the cost of each consulting engagement, Datanet uses a job order cost system. All costs traceable to specific clients are charged to individual client jobs. Other costs incurred by the firm, but not identifiable with specific clients, are charged to jobs via a predetermined overhead application rate. Clients pay Datanet for directly chargeable costs, overhead, and a markup. The markup is sufficient so the firm will earn its budgeted operating income for the year.

On the basis of past experience, Datanet has prepared the following budget for the upcoming year:

| *Cost* | *Total* | *Directly Traceable to Specific Jobs* | *Not Traceable to Specific Jobs* |
|---|---|---|---|
| Professional staff | $514,000 | $450,000 | $ 64,000 |
| Computer charges | 100,000 | 90,000 | 10,000 |
| Travel | 50,000 | 30,000 | 20,000 |
| Office costs | 68,000 | 40,000 | 28,000 |
| | $732,000 | $610,000 | $122,000 |

The budget also revealed expected revenues and operating income of $976,000 and $244,000, respectively.

**Instructions**

a Determine the company's overhead application rate. The rate is based on total costs traceable to client jobs.

b Compute Datanet's estimated income for the year as a percentage of costs traceable to client jobs.

c In February, Datanet completed an engagement for Mansfield Publishers. The following costs were directly chargeable to Mansfield:

| | |
|---|---|
| Professional staff | $32,000 |
| Computer charges | 26,000 |
| Travel | 2,600 |
| Office costs | 900 |

Compute the total billing to Mansfield Publishers.

d Would there be any benefit to Datanet if the firm tried to increase the percentage of costs that could be classified as direct (as opposed to indirect)? Briefly explain.

## Series B

### P22-B1 *Preparation of job cost sheet and journal entries*

Westex, Inc., manufactures items that are used in the plastics industry. The company, which uses a job costing system, has two departments: cutting and finishing. The cutting department applies overhead to products at the rate of $20 per machine hour; finishing, on the other hand, uses an application rate of 300% of direct labor cost.

On August 12, 19X4, Westex received an order from Arriva, Inc., for 450 wedge forms, model no. 19. Production began immediately, and the order (known as job no. 3434) was completed on August 31. Paperwork supporting the order revealed the following:

| *Document** | *Date* | *Department* | *Hours* | *Amount* |
|---|---|---|---|---|
| MR 2298 | 8/12 | Cutting | — | $1,500 |
| MR 2317 | 8/15 | Cutting | — | 6,400 |
| MUR 59 | 8/17 | Cutting | 80 | — |
| TT 1190-92 | 8/17 | Cutting | 30 | 300 |
| MR 6680 | 8/19 | Finishing | — | 800 |
| MUR 62 | 8/31 | Cutting | 140 | — |
| TT 1235-38 | 8/31 | Cutting | 50 | 500 |
| TT 6608-14 | 8/31 | Finishing | 200 | 1,800 |

* MR = materials requisition; TT = time ticket; MUR = machine usage report

Employees who supervised the order earned $2,800 of salaries from August 12 through month-end. Westex accounts for supervisory salaries as indirect labor.

**Instructions**

a Prepare a job cost sheet for the Arriva order as of August 31. Use the following column headings:

| | Direct Materials | | Direct Labor | | | Machine Usage | | Factory Overhead |
|---|---|---|---|---|---|---|---|---|
| *Date* | *Requisition* | *Amount* | *Ticket* | *Hours* | *Amount* | *Report* | *Hours* | *Amount* |

b Prepare journal entries to record (1) the issuance of direct materials, (2) direct labor incurred on the order, (3) the application of factory overhead, and (4) the supervisory salaries. All materials requisitions should be combined in one entry, all time tickets in another, and so forth.

c If company policy is to sell goods at a profit of 60% of total job cost, present the journal entries necessary to recognize completion and sale of the wedge forms.

**P22-B2** ***Basic job order costing with journal entries***

Tri-City Manufacturing uses a job order system to accumulate production costs. On May 1, the only job in process was job no. 406. Its cost sheet appears as follows:

| | *Job No. 406* |
|---|---|
| Direct materials | $14,100 |
| Direct labor | 28,600 |
| Applied overhead | 31,460 |
| | $74,160 |

The following costs were incurred during May:

| | *Job No. 406* | *Job No. 407* | *Job No. 408* | *Job No. 409* | *Total* |
|---|---|---|---|---|---|
| Direct materials | $3,100 | $9,500 | $12,500 | $15,800 | $40,900 |
| Indirect materials | | | | | 6,300 |
| Direct labor | 7,000 | 8,400 | 6,200 | 10,600 | 32,200 |
| Indirect labor | | | | | 7,000 |
| | | | | | $86,400 |

Overhead is applied on the basis of direct labor cost. During May, jobs no. 406 and no. 408 were completed, job no. 406 was sold on account for $104,000, and miscellaneous overhead incurred amounted to $36,900.

**Instructions**

a Determine Tri-City's overhead application rate by analyzing job no. 406.

b Prepare journal entries for May to record the following. (*Note:* Prepare summary entries by combining individual job data.)

(1) The issuance of direct and indirect materials
(2) The direct and indirect labor incurred
(3) The miscellaneous overhead charges
(4) The application of overhead to production
(5) The completion of jobs no. 406 and no. 408
(6) The sale of job no. 406

**P22-B3** ***Computations using a job order system***

Fresno Corporation employs a job order cost system. On July 1, the following balances were extracted from the general ledger:

| | |
|---|---|
| Work in process | $ 50,900 |
| Finished goods | 118,700 |
| Cost of goods sold | 185,400 |

Work in Process consisted of two jobs, no. 421 ($31,700) and no. 423 ($19,200). During July, direct materials requisitioned from the storeroom amounted to $73,700, and direct labor incurred totaled $87,500. These figures are subdivided as follows:

| *Direct Materials* | | *Direct Labor* | |
|---|---|---|---|
| ***Job No.*** | ***Amount*** | ***Job No.*** | ***Amount*** |
| 421 | $10,100 | 421 | $15,000 |
| 425 | 22,400 | 423 | 19,600 |
| 426 | 29,300 | 425 | 24,300 |
| Other | 11,900 | 426 | 11,100 |
| | $73,700 | Other | 17,500 |
| | | | $87,500 |

Job no. 425 was the only job in process by the end of the month. Job no. 421 and three other jobs (material cost, $9,400; labor cost, $14,500—the costs of job no. 421 are not included in these figures) were sold during July at a profit of 40% of cost.

Fresno applies overhead daily at the rate of 180% of direct labor cost as labor summaries are posted to job orders. The firm's fiscal year ends on July 31.

**Instructions**

a Compute the total overhead applied to production during July.
b Compute the cost of the ending work in process inventory.
c Compute the cost of jobs completed during July.
d Compute the cost of goods sold for the year ended July 31.

**P22-B4** ***Job order costing, overhead emphasis***

Toledo Company uses a job order system to accumulate manufacturing costs. On December 31, 19X1, the work in process inventory consisted of job no. 764, costed as follows:

| | |
|---|---|
| Direct materials | $ 4,800 |
| Direct labor | 12,500 |
| Applied overhead | 10,000 |
| | $27,300 |

Because of changing plant conditions and labor markets, the cost accounting department calculated a new overhead application rate for use throughout 19X2. Estimated totals for direct labor cost and factory overhead for 19X2 amounted to $300,000 and $270,000, respectively. Actual results follow.

| | |
|---|---:|
| Direct materials used | $259,600 |
| Direct labor | 316,000 |
| Indirect materials | 23,700 |
| Indirect labor | 144,900 |
| Factory depreciation | 55,300 |
| Factory taxes | 12,700 |
| Factory utilities | 55,200 |
| | $867,400 |

All jobs were completed and sold by December 31, 19X2, except for job no. 821, which contained direct material costs of $10,900 and direct labor charges of $22,500. This job was still in production and was anticipated to be completed in early January. The company charges any under- or overapplied overhead to Cost of Goods Sold.

**Instructions**

a Determine the 19X2 overhead application rate, using direct labor cost as the application base.

b Determine the total cost of the company's work in process inventory as of December 31, 19X2.

c Determine the amount of under- or overapplied overhead for the year. Be sure to indicate whether overhead was underapplied or overapplied.

d Compute the company's cost of goods sold. Toledo had no finished goods inventory on January 1, 19X2.

**P22-B5** ***Flow of costs: Finding unknowns***
Selected ledger accounts for the year ended December 31, 19X3, for Ormsby Manufacturing follow.

***Raw Materials***

| | | |
|---|---:|---:|
| Balance, 1/1 | 17,000 | 84,000 |
| | 92,000 | |

***Wages Payable***

| | | |
|---|---:|---:|
| | | 104,000 |

***Factory Overhead***

| | | |
|---|---:|---:|
| Indirect labor | 16,000 | 132,000 |
| Other | 120,000 | |

***Work in Process***

| | | |
|---|---:|---:|
| Balance, 1/1 | 26,000 | ? |
| Direct materials | 72,000 | |
| Direct labor | ? | |
| Applied overhead | ? | |

| Finished Goods | | | |
|---|---|---|---|
| Balance, 1/1 | 37,000 | | ? |
| | 286,000 | | |

| Cost of Goods Sold | |
|---|---|
| ? | |

The year-end count of completed goods on hand revealed the following:

| *Part No.* | *Quantity (Units)* | *Unit Cost* |
|---|---|---|
| 118 | 4,500 | $5.20 |
| 124 | 6,400 | 8.40 |
| 131 | 10,100 | 6.50 |

Ormsby applies overhead on the basis of direct labor cost.

**Instructions**

a Compute the amount of indirect materials used in operations.
b Compute total direct labor for the period.
c Determine Ormsby's overhead application rate.
d Compute the ending work in process balance.
e Determine total credits to the Finished Goods account.
f Compute the over- or underapplied overhead.

**P22-B6** ***Job costing in a service business***

Hartwell and Associates renders consulting services to a number of medical practices. To determine the cost of each consulting engagement, Hartwell uses a job order cost system. All costs traceable to specific clients are charged to individual client jobs. Other costs incurred by the firm, but not identifiable with specific clients, are charged to jobs via a predetermined overhead application rate. Clients pay Hartwell for directly chargeable costs, overhead, and a markup. The markup is sufficient so the firm will earn its budgeted operating income for the year.

On the basis of past experience, Hartwell has prepared the following budget for the upcoming year:

| *Cost* | *Total* | *Directly Traceable to Specific Jobs* | *Not Traceable to Specific Jobs* |
|---|---|---|---|
| Consulting staff | $200,000 | $180,000 | $20,000 |
| Office staff | 30,000 | 12,000 | 18,000 |
| Travel | 20,000 | 15,000 | 5,000 |
| Other office costs | 10,000 | 1,000 | 9,000 |
| | $260,000 | $208,000 | $52,000 |

The budget also revealed expected revenues and operating income of $364,000 and $104,000, respectively.

**Instructions**

a Determine the company's overhead application rate. The rate is based on total costs traceable to client jobs.

b Compute Hartwell's estimated income for the year as a percentage of costs traceable to client jobs.

c In January, Hartwell completed an engagement for the Ohio Medical Group (OMG). The following costs were directly chargeable to OMG:

| | |
|---|---|
| Consulting staff | $4,500 |
| Office staff | 300 |
| Travel | 1,100 |
| Other office costs | 100 |

Compute the total billing to OMG.

d Observe that part of the consulting staff's time is not directly traceable to specific jobs. List several possible underlying reasons.

## Beyond the Basics

**BB22-1** ***Overhead application and cost drivers***

Overhead allocation (i.e., application) is a fact of life in business. Overhead may be allocated to products, departments, divisions, and so forth via an application base, and the selection of that base is a crucial issue in accounting. Consider the five cases that follow.

- *Case A*—The Drury Manufacturing Company has extensive automated facilities, with many machines and robots being controlled by computers. The firm applies factory overhead to products on the basis of direct labor cost.
- *Case B*—Amber Company's corporate headquarters is occupied by five divisions. The firm's building maintenance cost is allocated (charged) to the five divisions on the basis of the square footage occupied by each division.
- *Case C*—Rent All rents a wide variety of equipment, including bulldozers, servingware for parties, small garden and workshop tools, and so forth. The servingware and small tools divisions generate a large number of rentals for short periods of time (e.g., a few days and/or hours). In contrast, the construction equipment division has fewer rentals, but the rentals produce more revenue and cover a longer period of time. The divisions vary greatly in terms of profitability and operating problems. Rent All allocates company administrative cost on the basis of the number of rental invoices written in each division.
- *Case D*—Rent All (from Case C) has a maintenance and repair department that furnishes repair services to the company's divisions. Periodically, the department totals all maintenance costs, including major parts, and divides by the total service calls made. The result is the cost per service call. Each division is then charged on the basis of the number of service calls requested during the period.
- *Case E*—Crossroads Company operates a cafeteria for the convenience of its personnel. The cafeteria offers meals at extremely low prices and operates at a loss. The loss is allocated to the firm's six departments on the basis of the number of employees in each department.

**Instructions**

Recall that in overhead allocation, the application base selected should have a strong bearing on the amount of overhead incurred. Consider the allocation bases and procedures used in the five cases presented and briefly evaluate whether the allocation described is acceptable or could be improved.

## Answers to Chapter Quiz

**1** c

**2** b

**3** a

**4** c [Application rate = 90% ($180,000 ÷ $200,000); applied overhead = $210,000 × 0.90 = $189,000; $189,000 − $185,000 = $4,000 overapplied]

**5** d

# Process Costing Systems

CHAPTER 23

## Learning Objectives

After reading this chapter you should:

1. Understand the basic features that are associated with a process cost accounting system.
2. Understand the meaning of equivalent units.
3. Be aware of the various factors that affect the computation of equivalent units.
4. Be able to construct a production cost report.
5. Understand the accounting issues related to units transferred to a second processing department.
6. (Appendix) Be familiar with the weighted-average process costing method.

As you saw in Chapter 22, many companies accumulate production costs (and service costs as well) by use of a job order system. These systems are often employed by businesses such as custom home builders, furniture manufacturers, and print shops, all of which typically operate in an environment that is subdivided into specific jobs or orders.

There are, as you can well imagine, numerous manufacturing applications that lack the job order "orientation." Picture the manufacture of paint, for example, where finished goods (e.g., one-gallon cans) continually roll off a production line. The manufacturing plant does *not* produce a batch of paint for the Decorating Den (say, job no. 376), then stop, and later resume operation to process the goods needed by Discount City (job no. 377). Manufacturing is ongoing and continuous; product costing by job or order thus becomes difficult, if not impossible.

In such situations, accountants turn to a **process costing system** to accumulate costs. Process costing systems are often employed in steel, petroleum, chemical, and flour production as well as in many assembly types of industries (e.g., appliances and bicycles).

## Process Costing Versus Job Order Costing

OBJECTIVE 1
Understand the basic features that are associated with a process cost accounting system.

To a great extent, process costing systems operate in much the same manner as job costing systems. Both systems are established to accumulate costs for a business and both use the same accounts. These accounts include Raw Materials, Work in Process, Finished Goods, Cost of Goods Sold, and Factory Overhead—all those introduced in the previous chapter. Furthermore, the flow of costs through these accounts is essentially the same no matter what system is used. The issuance of direct materials to production, for instance, would be recorded under process costing by a debit to Work in Process and a credit to Raw Materials; the cost of completed units is debited to Finished Goods and credited to Work in Process; and so forth. Should you need a refresher of production cost flows, we refer you to pages 795 through 801.

### How the Systems Differ

There are three basic differences between job-order and process cost accounting, all of which arise because of the nature of a continuous manufacturing environment. Such environments normally result in the manufacture of mass produced, homogeneous goods. In other words, the units are virtually identical, all having received the same amounts of direct material, direct labor, and factory overhead through the process.

Given the inability to subdivide activities by job and really no need to do so, costs under a process system are accumulated by *process or department* for a specified period of time (e.g., one month). Often a process and department are synonymous—the blending process takes place in the blending department, the assembly process in the assembly department, and so on. Then, since all units are identical, equal costs are assigned to each unit produced during the period.

A second difference between the two systems arises because in many manufacturing applications, several steps (i.e., processes) are required to complete a product. In our earlier paint illustration, for instance, various chemicals and colorings are combined in the mixing department. Cans are then filled and lids added in the filling department, the cans being passed along to a subsequent packaging opera-

## HIGHLIGHT

# A Continuous Process "Operation"

Job order and process costing systems have been used for many years to accumulate production costs. As noted in the text, process systems are used in environments where manufacturing activities are ongoing; that is, the activities do not stop when one batch of goods is completed and then restart when another is begun. The continuous process is well known in industry; it is a relative newcomer to—medicine? Yes, there are now surgical assembly lines, subject of a recent CBS *60 Minutes* episode.

An interesting application of the technique surfaced about 15 years ago in the Soviet Union. Dr. Svyatoslav Fyodorov, a top Soviet eye surgeon, started experimenting with the teamwork approach in surgery by operating on two patients at one time. After completing the operation at the first table, he quickly moved to the second one. In the beginning, Fyodorov's surgical "assembly line" performed 16 operations a day; time brings change, however, as we will note in a moment. In a country where specialized, high-technology instruments are often hard to come by, efficiency must be achieved. As the noted surgeon explains, "Our institute [the Moscow Research Institute of Eye Microsurgery] can serve as the model. Teamwork has enabled us to enhance our clinic's efficiency by 3.5 times. The number of operations has increased and their quality has improved."

So how does it work? Specialization is the key, with each of five surgeons responsible for one stage of an operation. Each stage takes from three to five minutes to perform, so approximately every three to five minutes a patient comes off the "eyesight restoring line." Using this system, Soviet ophthalmologists can perform about 100 cataract operations a day. Facilities are essential for this process and Dr. Fyodorov has them—right down to an operating room that has a floor-length rail.

Prior to the start of surgery, patients are kept in a holding room behind a series of glass doors. When a button is pressed the doors open, and a patient on an operating table attached to the rail rolls in. The surgeons are seated to the right of the rail and have their instruments in place. When the table reaches Surgeon No. 1, he begins his work: preparation of an eye for cataract removal. When No. 1 finishes, the table moves to Surgeon No. 2, who marks the places for several predetermined incisions. No. 2 then makes the first incisions and, once done, the table moves along to Surgeon No. 3. No. 3, the most experienced member of the team, performs further procedures. Since No. 3's instruments are connected to a large display monitor, everyone present in the operating room can observe the work being performed.

The operation continues with the work of Surgeon No. 4 and Surgeon No. 5, the latter of whom washes the incisions and administers antibiotics. At this time the table rolls out of the operating room and a new patient rolls in. What if there are complications? The line is stopped; the operating table is removed from the rail and taken to an adjoining room.

The main advantage of the surgical assembly-line system is that the most sophisticated part of the surgery is done by the best surgeons—people who don't have to worry about the more mundane procedures associated with the operation. Further, the division of duties among the specialists makes it possible to significantly reduce the time needed to train young, inexperienced surgeons. It also gives them the opportunity to master every stage of the operation.

SOURCE: Adapted from "The Surgical Assembly Line," *Soviet Life*, July 1985, pp. 6–7. Reprinted by permission of *Soviet Life*.

tion. Here, labels are attached and the containers packed four to a case. As a final step, the cases are transferred to a finished goods warehouse.

This sequence of events is depicted in the middle of Exhibit 23-1, which shows the basic differences between job order costing and process cost accounting. Notice that the separate operation and departmental orientation requires a separate Work in Process account for each major manufacturing activity. Direct materials and direct labor, costs easily traced to production, are charged to the department where consumed or incurred; factory overhead is then applied by using an overhead application rate.

The lack of cost accumulation by job or order does away with the use of job cost sheets. In their place, and the third basic difference between the two systems, are *production cost reports.* These reports, which document the units and costs that flow through a manufacturing department, will be shown later in the chapter.

## Measuring Production Volume

Earlier in the discussion we noted that process costing systems accumulate departmental costs *for a period of time.* Most businesses, of course, do not complete all production by the period's end; some units typically remain in process. As the following example reveals, in-process inventories create a measurement problem when calculating the costs assignable to manufactured goods.

The Paige Corporation, which uses a process cost system, began operations on January 2 of the current year. The following information pertains to the first month of activity:

| *Manufacturing Costs* | | *Production* | |
|---|---|---|---|
| Direct materials used | $ 90,000 | Units completed | 80,000 |
| Direct labor | 50,000 | Units in process, | |
| Applied factory overhead* | 60,000 | $\frac{1}{4}$ complete | 80,000 |
| Total manufacturing costs | $200,000 | | |

* 120% of direct labor cost.

Paige has a $200,000 cost pool that must be split between 80,000 completed units and 80,000 units in process, as shown in the accompanying diagram:

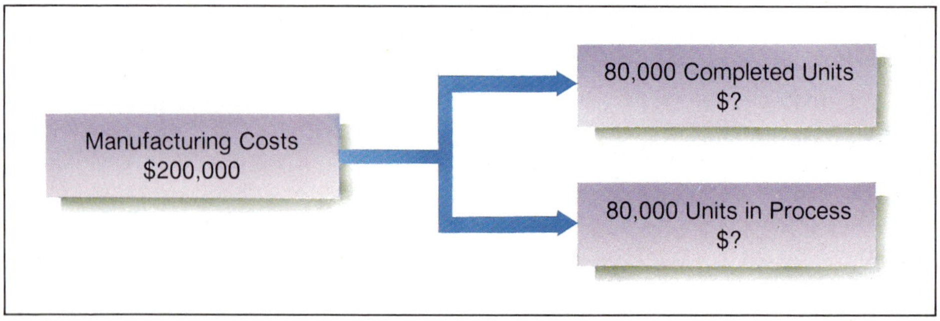


In more familiar terms, the cost pool is located in the Work in Process account at the end of January. So that direct materials, direct labor, and factory overhead follow the flow of production, a portion of the $200,000 must be removed from this account and transferred to Finished Goods.

**Exhibit 23-1**
**Job Order Costing vs. Process Cost Accounting**

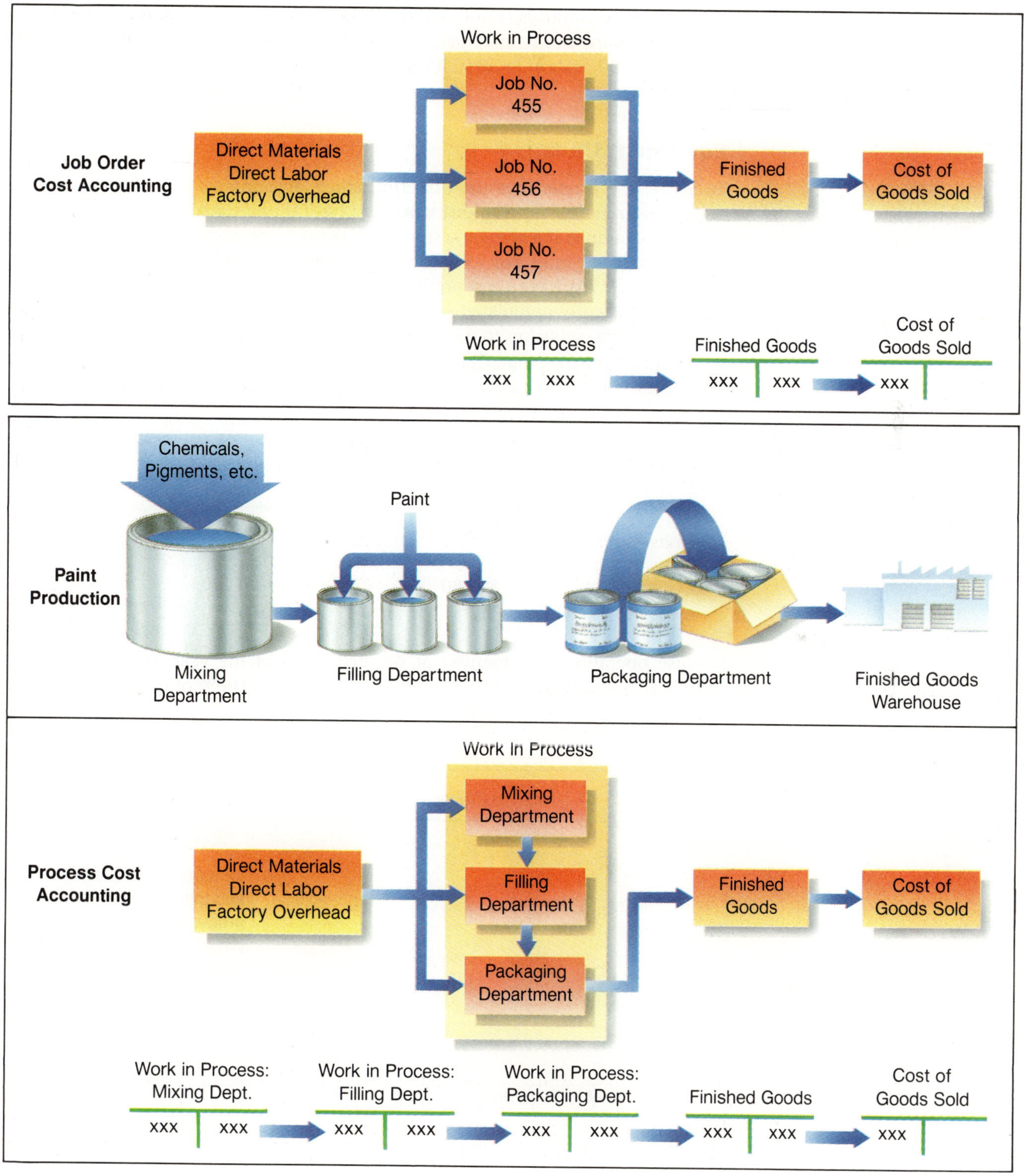

Some individuals would say that Work in Process should be credited for $100,000 (i.e., one-half of the cost pool) because 50% of Paige's total production is completed. Stated differently, since the average cost per unit is $1.25 ($200,000 ÷ 160,000 units), $100,000 (80,000 completed units × $1.25) should be transferred to the Finished Goods account. Although the preceding computation is straightforward, it is, at the same time, logically unsound. We cannot add 80,000 completed units to 80,000 units in process. It's like adding apples and oranges—a meaningless total is generated.

## Equivalent Units

OBJECTIVE 2
Understand the meaning of equivalent units.

To arrive at a proper measure of performance, accountants use a base known as equivalent units. An **equivalent unit** is a physical unit stated in terms of a finished unit. For example, if a company started work on 12 physical units (e.g., cars, tons, gallons) and the units are 75% complete at the end of the period,[1] 9 equivalent units (12 × 0.75) have been produced. It is important to note that *none* of these units are currently completed—all are still in process. The company has simply done the work *equivalent* to manufacturing nine finished units (see Exhibit 23-2).

Returning to the Paige Corporation example, 100,000 equivalent units of production took place in January:

| | *Physical Units* | | *% of Work Completed During January* | | *Equivalent Units* |
|---|---|---|---|---|---|
| Units completed | 80,000 | × | 100% | = | 80,000 |
| Units in process, ¼ complete | 80,000 | × | 25 | = | 20,000 |
| | | | | | 100,000 |

Because operations commenced at the beginning of the year, the 80,000 units completed were all started in January. Consequently, 100% of the work on these units occurred during the month.

**Exhibit 23-2**
**The Concept of Equivalent Units**

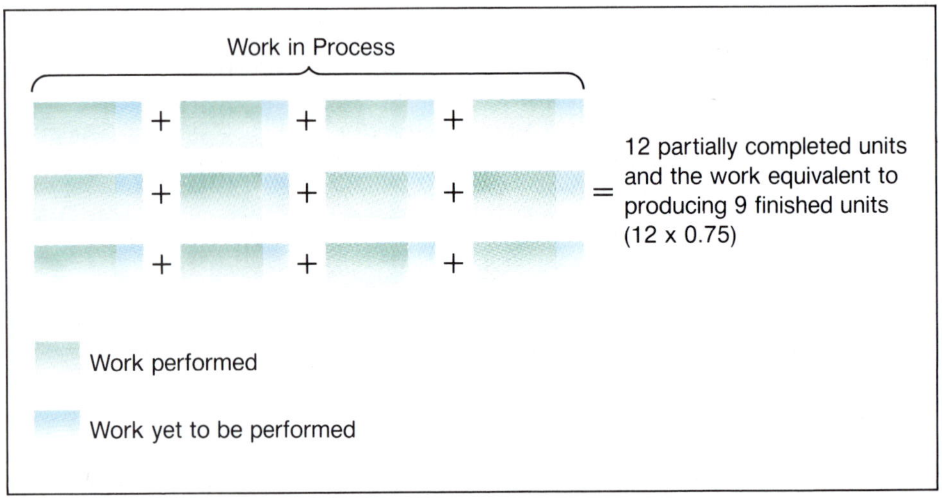


[1] The 75% figure refers to an average stage of completion in a continuous process.

## Factors That Affect Equivalent Production

OBJECTIVE 3
Be aware of the various factors that affect the computation of equivalent units.

Having introduced the concept of equivalent units, we must now become a bit more detailed. Three factors must be considered in all equivalent-unit computations:

- The presence of a beginning work in process inventory
- The introduction of production costs at different points in the manufacturing process
- The method of process costing used

### Beginning Work in Process Inventory

Should a firm have a beginning work in process inventory, the goods must be studied to determine the work performed in prior periods. Assume, for instance, that a company has 500 units in process at the start of May that are three-fifths complete. To finish the goods during the current accounting period (i.e., May), 200 equivalent units of production are needed ($500 \times \frac{2}{5} = 200$). Equivalent-unit calculations focus on the work performed during the *present* period because of the need to figure the current unit cost of manufacturing.

### Cost Incurrence in the Manufacturing Process

A second point to consider is that the three factors of production (direct materials, direct labor, and factory overhead) are generally introduced in different ways throughout manufacturing. Labor and overhead, collectively known as *conversion cost,* are often incurred uniformly through the process. Direct materials, however, can be introduced at different stages of production. In some products, for example, all materials enter manufacturing at the beginning. With other goods, materials are introduced at specific points after manufacturing has commenced (e.g., a part may be added at the 50% stage of completion, the product may be encased in protective packaging at the end of the process, and so forth).

The uniform introduction of conversion cost and the introduction of materials at specified points require the calculation of separate equivalent-unit figures. For example, assume that Sparks Company uses a process cost system. At the beginning of July the firm had a work in process inventory of 3,000 units, 30% complete. During July, the beginning work in process was completed along with 7,500 other units that had entered production. Finally, on July 31 the factory foreman determined that the ending work in process totaled 5,000 units, 20% complete. All materials are introduced at the start of manufacturing, and labor and overhead are incurred uniformly throughout the process. The equivalent units for July are calculated as follows:

| | | *Equivalent Units* | |
|---|---|---|---|
| | ***Physical Units*** | ***Materials*** | ***Conversion*** |
| Completed | | | |
| Beginning work in process | 3,000 | — | 2,100 |
| Units started and completed | 7,500 | 7,500 | 7,500 |
| Ending work in process | 5,000 | 5,000 | 1,000 |
| | 15,500 | 12,500 | 10,600 |

To explain, the beginning work in process inventory received no additional material. Remember, these units were begun last period, and all material is introduced at the start of production. To complete the beginning inventory, 70% of the work was performed in July, resulting in 2,100 (3,000 × 0.70) equivalent conversion units. Next, observe that 7,500 units were started and completed. Thus, all material for these units was introduced during the current month along with 100% of the processing (i.e., 7,500 equivalent units of materials and conversion must be tallied). Finally, we assume that the ending work in process was started in July, resulting in the introduction of 5,000 equivalent units of material. Because the ending inventory is only 20% complete, Sparks did 1,000 (5,000 × 0.20) equivalent units of conversion. These facts are depicted graphically in Exhibit 23-3.

## Process Costing Method

The third issue to address in the computation of equivalent units is the process costing method used by the firm. Two approaches are available: FIFO and weighted average.

Under the **FIFO method,** the beginning work in process inventory is assumed to be the first batch of goods completed (i.e., the first-in are the first-out). This batch is therefore treated as being separate and distinct from those units that are started and completed during the period. In addition, under the FIFO method, any work performed on the beginning work in process inventory in the previous accounting period must be considered when calculating the current period's equivalent units. These features are not new; they were both discussed and illustrated in the just-concluded Sparks Company example.

**Exhibit 23-3**
**Computation of Equivalent Units**

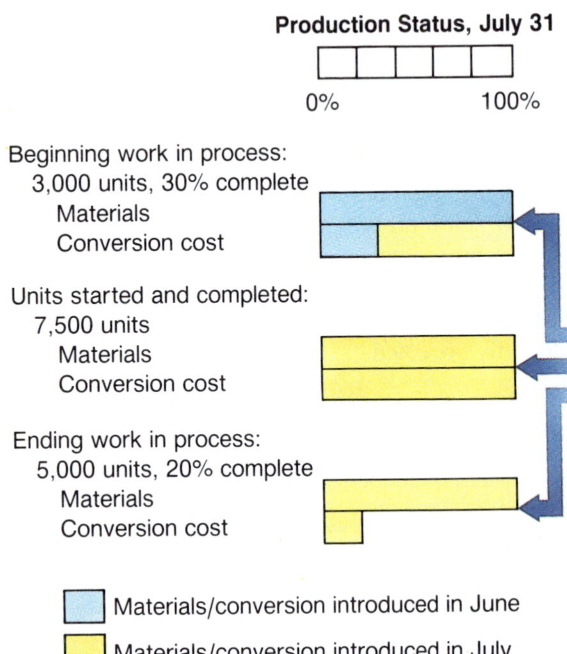


Production Figures for July

| | Physical Units | Equivalent Units Materials | Equivalent Units Conversion |
|---|---|---|---|
| Completed | | | |
| Beginning work in process | 3,000 | — | 2,100 |
| Units started and completed | 7,500 | 7,500 | 7,500 |
| Ending work in process | 5,000 | 5,000 | 1,000 |
| | 15,500 | 12,500 | 10,600 |

The remainder of our presentation will use the FIFO process costing approach. The weighted-average method, which results in different equivalent-unit figures, is introduced in an appendix to this chapter.

## Comprehensive Example

OBJECTIVE 4
Be able to construct a production cost report.

To bring together a number of the concepts thus far discussed, we will study the manufacturing operations of Berloff, Inc. The following information pertains to September:

- Beginning work in process inventory: 4,000 units, 75% complete; cost, $21,900
- Number of units started during September: 13,000
- Total units completed: 11,000
- Ending work in process inventory: 6,000 units, 40% complete
- September manufacturing costs: direct materials used, $32,500; conversion cost, $48,880

All materials are introduced at the start of the process, and conversion costs are incurred uniformly throughout manufacturing. The following approach is suggested to calculate the cost of goods completed during September and the cost of the ending work in process inventory.

### Step 1: Analyze the Physical Flow

Berloff must trace the units through the manufacturing process. On the basis of the information presented, the proper physical flow is as follows:

| | *Physical Units* |
|---|---|
| Beginning work in process | 4,000 |
| Units started | 13,000 |
| Units to account for | 17,000 |
| Completed | |
| Beginning work in process | 4,000 |
| Units started and completed | 7,000 |
| Ending work in process | 6,000 |
| Units accounted for | 17,000 |

Must be equal

The production manager has 17,000 units to account for during the month: the beginning work in process and the units started in September.

Assuming no spoilage, these units have either been completed by the company's manufacturing activities or are still in production at month-end. As you can see, the completed goods are really composed of two separate batches: the units in process on September 1 and an additional 7,000 units that were started and completed during the period. The latter batch is obtained by subtracting the beginning work in process from the total finished units manufactured (11,000 − 4,000 = 7,000).

### Step 2: Compute Equivalent Units

Once the physical flow is determined, current production is then translated into equivalent units. Because materials are introduced at the start of the process and labor and overhead incurred evenly throughout, the figures presented in Exhibit 23-4 are obtained (see the numbers in color type).

### Step 3: Compute Equivalent-Unit Costs

The cost per equivalent unit is calculated by dividing production costs by the equivalent units computed in Step 2. Just as the equivalent production figures are calculated for current activity, so, too, are the unit costs. The necessary procedures follow.

| *Costs* | *Total* | *Materials* | *Conversion* |
|---|---|---|---|
| Beginning work in process | $ 21,900 | $ — | $ — |
| Current | 81,380 | 32,500 | 48,880 |
| To account for | $103,280 | $32,500 ÷ | $48,880 ÷ |
| Equivalent units* | | 13,000 | 10,400 |
| Cost per equivalent unit | | $2.50 | $4.70 |

* From Step 2.

Note that the cost of the beginning work in process inventory ($21,900) is ignored in unit-cost computations—a logical procedure because this amount represents work performed in the previous period. The production manager, however, is still held accountable for the related expenditures; thus, $21,900 is reflected in the $103,280 total.

**Exhibit 23-4**
**Equivalent Production Figures for Berloff, Inc.**

| | *Physical Units* |
|---|---|
| Beginning work in process | 4,000 |
| Units started | 13,000 |
| Units to account for | 17,000 |

| | | *Equivalent Units* | |
|---|---|---|---|
| | | *Materials* | *Conversion* |
| Completed | | | |
| Beginning work in process* | 4,000 | — | 1,000 |
| Units started and completed† | 7,000 | 7,000 | 7,000 |
| Ending work in process‡ | 6,000 | 6,000 | 2,400 |
| Units accounted for | 17,000 | 13,000 | 10,400 |

* All materials were added last period; 25% of the conversion was performed in this period.
† All materials and conversion were introduced in this period.
‡ Units were started in this period; all materials were introduced plus 40% of the conversion.

### Step 4: Cost Assignment

Berloff's cost pool of $103,280 must now be assigned to the goods completed during the period and the ending work in process inventory. This assignment is accomplished by multiplying the cost per equivalent unit by the proper number of equivalent units. As shown in Exhibit 23-5, the cost of goods completed is $77,000, and the ending work in process is $26,280.

Because the prior period cost of $21,900 was not considered when computing equivalent-unit figures, it is attached entirely to the beginning work in process inventory. That is, no prior period cost is allocated to either the units started and completed or the partially completed production at the end of the period. Observe that the total cost accounted for ($103,280) agrees with the total cost to account for (as shown in Step 3).

### Production Cost Report

Companies that use a process costing system document the period's manufacturing activity on a **production cost report.** The report is a summary of the units and costs that have passed through a department; in actuality, it is the combined result of Steps 1–4 just discussed. Briefly review these steps and then focus on Exhibit 23-6—the end product of the entire process.

### The Work in Process Account

The production cost report is really a disclosure mechanism for various amounts contained in the general ledger. As evidence, we present Berloff's Work in Process account:

| *Work in Process* | | |
|---|---|---|
| Beginning balance | 21,900 | |
| Materials | 32,500 | |
| Conversion | 48,880 | |
| | **103,280** | |

**Exhibit 23-5**
**Cost Assignment of Berloff, Inc.**

| | *Equivalent Units* | |
|---|---|---|
| | *Materials* | *Conversion* |
| Completed | | |
| Beginning work in process | — | 1,000 |
| Units started and completed | 7,000 | 7,000 |
| Ending work in process | 6,000 | 2,400 |
| Units accounted for | 13,000 | 10,400 |

| | | |
|---|---|---|
| Completed | | |
| Beginning work in process | | |
| Prior period cost | $21,900 | |
| Conversion cost: | | |
| 1,000 × $4.70 | 4,700 | $ 26,600 |
| Units started and completed | | |
| Materials: 7,000 × $2.50 | $17,500 | |
| Conversion cost: 7,000 × $4.70 | 32,900 | 50,400 |
| Total cost of completed goods | | $ 77,000 |
| Ending work in process | | |
| Materials: 6,000 × $2.50 | $15,000 | |
| Conversion cost: 2,400 × $4.70 | 11,280 | 26,280 |
| Total cost accounted for | | $103,280 |

**Exhibit 23-6**
**Production Cost Report: FIFO**

**BERLOFF, INC.**
**Production Cost Report**
**For the Month Ended September 30, 19XX**

| | *Physical Units* | | | |
|---|---|---|---|---|
| Beginning work in process | 4,000 | | | |
| Units started | 13,000 | | | |
| Units to account for | 17,000 | | | |

STEP 1

| | | | *Equivalent Units* | |
|---|---|---|---|---|
| | | | *Materials* | *Conversion* |
| Completed | | | | |
| Beginning work in process | 4,000 | | — | 1,000 |
| Units started and completed | 7,000 | | 7,000 | 7,000 |
| Ending work in process | 6,000 | | 6,000 | 2,400 |
| Units accounted for | 17,000 | | 13,000 | 10,400 |

STEP 2

| *Costs* | | *Total* | | |
|---|---|---|---|---|
| Beginning work in process | | $ 21,900 | $ — | $ — |
| Current | | 81,380 | 32,500 | 48,880 |
| To account for | | $103,280 | $32,500 ÷ | $48,880 ÷ |
| Equivalent units | | | 13,000 | 10,400 |
| Cost per equivalent unit | | | $2.50 | $4.70 |

STEP 3

| *Cost Assignment* | | |
|---|---|---|
| Completed | | |
| Beginning work in process | | |
| Prior period cost | $21,900 | |
| Conversion cost: 1,000 × $4.70 | 4,700 | $ 26,600 |
| Units started and completed | | |
| Materials: 7,000 × $2.50 | $17,500 | |
| Conversion cost: 7,000 × $4.70 | 32,900 | 50,400 |
| Total cost of completed goods | | $ 77,000 |
| Ending work in process | | |
| Materials: 6,000 × $2.50 | $15,000 | |
| Conversion cost: 2,400 × $4.70 | 11,280 | 26,280 |
| Total cost accounted for | | $103,280 |

STEP 4

The balance of $103,280 coincides with the costs that Berloff's production manager had to account for during the period. Because the cost of completed units totals $77,000, the following journal entry is needed on September 30:

| | | |
|---|---|---|
| Finished Goods | 77,000 | |
| Work in Process | | 77,000 |
| To transfer the cost of completed units to finished goods | | |

This entry, identical to that shown in Chapter 22 for a job order system, makes the Work in Process account consistent with the figures disclosed on the production cost report.

## Accounting for a Second Processing Department

OBJECTIVE 5
Understand the accounting issues related to units transferred to a second processing department.

At the beginning of our presentation, we noted that goods manufactured in a continuous process must often pass through several departments. For example, goods may be started in the assembly department and then transferred to the finishing department for final processing. The presence of additional departments gives rise to some new terminology in the determination of both the cost of goods completed and the cost of the ending work in process inventory. This terminology is best understood if the manufacturing process is viewed from the second department's perspective.

The goods received by the second department (called **transferred-in units**) are very similar to raw materials, that is, materials to be worked on during the accounting period. Attached to these goods is a **transferred-in cost,** computed as the sum of the units' material, labor, and factory overhead charges from the previous process. After receipt, the second department will add its own labor and overhead (and perhaps still more material), complete the units, and transfer the goods either to another processing operation or to the finished goods warehouse.

### An Illustration

To illustrate the procedures related to multiple processing operations, we will continue (and slightly modify) the Berloff, Inc., example. Assume the company's production operation now consists of two departments, A and B. The 11,000 completed units, which cost $77,000 and previously went to the finished goods warehouse, will instead be transferred throughout the month to a second department (B) for further processing. The transfer requires the following journal entry:

| | | |
|---|---|---|
| Work in Process: Dept. B | 77,000 | |
| Work in Process: Dept. A | | 77,000 |
| To transfer 11,000 completed units to Department B | | |

In processing the units, department B incurs direct labor and overhead costs; no additional materials are added to the product. The data that follow pertain to the department's activities.

- Beginning work in process inventory: 3,000 units, 40% complete; cost, $16,500.
- Number of units started during the month: 11,000

- Total units completed: 13,000
- Ending work in process inventory: 1,000 units, 70% complete
- Conversion cost: $75,000

These data are summarized in department B's production cost report, which is shown in Exhibit 23-7. To explain, the 11,000 units started during the month are the goods transferred in from department A. Equivalent units are once again computed for the various factors of production, in this case transferred-in costs and conversion. The calculations that pertain to the first element are performed by remembering that transferred-in units are similar to raw materials—more specifically, materials introduced at the *start* of B's production activities. Because the beginning work in process inventory is already 40% complete on September 1, no additional department A cost is incurred with respect to these units.

The remainder of the report is completed in the same fashion as that shown earlier in the text. A careful review of the exhibit reveals that department B is really adding its own costs ($75,000, or $6 per equivalent unit) to charges that relate to activities previously performed in department A (i.e., transferred-in cost). Upon completion, the manufactured product will carry the sum of these amounts along to finished goods, as follows:

| | | |
|---|---|---|
| Finished Goods | 157,300 | |
| Work in Process: Dept. B | | 157,300 |
| To transfer the cost of completed units to finished goods | | |

## APPENDIX Process Costing and the Weighted-Average Method

**OBJECTIVE 6**
**Be familiar with the weighted-average process costing method.**

The physical flow of goods in many continuous manufacturing processes is on a first-in, first-out basis, with units in process at the beginning of a period being the first ones completed. As we explained in Chapter 9, the costing method used to account for inventory may be entirely different from the actual flow of goods through a warehouse (or in this case, a manufacturing plant). Accordingly, many companies have adopted weighted-average process costing.

### Features of Weighted-Average Costing

The thrust of **weighted-average costing** is that all goods completed during the period are carried at the same unit cost. This cost, a weighted average, is derived by combining costs that are present in the beginning work in process inventory with those that arise from current manufacturing activities. On a per-unit basis such amounts could differ because of newly granted wage increases, changes in supplier prices for materials, and other factors. Nevertheless, any differences are downplayed in favor of the weighted-average method's primary advantages: simplicity and reduced record keeping requirements.

Given the preceding cost treatment, there is no need to account for the units completed as two separate batches of goods: those from the beginning work in process and those actually begun during the period (see p. 834). These batches are lumped together in the weighted-average approach, and it is assumed that *all* units completed are started and completed during the period. As an outgrowth of this

**Exhibit 23-7**
**Production Cost Report: Department B (FIFO)**

**BERLOFF, INC.**
**Production Cost Report—Department B**
**For the Month Ended September 30, 19XX**

| | *Physical Units* | | |
|---|---|---|---|
| Beginning work in process | 3,000 | | |
| Units started (transferred-in) | 11,000 | | |
| Units to account for | 14,000 | | |
| | | | *Equivalent Units* |
| | | *Transferred-In* | *Conversion* |
| Completed | | | |
| Beginning work in process | 3,000 | — | 1,800 |
| Units started and completed | 10,000 | 10,000 | 10,000 |
| Ending work in process | 1,000 | 1,000 | 700 |
| Units accounted for | 14,000 | 11,000 | 12,500 |

| *Costs* | | *Total* | | |
|---|---|---|---|---|
| Beginning work in process | | $ 16,500 | $ — | $ — |
| Current | | 152,000 | 77,000 | 75,000 |
| To account for | | $168,500 | $77,000 ÷ | $75,000 ÷ |
| Equivalent units | | | 11,000 | 12,500 |
| Cost per equivalent unit | | | $7.00 | $6.00 |

| *Cost Assignment* | | |
|---|---|---|
| Completed | | |
| Beginning work in process | | |
| Prior period cost | $16,500 | |
| Conversion cost: 1,800 × $6.00 | 10,800 | $ 27,300 |
| Units started and completed | | |
| Transferred-in: 10,000 × $7.00 | $70,000 | |
| Conversion cost: 10,000 × $6.00 | 60,000 | 130,000 |
| Total cost of completed goods | | $157,300 |
| Ending work in process | | |
| Transferred-in: 1,000 × $7.00 | $ 7,000 | |
| Conversion cost: 700 × $6.00 | 4,200 | 11,200 |
| Total cost accounted for | | $168,500 |

assumption, any work performed previously on the beginning work in process inventory is ignored when computing equivalent units.

## An Example

To illustrate these features we will use data from Berloff, Inc., which appear in the body of the chapter. Key data from page 835 are reproduced here for your convenience.

- Beginning work in process inventory: 4,000 units, 75% complete; cost $21,900 (materials, $8,470; conversion, $13,430)[2]
- Number of units started during September: 13,000
- Total units completed: 11,000
- Ending work in process inventory: 6,000 units, 40% complete
- September manufacturing costs: direct materials used, $32,500; conversion cost, $48,880

All materials are introduced at the start of the process, and conversion costs are incurred uniformly throughout manufacturing.

The four steps that follow are required to figure the cost of finished goods manufactured and the cost of ending work in process inventory.

### Step 1: Analyze the Physical Flow

To ensure that all units are properly accounted for, the company must trace its goods through production activities. As shown by the following tabulation, the 17,000 units charged to the department (beginning work in process plus units started) have either been completed or are still in process:

| | *Physical Units* | |
|---|---|---|
| Beginning work in process | 4,000 | |
| Units started | 13,000 | |
| Units to account for | 17,000 | ← |
| Completed | 11,000 | Must |
| Ending work in process | 6,000 | be equal |
| Units accounted for | 17,000 | ← |

### Step 2: Compute Equivalent Units

Next, the preceding figures are converted into equivalent units, as shown in Exhibit 23-8. Because the 11,000 finished units are assumed to be *started and completed* during the month, these units have 100% of the materials and conversion introduced in September (and, thus, 11,000 equivalent units each). The fact that the

[2] The material and conversion cost figures ($8,470 and $13,430, respectively) are new here. These amounts are needed with the weighted-average method for the calculation of average cost figures.

| | Physical Units | Equivalent Units | |
|---|---|---|---|
| | | Materials | Conversion |
| Beginning work in process | 4,000 | | |
| Units started | 13,000 | | |
| Units to account for | 17,000 | | |
| Completed | 11,000 | 11,000 | 11,000 |
| Ending work in process | 6,000 | 6,000 | 2,400 |
| Units accounted for | 17,000 | 17,000 | 13,400 |

**Exhibit 23-8**
**Equivalent Production Figures: Weighted-Average Method**

beginning work in process inventory actually commenced production in the previous month, with 75% of the work performed at that time, is ignored under the weighted-average method. Finally, the ending work in process inventory was started in September and progressed through 40% of the manufacturing operation, giving rise to 6,000 and 2,400 equivalent units for materials and conversion cost, respectively.

## Step 3: Compute Equivalent-Unit Costs

The computation of the cost per equivalent unit is very straightforward: production costs are divided by equivalent-unit totals.

| *Costs* | *Total* | *Materials* | *Conversion* |
|---|---|---|---|
| Beginning work in process | $ 21,900 | $ 8,470 | $13,430 |
| Current | 81,380 | 32,500 | 48,880 |
| To account for | $103,280 | $40,970 ÷ | $62,310 ÷ |
| Equivalent units* | | 17,000 | 13,400 |
| Cost per equivalent unit | | $2.41 | $4.65 |

* From Step 2.

The combination of previous period and current costs and the related division procedure results in the calculation of *average* costs. These figures are now allocated to the month's total manufacturing output.

## Step 4: Cost Assignment

Berloff incurred $103,280 of production costs to complete 11,000 units and partially manufacture 6,000 units. The cost of these goods is determined by multiplying the amount of material consumed and work performed (i.e., the equivalent-unit figures) by the unit costs just computed. Step 4, the cost assignment process, is shown at the bottom of the company's production cost report in Exhibit 23-9.

**Exhibit 23-9**
**Production Cost Report: Weighted-Average Method**

**BERLOFF, INC.**
**Production Cost Report**
**For the Month Ended September 30, 19XX**

| | *Physical Units* | *Total* | *Equivalent Units: Materials* | *Equivalent Units: Conversion* |
|---|---|---|---|---|
| Beginning work in process | 4,000 | | | |
| Units started | 13,000 | | | |
| Units to account for | 17,000 | | | |
| Completed | 11,000 | | 11,000 | 11,000 |
| Ending work in process | 6,000 | | 6,000 | 2,400 |
| Units accounted for | 17,000 | | 17,000 | 13,400 |
| ***Costs*** | | | | |
| Beginning work in process | | $ 21,900 | $ 8,470 | $13,430 |
| Current | | 81,380 | 32,500 | 48,880 |
| To account for | | $103,280 | $40,970 ÷ | $62,310 ÷ |
| Equivalent units | | | 17,000 | 13,400 |
| Cost per equivalent unit | | | $2.41 | $4.65 |
| ***Cost Assignment*** | | | | |
| Completed | | | | |
| Materials: 11,000 × $2.41 | $26,510 | | | |
| Conversion cost: 11,000 × $4.65 | 51,150 | $ 77,660 | | |
| Ending work in process | | | | |
| Materials: 6,000 × $2.41 | $14,460 | | | |
| Conversion cost: 2,400 × $4.65 | 11,160 | 25,620 | | |
| Total cost accounted for | | $103,280 | | |

## Chapter Review

### Learning Objectives—The Key Points

**1 Understand the basic features that are associated with a process cost accounting system.** Process costing systems are used in continuous process and assembly-line types of industries. With such systems, the manufacturing costs incurred flow through the Raw Materials, Work in Process, Finished Goods, and Cost of Goods Sold accounts—the same as those established for a job order firm. In contrast, however, the cost accumulation method is significantly different, with costs being accumulated by department (or process) for a given time period. Furthermore, each department maintains its own Work in Process account and reports manufacturing activity on a production cost report.

**2 Understand the meaning of equivalent units.** Equivalent units are the basis for assigning inventoriable costs under a process costing system. Upon conclusion of a typical accounting period, many units have been fully manufactured while others are still in production. Because fully completed units cannot be combined with in-process units (i.e., the two batches are not the same), some common measurement base must be found. This base is equivalent units, or physical units that are stated in terms of finished units. If, for example, a company started 1,000 units into production and these goods are 70% complete at the end of the period, the firm has done the work equivalent to manufacturing 700 finished units. None of these goods are finished, however; they are all still in process.

**3 Be aware of the various factors that affect the computation of equivalent units.** Three factors must be considered in the calculation of equivalent units: the presence of a beginning work in process inventory, the introduction of various production factors at different points in the manufacturing process, and the method of process costing used by the firm. If a company has a beginning work in process inventory, then some manufacturing work occurred on these units in the previous accounting period. Should the FIFO method of costing be in use, as illustrated in the body of the chapter, the work performed last period must be considered when determining equivalent-unit totals. In addition, because materials tend to be introduced at specific points in a manufacturing operation and conversion costs are incurred uniformly throughout a process, separate equivalent-unit figures must be computed for these costs.

The final factor to consider is whether the firm is using FIFO or weighted-average costing. As just noted, previous period manufacturing activity affects equivalent-unit calculations under FIFO; with weighted average, however, as explained in the chapter appendix, such work is ignored.

**4 Be able to construct a production cost report.** A production cost report summarizes both units manufactured and production costs for a given accounting period. The physical flow of goods through the production process is reported as are the equivalent units of materials added and work performed. Further, equivalent-unit costs are disclosed along with the assignment of manufacturing costs to goods completed and the ending work in process inventory. The latter two amounts are the result of multiplying the equivalent-unit figures by the per-unit costs.

**5 Understand the accounting issues related to units transferred to a second processing department.** Units are frequently transferred from one department to another for further processing. The receiving department accounts for these goods as transferred-in units, which are viewed as raw materials introduced at the start of the receiving department's manufacturing process. These units have an associated transferred-in cost, namely, the direct materials, direct labor, and factory overhead from preceding production operations. The second (i.e., subsequent) department adds its own costs for work performed, and the total charges are passed along to either another department for still more processing or to finished goods.

**6 (Appendix) Be familiar with the weighted-average process costing method.** The weighted-average method is used by many businesses to simplify costing and reduce record keeping. Under this approach, all goods completed during a period are assumed to be started and completed during that period. Any previous manufacturing activity on the beginning work in process inventory is therefore ignored in the computation of equivalent units. This method is known as the weighted-average approach because the previous period costs in the beginning work in process are averaged together with current manufacturing costs, and all units produced during the period are carried at the same unit cost figure.

## Chapter Quiz

The five questions that follow relate to several issues raised in the chapter. Test your knowledge of the issues by selecting the best answer. (The answers appear on p. 858.)

**1** Process cost accounting systems:
- a use distinctly different general ledger accounts than job order systems.
- b frequently accumulate costs by department.
- c are seldom found in assembly-line manufacturing plants.
- d may, in selected cases, use job order cost sheets.

**2** Equivalent units:
- a are normally computed separately for direct materials and conversion cost.
- b are finished units stated in terms of physical units.
- c cannot be used to calculate the *cost* of the ending work in process inventory.
- d are generally equal (in total) for both completed goods and the ending work in process inventory.

**3** Harris Company introduces direct material at the beginning of its manufacturing operation. The following data pertain to July:

Beginning work in process: 4,000 units, 20% complete
Units started and completed: 7,000
Ending work in process: 3,000 units, 60% complete

Assuming the use of FIFO, the total equivalent units for direct materials amounted to:
- a 8,800.
- b 10,000.
- c 12,000.
- d 14,000.

**4** A production cost report:
- a documents manufacturing costs of companies that use process costing systems and job order systems.
- b discloses equivalent units but not the cost per equivalent unit.
- c discloses the cost of completed goods but not the cost of the ending work in process inventory.
- d summarizes equivalent-unit calculations, unit-cost calculations, and the assignment of manufacturing costs to goods completed and the ending work in process inventory.

**5** Transferred-in units:
- a have no cost to the firm.
- b should be treated as raw materials by the receiving department.
- c require no equivalent-unit calculations.
- d are often found in the accounting records of manufacturing companies that have one processing department.

## Summary Problem

Santa Fe Manufacturing uses a FIFO process costing system to accumulate production costs. Selected data applicable to January of the current year follow.

- Beginning work in process inventory: 8,000 units, $\frac{1}{4}$ complete; cost, $17,500
- Number of units started in January: 20,000
- Total units completed: 22,000
- Ending work in process inventory: 6,000 units, $\frac{2}{3}$ complete
- Direct materials used in January: $60,000
- January conversion cost: $42,000

**Instructions**

**a** Compute the equivalent production figures for January with respect to materials and conversion cost. Materials are added at the start of the process; conversion costs are incurred evenly throughout manufacturing.

**b** Compute the equivalent-unit costs for materials and conversion costs.

**c** Determine the cost of goods completed during January and the ending work in process inventory.

**d** Present the journal entry to transfer completed production to finished goods.

**Solution**

**a**

| | *Physical Units* |
|---|---|
| Beginning work in process | 8,000 |
| Units started | 20,000 |
| Units to account for | 28,000 |

| | | *Equivalent Units* | |
|---|---|---|---|
| | | *Materials* | *Conversion* |
| Completed | | | |
| Beginning work in process* | 8,000 | — | 6,000 |
| Units started and completed† | 14,000 | 14,000 | 14,000 |
| Ending work in process‡ | 6,000 | 6,000 | 4,000 |
| Units accounted for | 28,000 | 20,000 | 24,000 |

* All materials added last period; three-fourths of the conversion performed in this period.
† All materials and conversion introduced in this period; 14,000 units derived by subtracting the beginning work in process inventory from the total units completed (22,000).
‡ Units were started in this period; all materials were introduced plus two-thirds of the conversion.

**b**

| *Costs* | *Total* | *Materials* | *Conversion* |
|---|---|---|---|
| Beginning work in process | $ 17,500 | $ — | $ — |
| Current | 102,000 | 60,000 | 42,000 |
| To account for | $119,500 | $60,000 ÷ | $42,000 ÷ |
| Equivalent units | | 20,000 | 24,000 |
| Cost per equivalent unit | | $3.00 | $1.75 |

| | | |
|---|---|---|
| **c** Completed | | |
| Beginning work in process | | |
| Prior period cost | $17,500 | |
| Conversion cost: 6,000 units × $1.75 | 10,500 | $ 28,000 |
| Units started and completed | | |
| Materials: 14,000 units × $3.00 | $42,000 | |
| Conversion cost: 14,000 units × $1.75 | 24,500 | 66,500 |
| Total cost of completed units | | $ 94,500 |
| Ending work in process | | |
| Materials: 6,000 units × $3.00 | $18,000 | |
| Conversion cost: 4,000 units × $1.75 | 7,000 | 25,000 |
| Total cost accounted for | | $119,500 |

| | | |
|---|---|---|
| **d** Finished Goods | 94,500 | |
| Work in Process | | 94,500 |
| To transfer the cost of completed units to finished goods | | |

## Questions

**Q23-1** In what type of production setting is a process cost accounting system often found?

**Q23-2** How are job order systems and process costing systems similar?

**Q23-3** How are costs accumulated under a process costing system?

**Q23-4** Explain the concept of equivalent units to someone who has no background in cost accounting.

**Q23-5** The Gateway Company uses a process costing system. An examination of goods in production at the end of the accounting period revealed 6,000 units, two-thirds complete. Would it be correct to say that 4,000 finished units were manufactured? Why?

**Q23-6** Why is it usually necessary to compute separate equivalent-unit totals for direct materials and conversion cost?

**Q23-7** Explain the basic features that are associated with a FIFO process costing system.

**Q23-8** List the four steps that are required when preparing a production cost report.

**Q23-9** What are transferred-in units? How should these units be treated by the receiving department?

**Q23-10** What is meant by the term "transferred-in cost"?

**Q23-11** What journal entry is needed to record the transfer of completed goods from one processing department to another?

***Q23-12** What basic features are associated with weighted-average process costing?

***Q23-13** In comparison with FIFO, what benefits arise from the use of weighted-average process costing?

---

* An asterisk preceding an item indicates that the material is covered in the appendix to this chapter.

## Exercises

**E23-1** ***Industry characteristics and costing systems***

Consider the activities of the following businesses. Determine whether each business would be most likely to use a job order system or a process costing system.

a Shipbuilder
b Petroleum refiner
c Candy manufacturer
d Trophy shop
e Brick manufacturer
f Shopping mall developer
g Book publisher
h Manufacturer of nuts and bolts
i Brewery
j Motion picture studio
k Frozen orange juice producer
l Manufacturer of jet aircraft
m Manufacturer of washers and dryers
n Nuclear power plant

**E23-2** ***Overview of process costing***

Evaluate the comments that follow as being True or False. If the comment is false, briefly explain why.

a The basic objective of a process costing system is to determine the cost of goods completed during the period and the cost of the ending work in process inventory.
b Under a FIFO process costing system, all goods completed during May are assumed to be started and completed in May.
c Unit manufacturing costs are the result of dividing the period's production costs by the number of physical units (e.g., tons, gallons, and so forth) manufactured.
d Each manufacturing department that uses a process costing system will maintain its own Work in Process account.
e Process costing systems are normally found in continuous manufacturing environments.

**E23-3** ***Calculation of equivalent units***

Consider the following independent cases:

- *Case A* Beginning work in process: 1,200 units, $\frac{2}{3}$ complete
  Units started and completed: 4,000
  Ending work in process: 1,600 units, $\frac{1}{4}$ complete
- *Case B* Beginning work in process: 6,000 units, $\frac{1}{3}$ complete
  Total units completed during the period: 15,000
  Ending work in process: 3,000 units, $\frac{1}{6}$ complete

All materials are added at the start of the process, and conversion costs are incurred uniformly throughout manufacturing. Assuming use of FIFO, compute total equivalent units with respect to materials and conversion costs for each of the preceding cases.

**E23-4** ***Computation of physical and equivalent units***

Victory Manufacturing produces industrial chemicals and uses a FIFO process costing system. The data that follow relate to July operations.

| | Gallons | Percent Complete | |
|---|---|---|---|
| | | Materials | Conversion |
| Work in process, 7/1 | 10,000 | 80% | 70% |
| Work in process, 7/31 | 14,000 | 30 | 10 |

Eighty thousand gallons were started into production during the month.

a Compute the number of gallons of chemicals completed in July.

b Calculate Victory's equivalent units for materials and conversion cost.

**E23-5** ***Cost of goods completed and ending work in process***

Accutech Manufacturing's cost accounting department has calculated the following equivalent production figures for August:

| | Physical Units | Equivalent Units | |
|---|---|---|---|
| | | Materials | Conversion |
| Completed production | | | |
| Beginning work in process | 900 | — | 600 |
| Units started and completed | 2,600 | 2,600 | 2,600 |
| Ending work in process | 1,500 | 1,500 | 1,000 |
| | 5,000 | 4,100 | 4,200 |

Prior period costs pertaining to the August 1 work in process inventory amounted to \$4,500. Current costs per equivalent unit are: materials, \$3.50; conversion, \$5.00.

a Determine the cost of production completed in August.

b Determine the cost of the ending work in process inventory.

**E23-6** ***Accounting for a second processing department***

Alamo Manufacturing uses a FIFO process cost system to accumulate production costs. The following information pertains to department B—the second department of a two-stage operation:

- Beginning work in process: 4,000 units, $\frac{1}{4}$ complete; cost, \$42,000
- Units transferred in during the period from department A: 7,000
- Total units completed during the period: 8,000
- Ending work in process: 3,000 units, $\frac{2}{3}$ complete

All materials are introduced in the initial processing stages; department B adds only conversion cost. Transferred-in cost during the period amounted to \$70,000; conversion cost related to B's operations totaled \$36,000.

a Compute equivalent unit figures for transferred-in and conversion cost.

b Compute the cost of production completed during the period and the ending work in process inventory.

***E23-7** ***Equivalent units and unit cost computations***

Fittings Unlimited uses a weighted-average process costing system. The data that follow pertain to May.

| | |
|---|---|
| Units started into production | 19,000 |
| Units in process, May 31 (40% complete) | 7,000 |
| Units in process, May 1 (30% complete) | 6,000 |
| Units completed | 18,000 |

The beginning work in process contained material and conversion costs of $10,000 and $22,000, respectively. Current manufacturing costs amounted to: materials, $40,000; conversion, $264,000.

a Determine the company's equivalent units for May.

b Calculate the cost per equivalent unit for materials and conversion cost.

***E23-8** ***Cost of goods completed and ending work in process***

Westwood Corporation has a two-stage production operation. Goods pass from cleaning to milling to finished goods. The following information pertains to the cleaning department for December:

| | |
|---|---|
| Total goods completed | 4,000 units |
| Ending work in process (70% complete) | 800 units |
| Beginning work in process (20% complete) | 500 units |

All materials are added at the beginning of production; conversion costs are incurred uniformly throughout manufacturing. The weighted-average costs per equivalent unit are: materials, $2.10; conversion, $8.50.

a Calculate the cost of goods completed and prepare the journal entry to record the transfer of goods from the cleaning department.

b Calculate the cost of the ending work in process.

## Problems

### Series A

**P23-A1** ***Straightforward process costing***

Chief Manufacturing uses a FIFO process costing system to accumulate production costs. The following information pertains to August:

- Beginning work in process inventory: 6,000 units, 70% complete; cost, $34,650
- Costs incurred in August: direct materials used, $28,500; conversion cost, $22,800
- Total units completed: 9,000
- Ending work in process inventory: 7,000 units, 40% complete
- Number of units started during August: 10,000

All materials are introduced at the start of the process, and conversion costs are incurred uniformly throughout manufacturing. Units pass directly from Chief's sole production department to the finished goods warehouse.

**Instructions**

a Prepare a production cost report in good form.

b Prepare the necessary journal entry to record the completed production for August.

**P23-A2** ***Production cost report; partial computations for second month***

Dallas Electronics operates a FIFO process costing system. All materials enter production at the beginning of the process; conversion costs are incurred evenly throughout manufacturing. The data that follow pertain to April of the current year.

- Work in process, 4/1: 12,000 units, 60% complete; cost, $104,900
- Work in process, 4/30: 10,000 units, 30% complete
- Units started into production: 48,000
- Total units completed: 50,000

Materials consumed during the month totaled $211,200; conversion costs amounted to $343,500.

**Instructions**

a Prepare a production cost report for April.
b During the following month, the company began work on 48,000 new units and finished 51,000 units. If the work in process on May 31 is 20% complete, calculate May's equivalent units for materials and conversion cost.

**P23-A3** ***Production cost computations***

Singapore Electronics assembles various components that are used in the aircraft industry. The company's major product, a pressure gauge, is the result of assembling three parts: DR532, HB4-786, and 429GY. All parts are introduced at the beginning of Singapore's manufacturing process; labor and overhead (i.e., conversion cost) is incurred uniformly throughout production. During March, the following costs were incurred:

- Direct materials used: DR532, $100,500; HB4-786, $207,300; 429GY, $32,400
- Direct labor: 2,500 hours @ $8

The overhead application rate is 260% of direct labor cost.

The beginning work in process inventory (8,000 units, 80% complete) was carried in the accounting records at a cost of $85,000. The ending work in process amounted to 4,000 units, 60% complete. Singapore finished a total of 40,000 gauges during the period.

**Instructions**

Assuming use of a FIFO process costing system, determine:
a Total production costs for March.
b Cost of goods completed during the month.
c Cost of the work in process inventory on March 31.

**P23-A4** ***Process costing and cost flow***

Stillwater Corporation uses a FIFO process costing system. All materials are introduced at the start of the process, and conversion costs are incurred uniformly throughout manufacturing. The following T-accounts were extracted from the company's records as of March 31:

***Work in Process***

| | | | | |
|---|---|---|---|---|
| 3/1 | Balance 1,800 units, $\frac{1}{3}$ complete | 14,720 | To finished goods: 1,800 units from 3/1 inventory | ? |
| | Started 6,000 units | | 4,000 units started and completed in March | ? |
| | Materials | 9,000 | | |
| | Conversion | 37,700 | | |

***Finished Goods***

| | | | | |
|---|---|---|---|---|
| 3/1 | Balance 4,000 units | 30,800 | To cost of goods sold: ? units | 65,580 |
| | From work in process: 5,800 units | ? | | |

The ending work in process inventory is 30% complete.

**Instructions**

a Compute the following:
 (1) Total equivalent units and the cost per equivalent unit for both materials and conversion cost.
 (2) The cost of units started in February and completed in March.
 (3) The cost of units started and completed in March.
 (4) The cost of units transferred to finished goods.
 (5) The cost of Stillwater's ending work in process inventory.

b If 2,100 finished units were on hand on March 31, determine (1) the ending balance in the Finished Goods account and (2) the number of units sold during March.

**P23-A5** ***Process cost accounting—Two departments***

Viking Manufacturing uses a FIFO process cost system to accumulate production costs. Units pass from department A to department B and then to finished goods. All direct materials are introduced in the initial processing stages of department A. The following data pertain to February:

- Department A
 Work in process inventory, Feb. 1: 5,000 units, 70% complete; cost, $30,300
 Number of units started during February: 13,000
 Total units completed: 11,000
 Work in process inventory, Feb. 28: 7,000 units, 40% complete
 Direct materials used: $39,000
 Conversion cost: $51,500
- Department B
 Work in process inventory, Feb. 1: 4,000 units, 60% complete; cost, $39,500
 Number of units started during February: ?
 Total units completed: 10,000
 Work in process inventory, Feb. 28: 5,000 units, 30% complete
 Conversion cost: $34,580

**Instructions**

a Prepare a production cost report for department A.

b Present the necessary journal entry to reflect the transfer of production from department A to department B.

c Prepare a production cost report for department B.

d Present the necessary journal entry to reflect the completion of production in department B.

***P23-A6** ***Straightforward process costing: Weighted average***

Surfing Equipment uses a weighted-average process costing system. The following information relates to department A for March:

- Units started into production: 34,000
- Total units completed: 29,000
- March manufacturing costs
 Direct materials used: $299,250
 Conversion cost: $379,350
- Work in process
 March 1: 7,000 units, 70% complete; cost, $114,400 (materials, $59,500; conversion, $54,900)
 March 31: 12,000 units, 80% complete

All materials are introduced at the start of manufacturing; conversion cost is incurred uniformly throughout the process. Units pass directly from department A to department B and then to finished goods.

**Instructions**

a Prepare a production cost report for March.
b Prepare the journal entry necessary to record the month's completed goods.

## Series B

**P23-B1** ***Straightforward process costing***

University Company uses a FIFO process costing system to accumulate production costs. The following information pertains to department no. 1 for July:

- Number of units started during July: 12,000
- Total units completed: 9,000
- Ending work in process inventory: 5,000 units, 40% complete
- Beginning work in process inventory: 2,000 units, 25% complete; cost, $8,600
- Costs incurred in July: direct materials used, $38,400; conversion cost, $47,250

All materials are introduced at the start of the process, and conversion costs are incurred uniformly throughout manufacturing. Units pass directly from department no. 1 to department no. 2 and then to finished goods.

**Instructions**

a Prepare a production cost report in good form.
b Prepare the necessary journal entry to record the completed production for July.

**P23-B2** ***Production cost report; partial computations for second month***

HRS Assembly, Inc., operates a FIFO process costing system. All materials enter production at the beginning of the process; conversion costs are incurred evenly throughout manufacturing. The data that follow pertain to November of the current year.

- Work in process, 11/1: 20,000 units, 70% complete; cost, $81,500
- Units started into production: 70,000
- Total units completed: 85,000
- Direct materials consumed: $140,000
- Conversion costs: $240,500
- Work in process, 11/30: 5,000 units, 60% complete

**Instructions**

a Prepare a production cost report for November.
b The following data relate to December:
    New production started: 78,000 units
    Total units completed: 76,000
  If the ending work in process is 20% complete, calculate December's equivalent units for materials and conversion cost.

**P23-B3** ***Production cost computations***

Consumer Health Foods produces a variety of health food items that are available at retail stores throughout the country. One of the company's products is Fruit & Grain, a popular breakfast cereal. The cereal is a combination of grain, bananas, and raisins, all of which are introduced at the beginning of the blending process. During June, the company used the following: grain, $19,200; bananas, $20,000; and raisins, $16,900. Other data for June are:

- Conversion cost
  Direct labor: Five employees worked 160 hours each and were paid $12 per hour.
  Overhead: Overhead for this highly automated process is applied at the rate of $29 per labor hour.
- Beginning work in process: 20,000 pounds, 30% complete; cost, $7,900
- Ending work in process: 25,000 pounds, 40% complete
- Total production completed during the month: 160,000 pounds

Conversion cost is incurred uniformly throughout manufacturing; a FIFO process costing system is used.

**Instructions**

Compute:
a Total production costs for June.
b Cost of goods completed during the month.
c Cost of the work in process inventory on June 30.

**P23-B4** ***Process costing and cost flow***
Spare Parts, Inc., uses a FIFO process costing system. All materials are introduced at the start of the process, and conversion costs are incurred uniformly throughout manufacturing. The following T-accounts were extracted from the company's records as of December 31:

| Work in Process | | | | |
|---|---|---|---|---|
| 12/1 | Balance 4,000 units, $\frac{3}{4}$ complete | 33,500 | To finished goods: | |
| | Started 9,000 units | | 4,000 units from 12/1 inventory | ? |
| | Materials | 32,400 | 6,000 units started and completed in December | ? |
| | Conversion | 43,450 | | |

| Finished Goods | | | | |
|---|---|---|---|---|
| 12/1 | Balance 7,000 units | 63,000 | To cost of goods sold: | |
| | From work in process: 10,000 units | ? | ? units | 134,136 |

The ending work in process inventory is 30% complete.

**Instructions**

a Compute the following:
  (1) Total equivalent units and the cost per equivalent unit for both materials and conversion cost.
  (2) The cost of units started in November and completed in December.
  (3) The cost of units started and completed in December.
  (4) The cost of units transferred to finished goods.
  (5) The cost of the company's ending work in process inventory.
b If 2,400 finished units were on hand on December 31, determine (1) the ending balance in the Finished Goods account and (2) the number of units sold during December.

**P23-B5** ***Process cost accounting—Two departments***

Frisco Manufacturing uses a FIFO process cost system to accumulate production costs. Units pass from the assembly department to the finishing department and then to finished goods. All direct materials are introduced in the initial processing stages of the assembly department. The following data pertain to August:

| | *Assembly* | *Finishing* |
|---|---|---|
| Work in process inventory, August 1 | | |
| Assembly: 8,000 units, 40% complete | $71,800 | |
| Finishing: 5,000 units, 70% complete | | $124,500 |
| Units started during August | 15,000 | ? |
| Total units completed | 17,000 | 18,000 |
| Work in process inventory, August 31 | | |
| Assembly: 6,000 units, 30% complete | | |
| Finishing: 4,000 units, 80% complete | | |
| Direct materials used | $75,000 | — |
| Conversion cost | $171,600 | $247,800 |

**Instructions**

a Prepare a production cost report for the assembly department.
b Present the necessary journal entry to reflect the transfer of production from the assembly department to the finishing department.
c Prepare a production cost report for the finishing department.
d Present the necessary journal entry to reflect the completion of production in the finishing department.

***P23-B6** ***Straightforward process costing: Weighted average***

Red River, Inc., uses a weighted-average process costing system. The following information relates to operations of October:

- Work in process
  October 1: 10,000 units, 40% complete; cost $41,600 (materials, $18,000; conversion, $23,600)
  October 31: 4,000 units, 75% complete
- October manufacturing costs
  Direct materials used: $46,600
  Conversion cost: $174,400
- Units started into production: 24,000
- Total units completed: 30,000

All materials are introduced at the start of manufacturing; conversion cost is incurred uniformly throughout the process. Units pass directly from Red River's sole production department to the finished goods warehouse.

**Instructions**

a Prepare a production cost report for October.
b Prepare the journal entry necessary to record the month's completed goods.

## Beyond the Basics

**BB23-1** ***Process costing calculations: Partial data***

Dr. Laura Allen, an accounting professor, has just completed writing an examination that covers FIFO process costing. Unfortunately, while Laura was attending a birthday dinner with her spouse, the family dog became hungry and ate selected parts of problem no. 3.

Problem no. 3 deals with LBG Industries, which manufactures goods in a two-stage operation. Goods pass from assembly to finishing to the finished goods warehouse. All materials are introduced in the assembly department, with the exception of packaging material. Packaging is added at the end of the finishing process; conversion costs are incurred uniformly throughout production. Consider the following fragmented data that pertain to the finishing operation:

| | | *Equivale* | *ts* | |
|---|---|---|---|---|
| | *Physical Units* | *Transferred-In* | *Mate* | *Conversion* |
| Completed | | | | |
| Beginning work in process | 14,000 | — | | 12,600 |
| Units started and completed | 32,000 | 32,000 | 32,000 | 32,000 |
| Ending work in process | 10,000 | 10,000 | | 3,000 |
| Units accounted for | 56,000 | 42,000 | | 47,600 |

| *Costs* | *Total* | *Transferred-In* | *Mat* | *nversion* |
|---|---|---|---|---|
| Beginning work in process | $90,800 | — | | |
| Current costs | | $252,000 | | |
| Cost per equivalent unit | | $6 | $0.20 | $5.50 |

Dr. Allen has given the fragments to her student assistant to determine whether the examination questions can still be answered. The professor is considering use of the fragments alone as a new test problem.

### Instructions

Assume the role of the student assistant and determine answers to the following:

a What does the transferred-in cost of $252,000 represent?
b How many units were started into production during the period?
c How much finishing work was performed on the beginning work in process in the last accounting period?
d How far into the finishing process is the ending work in process inventory?
e Why has the finishing department established equivalent-unit columns for both transferred-in goods and materials?
f Calculate the total equivalent units for materials.
g Determine the total conversion cost for the period.
h Calculate the cost of goods completed during the period.

## Answers to Chapter Quiz

**1** b

**2** a

**3** b (Beginning work in process, 0; units started and completed, 7,000; ending work in process, 3,000)

**4** d

**5** b

# Budgeting

CHAPTER 24

## Learning Objectives

After reading this chapter you should:

1 Understand the benefits of budgeting.

2 Understand the distinction between top-down and bottom-up budgeting.

3 Be familiar with slack as it relates to the estimation process.

4 Understand the variations in budget periods.

5 Be familiar with the limitations of budgeting, especially in the human relations area.

6 Be able to prepare a master budget.

7 Be familiar with the adaptability of budgets to computers.

Businesses in this country continually strive to increase profitability. In an effort to boost net income, companies construct new facilities, undertake research programs, hire employees with needed skills, and introduce new product lines. These actions are usually not haphazard; rather, they are part of a carefully defined plan to achieve a certain objective.

Business planning may assume several different forms. When dealing with the long run, companies formulate generalized goals along with strategies and policies to achieve those goals. For example, suppose a manufacturer of household cleaning products desires to enter the car care market. Accordingly, the company could establish a strategy to acquire an existing manufacturer of car care products or perhaps engage in an extensive research program and develop new products internally. Planning of this nature is essential, because it helps chart an entity's operation over many future periods.

Another facet of planning involves budgets. A **budget** is a formal quantitative expression of management expectations. Unlike strategies and policies, budgets contain considerable detail. In effect, a budget can be likened to a blueprint, that is, an intricate plan that serves as a framework for future action.

Budgets are popular among businesses and numerous governmental units. As the following example shows, even not-for-profit entities find budgeting beneficial.

> The American Bar Association (ABA) is a national professional organization of practicing attorneys. The purpose of the organization is to advance the professional practice of law. This purpose is accomplished (1) through various committees that study specific legal issues, (2) by furnishing advice to the United States Congress on pending legislation, and (3) by disseminating various publications to members. Most of the ABA's revenues are received during a three-month period (June–August) when annual dues are billed to members. However, the organization's activities continue throughout the year. If the ABA did not engage in a budgeting program to forecast revenues and expenditures, it could easily run out of funds before the next billing period. For this reason the budgeting process at the ABA is quite formalized, and all units must carefully adhere to the approved budgetary plan.

## Benefits of Budgeting

OBJECTIVE 1
**Understand the benefits of budgeting.**

If done correctly, budgeting is a time-consuming and arduous process. It goes without saying that an in-depth look at the future requires numerous assumptions, much uncertainty, and often, considerable employee involvement. Furthermore, managers must frequently turn their thoughts away from current, pressing problems to devote full attention to the budget effort. With all these unattractive features, the question arises, "Why budget?" Normally, the benefits of budgeting outweigh the associated problems. Budgets formalize planning, serve as a basis for performance evaluation, and assist in communication and coordination within an entity.

### Formalize Planning

Budgets are an outgrowth of the planning process. Because budgets force managers to look ahead and study the future, a formalized "plan of attack" can be constructed. To picture the related benefits, imagine building a home without the availability of the previously mentioned blueprint. Walls may be encased in plasterboard, only for the contractor to discover that electrical outlets and heating vents were forgotten. Or the foundation may be laid and then found to be over the property line. Indeed, the building process would be chaotic at best. Similarly, the lack of a formal plan leads to considerable "fire fighting" on the part of management, thereby hampering the attainment of long-run goals and objectives.

The implementation of a budget enables companies (and individuals) to pinpoint potential problems before the problems occur. Operating distractions are thus greatly reduced, since anticipation often leads to the introduction of preliminary corrective action. The eventual outcome of planning is a direction-oriented entity—one that knows where it wants to go and how it wants to get there.

## Serve as a Basis for Performance Evaluation

Although best-noted for its role in planning, a budget also assists management in the appraisal of performance and control of operations. As explained in Chapter 21, organizations often prepare reports that compare actual results against a predetermined plan. The budget therefore serves as a yardstick in judging whether performance has been up to par. Should deficiencies arise, corrective action can be taken to bring the organization back on target.

Some businesses attempt to evaluate performance by comparing current results against the actual results of previous accounting periods. Unfortunately, this type of evaluation has an inherent deficiency. To illustrate, assume that a company's total operating expenses last year amounted to $200,000. If the company was subjected to a 10% inflation rate and current expenses total only $210,000, the immediate conclusion might be that management has done a creditable job in controlling costs. However, if last year's expenses were excessive because of significant inefficiencies, the entire evaluative picture could change. For instance, suppose last year's expenses would have been $180,000 under reasonably efficient operating conditions. Allowing for an $18,000 increase from inflation, current expenses would exceed the $198,000 target by $12,000 ($210,000 − $198,000).

Comparisons with past data simply do not reveal whether current performance is acceptable. Bear in mind that past data bring all that was bad about the past into the evaluation. Furthermore, if a company's operating environment has changed significantly because of new technology, a new management team, or other factors, studies of past versus present very quickly approach the meaningless level. Current performance is best judged against a budget for the same period. Although the budget relies on many assumptions, adequate appraisal can occur if due care has been exercised in budget formation and if all available information is considered.

## Assist in Communication and Coordination

Business operations dictate the performance of many diverse activities. These activities include the production and sale of goods and services, purchasing, credit extension and the collection of accounts, data processing, and the financing of operations. In very small enterprises these functions are often supervised by the same person. In larger organizations, however, operations are normally divided and are the responsibility of different managers.

To achieve company objectives, close coordination of activities is a necessity. Imagine the problems that could arise if coordination was lacking. For example, the marketing department could undertake a large advertising campaign for a new product and then find that production was halted from a shortage of needed raw materials. Or at a time when marketing was attempting to expand the company's market share, the credit department might be tightening credit standards because of recent problems with uncollectible accounts. In both of these cases embarrassment is sure to result.

Where do budgets fit in? When a budget for the overall organization is being constructed, individual managers must communicate their plans. The plans are then examined to determine whether they are feasible and consistent with the plans of other operating units. The budget process therefore serves as a gigantic blender that integrates and coordinates diverse activities to help attain company goals.

## Budget Construction

The construction of a budget varies dramatically from one business to the next. Many companies establish formal procedures that are followed to the letter. In contrast, other enterprises employ "seat of the pants" management and merely scribble some hastily derived projections on the back of an envelope. Because of the wide variety of approaches found in practice, any attempt at presenting a detailed discussion on how to budget or "The Ten Easy Steps to Budgeting" is fruitless. There are, however, several general construction concepts with which you should be familiar. A short discussion of these concepts follows.

### Construction Flows

Most medium- and large-size entities are composed of several management levels. See Exhibit 24-1, for example, which depicts a typical organizational hierarchy.

The budget-building process generally follows the organizational structure. That is, construction proceeds from higher- to lower-management levels, or vice versa.

OBJECTIVE 2
Understand the distinction between top-down and bottom-up budgeting.

#### Top-Down Approach

With the **top-down approach,** virtually all budget development takes place at the upper echelons of management. The budget is imposed on lower-level personnel, who rarely become involved in the construction process. On paper, the top-down

**Exhibit 24-1**
**Organizational Hierarchy**

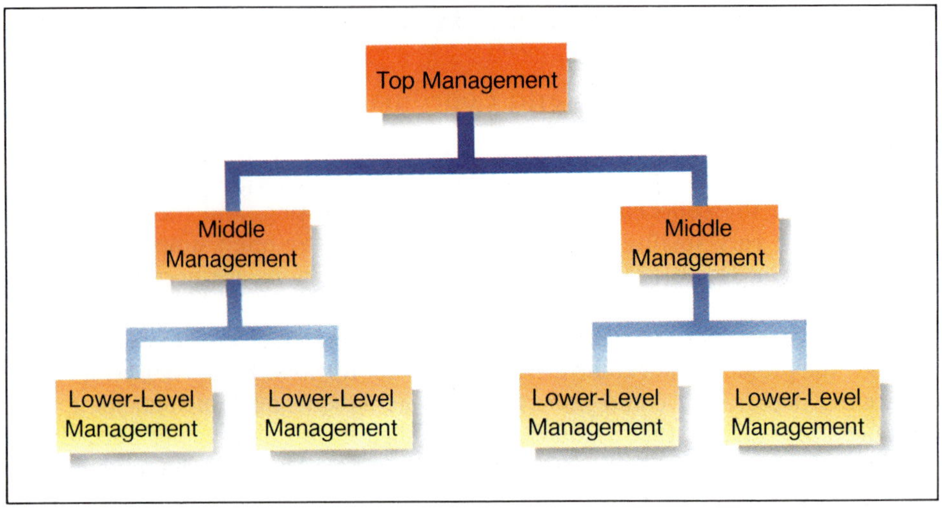

approach offers the advantage of sound budget preparation. A budget should reflect the overall goals of an organization; preparation in this instance is carried forth by those who have the best view of companywide operations, namely, top management. Upper-level executives can study the interactions of the lower units and determine the consistency of the units' plans and expectations.

In most cases this apparent advantage gives rise to a significant problem. When the budget is imposed from above, lower-level managers often feel that their opinions and operating perspectives lack importance. Although lower-level employees will be evaluated against the budget, they have done little to assist in its development. This "dictatorial" approach is generally met with resentment and a "who cares" attitude, both of which result in a negative stand toward budget achievement.

## Bottom-up Approach

Unlike the top-down approach, **bottom-up budgeting** centers on lower-level employee participation in the development process. The bottom-up approach usually begins with the issuance of general budget guidelines by top management or perhaps by a budget committee. The budget committee normally consists of company executives along with representatives from functional areas such as sales, production, and finance. The guidelines often include yearly goals, anticipated inflation rates, available resources, and other similar data.

Once this information is communicated, those employees held responsible for achieving the desired results assemble appropriate budgets. The process begins at the lower levels of the organizational structure and works its way upward. Individual budgets become grouped by major operating units, such as divisions and territories, and eventually reach top management or the budget committee. The budgets are reviewed, and suggestions for improvement are offered. Lower-level managers then make the necessary revisions, and ultimately, a compromise is reached.

The bottom-up approach offers several distinct advantages over a budget that is handed down from top management with a "meet it or else" attitude.

1 Bottom-up (i.e., *participative*) budgets are really self-imposed. By consulting with and incorporating the goals of lower-level employees, greater strides are made toward budget achievement. That is, individuals throughout the organization know their views are valued and considered by top management. As a result, employee morale and job satisfaction generally increase, and extensive efforts are made to meet the agreed-on targets.

2 The budget is constructed by employees who are close to the action and who know the intricate details of daily activity. The same cannot be said for a budget that is prepared solely by top management with no lower-level input. Consequently, the bottom-up approach usually results in a more realistic and accurate target of performance.

In terms of negative criticism, the bottom-up method is time-consuming and expensive to administer because of increased employee involvement. Nevertheless, it is a popular tool among progressive companies. Because the broad perspectives of top management are used in conjunction with the detailed operating knowledge of lower-level personnel, a powerful budget document is created—one that encompasses the views of all ranges of the organizational hierarchy.

## HIGHLIGHT

# Capitol Hill Budget Construction

During an otherwise routine White House meeting between President Reagan and Republican lawmakers several years ago, Sen. Jake Garn erupted in an emotional tirade against the congressional budget process. The procedure had broken down, the Utah lawmaker asserted. The American people were being ill served. Budget deficits weren't being restrained as they should. So heartfelt was his message, other participants recall, that tears rolled down his cheeks.

Not every member of Congress sheds tears over the budget process, but most do throw their hands up in frustration. The manner in which Congress decides how to spend taxpayers' money increasingly has come under attack for taking too much time and accomplishing too little, as well as for making the legislative lives of many members miserable. "A lot of people hate the budget process for a lot of reasons," acknowledges the chairman of the Senate Budget Committee. His House counterpart adds, "It is a pain."

Formerly, Congress had a two-tiered budget process. So-called authorizing committees would decide on the need for and specifics of government programs, while appropriations committees would vote the funds for them. But many found that system to be haphazard, and argued that creating a single, coherent spending blueprint would improve management of the government. Moreover, some thought such a system would increase Congress's control over the purse strings in the wake of its battles over President Nixon's attempted refusal to spend some funds appropriated by Congress.

So in 1974, Congress set up a third layer in the form of a new budget committee in both the House and Senate. These panels were charged with drafting a spending blueprint that the rest of Congress would follow. It often doesn't work that way. In some years, the blueprint is simply ignored. In others, it is composed only after the real budget decisions are already made. In the 186 years before the 1974 Budget Act, the U.S. accumulated $544 billion of debt; in the years since, the government has accumulated over $1 trillion of *additional* debt—though some argue that the deficit would be even greater without the budget process. [1]

Contrary to popular opinion, Congress (unlike most other legislatures) does not in fact approve a budget per sé. Since 1974, Congress (usually) adopts something called a budget *resolution,* which the press frequently calls a budget. It is not. It is a set of guidelines, of varying degrees of enforceability, for subsequent spending and revenue legislation. But the resolution does not enact anything and is not signed by the President.

There are various proposals for budget reform in the works, including anything from budgeting on a two-year rather than a one-year basis and imposing harsh spending cuts if budget deadlines aren't met. President Reagan himself expressed a desire for two amendments to the Constitution, one requiring a balanced budget, the other giving him the power to veto individual items in the budget. As one publication that focuses on our economy has noted, the prospects for these proposed changes are about as obscure as the existing process. [2]

SOURCES: Adapted from "Congress Pokes Again At Perennial Problem, The Budgetary System," *The Wall Street Journal*, February 26, 1987, pp. 1, 13 [1]; and "Not So Much a Budget, More a Mess," *The Economist*, June 27, 1987, p. 29 [2]. 

## Budget Estimation

By its nature, a budget is a series of future estimates. These estimates should not be arrived at haphazardly; instead, significant care should be exercised in their determination.

Normally, budget estimates are based on both the past and the future. Historical information is often a good starting point for prediction; however, because of changing conditions, modification of past trends may be necessary. As an example, suppose that a company is attempting to budget sales for a particular product. The company presently has a 26% market share and has increased its share by 1% in each of the past five years. Should business conditions remain relatively stable, the firm would be correct in anticipating a 27% share of total sales for the upcoming period. If, however, the operating environment changes because of, say, new competition or technological innovations, these factors must be considered if the sales estimate is to have much meaning.

### Estimation and Slack

OBJECTIVE 3
Be familiar with slack as it relates to the estimation process.

As noted earlier, budgets are frequently used in performance evaluation. Well aware of this fact, many managers build **slack,** or padding, into their budgets to avoid unfavorable appraisals. For example, sales and operating capabilities may be underestimated and expenses may be overestimated. Thus, when the actual results are tabulated and sales are "down" and expenses are "up," the manager is still deemed to have met his or her budget (and company objectives). In essence, slack has given the manager some leeway in the performance of daily activities.

Slack permeates the entire budgetary process and sometimes tends to perpetuate itself. As an example, in many not-for-profit entities, operating units are given a maximum spending limit for specific types of expenditures. A governmental entity, for instance, may be authorized to spend $5,000 for new equipment acquisitions during the fiscal year. If the year-end is rapidly approaching and considerable funds have yet to be used, the unit may undertake a buying spree. Why? If funds remain, administrators might take the position that the current equipment budget was apparently in excess of amounts really needed. Consequently, there could be a strong tendency for cutbacks in the next budget period. This "use it or lose it" philosophy often gives rise to status-quo or larger (i.e., slack-filled) budgets in future years and may result in questionable operating practices that conflict with an entity's goals.

Slack is a significant problem for many budget makers and is extremely difficult to eliminate. Although it is easier said than done, budget estimates should be realistic and should shy away from excessive optimism and pessimism. Unrealistic estimates defeat the entire purpose of the budgeting effort. The net result is aptly described by the acronym GIGO: garbage in, garbage out.

## The Budget Period

OBJECTIVE 4
Understand the variations in budget periods.

Budgets normally cover differing periods of time. Picture, for example, a company that is planning a major capital improvements program through acquisitions of needed property, plant, and equipment. These assets benefit many periods and usually involve substantial dollar outlays. Given the nature of the expenditure, the company should establish a budget for such acquisitions that extends several years into the future. In fact, capital expenditure budgets covering five to ten years are common. Such a long time horizon is necessary so that problems can be solved long before they occur. In the capital equipment area, for instance, a company may find itself in need of new assets but suddenly determine that insufficient funds are available to make the required purchases. Funding of this nature normally cannot be obtained overnight; thus, long-term planning is of utmost importance.

Budgets that pertain to *operations* are generally prepared for a one-year time frame and usually coincide with the period employed for external financial reporting. For purposes of control and evaluation these budgets are subsequently subdivided into quarters and months. The benefit of following this latter procedure is evident after studying Exhibit 24-2.

The exhibit depicts the budgeted monthly cash balances of a seasonal business. Notice that if the budget is viewed over a one-year period, we see a favorable cash position—the balance increases by $20,000 (from $80,000 in January to $100,000 in December). A breakdown by months, however, shows the need for short-term financing from the end of May through July because of seasonal cash needs and a drop below the $50,000 minimum. Generally stated, shorter budget periods usually enable a closer monitoring of operations.

In actuality, many businesses use a combination of monthly, yearly, and long-term budgets. In recent years a number of organizations have turned to continuous budgets. A **continuous budget** covers a one-year period, with a new month being added as the current month is completed. For example, assume that a budget for 19X1 operations is prepared. As soon as January 19X1 is completed, a budget is added on for January 19X2. Continuous budgets offer the advantage of forcing management to continually think about the future. The planning process is not confined to only a few months of each year but becomes an ongoing, stabilized activity.

## Budget Limitations and Human Relations

Critics contend that several limitations are associated with budgeting. First, a budget is only as good as the effort that goes into its preparation. Top management

**Exhibit 24-2**
**Cash Balances of a Seasonal Business**

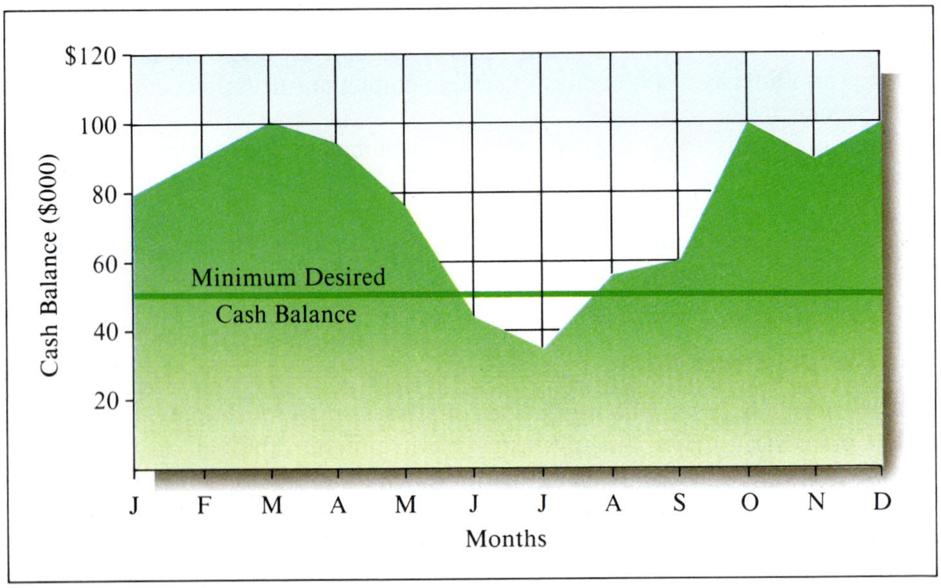

must thoroughly support the budget process, or else the entire exercise will be a lesson in futility. Second, budgeting cannot replace effective day-to-day management. That is, the budget is a tool to be used by managers; it is not an end in itself and will not automatically improve a faltering operation. Although the critics' observations are correct, the preceding comments really apply to all aspects of management, not just budgeting in isolation.

OBJECTIVE 5
Be familiar with the limitations of budgeting, especially in the human relations area.

Perhaps the most significant limitation of budgeting lies in the human relations and administration area. Many organizations overemphasize the use of budgets in control—and they often do so in an incorrect manner. To explain, employees are frequently disenchanted with tools used to evaluate performance. Budgets disclose weaknesses and are often studied by upper management when finding who's to blame in unfavorable times. To avoid possible negativism on the part of employees, management should educate personnel that budgeting is a positive tool that assists in achieving company goals, monitoring progress toward those goals, and setting standards of performance.

The administration of a budget program is a difficult task. Executives often become overly involved with the numerical aspects of budget construction and lose sight of the fact that employees are people. Employees have feelings and are sensitive to management looking over their shoulders to appraise performance. Unless the budget process considers human relations, even the best efforts will go for naught and be met with resistance.

## Comprehensive Budgeting

OBJECTIVE 6
Be able to prepare a master budget.

Earlier in the chapter we noted that budget preparation often follows a company's organizational structure. Budgets for the company's individual operating units (e.g., departments, divisions, territories, and so forth) are generated and later combined. This process culminates in the **master budget,** a comprehensive set of integrated budgets that serves as the financial plan for the entire organization. Although variations are found in practice, the master budget generally consists of the following:

1 Sales budget
2 Production budget
3 Direct material purchases budget
4 Direct labor budget
5 Factory overhead budget
6 Selling and administrative expense budget
7 Capital expenditures budget
8 Cash budget
9 Budgeted income statement
10 Budgeted balance sheet
11 Budgeted statement of cash flows

These budgets cannot be prepared independently. Sales levels, for example, influence production plans. The number of units produced affects direct material, direct labor, and overhead costs, and all the foregoing have a bearing on an entity's cash budget and financial statements. The relationships within a master budget are shown in Exhibit 24-3.

**Exhibit 24-3 Relationships Within the Master Budget**

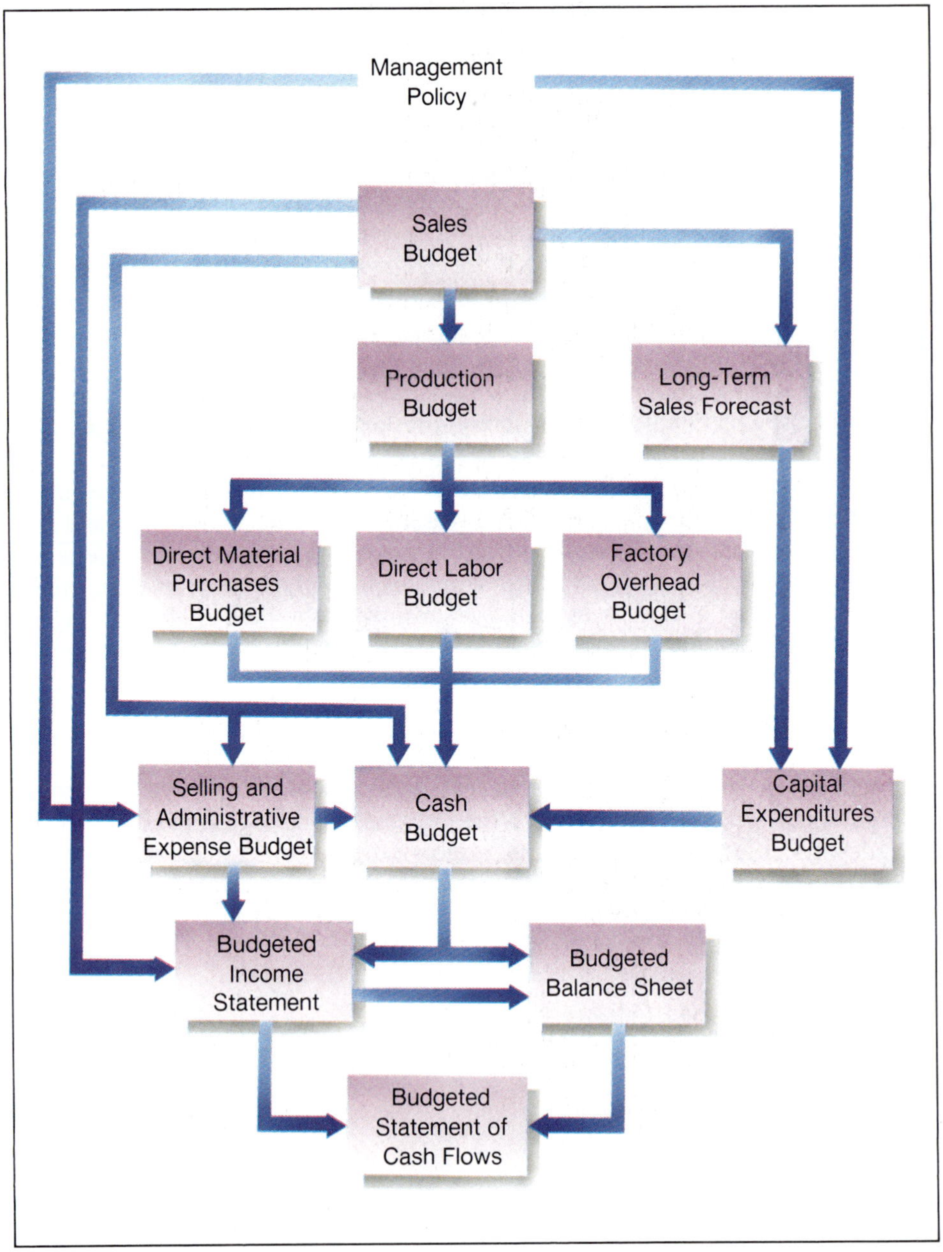


These relationships will become more apparent in the example that follows. At this point, observe how the sales budget is the starting point in the budgeting process. In addition, note how the cash budget and the budgeted financial statements serve as the focal point and summarization of the entire planning effort.

## Master Budget Illustration

To illustrate the construction of a master budget, we will focus on the Hillcroft Corporation. Hillcroft manufactures and sells a single product and desires to budget first-quarter activity for 19X2. Assume that Hillcroft's master budget is similar to that just discussed. For simplicity, however, we will exclude the capital expenditures budget and the statement of cash flows from our presentation. Hillcroft's December 31, 19X1, balance sheet appears in Exhibit 24-4.

## Sales Budget

The sales budget is probably the most important element of the master budget. Production, cash flow, the financial statements, and a number of other items all depend on sales, in terms of both units sold and revenues generated. A grossly incorrect sales budget will therefore be reflected throughout the entire budgeting process.

The sales budget is based on a forecast of sales volume. Forecasted volume is influenced by such factors as previous sales patterns, current and expected economic conditions, actions of competitors, and advertising and marketing strategies. Estimates of volume can be calculated by using several different techniques. For example, a company can (1) study the relationship of sales to various economic indicators (such as interest rates and disposable income), (2) use various statistical forecasting methods, or (3) probe its sales staff regarding customer purchase plans for the upcoming period.

Once the forecast is derived, the sales budget is prepared by multiplying the expected volume by the estimated selling price per unit. Hillcroft's sales budget is shown in Exhibit 24-5.

**Exhibit 24-4**

**HILLCROFT CORPORATION**
**Balance Sheet**
**December 31, 19X1**

| | | |
|---|---|---|
| ***Assets*** | | |
| Current assets | | |
| Cash | $ 7,000 | |
| Accounts receivable | 10,000 | |
| Finished goods (1,500 units × $7.00) | 10,500 | |
| Direct materials (6,900 units × $1.50) | 10,350 | $ 37,850 |
| Property, plant, & equipment | | |
| Plant & equipment | $70,000 | |
| Less: Accumulated depreciation | 5,000 | 65,000 |
| Total assets | | $102,850 |
| ***Liabilities & Stockholders' Equity*** | | |
| Current liabilities | | |
| Accounts payable | | $ 8,000 |
| Stockholders' equity | | |
| Common stock | $40,000 | |
| Retained earnings | 54,850 | 94,850 |
| Total liabilities & stockholders' equity | | $102,850 |

**Exhibit 24-5**

**HILLCROFT CORPORATION**
**Sales Budget**
**For the Quarter Ended March 31, 19X2**

| | *January* | *February* | *March* | *Total* |
|---|---|---|---|---|
| Expected sales (units) | 4,500 | 5,500 | 7,000 | 17,000 |
| Selling price per unit | × $10 | × $10 | × $10 | × $10 |
| Budgeted sales revenues | $45,000 | $55,000 | $70,000 | $170,000 |

***Schedule of Cash Collections*** Although not part of the formal sales budget, a schedule of expected cash collections is easily generated at this time. The schedule provides information that will be needed when preparing the cash budget. To illustrate the necessary procedures, assume Hillcroft's sales are all on account. Seventy percent of the sales are collected in the month of sale; the remaining 30% are collected in the following month. The corporation's cash collection schedule appears in Exhibit 24-6.

## Production Budget

Once the sales budget is completed, a company's production requirements can be determined. Aside from sales, the number of units scheduled for manufacturing depends on raw material and facilities availability and desired finished goods inventory levels. Finished goods are often budgeted in advance so that adequate stock levels can be maintained. Businesses try to avoid carrying excessive goods because of associated storage, insurance, taxes, and interest costs, and the possibility of deterioration and obsolescence. Further, these same entities shy away from precariously low inventories that could lead to stockouts, lost sales, and even lost customers.

**Exhibit 24-6**

**HILLCROFT CORPORATION**
**Schedule of Cash Collections**
**For the Quarter Ended March 31, 19X2**

| | *January* | *February* | *March* | *Total* |
|---|---|---|---|---|
| Accounts receivable, 12/31/X1 | $10,000* | | | $ 10,000 |
| January sales ($45,000) | 31,500 | $13,500 | | 45,000 |
| February sales ($55,000) | | 38,500 | $16,500 | 55,000 |
| March sales ($70,000) | | | 49,000 | 49,000 |
| Total budgeted cash collections | $41,500 | $52,000 | $65,500 | $159,000 |

* From Exhibit 24-4.

*Note:* Because only $49,000 of March sales are collected in March, the remaining $21,000 ($70,000 − $49,000) will appear on Hillcroft's end-of-quarter balance sheet as accounts receivable.

The budgeted units of production in any given period can be calculated as follows:

| Number of units to be produced | |
|---|---|
| Number of units sold | XXX |
| Add: Desired ending finished goods inventory (units) | XXX |
| Total finished units needed | XXX |
| Less: Beginning finished goods inventory (units) | XXX |
| Number of units to be produced | XXX |

By adding budgeted sales to the units desired for the ending finished goods inventory, we obtain the total units needed during the period. Because some of these units already exist via the beginning finished goods inventory, the remainder will have to be manufactured.

Hillcroft wishes to maintain an ending finished goods inventory that covers 50% of the following month's sales. This inventory policy gives rise to the production budget shown in Exhibit 24-7.

## Direct Material Purchases Budget

Now that production requirements are known, the direct material purchases budget can be prepared. Budgeted purchases are based on anticipated manufacturing schedules and desired ending raw material inventories. The latter amounts are sometimes influenced by supplier delivery schedules, the availability of "specials" and quantity discounts, and management's purchasing strategy in heading off price increases.

**Exhibit 24-7**

**HILLCROFT CORPORATION**
**Production Budget**
**For the Quarter Ended March 31, 19X2**

| | *January* | *February* | *March* | *Total* |
|---|---|---|---|---|
| Number of units sold (Exhibit 24-5) | 4,500 | 5,500 | 7,000 | 17,000 |
| Add: Desired ending finished goods inventory (50% × following month's sales) | 2,750 | 3,500 | 3,800† | 3,800‡ |
| Total finished units needed | 7,250 | 9,000 | 10,800 | 20,800 |
| Less: Beginning finished goods inventory* | 1,500 | 2,750 | 3,500 | 1,500‡ |
| Number of units to be produced | 5,750 | 6,250 | 7,300 | 19,300 |

* The beginning finished goods inventory is the ending finished goods inventory from the preceding month. January's beginning inventory of 1,500 units appears on the balance sheet presented in Exhibit 24-4.

† April's sales are assumed to be 7,600 units; thus, the desired ending finished goods inventory in March is 3,800 units (7,600 units × 50%).

‡ The ending and beginning inventories are used here, not the total of the inventories. Insertion of totals will result in incorrect calculations. As an example, summation of the ending inventory figures yields 10,050 units (2,750 + 3,500 + 3,800), which, when added to sales, produces total finished units needed of 27,050 (10,050 + 17,000). The result is misleading because Hillcroft needs only 20,800 units during the quarter: 17,000 units to cover sales and 3,800 units to generate the desired March 31 finished goods inventory.

The amount of materials to purchase can be computed in a fashion similar to that for finding the budgeted units of production, namely:

| Direct materials to be purchased | |
|---|---|
| Direct materials used in production (units) | XXX |
| Add: Desired ending direct materials inventory (units) | XXX |
| Total direct materials needed | XXX |
| Less: Beginning direct materials inventory (units) | XXX |
| Direct materials to be purchased (units) | XXX |

Assume that Hillcroft uses two units of direct material in each completed product and that each direct material unit costs $1.50. Management desires to maintain an ending materials inventory equal to 60% of the direct materials needed in the following month's production. The company's direct material purchases budget is shown in Exhibit 24-8.

***Schedule of Cash Disbursements for Material Purchases*** Given Hillcroft's purchasing program, we can now construct a schedule of the required cash disbursements. This schedule, like the schedule of cash collections, is useful when preparing the cash budget. To illustrate the necessary procedures, assume Hillcroft expects to pay 60% of a given month's purchases during the month of purchase; the remain-

**Exhibit 24-8**

**HILLCROFT CORPORATION**
**Direct Material Purchases Budget**
**For the Quarter Ended March 31, 19X2**

| | *January* | *February* | *March* | *Total* |
|---|---|---|---|---|
| Planned production in units (Exhibit 24-7) | 5,750 | 6,250 | 7,300 | 19,300 |
| Units of direct material per finished unit | × 2 | × 2 | × 2 | × 2 |
| Direct materials used in production (units) | 11,500 | 12,500 | 14,600 | 38,600 |
| Add: Desired ending direct materials inventory (units)* | 7,500 | 8,760 | 9,960 | 9,960 |
| Total direct materials needed | 19,000 | 21,260 | 24,560 | 48,560 |
| Less: Beginning direct materials inventory (units)† | 6,900 | 7,500 | 8,760 | 6,900 |
| Direct materials to be purchased (units) | 12,100 | 13,760 | 15,800 | 41,660 |
| Cost per unit | × $1.50 | × $1.50 | × $1.50 | × $1.50 |
| Cost of direct material purchases | $18,150 | $20,640 | $23,700 | $62,490 |

* The desired ending inventory equals 60% of the direct materials used in the following month's production. Ending inventories are computed as follows:

January: 60% × 12,500 = 7,500
February: 60% × 14,600 = 8,760
March: 60% × 16,600 (assumed) = 9,960

† The beginning direct materials inventory is the ending direct materials inventory from the preceding month. January's beginning inventory of 6,900 units appears on the balance sheet presented in Exhibit 24-4.

Exhibit 24-9

**HILLCROFT CORPORATION**
**Schedule of Cash Disbursements for Material Purchases**
**For the Quarter Ended March 31, 19X2**

| | *January* | *February* | *March* | *Total* |
|---|---|---|---|---|
| Accounts payable, 12/31/X1 | $ 8,000* | | | $ 8,000 |
| January purchases ($18,150) | 10,890 | $ 7,260 | | 18,150 |
| February purchases ($20,640) | | 12,384 | $ 8,256 | 20,640 |
| March purchases ($23,700) | | | 14,220 | 14,220 |
| Total disbursements for purchases | $18,890 | $19,644 | $22,476 | $61,010 |

* From Exhibit 24-4.

*Note:* Because only $14,220 of March purchases are paid in March, the remaining $9,480 ($23,700 − $14,220) will appear on Hillcroft's end-of-quarter balance sheet as accounts payable.

ing 40% will be paid in the following month. The schedule of cash disbursements for materials appears in Exhibit 24-9.

## Direct Labor Budget

The direct labor budget is also based on the production schedule. Direct labor must be budgeted so that management can determine if sufficient personnel are available to manufacture the company's product. A lack of proper planning could lead to labor shortages or overstaffing, both of which result in production inefficiencies. Furthermore, employee morale could suffer because of possible layoffs or extensive overtime to meet manufacturing schedules.

Direct labor requirements are determined by multiplying the number of direct labor hours per finished unit by the number of units to be produced. The result is then multiplied by the estimated direct labor cost per hour to generate total budgeted labor costs. For example, assume Hillcroft Corporation pays its workers $6.00 per hour and that each finished unit requires 0.5 hours of direct labor time. The necessary computations appear in Hillcroft's direct labor budget, which is shown in Exhibit 24-10.

Exhibit 24-10

**HILLCROFT CORPORATION**
**Direct Labor Budget**
**For the Quarter Ended March 31, 19X2**

| | *January* | *February* | *March* | *Total* |
|---|---|---|---|---|
| Planned production, in units (Exhibit 24-7) | 5,750 | 6,250 | 7,300 | 19,300 |
| Labor time per unit (hours) | × 0.5 | × 0.5 | × 0.5 | × 0.5 |
| Total labor hours needed | 2,875 | 3,125 | 3,650 | 9,650 |
| Direct labor cost per hour | × $6 | × $6 | × $6 | × $6 |
| Total budgeted direct labor cost | $17,250 | $18,750 | $21,900 | $57,900 |

## Factory Overhead Budget

The factory overhead budget incorporates all production costs other than direct materials and direct labor. Such costs include indirect materials, indirect labor, depreciation, maintenance, and utilities. To construct an accurate overhead budget, individual overhead costs are first studied in terms of their behavior. Observe, for example, that several of the preceding costs vary with changes in production volume, while others remain static. Once cost behavior is determined, we then compute overhead application rates similar to those described in Chapter 22.

Assume that Hillcroft's variable overhead application rate is $1.40 per direct labor hour. Fixed overhead charges are anticipated to be $1,930 per month, which includes $700 of straight-line depreciation. Exhibit 24-11 contains the company's factory overhead budget.

**TIPS & TECHNIQUES**

As the exhibit indicates, the overhead budget contains *total* fixed factory overhead costs of $1,930—*not* a fixed application rate multiplied by the number of monthly labor hours. The underlying reason for this treatment is that fixed costs are, indeed, fixed and do not vary with labor activity. Whether Hillcroft anticipates 2,875, 3,125, or 3,650 labor hours makes no difference because the same fixed charges will be incurred each month.

The overhead budget reveals that total estimated overhead for the quarter amounts to $19,300—a figure that is needed to cost Hillcroft's single product. Assuming the use of direct labor hours as an application base, the overhead application rate will equal $2.00 per hour ($19,300 ÷ 9,650 budgeted labor hours, from Exhibit 24-10). Further, notice there is a difference between total budgeted overhead and the required cash disbursements for overhead. Depreciation, although a factory cost, does not entail a cash outlay and is therefore subtracted to generate monthly cash payments. We are assuming that all other overhead is paid when incurred.

**Exhibit 24-11**

**HILLCROFT CORPORATION**
**Factory Overhead Budget**
**For the Quarter Ended March 31, 19X2**

| | *January* | *February* | *March* | *Total* |
|---|---|---|---|---|
| Budgeted direct labor hours (Exhibit 24-10) | 2,875 | 3,125 | 3,650 | 9,650 |
| Variable overhead rate | × $1.40 | × $1.40 | × $1.40 | × $1.40 |
| Budgeted variable overhead | $4,025 | $4,375 | $5,110 | $13,510 |
| Budgeted fixed overhead | 1,930 | 1,930 | 1,930 | 5,790 |
| Budgeted total overhead | $5,955 | $6,305 | $7,040 | $19,300 |
| Less: Depreciation | 700 | 700 | 700 | 2,100 |
| Cash disbursements for factory overhead | $5,255 | $5,605 | $6,340 | $17,200 |

## Selling and Administrative Expense Budget

All manufacturing organizations incur costs unrelated to production activities, namely, selling and administrative (S&A) expenses. Like factory overhead, S&A expenses consist of variable and fixed components and require an in-depth review (in terms of cost behavior) prior to budget preparation.

Hillcroft's variable selling and administrative costs are freight-out and sales commissions, which total $0.80 per unit. Fixed costs include salaries, advertising, insurance, and other miscellaneous items. The firm's S&A expense budget appears in Exhibit 24-12. It is important to note that a new activity base is employed because these expenses vary with *sales*, not production.

## Cash Budget

The cash budget, which is based on many of the budgets previously discussed, serves to summarize a considerable portion of the budgeting process. This important document provides substantial assistance to management when assessing a company's future cash needs. The cash budget is typically composed of four major sections:

- Cash receipts
- Cash disbursements
- Analysis
- Financing

The *receipts section* discloses the total cash available during the period before considering any disbursements. Total cash available is computed by adding an entity's beginning cash balance to total cash receipts. For most businesses the major sources of receipts are cash sales and collections from customers on account.

Exhibit 24-12

**HILLCROFT CORPORATION**
**Selling and Administrative Expense Budget**
**For the Quarter Ended March 31, 19X2**

| | *January* | *February* | *March* | *Total* |
|---|---|---|---|---|
| Expected sales, in units (Exhibit 24-5) | 4,500 | 5,500 | 7,000 | 17,000 |
| Variable S&A expense per unit | × $0.80 | × $0.80 | × $0.80 | × $0.80 |
| Budgeted variable expenses | $3,600 | $4,400 | $5,600 | $13,600 |
| Fixed S&A expenses | | | | |
| Salaries | $2,000 | $2,000 | $2,000 | $ 6,000 |
| Advertising | 600 | 600 | 600 | 1,800 |
| Insurance | 1,900 | — | — | 1,900 |
| Miscellaneous | 500 | 1,500 | 500 | 2,500 |
| Total fixed expenses | $5,000 | $4,100 | $3,100 | $12,200 |
| Total budgeted S&A expenses | $8,600 | $8,500 | $8,700 | $25,800 |

The cash *disbursements section* details expected cash payments during the budget period. Such payments include outlays for materials, labor, overhead, selling and administrative expenses, dividends, taxes, and capital improvements.

The *analysis section* combines the information presented in the receipts and disbursements sections and discloses whether an organization has an excess of cash or a cash deficiency. Excessive cash balances should be used to retire outstanding loans or be invested in safe short-term securities such as certificates of deposit and government notes. If the latter course of action is followed, a firm can generate a return on its investment and can reacquire the cash (if needed) in a short period of time. Should a deficiency arise, the need for additional cash is dictated. Because the deficiency is disclosed before it actually occurs, management can take corrective action to prevent possible loan defaults, past-due bills, and other undesirable outcomes.

Finally, the *financing section* provides a schedule of expected borrowings and repayments and also discloses the related interest payments on borrowed funds. Overall, this section enables companies to determine financing requirements and thereby give banks and other lending institutions advance notice of funding needs.

***Cash Budget Illustration*** To illustrate the cash budget, we will continue the Hillcroft Corporation example. Assume that Hillcroft requires a minimum cash balance of $6,000, with bank loans available in $1,000 multiples at a 15% interest rate. For simplicity we assume that loans are obtained at the beginning of a month and are repaid at the end of the month of repayment. Interest is paid at the time of repaying principal. Finally, the company will have a $3,000 quarterly tax payment in March and expects to distribute a $500 cash dividend on March 31. Hillcroft's cash budget appears in Exhibit 24-13.

To explain the financing section, management requires a $6,000 minimum cash balance. Because borrowings are in $1,000 multiples, $8,000 of funding is needed in January ($8,000 − $1,495 = $6,505). All borrowings are assumed to be repaid as soon as possible (also in $1,000 increments); thus, $2,000 of the loan obligation can be retired in March without reducing the cash balance below the desired minimum. Interest is figured for three months, because the obligation is outstanding from January 1 through March 31 ($\$2,000 \times 0.15 \times \frac{3}{12} = \$75$).

## Budgeted Income Statement

The preparation of budgeted financial statements, often called **pro forma statements,** is the final step in budget construction. The first of these statements, the income statement, projects the forecasted results of operations and serves as a useful tool against which actual performance can be measured. Information needed for its construction is taken from the various budgets discussed in preceding sections of the chapter. Hillcroft's budgeted income statement is shown in Exhibit 24-14.

The most difficult part of the statement is the computation of cost of goods manufactured and the ending finished goods inventory. As noted in Hillcroft's production budget (see Exhibit 24-7), the firm produced 19,300 units during the quarter. The cost per unit of $7 is computed as shown on page 878.

Exhibit 24-13

**HILLCROFT CORPORATION**
**Cash Budget**
**For the Quarter Ended March 31, 19X2**

| | *January* | *February* | *March* |
|---|---|---|---|
| Beginning cash balance* | $ 7,000 | $ 6,505 | $ 6,006 |
| Add receipts: customer collections (Exhibit 24-6) | 41,500 | 52,000 | 65,500 |
| Cash available before disbursements | $48,500 | $58,505 | $71,506 |
| Less disbursements | | | |
| Material purchases (Exhibit 24-9) | $18,890 | $19,644 | $22,476 |
| Direct labor (Exhibit 24-10) | 17,250 | 18,750 | 21,900 |
| Factory overhead (Exhibit 24-11) | 5,255 | 5,605 | 6,340 |
| S&A expenses (Exhibit 24-12) | 8,600 | 8,500 | 8,700 |
| Income taxes | — | — | 3,000 |
| Dividends | — | — | 500 |
| Total disbursements | $49,995 | $52,499 | $62,916 |
| Cash excess (deficiency) before financing | $ (1,495) | $ 6,006 | $ 8,590 |
| Financing | | | |
| Borrowing to maintain $6,000 minimum balance (at beginning of period) | $ 8,000 | $ — | $ — |
| Repayment (at end of period) | — | — | (2,000) |
| Interest at 15% per annum | — | — | (75) |
| Ending cash balance | $ 6,505 | $ 6,006 | $ 6,515 |

* January's beginning cash balance of $7,000 is obtained from Exhibit 24-4. Subsequent beginning balances are the ending cash balances of the preceding period.

Exhibit 24-14

**HILLCROFT CORPORATION**
**Budgeted Income Statement**
**For the Quarter Ended March 31, 19X2**

| | | |
|---|---|---|
| Sales (Exhibit 24-5) | | $170,000 |
| Cost of goods sold | | |
| Beginning finished goods inventory (Exhibit 24-4) | $ 10,500 | |
| Cost of goods manufactured (19,300 units × $7) | 135,100 | |
| Goods available for sale | $145,600 | |
| Less ending finished goods inventory (3,800 units × $7) | 26,600 | |
| Cost of goods sold | | 119,000 |
| Gross profit | | $ 51,000 |
| Less S&A expenses (Exhibit 24-12) | | 25,800 |
| Income before interest and taxes | | $ 25,200 |
| Less interest expense | | 300* |
| Income before taxes | | $ 24,900 |
| Income taxes (Exhibit 24-13) | | 3,000 |
| Net income | | $ 21,900 |

* Interest expense is calculated as follows:

| | |
|---|---|
| From Exhibit 24-13 | $ 75 |
| Accrued interest on remaining loan balance ($6,000 × 0.15 × $\frac{3}{12}$) | 225 |
| | $300 |

| | |
|---|---|
| Direct material (2 units of direct material @ \$1.50 per unit; see Exhibit 24-8) | \$3.00 |
| Direct labor (0.5 hours per unit @ \$6 per hour; see Exhibit 24-10) | 3.00 |
| Variable factory overhead (0.5 hours per unit @ \$1.40 per hour; see Exhibit 24-11) | 0.70 |
| Fixed factory overhead (see Exhibit 24-11 and the following discussion) | 0.30 |
| Manufactured cost per unit | \$7.00 |

The fixed factory overhead is calculated on the basis of estimated direct labor hours. Because Hillcroft anticipates \$5,790 of fixed overhead and 9,650 labor hours (both figures taken from Exhibit 24-11), the rate per hour is \$0.60 (\$5,790 ÷ 9,650 hours). As a result, each finished unit is charged with \$0.30 (0.5 labor hours × \$0.60) of fixed production cost.

Once the \$7-per-unit manufacturing cost is computed, the ending finished goods inventory can be determined. From information that appears in Exhibit 24-7, the company has estimated finished goods at 3,800 units as of March 31. The inventory is therefore costed at \$26,600 (3,800 units × \$7).

### Budgeted Balance Sheet

The budgeted balance sheet as of March 31 is derived by combining the beginning balance sheet (see Exhibit 24-4) with the information presented in the other budgets. Hillcroft's end-of-quarter balance sheet is shown in Exhibit 24-15.

## Budgeting and Computers

**OBJECTIVE 7**
**Be familiar with the adaptability of budgets to computers.**

No doubt you have gotten the impression that budget construction is extremely tedious and procedural. Furthermore, as discussed earlier in the chapter, the budget process usually consists of several rounds, with changes and refinements being added along the way. These characteristics make budgeting very adaptable to computers. Computers speed up the process and eliminate much of the drudgery for the accountant, thereby allowing more time for analysis and evaluation.

Computerized budgeting applications have expanded greatly in recent years, primarily because of the increased use of microcomputers and the availability of software packages known as *electronic spreadsheets* (see p. 215). The spreadsheet (i.e., work sheet) configures the memory of a computer to resemble an accountant's columnar pad, actually, a pad that is much larger than could be printed on a piece of paper. For instance, a popular spreadsheet at the time of this writing has in excess of 8,100 rows and 250 columns. This vast working area is employed to perform mathematical operations (e.g., the multiplication of data in cell D15 by that contained in cell D19, with the result being stored in cell E24) and to format various schedules and reports.[1]

### Use of a Spreadsheet

The act of budgeting with a spreadsheet requires that users enter mathematical formulas into the computer. The formulas express the financial relationships of the

[1] A cell is a spreadsheet component that stores data. Each cell is referenced by its address, as determined by a column and row location. Cell G37, for instance, is found at the intersection of column G and row 37.

Exhibit 24-15

**HILLCROFT CORPORATION**
**Budgeted Balance Sheet**
**March 31, 19X2**

| | | |
|---|---|---|
| ***Assets*** | | |
| Current assets | | |
| Cash (Exhibit 24-13) | $ 6,515 | |
| Accounts receivable (Exhibit 24-6) | 21,000 | |
| Finished goods (Exhibit 24-14) | 26,600 | |
| Direct materials (Exhibit 24-8) | 14,940* | $ 69,055 |
| Property, plant, & equipment | | |
| Plant & equipment (Exhibit 24-4) | $70,000 | |
| Less: Accumulated depreciation | 7,100† | 62,900 |
| Total assets | | $131,955 |
| ***Liabilities & Stockholders' Equity*** | | |
| Current liabilities | | |
| Accounts payable (Exhibit 24-9) | $ 9,480 | |
| Loan payable (Exhibit 24-13) | 6,000‡ | |
| Interest payable (Exhibit 24-14) | 225 | $ 15,705 |
| Stockholders' equity | | |
| Common stock (Exhibit 24-4) | $40,000 | |
| Retained earnings | 76,250§ | 116,250 |
| Total liabilities & stockholders' equity | | $131,955 |

* 9,960 units × $1.50 per unit = $14,940.

| | | |
|---|---|---|
| † Accumulated depreciation, Jan. 1 (Exhibit 24-4) | | $ 5,000 |
| Straight-line depreciation, Jan.–Mar. (Exhibit 24-11) | | 2,100 |
| Accumulated depreciation, Mar. 31 | | $ 7,100 |

‡ Original loan − repayment ($8,000 − $2,000 = $6,000).

| | | |
|---|---|---|
| § Retained earnings, Jan. 1 (Exhibit 24-4) | | $54,850 |
| Add: Net income (Exhibit 24-14) | $21,900 | |
| Deduct: Dividends (Exhibit 24-13) | 500 | 21,400 |
| Retained earnings, Mar. 31 | | $76,250 |

entity, for example, the fact that the ending cash balance is equal to the beginning cash balance + receipts − disbursements. Or that 70% of a firm's sales are on account, with the following collection pattern: 60% collected in the month after sale, 38% collected in the second month after sale, and 2% uncollectible. The company's data (e.g., expected monthly sales) are then keyed into the computer, and the computer performs the necessary calculations (as instructed by the formulas).

Once the formulas are developed, spreadsheets allow managers to perform "what if" testing. That is, a manager can study the financial impact of changes in specified budget variables. As an example, refer to Exhibit 24-5. Assume that Hillcroft Corporation is considering a decrease in its selling price. The company desires to know the impact on cash position and profitability of a $0.50-per-unit price reduction, coupled with new sales volumes of 5,800 and 7,200 units in February and March, respectively.

If the calculations were performed manually, the related mathematics would easily take hours to perform. And even then, management might not be satisfied with the results and may want to study a different pricing strategy. With the use of a spreadsheet, data (or formula) changes are entered into the computer by depressing a few keys; electronics does the rest. Newly generated reports and pro forma statements are produced in a matter of seconds, thereby giving executives additional business insights in a cost-effective and timely manner.

## Chapter Review

### Learning Objectives—The Key Points

**1 Understand the benefits of budgeting.** Budgets provide three basic benefits for an organization. First, a formalized plan of attack is created, allowing managers to pinpoint problems before the problems actually occur. Daily operating distractions are therefore reduced, because a close look at the future often leads to implementation of preliminary corrective actions. A second benefit is that budgets serve as a basis for performance evaluation. Actual performance is compared against budgeted amounts, giving management considerable insight when judging whether operations have been up to par. Finally, budgets assist in communicating and coordinating the diverse goals of different operating units (e.g., divisions, departments, and so forth). The budgets of these units are examined and integrated when developing a plan for attaining overall company objectives.

**2 Understand the distinction between top-down and bottom-up budgeting.** With top-down budgeting, virtually all budget development takes place at the higher managerial levels of the entity. This approach tends to reflect the goals of the entire firm as opposed to those of individual subunits (e.g., divisions). However, because of the lack of involvement, lower-level employees often resent the budget effort and do little when it comes to budget achievement.

In contrast, the bottom-up approach stresses active participation of lower-level employees in the budget construction process. Given their involvement, these employees usually make greater strides toward attaining budgetary goals. Further, more realistic budgets are constructed because people who best know the operation are providing valuable input to the development process.

**3 Be familiar with slack as it relates to the estimation process.** Slack refers to the use of padding in budget estimates to avoid unfavorable performance appraisals. As an example, a manager may underestimate sales and overestimate expenses when constructing a budget. Later, when actual sales are "down" and expenses are "up" and both amounts are compared against budgeted figures, the manager is deemed to have met his or her target for the period.

**4 Understand the variations in budget periods.** Different types of budgets tend to cover differing time periods. Budgets for capital expenditures are long-term in nature, often spanning five to ten years into the future. Operations budgets are typically prepared for a one-year period; budgets used primarily to assess actual performance are frequently subdivided into quarters and months.

**5 Be familiar with the limitations of budgeting, especially in the human relations area.** There are several limitations associated with budgets. Like other management tools, a budget is only as good as the effort that goes into its preparation. The degree of support by top management is a key factor in the success (or failure) of any budget program. In addition, budgets are not ends in themselves; they cannot replace effective day-to-day operating decisions.

Because budgets are used in the appraisal of performance, employees often become disenchanted with the budgetary effort and its end product. Employees should be educated that budgets are helpful tools that assist in the attainment of company goals, not a means to fix blame when evaluating personnel.

**6 Be able to prepare a master budget.** A master budget is a series of integrated budgets that serves as a financial plan for an organization. The starting point in the budget process is the sales budget, which logically flows into the production budget. Production levels, in turn, affect the direct material purchases budget, the direct labor budget, and the factory overhead budget. Other elements of the master budget include the selling and administrative expense budget, a capital expenditures budget, a cash budget, and pro forma (i.e., forecasted) financial statements.

**7 Be familiar with the adaptability of budgets to computers.** Budgets are extremely adaptable to computers, primarily because of the heavy computational emphasis. Computers eliminate much of the procedural drudgery for the accountant, thereby allowing more time for analysis and evaluation. An electronic spreadsheet (i.e., work sheet) is a helpful tool, one that allows exploration of different scenarios in budgeting by changing only a few key input variables.

## Chapter Quiz

The five questions that follow relate to several issues raised in the chapter. Test your knowledge of the issues by selecting the best answer. (The answers appear on p. 895.)

**1** Which of the following statements is false?
- a Budgets are used in both the planning and control of daily operations.
- b Budgets assist in coordinating the diverse goals of a company's different subunits (e.g., divisions, departments, and so forth).
- c Top-down budgeting is sometimes known as participative budgeting.
- d Budgets help to formalize a company's planning process.

**2** Bottom-up budgeting:
- a generally results in increased efforts by lower-level employees when it comes to budget attainment.
- b often results in less realistic (i.e., accurate) budgets than when top-down budgeting is used.
- c is used solely by manufacturing companies.
- d is another name for top-down budgeting.

**3** The first budget to be prepared is normally the:
- a cash budget.
- b production budget.
- c pro forma balance sheet.
- d sales budget.

**4** Which of the following listings is the most logical sequence of budget preparation?
- a Production budget, sales budget, cash budget, pro forma income statement.
- b Sales budget, cash budget, production budget, pro forma balance sheet.
- c Sales budget, production budget, direct labor budget, cash budget.
- d Production budget, direct material purchases budget, pro forma balance sheet, cash budget.

**5** The cash budget:
- a assists management in predicting both cash shortages and cash deficiencies.
- b is dependent on figures that are generated in other, previously-prepared budgets.
- c discloses any borrowings and loan repayments that are expected to occur.
- d possesses the characteristics noted in a, b, and c above.

## Questions

**Q24-1** Briefly discuss the advantages of budgeting.

**Q24-2** Is a budget a planning tool, a control tool, or both? Explain.

**Q24-3** When evaluating performance, many organizations compare current results with the actual results of previous accounting periods. Are any problems encountered when following this approach? Explain.

**Q24-4** Explain how a budget assists in coordinating the plans of an organization's various operating subunits (divisions, departments, and so forth).

**Q24-5** Define and fully explain the top-down approach to budgeting.

**Q24-6** Briefly explain the bottom-up approach to budgeting.

**Q24-7** Should budget data be based on the past, the future, or both? Explain.

**Q24-8** Briefly discuss the concept of slack as it pertains to budgeting.

**Q24-9** Calabro Corporation, a manufacturer with annual sales approaching $75 million, is beginning the budget process for the upcoming year. Should Calabro use long-term budgets, yearly budgets, or monthly budgets? Explain your answer.

**Q24-10** What is a continuous budget?

**Q24-11** Why is an accurate sales forecast so important in the preparation of a master budget?

**Q24-12** What factors influence a company's expected direct material purchases?

**Q24-13** Why is it necessary to carefully budget direct labor requirements for an upcoming period?

**Q24-14** Explain how a cash budget leads to effective management of an organization's cash balances.

**Q24-15** What is an electronic spreadsheet?

**Q24-16** Explain the concept of "what if" testing and how the computer can be of assistance.

## Exercises

**E24-1** ***Overview of the budgeting process***

Evaluate the comments that follow as being True or False. If the comment is false, briefly explain why.

a When assessing current performance, a comparison of actual results against a predetermined budget is generally preferred over a comparison of the current period's actual results with those of the preceding period.

b Lower-level managers are inclined to work harder to achieve budgeted targets if the top-down (rather than the bottom-up) budget approach is used.

c Virtually all budgets are one year in duration.

d Land & Sea plans to sell 36,700 units of its single product during the coming year. If the beginning and ending finished goods inventories are 15,900 and 17,700 units, respectively, the company's production budget will reveal that 38,500 units should be manufactured.

e The last step in the construction of a master budget is the preparation of a cash budget.

**E24-2** ***Sales budget; schedule of cash collections***

Willow Company anticipates opening a new facility in Pittsburgh on July 1 of the current year. Unit sales of the firm's two products, A106 and B324, are expected to be as follows:

| | July | August | September |
|---|---|---|---|
| A106 | 5,000 | 5,500 | 6,200 |
| B324 | 8,000 | 9,000 | 11,000 |

Willow has established a selling price for each unit of A106 and B324 at $10 and $30, respectively.

Twenty percent of all sales are for cash; the remaining 80% are on account. Credit sales have the following collection pattern:

- Seventy percent are collected in the month of sale.
- Thirty percent are collected in the month following sale.

a Prepare the company's sales budget for July through September.
b Prepare a schedule of cash collections for July through September.

**E24-3** ***Schedule of cash collections***

Mill Rose Enterprises will begin operation in Oregon on January 1, 19X4. Management has estimated sales as follows, which are subject to a 2% discount if paid within 10 days of billing: January, $100,000; February, $200,000; and March, $400,000. Gross sales, as judged by other Mill Rose businesses, are expected to be collected in the following pattern:

| | |
|---|---|
| Collected in the month of sale | 60% |
| Collected in the month following sale | 35 |
| Uncollectible | 5 |

Customers will take advantage of the discount on 80% of the collections in the month of sale and 30% of the collections in the month following sale.

Prepare a schedule of cash collections for January through March.

**E24-4** ***Production budget***

Paste Products anticipates the following unit sales during the first four months of the upcoming year:

| | |
|---|---|
| January | 30,000 |
| February | 35,000 |
| March | 38,000 |
| April | 40,000 |

The company desires to maintain its finished goods inventory at 40% of the following month's sales. The January 1 finished goods inventory will be 11,500 units.

Prepare a production budget for January through March.

**E24-5** ***Direct material purchases budget***

Bass Corporation manufactures a home video recorder that requires four no. S1326 circuit boards. Anticipated production of recorders for the upcoming year follows.

| Quarter | Production (Units) |
|---|---|
| First | 8,000 |
| Second | 10,000 |
| Third | 12,000 |
| Fourth | 16,000 |

Bass desires to stock enough circuit boards to meet 30% of the following quarter's production needs. Circuit boards cost $2.50 each; the cost has been fairly stable over the past six months.

Assuming a beginning circuit board inventory of $23,750, prepare a direct material purchases budget for the first three quarters of the year.

**E24-6** ***Production and cash-outlay computations***

RPR, Inc., anticipates that 120,000 units of product K will be sold during May. Each unit of product K requires four units of raw material A. Actual inventories as of May 1 and budgeted inventories as of May 31 follow.

| | *May 1* | *May 31* |
|---|---|---|
| Product K (units) | 55,000 | 60,000 |
| Raw material A (units) | 40,000 | 37,000 |

Each unit of raw material A costs $8; RPR pays for all purchases in the month of acquisition. Invoices that account for approximately 80% of the cost of materials acquired will be paid within 10 days of receipt, entitling the company to a 2% cash discount.

a Determine the number of units of product K to be manufactured in May.

b Compute the May cash outlay for purchases of raw material A.

**E24-7** ***Analysis of operations: Cash emphasis***

Lexington Wood Products manufactures and distributes wooden baseball bats. Business is seasonal, with a large portion of the sales occurring in late winter and early spring. Production is heavy during the last quarter of the year to meet demand, and Lexington experiences a temporary cash strain during this period. Payroll costs rise because considerable overtime is scheduled. Furthermore, customer collections are low because the fall season produces only modest sales. This year there are added problems because of high inflation rates and declining sales, the latter caused by the increased popularity of aluminum bats. Also, only 25% of the customers are paying their balances in the month of sale. The average collection period is approximately 62 days.

Fortunately, the cash strain arises only during the last quarter. The Cash account builds up during the first two quarters as sales exceed production. Excessive cash is subsequently invested in U.S. Treasury bills and certificates of deposit.

Assume that Lexington regularly experiences the preceding cash strain. What actions could the firm undertake to "ease the squeeze" on cash? Consider possible changes in operations when formulating your answer.

**E24-8** ***Cash budget***

Tennessee Merchandising has had continual problems with cash flow. The following information has come to your attention:

a The company has an opening cash balance on January 1 of $10,000. Management desires to maintain a minimum cash balance of $8,000 at all times.

b Budgeted sales for January total $200,000. Sales are expected to increase at the rate of 5% per month over the next six months. Sales from the preceding November and December amounted to $170,000 and $180,000, respectively.

c All sales are on credit and subject to the following collection pattern:

- Sixty percent collected in the month of sale.
- Thirty percent collected in the month following sale.
- Ten percent collected in the second month following sale.

d All merchandise purchases are paid for in the month of purchase. The cost of acquisitions is expected to average 70% of the month's sales revenues.

e Operating expenses are budgeted as follows:

| | *January* | *February* | *March* |
|---|---|---|---|
| Selling (excluding depreciation) | $16,000 | $20,000 | $25,000 |
| Administrative (excluding depreciation) | 12,000 | 12,000 | 12,000 |
| Depreciation | 6,000 | 6,000 | 7,000 |

f The company will acquire $28,000 of new equipment in March for cash.
g Additional financing is available in $1,000 multiples at a 16% interest rate. Assume that all borrowings take place at the beginning of the month and that repayments occur at the end of the month of repayment. Interest is paid at the time of repaying principal.

Analyze Tennessee's cash position by preparing a cash budget for January through March. Has the company solved its cash flow problems or will additional financing be necessary?

## Problems

### Series A

**P24-A1** ***Production and purchases budgets; purchasing policy***

O. I

Mason, Inc., manufactures and distributes various parts for lawn mowers. The company's main product, a bilateral assembly, requires five units of direct material at a cost of $0.60 per unit. To keep production moving smoothly, the firm must maintain a direct materials inventory equal to 70% of the following month's production needs.

Sales projections in units for the last six months of 19X6 follow.

| *Month* | *Estimated Sales* |
|---|---|
| July | 9,000 |
| August | 12,000 |
| September | 16,000 |
| October | 22,000 |
| November | 29,000 |
| December | 26,000 |

Management desires to carry a finished goods inventory equal to 40% of the following month's sales. On June 30, 19X6, the finished goods inventory totaled 3,200 assemblies. On the same date, 30,000 units of direct material were in the warehouse.

**Instructions**

a Prepare a production budget for July through September.
b Prepare a direct material purchases budget for July through September.
c List several factors that could cause a change in the company's present direct material inventory policy.

**P24-A2** ***Production budget and abbreviated cash budget***

The Redwood Company has gathered the following information in preparation of its first-quarter budget for the coming year:

*Sales and collections:*

| | *Units* | *Sales Revenues* |
|---|---|---|
| December sales (actual) | 7,800 | $117,000 |
| January sales (estimated) | 8,000 | 120,000 |
| February sales (estimated) | 8,500 | 136,000 |
| March sales (estimated) | 8,800 | 140,800 |
| April sales (estimated) | 9,000 | 153,000 |

Seventy percent of all sales are collected in the month of sale; the remaining 30% are collected in the following month.

*Production:*
Manufacturing costs are paid in the month incurred. The following costs relate to the 65,000 units produced during the current year:

| | |
|---|---|
| Direct materials | $130,000 |
| Direct labor | 325,000 |
| Variable factory overhead | 65,000 |
| Fixed factory overhead | 292,500 |

No significant changes in cost behavior are anticipated. The fixed factory overhead, which includes $52,500 of depreciation, is incurred evenly throughout the year.

*Inventory policies:*
1 All direct materials are acquired when needed (i.e., no direct material inventory is maintained).
2 Management desires finished goods inventories equal to 40% of the following month's sales. December's ending finished goods inventory is 3,200 units.

*Other data:*
1 Selling and administrative expenses amount to $2.50 per unit and are paid in the month following their incurrence.
2 The January 1 cash balance is $12,000.

**Instructions**

a Prepare a production budget (in units only) for January through March.
b Prepare a cash budget for January through March. *Note:* The budget should end with the cash excess (deficiency) before financing.

**P24-A3** ***Cash budget covering three months***
Atra Corporation is a distributor of recording equipment. Management is studying the company's cash needs for July through September and has assembled the following information:

| | *July* | *August* | *September* |
|---|---|---|---|
| Sales | $60,000 | $70,000 | $85,000 |
| Purchases of merchandise | 40,000 | 46,000 | 48,000 |
| Cash operating costs | 37,500 | 35,500 | 39,000 |
| Depreciation expense | 3,000 | 3,300 | 3,300 |
| Equipment acquisitions | 11,000 | — | — |
| Sale of delivery trucks | — | — | 20,000 |

The pro forma balance sheet on June 30 revealed the following account balances:

| | |
|---|---|
| Cash | $23,000 |
| Accounts receivable | 22,800 |
| Accounts payable | 15,900 |

Sixty percent of all customer accounts are collected in the month of sale; 35% are collected in the following month. Because of a liberal credit policy, bad debts amounting to 5% of sales are anticipated. Management feels that only $19,000 of the accounts outstanding on June 30 will be collectible.

Sixty percent of the merchandise purchases are paid for in the month of purchase to take advantage of a 2% discount. The remaining 40% are paid in the month following purchase.

Atra maintains a $5,000 minimum cash balance at all times. Should borrowing be necessary, financing is available in $1,000 multiples at a 16% interest rate. Assume all borrowings take place at the beginning of the month and all repayments (including interest) at the end of the month of repaying principal. Principal repayments are also made in multiples of $1,000.

**Instructions**

a Prepare a schedule of cash collections for July through September.
b Prepare a schedule of cash disbursements for merchandise purchases for July through September.
c Prepare a cash budget similar to that shown in Exhibit 24-13.

**P24-A4** ***Pro forma statements***
The Traxton Company's balance sheet as of December 31, 19X1, follows.

**TRAXTON COMPANY**
**Balance Sheet**
**December 31, 19X1**

| | | |
|---|---|---|
| ***Assets*** | | |
| Cash | | $ 17,500 |
| Accounts receivable | | 98,000 |
| Merchandise inventory | | 51,800 |
| Plant & equipment | $96,000 | |
| Less: Accumulated depreciation | 29,000 | 67,000 |
| Total assets | | $234,300 |
| ***Liabilities & Stockholders' Equity*** | | |
| Accounts payable | | $ 68,200 |
| Common stock, $10 par | $70,000 | |
| Retained earnings | 96,100 | 166,100 |
| Total liabilities & stockholders' equity | | $234,300 |

Traxton has gathered the following information relating to January 19X2:

1 Budgeted sales total $450,000. Historically, cash sales have averaged 30% of total sales. Sixty percent of the firm's credit sales are collected in the month of sale; the remainder are collected in the following month.
2 Merchandise purchases are expected to total $370,000. Obligations to suppliers are settled as follows:

- Forty percent are paid in the month of purchase, subject to a 2% discount.
- Twenty percent are paid in the month of purchase after the discount period has lapsed.
- Forty percent are paid in the month following purchase.

Management has budgeted the January 31 inventory at $74,900.

3 Monthly operating expenses are paid as incurred and subdivided as follows:

| | |
|---|---|
| Variable | 15% of sales |
| Fixed (includes depreciation) | $62,400 |

4 The plant and equipment have a 10-year service life. Traxton uses the straight-line method of depreciation.
5 The company plans to acquire $20,000 of land on January 31 by paying $9,000 down and signing a short-term note for the remaining balance.
6 Traxton will declare a $0.30-per-share cash dividend on January 21. The dividend will be distributed on February 21.

**Instructions**

a Determine Traxton's January 31 cash balance.
b Prepare a pro forma income statement for January. Disregard income taxes and earnings-per-share computations.
c Prepare a pro forma balance sheet as of January 31.

**P24-A5** ***Comprehensive budgeting***

The balance sheet of Watson Company as of December 31, 19X1, follows.

**WATSON COMPANY**
**Balance Sheet**
**December 31, 19X1**

| | | |
|---|---|---|
| ***Assets*** | | |
| Cash | | $ 4,595 |
| Accounts receivable | | 10,000 |
| Finished goods (575 units × $7.00) | | 4,025 |
| Direct materials (2,760 units × $0.50) | | 1,380 |
| Plant & equipment | $50,000 | |
| Less: Accumulated depreciation | 10,000 | 40,000 |
| Total assets | | $60,000 |
| ***Liabilities & Stockholders' Equity*** | | |
| Accounts payable to suppliers | | $14,000 |
| Common stock | $25,000 | |
| Retained earnings | 21,000 | 46,000 |
| Total liabilities & stockholders' equity | | $60,000 |

The following information has been extracted from the accounting records:

1 All sales are made on account at $20 per unit. Sixty percent of the sales are collected in the month of sale; the remaining 40% are collected in the following month. Forecasted sales for the first five months of 19X2 are: January, 1,500 units; February, 1,600 units; March, 1,800 units; April, 2,000 units; May, 2,100 units.
2 Management desires to maintain the finished goods inventory at 30% of the following month's sales.
3 Watson uses four units of direct material in each finished unit. The direct material price has been stable and is expected to remain so over the next six months. Management desires to maintain the ending direct materials inventory at 60% of the following month's production needs.
4 Seventy percent of all purchases are paid in the month of purchase; the remaining 30% are paid in the subsequent month.

5 Watson's product requires 30 minutes of direct labor time. Each hour of direct labor costs $7.

### Instructions

a Rounding computations to the nearest dollar, prepare the following for January through March:
(1) Sales budget
(2) Schedule of cash collections
(3) Production budget
(4) Direct material purchases budget
(5) Schedule of cash disbursements for material purchases
(6) Direct labor budget

b Determine the balances in the following accounts as of March 31:
(1) Accounts Receivable
(2) Direct Materials
(3) Accounts Payable

## Series B

**P24-B1** ***Production and purchases budgets; inventory policy***

Procraft, Inc., manufactures and distributes various parts for video cassette recorders. The company's main product, a switching device, requires two units of direct material at a cost of $1.50 per unit. To keep production moving smoothly, the company must maintain a direct materials inventory equal to 40% of the following month's production needs.

Sales projections in units for the first six months of 19X2 follow.

| *Month* | *Estimated Sales of Switching Devices* |
|---|---|
| January | 40,000 |
| February | 44,000 |
| March | 46,000 |
| April | 50,000 |
| May | 48,000 |
| June | 45,000 |

Management desires to carry a finished goods inventory equal to 30% of the following month's sales. On December 31, 19X1, the finished goods inventory totaled 11,000 switches. On the same date, 25,000 units of direct material were in the warehouse.

### Instructions

a Prepare a production budget for January through March.

b Prepare a direct material purchases budget for January through March.

c List several factors that could cause a change in the company's present finished goods inventory policy.

**P24-B2** ***Production budget and abbreviated cash budget***

Lambert Industries has gathered the information that follows in preparation of its second-quarter budget for 19X3.

*Sales and collections:*

| | *Units* | *Sales Revenues* |
|---|---|---|
| March sales (actual) | 15,000 | $150,000 |
| April sales (estimated) | 18,000 | 180,000 |
| May sales (estimated) | 20,000 | 240,000 |
| June sales (estimated) | 19,000 | 228,000 |
| July sales (estimated) | 22,000 | 242,000 |

Sixty percent of all sales are collected in the month of sale; the remaining 40% are collected in the following month.

*Production:*
Manufacturing costs are paid in the month incurred. The following costs relate to 200,000 units that were recently produced:

| | |
|---|---|
| Direct materials | $400,000 |
| Direct labor | 600,000 |
| Variable factory overhead | 300,000 |
| Fixed factory overhead | 408,000 |

No significant changes in cost behavior are anticipated. The fixed factory overhead, which includes $72,000 of depreciation, is incurred evenly throughout the year.

*Inventory policies:*
1 All direct materials are acquired when needed (i.e., no direct material inventory is maintained).
2 Management desires finished goods inventories equal to 70% of the following month's sales. March's ending finished goods inventory is 12,600 units.

*Other data:*
1 Selling and administrative expenses amount to $2.25 per unit and are paid in the month following their incurrence.
2 The April 1 cash balance is $9,400.

**Instructions**

a Prepare a production budget (in units only) for April through June.
b Prepare a cash budget for April through June. *Note:* The budget should end with the cash excess (deficiency) before financing.

**P24-B3** ***Cash budget covering three months***
Riverside Corporation is a distributor of medical supplies. Management is studying the company's cash needs for October through December and has assembled the following information:

| | *October* | *November* | *December* |
|---|---|---|---|
| Sales | $60,000 | $54,000 | $50,000 |
| Purchases of merchandise | 26,000 | 21,000 | 19,000 |
| Cash operating costs | 33,000 | 31,000 | 25,000 |
| Depreciation expense | 2,000 | 2,200 | 2,500 |
| Equipment acquisitions | 8,000 | 5,000 | — |

The pro forma balance sheet on September 30 revealed the following account balances:

| | |
|---|---|
| Cash | $ 6,500 |
| Accounts receivable | 21,000 |
| Accounts payable | 18,000 |

Seventy percent of all customer accounts are collected in the month of sale; 25% are collected in the following month. Because of a liberal credit policy, bad debts amounting to 5% of sales are anticipated. Management feels that only $20,000 of the accounts outstanding on September 30 will be collectible.

Forty percent of the merchandise purchases are paid for in the month of purchase to take advantage of a 2% discount. The remaining 60% are paid in the month following purchase.

Riverside maintains a $6,000 minimum cash balance at all times. Should borrowing be necessary, financing is available in $1,000 multiples at a 16% interest rate. Assume all borrowings take place at the beginning of the month and all repayments (including interest) at the end of the month of repaying principal. Principal repayments are also made in multiples of $1,000.

**Instructions**

a Prepare a schedule of cash collections for October through December.

b Prepare a schedule of cash disbursements for merchandise purchases for October through December.

c Prepare a cash budget similar to that shown in Exhibit 24-13.

**P24-B4** ***Pro forma statements***

Aircon Company's balance sheet as of December 31, 19X6, follows.

**AIRCON COMPANY**
**Balance Sheet**
**December 31, 19X6**

| | | |
|---|---|---|
| ***Assets*** | | |
| Cash | | $ 10,900 |
| Accounts receivable | | 31,200 |
| Merchandise inventory | | 64,500 |
| Plant & equipment | $84,000 | |
| Less: Accumulated depreciation | 16,000 | 68,000 |
| Total assets | | $174,600 |
| ***Liabilities & Stockholders' Equity*** | | |
| Accounts payable | | $ 56,000 |
| Common stock, $1 par | $30,000 | |
| Retained earnings | 88,600 | 118,600 |
| Total liabilities & stockholders' equity | | $174,600 |

Management has gathered the following information relating to January 19X7:

1 Budgeted sales total $200,000. Historically, cash sales have averaged 10% of total sales. Seventy percent of the firm's credit sales are collected in the month generated; the remainder are collected in the following month.

2 Merchandise purchases are expected to total $120,000. Obligations to suppliers are settled as follows:

- Sixty percent are paid in the month of purchase, subject to a 1% discount.
- Five percent are paid in the month of purchase after the discount period has lapsed.
- Thirty-five percent are paid in the month following purchase.

Management has budgeted the January 31 inventory at $47,800.

3 Monthly operating expenses are paid as incurred and subdivided as follows:

| | |
|---|---|
| Variable | 7% of sales |
| Fixed (includes depreciation) | $17,900 |

4 The plant and equipment have a 20-year service life. Aircon uses the straight-line method of depreciation.

5 The company plans to acquire $16,000 of land on January 31 by paying $3,000 down and signing a short-term note for the remaining balance.

6 Aircon will declare a $0.15-per-share cash dividend on January 24. The dividend will be distributed on February 24.

**Instructions**

a Determine Aircon's January 31 cash balance.

b Prepare a pro forma income statement for January. Disregard income taxes and earnings-per-share computations.

c Prepare a pro forma balance sheet as of January 31.

**P24-B5** ***Comprehensive budgeting***

The balance sheet of Mid-America Company as of December 31, 19X8, follows.

**MID-AMERICA COMPANY**
**Balance Sheet**
**December 31, 19X8**

| | | |
|---|---|---|
| ***Assets*** | | |
| Cash | | $ 14,800 |
| Accounts receivable | | 26,000 |
| Finished goods (1,200 units × $8.00) | | 9,600 |
| Direct materials (6,000 units × $1.50) | | 9,000 |
| Plant & equipment | $115,000 | |
| Less: Accumulated depreciation | 12,000 | 103,000 |
| Total assets | | $162,400 |
| ***Liabilities & Stockholders' Equity*** | | |
| Accounts payable to suppliers | | $ 12,000 |
| Common stock | $ 50,000 | |
| Retained earnings | 100,400 | 150,400 |
| Total liabilities & stockholders' equity | | $162,400 |

The following information has been extracted from the company's records:

1 All sales are made on account at $15 per unit. Forty percent of the sales are collected in the month of sale; the remaining 60% are collected in the following month. Forecasted sales for the first five months of 19X9 are: January, 2,600 units; February, 2,900 units; March, 3,100 units; April, 3,500 units; May, 3,200 units.

2 Management desires to maintain the finished goods inventory at 20% of the following month's sales.
3 Mid-America uses three units of direct material in each finished unit. The direct material price has been stable and is expected to remain so over the next six months. Management desires to maintain the ending direct materials inventory at 70% of the following month's production needs.
4 Eighty percent of all purchases are paid in the month of purchase; the remaining 20% are paid in the subsequent month.
5 Mid-America's product requires 20 minutes of direct labor time. Each hour of direct labor costs $9.

**Instructions**

a Rounding computations to the nearest dollar, prepare the following for January through March:
 (1) Sales budget
 (2) Schedule of cash collections
 (3) Production budget
 (4) Direct material purchases budget
 (5) Schedule of cash disbursements for material purchases
 (6) Direct labor budget

b Determine the balances in the following accounts as of March 31:
 (1) Accounts Receivable
 (2) Direct Materials
 (3) Accounts Payable

## Beyond the Basics

**BB24-1** ***Cash budget: Analysis of operations***

The Lincoln Tennis Club frequently experiences cash flow difficulties, with its checking account often below a desired minimum balance of $12,000. The following information pertains to club operations for the upcoming year (19X2):

1 The directors anticipate that 400 memberships will be sold. Family memberships ($150) will comprise 60% of this total; the remainder are individual memberships ($50).
2 Members are assessed hourly fees for court time, the rate dependent on whether usage occurs during "prime" time or "regular" time. The following hours and rates are expected:

| | *Prime Time* | *Regular Time* |
|---|---|---|
| Rate per hour | $10 | $7 |
| Hours of use | 4,300 | 7,200 |

3 As of January 1, 19X2, the accounts receivable balance stood at $22,600. Conversations with the club's directors indicate that $2,500 of these accounts will be written off the books as uncollectible. Amounts due from members as of December 31, 19X2, are expected to total $27,000.
4 John Connors, club pro, is paid a salary of $20,000 plus 20% of all court fee revenues. Connors gives private lessons and expects to earn an additional $3,500. Lesson fees are paid directly to Connors by the participating members.
5 Expenses incurred during 19X1 were: maintenance, $34,000; utilities, $13,500; and taxes, $6,200. Maintenance and utilities are expected to increase by 10% during 19X2; taxes should amount to $6,800. All expenses will be paid when incurred.

6 An examination of the club's records revealed outstanding accounts payable on January 1, 19X2, of $1,000. These amounts will be paid by the end of February.
7 The addition of one new court and improved lighting will cost $45,000. The club will pay $20,000 down, with the remaining balance financed by a short-term note. Interest and principal payments during 19X2 will amount to $3,600.
8 The cash balance on January 1, 19X2, amounts to $5,000.

**Instructions**

a Prepare a cash budget for 19X2 for the Lincoln Tennis Club. Disregard financing [except for that noted in item (7)] to meet minimum balance requirements.
b Assume that the budget revealed an ending cash balance of $4,400. In light of the club's target minimum of $12,000, what actions could the directors take to improve the ending cash position?

**BB24-2** ***Master budget relationships***

The data that follow pertain to Trinity Enterprises, which manufactures a single product.

1 All sales are on account, with 60% collected in the month of sale and 40% in the following month. The selling price is $20 per unit.
2 The schedule of cash collections for January through March of 19X5 revealed the following receipts for the period:

| | *Cash Receipts* | | |
|---|---|---|---|
| | ***January*** | ***February*** | ***March*** |
| December receivables | $32,000 | | |
| January sales | 54,000 | $36,000 | |
| February sales | | 66,000 | $44,000 |
| March sales | | | 72,000 |

3 Finished goods inventories are maintained at 30% of the following month's sales.
4 There are five units of direct material in each finished product, with each unit being purchased from a local supplier for $2. Delivery is within hours of placing an order; thus, Trinity stocks no direct material inventories.
5 Seventy percent of all direct material purchases are paid in the month of purchase, subject to a 2% discount. Ten percent are paid in the month of purchase but after the discount period has lapsed, and the remaining 20% are settled in the month following purchase.
6 Trinity desires to maintain a minimum cash balance of $15,000. Total payments in January are expected to be $106,500.
7 The December 31, 19X4, balance sheet revealed the following selected figures:

| | |
|---|---|
| Cash | $24,900 |
| Accounts receivable | 32,000 |
| Finished goods (? units) | 22,950 |

**Instructions**

Determine:

a Sales revenues earned in December 19X4.
b Total sales revenues to be reported on Trinity's pro forma income statement for the first quarter of 19X5.
c Accounts receivable to be reported on the March 31, 19X5, pro forma balance sheet.
d Number of units in the December 31, 19X4, finished goods inventory.

e Units of finished goods to be manufactured in January 19X5.
f Units of finished goods to be manufactured in February 19X5.
g February 19X5 payments for direct material purchases.
h Financing required in January, if any, to maintain the firm's minimum cash balance.

**BB24-3** ***Electronic spreadsheets; financial models***

Concord Enterprises, a service business, has just acquired a new microcomputer and electronic spreadsheet package. The company has experienced cash flow problems in recent years, and management is hopeful that the spreadsheet will assist in monitoring receipts and disbursements.

Scott Hemphill, a staff accountant, has been selected to computerize the firm's cash budget. Hemphill knows that before the spreadsheet can be used, he must first develop mathematical formulas that correctly express Concord's financial relationships. A review of the company's accounting records has revealed that 30% of the firm's sales are for cash, with the remaining 70% on account. Credit customers settle 60% of their balances due in the month following sale and 35% in the second month following sale. Five percent of the credit sales are uncollectible. Operating expenses, both variable and fixed, are paid when incurred. Variable costs average 40% of sales, and monthly fixed costs amount to $55,000.

Hemphill is constructing a formula that can be used to predict a month's ending cash balance. He has developed the following notation:

$$S = \text{sales for a month}$$
$$t = \text{time}$$

For example, $S_t$ would stand for sales in month t. If a cash flow was dependent on sales of the previous month, the appropriate notation would be $S_{t-1}$.

**Instructions**

a Explain what an electronic spreadsheet is and the benefits of using a spreadsheet package in cash budgeting applications.
b Develop a mathematical formula that would correctly express the change in Concord's cash balance (i.e., receipts minus payments) during any month. The receipts from cash sales, for instance, would be expressed as $0.3S_t$ because the amounts are collected in the period of sale.

## Answers to Chapter Quiz

**1** c

**2** a

**3** d

**4** c

**5** d

# Cost-Volume-Profit Analysis

CHAPTER 25

## Learning Objectives

After reading this chapter you should:

1 Be familiar with the characteristics of variable, step, fixed, and mixed (semivariable) cost functions.

2 Be able to use the scattergraph and high-low method for studying cost behavior.

3 Be able to perform various types of cost-volume-profit analysis, including calculation of the break-even point.

4 Be familiar with the computation and meaning of the contribution margin.

5 Be able to apply cost-volume-profit analysis to multiproduct firms.

6 Understand the limiting assumptions on which cost-volume-profit analysis is based.

During the past decade, many firms have felt the effects of increased operating costs and sharp (oftentimes foreign) competition. In an effort to maintain adequate earnings growth and cash-flow generation, many companies have been forced to alter existing business practices. Retailers have extended store hours and occasionally changed their image to appear more "lean and mean." Manufacturers have increased the use of "high-tech" production methods (e.g., robotics) to improve efficiency and product quality. And, in an example that may be very close to home, consider something as basic as the menu of your favorite fast-food restaurant. No doubt that menu has undergone considerable expansion, with the addition of breakfasts, salad bars, specialty sandwiches, and desserts to the standard fare.

Operating changes such as those just cited can be implemented only after extensive analysis. Businesses must determine how increases and decreases in revenue, cost, and volume affect net income. As you learned in an earlier chapter, certain costs fluctuate with changes in activity, while other costs remain constant. The study of interrelationships among the preceding factors is often termed **cost-volume-profit (CVP) analysis.** Like budgeting, CVP analysis is another useful planning tool.

## Cost Behavior

OBJECTIVE 1
Be familiar with the characteristics of variable, step, fixed, and mixed (semivariable) cost functions.

Effective CVP analysis requires a thorough understanding of cost behavior and calls for an expansion of the material presented in Chapter 21. Before we do so, however, a word of caution is necessary. It is important to understand that costs often exhibit different behavior patterns under differing sets of circumstances. For example, many costs do not change when small fluctuations in volume occur. Those same costs, however, may increase (or decrease) greatly when the activity change is more pronounced. Also, certain costs may follow a definite behavior pattern when closely monitored and controlled by management. Remove the controls and the predictable pattern may vary significantly from what was originally observed.

In sum, it is frequently difficult to generalize about the behavior of a given cost. An accounting educator once likened costs to people: they both have unique personalities and behave as individuals. Given this introduction, we will now explore four types of costs: variable, step, fixed, and mixed.

### Variable Costs

Recall that a **variable cost** varies in direct proportion to a change in an activity base (e.g., sales, production, miles driven, and so forth). As a result, if an activity base triples, a true variable cost should triple; if the base is halved, the cost should decrease by 50%. Common examples of variable costs include direct materials, direct labor, supplies, sales commissions, and fuel.

To determine whether a cost possesses variable characteristics, one should observe the cost's behavior over wide ranges of volume. Consider, for instance, the wear and tear on automobile tires. Short daily trips and even total monthly mileage will have little effect on tire wear and tread depth. Over time—say, several years—daily driving will take its toll. Eventually, the tires will have to be replaced after a substantial number of miles have been traveled.

Because variable costs change in direct proportion to fluctuations in an activity base, the variable cost *per unit* is constant. To illustrate, assume that Yellowstone Manufacturing normally produces 10,000 to 12,000 units each month. On the basis of the data in columns A and B, the accounting department has calculated labor cost at $8 per unit:

| *(A) Units Produced* | *(B) Total Labor Cost* | *(B) ÷ (A) Cost per Unit* |
|---|---|---|
| 10,000 | $80,000 | $80,000 ÷ 10,000 = $8 |
| 10,500 | 84,000 | $84,000 ÷ 10,500 = $8 |
| 11,000 | 88,000 | $88,000 ÷ 11,000 = $8 |
| 11,500 | 92,000 | $92,000 ÷ 11,500 = $8 |
| 12,000 | 96,000 | $96,000 ÷ 12,000 = $8 |

Notice that the $8 figure holds true at all volume levels.

## The Economist's View

Those readers who have taken an economics course may have noticed an apparent conflict in the economist's and accountant's views of variable cost behavior. Economic models generally assume that per-unit variable cost does not remain stable; rather, it changes with increases in activity. For example, picture a company that produces trucks by an assembly-line process. If the firm employed only two laborers, the number of trucks manufactured would surely be low. Furthermore, efficiency would be lacking, because the employees must each perform a multitude of tasks. As demand increases, the firm could raise its output by hiring more personnel. Instead of being a "jack of all trades," a worker could specialize, improve capital utilization, and become more efficient. The net result is a decreasing variable cost per unit. Naturally, a business can improve operations only so far. At some point production problems are encountered because of capacity constraints, lack of activity and departmental coordination, bottlenecks, and other factors. The culmination is a decrease in productivity and an accompanying rise in the variable cost per unit.

The accounting and economic views of variable cost behavior are graphed as shown in Exhibit 25-1. The accountant's variable cost is graphed as a straight-line,

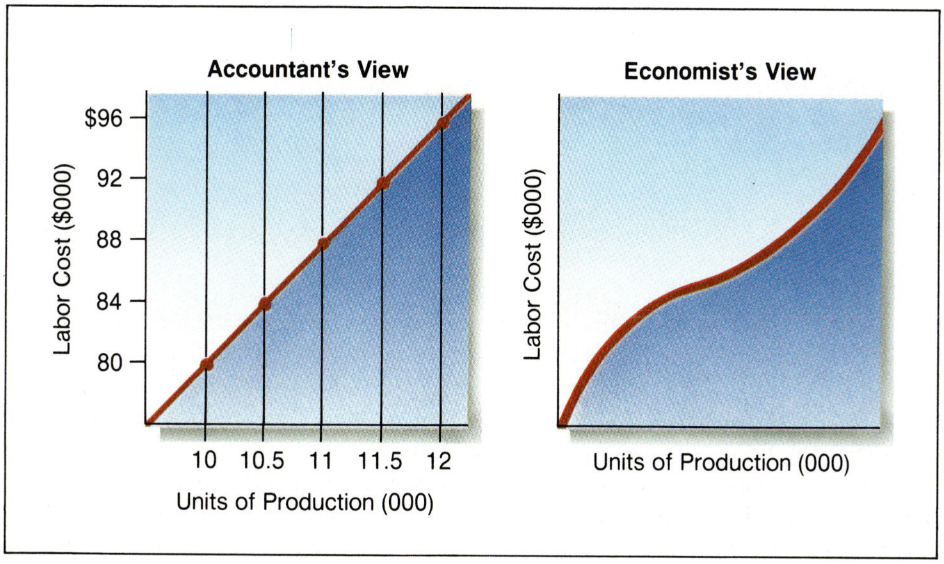


**Exhibit 25-1**
**Differing Views of Variable Cost**

linear function. The economist's curve, on the other hand, first depicts a decreasing cost per unit and later an increasing unit cost. The gradual upward slope to the right still indicates, however, that *total* variable cost increases with additional activity.

Both of the preceding views are correct. The accountant, however, normally studies costs over a smaller range of activity than does the economist. Examine Exhibit 25-2, which shows the behavior of a curvilinear cost function. Notice that within the narrow shaded band, linear behavior (i.e., a constant per-unit amount) is realistic. The band depicts the **relevant range,** or the area of activity where a specified cost relationship is expected to hold true. Normally, the relevant range is an area in which the entity has had some recent operating experience. Generally stated, the assumption of linearity within this narrow band is acceptable and not likely to result in substantial inaccuracies when analyzing costs.

## Step Cost

A careful inspection of specific variable cost functions will often reveal different behavior patterns. Although direct materials and sales commissions change in response to small changes in production and sales, respectively, other variable costs vary only when substantial increases or decreases occur in the activity base. For example, consider the clerical staff needed to process customer orders in a mail-order firm. By working at different paces, employees can usually handle a range of orders. The number of orders processed will be low if the office staff is working at a relaxed pace or high if efforts intensify. Thus, when small fluctuations in activity (i.e., orders) occur, the total cost of office personnel remains constant. If orders dramatically increase, however, additional staff will be hired, and the total office costs will rise.

Because the personnel cost increases in proportion to the number of sales orders, the cost is classified as variable. In this case, though, the cost function changes only when sizable changes are experienced in the activity base. Specifically, the office cost will rise in "chunks" as new workers are added to the payroll. Cost functions that behave in this manner are frequently termed **step costs** and tend to approximate the behavior of a "true" variable cost (see Exhibit 25-3).[1]

**Exhibit 25-2**
**Curvilinear Variable Cost and the Relevant Range**

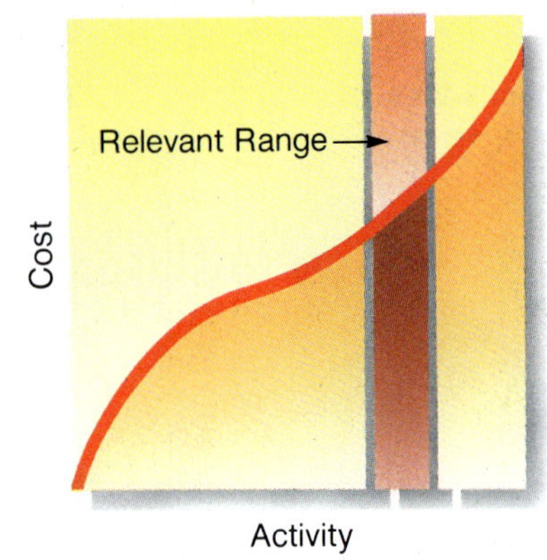


[1] Although our example has depicted a step cost as a type of variable cost, be aware that the step function may also resemble a fixed cost. This situation occurs when the steps become very wide or, in other words, when an extremely large activity change is needed to force an increase (or decrease) in cost. An explanation is provided on page 902.

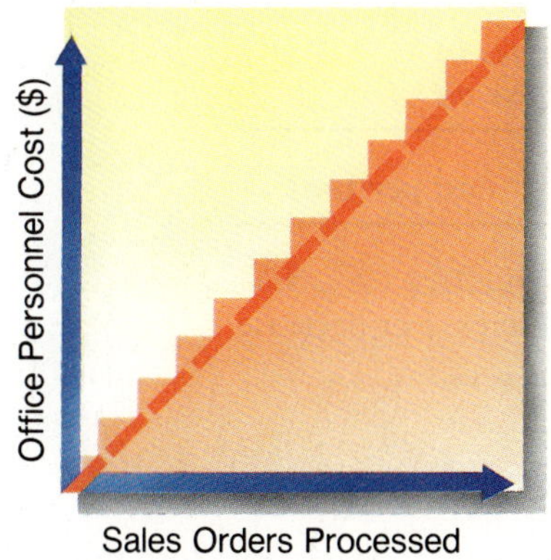


**Exhibit 25-3**
**Step Cost Function**

A careful review of the step cost function provides the underlying explanation of a popular business practice, that of operating at the rightmost portion of a step. By so doing, an organization gets the most for its money, that is, maximum activity just prior to a cost increase.

## Fixed Costs

**Fixed costs** are costs that do not change when the activity base fluctuates. To illustrate a fixed cost, assume Yellowstone Manufacturing leased machinery for $100,000 that is capable of producing from 40,000 to 60,000 units per year depending on utilization. Because the lease payment remains the same no matter how many units are produced, the following graph is appropriate.

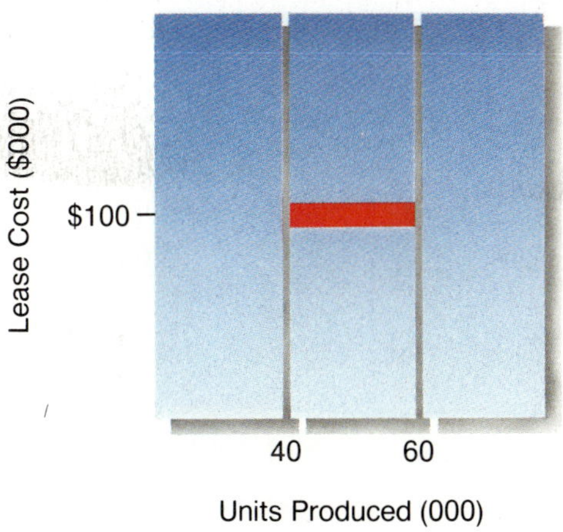


Constant dollars combined with changing activity cause variations in the fixed cost *per unit.* If Yellowstone manufactures only 40,000 units, the lease cost is $2.50 per unit ($100,000 ÷ 40,000 units). On the other hand, if production climbs to 60,000 units, the per-unit cost falls to $1.67 ($100,000 ÷ 60,000 units). In view of this behavior, we can summarize the movement of fixed and variable costs as shown in the accompanying chart.

| Type of Cost | *Effect of Changes in the Activity Base on* Total Cost | Cost per Unit |
|---|---|---|
| Variable | Increase or decrease | No effect |
| Fixed | No effect* | Increase or decrease |

* This is a general rule, as further explained in the next section.

## Total Fixed Costs Can Change

Although total fixed costs remain static, they can, in fact, vary. Both time and other ranges of activity will readily cause increases or decreases in this significant cost element. To explain, virtually all costs change over the years because of inflation and variations in business practices. In the previous illustration, for example, Yellowstone might have leased the same equipment in future years at an increased cost or perhaps have turned to another lessor to obtain newer technology. Whether a cost is, indeed, fixed depends on the time period under consideration. In the long run most costs change to match increases and decreases in manufacturing and sales activities.

Ranges of activity also affect fixed cost behavior. Notice that Yellowstone's equipment can manufacture up to 60,000 units per year. If production increases beyond this point, additional machinery must be leased, which forces fixed costs to rise. The additional machinery will allow the firm to handle a new range of activity, say 60,001 to 80,000 units. If production increases once again, then even more machinery must be acquired. Costs that behave in this manner can be graphed as shown in Exhibit 25-4. The graph reveals that fixed costs will change with wide fluctuations in activity. The shaded band represents Yellowstone's most recent manufacturing experience—in essence, the relevant range. If the relevant range

**Exhibit 25-4**
**Fixed Cost Behavior**

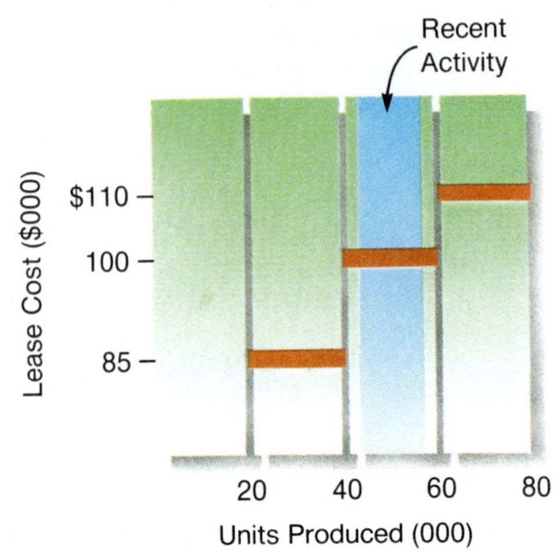

has been properly defined, normal operations should produce fixed costs that can be graphed as a single horizontal line.

## Committed and Discretionary Fixed Costs

Fixed costs are substantial for many companies, especially those engaged in manufacturing. Heavy capital equipment and inventory requirements generate sizable depreciation write-offs, lease costs, and various related outlays. For purposes of planning, fixed costs are often subdivided into two types: committed and discretionary.

**Committed fixed costs** arise from an organization's commitment to engage in operations. By opening its doors and commencing activities, a firm must secure a plant, equipment, and management team. Immediately, as a result, an obligation is made to incur such costs as depreciation, rent, insurance, property taxes, and executive salaries.

By their very nature, most committed costs are not easily changed by daily business activities and decisions. Even if activity slows because of a depressed economy, many of these costs will still be incurred. Obviously, executives can vote to take salary cuts, layoffs can be instituted, and certain operations may be sold or perhaps temporarily closed. However, significant cutbacks in committed costs normally prevent a firm from achieving its long-run goals and objectives.

**Discretionary fixed costs** are those that originate from top management's yearly spending decisions. That is, in preparing the annual operating budget, management will decide the amount it wishes to allocate to certain forthcoming activities. Fixed costs typically determined in this fashion include advertising, research and development, employee training, and contributions.

***The Underlying Differences*** Aside from the manner in which they originate, there are two major differences between committed and discretionary fixed costs. First, when a business decides to engage in or expand operations, a careful study is performed of both the current *and* future economic position of the firm. Buildings will not be built and equipment will not be acquired unless *long-run* profitability is anticipated. In view of their nature, it is apparent that committed costs are geared heavily to the future. Discretionary fixed costs, conversely, are short term in orientation and based on management's expectations for the forthcoming accounting period.

The second distinction between committed and discretionary costs concerns cost elimination. As noted, committed costs are not easily changed. Once the decision is made for their incurrence, an organization becomes locked-in and must live with its obligation for a number of years. Because of this relative stranglehold, companies strive for effective facility utilization as a means of coping with committed costs. Such a strategy is very logical; the associated inflexibility dictates an uphill battle if cost reduction is attempted in drives to improve earnings. In contrast, discretionary costs also lock in an organization; however, the period of commitment is normally much shorter. Frequently, for example, discretionary costs are set by yearly contracts. Should financial difficulties arise, cost cutbacks can be achieved more rapidly and possibly without significant damage to long-run objectives.

## Increased Fixed Costs

Over the years there has been a shift by businesses toward higher levels of fixed cost incurrence (relative to variable cost). Consider, for example, that labor unions have fought long and hard for guaranteed annual wages and workweeks, both of which have transformed direct labor (a variable cost) into a cost that is not totally responsive to changes in production. Another factor is an increased use of automated facilities and robots. Automation and its accompanying charges for depreciation, property taxes, leasing, and maintenance have added to a company's fixed costs while often, at the same time, reducing the firm's labor force.

Although guaranteed wages and workweeks may be attractive from a social viewpoint, and automation may lead to improved efficiency and product quality, operating flexibility will frequently suffer for reasons noted earlier in the discussion. The alternatives faced by a manager in daily business decisions would normally be greater and more diverse in a variable-cost environment—one where costs are readily changed and/or eliminated should the need arise.

## Mixed (Semivariable) Costs

Many cost functions contain both variable and fixed cost elements. Companies, for instance, often pay their salespeople a weekly salary plus a commission. The commission, generally a stipulated percentage of sales, varies with the revenues generated. As another example, electric utilities frequently bill their customers a fixed amount each month, plus a certain number of cents per kilowatt-hour used. Both of these cost functions are termed **mixed,** or **semivariable, costs.** Like a variable cost, a mixed cost changes in response to fluctuations in the activity base. Mixed cost movement, however, is not directly proportional because of the presence of a constant fixed charge. The elements of a mixed cost are shown graphically in Exhibit 25-5.

Observe that the variable and fixed cost elements are combined to generate the total mixed cost. To illustrate, assume that New England Products pays Howard Polk a $200 weekly salary plus a 10% sales commission. If Polk's sales for the week just ended total $2,450, New England's compensation cost of $445 would be computed in the following manner:

| | |
|---|---|
| Fixed salary cost | $200 |
| Variable cost: $2,450 × 0.10 | 245 |
| Total (mixed) cost | $445 |

**Exhibit 25-5**
**Mixed Cost**

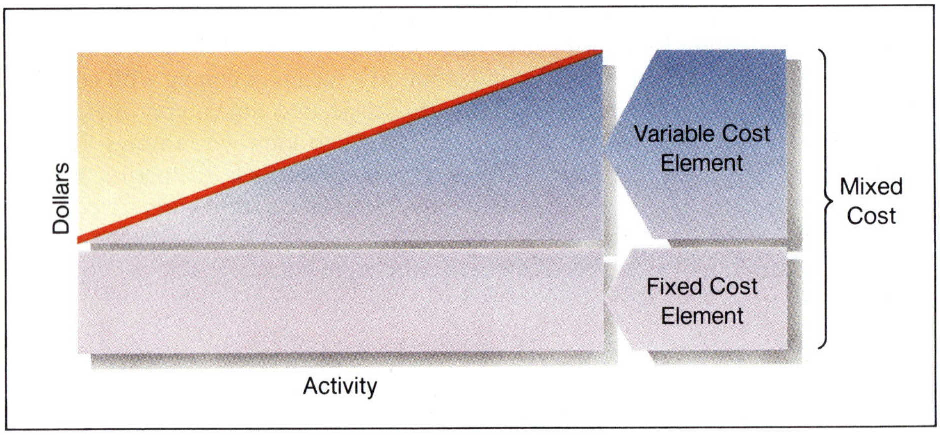

## Cost Analysis

Most accountants and cost analysts have little difficulty understanding the differences among variable, step, fixed, and mixed costs. The determination of how specific costs behave, however, is another matter. Recall our earlier warning—the same costs can behave differently in different situations. To further complicate the picture, many costs are influenced by more than one factor at a given time. Direct materials used, for example, is normally classified as a variable cost. Use varies with production but is also influenced by material quality and worker efficiency. Turning to another area, gasoline consumption increases with the number of miles driven. However, the exact consumption is also affected by the vehicle involved, wind conditions, the type of driving (city or highway), and other factors.

You are probably beginning to realize that cost analysis is an extremely difficult task. In practice, many companies assume that cost behavior can be sufficiently explained by concentrating on only one key factor rather than the many variables that may actually affect expenditure levels. Management, as a result, must exercise judgment when examining cost functions. Cost analysis in most organizations is heavily dependent on assumptions and estimates; perfection is the exception as opposed to the rule.

Several techniques have been developed to study cost behavior. These techniques include the scattergraph, the method of least squares, and the high-low method.

### Scattergraph

OBJECTIVE 2
Be able to use the scattergraph and high-low method for studying cost behavior.

A **scattergraph** is a graphical representation of observed relationships between costs and activity levels. By using operating data, one plots the costs incurred at various levels of activity. On the basis of the observed relationships, the costs are then identified as being fixed, variable, or mixed. To illustrate use of a scattergraph, assume that Zephyr Bus Lines desires to analyze the maintenance costs incurred to service its bus fleet. An examination of maintenance records for a recent six-month period revealed the following information:

| *Month* | *Maintenance Labor Hours* | *Maintenance Cost* |
|---|---|---|
| January | 1,400 | $25,000 |
| February | 1,200 | 22,400 |
| March | 1,600 | 24,500 |
| April | 1,800 | 24,700 |
| May | 1,900 | 28,000 |
| June | 2,000 | 30,000 |

A casual inspection of the data reveals that some variable cost is present, since higher levels of activity (labor hours) generate higher costs. This observation is confirmed by examining the scattergraph in Exhibit 25-6. The line through the data points, drawn by visual approximation, intersects the cost axis at $10,000—the fixed cost of Zephyr's maintenance operation. The variable cost per hour can now be found by studying the total cost of any point that falls on the line.[2] The computations that follow show the proper approach.

[2] The hourly variable cost is equal to the slope of the line.

**Exhibit 25-6**
**Scattergraph**

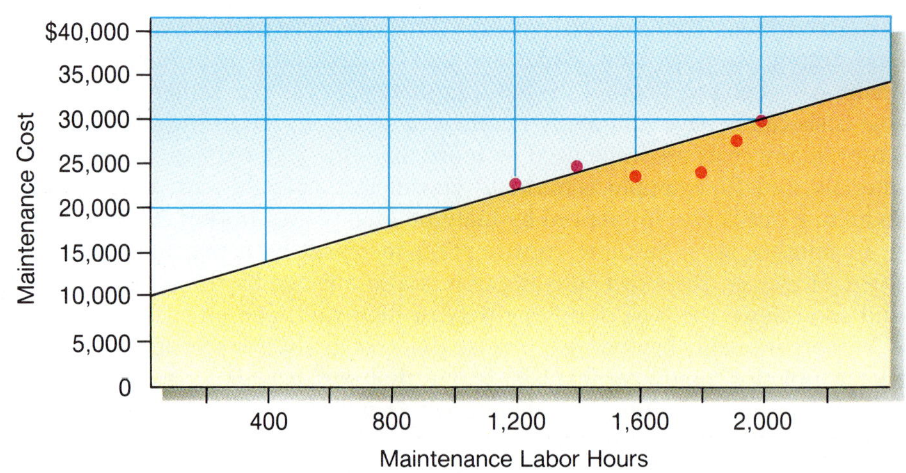


| | |
|---|---:|
| Total cost at 2,000 hours | $30,000 |
| Less fixed cost | 10,000 |
| Variable cost | $20,000 |

Variable cost per hour: $20,000 ÷ 2,000 hours = $10 per hour

The scattergraph is somewhat imprecise because of the manner in which the cost line is determined; yet it is a starting point for analyzing cost behavior. Further study is needed to ensure that the observed data points are representative of the cost function's normal behavior and not caused by unusual events such as worker slowdowns, an abnormally high number of breakdowns, and so forth.

## Method of Least Squares

The **method of least squares** is a statistical technique that overcomes the imprecision of the scattergraph. Rather than determine the cost line by approximation, the least-squares method relies on mathematical formulas to minimize the sum of the squares of the distances from the data points to the line. With this approach the best possible line fit is obtained, and higher accuracy is achieved. The details of the least-squares method are normally presented in most statistics courses and many advanced managerial accounting courses.

## High-Low Method

Unlike the scattergraph and the method of least squares, the **high-low method** focuses on only two data points when analyzing costs: those at the highest and lowest levels of activity within the relevant range. From these two points a generalization is made with regard to variable and fixed cost behavior.

To illustrate the related procedures, we will continue the Zephyr Bus Lines example. Observe that the highest and lowest activity occurred during June and February, respectively. By studying these two months, we see that an 800-hour increase in labor time caused maintenance cost to rise by $7,600. These figures are obtained from the following computations:

| | *Maintenance Labor Hours* | *Maintenance Cost* |
|---|---|---|
| Highest activity (June) | 2,000 | $30,000 |
| Lowest activity (February) | 1,200 | 22,400 |
| Difference | 800 | $ 7,600 |

The increase in total cost represents variable cost; thus, the variable maintenance cost per hour amounts to $9.50 ($7,600 ÷ 800 hours).

Once the variable portion is known, fixed cost can be determined by returning to either of the two months under study. Because total cost equals variable cost plus fixed cost, the latter amount is found by subtraction:

| | *High Point (2,000 Hours)* | *Low Point (1,200 Hours)* |
|---|---|---|
| Total cost | $30,000 | $22,400 |
| Less variable cost @ $9.50 per hour | 19,000* | 11,400† |
| Fixed cost | $11,000 | $11,000 |

* 2,000 hours × $9.50 = $19,000.
† 1,200 hours × $9.50 = $11,400.

As the calculations show, fixed costs are the same at both volume levels—an expected finding since we are working within one range of activity.

The high-low method is criticized by many accountants because only two points are analyzed; all other observed cost and activity relationships are ignored. It is therefore especially important that the data points selected for evaluation are representative of normal activity and not caused by unusual happenings. Because of the procedures employed, it is not surprising that the results obtained by the high-low method (fixed cost = $11,000; variable cost = $9.50 per hour) differ from those generated by use of the scattergraph (fixed cost = $10,000; variable cost = $10 per hour). Both methods have inherent deficiencies and should be used with care.

## Cost-Volume-Profit Analysis

OBJECTIVE 3
**Be able to perform various types of cost-volume-profit analysis, including calculation of the break-even point.**

Once variable and fixed costs are determined, cost-volume-profit analysis can begin. Managers utilize CVP analysis in many different ways. Various cost strategies can be explored, such as trade-offs between incurring fixed salary costs or variable sales commission expenses. CVP can also be used to examine pricing policies and the policies' impact on market share; profit strategies such as purposely incurring a loss on a product to generate additional customer traffic in a retail store; and other similar issues.

An important and highly publicized facet of cost-volume-profit analysis is break-even analysis. This popular management tool concentrates on finding the **break-even point**—the level of activity where revenues and expenses are equal. Net income, as a result, is zero.

The break-even point can be calculated by employing either an equation or a contribution approach. To illustrate both methods, we will assume that the University Bookstore is studying whether to add a collection of mugs to its product line.

Each mug costs \$7 and will be sold for \$10. The following additional monthly costs will be incurred:

| | |
|---|---|
| Rental cost of display case | \$300 |
| Salary of part-time salesperson | 600 |
| | \$900 |

## Equation Approach

As its name implies, the equation approach relies on a mathematical equation to compute the break-even point. The equation is based on the calculation of net income, that is:

| | | |
|---|---|---|
| Sales | | \$XXX |
| Less: Variable costs | \$XXX | |
| Fixed costs | XXX | XXX |
| Net income | | \$XXX |

Because net income equals zero at the break-even point, the following expression is constructed:

$$\text{Sales} - \text{Variable Costs} - \text{Fixed Costs} = 0$$

Transforming, we have

$$\text{Sales} = \text{Variable Costs} + \text{Fixed Costs}$$

The equation requires that variable costs be expressed as a percentage of sales. An examination of the University Bookstore data reveals that the \$300 display case rental and the \$600 salary are both fixed since neither amount changes with volume. The \$7 mug cost, on the other hand, is variable, making variable cost in our example 70% of sales (\$7 ÷ \$10 selling price).

The break-even point can now be found in the following manner:

$$\begin{aligned}\text{Sales} &= \text{Variable Costs} + \text{Fixed Costs}\\ S &= VC + FC\\ S &= 0.7S + \$900\\ 0.3S &= \$900\\ S &= \$3{,}000\end{aligned}$$

The calculations show that monthly sales must total \$3,000 to break even. Stated differently, sales in excess of 300 mugs (\$3,000 ÷ \$10 selling price) will generate net income; in contrast, sales of less than 300 mugs will produce a net loss. (See the Tips & Techniques feature on p. 909.)

## Contribution Approach

> **OBJECTIVE 4**
> Be familiar with the computation and meaning of the contribution margin.

The contribution approach focuses on unit profitability. Because mugs are purchased for \$7 and later sold for \$10, the bookstore is better off by \$3 for each mug sold. The \$3 figure is termed the **contribution margin,** namely, selling price minus variable cost per unit. In plain and simple terms, the contribution margin

**▶ TIPS & TECHNIQUES**

The break-even computation is easily verified:

| | | |
|---|---|---|
| Sales | | $3,000 |
| Less: Variable costs ($3,000 × 0.70) | $2,100 | |
| Fixed costs | 900 | 3,000 |
| Net income | | $ — |

This calculation shows that the variable cost element must, as its name implies, "be free" to vary with dollar sales. By expressing the mug's cost as a *percentage* of sales rather than a flat dollar amount (i.e., $7), the proper cost behavior pattern is achieved.

represents the amount that each mug contributes toward covering fixed costs and generating net income.

To illustrate, examine the data in the following chart.

| *Mugs Sold* | *Revenue* | *Total Variable Cost* | *Fixed Cost* | *Total Cost* | *Net Income* |
|---|---|---|---|---|---|
| 0 | $ 0 | $ 0 | $900 | $ 900 | $(900) |
| | | | | | >$3 |
| 1 | 10 | 7 | 900 | 907 | (897) |
| | | | | | >$3 |
| 2 | 20 | 14 | 900 | 914 | (894) |
| ⋮ | ⋮ | ⋮ | ⋮ | ⋮ | ⋮ |
| 300 | 3,000 | 2,100 | 900 | 3,000 | 0 |
| | | | | | > $3 |
| 301 | 3,010 | 2,107 | 900 | 3,007 | 3 |
| | | | | | > $3 |
| 302 | 3,020 | 2,114 | 900 | 3,014 | 6 |

The first line shows product line profitability immediately after the decision to carry the mugs. Specifically, the salesperson has been hired and the display case has been rented; however, no merchandise has been sold. Each sale then contributes $3 toward covering the fixed costs and decreases the overall loss. Although the decision to stock the goods will eventually prove profitable, the bookstore must first generate sufficient volume to completely offset the fixed costs and break even. The break-even point is computed in the following manner:

$$\frac{\text{Fixed Costs}}{\text{Unit Contribution Margin}} = \text{Break-Even Point in Units}$$

$$\frac{\$900}{\$3} = 300 \text{ mugs}$$

After the 300th mug is sold, income will be produced at the rate of $3 per unit.

The contribution margin is a very powerful business tool and should not be dismissed lightly. In addition to its use in profit planning, the contribution margin also assists in performance evaluation and decision making. These applications are explored in Chapter 27.

## HIGHLIGHT

# CVP Spells Big Bucks

In a contest for book title most likely to put buyers to sleep, who could resist nominating *The Visual Display of Quantitative Information*? And who could be more wrong? The book has developed a kind of cult following, and it is making its author and publisher a lot of money.

As it happens, the author and publisher are one and the same: Edward Tufte. Tufte is a professor of statistics, politics, and graphics at Yale University and proprietor of Graphics Press, which he runs out of his home. Not too long ago the 61,000th copy of *Visual Display* rolled from the bindery. So far Graphics Press, which has only this book in its catalog, has raked in $1.7 million in sales, and there is no sign of a slackening. On most of the books, which currently retail at $33, Tufte earns a pretax margin of 58%, and he is well on his way to netting $1 million from his one-book publishing enterprise. A full professor's salary at Yale: about $64,000.

Tufte had already written four books for established publishers and wanted his fifth to be a business venture. "I had the odd notion," he says, "that the author is the one who should mainly be rewarded . . ." Feeling this way puts Tufte in eminent company. Mark Twain distrusted publishers and set up his own firm to distribute *Huckleberry Finn*. John Maynard Keynes was more confident than his publisher that *Economic Consequences of the Peace* would be a major publishing event. So he issued the 1919 work himself and used the publisher primarily for distribution—at great profit to Lord Keynes. Still, Tufte is quick to warn that self-publishing is "a good way to wind up with a basement full of mildewing books."

The professor, though, has succeeded because he understands business and cost-volume-profit relationships. Tufte likes to say that the first copy of his book cost $105,000, and each additional copy $6. What he means is that he shelled out $105,000 to get started, and can now produce books at $6 each. The startup money included a $55,000 bill from the printer, mostly for high-grade camera work, and $30,000 for a book designer, an illustrator, page makeup, and permission fees to publications whose charts he reproduced. The other $20,000 was a downpayment on advertising and other costs.

Now that the process is up and running, Tufte incurs $14 of variable cost per volume (the $6 manufacturing cost just noted plus additional outlays for postage, labor, promotion, and so forth). The professor therefore pockets $19 pretax, on each $33 mail-order book he sells. Adding further attractiveness, the operation's overhead is kept very low. There are no fancy lunches or marketing studies. No computers, not even to keep track of orders. Envelopes on follow-up fliers are typed by hand. Tufte declines to say exactly how much money he has made, but there are hints of budding affluence. His hilltop home is adorned by a new swimming pool, surrounded by a visually striking fence of his own design. His newest toy is a costly 17th-century edition of Galileo.

Tufte insists that the point of the book was not to make money but to help people understand the difference between charts and graphs that inform and charts and graphs that are misleading. "Cosmetics are not going to rescue a bad chart," says Tufte. "If the numbers are boring, you've just got the wrong numbers." He might also add that if you've got an exciting product and a grasp of CVP relationships, the financial numbers will take care of themselves.

SOURCE: Adapted from "Publish and Prosper," *Forbes*, May 18, 1987, pp. 121–123. Reprinted by permission of *Forbes* magazine, © Forbes Inc., 1987.

## A Graphical Representation

The break-even point and CVP relationships are frequently presented in a graphical format known as a **break-even chart.** The graph is useful because it allows managers to (1) review earnings over a wide range of activity and (2) examine the effects on profitability of changes in sales and costs.

The break-even chart for our mug example appears in Exhibit 25-7. With sales volume graphed on the horizontal axis and dollars on the vertical axis, the chart is constructed in the following manner:

**1** Fixed costs are depicted by drawing a line parallel to the horizontal axis.

**2** Total costs are represented by first computing the total cost of an arbitrarily selected volume level. The calculations for a selected volume of 500 mugs follow.

| | |
|---|---|
| Variable cost (500 mugs × $7) | $3,500 |
| Fixed cost | 900 |
| Total cost | $4,400 |

The total cost line is then extended from the intersection of the fixed cost line and the vertical axis to $4,400 (point *A*).

**3** Sales revenues are plotted in a manner similar to that described in Step 2. A diagonal line is extended from the graph's origin through a point that represents the total revenues of an arbitrarily selected activity level. If we again choose 500 mugs, the line would be extended through point *B*, or $5,000 (500 mugs × $10).

Point *C* represents break-even operations: $3,000 of sales (300 mugs). The graph readily discloses that sales in excess of 300 mugs will be profitable, because

**Exhibit 25-7**
**Break-Even Chart**

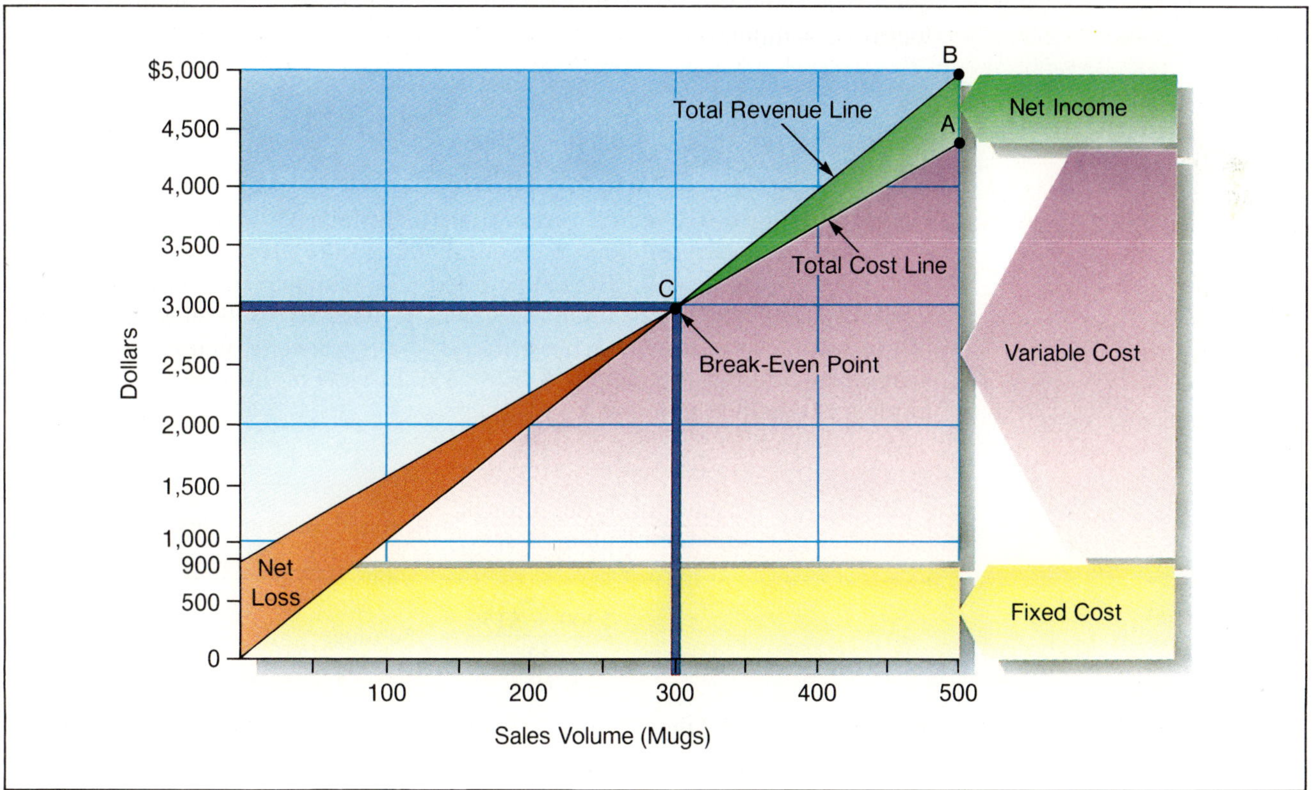

total revenues exceed total costs. In contrast, should volume drop below this figure, the University Bookstore will generate a loss from its new product line.

## Target Net Income

In addition to finding the break-even point, CVP analysis can also be used to identify the amount of sales necessary to produce a particular level of net income (often called the **target net income**). To illustrate the related procedures, we will continue the University Bookstore example. Assume that the mugs will be carried in stock only if they generate a monthly net income of $150. The sales required to achieve this level of profitability can be calculated by modifying the equation and contribution approaches to break-even analysis.

Focusing on the first approach, we noted earlier that the following relationship is true at the break-even point:

$$\text{Sales} - \text{Variable Costs} - \text{Fixed Costs} = 0$$

Because we now desire to earn a particular income figure, the equation becomes

$$\text{Sales} - \text{Variable Costs} - \text{Fixed Costs} = \text{Net Income}$$

or

$$\text{Sales} = \text{Variable Costs} + \text{Fixed Costs} + \text{Net Income}$$

Recall from the initial data that variable cost is 70% of sales and fixed costs total $900. The bookstore must therefore generate sales of $3,500, as shown in the following computation:

$$\begin{aligned} S &= VC + FC + NI \\ S &= 0.7S + \$900 + \$150 \\ 0.3S &= \$1{,}050 \\ S &= \$3{,}500 \end{aligned}$$

On the basis of the $10 selling price, volume must total 350 mugs ($3,500 ÷ $10).

Turning to the contribution method, the bookstore previously calculated that each mug contributes $3 ($10 selling price − $7 variable cost) toward covering fixed costs and producing a profit. As shown on page 909, 300 mugs must be sold just to break even. Now, to achieve the $150 target income figure, volume must increase by 50 units per month ($150 ÷ $3). In view of this fact, the break-even formula is modified as follows:

$$\frac{\text{Fixed Costs} + \text{Net Income}}{\text{Unit Contribution Margin}} = \text{Required Sales in Units}$$

$$\frac{\$900 + \$150}{\$3} = 350 \text{ mugs}$$

## Operating Changes

New technology, shifts in management, and variations in efficiency are commonplace for most businesses. These events and others are usually accompanied by changes in costs and revenues and thus affect an organization's CVP relationships. Consider, for example, the following break-even load factors[3] for several of this country's airlines:

| | *1988* | *1987* | *1986* | *1985* | *1984* |
|---|---|---|---|---|---|
| American Airlines | 56.0% | 58.5% | 59.3% | 57.3% | 57.1% |
| Braniff | 69.5 | 70.4 | 61.7 | 59.9 | 69.2 |
| Delta Air Lines | 52.7 | 51.1 | 56.0 | 51.6 | 48.5 |
| Midway Airlines | 54.4 | 53.5 | 56.5 | 58.1 | 54.3 |
| USAir | 58.7 | 57.3 | 56.4 | 54.2 | 51.7 |

Observe the variation over the years and among different carriers within the same year. Although there are a number of underlying causes, several of the more significant include fleet composition in terms of size, age, and fuel efficiency; route systems and structures (e.g., long haul vs. short haul, business vs. vacation); fleet financing methods; passenger fare composition (i.e., full-fare vs. discount traffic); and labor and jet fuel contracts.

Airlines must respond to changes in these factors to stay in the black. Some have done so successfully, while others have not. Those in the latter category have incurred significant operating losses (occasionally leading to bankruptcy) or, in some cases, been absorbed by another carrier. Airlines are not alone—all businesses are faced with variations in their cost and revenue patterns.

Because management's ability to analyze operating changes often spells the difference between prosperity or failure, it is desirable to focus on the impact of changes in CVP relationships. To do so, we will continue the University Bookstore example. As a refresher, recall the following data:

| | | | |
|---|---|---|---|
| Selling price per mug | $10 | Fixed costs | |
| Variable cost per mug | 7 | Display case rental | $300 |
| Contribution margin | $ 3 | Salary of salesperson | 600 |
| | | | $900 |

Sales necessary to reach break-even point: 300 mugs
Sales necessary to generate net income of $150: 350 mugs

## Change in Fixed Costs

Assume the bookstore is considering hiring a more experienced salesperson who requires a $720 monthly salary. Management wants to know the effect on the break-even point of this $120 increase in fixed cost. The desired information can be obtained in several different ways. Employing the contribution approach, we see the new break-even volume is 340 mugs:

$$\frac{\text{Fixed Costs}}{\text{Unit Contribution Margin}} = \frac{\$1{,}020}{\$3} = 340 \text{ mugs}$$

Or, since each mug contributes $3 toward fixed obligations, an additional 40 mugs must be sold to cover the $120 cost increase ($120 ÷ $3 = 40 mugs). Thus, the break-even point will jump from 300 to 340 units.

[3] The break-even load factor is the percentage of seats that must be filled on scheduled flights to break even.

## Changes in Fixed Costs and Variable Costs

Returning to the original data, assume the bookstore is exploring different compensation methods. Rather than a \$600 monthly salary, a plan is under consideration that calls for a base salary of \$200 plus a \$1-per-mug sales commission. Specifically, management desires to learn the sales volume required to yield the target monthly net income of \$150. In this case, total fixed costs fall to \$500 (\$200 + \$300 display case rental). Furthermore, because variable costs rise by \$1 from the commission, the mug's contribution margin decreases to \$2 (\$10 − \$8). These two changes are combined to generate the following results:

$$\frac{\text{Fixed Costs} + \text{Net Income}}{\text{Unit Contribution Margin}} = \text{Required Sales in Units}$$

$$\frac{\$500 + \$150}{\$2} = 325 \text{ mugs}$$

The change in salary structure shows the bookstore can suffer a drop in monthly sales of 25 mugs (350 − 325) and still produce the target income figure. The plan is therefore advantageous and should be implemented. Not only do the numbers support the change, but an important qualitative consideration is present as well. The compensation plan under study (i.e., reward via commission) often increases employee motivation. Higher motivational levels, in turn, frequently lead to improved sales performance.

## Changes in Fixed Costs and Sales Volume

Again returning to the original data, assume that operations have been quite profitable, with monthly sales averaging 400 mugs. Management is now considering a larger display case at an increased rental cost of \$75 per month. The added space will allow the bookstore to carry a greater selection of merchandise, and sales are expected to total 440 units. Should the new display case be acquired?

Because there are changes in both revenues and costs, management should compare the additional revenues that arise from the decision against the additional costs. If additional revenues exceed additional costs, the proposal should be accepted; if not, rejection is in order. The following analysis reveals a net benefit in favor of the larger display case:

| | | |
|---|---|---|
| Additional revenues: 40 mugs × \$10 | | \$400 |
| Less additional costs | | |
| Variable: 40 mugs × \$7 | \$280 | |
| Increased rental | 75 | 355 |
| Net monthly benefit | | \$ 45 |

Observe that we have ignored the present volume of 400 mugs in our analysis. No matter which alternative is selected (i.e., maintain the present situation or acquire the larger case), these goods will continue to be sold. The analysis should concentrate on those items that change as a result of the decision, namely, the 40-unit increase in sales and the higher rental charge. Decisions of this nature are explored further in Chapter 27.

## Changes in Sales Price and Sales Volume

Independent of the previous example that focused on a change in fixed costs and sales volume, assume that monthly sales have averaged 550 mugs. The bookstore is considering an increase in selling price from $10 to $12 despite a possible lowering of volume. Before the final decision is made, management desires information regarding the amount sales can decline before there is a detrimental effect on profitability.

Because current sales total 550 mugs, the present product-line net income is $750 per month:

| | |
|---|---|
| Sales (550 mugs × $10) | $5,500 |
| Less variable cost (550 mugs × $7) | 3,850 |
| Contribution margin | $1,650 |
| Less fixed cost | 900 |
| Net income | $ 750 |

With a new selling price of $12, the unit contribution margin becomes $5 ($12 − $7). Using the following technique, which was illustrated earlier in the chapter, we find that 330 mugs must be sold to maintain current profit levels.

$$\frac{\text{Fixed Costs} + \text{Net Income}}{\text{Unit Contribution Margin}} = \text{Required Sales in Units}$$

$$\frac{\$900 + \$750}{\$5} = 330 \text{ mugs}$$

Thus, the bookstore can suffer a monthly sales loss of 220 units (550 − 330) without any impact on net income.

**TIPS & TECHNIQUES**

The preceding illustrations have shown several different methods to examine and solve business problems. As more experience is gained you will find this topical area is full of variety, with the correct answer obtainable by using alternative approaches. As long as your logic is sound and the method of solution is not specified by the text or your instructor, feel free to use any of the approaches presented.

## Margin of Safety

In addition to the techniques thus far discussed, an analyst has other tools available to evaluate an entity and any contemplated operating changes. One such tool is the **margin of safety,** which shows the amount that sales can fall before a firm generates a net loss. Mathematically, the margin of safety is computed as the difference between anticipated (or actual) sales and break-even sales. If we assume the University Bookstore is presently selling 700 mugs at $10 each, the margin of safety (using the original data) would be $4,000 ($7,000 − $3,000).

Several options are available to management if the $4,000 amount is deemed inadequate. The alternatives that first come to mind include attempts to increase sales and/or lower the break-even point. Be cautioned, though, that something as simple as a sales increase may not accomplish the intended objective. Suppose, for instance, that the bookstore undertook a costly advertising campaign to stimulate volume. Because the advertising outlays are considered a fixed cost, the operation's break-even point is increased. It is possible that the margin of safety could actually fall, with the rise in break-even sales outpacing the additional mugs actually sold.

Overall, the margin of safety cannot be studied in isolation; it is used in conjunction with the other CVP tools when evaluating available alternatives.

## CVP Analysis for Multiproduct Firms

OBJECTIVE 5
Be able to apply cost-volume-profit analysis to multiproduct firms.

Most businesses engaged in retailing, wholesaling, and manufacturing activities sell more than one product, normally in differing volumes and at different markups. Although the University Bookstore example focused on the use of CVP analysis for a single item only, the procedures illustrated can, with minor modification, be employed when multiple goods are involved. As an example, assume that Stewart Distributors sells toasters, blenders, and mixers. The following data are anticipated for the upcoming year:

| *Product* | *Forecasted Sales (Units)* | *Selling Price* | *Variable Cost* |
|---|---|---|---|
| Toaster | 40,000 | $20 | $16 |
| Blender | 100,000 | 44 | 37 |
| Mixer | 60,000 | 34 | 26 |
| | 200,000 | | |

Fixed costs: $335,000

As before, the break-even point can be found by dividing fixed costs by the unit contribution margin. Rather than dealing with the contribution margin of one product, however, Stewart has three margins to consider. Adding a further complication, the margins are not expected to occur with the same frequency. For every toaster sold, for example, the firm anticipates selling $2\frac{1}{2}$ blenders and $1\frac{1}{2}$ mixers. In view of this situation, Stewart must weight the unit contribution margins by the **sales mix,** or the relative proportion of individual product sales to total sales. The computations that follow reveal a weighted "unit" contribution margin of $6.70:

| *Product* | *Forecasted Sales (Units)* | *Sales Mix** | | *Unit Contribution Margin†* | | *Weighted Contribution Margin* |
|---|---|---|---|---|---|---|
| Toaster | 40,000 | 20% | × | $4 | = | $0.80 |
| Blender | 100,000 | 50% | × | 7 | = | 3.50 |
| Mixer | 60,000 | 30% | × | 8 | = | 2.40 |
| | 200,000 | | | | | $6.70 |

* Forecasted individual product sales ÷ 200,000 units.
† Selling price minus variable cost for each product.

Stewart's break-even point is therefore 50,000 "units" ($335,000 ÷ $6.70). Because each "unit" is really a combination of the three products in the same proportions as the predicted sales mix, the following product line sales are necessary:

| *Product* | *Sales Mix* | | *Break-Even "Units"* | | *Break-Even Sales by Product (Units)* |
|---|---|---|---|---|---|
| Toaster | 20% | × | 50,000 | = | 10,000 |
| Blender | 50% | × | 50,000 | = | 25,000 |
| Mixer | 30% | × | 50,000 | = | 15,000 |

On the basis of the calculations presented, it is evident that if the sales mix varies, the "unit" contribution margin will differ. Consequently, the break-even volume will change.

## Limiting Assumptions of CVP Analysis

OBJECTIVE 6
Understand the limiting assumptions on which cost-volume-profit analysis is based.

The CVP model that we have presented is used to analyze the financial relationships within an organization. Businesses constantly change their operating practices, and many of the changes affect the relationships expressed in the model. CVP studies are therefore based on several limiting assumptions, a few of which have been touched upon in the preceding pages. The assumptions are:

1 All costs can be classified as fixed or variable.
2 Fixed costs remain constant through the range of analysis (i.e., the relevant range).
3 The behavior of costs and revenues is linear through the range of analysis.
4 Technology, efficiency, costs, and selling prices remain as predicted.
5 The sales mix remains as predicted (i.e., constant).
6 Inventory levels remain fairly stable.

Management must be fully aware of the preceding assumptions if CVP analysis is to be used properly. Given the dynamic nature of business, a failure to recognize the model's restrictive features could lead to serious deficiencies in the planning and decision processes.

# Chapter Review

### Learning Objectives—The Key Points

**1 Be familiar with the characteristics of variable, step, fixed, and mixed (semivariable) cost functions.** A variable cost is one that varies in direct proportion to a change in an activity base (e.g., sales, production, and so forth). As a result of this behavior, the total cost incurred increases or decreases and the per-unit amount remains constant. Sometimes, a sizable movement is needed in the activity base for a cost to change. A function that behaves in this manner is known as a step cost because the cost fluctuations really occur in "chunks."

Step functions are often viewed as a type of variable cost; however, when an extremely large activity change is needed to force a change in the dollar amount incurred, the function's behavior tends to approximate that of a fixed cost. A fixed cost remains constant in total over a range of activity; in contrast, the cost per unit fluctuates. Finally, a mixed (semivariable) cost fluctuates with a change in the activity base but does not move in direct proportion to the base. The mixed cost contains both variable and fixed elements.

**2 Be able to use the scattergraph and high-low method for studying cost behavior.** The scattergraph is a graph of past observations between an activity base and the level of cost incurred. Points are plotted and a straight-line is then fit through the points by visual approximation. The line's intersection with the cost axis is the amount of fixed cost incurred; the line's slope is the unit variable cost.

In contrast, the high-low method focuses only on the highest and lowest data observations. The variable cost per unit (or hour) is calculated by studying the cost change between the two points in question relative to the activity base change. Fixed cost is then determined by subtracting the variable cost incurred at the highest (or lowest) point from that point's total cost.

**3 Be able to perform various types of cost-volume-profit analysis, including calculation of the break-even point.** The study of CVP relationships is useful for most any business. One facet of cost-volume-profit analysis deals with finding the break-even point, or the level of activity where total revenues and total costs are equal. Net income is therefore zero. Break-even sales may be computed in both dollars and units, as follows:

- Dollars (equation method): Sales = Variable Costs + Fixed Costs
- Units (contribution approach): Fixed Costs ÷ Unit Contribution Margin

These same calculations, with a minor modification, are used to find the sales required to generate a particular level of income (known as the target net income). In both cases the desired income is added to the fixed cost figure and treated as a "dollar obligation" that must be covered by sales. The formulas, whether modified or not, are useful in studying the impact of numerous operating changes on the entity. Such changes include increases and decreases in sales prices, variable costs, and fixed costs; the addition of new product lines; and so forth.

**4 Be familiar with the computation and meaning of the contribution margin.** The contribution margin, calculated as the difference between selling price and variable cost, represents the amount that each unit will contribute toward covering fixed costs and generating income. That is, if the contribution margin is $8 per unit, overall income will rise by $8 for each unit that is sold by the firm.

**5 Be able to apply cost-volume-profit analysis to multiproduct firms.** CVP analysis can be used in single- or multiple-product settings. To compute the break-even point, fixed costs are once again divided by the contribution margin per unit. A "unit" in this instance, however, is really a combination of a company's various products in preset proportions known as a sales mix (i.e., the percentage of individual product sales to total unit sales). A weighted contribution margin is found by weighting (multiplying) individual product margins with the sales mix percentages, the result then being divided into total fixed costs.

**6 Understand the limiting assumptions on which cost-volume-profit analysis is based.** The cost-volume-profit model assumes that all costs can be classified as variable or fixed, with costs falling in the latter category being constant through the range of analysis. Further, costs and revenues have linear, straight-line relationships. The components used in the model (e.g., costs, revenues, and sales mix) must remain as predicted, and inventory levels must remain fairly stable during the accounting period.

## Chapter Quiz

The five questions that follow relate to several issues raised in the chapter. Test your knowledge of the issues by selecting the best answer. (The answers appear on p. 931.)

**1** Variable costs (from the accountant's viewpoint):
- a are graphed by means of a curvilinear line.
- b remain constant in total through the relevant range.
- c are constant on a per-unit basis through the relevant range.
- d are commonly divided into committed and discretionary classifications.

**2** The high-low method of analyzing cost behavior:
- a can be used to determine the variable and fixed components of a mixed cost function.
- b uses the same number of data observations as a scattergraph in the analysis process.
- c relies on the following computation to figure the variable cost per unit (or hour): Change in activity between the high and low points ÷ change in cost between the high and low points.
- d results in different amounts of fixed cost at the high and low data points.

**3** Foster Company has sales of $800,000, variable costs that total 60% of sales, and fixed costs of $180,000. The firm's break-even point is:
a $140,000.
b $300,000.
c $450,000.
d $560,000.

**4** The contribution margin:
a is the amount that each unit contributes toward covering variable costs and producing income.
b is the result of subtracting both the variable and fixed costs per unit from the selling price.
c may, in selected cases, be less than net income.
d is the difference between a unit's selling price and variable cost and, when divided into fixed costs, will produce the unit sales required to break even.

**5** The cost-volume-profit model:
a can only be used by single-product companies.
b assumes that the sales mix must remain as predicted.
c assumes that technology, efficiency, and costs can change.
d cannot be used to study operating changes of the firm.

## Summary Problem

Kennett Company manufactures and sells a single product. Sales peak in March and generally bottom out in October. The following cost and volume information was extracted from the accounting records:

| | *March* | *July** | *October* |
|---|---|---|---|
| Production and sales (units) | 25,000 | 19,000 | 14,000 |
| Total cost incurred | $195,300 | $176,200 | $156,800 |

*An average month.

The company's product sells for $9.00 per unit.

### Instructions

**a** By using the high-low method, compute Kennett's variable cost per unit and total monthly fixed cost.

**b** Compute the firm's contribution margin per unit.

**c** Determine the break-even point in terms of both units and dollar sales.

**d** Determine the sales volume (in units) required to generate a target net income of $29,150 per month.

**e** Assume that Kennett desires to add a second product (known as product no. 2). Data related to this product follow.

| | |
|---|---|
| Selling price per unit | $7.00 |
| Variable cost per unit | $4.20 |
| Additional fixed costs | $65,800 |

Management anticipates that product no. 2 will initially account for 20% of the company's total sales volume; the remaining 80% will be generated by the existing product (known as product no. 1). If Kennett adds the new product to its merchandise line, compute the new monthly break-even point (in units).

**Solution**

**a**

| | *Units* | *Total Cost* |
|---|---|---|
| Highest activity (March) | 25,000 | $195,300 |
| Lowest activity (October) | 14,000 | 156,800 |
| Difference | 11,000 | $ 38,500 |

Variable cost per unit = $38,500 ÷ 11,000 units = $3.50

| | *High Point (25,000 Units)* | *Low Point (14,000 Units)* |
|---|---|---|
| Total cost | $195,300 | $156,800 |
| Less variable cost @ $3.50 per unit | 87,500* | 49,000† |
| Fixed cost | $107,800 | $107,800 |

* 25,000 units × $3.50 = $87,500.
† 14,000 units × $3.50 = $49,000.

**b**

| | |
|---|---|
| Selling price | $9.00 |
| Less variable cost per unit | 3.50 |
| Contribution margin | $5.50 |

**c**

$$\frac{\text{Fixed Costs}}{\text{Unit Contribution Margin}} = \text{Break-Even Point in Units}$$

$$\frac{\$107{,}800}{\$5.50} = 19{,}600 \text{ units}$$

A break-even point of 19,600 units produces a sales level of $176,400 (19,600 units × $9).

**d**

$$\frac{\text{Fixed Costs + Net Income}}{\text{Unit Contribution Margin}} = \text{Required Sales in Units}$$

$$\frac{\$107{,}800 + \$29{,}150}{\$5.50} = 24{,}900 \text{ units}$$

**e**

| *Product* | *Selling Price* | | *Variable Cost* | | *Contribution Margin* | | *Sales Mix* | | *Weighted Contribution Margin* |
|---|---|---|---|---|---|---|---|---|---|
| 1 | $9.00 | − | $3.50 | = | $5.50 | × | 80% | = | $4.40 |
| 2 | 7.00 | − | 4.20 | = | 2.80 | × | 20% | = | 0.56 |
| | | | | | | | | | $4.96 |

Fixed costs now total $173,600 ($107,800 from product no. 1 + $65,800 from product no. 2). Therefore:

$$\frac{\text{Fixed Costs}}{\text{"Unit" Contribution Margin}} = \text{Break-Even Point in "Units"}$$

$$\frac{\$173{,}600}{\$4.96} = 35{,}000 \text{ "units"}$$

Each "unit" is a mixture of product no. 1 and product no. 2 in the 80:20 sales mix. The break-even point is thus computed as follows:

| *Product* | *Sales Mix* | | *Break-Even "Units"* | | *Break-Even Sales by Product (Units)* |
|---|---|---|---|---|---|
| 1 | 80% | × | 35,000 | = | 28,000 |
| 2 | 20% | × | 35,000 | = | 7,000 |

## Questions

**Q25-1** In evaluating the cost of operating his automobile, a professor once commented: "Fuel is a fixed cost and insurance is a variable cost. I always pay the same amount per gallon and my mileage is fairly constant. On the other hand, the cost per mile for insurance varies with the distance that I drive." Comment on the professor's observations.

**Q25-2** Differentiate between the accountant's and economist's views of variable cost behavior.

**Q25-3** What is meant by the relevant range of activity?

**Q25-4** Discuss the characteristics of a step cost function. In general, where is the best place to operate on a step?

**Q25-5** An accounting professor once commented: "In the long run even fixed costs are variable." Evaluate the professor's comment.

**Q25-6** Distinguish between committed and discretionary fixed costs. Which type can be cutback more easily without doing significant long-run harm to the organization? Explain.

**Q25-7** Briefly comment on the trend toward increased fixed cost incurrence by businesses during the past decade. How does this trend affect operating flexibility?

**Q25-8** Identify the inherent problems of the scattergraph and the high-low method.

**Q25-9** Define the break-even point.

**Q25-10** Define the contribution margin. What does the contribution margin represent, and how is it used in finding the break-even point?

**Q25-11** Product A has a negative contribution margin. Explain how a negative contribution margin can arise, and determine whether product A should continue to be sold.

**Q25-12** Discuss the benefits associated with using a break-even chart.

**Q25-13** Determine the effect on the break-even point of each of the following situations:

a An increase in variable cost
b A decrease in fixed cost
c An increase in sales price

**Q25-14** What is the margin of safety?

**Q25-15** What are the limiting assumptions of CVP analysis?

## Exercises

**E25-1** ***Cost behavior***

Melinda and Arthur Cooley own a fast-food restaurant in Salt Lake City. The following costs are under evaluation:

a Property taxes paid.
b Franchise fees paid ($10,000 per year plus 15% of gross sales).
c Food costs.
d Straight-line depreciation on restaurant equipment.
e Donations of food and supplies to charitable organizations.

f Local advertising.
g Paper supplies (napkins, cups, and so on).

Classify each of these costs as variable, committed fixed, discretionary fixed, or mixed.

**E25-2** ***Cost behavior patterns***

Consider the graphs that follow, each of which represents a different cost or expense of Society Jewelers, an operator of 22 jewelry stores throughout Illinois.

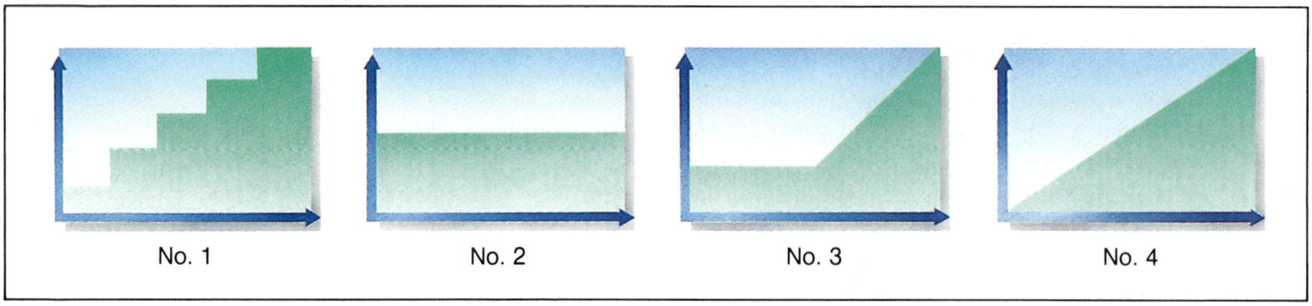


The vertical axis measures dollars and the horizontal axis represents an activity base (number of sales, clerks, and so forth). Select the graph that best describes the following items:

a Straight-line depreciation on store equipment.
b Store manager compensation. Each store manager is paid a monthly salary, plus a commission after a certain level of sales is reached.
c Cost of jewelry sold during the period.
d Weekly wages of store clerks who work a 40-hour week. One clerk is hired for every 100 sales made during the month.
e Rental charges on the firm's warehouse and distribution center.

**E25-3** ***High-low method***

The following data pertain to Jenkins, Inc., during a recent six-month period:

| | *January* | *February* | *March* | *April* | *May* | *June* |
|---|---|---|---|---|---|---|
| Maintenance cost | $99,300 | $91,500 | $87,100 | $105,600 | $105,800 | $94,200 |
| Direct labor hours | 7,420 | 6,370 | 5,950 | 7,980 | 8,150 | 6,740 |

a Determine the variable maintenance cost per direct labor hour by using the high-low method.
b Determine monthly fixed maintenance cost by using the high-low method.

**E25-4** ***High-low method; cost determination***

Dempsey and Associates experienced the following costs when manufacturing 800 and 900 units, respectively:

| | *800 Units* | *900 Units* |
|---|---|---|
| Direct material | $ 9,200 | $10,350 |
| Property taxes | 1,100 | 1,100 |
| Maintenance | 6,200 | 6,850 |
| | $16,500 | $18,300 |

Determine the anticipated outlays for direct material, property taxes, and maintenance cost if 880 units are produced. Dempsey uses the high-low method to analyze cost behavior.

**E25-5** ***Break-even and other CVP relationships***

Gamma Gamma Gamma sorority is in the process of planning its annual homecoming dinner and dance. The treasurer anticipates the following costs for the event, which will be held at the Regency Hotel:

| | |
|---|---|
| Room rental | $300 |
| Dinner cost (per person) | 25 |
| Chartered buses | 500 |
| Favors and souvenirs (per person) | 5 |
| Band | 900 |

Each person would pay $40 to attend; 200 attendees are expected.

a Will the event be profitable for the sorority? Show computations.

b How many people must attend for the sorority to break even?

c Suppose the sorority encouraged its members to drive to the hotel and did not charter the buses. Further, a planned menu change will reduce the cost per meal by $2. If each person will still be charged $40, compute the:

(1) Contribution margin per person.

(2) Margin of safety.

**E25-6** ***Break-even and other CVP relationships***

Cedars Hospital has average revenue of $180 per patient day. Variable costs are $45 per patient day; fixed costs total $4,320,000 per year.

a How many patient days does the hospital need to break even?

b What level of revenue is needed to earn a net income of $540,000?

c If variable costs drop to $36 per patient day, what increase in fixed costs can be tolerated without changing the break-even point as determined in part (a)?

**E25-7** ***Break-even and other CVP relationships***

The Hilltop Hotel has annual fixed costs of $4,496,800 for its 400-room facility. The average room rents for $80 per day; the daily variable cost is $24 for each room rented. The hotel is open 365 days per year.

a Compute Hilltop's net income if the hotel has a 60% occupancy rate throughout the year.

b How many rooms must be rented each year to break even?

c Given your answer in part (b), what percentage of rooms must be rented during the year to break even?

**E25-8** ***CVP relationships: Working backward***

Determine the missing amounts in each of the independent cases that follow.

| *Case* | *Units Sold* | *Sales* | *Variable Costs* | *Contribution Margin per Unit* | *Fixed Costs* | *Net Income* |
|---|---|---|---|---|---|---|
| A | ? | $70,000 | $ ? | $6 | $14,000 | $10,000 |
| B | 7,000 | ? | 42,000 | 5 | ? | 8,000 |
| C | 4,000 | 53,000 | ? | ? | 21,000 | (2,000) |
| D | 8,000 | 92,000 | 40,000 | ? | 24,000 | ? |

**E25-9** ***Overview of CVP relationships***

Evaluate the comments that follow as being True or False. If the comment is false, briefly explain why.

a The contribution margin is computed by subtracting the fixed cost per unit from the selling price.

b The margin of safety is essentially the same concept as target net income.

c An automobile dealer has a negative contribution margin on each auto sold. He nonetheless claims that he makes up for this situation on volume; with more cars sold than the competition, the dealership can be profitable. (Note: Ignore leasing, body shop, and service department considerations.)

d An increase in the number of units sold each month will decrease a company's break-even point.

e The sales mix is an important consideration when figuring the break-even point in a multiproduct company.

**E25-10** ***Break even with multiple products***

The following data pertain to recent operations of the Omni Company:

| | *Product* | | |
|---|---|---|---|
| | *X* | *Y* | *Z* |
| Sales (units) | 12,000 | 18,000 | 10,000 |
| Sales | $48,000 | $90,000 | $62,000 |
| Variable costs | $15,600 | $36,000 | $38,000 |

Fixed costs amounted to $96,600.

a Determine Omni's sales mix.

b Compute the company's weighted contribution margin.

c Calculate the number of Xs, Ys, and Zs that must be sold to break even.

# Problems

## Series A

**P25-A1** ***Scattergraph and high-low method***

Velez Manufacturing has a highly automated machine shop. The firm is studying utilities cost behavior and has gathered the following data for a recent six-month period:

| *Month* | *Machine Hours* | *Utilities Cost* |
|---|---|---|
| January | 22,000 | $26,100 |
| February | 24,000 | 28,500 |
| March | 25,000 | 29,000 |
| April | 27,000 | 31,200 |
| May | 26,000 | 29,900 |
| June | 28,000 | 32,100 |

**Instructions**

a Prepare a scattergraph by plotting machine hours on the horizontal axis and utilities cost on the vertical axis.

b By fitting a line through the plotted points, determine Velez's fixed cost per month and the variable cost per machine hour.

c Determine the variable and fixed costs by using the high-low method.

d In general, will the scattergraph and the high-low method yield identical results? Why?

**P25-A2** ***Cost behavior and analysis***

The chief accountant of Stevenson Corporation is studying certain costs (direct labor, plant security, utilities, and maintenance) in an effort to better control operations. Normal production activity ranges from 7,500 to 8,000 units per month. In the past three months the following cost behavior has been observed:

| | *Month 1* | *Month 2* | *Month 3* |
|---|---|---|---|
| Production (units) | 7,540 | 7,950 | 7,680 |
| Direct labor | $18,850 | $19,875 | $19,200 |
| Plant security | 14,600 | 14,600 | 14,600 |
| Utilities | 28,044 | 29,520 | 28,548 |

In addition, maintenance costs have displayed the following step behavior:

| *Activity Range (Units)* | *Cost* |
|---|---|
| Up to 7,600 | $ 8,000 |
| 7,601–7,800 | 9,500 |
| 7,801–8,000 | 11,000 |

Stevenson uses the high-low method to analyze cost behavior.

**Instructions**

a Production for next month is expected to total 7,850 units. Calculate the cost of direct labor, plant security, utilities, and maintenance for this level of activity.

b Comment on the cost-effectiveness of producing at a 7,850-unit level of activity with respect to maintenance costs. If you feel this is an ineffective production level, describe how effectiveness could be improved.

c There is a high probability that Stevenson's production volume will nearly double in forthcoming months because of a new customer. Can the data and methods used in part (a) for predicting the cost of 7,850 units be employed to estimate total costs for, say, 17,500 units? Why?

**P25-A3** ***Straightforward CVP analysis***

FRB, Inc., sells a single product for $40. The following costs and expenses were incurred at store no. 504:

| *Variable Costs per Unit* | | *Annual Fixed Costs* | |
|---|---|---|---|
| Invoice cost | $24 | Salaries | $60,000 |
| Sales commission | 4 | Advertising | 14,000 |
| | | Other | 16,000 |

The company sold 8,200 units during 19X4.

**Instructions**

a Compute the 19X4 break-even point in both dollar and unit sales.

b By how much will sales have to increase in 19X5 over 19X4 levels if management desires to earn a target net income of $14,400?

c At present, how much does each unit provide toward covering FRB's fixed costs and generating income? Assume that management feels this amount is too low. What alternatives are available to FRB?

d What would be the effect on the break-even point if management reduced salary costs by $11,600 and increased the $4 sales commission by 20%?

**P25-A4** ***Break-even and other CVP analysis***

Hodge and Best manufacture a single product. The information that follows relates to current operations.

| | | |
|---|---|---|
| Sales (80,000 units @ $15) | | $1,200,000 |
| Less: Variable cost | $720,000 | |
| Fixed cost | 360,000 | 1,080,000 |
| Net income | | $ 120,000 |

**Instructions**

a The sales outlook for next year is bleak. Calculate the number of units that must be sold to break even if current revenue and cost behavior patterns continue.

b If Hodge and Best wish to earn a target net income of $90,000 during the next accounting period, what level of dollar sales must be generated?

c Management is contemplating an increase in the selling price to $18 per unit. If consumers balk and volume drops, calculate the number of units that must be sold to earn the target net income of $90,000. Should the change be implemented? Why?

d Hodge and Best's projected break-even point and target net income are the result of interactions of numerous financial events and transactions. Determine the impact of the following operating changes by filling in the blanks below with "increase," "decrease," or "not affect."

(1) An increase in direct labor cost will ______________ total variable costs, ______________ the contribution margin, and ______________ the break-even point.

(2) An increase in plant insurance will ______________ the break-even point and ______________ the dollar sales level calculated in part (b).

**P25-A5** ***CVP and analysis of operations***

The Rocky Mountain Company is exploring two possible manufacturing methods to produce a short-lived, fad product. The following unit-cost data have been generated by the firm's accounting department:

| | *Process A* | *Process B* |
|---|---|---|
| Direct materials | $2.50 | $2.25 |
| Direct labor | 3.75 | 2.00 |
| Variable overhead | 2.75 | 1.75 |

The fixed manufacturing costs associated with processes A and B total $360,000 and $408,000, respectively. Management anticipates that regardless of which process is selected, the fad product will require the following selling and administrative expenses: advertising, $54,000; sales commissions, 10%. The marketing department has tentatively set a selling price of $30. Rocky Mountain will manufacture sufficient units to meet demand; no inventory will be carried.

**Instructions**

a Compute the number of units that Rocky Mountain will have to sell to break even if process B is selected.

b Which of the two processes will be more profitable for the company if sales total 31,000 units?

c Compute the dollar sales level necessary to generate a target net income of $36,000 if process A is selected.

d At what volume level (in units) will management be indifferent concerning the choice between process A and process B?

## Series B

**P25-B1** ***Scattergraph and high-low method***

P. Thurmond has a highly automated machine shop. The firm is studying maintenance cost behavior and has gathered the following data for a recent six-month period:

| *Month* | *Machine Hours* | *Maintenance Cost* |
|---|---|---|
| July | 18,000 | $36,000 |
| August | 20,000 | 39,600 |
| September | 18,500 | 37,000 |
| October | 19,000 | 38,200 |
| November | 22,000 | 36,400 |
| December | 17,000 | 35,400 |

**Instructions**

a Prepare a scattergraph by plotting machine hours on the horizontal axis and maintenance cost on the vertical axis.

b By fitting a line through the plotted points, determine Thurmond's fixed cost per month and the variable cost per machine hour.

c Determine the variable and fixed costs by using the high-low method.

d In view of Thurmond's cost behavior, which of the two methods (scattergraph or high-low) appears more accurate? Explain your answer.

**P25-B2** ***Cost behavior and analysis***

The chief accountant of Oak Meadows, Inc., is studying certain costs (direct materials, plant insurance, utilities, and plant supervision) in an effort to better control operations. Normal production activity ranges from 20,000 to 23,500 units per month. In the past three months the following cost behavior has been observed.

| | *Month 1* | *Month 2* | *Month 3* |
|---|---|---|---|
| Production (units) | 23,450 | 21,700 | 20,300 |
| Direct materials | $89,110 | $82,460 | $77,140 |
| Plant insurance | 4,200 | 4,200 | 4,200 |
| Utilities | 5,840 | 5,420 | 5,210 |

In addition, plant supervision costs have displayed the following step behavior:

| *Activity Range (Units)* | *Cost* |
|---|---|
| Up to 20,600 | $25,000 |
| 20,601–23,000 | 40,000 |
| 23,001–25,500 | 55,000 |

Oak Meadows uses the high-low method to analyze cost behavior.

**Instructions**

a Production for next month is expected to total 22,800 units. Calculate the cost of direct materials, plant insurance, utilities, and plant supervision for this level of activity.

b Comment on the cost-effectiveness of producing at a 22,800-unit level of activity with respect to plant supervision costs. If you feel this is an ineffective production level, describe how effectiveness could be improved.

c Frank Cisco, the company's chief accountant, has analyzed cost incurrence over the past six months by studying the highest and lowest levels of activity. The highest activity occurred when 23,450 units were produced (Month 1 data). The lowest activity took place five months ago when only 14,200 units were manufactured because of a strike. Comment on the use of these activity levels when employing the high-low method.

**P25-B3** ***Straightforward CVP analysis***

Imperial Enterprises sells a single product for $50. The following costs and expenses were incurred at store no. 118:

| *Variable Costs per Unit* | | *Annual Fixed Costs* | |
|---|---|---|---|
| Invoice cost | $21 | Salaries | $180,000 |
| Sales commission | 7 | Rent | 60,000 |
| | | Other | 13,000 |

The company sold 11,100 units during 19X6.

**Instructions**

a Compute the 19X6 break-even point in both dollar and unit sales.

b By how much will sales have to increase in 19X7 over 19X6 levels if management desires to earn a target net income of $9,900?

c Assume that management desires to cut salaries by $30,000 and increase sales commissions to $10 per unit. Determine the effect of these changes on the unit contribution margin and explain the meaning of the contribution margin to Imperial's president, who has a manufacturing background.

d Returning to the original data, assume that management is willing to pay an extra $3 commission on all units sold in excess of the company's break-even point. If 19X7 sales are expected to be 11,850 units, calculate the year's net income (or loss).

**P25-B4** ***Break-even and other CVP analysis***

Rosen and Tidwell manufacture a single product. The following information relates to current operations:

| | | |
|---|---|---|
| Sales (200,000 units @ $9) | | $1,800,000 |
| Less: Variable cost | $720,000 | |
| Fixed cost | 864,000 | 1,584,000 |
| Net income | | $ 216,000 |

**Instructions**

a The sales outlook for next year is bleak. Calculate the number of units that must be sold to break even if current revenue and cost behavior patterns continue.

b If Rosen and Tidwell wish to earn a target net income of $27,000 during the next accounting period, what level of dollar sales must be generated?

c Consider your answer in part (b). Management is contemplating a change in compensation methods during the next accounting period to boost sales. The firm presently employs five salaried salespeople who earn an average of $25,000 per year. Should a new plan be implemented that calls for a base salary of $7,000 per salesperson and a 7% commission based on gross sales? Why?

d Rosen and Tidwell's projected break-even point and target net income are the result of interactions of numerous financial events and transactions. Determine the impact of the following operating changes by filling in the blanks below with "increase," "decrease," or "not affect."

(1) A rise in property taxes will ______________ net income and ______________ the break-even point.

(2) A decrease in raw material cost will ______________ total fixed costs and ______________ the dollar sales level calculated in part (b).

**P25-B5** ***CVP and analysis of operations***

The Ditmar Company is exploring two possible manufacturing methods to produce a short-lived, fad product. The following unit cost data have been generated by the firm's accounting department:

| | ***Process A*** | ***Process B*** |
|---|---|---|
| Direct materials | $ 3.00 | $ 4.50 |
| Direct labor | 4.00 | 5.00 |
| Variable overhead | 10.00 | 12.50 |

The fixed manufacturing costs associated with processes A and B total $760,000 and $541,000, respectively. Management anticipates that regardless of which process is selected, the fad product will require the following selling and administrative expenses: advertising, $80,000; sales commissions, 10%. The marketing department has tentatively set a selling price of $50. Ditmar will manufacture sufficient units to meet demand; no inventory will be carried.

**Instructions**

a Compute the number of units that Ditmar will have to sell to break even if process A is selected.

b Which of the two processes will be more profitable for the company if sales total 35,000 units?

c Compute the dollar sales level necessary to generate a target net income of $69,000 if process B is selected.

d At what volume level (in units) will management be indifferent concerning the choice between process A and process B?

## Beyond the Basics

**BB25-1** ***CVP analysis and operating changes***

Huron Company released the following income statement in 19X1 when 40,000 gallons of product were manufactured and sold:

| | | |
|---|---|---|
| Sales | | $320,000 |
| Less: Variable costs | | |
| Manufacturing | $140,000 | |
| Selling & administrative | 60,000 | 200,000 |
| Contribution margin | | $120,000 |
| Less: Fixed costs | | |
| Manufacturing | $ 50,000 | |
| Selling & administrative | 40,000 | 90,000 |
| Net income | | $ 30,000 |

The volume, revenue, and cost behavior patterns are expected to continue in 19X2.

**Instructions**

a Determine the company's break-even point in gallons of product.
b Compute Huron's net income in 19X2 if 45,000 gallons will be produced and sold.
c Assume that Huron will acquire new machinery (cost = $240,000) at the beginning of 19X2 that promises to reduce variable manufacturing costs by $1 per gallon. If the machinery will be depreciated over a five-year life by the straight-line method, determine the number of gallons that must be sold in 19X2 to achieve a net income of $35,000.
d Independent of part (c), assume that Huron's sales orders and manufacturing capacity for the period each amount to 45,000 gallons. A foreign company has approached management with a special order request for 14,000 gallons at a selling price of $7.50. Calculate Huron's net income if management accepts the order and rejects some business from regular customers to avoid exceeding capacity.

**BB25-2** ***CVP relationships: Working backward***

Electra, Inc., manufactures and sells a single product. The selling price and variable cost per unit in 19X5 were $10 and $6.40, respectively. The company's accountant has calculated the break-even point to be 15,000 units and the year's net income at $7,920.

Management has determined the selling price must be raised in 19X6 to $12 to offset increases in the variable cost per unit and annual fixed costs. These latter amounts are expected to rise by 25% and 15%, respectively.

**Instructions**

a Compute the fixed costs incurred during 19X5.
b Determine the number of units manufactured and sold during 19X5.
c How many units must be sold during 19X6 to produce a target net income of $15,200?
d Compute Electra's 19X5 contribution margin per unit as a percentage of the 19X5 selling price. What selling price would have to be charged in 19X6 to maintain the same percentage as that generated in 19X5?

**BB25-3** ***Sales mix evaluation***

Michelle Williams operates the concession stand at the Roxy Theater. On the basis of last year's operating results, she has established the following budget for 19X2:

| | *Food* | *Beverage* | | *Total* |
|---|---|---|---|---|
| Expected number of sales | 80,000 | 120,000 | | 200,000 |
| Sales revenue | $100,000 | $96,000 | | $196,000 |
| Less: Variable costs | 72,000 | 12,000 | | 84,000 |
| Contribution margin | $ 28,000 | $84,000 | | $112,000 |
| Less: 20% of gross sales paid to theater | | | $39,200 | |
| Fixed costs | | | 60,000 | 99,200 |
| Net income | | | | $ 12,800 |

Patrons changed their buying habits during 19X2 and Williams had 120,000 food sales and 80,000 beverage sales. The average sale amount and contribution margin per sale remained as budgeted.

**Instructions**

a Williams achieved her budget of 200,000 sales; she therefore believes that 19X2 net income will approximate $12,800. Prepare an income statement to determine the concession stand's operating performance. Explain any significant variations from the budget.

b Refer to the original budget. Assume the fixed costs can be subdivided as follows: food, $16,000; beverage, $8,000; and general, $36,000. Williams is considering the elimination of food sales because, as she notes, "The food operation is more trouble than it's worth." Determine the budgeted net income for 19X2 if the food service had been dropped and the associated fixed costs could have been eliminated.

c What other factors should be considered when evaluating the possible elimination of the food operation?

## Answers to Chapter Quiz

**1** c

**2** a

**3** c (S = VC + FC; S = 0.6S + $180,000; S = $450,000)

**4** d

**5** b

CHAPTER 26

# Performance Evaluation via Flexible Budgets and Standard Costs

## Learning Objectives

After reading this chapter you should:

1 Understand the purpose and structure of a responsibility accounting system.

2 Know how to construct and use a flexible budget.

3 Know what a standard cost is and how standards are developed.

4 Understand the distinction between ideal and attainable standards.

5 Know how to calculate variances as related to direct materials, direct labor, and factory overhead.

6 Understand the problems encountered in the variance investigation process.

7 (Appendix) Know how to integrate standard costs and variances into an accounting system.

Throughout this text we have presented various measures of financial performance. Earnings per share, the current ratio, and cash provided by operating activities are among the many evaluative measures that interest investors, analysts, and managers. Although our presentation has been accounting-oriented, realize that performance analysis is widespread and affects virtually everyone. For example, economists continually study unemployment rates and changes in the Consumer Price Index. Sales personnel are constantly judged against budgeted sales quotas. Baseball players are ranked on batting averages, runs batted in, and fielding percentages. And finally, you are probably being evaluated in this course on the basis of examination scores. Naturally, our list of performance measures is far from complete. Suffice it to say, however, that in one form or another, performance measurement is a way of life.

This chapter introduces two popular tools that are used to study performance in a business organization: flexible budgets and standard costs. These tools allow a manager to monitor operations against a preset target and provide insight to the age-old question: "How am I doing?" Before we proceed with a discussion of flexible budgets and standard costs, it is helpful if we first present the underlying foundation of performance measurement—responsibility accounting.

## Responsibility Accounting

OBJECTIVE 1
Understand the purpose and structure of a responsibility accounting system.

**Responsibility accounting** is a reporting system that is based on the organizational structure of a firm. In essence, the firm is subdivided into various centers (i.e., segments) such as departments, plants, territories, or divisions. Managers are appointed to oversee individual center activities, are held accountable for operating results, and evaluated accordingly. The thrust of responsibility accounting is that centers are charged only for costs and credited only for revenues that are subject to their control. By operating in this manner, top management can better assess performance and monitor progress toward the attainment of specific company objectives.

### Responsibility Units

As noted, responsibility centers may be organized in different ways: by territories, by departments, and so forth. Each center, in turn, may be established as a cost, profit, or investment center.

#### Cost Center

A **cost center** is a responsibility unit in which a manager is held accountable for cost incurrence. Generally, cost centers are operations or departments that are not directly involved in revenue-generating activities. Managers are thus evaluated on the level of cost incurred, not net income. Common examples of cost centers include billing, purchasing, payroll, and janitorial departments.

Contrary to what many people believe, a cost center manager should not necessarily strive for cost minimization. Such a goal is actually inconsistent with the center's purpose. To explain, most cost centers render services (as opposed to manufacture and/or sell a product). With increased activity comes increased cost, namely, variable cost. A minimization philosophy would therefore dictate that the center provide "bare bones" service to the remainder of the organization, that is, just enough to get by. A more appropriate philosophy requires that the center furnish adequate assistance to other segments of the firm; in the process, the level of cost incurrence should be held reasonably low.

### Profit Center

A **profit center** is a responsibility unit in which a manager is held accountable for profit (i.e., revenues minus expenses). Because revenues now enter the evaluation process, profit centers must be involved in the sale of goods or services. Although it seems strange, the sales may be *intracompany,* that is, within the firm. For example, the filmmaking division of a large entertainment concern could produce and sell a "made-for-television" movie to the organization's broadcasting division. Although both divisions are part of the same company, one division is selling its output to the other. Further examples of profit centers include computer and repair centers, which charge other operating segments for data processing services and maintenance work, respectively.

### Investment Center

An **investment center** is the most complex of the responsibility centers. A manager is evaluated not only on revenues and expenses but also on asset investment. More specifically, the head of an investment center is concerned with both profitable operations *and* the effective use of capital funds. Capital funds are normally disbursed for long-term projects such as the acquisition of new buildings, machinery, or equipment; investment in other companies for purposes of control and affiliation; and entry into new product lines and markets. In effect, the investment center structure allows a manager to run his or her own small business; the business, however, is part of a larger organization.

To measure the success (or failure) of an investment center manager, most companies employ a measure known as **return on assets.** Sometimes referred to as *return on investment* (*ROI*), the measure shows the amount of income generated from a given level of assets. For example, if division A has operating income of $100,000 and an asset investment base of $500,000, the division is said to have an ROI of 20% ($100,000 ÷ $500,000).

Because the evaluation is done on a percentage basis, segments of different sizes can be compared more readily.[1] Comparative analysis might reveal, for example, that assets employed in a "low-return" division could be better used by another unit of the firm. Or perhaps that certain assets should be sold, with the proceeds invested in new and more profitable endeavors. We stress that any comparative studies be done with caution because segments often have vastly different operating characteristics.

## Reporting System

The responsibility accounting system established for cost, profit, and investment centers is typically tailored to the entity's organization chart. That is, performance reporting begins at lower levels of the firm and continues upward. This design approach is used to reflect the pyramiding of responsibility that exists in a typical management hierarchy. The system's reports therefore show an executive's own

[1] Further discussion of this topic is found on page 725.

performance plus the performance of lower-level employees in the chain of command.

To illustrate, we will focus on the organization chart of Sakowski Manufacturing Corporation (see Exhibit 26-1). Sakowski has divided its operations into divisions that are organized along territorial lines, with each division being composed of several plants. For purposes of simplicity, only the details of the Eastern Division are presented. In addition, smaller responsibility units that may be established at the plant level (e.g., departments and work stations) are omitted. Overall, our example will focus on three reporting levels: plant, division (vice-president), and president.

## Performance Reports

Sakowski, like most other organizations, provides its responsibility center managers with a series of **performance reports.** These reports furnish management with feedback of operating results and are used for purposes of evaluation and control.

The exact format and detail level of a performance report are determined by the needs and preferences of the user as well as by the type of responsibility center being evaluated. For example, the management of a manufacturing firm may desire feedback about the number of units produced during a given period. A sports enterprise, on the other hand, may be concerned with attendance and sales of particular seat classifications, such as reserved and general admission. Regardless of the report's specific content, most performance reports compare budgeted figures to actual figures. The differences, or *variances,* may be expressed in dollars or as percentages of budgeted amounts.

The series of reports used by Sakowski Manufacturing appears in Exhibit 26-2. Observe the bottom-up progression of operating information. The operating results at the plant level are compiled first and then included in the vice-president's report. The report of the vice-president summarizes all plants under his or her supervision and also reveals the cost of running the vice-president's office. The summarization process continues upward to the president. The president's report discloses the operating performance of the three vice-presidents (i.e., divisions) as well as the costs associated with the top administrative function.

**Exhibit 26-1**
**Sakowski Manufacturing Corporation Organization Chart**

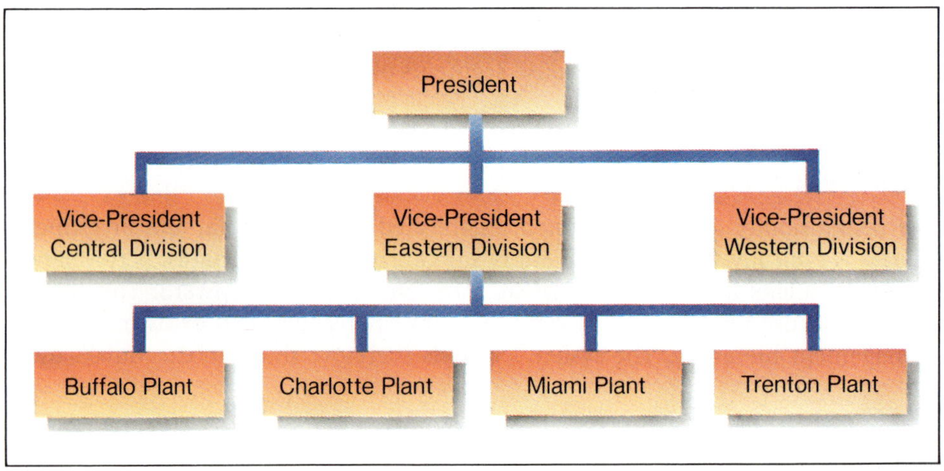

**Exhibit 26-2**
**Responsibility Accounting at Various Organizational Levels ($000 omitted)**

*PRESIDENT'S OCTOBER PERFORMANCE REPORT*

| | | | *Variance** | |
|---|---|---|---|---|
| | ***Budget*** | ***Actual*** | ***Dollars*** | ***Percentage of Budget*** |
| President's office | $ (100) | $ (95) | $ 5 | 5% |
| Central division | 490 | 485 | (5) | (1) |
| Eastern division | 400 | 416 | 16 | 4 |
| Western division | 350 | 360 | 10 | 3 |
| Operating income | $1,140 | $1,166 | $26 | 2 |

* ( ) = unfavorable

*EASTERN VICE-PRESIDENT'S OCTOBER PERFORMANCE REPORT*

| | | | *Variance** | |
|---|---|---|---|---|
| | ***Budget*** | ***Actual*** | ***Dollars*** | ***Percentage of Budget*** |
| Vice-president's office | $ (28) | $ (30) | $ (2) | (7)% |
| Buffalo plant | 66 | 70 | 4 | 6 |
| Charlotte plant | 75 | 85 | 10 | 13 |
| Miami plant | 55 | 61 | 6 | 11 |
| Trenton plant | 232 | 230 | (2) | (1) |
| Operating income | $400 | $416 | $16 | 4 |

* ( ) = unfavorable

*CHARLOTTE PLANT'S OCTOBER PERFORMANCE REPORT*

| | | | *Variance** | |
|---|---|---|---|---|
| | ***Budget*** | ***Actual*** | ***Dollars*** | ***Percentage of Budget*** |
| Sales | $360 | $365 | $ 5 | 1% |
| Cost of goods sold | $240 | $233 | $ 7 | 3 |
| Administrative expense | 25 | 25 | — | — |
| Selling expense | 20 | 22 | (2) | (10) |
| Total | $285 | $280 | $ 5 | 2 |
| Operating income | $ 75 | $ 85 | $10 | 13 |

* ( ) = unfavorable

It is now apparent that the responsibility reporting system is both consistent with Sakowski's organizational structure and reflects the progression of authority that exists in most businesses. Also, it is evident that as one goes higher and higher in the structure, the reports become more summarized. This summarization reflects upper-level management's unwillingness to sift through reams of detailed data that reflect activities for which subordinates are responsible. Given the nature of top management positions and the type of work performed, summarized information is normally satisfactory. If for some reason more detail is needed, the reporting system is structured so that the desired facts and figures are readily accessible.

### Controllability: The Key to Responsibility Accounting

When evaluating performance under a responsibility accounting system, management should consider only those revenues, expenses, and investments that a segment can control. To hold a segment and its employees accountable for uncontrollable items and events clearly diminishes the usefulness of the responsibility system. The end result is often low morale and high employee turnover. If a responsibility system is to be effective, reports should clearly distinguish between those performance factors that are controllable and those that are not.

Generally speaking, the ability to control means being able to influence or change. Consequently, if a responsibility center can significantly influence revenues, expenses, or investment funds through its own direct actions, the center's management should be held accountable for these items. Although this concept seems straightforward, it is extremely difficult to apply in practice. Stated simply, revenue generation and cost incurrence are frequently affected by two or more managers.

For example, the total cost of raw materials used in production is influenced by both the purchasing manager and the production manager. The production manager bears primary responsibility for raw material use since worker efficiency directly affects the materials consumed and the amount of waste incurred. The purchasing manager, on the other hand, is chiefly concerned about the prices paid to secure needed materials. Assume that in an effort to curb soaring costs in an inflationary economy, the head of purchasing has purposely acquired lower-quality goods. As a result of this situation, no matter how efficient the production workers are, overall consumption will be influenced by factors beyond their control.

Even though multiple influences are brought to bear, somebody is usually in the best position to explain the level of revenue generated and cost incurred and the reasons for variances from budgeted amounts. The goal of responsibility accounting is to trace revenues and costs to their source and thereby fix responsibility for their creation. An attempt is therefore made to associate control and accountability with the person or center that has the greatest potential influence over the item in question.

## Flexible Budgets

Given the framework of responsibility accounting, let us now become a bit more detailed. Suppose it is your first day on the job as assistant to the president of Coleman Industries. On the basis of figures provided by the accounting department, the president has constructed the performance report that appears in Exhibit 26-3 for the company's Oregon plant.

Exhibit 26-3

**COLEMAN INDUSTRIES**
**Oregon Plant Performance Report**
**For the Quarter Ended March 31, 19X3**

| *Cost* | *Budget, 50,000 Units* | *Actual, 54,000 Units* | *Variance** |
|---|---|---|---|
| Variable production costs | | | |
| Direct materials used | $150,000 | $159,300 | $ 9,300U |
| Direct labor | 350,000 | 367,200 | 17,200U |
| Variable factory overhead | 75,000 | 86,400 | 11,400U |
| Total | $575,000 | $612,900 | $37,900U |
| Fixed factory overhead | $215,000 | $212,500 | $ 2,500F |
| Total production costs | $790,000 | $825,400 | $35,400U |

* F = favorable; U = unfavorable.

The budget was based on an initial production target of 50,000 units; however, 54,000 units were actually manufactured during the quarter. The president has given you the report and desires to know whether Oregon's production manager should be praised for outstanding performance or called on the carpet for ineptness.

At first glance it appears that performance was not satisfactory, because actual costs were $35,400 in excess of budget. When we consider only the variable costs, unfavorable variances total 6.6% of budgeted amounts ($37,900 ÷ $575,000), an overrun that some managers would deem significant. Before proceeding with the production manager's termination from employment, though, we must consider one important underlying fact. The performance report compares the actual costs of producing 54,000 units against budgeted costs for only 50,000 units. By the nature of the comparison, a number of unfavorable variable cost variances are bound to arise because of the increase in activity.

Your conclusion about the production manager's performance? It's really impossible to tell how good or bad the manager performed given the report that has been prepared. What we have illustrated is one of the classic problems associated with using a static budget for evaluative purposes. A **static budget** is a budget developed for one level of activity. Should output vary from that which was anticipated (50,000 units in Oregon's case), comparisons with actual costs become meaningless. In plain and simple terms, we cannot compare expected costs against actual costs at different activity levels. An adjustment is needed for the change in volume.

## Constructing a Flexible Budget

OBJECTIVE 2
Know how to construct and use a flexible budget.

In order to overcome the above problem, performance reports normally incorporate the use of flexible budgets. A **flexible budget** covers a *range* of activity as opposed to a single level. Specifically, the relevant range of activity is determined for the forthcoming accounting period. Then, individual budgets are prepared for various levels within the anticipated range of operation.

To illustrate the concept of a flexible budget, we will continue the Coleman Industries example. The 50,000-unit budget that appears in Exhibit 26-3 was constructed after a thorough study of cost behavior, with the following costs judged to be realistic targets of performance:

| | |
|---|---|
| Direct materials used | \$3.00 per unit |
| Direct labor | \$7.00 per unit |
| Variable factory overhead | \$1.50 per unit |
| Fixed factory overhead | \$215,000 |

A review of past accounting records disclosed that quarterly production volume usually varies between 50,000 and 54,000 units. A flexible budget that covers this range of activity is presented in Exhibit 26-4.

The figures shown are the result of multiplying the unit variable costs by the different activity levels and then adding the fixed factory overhead. We did not calculate a fixed overhead cost per unit because the unit cost will fluctuate depending on the volume level used in the computation.

## Flexible Budgets and Performance Evaluation

Given the nature of flexible budgets, we can now appraise the performance of the Oregon plant's production manager. As shown in Exhibit 26-5, a properly prepared performance report enables management to compare the actual costs incurred in the manufacture of 54,000 units against budgeted costs for the same level of activity.

Once the impact of the 4,000-unit variation between the original static budget and actual production is eliminated, the manager appears to have done an acceptable job. With the exception of variable factory overhead, all costs were less than budgeted, and a total favorable variance was generated. Overall, the flexible budget provides a useful tool for performance evaluations, because like volumes are compared. Activity level fluctuations no longer influence the appraisal process.

**Exhibit 26-4**
**Flexible Budget**

**COLEMAN INDUSTRIES**
**Oregon Plant Flexible Budget**
**For the Quarter Ended March 31, 19X3**

| | | *Units of Activity* | | |
|---|---|---|---|---|
| *Cost* | *Cost per Unit* | *50,000* | *52,000* | *54,000* |
| Variable production costs | | | | |
| Direct materials used | \$ 3.00 | \$150,000 | \$156,000 | \$162,000 |
| Direct labor | 7.00 | 350,000 | 364,000 | 378,000 |
| Variable factory overhead | 1.50 | 75,000 | 78,000 | 81,000 |
| Total | \$11.50 | \$575,000 | \$598,000 | \$621,000 |
| Fixed factory overhead | | \$215,000 | \$215,000 | \$215,000 |
| Total production costs | | \$790,000 | \$813,000 | \$836,000 |

**COLEMAN INDUSTRIES**
**Oregon Plant Performance Report**
**For the Quarter Ended March 31, 19X3**

| *Cost* | *Budget, 54,000 Units* | *Actual, 54,000 Units* | *Variance** |
|---|---|---|---|
| Variable production costs | | | |
| Direct materials used | $162,000 | $159,300 | $ 2,700F |
| Direct labor | 378,000 | 367,200 | 10,800F |
| Variable factory overhead | 81,000 | 86,400 | 5,400U |
| Total | $621,000 | $612,900 | $ 8,100F |
| Fixed factory overhead | $215,000 | $212,500 | $ 2,500F |
| Total production costs | $836,000 | $825,400 | $10,600F |

* F = favorable; U = unfavorable.

**Exhibit 26-5**
**Performance Report Based on Flexible Budgets**

## A Common Misunderstanding

Before leaving this example, we wish to clear up a common misconception about flexible budgets. Careful study of Exhibit 26-4 normally leaves the impression that many different budgets must be prepared when using the flexible approach. This is not the case. Even if this practice were followed, an organization could establish budgets for numerous operating volumes and still miss the actual level of activity. For most entities, the likelihood that a budget prepared in advance will coincide precisely with the actual volume level is extremely slim.

The preceding discussion should not be taken to mean that flexible budgets have limited application. For instance, suppose the Oregon plant's output for the first quarter amounted to 53,000 units—an activity level that was not considered when establishing the budgets presented in Exhibit 26-4. Nonetheless, the manager's actual performance can still be compared against budgeted performance of $824,500, computed as follows:

| | |
|---|---|
| Variable production costs per unit | |
| Direct materials used | $ 3.00 |
| Direct labor | 7.00 |
| Variable factory overhead | 1.50 |
| Total | $11.50 |

| | |
|---|---|
| Budget for 53,000 units | |
| Variable production costs (53,000 units × $11.50) | $609,500 |
| Fixed production costs | 215,000 |
| Total | $824,500 |

It is apparent that flexible budgets can be prepared to coincide with any volume of operation. Companies determine the flexible budget characteristics (i.e., variable production costs of $11.50 per unit and fixed production costs of $215,000) in advance. The "proper" budget and accompanying performance report must then wait until after the fact, that is, after the actual activity level is known.

## Standard Costs

OBJECTIVE 3
Know what a standard cost is and how standards are developed.

Par on a golf course, a four-minute mile, a .300 batting average, and an eight-hour workday are well-recognized standards of performance. These measures and others are used to gauge one's accomplishments in a variety of diverse activities.

Standards are also popular among businesses as a means of measuring efficiency and monitoring cost incurrence. Defined as preset norms of what should occur under reasonably efficient operating conditions, **standards** normally refer to the expected quantity and cost of inputs required in producing a good or service. Typical standards include the cost per pound of direct materials, the wage rate for direct labor, and the number of hours needed to complete a task.

### Standard Costs and Budgets

The concept of a standard cost is really nothing new. Although they were not described as such, you were introduced to standard costs earlier in the chapter. Standard costs are used in the construction of both static and flexible budgets. Specifically, standard costs are a per-unit concept; budgets, on the other hand, deal in totals.

To illustrate the difference between standards and budgets, assume Centre Enterprises manufactures a single product that requires five gallons of direct material at an anticipated cost of $4 per gallon. The standard direct material cost per unit of output is computed as follows:

| *Standard Quantity per Finished Unit* | × | *Standard Price* | = | *Standard Cost per Unit of Output* |
|---|---|---|---|---|
| 5 gallons | | $4 per gallon | | $20 |

Once the standard cost is known, a budget (flexible in this case) can be prepared, as the accompanying figures show.

| *Production Component* | *Standard Cost per Unit of Output* | *Flexible Budget: Units of Activity* | | |
|---|---|---|---|---|
| | | *10,000* | *10,500* | *11,000* |
| Direct materials | $20 | $200,000 | $210,000 | $220,000 |

As our example illustrates, a standard cost is merely the budgeted cost for a single unit of activity.

### Setting Standards

The setting of standards is a complex process, one that requires skills that often surpass the expertise possessed by the average accountant. Generally, a team effort is needed and involves participation from many different areas within the organization. In a manufacturing entity, for example, all persons who have responsibility for prices and quantities of finished product inputs should assist in the standard-setting process.

Recall from Chapter 21 that manufactured products contain three cost elements: direct materials, direct labor, and factory overhead. Standards must be established for each of these elements in terms of both price and quantity. Beginning with direct materials, engineering and production employees should participate in the calculation of standard inputs by both type and quantity of materials used. Given these calculations, the purchasing department can then determine the proper dollar amounts. Standard material prices should include transportation charges and be net of any expected cash discounts.

Direct labor standards are determined jointly by production, engineering, and personnel staffs. Standards for labor time are established, often by using *time and motion studies*. Such studies require that individual manufacturing operations be monitored and clocked by industrial engineers. Once labor time is known, the cost standard can be computed from information furnished by the personnel department. Although wage rates will vary among employees because of differences in seniority, skill levels, and other factors, many companies use a single (average) rate to cost specific manufacturing procedures. The accountant's role in the area of labor is to formalize and coordinate the standard-setting process and to establish an effective system of performance reporting once the standards have been determined.

The development of an overhead standard parallels the calculation of an overhead application rate, a topic that was discussed in Chapter 22. Normally, however, separate standards are established for variable and fixed cost components. To explain the necessary procedures, we will again focus on Centre Enterprises, which applies factory overhead to products on the basis of direct labor hours. Management estimates that 10,000 units will be produced in the upcoming period, requiring 80,000 hours of labor time. Variable and fixed overhead at this level of activity are budgeted at $80,000 and $120,000, respectively. Centre must first compute the overhead standard per direct labor hour, as shown.

***Variable:***

$$\frac{\text{Estimated Variable Overhead}}{\text{Estimated Activity}} = \frac{\$80{,}000}{80{,}000 \text{ hours}} = \$1.00 \text{ per hour}$$

***Fixed:***

$$\frac{\text{Estimated Fixed Overhead}}{\text{Estimated Activity}} = \frac{\$120{,}000}{80{,}000 \text{ hours}} = \$1.50 \text{ per hour}$$

Since each unit requires 8 hours of production time (80,000 hours ÷ 10,000 units), the standard overhead cost per finished unit is derived in the following manner:

| | |
|---|---|
| Variable overhead: 8 hours × $1.00 per hour | $ 8.00 |
| Fixed overhead: 8 hours × $1.50 per hour | 12.00 |
| Standard overhead cost per finished unit | $20.00 |

The outcome of the standard-setting process is summarized in a *standard cost sheet* (see Exhibit 26-6).

**Exhibit 26-6**
**Standard Cost Sheet**

**CENTRE ENTERPRISES**
**Standard Cost Sheet**
**Product No. 626**

| *Production Component* | *Standard Quantity per Finished Unit* | × | *Standard Price* | = | *Standard Cost per Unit of Output* |
|---|---|---|---|---|---|
| Direct materials | 5 gallons | | $4.00 | | $20.00 |
| Direct labor | 8 hours | | 6.50* | | 52.00 |
| Variable factory overhead | 8 hours | | 1.00 | | 8.00 |
| Fixed factory overhead | 8 hours | | 1.50 | | 12.00 |
| Total standard cost | | | | | $92.00 |

* Assumed.

## Levels of Standards

Should a standard be set high, low, or somewhere in between? How much effort should workers put forth in attempting to achieve a standard? In many cases, the answers to these and other related questions are difficult to determine. Production supervisors, engineers, laborers, and other veterans of manufacturing activities have grappled with the preceding issues for years. Although there is a diversity of opinion, companies must address the problem and somehow derive a "correct" standard for each facet of their production operations.

The starting point for the development of standards is a look at the past. The costs incurred in prior years can provide considerable insight about a company's cost experience at different levels of activity. The past should be interpreted with care, however. Changes in the form of new suppliers, new technology, and employee training programs can rapidly make past data obsolete and not representative of the entity's current manufacturing environment. Further complicating matters is the fact that past inefficiencies are often built into the data under examination. Standards strive to reflect what *should be*, not what *has been*. Management must be aware of these deficiencies when analyzing earlier experiences and make appropriate adjustments to its findings.

### Ideal Standards

OBJECTIVE 4
Understand the distinction between ideal and attainable standards.

Despite the diversity that is encountered when setting standards, most standards can be classified as either ideal or attainable. An **ideal standard** is one that can be achieved under perfect operating conditions. By essentially assuming maximum efficiency at minimum cost, ideal standards make no allowances for spoilage, machine breakdowns, worker fatigue, inefficiency, human error, and other similar factors. In most applications, the perfection emphasis of these performance targets results in variances that have little meaning. Realize that nothing is perfect, and normal inefficiencies are a fact of life.

Managers who favor ideal standards feel that by setting goals that are difficult (if not impossible) to achieve, overall output and efficiency will increase because of the constant efforts made by employees to attain the standard. This outcome is in contrast to the situation that arises when using a loose standard, or one that is easily attained with minimal effort. Behavioral scientists have observed that ideal standards *do* cause an increase in productivity when first introduced, as employees strive for the unreachable. Subsequently, however, performance tends to fall after numerous failures and a constant barrage of unfavorable variances. Workers soon become frustrated and discouraged and adopt a "what the heck" attitude.

### Attainable Standards

To overcome the problems associated with ideal standards, most companies turn to attainable standards. An **attainable standard** is one that can be achieved by efficient, not perfect, operations. In the setting of standards for direct materials, for example, allowances are provided for *normal* scrap, waste, and spoilage. Similarly, in the establishment of direct labor targets, provision is made for *normal* worker inefficiencies, machine breakdowns, and so forth.

The level of attainable standards varies from firm to firm. Most organizations use a high but reachable standard and thereby encourage employees to achieve above-average levels of operating efficiency. The standard is not unreasonable and therefore avoids worker frustration and other behavioral problems.

Attainable standards offer the further benefits of improved planning and decision making. Realistic budgets can be prepared, and as we will show in the next chapter, decisions are facilitated because they are based on reasonable estimates of cost.

## Variance Analysis

Standard costs provide information to management that is useful in the control of an enterprise's affairs. Much of this information comes in the form of **variances,** or deviations from standard. Actual costs are compared against standard costs to determine whether operations are running according to plan or whether significant deviations exist. Management is then alerted to departures from established targets of performance, and appropriate corrective action can be implemented. With a focus on variances, managers can avoid spending countless hours in a review of what is going right; instead, their efforts can be devoted to problem areas that need attention. This process is frequently known as **management by exception.**

To illustrate the fundamentals of variance analysis, we will begin by concentrating on direct materials and direct labor. Suppose that a company reported the following results on conclusion of a recent month's activity:

| *Cost* | *Actual* | *Standard* | *Variance* |
|---|---|---|---|
| Direct materials used | $36,500 | $33,000 | $3,500U |
| Direct labor | 59,400 | 62,700 | 3,300F |

Notice that both direct material consumption and direct labor incurrence failed to conform to the original plan. The company spent $3,500 more than anticipated for materials, giving rise to an *unfavorable variance.* In contrast, direct labor cost was $3,300 less than planned and created a *favorable variance.*

## HIGHLIGHT

# Standards, Variances, and Paychecks

Standards and variances are starting to hit home for more and more employees. Home is defined as the paycheck, a desirable and sought-after piece of paper by virtually everyone in the workforce. It is a well-known fact that companies, seeking higher productivity, are shifting pay plans from rank and status based to pay-for-performance, even in non-sales and non-executive positions.

"There's more attention paid to pay-for-performance in the 1980s. It has always been of interest to personnel people, but the difference is a wider group of people have jumped on the bandwagon," says a business professor at Southern Methodist University. "Pay-for-performance fits in with the buzzwords that America has to be lean and mean." A recent survey of 1,598 companies, for example, showed that 70% supplemented or replaced annual increase systems with variable compensation and 69% of those businesses instituted their plans in the last five years.

Not too long ago, for instance, General Dynamics Corp., substituted lump-sum bonuses for annual increases in contracts for 10,000 machinists and aerospace workers at its Fort Worth plant. Government contractors have been forced to adopt pay-for-performance to meet cost-control standards. "Companies like LTV Corp., Texas Instruments, [and others] have merit-based plans in place in part because the taxpayers are paying for it and the government's investigators require proof that the money is earned," notes a director of executive compensation at an international accounting firm.

An example of such a plan is the reward system at Texas Instruments (TI), which is really a mix of traditional annual merit increases, recognition awards for outstanding effort and inventions, and a profit-sharing program that equitably distributes annual rewards based on overall company performance. Merit increases are a function of annual formal appraisals, but TI also emphasizes day-to-day coaching between supervisors and employees to improve performance understanding. For recognition, employee awards can range from $100 for good work to $50,000 for outstanding inventions.

Gain sharing, which offers unitwide bonus systems designed to reward members for improved performance, is another popular compensation tool. If a predetermined goal is met, the company or division returns a portion, sometimes 50%, of any gain as a lump-sum bonus to employees. Gain sharing includes some types of profit-sharing, but gains are also measured in terms of costs saved through higher productivity, minimized losses, or improved sales. These programs are more popular in small firms and manufacturing organizations, where production is easily quantified and employees can easily see the results of their efforts on company performance. A management consulting group reports that 84% of the businesses that use gain sharing say their employees view it favorably.

In sum, it is apparent that performance standards and an employee's ability to meet them will, if present trends continue, have an increased probability of affecting annual compensation. Although gripes are often heard about paycheck fairness and adequacy, managers can and are taking various steps to put the complaints to rest. Notes one personnel expert, "Everybody is searching for the right combination of rewards. Since there's no magical answer, you have to try different things every year."

SOURCE: Adapted from "New Ways to Pay," Dallas, Inc. section, *Dallas Times Herald*, June 20–June 26, 1988, pp. 1, 10–11. © Dallas Times Herald. Used with permission.

Management now desires to know why the variances arose. Material and labor costs will stray from standard because of deviations in the following factors:

**1** Direct materials:
   a The per-unit acquisition cost of materials
   b The quantity of materials consumed

**2** Direct labor:
   a The hourly wage rate
   b The number of hours worked

## Variance Calculation

OBJECTIVE 5
Know how to calculate variances as related to direct materials, direct labor, and factory overhead.

The impact of these price and quantity factors on the total variances can be determined by several relatively simple calculations. The calculations are perhaps best illustrated by the model that appears in Exhibit 26-7.

Careful study of the model reveals that the price variance is really the difference between the actual and standard prices, multiplied by the actual quantity of material or labor put into production. For direct materials the price variance is commonly known as the **materials price variance.** With labor, however, the name changes slightly to the **labor rate variance** to be more attuned to the area of study.

The quantity variance is slightly more difficult to understand. Exhibit 26-7 shows the quantity variance is calculated by comparing (Aq × Sp) and (Sq × Sp). If we take the difference between these two expressions, the following formula is derived:

$$\text{Quantity Variance} = \text{Sp}\ (\text{Aq} - \text{Sq})$$

The formula shows that by weighting the difference in quantities by the standard price, the quantity variance is measured in dollars.

Additionally, it is important to note that the standard quantity is subtracted from the actual quantity. The actual quantity represents the actual input (pounds, gallons, hours, and so on) placed in production. In contrast, *the standard quantity is*

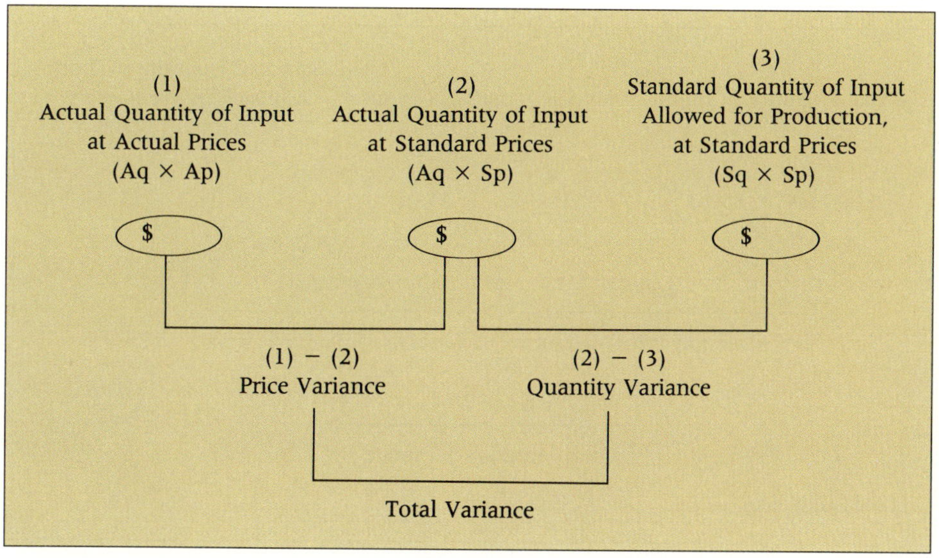


**Exhibit 26-7**
**General Model for Variance Analysis of Direct Materials and Direct Labor**

*the amount of input that should have been used in manufacturing activities during the period.* As an example, assume that a company manufactures a single product that requires three pounds of direct materials. Production totaled 4,000 completed units for the month just ended. If 11,800 pounds of materials were consumed, Aq would be 11,800 pounds and Sq would be 12,000 pounds (4,000 completed units × 3 pounds per unit).

The quantity variance is called the **materials quantity variance** when working with direct materials. For labor the name is changed to the **labor efficiency variance** to reflect the cause of the difference between actual and standard labor hours.

## An Illustration of Direct Material Variances

To illustrate use of the preceding model, assume that Sanco, Inc., has developed the following standard for one of its products:

- Direct materials: 3 pounds at $5.00 per pound

During a recent period the following activity took place:

- Direct materials purchased and used in production: 6,000 pounds at $5.10 per pound
- Production completed: 1,900 units

Exhibit 26-8 shows Sanco's price and quantity variances for direct materials, both of which are unfavorable. The unfavorable price variance arose because Sanco paid $0.10 in excess of the $5.00 standard price to acquire needed materials. The unfavorable quantity variance resulted from the company's usage of 300 pounds more than planned (6,000 vs. 5,700) in manufacturing activities.

## An Illustration of Direct Labor Variances

To explain the computation of direct labor variances, we will continue the previous example. Assume that Sanco has established the following labor standards for each unit of completed product:

**Exhibit 26-8**
**Sanco, Inc., Direct Materials Variances**

| Actual Quantity of Input at Actual Prices (Aq × Ap) | Actual Quantity of Input at Standard Prices (Aq × Sp) | Standard Quantity of Input Allowed for Production, at Standard Prices (Sq × Sp) |
|---|---|---|
| 6,000 lbs. × $5.10 | 6,000 lbs. × $5.00 | 5,700 lbs.* × $5.00 |
| $30,600 | $30,000 | $28,500 |

$600U — Materials Price Variance

$1,500U — Materials Quantity Variance

$2,100U — Total Materials Variance

* 1,900 units × 3 lbs. per unit.

- Direct labor: 2 hours at $6.00 per hour

In producing the 1,900 finished units, direct labor incurred totaled 4,100 hours at $5.80 per hour, or $23,780. The company's direct labor variances are shown in Exhibit 26-9.

As you can see, the labor variance computations are similar to those for materials. Rather than employ pounds and the material purchase price, labor calculations require the respective use of hours worked and the firm's wage rate. Sanco's labor rate variance was favorable because the actual rate paid ($5.80) was $0.20 less than standard. Labor efficiency was unfavorable, however, since actual hours worked exceeded the standard time allowed by 300 hours (4,100 − 3,800 = 300).

## Factory Overhead Variances

Variances for the third element of product cost, factory overhead, are generally more difficult to understand than those for direct materials and direct labor. Remember that for flexible budgeting and standard costing purposes, manufacturing overhead is divided into its fixed and variable components. In addition, recall that in the setting of overhead standards, an activity level is estimated to calculate the overhead rate per hour (or unit).

Although a minor modification is needed, we can compute overhead variances by using the model illustrated in Exhibit 26-7. To explain, a simplified version of the model follows.

Aq × Ap          Aq × Sp          Sq × Sp

Study the nature of the middle term Aq × Sp, which is the amount that the actual quantity of input should have cost. Observe that as activity increases or decreases, the Aq × Sp expression will fluctuate—a result that is easily seen by picturing the computations for direct materials and direct labor. As production

**Exhibit 26-9**
**Sanco, Inc., Direct Labor Variances**

| Actual Quantity of Input at Actual Prices (Aq × Ap) | Actual Quantity of Input at Standard Prices (Aq × Sp) | Standard Quantity of Input Allowed for Production, at Standard Prices (Sq × Sp) |
|---|---|---|
| 4,100 hrs. × $5.80 | 4,100 hrs. × $6.00 | 3,800 hrs.* × $6.00 |
| $23,780 | $24,600 | $22,800 |

Labor Rate Variance: $820F

Labor Efficiency Variance: $1,800U

Total Labor Variance: $980U

* 1,900 units × 2 hrs. per unit.

increases, for example, the actual quantity of materials consumed and labor incurred will rise because of the variable nature of the cost functions. With *fixed costs,* however, it is an entirely different story. No matter what the actual level of activity, the same amount of cost should be incurred.[2] The Aq × Sp expression must therefore remain constant.

Given the foregoing, we can now proceed with the calculation of overhead variances for Sanco, Inc. Assume that Sanco applies overhead to products on the basis of direct labor hours. The following information is available:

- Actual factory overhead incurred (fixed plus variable): $73,000
- Standard variable overhead rate per direct labor hour: $7
- Standard fixed overhead rate per direct labor hour: $10
- Budgeted fixed factory overhead for the period: $40,000
- Estimated activity in labor hours during the period: 4,000 hours

The company's overhead variances are shown in Exhibit 26-10.

### Spending Variance

The **spending variance** measures the difference between actual overhead incurred (both variable and fixed combined) and the total overhead budgeted for 4,100 direct labor hours of production. Because Aq × Ap must equal the actual overhead incurred, we merely inserted the $73,000 figure on the left-hand side of the exhibit. The planned amount of variable overhead for the activity level attained is computed in the same fashion as planned amounts for other variable cost elements (direct materials and direct labor), that is, Aq × Sp (4,100 hours × $7 = $28,700). Turning to fixed costs, Sanco has budgeted $40,000 of fixed factory overhead for the period. Given the nature of the expenditure, this figure should be incurred if direct labor input totals 4,100 hours, 4,200 hours, 4,000 hours, or for that matter, any level of activity within the relevant range.

Because actual overhead exceeded budgeted amounts by $4,300 [$73,000 − ($28,700 + $40,000)], better control of overhead costs is needed. For effective control to occur, the variance must be further subdivided into its individual cost components (i.e., specific variable and fixed costs) and further related to the proper responsibility centers.

### Variable Overhead Efficiency Variance

Sanco used 300 labor hours in excess of standard (4,100 hours − 3,800 hours), resulting in a $2,100 unfavorable **variable overhead efficiency variance.** This variance is somewhat misleading because it really has nothing to do with the use of overhead. Rather, the variance reflects inefficiencies experienced with the base used to apply the overhead—direct labor hours in this case. By reviewing the direct labor calculations in Exhibit 26-9, the relationship between the two efficiency variances becomes apparent.

### Fixed Overhead Volume Variance

The **fixed overhead volume variance** represents the fixed costs associated with an under- or overutilization of manufacturing facilities. To explain, Sanco has

[2] We are assuming that a firm is not moving from one activity range to another.

**Exhibit 26-10**
**Sanco, Inc., Factory Overhead Variances**

| Actual Quantity of Input at Actual Prices (Aq × Ap) | Amount the Actual Quantity of Input Should Have Cost: Variable: (Aq × Sp) Fixed: Budget for the Period | Standard Quantity of Input Allowed for Production, at Standard Prices (Sq × Sp) |
|---|---|---|
| | Variable: 4,100 hrs. × $7 $28,700 | 3,800 hrs.* × $7 $26,600 |
| | $2,100U Variable Overhead Efficiency Variance | |
| | Fixed: Budget = $40,000 | 3,800 hrs.* × $10 $38,000 |
| | $2,000U Fixed Overhead Volume Variance | |
| $73,000 | $68,700† | |
| $4,300U Spending Variance | | |

Summary

| | |
|---|---|
| Spending variance | $4,300U |
| Variable overhead efficiency variance | 2,100U |
| Fixed overhead volume variance | 2,000U |
| Total overhead variance | $8,400U |

Note: The following data were obtained from Exhibit 26-9:
Actual labor hours: 4,100
Actual production (units): 1,900
Labor standard: 2 hours per finished unit

* 1,900 units × 2 hrs. per unit.
† $28,700 + $40,000.

budgeted fixed overhead for the period of $40,000. This level of expenditure provides the company with an estimated capacity of 4,000 direct labor hours (see p. 950). As a result, each hour has an associated fixed cost of $10 ($40,000 ÷ 4,000). Observe that this amount is Sp—the standard fixed overhead rate per direct labor hour.

For the period just ended Sanco produced only 1,900 units. The standard hours allowed for these units total 3,800 (1,900 units × 2 hours per unit), leaving the company 200 hours shy of using its 4,000-hour capacity. Because each hour costs

$10, the volume variance amounts to $2,000. In this particular case the volume variance is unfavorable since utilization was less than capacity. Had utilization been greater than capacity, the variance would have been favorable, thereby indicating a theoretical "savings" in fixed costs.

Volume variances are caused by a number of factors, including an abnormally high number of machine breakdowns, strikes, sloppy production scheduling, changes in inventory policies, raw material shortages, and a lack of (or unanticipated) sales orders. In many instances volume variances are very difficult to control or eliminate. Top management, though, should do some analysis to determine the cause of the variance and whether operational changes are needed.

## Variance Investigation

> OBJECTIVE 6
> **Understand the problems encountered in the variance investigation process.**

The calculation of variances is only one step in the drive for effective cost control. Additional tasks, namely, variance investigation and the implementation of corrective action, are necessary to complete the process. Frequently, investigations are straightforward and relatively few problems are encountered. Sometimes, however, managers must assume the role of a detective to determine both the underlying cause and the correct party to hold accountable for a variance's creation.

In the simplest of cases, a variance arises because of problems directly identified with the production factor itself. For example, a direct labor rate variance may be caused by a temporary change in the labor mix required for production. Because of illness or perhaps a rush order, workers who earn $7 per hour may be temporarily shifted to jobs that are normally performed by lower-paid employees. Turning to another example, a labor efficiency variance may arise from a lack of proper employee training or morale problems among the workers.

A variance investigation is often complicated by the strong interrelationships that exist among manufacturing activities. Difficulties with machine operation, for instance, can destroy labor efficiency and cause excessive use of raw materials. In a multidepartment environment, sloppy performance in a production department may lead to unfavorable efficiency and unfavorable overhead spending variances in subsequent assembly work. Furthermore, variance trade-offs may be a factor. A manager may purposely acquire subpar materials in hopes the accompanying favorable price variance will exceed the costs of any excess usage or additional labor time.

Our discussion thus far has taken the position that actual operations are to blame for the creation of variances. It is possible, of course, that the standard is the problem. Variance investigators should examine standards to determine whether the standards are set correctly and up to date. Standards should be reviewed periodically, usually once each year, and adjusted if necessary.

> **TIPS & TECHNIQUES**
>
> Be aware that both unfavorable *and* favorable variances are candidates for investigation. Although a thorough examination of the latter may seem strange, such studies often prove beneficial. For instance, new production methods that have improved efficiency may be singled out and implemented elsewhere in the plant. As another example, favorable spending variances may be investigated in an effort to avoid long-term problems. Such variances in advertising and maintenance could indicate a need for management action to correct insufficient promotion and preventive maintenance programs, respectively.

## The Decision to Investigate

Realize that a variance is merely the mathematical difference between two numbers and serves as a gauge of performance. Like ratios, which were discussed earlier in the text, these measures present a hint that something is right or that something is wrong; only in rare circumstances can they tell the complete story.

The decision to investigate normally depends on the size of the variance involved. Large variances are of obvious concern to management; small variances are not. Most firms establish a general guideline, such as, "Review all variances that differ from standard amounts by 10% or $1,000, whichever is lower."

Bear in mind that variance investigation costs money. The cost of determining the cause of a variance and taking the necessary corrective action may very well exceed the amount of the variance under study. Consequently, variance review and correction should be based on the principle of cost-benefit analysis—making the evaluation and control of operations a profitable endeavor for the parties involved.

# APPENDIX Journal Entries for Variances

**OBJECTIVE 7**
Know how to integrate standard costs and variances into an accounting system.

Many companies have integrated standards and variances into their formal accounting systems to simplify bookkeeping. Firms can establish and carry a number of accounts at standard and need not keep track of daily fluctuations in input quantities and actual costs. The result is a reduction in record-keeping procedures.

To illustrate the journal entries used in a standard cost system, we will employ data from the Sanco, Inc., example that appears on pages 948–952.

### Direct Materials

Sanco purchased and consumed 6,000 pounds of direct materials in current production activities. The entry to record the purchase follows.

| | | |
|---|---|---|
| Raw Materials | 30,000 | |
| Materials Price Variance | 600 | |
| Accounts Payable | | 30,600 |
| To record purchase of direct materials | | |

The Accounts Payable account must be established at the actual amount owed to creditors, specifically, $30,600 (6,000 pounds × $5.10). The price variance is recognized at the time of acquisition to give management immediate feedback that a variance has occurred. Finally, the Raw Materials account is debited for $30,000: the actual quantity of materials purchased multiplied by the $5.00 standard price (6,000 pounds × $5.00 = $30,000).

Direct materials will eventually be taken out of the storeroom and used in manufacturing activities. Because the materials are carried in the accounts at the $5.00 standard price, the following entry is needed to record consumption of 6,000 pounds:

| | | |
|---|---|---|
| Work in Process | 28,500 | |
| Materials Quantity Variance | 1,500 | |
| Raw Materials | | 30,000 |
| To record direct materials used | | |

The quantity variance is recorded at this time because the excess use of 300 pounds (6,000 − 5,700) is now known. The net result of these two entries is that Work in Process is debited for $28,500—the standard quantity of input times the standard price (5,700 pounds × $5.00 = $28,500).

Note that both the Raw Materials and Work in Process accounts are carried at the standard price and have debit balances. As a result, any amounts in excess of standard (i.e., unfavorable variances) are recorded as additional costs and debited to the proper variance accounts. In contrast, favorable variances are entered as credits.

## Direct Labor

Consistent with the procedures just shown, Sanco would record direct labor incurrence in the following manner:

| | | |
|---|---|---|
| Work in Process | 22,800 | |
| Labor Efficiency Variance | 1,800 | |
| Labor Rate Variance | | 820 |
| Wages Payable | | 23,780 |
| To record direct labor for the period | | |

Once again, Work in Process is charged for the standard quantity of input multiplied by the standard price (3,800 hours × \$6.00 = \$22,800). In addition, Wages Payable is established at \$23,780, which represents Aq × Ap (the wages actually owed to employees).

## Factory Overhead

Actual factory overhead incurred is recorded as:

| | | |
|---|---|---|
| Factory Overhead | 73,000 | |
| Accounts Payable, Raw Materials, and so on | | 73,000 |
| To record actual factory overhead charges | | |

Recall from Chapter 22 that because of difficulties in tracing overhead to finished products, each unit manufactured is charged with an estimated amount of overhead via an application rate. The application rate corresponds to the standard price (Sp), as described in the preceding pages. Sanco's variable and fixed overhead rates per direct labor hour amounted to \$7 and \$10, respectively. To achieve consistency with the accounting treatments for materials and labor, the Work in Process account is again charged with the amount obtained by multiplying the standard quantity of input by the standard price. From the variances computed in Exhibit 26-10, the journal entry to apply overhead to the 1,900 units produced is as follows:

| | | |
|---|---|---|
| Work in Process | 64,600* | |
| Overhead Spending Variance | 4,300 | |
| Variable Overhead Efficiency Variance | 2,100 | |
| Fixed Overhead Volume Variance | 2,000 | |
| Factory Overhead | | 73,000 |
| To apply overhead to production | | |

* Variable + fixed (\$26,600 + \$38,000 = \$64,600).

## Subsequent Entries

Upon conclusion of production, an entry is needed to transfer the cost of the completed units to the Finished Goods account. In addition, the variance accounts are either closed to Cost of Goods Sold or, if significant, allocated on a proportional basis among Work in Process, Finished Goods, and Cost of Goods Sold. The latter treatment restates these three accounts from standard cost to actual cost and prevents the generation of misleading financial statements.

When a company experiences significant variances, the cause of the variances should be determined prior to undertaking any allocation procedure. If large variances are caused by abnormal levels of inefficiency, spoilage, and similar factors, allocation to inventory accounts is inappropriate. Such a procedure would result in carrying waste and ineptness as assets on the balance sheet, a treatment that is incompatible with the principles of sound financial accounting. Charging the variances as a loss of the current period may be more appropriate.

# Chapter Review

## Learning Objectives—The Key Points

**1 Understand the purpose and structure of a responsibility accounting system.** Responsibility accounting involves the division of a company into various segments (e.g., divisions, territories, and so forth), with a manager appointed to oversee the segment's activities. The manager is held accountable for the unit's operating results and is evaluated accordingly. Such a system assists in the attainment of company objectives.

The units in a responsibility accounting system may be organized as cost, profit, or investment centers. With a cost center (e.g., billing department), a manager is evaluated on the basis of costs incurred. Departmental heads strive to provide adequate service while keeping costs at a reasonably low level. In contrast, if the unit is organized as a profit center, the performance evaluation focuses on the level of profit generated. Finally, an investment center manager is concerned with the amount of income produced from a given level of asset investment, as measured by the segment's return on assets.

**2 Know how to construct and use a flexible budget.** A flexible budget is a budget constructed for different levels of operation within the relevant range of activity. Costs are normally subdivided into variable and fixed categories, with amounts often integrated into performance reports once the actual level of activity is known. Flexible budgets are extremely useful in performance evaluations because actual costs can be compared against budgeted amounts for the same volume level.

**3 Know what a standard cost is and how standards are developed.** Standard costs are preset targets of performance—targets that are reachable under reasonably efficient operating conditions. These per-unit amounts are easily incorporated into budgets.

Standards are normally established by using a team approach. Engineering and production personnel, for example, are often consulted when determining the amount of direct material that is consumed in a product. Once the proper quantities are known, the standard cost is calculated by using information obtained from the purchasing department. In a similar manner, engineering and production staffs work jointly to compute the direct labor time needed to perform a particular task. The figures are then converted to dollars on the basis of wage rate data furnished by the personnel department.

**4 Understand the distinction between ideal and attainable standards.** An ideal standard is one that can be achieved in a perfect operating environment (i.e., maximum efficiency at minimum cost). By setting standards at such tight levels, companies hope to improve output as employees increase their efforts to hit the target. Often, however, workers become frustrated in their attempts and morale may suffer. Most companies use attainable standards, or those achievable under efficient, not perfect, operating conditions. The standard is set high enough to motivate employees, but is not unreasonably high to cause frustration.

**5 Know how to calculate variances as related to direct materials, direct labor, and factory overhead.** The variances for direct materials and direct labor are easily computed by use of the general model:

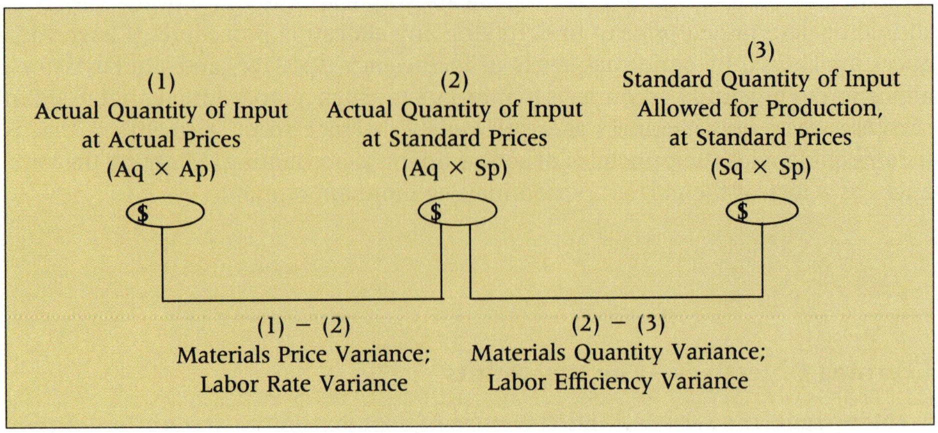


The calculations for factory overhead variances are slightly more complex and may be summarized as follows:

- *Spending variance*—The difference between the actual total overhead incurred (Aq × Ap) and the sum of the amounts budgeted for the actual hours worked (variable, Aq × Sp; fixed, budget for the period).
- *Variable overhead efficiency variance*—The difference between Aq × Sp and Sq × Sp for variable overhead.
- *Fixed overhead volume variance*—The difference between the fixed overhead budgeted for the period and the Sq × Sp computation.

**6 Understand the problems encountered in the variance investigation process.** A variance investigation involves a look at both actual *and* standard costs. Differences between these two amounts may arise from problems with the production factor itself (e.g., variable overhead) or interrelationships that exist among manufacturing activities. As an example of the latter, problems with labor efficiency may affect the amount of direct materials used during the period. Given that variance investigations are often time consuming and costly, the decision to investigate is generally made on a cost-benefit basis.

**7 (Appendix) Know how to integrate standard costs and variances into an accounting system.** Standard costs and variances are integrated into an accounting system by the use of journal entries. Variances are recorded in their own accounts (unfavorable variances by debits and favorable variances via credits). In addition, the entries are structured so that Work in Process, Finished Goods, and Cost of Goods Sold are generally carried at Sq × Sp amounts.

## Chapter Quiz

The five questions that follow relate to several issues raised in the chapter. Test your knowledge of the issues by selecting the best answer. (The answers appear on p. 972.)

1 Which of the following statements about responsibility accounting is false?
   a An investment center manager is usually evaluated on the basis of return on assets.
   b Managers should be held accountable for controllable costs.
   c Performance reports tend to be summarized at lower levels of an organization and more detailed at higher levels.
   d Normally, cost centers are not involved with revenue-generating activities.

**2** Flexible budgets:
a tend to result in improved performance reporting.
b are the same as static budgets.
c are constructed for one level of activity.
d normally exclude fixed manufacturing costs.

**3** Standard costs:
a are inconsistent with budgets.
b should be based on attainable levels of performance.
c are usually calculated by the accountant without any other departmental input.
d are calculated for direct materials and direct labor but not factory overhead.

**4** Ace Corporation recently completed the manufacture of 4,000 computer tables. Each table's standard direct labor cost is $16 (2 hours at $8 per hour). If the actual payroll totaled $63,990 (8,100 hours at $7.90), the company's labor efficiency variance is:
a $800F.
b $800U.
c $810F.
d $810U.

**5** The difference between the actual factory overhead incurred during the period and the overhead budgeted for the actual hours worked is known as the:
a overhead spending variance.
b variable overhead efficiency variance.
c fixed overhead volume variance.
d total overhead variance.

## Summary Problem

Mahoney, Inc., manufactures a single product and uses a standard costing system. A conversation with the firm's accountant revealed that each unit of finished product has the following material and labor standards:

- Direct materials: 4 units @ $2.50
- Direct labor: 2 hours @ $6.50

Mahoney applies factory overhead on the basis of direct labor hours. Management estimates that budgeted production levels during the upcoming period will require a total of 50,000 direct labor hours. Variable and fixed overhead at this level of activity are estimated at $150,000 and $275,000, respectively. Additional data follow.

1 Direct materials purchased and consumed during the period totaled 100,000 units at a cost of $2.65 per unit.
2 Direct labor incurred totaled 51,000 hours at a rate of $6.70 per hour.
3 Total overhead incurred amounted to $436,000.
4 Actual production totaled 26,000 units, all of which were completed.

### Instructions

**a** Compute the company's variable and fixed overhead rates per direct labor hour.

**b** Compute the total standard cost of a finished unit.

**c** Determine Mahoney's direct materials variances.

**d** Determine Mahoney's direct labor variances.

**e** Determine Mahoney's factory overhead variances.

**Solution**

**a**

$$\text{Variable Overhead Rate} = \frac{\text{Estimated Variable Overhead}}{\text{Estimated Activity}}$$

$$= \frac{\$150{,}000}{50{,}000 \text{ direct labor hours}}$$

$$= \$3 \text{ per direct labor hour}$$

$$\text{Fixed Overhead Rate} = \frac{\text{Estimated Fixed Overhead}}{\text{Estimated Activity}}$$

$$= \frac{\$275{,}000}{50{,}000 \text{ direct labor hours}}$$

$$= \$5.50 \text{ per direct labor hour}$$

**b**

| | |
|---|---|
| Direct materials: 4 units @ $2.50 | $10.00 |
| Direct labor: 2 hours @ $6.50 | 13.00 |
| Variable overhead: 2 hours @ $3.00* | 6.00 |
| Fixed overhead: 2 hours @ $5.50* | 11.00 |
| Total standard cost per finished unit | $40.00 |

* From part (a).

**c**

| Actual Quantity of Input at Actual Prices (Aq × Ap) | Actual Quantity of Input at Standard Prices (Aq × Sp) | Standard Quantity of Input Allowed for Production, at Standard Prices (Sq × Sp) |
|---|---|---|
| 100,000 units × $2.65 | 100,000 units × $2.50 | 104,000 units* × $2.50 |
| $265,000 | $250,000 | $260,000 |

$15,000U — Materials Price Variance

$10,000F — Materials Quantity Variance

$5,000U — Total Materials Variance

* 26,000 finished units × 4 units of direct materials.

**d**

| Actual Quantity of Input at Actual Prices (Aq × Ap) | Actual Quantity of Input at Standard Prices (Aq × Sp) | Standard Quantity of Input Allowed for Production, at Standard Prices (Sq × Sp) |
|---|---|---|
| 51,000 hrs. × \$6.70 | 51,000 hrs. × \$6.50 | 52,000 hrs.* × \$6.50 |
| \$341,700 | \$331,500 | \$338,000 |

\$10,200U — Labor Rate Variance

\$6,500F — Labor Efficiency Variance

\$3,700U — Total Labor Variance

* 26,000 finished units × 2 hrs. per unit.

**e**

| Actual Quantity of Input at Actual Prices (Aq × Ap) | Amount the Actual Quantity of Input Should Have Cost: Variable: (Aq × Sp) Fixed: Budget for the Period | Standard Quantity of Input Allowed for Production, at Standard Prices (Sq × Sp) |
|---|---|---|
| | Variable: 51,000 hrs. × \$3* \$153,000 | 52,000 hrs.† × \$3* \$156,000 |
| | Fixed: Budget = \$275,000 | 52,000 hrs.† × \$5.50* \$286,000 |
| \$436,000 | \$428,000‡ | |

\$3,000F — Variable Overhead Efficiency Variance

\$11,000F — Fixed Overhead Volume Variance

\$8,000U — Spending Variance

* See part (a).
† 26,000 finished units × 2 hrs. per unit.
‡ \$153,000 + \$275,000.

## Questions

**Q26-1** Briefly discuss the features associated with a responsibility accounting system.

**Q26-2** Should a cost center manager strive for cost minimization? Why?

**Q26-3** Differentiate between a profit center and an investment center.

**Q26-4** Describe the flow of information in a typical responsibility reporting system.

**Q26-5** Differentiate between a static budget and a flexible budget.

**Q26-6** Explain the relationship, if any, between a standard cost and a flexible budget.

**Q26-7** Identify the parties normally involved in establishing the following:
a Quantity standards for materials
b Rate standards for direct labor

**Q26-8** An engineer once commented: "Standards must be based on a perfect operating environment, as anything less assumes inefficient working conditions." Evaluate the engineer's comment.

**Q26-9** Why do some companies use ideal standards? What often occurs shortly after the introduction of ideal standards?

**Q26-10** What is meant by an attainable standard?

**Q26-11** Explain the concept known as "management by exception." Is variance analysis consistent or inconsistent with management by exception? Why?

**Q26-12** Should managers investigate all variances? Why?

***Q26-13** Are favorable variances recorded in the accounts as debits or credits?

***Q26-14** List two possible methods of accounting for variances at the end of a reporting period. When is each method appropriate?

## Exercises

**E26-1** ***Cost centers and profit centers***

Crest Manufacturing produces a single product at its Albany plant. Units are processed through departments A and B and then to finished goods. The firm has a maintenance department that performs repair jobs for the manufacturing departments.

The maintenance operation has always been evaluated as a cost center. Now with a change in management, a switch to a profit center setup is being considered. Prices charged for repair jobs would be based on the maintenance department's cost of operations.

a Discuss the difference between a cost center and a profit center.
b Mike Mizer, the head of maintenance, has always operated with a cost minimization philosophy. Will the change to a profit center likely alter the quality of service provided by the maintenance department? Explain your answer.
c What will be the reaction of the manufacturing departments to the change to a profit center? Consider the probable effect on the number of service requests when structuring your answer.

**E26-2** ***Flexible budgets and performance reports***

The following performance report of production costs was prepared by a staff assistant of the Carnahan Company:

---

* An asterisk preceding an item indicates that the material is covered in the Appendix to this chapter.

**CARNAHAN COMPANY**
**Performance Report**
**For the Month Ended January 31, 19X2**

| *Cost* | *Budget* | *Actual* | *Variance* |
|---|---|---|---|
| Direct materials used | $ 33,000 | $ 32,400 | $ 600F |
| Direct labor | 75,000 | 71,550 | 3,450F |
| Variable factory overhead | 18,000 | 15,120 | 2,880F |
| Fixed factory overhead | 48,000 | 49,300 | 1,300U |
| Total production costs | $174,000 | $168,370 | $5,630F |

The budget was based on a production level of 30,000 units. Because of several snowstorms in the area, Carnahan's plant was closed for four working days and only 27,000 units were manufactured.

Management desires a performance report that uses the flexible budgeting approach.

a Explain the major cause of the total favorable variance for the period.
b Prepare a performance report by using the flexible budgeting approach.

**E26-3** ***Flexible budgets and performance reports***

Home Products, Inc., uses flexible budgeting for cost control and performance evaluations. A review of the company's master budget found that management expects to produce 8,000 units each month, resulting in annual expenditures for direct labor and supervisory salaries of $307,200 and $806,400, respectively. Supervisory salaries, a fixed cost, are spread evenly throughout the year. If October's production amounted to 7,800 units and a $2,900 unfavorable direct labor variance was reported, determine:

a The actual direct labor cost that appeared in the October performance report.
b The budgeted amount for supervisory salaries that appeared in the October performance report.

**E26-4** ***Variances for direct materials and direct labor***

Advanced Manufacturing Corporation has established the following standards for one of its products.

| | |
|---|---|
| Materials: 5 gallons @ $7 | $35 |
| Labor: 1.5 hours @ $10 | 15 |

During a recent month 9,000 finished units were produced. Materials purchased and consumed in operations totaled 47,000 gallons at a cost of $6.80 per gallon. In addition, Advanced paid $10.25 per hour for 13,300 hours of factory labor. Compute variances for the following:

a Direct materials
b Direct labor

**E26-5** ***Variances for direct materials and direct labor***

Banner Company manufactures flags of various countries. Each flag has a standard of eight square feet of fabric and three hours of direct labor time. Information about recent production activity follows.

- Actual cost of fabric: $4.50 per square foot
- Fabric consumed: 32,080 square feet
- Standard price per square foot of fabric: $4.25
- Standard direct labor rate: $10.00 per hour
- Actual direct labor rate: $10.20 per hour
- Actual labor hours worked: 11,940
- Actual production completed: 4,000 flags

a Compute the materials price variance and the materials quantity variance.
b Compute the labor rate variance and the labor efficiency variance.

**E26-6** ***Analysis of direct labor variances***

North Central Manufacturing was in the midst of completing an order for a valued customer when a flu epidemic occurred. To finish the order on time, the production supervisor substituted skilled tool and die personnel on a job normally performed by apprentices. The job was completed in 430 hours, which was 95 hours less than the standard time allowed. The tool and die personnel earn $10.50 per hour; apprentices normally earn $7.00 per hour.

a Compute the labor rate and labor efficiency variances for this job.
b Was the production supervisor's substitution decision correct? Explain your answer.

**E26-7** ***Variance analysis: Working backward***

Auto Lube performs oil changes and other minor maintenance services (e.g., tire pressure checks, fluid checks, and so forth). The company advertises that all services are completed in 15 minutes. Eighty cars were serviced on a recent Saturday, resulting in the following labor variances: rate, $18U; efficiency, $64U. If the labor rate standard is $4 per hour, determine the:

a Standard hours allowed for Saturday's work.
b Actual hours worked.
c Actual wage rate.

**E26-8** ***Determining the effect on variances***

Consider the following events that relate to Consolidated Industries:

a A machine malfunction caused higher-than-normal spoilage rates and required increased attention by the machine operator.
b The company had to absorb unexpected air freight charges on a rush order of direct materials.
c A slowdown occurred on the production line because of low morale among the workers.
d The local power company raised its rates by 5%.
e The firm hired 10 part-time workers to meet an increase in production levels. Consolidated had to pay premium wages because of a shortage of qualified help.

Picture the nature of the materials variances (price and quantity) and labor variances (rate and efficiency). Determine which variances, if any, are affected by each event and whether the variance will be favorable or unfavorable. *Note:* If a revision of standards is necessary, assume that no revision occurs until the next accounting period.

**E26-9** ***Overview of standards and variances***

Evaluate the comments that follow as being True or False. If the comment is false, briefly explain why.

a The direct labor rate variance is computed as the difference between the actual and standard pay rates, multiplied by the actual hours worked.
b By hiring employees who possess below average skill levels, a company is likely to generate favorable labor rate variances and unfavorable labor efficiency variances.

c In most cases, ideal standards are preferred rather than attainable standards.
d Standard costs are generally integrated into a company's budgets.
e An unfavorable volume variance indicates that fixed overhead incurred exceeded budgeted amounts.

**E26-10** ***Overhead variances***

Nova Manufacturing applies factory overhead to products on the basis of direct labor hours. At the beginning of the current year, the company's accountant made the following estimates for the forthcoming period:

- Estimated variable overhead: $500,000
- Estimated fixed overhead: $400,000
- Estimated direct labor hours: 40,000

It is now twelve months later. Actual total overhead incurred in the manufacture of 7,900 units amounted to $895,100. Actual labor hours totaled 39,800. Assuming a direct labor standard of five hours per finished unit, calculate the following:
a Variable overhead efficiency variance
b Fixed overhead volume variance
c Overhead spending variance

**E26-11** ***Overhead variances***

Chen Company employs a standard costing system. The standard cost sheet for one of its products follows.

| | |
|---|---|
| Direct materials: 3 pounds @ $5.00 | $ 15.00 |
| Direct labor: 6 hours @ $6.50 | 39.00 |
| Variable factory overhead: 6 hours @ $7.00 | 42.00 |
| Fixed factory overhead: 6 hours @ $3.00 | 18.00 |
| Total | $114.00 |

Total overhead incurred during June amounted to $445,000, of which $295,000 was variable. Budgeted fixed overhead of $1.8 million is spread evenly throughout the year. Finally, Chen's labor force worked a total of 40,000 hours during the month in producing 7,000 finished units.

Determine Chen's spending variance, variable overhead efficiency variance, and fixed overhead volume variance. Be sure to label the variances as favorable or unfavorable.

***E26-12** ***Standard costs and journal entries***

Hutchins, Inc., has established the following standards for direct materials and direct labor for product no. 781:

| | |
|---|---|
| Direct materials: 4 pounds @ $2.50 per pound | $10.00 |
| Direct labor: 2 hours @ $8.00 per hour | 16.00 |

The information below pertains to a recent month.
1 Purchases of direct materials amounted to 9,000 pounds at a total cost of $23,850.
2 Nine thousand pounds of direct materials were consumed in operations to manufacture 2,300 finished units.
3 Direct labor charges totaled 4,750 hours at $7.90 per hour.

a Compute the price and quantity variances for direct materials.
b Determine the rate and efficiency variances for direct labor.
c Prepare journal entries to record the transactions that relate to direct materials and direct labor.

## Problems

### Series A

**P26-A1** ***Basic flexible budgeting***

Centron, Inc., has the following budgeted production costs:

| | |
|---|---|
| Direct materials | $0.40 per unit |
| Direct labor | 1.80 per unit |
| Variable factory overhead | 2.20 per unit |
| Fixed factory overhead | |
| Supervision | $24,000 |
| Maintenance | 18,000 |
| Other | 12,000 |

The company normally manufactures between 20,000 and 25,000 units each quarter. Should output exceed 25,000 units, maintenance and other fixed costs are expected to increase by $6,000 and $4,500, respectively.

During the recent quarter ended March 31, Centron produced 25,500 units and incurred the following costs:

| | |
|---|---|
| Direct materials | $ 10,710 |
| Direct labor | 47,175 |
| Variable factory overhead | 51,940 |
| Fixed factory overhead | |
| Supervision | 24,500 |
| Maintenance | 23,700 |
| Other | 16,800 |
| Total production costs | $174,825 |

**Instructions**

a Prepare a flexible budget for 20,000, 22,500, and 25,000 units of activity.

b Was Centron's experience in the quarter cited better or worse than anticipated? Prepare an appropriate performance report and explain your answer.

c Explain the benefit of using flexible budgets (as opposed to static budgets) in the measurement of performance.

**P26-A2** ***Flexible budgeting and performance appraisal***

Royal Company has just completed an in-depth study of overhead costs. The firm normally operates between 20,000 and 22,000 labor hours each month. Budgeted costs for this range of activity are:

| | |
|---|---|
| Maintenance | $40,000 plus $0.30 per direct labor hour |
| Supplies | $0.50 per direct labor hour |
| Power | $9,000 plus $0.18 per direct labor hour |
| Depreciation | $20,800 |
| Overtime | $0.70 for each direct labor hour worked in excess of 21,500 direct labor hours per month |
| Indirect labor | $18,000 plus $1.00 per direct labor hour |

During March, Royal had planned to operate at 21,800 direct labor hours. Actual activity, however, amounted to only 21,300 hours at the following costs:

| | |
|---|---|
| Maintenance | $49,050 |
| Supplies | 10,800 |
| Power | 12,900 |
| Depreciation | 20,800 |
| Overtime | 150 |
| Indirect labor | 39,600 |

All fixed cost elements remained as budgeted except for maintenance, which increased by $2,600.

**Instructions**

a Prepare a performance report for March that compares actual activity against a static budget. The report should list all variable costs and then all fixed costs. Split mixed costs into their variable and fixed components.
b Repeat part (a), using a flexible budgeting approach.
c Given the nature of the flexible budget, why is an in-depth study of cost behavior necessary prior to the budget's preparation?

**P26-A3** ***Straightforward variance analysis***
Australian Collectibles (AC) uses a standard costing system. The standard cost sheet for product no. XJ36 is shown below.

| | |
|---|---|
| Direct materials: 2 pounds @ $2.75 | $ 5.50 |
| Direct labor: 4 hours @ $7.50 | 30.00 |
| Variable factory overhead: 4 hours @ $2.00 | 8.00 |
| Fixed factory overhead: 4 hours @ $5.00 | 20.00 |
| Total standard cost per unit | $63.50 |

The following information pertains to activity for April:
1 Direct materials acquired during the month amounted to 3,160 pounds at $2.80 per pound. All materials were consumed in operations.
2 AC incurred an average wage rate of $7.40 for 6,500 hours of activity.
3 Total overhead incurred amounted to $38,900. Budgeted fixed overhead totals $264,000 and is spread evenly throughout the year.
4 Actual production amounted to 1,600 completed units.

**Instructions**

a Compute AC's direct materials variances.
b Compute AC's direct labor variances.
c Compute AC's variances for factory overhead.

**P26-A4** ***Variance analysis and interpretation***
Cisco Industries uses a standard costing system to assist in the control of operations. The company's May performance report for variable manufacturing costs follows.

**CISCO INDUSTRIES**
**Performance Report**
**For the Month Ended May 31, 19X7**

| | |
|---|---|
| Direct materials variance, favorable | $ 300 |
| Direct labor variance, favorable | 600 |
| Variable overhead variance, favorable | 100 |
| Total variances, favorable | $1,000 |

The president is extremely satisfied with the figures. He notes: "It looks like we've finally gotten operations under control. Apparently the change to a new supplier did the trick. In addition, I think the new supervisor is working out well. I've noticed a much happier and more efficient work force on my daily tours through the plant."

Assume that the following information has come to your attention.

1 Standard variable costs per unit of finished product:

| | |
|---|---|
| Direct materials: 2.5 pounds @ $2.00 | $ 5.00 |
| Direct labor: 3.2 hours @ $7.00 | 22.40 |
| Variable overhead: 3.2 hours @ $5.00 | 16.00 |
| Total standard variable cost per unit | $43.40 |

2 Direct materials purchased and consumed amounted to 8,400 pounds at $1.75 per pound.
3 Direct labor incurred in the manufacture of 3,000 completed units totaled 11,100 hours at $6.00 per hour.
4 Variable factory overhead incurred amounted to $47,900.

**Instructions**

a Criticize the format and content of the performance report as presently constructed.
b Prepare a complete variance analysis for direct materials, direct labor, and variable overhead. *Note:* Compute the overhead spending variance with regard to variable overhead only.
c Explain the results of your findings to the president. Are things going as smoothly as the president believes? Discuss.

**P26-A5** ***Variance analysis: Working backward***

Falcon Company has a single manufacturing department that applies factory overhead on the basis of direct labor hours. Selected department information follows.

| | |
|---|---|
| Cost of materials purchased and consumed | ? |
| Materials standard per finished unit | 3 pounds |
| Standard material cost per pound | $4 |
| Materials price variance | $3,500U |
| Materials quantity variance | $8,600F |
| Actual labor hours worked | ? |
| Labor standard per finished unit | 5 hours |
| Standard labor rate per hour | $7 |
| Labor rate variance | $22,000U |
| Labor efficiency variance | $14,000F |
| Total actual overhead incurred | ? |
| Standard variable overhead rate | $2 per hour |
| Standard fixed overhead rate | $6 per hour |
| Budgeted fixed overhead | ? |
| Variable overhead efficiency variance | ? |
| Fixed overhead volume variance | $11,000U |
| Overhead spending variance | $4,800U |
| Number of units manufactured | 8,000 |

**Instructions**

Determine each of the unknowns. *Hint:* It is helpful to solve separate models simultaneously for materials, labor, and overhead by filling in the given information.

***P26-A6** ***Variance analysis and journal entries***

Southeast Manufacturing has integrated standard costs and variance reporting into its formal accounting system. The standard costs per finished unit follow.

| | |
|---|---|
| Direct materials: 2 gallons @ $7.40 | $14.80 |
| Direct labor: 3 hours @ $10.00 | 30.00 |
| Variable overhead* | 6.00 |
| Fixed overhead* | 4.50 |
| Total | $55.30 |

* Applied on the basis of direct labor hours.

Other data are:

Purchases of direct materials: 20,000 gallons at $7.35 per gallon
Direct labor incurred: 29,900 hours at a cost of $304,980
Total overhead incurred amounted to $109,400; overhead variances were as follows:

| | |
|---|---|
| Spending variance | $ 400F |
| Variable overhead efficiency variance | 200F |
| Fixed overhead volume variance | 5,000U |

Actual production amounted to 10,000 finished units, and direct materials consumption conformed to original predictions.

**Instructions**

a Determine Southeast's variances for direct materials.
b Determine Southeast's variances for direct labor.
c Prepare journal entries to record the following:
  (1) Direct materials purchases
  (2) Direct materials issued to production
  (3) Direct labor incurred
  (4) Factory overhead incurred
  (5) Factory overhead applied to production

## Series B

**P26-B1** ***Basic flexible budgeting***

Seagate Lighting has the following budgeted production costs:

| | |
|---|---|
| Direct materials | $1.50 per unit |
| Direct labor | 4.60 per unit |
| Variable factory overhead | 7.40 per unit |
| Fixed factory overhead | |
| Supervision | $42,000 |
| Machinery leasing | 88,000 |
| Other | 26,000 |

The company normally manufactures between 25,000 and 29,000 units each quarter. Should output be less than 25,000 units, supervision and other fixed costs are expected to decrease by $12,000 and $4,000, respectively.

During the recent quarter ended June 30, Seagate produced 24,600 units and incurred the costs that follow.

| | |
|---|---|
| Direct materials | $ 36,750 |
| Direct labor | 112,500 |
| Variable factory overhead | 182,350 |
| Fixed factory overhead | |
| Supervision | 35,800 |
| Machinery leasing | 89,300 |
| Other | 19,100 |
| Total production costs | $475,800 |

**Instructions**

a Prepare a flexible budget for 25,000, 27,000, and 29,000 units of activity.
b Was Seagate's experience in the quarter cited better or worse than anticipated? Prepare an appropriate performance report and explain your answer.
c Explain the flexibility associated with a flexible budget.

**P26-B2** ***Flexible budgeting and performance appraisal***

All Star Plastics has just completed an in-depth study of overhead costs. The firm normally operates between 12,000 and 14,000 labor hours each month. Budgeted costs for this range of activity are:

| | |
|---|---|
| Maintenance | $30,000 plus $0.15 per direct labor hour |
| Supplies | $0.40 per direct labor hour |
| Power | $12,000 plus $0.10 per direct labor hour |
| Machinery leasing | $28,000 |
| Overtime | $2.50 for each direct labor hour worked in excess of 13,500 direct labor hours per month |
| Indirect labor | $15,000 plus $2.00 per direct labor hour |

During May, All Star had planned to operate at 13,800 direct labor hours. Actual activity, however, amounted to only 13,300 hours at the following costs:

| | |
|---|---|
| Maintenance | $32,050 |
| Supplies | 5,500 |
| Power | 13,420 |
| Machinery leasing | 28,000 |
| Overtime | 200 |
| Indirect labor | 38,900 |

All fixed cost elements remained as budgeted except for indirect labor, which decreased by $2,400.

**Instructions**

a Prepare a performance report for May that compares actual activity against a static budget. The report should list all variable costs and then all fixed costs. Split mixed costs into their variable and fixed components.
b Repeat part (a), using a flexible budgeting approach.
c The president of All Star prefers the static budgeting approach, "because there's no way we can predict our actual activity in advance. Furthermore, once a budget is set, it should remain in force until the month is past." Explain the problems associated with using a static budget in performance evaluations.

**P26-B3** ***Straightforward variance analysis***

Arrow Enterprises uses a standard costing system. The standard cost sheet for product no. 549 follows.

| | |
|---|---|
| Direct materials: 4 units @ $6.50 | $ 26.00 |
| Direct labor: 8 hours @ $8.50 | 68.00 |
| Variable factory overhead: 8 hours @ $7.00 | 56.00 |
| Fixed factory overhead: 8 hours @ $2.50 | 20.00 |
| Total standard cost per unit | $170.00 |

The following information pertains to activity for December:

1 Direct materials acquired during the month amounted to 26,350 units at $6.40 per unit. All materials were consumed in operations.
2 Arrow incurred an average wage rate of $8.75 for 51,400 hours of activity.
3 Total overhead incurred amounted to $508,400. Budgeted fixed overhead totals $1.8 million and is spread evenly throughout the year.
4 Actual production amounted to 6,500 completed units.

Instructions

a Compute Arrow's direct materials variances.
b Compute Arrow's direct labor variances.
c Compute Arrow's variances for factory overhead.

**P26-B4** ***Variance analysis and interpretation***

Imtex Manufacturing uses a standard costing system. The variable cost standards for product no. 628 follow.

| | |
|---|---|
| Direct materials: 3.2 pounds @ $5 | $16.00 |
| Direct labor: 8.5 hours @ $8 | 68.00 |
| Variable overhead: 8.5 hours @ $3 | 25.50 |

The company has been experiencing rough times of late, with constant complaints from customers about poor product quality. In addition, the production supervisor is very unhappy with the performance reports that he receives to monitor factory operations. A typical report appears as shown.

**IMTEX MANUFACTURING**
**Performance Report**
**For the Month Ended June 30, 19X3**

| | *Actual* | *Standard* | *Variance* |
|---|---|---|---|
| Direct costs* | $XX,XXX | $XX,XXX | $XX,XXX |
| Factory overhead | XX,XXX | XX,XXX | XX,XXX |
| Total | $XX,XXX | $XX,XXX | $XX,XXX |

* Direct materials + direct labor.

In an effort to improve product quality, the supervisor has fought long and hard for a change to a better supplier and the hiring of more competent employees. He has recently been given permission to pursue both of these alternatives. Actual data follow.

1 Direct materials purchased and consumed amounted to 6,000 pounds at $5.80 per pound.
2 Direct labor incurred in the manufacture of 2,000 completed units totaled 15,400 hours at $10.50 per hour.
3 Variable overhead incurred totaled $47,200.

**Instructions**

a Suggest several ways that Imtex's performance report could be improved to provide better information to the supervisor.

b Prepare a complete variance analysis for direct materials, direct labor, and variable overhead. *Note:* Compute the overhead spending variance with regard to variable overhead only.

c Does the production supervisor's plan seem to be working? Discuss.

**P26-B5** ***Variance analysis: Working backward***

Vermont, Inc., has a single manufacturing department that applies factory overhead on the basis of direct labor hours. Selected departmental information follows.

| | |
|---|---|
| Cost of materials purchased and consumed | $46,000 |
| Materials standard per finished unit | 4 pounds |
| Standard material cost per pound | ? |
| Materials price variance | $5,000U |
| Materials quantity variance | $3,000F |
| Actual labor hours worked | 6,000 hours |
| Labor standard per finished unit | 1.5 hours |
| Standard labor rate per hour | $6 |
| Labor rate variance | $4,000U |
| Labor efficiency variance | ? |
| Total actual overhead incurred | $80,500 |
| Standard variable overhead rate per hour | ? |
| Standard fixed overhead rate | $8 per hour |
| Budgeted fixed overhead | $64,000 |
| Variable overhead efficiency variance | $4,500F |
| Fixed overhead volume variance | ? |
| Overhead spending variance | ? |
| Number of units manufactured | 5,000 |

**Instructions**

Determine each of the unknowns. *Hint:* It is helpful to solve separate models simultaneously for materials, labor, and overhead by filling in the given information.

***P26-B6** ***Variance analysis and journal entries***

Evergreen Manufacturing has integrated standard costs and variance reporting into its formal accounting system. The standard costs per finished unit follow.

| | |
|---|---|
| Direct materials: 2 pounds @ $3.25 | $ 6.50 |
| Direct labor: 0.75 hours @ $8.00 | 6.00 |
| Variable overhead* | 3.00 |
| Fixed overhead* | 5.25 |
| Total | $20.75 |

* Applied on the basis of direct labor hours.

Other data are:

- Purchases of direct materials: 30,000 pounds at $3.35 per pound
- Direct labor incurred: 11,400 hours at a cost of $90,630
- Total overhead incurred amounted to $125,000; overhead variances were as follows:

| | |
|---|---|
| Spending variance | $4,600F |
| Variable overhead efficiency variance | 600U |
| Fixed overhead volume variance | 5,250U |

Actual production amounted to 15,000 finished units, and direct materials consumption conformed to original predictions.

**Instructions**

a Determine Evergreen's variances for direct materials.
b Determine Evergreen's variances for direct labor.
c Prepare journal entries to record the following:
  (1) Direct materials purchases
  (2) Direct materials issued to production
  (3) Direct labor incurred
  (4) Factory overhead incurred
  (5) Factory overhead applied to production

## Beyond the Basics

**BB26-1** ***Responsibility accounting and variances***

Burdick Manufacturing is a small producer of decorative accessories used in the home. Various materials are carefully shaped and formed by skilled craftsmen, with the final product being sold in fine furniture stores and specialty shops. The company uses responsibility accounting and has recently installed a new computerized standard cost system. The system has been tested thoroughly and is operating correctly.

Six weeks ago, the firm's sales manager accepted a large rush order for a nonstock item from a valued customer. The sales manager forwarded the order to Joe Perry, the production supervisor. Perry, in turn, filed the necessary paperwork with the purchasing department so that needed raw materials could be acquired. Unfortunately, a purchasing clerk temporarily lost the paperwork, and by the time it was located, it was too late to order from the normal supplier. A new supplier was found, who quoted a very attractive price. The materials arrived and production personnel found them to be of poor quality.

Perry has recently returned from vacation, only to be confronted by Burdick's manufacturing vice-president about "inept performance in the period just ended." A heated discussion took place, with Perry being told to shape up or ship out.

**Instructions**

a Briefly explain the essence of a responsibility accounting system.
b What variances for materials and labor would *ordinarily* be controllable by and appear on a production supervisor's performance report?
c Briefly explain the probable reason behind the heated confrontation between Perry and the manufacturing vice-president. Does the manufacturing vice-president have a valid reason to be upset? Why?
d Given that the company has a responsibility accounting system, what could be done to correct the situation? Briefly discuss.

**BB26-2** ***Setting standards***

Starr Manufacturing Corporation is considering the implementation of a standard costing system. The information that follows pertains to one of the company's products, HD-24.

| | | |
|---|---|---|
| Direct materials used* | | $1,020,000 |
| Direct labor† | | 348,000 |
| Other traceable variable costs | | |
| Blending costs | $148,000 | |
| Packaging materials | 40,700 | |
| Miscellaneous | 74,000 | 262,700 |
| Total variable costs | | $1,630,700 |

* 240,000 gallons at $4.25 per gallon.
† 58,000 hours at $6.00 per hour.

These costs were incurred in the production of 185,000 gallons of HD-24, which were packaged four gallons to a case. Starr has been experiencing problems with the quality of materials used and plans to change suppliers in the forthcoming period. The price per gallon of direct materials is expected to rise to $4.40. Starr anticipates that HD-24 output will total 80% of the direct materials used in production; the remainder is lost through evaporation.

Management estimates that abnormal production problems in the prior period led to the incurrence of an additional 2,500 labor hours. These problems have been corrected and are not expected to recur. Other variable costs are anticipated to remain stable, with the exception of packaging materials. Packaging cost is expected to increase by $0.04 per gallon.

**Instructions**

a By analyzing the data presented, compute an attainable standard variable cost for a case of HD-24.

b Compare and contrast ideal and attainable standards. What benefits normally result from the use of attainable standards?

c Discuss several problems that may be encountered in the standard-setting process by relying too heavily on past experience.

## Answers to Chapter Quiz

**1** c

**2** a

**3** b

**4** b [(Aq × Sp) − (Sq × Sp) = (8,100 hours × $8) − (8,000 hours × $8) = $800. The variance is unfavorable because actual hours exceeded standard hours.]

**5** a

# Decision Making and Contribution Reporting

CHAPTER 27

## Learning Objectives

After reading this chapter you should:

1 Understand the effect of relevant costs and sunk costs on decision making.

2 Know how to evaluate different types of decision situations (e.g., make or buy).

3 Know why the contribution margin must be analyzed in terms of capacity constraints.

4 Be able to distinguish between direct costs and indirect costs.

5 Know how to prepare and use a contribution income statement.

6 Be familiar with the features of direct (variable) costing and absorption costing.

Managers make a variety of decisions that are critical to the short- and long-term profitability and solvency of an enterprise. As evidence, examine the recent decisions of several well-known corporations that are shown in Exhibit 27-1. Future events and conditions will determine whether these actions were wise or whether other alternatives would have been preferable.

Accountants play a significant role in decision making. Accounting information is continually generated to assist management in the problem-solving process and to evaluate subsequent performance. Furthermore, in many firms the accountant actually assumes the role of a decision maker and selects from among alternative courses of action. The extent of this role is dependent on the overall philosophy of top management and the accountant's position in the organizational hierarchy.

This chapter is the first of a two-chapter sequence that explores the fundamentals of decision making. Although much of our presentation will focus on the decision process from a business viewpoint, many of the concepts illustrated have considerable relevance to individuals as well. Students, employees, and family members are continually confronted with financial problems or issues that need attention. Knowledge of how to correctly evaluate alternatives is therefore of utmost importance in any attempts made to improve financial position and well-being.

## General Approach to Decision Making

OBJECTIVE 1
Understand the effect of relevant costs and sunk costs on decision making.

Over time, management is faced with a number of different decisions. Certain decisions, such as the selection of a supplier for raw materials, are fairly routine; others occur with less regularity and are relatively complex (e.g., the addition or deletion of a product line). Some decisions affect only current operations, while others will have a significant impact for years to come. No matter what the decision, cost is bound to be a major factor. Stated simply, the costs related to one course of action must be compared against those of alternative strategies and policies.

Because of the variety inherent in the decision process, a general approach to decision making is extremely useful. The general approach first involves the identification of future costs, specifically, those associated with the decision at hand. To

**Exhibit 27-1**
**Recent Business Decisions**

| *Corporation* | *Decision* |
|---|---|
| Consolidated Freightways | To purchase eight DC-8 cargo jets |
| Bristol-Myers | To introduce Tri-Buffered Bufferin |
| Campbell Soup | To acquire a new product line: "Marie's" salad dressings |
| Paramount Communications | To sell its financial services subsidiary |
| Compaq Computer | To build additional manufacturing facilities in Houston and Scotland |
| The Limited | To open 311 new stores and close 50 under-performing stores |
| Monsanto | To undertake an informational campaign in Brazil through The NutraSweet Company |

illustrate, assume that management is studying whether to replace an existing machine with a newer, more efficient model. Expected future costs must be evaluated, because these amounts will be the only ones incurred as a result of making the decision. Past historical costs may serve as a basis for predicting what the future costs will be, but *old costs are just memories and are not considered in the selection of alternatives.*

The next step in the general approach is to focus on **relevant costs,** or future costs that differ among alternative courses of action. In the replacement decision just cited, for example, any differences in maintenance costs between the old machine and the new machine are relevant and must be considered. Future costs that are identical for both pieces of equipment can be ignored, as such amounts have no impact on the ultimate selection.

## Full Project or Incremental Approach?

Relevant costs can be studied by using either a full project or an incremental approach. As an example, assume that Merchants Company must make a delivery 150 miles from its warehouse (300 miles for a round trip). Two trucks are available: A and B. Truck A gets 10 miles per gallon and consumes one quart of oil every 100 miles. Truck B gets 7.5 miles per gallon and uses one quart of oil every 150 miles. Other data are as follows:

| | |
|---|---|
| Gasoline | $0.90 per gallon |
| Oil | $1.00 per quart |
| Driver's wage | $6.00 per hour |
| Trip time | 8 hours |
| Road tolls | $10.00 |

The costs of operating the two trucks are shown below.

| | *Truck A* | *Truck B* | *Difference* |
|---|---|---|---|
| Gasoline* | $27 | $36 | $ 9 |
| Oil† | 3 | 2 | (1) |
| Driver's wage (8 hours × $6) | 48 | 48 | – |
| Tolls | 10 | 10 | – |
| Total cost | $88 | $96 | $ 8 |

* Truck A: [(300 miles ÷ 10 miles per gallon) × $0.90] = $27.
Truck B: [(300 miles ÷ 7.5 miles per gallon) × $0.90] = $36.

† Truck A: [(300 miles ÷ 100 miles per quart) × $1] = $3.
Truck B: [(300 miles ÷ 150 miles per quart) × $1] = $2.

On the basis of the expected costs of delivery, the company should use truck A. Notice that the driver's wage and road tolls are the same for both vehicles, making these two items "nonfactors" in the selection process. Given this situation, the proper approach would have been to focus solely on the costs of gasoline and oil. These costs are relevant because they will be incurred in the future and will differ between the trucks.

Using the **full project approach,** management would compare $30 against $38 (gasoline + oil cost) to make the proper decision. Specifically, the total relevant costs associated with each alternative are evaluated. Conversely, with the **incremental approach,** only the net differences are considered. Management would therefore focus its attention on the $8 variation that appears in the right-hand column, which favors vehicle A.[1]

Although the incremental approach is often used in practice, it has two serious drawbacks. The method is cumbersome when more than two alternatives are being evaluated, and the act of netting often leads to mathematical errors. For these reasons we will stress the full project approach throughout the remainder of this chapter.

## Decision Making: An Emphasis on the Future

Observe that the thrust of decision making is a focus on the future. Let us expand on this idea by concentrating on a problem faced by Malibu Construction, a builder of custom homes in southern California. Recently, the company agreed to build a spacious estate for a valued customer. Work on the project began several months ago and is nearing completion. Most of the remaining work involves optional decorative accessories, landscaping, and the construction of a swimming pool and a tennis court. To date, Malibu has spent $650,000 on the project in the form of materials, labor, and overhead. Much to the dismay of management, the customer has just declared bankruptcy and must back out of the contract.

A thorough study of available alternatives was performed and two courses of action have been identified:

1 Sell the unfinished residence as is for $610,000.

2 Make several design changes at a cost of $80,000 and complete the project. The company has found a buyer who is willing to pay $700,000 for the home if the changes are made.

Interestingly, a conventional "income statement" analysis reveals the undesirability of both alternatives. As the following figures show, losses will be incurred regardless of the selected option:

| | *Sell As Is* | | *Redesign* | |
|---|---|---|---|---|
| Revenue | | $610,000 | | $700,000 |
| Costs | | | | |
| Existing | $650,000 | | $650,000 | |
| Additional | — | 650,000 | 80,000 | 730,000 |
| Loss | | $ (40,000) | | $ (30,000) |

Malibu's president, obviously displeased, was overheard saying: "We've already got $650,000 in this venture; incurring a loss on top of all this would be foolish."

### The Concept of Sunk Cost

A careful inspection of the preceding figures will reveal inconsistency with the general approach to decision making that was illustrated earlier. Notice that the existing cost of $650,000 is common to both alternatives and, therefore, should have no effect on the eventual selection.

[1] Costs that differ among alternatives are sometimes called **differential costs.**

More important, however, this amount is properly considered a **sunk cost**—a past cost that has already been incurred. Regardless of whether Malibu sells the residence as is or pursues the redesign option, the existing costs are like "water under the bridge" and cannot be changed by management's actions, both present and future. *Sunk costs are thus an irrelevant consideration in decision making.*

How, then, should the evaluation be made? A more appropriate analysis would be as follows:

| | *Sell As Is* | *Redesign* |
|---|---|---|
| Revenue | $610,000 | $700,000 |
| Additional future costs | — | 80,000 |
| Net benefit from sale | $610,000 | $620,000 |

With a focus on future revenues and costs that differ among the alternatives (i.e., those that are *relevant*), the analysis reveals that Malibu should spend $80,000 for the redesign work and then sell the estate for $700,000. In comparison with the "as is" sale, the company will be better off by $10,000 ($620,000 − $610,000).

## Qualitative Factors

In addition to quantitative considerations, various qualitative factors must be addressed in the decision-making process. **Qualitative factors** are those whose evaluation in terms of dollars is impossible, or at best, difficult. As an example, the manager in the Merchants Company truck illustration may decide to send truck B on the delivery because the vehicle is brand new and customer impressions are important. Or, in another situation, machine operators may rebel if given no say in the proposed acquisition of new equipment. Such action would be detrimental to the firm and could lead to low morale and decreased productivity.

The preceding factors, although not quantifiable, can be important and should not be disregarded. Quite honestly, however, most business decisions are based primarily on dollars. Qualitative issues are perhaps most significant when the mathematical difference between alternatives is small and management is in need of a "tie breaker."

## A Summary of the Decision-Making Approach

The general approach to decision making can be summarized as follows:

1. Identify each alternative and examine the future costs and revenues.
2. Disregard items that are the same among the alternatives.
3. Identify and consider the qualitative factors.
4. Make a decision after a thorough study of both the quantitative analysis and the related qualitative concerns.

These steps can be applied to many different decision-making areas. The next few sections of the chapter will explore several of these areas, including make or buy decisions, special order pricing, and the addition or deletion of products or departments.

HIGHLIGHT

## Good Decisions = High Earnings + Green Stuff

Tadd Seitz still remembers the apprehension that gripped him when Martin Dubilier showed up. Mr. Seitz ran a profitable ITT Corp. division that made lawn fertilizer and grass seed: O. M. Scott & Sons. ITT wanted to sell Scott in late 1986, and Mr. Dubilier's firm was about to acquire it. "Your standards are going to change drastically," Mr. Seitz remembers the blunt New York financier warning him over dinner. Overhead costs were too high, inventories were too big, and management was too relaxed about winning new customers, Mr. Dubilier complained. "If you don't think you're the guy to solve this, let me know, and we'll get someone else," he added. At their first dinner, Mr. Seitz, a likable 47-year-old, could have been offended by Mr. Dubilier's regimen. But instead, he was won over. "Martin made a lot of good suggestions," he recalls.

Dubilier's firm bought Scott for $211 million. Lenders provided $191 million of funding; only the final $20 million came from Scott's new owners—mostly Dubilier's company and also Scott's top executives. "We didn't have a whole lot of margin for error," Scott's financial vice president recalls. He ordered accountants to tell him the company's cash position each day at 8 a.m. so that he could be sure that Scott was not running low. That hadn't ever mattered when Scott was part of ITT; it could always get an intracompany loan. Now, Scott faced annual interest bills of about $20 million—and no one was about to give it more credit.

How do you survive in such a situation? It's called one good decision after another. Scott acted quickly. It sold off a related seed company, Burpee, within four months. ITT once thought Burpee and Scott would be a good fit, but Dubilier wanted cash fast. To raise even more funds, Scott next started slashing inventory. It stepped up a $4-a-bag rebate program to empty out a warehouse full of Turf Builder fertilizer. It unloaded obsolete sprinklers by slashing prices. Scott also made plans to close some production lines in the slow summer season and then hired temporary workers—at about $4 an hour less than regular wages—to deliver peak output in the fall.

The company also worked out better terms with suppliers. Under ITT, Scott had spread its orders among three suppliers. Now, it went to one and offered it more business if Scott could buy in the fall and winter and pay only after the fertilizer was sold in the spring. The supplier reluctantly agreed. To further strengthen its earnings, Scott didn't touch its $4 million research budget. It didn't cut charitable contributions. But it leaned hard in other areas. Employees were cut to 782 from 828, mostly through attrition. The computer department was told to stop adding staff, even though the data load was rising. And temporarily idle secretaries were sent to fill in as order clerks during peak seasons.

The result? Scott finished its first year under new ownership with a flourish. The company had reduced bank debt by $41 million; earnings before interest, taxes, and depreciation rose 30%; and working capital declined by $15 million—in this case a sign that cash was being used better. Mr. Seitz earned $378,000 for the year, well above his $220,000 base salary. Other officials reaped bonuses running from 20% to 50% of their pay. Good decisions obviously played a key role. As an ex-ITT employee notes, "ITT got a good price," and a lot of the changes at Scott "couldn't have happened any other way" except under the Dubilier acquisition.

SOURCE: Adapted from "Leveraged Buy-Outs Make Some Companies Tougher Competitors," *The Wall Street Journal*, September 15, 1988, pp. 1, 18. Reprinted by permission of *The Wall Street Journal*, 

## Make or Buy Decisions

OBJECTIVE 2
Know how to evaluate different decision situations (e.g., make or buy).

Manufacturing firms often purchase needed parts for their operations from outside suppliers. For example, Ford and McDonnell Douglas contract other companies to make many of the components used in their cars and planes.[2] Even Burger King acquires its hamburger meat from outsiders. Interestingly, many of the firms that rely on external sources of supply have the technical abilities to produce the needed parts and materials themselves. Apparently, an analysis has deemed the purchase alternative preferable.

The choice to produce internally or to rely on external suppliers is commonly known as a *make or buy* decision. To illustrate the proper approach to follow in this decision situation, assume that Crane Company, a manufacturer of mopeds, is now producing all of its own motors. As shown in the following analysis, the motors cost $75 each, based on an output of 10,000 units per year.

| | *10,000 Motors* | *Per Motor* |
|---|---|---|
| Direct materials | $180,000 | $18 |
| Direct labor | 390,000 | 39 |
| Variable factory overhead | 100,000 | 10 |
| Fixed factory overhead* | 80,000 | 8 |
| Total cost | $750,000 | $75 |

* Allocated on the basis of capacity used.

Crane has solicited an offer from an external supplier to provide 10,000 motors at a set price of $72 each. To determine whether the motors should be manufactured internally or purchased externally, management must isolate the relevant costs. Future costs that differ between the make and buy alternatives must be studied; sunk costs, on the other hand, should be ignored.

In reviewing the previous information, we see that motor production was charged with $670,000 of variable costs, specifically, direct materials, direct labor, and variable factory overhead. Being variable, these costs will be eliminated if the motors are acquired from an outside supplier. The variable costs are thus relevant in an analysis of the make and buy alternatives. Turning to the fixed costs, Crane has allocated $80,000 of fixed factory overhead to motor production. In view of their fixed nature, these costs will be incurred even if the company decides in favor of an external purchase. As you already know, amounts that are the same among the alternatives can be disregarded.

### Avoidable Fixed Overhead

Frequently, when operations undergo a significant change, total fixed costs do not remain static. If manufacturing activities are discontinued, for example, it is con-

[2] The University of Michigan Office for the Study of Automotive Transportation recently reported the following sources of parts for the big three domestic auto producers:

| | *Manufacture Internally* | *External Purchase* |
|---|---|---|
| General Motors | 72% | 28% |
| Ford | 54 | 46 |
| Chrysler | 39 | 61 |

ceivable that a production supervisor would be dismissed and some equipment leases terminated. Naturally, any future fixed costs that change should be included in the analysis. In Crane's case, we assume that fixed factory overhead can be reduced by $20,000 if production is stopped.

The following analysis indicates that management should reject the supplier's offer, because there is a $30,000 advantage in favor of manufacturing internally.

| | *10,000 Motors* | |
|---|---|---|
| | ***Make*** | ***Buy*** |
| Purchase | | $720,000 |
| Direct materials | $180,000 | |
| Direct labor | 390,000 | |
| Variable factory overhead | 100,000 | |
| Avoidable fixed factory overhead | 20,000 | |
| Total cost | $690,000 | $720,000 |

$30,000 difference

The preceding evaluation is straightforward with the possible exception of the avoidable fixed overhead. Realize that Crane will incur $80,000 of fixed overhead if the motors are produced internally and $60,000 of fixed overhead if they are acquired from suppliers. Thus, $20,000 of fixed costs must be associated with the manufacturing option.

Looking at the analysis from a slightly different perspective, we observe a $20,000 savings in fixed costs if the purchase alternative is selected. Therefore the net cost of dealing with an outside supplier is $700,000 ($720,000 − $20,000). Manufacturing costs would now consist solely of variable items and would total $670,000, which still maintains the $30,000 difference in favor of production ($700,000 − $670,000 = $30,000).

## Qualitative Considerations

Given the quantitative outcome, we must also explore the qualitative factors that surround each alternative. In make or buy decisions, the decision to purchase externally means more dependence on suppliers and the attendant worry about product quality, strikes against suppliers, transportation strikes and hazards, personnel changes at suppliers' offices, and product discontinuance. To many companies, the quality concern alone would dictate rejection of the purchase alternative.

## Opportunity Cost

In performing a complete analysis of make versus buy, management must also evaluate alternative uses of manufacturing facilities. If, for example, a decision is made to acquire goods externally, the purchaser's factory and equipment may remain idle. On the other hand, such decisions frequently release facilities for use in other production applications. In the Crane Company illustration, for instance, suppose the resources committed to motor production could be redirected toward making a new line of golf carts. Naturally, any income from the golf cart line would be lost if the firm continues its motor operation.

The cost of a forgone alternative is termed **opportunity cost.** If the golf carts promise to generate a *contribution margin* (i.e., sales minus variable costs) of $75,000, the make or buy decision will assume the following form:

| | *Make* | *Buy* |
|---|---|---|
| Cost of buying | | $720,000 |
| Cost of making | $690,000 | |
| Forgone contribution on golf carts | 75,000 | |
| Total cost | $765,000 | $720,000 |

$45,000 difference

The analysis now shows that the company would benefit by $45,000 if it acquired the motors from the outside supplier. Explained differently, Crane is willing to pay an additional $30,000 per year to purchase the motors, in exchange for $75,000 of contribution margin provided by the golf carts. This decision, like the others, assumes that the appropriate qualitative considerations have been met.[3]

**TIPS & TECHNIQUES**

Be aware that opportunity costs are not restricted to make or buy decisions. Such amounts arise in many different settings (e.g., the evaluation of competing job offers) and must be considered if the proper alternative is to be selected. Despite their importance, opportunity costs are *not* entered in the accounting records nor do they appear on a company's financial statements. Financial accounting reports transactions and events that have occurred, not those that have been rejected.

## Special Order Pricing

The pricing of special orders is another decision faced by many firms. Although businesses prefer to sell their products at the highest prices possible, economic conditions sometimes dictate otherwise. Various situations may arise where special orders are considered at prices that are less than optimum. In an effort to reach the proper decision, management must again focus on the differential (or incremental) costs and revenues involved.

As an example, assume that Smithfield Bicycle Company received an inquiry from a large national retailer to provide 20,000 R-18 racing bicycles at a price of $77 each. The bicycles will be marketed under the retailer's brand name. Although Smithfield has sufficient (idle) manufacturing capacity, management is reluctant to accept the order because the price is well below the company's normal selling price of $119. The costs that follow pertain to the R-18 bicycle.

[3] The same analysis in another format would show the net cost of buying to be $645,000 ($720,000 purchase cost − $75,000 contribution generated). The decision maker would then compare $645,000 against $690,000, still noting a $45,000 advantage in favor of the buy alternative.

| | |
|---|---|
| Materials | $ 42.80 |
| Labor | 24.50 |
| Factory overhead* | 24.70 |
| Variable selling costs | 10.00 |
| Total | $102.00 |

* Eighty percent of the factory overhead represents fixed cost.

At first glance it appears that the retailer's offer should be rejected because of a failure to cover the $102 total cost. However, further investigation reveals that variable selling costs will not be incurred on the order. Furthermore, in view of the fact that Smithfield presently has idle facilities, total fixed costs are not expected to change. As a result, 80% of the factory overhead ($24.70 × 0.80 = $19.76) will be present even if the offer is refused and can be disregarded. The following analysis shows that Smithfield would benefit by doing business with the retailer:

| | | |
|---|---|---|
| Special selling price | | $77.00 |
| Less variable costs | | |
| Materials | $42.80 | |
| Labor | 24.50 | |
| Variable factory overhead ($24.70 − $19.76) | 4.94 | 72.24 |
| Contribution margin per bicycle | | $ 4.76 |

Recall from Chapter 25 that the contribution margin is the amount that each unit generates toward covering fixed costs and producing net income. Given the preceding figures, acceptance of the special order will result in an overall profitability boost of $95,200 (20,000 bicycles × $4.76). Although each unit yields less than the normal R-18 sale, Smithfield has machines and other productive resources already in place that are not being used to the fullest extent possible. Thus, some extra business is really "icing on the cake."

Several qualitative considerations must be addressed in this decision, including the following:

- Will there be a decrease in sales of Smithfield's own brand of R-18 bicycle?
- Are future orders from the retailer likely?
- Will plant capacity devoted to the special order soon be needed for Smithfield's regular production activity?

## Contribution Margin in Relation to Capacity

OBJECTIVE 3
Know why the contribution margin must be analyzed in terms of capacity constraints.

In addition to the special order situation, managers frequently study contribution margins when dealing with capacity constraints. Consider a multiple-product firm, for example, that is operating at capacity. The firm must evaluate which orders to accept and which to reject, which products to promote and which to de-emphasize, and other similar issues. The goal is to maximize contribution margin of the entire business, not just of one small facet. A common error in pursuing this goal is that given the resources available, items with the highest contribution margin per sales dollar are considered to be the most attractive.

To illustrate, assume that Beltline Manufacturing produces two models of computer furniture: Deluxe and Regular. The following information has been gathered:

| | *Deluxe* | *Regular* |
|---|---|---|
| Selling price | $120 | $110 |
| Variable cost | 60 | 66 |
| Contribution margin | $ 60 | $ 44 |
| Contribution margin ratio (contribution margin ÷ selling price) | 50% | 40% |

It appears that the company should concentrate its activity on the Deluxe model. Before we decide for certain, however, let us introduce some additional information. Suppose the furniture is extremely popular, with demand far exceeding the company's production capabilities. Further, it takes three hours to produce a Deluxe model and two hours to manufacture a Regular model. If only 30,000 labor hours are available during the period, Beltline would be better off to focus its efforts on the Regular model because of a higher payoff *per labor hour.*

| | *Deluxe* | *Regular* |
|---|---|---|
| Contribution margin per labor hour | | |
| Deluxe: $60 ÷ 3 hours | $20 | |
| Regular: $44 ÷ 2 hours | | $22 |
| Available labor hours | 30,000 | 30,000 |
| Contribution margin per labor hour | × $20 | × $22 |
| Total contribution margin | $600,000 | $660,000 |

The analysis shows that the Regular model provides the greatest total contribution given the firm's limited manufacturing resources. It should now be apparent that when a firm is operating at capacity, management may be in error by emphasizing products or services that provide the greatest contribution per unit or per sales dollar. Stated simply, *contribution margin must be analyzed in terms of factors that limit its generation.*

Limiting factors assume many different forms, depending on the type of business. In heavily automated manufacturing companies, for example, the limiting factor is often the machine hours available for production. In entertainment situations it is the number of seats in a theater or an arena. Finally, in retail operations it is floor space.

The limiting-factor (i.e., floor space) problem is particularly acute for supermarkets and drugstores where, in a recent year alone, some 12,000 new items were introduced to the marketplace. These entities have found themselves in the business of managing increasingly valuable in-store real estate to an extent never imagined. Adding further complications, their customers want one-stop shopping, which can mean putting in a deli, bakery, salad bar, flower stand, and even a videotape department. Such actions generally result in stocking fewer brands of corn flakes or soft drinks to make room for potted chrysanthemums and three varieties of croissants. Notes an executive, "Retailers are constantly asking whether each category needs as much space as it's got. Are the sizes too large? Can I make more money with something else?"[4]

[4] Part of this discussion is based on "Profit by the Square Foot," *Forbes,* November 28, 1988, p. 248.

## Addition or Deletion of Products or Departments

Decisions to add or delete products, departments, and other major operating units (e.g., stores, plants, or divisions) are critical. Any errors that are made can normally be corrected only after suffering years of financial strife. In-depth analysis is therefore of utmost importance.

When a business unit is eliminated, the unit's sales are lost and there is a savings in variable costs. As a result, if a positive contribution margin is being generated and the unit is discontinued, overall profitability will suffer. One additional factor must be considered, however, and that is the behavior of fixed costs. As we noted earlier in the chapter, a significant change in operations will often influence the amount of fixed costs incurred by an enterprise. If a department or segment is eliminated, some fixed costs can normally be avoided. Those costs that can be avoided are really differential costs and, therefore, relevant to the decision.

To illustrate addition and deletion decisions, we will study the operations of Foodway, Inc., which owns a chain of supermarkets. Each Foodway store has four major departments: groceries, meat, produce, and hardware. Earnings data for store no. 175 during the past year are shown in Exhibit 27-2. On the basis of the reported $1.1 million loss, management believes that total profitability will increase if the hardware department is closed. A deeper probe of the figures and overall operation is needed, though, prior to any action being taken.

If customers remain loyal and sales in the other departments are not affected by the discontinuance of hardware, Foodway's profit will immediately decline by $1 million because of the loss in contribution margin. Notice, though, that the hardware department has four types of fixed costs: salaries, utilities, depreciation, and general and administrative. Specific information about these costs follows.

1 The salaries represent amounts paid to employees who work in the department. If hardware is dropped, employees who earn 40% of the salary amounts will be shifted to other areas; all other personnel in hardware will be discharged.

2 Utilities expense is allocated to each department on the basis of square feet. Total utilities cost is not expected to change significantly if the hardware operation is closed.

3 Depreciation relates to the building and also to the fixtures used in each department. If hardware is eliminated, the department's display racks and equipment

**Exhibit 27-2**
**Foodway, Inc., Store no. 175: Departmental Income Statements**

| | *Groceries* | *Meat* | *Produce* | *Hardware* | *Total* |
|---|---|---|---|---|---|
| Sales | $42,000,000 | $14,000,000 | $7,000,000 | $ 7,000,000 | $70,000,000 |
| Less variable costs | 33,000,000 | 9,000,000 | 4,000,000 | 6,000,000 | 52,000,000 |
| Contribution margin | $ 9,000,000 | $ 5,000,000 | $3,000,000 | $ 1,000,000 | $18,000,000 |
| Less fixed costs | | | | | |
| Salaries | $ 2,000,000 | $ 2,500,000 | $1,900,000 | $ 1,100,000 | $ 7,500,000 |
| Utilities | 400,000 | 50,000 | 100,000 | 150,000 | 700,000 |
| Depreciation | 100,000 | 50,000 | 100,000 | 50,000 | 300,000 |
| General & administrative | 4,800,000 | 1,600,000 | 800,000 | 800,000 | 8,000,000 |
| Total fixed costs | $ 7,300,000 | $ 4,200,000 | $2,900,000 | $ 2,100,000 | $16,500,000 |
| Net income (loss) | $ 1,700,000 | $ 800,000 | $ 100,000 | $(1,100,000) | $ 1,500,000 |

will be utilized by other segments of the firm. Again, total cost is not expected to change.

**4** General and administrative charges represent the costs of functions common to all departments, including purchasing, accounting, and personnel. These costs, allocated to each department on the basis of sales, will be reduced by $120,000 because of employee terminations.

In view of this information, the following analysis can be made:

| | | |
|---|---|---|
| Contribution margin lost if hardware is dropped | | $1,000,000 |
| Less avoidable costs | | |
| Salaries ($1,100,000 × 60%) | $660,000 | |
| General & administrative | 120,000 | 780,000 |
| Decrease in total company profit | | $ 220,000 |

Although hardware's present bottom line indicates a loss of $1.1 million, it is still beneficial to retain the department, because the contribution produced is greater than the avoidable costs.

If desired, the same conclusion could have been reached by using an evaluation of Foodway's earnings with and without the hardware department:

| | *With Hardware* | *Without Hardware* |
|---|---|---|
| Sales | $70,000,000 | $63,000,000 |
| Less variable costs | 52,000,000 | 46,000,000 |
| Contribution margin | $18,000,000 | $17,000,000 |
| Less fixed costs | | |
| Salaries | $ 7,500,000 | $ 6,840,000 |
| Utilities* | 700,000 | 700,000 |
| Depreciation* | 300,000 | 300,000 |
| General & administrative | 8,000,000 | 7,880,000 |
| Total fixed costs | $16,500,000 | $15,720,000 |
| Net income (loss) | $ 1,500,000 | $ 1,280,000 |

→ $220,000 difference ←

* These amounts are actually irrelevant to the decision and could have been omitted from the analysis.

## Improvements in Performance Reporting

OBJECTIVE 4
Be able to distinguish between direct costs and indirect costs.

The departmental income statements prepared for Foodway, Inc., are fairly traditional in scope and format. By a slight restructuring of the data, it is possible to significantly improve the statements' usefulness in performance evaluation and decision making. Before we explain the underlying procedures, it is necessary to first introduce a cost classification scheme that is based on traceability.

Many costs within an organization are easily traced to and associated with a business segment, while other costs are not. Amounts that fall in the first category are called **direct costs;** those in the latter classification are **indirect costs.** A business segment normally refers to a responsibility center of the firm, such as a territory, division, department, and so on.

Because a segment can be defined in different ways, a given cost may be direct with respect to certain segments and indirect with respect to others.[5] In the Foodway example, for instance, utilities expense was easily traced to store no. 175. However, it was an entirely different story when the store tried to associate the expense with smaller segments—in this case, departments. Traceability was much more difficult, leading management to adopt cost allocation procedures. Total utilities expense was related to the total square feet in the store, yielding a cost per square foot. Each department was then charged an appropriate amount, based on the area occupied.

## Cost Allocations

Companies have adopted a variety of allocation procedures that range from the simple to the complex. The reason normally advanced for such procedures is that indirect costs are incurred to benefit multiple responsibility centers (e.g., departments). As such, each center should absorb its "fair share" of the expenditures.

Although this argument is sound, most accountants recognize that cost allocations have two serious deficiencies. First, as you saw earlier in the text with depreciation, the same cost can be allocated in several different ways. At best, then, allocations are arbitrary. A given allocation method is generally viewed as adequate or inadequate by a responsibility center, depending on the amount charged. Large cost allocations are branded as unfair; small cost allocations, on the other hand, receive few complaints. Turning to the second deficiency, the total cost to be allocated normally results from the decisions of other managers in the organizational hierarchy. Thus, to a large degree, the amount of cost charged to a center is beyond the center's control.

## Contribution Income Statement

OBJECTIVE 5
Know how to prepare and use a contribution income statement.

It appears that when costs are allocated to business segments, the final income figure does not always present a clear measure of the segment's operating results. In recognition of this fact, accountants have developed the **contribution income statement.** This statement provides top management with an understanding of how individual responsibility centers affect total firm profitability and serves as a useful tool in performance evaluation and decision making. Consistent with responsibility accounting, the statement incorporates the following features:

1 The contribution margin is disclosed.
2 Fixed costs directly identifiable with a segment are divided into two classifications: controllable and uncontrollable.
3 Allocations of nontraceable costs are disregarded.[6]

To illustrate the contribution income statement, we will study EXOIL Corporation. EXOIL is divided into two divisions: Refining and Retailing. Retailing, in turn, has two major product lines: Parts and Fluids. Exhibit 27-3 contains the firm's contribution statements. The top half of the exhibit shows EXOIL's divisional operations; the bottom half displays Retailing's product lines.

[5] The classification of costs into direct and indirect categories was first discussed in Chapter 22, where the term "segment" represented individual jobs in a job costing system.

[6] Although departmental contributions are disclosed, Exhibit 27-2 falls short of being a "true" contribution margin income statement. The upcoming discussion should substantiate this point.

**Exhibit 27-3**
**EXOIL Corporation Contribution Income Statements (in thousands)**

| | Total Company | Divisions: Refining | Divisions: Retailing |
|---|---|---|---|
| Net sales | $3,000 | $2,080 | $920 |
| Less variable costs | | | |
| Cost of goods sold | $2,000 | $1,390 | $610 |
| Variable selling & administrative expense | 240 | 85 | 155 |
| Total variable costs | $2,240 | $1,475 | $765 |
| Contribution margin | $ 760 | $ 605 | $155 |
| Less controllable fixed costs | 290 | 225 | 65 |
| Controllable contribution margin | $ 470 | $ 380 | $ 90 |
| Less uncontrollable fixed costs | 210 | 168 | 42 |
| Segment margin | $ 260 | $ 212 | $ 48 |
| Less nontraceable costs | 115 | | |
| Net income | $ 145 | | |

| | Retailing Division | Product Lines: Parts | Product Lines: Fluids | Non-traceable Costs |
|---|---|---|---|---|
| Net sales | $920 | $645 | $275 | |
| Less variable costs | | | | |
| Cost of goods sold | $610 | $440 | $170 | |
| Variable selling & administrative expense | 155 | 100 | 55 | |
| Total variable costs | $765 | $540 | $225 | |
| Contribution margin | $155 | $105 | $ 50 | |
| Less controllable fixed costs | 65 | 30 | 10 | $ 25 |
| Controllable contribution margin | $ 90 | $ 75 | $ 40 | $(25) |
| Less uncontrollable fixed costs | 42 | 13 | 7 | 22 |
| Segment margin | $ 48 | $ 62 | $ 33 | $(47) |

The contribution statement begins with a display of a segment's contribution margin, that is, sales minus variable costs. Variable costs are considered to be controllable by (and traceable to) responsibility centers because the costs vary with center activity. The calculation of the contribution margin is helpful not only for performance evaluation but also for cost-volume-profit (CVP) analysis, such as determination of the break-even point.

***Controllable Contribution Margin*** Next, the **controllable contribution margin** is computed by subtracting fixed costs that are both controllable by the segment's management *and* directly traceable to the segment. Such costs are normally discretionary fixed costs (i.e., those that arise from management's decision-making process) and include certain supervisory salaries, local sales promotion costs, and outlays for research and development activities.

The controllable contribution margin is often considered the heart of the entire statement. This important measure represents the contribution to profit that is under the direction of the responsibility center manager and is probably the best overall indicator of a manager's performance.

***Segment Margin*** The controllable contribution margin minus uncontrollable fixed costs yields the **segment margin.** The uncontrollable costs used in this calculation are incurred for the benefit of a specific responsibility center but are only minimally affected by the center's management during the reporting period. Typical examples of such costs include committed costs (such as property taxes and depreciation on factory buildings) and costs that result from decisions made at higher levels in the organizational structure (e.g., the salary of the center's manager).

The segment margin shows the contribution of each responsibility center to company income after considering all traceable costs. Many accountants feel the segment margin is a good indicator of ongoing profitability because a center's entire fixed cost obligation is considered in the computation.

***Controllable Margin Versus Segment Margin*** Beginning accounting students often see little difference between the controllable contribution margin and the segment margin. Actually, these two performance measures serve distinctly different purposes. To explain, outstanding managers are frequently transferred to weak divisions to improve operations. Would you accept such an assignment if the company evaluated personnel and awarded bonuses on the basis of the "bottom line," namely, the segment margin? Probably not. No matter how hard you try, many uncontrollable factors would influence your performance appraisal. In addition, if the division was extremely weak, a heroic effort would be needed to show significant improvement in overall profitability. Thus, two performance measures are utilized. The controllable contribution margin is used for personnel evaluations, such as raises, promotions, and so forth. The segment margin, in contrast, is employed in exploring the long-run advisability of keeping a segment as an operating center of the business.

***Nontraceable Costs*** As we noted, the contribution approach disregards allocations of indirect costs. By studying the top half of Exhibit 27-3, for example, you will notice that EXOIL incurred $115,000 of nontraceable costs; yet not a single penny was charged against the segment margins of Refining and Retailing via allocations. These costs could represent corporate administrative overhead incurred by the firm as a whole and not readily identifiable with either of the divisions.

In a similar manner, the bottom half of the exhibit reveals that Retailing's divisional manager had control over $65,000 of fixed costs. However, when the division was further segmented by product line, only $40,000 ($30,000 + $10,000) could be traced to Parts and Fluids. The remaining $25,000 was incurred jointly by the two product lines, making traceability difficult. As an example, the Retailing division may have employed an office manager who handled clerical work that related to both areas of activity. Once again, no attempt is made to charge indirect cost to segments; to do so would result in arbitrary, noncontrollable allocations.

## Direct and Absorption Costing

**OBJECTIVE 6**
**Be familiar with the features of direct (variable) costing and absorption costing.**

By viewing Exhibit 27-3, you will notice that (1) cost of goods sold is included under the variable cost caption and (2) fixed costs are written off entirely in the current reporting period. This accounting treatment appears to contradict the material introduced in Chapters 21 and 22. Specifically, both variable *and* fixed overhead were included in the cost of a manufactured product and thus incorporated into the cost-of-goods-sold calculation.

Over the years, two product costing methods have evolved: absorption costing and direct costing. The more traditional approach (and that illustrated in earlier chapters) is full or **absorption costing.** Under absorption costing, all manufacturing costs are considered product costs and are included in the valuation of inventory.

An alternate approach is the **direct costing** method. Direct costing is more accurately called **variable costing,** because only variable manufacturing costs (direct materials, direct labor, and variable factory overhead) are assigned to products. Fixed manufacturing costs are regarded as period costs and charged against revenues when incurred.

### Fixed Manufacturing Overhead: The Key Difference

Observe that the treatment of fixed manufacturing overhead is the basic difference between direct and absorption costing. Companies that employ absorption costing place fixed overhead in inventory on the balance sheet. At the time of sale, product cost (including fixed overhead) is transferred from the balance sheet to the income statement via cost of goods sold. Firms that use direct costing, on the other hand, write off fixed manufacturing overhead immediately. This difference in timing is depicted in Exhibit 27-4.

### A Basic Illustration

To illustrate the procedures that accompany these two methods, examine the following information, which was obtained from the records of the Harris Corporation for the year ended December 31, 19X4.

Sales: 9,500 units at $9
Selling and administrative costs: fixed, $5,000; variable, $2 per unit
Variable production costs per unit:

| | |
|---|---|
| Direct materials | $1.00 |
| Direct labor | 1.50 |
| Variable factory overhead | 0.50 |
| Total | $3.00 |

Fixed factory overhead: $10,000
Production: 10,000 units

Under absorption costing the unit product cost is $4.00:

| | |
|---|---|
| Variable production costs | $3.00 |
| Fixed factory overhead ($10,000 ÷ 10,000 units produced) | 1.00 |
| Total | $4.00 |

**Exhibit 27-4**
**Comparison of Absorption Costing and Direct Costing**

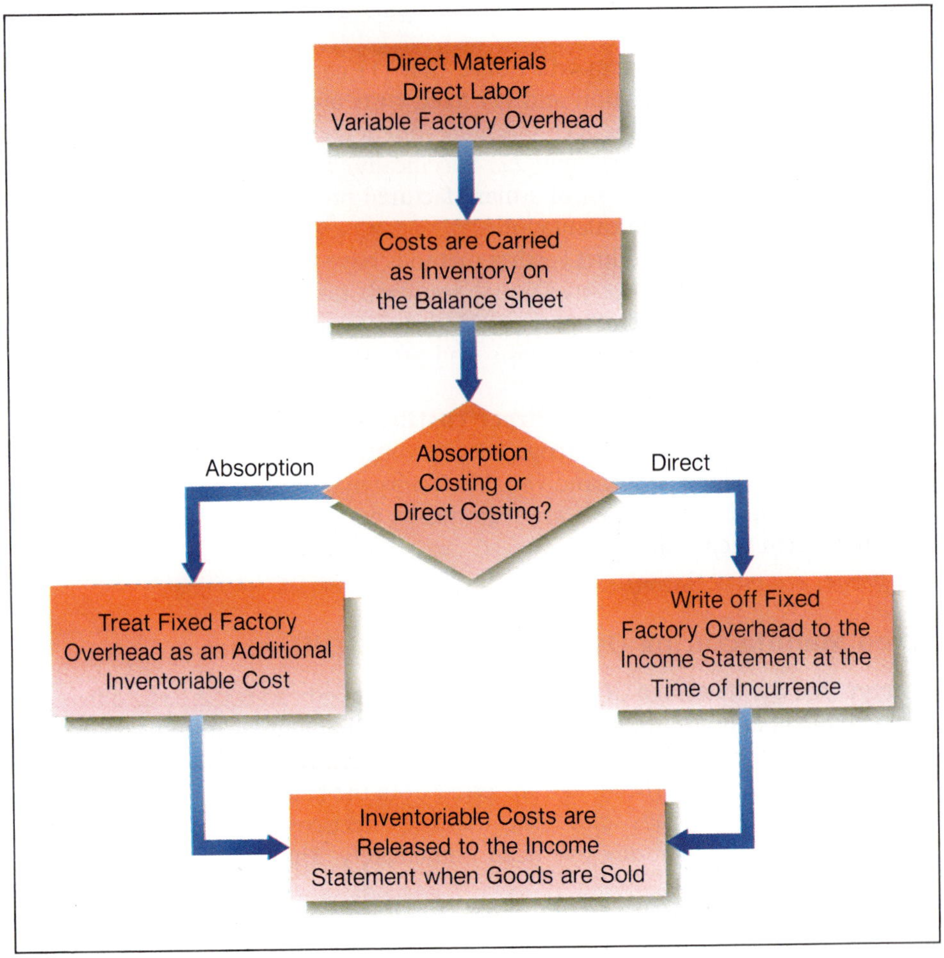


With direct costing the product cost per unit drops to $3.00, because only variable production costs are inventoried. Remember from previous chapters that selling and administrative costs are never attached to manufactured units; these amounts are treated as expenses of the period.

Given the preceding calculations, the company's income statements under both absorption costing and direct costing appear as shown in Exhibit 27-5. Two important observations should be made. First, notice the similarity between the direct costing income statement and the contribution approach shown earlier in the chapter. Direct costing produces a cost of goods sold that is comprised solely of variable costs, thereby giving management the ability to figure the contribution margin. In practice, the fixed costs that appear on the statement would be divided into two categories: those controllable by the segment manager and those that are uncontrollable.

Second, observe that a $500 difference arises between the two net income figures. Although both methods used the same data, keep the differing treatments of fixed manufacturing overhead in mind. Under direct costing, the entire pool of fixed production cost ($10,000) was deducted from current period revenues. With

**Exhibit 27-5**
**Absorption Costing and Direct Costing Income Statements**

**HARRIS CORPORATION**
**Absorption Costing Income Statement**
**For the Year Ended December 31, 19X4**

| | | |
|---|---|---|
| Sales (9,500 units × $9) | | $85,500 |
| Cost of goods sold (9,500 units × $4) | | 38,000 |
| Gross profit | | $47,500 |
| Less selling & administrative costs | | |
| Fixed | $ 5,000 | |
| Variable (9,500 units × $2) | 19,000 | 24,000 |
| Net income | | $23,500 |

**HARRIS CORPORATION**
**Direct Costing Income Statement**
**For the Year Ended December 31, 19X4**

| | | |
|---|---|---|
| Sales (9,500 units × $9) | | $85,500 |
| Less variable costs | | |
| Cost of goods sold (9,500 units × $3) | $28,500 | |
| Selling & administrative (9,500 units × $2) | 19,000 | 47,500 |
| Contribution margin | | $38,000 |
| Less fixed costs | | |
| Manufacturing | $10,000 | |
| Selling & administrative | 5,000 | 15,000 |
| Net income | | $23,000 |

the absorption approach, however, $1 of fixed overhead ($10,000 ÷ 10,000 units manufactured) was attached to each unit produced. Because Harris completed 10,000 units but sold only 9,500, the fixed overhead charges were actually divided as follows:

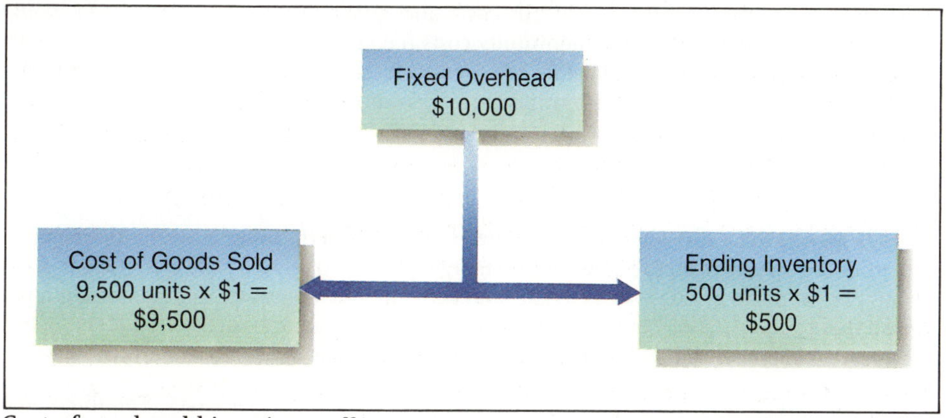


Cost of goods sold is written off in 19X4 and matched against sales. In contrast, the $500 of fixed overhead in ending inventory is carried as an asset on the balance sheet. The write-off of this latter amount is deferred until such time that the units are sold—probably 19X5. In sum, then, absorption costing would result in a higher income figure than direct costing because of the smaller charge against revenues ($9,500 vs. $10,000). The opposite situation would occur in those periods where the number of units sold exceeds the number of units produced.

### An Overview

Companies are free to use either of the preceding methods for internal reporting to management. Direct costing is generally preferred, however, because of its consistency with contribution reporting and the fact that the contribution margin is employed in performance evaluation and decision making—two internal, management functions. Additionally, direct costing usually results in a "cleaner" measure of income than absorption costing, with the bottom line influenced by changes in sales and not by changes in inventory levels.

Despite these attributes, direct costing cannot be used for external financial reporting. The absorption method's approach of inventorying fixed manufacturing costs normally yields a better match on the income statement. At the time of sale, fixed costs are released to the income statement (via cost of goods sold) and matched against the sales revenues that have just been realized. Direct costing, on the other hand, dictates that all fixed production costs be written off at the time of incurrence. This procedure thereby ignores the fact that future revenues may result from the expenditure (and the units manufactured).

## Chapter Review

### Learning Objectives—The Key Points

**1 Understand the effect of relevant costs and sunk costs on decision making.** Decision making is concerned with the future, as the past is history and cannot be changed. Thus, the focus is on relevant costs, or those future costs that differ among alternatives. Sunk costs, which are past costs that have already been incurred, are therefore ignored when reviewing possible options.

**2 Know how to evaluate different decision situations (e.g., make or buy).** The evaluation of decisions such as make or buy and the acceptance of special orders requires an identification of the associated relevant costs and qualitative factors. Such costs would normally include variable costs, opportunity costs (i.e., the benefits associated with forgone alternatives), and also any avoidable fixed costs. Both special orders and addition and deletion decisions focus on the contribution margin, or the amount that a unit contributes toward covering fixed costs and generating income. The unit in this case is an order or perhaps a department.

**3 Know why the contribution margin must be analyzed in terms of capacity constraints.** When a business is constrained in terms of performing its activities, management should not focus on the contribution margin per unit of product. Rather, the emphasis should be on those products or activities that generate the highest contribution margin per constraining factor (labor hour, machine hour, square foot, and so forth). By following this strategy, a company will make the most profitable use of its available resources.

**4 Be able to distinguish between direct costs and indirect costs.** The direct and indirect classification scheme deals with traceability. Direct costs are easily traced to a business segment, whereas indirect costs are not. A business segment may be defined in several different ways; for example, it may be a division, a department, or a product line. In an attempt to charge each segment with a fair share of the costs incurred, management often uses a chargeback procedure and allocates indirect costs to the units in question.

**5 Know how to prepare and use a contribution income statement.** A contribution income statement discloses a segment's contribution toward the overall profit of the firm. All variable and direct fixed costs are charged to the segment where incurred, with the latter costs often categorized in terms of the degree of control exercised by the segment manager. Most important, the contribution statement contains no arbitrary allocations of indirect costs.

The statement reveals three performance measures: the contribution margin (sales minus variable costs), the controllable contribution margin, and the segment margin. The second measure, calculated by subtracting controllable fixed costs from the contribution margin, focuses on the margin controllable by a manager and is often used in personnel decisions (raises, bonuses, and so forth). The segment margin, a good indicator of long-run profitability, is the result of subtracting a segment's uncontrollable fixed costs from the controllable contribution margin.

**6 Be familiar with the features of direct (variable) costing and absorption costing.** These two methods of inventory costing differ in their treatment of fixed factory overhead. Under absorption costing, a specified amount of fixed overhead is attached to each unit produced; in contrast, with direct (i.e., variable) costing, fixed manufacturing charges are written off to the income statement when incurred. Direct costing is consistent with the contribution income statement and is therefore preferred for internal reporting. For external financial reporting, however, absorption costing must be used.

## Chapter Quiz

The five questions that follow relate to several issues raised in the chapter. Test your knowledge of the issues by selecting the best answer. (The answers appear on p. 1008.)

**1** Which of the following statements is false?
- a Decision making focuses on future costs.
- b If a cost is identical for two alternatives under study, the cost can be ignored when making a decision.
- c Sunk costs are the key to decision making.
- d Fixed costs can be relevant when making a decision.

**2** Martin Company has idle capacity and is studying whether to accept a special order for 1,000 units of its sole product. The product normally sells for $20 and has related variable and fixed manufacturing costs of $12 and $4, respectively. If the special order is accepted at a price of $15 per unit, Martin's overall profitability will:
- a decrease by $1,000.
- b increase by $3,000.
- c increase by $11,000.
- d increase by $15,000.

**3** CEN Manufacturing has limited production time in its heavily automated factory. When determining which products to manufacture, management should study each product's:
- a contribution margin.
- b contribution margin ratio.
- c total cost.
- d contribution margin per machine hour.

**4** Contribution income statements:
- a disclose a segment's controllable contribution margin and the segment margin.
- b contain allocations of nontraceable costs.
- c make no distinction between direct costs and indirect costs.
- d charge only controllable costs to the segment in question.

5 A company that uses absorption costing procedures:
a is in violation of generally accepted accounting principles.
b attaches fixed manufacturing overhead to each unit produced.
c normally generates the same amount of net income that would be calculated by using direct costing.
d attaches a selected amount of the firm's total fixed costs (including selling and administrative) to each unit manufactured.

## Questions

**Q27-1** Discuss the general approach to decision making.

**Q27-2** Are all future costs relevant for decision-making purposes? Explain.

**Q27-3** An educator once commented, "Not all future costs are relevant to decisions, but costs are not relevant unless they occur in the future." Evaluate the educator's comment.

**Q27-4** What is meant by the term "sunk cost"?

**Q27-5** Fred Holtz recently experienced a $16,000 opportunity cost. Discuss the concept of an opportunity cost.

**Q27-6** The Crandall Corporation has been offered $34 per unit for a one-time special order. Variable cost and fixed cost per unit amount to $27 and $10, respectively. If Crandall has available facilities, should the order be accepted? Why?

**Q27-7** If a retailer has limited square footage in its store, what guideline should be used in deciding which new products to carry?

**Q27-8** Differentiate between a direct cost and an indirect cost. As segments become smaller and smaller, what generally happens to cost traceability?

**Q27-9** Should a departmental manager be held accountable for allocations of corporate overhead? Briefly discuss.

**Q27-10** What features are associated with a contribution margin income statement?

**Q27-11** Discuss the computations and meaning associated with the controllable contribution margin and the segment margin.

**Q27-12** Differentiate between direct costing and absorption costing.

**Q27-13** Creekside, Inc., began business on January 1 of the current year. The company produced 42,000 units but sold only 35,000 by December 31. Would direct costing net income be greater than absorption costing net income? Why?

**Q27-14** Can direct costing be used for internal reporting? For external financial reporting?

## Exercises

**E27-1** ***Relevant decision factors***

Consider the following:
a The cost of special electrical wiring in an equipment acquisition decision.
b The sales revenues generated with an existing machine, which are not expected to change, in deciding whether to keep or replace the machine.
c Avoidable fixed manufacturing overhead in a make-versus-buy decision.
d The salary cost of a production supervisor who is already on the payroll, in a special order acceptance decision.
e The direct materials cost in a make-versus-buy decision.
f Product development costs incurred several months ago, in a product-introduction decision.

g Alternative uses of your time, in a job acceptance decision.
h The cost of an old vehicle, in a keep-versus-disposal decision.
i Fixed corporate overhead, in the acceptance or rejection of a special order.

Evaluate each of the factors listed as being relevant or irrelevant to the decision situation noted. If the factor is irrelevant, briefly explain why.

**E27-2** ***Introductory decision making***

Metro Manufacturing recently produced 14,000 units at a cost of $18.40 per unit. The goods do not meet quality standards and can be sold as seconds to a discount chain for $14.75 each. Alternatively, Metro can reprocess the units at an additional cost of $5.60. The reprocessed units can then be sold for $21.00.

After evaluating the two alternatives, an assistant in the accounting department concluded: "We'd be better off to keep the units. We'll incur a loss no matter which alternative is selected."

a Show the computations that formed the basis for the assistant's remarks.
b Is the assistant's conclusion correct? Why?

**E27-3** ***Make or buy***

The Ranco Corporation makes small plastic cases with built-in mirrors for sale to cosmetics manufacturers. The company's production costs for an annual volume of 300,000 cases (including mirrors) follow.

| | |
|---|---|
| Direct materials | $ 45,000 |
| Direct labor | 18,000 |
| Variable factory overhead | 21,000 |
| Fixed factory overhead | 30,000 |
| | $114,000 |

Because of various problems, Ranco desires to discontinue the mirror production and purchase the mirror from East Coast Glass for $0.11. If Ranco does business with East Coast Glass, material, labor, and variable overhead costs will decline by 40%, 30%, and 20%, respectively.

a Should Ranco make or buy the mirror? Why?
b Assume that if the mirror is purchased, the mirror's production space will be leased to a small manufacturer for $1,300 per month. Discuss the proper treatment of this revenue and its impact on Ranco's make or buy decision. *Note:* The amount of fixed overhead incurred will remain constant.

**E27-4** ***Special order***

Springfield Corporation produces house paint and supplies and sells most of its paint through company-owned stores or franchises. A recent income statement of the latex division follows.

| | |
|---|---|
| Sales (400,000 gallons @ $7) | $2,800,000 |
| Cost of goods sold | 1,960,000 |
| Gross profit | $ 840,000 |
| Selling & administrative expenses (fixed) | 680,000 |
| Net income | $ 160,000 |

Fixed costs included in cost of goods sold total $336,000.

Bargain Barn, a discount chain, recently approached Springfield with a request to purchase 24,000 gallons of latex at $4.50 per gallon. Bargain Barn will attach its own label to the can and thereby prevent disclosure of the paint's manufacturer. Springfield presently has idle capacity and will experience no change in fixed costs as a result of accepting the order. Per-unit variable costs are expected to remain stable.

Should Springfield accept the special order? Why?

**E27-5** ***Analysis of special order***

William Row builds custom homes that range in price from $125,000 to $300,000. The price of a home is determined by summing the estimated costs of materials, labor, and overhead, and then adding 15% for a profit margin. As an example, a home designed for Mr. and Mrs. David Presley was priced as follows:

| | |
|---|---|
| Materials | $ 70,000 |
| Labor | 100,000 |
| Overhead (20% of labor) | 20,000 |
| | $190,000 |
| Profit—15% | 28,500 |
| Selling price | $218,500 |

Total overhead for the year has been estimated at $200,000, of which $120,000 is fixed and the remainder is variable in direct proportion to labor.

Business is currently very slow. The Presleys, feeling that the $218,500 price was too high, countered with an offer of $205,000.

a Determine the contribution margin on the home if Row accepted the Presleys' offer of $205,000.

b What is the minimum price that Row could have quoted without reducing or increasing his firm's net income?

**E27-6** ***Capacity constraint***

Moss Port Enterprises manufactures three products known as X, Y, and Z. Pertinent data about the products follow.

| | *X* | *Y* | *Z* |
|---|---|---|---|
| Selling price | $50 | $48 | $80 |
| Less variable costs | | | |
| Direct materials | $ 2 | $24 | $30 |
| Direct labor | 24 | 9 | 30 |
| Variable factory overhead | 8 | 3 | 10 |
| Total | $34 | $36 | $70 |
| Contribution margin | $16 | $12 | $10 |

Direct laborers are paid $6 per hour. The demand for these products is very strong; unfortunately, Moss Port has experienced a severe shortage of qualified workers. As a result, the company's labor force is working close to capacity and only 2,000 hours of labor time are available in the upcoming accounting period.

a Determine the amount of labor time needed to manufacture a single unit of X, Y, and Z.

b Does Moss Port face any constraints that limit the amount of contribution margin it can generate? If so, what strategy should the company follow when deciding which product to manufacture.

c Determine which product should be selected for manufacture in the upcoming accounting period.

**E27-7** ***Dropping a product***

Nelson Company manufactures three products. The following figures reveal that product B generated a net loss of $46,000 for the year just ended:

| | |
|---|---|
| Sales | $310,000 |
| Cost of goods sold | 230,000 |
| Gross profit | $ 80,000 |
| Selling & administrative expenses | 126,000 |
| Net income (loss) | $ (46,000) |

Fixed manufacturing costs total 25% of cost of goods sold. Selling and administrative (S&A) expenses include a 15% sales commission; all other S&A costs are fixed. Management desires to drop product B because of the loss. If B is dropped, fixed production costs will decrease by $42,000.

Should product B be discontinued? Why?

**E27-8** ***Overview of decision making***

Evaluate the comments that follow as being True or False. If the comment is false, briefly explain why.

a Decisions should be based solely on quantitative factors.
b Unavoidable fixed costs can be ignored in decision making.
c The cost of obsolete inventory can be disregarded when deciding whether to keep or dispose of the goods.
d If Dixon Company stops the production of a particular component, it can lease presently-used factory space to another firm. The lease revenue is properly viewed as an opportunity cost should Dixon continue its manufacturing activities.
e Special orders are frequently accepted even though an order's selling price may be less than the sum of direct material, direct labor, variable factory overhead, and fixed factory overhead charges.

**E27-9** ***Controllable costs***

Consider the following costs of the Spirit Company:

a Allocated corporate overhead: $20,000.
b Local advertising expense: $6,600.
c Wages of part-time divisional workers: $3,200.
d Cost of goods sold (variable): $217,800.
e Salary of division manager: $23,600.
f Charges for divisional use of the corporate computer facility: $12,400.
g Sales commissions paid: $34,500.

Which of these costs would most likely be considered in the computation of the controllable contribution margin of a divisional manager? For those costs that are not considered, briefly explain why.

**E27-10** ***Contribution margin income statement***

The following information pertains to the Fairfax Division of Santa Monica Industries:

| | |
|---|---|
| Net sales | $2,200,000 |
| Controllable fixed costs traceable to the division | 640,000 |
| Allocated corporate overhead | 150,000 |
| Variable costs | |
| Cost of goods sold | 510,000 |
| Selling & administrative | 440,000 |
| Uncontrollable fixed costs traceable to the division | 190,000 |

a Compute the Fairfax Division's:
(1) Contribution margin.
(2) Controllable contribution margin.
(3) Segment margin.
b Which of the preceding measures (contribution margin, controllable contribution margin, or segment margin) should be used when making long-term decisions about divisional operations?
c Which of the preceding measures should be used in pay-raise decisions for divisional managers?

**E27-11** ***Direct and absorption inventory costing***

The Arnez Company began operations on January 1 of the current year. The following information pertains to the firm's sole product:

Material cost per unit: $4.00
Labor cost per unit: $7.00
Variable overhead per unit: $3.50
Variable selling cost per unit: $1.50
Fixed manufacturing overhead: $160,000
Fixed selling costs: $48,000

During the year, 20,000 units were produced and 16,000 units were sold.

a Compute the cost of Arnez's ending inventory by using absorption costing.

b Compute the cost of Arnez's ending inventory by using direct costing.

**E27-12** ***Direct and absorption income computations***

Crawford Company began operations on January 1 of the current year. The following information has been gathered from the accounting records:

Variable costs per unit
  Manufacturing: $12.50
  Selling & administrative: $1.10
Fixed costs
  Manufacturing: $120,000
  Selling & administrative: $60,000

Production and sales amounted to 80,000 units and 75,000 units, respectively. The selling price is $17.

a Compute net income for the year just ended by using the direct costing method.

b Compute net income for the year just ended by using the absorption costing method.

# Problems

## Series A

**P27-A1** ***Make or buy***

Cosby, Inc., manufactures a full line of workshop tools. The manufactured cost of one of the company's products, an electric sander, follows.

| | |
|---|---|
| Direct materials | $10.00 |
| Direct labor | 9.00 |
| Total factory overhead | 10.80 |
| Total | $29.80 |

Fixed overhead generally averages 30% of direct labor cost.

Cosby is presently producing all of the sander's components. One of the components, part no. C312, has created a number of manufacturing problems. The company is therefore considering an outside supplier. A supplier has agreed to provide C312s in lots of 1,000 for $5,300. If Cosby accepts the supplier's offer, it is estimated that the sander's direct labor and variable overhead cost will decline by 20%. In addition, direct material cost should fall by approximately 15%.

### Instructions

a Should Cosby make or buy the component? Show computations to support your answer. *Note:* Each sander uses one of the C312 components.

b What is the maximum purchase price that Cosby would be willing to pay an outside supplier for the 1,000 components?

c Assume that Cosby can manufacture and sell 30,000 electric sanders per year. To eliminate the production problems, top management has proposed hiring an additional supervisor for $20,000. In addition, $9,000 of existing fixed administrative costs would be allocated to the electric sander line. If both of these actions take place, should Cosby make or buy the component? Show computations to support your answer.

d List several reservations that Cosby might have about dealing with an outside supplier.

**P27-A2** ***Special order and pricing policy***

The Suzuki Company makes several products that are used in the computer industry. Revenues and costs of the Advanced Digital Laser Chip follow.

| | | |
|---|---|---|
| Sales | | $240,000 |
| Less: | | |
| Direct materials used | $55,000 | |
| Direct labor | 24,000 | |
| Total factory overhead | 82,000 | |
| Variable selling & administrative expenses | 20,000 | |
| Fixed selling & administrative expenses | 31,000 | 212,000 |
| Net income | | $ 28,000 |

The figures shown are for the production and sale of 20,000 chips. Factory overhead is applied on the basis of direct labor cost.

Seaside Technologies has submitted an offer to purchase 1,500 chips at $9 each. Seaside will market the product under its own brand name, and Suzuki's normal sales are not expected to suffer. Suzuki's president feels that the offer should be rejected because the price is below the current unit cost of $10.60 ($212,000 ÷ 20,000 units). An in-depth study revealed the following information:

1 Variable selling and administrative costs fluctuate with units sold. Because no commissions will be paid on this order, costs are expected to drop by 70%.

2 Budgeted fixed factory overhead represents 60% of Suzuki's total factory overhead.

3 Seaside's chips have slightly different specifications than those now produced by Suzuki. As a result, a one-time design and engineering fee of $3,300 will be incurred by Suzuki if the order is accepted.

4 Fixed selling and administrative expenses are allocated to product lines on the basis of sales dollars. Because of the special order, an additional $2,000 will be charged to the laser chip line. Suzuki's total fixed selling and administrative costs will remain the same, however.

**Instructions**

Should Suzuki reject Seaside's offer? Why?

**P27-A3** ***New product introduction***

The Estrada Corporation is a small firm engaged in the manufacture of garden tools. During the past 12 months, two new products have been under development: a timer system for lawn watering and a lawn weeder. Research and development costs for the timer and the weeder have totaled $72,000 and $18,000, respectively.

Company policy is to introduce only one new product each year. Customer acceptability studies performed in the past few months indicate that both products would be successful. Estrada's accounting department has gathered the information that follows.

| | *Timer System* | *Lawn Weeder* |
|---|---|---|
| Customer acceptability studies | $17,000 | $24,000 |
| Projected advertising | $30,000 | $27,000 |
| Projected sales (units) | 10,000 | 18,000 |
| Selling price | $48 | $42 |
| Sales commission (expressed as a percentage of sales) | 5% | 10% |
| Unit production costs | | |
| Direct materials | $11.00 | $12.00 |
| Direct labor | $10.00 | $10.50 |
| Variable overhead | $15.50 | $10.10 |

**Instructions**

a List those costs that are irrelevant to the product introduction decision and explain why each is irrelevant.

b Compute the contribution margin per unit for each product.

c Which of the two products should be introduced? Why?

**P27-A4** ***Dropping an unprofitable segment***

Bargain Mart operates a chain of discount stores in large metropolitan areas of the United States. An abbreviated income statement for store no. 2104 for the year just ended follows.

| | *Total* | *General Merchandise* | *Patio* | *Lunch Counter* |
|---|---|---|---|---|
| Sales | $940,000 | $500,000 | $280,000 | $160,000 |
| Less variable expenses | 598,000 | 310,000 | 168,000 | 120,000 |
| Contribution margin | $342,000 | $190,000 | $112,000 | $ 40,000 |
| Less fixed expenses | 256,000 | 130,000 | 77,000 | 49,000 |
| Net income (loss) | $ 86,000 | $ 60,000 | $ 35,000 | $ (9,000) |

Because of poor performance, management desires to drop the lunch counter. If the lunch counter is closed, the vacated space will be divided between general merchandise and patio, with the following results:

1 General merchandise and patio sales are expected to increase by $35,000 and $12,000, respectively.

2 Fixed expenses include $31,000 of salaries earned by lunch counter employees. Employees who earn $19,000 would be transferred to other departments; remaining counter people will be terminated.

3 All other fixed costs incurred by the lunch counter will continue to be incurred.

4 The lunch counter's equipment will be removed and transferred to another store. Removal and transportation costs will amount to $2,700.

**Instructions**

a Should the lunch counter be dropped? Show computations to support your answer.

b Assume that Quality Caterers has approached Bargain Mart about taking over the lunch counter operation. Quality will pay Bargain Mart $1,400 per month and assume all costs of operation, with the exception of $12,200 of fixed costs. Should the lunch counter be retained in its present form or be turned over to Quality Caterers? Show computations to support your answer.

**P27-A5** ***Contribution income statement: Preparation and analysis***

Marsha Warren, president of Warren Distributors, has just finished her review of the current year's operations. She noted, "We've been lucky. Given the state of the economy, I'm really pleased with these figures. A 3% return on sales will probably beat the competition."

Marsha's comments were based on the following income statement, which was prepared by a new employee. The employee summarized information that pertains to the company's three product lines: X, Y, and Z.

**WARREN DISTRIBUTORS**
**Income Statement**
**For the Year Ended December 31, 19XX**

| | | |
|---|---|---|
| Net sales | | $690,000 |
| Less: Cost of goods sold | $444,000 | |
| Sales commissions | 63,300 | |
| Local advertising | 60,000 | |
| Sales salaries | 30,000 | |
| Other | 72,000 | 669,300 |
| Net income | | $ 20,700 |

Supplementary records revealed the following data:

1 Sales: X, 60,000 units at $5.00; Y, 70,000 units at $3.00; and Z, 40,000 units at $4.50.
2 Warren purchases units from various manufacturers. The prices paid per unit were as follows: X, $3.00; Y, $2.20; Z, $2.75.
3 Sales personnel of X and Z are paid on a commission basis. Commissions total 10% and 15% of each product's respective gross sales. Sales of Y are handled by one salesperson who receives a 3% commission plus a $30,000 salary. The salary is set by Y's management.
4 Local advertising is handled by product line managers. Advertising costs for the product lines were: X, $25,000; Y, $20,000; Z, $15,000.
5 Other costs of $72,000 are subdivided as follows:
   Uncontrollable costs traceable to product lines: X, $20,000; Y, $16,000; and Z, $12,000.
   Administrative overhead not traceable to product lines: $24,000.

**Instructions**

a Give Warren more insight into operations by preparing a contribution income statement for the three product lines. Are things going as well as she believes or could operations be improved? Explain.
b If any of the product lines have a negative segment margin, present an analysis of the probable causes of poor performance.

**P27-A6** ***Direct and absorption costing***

The information that follows pertains to Consumer Products for the year ended December 31, 19X6.

| | |
|---|---|
| Inventory, 1/1/X6 | 24,000 units |
| Units manufactured | 80,000 |
| Units sold | 82,000 |
| Inventory, 12/31/X6 | ? units |
| Manufacturing costs: | |
| Direct materials | $ 3 per unit |
| Direct labor | 5 per unit |
| Variable factory overhead | 9 per unit |
| Fixed factory overhead | 280,000 |
| Selling & administrative expenses: | |
| Variable | $ 2 per unit |
| Fixed | 136,000 |

The unit selling price is $26. Assume that costs have been stable in recent years.

**Instructions**

a Compute the number of units in the ending inventory.
b Calculate the cost of a unit assuming use of:
  (1) Direct costing.
  (2) Absorption costing.
c Prepare an income statement for the year ended December 31, 19X6, by using direct costing.
d Prepare an income statement for the year ended December 31, 19X6, by using absorption costing.

## Series B

**P27-B1** ***Make or buy***

Micron, Inc., manufactures a full line of small home appliances. The manufactured cost of one of the company's products, a toaster oven, follows.

| | |
|---|---|
| Direct materials | $ 5.60 |
| Direct labor | 9.00 |
| Total factory overhead | 13.50 |
| Total | $28.10 |

Fixed overhead generally averages 70% of the total overhead charge.

Micron is presently producing all of the toaster oven's components. One of the components, part no. XY368, has created a number of manufacturing problems. The company is therefore considering an outside supplier. A supplier has agreed to provide XY368s in lots of 20,000 for $84,000. If Micron accepts the supplier's offer, it is estimated that the oven's direct labor and variable overhead cost will decline by 20%. In addition, direct material cost should fall by approximately 10%.

**Instructions**

a Should Micron make or buy the component? Show computations to support your answer. *Note:* Each oven uses one of the XY368 components.
b What is the maximum purchase price that Micron would be willing to pay an outside supplier for the 20,000 components?
c Assume that Micron can manufacture and sell 60,000 toaster ovens per year. To eliminate the production problems, top management has proposed transferring Phil Hartley from the company's microwave division to oversee manufacturing. Hartley is presently earning an annual salary of $43,000. In addition, new equipment would be leased at a cost of $3,100 per month. If both of these

actions take place, should Micron make or buy the component? Show computations to support your answer.

d List several qualitative factors that Micron should consider in deciding whether to make or buy the component.

**P27-B2** ***Special order and pricing policy***

Regal Company makes several products that are used in the home. Revenues and costs of the Portable Vacuum System follow.

| | | |
|---|---|---|
| Sales | | $290,000 |
| Less: | | |
| Direct materials used | $88,000 | |
| Direct labor | 80,000 | |
| Total factory overhead | 56,000 | |
| Sales commissions, 10% | 29,000 | |
| Allocated administrative expense | 15,500 | 268,500 |
| Net income | | $ 21,500 |

The figures shown are for the production and sale of 5,000 units. Factory overhead is applied on the basis of direct labor cost.

The Brower Corporation, which advertises heavily on television, has submitted an offer to purchase 2,200 vacuums at $51 each. Brower will market the product under its own brand name, and Regal's normal sales are not expected to suffer. Regal's president feels that the offer should be rejected because the price is below the current unit cost of $53.70 ($268,500 ÷ 5,000 units). An in-depth study revealed the following information:

1 Brower's units will require overtime at time and one-half the regular wage rate. *Note:* The overtime premium will be accounted for as direct labor.

2 Fixed factory overhead is applied by using a rate of 42% of direct labor cost.

3 No sales commissions will be paid on these units.

4 Administrative expenses are allocated to product lines on the basis of sales dollars. Because of the special order, an additional $6,000 will be charged to the vacuum line. Regal's total administrative costs will remain the same, however.

**Instructions**

Should Regal reject Brower's offer? Why?

**P27-B3** ***New product introduction***

The FHR Corporation is engaged in the manufacture of communications equipment. During the past 18 months, two new products have been developed: a voice module and a decoder unit.

FHR recently conducted market surveys for the voice module and the decoder at a cost of $42,000 each. Although the surveys indicate that both products could be introduced at this time, the firm has encountered difficulty in obtaining the required electronic components. Thus, only one product will be manufactured. FHR's accounting department has gathered the information that follows.

| | *Voice Module* | *Decoder Unit* |
|---|---|---|
| Development costs over the past 18 months | $115,000 | $135,000 |
| Production costs per unit | | |
| Direct materials | $22.50 | $27.80 |
| Direct labor | $15.00 | $20.00 |
| Variable overhead | $18.00 | $24.00 |
| Sales commissions (expressed as a percentage of sales) | 10% | 5% |
| Selling price | $85 | $95 |
| Projected sales (units) | 35,000 | 41,000 |
| Projected advertising | $25,000 | $30,000 |

**Instructions**

a List those costs that are irrelevant to the product introduction decision and explain why each is irrelevant.
b Compute the contribution margin per unit for each product.
c Which of the two products should be introduced at this time? Why?

**P27-B4** ***Dropping an unprofitable segment***

Handy Mart, Inc., operates a chain of discount stores in large metropolitan areas of the United States. An abbreviated income statement for store no. 134 for the year just ended follows.

| | *Total* | *General Merchandise* | *Lawn and Garden* | *Snack Bar* |
|---|---|---|---|---|
| Sales | $1,144,000 | $700,000 | $360,000 | $ 84,000 |
| Less variable expenses | 769,400 | 455,000 | 255,600 | 58,800 |
| Contribution margin | $ 374,600 | $245,000 | $104,400 | $ 25,200 |
| Less fixed expenses | 304,200 | 194,000 | 68,900 | 41,300 |
| Net income (loss) | $ 70,400 | $ 51,000 | $ 35,500 | $(16,100) |

Because of poor performance, management desires to drop the snack bar. If the snack bar is closed, the vacated space will be divided between general merchandise and lawn and garden, with the following results:

1 General merchandise and lawn and garden sales are expected to increase by $30,000 and $40,000, respectively.
2 Fixed expenses include $28,000 of salaries earned by snack bar employees. Employees who earn $19,000 would be transferred to other departments; remaining snack bar employees will be terminated.
3 All other fixed costs incurred by the snack bar will continue to be incurred.
4 The snack bar's equipment will be removed and transferred to another store. Removal and transportation costs will amount to $8,400.

**Instructions**

a Should the snack bar be dropped? Show computations to support your answer.
b Assume that Midvale Caterers has approached Handy Mart about taking over the snack bar operation. Midvale will pay Handy Mart $1,200 per month and assume all costs of operation, with the exception of $17,000 of fixed costs. Should the snack bar be retained in its present form or be turned over to Midvale Caterers? Show computations to support your answer.

**P27-B5** ***Contribution income statement: Preparation and analysis***

Harold Brandt, president of Brandt Distributing, has just finished a review of the current year's operations. He noted, "These figures look great. I was expecting overall performance to suffer, given the problems we've had with the Urbana Division. However, I believe we're now on sound footing and have few financial problems."

Harold's comments were based on the following income statement, which was prepared by a new employee. The employee summarized information that pertains to the firm's three divisions: Barrington, Springfield, and Urbana.

**BRANDT DISTRIBUTING**
**Income Statement**
**For the Year Ended December 31, 19XX**

| | | |
|---|---|---|
| Net sales | | $994,000 |
| Less: Cost of goods sold | $632,000 | |
| Sales commissions | 49,700 | |
| Salaries | 130,000 | |
| Advertising | 80,000 | |
| Other | 75,000 | 966,700 |
| Net income | | $ 27,300 |

Supplementary records revealed the following information:

1 Sales: Barrington, 29,000 units at $10; Springfield, 34,000 units at $8; and Urbana, 48,000 units at $9.
2 Each division purchases units from various manufacturers. The prices paid per unit were as follows: Barrington, $6; Springfield, $5; Urbana, $6.
3 Each division pays a 5% commission to its sales force. In addition, the Urbana Division employs a sales manager who earns $30,000 per year. The sales manager's salary is set by Urbana's divisional manager. Other salaries for executives are established by Brandt and subdivided as follows:

| | |
|---|---|
| Barrington | $ 25,000 |
| Springfield | 40,000 |
| Urbana | 35,000 |
| Total | $100,000 |

4 Advertising is handled by divisional managers. The following costs were incurred: Barrington, $10,000; Springfield, $20,000; Urbana, $50,000.
5 Other costs of $75,000 consisted of the following:
Uncontrollable costs traceable to divisions: Barrington, $8,000; Springfield, $6,000; and Urbana, $27,000.
General corporate overhead: $34,000.

**Instructions**

a Give Brandt more insight into operations by preparing a contribution income statement for the three divisions. Are things going as well as he believes or could operations be improved? Explain.
b If any of the divisions have a negative segment margin, present an analysis of the probable causes of poor performance.

**P27-B6** ***Direct and absorption costing***

The following information pertains to Turbo Enterprises for the year ended December 31, 19X8:

| | |
|---|---|
| Variable cost per unit: | |
| Direct materials | $ 6 |
| Direct labor | 4 |
| Factory overhead | 9 |
| Selling & administrative expense | 3 |
| | $22 |
| Annual fixed costs: | |
| Factory overhead | $600,000 |
| Selling & administrative expense | 115,000 |
| | $715,000 |
| Other data (units): | |
| Sales | 21,000 |
| Production | 25,000 |
| Inventory, 12/31/X8 | 11,000 |

The unit selling price is $62. Assume that costs have been stable in recent years.

**Instructions**

a Compute the number of units in the beginning inventory on January 1, 19X8.
b Calculate the cost of the December 31 inventory assuming use of:
  (1) Direct costing.
  (2) Absorption costing.
c Prepare an income statement for the year ended December 31, 19X8, by using direct costing.
d Prepare an income statement for the year ended December 31, 19X8, by using absorption costing.

## Beyond the Basics

**BB27-1** ***Analysis of costs; decision making****

Paradise Inc., is a developer of hotels in Hawaii and other resort-type locations. The company is studying construction of a new facility on the island of El Reno, and two alternatives are under consideration:

- *Alternative A*—Build a "commercial class" hotel similar to Holiday Inn or Ramada, with an average room area of 550 square feet (including public spaces). There would be minimal meeting and banquet facilities.
- *Alternative B*—Build an "executive class" hotel similar to a Hyatt or a Hilton. The average room size would be 700 square feet; ample meeting and banquet facilities would be available for conventions, conferences, and so forth.

Paradise's accounting department has generated the following data:

- Land cost: $25 per square foot of floor area
- Construction cost: $80 per square foot
- Real estate taxes, interest, and other overhead during construction: 30% of land and construction costs

* This problem is adapted from "Room at the Top," *Forbes,* March 12, 1984, pp. 58, 59, 61.

Per-room outlays for furnishings and equipment, supplies, and opening advertising and marketing costs are estimated as follows:

| | *Commercial* | *Executive* |
|---|---|---|
| Furnishings and equipment | $8,000 | $12,500 |
| Supplies | 1,000 | 2,000 |
| Advertising and marketing | 2,000 | 4,000 |

The accounting department recommends adding 10% to the total of all preceding costs to allow for contingencies and estimation errors. Construction is expected to take two years.

Paradise sets a room rental rate equal to $1 per $1,000 of cost. Upon completion, the going rates for similar rooms are anticipated to be: commercial, $79 per day; executive, $135.

**Instructions**

a Compute the cost per room of building a commercial class hotel and an executive class hotel.

b Consider all information presented and determine the type of hotel that Paradise should construct. What factors should be evaluated in reaching the proper decision?

**BB27-2** ***Productive capacity; make or buy***

The Viceroy Corporation is a small manufacturer of workshop tools. The company generates an adequate profit by operating a single eight-hour shift at its Lincoln plant. Presently, the plant manufactures 380,000 units of finished product per year. Although various goods are involved, production personnel estimate that the average direct labor time to complete one unit is 15 minutes. Viceroy currently uses 95% of its operating capacity.

Management is considering a change in operations. Part no. A402 is now purchased from outside suppliers at $4.25 per unit. Viceroy has had significant problems with supplier reliability; thus, the firm is studying the feasibility of producing the part itself. The following information has been gathered:

- Annual volume needed: 36,000 units
- Estimated direct material cost per unit: $1.45
- Estimated direct labor cost per unit: $\frac{1}{6}$ hour @ $6.00 = $1.00
- Estimated variable factory overhead per unit: $0.75
- Estimated fixed factory overhead: annual rental of special machine, $12,500; salary of newly hired production supervisor, $18,000

In addition to processing on the special machine, part no. A402 will require machine time on existing equipment. The related costs are reflected in the preceding figures. The new machine will not significantly affect Viceroy's productive capacity.

**Instructions**

a From a productive capacity viewpoint, should Viceroy begin to manufacture part no. A402? Why?

b If your answer to part (a) was "no," what alternatives should be considered so that manufacturing activities could commence?

c From a purely financial viewpoint, should Viceroy begin to manufacture part no. A402? Why?

d What qualitative factors should be considered in reaching the proper decision?

## Answers to Chapter Quiz

**1** c

**2** b [Each unit has a $3 contribution margin ($15 − $12); thus, 1,000 units × $3 = $3,000]

**3** d

**4** a

**5** b

# Capital Budgeting

CHAPTER 28

## Learning Objectives

After reading this chapter you should:

1 Understand the capital budgeting process.

2 Know the factors that management considers in the evaluation of capital expenditure proposals.

3 Be familiar with the concept of the time value of money.

4 Understand the distinction between compound interest and present value.

5 Be familiar with net present value, the internal rate of return, payback, and the accounting rate of return.

6 (Appendix) Have a basic knowledge of how income taxes complicate cash-flow calculations.

OBJECTIVE 1
Understand the capital budgeting process.

Each year, American businesses spend vast sums of money on a variety of long-term investments. As evidence, consider the following excerpts from recent annual reports of General Electric and NWA (Northwest Airlines):

**General Electric**

GE's total expenditures for new plant and equipment during [the year] were $2.3 billion, bringing the total for the last five years (excluding the unusually large addition by acquisition of RCA in 1986) to $10.5 billion. Of that five-year total, 33% was to increase capacity; 25% was to increase productivity; 13% was to support new business start-ups; 13% was to replace and renew older equipment; and 16% was for such other projects as improving R&D facilities and safety and environmental protection.

**NWA**

During [the year] the Company invested $585,653,000 in property and equipment. The major components of this total were the purchase of five Boeing 757 aircraft and one McDonnell Douglas DC9-30 aircraft, additional deposits and capitalized interest relating to aircraft, spare engine and flight simulator purchases, aircraft and flight simulator modifications and the purchase of rights to additional gates. . . . Capital commitments for [next year] and thereafter principally consist of scheduled aircraft acquisitions. In addition, the Company continues to acquire property and equipment to support its airline operations and to make improvements to ground facilities including terminal improvements and modifications to office buildings. Major additions planned include 11 new flight simulators and upgrades for 12 existing simulators; expansion of facilities at Minneapolis/St. Paul, Tokyo, San Francisco and London; and additional ground support and computer equipment to replace and upgrade existing equipment.

Most executives will agree that a company's long-term investments often spell the difference between financial prosperity or lengthy periods of unprofitable performance. Investments such as those cited in the excerpts are costly and require the commitment of resources for many years. As a result, poor decisions are usually very difficult to reverse.

This chapter focuses on the evaluation of programs and projects that influence the financial performance of more than a single accounting period. Outlays for such undertakings are commonly called *capital expenditures*; the related planning and decision making is appropriately labeled **capital budgeting.**

## Capital Budgeting Decisions

Most firms face the same problem when evaluating long-term investments: too many investment opportunities and not enough money. Management must therefore exercise extreme care in the analysis of alternative courses of action. This analysis process gives rise to two basic types of capital budgeting decisions. The first type involves *project screening* to determine whether an investment proposal meets certain preset criteria. Examples of such criteria include a specified rate of return or perhaps the recovery of invested funds within a certain number of years. If the screening tests are met, the proposal is considered for acceptance; if not, rejection is in order.

The second type of decision concerns *ranking*. Given that a number of projects will probably be acceptable, ranking must occur because of the limited availability of investment dollars. A distinction is necessary to determine the most attractive project, the second most attractive project, and so forth. Our discussion will concentrate on screening decisions, with ranking decisions more appropriately left for advanced accounting and finance courses.

## Decision Factors to Consider

Assume that you recently inherited $10,000 from a wealthy relative and are now exploring various investment possibilities. Three opportunities appear particularly attractive:

**OBJECTIVE 2**
**Know the factors that management considers in the evaluation of capital expenditure proposals.**

1 Purchase a six-month, $10,000 money market certificate that carries an interest rate of 10%.

2 Acquire $10,000 of stock in several so-called growth companies. The shares promise significant appreciation in market value but pay no dividends.

3 Purchase a $70,000 home by paying $9,000 down and securing a $61,000 mortgage loan. The loan will require payments over the next 30 years and carries a 12% interest rate.

Somehow you must decide which of the three investments to select. As a starting point, the following thoughts might be running through your mind:

- The first two investments require an immediate cash outlay of $10,000; the third requires only $9,000.
- The money market certificate yields a guaranteed interest rate of 10%.
- The stocks generate no dividends; however, the long-run income may be attractive if market prices increase substantially.
- The house requires monthly payments for mortgage principal and interest along with outlays for insurance, utilities, and property taxes. Furthermore, under laws and regulations that exist at the time of this writing, interest and property taxes are deductible for federal income tax purposes. In addition, appreciation in housing prices has been substantial over the years.

Although our list of decision factors is far from complete, these factors coincide with those studied by managers in the evaluation of capital expenditure proposals. Specifically, management is concerned with (1) the amount of an investment, (2) the periodic returns from an investment, and (3) the lowest rate of return acceptable to the company.

### Initial Investment

The amount of an investment is measured by the cash outlays necessary for acquisition. These outlays usually coincide with the purchase cost of the acquired assets (e.g., buildings, machinery, and so forth). Be aware, however, that in addition to this type of investment, some projects may require a further commitment of funds to simply get "up and running." Consider, for example, a company that desires to expand its market area and customer base. In most cases, this type of business decision is accompanied by a rise in the level of cash needed to support daily operations, along with buildups in accounts receivable and inventory levels. This situation requires an *investment in working capital* by the firm, with related dollar amounts treated as part of the project's initial cost.

Most companies are able to generate a partial recovery of invested funds on conclusion of a project's life. For instance, equipment and other assets may be sold in secondhand markets. In addition, the working capital investment just mentioned may be recovered via the sale of inventory, the collection of receivables, and the return of cash for use in other business activities. Amounts received from these events are properly treated as cash inflows in the year of occurrence.

### Periodic Returns

Investments are made to increase an organization's profitability. Added profitability results from projects that (1) produce income by generating revenues in excess of expenses or (2) decrease costs. Income-producing investments include the addition of new product lines, an expansion of plant capacity, and the implementation of successful marketing and advertising programs. Cost reduction endeavors, on the other hand, often involve the installation of more efficient equipment and the acquisition of assets to perform services presently handled by outside entities. For instance, a company could acquire its own computer to eliminate dependence on an outside service bureau.

For both income-producing and cost-saving projects, managers desire a return. That is, managers seek to recover their initial outlays *and* to provide the company with a reward for the risk associated with the investment. Returns can be measured in terms of accounting profits or net cash flows (cash inflows minus cash outflows). *For long-term decisions cash flow is preferred.* Bear in mind that accounting net income is accrual-based and thereby focuses on when revenues are earned and expenses are incurred. The actual receipt and disbursement of cash is ignored.

As we explained in the Appendix to Chapter 17 and as we will explore later in this chapter, the timing of cash flows is extremely important. Stated succinctly, a dollar received today is worth more than a dollar to be received in the future. The dollar received today can be reinvested to earn additional returns for the enterprise. Naturally, additional returns are not possible with future dollars until such amounts are actually in hand. Given the time value of money and the fact that *cash* is invested and *cash* earns a return, cash flow is normally used for the evaluation of long-term investments.

### The Cost of Capital

The analysis of investment opportunities requires the establishment of a cutoff rate for project acceptance or rejection. The cutoff rate (i.e., the minimum return acceptable to the firm) depends on the cost of obtaining investment funds. For example, if the cost of funds is 12%, a firm would ordinarily invest only in those projects that promise a return in excess of 12%.

As you are aware, funds for long-term investments are obtained from a variety of sources such as bonds, mortgages, stock issuances, and operations. The collective cost of these funds (which includes outlays for interest expense and dividends) is commonly referred to as the **cost of capital.**

Most managers will agree that proper determination of this measure is controversial and a topic related more to finance than to accounting. Thus, the underlying calculations are not considered here. Be aware, though, that the minimum desired return for investments is typically set several percentage points higher than the cost of capital. Such a procedure helps to offset any errors that may occur in the cost of capital's accompanying assumptions and estimates. The illustrations and problems that follow this discussion assume that the cost of capital has already been determined and is ready for use in the decision-making process.

## The Time Value of Money[1]

Suppose that a manager has an option of receiving $1,000 today or $1,000 one year from now. Virtually every executive would prefer the first alternative for two

[1] The presentation on the next few pages is an expansion of the Appendix to Chapter 17.

basic reasons. Receipt of the money today offers the advantage of reduced risk. The future, of course, is full of uncertainty. As time passes, more and more events can occur that imperil the inflow of future dollars. Because the $1,000 is in hand, the executive is exposed to less risk and becomes less concerned about changing conditions in the forthcoming months.

The first alternative is also preferred because of the **time value of money.** As explained earlier, a cash receipt today is worth more than an inflow that occurs in the future. Remember, money in hand can be reinvested to earn additional returns.

OBJECTIVE 3
Be familiar with the concept of the time value of money.

We caution that the preceding example is overly simplistic. When one compares equal sums of money (e.g., $1,000) at two different times, the preferred alternative is readily apparent. What happens, however, if we change the illustration? Assume that the second alternative now calls for an inflow of $1,050 or even $1,100 in one year. The decision becomes more difficult. Maybe the extra $50 or $100 is worth the wait; maybe not. An important influence would surely be the investment opportunities available for the immediate $1,000 receipt.

Decisions such as those just cited are facilitated if the time value of money is quantitatively incorporated into the evaluation process. This integration is accomplished by the use of present value, a derivation of compound interest.

## Compound Interest

With **compound interest,** the interest is computed on principal plus previously accumulated interest. For example, assume that you deposited $1,000 in a 6% savings account. If the interest is compounded annually, the deposit will grow to $1,191.02 by the end of three years, as the following figures show.

OBJECTIVE 4
Understand the distinction between compound interest and present value.

| *Year* | *Beginning Balance* | + | *Interest at 6%* | = | *Ending Balance* |
|---|---|---|---|---|---|
| 1 | $1,000.00 | | $60.00 | | $1,060.00 |
| 2 | 1,060.00 | | 63.60 | | 1,123.60 |
| 3 | 1,123.60 | | 67.42 | | 1,191.02 |

Observe that the interest rate remains constant at 6%; however, the amount of interest earned each year has grown. This situation arises because the interest is based on principal and also on previously computed interest that is left on deposit.

Despite the apparent simplicity, the calculations become quite burdensome when many years are involved. Fortunately, a formula is available to determine the *future value* (i.e., ending value) of an investment at a given rate of interest (return). The formula is:

$$V = P(1 + r)^n$$

where

V = future value of the investment
P = present value of the investment
r = interest rate
n = number of periods

To calculate the value of the previous deposit at the end of, say, two years, the formula is used as follows:

$$\begin{aligned} V &= P(1 + r)^n \\ &= \$1{,}000(1 + 0.06)^2 \\ &= \$1{,}000(1.1236) \\ &= \$1{,}123.60 \end{aligned}$$

## Present Value

An investment such as the foregoing can also be evaluated from a different perspective. Restudy the preceding example. Assume that an opportunity is available that promises a cash inflow of $1,060 at the end of one year. If you are willing to accept a 6% return on your money, how much would you spend today to receive this cash flow? The answer is $1,000. Why? If $1,000 is invested immediately at a 6% interest rate, the outlay will grow to the $1,060 that you can receive.

In essence we found this amount by working backward. Rather than take a present amount and extend it out to the future, as we would with compound interest, we took a future amount and brought it back to today (a process often called **discounting**). The $1,000 is termed the **present value** of the investment, or the amount an investor is willing to pay to secure a specified cash flow ($1,060) on a future date (one year from now) at a given rate of return (6%). Compound interest and present value can be contrasted as shown in Exhibit 28-1.

In view of this relationship, the present value of a future cash flow can be found by solving the compound interest formula for P. Since

$$V = P(1 + r)^n$$

then

$$P = \frac{V}{(1 + r)^n}$$

Using numbers from the preceding illustration, the $1,000 present value is determined as follows:

$$P = \frac{V}{(1 + r)^n}$$

$$= \frac{\$1,060}{(1.06)^1}$$

$$= \$1,000$$

### Present Value Tables

Fortunately, tables have been developed to assist in present value computations. Examine Table 1 in Appendix C at the end of the text. The table shows the present value factors of $1 at different rates of interest and for different time periods. Continuing our previous example, the factor for $1 to be received in one year given a 6% interest rate is 0.94340. Because we are trying to find the present value of $1,060, the calculation that follows is necessary.

**Exhibit 28-1**
**Compound Interest Versus Present Value**

| | *Today* | | *End of Year 1* |
|---|---|---|---|
| Compound interest | $1,000 | 6% → | $1,060 |
| Present value | $1,000 | ← 6% | $1,060 |

| Cash Flow | | Present Value Factor | | Present Value |
|---|---|---|---|---|
| $1,060 | × | 0.94340 | = | $1,000 |

A quick review of the table reveals that as we go further into the future, the present value factors become smaller. Notice the impact of time on the receipt of $1,060.

| If Received at the End of Year | The 6% Present Value Factor Would Be | Producing a Present Value of* |
|---|---|---|
| 1 | 0.94340 | $1,000 |
| 3 | 0.83962 | 890 |
| 5 | 0.74726 | 792 |
| 7 | 0.66506 | 705 |
| 9 | 0.59190 | 627 |

* $1,060 × present value factor.

These factors reflect the time value of money—the sooner cash inflows are received, the more valuable they are to the recipient. All other things being equal, companies are willing to pay greater sums of money for those investments that promise quicker dollar returns.

## Multiple Cash Flows and Annuities

Most long-term investments affect cash flows for more than a single year. To illustrate the necessary procedures, assume Target Industries acquired a machine that promised annual savings in cash operating costs of $2,000 over the next five years. Management requires a return on investment of 10%. For capital budgeting purposes, reductions in operating costs are viewed as cash inflows. Using the factors from Table 1, the present value of the machine's savings is $7,582:

| Year | Cash Flow | × | Present Value Factor | = | Present Value |
|---|---|---|---|---|---|
| 1 | $2,000 | | 0.90909 | | $1,818 |
| 2 | 2,000 | | 0.82645 | | 1,653 |
| 3 | 2,000 | | 0.75132 | | 1,503 |
| 4 | 2,000 | | 0.68301 | | 1,366 |
| 5 | 2,000 | | 0.62092 | | 1,242 |
| Total present value | | | | | $7,582 |

These computations result in each of the individual cash flows being discounted back to the beginning of Year 1 (i.e., the "present"), as depicted in Exhibit 28-2.

A review of this process shows that in each year a present value factor is multiplied by the $2,000 cash flow. The calculations would have required less work had the savings been multiplied by the summation of the individual factors (0.90909 + 0.82645 + 0.75132 + 0.68301 + 0.62092 = 3.79079). As the following figures show, the same result is achieved:

$$\$2,000 \times 3.79079 = \$7,582$$

**Exhibit 28-2**
**The Discounting of Multiple Cash Flows**

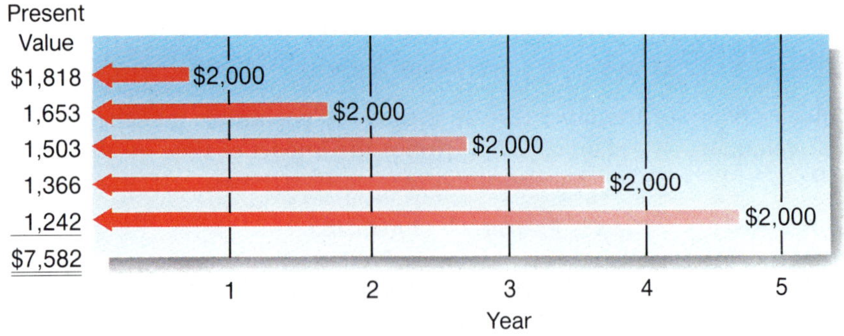


Our example has focused on an **annuity**—a series of equal cash flows over a number of years. To further simplify procedures in this type of situation, accountants often use an annuity table (see Table 2 in Appendix C). The factor in Table 2 for a $1 annuity over the next five years, discounted at 10%, is 3.79079. As before, the factor is multiplied by the cash flow to derive the appropriate present value.

***An Added Complexity*** Sometimes, annuity calculations are needed to discount cash flows that *begin* several years into the future. Suppose, for instance, that the machine in our illustration promises annual operating savings of $2,000 for the first two years and $1,000 for each of the next three years. Target now has two separate annuities, and the present value is found as follows:

| *Years* | *Cash Flow* | × | *Present Value Factor* | = | *Present Value* |
|---|---|---|---|---|---|
| 1–2 | $2,000 | | 1.73554 | | $3,471 |
| 3–5 | 1,000 | | 2.05525* | | 2,055 |
| Total present value | | | | | $5,526 |

* 3.79079 − 1.73554

Table 2 is once again the source of our data. The factor of 1.73554 is needed to discount the savings that occur during the first two years. The second factor, computed as the difference between 3.79079 (an annuity factor that covers Years 1–5) and 1.73554, permits Target to discount the cash flows for Years 3–5.

### TIPS & TECHNIQUES

The authors have found that many students disregard annuities in favor of a series of yearly multiplications with Table 1 factors. We feel this practice is unwise. Because an annuity factor is nothing more than the total of individual present value factors, problem solution time can be greatly reduced by mastering Table 2. Use the annuity factors whenever you are confronted with a series of equal cash inflows or outflows. The study time expended is more than offset by the benefits derived.

## Capital Budgeting Evaluation Methods

Four methods are frequently encountered in practice to evaluate capital budgeting proposals. The methods are:

**1** Net present value
**2** Internal rate of return
**3** Payback
**4** Accounting rate of return

Several recent surveys of industry practices have shown that these evaluation tools are normally used in conjunction with one another. This situation occurs because each of the techniques listed has strengths and weaknesses and provides different information to management.

The majority of our discussion will center on the discounted cash flow methods of net present value and the internal rate of return. Both of these approaches have conceptual advantages over the others cited and have seen increased use in recent years.

### Net Present Value

OBJECTIVE 5
**Be familiar with net present value, the internal rate of return, payback, and the accounting rate of return.**

The **net-present-value method** requires the present value of an investment's cash inflows be netted against the present value of the cash outflows. The rate of return used for discounting corresponds to or is slightly in excess of the firm's cost of capital.

As an example of the necessary procedures, assume that Alpine Delivery is considering an expansion of service to the cities of High Point and Beeville. Two trucks must be acquired at a total cost of $95,000. The trucks have an eight-year life, will be depreciated by using the straight-line method, and are expected to generate annual net cash inflows from new business of $18,000. Alpine requires a 10% minimum return on all investments.

Some managers may be tempted to evaluate the truck acquisition as follows:

| | |
|---|---|
| Initial investment | $(95,000) |
| Annual net cash inflows ($18,000 × 8 years) | 144,000 |
| Difference in favor of acquisition | $ 49,000 |

This analysis is incorrect for two reasons. First, the computations imply that all of the cash inflows are equivalent when, in fact, they are not. Inflows that occur in earlier years can naturally be reinvested for longer periods of time. Second, we cannot compare an immediate cash outflow with cash inflows that are spread over the next eight years. Since the timing differs, the result is a comparison of dollars of unequal values—basically a study of apples and oranges.

The proper approach is to discount the cash flows at 10%. The correct computations follow.

| | *Cash Flow* | × | *Present Value Factor* | = | *Present Value* |
|---|---|---|---|---|---|
| Initial investment | $(95,000) | | 1.00000 | | $(95,000) |
| Annual net cash inflows | 18,000 | | 5.33493 | | 96,029 |
| Net present value | | | | | $ 1,029 |

A factor of 1.0 is used for the initial investment because the outlay takes place immediately; the other factor (5.33493) is obtained from the annuity table (Table 2) at the intersection of the 8-period row and 10% column.

The net present value of $1,029 indicates the present value of the inflows exceeds the present value of the outflows. The trucks are therefore an attractive investment and should be acquired if funds are available. Projects that produce a positive net present value are acceptable; those with a negative net present value should be rejected. A positive net present value means the returns from an investment exceed a company's minimum desired rate of return (10% in Alpine's case).

Before leaving this example, it is important to note the impact of the discounting process on the decision. Actual cash inflows exceed actual cash outflows by $49,000; yet when discounting is introduced, the present value of the inflows and outflows differs by only $1,029. The time value of money has certainly diminished the attractiveness of the investment. With little hesitation we can conclude that present value is a significant consideration in the evaluation of long-term alternatives.

## Omission of Depreciation Expense

Although the trucks had an eight-year life, management disregarded depreciation expense when making the acquisition decision. Depreciation is excluded from present value calculations because of the emphasis on cash flows and depreciation's noncash nature. The cost of the trucks took the form of a single cash outflow of $95,000 at the time of acquisition. An additional deduction for depreciation would therefore result in a double counting of the assets' cost.

Despite its noncash character, depreciation expense does affect the amount of income taxes paid to federal and state governments. As a result, there is some impact on a firm's cash flows. Income taxes, which were ignored in the Alpine example, are discussed in the Appendix to this chapter.

## An Expanded Example Using Net Present Value

The illustration that follows shows how a business can integrate present value into a keep-versus-replace decision. As you progress through the presentation, observe how the relevancy concept (as introduced in Chapter 27) continues to play an important role in the evaluation of alternatives.

Assume the Delicious Baking Company is studying the replacement of some equipment acquired four years ago at a cost of $55,000. The equipment is expected to provide six more years of service if $4,000 of major repairs are performed two years from now. Annual cash operating costs total $13,000 and are not expected to change in future periods. Delicious can sell the equipment now for $24,000; the estimated residual value in six years is $5,000.

Management can acquire new equipment that costs $62,000. The new equipment has a service life of six years, is expected to reduce cash operating costs by $6,000 annually, and has an estimated residual value of $18,000. Annual company sales will total $240,000 regardless of the decision.

If Delicious has a minimum desired rate of return of 14%, what should the firm do? To determine the proper course of action, we must first identify all *relevant* cash flows, namely, those that occur in the future and differ among the alternatives. Such an analysis reveals that we can disregard the $55,000 cost of the old equipment (it is sunk) and the future sales revenues of $1,440,000 ($240,000 × 6 years), which are common to both the keep and the replace options. Once the relevant cash flows are decided, the amounts are discounted by using the 14% present value factors that appear in Tables 1 and 2. The appropriate computations are shown in Exhibit 28-3.

The analysis reveals a negative net present value for both the keep and the replace alternatives. According to the guidelines presented earlier, a negative net present value calls for rejection; however, it is impossible to reject both "keep" *and* "replace." Because one alternative must be selected in this type of situation, Delicious Baking should keep the present equipment. On a discounted cash flow basis, the company stands to benefit by $5,667 [$(51,353) vs. $(57,020)].[2]

## Internal Rate of Return

The net-present-value method is only one of several tools that a company can employ to evaluate capital budgeting proposals. Another tool that incorporates discounted cash flows is the **internal rate of return (IRR).** Sometimes called the time-adjusted rate of return, the IRR represents the actual yield on a project. It is computed by finding the discount rate that equates the present value of a project's cash inflows with the present value of the cash outflows. As a result of this calculation, the net present value is zero.

To illustrate the related procedures, let us assume that Kim Enterprises is confronted with an investment opportunity that costs $12,009 and promises net cash inflows of $5,000 for each of the next three years. The following computation,

**Exhibit 28-3**
**Delicious Baking Company's Analysis of Keep and Replace Alternatives**

| | *Year(s) of Occurrence* | *Cash Flow* | × *Present Value Factor* | = *Present Value* |
|---|---|---|---|---|
| **Keep the present equipment** | | | | |
| Cash operating costs | 1–6 | $(13,000) | 3.88867 | $(50,553) |
| Major repairs | 2 | (4,000) | 0.76947 | (3,078) |
| Disposal | 6 | 5,000 | 0.45559 | 2,278 |
| Net present value | | | | $(51,353) |
| **Replace the present equipment** | | | | |
| Initial investment | Immediate | $(62,000) | 1.00000 | $(62,000) |
| Sale of old equipment | Immediate | 24,000 | 1.00000 | 24,000 |
| Cash operating costs ($13,000 − $6,000) | 1–6 | (7,000) | 3.88867 | (27,221) |
| Disposal | 6 | 18,000 | 0.45559 | 8,201 |
| Net present value | | | | $(57,020) |
| Net present value in favor of keeping the present equipment | | | | $ 5,667 |

[2] The negative net present values arise in this case because the company's sales revenues (a significant cash inflow) were omitted from the analysis.

where $F$ is defined as the discount factor that equates the project's inflows and outflows, is needed:

$$\$5{,}000 \times F = \$12{,}009$$

$$F = \frac{\$12{,}009}{\$5{,}000}$$

$$F = 2.4018$$

The return on Kim's investment can now be found by determining the rate represented by a factor of 2.4018. Because the investment involves a three-year annuity, we must examine Table 2, part of which is reproduced below.

| *Periods* | *8%* | *10%* | *12%* | *14%* | *16%* |
|---|---|---|---|---|---|
| ⋮ | ⋮ | ⋮ | ⋮ | ⋮ | ⋮ |
| 3 | 2.57710 | 2.48685 | 2.40183 | 2.32163 | 2.24589 |
| ⋮ | ⋮ | ⋮ | ⋮ | ⋮ | ⋮ |

Except for an extremely small rounding error, the 2.4018 discount factor coincides with a 12% interest rate. Thus, Kim's investment yields a 12% rate of return. As noted earlier, this particular rate will produce a zero net present value:

| | |
|---|---|
| Initial investment [$(12,009) × 1.00000] | $(12,009) |
| Annual net cash inflows discounted at 12% ($5,000 × 2.4018) | 12,009 |
| Net present value | $ — |

Should the investment be pursued? Is a 12% return attractive to Kim? The answers to these questions depend on the company's cost of capital. If the internal rate of return is equal to or greater than the cost of capital, then the project should be considered for acceptance. If not, rejection is in order.

## Two Complications

Two complications are normally encountered when figuring the internal rate of return. First, the factor that equates the present value of the inflows and outflows usually does not coincide with the factors that appear in the annuity table. Returning to the Kim example, for instance, suppose the investment called for an initial outlay of $11,775 rather than $12,009. The factor for the project would now be 2.355, calculated as follows:

$$\$5{,}000 \times F = \$11{,}775$$

$$F = \frac{\$11{,}775}{\$5{,}000}$$

$$F = 2.355$$

Scanning Table 2 for a three-period annuity, we find that the factor falls between a return of 12% and 14%. The actual return is found by using the mathematical process of *interpolation,* with the necessary procedures shown on page 1021.

| | *Present Value Factors* | |
|---|---|---|
| 12% return | 2.40183 | 2.40183 |
| Return on Kim's investment | 2.35500 | |
| 14% return | | 2.32163 |
| Difference | 0.04683 | 0.08020 |

$$\text{Internal Rate of Return} = 12\% + \frac{0.04683}{0.08020}(2\%)^*$$

$$= 13.17\%$$

* 14% − 12%.

The second complication relates to uneven cash flows. The Kim illustration had an immediate single outflow followed by three inflows of $5,000 each. Picture the difficulties that would arise if there were additional flows of, say, an extra payment in the second year and the receipt of a salvage value in the third year. Finding the one factor that equates the present value of all inflows and outflows would be burdensome, to say the least, and would require numerous rounds of trial and error. Fortunately, computer programs and hand-held calculators are available that perform the required computations. The accountant is thereby freed to concentrate on the analysis of results rather than the drudgery of procedure.

## The Payback Method

Few accountants question the superiority of the discounted cash flow methods for investment analysis. Yet, as explained earlier in the chapter, methods other than net present value and the internal rate of return are in widespread use. Discounted cash flow began to gain popularity in the 1950s and is a relative newcomer on the project evaluation scene. For a number of reasons many managers still favor the older approaches, which ignore the time value of money. A brief overview of these approaches is therefore in order.

The **payback method** measures the amount of time it takes to recover a project's initial cash investment. To illustrate the necessary calculations, assume that Hill Corporation is examining the possibility of manufacturing a new product. Plant and equipment that cost $200,000 must be purchased and should result in net cash inflows of $60,000 for each of the next five years. When the cash flows are uniform, as they are in this example, the payback period is derived by use of the following formula:

$$\text{Payback Period} = \frac{\text{Initial Investment}}{\text{Annual Net Cash Inflow}}$$

$$= \frac{\$200{,}000}{\$60{,}000}$$

$$= 3.33 \text{ years}$$

## Uneven Cash Flows

The formula just shown can only be used with uniform, or even, net cash inflows. In those situations where the annual inflows are unequal, the flows are summed until the amount of the original investment is reached. For example, assume the inflows associated with Hill's $200,000 investment are now as follows: Year 1, $70,000; Year 2, $70,000; Year 3, $80,000; Year 4, $50,000; and Year 5, $30,000. The required computations are:

| *Year* | *Annual Net Cash Inflow* | *Cumulative Net Cash Inflow* |
|---|---|---|
| 1 | $70,000 | $ 70,000 |
| 2 | 70,000 | 140,000 |
| 3 | 80,000 | 220,000 |
| 4 | 50,000 | 270,000 |
| 5 | 30,000 | 300,000 |

The computations reveal that $140,000 is recovered by the end of Year 2 and $220,000 by the conclusion of Year 3. Thus, the 200,000th dollar arrives sometime during Year 3 as a result of the $80,000 net cash inflow. The payback method assumes that cash flows are spread evenly throughout a period. Consequently, the additional $60,000 that must be recovered to reach the payback ($200,000 − $140,000) is assumed to be received three quarters of the way through the year ($60,000 ÷ $80,000). The payback, then, is 2.75 years.

## Use of Payback: Pros and Cons

The payback method provides its users with a very simple tool for evaluation purposes. By comparing a project's payback period against a preestablished standard, a manager can easily determine project acceptability. This type of comparison is especially useful for those companies that have limited cash balances and desiring a rapid recovery of investment dollars. Short paybacks allow cash-starved businesses to undertake additional opportunities: the sooner cash is received, the sooner reinvestment can occur.

Unfortunately, the use of payback is not problem-free. In addition to ignoring the time value of money, the payback method exhibits a serious weakness by disregarding project profitability. As an example, assume that a company can invest in one of the following projects:

| *Project* | *Initial Investment* | *Annual Net Cash Inflow* | *Project Life* |
|---|---|---|---|
| A | $100,000 | $50,000 | 3 years |
| B | 100,000 | 40,000 | 6 years |

If the decision is based solely on payback, project A would be selected, because the initial investment is recovered more quickly.

$$\text{Project A Payback} = \frac{\$100{,}000}{\$50{,}000} = 2.0 \text{ years}$$

$$\text{Project B Payback} = \frac{\$100{,}000}{\$40{,}000} = 2.5 \text{ years}$$

HIGHLIGHT

# Payback and a Midlife Crisis

Periodically, most everyone steps back and studies his or her career choice—especially when things are not going smoothly. Included in this group are lawyers who haven't made partner, teachers whose careers have peaked, and artists who grow tired of poverty. Many of these individuals think about dropping it all for a job switch, often by pursuing a graduate degree in business administration (more commonly known as an M.B.A.). Getting such a degree may well be a road to a new career. It might even be an intellectual challenge. But in financial terms, it may *not* be a good investment, especially for mid-career professionals.

The problem is the cost—and not just the cost of tuition. Getting an M.B.A. often means a career-switcher has to forgo two years of a substantial salary to study full-time, since part-time studies are considered inadequate for students who need to be immersed in a new field. Analyzing the cost and return of investing in an M.B.A. degree, two tax planners with a large public accounting firm calculated how long it would take a career-switcher to pay for the degree with earnings from a new job. Their conclusion: Even with an above-average starting salary, the investment would be earned back only with superstar raises.

The conclusion is based on the following table, which shows the number of years required to recoup the two years of lost earnings and the cost of private-school education (the latter estimated at $28,000). The calculations assume that the career changers were 35 years old, had 10 years' work experience, and were earning $50,000 a year before the switch. Two further assumptions: their salaries would have increased 5% a year if they had stayed on the job, and the switchers could have earned 6% a year on the forgone income. The table shows a range of starting salaries—and annual increases—after graduation.

| | *Starting Salary* | | |
|---|---|---|---|
| ***Annual Salary Increases*** | ***$40,000*** | ***$50,000*** | ***$60,000*** |
| 5% | Never | Never | Never |
| 10% | 22 years | 16 years | 11 years |
| 15% | 17 years | 11 years | 9 years |

As you can see, the fastest payback would be nine years—at a $60,000 starting salary and 15% annual raises. At a $40,000 starting salary and 10% annual raises, it would take 22 years to recoup the investment.

Not everyone would fare so badly, of course. Someone making a lower salary to begin with would lose less money by quitting work. And students at taxpayer-supported state schools would pay substantially less tuition than at a private school. Students who would have to leave home and live on campus, on the other hand, would face additional expenses that could run over $10,000 a year.

Some M.B.A. candidates are fortunate and can manage to keep income flowing while attending school full time. Jeff Zahn, a 33-year-old New York musician, was earning between $45,000 and $50,000 annually as an electronic keyboard and cello player, but the unpredictability of the musician's life made him opt for business school. "A Broadway show can open and close in a night," he says. At the time this article was written Zahn worked while studying full time at New York University. During the day, he was a business student. At night, he played in the orchestra for the Broadway musical "Cats."

SOURCE: Adapted from "MBA May Not Be Worth It for Many Career-Switchers," *The Wall Street Journal*, July 20, 1988, p. 25. Reprinted by permission of *The Wall Street Journal*, 

Is this the correct choice, however? Most companies make investments to generate profit, not to see how fast funds can be returned. Project B is really a better selection, because inflows will total \$140,000 (\$40,000 × 3.5 years) versus \$50,000 (\$50,000 × 1 year) for project A *after* the respective payback periods are reached. Stated differently, the payback method considers net cash inflows up until the time the initial investment is recovered. Any receipts that occur after this point are disregarded in the computational process.

## Accounting Rate of Return

A fourth evaluation tool, the **accounting rate of return,** focuses on the average income generated by a project in relation to the project's initial investment outlay. Unlike the methods discussed earlier, this capital budgeting technique emphasizes income and *not* cash flows. A proper measure of profit, of course, includes a deduction for depreciation expense.

The accounting rate of return is computed by the following formula:

$$\text{Accounting Rate of Return} = \frac{\text{Average Annual Increase in Income}}{\text{Initial Investment}}$$

To illustrate the related calculations, assume that a company is considering the acquisition of some new machinery that costs \$80,000. The machinery has a service life of 10 years, no residual value, and will be depreciated by using the straight-line method. Average annual net cash inflows from operations are expected to increase by \$28,000. The accounting rate of return is 25%, derived as follows:

$$\text{Accounting Rate of Return} = \frac{\$28{,}000 - \$8{,}000}{\$80{,}000} = 25\%$$

The numerator is computed by subtracting depreciation expense of \$8,000 (\$80,000 ÷ 10 years) from the operating cash flows.

Because the machinery will be depreciated, some companies feel the accounting rate of return is more appropriately based on an average investment figure rather than on the initial outlay. The average investment can be calculated by adding the beginning and ending investment and dividing by 2, specifically, (\$80,000 + \$0) ÷ 2, or \$40,000.

### Evaluation of the Accounting Rate of Return

The accounting rate of return remains popular primarily because of its consistency with the techniques employed to evaluate companywide and divisional performance. Further, most users agree that the accounting rate of return is a simple tool and easy to understand. The calculated return on an investment is merely compared against a cutoff that has been established by management to judge project attractiveness.

Like payback, however, this method has several serious drawbacks. The time value of money is ignored as is the timing of an investment's earnings. Two projects, for example, may produce identical rates of return over a period of, say, three years. One of these projects may generate uniform earnings through the three-year period; the other may actually produce negative returns in the first two years and a substantial payoff in Year 3. These problems require that management closely study the data that underlie the calculation and not rely totally on the rate of return itself.

## APPENDIX Cash Flows and Income Taxes

Businesses pay a substantial amount of their income to governmental authorities. In light of this fact, the revenues and expenses that accompany an investment must be examined to determine the effect on a company's taxes and related cash flows. In practice, the cash flows used with the evaluation methods discussed earlier are normally calculated on an aftertax basis.

### The Aftertax Concept

OBJECTIVE 6
Have a basic knowledge of how income taxes complicate cash-flow calculations.

The aftertax concept is probably best explained by means of a simplified illustration. Assume that San Juan Enterprises, a service business, is studying the effect of adding a new administrative assistant to the payroll. Yearly salary and fringe benefit costs are expected to amount to $25,000; the company is subject to a 40% income tax rate. Management has prepared the following profitability analysis:

| | *Present Situation* | *Proposed Situation* |
|---|---|---|
| Revenues | $200,000 | $200,000 |
| Operating expenses | | |
| Existing | $130,000 | $130,000 |
| Administrative assistant | — | 25,000 |
| Total | $130,000 | $155,000 |
| Income before taxes | $ 70,000 | $ 45,000 |
| Income taxes at 40% | 28,000 | 18,000 |
| Net income | $ 42,000 | $ 27,000 |

Observe the impact of the hiring decision on the company's income taxes. The increased salary and fringe benefit cost has reduced San Juan's taxes by $10,000 ($28,000 − $18,000). The true, *aftertax cost* of the administrative assistant, then, is $15,000 ($25,000 − $10,000).

In terms of cash flow, an analysis could have been made as follows:

| | |
|---|---|
| Cash outflow for salaries and benefits | $(25,000) |
| Tax savings* | 10,000 |
| Net cash outflow | $(15,000) |

* Recall that cost savings are treated as cash inflows.

The $15,000 net cash outflow would be employed in any type of capital budgeting analysis performed by the company (e.g., payback, net present value, and so forth).

Although our example has focused on an expense, the same concept could have been illustrated with an increase in revenue. Because revenues increase income (and related tax payments), we can say the following:

| | |
|---|---|
| Cash inflow from added revenue | $ XX,XXX |
| Added taxes (a cash outflow) | (XX,XXX) |
| Net cash inflow | $ XX,XXX |

Fortunately, the net cash flow computations can be simplified by use of the formula shown.

| (Cash Inflow or Outflow) × (1 − Tax Rate) = Net Cash Flow |
|---|

In San Juan's case, for example, the $15,000 figure could have been derived as:

$$\$25{,}000 \times (1 - 0.40) = \$15{,}000$$

### Depreciation: Why Special Treatment is Needed

On page 1018, we emphasized that depreciation is ignored in present value calculations because of its noncash nature. Bear in mind that depreciation (more specifically, a cost recovery write-off under the Modified Accelerated Cost Recovery System) is a deductible item in the computation of a company's tax obligation to the federal government. Such amounts, like the salary and fringe benefit costs shown earlier, therefore give rise to tax savings. However, special treatment is needed because depreciation itself is a noncash charge.

To illustrate this treatment, let us assume that San Juan's management is now considering an investment that will increase the firm's depreciation expense by $25,000. (This figure was purposely selected to coincide with the cost of the administrative assistant for ease in understanding.) Similar to the company's other expenditure, depreciation will produce a tax savings of $10,000. Unlike the earlier example, however, it would be improper to net the tax savings against the $25,000 figure—to do so would result in the offset of a cash flow against a noncash item. Hence, *the only cash flow related to depreciation is the tax savings.*

We can conclude that depreciation has given San Juan a *tax shield* of $10,000. That is, the deduction has shielded ("protected") the company's revenues from taxation and has lowered the firm's tax payments to the government. If desired, this concept could be expressed in a formula, as follows:

| Depreciation Deduction × Tax Rate = Cash Savings |
|---|

$$\$25{,}000 \times 0.40 = \$10{,}000$$

## Chapter Review

### Learning Objectives—The Key Points

**1 Understand the capital budgeting process.** Capital budgeting is concerned with the planning and decision making related to long-term investments. Examples of long-term investments would include equipment acquisitions, building construction, and the addition of new product lines. The evaluation of such projects is performed by comparing various project characteristics (e.g., the rate of return) against guidelines that have been established by management. Such evaluations are commonly known as screening decisions. Given that most companies have many acceptable projects but limited funds, a determination must be made of the most attractive investment, the second most attractive investment, and so forth. This process is known as project ranking.

**2 Know the factors that management considers in the evaluation of capital expenditure proposals.** Three factors are normally evaluated when analyzing an investment. First, there is the amount of the initial investment, which may include an investment in working capital (e.g., buildups in cash, accounts receivable, and inventory). Second, the returns from the investment must be considered. Project returns are usually measured in terms of net cash flows, or cash inflows minus cash outflows. For those investments that produce savings in operating costs, such savings are given the same accounting treatment as cash inflows. Finally, companies must consider the minimum rate of return acceptable on a project. This rate is typically set equal to or slightly in excess of the firm's cost of capital.

**3 Be familiar with the concept of the time value of money.** The time value of money recognizes that a dollar received today is worth more to an investor than a dollar received in the future. Earlier inflows can be reinvested to generate additional returns. This concept is integrated in the evaluation of capital projects by use of present value, as described by the next learning objective.

**4 Understand the distinction between compound interest and present value.** Compound interest and present value are two different tools that are used to evaluate an investment. Compound interest is employed to figure the amount to which a given sum will grow by the end of a designated time period. The underlying procedures involve the calculation of interest on the original amount invested as well as on previously computed interest that is left "on deposit."

Present value, on the other hand, discounts a future cash sum and figures its "current worth" to an investor. Stated differently, present value is the amount an investor is willing to pay today to receive specified future cash flows. The related computations recognize the time value of money by weighting the cash flows that occur in earlier years more heavily than those that occur in later years.

**5 Be familiar with net present value, the internal rate of return, payback, and the accounting rate of return.** As its name implies, the net-present-value method focuses on netting (i.e., offsetting) the present value of an investment's cash inflows against the present value of the cash outflows. If the result of this process is positive, the project should be considered for acceptance; if negative, rejection is in order. The internal rate of return is another present-value-based evaluation approach. This method finds the actual yield on an investment by equating the present value of an investment's cash inflows and cash outflows. The underlying calculations are sometimes complicated by uneven cash flow streams and the need for interpolation.

Unlike the first two approaches, payback and the accounting rate of return do not consider the time value of money. Payback shows how rapidly an initial investment is recovered. This method of project evaluation, although simple, ignores all cash flows that occur after the payback point has been reached. The accounting rate of return, also considered very easy to use, focuses on a project's return in relation to the amount invested or perhaps an average investment amount. The return in this case is measured in terms of income and not cash flow.

**6 (Appendix) Have a basic knowledge of how income taxes complicate cash-flow calculations.** Capital budgeting models normally use aftertax amounts. Because many cash inflows and outflows (e.g., those from revenues and those for deductible expenses) affect a company's tax obligation, the tax implications for these items must be considered when analyzing a long-term investment. Deductible expenses result in a tax savings; conversely, revenues produce added tax for the firm. The tax effect is subtracted from the cash flow itself, with the net amount then used with the various capital budgeting evaluation tools. Be aware that netting is not required for depreciation, which is a noncash expense.

## Chapter Quiz

The five questions that follow relate to several issues raised in the chapter. Test your knowledge of the issues by selecting the best answer. (The answers appear on p. 1040.)

**1** Which of the following is rarely a consideration when analyzing a long-term project?
- a The cost of the investment.
- b The lowest rate of return acceptable to management.
- c The company's current ratio.
- d The investment's cash inflows and cash outflows.

**2** The time value of money:
- a is integrated in present-value computations.
- b weights cash flows that occur in five years more heavily than cash flows that occur in two years.
- c is reflected by the accounting rate of return.
- d should not be considered when analyzing an investment.

**3** Hughes Corporation is considering a $200,000 machine that promises savings in cash operating costs of $40,000 over each of the next six years. The company requires a 10% return on its investments. Appropriate present value factors follow.

| *Present Value of $1* | *Present Value of a $1 Annuity* |
|---|---|
| 0.56447 | 4.35526 |

Ignoring income taxes, the machine's net present value is:
- a $(5,790).
- b $(25,790).
- c $(177,421).
- d some amount other than those listed above.

**4** The internal rate of return:
- a ignores the time value of money.
- b is another name for the accounting rate of return.
- c results in a net present value of zero.
- d cannot be used when the payback period is less than three years.

**5** The payback method:
- a normally incorporates the use of discount factors.
- b cannot be used with uneven cash flows.
- c generally results in attractive projects from management's perspective, especially when the payback is "long" as opposed to "short."
- d fails to consider all cash flows related to a project.

## Summary Problem

The Ellison Corporation is studying the following investment opportunity:

| | |
|---|---|
| Initial outlay required | $225,000 |
| Net cash inflows, Years 1–5 | 75,000 |
| Disposal value at the end of Year 5 | 5,000 |

Ellison desires a minimum return of 12% on all investments.

**Instructions**

**a** Compute the investment's payback period.

**b** Compute the net present value. Should the investment be considered for acceptance? Explain.

**c** Compute the internal rate of return. For simplicity, disregard the $5,000 disposal value.

**Solution**

**a**

| Year | *Annual Net Cash Inflow* | *Cumulative Net Cash Inflow* |
|---|---|---|
| 1 | $75,000 | $ 75,000 |
| 2 | 75,000 | 150,000 |
| 3 | 75,000 | 225,000 |
| 4 | 75,000 | 300,000 |
| 5 | 80,000 | 380,000 |

The payback period is three years.

**b**

| | *Cash Flow* | × | *Present Value Factor at 12%* | = | *Present Value* |
|---|---|---|---|---|---|
| Initial investment | $(225,000) | | 1.00000 | | $(225,000) |
| Annual net cash inflows | 75,000 | | 3.60478 | | 270,359 |
| Disposal value | 5,000 | | 0.56743 | | 2,837 |
| Net present value | | | | | $ 48,196 |

The net present value is positive, which means the investment should be considered for acceptance.

**c** Let F = the discount factor that equates the present value of the investment's cash inflows and cash outflows

$$\$75{,}000 \times F = \$225{,}000$$
$$F = 3.0$$

Table 2 reveals that for a five-year annuity, a 3.0 factor lies between 18% and 20%. The internal rate of return is 19.86%, as shown by the following calculations:

| | *Present Value Factors* | |
|---|---|---|
| 18% return | 3.12717 | 3.12717 |
| Return on Ellison's investment | 3.00000 | |
| 20% return | | 2.99061 |
| Difference | 0.12717 | 0.13656 |

$$\text{Internal Rate of Return} = 18\% + \frac{0.12717}{0.13656}(2\%)^*$$
$$= 19.86\%$$

* 20% − 18%.

## Questions

**Q28-1** Why must businesses exercise extreme care in the selection of long-term investments?

**Q28-2** Describe the screening and ranking processes as related to capital budgeting.

**Q28-3** What three factors should be considered in the evaluation of an investment opportunity?

**Q28-4** What is meant by an investment in working capital? Are such investments ever recovered? Briefly explain.

**Q28-5** In general, are net cash flows or accounting profits preferred in the evaluation of long-term investment proposals? Why?

**Q28-6** What is the lowest rate of return acceptable to a company?

**Q28-7** Explain what is meant by the time value of money.

**Q28-8** Explain the relationship, if any, between compound interest and present value.

**Q28-9** What is meant by the term "present value"?

**Q28-10** What is an annuity?

**Q28-11** Four methods are frequently used to evaluate capital budgeting proposals. Are these methods normally used by themselves or in conjunction with each other? Why?

**Q28-12** When examining a project's cash inflows and outflows, what present-value relationship holds true at the internal rate of return?

**Q28-13** Aside from ignoring the time value of money, what is another inherent problem associated with the payback method?

**Q28-14** Does the accounting rate of return focus on income or cash flows?

***Q28-15** Should cash flows be expressed on a beforetax or an aftertax basis?

***Q28-16** Briefly discuss the concept of a depreciation tax shield.

## Exercises

**E28-1** ***Basic present value calculations***

Calculate the present value of the following cash flows, rounding to the nearest dollar:

a A single cash inflow of $12,000 in five years given a 12% rate of return.

b An annual receipt of $16,000 over the next 12 years given a 14% rate of return.

c A single receipt of $15,000 at the end of Year 1 followed by a single receipt of $10,000 at the end of Year 3. The company has a 10% rate of return.

d An annual receipt of $8,000 for three years followed by a single receipt of $10,000 at the end of Year 4. The company has a 16% rate of return.

**E28-2** ***Present value analysis: Working backward***

The following information pertains to four independent investments:

| | *A* | *B* | *C* | *D* |
|---|---|---|---|---|
| Present value | ? | $19,646 | $34,625 | $50,852 |
| Interest rate | 10% | ? | 14% | 12% |
| Investment period | 4 years | 5 years | ? | 10 years |
| Annual cash inflows | $8,000 | $6,000 | $7,000 | ? |

* An asterisk preceding an item indicates that the material is covered in the Appendix to this chapter.

Determine the unknown for each of the investments. (*Note:* Amounts have been rounded to the nearest dollar; please consider this procedure in your calculations. Do *not* interpolate.)

**E28-3** ***Straightforward net present value calculations***

Contempo, Inc., is considering the acquisition of some new labor-saving equipment. Management estimates that the equipment will cost $42,000 and will produce the following savings in cash operating costs over the next five years: Year 1, $15,000; Year 2, $13,000; Year 3, $10,000; Year 4, $10,000; and Year 5, $6,000. The company uses the net-present-value method to analyze investments and desires a minimum rate of return of 12%.

a Compute the net present value of the proposed investment. Ignore income taxes and round to the nearest dollar.

b Considering the time value of money, should Contempo acquire the new equipment? Why?

**E28-4** ***Cash flow calculations and net present value***

On January 2, 19X1, Bruce Greene invested $10,000 in the stock market and purchased 500 shares of Heartland Development, Inc. Heartland paid cash dividends of $2.60 per share in 19X1 and 19X2; the dividend was raised to $3.10 per share in 19X3. On December 31, 19X3, Greene sold his holdings and generated proceeds of $13,000. Greene uses the net-present-value method and desires a 16% return on investments.

a Prepare a chronological list of the investment's cash flows. *Note:* Greene *is* entitled to the 19X3 dividend.

b Compute the investment's net present value, rounding calculations to the nearest dollar.

c Given the results of part (b), should Greene have acquired the Heartland stock? Briefly explain.

**E28-5** ***Straightforward net present value and internal rate of return***

The following items are independent of one another; round all calculations to the nearest dollar.

a You have $8,000 to invest and require a 10% minimum rate of return. Two proposals are under consideration. Investment A will generate $2,000 for each of the next six years; investment B promises $2,500 at the end of Years 1 and 2 and $1,700 for each of the following four years. By using the net-present-value method, determine which investment is preferable.

b You have $9,000 to invest. An opportunity is available that produces a stream of six annual inflows of $2,000 each. Compute the investment's internal rate of return.

**E28-6** ***Net present value and payback***

Collins Corporation is considering the acquisition of a new delivery truck that costs $26,000, to expand its service area. Annual cash inflows are expected to increase by $6,000 over the next two years, $8,000 over the following two years, and $11,000 over the final three years of the truck's service life. The truck will be depreciated by the straight-line method and is expected to have a $2,000 disposal value.

Management evaluates investment opportunities by using payback and the net-present-value method. Collins desires a minimum payback of four years and a minimum rate of return of 12%. Ignore income taxes and round calculations to the nearest dollar.

Should the truck be acquired? Explain your answer.

**E28-7** ***Payback and cash flow analysis***

Elway and Associates uses the payback method to evaluate investment opportunities. Two investment proposals are under consideration, each requiring an initial outlay of $150,000. Cash flow information follows.

| Investment A | | Investment B | |
|---|---|---|---|
| ***Year*** | ***Net Cash Inflow*** | ***Year*** | ***Net Cash Inflow*** |
| 1 | $45,000 | 1–3 | $35,000 |
| 2 | 60,000 | 4 | 40,000 |
| 3 | 35,000 | 5 | 10,000 |
| 4 | 10,000 | 6 | 40,000 |
| 5 | 15,000 | | |
| 6 | 27,000 | | |

a Compute the payback period of each investment.

b Solely on the basis of payback, which of the two investments is the more attractivc? Why?

c From a total cash flow viewpoint, which of the two investments is really the more attractive? Disregard the time value of money.

d To provide the decision maker with additional information, what could Elway do to the cash inflows? Why would this process be helpful?

**E28-8** ***Comprehensive capital budgeting***

Castle, Inc., is considering the purchase of a machine that costs $69,952. The machine has a six-year life and will result in net cash inflows of $20,000 per year. Assume the use of straight-line depreciation, no residual value, and no income taxes, and round calculations to the nearest dollar.

a Determine the machine's net present value if Castle has a 16% rate of return.

b Compute the machine's internal rate of return.

c Determine the payback period.

d Determine the accounting rate of return on the company's initial investment.

**E28-9** ***Capital budgeting methods***

Consider the following capital budgeting evaluation tools:

1—Net present value
2—Internal rate of return
3—Payback method
4—Accounting rate of return

Match these tools with the comments that follow. In some cases more than one tool may apply.

______a Focuses on income, not cash flows.

______b Integrates the time value of money into the evaluation process.

______c Equates the present value of a project's cash inflows and cash outflows.

______d Stresses the recovery of the initial investment outlay.

______e Discounts cash flows by employing factors that relate to a company's minimum acceptable return.

______f A cash-flow-based approach that ignores selected cash flows on a project.

**E28-10** ***Overview of capital budgeting***

Evaluate the comments that follow as being True or False. If the comment is false, briefly explain why.

a Generally speaking, cash flows are preferred over accounting income when evaluating long-term investments.

b Present value is actually the "reverse" of compound interest.

c Annuity factors can be derived by summing the present value factors for individual, yearly cash flows.

d A project's internal rate of return will result in a zero net present value for the project.

e If income taxes are ignored, depreciation expense amounts should be used when figuring an investment's net present value.

***E28-11** ***Aftertax cash flows and payback***

Dayton Industries is considering the acquisition of a machine that costs $50,000. The machine is expected to provide annual beforetax savings in cash operating costs of $10,000 over its 10-year service life. Dayton uses straight-line depreciation on all assets and is subject to a 40% income tax rate.

a Determine the aftertax cash flows related to the machine. *Hint:* Be sure to include the tax savings from depreciation.

b Compute the machine's payback.

## Problems

### Series A

**P28-A1** ***Straightforward net-present-value and payback computations***

STL Entertainment is considering the acquisition of a sight-seeing boat for summer tours along the Mississippi River. The following information is available:

| | |
|---|---|
| Cost of boat | $500,000 |
| Service life | 10 summer seasons |
| Disposal value at the end of 10 seasons | $100,000 |
| Capacity per trip | 300 passengers |
| Fixed operating costs per season (including straight-line depreciation) | $160,000 |
| Variable operating costs per trip | $1,000 |
| Ticket price | $5 per passenger |

All operating costs, except depreciation, require cash outlays. On the basis of similar operations in other parts of the country, management anticipates that each trip will be sold out and that 120,000 passengers will be carried each season. Ignore income taxes.

#### Instructions

a Compute the payback period of the boat.

b By using the net-present-value method, determine whether STL Entertainment should acquire the boat. Assume a 14% desired return on all investments; round calculations to the nearest dollar.

**P28-A2** ***Make or buy; net present value; working capital investment***

Equity Products is a manufacturer of electronic components used in the appliance industry. The company currently purchases a particular part for $1.75. Because of problems with product quality and supplier reliability, Equity is studying whether to manufacture the part internally.

To begin production, new machinery must be acquired that costs $380,000. The machinery, which has a six-year life and an estimated residual value of $50,000, will be depreciated by the straight-line method. Art Sanchez, a current Equity employee, will oversee manufacturing activities and will be given a $7,000 raise because of increased responsibilities. Sanchez's original position will remain unfilled.

The company's cost accountants and engineers have estimated the unit variable production costs that follow.

| | |
|---|---|
| Direct materials | $0.22 |
| Direct labor | 0.40 |
| Variable factory overhead | 0.32 |

Equity must make an immediate $30,000 working capital investment to build needed direct materials inventories. Annual production should total 120,000 units over each of the next six years. Manufacturing activities will then be discontinued and the materials inventories depleted (i.e., working capital recovered) because of a planned change in Equity's product line. The machinery will be sold because of its specialized nature.

Management uses the net-present-value method to analyze investment opportunities, requiring a 10% minimum rate of return. Ignore income taxes, and round calculations to the nearest dollar.

**Instructions**

Determine whether Equity should make or buy the part.

**P28-A3** ***Basketball player decision***

The Phoenix Kings of the United Basketball League have a moody center by the name of Orlando Dawkins. Dawkins is under contract with the team and is scheduled to earn $650,000 in both 19X3 and 19X4. A $75,000 salary increase will take effect in 19X5.

Dawkins has not gotten along with several of his teammates and, as a result, management is exploring the possibility of a trade with the Philadelphia Rockets to acquire George Harper, a star player. The Kings would pay the Rockets $350,000 immediately for the trade to take place. Harper would be paid a $270,000 signing bonus at the beginning of 19X3 that management plans to expense over the next three years by using straight-line amortization. Harper's annual salary would be $950,000 from 19X3–19X5, highest on the team because of his ability to attract fans. The Kings expect that increased attendance will produce added annual net cash inflows of $525,000.

Phoenix officials feel that both players will play three more years for the Kings, at which time they would become free agents and move along to other clubs. Compensation to be received from the other club for Dawkins will be $380,000; for Harper the figure would increase to $500,000. Regardless of whether the trade takes place, the Kings are obligated to pay Dawkins $200,000 at the end of 19X4 per terms of his original contract.

The Kings desire a rate of return of 14% and use the net-present-value method to analyze investments. Round all calculations to the nearest dollar and ignore income taxes.

**Instructions**

a Determine whether the Kings should keep Dawkins or trade for Harper. Assume the trade would occur on January 1, 19X3.
b Future cash flows are, in many cases, subject to change. List several events that could occur that might influence the cash flows in this situation.

**P28-A4** ***Accounting and internal rates of return***

Triple-A Storage, Inc., is studying two investments in depreciable assets. Each asset requires an initial outlay of $180,000. The following schedules of cash flows are applicable:

| | Investment No. 113 | | | Investment No. 114 | |
|---|---|---|---|---|---|
| *Year* | *Cash Inflows* | *Cash Outflows* | *Year* | *Cash Inflows* | *Cash Outflows* |
| 1 | $ — | $ — | 1 | $86,900 | $35,600 |
| 2 | — | — | 2 | 94,300 | 43,000 |
| 3 | — | — | 3 | 98,000 | 46,700 |
| 4 | — | — | 4 | 90,000 | 38,700 |
| 5 | 501,900 | 245,400 | 5 | 80,000 | 28,700 |

The company will depreciate the assets by the straight-line method over a five-year life. Disregard residual values and income taxes.

**Instructions**

a Compute the accounting rate of return for each investment. Triple-A calculates the rate of return on the investment's initial acquisition cost.
b Compute the internal rate of return for investment no. 114.
c Assume that the internal rate of return for investment no. 113 amounts to 7.4%. Explain why the internal rate of return differs between investments 113 and 114.

**P28-A5** ***Payback analysis; accounting rate of return***

Jimmy's Pizza is studying the acquisition of a small truck for after-hours food service to dorm students. The truck and necessary equipment, which have a 10-year service life and $5,000 residual value, are expected to cost $25,000. Jimmy anticipates that annual dorm sales will total $27,000; however, restaurant sales will fall by $6,000 per year if the acquisition occurs. Annual operating costs will be: gasoline, $2,500; maintenance and repair, $800; driver's salary, $5,500; and insurance, $600. The cost of food and drinks generally averages 30% of sales. Ignore income taxes.

**Instructions**

a Compute the annual net cash inflow from operation of the food service.
b If Jimmy requires a payback of five years on all new investments, should the truck be acquired?
c Determine the accounting rate of return on the initial investment.

***P28-A6** ***Cash flow; taxes; net present value***

Central Plains Freight Company is studying the possibility of adding a new truck to its fleet. The vehicle will cost $80,000 and is expected to generate annual sales revenues of $70,000. Central depreciates all vehicles by the straight-line method over a six-year service life. An $8,000 residual value is anticipated.

Management expects that the truck will be driven approximately 25,000 miles each year. Cash operating costs will average $0.22 per mile in Years 1–3 and then jump to $0.26 in Years 4–6. A driver will be paid a $35,000 annual salary.

Central Plains is subject to a 40% tax rate on all items of revenue and expense and requires a 16% return on all investments. The company employs the net-present-value method to evaluate long-term projects.

**Instructions**

a The following schedule has been designed to identify the net cash flows related to the truck. The first two items are done as examples.

| Item | Amount | Tax Effect, If Any* | Aftertax Cash Flow |
|---|---|---|---|
| Truck cost | $(80,000) | None | $(80,000) |
| Revenues | 70,000 | $(28,000) | 42,000 |

* Parentheses denote an increase in taxes.

Complete the schedule for the remaining items that result in an aftertax cash flow.

b Use the aftertax cash flow amounts in a net-present-value analysis and determine whether Central Plains should acquire the truck. Round all computations to the nearest dollar.

## Series B

**P28-B1** ***Straightforward net-present-value and payback computations***

Buckeye Cruises is considering the acquisition of a sight-seeing boat for summer tours along the Ohio River. The following information is available:

| | |
|---|---|
| Cost of boat | $360,000 |
| Service life | 8 summer seasons |
| Disposal value at the end of 8 seasons | $80,000 |
| Variable operating costs per trip | $850 |
| Fixed operating costs per season (including straight-line depreciation) | $65,000 |
| Capacity per trip | 250 passengers |

All operating costs, except depreciation, require cash outlays. On the basis of similar operations in other parts of the country, management anticipates that each trip will be sold out and that 75,000 passengers will be carried each season. Each passenger pays $5; ignore income taxes.

**Instructions**

a Compute the payback period of the boat.

b By using the net-present-value method, determine whether Buckeye Cruises should acquire the boat. Assume a 12% desired return on all investments; round calculations to the nearest dollar.

**P28-B2** ***Make or buy; net present value; working capital investment***

Fairbanks, Inc., manufactures various components that are used in the production of motorcycle engines. The company is presently purchasing a particular valve assembly from Medford Machining for $14.80. Because of reliability problems with Medford and the fact that a price increase is imminent, Fairbanks is studying whether to produce the assembly itself. The following information is available:

a The company will need 7,500 valve assemblies annually over each of the next four years.

b Variable production costs are anticipated to be: direct materials, $1.10; direct labor, $1.50; and factory overhead, $0.60.

c A new supervisor would be hired to oversee production. Estimated annual wages will be $37,000, plus an additional 20% for fringe benefit costs.

d Specialized machinery that costs $140,000 would be acquired at the start of manufacturing. The machinery has a four-year life, a projected disposal value of $20,000, and will be depreciated by the straight-line method.

e Fairbanks must make an immediate $15,000 investment in working capital to acquire needed raw materials inventories. This investment will be recovered at the end of four years when production is anticipated to be discontinued. The machinery (see item (d)) will be sold at this time as well.

f Management uses the net-present-value method to analyze investments, requiring a 14% rate of return. Ignore income taxes and round calculations to the nearest dollar.

**Instructions**

Determine whether Fairbanks should make or buy the valve assemblies.

**P28-B3** ***Equipment replacement decision***

Columbia Enterprises is studying the replacement of some equipment that originally cost $74,000. The equipment is expected to provide six more years of service if $8,700 of major repairs are performed in two years. Annual cash operating costs total $27,200. Columbia can sell the equipment now for $36,000; the estimated residual value in six years is $5,000.

New equipment is available that will reduce annual cash operating costs to $21,000. The equipment costs $103,000, has a service life of six years, and has an estimated residual value of $13,000. Company sales will total $430,000 per year with either the existing or the new equipment.

Columbia has a minimum desired return of 12% and depreciates all equipment by the straight-line method.

**Instructions**

a By using the net-present-value method, determine whether Columbia should keep its present equipment or acquire the new equipment. Round all calculations to the nearest dollar, and ignore income taxes.

b Columbia's management feels that the time value of money should be considered in all long-term decisions. Briefly discuss the rationale that underlies management's belief.

**P28-B4** ***Accounting and internal rates of return***

Flowerville, Inc., is studying two investments in depreciable assets. Each asset requires an initial outlay of $60,000. The following schedules of cash flows are applicable:

| *Investment A* | | | *Investment B* | | |
|---|---|---|---|---|---|
| *Year* | *Cash Inflows* | *Cash Outflows* | *Year* | *Cash Inflows* | *Cash Outflows* |
| 1 | $32,800 | $11,800 | 1 | $ — | $ — |
| 2 | 35,000 | 14,000 | 2 | — | — |
| 3 | 38,700 | 17,700 | 3 | — | — |
| 4 | 40,000 | 19,000 | 4 | 186,800 | 102,800 |

The company will depreciate the assets by the straight-line method over a four-year life. Disregard residual values and income taxes.

**Instructions**

a Compute the accounting rate of return for each investment. Flowerville calculates the rate of return on the investment's initial acquisition cost.

b Compute the internal rate of return for investment A.

c Assume that the internal rate of return on investment B is 8.8%. Compare the results obtained in parts (a) and (b). Comment on any differences that arose, and explain an underlying problem associated with the accounting rate of return.

**P28-B5** ***Payback analysis; accounting rate of return***

Tasty Treats is studying the acquisition of a new vehicle to expand its fleet of ice-cream trucks for service in suburban neighborhoods. The truck, which has an eight-year service life and $2,000 residual value, is expected to cost $20,000. The company's owner anticipates that annual sales will increase by $25,000 if the acquisition occurs. Annual operating costs will be: gasoline, $2,000; license, $100; maintenance and repair, $1,200; driver's salary, $6,800; and insurance, $900. The cost of ice cream generally averages 40% of sales. Ignore income taxes.

**Instructions**

a Compute the annual net cash inflow from operation of the additional truck.
b Determine the payback period.
c If Tasty Treats requires an accounting rate of return on initial investment of 12%, should the truck be acquired?

***P28-B6** ***Cash flow; taxes; net present value***

Overnight Freight Company is studying the possibility of adding a new truck to its fleet. The vehicle will cost $60,000 and is expected to generate annual sales revenues of $50,000. Overnight depreciates all vehicles by the straight-line method over a five-year service life. A $5,000 residual value is anticipated.

Management expects that the truck will be driven approximately 20,000 miles each year. Cash operating costs will average $0.20 per mile in Years 1–3 and then jump to $0.24 in Years 4 and 5. A driver will be paid a $30,000 annual salary.

Overnight is subject to a 40% tax rate on all items of revenue and expense and requires a 12% return on all investments. The company employs the net-present-value method to evaluate long-term projects.

**Instructions**

a The following schedule has been designed to identify the net cash flows related to the truck. The first two items are done as examples.

| *Item* | *Amount* | *Tax Effect, If Any** | *Aftertax Cash Flow* |
|---|---|---|---|
| Truck cost | $(60,000) | None | $(60,000) |
| Revenues | 50,000 | $(20,000) | 30,000 |

* Parentheses denote an increase in taxes.

Complete the schedule for the remaining items that result in an aftertax cash flow.

b Use the aftertax cash flow amounts in a net-present-value analysis and determine whether Overnight should acquire the truck. Round all computations to the nearest dollar.

## Beyond the Basics

**BB28-1** ***Net present value; algebra; analysis***

Ron Horstmann is considering various investment opportunities for his employer. One possible opportunity involves obtaining a five-year franchise from CC Cookies to operate a store at Pepperwood Mall. CC Cookies requires a $40,000 immediate up-front payment. In addition, each store must be furnished with $200,000 of equipment that has a five-year life and a $20,000 disposal value. Additional information follows.

| | |
|---|---|
| Anticipated annual sales | 16,000 dozen |
| Annual franchise fee | 5% of sales revenue |
| Variable cost per dozen | $2.25 |
| Annual mall rent | |
| Years 1–2 | $12,000 |
| Years 3–5 | 13,500 |

CC Cookies will allow each franchise to set its own selling price on the basis of regional factors, local competition, and so forth. The price can range from $6.75 to $7.50 per dozen. In an effort to maximize sales, Horstmann's employer would charge $6.75.

Assume a 10% rate of return is required on all investments. Ignore income taxes.

**Instructions**

a Compute the net present value of the cookie franchise, rounding calculations to the nearest dollar. Should the store be opened? Why?

b At what selling price would the franchise produce a zero net present value? What has a strong possibility of changing if this selling price is charged?

c Would the net present value from part (a) increase or decrease if payment of the $40,000 franchise fee could be postponed until a later date? No calculations are necessary.

***BB28-2** ***Focus on internal rate of return and cash flows***

This problem consists of two unrelated parts.

**Part I** Assume that an investment requires an immediate $86,000 outflow. The investment will generate annual cash inflows of $17,500 over each of the next eight years along with a single $3,000 cash inflow in Year 3.

a Compute the investment's net present value, assuming a 12% rate of return.

b Compute the investment's net present value, assuming a 14% rate of return.

c What is the net present value at the investment's internal rate of return? Briefly explain.

d By interpolating on the basis of net present values, compute the investment's internal rate of return.

**Part II** Virginia Tool & Die desires a 10% rate of return on all investments and is subject to a 40% income tax rate. The company will dispose of a machine at the end of Year 5, generating the following figures:

| | |
|---|---|
| Machine cost | $85,000 |
| Accumulated depreciation | 60,000 |
| Book value | $25,000 |
| Cash disposal value | 28,000 |
| Gain on disposal | $ 3,000 |

a Virginia Tool & Die is taxed on its income, which includes gains and losses. Determine the cash flow from this disposal that would be used in a capital budgeting analysis.

b Compute the discounted cash flow amount for the disposal.

## Answers to Chapter Quiz

**1** c

**2** a

**3** b

| | | |
|---|---|---|
| $(200,000) | × 1.00000 = | $(200,000) |
| 40,000 | × 4.35526 = | 174,210 |
| | | $ (25,790) |

**4** c

**5** d

# An Introduction to Federal Income Taxes

APPENDIX A

The dates of April 15 and May 4 have a unique meaning to many people in this country. April 15, of course, is the usual deadline for settling one's tax obligation with the U.S. government. May 4, on the other hand, represents a recent Tax Freedom Day—the day on which the average American will have earned enough money to pay his or her federal, state, and local tax bills for the year. Tax Freedom Day is calculated by The Tax Foundation, Inc., by assuming that every dollar the average worker earns starting on January 1 goes to the government.

Income taxes also have a "special meaning" to corporate management. Tax payments to various government authorities represent a significant cost of doing business and can severely limit an entity's plans for growth and expansion. In view of the magnitude of these assessments, companies (and individuals too) often devote considerable efforts in trying to reduce or postpone taxes. Tax planning and decision making is therefore of utmost importance.

This appendix presents an introduction to federal income taxes. Be aware while reading these pages that tax law is complex, full of exceptions, and often studied in advanced accounting courses. Our goal, thus, is to focus on the basic issues only.[1]

## Federal Income Tax: Background and Administration

The first federal income tax was enacted to help finance the Civil War. Our present income tax, however, is derived from the Sixteenth Amendment to the Constitution, which was ratified in 1913. The amendment states:

> The Congress shall have power to lay and collect taxes on incomes, from whatever source derived, without apportionment among the several States, and without regard to any census or enumeration.

Over the years, various tax-related laws have been passed by Congress. Some of these laws have led to sweeping changes in our country's approach to the taxation of income. Not too long ago, for example, Congress enacted the Tax Reform Act of 1986—the culmination of efforts to provide "relief" for the taxpaying public. The Act called for substantial reductions in both individual and business income tax rates, while broadening the base on which taxes are computed. In addition, this legislation attempted to shift more of the tax burden from individuals to corporations.

[1] Our discussion reflects the tax rules and rates that are in effect at the time of this writing.

### Administration of the Tax Law

The tax laws passed by Congress are administered by the **Internal Revenue Service (IRS),** an agency of the Treasury Department. Probably best noted for the processing of tax returns, the IRS also interprets tax law, answers taxpayer questions, processes tax payments and refunds, and sometimes initiates legal action. Let us dwell on return processing for a moment, since this is the area of tax with which you may have had some interaction.

All returns filed with the IRS are checked for mathematical and mechanical accuracy. If a return is found to contain an error that overstates tax, any excess is either refunded or held as a credit against the next period's tax liability. For inaccuracies that result in an underpayment of tax, a bill is sent to the erring taxpayer.

The IRS often goes one step further in the examination of returns by performing an audit. Returns are selected for audit on the basis of several factors, including errors contained within the return, requests for abnormally large refunds, disclosure of income and expenses in excess of certain specified limits, and simply on a random basis to encourage correct reporting by taxpayers. The number of returns selected for review varies and often depends on the availability of audit personnel. In a recent fiscal year such examinations resulted in the collection of $19.2 billion of additional taxes and penalties.[2]

## Classes of Taxpayers

According to tax law, there are four classes of taxpayers: individuals, corporations, estates, and trusts. Missing from this list are the proprietorship and partnership forms of business organization. These latter entity forms are not considered as separate taxable units apart from their owners; consequently, any income generated is taxed to the owner or partners whether or not such amounts have been withdrawn from the business. As we will show later in the discussion, the owner of a proprietorship reports business income from the enterprise on his or her individual tax return, together with salaries and income from other sources, and is taxed accordingly. Members of a partnership report their respective share of business income in a similar fashion.

In contrast to the proprietorship and partnership, the corporation is a separate taxable entity and is required to pay taxes on its income. Additionally, individual stockholders must report any dividends received as part of their annual income. These procedures result in "double taxation" because income is taxed first to the corporation at the time of generation and then later to stockholders when dividends are distributed. Taxation of estates and trusts is extremely specialized and will not be discussed in this text.

### Taxpayer Accounting Methods: Cash Versus Accrual

Virtually all individual taxpayers and most small businesses use the **cash basis** of accounting when reporting to the IRS. Although not in accord with generally accepted accounting principles, the cash basis is often acceptable for figuring in-

[2] *Annual Report of the Commissioner of the Internal Revenue Service and Chief Counsel: 1988* (Washington, D.C.: Government Printing Office, 1988), p. 10.

come subject to taxation. With the cash basis, revenues are recognized when cash is collected or *constructively received* (i.e., made available to the taxpayer). To explain constructive receipt, income is considered taxable when it is within the taxpayer's control. As a result, interest credited to a savings account on December 31, 19X1, is 19X1 income even if the amount is not entered in the savings passbook or withdrawn until 19X2.

Turning to expenses, the general rule under the cash basis is that expenses are recognized in the period of payment. There are exceptions, however. For example, disbursements for long-lived assets such as plant and equipment must be capitalized upon acquisition. Subsequently, if the assets are used for business purposes, a depreciation (i.e., cost recovery) deduction is allowed. Similarly, prepayments for business services (such as rent and insurance) are expensed not when paid but rather in the period(s) when benefits are received.

If they desire, taxpayers may elect to use the accrual basis of accounting. Under the **accrual basis,** revenues are recognized when earned, and expenses are entered in the records when incurred. Accrual accounting must be used by large corporations and businesses in which inventories play a major role in operating activities.

Individual taxpayers generally voice a strong preference for cash basis accounting because of the method's simplicity. In addition, cash basis taxpayers are able to defer taxes into future accounting periods. A doctor, for instance, could delay billing patients seen in December until January and thereby transfer revenue into the next taxable year. Lower revenues, of course, mean lower taxes. Naturally, this action will catch up with the doctor in the next period; however, if the same practice is repeated, the postponement of taxes will continue. The end result is the generation of additional cash for investment purposes or to cover business expenses. Use of accrual accounting would prevent this postponement from occurring.

## Tax Accounting for Individuals

Forms and instructions for the computation and filing of income taxes are available from the IRS. Although the standard forms will not be illustrated here, the calculation of an individual's tax liability can be visualized in terms of the general formula shown in Exhibit A-1. The manner in which the formula's components actually appear on a tax return varies somewhat from that shown in our illustration. Nevertheless, the formula is a useful tool for understanding the structure of our income tax system. Each of the components in the exhibit will now be explained.

### Gross Income

A taxpayer can receive income from hundreds of different sources. In all likelihood even the most comprehensive listing of income sources would be incomplete. The Internal Revenue Code therefore presumes that all income is reportable and taxable *unless specifically excluded by law.* A taxpayer's **gross income,** then, is his or her total income less allowable exclusions. Typical items of gross income include, but are not limited to, compensation for services (e.g., wages, salaries, tips, and bonuses), interest, dividends, rents, alimony, pensions, most prizes and awards, income from a proprietorship or partnership, and gains from dealings in property and securities. Even proceeds from embezzlement, gambling winnings, and unemployment compensation are taxable!

**Exhibit A-1**
**General Tax Formula for Individuals**

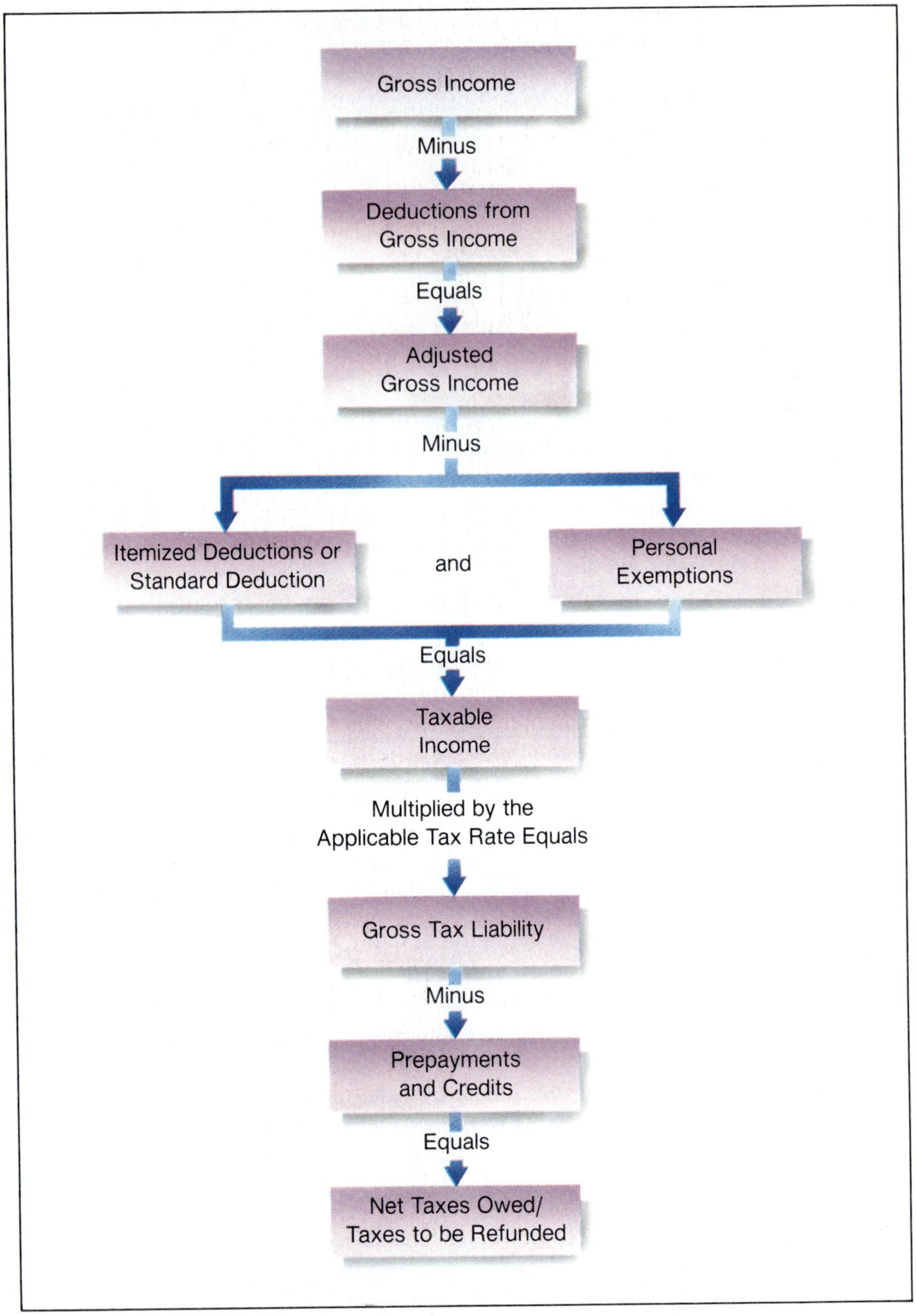


Items excludable from gross income include certain life insurance proceeds, gifts and inheritances, certain scholarships, benefits from workers' compensation, and interest on state and local obligations such as municipal bonds. Thus, if a single taxpayer received a $24,000 salary, a $6,000 inheritance, $900 of dividends, and a $400 prize from a quiz show, gross income would be figured as follows:

| | *Income Received* | *Exclusions* | *Gross Income* |
|---|---|---|---|
| Salary | $24,000 | $ — | $24,000 |
| Inheritance | 6,000 | 6,000 | — |
| Dividends | 900 | — | 900 |
| Prize | 400 | — | 400 |
| | $31,300 | $6,000 | $25,300 |

## Deductions from Gross Income

As shown in Exhibit A-1, a taxpayer is entitled to several types of deductions. The first type, called **deductions from gross income,** are subtracted from gross income to yield **adjusted gross income.** These deductions often relate to an individual's trade or business and include certain expenses incurred in the generation of gross income. No matter where a deduction appears on a tax return, the rules for deductibility are the opposite of those for income. That is, nothing is deductible *unless specifically stated in the tax laws.*

Deductions from gross income include, but are not limited to, the following:

1 *Trade and business expenses*—Most ordinary and necessary expenses attributable to a taxpayer's trade or business are deductible. Such expenses include employee salaries, advertising, rent, utilities, and 80% of the amounts spent for business meals and entertainment. In the actual tax computation, business expenses are deducted from business revenues, and the net income figure is reflected in the taxpayer's adjusted gross income.

2 *Losses on the sale or exchange of property and securities*—Subject to certain limits and conditions, losses incurred on the sale or exchange of selected assets are deductible from gross income if such assets were acquired and held for investment purposes. Examples of qualifying items include stocks, bonds, stamps, coins, and art. It is important to note that losses on the sale or exchange of *personal* property (e.g., a personal automobile or home) are not deductible.

3 *Contributions to retirement plans*—Taxpayers are eligible to establish their own retirement plans (such as an Individual Retirement Account, better known as an IRA). Subject to certain restrictions and limits, amounts contributed to these plans are deductible from gross income.

4 *Other deductions*—Other items that may be deducted from gross income include limited amounts of rental property expenses (e.g., repairs, interest, taxes, and depreciation) and certain alimony payments.

## Deductions from Adjusted Gross Income

Exhibit A-1 reveals two groups of **deductions from adjusted gross income:** (1) itemized deductions or the standard deduction and (2) personal exemptions. Focusing on the first group, all taxpayers are given a tax break for selected expenses, most of which are personal in nature. These expenses may be "claimed" by using either the standard deduction or by itemizing.

The **standard deduction** is a preset amount, namely, $3,100 for single individuals and $5,200 for married couples who file a joint return.[3] These figures are

[3] A **joint return** reports the combined income and deductions of a husband and wife.

raised if the taxpayers meet certain age and sight requirements. The benefit of using the standard deduction is that the deduction is automatic. Consequently, the taxpayer need not furnish proof that allowable expenses equal to the preset amounts were actually incurred.

### Itemized Deductions

If taxpayers have allowable expenses that exceed the standard deduction, a lower taxable income is produced by using an alternate procedure known as **itemizing.** With itemizing, the taxpayer lists (i.e., deducts) *actual* allowable expenses that have been incurred during the year.

For example, if a married couple filing a joint return has allowable itemized deductions of $8,500, it would be advantageous to subtract this amount from adjusted gross income as opposed to using the $5,200 standard deduction. Alternatively, if itemized deductions total only $4,500, the couple should employ the standard deduction to reduce taxable income by an additional $700 ($5,200 − $4,500).

Unlike the standard deduction, itemizing is not automatic. Thus, the burden of proof shifts to the taxpayer that the expenses deducted were both incurred and allowable. Accurate record keeping along with retention of invoices, canceled checks, and other documentation is therefore necessary when using this method.

Deductions from adjusted gross income are permitted for the following:

1 *Medical and dental expenses*—Medical and dental expenses paid by the taxpayer are deductible to the extent such amounts exceed 7.5% of adjusted gross income. Deductible expenses include fees paid to hospitals and doctors, outlays for medical appliances such as wheelchairs and glasses, the costs of any medical insurance premiums paid, and the costs of prescription drugs.

2 *Taxes*—Real estate taxes, personal property taxes, and state and local income taxes are deductible. Nondeductible items include most federal taxes, taxes on gasoline and other motor fuels, state and local sales tax, and most licensing fees (such as driver's licenses).

3 *Interest*—Interest that results from a mortgage on a principal or second residence is fully deductible. In contrast, under 1989 law, only 20% of interest incurred on personal debt (e.g., car loans and credit card balances) can be deducted. The deductibility of such personal interest is being phased out and will be totally eliminated after 1990.

4 *Charitable contributions*—Subject to certain limits, contributions of money and property made to charitable, religious, educational, and other qualified organizations (usually nonprofit in nature) are deductible.

5 *Casualty losses*—A taxpayer can deduct the nonreimbursed portion of certain personal property losses that result from casualties such as fire and theft. A deduction is permitted to the extent that a given casualty loss exceeds $100 *and* the total of such net losses exceeds 10% of adjusted gross income. A taxpayer who has adjusted gross income of $25,000 and losses of $1,900 and $1,200 is therefore entitled to a $400 deduction: [($1,900 − $100 + $1,200 − $100) − 0.10($25,000)].

6 *Miscellaneous deductions and employee business expenses*—Itemized expenses related to investments and the production of income, such as those for safe deposit box

rentals, certain legal and accounting fees, and investment counsel fees, are deductible. In addition, taxpayers can deduct some nonreimbursed costs that pertain to employment (e.g., uniform costs, union dues, dues to professional societies, subscriptions to professional journals, certain employment agency fees, job-related travel, 80% of entertainment costs, and moving expenses). With the exception of moving costs, the allowable deduction for the total of investment expenses, income-producing expenses, and employee expenses is limited to that amount which exceeds 2% of adjusted gross income.

### Personal Exemptions

In addition to itemized deductions or the standard deduction, taxpayers are entitled to reduce adjusted gross income for **personal exemptions.** A $2,000 reduction is allowed for each exemption. Tax laws permit one exemption for the taxpayer and additional exemptions for the taxpayer's spouse and each dependent claimed.

Generally stated, a **dependent** is a person who (1) has received over one-half of his or her support (food, clothing, lodging, and other similar expenses) from the taxpayer, (2) is closely related to the taxpayer or has lived in the taxpayer's home for the entire year, and (3) has less than $2,000 of gross income. This last test is waived for children of the taxpayer who are under nineteen years of age or full-time students.[4]

## Taxable Income and the Gross Tax Liability

Adjusted gross income minus itemized deductions (or the standard deduction) and personal exemptions equals **taxable income.** Taxable income is used in conjunction with rate schedules similar to those shown in Exhibit A-2 to determine an individual's gross tax liability.[5]

**Exhibit A-2**
**Tax Rate Schedules**

| *SINGLE TAXPAYERS* | | | | *MARRIED TAXPAYERS FILING A JOINT RETURN* | | | |
|---|---|---|---|---|---|---|---|
| *Taxable Income* | | *Gross Tax Liability* | | *Taxable Income* | | *Gross Tax Liability* | |
| *From* | *To* | *Rounded Amount* | *Of Taxable Income in Excess of* | *From* | *To* | *Rounded Amount* | *Of Taxable Income in Excess of* |
| $ 0 | $18,550 | $ 0 + 15% | $ 0 | $ 0 | $ 30,950 | $ 0 + 15% | $ 0 |
| 18,550 | 44,900 | 2,783 + 28% | 18,550 | 30,950 | 74,850 | 4,643 + 28% | 30,950 |
| 44,900 | 93,130 | 10,161 + 33% | 44,900 | 74,850 | 155,320 | 16,935 + 33% | 74,850 |
| 93,130+ | | 26,077 + 28% | 93,130* | 155,320+ | | 43,490 + 28% | 155,320† |

* The result of this computation [$26,077 + 0.28 (Taxable Income − $93,130)] is then increased by the lesser of (1) $560 × number of exemptions claimed or (2) 5% of taxable income in excess of $93,130.

† The result of this computation [$43,490 + 0.28 (Taxable Income − $155,320)] is then increased by the lesser of (1) $560 × number of exemptions claimed or (2) 5% of taxable income in excess of $155,320.

[4] Full-time students must be under age 24.

[5] In certain instances taxpayers use simplified tax tables to figure their tax obligation.

A review of the exhibit reveals that single taxpayers attain higher tax rates faster (i.e., at a lower taxable income) than their married counterparts. For example, assuming $40,000 of taxable income, a single taxpayer would pay $8,789 to the federal government, while a married couple would pay $7,177. The computations follow.

| | |
|---|---|
| Single taxpayer | |
| Tax on $18,550, per schedule | $2,783 |
| Tax on $21,450 excess ($40,000 − $18,550) at 28% | 6,006 |
| Total tax | $8,789 |

| | |
|---|---|
| Married couple | |
| Tax on $30,950, per schedule | $4,643 |
| Tax on $9,050 exccss ($40,000 − $30,950) at 28% | 2,534 |
| Total tax | $7,177 |

You may have noticed from reading the exhibit that the tax computation becomes more complex when high levels of income are reached (namely, amounts in excess of $93,130 for single taxpayers and $155,320 for married couples). Although an explanation of the rationale behind these computations is clearly beyond the scope of this text, the related mechanics are easily seen via the following example.

Richard and Barbara Taylor file a joint tax return and have three dependent children. Assuming a taxable income of $180,000, the Taylor's tax bill will amount to $51,634:

| | | |
|---|---|---|
| Tax on $155,320, per schedule | | $43,490 |
| Tax on $24,680 excess ($180,000 − $155,320) at 28% | | 6,910 |
| Add the lesser of: | | |
| $560 × number of exemptions claimed* | $2,800 | |
| 5% × taxable income in excess of $155,320 ($24,680) | 1,234 | 1,234 |
| Total tax | | $51,634 |

* The Taylors are entitled to five personal exemptions: one for the taxpayer, one for the spouse, and three for the children.

## Prepayments and Tax Credits

Once the income tax is determined, two further items must be considered: tax prepayments and tax credits. Recall that our tax system operates on a pay-as-you-go basis; specifically, income taxes are withheld from employees' wages throughout the accounting period. These withholdings are made for two reasons. First, governmental expenditures occur during the year, so it is convenient to collect taxes on the same basis. Second, few taxpayers could (or would) pay their entire tax bill on a single date (usually April 15) because considerable savings would be necessary. Such withholdings are really tax prepayments and are therefore deducted from the gross tax liability when figuring the balance due the government.

Taxpayers who anticipate owing large amounts of tax and who meet other requirements must pay estimated taxes in quarterly installments throughout the year. Estimated payments are also viewed as prepayments and are deducted from the taxpayer's gross liability.

In addition to withholdings and estimated payments, taxpayers are permitted certain **tax credits.** Such amounts are direct dollar-for-dollar reductions from a taxpayer's total yearly tax bill. Credits currently exist, subject to specific limits and conditions, for low-income taxpayers, dependent child care expenses, and other selected items.

After withholdings, estimated payments, and tax credits are subtracted, the additional balance owed to the federal government or a taxpayer's expected refund becomes known. Sound money management dictates that requests for refunds be filed as soon as possible while taxes due be paid as late as possible. By following these practices, the taxpayer has more funds available for longer periods of time.

## Individual Tax Return Illustration

At this point it is helpful to review the preceding discussion in terms of a comprehensive illustration. Assume that George and Susan McGee and their three small children recently moved from another state for job-related reasons. Susan's father lives with the family and is totally dependent on the McGees for his support. George earned $44,000 working as an accountant. Susan operates a small gift shop that had sales of $57,000 and expenses (including cost of goods sold) of $39,500. The McGees earned $2,600 of interest on various savings accounts, $900 of dividends from a common stock investment, and $100 of interest on a municipal bond. During the year they generated a $2,000 deductible loss on the sale of investment property. Itemized deductions included medical expenses of $2,000, mortgage interest of $10,000, state income taxes of $1,500, $1,200 of nonreimbursed employee business expenses, and moving costs of $2,400.

Total withholdings for federal income taxes amounted to $7,100. The McGees also paid estimated taxes of $2,200 and are entitled to a $75 tax credit for dependent child care expenses. On the basis of the preceding information and the filing of a joint return, the couple is due a tax refund of $3,010, as shown in Exhibit A-3.

## A Further Probe of Tax Rates

The mechanics of using tax rates when determining an individual's tax obligation are fairly straightforward. A deeper understanding of rate structures and their impact is necessary, however, for achieving financial success. In discussing tax rates, we must distinguish between the average rate of tax and the marginal rate of tax. Assume, for a moment, that Linda Newton is a single taxpayer with taxable income of $44,900. Using the data that appear in Exhibit A-2, her tax obligation would amount to $10,161. Stated differently, the tax **averages** 22.6% of taxable income ($10,161 ÷ $44,900).

Suppose that Newton has been offered a new job with a $4,000 salary increase. Assuming her deductions remain fairly constant, the salary increase would be taxed at the rate of 33% (from Exhibit A-2). Thirty-three percent is termed the **marginal rate of tax,** or the tax rate applied to each dollar of additional taxable income. From this simple example you can see the importance of the marginal tax rate in planning and decision making. If the government has a 33% "bite," Newton would keep only 67¢ of each additional dollar earned. She could easily decide that the incremental take-home pay is simply too small, given the numerous problems associated with a change in employment. Should she be in a location where state and local income taxes have been enacted, these, too, must be considered, as such amounts further diminish the attractiveness of the increased salary.

**Exhibit A-3**
**Individual Tax Return Filed Jointly by George and Susan McGee**

| | | | |
|---|---|---|---|
| Gross income | | | |
| George's salary | | $44,000 | |
| Gift shop sales | $57,000 | | |
| Less: Gift shop expenses | 39,500 | 17,500 | |
| Interest on savings | | 2,600 | |
| Dividends | | 900 | |
| Municipal bond interest (excluded) | | — | |
| Total gross income | | | $65,000 |
| Deductions from gross income | | | |
| Loss on investment property | | | 2,000 |
| Adjusted gross income | | | $63,000 |
| Deductions from adjusted gross income | | | |
| Medical expenses | $ 2,000 | | |
| Less: 7.5% of adjusted gross income | 4,725 | $ — | |
| Mortgage interest | | 10,000 | |
| State income taxes | | 1,500 | |
| Employee business expenses | $ 1,200 | | |
| Less: 2% of adjusted gross income | 1,260 | — | |
| Moving expenses | | 2,400 | |
| Total itemized deductions | | $13,900 | |
| Personal exemptions ($2,000 × 6) | | 12,000 | 25,900 |
| Taxable income | | | $37,100 |
| Tax computation based on rates in Exhibit A-2: | | | |
| Tax on $30,950, per schedule | | $ 4,643 | |
| Tax on $6,150 excess ($37,100 − $30,950) at 28% | | 1,722 | |
| Gross tax liability | | | $ 6,365 |
| Less: Child care tax credit | | $ 75 | |
| Taxes withheld | | 7,100 | |
| Estimated payments | | 2,200 | 9,375 |
| Taxes owed (refund) | | | $ (3,010) |

## Tax Accounting for Corporations

Corporate taxation is based on the same philosophy as that for individuals. Namely, all income is reportable and taxable unless specifically excluded by tax law, while no expense is deductible unless explicitly authorized. Although the philosophies are identical, numerous differences are encountered when dealing with the various components of taxable income.

Study Exhibit A-4, which is the general tax formula for corporate entities. As you can see, corporations lump all deductions together and make no attempt to divide their costs into "from gross income" and "from adjusted gross income" categories. Further, notice the absence of personal exemptions. And, as the following figures show, corporate tax rates differ from those of individual taxpayers.[6]

[6] These rates do not apply to professional service corporations (accountants, lawyers, doctors, and so forth).

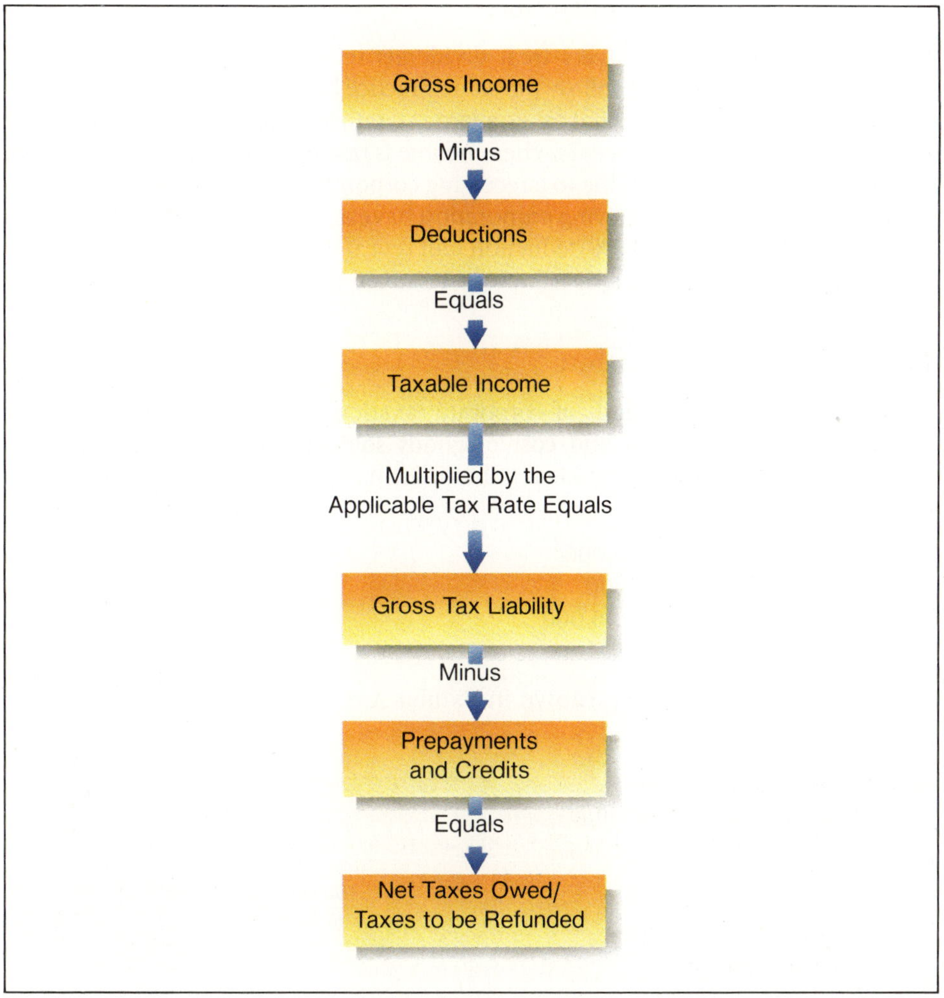


**Exhibit A-4**
**General Tax Formula for Corporations**

| *Taxable Income* | | *Gross Tax Liability* | |
|---|---|---|---|
| *From* | *To* | *Amount* | *Of Taxable Income in Excess of* |
| $ 0 | $50,000 | $ 0 + 15% | $ 0 |
| 50,000 | 75,000 | 7,500 + 25% | 50,000 |
| 75,000+ | | 13,750 + 34% | 75,000 |

Note: For taxable income levels in excess of $100,000 there is an additional tax of 5% on the excess. That tax, however, cannot exceed $11,750.

An overview of the similarities and differences between individual and corporate taxation is more appropriately left for advanced accounting courses. There is one feature, though, that deserves mention at this time: the dividends-received deduction.

## Dividends-Received Deduction

Recall that individual taxpayers treat dividends received in the computation of gross income. Corporations follow the same practice but are entitled to deduct 80% of such amounts, a practice that takes a large step toward the prevention of "triple taxation."[7] Triple taxation occurs when income is taxed to the earning corporation, taxed again as dividend income to a receiving corporation, and taxed a third time to stockholders should the receiving corporation have any dividend distributions of its own. Careful study of the 80% deduction will reveal the deduction's true objective: that only 20% of the related distributions be taxed to the recipient organization.

## Corporate Tax Illustration

To illustrate the fundamentals of corporate taxation, let us assume that Century Corporation reported sales and cost of goods sold of $565,000 and $300,000, respectively, for the year just ended. Other information pertaining to the company follows.

Operating expenses, $200,000
Dividends received, $10,000
Estimated tax payments, $8,000
Tax credits, $2,000

Century's tax computation is shown in Exhibit A-5.

**Exhibit A-5**
**Century Corporation Tax Computation**

| | | | |
|---|---|---|---|
| Gross income | | | |
| Sales | $565,000 | | |
| Less: Cost of goods sold* | 300,000 | $265,000 | |
| Dividends received | | 10,000 | |
| Total gross income | | | $275,000 |
| Deductions | | | |
| Operating expenses | | $200,000 | |
| Dividends-received deduction ($10,000 × 80%) | | 8,000 | |
| Total deductions | | | 208,000 |
| Taxable income | | | $ 67,000 |
| Tax on $50,000 (see p. 1051) | | | $ 7,500 |
| Tax on $17,000 excess ($67,000 − $50,000) at 25% | | | 4,250 |
| Gross tax liability | | | $ 11,750 |
| Less: Estimated payments | | $ 8,000 | |
| Tax credits | | 2,000 | 10,000 |
| Taxes owed (refund) | | | $ 1,750 |

* According to income tax regulations, cost of goods sold is considered in the computation of gross income.

[7] In some cases, the amount of the deduction depends on whether the receiving firm meets certain percentage-of-ownership tests. We will ignore these tests for the sake of simplicity.

## Tax Planning

The payment of income taxes often drains businesses (and individuals) of money needed for operations, growth, and perhaps even survival. As a result, taxpayers constantly strive to minimize their tax liability to the government by careful planning.

Tax liability may be reduced by following two courses of action: tax avoidance and tax evasion. **Tax avoidance** is achieved by the proper planning of financial events, affairs, and transactions within the legal confines of the tax statutes passed by Congress. In contrast, **tax evasion** represents a deliberate attempt to understate taxable income by the manipulation of income and expenses. For example, income may be intentionally understated, while fictitious and fraudulent deductions are claimed for expenses or exemptions. Tax evasion, of course, is illegal and accompanied by severe penalties.

### Tax Avoidance: Areas to Consider

Taxpayers can reduce their liability to the government in many different ways. Small service businesses, for instance, that use the cash basis of accounting can enjoy delays in the recording of revenue, thereby reducing taxable income and postponing income taxes.

Taxes can be deferred into future periods by using accelerated cost recovery write-offs of long-term assets and, in periods of rising prices, the LIFO method of inventory costing. Recall that under LIFO, the higher costs of recently acquired goods are matched against revenues, resulting in a lowering of taxable income. An additional method of avoidance is the acquisition of certain investments that generate tax-exempt income (such as state and local municipal bonds).

Suffice it to say that as long as there is an income tax, tax avoidance will be popular. Good business practice dictates that both companies and individuals conduct their activities mindful of tax implications. By so doing, significant strides will generally be made toward cash retention and economic prosperity.

## Exercises

**EA-1** ***Treatment of deductions and credits***

Classify items (a)–(h) as one of the following:

1 A deduction from gross income to arrive at adjusted gross income.

2 A deduction from adjusted gross income to arrive at taxable income.

3 A tax credit deductible from the gross tax liability.

4 A cost not deductible anywhere on the tax return.

Ignore possible limitations on the amount of the deduction or credit.

_____ a Amounts paid for dependent child care expenses.

_____ b Uninsured portion of fire loss on personal residence.

_____ c State income taxes.

_____ d Nonreimbursed moving expenses from New York to Denver related to a change in employment.

_____ e Contribution to a retirement plan by a self-employed person.

_____ f Sales taxes paid on the purchase of a new fishing boat.

_____ g Subscription to a professional, work-related journal.

_____ h Dental expenses.

**EA-2** ***Itemized deductions versus standard deduction***

Bob and June Pryor, a married couple, file a joint return and have the following expenditures for the year just ended:

| | |
|---|---|
| Hospital bills | $ 400 |
| Medical insurance costs | 750 |
| Physician bills | 150 |
| Dentist bills | 700 |
| Prescription drugs | 300 |
| Cash donations to church | 530 |
| Real estate taxes on personal residence | 600 |
| Miscellaneous employee expenses | 250 |
| Cost recovery (i.e., depreciation) on rental property | 3,000 |
| Mortgage interest on personal residence | 1,100 |
| Casualty loss on car accident (uninsured amount) | 450 |

Assuming an adjusted gross income of $30,000, should the couple itemize their deductions? Show calculations to support your answer.

**EA-3** ***Calculation of key tax amounts***

Pam and Wayne Moore have two small children. The following information was extracted from the couple's joint tax return:

| | |
|---|---|
| Gross income | $50,000 |
| Deductions from gross income | 4,500 |
| Itemized deductions | 13,500 |
| Taxes withheld from salaries | 2,900 |
| Estimated tax payments | 500 |
| Tax credits | 600 |

Determine the following:

a Adjusted gross income.

b Taxable income.

c The couple's gross tax liability, using the rates presented in Exhibit A-2.

d The balance owed the federal government or the refund due. Indicate which and the amount.

**EA-4** ***Tax computation for individuals***

The following information was extracted from the accounting records of Bob and Anita Sharkey:

| | |
|---|---|
| Bob's salary | $91,000 |
| Inheritance from deceased relative | 5,000 |
| Interest on savings account | 1,100 |
| Deductions from gross income | 14,500 |
| Itemized deductions | 10,700 |
| Income taxes withheld | 14,400 |

The Sharkeys file a joint return and have three small children. Using the tax rates that appear in Exhibit A-2, compute the amount of tax the couple owes to the federal government (or the refund due).

**EA-5** ***Tax rate analysis***

Dick Etlinger is married and the father of two small children. He has adjusted gross income of $90,000 and itemized expenses of $21,000.

a Using the tax rate schedule that appears in Exhibit A-2, compute Dick's gross tax liability to the government. Dick files a joint return with his wife.

b Compute the average tax rate.

c Compute the marginal tax rate.

d Assume that Dick is considering a new job that will pay an additional $1,000 per month. If itemized expenses remain fairly constant, how much additional cash will Dick have to meet living expenses during the upcoming year? Express your answer on an after-tax basis.

**EA-6** ***Corporate tax computations***
The following information was extracted from the records of Stone, Inc.

| | |
|---|---|
| Gross profit | $600,000 |
| Operating expenses | 550,000 |
| Dividends received during the year | 60,000 |
| Prepayments of income tax | 8,000 |
| Tax credits | 1,500 |

Using the tax rates presented on page 1051, compute the amount of tax the corporation owes the federal government (or the refund due).

## Problems

**PA-1** ***Tax computations for individuals***
Howard and Janice Wexler have three small children and file a joint tax return. Howard is employed as a manufacturer's representative and earns $65,000 per year. Janice is self-employed and conducts cooking classes in a rented facility across town. Revenues and expenses from her business, which is organized as a sole proprietorship, amounted to $24,200 and $18,700, respectively. (Note: No expenses were incurred for business meals or entertainment.) The couple earned $1,100 of interest and $700 of dividends from investments made throughout the year. The interest includes $100 from bonds issued by the state of Iowa. Additional information relating to the Wexlers follows.

| | |
|---|---|
| Hospital and doctor bills | $ 2,600 |
| Health insurance premiums | 900 |
| Prescription drugs | 400 |
| Interest on personal residence | 6,400 |
| Nonreimbursed moving expenses related to change in employment | 1,800 |
| Property taxes on personal residence | 3,200 |
| Contribution to Mid State University | 500 |
| Federal taxes withheld | 10,300 |
| Estimated tax payments during the year | 1,900 |

**Instructions**

Compute the amount of tax the couple owes the federal government (or the refund due). Use the tax rate schedule that appears in Exhibit A-2.

**PA-2** ***Tax computations for individuals***
Ken and Sharon Ziegler are married and support four young children. The couple also provides all the support for Ken's father, who lives in a neighboring city. The following information has been extracted from the Zieglers' accounting records:

| | |
|---|---|
| Ken's salary | $90,000 |
| Rental income | 7,200 |
| Interest on savings accounts | 2,400 |
| Prize won at raffle | 3,600 |
| Dividends from stock investments | 800 |
| Expenses on rental property | 5,000 |
| Medical insurance premiums | 1,800 |
| Hospital costs | 900 |
| Prescription drugs | 1,400 |
| Property taxes on personal residence | 1,900 |
| State income taxes | 400 |
| Mortgage interest on personal residence | 6,200 |
| Charitable contributions | 1,700 |
| Food and clothing costs | 9,700 |
| Income tax withholdings | 11,000 |
| Estimated tax payments | 2,000 |
| Tax credits | 400 |

The couple plans to file a joint tax return.

### Instructions

Determine:

a Adjusted gross income. (*Hint:* The rental property transactions should be listed with other items of gross income.)

b Taxable income.

c The balance owed the federal government or the refund due. Indicate which and the amount; use the tax rate schedule that appears in Exhibit A-2.

**PA-3** ***Tax computations for corporations***

The following information pertains to Ventura Corporation:

| | |
|---|---|
| Net sales | $2,075,000 |
| Cost of goods sold | 1,400,000 |
| Selling expenses | 180,000 |
| Administrative expenses | 210,000 |
| Other income* | 47,000 |
| Other expense | 35,000 |
| Estimated tax payments | 50,000 |
| Tax credits | 9,500 |

* Other income includes $7,000 of interest revenue and $40,000 of dividends.

### Instructions

From the preceding information, calculate the amount of tax that Ventura owes the federal government (or the refund due). Use the tax rates presented on page 1051.

# Specimen Financial Statements

APPENDIX B

The next few pages contain recent financial statements of the Alberto-Culver Company, a firm engaged in the manufacture and sale of consumer products. These statements are representative of those issued by other large corporations and reflect many of the topics discussed in this text.

Also included in these pages is a comprehensive set of footnotes. The footnotes expand upon the material presented in the statements and enlighten readers who desire further information about the firm's resources, obligations, transactions, and financial reporting practices. In addition, on page 1065, you will find an audit report to Alberto-Culver's stockholders from Peat Marwick Main & Co., a large public accounting firm. The audit report indicates that the statements present fairly the company's financial position, cash flows, and results of operations.

ALBERTO CULVER

## Consolidated Statements of Earnings

Alberto Culver Company and Subsidiaries

| | Year ended September 30, | | |
|---|---|---|---|
| | **1988** | 1987 | 1986 |
| Net sales | **$604,708,002** | 514,491,442 | 435,355,255 |
| Costs and expenses: | | | |
| Cost of products sold | **275,893,896** | 240,006,380 | 204,659,074 |
| Advertising, promotion, selling and administrative | **282,520,171** | 236,950,979 | 201,609,252 |
| Interest expense | **5,926,771** | 4,509,732 | 5,801,542 |
| Total costs and expenses | **564,340,838** | 481,467,091 | 412,069,868 |
| Earnings from continuing operations before gain on sale of investment and provision for income taxes | **40,367,164** | 33,024,351 | 23,285,387 |
| Gain on sale of investment (note 11) | **3,676,709*** | — | — |
| Earnings from continuing operations before provision for income taxes | **44,043,873*** | 33,024,351 | 23,285,387 |
| Provision for income taxes (note 7) | **17,153,000*** | 14,861,000 | 10,025,000 |
| Earnings from continuing operations | **26,890,873*** | 18,163,351 | 13,260,387 |
| Loss from discontinued operations (note 2) | **—** | — | (4,629,420) |
| Net earnings | **$ 26,890,873*** | 18,163,351 | 8,630,967 |
| Earnings per share of common stock: | | | |
| Continuing operations | **$1.99*** | 1.28 | 1.05 |
| Discontinued operations | **—** | — | (.37) |
| Net earnings | **$1.99*** | 1.28 | .68 |

*The sale of an investment in 1988 resulted in a pre-tax gain of $3,676,709. The nonrecurring gain increased net earnings by $2,268,709 or $.16 per share after deducting income taxes of $1,408,000.

See accompanying notes to consolidated financial statements.

## Consolidated Statements of Retained Earnings

Alberto Culver Company and Subsidiaries

| | Year ended September 30, | | |
|---|---|---|---|
| | **1988** | 1987 | 1986 |
| Retained earnings, beginning of year | **$ 93,483,029** | 78,552,613 | 73,187,791 |
| Net earnings | **26,890,873** | 18,163,351 | 8,630,967 |
| | **120,373,902** | 96,715,964 | 81,818,758 |
| Stock dividends (note 6) | **—** | — | (767,944) |
| Cash dividends (note 6) | **(3,826,272)** | (3,232,935) | (2,498,201) |
| Retained earnings, end of year | **$116,547,630** | 93,483,029 | 78,552,613 |

See accompanying notes to consolidated financial statements.

## Consolidated Balance Sheets

Alberto Culver Company and Subsidiaries

| Assets | 1988 | September 30, 1987 |
|---|---|---|
| Current assets: | | |
| Cash and cash equivalents | $ 24,020,242 | 29,684,399 |
| Short-term investments | 10,108,010 | 7,322,152 |
| Receivables, less allowance for doubtful accounts (1988—$2,740,000; 1987—$2,872,000) | 73,939,031 | 69,345,764 |
| Inventories: | | |
| Finished goods | 82,476,845 | 67,796,655 |
| Work-in-process | 3,672,054 | 3,088,258 |
| Raw materials | 18,132,075 | 15,235,457 |
| Total inventories | 104,280,974 | 86,120,370 |
| Prepaid expenses | 4,267,129 | 4,178,831 |
| Total current assets | 216,615,386 | 196,651,516 |
| Property, plant and equipment (note 8): | | |
| Land | 3,194,540 | 3,186,863 |
| Buildings | 33,215,686 | 30,520,316 |
| Machinery and equipment | 62,797,645 | 48,117,010 |
| Total property, plant and equipment | 99,207,871 | 81,824,189 |
| Accumulated depreciation | 35,399,184 | 31,208,976 |
| Property, plant and equipment, net | 63,808,687 | 50,615,213 |
| Goodwill and trade names, net | 12,898,382 | 12,654,705 |
| Long-term notes receivable and other assets | 10,025,915 | 11,903,645 |
| | $303,348,370 | 271,825,079 |

| Liabilities and Stockholders' Equity | 1988 | 1987 |
|---|---|---|
| Current liabilities: | | |
| Short-term borrowings | $ 4,716,973 | 3,205,805 |
| Current maturities of long-term debt | 7,312,186 | 16,408,970 |
| Accounts payable | 67,481,968 | 57,193,127 |
| Accrued expenses (note 3) | 35,259,511 | 29,436,480 |
| Income taxes | 7,023,789 | 5,950,649 |
| Total current liabilities | 121,794,427 | 112,195,031 |
| Long-term debt (note 4) | 44,787,237 | 23,643,568 |
| Deferred income taxes (note 7) | 1,099,689 | 2,495,512 |
| Other liabilities | 976,857 | 553,528 |
| Stockholders' equity (note 6): | | |
| Common stock, par value $.22 per share: | | |
| Class A authorized 25,000,000 shares; issued 5,730,729 shares | 1,260,760 | 1,260,736 |
| Class B authorized 15,000,000 shares; issued 10,472,795 shares | 2,304,015 | 2,304,039 |
| Additional paid-in capital | 46,230,704 | 46,190,899 |
| Retained earnings | 116,547,630 | 93,483,029 |
| Foreign currency translation (note 1) | (2,327,821) | (2,723,003) |
| | 164,015,288 | 140,515,700 |
| Less treasury stock, at cost (Class A common shares: 900,626 in 1988 and 570,977 in 1987; Class B common shares: 2,254,722 in 1988 and 1,712,930 in 1987) | 29,325,128 | 7,578,260 |
| Total stockholders' equity | 134,690,160 | 132,937,440 |
| | $303,348,370 | 271,825,079 |

See accompanying notes to consolidated financial statements.

## Consolidated Statements of Cash Flows

Alberto Culver Company and Subsidiaries

| | Year ended September 30, | | |
|---|---|---|---|
| | **1988** | 1987 | 1986 |
| **Cash Flows from Operating Activities:** | | | |
| Net earnings | **$26,890,873** | 18,163,351 | 8,630,967 |
| Adjustments to reconcile net earnings to net cash provided by operating activities: | | | |
| Depreciation | **7,483,597** | 6,088,789 | 4,638,330 |
| Amortization of goodwill and other assets | **2,496,872** | 2,608,140 | 2,529,022 |
| Short-term investments | **(9,917,699)** | (6,889,261) | (366,113) |
| Receivables, net | **(4,597,619)** | (6,069,028) | (2,758,375) |
| Inventories | **(17,486,842)** | (8,955,382) | (2,329,408) |
| Prepaid expenses | **(61,473)** | 504,715 | (985,639) |
| Accounts payable and accrued expenses | **16,036,011** | 7,511,452 | 11,903,381 |
| Income taxes | **1,072,643** | 2,842,942 | (551,460) |
| Deferred income taxes | **(1,693,000)** | (115,000) | (318,000) |
| Gain on sale of investment | **(3,676,709)** | — | — |
| Loss from discontinued operations | **—** | — | 4,629,420 |
| Other, net | **495,242** | (1,100,190) | (301,348) |
| Net cash provided by operating activities | **17,041,896** | 14,590,528 | 24,720,777 |
| **Cash Flows from Investing Activities:** | | | |
| Capital expenditures | **(19,699,011)** | (16,661,826) | (11,163,638) |
| Additions to other assets | **(1,204,931)** | (269,037) | (852,026) |
| Payments for acquisitions | **(339,224)** | (1,189,443) | (12,250,000) |
| Proceeds from disposals of assets | **11,587,874** | 7,766,064 | 1,411,798 |
| Net cash used by investing activities | **(9,655,292)** | (10,354,242) | (22,853,866) |
| **Cash Flows from Financing Activities:** | | | |
| Proceeds from long-term debt | **30,000,000** | 12,166,973 | 477,596 |
| Retirements of long-term debt | **(19,349,755)** | (4,569,289) | (25,398,980) |
| Short-term borrowings | **1,717,550** | (2,928,735) | (5,310,756) |
| Proceeds from exercise of stock options | **751,829** | 290,023 | 272,219 |
| Net proceeds from issuance of common stock | **—** | — | 40,064,969 |
| Cash dividends paid | **(3,826,272)** | (3,232,935) | (2,498,201) |
| Stock purchased for treasury | **(22,458,892)** | — | (4,438) |
| Net cash provided (used) by financing activities | **(13,165,540)** | 1,726,037 | 7,602,409 |
| Effect of foreign exchange rate changes on cash | **114,779** | 59,015 | (24,685) |
| Net increase (decrease) in cash and cash equivalents | **(5,664,157)** | 6,021,338 | 9,444,635 |
| Cash and cash equivalents at beginning of year | **29,684,399** | 23,663,061 | 14,218,426 |
| Cash and cash equivalents at end of year | **$24,020,242** | 29,684,399 | 23,663,061 |

See accompanying notes to consolidated financial statements.

# Notes to Consolidated Financial Statements

## (1) Summary of Significant Accounting Policies

PRINCIPLES OF CONSOLIDATION
The consolidated financial statements include accounts of the company and its subsidiaries. All significant inter-company accounts and transactions have been eliminated.

CASH EQUIVALENTS
All highly liquid investments purchased with a maturity of three months or less are considered to be cash equivalents. These investments are stated at cost which approximates market value. Cash, cash equivalents and short-term investments for 1987 have been restated to conform to the 1988 presentation.

SHORT-TERM INVESTMENTS
Short-term investments are stated at cost. The market value of short-term investments was $10.1 million and $11.3 million at September 30, 1988 and 1987, respectively.

INVENTORIES
Inventories are stated at the lower of cost (first-in, first-out method) or market (net realizable value).

PROPERTY, PLANT AND EQUIPMENT
Property, plant and equipment are carried at cost. Depreciation is provided primarily on the straight-line method based on the estimated useful lives of assets. Expenditures for maintenance and repairs are expensed as incurred.

GOODWILL AND TRADE NAMES
The cost of goodwill and trade names is amortized over periods ranging from five to forty years.

FOREIGN CURRENCY TRANSLATION
Foreign currency balance sheet accounts are generally translated at rates of exchange in effect at the balance sheet date. Results of operations are translated using the average exchange rates prevailing throughout the period.

Translation effects for operations in countries which do not have hyperinflationary economies are recorded as foreign currency translation in stockholders' equity. The following is an analysis of changes in the foreign currency translation account in 1988 and 1987:

| | **1988** | 1987 |
|---|---|---|
| Balance, beginning of year | **$2,723,003** | 4,373,597 |
| Foreign currency translation | **(395,182)** | (1,650,594) |
| Balance, end of year | **$2,327,821** | 2,723,003 |

Translation effects for operations in countries considered to be hyperinflationary and realized gains and losses from foreign currency transactions included in the consolidated statements of earnings resulted in losses of $776,000, $721,000 and $1,338,000 in 1988, 1987 and 1986, respectively.

INCOME TAXES
Provision is made for deferred income taxes resulting from timing differences in the recognition of revenue and expense for tax and financial statement purposes. During 1986, investment tax credits were accounted for as a reduction of the provision for income taxes in the year the credits arose. Investment tax credits were not available in 1988 or 1987 due to a change in the income tax law.

Statement of Financial Accounting Standards No. 96, entitled "Accounting for Income Taxes," was issued by the Financial Accounting Standards Board (FASB) in December, 1987. The new pronouncement requires a change from the deferred method to the asset and liability method of accounting for income taxes. Statement 96 must be adopted by the company no later than October 1, 1989. However, the FASB is considering an extension of the implementation date.

The company elected not to adopt the provisions of Statement No. 96 in fiscal year 1988. However, the company estimates the cumulative effect of applying the provisions of the Statement would not have had a material effect on the consolidated financial statements.

STATEMENTS OF CASH FLOWS
Effective September 30, 1988, the company adopted Statement of Financial Accounting Standards No. 95, entitled "Statements of Cash Flows." The consolidated financial statements for 1987 and 1986 have been restated to reflect the requirements of Statement No. 95.

CALCULATION OF EARNINGS PER SHARE
Earnings per share are based on the following weighted average shares outstanding: 1988—13,500,000; 1987—14,202,000; 1986—12,630,000.

## (2) Discontinued Operations

During 1986, the company sold the assets of Phillippe of California, Inc. for cash. Net sales of the discontinued operation in 1986 were $3,694,023. The loss from operations was $689,958, net of income tax benefit of $529,000. The loss from disposal was $3,939,462, net of income tax benefit of $1,125.000.

## (3) Accrued Expenses

Accrued expenses consist of the following:

| | **1988** | 1987 |
|---|---|---|
| Compensation and payroll taxes | **$ 9,175,184** | 7,333,350 |
| Promotional allowances | **13,808,409** | 11,307,333 |
| Other | **12,275,918** | 10,795,797 |
| | **$35,259,511** | 29,436,480 |

# Notes Continued

## (4) Long-Term Debt

Long-term debt, exclusive of current maturities, consists of the following:

| | 1988 | 1987 |
|---|---|---|
| Installment notes payable: | | |
| 9% due July, 1990 | $ 342,785 | 676,732 |
| 8% due June, 1992 | 300,000 | 400,000 |
| Term notes payable: | | |
| 11.1% due May, 1989 | — | 5,000,000 |
| 8% due April, 1990 | 2,958,468 | 4,063,750 |
| 7.875% due March, 1992 | 10,000,000 | 10,000,000 |
| 8.95% due February, 1993 | 10,000,000 | — |
| 9% due February, 1993 | 20,000,000 | — |
| Revolving credit note | — | 2,443,500 |
| Capitalized leases at weighted average interest rates of 11.7% in 1988 and 10.1% in 1987 | 1,023,579 | 847,043 |
| Other | 162,405 | 212,543 |
| | $44,787,237 | 23,643,568 |

Maturities of long-term debt for the next five years are as follows: 1989—$7,312,000; 1990—$2,749,000; 1991—$1,788,000; 1992—$10,222,000; 1993—$30,027,000.

Various borrowing arrangements impose restrictions on such items as total debt, working capital, dividend payments, treasury stock purchases and interest expense. At September 30, 1988, the company was in compliance with these arrangements and $30.0 million of consolidated retained earnings was not restricted as to the payment of dividends and purchases of treasury stock.

The company had unused lines of credit of approximately $150 million with various banks at September 30, 1988. The credit lines, which required no compensating balances, may be terminated at the option of the banks or the company.

## (5) Stock Option Plans

The company has stock option plans which authorize the issuance of options to purchase a limited number of shares of the company's common stock at a price not less than the fair market value of the stock at the date of grant. Options under the plans expire five years from date of grant and are exercisable in sequence on a cumulative basis in four equal annual increments commencing one year after the date of grant.

Shares under option at September 30, 1988 are summarized below:

| Year Granted | Shares Under Option | Per Share Option Price | Total Option Price |
|---|---|---|---|
| 1984 | 2,402 | $5.63 | $ 13,523 |
| 1985 | 234,685 | 7.04 to 10.09 | 2,263,452 |
| 1986 | 38,500 | 14.69 | 565,565 |
| 1987 | 81,700 | 16.50 | 1,348,050 |
| 1988 | 90,700 | 13.19 | 1,196,333 |
| | 447,987 | | $5,386,923 |

Options for 126,844 shares were exercised in 1988 whereas options for 49,223 shares were exercised in the prior year. During 1988 and 1987, options for 12,927 and 58,776 shares, respectively, were terminated. Options for 216,885 shares were exercisable at September 30, 1988.

## (6) Treasury Stock and Additional Paid-In Capital

Changes in treasury stock and additional paid-in capital during 1988, 1987 and 1986 were as follows (in thousands):

| | Treasury Stock | | Additional Paid-In Capital |
|---|---|---|---|
| | Shares | Amount | |
| Balance at September 30, 1985 | 2,384 | $7,910 | $ 7,180 |
| Stock options exercised | (52) | (172) | 100 |
| Stock purchased for treasury | 1 | 4 | — |
| 4-for-3 stock split | — | — | (788) |
| Net proceeds from issuance of stock | — | — | 39,572 |
| Balance at September 30, 1986 | 2,333 | 7,742 | 46,064 |
| Stock options exercised | (49) | (164) | 127 |
| Balance at September 30, 1987 | 2,284 | 7,578 | 46,191 |
| Stock options exercised | (127) | (712) | 40 |
| Stock purchased for treasury | 998 | 22,459 | — |
| Balance at September 30, 1988 | 3,155 | $29,325 | $46,231 |

The company has two classes of common stock, both of which are listed on the New York Stock Exchange. Except for voting, dividend and conversion rights, the Class A and Class B common stock are identical. Class A has one-tenth vote per share and Class B has one vote per share. No dividend may be paid on the Class B unless an equal or greater dividend is paid on the Class A, and dividends may be paid on the Class A in excess of dividends paid, or without paying dividends, on the Class B. All, and not less than all, of the Class A may at any time be converted into Class B on a share-for-share basis at the option of the company. The Class B is convertible into Class A on a share-for-share basis at the option of the holders.

In June, 1986, the company sold 2,240,000 shares of previously unissued Class A common stock. Net proceeds after related expenses were $40.1 million. An amount equal to the par value of the shares was credited to common stock with the remaining net proceeds being credited to additional paid-in capital.

# Notes Continued

Cash dividends for Class B common stock in 1988, 1987 and 1986 were $2,414,890 or $.285 per share, $2,034,172 or $.2325 per share and $2,075,464 or $.205 per share, respectively. Cash dividends for Class A common stock in 1988, 1987 and 1986 were $1,411,382 or $.285 per share, $1,198,763 or $.2325 per share and $422,737 or $.105 per share, respectively. Class A common stock dividends per share have been equal to those of Class B common stock since the Class A shares were issued in April, 1986.

The board of directors declared a three-for-two stock split in the form of a stock dividend effective February, 1986. In April, 1986, stockholders approved a reclassification of each three shares of common stock issued and outstanding or held in the company's treasury as three shares of Class B common stock and one share of Class A common stock. All common stock and per share figures included in this report, except the twenty-two cents per share par value, have been adjusted for the stock split and reclassification.

## (7) Income Taxes

The provisions for income taxes consist of the following:

| | 1988 | 1987 | 1986 |
|---|---|---|---|
| Currently payable: | | | |
| Federal | **$13,263,000** | 11,311,000 | 7,200,000 |
| Foreign | **3,651,000** | 2,076,000 | 2,542,000 |
| State | **1,932,000** | 1,589,000 | 601,000 |
| | **18,846,000** | 14,976,000 | 10,343,000 |
| Deferred: | | | |
| Federal | **(1,369,000)** | (371,000) | (443,000) |
| Foreign | **(324,000)** | 256,000 | 125,000 |
| | **(1,693,000)** | (115,000) | (318,000) |
| | **$17,153,000** | 14,861,000 | 10,025,000 |

The deferred income tax provisions include the following components:

| | 1988 | 1987 | 1986 |
|---|---|---|---|
| Accelerated tax depreciation | **$ 539,000** | 265,000 | 340,000 |
| Prepaid expenses | **(242,000)** | (275,000) | (97,000) |
| Foreign exchange | **41,000** | (228,000) | 560,000 |
| Inventory adjustments | **(357,000)** | (135,000) | (180,000) |
| Promotional accruals | **(1,414,000)** | (119,000) | (561,000) |
| Other | **(260,000)** | 377,000 | (380,000) |
| | **$(1,693,000)** | (115,000) | (318,000) |

The difference between the effective income tax rate on earnings for financial statement purposes and the United States statutory federal income tax rate is summarized below:

| | 1988 | 1987 | 1986 |
|---|---|---|---|
| Statutory tax rate | **34.0%** | 43.0% | 46.0% |
| Effect of foreign income tax rates | **.9** | 2.6 | (1.2) |
| State income taxes, net of federal tax benefit | **2.9** | 2.7 | 1.4 |
| Utilization of capital loss carryforward | **(.1)** | (4.5) | — |
| Investment and other tax credits | — | — | (1.2) |
| Other, net | **1.3** | 1.2 | (1.9) |
| Effective tax rate | **39.0%** | 45.0% | 43.1% |

Domestic earnings from continuing operations before income taxes were $39.6 million, $37.7 million and $24.1 million in 1988, 1987 and 1986, respectively. Foreign operations had earnings before income taxes of $4.4 million in 1988 and losses before income taxes of $4.7 million and $.8 million in 1987 and 1986, respectively.

Undistributed earnings of the company's international operations are intended to remain permanently invested to finance future growth and expansion. Accordingly, no U.S. income taxes have been provided on those earnings which aggregated $28.3 million at September 30, 1988. Should such earnings be distributed, the credit for foreign income taxes paid would substantially offset applicable U.S. income taxes.

## (8) Lease Commitments

The major portion of the company's leases are for beauty supply stores. Other leases cover certain manufacturing and warehousing properties, office facilities, data processing equipment and automobiles. At September 30, 1988, future minimum payments under noncancellable leases are as follows:

| | Capital Leases | Operating Leases |
|---|---|---|
| 1989 | $ 730,600 | 12,122,038 |
| 1990 | 588,449 | 10,364,622 |
| 1991 | 420,320 | 8,508,349 |
| 1992 | 130,255 | 5,765,345 |
| 1993 | 21,252 | 3,184,116 |
| 1994 and later | 7,039 | 10,439,513 |
| Total minimum lease payments | 1,897,915 | 50,383,983 |
| Less interest | (301,549) | |
| Present value of net minimum lease payments | $1,596,366 | |

Capital leases included in the consolidated balance sheets at September 30, 1988 and 1987 are summarized below:

| | 1988 | 1987 |
|---|---|---|
| Machinery and equipment | **$2,917,825** | 2,432,410 |
| Accumulated depreciation and amortization | **1,042,711** | 1,029,818 |
| Obligations under capital leases: | | |
| Current | **572,787** | 433,974 |
| Long-term | **1,023,579** | 847,043 |

Certain leases require the company to pay real estate taxes, insurance, maintenance and special assessments.

Total rental expense for operating leases amounted to $17,833,000 in 1988, $13,707,000 in 1987 and $11,328,000 in 1986.

# Notes Continued

## (9) Business Segments and Geographic Area Information

The principal business of Alberto Culver Company and its subsidiaries is developing, manufacturing, promoting and marketing products which are designed for sale at retail and ultimately for personal use or use in the home (referred to as "mass marketed personal use products").

Another segment of the company's business is "institutional and industrial products" which includes hair care products sold through beauty and barber distributors to the professional trade and specialty foods sold to institutions and restaurants. Prior to fiscal year 1988, this segment also included cleaning aid products intended for end-use by institutions and industries.

The "other products—Sally" business segment principally represents the operations of Sally Beauty Company which sells the company's and other manufacturers' professional beauty and barber products through Sally outlet stores. This segment also includes contract packaging services performed for other companies which are provided through the company's own production facilities.

Segment and geographic data for the years ended September 30, 1988, 1987 and 1986 are as follows:

| Business Segments Information | 1988 | 1987 | 1986 |
|---|---|---|---|
| Net sales: | | | |
| Mass marketed personal use products | **$317,801,907** | 256,287,906 | 214,374,239 |
| Institutional and industrial products | **73,546,017** | 84,631,923 | 84,396,653 |
| Other products—Sally | **219,322,680** | 178,552,232 | 140,829,030 |
| Eliminations | **(5,962,602)** | (4,980,619) | (4,244,667) |
| | **$604,708,002** | 514,491,442 | 435,355,255 |
| Earnings from continuing operations before income taxes: | | | |
| Operating profit: | | | |
| Mass marketed personal use products | **$ 32,954,176** | 27,887,371 | 18,558,104 |
| Institutional and industrial products | **9,860,423** | 6,395,429 | 9,335,081 |
| Other products—Sally | **12,880,204** | 9,427,420 | 6,312,443 |
| | **55,694,803** | 43,710,220 | 34,205,628 |
| Unallocated expenses, net | **(5,724,159)** | (6,176,137) | (5,118,699) |
| Interest expense | **(5,926,771)** | (4,509,732) | (5,801,542) |
| | **$ 44,043,873** | 33,024,351 | 23,285,387 |
| Identifiable assets: | | | |
| Mass marketed personal use products | **$113,492,166** | 103,982,678 | 87,344,030 |
| Institutional and industrial products | **56,878,290** | 50,798,993 | 49,959,766 |
| Other products—Sally | **101,570,632** | 83,084,434 | 60,003,552 |
| Corporate | **31,407,282** | 33,958,974 | 30,434,223 |
| | **$303,348,370** | 271,825,079 | 227,741,571 |
| Depreciation and amortization expense: | | | |
| Mass marketed personal use products | **$ 3,108,337** | 3,007,171 | 2,326,734 |
| Institutional and industrial products | **1,331,011** | 880,177 | 679,697 |
| Other products—Sally | **4,736,713** | 3,880,045 | 3,590,484 |
| Corporate | **804,408** | 929,536 | 570,437 |
| Discontinued operations | **—** | — | 282,799 |
| | **$ 9,980,469** | 8,696,929 | 7,450,151 |
| Capital expenditures: | | | |
| Mass marketed personal use products | **$ 3,329,771** | 6,716,578 | 2,677,459 |
| Institutional and industrial products | **1,368,586** | 2,514,627 | 936,090 |
| Other products—Sally | **6,928,444** | 8,027,889 | 2,190,333 |
| Corporate | **9,092,395** | 72,547 | 6,133,925 |
| | **$ 20,719,196** | 17,331,641 | 11,937,807 |

| Geographic Area Information | 1988 | 1987 | 1986 |
|---|---|---|---|
| Net sales: | | | |
| United States | **$457,131,655** | 404,073,006 | 341,127,775 |
| Foreign | **149,757,532** | 112,482,178 | 96,172,260 |
| Eliminations | **(2,181,185)** | (2,063,742) | (1,944,780) |
| | **$604,708,002** | 514,491,442 | 435,355,255 |
| Operating profit (loss): | | | |
| United States | **$ 53,311,343** | 46,316,493 | 33,969,297 |
| Foreign | **2,383,460** | (2,606,273) | 236,331 |
| | **$ 55,694,803** | 43,710,220 | 34,205,628 |
| Identifiable assets: | | | |
| United States | **$204,769,465** | 176,822,525 | 143,155,018 |
| Foreign | **67,171,623** | 61,043,580 | 54,152,330 |
| Corporate | **31,407,282** | 33,958,974 | 30,434,223 |
| | **$303,348,370** | 271,825,079 | 227,741,571 |

"Unallocated expenses, net" principally consist of general corporate expenses and foreign exchange gains and losses. Corporate assets are primarily cash, cash equivalents, short-term investments, equipment and long-term receivables.

## Notes Continued

### (10) Quarterly Financial Data

Unaudited quarterly statement of earnings information for the years ended September 30, 1988 and 1987 is summarized below (in thousands, except per share amounts):

| 1988 | 1st Quarter | 2nd Quarter | 3rd Quarter | 4th Quarter |
|---|---|---|---|---|
| Net sales | $133,536 | 151,767 | 154,158 | 165,247 |
| Cost of products sold | 63,803 | 69,030 | 72,325 | 70,736 |
| Earnings before nonrecurring gain* | 4,540 | 4,928 | 7,010 | 8,144 |
| Earnings per share before nonrecurring gain* | .32 | .36 | .53 | .62 |
| **1987** | | | | |
| Net sales | $112,737 | 124,744 | 132,716 | 144,294 |
| Cost of products sold | 53,607 | 57,633 | 63,309 | 65,457 |
| Net earnings | 3,281 | 3,534 | 5,234 | 6,114 |
| Earnings per share | .23 | .25 | .37 | .43 |

*Earnings before nonrecurring gain and net earnings are equivalent except in the first quarter during which the sale of an investment resulted in a nonrecurring net gain of $2,268,709 or $.16 per share (note 11). The nonrecurring gain is included in net earnings in the consolidated statement of earnings for the year ended September 30, 1988.

### (11) Sale of Investment

During 1988, the company sold its investment in the common stock of another company. The investment had been made pursuant to an unsuccessful merger proposal. The sale resulted in a nonrecurring gain of $2,268,709 or $.16 per share after deducting income taxes of $1,408,000.

### (12) Supplemental Cash Flow Information

| | Year ended September 30, | | |
|---|---|---|---|
| | **1988** | 1987 | 1986 |
| Cash paid for: | | | |
| Interest | **$ 5,752,000** | 4,332,000 | 6,089,000 |
| Income taxes | **17,476,000** | 11,661,000 | 9,373,000 |
| Capital lease obligations assumed | **1,020,185** | 669,815 | 774,169 |
| Liabilities incurred in conjunction with acquisitions: | | | |
| Fair value of assets acquired | **$ 408,851** | 11,339,252 | 19,310,766 |
| Cash paid | **339,224** | 1,189,443 | 12,250,000 |
| | **$ 69,627** | 10,149,809 | 7,060,766 |

### (13) Subsequent Event

During October, 1988, the company purchased all of the assets of Save-Way Beauty Supply for cash and notes totaling approximately $23 million. Save-Way operates 175 beauty supply stores in the southeastern section of the United States. The acquisition will be accounted for as a purchase.

## Auditors' Report

The Board of Directors and Stockholders
Alberto Culver Company:

We have audited the accompanying consolidated balance sheets of Alberto Culver Company and subsidiaries as of September 30, 1988 and 1987, and the related consolidated statements of earnings, retained earnings, and cash flows for each of the years in the three year period ended September 30, 1988. These consolidated financial statements are the responsibility of the company's management. Our responsibility is to express an opinion on these consolidated financial statements based on our audits.

We conducted our audits in accordance with generally accepted auditing standards. Those standards require that we plan and perform the audits to obtain reasonable assurance about whether the financial statements are free of material misstatement. An audit includes examining, on a test basis, evidence supporting the amounts and disclosures in the financial statements. An audit also includes assessing the accounting principles used and significant estimates made by management, as well as evaluating the overall financial statement presentation. We believe that our audits provide a reasonable basis for our opinion.

In our opinion, the consolidated financial statements referred to above present fairly, in all material respects, the financial position of Alberto Culver Company and subsidiaries at September 30, 1988 and 1987, and the results of their operations and their cash flows for each of the years in the three year period ended September 30, 1988 in conformity with generally accepted accounting principles.

Chicago, Illinois
November 7, 1988

Peat Marwick Main & Co.

Peat Marwick Main & Co.

## Management's Discussion and Analysis of Results of Operations and Financial Condition

RESULTS OF OPERATIONS

Fiscal year 1988 marked the company's fifth consecutive year of record sales and earnings. Net sales for the year were $604.7 million or 17.5% higher than 1987 sales of $514.5 million. Sales in 1987 increased 18.2% compared to the prior year.

Earnings from continuing operations in 1988 increased 48.1% to an all-time high of $26.9 million or $1.99 per share. Excluding a nonrecurring gain on the sale of an investment in another company, earnings for 1988 still set a new record, up 35.6% to $24.6 million or $1.83 per share. Earnings from continuing operations in 1987 and 1986 were $18.2 million or $1.28 per share and $13.3 million or $1.05 per share, respectively.

During the first quarter of fiscal year 1988, the company sold its investment in the common stock of another company. The investment had been made pursuant to an unsuccessful merger proposal. The sale resulted in a nonrecurring gain of $2.3 million or $.16 per share, after deducting income taxes of $1.4 million.

During 1988, the "mass marketed personal use products" business segment achieved a 24.0% increase in sales, growing to $317.8 million compared to $256.3 million in 1987. VO5 Shampoo, VO5 Instant Conditioner, VO5 Hot Oil Treatment, VO5 Styling Mousse and Mrs. Dash low-sodium products were among the established brands contributing to the current year's sales improvement. The segment's sales gain was also aided by the successful introductions of Molly McButter Butter Flavored Sprinkles and the Bold Hold styling line. Sales of "mass marketed personal use products" increased 19.6% in 1987 compared to 1986.

Sales for the "institutional and industrial products" business segment decreased in 1988 due to the sale of the company's chemical maintenance business in the fourth quarter of fiscal year 1987. Sales for the "institutional and industrial products" segment, exclusive of the chemical maintenance business, were $73.5 million in 1988 versus $73.3 million in 1987 and $70.8 million in 1986.

The "other products—Sally" business segment rose to $219.3 million in sales in 1988 compared to $178.6 million and $140.8 million in 1987 and 1986, respectively. The sales growth was due to a 128% increase in the number of Sally stores over the three year period. Sally stores as of the fiscal year-end totaled 593 in 1988 compared to 470 stores in 1987, 350 stores in 1986 and 260 stores in 1985.

Cost of products sold as a percentage of sales was 45.6% in 1988 compared to 46.6% in 1987 and 47.0% in 1986. Variances between the periods are principally due to changes in product sales mix.

Advertising, promotion, selling and administrative expenses increased 19.2% in 1988 and 17.5% in 1987. The higher expenditures were due to greater investments in advertising and promoting "mass marketed personal use products" and higher administrative expenses related to the growth of Sally Beauty Company. Advertising, promotion and market research expenditures were $113.5 million, $91.4 million and $74.7 million in 1988, 1987 and 1986, respectively.

Interest expense was $5.9 million in 1988 versus $4.5 million in 1987 and $5.8 million in 1986. The increase in interest expense in 1988 was mainly attributable to higher long-term borrowings.

The provision for income taxes as a percentage of earnings from continuing operations before income taxes was 39.0% for 1988 compared to 45.0% and 43.1% in 1987 and 1986, respectively. The effective tax rate for 1988 was less than the 1987 rate primarily due to a lower U.S. federal statutory tax rate and foreign income taxed at lower rates. Factors which influenced the effective tax rates for 1988, 1987 and 1986 are described in "note 7" to the consolidated financial statements.

During 1986, the company sold the assets of Phillippe of California, Inc. The loss on the sale combined with Phillippe's loss from operations resulted in a 1986 loss from discontinued operations of $4.6 million or $.37 per share after deducting applicable income tax benefits.

FINANCIAL CONDITION
Record sales and earnings in 1988 contributed to the continued strengthening of the company's financial condition. Earnings from continuing operations as a percentage of average stockholders' equity showed a return of 18.6% in 1988, excluding the nonrecurring gain on the sale of an investment, compared to 14.6% in 1987 and 14.3% in 1986.

Working capital of $94.8 million at September 30, 1988 represented an increase of $42.8 million or 82.3% for the three year period. The improvement includes the $40.1 million of net proceeds from the sale of 2,240,000 shares of Class A common stock in April, 1986. During 1988, working capital of $22.5 million was used to purchase 998,000 shares of the company's common stock.

Working capital invested in accounts receivable and inventories less accounts payable amounted to $110.7 million at September 30, 1988, which was $23.4 million greater than the comparable investment at the beginning of 1986. The company's current ratio increased to 1.78 to 1.0 in 1988 compared to 1.59 to 1.0 in 1985. Cash, cash equivalents and short-term investments were $34.1 million at September 30, 1988 compared to $14.3 million at September 30, 1985.

Over the last three years, short-term borrowings were reduced $3.7 million while long-term debt, including current maturities, increased $4.4 million. At September 30, 1988, the company had available approximately $150 million of unused lines of credit with various banks.

Investments in fixed assets and acquired businesses totaled $69.7 million for the three years ended September 30, 1988. Also, the company paid cash dividends on Class B common stock of 28.5¢ per share in 1988 compared to 23.25¢ in 1987 and 20.5¢ in 1986. Class A common stock cash dividends per share have been equal to those of Class B common stock since the Class A shares were issued in April, 1986. Total cash dividends paid during the three year period were $9.6 million.

INFLATION
The company was not significantly affected by inflation during the last three years. Using constant dollar accounting, net sales would have been $604.7 million, $536.2 million and $473.2 million in 1988, 1987 and 1986, respectively. It is estimated that 1988 earnings from continuing operations would have been lower than reported if current costs had been used to compute inventories and depreciation.

## Market Price of Common Stock and Cash Dividends Per Share

Alberto Culver Company and Subsidiaries

The high and low sales prices of both classes of the company's common stock on the New York Stock Exchange and cash dividends per share in each quarter of fiscal year 1988 and 1987 are as follows:

| | Market Price Range | | | | Cash Dividends Per Share | |
|---|---|---|---|---|---|---|
| | 1988 | | 1987 | | | |
| | **High** | **Low** | High | Low | **1988** | 1987 |
| Class A: (NYSE symbol ACVA) | | | | | | |
| First Quarter | **$21¾** | **12⅝** | 18¾ | 13½ | **$.0600** | .0525 |
| Second Quarter | **28¼** | **15½** | 22 | 16¾ | **.0750** | .0600 |
| Third Quarter | **26¾** | **21** | 22⅜ | 17¾ | **.0750** | .0600 |
| Fourth Quarter | **27½** | **23** | 24 | 19⅛ | **.0750** | .0600 |
| | | | | | **$.2850** | .2325 |
| Class B: (NYSE symbol ACV) | | | | | | |
| First Quarter | **$24⅞** | **14¾** | 22⅛ | 14½ | **$.0600** | .0525 |
| Second Quarter | **38** | **19⅜** | 26 | 19¾ | **.0750** | .0600 |
| Third Quarter | **36½** | **28** | 27½ | 21¾ | **.0750** | .0600 |
| Fourth Quarter | **37** | **30½** | 28¼ | 22½ | **.0750** | .0600 |
| | | | | | **$.2850** | .2325 |

As of November 21, 1988, stockholders of record totaled 1,586 for Class A and 1,811 for Class B.

## Selected Financial Data
Alberto Culver Company and Subsidiaries

| | Year ended September 30, | | | | |
|---|---|---|---|---|---|
| | **1988** | 1987 | 1986 | 1985 | 1984 |
| Net sales | **$604,708,002** | 514,491,442 | 435,355,255 | 363,275,265 | 322,670,675 |
| Cost of products sold | **275,893,896** | 240,006,380 | 204,659,074 | 162,870,260 | 146,115,250 |
| Interest expense | **5,926,771** | 4,509,732 | 5,801,542 | 7,355,397 | 7,363,544 |
| Earnings from continuing operations before gain on sale of investment and income taxes* | **40,367,164** | 33,024,351 | 23,285,387 | 15,238,635 | 12,720,533 |
| Provision for income taxes* | **15,745,000** | 14,861,000 | 10,025,000 | 6,367,000 | 4,784,000 |
| Earnings from continuing operations before gain on sale of investment* | **24,622,164** | 18,163,351 | 13,260,387 | 8,871,635 | 7,936,533 |
| Earnings per share from continuing operations before gain on sale of investment* | **1.83** | 1.28 | 1.05 | .76 | .68 |
| Cash, cash equivalents and short-term investments | **34,128,252** | 37,006,551 | 24,095,952 | 14,285,204 | 2,988,254 |
| Working capital | **94,820,959** | 84,456,485 | 79,956,599 | 52,028,349 | 30,287,237 |
| Current ratio | **1.78 to 1** | 1.75 to 1 | 1.93 to 1 | 1.59 to 1 | 1.35 to 1 |
| Property, plant and equipment, net | **63,808,687** | 50,615,213 | 39,535,109 | 29,203,040 | 26,663,085 |
| Total assets | **303,348,370** | 271,825,079 | 227,741,571 | 190,211,857 | 183,664,126 |
| Long-term debt | **44,787,237** | 23,643,568 | 22,780,367 | 29,660,658 | 22,874,206 |
| Stockholders' equity | **134,690,160** | 132,937,440 | 116,066,407 | 69,404,449 | 69,354,118 |
| Cash dividends per share: | | | | | |
| Class A common stock** | **.285** | .2325 | .105 | — | — |
| Class B common stock | **.285** | .2325 | .205 | .1875 | .18 |

Reference is made to "note 2" to the consolidated financial statements for a description of the company's discontinued operations and "note 6" pertaining to changes in common stock.

*Earnings from continuing operations before gain on sale of investment are equivalent to earnings from continuing operations for the respective year except for 1988. In 1988, the sale of an investment resulted in a nonrecurring gain of $2,268,709 or $.16 per share after deducting income taxes of $1,408,000 (note 11).

**Dividends on Class A common stock have been equal to those of Class B common stock since the Class A shares were issued in April, 1986.

Annual 10-K Report

Stockholders may obtain a copy of the company's 1988 Form 10-K Report filed with the Securities and Exchange Commission without charge by writing to the Corporate Secretary, Alberto Culver Company, 2525 Armitage Avenue, Melrose Park, Illinois 60160.

# Corporate Data

## Directors:

**Leonard H. Lavin**(1)(3)
Chairman and Chief Executive Officer of the company

**Howard B. Bernick**
President and Chief Operating Officer of the company

**Carol L. Bernick**
Group Vice President of the company

**Archie R. Boe**(1)(2)
Former President, Sears, Roebuck and Co.

**Robert P. Gwinn**(2)
Chairman of the Board, Chief Executive Officer and Director, Encyclopaedia Britannica, Inc.

**Bernice E. Lavin**(1)(3)
Vice President, Secretary and Treasurer of the company

**W. Clement Stone**
Chairman of the Board, Aon Corporation

**William W. Wirtz**(2)(3)
President, The Wirtz Corporation

(1)Member of Executive Committee
(2)Member of Audit Committee
(3)Member of Compensation Committee

## Corporate Officers:

**Leonard H. Lavin**
Chairman and Chief Executive Officer

**Howard B. Bernick**
President and Chief Operating Officer

**Carol L. Bernick**
Group Vice President

**William J. Cernugel**
Vice President, Finance-Controller

**Stephen G. Crews**
Vice President, Public Affairs and Communication

**Bernice E. Lavin**
Vice President, Secretary and Treasurer

**David D. Lewis**
Group Vice President

**Malcolm R. Lloyd**
President, International Group

**Nicholas Z. Malham**
Vice President, Information Systems

**Raymond A. Maslanka**
Vice President, Operations

**P. Douglas McAuley**
Group Vice President

**Thomas J. Pallone**
Vice President, Research and Development

**Norman R. Solberg**
Vice President and General Counsel

**A. M. Swayne, Jr.**
Vice President, Personnel

**John J. Trakselis**
Vice President, Corporate Administration

## Other Officers:

**David D. DeTomaso**
Vice President, Professional Domestic Division

**Ronald M. Kirshbaum**
Vice President, Milani Foods Division

**Robert C. Maurer**
Vice President, U.S. Household/Grocery Products Division

**Janice J. Miller**
Vice President, Market Research

**Cecilia M. Odziomek**
Vice President, Draper Daniels Media Services, Inc.

**Michael H. Renzulli**
President, Sally Beauty Company, Inc.

**Ralph M. Sutherland**
Vice President, U.S. Toiletries Division

## Corporate Office:

Alberto Culver Company
2525 Armitage Avenue
Melrose Park, IL 60160
(312) 450-3000

## Stock Transfer Agent and Registrar:

The First National Bank of Boston
Box 644
Boston, MA 02102
(617) 929-6851

## Auditors:

Peat Marwick Main & Co.
303 East Wacker Drive
Chicago, IL 60601

# Present Value Tables

## APPENDIX C

**Table 1**
**Present Value of $1**

| *Periods* | *2%* | *4%* | *5%* | *6%* | *8%* | *9%* | *10%* | *12%* | *14%* | *16%* | *18%* | *20%* |
|---|---|---|---|---|---|---|---|---|---|---|---|---|
| 1 | .98039 | .96154 | .95238 | .94340 | .92593 | .91743 | .90909 | .89286 | .87719 | .86207 | .84746 | .83333 |
| 2 | .96117 | .92456 | .90703 | .89000 | .85734 | .84168 | .82645 | .79719 | .76947 | .74316 | .71818 | .69444 |
| 3 | .94232 | .88900 | .86384 | .83962 | .79383 | .77218 | .75132 | .71178 | .67497 | .64066 | .60863 | .57870 |
| 4 | .92385 | .85480 | .82270 | .79209 | .73503 | .70843 | .68301 | .63552 | .59208 | .55229 | .51579 | .48225 |
| 5 | .90573 | .82193 | .78353 | .74726 | .68058 | .64993 | .62092 | .56743 | .51937 | .47611 | .43711 | .40188 |
| 6 | .88797 | .79031 | .74622 | .70496 | .63017 | .59627 | .56447 | .50663 | .45559 | .41044 | .37043 | .33490 |
| 7 | .87056 | .75992 | .71068 | .66506 | .58349 | .54703 | .51316 | .45235 | .39964 | .35383 | .31393 | .27908 |
| 8 | .85349 | .73069 | .67684 | .62741 | .54027 | .50187 | .46651 | .40388 | .35056 | .30503 | .26604 | .23257 |
| 9 | .83676 | .70259 | .64461 | .59190 | .50025 | .46043 | .42410 | .36061 | .30751 | .26295 | .22546 | .19381 |
| 10 | .82035 | .67556 | .61391 | .55839 | .46319 | .42241 | .38554 | .32197 | .26974 | .22668 | .19106 | .16151 |
| 11 | .80426 | .64958 | .58468 | .52679 | .42888 | .38753 | .35049 | .28748 | .23662 | .19542 | .16192 | .13459 |
| 12 | .78849 | .62460 | .55684 | .49697 | .39711 | .35554 | .31863 | .25668 | .20756 | .16846 | .13722 | .11216 |
| 13 | .77303 | .60057 | .53032 | .46884 | .36770 | .32618 | .28966 | .22917 | .18207 | .14523 | .11629 | .09346 |
| 14 | .75788 | .57748 | .50507 | .44230 | .34046 | .29925 | .26333 | .20462 | .15971 | .12520 | .09855 | .07789 |
| 15 | .74301 | .55526 | .48102 | .41727 | .31524 | .27454 | .23939 | .18270 | .14010 | .10793 | .08352 | .06491 |
| 16 | .72845 | .53391 | .45811 | .39365 | .29189 | .25187 | .21763 | .16312 | .12289 | .09304 | .07078 | .05409 |
| 17 | .71416 | .51337 | .43630 | .37136 | .27027 | .23107 | .19785 | .14564 | .10780 | .08021 | .05998 | .04507 |
| 18 | .70016 | .49363 | .41552 | .35034 | .25025 | .21199 | .17986 | .13004 | .09456 | .06914 | .05083 | .03756 |
| 19 | .68643 | .47464 | .39573 | .33051 | .23171 | .19449 | .16351 | .11611 | .08295 | .05961 | .04308 | .03130 |
| 20 | .67297 | .45639 | .37689 | .31180 | .21455 | .17843 | .14864 | .10367 | .07276 | .05139 | .03651 | .02608 |
| 21 | .65978 | .43883 | .35894 | .29416 | .19866 | .16370 | .13513 | .09256 | .06383 | .04430 | .03094 | .02174 |
| 22 | .64684 | .42196 | .34185 | .27751 | .18394 | .15018 | .12285 | .08264 | .05599 | .03819 | .02622 | .01811 |
| 23 | .63416 | .40573 | .32557 | .26180 | .17032 | .13778 | .11168 | .07379 | .04911 | .03292 | .02222 | .01509 |
| 24 | .62172 | .39012 | .31007 | .24698 | .15770 | .12641 | .10153 | .06588 | .04308 | .02838 | .01883 | .01258 |
| 25 | .60953 | .37512 | .29530 | .23300 | .14602 | .11597 | .09230 | .05882 | .03779 | .02447 | .01596 | .01048 |

**Table 2**
**Present Value of Ordinary Annuity of $1**

| Periods | 2% | 4% | 5% | 6% | 8% | 9% | 10% | 12% | 14% | 16% | 18% | 20% |
|---|---|---|---|---|---|---|---|---|---|---|---|---|
| 1 | .98039 | .96154 | .95238 | .94340 | .92593 | .91743 | .90909 | .89286 | .87719 | .86207 | .84746 | .83333 |
| 2 | 1.94156 | 1.88609 | 1.85941 | 1.83339 | 1.78326 | 1.75911 | 1.73554 | 1.69005 | 1.64666 | 1.60523 | 1.56564 | 1.52778 |
| 3 | 2.88388 | 2.77509 | 2.72325 | 2.67301 | 2.57710 | 2.53130 | 2.48685 | 2.40183 | 2.32163 | 2.24589 | 2.17427 | 2.10648 |
| 4 | 3.80773 | 3.62990 | 3.54595 | 3.46511 | 3.31213 | 3.23972 | 3.16986 | 3.03735 | 2.91371 | 2.79818 | 2.69006 | 2.58873 |
| 5 | 4.71346 | 4.45182 | 4.32948 | 4.21236 | 3.99271 | 3.88965 | 3.79079 | 3.60478 | 3.43308 | 3.27429 | 3.12717 | 2.99061 |
| 6 | 5.60143 | 5.24214 | 5.07569 | 4.91732 | 4.62288 | 4.48592 | 4.35526 | 4.11141 | 3.88867 | 3.68474 | 3.49760 | 3.32551 |
| 7 | 6.47199 | 6.00205 | 5.78637 | 5.58238 | 5.20637 | 5.03295 | 4.86842 | 4.56376 | 4.28830 | 4.03857 | 3.81153 | 3.60459 |
| 8 | 7.32548 | 6.73274 | 6.46321 | 6.20979 | 5.74664 | 5.53482 | 5.33493 | 4.96764 | 4.63886 | 4.34359 | 4.07757 | 3.83716 |
| 9 | 8.16224 | 7.43533 | 7.10782 | 6.80169 | 6.24689 | 5.99525 | 5.75902 | 5.32825 | 4.94637 | 4.60654 | 4.30302 | 4.03097 |
| 10 | 8.98259 | 8.11090 | 7.72173 | 7.36009 | 6.71008 | 6.41766 | 6.14457 | 5.65022 | 5.21612 | 4.83323 | 4.49409 | 4.19247 |
| 11 | 9.78685 | 8.76048 | 8.30641 | 7.88687 | 7.13896 | 6.80519 | 6.49506 | 5.93770 | 5.45273 | 5.02864 | 4.65601 | 4.32706 |
| 12 | 10.57534 | 9.38507 | 8.86325 | 8.38384 | 7.53608 | 7.16073 | 6.81369 | 6.19437 | 5.66029 | 5.19711 | 4.79322 | 4.43922 |
| 13 | 11.34837 | 9.98565 | 9.39357 | 8.85268 | 7.90378 | 7.48690 | 7.10336 | 6.42355 | 5.84236 | 5.34233 | 4.90951 | 4.53268 |
| 14 | 12.01625 | 10.56312 | 9.89864 | 9.29498 | 8.24424 | 7.78615 | 7.36669 | 6.62817 | 6.00207 | 5.46753 | 5.00806 | 4.61057 |
| 15 | 12.84926 | 11.11839 | 10.37966 | 9.71225 | 8.55948 | 8.06069 | 7.60608 | 6.81086 | 6.14217 | 5.57546 | 5.09158 | 4.67547 |
| 16 | 13.57771 | 11.65230 | 10.83777 | 10.10590 | 8.85137 | 8.31256 | 7.82371 | 6.97399 | 6.26506 | 5.66850 | 5.16235 | 4.72956 |
| 17 | 14.29187 | 12.16567 | 11.27407 | 10.47726 | 9.12164 | 8.54363 | 8.02155 | 7.11963 | 6.37286 | 5.74870 | 5.22233 | 4.77463 |
| 18 | 14.99203 | 12.65930 | 11.68959 | 10.82760 | 9.37189 | 8.75563 | 8.20141 | 7.24967 | 6.46742 | 5.81785 | 5.27316 | 4.81219 |
| 19 | 15.67846 | 13.13394 | 12.08532 | 11.15812 | 9.60360 | 8.95012 | 8.36492 | 7.36578 | 6.55037 | 5.87746 | 5.31624 | 4.84350 |
| 20 | 16.35143 | 13.59033 | 12.46221 | 11.46992 | 9.81815 | 9.12855 | 8.51356 | 7.46944 | 6.62313 | 5.92884 | 5.35275 | 4.86958 |
| 21 | 17.01121 | 14.02916 | 12.82115 | 11.76408 | 10.01680 | 9.29224 | 8.64869 | 7.56200 | 6.68696 | 5.97314 | 5.38368 | 4.89132 |
| 22 | 17.65805 | 14.45112 | 13.16300 | 12.04158 | 10.20074 | 9.44243 | 8.77154 | 7.64465 | 6.74294 | 6.01133 | 5.40990 | 4.90943 |
| 23 | 18.29220 | 14.85684 | 13.48857 | 12.30338 | 10.37106 | 9.58021 | 8.88322 | 7.71843 | 6.79206 | 6.04425 | 5.43212 | 4.92453 |
| 24 | 18.91393 | 15.24696 | 13.79864 | 12.55036 | 10.52876 | 9.70661 | 8.98474 | 7.78432 | 6.83514 | 6.07263 | 5.45095 | 4.93710 |
| 25 | 19.52346 | 15.62208 | 14.09394 | 12.78336 | 10.67478 | 9.82258 | 9.07704 | 7.84314 | 6.87293 | 6.09709 | 5.46691 | 4.94759 |

# Ethics and the Accountant

APPENDIX D

Not too long ago, a survey was conducted of the 500 largest corporations in a five-state region.[1] The topic was **ethics:** a broad set of moral principles that groups adopt as behavior standards. The survey involved a mail questionnaire, which was ultimately completed by the firms' chief executive officers or by other senior managers. The findings were eye-opening, with a significant number of the business leaders reporting concerns. Consider that:

Thirty percent said they had inherited problems from a predecessor who was "too lenient, allowing questionable practices to become part of doing business."

Thirteen percent said they had "high concern" that employees who have access to confidential information might be misusing that information.

Nine percent were at least somewhat concerned that *directors* of their corporate boards might be profiting from inside information.

Without a doubt, ethics has become an extremely hot topic. A day rarely goes by without the media reporting that companies and employees have engaged in some type of marginal behavior—doing things that they clearly should have avoided. In an effort to address these problems, a number of businesses have implemented ethics policies. The questionnaire just cited found that 76% of the surveyed companies had done so. Further, the respondents reported that various steps had been taken to inform employees about the companies' standards.

## A Case Study

An example of an ethics policy is that implemented by General Dynamics, an engineering-based manufacturer that does considerable work for the military and government.[2] The firm's program has three goals: to support individual employees in their daily business conduct; to enhance the administrative performance of the company in basic business relationships; and to build the bond of trust between the company and its customers, suppliers, employees, shareholders, and the communities in which it functions.

General Dynamics has established a series of broadreaching standards to achieve these goals. Several of the standards follow.

- *Gifts, gratuities, and entertainment to customers*—It is a serious violation of standards for any employee to seek a competitive advantage through the use of gifts,

[1] "Southwest Firms Concerned About Ethics, Survey Finds," *The Dallas Morning News,* October 10, 1989, pages 5D, 6D.

[2] See *General Dynamics Standards of Business Ethics and Conduct, Second Edition;* and *The General Dynamics Ethics Program Update.* Both of these sources are published by General Dynamics Corporation, St. Louis, Missouri, Copyright 1988.

gratuities, entertainment, or other favors. (An exception may apply in some foreign countries, where custom requires the exchange of gifts.)

- *Inside information*—Employees may not use or share inside information that is not otherwise available to the general public for any type of personal gain (e.g., trading in the stock of General Dynamics or other firms).
- *Outside interests*—Certain outside interests are "not desirable," such as when an employee has a significant investment in or is an official, director, or employee of another firm, particularly if that firm is a supplier of General Dynamics.
- *Time card reporting*—Prompt and accurate completion of time cards is essential. A cost must not be allocated to a government contract if it (the cost) is unallowable, contrary to the contract or related regulations, or otherwise improper.
- *Quality and testing*—All inspection and testing documentation that relate to design and manufacturing activities must be complete, accurate, and truthful.
- *Expense reports*—Business expenses must be properly and promptly disclosed on expense reports. Further, employees must distinguish between personal expenses, and travel and conference expenses that pertain to business activity.
- *Cash and bank accounts*—All transactions that involve cash and bank accounts must be handled in such a way to avoid any questions of bribery, kickbacks, and any other types of illegal or improper payments.

As General Dynamics so properly notes, communication is the key to maintaining an effective ethics program. In a recent year the ethics program directors received nearly 5,800 communications. Approximately 60% involved individuals who sought information or asked advice; the remaining 40% voiced concerns or raised allegations concerning meaning or application of the standards. Preliminary assessments were made of each communication's significance, with a priority rating being assigned. To illustrate:

> Priority 1 communications involve concerns or allegations, which because of their potential seriousness, could lead to criminal or civil prosecution, congressional investigation, or investigation by other government bodies. Such issues could also cause negative national notoriety, or could lead to suspension . . . or other serious damage to the company reputation. Examples include allegations of bribes, kickbacks, fraud, mischarging, falsification of records or other misrepresentations, security breaches, political payoffs, environmental or safety violations, and other violations of laws or regulations including antitrust or insider trading statutes.

Less than 1% of the 5,800 communications received were classified as Priority 1. Eighty-seven percent fell in the Priority 3 category [those events that had the lowest potential for firm-wide problems (financial or otherwise)].

## The Accountant

Accountants, through certain professional organizations, have developed ethical standards that pertain to financial record keeping and reporting. For example, all accountants should be objective, maintain a high degree of integrity, and not knowingly misrepresent facts to others. In addition, acts should not be committed that reflect poorly on the profession.

As discussed in Chapter 1, accountants may be employed in such diverse areas as public accounting, industry, and government. Those involved in public practice are faced with the further ethical issues of independence, and contingent fees and commissions. (Note: Certain aspects of these issues were addressed in the General Dynamics illustration from the company viewpoint; we now focus on the "outsider's" perspective.)

### Independence

Independence requires that the accountant be free from the influence of others when performing his or her duties. Such independence, which helps protect the public interest, must be maintained in both fact and appearance. Certain activities that would impair independence would include an accountant having a financial interest in a company for which he or she provides services; an accountant having a relative in a high-level management position with a client organization; and an accountant serving as trustee of a client organization.

### Contingent Fees and Commissions

Certified public accountants (CPAs) in public practice are allowed to charge fees that are based on the complexity of the services rendered and the time needed to perform the services. Contingent fees, however, are not permitted. Contingent fees are those that depend on the occurrence of an event or those calculated on some other value. For example, if a tax accountant based a fee on the amount of client taxes paid (or not paid), this fee arrangement might have an influence on the accountant's judgment.

In addition, CPAs are not allowed to accept commissions for the referral of products or services. If, say, an accountant recommends a computer software package that is produced by a client, the accountant may not receive a commission if the client makes a sale from that referral. As you may have gathered, commissions (and contingent fees as well) may affect independence.

## Ethical Challenges for the Accountant

The accountant is continually faced with a number of ethical challenges that affect different accountants in different ways. As evidence, let us consider an independent outside auditor and an accountant employed in industry (i.e., a managerial accountant).

Focusing on the independent auditor, suppose an accountant is hired by a company to perform an audit. He or she has a responsibility to the client company to perform quality work and maintain professional standards. But this same auditor has a responsibility to the stockholders (assuming the firm is organized as a corporation) to adequately disclose any significant information that would be of interest to them. To further complicate matters, the auditor may also be responsible to third parties such as lenders, who will rely on the auditor's work to see that assets the company claims it owns actually exist. In addition, certain regulatory agencies may look to the auditor for a particular level of professional performance. These multiple responsibilities may place the accountant in a decision dilemma; hopefully, though, the rules of ethical conduct will help the auditor in determining priorities and making the correct decision.

The managerial accountant faces the challenge of balancing a commitment to a particular employer with the ethical rules of the profession. As an employee, the managerial accountant has a direct financial interest in the company as the source of his or her well-being (e.g., salary, fringe benefit plans, and so forth). Consider the difficulty that would arise for the accountant when, in complying with ethical standards of the profession, the financial security of the company is endangered. This situation could arise if the accountant discloses that the firm is in violation of the terms of a loan agreement (such as the maintenance of certain financial ratios). The loan's due date could be accelerated, forcing the company to immediately settle any outstanding balances. For many businesses this action would lead to bankruptcy (and eventual unemployment for the "whistle blower").

## A Concluding Comment

Ethics is big news in the business world, with many companies and professions having established ethics programs. Unfortunately, though, such programs do little to change individuals who deliberately engage in misconduct. As far as accounting is concerned, the profession has taken steps to set ethical guidelines for its members. However, the practice of accounting is not always black and white, and no set of standards can ensure the ethical behavior of all participants. Each accountant must therefore overcome the pressures to which he or she is subject and practice the profession in an objective, moral, and dignified manner.

### *Who's the Most Ethical?*

A nationwide survey of business people ranked the corporate ethics of various professions or occupations in the following order:

**1** Accountants
**2** Dentists
**3** Doctors
**4** Officers of large corporations
**5** Public relations practitioners
**6** Lawyers
**7** Funeral home operators
**8** Advertising practitioners
**9** TV repairmen
**10** Realtors
**11** Newspaper reporters
**12** Stockbrokers
**13** Union leaders
**14** Politicians
**15** TV evangelists
**16** Used car salesmen

SOURCE: "Ethics Survey Ranks Accountants First," *Journal of Accountancy,* October 1989, p. 110.

# Checklist of Key Figures

APPENDIX E

This list presents key figures for use when solving the problems (including "Beyond the Basics") in the text. Some of the key figures represent intermediate checkpoints so you can determine if you are on the right track. Other key figures represent a portion of the final solution. If your solution does not agree, you will want to review your calculations to find the error(s).

### CHAPTER 1

**P1-A2** (c2) Ending owner's equity, $25,400
**P1-A3** (a) Net income, $13,000
**P1-A4** (b) Net income, $925
**P1-A5** (c) Total assets, $97,000
**P1-B2** (c2) Ending owner's equity, $20,300
**P1-B3** (a) Net income, $6,850
**P1-B4** (b) Net income, $550
**P1-B5** (c) Total assets, $51,700
**BB1-1** (a) Net income, $73,850

### CHAPTER 2

**P2-A1** (b) Trial balance totals, $32,800
**P2-A2** (b) Trial balance totals, $31,525
**P2-A3** (d) Trial balance totals, $76,100
**P2-A4** (b) Cash balance (February 28), $21,650
**P2-A5** (b) Ending cash balance, $50,600
**P2-A6** Trial balance totals, $168,400
**P2-B1** (b) Trial balance totals, $26,600
**P2-B2** (b) Trial balance totals, $23,340
**P2-B3** (d) Trial balance totals, $98,100
**P2-B4** (b) Cash balance (August 31), $39,300
**P2-B5** (b) Ending cash balance, $44,100
**P2-B6** Trial balance totals, $226,500
**BB2-1** (a) May repair revenue, $13,200
**BB2-2** (b) Ending cash balance, $17,705

### CHAPTER 3

**P3-A1** (b) Net income, $5,810
**P3-A4** (b) Adjusted trial balance totals, $73,325
**P3-A6** (c1) Prepaid advertising, $2,600
**P3-B1** (b) Net income, $3,015
**P3-B4** (b) Adjusted trial balance totals, $50,125
**P3-B6** (c1) Consulting revenue, $27,750
**BB3-1** Case B, salaries paid, $28,780
**BB3-2** (b) Net loss for May, $100

### CHAPTER 4

**P4-A1** (b) Ending capital balance, $64,300
**P4-A2** (a) Net income, $9,300
**P4-A3** (a) Net income, $13,900
**P4-A4** (c) Adjusted trial balance totals, $116,730
**P4-A5** Total assets, $245,445
**P4-A6** (a) Total wage expense, $35,330
**P4-B1** (b) Ending capital balance, $88,520
**P4-B2** (a) Net income, $8,200
**P4-B3** (a) Net income, $4,400
**P4-B4** (c) Adjusted trial balance totals, $36,820
**P4-B5** Total assets, $272,890
**P4-B6** (a) Total wage expense, $55,970
**BB4-2** (b) Current ratio for American Products, 2.8

### CHAPTER 5

**P5-A3** (a) Adjusted trial balance totals, $304,100
**P5-A4** (a) Adjusted trial balance totals, $383,970
**P5-A6** (a) Net income, $100,452
**P5-A7** (a) Adjusted trial balance totals, $363,900
**P5-A8** (a) Adjusted trial balance totals, $415,470
**P5-B3** (a) Adjusted trial balance totals, $238,200
**P5-B4** (a) Adjusted trial balance totals, $484,100
**P5-B6** (a) Net income, $44,520
**P5-B7** (a) Adjusted trial balance totals, $274,200
**P5-B8** (a) Adjusted trial balance totals, $535,700
**BB5-1** (b2) Cost of goods sold, $300,270
**BB5-2** (b) Gross profit percentage for Q-Mart, 37.5%

### CHAPTER 6

**P6-A5** (b) Trial balance totals, $16,872
**P6-A6** (c) Trial balance totals, $256,947
**P6-B5** (b) Trial balance totals, $58,732
**P6-B6** (c) Trial balance totals, $120,561

## CHAPTER 7

**P7-A1** (a) Total cash balance, $32,685
**P7-A2** (a) Adjusted cash balance, $11,231.60
**P7-A3** (a) Adjusted cash balance, $8,845
**P7-A5** (b) Total check register debits to Vouchers Payable, $6,390
**P7-A6** (d) Short-term investments at lower of cost or market, $82,150
**P7-B1** (a) Total cash balance, $11,480
**P7-B2** (a) Adjusted cash balance, $7,904.15
**P7-B3** (a) Adjusted cash balance, $4,380
**P7-B5** (b) Total check register debits to Vouchers Payable, $2,000
**P7-B6** (d) Short-term investments at lower of cost or market, $54,100
**BB7-2** (b) Short-term investments at lower of cost or market (Ace, Inc.), $34,200

## CHAPTER 8

**P8-A2** (c) Bad debts expense, $855
**P8-A3** (b) Estimated amount of uncollectibles, $87,250
**P8-A4** (b) Net realizable value of accounts receivable, $69,100
**P8-B2** (c) Bad debts expense, $510
**P8-B3** (b) Estimated amount of uncollectibles, $75,000
**P8-B4** (b) Net realizable value of accounts receivable, $83,800
**BB8-1** (c) Estimated amount of uncollectibles, $5,750

## CHAPTER 9

**P9-A1** (a) Correct 19X2 net income, $27,000
**P9-A2** (b) Cost of goods sold, $27,850
**P9-A3** (a) Cost of goods sold, $77,743
**P9-A4** (b) Fire loss, $284,720
**P9-A5** (a) Estimated ending inventory, at cost, $41,860
**P9-A6** (b) Debit to Cost of Goods Sold, $46,110
**P9-A7** (b) Cost of goods sold, $46,170
**P9-B1** (a) Correct 19X5 net income, $20,840
**P9-B2** (b) Cost of goods sold, $11,670
**P9-B3** (a) Cost of goods sold, $8,380
**P9-B4** (b) Tornado loss, $115,860
**P9-B5** (a) Estimated ending inventory, at cost, $120,060
**P9-B6** (b) Debit to Cost of Goods Sold, $1,395,000
**P9-B7** (b) Cost of goods sold, $1,399,600
**BB9-2** (a) Estimated ending inventory, at cost (Month 2), $166,000

## CHAPTER 10

**P10-A2** Total land improvements, $212,000
**P10-A3** (a) 19X4 double-declining balance method depreciation, $3,456
**P10-A4** (a) 19X3 depreciation expense, $9,390
**P10-A5** 19X1 sum-of-the-years'-digits depreciation, $1,909,091
**P10-B2** Total land improvements, $102,000
**P10-B3** (a) 19X6 double-declining balance method depreciation, $4,320
**P10-B4** (a) 19X3 depreciation expense, $22,100
**P10-B5** 19X1 sum-of-the-years'-digits depreciation, $20,455
**BB10-1** (d) Total property, plant, & equipment, $533,500

## CHAPTER 11

**P11-A1** (b) 19X2 total depreciation expense, $20,600
**P11-A2** (b2) Loss on exchange of van, $3,000
**P11-A3** (a) Income after disposals and exchanges, $58,100
**P11-A4** (c) Revised depletion rate per ton, $0.68
**P11-A5** (b) 19X1 amortization expense, $11,070
**P11-A6** (a) Goodwill, $14,400
**P11-B1** (b) 19X4 total depreciation expense, $24,420
**P11-B2** (b1) Loss on exchange of computer, $11,800
**P11-B3** (a) Income after disposals and exchanges, $81,900
**P11-B4** (c) Revised depletion rate per ton, $0.90
**P11-B5** (b) 19X3 amortization expense, $8,775
**P11-B6** (a) Goodwill, $29,600
**BB11-1** (a) Loss on exchange, $5,250

## CHAPTER 12

**P12-A1** (b) Total current liabilities, $138,220
**P12-A2** (c) Total current liabilities, $57,378
**P12-A3** (c) Total current liabilities, $491,900
**P12-A4** (c) Total payroll expense, $329,235
**P12-A5** (a) Total net pay, $6,853.60
**P12-A6** (c) Payroll tax increase, $7,110.60
**P12-B1** (b) Total current liabilities, $174,625
**P12-B2** (c) Total current liabilities, $45,198
**P12-B3** (c) Total current liabilities, $322,560
**P12-B4** (c) Total payroll expense, $176,064
**P12-B5** (a) Total net pay, $7,038.85
**P12-B6** (c) Payroll tax increase, $7,170.20
**BB12-1** (a) Corrected net income, $68,900

## CHAPTER 13

**P13-A2** (a) Corrected owner's equity, $34,450
**P13-A4** (b) Profit recognized in 19X7, $1,450,000
**P13-A5** (a) Net income, $12,513
**P13-A6** Part I (c) Constant purchasing power net income, $10,400
**P13-B2** (a) Corrected owner's equity, $30,200
**P13-B4** (b) Profit recognized in 19X3, $100,000

**P13-B5** (b) Net income, $9,088
**P13-B6** Part II (c) Constant purchasing power net loss, $63,000
**BB13-2** (a) Profit to recognize on installment basis, $1,248,000

## CHAPTER 14

**P14-A1** (c) Total partners' equity (Dec. 31), $190,000
**P14-A2** (b) December 31, 19XX, ending partner's equity for Rambo, $81,600
**P14-A3** (c) Rice's capital balance, $91,600
**P14-A4** (a3) Credit to Ogden's capital account, $69,000
**P14-A5** (b) Total partners' equity, $1,260,000
**P14-A6** (b1) Cash balance after settlement of liabilities, $35,000
**P14-B1** (c) Total partners' equity (Dec. 31), $212,100
**P14-B2** (b) December 31, 19XX, ending partner's equity for Tyree, $50,300
**P14-B3** (c) Wiley's capital balance, $2,400
**P14-B4** (a3) Credit to Richardson's capital account, $112,000
**P14-B5** (b) Total partners' equity, $265,000
**P14-B6** (b1) Cash balance after settlement of liabilities, $50,000
**BB14-2** Perini's share of net income on July 31, $5,600

## CHAPTER 15

**P15-A1** (b) 19X4 dividends to preferred, $55,000
**P15-A2** (b) Total stockholders' equity, $304,100
**P15-A3** Total paid-in capital, $10,550,000
**P15-A4** (b) Total stockholders' equity, $80,400
**P15-A6** (a) Book value per common share, $16.74
**P15-B1** (a) 19X7 dividends to common, $242,250
**P15-B2** (b) Total stockholders' equity, $1,294,200
**P15-B3** Total paid-in capital, $344,000
**P15-B4** (b) Total stockholders' equity, $310,800
**P15-B6** (a) Book value per common share, $9.90

## CHAPTER 16

**P16-A1** (b) Total stockholders' equity, $612,900
**P16-A2** (b) Total stockholders' equity, $761,100
**P16-A3** (b) Total stockholders' equity, $1,075,500
**P16-A4** (b) Net income, $90,000
**P16-A5** Net income, $1,152,000
**P16-A6** (b) Fully diluted earnings per share, $1.60
**P16-B1** (b) Total stockholders' equity, $751,800
**P16-B2** (b) Total stockholders' equity, $711,097
**P16-B3** (b) Total stockholders' equity, $751,700
**P16-B4** (b) Net income, $4,050,000
**P16-B5** Net income, $1,584,000
**P16-B6** (b) Fully diluted earnings per share, $3.61
**BB16-3** (c) Retained earnings, December 31, $4,699,000

## CHAPTER 17

**P17-A1** (c) Total bond carrying value, $298,360
**P17-A2** (h) Bond carrying value, Case B, $777,800
**P17-A3** (c) Bond carrying value, $605,995
**P17-A4** (c) 11%
**P17-A5** (b1) Amortization (June 30, 19X2), $314
**P17-A6** (b) Unpaid note balance, December 31, 19X3, $587,919
**P17-B1** (c) Total bond carrying value, $148,720
**P17-B2** (h) Bond carrying value, Case B, $622,000
**P17-B3** (c) Bond carrying value, $295,000
**P17-B4** (c) 10%
**P17-B5** (b1) Amortization (June 30, 19X4), $2,707
**P17-B6** (b) Unpaid note balance, December 31, 19X7, $208,736
**BB17-1** (c1) Net income with stock alternative, $20,400

## CHAPTER 18

**P18-A1** (f) Total interest revenue for 19X1 (Case B), $19,415
**P18-A2** (c) Bond carrying value, $847,398
**P18-A3** (c) Investment carrying value, $70,000
**P18-A5** (b) Total consolidated assets, $566,000
**P18-A6** (a) Total consolidated assets, $1,887,700
**P18-B1** (f) Total interest revenue for 19X2 (Case B), $71,151
**P18-B2** (c) Bond carrying value, $632,479
**P18-B3** (c) Investment carrying value, $204,500
**P18-B5** (b) Total consolidated assets, $735,000
**P18-B6** (a) Total consolidated assets, $1,135,500

## CHAPTER 19

**P19-A2** (a) Net cash provided by operating activities, $215,000
**P19-A3** (a) Net cash used by investing activities, $115,000
**P19-A4** (a) Net cash used by investing activities, $65,600
**P19-A5** (a1) Net cash used by operating activities, $128,000
**P19-A6** Net cash provided by operating activities, $439,000
**P19-A7** (b) Net cash provided by operating activities, $439,000
**P19-B2** (a) Net cash provided by operating activities, $11,900
**P19-B3** (a) Net cash used by investing activities, $361,000
**P19-B4** (a) Net cash used by financing activities, $7,185
**P19-B5** (a1) Net cash used by operating activities, $6,000
**P19-B6** Net cash used by operating activities, $26,000

**P19-B7** (b) Net cash used by operating activities, $26,000
**BB19-1** Total assets, $170,000

## CHAPTER 20

**P20-A2** (d) Accounts receivable turnover, 13.33 times
**P20-A3** Net income, $1,950,000
**P20-A5** (b) Filmed entertainment, 14.92%
**P20-B2** (d) Inventory turnover, 8 times
**P20-B3** Net income, $2,250,000
**P20-B5** (b) Toiletries & cosmetics, 16.89%
**BB20-1** Question 3, part a, inventory turnover (Dayton), 2.31 times

## CHAPTER 21

**P21-A2** (b) Net income, $75,400
**P21-A3** (b) Cost of goods manufactured, $168,250
**P21-A4** (b) Net income, $82,000
**P21-A5** (b) Net income, $106,000
**P21-A6** (a) Cost of goods manufactured, $413,000
**P21-B2** (b) Net loss, $3,200
**P21-B3** (b) Cost of goods manufactured, $102,900
**P21-B4** (b) Net loss, $50,000
**P21-B5** (b) Net income, $14,500
**P21-B6** (a) Cost of goods manufactured, $388,000
**BB21-1** (a) 19X1 understatement of net income, $5,200
**BB21-2** Ending finished goods inventory, $52,000

## CHAPTER 22

**P22-A1** (a) Total job cost, $19,825
**P22-A2** (b5) Cost of jobs completed during March, $84,150
**P22-A3** (d) Total cost of goods sold, $238,100
**P22-A4** (d) Cost of goods sold, $2,451,060
**P22-A5** (e) Ending finished goods inventory, $58,000
**P22-A6** (c) Total billing, $98,400
**P22-B1** (a) Total job cost, $21,100
**P22-B2** (b5) Cost of jobs completed during May, $117,480
**P22-B3** (d) Total cost of goods sold, $319,200
**P22-B4** (d) Cost of goods sold, $841,050
**P22-B5** (d) Ending work in process, $32,000
**P22-B6** (c) Total billing, $10,500

## CHAPTER 23

**P23-A1** (a) Total cost of completed goods, $57,600
**P23-A2** (a) Ending work in process, $66,500
**P23-A3** (a) Total production costs for March, $412,200
**P23-A4** (b1) Ending finished goods, $19,740
**P23-A5** (a) Ending work in process, $35,000
**P23-A6** (a) Ending work in process, $213,000
**P23-B1** (a) Total cost of completed goods, $69,250
**P23-B2** (a) Ending work in process, $19,750
**P23-B3** (a) Total production costs for June, $88,900
**P23-B4** (b1) Ending finished goods, $22,464
**P23-B5** (a) Ending work in process, $49,800
**P23-B6** (a) Ending work in process, $25,600
**BB23-1** (h) Total cost of completed goods, $537,300

## CHAPTER 24

**P24-A1** (b) Cost of direct material purchases for August, $50,880
**P24-A2** (b) Cash excess before financing (March), $75,310
**P24-A3** (c) September ending cash balance, $5,008
**P24-A4** (b) Net loss, $23,840
**P24-A5** (a4) Cost of direct material purchases for March, $3,924
**P24-B1** (b) Cost of direct material purchases for February, $136,920
**P24-B2** (b) Cash excess before financing (June), $34,250
**P24-B3** (c) December ending cash balance, $6,608
**P24-B4** (b) Net income, $32,120
**P24-B5** (a4) Cost of direct material purchases for March, $15,129
**BB24-1** (a) Ending cash balance, $13,170
**BB24-2** (e) Units of finished goods to be manufactured in January 19X5, 4,800

## CHAPTER 25

**P25-A1** (c) Fixed cost, $4,100
**P25-A2** (a) Total utilities cost for 7,850 units, $29,160
**P25-A3** (b) Sales increase, $20,000
**P25-A4** (b) Required sales, $1,125,000
**P25-A5** (b) Net income, process B, $189,000
**P25-B1** (c) Fixed cost, $11,600
**P25-B2** (a) Total utilities cost for 22,800 units, $5,710
**P25-B3** (b) Sales increase, $42,500
**P25-B4** (b) Required sales, $1,485,000
**P25-B5** (b) Net income, process B, $184,000
**BB25-1** (b) Net income, $45,000
**BB25-2** (b) Units manufactured and sold during 19X5, 17,200
**BB25-3** (b) Budgeted net income, $20,800

## CHAPTER 26

**P26-A1** (b) Total budgeted production costs for 25,500 units, $176,700
**P26-A2** (b) Total budgeted overhead costs for 21,300 hours, $129,974

**P26-A3** (c) Variable overhead efficiency variance, $200U
**P26-A4** (b) Labor rate variance, $11,100F
**P26-A5** Labor hours worked, 38,000
**P26-A6** (a) Total materials variance, $1,000F
**P26-B1** (b) Total budgeted production costs for 24,600 units, $472,100
**P26-B2** (b) Total budgeted overhead costs for 13,300 hours, $120,245
**P26-B3** (c) Variable overhead efficiency variance, $4,200F
**P26-B4** (b) Labor rate variance, $38,500U
**P26-B5** Labor efficiency variance, $9,000F
**P26-B6** (a) Total materials variance, $3,000U
**BB26-2** (a) Total standard variable cost, $35.04

## CHAPTER 27

**P27-A1** (b) Maximum price to outside supplier, $4,920
**P27-A2** Contribution margin per chip, $3.11
**P27-A3** (c) Lawn weeder net income, $66,600
**P27-A4** (a) Net income without lunch counter, $73,400
**P27-A5** (a) Total company controllable contribution margin, $92,700
**P27-A6** (d) Net income, $151,000
**P27-B1** (b) Maximum price to outside supplier, $63,400
**P27-B2** Contribution margin per vacuum, $2.68
**P27-B3** (c) Decoder net income, $726,450
**P27-B4** (a) Net income without snack bar, $67,900
**P27-B5** (a) Total company controllable contribution margin, $202,300
**P27-B6** (d) Net income, $221,000
**BB27-1** (a) Executive class cost per room, $125,455
**BB27-2** (c) Cost to produce 36,000 units, $145,700

## CHAPTER 28

**P28-A1** (b) Net present value, $(55,736)
**P28-A2** Savings by making the part, $28,003
**P28-A3** (a) Net present value in favor of trading, $33,985
**P28-A4** (b) Internal rate of return, 13.12%
**P28-A5** (a) Net cash inflow, $5,300
**P28-A6** (b) Net present value, $5,327
**P28-B1** (b) Net present value, $119,398
**P28-B2** Savings of buying the valve, $10,153
**P28-B3** (a) Net present value in favor of keeping the equipment, $30,521
**P28-B4** (b) Internal rate of return, 14.98%
**P28-B5** (a) Net cash inflow, $4,000
**P28-B6** (b) Net present value, $(7,273)
**BB28-1** (a) Net present value, $(23,687)
**BB28-2** Part I, (d) Internal rate of return, 13.05%

## APPENDIX A

**PA-1** Taxable income, $50,300
**PA-2** (b) Taxable income, $74,800
**PA-3** Taxable income, $265,000

# Glossary

**absorption costing** A method under which all manufacturing costs are assigned to products; used for external financial reporting purposes. (Chapter 27)

**Accelerated Cost Recovery System (ACRS)** A system used to write off (i.e., depreciate) the cost of long-term assets; employed for tax purposes only. (Chapter 10)

**accelerated depreciation methods** Methods that generate relatively large amounts of depreciation in the early years of asset use and smaller amounts in later years. (Chapter 10)

**account** A record that is kept for the individual asset, liability, and owner's equity components of an organization. (Chapter 2)

**accounting** A set of theories, concepts, and techniques that collectively measure, summarize, and report financial information about an economic unit. (Chapter 1)

**accounting cycle** The various tasks performed during an accounting period to process transactions, including (1) recording transactions in the journal; (2) posting; (3) preparing a trial balance, work sheet, and financial statements; (4) recording adjusting and closing entries; and (5) preparing a post-closing trial balance. (Chapter 4)

**accounting equation** A mathematical relationship: Assets = Liabilities + Owner's Equity. (Chapter 1)

**accounting information system** The network that processes transactions and ultimately produces financial statements and other reports. (Chapter 6)

**Accounting Principles Board (APB)** A former policy-making body of the AICPA charged with the responsibility of developing generally accepted accounting principles. (Chapter 13)

**accounting rate of return** A method of evaluating long-term projects or investment centers that focuses on the average net income generated in relation to the investment; sometimes called return on investment (ROI). (Chapters 26, 28)

**accounts payable** Amounts owed to suppliers for the purchase of goods or services. (Chapter 12)

**accounts receivable** Amounts that are due an entity from credit sales of goods and services. (Chapter 8)

**accounts receivable turnover** An activity ratio that shows the number of times each year a company's receivables turn into cash; computed by dividing net credit sales by average accounts receivable. (Chapter 20)

**accrual** Revenues and expenses that gradually accumulate throughout an accounting period. (Chapter 3)

**accrual basis** The accounting basis that recognizes revenues when earned and, for income determination purposes, matches expenses against the revenues generated. (Chapter 3, Appendix A)

**accrued expenses** Unpaid expenses that are matched against revenues under the accrual basis of accounting. (Chapter 3)

**accrued liability** The amount owed for an accrued expense. (Chapter 12)

**accrued revenues** Revenues recognized under the accrual basis of accounting as being earned although such amounts have not yet been received. (Chapter 3)

**activity ratios** Ratios used to analyze a firm's effectiveness in using specific resources; often called turnover ratios. (Chapter 20)

**additions** Items that provide future benefits and are affixed to existing plant and equipment. (Chapter 11)

**adjusted gross income** Gross income of a taxpayer minus allowable deductions from gross income. (Appendix A)

**adjusted trial balance** A trial balance prepared after adjusting entries have been made and posted to the ledger accounts. (Chapter 3)

**adjusting entry method of handling inventory** An end-of-period procedure by which the Inventory account is updated through a series of adjusting entries. (Chapter 5)

**adjusting process** A process performed at the end of the period in which the accounts are analyzed and updated, if necessary. (Chapter 3)

**aging accounts receivable** Segregation of individual accounts receivable based on the length of time outstanding; used in the balance sheet approach to estimating bad debts. (Chapter 8)

**allowance method of bad debts** A method of accounting for bad debts that employs a contra asset (Allowance for Bad Debts) for use in the valuation of accounts receivable. (Chapter 8)

**American Institute of Certified Public Accountants (AICPA)** A national organization of licensed CPAs. (Chapter 13)

**amortization** The allocation of the cost of intangible assets to the accounting periods benefited. (Chapter 11)

**annuity** A series of equal cash flows over a number of years. (Chapters 17, 28)

**appropriation of retained earnings** A separation of the Retained Earnings account to inform financial statement readers that a portion of retained earnings is unavailable for dividend distributions. (Chapter 16)

**articles of partnership** The agreement in a partnership that details the rights, responsibilities, and duties of each of the partners. (Chapter 14)

**assessments** Amounts charged to property owners by government agencies for improvements such as new streets, sewers, and sidewalks. (Chapter 11)

**assets** The economic resources owned by a company that are expected to benefit future time periods. (Chapter 1)

**attainable standard** A standard that can be achieved by efficient, not perfect, operations; allows for normal scrap, waste, and spoilage. (Chapter 26)

**auditing** The investigation and examination of transactions that underlie an organization's financial statements. (Chapter 1)

**authorized stock** The number of shares of stock a corporation is permitted to issue as specified in its charter. (Chapter 15)

**average rate of tax** A taxpayer's gross tax liability divided by total taxable income. (Appendix A)

**bad debts** Uncollectible accounts receivable. (Chapter 8)

**balance sheet** A financial statement that presents a firm's assets, liabilities, and owner's equity at a particular point in time. (Chapter 1)

**balance sheet approach of accounting for bad debts** A method that employs estimates of bad debts based on accounts receivable and focuses on reporting accounts receivable at net realizable value. (Chapter 8)

**bank reconciliation** A process for determining the amount of cash that a company has control over and reports on its balance sheet. (Chapter 7)

**bank statement** A document that summarizes the activity in a checking account. (Chapter 7)

**betterments** Expenditures that improve or increase the future service potential of an item of plant and equipment. (Chapter 11)

**bond** A formal written document that provides evidence of long-term indebtedness. (Chapter 17)

**bond discount** The difference between the face value of bonds and the issue price, when issuance occurs below face value. (Chapter 17)

**bond indenture** A document that stipulates the provisions of a bond issue. (Chapter 17)

**bond premium** The difference between the face value of bonds and the issue price, when issuance occurs above face value. (Chapter 17)

**bond refunding** The replacement of a bond issue with other bonds that carry a lower interest rate. (Chapter 17)

**bond retirement** The cancellation of bonds that have been called. (Chapter 17)

**book value** The amount that an asset is carried at in the accounting records—namely, cost minus any offsetting contra accounts. (Chapters 3, 10)

**book value per share** The amount of stockholders' equity allocable to an individual share of stock. (Chapter 15)

**bookkeeping** A discipline heavily involved with record keeping and various mechanical tasks. (Chapter 1)

**bottom-up budgeting** A budgeting approach that centers on lower-level employee participation in the development of a budget. (Chapter 24)

**break-even chart** A presentation of the break-even point and other CVP relationships in a graphic format. (Chapter 25)

**break-even point** The level of activity where revenues and expenses are equal and net income is zero. (Chapter 25)

**budget** A formal quantitative expression of management expectations generated for any area that management deems critical. (Chapters 21, 24)

**callable bond** A bond that can be reacquired by the issuing firm prior to the maturity date. (Chapter 17)

**callable preferred stock** Preferred stock that can be reacquired by the issuing corporation at a preset price. (Chapter 15)

**capital budgeting** Planning and decision making related to long-term programs and projects. (Chapter 28)

**capital deficiency** A debit balance in a partner's capital account. (Chapter 14)

**capital expenditure** An expenditure that provides long-term benefits to a company. (Chapter 10)

**capital lease** A lease by which the lessee is really acquiring an asset via an installment purchase plan. (Chapter 17)

**carrying value of a bond** The face value of a bond minus the unamortized bond discount (or plus the unamortized bond premium). (Chapter 17)

**cash** Items acceptable to a bank for deposit and free from restriction for use in satisfying current debts. (Chapter 7)

**cash basis** The basis of accounting that focuses on the cash flows connected with revenues and expenses. Revenues are recognized when received, and expenses are recognized when paid. (Chapters 3, 13, Appendix A)

**cash budget** An overall plan of activity that depicts cash inflows and outflows for a stated period of time. (Chapters 7, 24)

**cash control system** Procedures adopted to ensure the safeguarding of an organization's funds. (Chapter 7)

**cash discount** A discount offered to credit customers to encourage prompt payment of invoices. (Chapter 5)

**cash payments journal** A special journal used to record virtually all cash disbursements made by a business. (Chapter 6)

**cash planning system** Those procedures adopted to ensure that adequate cash is available to meet normal business obligations and that any excess cash is invested. (Chapter 7)

**cash receipts journal** A special journal used to record all cash received by a business. (Chapter 6)

**certified public accountant (CPA)** An individual who is licensed by a state to practice public accounting. (Chapter 1)

**change in accounting principle** A change from one generally accepted accounting principle to another. (Chapter 16)

**chart of accounts** A detailed listing of a company's accounts and associated account numbers. (Chapter 2)

**charter** A document that specifies a corporation's business purpose, organizational structure, and the types and amounts of stock that can be issued. (Chapter 15)

**check register** A journal used in a voucher system to record each check written. (Chapter 7)

**closely held corporation** A corporation owned by only a few persons. (Chapter 15)

**closing entry method of handling inventory** An end-of-period procedure by which the Inventory account is updated through the closing process. (Chapter 5)

**closing process** A process in which the balances in all temporary accounts are transferred to the owner's capital account. (Chapter 4)

**committed fixed cost** A cost arising from an organization's commitment to engage in operations—for example, property taxes, rent, and depreciation. (Chapter 25)

**common-size financial statements** Statements that reveal account balances in both dollars and percentages, thereby facilitating different types of comparative analysis. (Chapter 20)

**common stock** A corporate ownership interest that controls management by exercising voting rights. (Chapter 15)

**comparability** A characteristic of financial information that allows users to make comparative evaluations among firms and within the same firm at different points in time. (Chapter 13)

**compensating balance** A portion of an amount loaned to a customer that remains on deposit in the bank during the loan period. (Chapter 7)

**compound interest** Interest that is calculated on both principal and previously accumulated interest. (Chapters 17, 28)

**computer fraud** A scheme that involves a computer to aid and abet in a fraud or embezzlement. (Chapter 6)

**conservatism** A concept stipulating that when alternative valuations and measurements are possible, the alternative selected should be that which is least likely to overstate assets and/or net income. (Chapters 7, 13)

**consignment** The process of transferring goods to a sales agent. (Chapter 9)

**consistency principle** A principle stipulating that entities employ the same accounting practices in each reporting period. (Chapter 13)

**consolidated financial statements** A set of financial statements that combines the activities of the parent and controlled subsidiaries as if only one company existed. (Chapter 18)

**constant purchasing power accounting** An approach used to account for inflation in which historical-cost data are adjusted for changes in the purchasing power of the dollar by using a general price level index. (Chapter 13)

**contingent liability** A potential liability whose outcome hinges on the future. (Chapters 8, 12)

**continuous budget** A budget that covers a one-year period; a new month is added when the current month is completed. (Chapter 24)

**contra asset** An account used to reduce asset balances in the financial statements. (Chapter 3)

**contra liability** An account used to reduce liability balances in the financial statements. (Chapter 12)

**contra revenue** An account that is deducted from revenues and used in the computation of net revenues on the income statement. (Chapter 5)

**contract interest rate** The interest rate printed on the face of a bond certificate. (Chapter 17)

**contribution income statement** An income statement that features disclosure of the contribution margin and fixed costs (both controllable and uncontrollable) directly identifiable with a segment. (Chapter 27)

**contribution margin** Selling price minus variable cost per unit. (Chapter 25)

**control** An activity that helps bring an organization back on target in terms of achieving its original plans. (Chapter 21)

**control account** A general ledger account that is composed of various subsidiary ledger accounts. (Chapter 6)

**controllable contribution margin** A performance measure computed by subtracting a segment's controllable fixed costs from its contribution margin. (Chapter 27)

**controller** The chief accounting officer of a company. (Chapter 15)

**controlling interest** A greater-than-50% ownership interest in a subsidiary company. (Chapter 18)

**conversion cost** The cost to convert raw material into finished product—namely, direct labor plus factory overhead. (Chapter 21)

**convertible bond** A bond that can be converted into common stock at the option of the bondholder. (Chapter 17)

**convertible preferred stock** Preferred stock that can be converted into common stock at the option of the stockholder. (Chapter 15)

**copyright** An intangible asset that gives its owners or heirs the exclusive right to produce and sell an artistic, musical, or published work for a stipulated period of time. (Chapter 11)

**corporation** A form of business organization that is a separate legal entity from its owners. Ownership is in the hands of investors who have acquired shares of the corporation's stock. (Chapters 1, 4, 15)

**cost accounting** An area of accounting that deals with the collection, assignment, control, and evaluation of costs. (Chapters 1, 21)

**cost center** A responsibility unit in which a manager is held accountable for cost incurrence. (Chapter 26)

**cost driver** A factor that causes given costs to be incurred within an organization. (Chapter 22)

**cost flow assumption** An assumption regarding the flow of inventory costs through a firm's accounting system. (Chapter 9)

**cost of capital** The cost of investment funds. (Chapter 28)

**cost of goods manufactured** The total of direct materials used, direct labor, and factory overhead, plus the beginning work in process inventory minus the ending work in process inventory. (Chapter 21)

**cost of goods sold** The total cost of inventory that a company has sold during an accounting period. (Chapter 5)

**cost-volume-profit analysis** The study of price, cost, volume, and profit interrelationships. (Chapter 25)

**coupon bonds** Bonds having small detachable coupons that correspond to each interest period and are payable to the bearer. (Chapter 17)

**coverage ratios** Ratios used to judge the solvency of an entity. (Chapter 20)

**credit** A tool used to increase and decrease account balances; also, the right-hand side of a T-account. (Chapter 2)

**credit memorandum** A document prepared by the seller for an allowance or an authorized return of merchandise. (Chapter 5)

**cumulative effect** The difference in the net income reported in prior years and the income that would have been reported using a new accounting principle. (Chapter 16)

**cumulative preferred stock** Preferred stock where the rights to dividends omitted in a given year accumulate. These dividends must be paid before any subsequent dividends are distributed to common stockholders. (Chapter 15)

**current assets** Those assets that management intends to convert into cash or consume in the normal course of business within one year or the operating cycle, whichever is longer. (Chapter 4)

**current cost** The present cost of replacing an asset with a similar asset in similar condition. (Chapter 13)

**current cost accounting** An approach to accounting for inflation that recognizes price changes in the individual assets owned by an enterprise and restates the assets in terms of their current cost. (Chapter 13)

**current liabilities** Debts or obligations that will be paid within one year or the operating cycle, whichever is longer. (Chapters 4, 12)

**current ratio** A measure of liquidity that relates total current assets to total current liabilities. (Chapters 4, 20)

**date of declaration** The date when a dividend is formally declared (approved) by the board of directors. (Chapter 16)

**date of payment** The date when a dividend will be distributed to stockholders. (Chapter 16)

**date of record** The date used to determine the stockholders entitled to receive a declared dividend. (Chapter 16)

**debenture bond** A bond that has no assets pledged as security and is issued on the general credit of the corporation. (Chapter 17)

**debit** A tool used to increase and decrease account balances; also, the left-hand side of a T-account. (Chapter 2)

**debit memorandum** A document prepared by the purchaser for either an allowance or an authorized return of merchandise. (Chapter 5)

**debt to total assets ratio** A coverage ratio that shows the percentage of total capital provided by the creditors of a business; computed as total debt divided by total assets. (Chapter 20)

**decision making** An integral part of the planning and control process that requires managers to choose from among alternative courses of action. (Chapter 21)

**declining-balance method** A method of depreciation by which a fixed depreciation rate is applied to the remaining book value each period. (Chapter 10)

**deductions from adjusted gross income** Subtractions from adjusted gross income for certain personal expenses—specifically, itemized deductions (or the standard deduction) and personal exemptions. (Appendix A)

**deductions from gross income** Subtractions from a taxpayer's income that generally relate to the generation of gross income. (Appendix A)

**deferred taxes** A postponement of income taxes that arises from temporary differences. (Chapter 17)

**deficit** A debit (negative) balance in the Retained Earnings account. (Chapter 16)

**dependent** A person who (1) has received more than one-half of his or her support from the taxpayer, (2) is closely related to the taxpayer or has lived in the taxpayer's home for the entire year, and (3) has earned less than $2,000 of income (unless 19 years of age or a full-time student). (Appendix A)

**depletion** The allocation of natural resource cost to the resources extracted during an accounting period. (Chapter 11)

**deposit in transit** Receipts entered on company records but not yet processed by the bank. (Chapter 7)

**depreciable base** The cost of an item of plant and equipment minus any residual value. (Chapter 10)

**depreciation** The process used to allocate the cost of long-lived items of plant and equipment to the accounting periods benefited. (Chapters 3, 10)

**differential cost** A cost that differs among alternatives. (Chapter 27)

**direct cost** Any cost that is easily traced to and associated with a business segment. (Chapters 22, 27)

**direct costing** A method that assigns only variable manufacturing costs (direct materials, direct labor, and variable manufacturing overhead) to products; more appropriately termed variable costing. (Chapter 27)

**direct labor** The gross wages of personnel who work directly on the goods being produced. (Chapter 21)

**direct materials** All materials that form an integral part of the finished product and that can be easily traced to the finished product. (Chapter 21)

**direct method to construct statement of cash flows** An approach whereby individual income statement items are converted from the accrual basis to the cash basis of accounting. (Chapter 19)

**direct write-off method of bad debts** A method of accounting for bad debts whereby customer accounts are written off (expensed) when determined to be uncollectible. (Chapter 8)

**disclosure principle** A principle holding that an entity must provide a complete reporting of all facts important enough to influence the judgment of an informed user of financial information. (Chapters 4, 13)

**discontinued operations** A segment of a business that is sold, abandoned, or otherwise disposed of. (Chapter 16)

**discount amortization** The process of reducing a discount on notes payable (or bonds payable) by recognizing interest expense; also refers to the process of reducing a discount on bond investments by recognizing interest revenue. (Chapters 12, 17, 18)

**discount on capital stock** The difference between the par (or stated) value of stock and the issue price, when issuance occurs below par or stated value. (Chapter 15)

**discount on notes payable** A contra-liability account that represents future interest expense. (Chapter 12)

**discounting** The process of taking a future amount and bringing it back to its value today. (Chapter 28)

**discounting notes receivable** A means of generating cash by presenting notes receivable to a bank before the maturity date and receiving the maturity value minus a discount (interest) assessed by the bank. (Chapter 8)

**discretionary fixed cost** A fixed cost that originates from top management's yearly appropriation decisions—for example, advertising expense and research and development expense. (Chapter 25)

**dishonoring a note** The process of failing to pay a note receivable as of the maturity date. (Chapter 8)

**dissolution** The termination of a partnership's life. (Chapter 14)

**dividend payout ratio** A profitability ratio; annual dividend per share divided by earnings per share. (Chapter 20)

**dividend yield** A profitability ratio that is calculated by dividing the annual cash dividend per share by the current market price of the stock. (Chapter 20)

**dividends** A distribution of income by a corporation to its stockholders. (Chapters 4, 16)

**dividends in arrears** Dividends that have been omitted on cumulative preferred stock. (Chapter 15)

**double-declining balance depreciation** A method of accelerated depreciation in which the straight-line depreciation rate is doubled and applied against the remaining book value (i.e., a declining balance) each period. (Chapter 10)

**double taxation** The taxing of income to a corporation and the subsequent taxing of dividends to stockholders. (Chapter 15)

**drawing account** An account used to accumulate withdrawals of sole proprietors or partners. (Chapter 2)

**earnings deficiency** The condition that exists when a partnership incurs a net loss or has insufficient earnings to cover salary and interest allowances. (Chapter 14)

**earnings per share (EPS)** A widely used profitability ratio; computed as earnings available to common stockholders (net income minus any preferred dividend requirements) divided by the weighted-average common shares outstanding. (Chapters 16, 20)

**economic entity** A group of companies that function as a single entity to pursue the objectives of operational efficiency and profit. (Chapter 18)

**effective-interest amortization** A method of bond discount and premium amortization by which interest expense (or revenue in the case of investments) is calculated as a constant percentage of bond carrying value. (Chapters 17, 18)

**effective interest rate** The actual interest rate on a bond, which may be different from the contract interest rate. (Chapter 17)

**electronic spreadsheet** Computer software that resembles a huge columnar work sheet; useful in a variety of accounting applications. (Chapters 6, 24)

**elimination entry** An entry made on the consolidated work sheet to eliminate intercompany transactions from consolidated financial statements. (Chapter 18)

**employee** A person who works for a specific business and is directly and closely supervised by that business. (Chapter 12)

**entity assumption** An assumption that a business is viewed as a unit that is separate and apart from its owners and from other firms. (Chapters 1, 13)

**equity method** A method of accounting for long-term investments in common stock, where the Investment account includes the acquisition cost and a share of the investee's net income, net losses, and dividends. (Chapter 18)

**equivalent unit** A physical unit stated in terms of a finished unit. (Chapter 23)

**ethics** A broad set of practices that groups follow as behavior standards. (Appendix D)

**expenses** The costs incurred in producing revenues. (Chapter 1)

**extraordinary gains and losses** Gains and losses that are both unusual in character and infrequent in occurrence. (Chapter 16)

**factory overhead** All factory-related costs other than direct materials used and direct labor. (Chapter 21)

**fair market value** The current market price of an asset. (Chapter 11)

**Federal Insurance Contributions Act (FICA)** An act, commonly called Social Security, that requires employers to withhold a portion of each employee's gross earnings and to match the employee's contribution. (Chapter 12)

**Federal Unemployment Tax Act (FUTA)** Federal legislation that requires employers to pay taxes to assist the unemployed. (Chapter 12)

**FIFO process costing** A method whereby the beginning work in process inventory is assumed to be the first batch of goods completed. (Chapter 23)

**financial accounting** An area of accounting concerned primarily with external reporting—that is, reporting the results of financial activities to parties outside the firm. (Chapters 1, 21)

**Financial Accounting Standards Boards (FASB)** The private sector organization presently in charge of formulating standards of financial reporting in the United States. (Chapters 1, 13)

**financial position** A determination of the resources owned by a company and the claims on those resources at a particular point in time. (Chapter 1)

**financial statements** Financial reports that are compiled and distributed by companies. (Chapter 1)

**financing activities** Those activities that supply a company with funds from the company's owners or creditors. (Chapter 19)

**finished goods** The inventory of completed production that is owned by a firm. (Chapter 21)

**first-in, first-out (FIFO)** An inventory accounting method based on the premise that costs are matched against revenues in the order of incurrence. (Chapter 9)

**fiscal year** Any one-year period other than a calendar year—for example, July 1–June 30. (Chapter 3)

**fixed cost** A cost that remains constant in total when changes occur in an activity base. (Chapters 21, 25)

**fixed overhead volume variance** A variance that discloses the fixed costs associated with an under- or overutilization of manufacturing facilities. (Chapter 26)

**flexible budget** A budget that covers a range of activity as opposed to a single level. (Chapter 26)

**F.O.B. destination** Freight terms indicating that transportation charges are borne by the seller. (Chapter 5)

**F.O.B. shipping point** Freight terms indicating that transportation charges are borne by the purchaser. (Chapter 5)

**footnotes** A supplemental, yet integral, part of the financial statements that provides an expansion of the information contained in the body of the statements. (Chapters 4, 20)

**Foreign Corrupt Practices Act (FCPA)** An act that outlaws bribes and questionable payments to foreign firms, governments, and political officials and makes such payments a criminal offense. (Chapter 6)

**franchise** An intangible asset representing rights that authorize the manufacture or sale of certain products and/or the performance of certain services. (Chapter 11)

**full project approach** An evaluation of the total relevant costs associated with a decision alternative. (Chapter 27)

**fully diluted earnings per share** A calculation of earnings per share based on the assumption that potentially dilutive securities were converted into common shares at the beginning of the accounting period. (Chapter 16)

**future value** The amount an original sum will increase to, given an interest rate and a designated time period. (Chapter 17)

**General Accounting Office (GAO)** A government agency that evaluates programs and other government agencies for the U.S. Congress. (Chapter 1)

**general ledger** A book or computer file that houses an entity's financial-statement accounts. (Chapter 2)

**generally accepted accounting principles (GAAP)** A set of assumptions, concepts, and practices that provides a foundation for measuring and disclosing the results of business transactions and events. (Chapter 13)

**going-concern assumption** An assumption that a business will continue to operate for an indefinite period of time unless there is substantial evidence to the contrary. (Chapter 13)

**goods available for sale** The beginning balance of inventory plus net purchases. (Chapter 5)

**goodwill** The amount paid by the purchaser of a business in excess of the current value of the assets and liabilities acquired. (Chapter 11)

**gross earnings** The total earnings of an employee before any deductions are made. (Chapter 12)

**gross income** A taxpayer's total income minus allowable exclusions. (Appendix A)

**gross method of recording purchases** A method of accounting for merchandise in which both Purchases and Accounts Payable are recorded at the total invoice cost of the merchandise acquired. (Chapter 5)

**gross profit** Net sales minus cost of goods sold. (Chapter 5)

**gross profit method** An inventory estimation method based on a company's gross profit rate—that is, gross profit expressed as a percentage of net sales. (Chapter 9)

**high-low method** A method of cost analysis that uses two data observations (the highest and lowest) to make generalizations about variable and fixed cost behavior. (Chapter 25)

**historical-cost method.** A method of accounting for securities by which securities are initially recorded and subsequently maintained at cost. (Chapter 7)

**historical-cost principle** The principle of recording goods, resources, and services acquired at cost, with cost defined as the exchange or transaction price. (Chapters 1, 13)

**holding gains and losses** The difference between an asset's acquisition cost and current cost. (Chapter 13)

**horizontal analysis** The calculation of dollar and percentage changes for corresponding items in comparative financial statements. (Chapter 20)

**ideal standard** A standard that can be achieved only under perfect operating conditions. (Chapter 26)

**inadequacy** The inability of a depreciable asset to meet the competitive needs of a business. (Chapter 10)

**income statement** A financial statement that summarizes the results of a company's operation for a given time period by disclosing the revenues earned and the expenses incurred. (Chapter 1)

**income statement approach of accounting for bad debts** A method that employs estimates of bad debts based on total sales or credit sales. (Chapter 8)

**income tax withholdings** The portion of an employee's gross earnings withheld by the employer to satisfy federal (and sometimes state and local) income tax laws. (Chapter 12)

**incremental approach** An evaluation of the net difference in relevant costs associated with decision alternatives. (Chapter 27)

**independent contractor** A person who frequently performs services for many different organizations at the same time, or perhaps finishes a project for one entity and then moves on to service another. (Chapter 12)

**independent review** An internal control feature that involves the review and evaluation of accounting controls by an independent external auditor. (Chapter 6)

**indirect cost** A cost that is not easily traced to a business segment. (Chapters 22, 27)

**indirect labor** The wages of factory employees who do not work directly on the product; treated as part of factory overhead. (Chapter 21)

**indirect materials** Minor materials (such as glue, varnish, and nails) used in manufacturing a product; treated as part of factory overhead. (Chapter 21)

**indirect method to construct statement of cash flows** An approach whereby cash flows from operations is derived by making certain adjustments to accrual-basis net income. (Chapter 19)

**inflation** A rise in the general price level that causes a decline in the purchasing power of the dollar. (Chapter 13)

**installment method** A method of revenue recognition by which a sale's profit is allocated to different accounting periods. The allocation is based on the amount of cash received from customers. (Chapter 13)

**installment receivable** Amounts due an entity from sales made on an installment plan. Such plans require specified, uniform payments over a predetermined number of months. (Chapter 8)

**intangible assets** Long-term assets that lack physical existence—for example, patents, copyrights, and trademarks. (Chapters 4, 11)

**intercompany transaction** A transaction between two affiliated companies such as a parent and a subsidiary. (Chapter 18)

**interest** A charge made for the use of borrowed funds. (Chapter 8)

**interest allowances** A consideration used in the division of net income of many partnerships. The allowances recognize differences in capital provided to the firm by the partners. (Chapter 14)

**interest period** The time that elapses between cash flows in future value and present value computations. (Chapter 17)

**internal auditors** Individuals in large organizations who review and monitor the organization's accounting procedures and controls. (Chapter 1)

**internal control** The various measures adopted by a company to safeguard assets, check the reliability and accuracy of financial information, ensure compliance with management policies, and evaluate operating performance and efficiency. (Chapter 6)

**internal rate of return** A discounted cash flow method of evaluating long-term projects that derives the actual return on an investment. (Chapter 28)

**Internal Revenue Service (IRS)** An agency of the U.S. Treasury Department that administers the tax laws passed by Congress and the rulings handed down by the courts. (Chapters 1, 13, Appendix A)

**intraperiod tax allocation** The practice of relating income tax expense to the items that give rise to the tax. (Chapter 16)

**inventory** Goods acquired for resale to customers. (Chapters 5, 9)

**inventory turnover ratio** An activity ratio that lends insight into a firm's inventory management policies; computed by dividing the cost of goods sold by average inventory. (Chapter 20)

**investee** A company whose shares have been acquired by an investor. (Chapter 18)

**investing activities** Those activities that involve investment of an entity's resources. (Chapter 19)

**investment center** A responsibility unit in which a manager is evaluated on profit and the effective use of asset investment. (Chapter 26)

**invoice price** List price minus applicable trade discounts. (Chapter 5)

**itemizing** A process performed by a taxpayer; involves listing the actual allowable personal expenses that have been incurred during the year. (Appendix A)

**job order system** A system of cost accumulation that gathers costs by job or order. (Chapter 22)

**joint return** A filing status for tax purposes that combines the income and deductions of a husband and wife. (Appendix A)

**journal** A chronological record that serves as the entry point for transactions into a company's formalized accounting system. (Chapter 2)

**journalizing** The process of recording transactions in a journal in the form of debits and credits. (Chapter 2)

**labor efficiency variance** The difference between actual and standard labor hours, multiplied by the standard wage rate. (Chapter 26)

**labor rate variance** The difference between actual and standard wage rates, multiplied by the actual hours of labor used in production. (Chapter 26)

**land improvements** Improvements made to land, such as parking lots and lawn sprinkler systems. (Chapter 10)

**last-in, first-out (LIFO)** An inventory accounting method based on the premise that costs are matched against revenues in the reverse order of incurrence. (Chapter 9)

**lease** An agreement allowing one party, the lessee, to use the assets of another party, the lessor, for a stated period of time. (Chapter 17)

**leasehold improvements** Improvements made to leased property by the lessee. (Chapter 11)

**legal capital** The minimum amount of owners' equity that must be maintained for the protection of creditors; obtained by multiplying the par value per share times the number of shares issued. (Chapter 15)

**legal entity** A unit authorized by the relevant government authority to conduct business. (Chapter 18)

**liabilities** Debts that are owed by an enterprise. (Chapters 1, 12)

**liquidation** The process of terminating a partnership and discontinuing operations. (Chapter 14)

**liquidity** How close an asset is to becoming cash. (Chapter 4)

**liquidity ratios** Ratios that measure the ability of a business to meet current debts as the obligations come due. (Chapter 20)

**list price** The basic catalog price for merchandise. (Chapter 5)

**long-term liabilities** Obligations expected to be paid after one year or the operating cycle, whichever is longer. (Chapters 4, 17)

**lower-of-cost-or-market methods** Methods that allow investments and inventories to be accounted for at acquisition cost or market value, whichever is lower. (Chapters 7, 9, 18)

**lump-sum purchase** The purchase of a number of assets together for a single amount. (Chapter 10)

**maker** The person or firm that promises to pay the stipulated amount of a note. (Chapter 8)

**management advisory services (MAS)** "Consulting" services performed by public accounting firms that are often unrelated to traditional accounting matters. (Chapter 1)

**management by exception** The practice of focusing a manager's attention on those aspects of operations that deviate from planned or expected results. (Chapter 26)

**managerial accounting** An area of accounting oriented toward reporting the results of operations to managers and other interested parties within an organization. (Chapters 1, 21)

**margin of safety** The amount that sales can fall before a net loss is generated; computed as the difference between sales and break-even sales. (Chapter 25)

**marginal rate of tax** The tax rate applied to each additional dollar of taxable income. (Appendix A)

**market value** For inventory: the replacement cost of a unit of merchandise. For stock: the price at which a share can be bought or sold. (Chapters 9, 15)

**master budget** A comprehensive set of integrated budgets that serves as the financial plan for the entire organization. (Chapter 24)

**matching principle** The principle that all costs and expenses associated with the production of revenue are recognized when the revenue is recognized. (Chapters 3, 13)

**materiality** A concept dictating that an accountant must judge the impact and importance of each transaction (or event) to determine its proper handling in the accounting records. Minor items are treated in the most expedient manner possible. (Chapters 10, 13)

**materials price variance** The difference between the actual and standard prices, multiplied by the actual quantity of materials purchased and put into production. (Chapter 26)

**materials quantity variance** The difference between actual and standard quantities of materials used, multiplied by the standard price. (Chapter 26)

**materials requisition** An order for materials to be issued from the storeroom. (Chapter 22)

**maturity date** The date that a note or obligation becomes due. (Chapter 8)

**maturity value** The amount due on the maturity date (principal plus interest). (Chapter 8)

**menu** A computerized listing that shows the various program options available to a user. (Chapter 6)

**merchandise inventory** Goods held by a merchandising business for resale to others. (Chapters 5, 9)

**method of least squares** A statistical technique for determining cost behavior. (Chapter 25)

**minority interest** The portion of a subsidiary entity owned by parties other than the parent (controlling) company. (Chapter 18)

**mixed (semivariable) cost** A cost that contains both fixed and variable elements. (Chapter 25)

**modified cash basis** A method that utilizes features from both the cash and accrual bases of accounting. (Chapter 3)

**monetary assets** Contractual claims to receive a fixed amount of cash in the future; include cash, accounts receivable, and notes receivable. (Chapter 13)

**monetary liabilities** Contractual claims to pay a fixed amount of cash in the future; include accounts payable, salaries payable, and bonds payable. (Chapter 13)

**monetary unit assumption** An assumption that an entity's transactions can be expressed in terms of a common measuring unit, such as the U.S. dollar. (Chapters 1, 13)

**mortgage note** A long-term note issued to finance the purchase of real estate. (Chapter 17)

**moving-average method** A perpetual inventory costing system under which a new average cost is computed after each purchase. (Chapter 9)

**multiple-step income statement** A type of income statement in which accounts are presented by association, thereby revealing important relationships to readers. (Chapter 5)

**mutual agency** A feature of partnerships whereby each partner acts as an agent of the partnership in business transactions. (Chapter 14)

**natural business year** A year that concludes at the end of "seasonal activity"—for example, October 31 for a professional baseball club, which is after the play-offs and World Series. (Chapter 3)

**net income** The excess of a company's revenues over expenses for a given time period. (Chapter 1)

**net loss** The excess of a company's expenses over revenues for a given time period. (Chapter 1)

**net method of recording purchases** A method of accounting for merchandise in which both Purchases and Accounts Payable are recorded at the net cost of the purchase—that is, total invoice cost minus the anticipated cash discount. (Chapter 5)

**net-present-value method** A method used to evaluate long-term investments in which the present value of an investment's cash inflows and cash outflows are netted against each other. (Chapter 28)

**net realizable value** For receivables: the amount of cash expected from the collection of present customer balances. For inventory: an item's selling price minus completion and disposal costs. (Chapters 8, 9)

**nonmonetary items** Asset, liability, and owner's equity items whose prices can change over time—for example, land, equipment, inventory, and warranty obligations. (Chapter 13)

**nontrade receivables** Those receivables that arise from transactions and events not directly related to the sale of goods and services. (Chapter 8)

**normal balance** The type of balance (debit or credit) usually found in a ledger account; for example, assets usually have debit balances, liabilities normally have credit balances, and so forth. (Chapter 2)

**notes payable** Written promises to pay a definite amount of money on a specific future date. (Chapter 12)

**notes receivable** Written promises owned by a firm that specify the receipt of a definite sum of money on some future date. (Chapter 8)

**NSF check (nonsufficient funds)** A customer's check returned by the bank because of a lack of funds. (Chapter 7)

**objectivity principle** A principle requiring that accounting information be free from bias and verifiable by an independent party, such as an external auditor. (Chapters 1, 13)

**operating activities** Company activities primarily related to the production and sale of goods and services, and that enter into the determination of net income. (Chapter 19)

**operating cycle** The period of time it takes a firm to buy merchandise inventory, sell the inventory, and collect the related receivables. (Chapter 4)

**operating expenses** Expenses that relate to the principal selling and administrative activities of a business. (Chapter 5)

**operating lease** A lease by which the lessee obtains the right to use leased property for a very limited period of time. (Chapter 17)

**opportunity cost** The cost of a forgone alternative. (Chapter 27)

**organization costs** Costs incurred to organize a corporation, such as state incorporation fees and legal costs. (Chapter 15)

**outstanding checks** Checks written but not yet processed by the bank. (Chapter 7)

**outstanding shares** Shares issued by a firm and held by the stockholders. (Chapter 15)

**overapplied overhead** A situation arising when the factory overhead applied to production is greater than the amount of factory overhead actually incurred. (Chapter 22)

**overhead application rate** The rate used to apply factory overhead to jobs or products; estimated factory overhead divided by the estimated application base. (Chapter 22)

**owner investments** Personal assets put into a business by the owner. The owner is relinquishing asset control and ownership to the enterprise. (Chapter 1)

**owner withdrawals** The removal of assets from the business by the owner for personal use. (Chapter 1)

**owner's equity (capital)** The owner's net worth of "interest" in the assets of a business; equal to the company's net assets (assets minus liabilities). (Chapter 1)

**paid-in capital** The amount of stockholder investments in a corporation. (Chapter 15)

**parent** A company that is the majority owner of another company. (Chapter 18).

**participating preferred stock** Preferred stock that participates in excess dividend distributions after specified distributions to common stockholders. (Chapter 15)

**partnership** A company formed by two or more persons to carry on, as co-owners, profitable business activity. (Chapters 1, 4, 14)

**par-value stock** Stock that has an arbitrary fixed amount per share specified in the corporate charter. (Chapter 15)

**patent** An exclusive right that permits its owner to use, manufacture, and sell a product or process. (Chapter 11)

**payback method** A method of analysis that measures the amount of time necessary to recover a project's initial cash investment. (Chapter 28)

**payee** The party to whom a note is made payable. (Chapter 8)

**payroll register** A journal-like record that summarizes a firm's entire payroll. (Chapter 12)

**percentage-of-completion method** A method of revenue recognition by which profit is allocated to different accounting periods based on the percentage of the total project completed. (Chapter 13)

**performance report** A report designed to provide the manager of a responsibility center with timely feedback of operating results. (Chapter 26)

**period cost** A cost unrelated to the acquisition or manufacture of inventory; it is expensed when incurred. (Chapter 21)

**periodic inventory system** A system of accounting in which purchases and sales of inventory are not recorded in the Inventory account. (Chapters 5, 9)

**periodicity assumption** An assumption stipulating that for reporting purposes, an entity's life can be divided into discrete time periods such as months, quarters, or years. (Chapters 3, 13)

**perpetual inventory system** A system of accounting for inventory in which the Inventory account is respectively increased and decreased for each purchase and sale of inventory made during the period. (Chapters 5, 9)

**personal exemption** A $2,000 deduction from adjusted gross income that is allowed for the taxpayer, the spouse, and each dependent claimed. (Appendix A)

**petty cash system** A fund used to make small payments that are impractical or uneconomical to make by check. (Chapter 7)

**planning** The formulation of methods and strategies that implement a company's objectives in definite terms. (Chapter 21)

**pooling-of-interests method** A method of accounting for business combinations; applicable when one company acquires virtually all the outstanding voting shares of another company in exchange for its own common stock. (Chapter 18)

**post-closing trial balance** An internal report that examines ledger account balances after the closing process has been completed to determine if total debits equal total credits. (Chapter 4)

**posting** The process by which the transactions in a journal are transferred to the appropriate ledger accounts. (Chapter 2)

**preemptive right** The right of existing stockholders to maintain their respective interests in a corporation by acquiring additional shares of new stock issues on a pro rata basis. (Chapter 15)

**preferred stock** Stock that gives its holders preference over common stockholders in dividend distributions and distributions of assets upon liquidation. (Chapter 15)

**premium on capital stock** The difference between the par (or stated) value of stock and the issue price, when issuance occurs above par or stated value. (Chapter 15)

**prepaid expenses** Goods or services purchased for future consumption and paid for in advance. (Chapter 3)

**present value** The amount an investor is willing to pay to secure a specified cash flow on a future date at a given rate of return. (Chapters 17, 28)

**pretax financial income** Pretax income reported in the financial statements. (Chapter 17)

**price-earnings (P/E) ratio** A profitability ratio calculated by dividing the current market price of a share of common stock by the annual earnings per share. (Chapters 16, 20)

**primary earnings per share** A calculation of earnings per share for firms with potential dilution; the calculation ignores the dilutive effect of convertible securities. (Chapter 16)

**prime cost** Those costs easily traced to the finished product—namely, direct materials used plus direct labor. (Chapter 21)

**principal** The amount on which interest is computed. (Chapter 8)

**prior period adjustments** Corrections of errors that affect the net income of previous accounting periods. (Chapter 16)

**process costing system** A system of cost accumulation that gathers costs by process or department. (Chapter 23)

**product cost** A cost that goes into inventory—namely, direct materials, direct labor, and factory overhead. (Chapter 21)

**production cost report** A report that is used in a process costing system; shows costs and units, classified by department. (Chapter 23)

**profit center** A responsibility unit in which a manager is held accountable for profit. (Chapter 26)

**profit margin on sales** A measure of profitability that relates net income to net sales. (Chapter 20)

**profitability ratios** Ratios that examine an organization's operating success (or lack of success) during an accounting period. (Chapter 20)

**pro-forma financial statements** Forecasted financial statements that are prepared as the final step of the budgeting process. (Chapter 24)

**property dividends** Dividends paid in assets other than cash. (Chapter 16)

**property, plant, and equipment** Assets with long lives acquired for use in business operations and not held for resale to customers. (Chapters 4, 10)

**prospectus** A document related to new stock issues that is required by the SEC; contains information about the corporation's products, management, and financial affairs. (Chapter 15)

**protest fee** A bank service charge associated with dishonored notes. (Chapter 8)

**public accounting** A branch of accounting in which an accountant provides services to all types of enterprises for fees. (Chapter 1)

**publicly held corporation** A corporation that sells its stock to the general public. (Chapter 15)

**purchase method** A method of accounting for business combinations. The parent acquires shares of the subsidiary's stock, and the subsidiary's stockholders terminate their interest in the company. (Chapter 18)

**purchases discount** A discount secured by the purchaser of merchandise for prompt payment of invoices. (Chapter 5)

**purchases journal** A special journal used to record purchases of merchandise on account. (Chapter 6)

**purchasing power gains and losses** Gains and losses that result from changes in the purchasing power of the dollar for holders of monetary assets and monetary liabilities. (Chapter 13)

**quick ratio** A severe measure of short-term debt paying ability that relates the total of cash, short-term investments, and accounts receivable to total current liabilities. (Chapter 20)

**ratio analysis** The use of mathematical relationships to study a firm's liquidity, activity, profitability, and coverage of obligations. (Chapter 20)

**raw materials** The items to be processed into salable goods—specifically, the direct and indirect materials owned. (Chapter 21)

**real accounts** Accounts whose balances are carried forward from period to period. (Chapter 4)

**realized holding gains and losses** Holding gains and losses that are calculated on the basis of assets sold or consumed. (Chapter 13)

**receivables** Amounts that a business expects to collect at some future date from claims against customers and other parties. (Chapter 8)

**registered bond** A bond whereby the issuing company maintains a record of the purchaser's name and address and mails interest to the registered bond owner. (Chapter 17)

**relevancy** A characteristic of financial information. Information is deemed relevant if it influences the actions of a decision maker. (Chapter 13)

**relevant cost** A future cost that differs among alternatives. (Chapter 27)

**relevant range** The area of activity where a cost relationship is expected to hold true. (Chapter 25)

**reliability** A characteristic of financial information. Information is deemed reliable if it accurately depicts the conditions it purports to represent. (Chapter 13)

**repairs** Amounts spent to maintain the normal operating condition of an asset. (Chapter 11)

**residual value** The amount that a business expects to receive upon disposal of an asset at the end of the asset's life. (Chapter 10)

**responsibility accounting** A reporting system based on the organizational structure of a firm. Managers of each segment are held accountable for operating results and evaluated accordingly. (Chapter 26)

**retail method** An inventory estimation method widely used by retail establishments; derives a cost to retail ratio and applies the ratio to the total retail value of inventory. (Chapter 9)

**retained earnings** The portion of stockholders' equity that has been generated by profitable operations and retained in the business. (Chapters 4, 15, 16)

**return on assets** A ratio that measures company profitability from a given level of asset investment; net income plus interest expense divided by average total assets. Also called return on investment (ROI). (Chapters 20, 26)

**return on common stockholders' equity** A profitability ratio that measures the profits generated on funds provided by common stockholders; calculated by dividing net income minus preferred dividends by the average common stockholders' equity. (Chapter 20)

**revenue** Amounts charged to customers for goods sold or services rendered. (Chapter 1)

**revenue expenditure** An expenditure that benefits only the current accounting period. (Chapter 10)

**revenue realization principle** The principle that revenue is earned when (1) the earnings process is complete or virtually complete and (2) the amount of revenue can be objectively measured. (Chapter 13)

**revenue recognition** The point at which revenue is entered into the accounting records; generally when goods are sold or services rendered. (Chapter 3)

**reversing entry** A journal entry made on the first day of the following period that is the exact opposite of an adjustment. (Chapter 4)

**running balance account** An account format that offers the advantage of maintaining an up-to-date balance after each transaction is posted. (Chapter 2)

**salary allowances** A consideration used in the division of net income in many partnerships. The allowances recognize differences in seniority, reputation, business contacts, and time devoted to the firm by the partners. (Chapter 14)

**sales discount** A cash discount from the seller's point of view. (Chapter 5)

**sales journal** A special journal used to record sales of merchandise on account. (Chapter 6)

**sales mix** The relative combination of individual product sales to total sales. (Chapter 25)

**scattergraph** A graphic representation of observed relationships between costs and activity levels. (Chapter 25)

**secured bond** A bond by which specific assets are pledged as security for the bondholders. (Chapter 17)

**Securities and Exchange Commission (SEC)** An agency of the federal government that administers several securities acts and prescribes accounting principles and reporting practices for companies that issue publicly traded securities. (Chapter 13)

**segment** A component of a company whose activities represent a major line of business or class of customer. (Chapters 16, 20)

**segment margin** The controllable contribution margin minus uncontrollable fixed costs. This measure, which shows the contribution of each responsibility center to company profits after considering all traceable costs, is a good indicator of a center's long-run profitability. (Chapter 27)

**segment reporting** The disclosure of selected information when a company is involved in several distinct business activities. (Chapter 20)

**separation of duties** An internal accounting control that requires separation of transaction authorization, transaction recording, and asset custody. (Chapter 6)

**serial bond** A bond issue in which bonds mature at different dates. (Chapter 17)

**service life** The period of time that depreciable assets provide service to a business; also known as the economic or useful life. (Chapter 10)

**shares of capital stock** Transferable units of ownership in a corporation. (Chapters 4, 15)

**short-term investments** Investments made in readily marketable securities with the intention of conversion back to cash within the operating cycle or one year, whichever is longer. (Chapter 7)

**single-step income statement** A type of income statement in which there is one section for revenues and another section for costs and expenses. (Chapter 5)

**sinking fund** A fund established to ensure that sufficient funds are available to pay bondholders at maturity. (Chapter 17)

**sinking-fund debentures** Bonds that are retired by using the proceeds from a sinking fund. (Chapter 17)

**slack** The use of padding in budgeting to avoid unfavorable appraisals. (Chapter 24)

**slide** An error that occurs when the decimal point of a number is improperly moved to the left or right. (Chapter 2)

**sole proprietorship** A business owned by one individual. (Chapters 1, 4)

**source document** A document, such as an inventory receiving report, bill from supplier, or customer sales slip, that provides evidence that a transaction has occurred. (Chapter 2)

**special journals** Journals that handle specialized (specific) types of transactions (cash receipts, sales, and so forth). (Chapter 6)

**specific identification method** An inventory method that requires a business to identify each unit of merchandise with the unit's cost and retain that identification until the inventory is sold. (Chapter 9)

**spending variance** The difference between actual overhead incurred and the total overhead budgeted for production. (Chapter 26)

**spot rate** The rate that is used to convert one currency into another. (Chapter 20)

**standard** A norm used by businesses to measure what should occur under reasonably efficient operating conditions. (Chapter 26)

**standard deduction** A preset amount that is used in place of a taxpayer's itemized deductions. (Appendix A)

**state unemployment taxes** Taxes paid by employers to state governments. The taxes are disbursed to the unemployed through the various state programs. (Chapter 12)

**stated-value stock** No-par stock that has had a minimum issue price established to allow for protection of the creditors in terms of legal capital. (Chapter 15)

**statement of cash flows** A financial statement that reveals the operating, investing, and financing cash flows of a company. (Chapter 19)

**statement of owner's equity** A financial statement that discloses the changes in owner's equity during an accounting period. (Chapter 1)

**statement of retained earnings** A financial statement that discloses the changes in the Retained Earnings account during an accounting period. (Chapter 16)

**static budget** A budget developed for one level of activity. (Chapter 26)

**step cost** A cost function that increases or decreases in "chunks," namely, when substantial changes occur in the activity base. (Chapter 25)

**stock dividend** A dividend that involves a distribution of a company's own shares of stock. (Chapter 16)

**stock split** An increase in the number of outstanding shares and an accompanying reduction of the stock's par or stated value per share. (Chapter 16)

**stock subscriptions** Agreements with investors to purchase stock at a given price, with payment taking place on a future date or via installments. (Chapter 15)

**stockholders** The owners of a corporation. (Chapter 15)

**stockholders' equity** The summation of a corporate entity's capital stock and retained earnings. (Chapter 15)

**straight-line amortization** A method by which an equal amount of bond discount or premium is allocated to each interest period. (Chapter 17)

**straight-line depreciation** A depreciation method by which the cost of a depreciable asset, minus residual value, is allocated equally over the estimated service life. (Chapter 10)

**subsidiary** A company that has another company as its majority stockholder. (Chapter 18)

**subsidiary ledger** A group of lower-level accounts that compose a general ledger account. (Chapter 6)

**sum-of-the-years'-digits depreciation** An accelerated method of depreciation in which a smaller fraction is applied against an asset's cost, minus residual value, each period. (Chapter 10)

**sunk cost** A past cost that is irrelevant for decision making. (Chapter 27)

**T-account** A form of account named for its shape; the left side is the debit side, and the right side is the credit side. (Chapter 2)

**take-home (net) pay** The amount of cash available to an employee after all appropriate payroll deductions are subtracted from gross pay. (Chapter 12)

**taking a physical inventory** The process of counting or measuring the goods in a company's possession upon conclusion of an accounting period. (Chapter 9)

**tax avoidance** The planning of financial events, affairs, and transactions within the confines of tax law to minimize the tax liability. (Appendix A)

**tax credit** A direct dollar-for-dollar reduction from a taxpayer's total tax bill. (Appendix A)

**tax evasion** The deliberate attempt to understate taxable income by the manipulation of revenues and expenses; an illegal activity. (Appendix A)

**taxable income** Income reportable to the IRS; computed as adjusted gross income minus itemized deductions (or the standard deduction) and personal exemptions. (Chapter 17, Appendix A)

**temporary differences** Differences in the timing of revenues and expenses for tax and accounting purposes; that is, revenues and expenses are recognized in different accounting periods for income tax and financial reporting purposes. (Chapter 17)

**temporary (nominal) accounts** Accounts that are reduced to zero at the end of the accounting period via the closing process. (Chapter 4)

**time ticket** A ticket used to gather labor time that shows the specific job or jobs to which an employee was assigned. (Chapter 22)

**time value of money** A concept based on the fact that a dollar received today is worth more than a dollar received in the future. (Chapter 28)

**times interest earned** A coverage ratio computed by dividing net income before taxes and interest by a firm's interest charges. (Chapter 20)

**top-down budgeting** An approach in which virtually all budget development takes place at the upper echelons of management and the budget is imposed on lower-level personnel. (Chapter 24)

**trade discount** A discount frequently offered to customers—specifically, a reduction from the list price of merchandise. (Chapter 5)

**trade receivables** Receivables that result from the sale of a company's products or services to customers. (Chapter 8)

**trademark** An exclusive right to use specific brand names and symbols for a period of 10 years, with renewals possible if certain conditions are met. (Chapter 11)

**trading on the equity** The process of securing funds at fixed interest and preferred dividend rates and investing the funds to earn a return greater than their cost; also called leverage. (Chapter 20)

**transferred-in cost** The cost of transferred-in units that is incurred in a previous manufacturing process. (Chapter 23)

**transferred-in units** Goods received by a second processing department. (Chapter 23)

**transactions approach** An approach to determining and measuring net income by focusing on business transactions, which have produced changes in the entity's assets, liabilities, and/or owner's equity. (Chapter 3)

**transposition** An error that occurs when two digits of a given number have been accidentally reversed. (Chapter 2)

**treasury stock** Shares of stock reacquired by the issuing corporation. (Chapter 16)

**trial balance** An internal report that is used to check the equality of the debits and credits in the ledger. (Chapter 2)

**underapplied overhead** A situation arising when the factory overhead applied to production is less than the amount of factory overhead actually incurred. (Chapter 22)

**understandability** A characteristic of financial information. Information is deemed understandable if it is comprehensible to those who (1) have a reasonable understanding of business and economic activities and (2) are willing to study the information with reasonable diligence. (Chapter 13)

**unearned revenue** Future revenue that has been collected but not as yet earned. (Chapter 3)

**units-of-output depreciation** A depreciation method by which the cost of a depreciable asset, minus residual value, is allocated to the accounting periods benefited based on output (miles, hours, numbers of times used, and so forth). (Chapter 10)

**unlimited liability** The fact that each partner is held personally liable for the debts of the enterprise. (Chapter 14)

**unrealized holding gains and losses** Holding gains and losses on assets still owned at the end of the accounting period. (Chapter 13)

**variable cost** A cost that varies in direct proportion to a change in an activity base. (Chapters 21, 25)

**variable costing** See "direct costing." (Chapter 27)

**variable overhead efficiency variance** A variance that reflects inefficiencies experienced with the base used to apply variable overhead cost to production. (Chapter 26)

**variances** Deviations from a budget or standard. (Chapters 21, 26)

**vertical analysis** An analysis in which each figure on a financial statement is related to a relevant total and stated as a percentage of that total. (Chapter 20)

**voucher** An internal document used in a voucher system that summarizes the details of each cash payment. (Chapter 7)

**voucher register** A multicolumn journal in which vouchers are recorded. (Chapter 7)

**voucher system** A detailed cash payments system that improves control over all cash disbursements made by check. (Chapter 7)

**Wage and Tax Statement (W-2)** A statement the employer must provide each employee regarding gross wages and salaries earned and taxes withheld. (Chapter 12)

**warranty** A promise made by a seller or manufacturer to remedy defects in product quality and performance. (Chapter 12)

**weighted-average method** A method of accounting for inventory under a periodic inventory system that requires the computation of a weighted-average cost for goods purchased or manufactured. The average is used to value the ending inventory and to determine cost of goods sold. (Chapter 9)

**weighted-average process costing** A process costing method under which all goods manufactured during a period are carried at the same unit cost. (Chapter 23)

**withholding allowance** A numerical amount used in computing the amount of federal income taxes withheld from an employee's paycheck. (Chapter 12)

**work in process** The inventory of goods started but not completed during the period. (Chapter 21)

**work sheet** A columnar form that aids in the construction of the financial statements and assists in the performance of other end-of-period tasks. (Chapter 4)

**working capital** The excess of total current assets over total current liabilities. (Chapter 4)

# Index